THE CAMBRIDGE HISTORY OF ANCIENT CHINA

In *The Cambridge History of Ancient China* fourteen leading scholars provide a survey of the cultural, intellectual, political, and institutional developments of pre-imperial China (from the beginnings of civilization to 221 B.C.). Drawing on both traditional and newly discovered sources, specialists in history, archaeology, palaeography and art history write the eight core chapters treating the Shang, Western Zhou, Spring and Autumn, and Warring States periods. Chapters on the pre-historic background and the growth of language provide the major context of China's achievements during the 1500 years under review. The teachings of China's early masters are set alongside what is known of the methods of astronomers, physicians, and diviners (including discussion of technical skills revealed in recently discovered manuscripts of the fourth and third centuries B.C.). Two final chapters show how China's developments relate to the growth of independent cultures in Central Asia and how many of the characteristic elements of the early empires (the Qin and Han) are indebted to pre-imperial precedents. The last chapter leads the reader forward to imperial times as described in the volumes of *The Cambridge History of China*.

Michael Loewe, retired Lecturer in Chinese at the University of Cambridge, is one of the world's leading authorities on China's Han dynasty (202 B.C.–A.D. 220). He is the author of numerous books, including *Ways to Paradise: The Chinese Quest for Immortality* (1994); *Divination, Mythology and Monarchy in Han China* (1994); and *Early Chinese Texts: A Bibliographic Guide* (1993). He is co-editor of *The Cambridge History of China, Vol. 1: The Ch'in and Han Empires 221 B.C.–A.D. 220* (1986).

Edward Shaughnessy is Lorraine J. and Herrlee G. Creel Professor of Early China at the University of Chicago. He specializes on Bronze Age China, with special interests in the Chinese classics and in palaeography. Long-time editor of *Early China*, he is also the author of *Before Confucius: Studies in the Creation of the Chinese Classics* (1997), *I Ching: The Classic of Changes, The First English Translation of the Newly Discovered Second-Century BC Mawangdui Texts* (1996), and *Sources of Western Zhou History: Inscribed Bronze Vessels* (1991).

THE CAMBRIDGE
HISTORY OF
ANCIENT CHINA

From the Origins of
Civilization to 221 B.C.

Edited by
MICHAEL LOEWE
and
EDWARD L. SHAUGHNESSY

CAMBRIDGE
UNIVERSITY PRESS

CAMBRIDGE UNIVERSITY PRESS
Cambridge, New York, Melbourne, Madrid, Cape Town, Singapore, São Paulo, Delhi

Cambridge University Press
32 Avenue of the Americas, New York, NY 10013-2473, USA

www.cambridge.org
Information on this title: www.cambridge.org/9780521470308

First published 1999
Reprinted 2004, 2006, 2007

Printed in the United States of America

A catalog record for this publication is available from the British Library.

Library of Congress Cataloging in Publication Data
The Cambridge history of ancient China / edited by Michael Loewe,
Edward L. Shaughnessy.
p. cm.
Includes bibliographical references and index.
ISBN 0-521-47030-7
1. China — History — To 221 B.C. 2. China — Civilization —
To 221 B.C. 3. China — Antiquities. 1. Shaughnessy, Edward L., 1952–
II. Loewe, Michael.
DS741.5.C35   1998
931 — dc21   97-33203
CIP

ISBN 978-0-521-47030-8 hardback

CONTENTS

MAPS, TABLES, AND FIGURES

MAPS

TABLES

FIGURES

TYPES OF BRONZE VESSELS

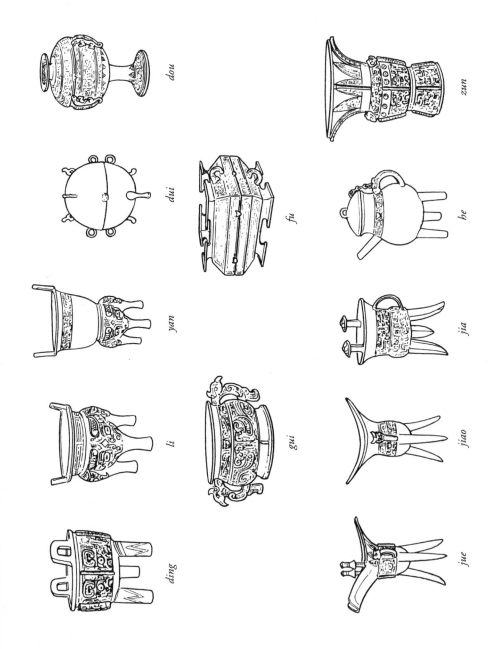

dou

zun

dui

fu

he

yan

jia

li

gui

jiao

ding

jue

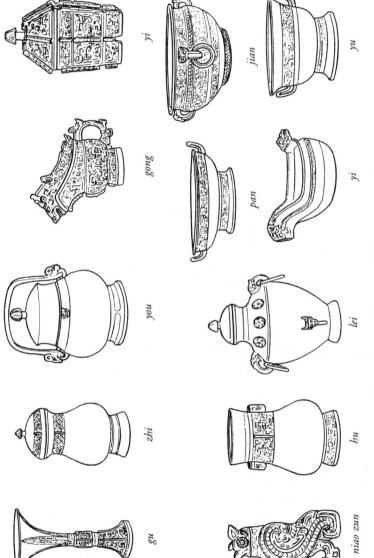

yi

jian

yu

gong

pan

yi

you

lei

zhi

hu

gu

niao zun

Principal types of Shang and Zhou bronze vessels

CONVENTIONS

The editors believe that there is no place in this volume for full accounts of
the stages whereby historians, whether of Eastern or Western traditions, have
accepted or rejected their predecessors' findings before reaching their conclusions. Certain differences will undoubtedly become manifest in the book.
In a jointly authored work that treats a historical period of a thousand years,
it is only to be expected that certain topics, which sometimes span different
periods of time and involve differences of interpretation and approach, have
required mention in several chapters. While attempts have been made to correlate the various chapters, the editors have felt that it would be improper
to insist on consistent translations of all terms or to exclude interpretations
by different contributors. While cross-references have been reduced to a
minimum, it is hoped that the index will suffice for purposes of contrast and
comparison.

REFERENCES

English translations of the titles of pre-imperial texts are provided on their first occurrence in
each chapter; they are not included in the footnotes.

The Thirteen Classics: references are to the *Shisan jing zhushu* 十三經注疏 (1816; variously
reprinted and easily available in facsimile form), except that, as is general practice, those
to the *Analects* and *Mencius* are to the chapters and divisions in Legge's edition, with
translation (2d edition 1893–94).

The Twenty-five Histories: references are to the punctuated edition of Beijing: Zhonghua
shuju (from 1959); where necessary, reference is added to editions that include other
commentaries.

Philosophical and other texts: references are to the *Si bu congkan*, *Si bu beiyao*, or *Congshu
jicheng* editions, as stated, with further reference to other scholarly editions as occasion
may demand.

Translations: unless otherwise stated, translations from primary sources are those of the contributors to the volume. To enable readers to place passages in context, these are sup-

ported by references to well-known and easily available translations of the complete works
that are cited; these are for comparison only.

Secondary publications: references cannot be expected for items that appeared after the presentation of the draft chapters in December 1995.

Archaeological reports: references in the notes to articles whose authorship is attributed simply
to instititional units are restricted to the date and pages of the periodical of publication.
Complete citations for these articles are given in the bibliography.

CHINESE CHARACTERS AND ROMANIZATION

Chinese characters in full, traditional forms are provided on the first occurrence in each chapter for all Chinese place names, proper names, and Chinese
terms, except where these appear in extended translations. Reference thereafter is provided in *pinyin* romanization, with the conventional usage of Han
漢, Hann 韓, Wei 魏, Wey 衛, Yi wang 夷王, Yih wang 懿王, Jing wang 敬
王, Jiing wang 景王, and Shaanxi 陝西. Where individual writers prefer other
forms for their names, these have been retained. Tones are marked, and
reconstructed forms of premodern forms of Chinese are given, only where
these are essential to the topic under-discussion.

TITLES AND TERMS

Since the English equivalents that have been adopted hitherto are often
varied, unsatisfactory, or even misleading, Chinese terms have in many cases
been retained, provided that the context makes their meaning clear (e.g., *Ba*
霸 is given in place of "Hegemon"), except that the well-established "king"
for *wang* 王 and "duke" for *Gong* 公 have often been kept as such. In general,
names of the rulers of some of the states thus appear in the form of Zheng
Huan Gong. A distinction is drawn between Du Bo 杜伯, where *Bo* 伯 is the
title of a nobility, and Dubo, where *bo* 伯 simply marks the appropriate generation of the man mentioned. Regrettably, it has not been possible to suggest
terms that would preclude the use of "state" or "fief" with their somewhat
misleading overtones.

ABBREVIATIONS

AM	*Asia Major*
BIHP	*Bulletin of the Institute of History and Philology*
BMFEA	*Bulletin of the Museum of Far Eastern Antiquities*
BSOAS	*Bulletin of the School of Oriental and African Studies*
EC	*Early China*
HJAS	*Harvard Journal of Asiatic Studies*
JA	*Journal asiatique*
JAS	*Journal of Asian Studies*
JAOS	*Journal of the American Oriental Society*
JESHO	*Journal of the Economic and Social History of the Orient*
JRAS	*Journal of the Royal Asiatic Society*
MS	*Monumenta Serica*
TP	*T'oung Pao*

ACKNOWLEDGMENTS

The editors are glad to express their thanks to a number of scholars who have supported this project from the outset, and name especially Li Xueqin and Denis Twitchett in this context. They are grateful to Fangpei Cai, Feng Li, Ke Peng, and David Sena for their help in preparing the final copy for press; to the Chiang Ching-kuo Foundation for International Scholarly Exchange, whose grant made it possible to hold a conference of the contributors; to Clare Hall, Cambridge, England, for thirty years the academic home of one of the editors and generous with the hospitality that it provided for the other; to Charles Aylmen of the University Library, Cambridge, England, and to the Needham Research Institute, Cambridge, England, and especially its librarian John Moffett, for making its collection and offices available to us during much of our work. They also wish to thank the contributors for their active cooperation and readiness to accord with the requirements of a corporate volume.

The editors wish to thank Mr. Li Xiating 李夏廷 of Taiyuan, China, for preparing very skillfully and at short notice many of the line drawings that grace this book.

We are also grateful to the Department of East Asian Languages and Civilizations and to the Division of the Humanities of the University of Chicago for considerable logistical help and for making it possible for Professor Shaughnessy to spend time in Cambridge during the editing of the volume.

ACKNOWLEDGMENTS FOR ILLUSTRATIONS

Yale University Press
Harry N. Abrams, New York
The Trustees of the British Museum
Wenwu chubanshe, Beijing

Harvard University Art Museums
The Fogg Museum, Harvard University
The Jinbun kakagu kenkyûjo, Kyoto
Kaogu Chunbanshe, Beijing
Museum Rietberg, Zurich
Arthur M. Sackler Museum, Cambridge, MA
Nihon keizai shinbunsha, Tokyo
Hong Kong University Press (Chinese University of Hong Kong)
Tokyo National Museum
The Metropolitan Museum of Art, New York
The Freer Gallery of Art, Washington
Kexue chubanshe, Beijing

San Qin chubanshe, Xi'an

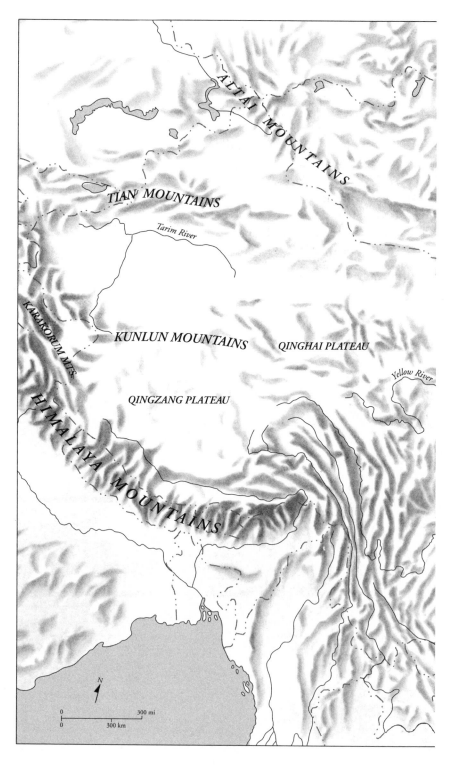

Topography of China

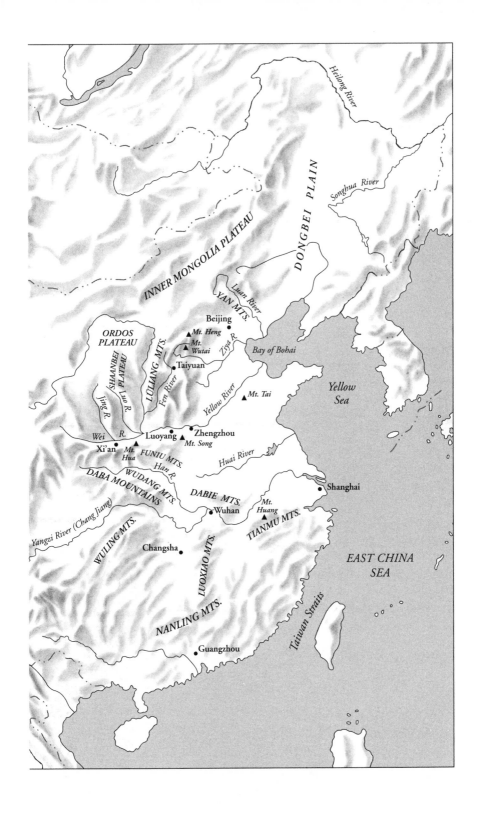

INTRODUCTION

Michael Loewe and Edward L. Shaughnessy

In their general introduction to the first volume of the *Cambridge History of China* (*The Ch'in and Han Empires*), John K. Fairbank and Denis Twitchett, general editors of the series, explained why, when they were planning the series in the 1960s, they had felt obliged to start their coverage with the first empires, omitting earlier developments. After noting the transformation brought about by archaeological discoveries, they wrote:[1]

This flood of new information has changed our view of history repeatedly, and there is not yet any generally accepted synthesis of this new evidence and the traditional written record. In spite of repeated efforts to plan and produce a volume or volumes that would summarize the present state of our knowledge of early China, it has so far proved impossible to do so.

However, by the time that first volume was published (1986), some twenty years after Fairbank and Twitchett had initiated the *Cambridge History of China* project, the "flood of new information" that they mentioned had already revitalized the study of ancient China. A large number of scholars, both in East Asia and in the West, had been drawn to consider the new archaeological evidence and, in its light, to reconsider China's traditional written record and many of the historiographical assumptions based thereon. In the light of these developments in the field, and with the active encouragement of Denis Twitchett, Cambridge University Press determined to repair the omission, the result being the present *Cambridge History of Ancient China*.

This title is intended to suggest that the volume can, and indeed should, be read as part of the larger, multivolume *Cambridge History of China*, but that at the same time it is independent of that series. This independence has

---

[1] *The Cambridge History of China. Vol. 1: The Ch'in and Han Empires, 221 B.C.–A.D. 220*, ed. Denis Twitchett and Michael Loewe (Cambridge University Press, 1986), p. v.

afforded us a measure of flexibility in organization and presentation that is welcome for two reasons. First, we cover a much longer period than any single volume in the *Cambridge History of China*, beginning with the Shang period (ca. 1570–1045 B.C.), when China's first written records appear, and extending until the Qin unification (221 B.C.) of the independent states of the Warring States period (480–221 B.C.), with other chapters providing transitions from and to earlier and later periods as well. Second, this measure of independence has freed us to treat the material culture of the period with the same degree of importance as the textual record. This enhanced focus on material culture is manifested in the design of the volume; unlike the volumes of *The Cambridge History of China*, which include no illustrations other than maps, this volume is illustrated with many of the recent archaeological discoveries that have transformed the field so markedly. But, of greater importance, in addition to requiring a different mode of presentation, the archaeological discoveries of ancient China have required a new approach to history, one that self-consciously seeks to integrate material and textual sources. This historiography now plays such an important role in the study of all aspects of ancient China, certainly including those that are treated in the fourteen chapters of the present volume, that we feel it is important to reflect upon its development, if only briefly.

THE DEVELOPMENT OF HISTORICAL APPROACHES AND THE IMPACT OF ARCHAEOLOGY IN THE STUDY OF ANCIENT CHINA

Two hundred years ago, when Joseph de Mailla wrote the first comprehensive history of China to appear in a Western language (*Histoire génerale de la Chine ou annales de cet empire*, 1777–83),[2] he relied on, and indeed simply paraphrased, the *Tongjian gangmu* 通鑑綱目, a synthetic and secondary piece of writing that was compiled by Zhu Xi 朱熹 (1130–1200). By the nineteenth century, Western sinologists started going straight to the texts that had served as the primary sources used by Zhu Xi and other writers. There followed translations of early works such as the *Zhou li* 周禮 (Rituals of Zhou), in Édouard Biot's French version (*Le Tcheou-li ou rites des Tcheou*, 1851),[3] and much of the rest of the Confucian canon, in James Legge's monumental work *The Chinese Classics* (originally published 1861–72).[4] Such work culminated at the end of the century in Édouard Chavannes's translation of fifty-two

[2] *Histoire génerale de la Chine ou annales de cet empire* (Paris: 1777–83).
[3] *Le Tcheou-li ou rites des Tcheou*, 3 vols. (Paris: Imprimerie Nationale, 1851).
[4] James Legge, *The Chinese Classics*, vols. 1–3 (Hong Kong: At the author's; and London: Trübner, 1861–5); vols. 4–5 (Hong Kong: Lane Crawford; and London: Trübner, 1871–2; 2nd rev. ed. Oxford: Clarendon Press, 1893–4).

chapters of the *Shi ji* 史記 (Records of the historian).[5] At the end of the twentieth century many of these translations are still unsurpassed.

With Chavannes (1865–1918), the study of Chinese history entered a new era. Throughout the nineteenth century, Western historians had been extending the scope of their interests to include, first, archival sources and, later, also artifactual evidence. By the end of the century, sinologists – now often professional scholars – added expertise in traditional Chinese philology, as well as first-hand experience of living in China, to their training in the developing discipline of history. Chavannes put all of these advantages to good use. His translation of the *Shi ji* was initiated by an early interest in religion, particularly of the *feng* 封 and *shan* 禪 rites said to have been performed upon the successful establishment of a new dynasty; his first scholarly publication was an annotated translation of the chapter that is devoted to these rites in the *Shi ji*.[6] More than two decades later he returned to this topic, according it a much broader treatment. In his masterly study *Le T'ai chan: Essai de monographie d'un culte chinois*,[7] which might be described as an ethno-archaeological history of the cult surrounding Mount Tai 泰 in Shandong, Chavannes not only traced mention of these rites throughout the Chinese historical record, demonstrating how they changed both in performance and in the significance that they had in the minds of Chinese scholars and statesmen, but he also cataloged the hundreds of steles erected all over the mountain by devout pilgrims, dating them, translating their inscriptions, and discussing their importance.

Chavannes's work could well be said to be modern Western sinology's first great original achievement. Its combination of historical awareness and archaeological sources anticipated what would be the main trend in the study of ancient China, both in the West and in China itself, throughout the succeeding century. It certainly characterized the approach of the sinological giants of the next generation, including Chavannes's own students, Paul Pelliot (1878–1945), Henri Maspero (1883–1945), Marcel Granet (1884–1940), and Paul Demiéville (1894–1979), as well as others outside France such as Bernhard Karlgren (1889–1978) and Berthold Laufer (1874–1934).

This generation of scholars was fortunate to have matured just as archaeology, a discipline that was new to China, was beginning to exercise a profound influence on native Chinese scholarship. Two signal discoveries at the turn of the century announced the potential influence that this discipline

---

[5] *Les mémoires historiques de Se-ma Ts'ien*, 5 vols. (Paris: Ernest Leroux, 1895–1905; rpt., with vol. 6, Paris: Adrien Maisonneuve, 1967).

[6] "Le traité sur les sacrifices Fong et Chan de Se ma Ts'ien traduit en Français par Édouard Chavannes," *Journal of the Peking Oriental Society* (Peking: Typographie du Pei-T'ang, 1890), in-8: xxxi–95.

[7] Édouard Chavannes, *Le T'ai chan: Essai de monographie d'un culte chinois* (Paris: Annales du Musée Guimet, 1910).

would exert on the historiography of ancient China. The first of these was that of archaic Chinese characters inscribed on bones, the so-called oracle-bone inscriptions, that were ultimately traced to Anyang 安陽, in the present day province of Henan, the site of one capital of the Shang dynasty. This discovery, and the century of scholarship and further discovery that has been attendant upon it, is the topic of Chapter 4 in the present volume, and thus requires no discussion here; however, it can perhaps easily be appreciated how important the discovery of written material, hundreds of years earlier than any examples previously known, was to Chinese historians, steeped as they were in a supremely literate historical tradition.

Just a few years after the oracle bones were discovered, there came another momentous discovery on the other side of China. This was at Dunhuang 敦煌 (present day Gansu province), an oasis town that had been the site of an important Buddhist community in medieval China. The finds included a large cache of manuscripts, dating from the fifth through the tenth centuries A.D. This site and its finds are of principal concern to periods later than that to which the present volume is addressed.[8] However, because the initial attention that they received came from Western scholars, notably Pelliot, the discovery did much to spark Western interest in the archaeological exploration of China. Subsequent achievements of archaeologists who worked in China included J. G. Andersson's excavations at Yangshao 仰韶 village in Mianchi 澠池 county, Henan, in 1920, where the first neolithic cultures were found, and some years later the discovery of Peking Man (*Sinanthropus pekinensis*) at Zhoukoudian 周口店 (southwest of Beijing) by a joint Chinese–European team. Both of these discoveries are discussed in Chapter 1 of the present volume.

Readiness to take full account of archaeology to reconsider the history of ancient China was by no means confined to Western scholars. Indeed, the first project of the newly established (1926) Academia Sinica's Institute of History and Philology was the excavation of Anyang. The explicit combination of history and archaeology to which this excavation attests continues to this day to inform the missions of the Institute of History and Philology in Taiwan and also its successor in the People's Republic of China, the Institute of Archaeology of the Chinese Academy of Social Sciences. This latter institution, in particular, has played the leading role in directing virtually all archaeological work in China over the last half century, and its publications are cited in every chapter of the present volume.

[8] These documents have attracted a considerable output of scholarly effort; for a preliminary general appreciation, see *The Cambridge History of China. Vol. 3: Sui and T'ang China, 589–906, Part 1*, ed. Denis Twitchett (Cambridge University Press, 1979), pp. 46–7. The discoveries are due to be treated in greater detail in *The Cambridge History of China*, vol. 4.

The initial archaeological discoveries led textual historians as well to question and overturn many of the traditions that Chinese historians had accepted, more or less uncritically, for two millennia. Certainly the most prominent manifestation of this historiographical revolution was the series of articles that appeared in the series *Gu shi bian* 古史辨 (Discriminations on ancient history). Published between 1926 and 1941, and edited for the most part by Gu Jiegang 顧頡剛 (1893–1980), *Gu shi bian* included contributions by most of the younger historians then active in China. Employing a methodology which, in a conscious borrowing from archaeology, he termed "stratigraphy," Gu proposed that China's traditional historical sources had come to be successively elaborated as they passed through time. By digging back through the accumulated textual layers, Gu argued, it should be possible to arrive back at the pristine origins of these historical sources. Furthermore, Gu and most of his collaborators believed that those origins would be far less grandiose than tradition held them to be; indeed, they argued that much of the work of that tradition had been engaged in fabricating sources that purported to be ancient. Thus, not only the sanctity but even the authenticity of parts of such classics as the *Yi jing* 易經 (Classic of changes) and the *Shu jing* 書經 (Classic of documents; also known as the *Shang shu* 尚書, Venerated documents) were called into question, as were many of the philosophical works traditionally held to have been written in the Warring States period. The iconoclasm of this new historiography found a ready welcome among Western sinologists, who, it is fair to say, were, at the time, inclined in any event to suspect any dogma, and certainly that of traditional China.

With the establishment of the People's Republic of China in 1949, political considerations came to constrain most work of historical interpretation by Chinese scholars, and from 1966 to 1972, even archaeological reporting was curtailed. The frustration of John Fairbank and Denis Twitchett, who were formulating their plans for the *Cambridge History of China* just as the Cultural Revolution raged, can readily be appreciated. However, the resumption of academic publishing in 1972 brought a flood of archaeological discoveries to the attention of sinologists everywhere. The numerous unprecedented finds made during those years inform virtually every chapter of the present volume, and there is thus no need to anticipate those discussions here. It does however bear mentioning that when, in 1979, relaxed political conditions once again freed Chinese scholars to publish the results of original research, the archaeological discoveries of the previous decade or so provided them with ready, and abundant, new data. As a result, whereas until 1979 there had been just the three national journals, *Wenwu* 文物 (Cultural relics), *Kaogu* 考古 (Archaeology), and *Kaogu xuebao* 考古學報 (Archaeological research), whose publication had also been suspended during the Cultural Revolution, there are today over sixty journals devoted to various topics in archaeology, published mostly at the local level and dedicated to the archaeology of specific areas.[9] Similarly, new monographs on particular subjects, which had hardly ever appeared in the 1960s and 1970s, are now forthcoming in such numbers that it is all but impossible to maintain bibliographical control.

The revival of Chinese historiography on ancient China was matched by a similar revival in the West. Just as mainland China was reopened to cultural contacts (beginning in the mid-1970s), a large number of young scholars who had benefited from extensive training first in Taiwan and then, more usually, on the mainland, turned their attention to the great archaeological discoveries of the early 1970s. For the first time in more than a generation, it now became possible to study and travel comparatively freely in China, to meet Chinese colleagues who were themselves traveling abroad to attend international conferences on scholarly topics, and, more recently, to engage in collaborative projects with Chinese scholars. The results of this scholarly communication will also be apparent in virtually every chapter of the present volume, where by far the greatest portion of the notes and bibliographic entries refer to scholarly results published in China over the past two decades. For their part Western scholars have been heartened by the readiness with which their Chinese colleagues have welcomed them to their institutions and been ready to consider and criticize their work. Plans are already in place to translate the present volume into Chinese, as has already been undertaken for some volumes of the *Cambridge History of China* both in the People's Republic and in Taiwan.

In addition to the unprecedented access to the active scholarly world of China that has become available to Western scholars, particularly in the past fifteen years, there must be added the great benefits that they have received from contacts with historians and archaeologists of Japan. Groups of Japanese archaeologists had indeed been engaged in investigating and excavating some of the sites in China from the beginning of the twentieth century and particularly during the 1940s, and the publication of whole series of Japanese monographs and journals has exerted an immense influence on all aspects of sinology. If one single work may be mentioned, the appearance of Morohashi Tetsuji's 諸橋轍次 (1883–1982) multivolume *Dai Kanwa jiten* 大漢和辭典 made an impact that was little less than dramatic, providing

---

[9] For an overview of these journals, see Lothar von Falkenhausen, "Serials on Chinese Archaeology Published in the People's Republic of China: A Bibliographical Survey," *EC* 17 (1992): 247–95.

researchers with immediate access to many unexplored riches of Chinese literature and to references to the scholarly output of the Qing period.[10]

THE SOURCES

In the view of the editors neither textual nor archaeological evidence is by itself necessarily of greater validity than the other. It is only by treating the two types of evidence as being complementary to each other, and with a full realization of the accidental circumstances of their survival, that either type can be handled with the criticism that is its due. If the written accounts can in no way be regarded as being comprehensive or free of bias, so must the excavated sites and materials be seen only as examples of much that may yet lie underground. Just as historians necessarily discriminate between archive and chronicle, or between contemporary documents and later statements, so too do archaeologists need to distinguish between contemporary products and heirlooms, or between local manufactures and imports. It would be as absurd for an archaeologist to dismiss documentary evidence as irrelevant as it would be for a historian to insist on the veracity of the written word in fundamentalist fashion. Just as the inferences drawn from archaeological evidence must always be subject to revision in the light of further discoveries and research, so are inferences that historians draw from their texts likewise ever open to reinterpretation.

Literary Sources

As with all historical studies, so here it is appropriate to consider the kinds of sources, both old and new, that are available and the ways in which they can be exploited. In the first place there are those works that have long been available: classics such as the *Yi jing, Shang shu, Shi jing* 詩經 (Classic of poetry), *Chunqiu* 春秋 (Spring and Autumn [annals]) and *Zuo zhuan* 左傳 (Zuo's tradition), *Zhou li* (Rituals of Zhou), *Li ji* 禮記 (Records of ritual); philosophical essays such as the *Analects* of Confucius, writings of the "Hundred Schools" of the Warring States period, which begin with the *Mozi* 墨子 and extend to the *Han Feizi* 韓非子; and later, noncontemporary historical accounts of the ancient period such as can be found in the *Zhushu*

---

[10] Morohashi Tetsuji, *Dai Kan Wa jiten* (Tokyo: Suzuki ippei, 1955–60). This work has now been complemented by two Chinese dictionaries that are of comparable scope and that draw attention among other things to the archaeological discoveries of the past thirty years: Xu Zhongshu, ed., *Han yu da zi dian*, vols. 1–7 and index (Chengdu: Sichuan cishu and Hubei cishu, 1986–90); and Luo Zhufeng, ed., *Han yu da ci dian*, vols. 1–12 and index (Shanghai: Shanghai cishu, 1986–93).

jinian 竹書紀年 (Bamboo annals) and the *Shi ji*. We also possess unquestionably authentic records in the form of oracle-bone and bronze inscriptions that derive directly from the hands of scribes of the Shang or Western Zhou periods. In addition, excavations of recent years have yielded texts from the Warring States period, written either on bamboo or wooden strips or on silk, some of which are discussed in Chapter 12.

There are also native historiographical traditions that inevitably influence our view of Chinese history. All Western scholars who study ancient China owe an immense debt to China's traditional historians. Few Westerners – or modern Chinese, for that matter – can hope to emulate the feats of memory whereby they were able to cite from the wealth of Chinese literature in support of an argument. If the material evidence now available to us but not to them, or the types of questions that historians now ask but did not do so previously, call for a rejection or reassessment of parts of China's historical tradition, this is hardly reason to criticize historians of centuries past.

At times some scholars have been tempted to reject the authority of all the received literary sources, on the grounds that their editing, or even their composition, was not contemporary with the times that they treat. But severe as the hazards of transmission, and important as such reservations, are, they are not necessarily strong enough to support such an overall view. Fundamental questions about this traditional textual heritage indeed arise because of the way in which it has come into our hands, transmitted through the ages, copied and recopied, with errors, additions, or deletions, whether deliberate or accidental. In addition, there is a real concern that the traditional scholars and historians consciously chose to transmit only those texts that they perceived to contribute in some way to their view of what they claimed to be their own culture; there is more than a chance that they deliberately discarded many other texts, which reflected other aspects of ancient China's ways that were perhaps inconvenient or unsavory. For the available sources too, it remains essential to inquire into the motives that lay behind the production. The nature and extent of the material at our disposal is such that it would be perilous to claim that all such motives can be identified with certainty. The difficulty is compounded by the absence of material from external sources with which to counterbalance or control the evidence of our surviving documents, deriving as these mainly do from the members or heirs of a Zhou polity. Historians would dearly welcome the discovery of a set of annals that originated from a regime that was both antagonistic to Zhou and sufficiently sophisticated to produce its own literature.

These are legitimate concerns, of which the scholars who study these texts are well aware. Much work in China, Japan, and the West has been and is being devoted to the exacting study of textual history and the production of authoritative versions.[11] Other scholars, familiar both with the traditional texts and the newly discovered inscriptions on durable materials that have not suffered the vagaries of transmission above ground, have been able to compare the writings that derive from the two media, demonstrating how far the grammar and vocabulary of the received texts are consistent with the period to which they have been traditionally attributed. Two cases may serve as examples of this type of inquiry.

The "Pan Geng" 盤庚 chapter of the *Shang shu* is traditionally supposed to have been the text of a speech delivered by the Shang king Pan Geng (r. ca. 1250 B.C.). Pan Geng was the uncle of King Wu Ding 武丁 (d. ca. 1189 B.C.), the first king for whose reign we possess written records in the form of the oracle-bone inscriptions. The language of these oracle-bone inscriptions differs so starkly from that of the "Pan Geng" chapter that it is very unlikely that the latter could have been written during the Shang dynasty at all; for this reason it is not mentioned in the account of the Shang Dynasty in Chapter 4, below.

By contrast, the discovery of the oracle-bone inscriptions, as well as advances in the understanding of Western Zhou bronze inscriptions, have shown that the "Shi fu" 世俘 (Great capture) chapter of the *Yi Zhou shu* 逸周書 (Remainder of the Zhou documents), an account of the Zhou conquest of Shang, is written for the most part in the language of the late Shang and early Western Zhou.[12] For this reason it is cited extensively in the account of the Zhou conquest given in Chapter 5, even though traditional Chinese historians largely ignored it because its description of bloody battles was anathema to their view of a pacifistic Zhou founding.

Comparisons of this type between traditional texts and epigraphic sources have been even more important in evaluating the literary heritage of the Late Warring States period. Texts such as the *Yu Liaozi* 尉繚子 (also referred to as the *Wei Liaozi*), *Heguanzi* 鶡冠子, and *Wenzi* 文子, long suspected of being forgeries of Han times or later, can now be shown, at least in part, to date from before the Han dynasty.[13]

No estimate can be made of the extent of the literary material that had been produced and was actively circulating during pre-imperial times. From the first of China's bibliographical lists, a resumé of the catalog of works preserved in the imperial library at the end of the Former Han period, it may

---

[11] For the most recent views regarding most early Chinese texts, see Michael Loewe, ed., *Early Chinese Texts: A Bibliographical Guide* (Berkeley: Society for the Study of Early China and Institute of East Asian Studies, University of California, 1993).

[12] Gu Jiegang, "*Yizhoushu* Shifu pian jiaozhu xieding yu pinglun," *Wenshi* 2 (1962): 1–42; Edward L. Shaughnessy, "'New' Evidence on the Zhou Conquest,' *EC* 6 (1980–1): 57–79.

[13] For a discussion of these texts, as well as a general argument for the authenticity of much of our received literature, see Li Xueqin, *Jianbo yi ji yu xueshu shi* (Taibei: Shibao wenhua, 1994).

be seen that we possess today no more than a small portion of the total of 677 titles that are named therein. But how far those works were available to China's traditional historians can only remain open to question. Certainly some texts, now long since lost, were read and cited by scholars of the Tang and Song periods, and it is to their comments that we owe what fragments that we have of a number of early works. As against this, copies of texts that have been brought to light from tombs in comparatively recent excavations, and which cannot necessarily be identified with items mentioned in that list, suggest that the imperial library contained no more than a part, and perhaps a very small part, of the texts that were in circulation by the third and second centuries B.C. These texts demonstrate the persistent habit whereby historical or other records (e.g., legal or astronomical writings) were being kept; many of them show how accurate those records often were. Taken together, these conclusions lend support to the validity of much of the surviving historical detail that is recorded for the Spring and Autumn and Warring States periods in, for example, the chronological or genealogical tables of the *Shi ji.*

This archaeological verification of some received texts has given rise, especially in China, to a scholarly view which affirms the antiquity of most significant aspects of Chinese culture. This view is now referred to as that of the *Xingu pai* 信古派 (Believing in Antiquity School), in conscious distinction from the *Yigu pai* 疑古派 (Doubting in Antiquity School) which had contributed to the *Gu shi bian* series of the 1930s. In some of its expressions this belief in antiquity is doubtless exaggerated, owing as much to contemporary cultural chauvinism as to scholarly evidence; but such opinions are probably no more biased than those of many Western attempts to negate this view, and each of its proposals needs consideration on its own merits. Despite all these reservations, it is hard to deny the conclusion that the archaeological discoveries of the past generation have tended to authenticate, rather than to overturn, the traditional literary record of ancient China.

Material Sources

Historians of China are today fortunate in being able to call on a number of sources of material culture that are contemporary with the period under study, having been brought to light only recently. The importance of the ever expanding evidence of the sites of cities, buildings, and tombs, and of the vast number of artifacts that they included, cannot be overstated. The scholarly world has been thrilled by discoveries from all periods of ancient China and from many different geographical regions. For the Shang period, excavations have continued at Anyang, adding greater depth to our understanding of the Shang dynasty; on the other hand, the bronze statues from San-xingdui 三星堆 at Guanghan 廣漢 in Sichuan were entirely unprecedented. The tomb of Zeng Hou Yi 曾侯乙 (buried ca. 433 B.C.), found at Suixian 隨縣, Hubei, suggests some of the wealth available to rulers of Zhou states, while the mausoleum of the king of Zhongshan 中山 (ca. 300 B.C.), located in the northern province of Hebei, has shown that similar riches were also available on the very periphery of Zhou China. But the contributions of archaeology have gone far beyond these sensational discoveries. Each pottery vessel and every tomb fills in a little more of the picture of what life was like in ancient China; that picture is far richer today than ever before.

Yet, just as in the case of the textual record, the archaeological record is also bound by biases of its own. Only rarely does the evidence result from a deliberate and sustained search, identification, and excavation of a site whose existence is to be inferred from other sources. Thus, the great bulk of what has now been found results from the dual accidents of preservation and discovery. In almost all cases, artifacts had to be buried if they were to survive: above ground they would have been susceptible to the hazards of nature, accidental destruction, and the ravages wrought by man; the choice of articles for burial was subject to differing motives; and of the articles selected for burial, only those of inert substance have usually survived decay. In addition, most of the archaeological work in China is in the nature of salvage, started either thanks to an accidental find or in advance of a basic construction project. The artifacts that have been found surely represent only a small percentage of those that had been in use in ancient China, and they just as surely derive very largely from the lives of the most privileged members of society; but as they are all that we possess of such evidence, we may well run the risk of exaggerating their importance. In addition, as several of the contributors to this volume point out, archaeology in China is subject to contemporary political and cultural concerns, perhaps chief among which has been the desire to demonstrate the grandeur of Chinese civilization.

Despite these methodological concerns, of which the contributors to this volume are all acutely aware, there can be no doubt that archaeology has transfigured – and very greatly enriched – our understanding of ancient China. We all look forward to the future discoveries that will almost surely render the present volume obsolete before too long.

CHINA'S IDEALIZED PAST

The political concerns that affect the contemporary practice of history and archaeology in China are not new. As may be seen in much of China's official writings, many of the rulers and officials who have governed the land

and its people have sought cultural precedents for their policies. They reiterated tales, sometimes strange, to which they traced their beginnings; they satisfied their pride in their own institutions by a belief that these harked back to many centuries before; and they idealized and respected the behavior that they saw depicted in the deeds of culture heroes, model kings, or exemplary ministers of state. A deep-seated veneration for the remote past (*Shang gu* 上古) or for the Three Royal Ages (*San wang* 三王) colored much of the training to which the scholars and civil servants of the imperial age were subjected, even though common sense may well have suggested to them – as it does to us today – that the Neolithic, Bronze, or Early Iron Ages were probably marked by material want, suffering, violence, and bloodshed. In particular, the house of Zhou was treated with a degree of respect and admiration that few of China's men of letters would care to gainsay. The force of such a view was of sufficient strength to color intellectual opinion, to affect the decisions of government, and to act as a fundamental obstacle to initiative.

According to this idealized view of the past, throughout these changes, and those of the ensuing two thousand years of imperial rule, there persisted a monolithic unity, grounded in one family or locality that could be identified and named. More recently historians have been concerned to redress the balance, by pointing to the wide gap between a mythological view of China's glorious past and a more critical assessment. The volumes of the *Cambridge History of China* that have already been published demonstrate that in the imperial ages reality was different from the ideal; effective unity was maintained for perhaps half of the two millennia of the imperial dynasties, and for lengthy periods the dynasties that ruled parts of China had arisen from alien houses. Readers of this volume may be tempted to ask how far, following the emergence of the several Neolithic cultures, China may properly be seen as a unity in the pre-imperial period. Others may seek the origin and growth of some of the essential elements that were necessary for the formation of such a unity. Such elements include a recognition of an authority's right to govern; obedience thereto; and the religious beliefs, ritual practices, and intellectual arguments required in its support. They resulted in the establishment of social hierarchies and of administrative institutions that were capable of wide application; they involved the admixture of foreign elements and their assimilation to an accepted way of life; and they produced a highly respected class of men, whose prestige depended on their literary skills, rather than on their position as religious functionaries. As compared with other cultures, some of these elements were indeed unique, contributing to an unparalleled cultural continuity which, despite the variations in the area that was effectively governed, may be seen to have persisted from at least Spring and Autumn times onward.

But with respect to ancient China this cultural continuity can no longer be accepted unquestioningly. Whereas China's traditional historians tended to see the past as moving from one house to another in an ordained series, with influences spreading outwards to encapsulate peoples of different styles of living or cultural habits, more recent appraisals suggest a different view, seeing developments arising independently in various parts of the land. Discoveries from throughout China have given the lie to the traditional view of a monolithic culture that originated in the Yellow River valley and then radiated out to the outlying areas. In place of such a supposition, there can be no escape from acknowledging the existence of a whole variety of cultures, discriminated by time and place, whose limitations have yet to be determined. Far from detracting from the wonder of Chinese culture, in our view this new awareness of its diversity can only lend it strength and enhance its historical richness.

THE SCOPE OF THE PRESENT VOLUME

The effect that the newly found evidence has exercised over the study of ancient China may be said to be explosive, even though when compared with later periods of history the amount that is available for any particular topic is still meager. Thus, some historians of ancient China might look with envy at the modern historian with file upon file of archives resting on a library's shelves. But our paucity of evidence can also be of real advantage. With what is relatively so little evidence, we have been discouraged from drawing our disciplinary boundaries too narrowly. The historian who disregards archaeological evidence soon finds that the field has passed him or her by; the archaeologist who is unfamiliar with traditional literature will miss much of the spirit that gives life to his or her artifacts.

The multidisciplinary approach that is essential to the study of ancient China can call on a tradition that stretches back to the great masters such as Chavannes and Pelliot. Its continuing strength is reflected in the organization of this volume. For each of the four periods into which ancient China's history is traditionally divided, Shang, Western Zhou, Spring and Autumn, and Warring States, the reader will find two chapters apiece, one based primarily on written sources, whether traditional or from inscriptions, and one based primarily on the record of archaeology and its artifacts. That both approaches should be represented was the editors' first desideratum in planning the book. Despite the inevitable redundancy and occasional contradictions that this dual organization may produce, we felt it essential that both approaches should be represented by their strongest possible advocates. Fully cognizant that once the book leaves the publishing plant we relinquish all control, and cognizant also that archaeologists and art historians will turn first to the chapters on material culture, while textualists will turn to the more traditional historical chapters, we take the opportunity to urge all readers to take the chapters in tandem. And while we do not wish to make any claim here regarding a continuous "Chinese" culture, we would also urge readers to study the chapters that concern the periods both before and after that one in which they are primarily interested; such steps will provide some of the context in which to understand the historical dynamic that wove its way throughout this thousand-year period.

The central core of this volume consists of the eight chapters that present the dual, complementary approach of the historian and the archaeologist to the four periods of Shang, Western Zhou, Spring and Autumn, and Warring States. By way of introduction two initial chapters place these detailed studies within their context. The first of these reminds the reader of the long prehistory from which the Neolithic and Bronze ages developed, and of the need to review these early stages in the light of a number of disciplines, such as geophysical science, human genetics, and anthropology. The second is concerned with the nature and growth of the Chinese language and script, the single characteristic element that informed the cultural developments of pre-imperial and imperial ages alike.

Until recently historical interest in the second millennium B.C. focused on the kingdom of Shang and its capital at Anyang 安陽. As the second of China's traditional Three Dynasties, and the first culture for which there is evidence of writing, it is natural that the Shang should receive intense scrutiny. Inscriptions on oracle bones and bronze vessels show that it had well-organized governmental administrations and religious rituals that may well have influenced the institutions of the later dynasties. Its fully developed bronze culture, including the first evidence in China of the horse-drawn chariot, has attracted great archaeological attention throughout the twentieth century. Ongoing excavations at Anyang continue to reveal greater detail about the capital area of this kingdom, and new advances in the study of the oracle-bone inscriptions over the past two decades now allow its historical development to be seen with greater clarity than has heretofore been possible. However, discoveries elsewhere in China now show that other contemporary cultures also deserve great attention. Archaeological sites as far flung as Xin'gan 新淦 in Jiangxi and Guanghan 廣漢 in Sichuan have yielded impressive finds showing some signs of contact with Shang but also being unmistakably distinct. While the absence of textual records from these sites

precludes identifying the names of the peoples who lived there, their existence serves as a forceful reminder that Shang was but one of several contemporary communities. How far these cultures influenced each other and
also how they influenced later cultures in China is just now beginning to
be traced.

In the Chinese tradition, the Western Zhou (1045–771 B.C.), the conqueror
of and successor to Shang as the third of the Three Dynasties, was always
regarded as China's finest and most noble age. In comparison to Shang, it
boasts a richer array of evidence, both textual and artifactual, on which the
historian may call: bronze inscriptions, poetry, speeches by the rulers, as well
as artifacts from sites throughout North China. By weaving all of these
sources together, it is now becoming possible to show just how much has
been left out of the traditional "dynastic cycle" model that focused almost
exclusively on virtuous founders and evil last kings. Political rivalries now
show through the cracks of the monolithic textual tradition, suggesting the
first conflict between royal rule ordained by Heaven and government by
worthy administrators – a conflict that would long beset China's rulers.
Poetry no less than bronze vessels tells the tale of a major reform of ritual
practice that took place ca. 900 B.C., a reform that not only had broad implications for contemporary intellectual and social development, but that would
continue to influence conceptions of social status for many centuries thereafter. Excavations at the capitals of the states of Jin 晉, Guo 虢, Lu 魯, and
Yan 燕, all states established in the eastern part of the Zhou realm to serve
Zhou interests there, are now suggesting how the multistate system of the
Spring and Autumn period (770–481 B.C.) began to develop.

Following the sacking of the Zhou capital in 771 B.C. and the subsequent
flight of the Zhou rulers to their eastern capital at Luoyang 洛陽, there was
no longer any predominant ruler who could command general respect and
loyalties. States that had hitherto maintained allegiance to the Zhou kings
now became fully independent; new leaders seized control of these states and
established new forms of government; men came to be valued for their professional abilities rather than for the circumstances of their birth; and ties of
kinship lost their power within society. There arose a recognition of the need
for some formal relationship between the many states of the day, partially as
a result of new influences from the south. The growth in interstate politics
is reflected also in the archaeological record of the period. Tombs have been
excavated in more widely separated areas than is the case for previous periods,
though their contents – especially ritual bronze vessels – suggest a surprising
degree of cultural uniformity, at least at the elite level. While reflecting a continued respect for social rank, the material culture of the time was by no
means conservative: bronze vessels and other bronze artifacts began to be

made by lost-wax casting in addition to the piece-mold casting used exlu-
sively theretofore; iron was introduced and achieved rather widespread use;
and new artistic motifs covered all types of artifacts. It is perhaps ironic
that an age that traditional Chinese historiography has seen as culturally
disjointed and stagnant should now seem both more uniform and also
progressive.

With the coming of the Warring States (480–221 B.C.) period, fuller and
more varied literary sources now allow the history of the large kingdoms that
formed out of the multistate system of the Spring and Autumn period to be
defined with greater certainty than is possible for earlier periods. The large-
scale interstate wars of the time demanded a more cohesive governmental
administration than ever before, with secure bases of tax income and manpower, while the greatly expanded armies of infantry required professional
officers to train and lead them. Projects for larger-scale public works are also
revealed in the material traces of buildings and walls and in the size and
design of mausoleums, the monumentality of which served to symbolize the
greater power of the states' rulers. This power would culminate in the empire
founded by the state of Qin 秦 (221–207 B.C.).

In addition to its evidence for institutional and cultural history, the
Warring States period provides for the first time broad evidence of the intellectual life of the time, at both the elite and popular levels. The *Analects* (*Lun
yu* 論語) of Confucius 孔子, compiled in the generations after his death (479
B.C.) and the works of Mozi 墨子 (ca. 480–390 B.C.), Mencius 孟子 (ca.
382–300 B.C.), Zhuangzi 莊子 (ca. 365–280 B.C.), Xunzi 荀子 (ca. 310–215
B.C.), as well as those of the other of the "Hundred Schools" of philosophers,
display a rich intertextual discourse showing the best minds of the day con-
versing with each other. This discourse has influenced all subsequent thought
in China, and the story of it is well known to most readers interested in
ancient China. But here too archaeology has made available a new perspective. In recent decades excavators have unearthed records of the popular religion of the time – rites of divination, medical recipes, ghost stories,
astrological almanacs – showing that intellectual exchange was even more
varied than hitherto imagined. But more than this, these new records show
the great extent to which intellectual elites were influenced by these popular
conceptions. Indeed, it was this popular religion, perhaps even more than
any of the philosophical schools, including that associated with the person
of Confucius, that provided the foundation for the intellectual synthesis of
the imperial age.

The volume closes with two chapters that seek, in very different ways, to
define the long duration of ancient Chinese history: one by looking outside
of the Central China plain to the great steppe land that stretches from

Xinjiang in the west through Mongolia to Manchuria in the east to see how other civilizations developed, often in close contact with those of China. The rise of a pastoral way of life in this steppe land contrasts sharply with the agrarian lifestyle adopted throughout China proper. This contrast was apparent already to the people of ancient China (and was marked by them physically by the construction, beginning in the Warring States period, of "great walls" along their northern border) and was instrumental in helping them to define a coherent view of themselves. Whether this coherent self-image was a cause or an effect of the empire created by the state of Qin at the end of the Warring States period, and then consolidated by the subsequent Han dynasty (206 B.C.–A.D. 220) is one of the questions addressed in the final chapter of the volume, which serves too as a bridge to Volume 1 of the *Cambridge History of China: The Ch'in and Han Empires.*

Two themes in particular recur throughout both pre-imperial and imperial times: the interplay between unity and diversity, and the conflict between the ties of kinship and the demands of administrative control. In both of these issues, religious belief and practice took a place of paramount importance.

Although acceptance of a king's right to exercise authority is taken for granted in our primary sources, its practice was often subject to dispute and has been taken as a criterion whereby China should be seen as a single realm or as a land split among a number of units. Long intervals passed between the days of the kings of Shang and Zhou and the claims of the Qin and Han emperors that they were rulers of the single, united empire under the skies. During the centuries of that interval no single one of the kings that had been set up could claim that he stood possessed both of inherited spiritual authority to rule and of sufficient material strength to do so effectively. Only after the passage of several decades were the Han emperors and statesmen ready and able to reassert a claim to be ruling as the Sons of Heaven, in the same way as had the kings of Zhou. Imperial sovereignty drew strength by appealing to the religious tenets of the kings of Zhou, by learning from the experience of the Spring and Autumn period, and by adopting the administrative institutions evolved in the Warring States period.

Recognition of the ties of kinship could and did convey a sense of permanency that outlasted the lives of individuals and prolonged the existence of clan or state. But a conflict could arise between the value of asserting these ties as an integral element of government and a need to override the demands of family solidarity in order to reinforce a government's authority. The distinction reverberates throughout Chinese history. It involved a choice between delegating power to members of a royal or imperial house, in the belief that their loyalties would be ensured, or commissioning talented individuals to perform administrative tasks effectively, on pain of dismissal or punishment. The different solutions that were adopted in the face of this problem in imperial times owed much to the precedents set in the pre-imperial age.

The editors are well aware that it has not been possible to include accounts of all aspects of the history of ancient China in this volume. In some cases research is not sufficiently far advanced to permit a satisfactory statement; owing to other commitments, specialists in some topics may not have been able to accept a commission to describe their findings in the volume, whose size imposes a further limit on what may be included. For these reasons it has not been possible to treat basic questions such as the rise or fall of the population, the impact of plague and other natural disasters, or the way of life at the lower strata of humanity. For other reasons little or no attention has been possible for the advances made in astronomy, mathematics, or for some of the technological achievements of the time, such as ceramics and sericulture, to name but two, which have been of major significance in molding the character of Chinese civilization. Other omissions that will be apparent are due to the nature of the sources at our disposal. The fuller documentation that is available for imperial times permits attempts to take account of some of the personalities who took decisions, to note the controversies that arose over policy, or to observe the moments when the strength of a religious movement was rising or falling; for pre-imperial times it is rare that we can individualize history in this way or put events under a microscope. Orthodox Chinese historiography has tended to concentrate attention on the Yellow River valley; although archaeology has begun to shed new light on the civilizations of the south, it is still not possible to provide a single systematic survey of those developments. Only rarely can it be suggested how a major aspect of human thought or activity developed throughout all the time that is under consideration, and in no more than a few cases can a statement or conclusion rest on statistical considerations.

The editors are confident that future generations of historians will be in a position to repair these omissions, treating social, economic, or institutional problems with full respect to scholarly advances and the wider context in which such specialist studies should be placed. We are also confident that the volume that we are now able to place before the reader represents the variety of life that existed in ancient China and the maturity of the field of scholarship as we approach the close of the twentieth century.

CALENDAR AND CHRONOLOGY

Edward L. Shaughnessy

In ancient China time was a pervasive concern: one of the first responsibilities of a new dynasty was to reform the calendar; the first passage of the *Analects* of Confucius enjoins the reader to put into practice in a "timely" manner the learning that he has; and most historical records are provided with notations of the date, even if the dates are not always as complete as modern historians would like. However, notions of time vary, and those in ancient China were sufficiently different from ours today to call for some preliminary description.

Throughout the thousand-year period under consideration in this volume, time was based in the first place on natural changes: the seasons of the year, the waxing and waning of the moon, and the cycle of days and nights. In addition to these natural periods, there were also divisions based on social changes, the most important of which were the reigns of kings. These various segments of time were woven together into a cycle broken only by the establishment of a new dynasty, which happened only once in this period (at least according to traditional Chinese historiography) – after the Zhou conquest of Shang.

The ancient Chinese day, like ours, was based on the sun, the word for "day" (*ri* 日) in fact being the same word as that for "sun." The day seems to have begun and ended about midnight[1] and to have been subdivided into smaller segments according to the major events of the day, especially meals.[2] Days were enumerated in a recurring cycle of sixty, formed by combining the names of ten "stems" (*gan* 干: *jia* 甲, *yi* 乙, *bing* 丙, *ding* 丁, *wu* 戊, *ji* 己, *geng* 庚, *xin* 辛, *ren* 壬, and *gui* 癸) with twelve "branches" (*zhi* 支: *zi* 子,

---

[1] The earliest sure evidence for midnight being the beginning point of the day does not come until the Han period (206 B.C.–A.D. 220), but there seems to be evidence for it already in the Shang; see H. H. Dubs, "The Date of the Shang Period," *TP* 40 (1951): 332.

[2] For the periods within the day as noted in Shang oracle-bone inscriptions, see Chen Mengjia, *Yinxu buci zongshu* (Beijing: Kexue, 1956), pp. 229–33.

chou 丑, *yin* 寅, *mao* 卯, *chen* 辰, *si* 巳, *wu* 午, *wei* 未, *shen* 申, *you* 酉, *xu* 戌, and *hai* 亥), namely, *jiazi* (day 1), *yichou* (day 2), *bingyin* (day 3), *dingmao* (day 4), and so on through sixty combinations,[3] the ten days of a single *gan* cycle serving as one "week."

The month was correlated with the moon, the word for "month" (*yue* 月) being the same as that for "moon." However, because the mean period of a single lunation is 29.53 days, the length of months regularly alternated between twenty-nine ("short") and thirty ("long") days, with two consecutive long, or thirty-day, months coming about every fifteen months.

The year included twelve months, usually simply numbered with the cardinal numbers (though the first month was often called the "upright" or "correct" month [*zheng yue* 正月]). The choice of which month would be regarded as the first month of the civil year varied in different places and different times: according to tradition, the Xia, Shang, and Zhou dynasties each had their own calendars, the Xia year beginning with the second new moon after the winter solstice, the Shang year beginning with the first new moon after the winter solstice, and the Zhou year beginning with the lunar month that contained the winter solstice. Regardless of the definition of the first month of the year, since the 354 days of twelve lunar months were appreciably fewer than the $365^1/_4$ days of the solar or tropical year, it was necessary roughly every third year to add an extra "intercalary" month (*run yue* 潤月). While the earliest Shang oracle-bone inscriptions indicate that this intercalary month was added as a "thirteenth" month at the end of the year, by the end of that dynasty and throughout the Zhou period intercalary months seem to have been interpolated into the year after any month that had drifted thirty days out of its proper placement in the tropical year. Various modern almanacs offer correlations between the lunisolar years of ancient China and the tropical year;[4] while there is no contemporary evidence to attest to their accuracy (and this is especially true of their schedule of intercalary months), it is unlikely that any actual civil calendar strayed too far from the ideal that these almanacs portray. Nevertheless, it should always be borne in mind that there is no exact equivalence in these almanacs between the lunisolar years of ancient China and the solar years to which they are correlated.

In addition to these natural divisions of time, civil time was also enumerated according to the year of the king's reign with notations such as "it was the king's thirteenth year." Two factors detract from the usefulness of these notations. First, the king was usually not named (even the titles by

---

[3] Only one-half of the possible combinations of these cycles of ten and twelve were used; thus, there is no day *jiachou* 甲丑 or *yiyin* 乙寅, for example.

[4] For the two most recent such almanacs, see Dong Zuobin, *Zhongguo nianli zongpu* (Hong Kong: Hong Kong University Press, 1960); Zhang Peiyu, *Zhongguo xian Qin shi libiao* (Jinan: Qi Lu, 1987).

which kings are known to history having been posthumously bestowed).[5] Second, while there is little question about the royal succession of the Shang and Zhou kings (or the rulers of the various Eastern Zhou states),[6] for nearly half of the period covered by this volume there is no agreement as to how long individual reigns lasted. The year 842 B.C. is the earliest commonly accepted "absolute" date in Chinese history. According to the *Shi ji* 史記 of Sima Qian 司馬遷 (ca. 145–86 B.C.), it was in this year that King Li of Zhou 周厲王 (r. 857–828, according to the chronology used in this book) was forced to vacate the Zhou capital near present-day Xi'an 西安 and go into exile at Zhi 彘 (in present-day Shanxi province); it is this event that the *Shi ji* uses as a touchstone for the genealogies (*shi jia* 世家) of the various local lineages that were then developing into what would be the independent states of the Eastern Zhou period (e.g., Qi 齊, Jin 晉, Qin 秦). With only relatively minor exceptions, dates of reign for the Zhou kings and the rulers of the major states after 842 appear to be correct as given in the "Shier zhuhou nianbiao" 十二諸侯年表 (Chronology of the rulers of the twelve states) and the "Liu guo nianbiao" 六國年表 (Chronology of the six states) chapters of the *Shi ji* (*juan* 14 and 15, respectively), and those mistakes that are apparent can often be corrected by comparison with the *Zhushu jinian* 竹書紀年 (Bamboo annals).

There are certain errors in the *Shi ji*'s chronology of the states of Wei 魏 and Qi in the fourth century B.C. that have significant implications for Warring States intellectual history, especially for the dating of the *Mencius*. These errors can be traced to unusual circumstances in the states' regnal calendars. For instance, with respect to the state of Wei, the *Shi ji* indicates reigns of thirty-six years for King Hui 惠 (370–335 B.C.), sixteen years for King Xiang 襄 (334–319 B.C.), and twenty-three more years for a King Ai 哀 (318–296 B.C.). In fact, there was no King Ai (though the term "Ai" may have been part of the reign name of King Xiang; i.e., King Ai Xiang). It is clear that this error stems from King Hui's having declared a new first year of reign in the thirty-sixth year after his initial accession (334 B.C., his first year of reign thus being 369 and not 370 B.C., as given in the *Shi ji*), after which he – and not King Xiang – reigned for sixteen more years (until 319 B.C.). It was not until 318 B.C. that King Xiang succeeded to power. One reason why this is important is because the *Mencius* relates conversations between Mencius and King Hui (referred to there as King Hui of Liang 梁, Liang being the

---

[5] This is surely the case from the middle of the Western Zhou on, though there is some evidence that reign titles were used during the lives of Zhou kings up until that point.

[6] For discussion of whether the Shang king Lin Xin 廩辛 (r. 1157–1149 B.C., according to the chronology adopted in this volume) reigned or not, see David N. Keightley, *Sources of Shang History: The Oracle-Bone Inscriptions of Bronze Age China* (Berkeley: University of California Press, 1978), p. 187, n. h; for discussion of questions about royal successions in the Warring States period, see below.

capital of Wei); according to the *Shi ji* chronology these conversations would have had to have taken place no later than 335 B.C., but in actuality they could have taken place – and doubtless did – as late as 319 B.C.

In a similar fashion, the *Shi ji* chronology for the state of Qi has King Wei 威 reigning from 378 to 343 B.C., King Xuan 宣 from 342 to 324, and King Min 湣 from 323 to 284, even though events in the reign of King Xuan, another of the rulers with whom Mencius had audience, certainly took place in 314 B.C. This confusion is due in the first place to the *Shi ji*'s failure to recognize the (illegitimate) reign of Tian Hou Yan 田侯剡 (383–375 B.C.), which for five years ran concurrently with the reign of Qi Kang Gong 齊康公 (404–379 B.C.), the last of the Qi rulers from the original ruling Jiang 姜 family. This confusion led to other errors, eventually producing a twenty-three-year error in the dates of reign for King Xuan (whose dates of reign are actually 319–301 B.C.).[7]

For the period before 842 B.C., the *Shi ji* does not provide fixed dates. This is not to say that there are no sources available for the dates of this earlier period; rather, Sima Qian was obviously confused by the sources – many apparently contradictory – that were available to him. Many other historians in the last two thousand years have attempted to make sense of those sources, sometimes using new evidence that was not available to Sima Qian. Of this new evidence, three types have been particularly important:

1.   The *Zhushu jinian*, an annalistic account of Chinese history through 299 B.C. This text was buried in the tomb of King Xiang of Wei in 296 B.C. and was then brought to light only when that tomb was plundered in A.D. 279.[8] Since its discovery, this text has been used both to correct mistakes in the *Shi ji* and also as the basis for reconstructing chronology before 842 B.C.[9]

2.   Bronze inscriptions from the Western Zhou period (1045–771 B.C., accord-

---

[7] For a full discussion of these and other errors in the *Shi ji*'s chronology of the Warring States period and how they can be corrected using the *Zhushu jinian*, see Yang Kuan, *Zhanguo shi* (Shanghai: Shanghai Renmin, 1955), pp. 273–80; see too D. C. Lau, *Mencius: Translated with an Introduction* (Harmondsworth: Penguin, 1970), pp. 205–6; Henri Maspero, "La chronologie des rois de Ts'i au Ive siècle avant notre ère," *TP* 25 (1928): 367–86; Jeffrey K. Riegel, "Ju-tzu Hsi 孺子瘊 and the Genealogy of the House of Wei 魏," *EC* 3 (1977): 46–51.

[8] For the *Zhushu jinian*, see Loewe, ed., *Early Chinese Texts: A Bibliographical Guide* (Berkeley: Society for the Study of Early China and the Institute of East Asian Studies, University of California, 1993), pp. 39–47.

[9] For the earliest attempt to use the *Zhushu jinian* to correct earlier chronologies, see the *Jin shu* 晉書 (History of the Jin dynasty) biography of Shu Xi 束皙, one of the persons responsible for putting in order the strips on which these annals were originally written (*Jin shu*, 51, p. 1432). An early attempt to use the *Zhushu jinian* as the basis for a systematic chronology of ancient China appears to be a *Di wang nianli* 帝王年曆, compiled by Tao Hongjing 陶弘景 (456–536), the famous Daoist pharmacologist; although this work is no longer extant, it is described in the Tang period *Yun ji qi qian* 雲笈七籤 (*j.* 107).

ing to the chronology adopted in this book), including especially inscriptions that contain a complete date notation: that is, the year of reign (the reigning king, however, usually being unspecified); the month (for which, see above); the phase of the moon [denoted in four quarters, each about seven or eight days in length: *chuji* 初吉 (first auspiciousness), from the new moon until the waxing half moon, roughly the first seven days of a lunar month; *jishengpo* 既生霸 (after the growing brightness), from the waxing half moon until the full moon; *jiwang* 既望 (after the full moon), from the full moon until the waning half moon; and *jisipo* 既死霸 (after the dying brightness) from the waning half moon until the disappearance of the moon again]; and the day in the Chinese cycle of sixty *ganzhi*. These inscriptions have been the most important sources for most recent attempts to reconstruct this earlier chronology.[10]

3. Records of astronomical phenomena, including lunar and solar eclipses and also conjunctions of the five visible planets.[11]

While no chronological reconstruction has yet achieved general acceptance, all three of these types of evidence, as well as the evidence preserved in the *Shi ji* and other early sources, do suggest that the date of the Zhou conquest of Shang – the pivotal date in ancient Chinese history – must be slightly later than 1050 B.C.; for the purposes of this volume, we give the year of the Zhou conquest as 1045 B.C.[12] Lengths of reign for Zhou kings from King Wu 周武王 (r. 1049/45–1043 B.C.) through King Li can then be deduced on the basis of dated bronze inscriptions and other evidence, one such deduction being given in Table 1. In this volume, references to Shang and Western Zhou kings will also include these dates for their reigns, but they are intended primarily as a convenience to the reader and should be regarded as provisional.

Dates for the nine Shang kings from whose reigns we have written records,

[10] For a recent overview of this question, including both an attempt to reconstruct the chronology of the Western Zhou and a tabulation of sixteen other recent attempts, see Edward L. Shaughnessy, *Sources of Western Zhou History: Inscribed Bronze Vessels* (Berkeley: University of California Press, 1991), esp. pp. 237–8.

[11] For notations of five lunar eclipses in oracle-bone inscriptions from the reign of Shang king Wu Ding, see Dubs, "The Date of the Shang Period." For the date of a solar eclipse in the reign of King Yih of Western Zhou, see Fang Shanzhu, "Xi Zhou niandai xue shang de jige wenti," *Dalu zazhi* 51, 1 (1975): 15–23. And for records of a conjunction of the five visible planets in 1059 B.C., see David W. Pankenier, "Astronomical Dates in Shang and Western Zhou," *EC* 7 (1981–2): 2–37.

[12] This date was first suggested in David S. Nivison, "The Dates of Western Chou," *HJAS* 43, 2 (1983): 481–580. Although Nivison subsequently repudiated his own conclusion, arguing for 1040 B.C. as the date of the Zhou conquest (David S. Nivison, "1040 as the Date of the Chou Conquest," *EC* 8 [1982–3]: 76–8), Shaughnessy later accepted the date with some elaboration (*Sources of Western Zhou History*, 217–87). Since then it has been accepted in a growing number of publications (see, e.g., *Beijing wenbo* 1995.1, with articles stemming from a conference held in 1995 commemorating the 3040th anniversary of the founding of the city of Beijing [supposing the founding of the city to have been in the same year as the Zhou conquest]).

especially oracle-bone inscriptions, can be similarly deduced. Especially useful in this regard are records of five different lunar eclipses among the inscriptions of the Bin 賓 group of diviners (i.e., from the reign of King Wu Ding 武丁 [d. 1189 B.C.] and probably also that of King Zu Geng 祖庚 [1188–1178 B.C.]). Correlations of dates that are expressed in terms of "stem" and "branch" (*ganzhi*) for these eclipses and canons of eclipses visible in the vicinity of Anyang, the Shang capital, suggest that the reign of King Wu Ding probably included the years 1198–1189 B.C., and that the end of his reign must have been near the last of these years.[13] In this book, lengths of generations for the following six reigns (two generations of which include two reigns apiece, since the Shang generally observed fraternal succession) are estimated at about thirty years, giving the estimated reign dates in Table 1. Dates for the reigns of kings Di Yi (1106–1087 B.C.) and Di Xin (1086–1046 B.C.), the last two kings of Shang, can be deduced from the date of the Zhou conquest of Shang, annals recorded in the *Zhushu jinian*, and year notations in Shang bronze inscriptions and late (Huang 黃 Group) oracle-bone inscriptions.[14] It cannot be stressed too much that these dates are provisional and will almost surely be subject to revision as new data become available.

---

[13] See Dubs, "The Date of the Shang Period"; David N. Keightley, "Shang China Is Coming of Age," *JAS* 41 (1982): 549–57; and Fan Yuzhou, "Jiaguwen yueshi jishi keci kaobian," *Jiaguwen yu Yin Shang shi* 2 (1986): 310–37.

[14] For a more detailed discussion of this chronology, see Table 4.1.

Table 1. *Reign dates*

(a) Shang*

Wu Ding	武丁	?–1189
Zu Geng	祖庚	1188–1178
Zu Jia	祖甲	1177–1158
Lin Xin	廩辛	1157–1149
Kang Ding	康丁	1148–1132
Wu Yi	武乙	1131–1117
Wen Wu Ding	文武丁	1116–1106
Di Yi	帝乙	1105–1087
Di Xin	帝辛	1086–1045

(b) Western Zhou

King Wen	文王	1099/56–1050
King Wu	武王	1049/45–1043
Duke of Zhou	周公	1042–1036
King Cheng	成王	1042/35–1006
King Kang	康王	1005/3–978
King Zhao	昭王	977/75–957
King Mu	穆王	956–918
King Gong	共王	917/15–900
King Yih	懿王	899/97–873
King Xiao	孝王	872?–866
King Yi	夷王	865–858
King Li	厲王	857/53–842/28
Gong He	共和	841–828
King Xuan	宣王	827/25–782
King You	幽王	781–771

*All years are B.C.

25

Table 1. *(cont.)*

(c) Spring and Autumn

ZHOU 周	LU 魯	QI 齊	JIN 晉	QIN 秦	CHU 楚	SONG 宋	WEY 衛	ZHENG 鄭	YAN 燕	WU 吳
770–720 Ping Wang 平王	796–769 Xiao Gong 孝公	794–731 Zhuang Gong 莊公	780–746 Wen Hou 文侯	777–766 Xiang Gong 襄公	790–764 Ruo Ao 若敖	799–766 Dai Gong 戴公	812–758 Wu Gong 武公	806–771 Huan Gong 桓公	790–767 Qing Hou 頃侯	
720–697 Huan Wang 桓王	768–723 Hui Gong 惠公	730–698 Xi Gong 僖公	745–740 Zhao Hou 昭侯	765–716 Wen Gong 文公	763–758 Xiao Ao 霄敖	765–748 Wu Gong 武公	757–735 Zhuang Gong 莊公	770–744 Wu Gong 武公	766–765 Ai Hou 哀侯	
696–682 Zhuang Wang 莊王	722–712 Yin Gong 隱公	697–686 Xiang Gong 襄公	739–724 Xiao Hou 孝侯	715–704 Ning Gong 寧公	757–741 Fen Mao 蚡冒	747–729 Xuan Gong 宣公	734–719 Huan Gong 桓公	743–701 Zhuang Gong 莊公	764–729 Zheng Hou 鄭侯	
681–677 Xi Wang 僖王	711–694 Huan Gong 桓公	685–643 Huan Gong 桓公	723–718 E Hou 鄂侯	703–698 Chu Gong 出公	740–690 Wu Wang 武王	728–720 Mu Gong 穆公	718–700 Xuan Gong 宣公	700–697 Li Gong 厲公	728–711 Mu Hou 穆侯	
676–652 Hui Wang 惠王	693–662 Zhuang Gong 莊公	642–633 Xiao Gong 孝公	717–710 Ai Hou 哀侯	697–678 Wu Gong 武公	689–677 Wen Wang 文王	719–711 Shang Gong 殤公	699–669 Hui Gong 惠公	696–695 Zhao Gong 昭公	710–698 Xuan Hou 宣侯	
								694 Zi Wei 子亹		
651–619 Xiang Wang 襄王	661–660 Min Gong 閔公	632–613 Zhao Gong 昭公	709–707 Xiaozi 小子	677–676 De Gong 德公	676–675 Du Ao 堵敖	710–692 Feng 馮	668–661 Yi Gong 懿公	693–680 Zi Yi 子儀	697–691 Huan Hou 桓侯	
618–613 Qing Wang 頃王	659–627 Xi Gong 僖公	612–609 Yi Gong 懿公	706–679 Jin Hou Min 晉侯緡	675–664 Xuan Gong 宣公	674–626 Cheng Wang 成王	691–682 Min Gong 閔公	660 Dai Gong 戴公	679–673 Li Gong 厲公	690–658 Zhuang Gong 莊公	
612–607 Kuang Wang 匡王	626–609 Wen Gong 文公	608–599 Hui Gong 惠公	678–677 Wu Gong 武公	663–660 Cheng Gong 成公	625–614 Mu Wang 穆王	681–651 Huan Gong 桓公	659–635 Wen Gong 文公	672–628 Wen Gong 文公	657–618 Xiang Gong 襄公	
606–586 Ding Wang 定王	608–591 Xuan Gong 宣公	598–582 Qing Gong 頃公	676–651 Xian Gong 獻公	659–621 Mu Gong 穆公	613–591 Zhuang Wang 莊王	650–637 Xiang Gong 襄公	634–600 Cheng Gong 成公	627–606 Mu Gong 穆公	617–602 Huan Gong 桓公	
585–572 Jian Wang 簡王	590–573 Cheng Gong 成公	581–554 Ling Gong 靈公	650–637 Hui Gong 惠公	620–609 Kang Gong 康公	590–560 Gong Wang 共王	636–620 Cheng Gong 成公	599–589 Mu Gong 穆公		601–587 Xuan Gong 宣公	585–561 Shou Meng 壽夢

ZHOU 周	LU 魯	QI 齊	JIN 晉	QIN 秦	CHU 楚	SONG 宋	WEY 衛	ZHENG 鄭	YAN 燕	WU 吳
Ling Wang 靈王 571~545	Xiang Gong 襄公 572~542	Zhuang Gong 莊公 553~548	Wen Gong 文公 636~628	Gong Gong 共公 608~604	Kang Wang 康王 559~545	Zhao Gong 昭公 619~611	Ding Gong 定公 588~577	Ling Gong 靈公 605	Zhao Gong 昭公 586~574	Zhu Fan 諸樊 560~548
Jing Wang 景王 544~520	Zhao Gong 昭公 541~510	Jing Gong 景公 547~490	Xiang Gong 襄公 627~621	Huan Gong 桓公 603~577	Jia Ao 郟敖 544~541	Wen Gong 文公 610~589	Xian Gong 獻公 576~559	Xiang Gong 襄公 604~587	Wu Gong 武公 573~555	Yu Ji 餘祭 547~544
Jing Wang 敬王 519~476	Ding Gong 定公 509~495	Yan Ruzi 晏孺子 489	Ling Gong 靈公 620~607	Jing Gong 景公 576~537	Ling Wang 靈王 540~529	Gong Gong 共公 588~576	Shang Gong 殤公 558~547	Dao Gong 悼公 586~585	Wen Gong 文公 554~549	Yi Mei 夷眛 543~527
	Ai Gong 哀公 494~477	Dao Gong 悼公 488~485	Cheng Gong 成公 606~600	Ai Gong 哀公 536~501	Ping Wang 平王 528~516	Ping Gong 平公 575~532	Xian Gong 獻公 546~544	Cheng Gong 成公 584~571	Yi Gong 懿公 548~545	Liao 僚 526~515
		Jian Gong 簡公 484~481	Jing Gong 景公 599~581	Hui Gong 惠公 500~491	Zhao Wang 昭王 515~489	Yuan Gong 元公 531~517	Xiang Gong 襄公 543~535	Xi Gong 僖公 570~565	Hui Gong 惠公 544~536	He Lü 闔閭 514~496
		Ping Gong 平公 480~456	Li Gong 厲公 580~573	Dao Gong 悼公 490~477	Hui Wang 惠王 488~432	Jing Gong 景公 516~477	Ling Gong 靈公 534~493	Jian Gong 簡公 564~530	Dao Gong 悼公 535~529	Fu Chai 夫差 495~477
			Dao Gong 悼公 572~558				Chu Gong 出公 492~481	Ding Gong 定公 529~514	Gong Gong 共公 528~524	
			Ping Gong 平公 557~532				Zhuang Gong 莊公 480~478	Xian Gong 獻公 513~501	Ping Gong 平公 523~505	
			Zhao Gong 昭公 531~526					Sheng Gong 聲公 500~477	Jian Gong 簡公 504~493	
			Qing Gong 頃公 525~512						Xian Gong 獻公 492~465	
			Ding Gong 定公 511~475							

Table 1. (cont.)
(d) Warring States

ZHOU 周	QIN 秦	JIN 晉	WEI 魏	HANN 韓	ZHAO 趙	CHU 楚	JIANG QI 姜齊	TIAN QI 田齊	YAN 燕
Jing Wang 敬王 519–476	Dao Gong 悼公 490–477	Ding Gong 定公 511–475				Hui Wang 惠王 488–432	Ping Gong 平公 481–456		Xiao Gong 孝公 497–455
Yuan Wang 元王 475–469	Ligong Gong 厲共公 476–443	Chu Gong 出公 474–450			Xiangzi 襄子				Cheng Gong 成公 454–439
Zhending Wang 貞定王 468–441	Zao Gong 躁公 442–429	Jing Gong 敬公 451–434	Wen Hou 文侯 445–396		Huanzi 桓子 475–425	Jian Wang 簡王 431–408	Xuan Gong 宣公 455–405		Min Gong 閔公 438–415
Kao Wang 考王 440–426	Huai Gong 懷公 428–425	You Gong 幽公 433–416		Wu Hou 武侯 424–409	424				
Weilie Wang 威烈王 425–402	Ling Gong 靈公 424–415	Lie Gong 烈公 415–389		Jing Hou 景侯 408–400	Xian Hou 獻侯 423–409	Sheng Wang 聲王 407–402	Kang Gong 康公 404–379	Daozi 悼子	Jian Gong 簡公 414–370
An Wang 安王 401–376	Jian Gong 簡公 414–400	Huan Gong 桓公 388–369	Wu Hou 武侯 395–370	Lie Hou 烈侯 399–387	Lie Hou 烈侯 408–387	Dao Wang 悼王 401–381		He Hou 和侯 410–405	
	Hui Gong 惠公 399–387			Wen Hou 文侯 386–377	Jing Hou 敬侯 386–375	Su Wang 肅王 380–370		Hou Yan 侯剡 404–384	
Lie Wang 烈王 375–369	Chuzi 出子 386–385		Hui Hou 惠侯 369–345	Ai Hou 哀侯 376–375	Cheng Hou 成侯 374–350	Xuan Wang 宣王 369–340		Huan Gong 桓公 383–375	Huan Gong 桓公 369–362
	Xian Gong 獻公 384–362			Yi Hou 懿侯 374–363				Wei Hou 威侯 374–357	Wen Gong 文公 361–337
								356–335	

ZHOU 周	QIN 秦	JIN 晉	WEI 魏	HANN 韓	ZHAO 趙	CHU 楚	JIANG QI 姜齊	TIAN QI 田齊	YAN 燕
Xian Wang 顯王 368–321	Xiao Gong 孝公 361–338		Hui Wang 惠王 344/34–319	Zhao Hou 昭侯 362–333	Su Hou 肅侯 349–326	Wei Wang 威王 339–329		Wei Wang 威王 334–320	Yi Wang 易王 332–321
	Huiwen Wang 惠文王 337/24–311			Xuanhui Wang 宣惠王 332–312	Wuling Wang 武靈王 325–299	Huai Wang 懷王 328–299		Xuan Wang 宣王 319–301	Wang Kuai 王噲 320–312
Shenjing Wang 慎覯王 320–315			Xiang Wang 襄王 318–296	Xiang Wang 襄王 311–296					Zhao Wang 昭王 311–279
Nan Wang 赧王 314–256	Wu Wang 武王 310–307				Huiwen Wang 惠文王 298–266	Qingxiang Wang 頃襄王 298–263		Min Wang 湣王 300–284	
	Zhao Wang 昭王 306–251		Zhao Wang 昭王 295–277	Xi Wang 釐王 295–273				Xiang Wang 襄王 283–265	Hui Wang 惠王 278–272
			Anxi Wang 安釐王 276–243	Huanhui Wang 桓惠王 272–239	Xiaocheng Wang 孝成王 265–245	Xiaolie Wang 孝烈王 262–238		Wang Jian 王建 264–221	Wuxiao Wang 武孝王 271–258
									Xiao Wang 孝王 257–255
Dongzhou Jun 東周君 255–249	Xiaowen Wang 孝文王 250		Jingmin Wang 景湣王 242–228	Wang An 王安 238–230	Daoxiang Wang 悼襄王 244–236	You Wang 幽王 237–228			Wang Xi 王喜 254–222
	Zhuangxiang Wang 莊襄王 249–247				Wang Qian 王遷 235–228				
	Zheng Wang 正王 246–221		Wang Jia 王假 227–225		Daiwang Jia 代王嘉 227–222	Wang Fuchu 王負芻 227–223			

Sources: For Shang dates, see Table 4.1, this volume; Western Zhou dates are as given in Edward L. Shaughnessy, *Sources of Western Zhou History: Inscribed Bronze Vessels* (Berkeley: University of California Press, 1991). Appendix 3. Spring and Autumn dates are adapted, with some revisions, from Rong Mengyuan, *Zhongguo lishi jinian* (Beijing: Sanlian, 1956), pp. 126–48. Warring States dates are adapted from Yang Kuan, *Zhanguo shi* (Shanghai: Shanghai Renmin, 1955), pp. 247–72.

THE ENVIRONMENT OF ANCIENT CHINA

David N. Keightley

Many aspects of early Chinese history were affected, if not determined, by the Neolithic and Bronze Age environment, whose evolving climate and landscape influenced a series of cultural decisions at the regional level, involving such matters as hunting, diet, health, housing, clothing, exchange, and the development of agriculture. Reconstruction of the early environment provides fresh ways to understand the origins and character of ancient Chinese civilization.

GEOGRAPHY

The Coastline

During the drier and colder period of the Last Glacial Maximum (ca. 18000–15000 B.C.), the sea level had fallen radically, exposing much of the continental shelf of East China, so that the coast lay anywhere from 200 to 1,000 km to the east of its present location, with Japan, Taiwan, and Hainan Island all linked to the mainland. Following the end of the glaciation (ca. 13000 B.C.), however, the sea level rose rapidly. In North China, it reached, with occasional fluctuations, its highest point between 4000 and 3000 B.C., when it was 5–10 m higher than at present; in the Yangzi 揚子 delta, by contrast, the maximum transgression had, due to local tectonic movements, taken place ca. 5500 B.C. After further fluctuations, the coastline came to approximate its present position toward the end of the Former Han dynasty in A.D. 9.[1]

[1] Shi Yafeng and Wang Jingtai, "The Fluctuations of Climate, Glaciers, and Sea Level Since Late Pleistocene in China," in *Sea Level, Ice, and Climatic Change*, ed. I. Allison (Washington, D.C.: International Association of Hydrological Sciences, 1981; Publication no. 131), pp. 281, 287, 292; Kwang-chih Chang, *The Archaeology of Ancient China*, 4th ed. (New Haven, Conn: Yale University Press, 1986), pp. 72, 73, fig. 35; Yang Huaijen, Chen Xiqing, and Xie Zhiren, "Sea Level Changes Since the Last Deglaciation and Their Impact on the East China Lowlands," in *The Palaeoenvironment of East Asia from the*

The changes in sea level affected the habitation sites and subsistence patterns of a large number of Neolithic coastal cultures. To the northeast, the Liaodong shore experienced marine transgressions that, ca. 2000–1000 B.C., appear to have forced the Neolithic coastal inhabitants to move inland to higher ground.[2] Further south, the Bo Hai 渤海 coastline, ca. 5000–4000 B.C., lay as much as 100 km west of its present location, with many large lakes, some linked to the sea, forming in the depressed area, which is still filled with lakes and marshes, some 110 km south of modern Beijing.[3] The coastline to the south of Shandong also experienced periods of marine transgression and regression.[4]

Still further to the south, much of the land around Hangzhou Bay (Hangzhou wan 杭州灣) emerged from the sea after 5000 B.C. to form a plain filled with numerous lakes; notable Neolithic sites, like those of Songze 崧澤 and Jiaxing 嘉興, appear to have been located on what had once been a large island, with the mainland coast lying some distance to the west in the vicinity of modern Hangzhou. The waters of Lake Tai (Tai hu 太湖) connected at many places with the sea and reflected, accordingly, the changes in sea level, with the period from 3000 to 2500 B.C. witnessing the greatest spread of the lakes and marshes.[5]

The Major Rivers

The impact of rising sea levels on the North China coast was mitigated by the riverine transfer of eolian loess from the northwest regions. Initially

Mid-Tertiary: Proceedings of the Second Conference. Vol. 1: Geology, Sea Level Changes, Palaeoclimatology and Palaeobotany, ed. Pauline Whyte et al. (Hong Kong: Center of Asian Studies, University of Hong Kong, 1988), p. 366, fig. 4; An Zhisheng et al., "Changes in the Monsoon and Associated Environmental Changes in China Since the Last Interglacial," in *Loess, Environment and Global Change (The Series of the XIII Inqua Congress)*, ed. Tungsheng Liu (Beijing: Science Press, 1991), pp. 13, 24; Marjorie G. Winkler and Pao K. Wang, "The Late Quaternary Vegetation and Climate of China," in *Global Climates Since the Last Glacial Maximum*, ed. H. E. Wright, Jr. et al. (Minneapolis: University of Minnesota Press, 1993), pp. 234, 247.

[2] Xu Yu-lin, "The Houwa Site and Related Issues," in *The Archaeology of Northeast China: Beyond the Great Wall*, ed. Sarah Milledge Nelson (London: Routledge, 1994), pp. 86–7.

[3] Xing Jiaming, "The Relationship Between Environment Changes and Human Activities Since Late Quaternary in North China," in *The Palaeoenvironment of East Asia from the Mid-Tertiary: Proceedings of the Second Conference. Volume 2: Oceanography, Palaeozoology and Palaeoanthropology*, ed. coordinator, Pauline Whyte (Hong Kong: Center of Asian Studies, University of Hong Kong, 1988), p. 1080; Winkler and Wang, "The Late Quaternary Vegetation and Climate of China," p. 234.

[4] For a map, see Wang Pinxian, Min Qiubao, Bian Yunhua, and Cheng Xinrong, "Wo guo dongbu disiji haiqin diceng de chubu yanjiu," *Dizhi xuebao* 1981.1: 8; Chang, *The Archaeology of Ancient China*, pp. 72, 73 (map); Huang Yukun and Chen Jiajie, "Sea Level Changes Along the Coast of the South China Sea Since Late Pleistocene," in *Geology, Sea Level Changes, Palaeoclimatology and Palaeobotany*, ed. Pauline Whyte et al., pp. 289–318.

[5] Shi Yafeng and Wang Jingtai, "The Fluctuations of Climate, Glaciers, and Sea Level," pp. 281, 287, 292; Wu Weitang, "Cong xinshiqi shidai wenhua yizhi kan Hangzhou wan liang an de quanxinshi gu dili," *Dili xuebao* 38, 2 (1983): 113–27.

deposited by the winter winds sweeping off the Mongolian steppe, and subsequently transported as sediment by the Yellow River (Huang Ho 黃河), the
alluvial loess, deposited in the plain and delta region, served to extend the
shoreline into the Bo Hai. Starting about 4000 B.C., the Yellow River delta
expanded eastward in a series of stages as the rate of sedimentation exceeded
the rate at which the sea level had been rising.[6] The muddiness of this great
watercourse, originally known simply as Ho 河, "River," had been explicitly
noted in Eastern Zhou texts, and its silt content had earned it the name of
"Yellow" by Han times.[7] The Yangzi – first known as the Jiang 江, "River"
(on the Austroasiatic origins of this word, see p. 82 below), and, by Han
times, as Chang Jiang 長江, "Long River" – also flowed through a loessic
plain. It too gradually extended its flood plain into the Yellow Sea (Huang
Hai 黃海), but the continuing subsidence of the Lower Yangzi Plain slowed
the extent of the delta's buildup.[8]

The Yellow River shifted its main course in the North China plain at least
twice during Neolithic times.[9] For much of the period, the river, making its
turn in the vicinity of Zhengzhou 鄭州, flowed northeast through modern
Hebei, running north of the Shandong Massif and pouring into the Bo Hai.
In about 2600 B.C., however, the river shifted to the southeast, flowing into
the Huai 淮 River drainage through eastern Henan, northern Anhui, and
northern Jiangsu on its way to the Yellow Sea. Then, in ca. 2000 B.C., it
returned to its former, northeastern route, roughly the route that it follows
today.[10] These cataclysmic events would have disrupted or destroyed the lives
of the Neolithic inhabitants as the thick beds of Yellow River silt, which have
concealed many Neolithic and Bronze Age sites from the eyes of modern
archaeologists, flattened out the landscape. It is likely, moreover, that the
shifting of the river, coupled with changes in climate, influenced both

---

[6] Li Cong-xian, Li Ping, and Wang Li, "Postglacial Marine Beds in the Coastal and Deltaic Areas in
East China," in *Quaternary Geology and Environment of China*, ed. in chief, Liu Tung-sheng (Beijing:
China Ocean Press; and Berlin: Springer, 1985), p. 32.

[7] Qu Wanli, "He zi yiyi de yanbian," *BIHP* 30 (1959): 143–55; Li Xingjian, "Ye shuo jiang he – cong
jiang he hanyi de bianhua kan ciyi de fazhan he ciyu de xunshi," *Yuyanxue luncong* 14 (1987): 70–4.

[8] Wu Weitang, "Cong xinshiqi shidai wenhua yizhi kan Hangzhou wan," 118, fig. 2, 120, fig. 3, 122; You
Lian-yuan, "Characteristics and Evolution of the Longitudinal Profiles in the Middle and Lower
Reaches of the Changjiang (Yangtze) River Since Late Pleistocene," in *Quaternary Geology and Envi-
ronment of China*, ed. in chief Liu Tung-sheng, p. 267; Nie Gaozhong and He Deming, "A New Expla-
nation Regarding the Provenances of Materials of China's Xiashu Loess," in *Loess, Environment and
Global Change*, ed. Liu Tung-sheng, pp. 213–27.

[9] For the changing courses of the Yellow River and the expansion of the Bo Hai and Yellow Sea coast-
lines in protohistoric and historic times, see Joseph Needham, with the research assistance of Wang
Ling and Lu Gwei-djen, *Science and Civilisation in China. Vol. 4: Physics and Physical Technology. Part
3: Civil Engineering and Nautics* (Cambridge University Press, 1971), fig. 859 and p. 242, table 69; Caroline Blunden and Mark Elvin, *Cultural Atlas of China* (New York: Facts on File, 1983), p. 16.

[10] Wang Qing, "Shilun shiqian Huanghe xiayou de gaidao yu gu wenhua de fazhan," *Zhongyuan wenwu*
1993.4: 63–72; Liu Li, "Settlement Patterns, Chiefdom Variability, and the Development of Early States
in North China," *Journal of Anthropological Archaeology* 15 (1996): 243, 245.

Neolithic settlement patterns and cultural developments, with the Yellow River and its various shifts in course serving to facilitate or hamper cultural interaction between, say, Dawenkou 大汶口 sites in Shandong and Yangshao 仰韶 sites in the Central Plain. The memory of these early inundations may have been preserved in later legends about the labors of Yu 禹, the sage-emperor and founder of the Xia 夏 dynasty, who is reputed to have cleared away the floods, making the north China plain habitable.[11] Further to the west, shifts in the courses of the Wei 渭 River and its tributaries have also left archaeological traces; so have the floods that inundated some Neolithic settlements in the upper reaches of the Han 漢 River.[12]

CLIMATE AND ENVIRONMENT

Initial reconstructions – based upon palynological and archaeological evidence – generally tell confirming stories of a paleoclimate that after the coldness and dryness of the last glacial maximum, gradually grew warmer and wetter, with the period from ca. 6000 to 1000 B.C. being the warmest and wettest in the last 18,000 years. It is no coincidence that the inhabitants of Neolithic China were able to expand their settlement range and develop their cultures during this Holocene Climatic Optimum (ca. 7500–3000 B.C.). After that period, the climate underwent, with fluctuations, a gradual drying and cooling that, consistent with changes in the contemporary global climate, has continued until modern times.[13] The environmental history of the Late Holocene in China involves the gradual southward retreat of the subtropical flora and fauna that had flourished in north China in earlier times.

In the northeast, for example, palynological studies in southern Liaoning indicate that between ca. 8300 and 6000 B.C., the climate had been both drier and colder, by some 6 °C, than it is today; the forests were mainly of birch, with some elm, oak, and pine. The climate grew considerably warmer by ca. 6000 to 5000 B.C., with oak and alder abundant in the forests, birch

---

[11] Shi Nianhai, *He shan ji*, vol. 2 (Beijing: Sanlian, 1981), pp. 63–77; Wu Hung, "The Art of Xuzhou: A Regional Approach," *Orientations* 21, 10 (1990): 40–5; Tang Lingyu, Li Minchang, and Shen Caiming, "Jiangsu Huai bei diqu xinshiqi shidai renlei wenhua yu huanjing," in *Huanjing kaogu yanjiu*, ed. Zhou Kunshu and Gong Qiming (Beijing: Kexue, 1991), pp. 164–72; Wang Qing, "Shilun shiqian Huanghe xiayou," pp. 64–9; Cao Bingwu, "Henan Huixan ji qi fujin diqu huanjing kaogu yanjiu," *Hua Xia kaogu* 1994.3: 65; Liu Li, "Settlement Patterns," pp. 260, 261, 270, 275.

[12] Duan Qingbo and Zhou Kunshu, "Chang'an fujin hedao bianqian yu wenhua fenbu," in *Huanjing kaogu yanjiu*, ed. Zhou Kunshu and Gong Qiming, pp. 47–55; Wei Jingwu and Wang Weilin, "Hanjiang shangyou diqu xinshiqi shidai yizhi de dili huanjing yu renlei de shengcun," in ibid., pp. 85–95.

[13] The scholarship is summarized in Winkler and Wang, "The Late Quaternary Vegetation and Climate of China," pp. 221–64. For studies of these environmental changes at the regional level, see the articles in Zhou Kunshu and Gong Qiming, eds., *Huanjing kaogu yanjiu*. See too An Zhisheng et al., "Changes in the Monsoon," p. 23; Li Bing-yuan et al., "On the Environmental Evolution of Xizang (Tibet) in Holocene," in *Quaternary Geology and Environment of China*, ed. Liu Tung-sheng, p. 236.

decreasing, and pine increasing.[14] In the period that followed (ca. 3000–1000 B.C.), however, mean annual temperature fell and remained relatively constant, standing at 2–4 °C warmer than it is today. After approximately 1000 B.C. a further fall in temperature, gradual and prolonged, began.[15]

In the Central Plain, at ca. 6000 B.C., the climate, in the last stages of the Postglacial Climatic Optimum, had also grown wetter and warmer; more oaks appeared in the forest, several varieties of evergreen tree and brake fern were present. The remains of herbivores, like cattle, deer, and sheep, in Peiligang 裴李岡 Neolithic sites indicate the presence of extensive grasslands; and the remains of numerous acquatic animals, like fish, alligators, freshwater mussels, and snails, together with marshy sediments, reveal the widespread existence of rivers, lakes, and marshes.[16] Most of the fauna were those of the temperate zone, indicating that the climate generally resembled that of the present day. During the Yangshao stage (ca. 5000–3000 B.C.), the presence of carnivores, like the tiger, black bear, and leopard, indicate a hinterland of mountains and forests, and the presence of the Giant Panda, the bamboo rat, and abundant traces of bamboo further indicate an environment in which bamboo flourished. The remains of subtropical animals like the Sumatran rhinoceros, Asian elephant, Macaque monkey, musk deer, jackal, and peacock – animals that today are generally found to the south of the Qinling Mountains, in the Yangzi Valley, or still further south – further reveal that the climate was warmer than it had been earlier. The existence of a climatic optimum at this time is also supported by reconstructions from Beijing, Shanghai, and Taiwan.[17]

From ca. 4000 to 3000 B.C., however, the climate in the Henan region gradually turned cooler and drier, as indicated by the disappearance of the tropical and subtropical animals, by the smaller number of aquatic animals, and by the predominance of yellow eolian soil in the deposits. The change in the climate, however, was gradual and gentle. By the Longshan 龍山 period (ca. 3000–2000 B.C.), the remains of herbivores like horse, cattle, sheep, and

---

[14] Winkler and Wang, "The Late Quaternary Vegetation and Climate of China," p. 229. The changes in the Chinese climate correspond here, as elsewhere, to a period of global cooling that appears to have set in after ca. 4800 B.C. (Feng Xiahong and Samuel Epstein, "Climatic Implications of an 8000-Year Hydrogen Isotope Time Series from Bristlecone Pine Trees," *Science* 265 [August 19, 1994]: 1080).

[15] *Zhongguo kexue* 1977.6: 603–14; *Scientia Sinica* 21, 4 (1978): 516–32; Kwang-chih Chang, *The Archaeology of Ancient China*, pp. 71–2, 76–8. Pollen studies from central Liaoning also reveal a gradual change from a climate that was warm and moist to one that was growing cooler and drier (Liu Muling, "Xinle yizhi de gu zhibei he gu qihou," *Kaogu* 1988.9: 846–8).

[16] Zhang Juzhong, "Huanjing yu Peiligang wenhua," in *Huanjing kaogu yanjiu*, ed. Zhou Kunshu and Gong Qiming, pp. 122–9.

[17] Gong Qiming and Wang Shejiang, "Jiangzhai yizhi zaoqi shengtai huanjing de yanjiu," in *Huanjing kaogu yanjiu*, ed. Zhou Kunshu and Gong Qiming, pp. 78–84; Winkler and Wang, "The Late Quaternary Vegetation and Climate of China," pp. 229–33; Zhou Feng, "Quanxinshi shiqi Henan de dili huanjing yu qihou," *Zhongyuan wenwu* 1995.4: 112–13.

deer indicate the continuing presence of abundant water, grass, and dense forests; and the presence of a small number of southern deer suggests that the temperature may still have been warmer than it is today.[18] Similar evidence reveals that the Yangzi Valley was also generally warmer and wetter in the middle Holocene than it is at present, with mangrove forests, which are now found only on the South China coast, growing in the coastal areas.[19]

Just as the shifts in the coastline and the course of the Yellow River had influenced settlement patterns, so did these changes in climate. The reduction in the size of the lakes and marshes, whose presence in the earlier period had rendered the low-lying areas less hospitable to the Yangshao inhabitants, evidently rendered more land habitable and may have contributed to a marked increase in the size of the Longshan population and the density of its settlements in various regions.[20]

When we come to the Bronze Age, the archaeological evidence provides further indication of a cooling trend in Henan, as temperate-zone animals, like horse and cattle, increasingly replaced the subtropical fauna that are now found only to the south.[21] In the Wei 渭 River valley, pollen samples from ca. 1000 B.C. also indicate that during the early years of the Western Zhou, the climate was growing colder and drier.[22] Historical texts confirm this trend. The *Zhushu jinian* 竹書紀年 (Bamboo annals), for example, records that at various times in the mid–Western Zhou, the Han 漢 and Yangzi Rivers froze, that there was a major drought, and that the Jing 涇, Wei, and Luo 洛 Rivers all ran dry.[23] Although Zhou temperatures were still generally warmer than those known today – as indicated by references to a lack of ice in winter, the presence of bamboo and plum in north China, and the possibility of double cropping in the regions of southern Hebei and southern Shandong – the general trend was one of increasing coolness and aridity.[24]

The landscape itself, whether dominated by temperate, subtropical, or tropical forest, would, in the earlier periods, have been far more densely

[18] Zhou Feng, "Quanxinshi shiqi," p. 112.
[19] Winkler and Wang, "The Late Quaternary Vegetation and Climate of China," p. 233.
[20] Yuan Guangkuo, "Guanyu Peiligang wenhua yizhi xiqian de jige wenti," *Hua Xia kaogu* 1994.3: 41–8; Cao Bingwu, "Henan Huixan," pp. 61–7, 78. For the situation in Jiangsu, see Xiao Jiayi, "Jiangsu Wujiang xian Longnan yizhi baofen zuhe yu xianmin shenghuo huanjing de chube yanjiu," *Dongnan wenhua* 1990.5: 259–63.
[21] Zhou Feng, "Quanxinshi shiqi," p. 114.
[22] Wang Shihe et al., "Anban yizhi baofen fenxi," in *Huanjing kaogu yanjiu*, ed. Zhou Kunshu and Gong Qiming, p. 64.
[23] *Zhushu jinian* (*Sibu beiyao* ed.), 2, pp. 7a, 8a, 10b (James Legge, *The Chinese Classics. Vol. 3: The Shoo King, or The Book of Historical Documents* [1865; rpt. Hong Kong: Hong Kong University Press, 1960], Prolegomena, p. 152 [Legge provided the words in his Chinese text, but omitted their translation], pp. 154, 157).
[24] Chu Ko-chen, "A Preliminary Study on the Climatic Fluctuations During the Last 5,000 Years in China," *Cycles* 25 (1974): 246–7; Zhu Kezhen, "Zhongguo jin wuqian nian lai qihou bianqian de chubu yanjiu," *Kaogu xuebao* 1972.1: 20–1, 36, fig. 2.

wooded and covered with brush and other vegetation than it is today.[25] Early
farmers would have had to clear such cover before they could grow their
crops; they would also have had to confront the numerous wild animals that
took such forest and brush for their habitat, preying upon both man and his
crops. The denudation of the Chinese landscape, so notable a feature of
modern China, was only beginning in the ancient period.[26]

The general conclusion to be drawn from the evidence, both archaeological and textual, is that the rainfall in Neolithic and early Bronze Age China
would have extended further north and for longer periods than it does today,
and that the climate, with fluctuations, was more temperate and hospitable
than it was to be in imperial and modern times, thus providing for a longer
growing season. The different regional environments help to explain the
various adaptational strategies adopted by the emerging Neolithic cultures
when, for example, they chose to focus their food-gathering and early agricultural efforts on millet, or rice, or other aquatic plants. The benevolence
of the climate and the fecundity of the environment also help to explain the
increasing prosperity of the Neolithic and Bronze Age cultures that were
emerging in China at this time. And it is not implausible to suppose that
such a favorable environment also contributed to the general optimism about
the human condition and human nature that characterizes much early
Chinese religion, legend, and philosophy.

---

[25] For maps that show the distribution of paleovegetation in China for 16000, 12000, 7000, and 4000
B.C. (together with a map showing the present situation) and that reveal the general northern shift of
vegetational zones at 4000 B.C., see Winkler and Wang, "The Late Quaternary Vegetation and Climate
of China," p. 245, fig. 10.11.

[26] Wang Shihe et al. ("Anban yizhi baofen fenxi," p. 64) conclude that Chinese farmers began to have a
significant impact on the environment at the start of the Western Zhou, ca. 1000 B.C.

CHAPTER ONE

CHINA ON THE EVE OF THE HISTORICAL PERIOD

Kwang-Chih Chang

This volume describes a history of ancient China, though the term China, as the name of a modern country, did not exist until recent times. The civilization that we have come to identify with present-day China began to be formed perhaps a few thousand years ago, but its geographic scope has undergone continuous change, at no other time coinciding with the present political borders. Therefore, it should be borne in mind that in this chapter the geographical stage here called China is more like a short-hand name for one part of East Asia, east of the Altai Mountains and the Tibetan Plateau. This is an area where early hominids came to settle, as they did in the rest of Eurasia, furnishing the basic populations among which an agricultural way of life began some ten thousand years ago. It is only then that one begins to recognize within this area a distinctive civilization later to be called Chinese. When we describe the beginnings of the area's human history, we cannot describe it totally separately from the rest of the human world before 10,000 years ago.

THE PALAEOGRAPHIC STAGE OF EAST ASIA AND ITS SETTLEMENT BY HUMANS

In 1859 Charles Darwin presented his theory of evolution by natural selection, immediately generating an impassioned debate on the "antiquity of man." He called on evidence from stratigraphical and faunal correlations, and although in the subsequent century and a half scientists in a number of disciplines have accumulated a great deal of new information, even now only a sketchy and controversial story can be told.[1] The animal order to which

[1] For up-to-date and comprehensive accounts, see *The Cambridge Encyclopedia of Human Evolution*, ed. Steve Jones, Robert Martin, and David Pilbeam (Cambridge University Press, 1992, pp. 86–107); van

humans belong, the Primate, became separated from the other mammals between 90 and 65 million years ago, though well-documented fossils are available only for the period since the early Eocene, about 57 million years ago. A common ancestor of the higher primates – cercopithecoid monkeys and hominoid apes – appeared in the Eocene of Africa at least 40–50 million years ago, and monkeys and apes became separated perhaps in the early Miocene between 23 and 17 million years ago. All of this earliest evolution took place on the continent of Africa; hominoid fossils begin to appear in eastern Europe and Asia as far as China by the middle Miocene, 17–11 million years ago.[2] Between 11 and 7 million years ago, in the late Miocene, there was at least one genus of big ape in the area of China, the *Lufengpithecus*, found in Lufeng 祿豐, Yunnan.[3] The next to branch off, between 10 and 6 million years ago, was probably the gorilla, while the closest relative to humans, according to the latest genetic studies, was the chimpanzee, which branched off as late as between 8 and 6 million years ago[4] or, as calibrated in the most recent study, just 4.9 million years ago.[5]

The last of the primates to evolve were the early humans. Their fossils discovered thus far have been grouped into two major genera, *Australopithecus* and *Paranthropus*, which begin to appear between late Miocene and Pliocene, and certainly by 4.5 million years ago, when a date for *Austrolopithecus* in this neighborhood was bolstered by the study which uses mitochondrial DNA to determine the above-mentioned 4.9-million-years-old date for the chimpanzee split. They are called human instead of ape because their canine teeth are reduced in size and are chisellike, and because they began to engage in bipedal walking like later humans (*Homo*). Of the two, *Australopithecus* is the

Riper and A. Bowdoin, *Men Among Mammoths* (Chicago: University of Chicago Press, 1993); Richard G. Klein, *The Human Career: Human Biological and Cultural Origins* (Chicago: University of Chicago Press, 1989); William Howells, *Getting Here: The Story of Human Evolution* (Washington, D.C.: Compass, 1993); L. Luca Cavalli-Sforza, Paolo Menozzi, and Alberto Piazza, *The History and Geography of Human Genes* (Princeton, N.J.: Princeton University Press, 1994).

[2] For the fossil record of prehuman early primates, see G. C. Conroy, *Primate Evolution* (New York: Norton, 1990); J. G. Fleagle, *Primate Adaptation and Evolution* (San Diego: Academic, 1988); R. D. Martin, *Primate Origins and Evolution: A Phylogenetic Reconstruction* (London: Chapman & Hall, 1990).

[3] The earlier notion regarding *Lufengpithecus* as an ancestor of the orangutans has now been rejected, the orangutan (Pongo) probably having branched off from the common ancestor of humans and apes between 12 and 16 million years ago, earlier than the age of *Lufengpithecus*. See Wu Rukang, "A Revision of the Classification of the Lufeng Great Apes," *Acta Anthropologica Sinica* 6 (1987): 265–71.

[4] L. Martin, "Relationships Among Extant and Extinct Great Apes and Humans," in *Major Topics in Primate and Human Evolution*, B. Wood, L. Martin, and P. Andrews, eds. (Cambridge University Press, 1986), pp. 161–87; M. Ruvolo, T. R. Disotell, M. W. Allard, W. M. Brown, and R. L. Honeycutt, "Resolution of the African Hominoid Trichotomy by the Use of a Mitochondrial Gene Sequence," *Proceedings of the National Academy of Sciences, USA*, 88 (1991): 1570–74.

[5] Satoshi Horai, Kenji Hayasaka, Rumi Kondo, Kazuo Tsugane, and Naoyuki Takahata, "Recent African Origin of Modern Humans Revealed by Complete Sequences of Hominoid Mitochondrial DNA," *Proceedings of the National Academy of Sciences, USA* 92 (1995): 532–6.

earlier and the more apelike, while members of *Paranthropus* may have been able to make and use crude stone tools. Significantly, these creatures are again known only in Africa, as is the first fossil classified into the genus *Homo*, *Homo habilis*, dated to 2.5 millions years ago. This fossil is placed into a new genus because, compared with the australopithecines, its dentition is finer (reflective of an improved diet), its bipedal walking is sturdier, and its brain is larger.[6]

Until now, the story of the evolution of the big primates, humans, and apes alike, is largely an African story, most of it having taken place in tropical East and South Africa. The only notable exception was during the middle and late Miocene, when primate fossils, some once regarded as ancestral to orangutans, were found in Eurasia. Significantly, the great apes closest to the genus *Homo*, chimpanzee and gorilla, have not been found outside of Africa in any form. Unless future finds prove otherwise, this could mean that the earliest humans, like the chimpanzees and gorillas, were so tightly adapted to the tropical forest environment of East and South Africa that they were unable to migrate out of this, their original habitat.

The first humans to achieve worldwide distribution are members of a new species, *Homo erectus*; they populated the eastern part of Asia and the rest of Eurasia, as well as Africa. Fossils of this species were in fact among the earliest human fossils to have been discovered and are still the best known throughout the world. The first such fossil was found in 1890 by a Dutch military doctor, Eugene DuBois, in Java. At that time, the only human fossils that scholars had ever seen were those of the Neanderthals, but the specimens DuBois acquired, a tooth and a skullcap in 1890 and a femur in 1892, were different.[7] Because they looked even more "primitive" than the Neanderthal bones, DuBois believed that he had found the "missing link" between man and the apes, calling his new find *Pithecanthropus erectus*, or the Erect Ape Man. Thirty years later, the Swedish geologist J. G. Andersson located the fossiliferous locality at Zhoukoudian 周口店 southwest of Beijing [Peking]. Since 1927, continuous excavations have been taking place at Zhoukoudian's locality 1, the Ape Man's Cave, and have resulted in the recovery of several skulls and postcranial skeletons (Fig. 1.1). These fossils were studied by Davidson Black and Franz Weidenreich, Black giving the population represented by the fossils a new Latin name, *Sinanthropus*

[6] D. E. Lieberman, D. R. Pilbeam, and B. A. Wood, "A Probabilistic Approach to the Problem of Sexual Dimorphism in *Homo Habilis*: A Comparison of KNM-ER 1470 and KNM-ER 1813," *Journal of Human Evolution* 17 (1988): 503–12.

[7] Eugene DuBois, *Pithecanthropus Erectus: Eine Menschenahnliche Ubergangsform aus Java* (Batavia). Rpt. in *Jaarboek van het Mijnwezen* 24 (1894): 5–77; idem, "On Pithecanthropus Erectus: A Transitional Form Between Man and the Apes," *Scientific Transactions of the Royal Dublin Society* 6 (1896): 1–18.

Figure 1.1. The site of Zhoukoudian, Beijing. The upper part of Locality 1 (The Ape-Man's Cave), marked for excavation, 1988. (Photograph by K. C. Chang.)

pekinensis, the Chinese Man at Peking.[8] Later researchers, who had not only both the Java and the Peking fossils at their disposal, but also other fossils from Africa and Europe, as well as other localities in China, came to the conclusion that these fossils represent humans in various parts of the world at a comparable level of morphological development and genetic makeup; they include all such fossils under the single name *Homo erectus*.

Until several years ago, paleoanthropologists agreed that *Homo erectus* first emerged in East Africa, where a find in Kenya was securely dated to 1.75 million years ago. A similar fossil of the same time period was found in South Africa, as was another in Ethiopia somewhat later. The Indonesian fossils of DuBois were dated to just around a million years ago, while the Zhoukoudian fossils dated to much later, about half a million years ago. Thus, the consensus held that the spread of *Homo erectus* out of Africa represented a migration of bands armed with a new technology, the Acheulean hand-axe complex, which equipped *Homo erectus* with the ability to break out of his pristine ecological niche to populate the subtropical and temper-

---

[8] The literature reporting and discussing these fossil and archaeological data is too long to list even the most important. A recent comprehensive monograph is Wu Rukang et al., *Beijing yuanren yizhi zonghe yanjiu* (Beijing: Kexue, 1985).

ate areas of Eurasia. Both Java Man and Peking Man were thus descendants of African ancestors.[9]

There are, however, two major difficulties with this hypothesis. The first is that a large number of *Homo erectus* fossils has been brought to light in China, none of which is associated with an Acheulean industry.[10] The second is that secure new dates now place the Java fossils to nearly 2 million years old, making them contemporary with the Kenyan *Homo erectus* populations.[11] If these dates stand, and every specialist seems to believe that they will, then it would seem that the 2-million-year-old *Homo erectus* emigrated out of Africa in a great hurry, even before an Acheulean industry had developed.

Time and again the theme of the African origin of human evolution has been put forward only to be retracted later. After *Homo erectus* spread, the next wave of migrations out of Africa are of the "anatomically modern" populations known as *Homo sapiens*. Two contrasting theories are now offered by scientists to account for their origins: the African hypothesis and the "multiregional" hypothesis.[12] The African hypothesis, based primarily upon recent genetic studies of mitochondrial DNA, holds that all modern humans derived from a small population in eastern or southern Africa, either 290,000–140,000 years ago,[13] 143,000 ± 18,000 years ago,[14] or 270,000 years ago,[15] according to three different studies. The other hypothesis, the multiregional model, initially formulated by Franz Weidenreich but recently most forcefully defended by M. H. Wolpoff,[16] posits parallel evolutions from *Homo erectus* to *Homo sapiens* in various regions of the Old World, with continuous gene flows among the populations of the various regions.

In this debate, fossil data from the area of China are playing a very significant role. As Geoffrey G. Pope has pointed out, the African hypothesis

[9] Klein, *The Human Career*, pp. 183ff.

[10] The main literature on Chinese *Homo erectus* fossils and their associated lithic industries is too voluminous to list here. For a recent comprehensive synthesis, see Wu Rukang, Wu Xinzhi and Zhang Senshui, *Zhongguo yuangu renlei* (Beijing: Kexue, 1993).

[11] C. C. Swisher III, G. H. Curtis, T. Jacob, A. G. Getty, A. Suprijo, and Widiasmoro, "Age of the Earliest Known Hominids in Java, Indonesia," *Science* 263 (1994): 1118–21.

[12] Robert Sussman, "A Current Controversy in Human Evolution," *American Anthropologist* 95 (1993): 9–96.

[13] R. L. Cann, M. Stoneking, and A. C. Wilson, "Mitochondrial DNA and Human Evolution," *Nature* 325 (1987): 31–6.

[14] Horai et al. "Recent African Origin of Modern Humans," pp. 532–6.

[15] Robert L. Korit, Hiroshi Akashi, and Walter Gilbert, "Absence of Polymorphism at the ZFY Locus on the Human Y Chromosome," *Science* 268 (1995): 1183–5.

[16] Franz Weidenreich, *Apes, Giants, and Men* (Chicago: University of Chicago Press, 1957); M. H. Wolpoff, "Multiregional Evolution: The Fossil Alternative to Eden," in *The Human Evolution: Behavioural and Biological Perspectives on the Origin of Modern Humans*, ed. P. Mellars and C. Stringer (Edinburgh: Edinburgh University Press, 1989), pp. 62–108; M. H. Wolpoff et al., "Modern Human Origins," *Science* 241 (1988): 772–3.

has "been made largely in ignorance of the fossil and archaeological record
of the Far East," and "the paleoanthropological evidence from the Far East
is squarely at odds with a replacement model for the origin of anatomically
modern *Homo sapiens* favored by the results of some mitochondrial DNA
studies."[17] Pope argues:

The archaeological record of the last one million years provides no evidence of the
rapid introduction of technological innovation or a major shift in adaptational or
exploitative strategies. Recently recovered evidence strongly suggests that regional
archaeological differences within the Far East may date back to the earliest hominid
colonization of the region and extend, only slightly altered, until well into the late
Pleistocene. Furthermore, the evidence from the facial morphology of fossil and
extant Asian hominids suggests that certain facial characteristics . . . also unite early
Asian *Homo erectus* and extant Far Eastern populations.[18]

Important as this debate is in the study of human evolution, what is relevant for our present purposes remains the same under either hypothesis. By
the end of the Pleistocene, East Asia, including the area now known as China,
had been occupied by people of great technological skill in the making of
lithic and microlithic varieties of blades; these were people whose intellectual
levels were on a par with the Magdalenians and Perigordians, the groups of
people in western Europe responsible for cave arts the artistic level of which
many consider not to have been surpassed even to this date. In this chapter
I will attempt to describe the probable process by which the descendants of
the Late Palaeolithic people of China gradually began to build a remarkable
civilization.

BEGINNINGS OF THE AGRICULTURAL WAY OF LIFE

The beginning of plant cultivation and animal domestication, one of the
truly important divides in the course of human history, was, again, a worldwide event, and the agricultural beginnings in China must be studied in this
context. However, from this time forward, such events become issues of the
area; that is, they are also Chinese issues, the word "Chinese" being used here
in a geographic rather than a cultural sense. This is because plants and
animals were parts of ecosystems with characteristic faunal and floral components of specific geographic areas.[19]

---

[17] Geoffrey G. Pope, "Replacement Versus Regionally Continuous Models: The Paleobehavioral and Fossil
Evidence from East Asia," in *The Evolution and Dispersal of Modern Humans in Asia*, ed. Takeru
Akazawa, Kenichi Aoki, and Tasuku Kimura (Tokyo: Hokusensha, 1992), pp. 3–14.
[18] Ibid., p. 3.
[19] David K. Ferguson, "The Impact of Late Cenozoic Environmental Changes in East Asia on the
Distribution of Terrestrial Plants and Animals," in *Evolving Landscapes and Evolving Biotas of East
Asia Since the Mid-Tertiary*, ed. Nina G. Jablowski and So Chak-lam (Hong Kong: Centre of Asian
Studies, University of Hong Kong, 1993), pp. 145–96.

A great deal of data and many studies have already made it clear that toward the end of the Pleistocene and during the several thousand years both before and after the Pleistocene–Holocene boundary, the climate throughout East Asia was warm and moist and the vegetation cover was much heavier than it is at present. In the river valleys and lowlands of North China, where now there is only loess land surface or bushes, there were dense forests and many bogs, marshes, and lakes, supporting such animals as tapir, elephant, water deer, elaphure, crocodile, and other species that are now found in South China and Southeast Asia but are no longer in the north. Pollen profiles from many cores drilled by palynologists give the same picture: trees that now live in the deciduous forests of South China are found to have occurred in the north. Near the waters and the trees were many grasses from the family Gramineae (especially the genera *Panicum* and *Setaria*) and from the genus *Oryza*. In and near the freshwater ponds and lakes were many water plants and many species that grew in wet soil, such as taro and yam.[20] This was an environment very rich in food resources, and the Palaeolithic people who lived on them (acquiring them by nets, bows and arrows, spears, harpoons, and other implements fitted with microliths) undoubtedly had long been familiar with the nature, the character, and the properties of each animal and each plant. As Carl Sauer emphasizes, "Man learned to plant before he grew crops by seeding."[21] The major purpose of seeding crops is to grow food. But before plants were grown for food, they undoubtedly had for a long, long time been gathered for fiber, fuel, poison for hunting and fishing, and herbs for medicine. The last of these was probably the most important use of plants, at least in China, before the cultivation of food plants; the legendary Chinese hero Shen Nong 神農 (the Divine Farmer) was also credited with the creation of Chinese pharmacology.

Around 10,000 years ago, geologically shortly before or after the transition from the Pleistocene to the Holocene, some as yet undetermined factor or factors seem to have compelled many peoples of the whole world to turn to plant resources for food at much the same time. There were four major seed plants that were used most extensively by the people of the world's ancient civilizations: wheat, millet, rice, and maize. Recent archaeological work indicates that their first cultivation by humans all took place at this time. There are many hypotheses to account for this extremely important

---

[20] For the most important features in landscape, climate, animals, plants, and other environmental elements with which the ancient people of this area had interacted in significant ways, consult K. C. Chang, *The Archaeology of Ancient China*, 4th ed. (New Haven, Conn.: Yale University Press, 1985), pp. 61–71. For the unique significance of water plants in early Chinese agriculture, see Hui-lin Li, "The Domestication of Plants in China: Ecogeographical Considerations," in *The Origins of Chinese Civilization*, ed. David N. Keightley (Berkeley: University of California Press, 1983), pp. 21–63.

[21] Carl O. Sauer, *Agricultural Origins and Dispersals* (New York: American Geographical Society, 1952), p. 27.

Figure 1.2. Ripened ears of foxtail millet (left, upper), common millet (right), and rice (left, lower) (photograph by K. C. Chang).

event, which Gordon Childe referred to as the Neolithic Revolution.[22] No hypothesis has been universally accepted to account for the initiation of cultivation, but all agree that fully charged ecological interaction provided the spark that started the system moving; that is, cultures in which people had full knowledge of plants needed only an incentive to put that knowledge to use. In other words, by the beginning of the Holocene Palaeolithic people all over the world had knowledge of the plants and the implements to manipulate them. Some worldwide event, perhaps population increase, a climatic optimum, or botanical mutation, must have provided the spark.

Whatever the cause, around 10,000 years ago agriculture in the form of seed cultivation began in both North and South China (Fig. 1.2). In the north, the earliest cultivated millets discovered in the world have been unearthed at a number of sites classified as Cishan 磁山, or Peiligang 裴李

[22] V. Gordon Childe, *Man Makes Himself* (1936; New York: New American Library Edition, 1951), pp. 59ff.

Figure 1.3. Pottery vessels, stone mortar and pestle, and clay figures of pig and sheep of the Cishan and Peiligang cultures of early millet farmers in North China. In the collections of the Arthur M. Sackler Museum, Peking University.

崗, culture.[23] The earliest site of this culture found so far was excavated in 1986 near Nanzhuangtou 南莊頭 village in Xushui 徐水 county in southern Hebei. Several radiocarbon dates from charcoal samples place the site very close to 10,000 years ago.[24] Although there are no crop remains at this site, there are seed-processing tools, such as pestles and mortars, similar to those found at other sites with seed remains identified as *Setaria italica* (Fig 1.3). Another kind of millet found in later sites is *Panicum miliaceum*; these were the two pillars of Old World millet culture.[25] Although wild species of both genera are found throughout Eurasia, and paleobotanical research of the initial cultivation of millets has not yet even been started, we can say that in view of the great antiquity of known millet remains in North China, there

[23] Chang, *The Archaeology of Ancient China*, pp. 87–95.
[24] Zhou Benxiong, "Hebei Xushui xian Nanzhuangtou yizhi shijue jianbao," *Kaogu* 1992.11: 961–7.
[25] N. I. Vavilov, *The Origin, Variation, Immunity and Breeding of Cultivated Plants*, trans. K. Starr Chester (New York: Ronald, 1952), pp. 63 and 69; Robert O. Whyte, "The Gramineae, Wild and Cultivated, of Monsoonal and Equatorial Asia," *Asian Perspectives* 15 (1972); 127–51; 21 (1978): 182–205.

is a strong presumption that both may have been first cultivated in the Yellow River valley. At the Nanzhuangtou site, dog and pig were domesticated, but a large amount of wild animal bones and shells, including crane, wolf, elaphure, several kinds of deer, turtle, clam, and snail, indicates that hunting and collecting were still of considerable importance. Nevertheless, we would be very much mistaken to underestimate the cultural sophistication of these farmer-hunter-collectors: at the Jiahu 賈湖 site in Wuyang 舞陽, central Henan, a seven-hole bone flute and two pieces of turtle shell inscribed with one symbol each were discovered. Both symbols closely resemble graphs in the oracle-bone inscriptions of the Shang dynasty 6,000 years later.[26]

In the south, remains of rice (*Oryza sativa*) have been discovered from increasingly earlier sites. In the 1970s, rice remains from the Hemudu 河姆渡 site in Hangzhou 杭州, Zhejiang, were securely dated to the early sixth millennium B.C.[27] In the 1980s, long series of radiocarbon and thermoluminescence dates became available to place several sites found in limestone cave deposits in Guangxi and Jiangxi (e.g., Zengpiyan 甑皮岩 and Xianrendong 仙人洞) in the period from 9000 to 5000 B.C., but many archaeologists used to the idea of the chronological precedence of the north over the south have not accepted these early dates, attributing them to contamination from the limestone of the caves.[28] In 1988, an open site was excavated on a small hill in a plain north of the Li 澧 River in the northwestern corner of Hunan, in the middle Yangzi River valley. At this site, called Pengtoushan 彭頭山, both residential and burial remains were found. The pottery was coarsely cord-marked, with most vessels being round-bottomed urns and bowls. In the urns there were huge quantities of carbonized rice remains; judging from their size and shape, the rice was undoubtedly domesticated. A series of radiocarbon dates places this site to the period of 8200–7800 B.C., lending credence to the similar dates of Zengpiyan.[29] The most recent investigations of rice and related flora have been jointly undertaken by a Sino-American team headed by Yan Wenming 嚴文明 and Richard S. MacNeish. Examining two caves in Wannian 萬年 county, northern Jiangxi, downstream along the Yangzi River from Hunan, they have brought to light rice pollen and phytoliths of *Oryza sativa*, both domesticated and wild, from layers of both caves tentatively dated by radiocarbon to just under 10,000 years ago.[30] The reso-

---

[26] *Wenwu* 1989.1: 1–14, 47.

[27] Chang, *The Archaeology of Ancient China*, pp. 208–14.

[28] On the early dates of the Xianrendong and Zengpiyan caves and the controversy surrounding these dates, see ibid., pp. 95–100.

[29] Pei Anping and Cao Chuansong. "Hunan Lixian Pengtoushan xinshiqi shidai zaoqi yizhi fajue baogao," *Wenwu* 1990.8: 17–29.

[30] Richard S. MacNeish and Jane Libby, eds., *Preliminary (1994) Report of the Sino-American Jiangxi (PRC) Origin of Rice Agriculture Project* (draft copy), Publication in Anthropology, no. 13. El Paso: El Paso Centennial Museum, University of Texas at El Paso, 1995.

lution of the long-outstanding question concerning the origin of the rice cultivation may now be near.[31]

REGIONAL CULTURES OF THE EARLY FARMERS

With agriculture, human settlements tend to be tied to a fixed place for longer than is the case for hunters; hence, many farming cultures throughout the world adopted pottery as the container of choice for their crops, seeds, and other foodstuffs, as well as for cooking utensils. Farmers also need sharp and durable axes so that they can cut down trees to clear fields for cultivation; as a result their axes and other lithic implements tend to be manufactured by polishing and grinding rather than flaking and chipping like those of their Paleolithic antecedents. For these reasons, agriculture, pottery, and stone polishing tend to occur together, and many archaeologists define the "Neolithic" period as the time when polished stone implements and/or pottery are found, and they regard the presence of these as sufficient evidence of agriculture. This is not necessarily the case everywhere. For example, in prehistoric Japan, pottery was used for at least seven thousand years before agriculture was adopted as a main strategy to sustain life. Conversely, in the prehistoric Levant, an agricultural life had been in existence for several thousand years before pottery was used.

In prehistoric China, the period of transition from hunting to farming is not yet adequately known, but from the data mentioned in the preceding section it appears that agriculture, pottery, and stone polishing occurred approximately at the same time, both in north and in south China, some 10,000 years ago. With pottery, it becomes possible to distinguish human groups by their cultural differences. However, since so few items of material culture survive, pottery alone may not suffice for cultural classification. Insofar as pottery is concerned, in the north it is characterized by fine cord marks and rocker impressions made with the edge of shells; a round-bottomed bowl with three small legs attached is the distinguishing vessel type. In the south, both cord-marked and shell-edge impressions also prevail, but the cord marks are coarser, while the impressions are not often rocker-stamped; what is more, the round-bottomed bowls lack the three legs. To say that these differences suggest a division into two cultures is overly simplistic. The pottery of both the north and the south may have derived from a

---

[31] T. T. Chang, "Domestication and Spread of the Cultivated Rices," in *Foraging and Farming: The Evolution of Plant Exploitation*, ed. D. R. Harris and G. C. Hillman (London: Unwin Hyman, 1989), pp. 408–17; idem, "Rice: *Oryza sativa* and *Oryza glaberrima* (Gramineae-Oryzeae)." in *Evolution of Crop Plants*, ed. J. Smartt and N. W. Simmonds (London: Longman Scientific & Technical, 1995), pp. 147–55.

single source and thus share their principal features, while other features of the material culture may have been vastly different. One fact points in this direction: by 5000 B.C. a number of regional cultures can be clearly identified in the archaeological record.

Regional cultures are usually defined by natural borders: river valleys, mountain valleys, coastal plains, and other ecological enclaves. But cultures are also hierarchically related; that is, several cultures may coexist within one very small area, or many such small-area cultures may be grouped into a single large culture defined, for instance, by a large river valley. For ease of description here, I will use large-scale geographic areas to summarize the principal regional cultures identifiable in the current available archaeological record. Six such regional cultures are highly distinctive. I will discuss them in geographic order from north to south (Map 1.1).

Xinglongwa, Xinle, and Hongshan Cultures

The Liao 遼 River of northern North China originates in the eastern part of the Mongolian plateau, flows east into the southern Manchurian plains, then takes a sharp turn south draining into the Bay of Bohai. In the early Holocene, the valley had a heavy vegetation cover in which a great variety of animals and plants lived. Millet farming and domestic cattle and sheep were common. Dessication since about the time of the Han dynasty (206 B.C.–A.D. 220) has now made this area barren. Today it is characterized by a mixed farming and herding economy and marks the divide between the northern nomads and the Han Chinese agrarians. In the early Holocene, a succession of three cultures occupied this area: Xinglongwa 興隆洼 (8500–7000 B.C.),[32] Xinle 新樂 (7000–5000 B.C.),[33] and Hongshan 紅山 (3000–2500 B.C.).[34] Many outstanding art objects whose material and motifs anticipated later Chinese elements south of this area have been brought to light here. Foremost among these are jade objects and the dragon motif. The most characteristic pottery wares are rocker-stamped flat-bottomed vessels in the earlier period, and red-striped red bowls and tubes in the latter period.[35]

[32] *Kaogu* 1985.10: 865–74; Ren Shinan, "Xinglongwa wenhua de faxian ji qi yiyi," *Kaogu* 1994.8: 710–18.
[33] *Kaogu xuebao* 1978.4: 449–66; *Kaogu xuebao* 1985.2: 209–22.
[34] Sun Shoudao and Guo Dashun, "Niuheliang Hongshan wenhua nüshen touxiang de faxian yu yanjiu," *Wenwu* 1986.8: 18–24; "Liaoning Niuheliang Hongshan wenhua nüshenmiao yu jisi zhongqun fajue jianbao," *Wenwu* 1986.8: 1–17.
[35] Dashun Guo, "Hongshan and Related Cultures," in Sarah M. Nelson, ed., *The Archaeology of Northeast China Beyond the Great Wall* (London: Routledge, 1995), pp. 21–65.

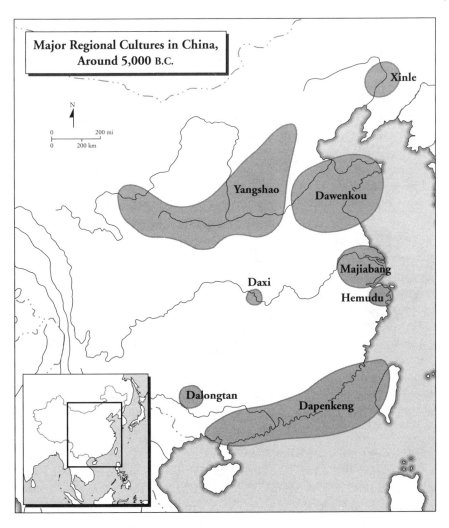

Map 1.1 Major regional cultures in China around 5000 B.C. recognized by archaeology.

Yangshao Culture (5000–3000 B.C.)

Discovered by the Swedish geologist J. G. Andersson in 1920 at Yangshao 仰韶 village in Mianchi 澠池 county, Henan, this was the first Neolithic culture to be found in China and is still the best known.[36] More than a thousand archaeological sites of this culture have been found distributed in the Yellow

---

[36] J. G. Andersson, "An Early Chinese Culture," *Bulletin of the Geological Society of China*, Series A, 5, 1 (1923): 1–68. For the most recent summary of the Yangshao culture, see Yan Wenming, *Yangshao wenhua yanjiu* (Beijing: Wenwu, 1989).

Figure 1.4. Painted pottery vessels of the Yangshao culture. Photographs reproduced by permission of Wenwu Press.

River valley from Zhengzhou 鄭州 in the east to the upper reaches in Gansu
and Qinghai. Within this vast area, the culture can be divided into several
phases on the basis of ceramic styles. All of these, however, are of reddish
color and are painted with various designs in black or dark brown (Fig. 1.4).
Major vessel types include the bowl, water bottle, jar, and urn. Tripods (*ding*
鼎) and bowls on ring stands (*dou* 豆) are seen in the east only, possibly being
forms introduced from the eastern coastal areas.

The Yangshao was a culture of millet farmers, already planting both *Setaria*
and *Panicum* millets. The people lived in lineage units regularly laid out in
villages. One major feature of Yangshao worth noting is that it has yielded
many remains that are indicative of shamanistic beliefs and practices. These
include, for example, a skeletal (or X-ray) style of art, bisexualism in ceramic
art, and, above all, the tomb of a figure, presumably religious, flanked by
a dragon to his left and a tiger to his right, both formed with clam shells
(Fig. 1.5).[37] This seems to resemble descriptions in such later sources

[37] Zhang Guangzhi, "Yangshao wenhua zhong de wuxi ziliao," *BIHP* 64 (1993): 611–25.

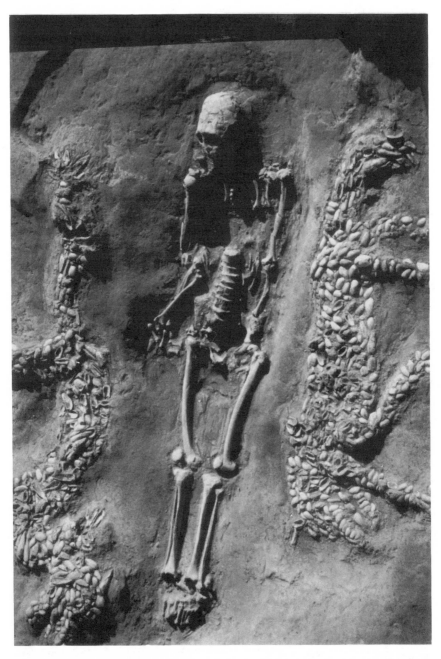

Figure 1.5. The Puyang shaman and two animals. Photograph by Henan Provincial Museum.

as *Baopuzi* 抱朴子 (third century A.D.) of Daoist priests who employed dragons, tigers, or deer as helpers in their journeys to Heaven, where they met with deities and ancestors to acquire wisdom, medical cures, and other benefits. The Yangshao culture, however, definitely is not the only regional Neolithic culture with a shamanistic orientation. Large dragon images laid out on the ground with stones have come to light recently from both the Xinglongwa and Daxi 大溪 cultures. These three cultures have very little in common in terms of material artifacts, so it is likely that shamanism is a substratal feature.

Dawenkou Culture (5000–3000 B.C.)

The Dawenkou 大汶口 culture, another millet-farming culture, was located on the low hills and lakeshores of the Shandong highland. Many of the sites are of burials with elongated pit graves often dug deeper at the center, forming a smaller pit at the bottom of the first pit. The encoffined body was placed into the smaller pit, filling it; grave furnishings were then placed alongside the coffin at the bottom of the larger pit, which is now referred to as the *ercengtai* 二層臺, "second level ledge." The abundance of grave furnishings on the *ercengtai* is a distinctive feature of the Dawenkou culture; they include pottery vessels, bone and ivory eating and drinking utensils, ritual instruments such as rattles made of turtle shells, and bone carvings. Among the pottery, often buff or reddish in color, there are many *ding*-tripods, *dou*-stands, water jars (some in the shape of animals and birds), and very tall cups on thin stands.[38]

Majiabang and Hemudu Cultures (5000–3500 B.C.)

The discovery of Majiabang 馬家濱 and Hemudu cultures, early rice-growing cultures along the Yangzi River in Jiangsu and northern Zhejiang, gave the first indications that in China all that is early and refined was not necessarily confined to the Yellow River valley. In addition to rice, the people of these cultures made extensive use of the area's freshwater plants such as the water caltrop, fox nut, lotus seed and stem, arrowhead, water chestnut, wild rice, water dropwort, water shield, water spinach, cattail, and rush.[39] Many dwellings were timber structures built on piles along river banks or lakeshores, with floors above the water. Fish, shellfish, and animal remains, including domestic dog, pig, and water buffalo, are extremely abundant in

---

[38] *Dawenkou* (Beijing: Wenwu, 1974); Gao Guangren, "Shilun Dawenkou wenhua de fenqi," *Kaogu xuebao* 1978.4: 399–419; "1987 nian Jiangsu Xinyi Huating yizhi de fajue," *Wenwu* 1990.2: 1–28.
[39] Li, "The Domestication of Plants in China," pp. 43–6.

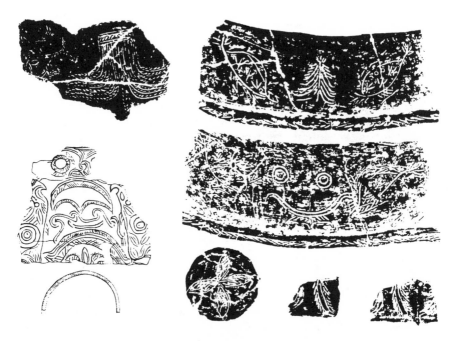

Figure 1.6. Engraved designs on Hemudu pottery vessels. From K. C. Chang, *The Archaeology of Ancient China*, 4th ed. (New Haven, Conn.: Yale University Press, 1986), p. 217.

the kitchen middens. The pottery is predominantly brown in the Majiabang culture but black in the Hemudu; both feature cord marking and incised designs of birds and other ritual or realistic motifs; most distinctive is a type of round-bottomed food cooker with a ridge around the neck so that it can be suspended from a ring in an oven. Some of the incised pottery designs have been interpreted as having a shamanistic significance (Fig. 1.6).[40]

Daxi Culture (5000–3000 B.C.)

Another of the Yangzi Valley rice-growing cultures, the Daxi culture, features abundant storage facilities, highly polished stones and perforated slate sickles, and even occasional village walls, all testifying to an advanced degree of agriculture. The characteristic ceramics are tall, thin stemmed, and painted with black or dark brown zoned bands; they served as stands for flat dishes. They were likely used in rituals. As mentioned earlier, Daxi is among the cultures with substratal dragon designs.[41]

[40] *Kaogu* 1961.7: 345–54; *Kaogu xuebao* 1978.1: 39–93; *Zhejiang sheng Wenwu kaogusuo xuekan* (1981): 1–34.
[41] He Jiejun, "Shilun Daxi wenhua," *Zhongguo kaogu xuehui di er ci nianhui lunwenji* (1982): 116–23; Meng Huaping, "Lun Daxi wenhua," *Kaogu xuebao* 1992.4: 293–412.

Dapenkeng Culture (5000–2500 B.C.)

In view of the abundant wild but potentially cultivable plants in South China during the sixth and fifth millennia B.C., we can confidently assume that there were a large number of regional cultures in its mountain valleys, river valleys, estuary lagoons, and coastal plains. But the archaeological investigation of South China has barely begun. At the present, aside from the Daxi and Majiabang–Hemudu cultures, the only other well-defined regional culture is Dapenkeng 大坌坑, the name being derived from the site of that name in Taipei 台北, excavated in 1964.[42] Similar but by no means identical sites are found widely scattered along the western coast of the Formosa Strait, from southern Zhejiang, along Fujian and Guangdong, all the way to Guangxi and Vietnam.[43] Most sites have yielded coarse cord-marked potsherds, and many have sherds that are shell–impressed, comb-impressed, or incised. Among the lithics are chipped and polished axes and adzes, perforated triangular arrowheads, and grooved tapa beaters. Sherds and stones are found in the kitchen middens full of molluscan shells, fish bones, and animal bones. This was a coastal culture that depended on farming, hunting, fishing, watercraft, and multiple uses of plants. In many ways this culture reminds us of the hearth of early plant domestication about which Carl Sauer had speculated.[44]

The Dapenkeng culture is important in Pacific prehistory. In Taiwan there are over 200,000 Austronesian speakers. Archaeology and history combine to manifest a continuous cultural development from the Dapenkeng culture, if not earlier, to the ethnographic present. This 4,000- to 5,000-year continuum, added to the many similarities of the Dapenkeng culture to the Proto-Austronesian culture reconstructed by linguists, has led many Malayo-Polynesian linguists to believe that Taiwan and the nearby coasts of southeastern China were the homeland of this large family of languages.[45]

FORMATION OF A CHINESE INTERACTION SPHERE AND THE DEVELOPMENT OF REGIONAL CULTURES

Regional cultures such as those described in the preceding section and probably many others that are not yet known archaeologically are the fundamental

---

[42] K. C. Chang et al., *Fengpitou, Tapenkeng, and the Prehistory of Taiwan*, Yale University Publications in Anthropology, no. 73 (New Haven, Conn.: Yale University Press, 1969).

[43] Zhang Guangzhi, "Xinshiqi shidai de Taiwan haixia," *Kaogu* 1989.6: 541–50, 569.

[44] Sauer, *Agricultural Origins and Dispersals*, pp. 5, 24.

[45] V. H. Misra and Peter Bellwood, eds., *Recent Advances in Indo-Pacific Prehistory: Proceedings of the International Symposium Held at Poona, Dec. 19–23, 1978* (Leiden: Brill, 1985); Zhang Guangzhi, "Zhongguo dongnan haian yuangu wenhua yu Nandao minzu qiyuan wenti," *Nanfang minzu kaogu* 1987.1: 1–14.

elements with which megacivilizations everywhere were formed. In China, the formation of the megacivilization began around the beginning of the fourth millennium B.C., the process of its formation being now fairly clearly understood. But the understanding of that process has not been achieved without many twists and turns.

Traditional Chinese historiography is the longest continuous historiographical tradition in the world, beginning when writing began. Writing, however, has not survived everywhere, so that the areas of China where written records are the most abundant have inevitably acquired a greater significance than those areas where fewer or even no written records survive. The Yellow River valley of North China has the longest continuous historical record, beginning with the first available writings, the oracle-bone inscriptions of the Shang dynasty. Records continued to be written in this area in the form of bronze inscriptions, on bamboo or wooden strips, and finally on paper. Consequently, throughout Chinese history the Yellow River valley, especially the middle courses in the northwestern portion of Henan, southwestern Shanxi, and the Wei 渭 River valley of Shaanxi, were regarded by historians and common people alike as the cradle of Chinese civilization. It was in the *Zhongyuan* 中原 (Central Plain) that one finds the greatest achievement of Chinese civilization. Traditional Chinese history begins with the *San huang* 三皇 (Three Sovereigns), followed by the *Wu di* 五帝 (Five Emperors). These are followed by the Three Dynasties: Xia, Shang, and Zhou. All of these ancient heroes, sages, and rulers originated in and were located in the Central Plain. As the *Shi ji* observes: "The kings of all three dynasties were between the Yellow River and the Luo 洛 (River)."[46]

This traditional view of the importance of the "center" definitely colored the initial interpretation of the archaeological data obtained after archaeology was introduced from the West in the 1920s. When J. G. Andersson discovered the first Chinese Neolithic site at Yangshao village in 1920, he immediately pronounced the painted pottery and polished stone celt at the site as coming from western Asia.[47] This ran against the traditional Chinese view of center-to-periphery diffusion of civilization, and few Chinese scholars supported it; the availability or absence of evidence was beside the point. In 1930–1, the excavation of the Black Pottery culture of Chengziyai 城子崖, in Zhangqiu 章丘, Shandong, with its scapulimancy and *hangtu* 夯土 (stamped-earth) construction, provided Chinese scholars with evidence of the native roots of two of the most characteristic features of Shang civilization, namely, inscribed oracle bones and *hangtu* construction.[48] In 1933, in his bril-

[46] *Shi ji*, 28, p. 1371.   [47] Andersson, "An Early Chinese Culture."
[48] Fu Sinian, Li Ji, et al., *Chengziyai* (Nanjing: Institute of History and Philology, Academia Sinica, 1934).

liant essay "Yi Xia dong xi shuo" 夷夏東西説 (The hypothesis of the Yi in the east and the Xia in the west),[49] Fu Sinian 傅斯年 used textual information to suggest that the ancient peoples of China were mainly divided into two groups: an Eastern Yi 夷 group located along the eastern coastal areas, and a Xia 夏 group located in the western interior of the loess plateaus. Seizing upon the coincidence of the newly discovered archaeological cultures of Yangshao and Longshan 龍山 with textual records, others then suggested that the western Yangshao culture was a manifestation of the western Xia, and that the eastern, coastal Longshan culture must have been representative of the Yi peoples of the east.[50] This in fact became the prevailing doctrine to interpret Chinese prehistory during the rest of the 1930s, 1940s, and 1950s.[51]

Beginning in 1959, a major revision of this Neolithic hypothesis took place. This was largely as a result of the excavation of the stratified site of Miaodigou 廟底溝, in Shanxian 陝縣, Henan. At this site, there was a stratified sequence of Yangshao, early Longshan (Miaodigou II), and Eastern Zhou cultures.[52] A most significant new situation was created since it appeared that the early Longshan culture at this site developed out of its Yangshao culture, a suggestion that the authors of the site report did indeed make. This remarkable new finding led a number of Chinese scholars to revise the earlier two-culture Neolithic hypothesis and turn instead to a new "nuclear area" hypothesis. In part inspired by Robert Braidwood with his "nuclear area" of "hilly flanks" in the Near Eastern hearth of agricultural origins,[53] K. C. Chang proposed the existence of a "nuclear area" in northwestern Henan, southwestern Shanxi, and eastern Shaanxi, with the Longshan growing out of the Yangshao and then spreading east to populate the eastern seaboard.[54] In the same year, several prominent archaeologists on the Chinese mainland came to the same conclusion.[55] For the next twenty years, the nuclear hypothesis – that the earliest agricultural life and the earliest civilizations first appeared in a nuclear area in the Central Plain – dominated the thinking of most

[49] Fu Sinian, "Yi Xia dong xi shuo," in *Qingzhu Cai Yuanpei xiansheng liushiwusui lunwenji* (Nanjing: Institute of History and Philology, Academia Sinica, 1933), pp. 1093–134.

[50] Liang Siyong, "Xiaotun Longshan yu Yangshao," in *Qingzhu Cai Yuanpei xiansheng liushiwusui lunwenji*, pp. 555–67.

[51] Liu Yao, "Longshan wenhua yu Yangshao wenhua zhi fenxi," *Zhongguo kaogu xuebao* 2 (1947): 251–82; J. G. Andersson, "Researches into the Prehistory of the Chinese," *BMFEA* 15 (1943): 29–91.

[52] *Miaodigou yu Sanliqiao* (Beijing: Kexue, 1959).

[53] Robert Braidwood, *Prehistoric Man*, 6th ed. (Chicago: Natural History Museum, 1964), pp. 86–101.

[54] Zhang Guangzhi, "Zhongguo xinshiqi shidai wenhua duandai," *BIHP* 20 (1959): 259–309.

[55] Shi Xingbang, "Huanghe liuyu yuanshi shehui kaogu shang de ruogan wenti," *Kaogu* 1959.10: 568. Note, however, that An Zhimin qualified this by pointing out that the black pottery found in Shandong probably had a separate origin; An Zhimin. "Shilun Huanghe liuyu xinshiqi shidai wenhua," *Kaogu* 1959.10: 565; idem, "Zhongguo xinshiqi shidai kaoguxue shang de zhuyao chengjiu," *Wenwu* 1959.10: 21. This qualification was strongly supported by Li Ji; Li Ji, "Heitao wenhua zai Zhongguo shanggushi zhong suo zhan de diwei," *Bulletin of the Department of Archaeology and Anthropology* 21–2 (1963): 1–12.

archaeologists,[56] a view obviously not unrelated to the traditional sinocentrism of Chinese historiography. In this connection, credit must be given to those archaeologists, many Westerners, who, while not neglecting the great contribution made by the Central Plain, insisted upon the highly important roles that each of the geographic regions described in the preceding section had played in the formation of Chinese civilization.[57] While this insistence was based more upon faith in ecological principles than in actual archaeological evidence, which at the time was scanty at best, it doubtless owes its origin in part to the absence of the burden of historical sinocentrism in the intellectual baggage of these Western authors.

By the mid-1970s, archaeological evidence was no longer scanty. There was for the first time a large number of radiocarbon dates determined for the most part by a half dozen laboratories; among these dates many from the peripheries were as early as or earlier than those from the nuclear area. Next, archaeological assemblages from many regions outside the nuclear area were found to contain art objects comparable or even superior in quality to those from the Central Plain. Thus, no more than a few years after the resumption of archaeological publications that followed the hiatus caused by the Cultural Revolution, the nuclear area hypothesis became no longer tenable, a regional approach taking its place. This is now referred to as the "regional systems and cultural types" (*quxi leixing* 區系類型) approach. It was first proposed by Su Bingqi 蘇秉琦 in a paper delivered in 1979 and subsequently published in 1981 in *Wenwu*, in which Su noted:[58]

In the past there was a point of view holding that the Yellow River valley was the cradle of the Chinese people and that the peoples and cultures of our country first developed here and only subsequently spread toward the four directions. The cultures of the other regions were relatively backward and were able to develop only under its [i.e., the Yellow River valley's] influence. This view is incomplete. In historical terms, the Yellow River valley did indeed play an important part, frequently occupying a leading position during periods of civilization. Nevertheless, during the same periods the ancient cultures of the other regions were also developing in accordance with their own respective characteristics and courses, as is increasingly proven

[56] Noel Barnard and Sato Tamotsu, *Metallurgical Remains of Ancient China* (Tokyo: Nichiosha, 1975), pp. 72–5; K. C. Chang, *The Archaeology of Ancient China*, 1st ed., pp. 54–6; Cheng Te-k'un *Archaeology in China. Vol. 1: Prehistoric China* (Cambridge: Heffer, 1959), pp. 64–7; Cheng Te-k'un, *Archaeology in China. Vol. 2: Shang China* (Cambridge: Heffer, 1960), pp. 243–9; William Watson, *Archaeology in China* (London: Parrish, 1960), p. 9; idem, *China Before the Han Dynasty* (New York: Praeger, 1961), pp. 36–7.

[57] Judith M. Treistman, "China at 1000 B.C.: A Cultural Mosaic," *Science* 160 (1968): 853–6; idem, *Prehistory of China* (Garden City, N.Y.: Natural History Press, 1972), pp. 23–50; William Meacham, "Continuity and Local Evolution in the Neolithic of South China: A Non-Nuclear Approach," *Current Anthropology* 18 (1977): 419–40.

[58] Su Bingqi and Yin Weizhang, "Guanyu kaoguxue wenhua de quxi leixing wenti," *Wenwu* 1981.5: 10–17; rpt. in *Su Bingqi kaoguxue lunshu xuanji* (Beijing: Wenwu, 1984), pp. 225–34.

by the archaeological data from various places. In the meantime, influence was always mutual; the Central Plain gave influence to the various places, and the various places gave influence to the Central Plain.

Among the "various places" (*quxi* 區系) to which Su refers, he singled out six. They are: (1) the area where Shaanxi, Henan, and Shanxi join together; (2) Shandong and some regions in neighboring provinces; (3) Hubei and its neighboring areas; (4) the lower reaches of the Yangzi River; (5) the southern region, with Lake Boyang and the Pearl River delta as an axis; (6) the northern region, principally the lands along the Great Wall. Within each region there may be many cultural types (*leixing* 類型).

Su's scheme of classification is obviously transitional, subject to continued expansions and modifications as the data from the field increase and require more sophisticated methods. Nevertheless, it gave legitimacy to a view of ancient China heretofore regarded as heresy: that Chinese civilization, rather than being the end result of a radiating process from the core (the Central Plain) to the "land of the barbarians," in fact had many origins. "Multiple origins," "pluralism," "diversity," "interaction," and terms such as these are now very much in vogue in Chinese archaeology. This is but one example of the numerous changes archaeology has brought to the study of ancient China.

The publication history of K. C. Chang's *The Archaeology of Ancient China* illustrates well the nature and extent of the changes in what most scholars regard as the most important issue facing students of ancient China: the origin of Chinese civilization. When it was first published in 1963, the available archaeological data were concentrated in the Central Plain of the Yellow River valley; consequently, the interpretive framework the book adopted was consistent with the sinocentric tradition. In 1968, the year of the second edition, there was a greater emphasis upon South China, but the basic view remained the same. By 1977, the year of the third edition, the nuclear hypothesis had to be rejected in the face of new information, such that extensive changes were made in the book's fundamental approach. The fourth edition of 1985 was written completely anew, fully reflective of the extent of changes that had to be made. In this edition, a new concept, that of the interaction sphere, was introduced to characterize the dynamics of the regionalist process of cultural development.

When the chronologies of the various cultural types and systems are carefully traced, it becomes apparent that by approximately 4000 B.C. some of the adjacent regional cultures had come into contact as an inevitable result of expansion and that a number of ceramic styles began to assume a sphere-wide instead of merely a region-wide distribution. For example, among pottery vessel types, the *ding* and the *dou* are found in every region, often in large numbers, suggesting the wide distribution of a style of cooking formerly prevailing only in the Dawenkou and Daxi cultures. The perforated slate rectangular and semilunar knives represent another horizon marker, as do some pottery and jade art motifs that, as pointed out earlier, may reflect deeper substratal commonalities than recent contact.

With the definition of "interaction spheres," for the first time we can discuss the issue of the name "China." I suggest that from this point on, as the regions with which we are concerned came to be joined together in archaeological terms and exhibit increasing similarities, the interaction sphere may be referred to as "Chinese." It is obvious that this became the most important geographic region of the country; and it is unquestionable that later on, but certainly as early as Han, the cultural entity consisting of Su Bingqi's six regions became the core of what was subsequently called China. There is no other name aside from Chinese that would be as suitable. On the other hand, I suggest that the cultural types and culture systems within each region that were to be passed into the other regions were to be large in number and clear-cut in identification. By 3000 B.C., the Chinese interaction sphere can properly and appropriately be called China, as it became the stage where Chinese history began to play out, with its clearly defined actors, events, motivations, and story lines.

THE "TEN THOUSAND STATES" ON THE EVE OF THE HISTORICAL PERIOD

The so-called Longshan cultures are among the most significant discoveries that archaeology has made during the twentieth century. Very rich in themselves, they are also of great importance in the comparative study of Chinese cultures of the third millennium B.C., providing tangible and reliable clues to the reasons why and how civilizations and states first came into being. The Longshan culture was first discovered in 1931–2 at Chengziyai, near the former Longshan district of Licheng 歷城 county, Shandong. Its characteristics included a town enclosure built with the *hangtu*, or rammed-earth, technique; very thin and polished black pottery made with the wheel, apparently for ritual purposes; and deer scapulas burned and cracked, undoubtedly antecedent to the inscribed oracle bones of the Shang dynasty. Such remains obviously indicate a society at a stage of development between that of the Yangshao culture, which until the 1950s was the only known Neolithic culture earlier than the Longshan, and the later Shang civilization. However, the mechanism of this Longshan transition did not become clear until much more evidence was discovered in many more provinces over the course of the

past two or three decades. The most important of these new data consist of
the settlement patterns of the Longshan towns excavated in Shandong and
Henan;[59] the gradations of furnishings and spatial distributions of graves in
Shanxi, Shandong, Jiangsu, and Zhejiang provinces;[60] and the remains of
ritual objects, especially ritual jades, found mostly in the Liangzhu 良渚
culture, a "Longshan" culture distributed throughout the Lake Taihu 太湖
area of southern Jiangsu and northern Zhejiang.[61] These remains show clearly
that, by the Longshan period, societies in China had become stratified; that
the existence of a large number of ordered communities known in Chinese
terms as *wan guo* 萬國 (10,000 states) is a prerequisite for stratified societies;
and that in China the way societies became stratified explains why jade and
bronze ritual objects decorated with animal designs were characteristic.

In Longshan graves, for the first time since farmers built villages and
buried their dead in cemeteries outside those villages, material wealth that
was buried with the dead became concentrated into the graves of a small
number of presumably special people. At a very important Shanxi Longshan
site, Taosi 陶寺, in Xiangfen 襄汾 county, southern Shanxi, archaeological
remains stretched over an area 1.5 by 2 km. In the small area that has been
excavated, the major find was a gigantic cemetery believed to contain several
thousand graves. Among the graves already excavated, there were only 6 large
graves, about 80 medium-size graves, but over 600 small graves. In the small
graves, the corpses were seldom accompanied with any material goods. In
the medium-size ones, the dead were encased in painted wooden coffins and
were furnished with pottery vessels; wooden, stone, and jade ornaments; and
ritual objects such as *cong* 琮 tubes and some pig mandibles. The large graves
were much more richly furnished. Sets of ritual pottery vessels; musical
instruments made of wood, crocodile skins, and copper (bells); and painted
murals in the grave chambers were all found (Fig. 1.7).[62] Such hierarchical
order is seen in each cluster of tombs, suggesting a segmentary lineage type
of kinship organization, in which each lineage is stratified according to the
distance from its stem. Similar cemeteries were also found in Shandong.[63]

In the Liangzhu culture cemeteries of southern Jiangsu and northern Zhejiang, the concentration of wealth took the form of even more abundant and
exclusively ritual objects (Fig. 1.8). In tomb 20 of the Fanshan 反山 site, on
top of an artificial mound in Yuyao 余姚, northern Zhejiang, for example, a

---

[59] Liu Li, "Chiefdoms in the Longshan Culture," Ph.D. dissertation, Harvard University, 1994.
[60] Chang, *The Archaeology of Ancient China*, pp. 248–9, 255, 276–7.
[61] *Liangzhu wenhua yuqi* (Beijing: Wenwu and Liangmu, 1990).
[62] *Kaogu* 1980.1: 18–31; 1983.1: 30–42; 1983.6: 531–6; 1984.12: 1069–71.
[63] *Kaogu xuebao* 1980.3: 329–85.

Figure 1.7. A "large grave" in the Taosi cemetery, Xiangfen, Shanxi, a Longshan culture site. (Photograph by the Institute of Archaeology, Chinese Academy of Social Sciences.)

single skeleton was found with 547 artifacts, including 2 pottery vessels, 24 lithic implements, 9 ivory objects, 1 shark's tooth, and 170 sets, or 511 single pieces, of jade.[64] At Yaoshan 瑤山, only about 5 km northeast of Fanshan, an earthen altar, square in shape and constructed of three layers of earth of different colors, was built; it served a small cemetery, probably devoted to persons engaged in religious rituals. Among the 11 Liangzhu culture tombs here, tomb 7 produced 160 sets and pieces of jade, 3 stone axes, 4 pottery vessels, 1 piece of lacquerware, and 4 shark's teeth.[65] Almost all of the jades from these and other similar tombs belong, in terms of the terminology commonly employed in Chinese antiquarianism, to the *ruiyu* 瑞玉 (ritual jades) category. The excavator of the Yaoshan site was certainly right to speculate that these were graves of shamans or religious leaders. Since there are no graves of any other "leaders," these religious leaders in all probability were also political and military leaders, a point supported by the presence amidst

[64] *Wenwu* 1988.1: 3.
[65] *Wenwu* 1988.1: 32–3.

Figure 1.8. A Liangzhu culture burial with many ritual jades. Burial M-3 at Sidun site in
Changzhou, Jiangsu. After *Kaogu* 1984.2: pl. 2.

Figure 1.9. Liangzhu jades engraved with shaman's animals. Upper left: A *cong* from Yaoshan, Yuyao, Jiangsu. Upper right: detail of the central figure at left. After *Wenwu* 1988.1: color pl. 1, pl. 1. Lower left: From Sidun, Changzhou, Jiangsu. After *Kaogu* 1984.2: pl. 2.

the grave goods of ritual axes of jade. (This type of axe, called *yue* 鉞 in Chinese antiquarianism, was used in the early historical periods as the instrument for beheading people.)

The Liangzhu burials, with their concentration of ritual objects, were apparently those of the small group of people within each community who were privileged to perform shamanistic rituals and were allowed to visit Heaven. The most common ritual jades are *bi* 璧 and *cong*. These are now regarded by many scholars as shamanic paraphernalia endowing the bearer with the power to ascend from Earth (symbolized by the square shape of the *cong*) to Heaven (symbolized by the round shape of the *bi* and *cong*) with the assistance of the shaman's animals (which are engraved on all kinds of ritual jades; Fig. 1.9).[66] It is clear that in ancient China political power, derived

[66] K. C. Chang, "An Essay on *Cong*," *Orientations* 20, 6 (1989): 37–43.

from the concentration of shamanic paraphernalia, was the principal means to accumulate and divide material wealth. Among these paraphernalia, the most important were made of jade, a rock that is both rare and requires political power to quarry. This political power manifests itself in two aspects of ancient Chinese life: ritual and war. "Ritual and war," says the *Zuo zhuan* 左 傳 (Zuo's tradition), "are the affairs of the state."[67] Archaeologically, the most conspicuously manifest aspects of the life of the Longshan elite are none other than ritual and war.

These elites and their followers no longer lived in villages, but in nodes with centers of power woven into networks large and small. The Liangzhu site itself, in fact, consists of more than a dozen localities distributed over an area of several square kilometers.[68] Recent intensive surveys in Shandong and Henan have disclosed clusters of ruins of walled Longshan culture towns of different sizes, forming settlement hierarchies of at least two levels, some stretching over an area of several hundred square kilometers.[69] Additional studies of other areas in China may substantiate the speculation that hundreds or even thousands of such clusters were laid out over the landscape, competing for political survival, power, or even episodic supremacy. The late Longshan period, that is, the latter part of the third millennium and the earlier part of the second millennium B.C., was the period of the legendary *wan guo* (ten thousand states), a term often seen in the later, classical period. The surge in interactions among these many states made the Longshan one of the most active periods in ancient Chinese history. Not only did political chiefdoms, hierarchical settlements, and high shamanism begin in this period, but it may have witnessed the invention of true writing as well; many inscribed but yet to be deciphered pottery pieces have come to light (Fig. 1.10).[70]

It was within such a context that the earliest Chinese historical period began. This was the Three Dynasties, the Xia, Shang, and Zhou. These three states arose from the Longshan base to a still higher social level. With bronze instruments of ritual and war, and further armed with a full-fledged writing system, they went on to subdue many of the *wan guo* and to achieve supremacy in successive periods.

[67] *Zuo zhuan*, 27 (Cheng 13), 10b, 11a (note).

[68] Zhang Zhongpei, "Liangzhu wenhua de niandai he qi suo chu shehui jieduan," *Wenwu* 1995.5: 47–57.

[69] Zhang Zhiheng, "Huanghe zhongxiayou jizuo Longshan wenhua chengzhi de xingzhi," in Zhang Xuehai, ed., *Jinan Chengziyai yizhi fajue liushi zhounian guoji xueshu taolunhui wenji* (Jinan: Qi Lu, 1993), pp. 90–8; Gong Qiming and Jiang Jie, "Shi wen Longshan wenhua de shehui xingzhi," in ibid., pp. 77–89.

[70] For more discussion of these pottery inscriptions, including a different view of their nature, see Chapter 2.

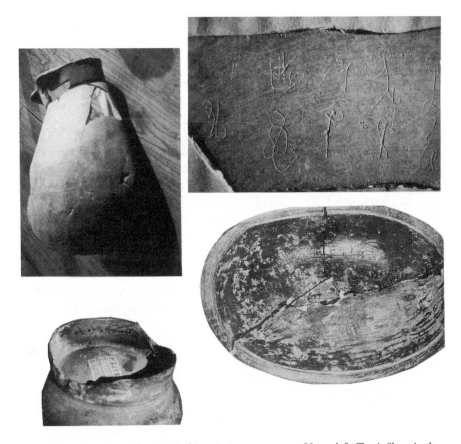

Figure 1.10. Longshan culture period inscriptions on pottery. Upper left: Taosi, Shanxi; photograph by the Institute of Archaeology, Chinese Academy of Social Sciences. Upper right: Dinggong, Zouping, Shandong. After *Kaogu* 1993.4: pl. 1. Lower left: Liangzhu, Zhejiang; in the collections of the Arthur M. Sackler Museum, Harvard University. Lower right: Liangzhu; published in He Tianxing, *Kangxian Liangzhu zhen zhi shiqi yu heitao* (Shanghai: Wu Yue yanjiuhui, 1937), pl. 1.

MYTHOLOGY, CHINA'S ORIGINS, AND
THE XIA DYNASTY

Before we move on to the other chapters of this book, all of which will deal in large part with the historical period, a brief account of traditional Chinese views of the period just discussed would be appropriate. Before the 1920s when scientific archaeology was introduced into China, there was already an account of the origins of Chinese civilization, an account recorded in myths, legends, and historical texts. These accounts record events that are supposed to have occurred at three different periods: remote antiquity; the ancient period when men had barely begun to organize and to invent; and the beginning of the political period when kings ruled. The first period was populated by gods, the second by demigods, and the third by the legendary kings.

The Cosmogony of the Ancient Periods

Scholars used to the mythology of the Judeo-Christian tradition observe that China lacks myths in general and creation myths in particular.[71] It is true that one finds in China no myth of the kind that is found in *The Book of Genesis*. No god or gods in China created, ex nihilo or in vacuo, Heaven, Earth, people, or animals. But in primordial antiquity there were a small number of supernatural creatures who were involved in a transformation process of a cataclysmic nature; this transformation closed an earlier world and opened a modern one. The most renowned of these creatures was Pan Gu 盤古. According to two different myths related by Xu Zheng 徐整 of the Three Kingdoms period (early third century A.D.), Pan Gu transformed the world in two ways. One of these myths says that

the world was opaque like the inside of an egg, and Pan Gu was born inside it. In 18,000 years, Heaven and Earth split open; the *yang*, which was clear, became Heaven, and the *yin*, which was murky, became Earth. Pan Gu was in the middle, transforming himself nine times every single day [and he performed] like a god in Heaven and like a sage on Earth. Heaven rose by one *zhang* 丈 every day, Earth thickened by one *zhang* every day, and Pan Gu grew by one *zhang* every day. It was like this for 18,000 years. Heaven was exceedingly high, Earth exceedingly deep, and Pan Gu exceedingly tall. . . . Thus, Heaven's distance from Earth was 90,000 *li*.[72]

In the other version, the transformation was not that of the universe but that of Pan Gu himself. In a fragment of Xu Zheng's *Wu yun li nianji* 五運歷年記, it is stated:

First born was Pan Gu, who as he was moribund became transformed. [His] breath became the wind and the clouds; his voice became the thunder; his left eye became the sun, and his right eye became the moon; his four limbs and five torsos became the four poles and the five mountains; his blood became the rivers; his sinews became geographic features; his muscles became the soils in the field; his hair and beard became stars and planets; his skin and skin-hairs became grasses and trees; his teeth and bones became bronzes and jades; his essence and marrow became pearls

[71] Derk Bodde, "Myths of Ancient China," in *Mythologies of the Ancient World*, ed. Samuel Noah Kramer (Garden City, N.Y.: Doubleday, 1961), pp. 367–408.
[72] *San Wu Li ji*, as quoted in *Taiping yulan*, 2, p. 4b.

and gemstones; his sweat became rain and lakes; and the various worms in his body, touched by the wind, became the black-haired commoners.[73]

To what extent these two stories of the third century can be said to be a part of the native Chinese culture described in this chapter is not yet knowable. Many scholars believe that Pan Gu was originally a god of certain southern Chinese peoples and did not attain supreme status in the Yellow River valley until about the Han (206 B.C.–A.D. 220) period.[74] But there is no compelling reason why these stories could not have been known much earlier in the Yellow River valley as well as in the Yangzi River valley. The *Shan hai jing* 山海經 (Classic of mountains and seas), compiled in part during the Warring States period, describes a creature named Zhuyin 燭陰 as "the god of Zhong 鍾 Mountain. [When Zhuyin] opens his eyes there comes the day; when he closes them there is the night. When he exhales he brings forth winter, and when he inhales there is the summer."[75] Still earlier, the separation of Heaven from Earth in the first Pan Gu myth describes a cosmic structure not only found in the oracle-bone inscriptions of the Shang dynasty,[76] but also represented by the layout of the Yangshao culture burial in Puyang 濮陽, Henan, commonly agreed to be that of a fifth millennium B.C. shaman. Many scholars interpret this layout to represent a cosmogram with a round Heaven and a square Earth.[77]

Two other cataclysmic events that took place in post-primordial times are recorded in the myths of the ten suns and the repair of Heaven by Nü Wa 女媧. The first of these myths describes a time when ten suns came out simultaneously, causing a drought. Archer Yi 羿 used his bow and arrows to shoot nine of the suns out of the heavens. This story appears in both the *Shan hai jing* and in the "Heavenly Questions" (*Tian wen* 天問) section of the *Chu ci* 楚辭 (Verses of Chu), both texts datable to the Warring States period.[78] Some scholars believe the story of the ten suns is related to the *xun* 旬 or ten-day week of the Shang calendar.[79] There is also a view that considers the earlier

[73] Xu Zheng, *Wu yun li nianji*, as quoted in Ma Su, *Yi shi*, 1, p. 2a.

[74] Rui Yifu, "Miaozu de hongshui gushi yu Fuxi Nüwa de chuanshuo," *Renleixue jikan* 1 (1938): 155–94.

[75] *Shanhai jing* ("Hainei beijing"), 8 (Yuan Ke, *Shan hai jing jiaozhu* [Shanghai: Guji, 1980], p. 230). For the authorship and dates of this text, see Michael Loewe, ed., *Early Chinese Texts: A Bibliographical Guide* (Berkeley: Society for the Study of Early China and the Institute of East Asian Studies, University of California, 1993), pp. 357–67.

[76] Chen Mengjia, *Yinxu buci zongshu* (Beijing: Kexue, 1956), pp. 584–94.

[77] Pang Pu, "Huo li gouchen," *Zhongguo wenhua* 1 (1989): 3–23; Feng Shi, "Henan Puyang Xishuipo 46 hao mu de tianwenxue yanjiu," *Wenwu* 1990.3: 52–60, 69.

[78] For the *Shan hai jing*, see note 81; *Chu ci* ("Tian wen"), 3. 9b (*Chu ci buzhu* [Sibu beiyao ed.]) (David Hawkes, *The Songs of the South: An Ancient Chinese Anthology of Poems by Qu Yuan and Other Poets* [Harmondsworth: Penguin, 1985], p. 129). For the authorship and dates of this text, see Loewe, ed., *Early Chinese Texts*, pp. 48–55.

[79] Guan Donggui, "Zhongguo gudai shi ri shenhua zhi yanjiu," in *Cong bijiao shenhua dao wenxue*, ed. Gu Tianhong and Chen Huihua (Taipei: Dongda, 1977), pp. 83–149; Sarah Allan, "The Myth of the Xia Dynasty," *JRAS* 2 (1984): 242–56.

animal motifs in the decorations of the Neolithic Hemudu culture as deriving from the sun myth, thus pushing its origin back even farther.[80]

The second myth concerns the villain Gong Gong 共工. Competing
with Zhuan Xu 顓頊 for power, when Gong Gong lost he knocked his head
against Buzhou 不周 Mountain, one of the mountains serving as a pillar supporting the heavens. The mountain fell, causing a hole to appear in the
northwestern corner of the heavens and water to flood to the southeast on
the earth. Nü Wa melted rocks of the five colors to mend this break, thus
restoring the dome to good shape. The earliest text in which this story
appears is the *Huainanzi* 淮南子, of the second century B.C.[81] However, the
other cosmogonic myths – the two versions of Pan Gu's creation and the
story of the ten suns – could be at least as early as the time of the Three
Dynasties, or, as I believe to be more likely, even earlier still, going well back
into the Upper Paleolithic period. In the Upper Paleolithic period, among
the inhabitants of the northern and eastern parts of Asia, the ancestors of
both the Chinese people and many New World peoples, there was undoubtedly a common cosmology in which Heaven was rounded like a dome and
Earth was square and oriented according to the four cardinal directions, each
of which had a name and a color. These could be represented by a ritual
chamber, with sacred trees at the four corners. In this ritual chamber,
shamans used such means as sacred animals, mountains and trees serving as
an *axis mundi*, and music, dance, and hallucinogens to ascend to Heaven to
meet with the deities and the ancestors. These shamans were capable of
transforming the world.[82]

The Heroes

The largest category of Chinese myths concerns hero myths, described by
Derk Bodde as "those of the culture heroes who enjoy supernatural birth, are
sometimes aided by protective animals, become sage rulers or otherwise
perform great deeds for mankind."[83] Within this category, those heroes who
"become sage rulers" appear in much later times in human history and within
the context of ancestral origins of clans or sibs, while those who "otherwise
perform great deeds" are more likely to be remnants of hero myths told by
the Paleolithic and Neolithic peoples.

[80] Hayashi Minao, *In Shû seidôki moyô no kenkyû* (Tokyo: Yoshikawa kôbunkan, 1986), pp. 43–53.
[81] *Huainanzi*, 6 (Liu Wendian, *Huainan honglie jijie* [Shanghai: Shangwu, 1926; rpt. Taipei: Shangwu,
1968], 6.10b. Nü Wa also appears in a brief passage of the *Shan hai jing* as a Pan Gu–like creature
whose intestines were transformed into ten spirits (*Shan hai jing*, 16, p. 389).
[82] Kwang-chih Chang, "Shamanism in Human History," *Bulletin of the Department of Archaeology and
Anthropology* 49 (1993): 1–6.
[83] Bodde, "Myths of Ancient China," p. 370.

The stories of these heroes are not very detailed. Most of them are collected in the chapter "Zuo" 作 (Inventions) of the *Shi ben* 世本 (Roots of the generations), a text available already to Sima Qian 司馬遷 (ca. 145–86 B.C.). Although the book was largely lost after the Southern Song (1127–1278), various editors used quotations of it in other early texts to reconstruct it. The *Shi ben* usually records only the name of a hero and a word or phrase about the deed with which he is credited. The most important heroes are the following:[84]

Hero's name	*Hero's activities or inventions*
Sui Ren 燧人	First use of fire
Bao Xi 庖犧 (Fu Xi 伏犧)	Wedding ritual; *se*-zither 瑟
his official Mang 芒	Hunting and fishing nets
Shen Nong 神農	*Qin*-zither 琴; medicinal plants
Huang Di 黃帝 (Yellow Emperor)	Cooked meals; crown
his official Xihe 羲和	Divination by the sun
his official Changyi 常儀	Divination by the moon
his official Qu 區	Divination by the stars
his official Linglun 伶倫	Musical notes
his official Darao 大撓	Calendar by *jiazi* 甲子
his official Lishou 隸首	Arithmetic
his archivists Quyong 沮誦 and Cangjie 倉頡	Writing
his official Shi Huang 史皇	Graphics
Yong Fu 雍父	Stone and wooden mortars; pestles
Hai 胲	Domesticated cattle
Xiangtu 相土	Horse carriage
Nü Wa 女媧	The Jew's harp
Hui 揮	Bow
Yimou 夷牟	Arrow
Chiyou 蚩尤	The five weapons
Zhurong 祝融	The market
Hou Ji 后稷	Plant cultivation
Wu 巫 (shaman) Peng 彭	Medicine
Wu Xian 巫咸	Yarrow divination; drum
Shun 舜	Pottery
Chui 垂	Wooden digging sticks; bell
Kui 夔	Music
Gun 鯀	The town wall
Yao 堯	The palace

[84] *Shi ben bazhong* (Shanghai: Shangwu, 1977), pp. 355–64.

Although different reconstructions of the *Shi ben* sometimes give different attributions of the same inventions, the major heroes are invariably Fu Xi, Sui Ren, and Shen Nong. They were, respectively, the inventors of hunting, fire, and agriculture (and medicine). They were followed by the Yellow Emperor (Huang Di), who established rule and most of its trappings. In the historiographic sources of the Later Han dynasty, these heroes were systematized into the *San huang* 三皇 (Three August Ones), and the *Wu di* 五帝 (Five Emperors). In the three-period system adopted here, we may place the creation heroes into the category of gods, the *San huang* into that of the demigods, and the *Wu di* into that of the legendary kings.

The Legendary Kings

As just described, some of the heroes in ancient Chinese myths correspond to later periods in human (Chinese) history and their inventions are often markers of civilization. For example, the Yellow Emperor and his court officials are credited with the institutions of rule, sophisticated calendars, and writing. The second of the Five Emperors, Zhuan Xu, is associated with the extremely important myth of the separation of Heaven from Earth. This myth is first mentioned in the "Lü xing" 呂刑 chapter of the *Shang shu* 尚書 (Venerated documents), which dates to approximately the fourth century B.C.:

We are told that the Miao . . . created oppressive punishments which threw the people into disorder. Shang Ti [Di], the Lord on High . . . surveyed the people and found them lacking in virtue. Out of pity for those who were innocent, the August Lord . . . had the Miao exterminated. "Then he charged Ch'ung [Chong] and Li to cut the communication between Heaven and Earth so that there would be no descending and ascending." After this had been done, order was restored and the people returned to virtue.[85]

A longer version of the same story is recorded in the *Guo yu* 國語 (Sayings of the states), and some fragments of it are also preserved in the *Shan hai jing*.[86] Several Chinese mythologists have correctly interpreted this myth as symbolizing the defining threshold in the rise of a stratified society on China's way to civilization.[87] Before Zhuan Xu and his two gods Chong 重 and Li 黎 made Heaven inaccessible, in the Yangshao period, for example, it was open to every household that had or could hire a shaman. In the Longshan period, shamanic paraphernalia came to be concentrated in the hands of just

[85] Bodde, "Myths of Ancient China," pp. 389–90; *Shang shu*, 19 ("Lü xing"), 18a–20b.
[86] *Guo yu* (Shanghai: Guji, 1978), p. 562; *Shan hai jing* ("Dahuang xijing"), 16, p. 402.
[87] Xu Xusheng, *Zhongguo gushi de chuanshuo shidai*, rev. ed. (Beijing: Kexue, 1960), pp. 79–80; Yang Xiangkui, *Zhongguo gudai shehui yu gudai sixiang yanjiu* (Shanghai: Renmin, 1964), pp. 162–3.

a few people, suggesting a monopoly of the ability to ascend to and descend from Heaven. In this sense, the Longshan period coincided with the period when Zhuan Xu caused Heaven and Earth to become separated. This myth, thus, not only marks the start of social stratification, but also indicates clearly the mechanism whereby wealth came to be concentrated.

The three "emperors" following Zhuan Xu were Yao, Shun, and Yu 禹. Their common distinctive feature is that each wanted to abdicate to the next in view of the latter's virtues, and the latter eventually succeeded to their high positions despite their intent of yielding to the sons of the former ruler. Their inability to yield was due to the public's insistence on their accession because these designated heirs were considered more virtuous than the former rulers' sons. Thus, Yao was succeeded by Shun, despite Shun's efforts to yield to Dan Zhu 丹朱, the son of Yao. Shun, in his turn, was succeeded by Yu, in spite of Yu's effort to have Yi, the son of Shun, rule. But many historians of ancient China dismiss this refusal to serve, seeing instead sinister plots in relation to the succession question.[88]

THE QUESTION OF THE XIA DYNASTY

The last hero, who is also the last of the Three Emperors, was Yu. Yu was a bona fide hero, because he succeeded where his father, Gun, had failed, in resolving a flood crisis that China had faced for a long time. Gun's strategy was to build dikes to stem the water's advance. Yu, however, opened drainage channels, allowing the water a controlled flow to the seas. With this technique he finally succeeded. The people were so enormously grateful to Yu that their gratitude extended even to his son Qi 啟, whom they caused to succeed Yu.

China's traditional historiography treats Yu somewhat differently from the earlier heroes. The first chapter of the *Shi ji* concerns the Five Emperors, from the Yellow Emperor to Shun. But the second chapter, which begins its account with Yu, is entitled "Xia benji" 夏本紀 (Basic annals of Xia), thus ascribing to Yu and his successors the same authority and status as the rulers of the Shang (Yin) and Zhou dynasties. In this way, Xia is represented as a "dynasty," Yu being succeeded by his son Qi, the first instance wherein rule was handed down on the basis of heredity.

Xia, however, was not the only such state at the time. Yu is said once to have summoned his contemporaries to Tushan 塗山, his wife's home state. Those who gathered are said to have come from 10,000 states.[89] In singling out Xia, the *Shi ji* describes the genealogy, capital cities, major political

[88] See, e.g., Sarah Allan, *The Heir and the Sage* (San Francisco: Chinese Materials Center, 1981).
[89] Gu Zuyu, *Dushi fangyu jiyao* (Shanghai: Shangwu, 1936), 1, p. 9.

events, and other issues concerning this "dynasty" and its history. There are no other chapters describing any of the other contemporary states.

Does this mean that there was indeed a "Xia dynasty" at the head of Chinese "history"? In traditional Chinese historiography, this could not be questioned, because the sequence of the Three August Ones, the Five Emperors, and the Three Dynasties lay at the root of every educated Chinese person's idea of the beginning of Chinese history. But beginning in the 1920s, a group of Chinese historians influenced by Western historiographical methods began to question the evidence on which this traditional view of ancient history was based. This led to the formation of an *Yigu pai* 疑古派 (Doubting Antiquity School), headed by Gu Jiegang 顧頡剛 and Qian Xuantong 錢玄同.[90] Their first target was Yu, the alleged founder of the Xia dynasty; they successfully demonstrated the mythical nature of this supposedly historical figure. Following this, some scholars have even regarded the entire Xia dynasty as sheer invention.[91] On the other hand, since the genealogy of the Shang dynasty given in the *Shi ji* has been essentially validated by the newly discovered oracle-bone inscriptions, there would seem to be good reason to accept its genealogy of the Xia dynasty as well.

The sequential view of the interrelationship among the Three Dynasties – Xia, Shang, and Zhou – is increasingly viewed by contemporary historians as inappropriate. Instead, a horizontal view has taken its place.[92] In this perspective, early Shang, early Zhou, and Xia were among the 10,000 states that were distributed throughout North China's Yellow River valley during the 2,000 years leading up to the establishment of imperial China. Many of these states were ruled by dynasties and could have left behind genealogical records. How many of these states deserve to be mentioned in a historical account ultimately depends on the historian's judgment. That Sima Qian selected Xia alone for treatment as a ruling dynasty is evidence of his great judgment, because it is now becoming increasingly clearer that the Xia state is represented archaeologically: since 1959, evidence of its culture has been continuously unearthed at the type site Erlitou 二里頭, just east of Luoyang 洛陽 in northwestern Henan province. The archaeological remains of this Erlitou culture are now found scattered throughout southern Shanxi and northwestern Henan and are dated to 1900–1350 B.C.,[93] coinciding in time and in space with the Xia dynasty as described in ancient texts. Was there a Xia

[90] See Gu Jiegang, ed., *Gu shi bian*, vol. 1 (Shanghai: Pushe, 1926).

[91] Allan, "The Myth of the Xia Dynasty."

[92] See, e.g., K. C. Chang, "Sandai Archaeology and the Formation of States in Ancient China: Processual Aspects of the Origin of Chinese Civilization," in *The Origins of Chinese Civilization*, ed. David N. Keightley (Berkeley: University of California Press, 1984), pp. 495–521.

[93] Xu Xusheng, "1959 nian xia Yuxi diaocha Xiaxu de chubu baogao," *Kaogu* 1959.11: 592–600.

dynasty? Present evidence suggests that there indeed was a Xia dynasty. That Sima Qian selected Xia from among many contemporary polities was probably because during the earliest part of the Chinese Bronze Age or the Three Dynasties period, Xia was most powerful. If Erlitou can be identified with Xia, this is indeed true.

CHAPTER TWO

LANGUAGE AND WRITING

William G. Boltz

No one needs to be persuaded that language plays a fundamental part in any society's everyday activities and constitutes one of the most durable fibers in the tapestry of human history. Indeed, language is a defining feature of our species. The present chapter describes the structure, history, and setting of the Chinese language, as well as the first appearance and subsequent development of its script, over the millennium from 1200 B.C., the time of the earliest known written record of Chinese, down to the beginning of the imperial era, ca. 200 B.C. While this is primarily a linguistically slanted presentation, it is important to remain aware of the extent to which language history is intertwined with fundamental issues of cultural history in general. The historian may see in language history a rich record of the lives of real people played out in a real world setting and may find clues even to a people's prehistory. These kinds of broad historical considerations depend on the narrower work of the linguist.

For the linguist, language history is the sum of a painstakingly assembled collection of internal analyses of speech forms and phonetic formulas. The historical linguist is concerned with the evolution of sounds, words, and structures of language, and with linguistic affinities per se. The fact that the linguist's work is accomplished with little reference to the associated nonlinguistic culture enables the linguist to make an especially valuable contribution to the overall historical study of a people by providing a body of evidence largely independent of the historian's other sources.

We have no record of language, of course, until the invention of writing. History is in fact conventionally defined as beginning with the first appearance of writing, because the availability of written evidence makes a dramatic difference in what we can know about the past. This applies with special force when what interests us about the past is language itself. In the first part of what follows we will focus on the nature of the Chinese language in the pre-imperial period and in the second part we will focus on the origin and evolution of the Chinese writing system, seeing both of these subjects as central features of early Chinese civilization.

THE CHINESE LANGUAGE

The Chinese language is unambiguously documented no earlier than the time of the late Shang state, about 1200 B.C. The earliest written Chinese texts presently known are the so-called oracle-bone inscriptions from Anyang 安陽 in modern Henan province, the site of the last Shang capital. In spite of formidable difficulties in reading these documents, it is clear that the language in which they are written is directly ancestral to what we know as "Chinese" in both a classical and a modern context. This marks the beginning of Chinese history, and our inference is that the people who spoke and wrote that language were Chinese and are the ancestors of the people we now know as Chinese.

Neither the Chinese language nor the Chinese people appeared out of nowhere in the second half of the second millennium B.C. Both surely were present in North China, and perhaps across most of Central China as well, from much earlier times. But, for want of linguistic artifacts, we can know very little about the Chineseness of that presence, and insofar as we intend to use the ethnonym "Chinese" meaningfully, rather than as a simple taxonomic convenience, we can speak of Chinese history, both of people and of language, only from the comparatively late date of around 1200 B.C. and from the comparatively limited area of the Anyang region.

The name "Chinese," designating the language, not the people, is at once both convenient and inconvenient, precise and imprecise. It is convenient and precise as a single term referring to all varieties of Chinese, past and present alike, without regard to changes over time or space or to degree of mutual intelligibility. It is inconvenient and imprecise for just the same reason; it fails to distinguish among the diverse forms of Chinese, either synchronically or diachronically. Considering only those languages and dialects that we call "Chinese," and disregarding the languages of non-Chinese minorities, modern China is fully comparable in linguistic diversity to that great arc of modern Europe from Hispania to Moldavia in which one or another of the Romance languages is spoken. For the earliest historical period in ancient China, by contrast, we have no documentary record of anything comparable to the great richness of languages that characterizes early European history from its Mesopotamian and Aegean origins down to the end of the classical age. All the same, it is reasonable to suppose that Chinese did not exist for the first millennium of its recorded history in a linguistic vacuum, untouched by the sounds of other tongues, but rather that it was in contact to some indeterminable extent with non-Chinese-speaking neighbors. Written records of such contact unfortunately do not exist, because either none of those non-Chinese-speaking neighbors had a writing system, or if they did, it has disappeared without trace (so far) in the subsequent dominance of an expanding Chinese culture. If the Chinese themselves, prior to the Han period, saw fit to record anything substantial of or about their neighbors' languages, it has not survived.

What we do have as evidence of speakers of non-Chinese languages in the vicinity of, and in contact with, Chinese in the ancient period is a residue of foreign words and names registered in Chinese texts, and in some cases recognized as standard vocabulary items in the Chinese language. When these last-mentioned items can be identified as non-Chinese in origin, they are called "loanwords" and attest to linguistic contact between the Chinese speakers and the speakers of the source language of the loans. In some cases we find words that may seem related by the simple criterion of phonetic similarity to words of a non-Chinese language, but that also seem to constitute an intrinsic part of the original Chinese vocabulary. This makes it uncertain whether they are loanwords and raises instead the possibility of what linguists typically call a "genetic," or "cognate," relation between the languages in question.

When linguists refer to a language as "genetically" related to other languages, they mean that it has devolved from the same stock as the others. The biological metaphor is maintained to the extent that we speak of related languages as constituting a "family" and having arisen from a common "parent" language.

While there is clearly some degree of objective validity to statements about languages being related to one another in a way that depends conceptually on a "family tree" structure (what linguists have traditionally called a *Stammbaum* model), the taxonomic thinking taken over from the classificatory constructs and evolutionary models associated with nineteenth-century Darwinism is ultimately inappropriate when applied to linguistic evolution. It can distort the true picture of language relation by making it look clear-cut and ideal, as if all linguistic evolution were codifiable as a sequence of diachronic, or "vertical," developments in which one form of a language derives only from a single immediate predecessor. Even worse, the evolutionary model is sometimes allowed to suggest or imply a kind of "progressive" development from "imperfect" to "perfect," or "less perfect" to "more perfect," the nature of perfection never being clearly specified. In fact synchronic, or "lateral," influences across language boundaries at virtually every stage will have significantly affected the degree to which a given language can be said to be a pristine offshoot of an earlier form. There is in any case no such thing as linguistic perfection or imperfection; these are meaningless attributes in the context of language history.

In theory at least, even if not recognized much in practice, questions arise when the extent of lateral influences, particularly those from noncognate neighboring languages, reaches a certain level. It becomes necessary to ask whether the cognate relation of the language in question to its "language-family forebears" should still be regarded as the primary defining relation or whether instead the sum of influences over time from noncognate languages has affected it so substantially that it is no longer accurately or meaningfully defined by its cognate affinity alone. The practical consequence of this theoretical concern is that family tree models give an artificial and oversimplified picture of language evolution, and statements about cognate relations of languages based on such models should be taken as idealized approximations at best.

With these definitions and caveats in mind, we can identify Chinese as a part of a large Sino-Tibetan language family. As the name partly suggests, Sino-Tibetan is divided into two major branches, Chinese and Tibeto-Burman. In the past the Tai languages were often included on the Chinese-branch side, which was then called Sino-Tai, but current accepted wisdom has removed them from the Sino-Tibetan language family altogether. Lexical similarities between Tai and Chinese are deemed the result of borrowing, and typological similarities are called "areal features", that is, features that come to characterize most if not all languages spoken in a given area irrespective of cognate relation.

Reference is often made to the Sino-Tibetan language family and to the position of Chinese within it as if these were established facts, when they are actually parts of a still unproven and conjectural hypothesis. The hypothesis of a Sino-Tibetan language family is based almost entirely on lexical evidence, that is, on a body of individual words in Chinese, usually a reconstructed form of Middle Chinese (MC) or Old Chinese (OC) (100–06) see pp. 100–06 and a body of words in one or more Tibeto-Burman languages, usually including classical Written Tibetan (WT) and Written Burmese (WB), that seem to match the Chinese words phonetically. The words in the table on page 79 are typical of such evidence.[1]

---

[1] The table is taken from Jerry Norman, *Chinese* (Cambridge University Press, 1988), p. 13. Norman uses the Middle and Old Chinese reconstructions of the late F. K. Li. For Li's Middle Chinese I have substituted the Early Middle Chinese (EMC) forms as reconstructed by E. G. Pulleyblank in order to be consistent with my use of Pulleyblank's reconstructions generally throughout. So as not to alter the impression of phonetic similarity that Norman wishes to convey via this chart, I have maintained Li's Old Chinese (OC) forms as Norman gives them. All WT, WB, Bodo, and Trung forms are transcribed exactly as Norman has them. I have omitted two items from Norman's chart: "worm/insect" and

Morphological or syntactic considerations are rarely invoked in support of the Sino-Tibetan hypothesis, and then only in a very tentative way, because the differences between Chinese and Tibeto-Burman in both of these categories are formidable and not easily explained.[2] This gives the hypothesis the appearance of standing unsurely on only one leg. At the present stage of our still somewhat rudimentary knowledge, the belief that Chinese and Tibeto-Burman are cognate language groups may seem more persuasive than that they are not, and may even be correct. All the same, as recently as 1988 Jerry Norman, while describing the Sino-Tibetan hypothesis as "unassailable" and pronouncing the list of words given in Table 2.1 "by itself virtually sufficient to establish a genetic link between Chinese and the other languages given," was obliged at the same time to acknowledge that "surprisingly little has been done in the field of Sino-Tibetan linguistic comparison" and that "the phonological correspondences between Chinese and Tibeto-Burman have never been worked out in detail."[3] To believe in the Sino-Tibetan hypothesis in these circumstances is as much an act of faith as it is adherence to a representation of demonstrable linguistic fact.[4]

The Tibeto-Burman half of the Sino-Tibetan family is further bifurcated into Tibetan and Burman, each of which in its turn comprehends a multitude of derivative languages and dialects. We might naturally assume that the closest linguistic neighbors of the Chinese would be speakers of related Tibeto-Burman languages, but this cannot be shown directly because the ear-

"poison". I have also added the Chinese characters for convenience in identifying the Chinese word in question. For Pulleyblank's reconstructions, see Pulleyblank, *Middle Chinese: A Study in Historical Phonology* (Vancouver: University of British Columbia Press, 1984), and idem, *Lexicon of Reconstructed Pronunciation in Early Middle Chinese, Late Middle Chinese, and Early Mandarin* (Vancouver: University of British Columbia Press, 1991).

[2] The exception to this generalization is the work of E. G. Pulleyblank, whose speculation about the nature of Old Chinese morphology derives significantly from the model of Classical Tibetan. See, e.g., Pulleyblank, "Close/Open Ablaut in Sino-Tibetan," *Lingua* 14 (1965): 230–40; and idem, "Some New Hypotheses Concerning Word Families in Chinese," *Journal of Chinese Linguistics* 1 (1973): 111–25.

[3] Norman, *Chinese*, p. 13. Two studies stand out as recent examples of substantial efforts to establish the Chinese/Tibeto-Burman relation through identifying sound correspondences in the traditional neogrammarian way: Nicholas C. Bodman, "Proto-Chinese and Sino-Tibetan: Data Towards Establishing the Nature of the Relationship," in *Contributions to Historical Linguistics*, ed. Frans van Coetsem and Linda R. Waugh. Cornell Linguistic Contributions, vol. 3 (Leiden: Brill, 1980), pp. 34–199; and W. South Coblin, *A Sinologist's Handlist of Sino-Tibetan Lexical Comparisons*, Monumenta Serica Monograph series, no. 18 (Nettetal: Steyler, 1986).

[4] One of the most recently studied alternatives to the Sino-Tibetan hypothesis is the proposal that Chinese is genetically related to Austronesian languages. See, e.g., Laurent Sagart, "Chinese and Austronesian: Evidence for a Genetic Relationship," *Journal of Chinese Linguistics* 21, 1 (1993): 1–62. For a critical evaluation of this proposal, see Paul Jenkuei Li, "Is Chinese Genetically Related to Austronesian?" in *The Ancestry of the Chinese Language*, ed. William S.-Y. Wang. Journal of Chinese Linguistics monograph series, no. 8 (Berkeley, 1995), pp. 93–112.

The most recent examination of the proposal that Chinese is related genetically to the Tibeto-Burman languages is William H. Baxter, "'A Stronger Affinity . . . than Could Have Been Produced by Accident': A Probabilistic Comparison of Old Chinese and Tibeto-Burman," in *The Ancestry of the Chinese Language*, ed. William S-Y. Wang, pp. 1–39.

Table 2.1. *Comparisons of words in the Sino-Tibetan language family*

Character	English	Early Middle Chinese	Old Chinese	Written Tibetan	Written Burmese	Bodo	Trung
吾	I	ŋɔ	ngag	nga	ŋa	aŋ	ŋà
汝	you	nɨə'	njag	—	naŋ	nəŋ	nă
無	not	muə̌	mjag	ma	ma'	—	mà
二	two	nɨʰ	njid	gnyis	hnac	nəy	ǎ-ni
三	three	sam	səm	gsum	sûm	tam	ǎ-səm
五	five	ŋɔ'	ngag	lnga	ŋâ	ba	pə́ŋ-ŋà
六	six	luwk	ljəkw	drug	khrok	—	khlu
九	nine	kuw'	kjəgw	dgu	kûi	—	də-gə̀
日	sun/ day	ɲit	njit	nyi-ma	ne	—	nì
薪	tree/ wood	sin	sjin	shing	sac	—	—
年	year	nɛn	nin	-ning	hnac	—	nin
名	name	mjiajŋ	mjing	ming	ə-mañ	muŋ	—
目	eye	muwk	mjəkw	mig	myak	megón	miè
耳	ear	nɨʔ/ni'	njəg	rna-ba	na	na:-	ǎ-nà
乳	breast	nuə̌'	njug	nu-mu	nui'	—	nuŋ
節	joint	tsɛt	tsit	tshigs	ə-chac	—	tsi
魚	fish	ŋɨǎ	ngjag	nya	ŋâ	ná	ŋa
犬	dog	kʰwɛn'	khwin	khyi	khwe	—	də-gəi
苦	bitter	kʰɔ'	khag	kha	khâ	ká	kha "salty"
涼	cold	liaŋ	gljang	grang	—	gazaŋ	glaŋ
殺	kill	ʂəɨt~ ʂɛ:t	srat	bsat	sat	—	sat
死	die	si'	sjid	shi-ba	se	təy	çi

liest written records of any Tibeto-Burman language are the Old Tibetan texts (many known only from the Dunhuang 敦煌 finds of the turn of the century), and these date no earlier than the eighth century A.D.

The hypothesis of a cognate relation between the Chinese and Tibeto-Burman languages entails the claim not only of a close geographic proximity of speakers at some undetermined early time, but also of a common ultimate source. This putative common source would account for lexical similarities of the kind exemplified in Table 2.1 and would belong to a time much earlier than the historical period with which we are concerned here. One of the major causes of linguistic differentiation is generally assumed to be the splitting of the community of speakers into separate groups that move out of contact. It is entirely possible that the groups that spoke the nascent Chinese and Tibeto-Burman languages had moved long distances away from each other by the beginning of the historical era. Indeed, to the extent that geographic separation is regarded as a cause of language differentiation, the degree of difference between the Chinese and Tibeto-Burman languages argues strongly for a prolonged period of no direct contact between the two, a period that could well have included the millennium between 1200 and 200 B.C. Although we cannot use the *argumentum ex silentio* to rule out the presence of speakers of Tibeto-Burman languages in North Central China in pre-imperial historical times, we must acknowledge that within the framework of the Sino-Tibetan hypothesis, there is no direct or tangible evidence attesting to such a presence. And we must acknowledge further that the ideal model of diachronic language differentiation would suggest to the contrary that Chinese speakers and Tibeto-Burman speakers were not in close proximity to each other at this comparatively late time.

Disavowal of the Sino-Tibetan hypothesis, on the other hand, means that all of the seeming cognates (e.g., the words in Table 2.1) must be explained as *borrowings*, that is, as loanwords either into Chinese from one or another Tibeto-Burman language or into the Tibeto-Burman language(s) from Chinese (except for the very limited possibility of chance similarity). This entails the assumption that Chinese speakers were in contact with speakers of Tibeto-Burman languages in the period between 1200 and 200 B.C. or, less likely, that the borrowings all predate the beginning of the historical era or postdate the beginning of the Chinese empire in the late third century B.C. Implicit in accepting the Sino-Tibetan hypothesis is the corollary that on linguistic evidence alone we cannot demonstrate contact between Chinese speakers and Tibeto-Burman speakers during the first millennium of the historical era, because all such evidence can be differently explained by the hypothesis. Rejecting it leaves us with a body of evidence that implies the likelihood of (but does not prove the fact of) contact between Chinese and Tibeto-Burman speakers during this time.[5]

Apart from Tibeto-Burman, the languages that we can identify with some confidence as having made up parts of the linguistic milieu in which the

[5] It may happen, of course, that cognate languages share one group of words inherited from their common source and another group that are later borrowings in one direction or another among the languages. Ideally the two kinds can be distinguished on the basis of differing sound correspondence patterns for each. Present knowledge of the sound correspondences that characterize the putative Sino-Tibetan language family is far from precise enough to be able to distinguish two such groups of shared words, and without the ability to make such distinctions we are unable to identify with confidence a given word as an inherited cognate or a loan.

The most recent attempt to establish a set of Sino-Tibetan sound correspondences is Gong Hwang-cherng, "The System of Finals in Proto-Sino-Tibetan," in *The Ancestry of the Chinese Language*, ed. William S-Y. Wang, pp. 41–92.

Chinese found themselves in the ancient period are Austroasiatic in the south and east and Indo-European in the northwest.

Austroasiatic

Austroasiatic is the name of a widespread language family stretching from the Munda languages in northwestern India and Khasi in Assam to Vietnamese and Muong in Vietnam, and including, among other languages, the Mon-Khmer languages in Lower Burma and parts of Indo-China. Jerry Norman and Mei Tsu-lin have identified a stratum of what appear to be early Austroasiatic loanwords in Chinese and have thus demonstrated the strong likelihood of an Austroasiatic presence in south China in pre-imperial times. They suggest that the data they have assembled point to Austroasiatic–Old Chinese language contact between 1000 and 500 B.C. in the area of the old state of Chu 楚, that is, in modern Hubei and northern Hunan provinces.[6]

There are three reasons for supposing that early contact with the Austroasiatic languages took place predominantly in the south. The most obvious reason is that modern Austroasiatic languages are found, apart from those on the Indian subcontinent, in the southernmost parts of China and in Southeast Asia. There is no good reason not to project that general geographical distribution back in time, although this should not preclude the possibility that Austroasiatic languages were also spoken further up into South Central China and along the eastern coast. E. G. Pulleyblank has recently suggested that in pre-imperial times the language of the Yi 夷 people in the east was non-Chinese and was probably related to the Austroasiatic languages known from areas to the south.[7] If correct, this would extend the domain of likely contact between Chinese and the Austroasiatic languages considerably further up the eastern coast than heretofore assumed. Second, it is probable that the peoples called by the Chinese name Yue 越 (also written 粵, both characters standing for the name Yue < EMC *wuat*, the source of the *Viet* part of the modern name "Vietnam") or referred to collectively as *bai yue* 百越 in early historical texts were Austroasiatic speakers, and Chinese historical records invariably place the Yue, including the pre-Han state of Yue, in the south.[8]

Mei and Norman substantiate the identification of the traditional Yue as Austroasiatic by giving two examples of words said in Han period Chinese texts to be from the Yue language that match words with the same meaning

[6] Tsu-lin Mei and Jerry Norman, "The Austroasiatics in Ancient South China: Some Lexical Evidence," *Monumenta Serica* 32 (1976): 274–301.

[7] E. G. Pulleyblank, "Zou 鄒 and Lu 魯 and the Sinification of Shandong," in *Chinese Language, Thought and Culture: Nivison and His Critics*, ed. P. Ivanhoe (La Salle, Ill.: Open Court, 1996), pp. 39–57.

[8] See Mei and Norman, "The Austroasiatics in Ancient South China," pp. 276–7.

in several of the modern Austroasiatic languages. These are not borrowings *sensu stricto*, but are simply indigenous Austroasiatic words registered in Chinese texts.

1. Zheng Xuan's 鄭玄 (A.D. 127–200) commentary to the *Zhou li* explains the word 札 *zha* < EMC *ʈṣɛːt* as 越人謂死為札 "the Yue people say *zha* < *ʈṣɛːt for 'die'."[9] Mei and Norman identify this with modern Vietnamese *chêt* and Mon *chɒt*, both meaning "die", as well as with similar words for "die" in a number of other Austroasiatic languages.

2. The *Shuowen jiezi* explains the character 獀 *sou* as 南越名犬玃獀: "In Nan-Yue the word for 'dog' is *nao-sou* < EMC *nuw-ṣuw*."[10] Mei and Norman identify the single-syllable entry word *sou* with Vietnamese *chɔ* "dog" and similar forms in a number of other Austroasiatic languages.

The third reason for supposing that Austroasiatic words came into Chinese via the south is that many of the borrowings are associated in some way with southern Chinese dialects or with southern features or products. The following examples are words that have become standard vocabulary items throughout Chinese.

3. One of the first Austroasiatic loanwords in Chinese to be recognized, and now perhaps the best known example, is the word *jiang* 江 "river", but especially "the Yangzi River", that is, the major river in the south of China, whence the loan presumably was introduced into Chinese. It has long been assumed that *jiang* < EMC *kæːŋ* with an OC **kl-* or **kr-* initial cluster reflects Thai *khlɔːŋ* "canal" in some way.[11] Mei and Norman give Austroasiatic forms for "river" such as Bahnar and Sedang *krong*, Katu *karung*, Bru *klong*, and Old Mon *krung*, making it clear that the word is not Thai alone but occurs widely in Austroasiatic languages.

4. Mei and Norman compare the Chinese word for "crossbow" 弩 *nu* < EMC *nɔ'* < OC **xná?* or perhaps **sná?*, with Vietnamese *ná*, and Proto-Muong **so'na*, and claim that the crossbow is traditionally associated with the south and southwest.[12]

5. They match Chinese 虎 *hu* < EMC *xɔ'* < OC **xlá?* "tiger" with Mon *kla*, Khmer *khla* ("felines"), Khasi *khla*, and Vietnamese *khát* and note that apart from the comparatively uncommon Manchurian tiger, the

[9] *Zhou li*, 15 ("Si guan"), 9b. Here and later I have replaced the reconstructions that Mei and Norman give with the Early Middle Chinese forms from Pulleyblank, *Lexicon of Reconstructed Pronunciation*.
[10] See *Shuowen jiezi gulin*, ed. Ding Fubao (Shanghai: Shangwu, 1937), p. 4382.
[11] Old Chinese reconstructions, marked OC, here and in the next several examples are my own ad hoc conjectures, based on the general features of Old Chinese established by Pulleyblank, Norman, and others, but possibly differing from the Old Chinese forms that any one of those authorities might endorse.
[12] Mei and Norman, "The Austroasiatics in Ancient South China," pp. 293–4.

tiger is a beast predominantly associated with the south and the Indian subcontinent.

Mei and Norman also give examples of Austroasiatic loanwords that are found only in southern, usually Min, dialects and that do not occur in dialects in the north. These are often colloquial words that have only an ad hoc invented character as their written form or that have no written form at all.

6. The common Min word for "son, child", Foochow *kiaŋ³*, Amoy *kiă³*, matches closely Vietnamese *con* "child", Khmer *koun*, Mon *kon*, Khasi *khu:n*, and several other Austroasiatic forms, all meaning "son" or "child".[13]

7. Foochow *pai?⁷* and Amoy *bat⁷* "to know, recognize" match Vietnamese *biĕt* "to know".

8. Foochow *p'iu²* and Amoy *p'io²* "duckweed" match Vietnamese *bèo* "duckweed".

In spite of the preponderance of data suggesting the linguistic influence of Austroasiatic on Chinese to be a consequence of contact in the south, Pulleyblank's identification of the ancient Yi people in the east as far north as the Shandong Peninsula as Austroasiatic speakers seems defensible, though inevitably more speculative than the Mei–Norman hypothesis of Austroasiatic contact in the south. Because there is no direct documentation of the Yi language, Pulleyblank is forced to rely on indirect indications, chiefly Yi place-names written in Chinese characters. In one important example he shows that the same name occurs in one text as a Yi place-name and in another as a place-name in the state of Yue. This suggests an identification of the Yi in the east with the Yue in the south and implies that the Yi language should be of the same kind as the Yue, which from independent evidence Mei and Norman have concluded, undoubtedly correctly, to be Austroasiatic. The time that Pulleyblank proposes for an Yi presence in the east, Shang and early Zhou, coincides closely with the time that Mei and Norman propose for Chinese contact with Austroasiatics in the south.[14]

Indo-European

The discovery early in this century of manuscript texts from the Tarim Basin written in a form of Indic script recognized as derived from Brahmi but recording a distinctive, and until then unknown, Indo-European language,

---

[13] Modern Foochow *-ŋ* can come from earlier *-n* and *-m*, as well as from *-ŋ*; thus the form *kiaŋ* is entirely compatible with Austroasiatic cognates in *-n*. This word is attested already in the eighth century, in the poetry of Gu Kuang 顧況, written 囝, and explained as the colloquial Foochow word for "son". See Mei and Norman, "The Austroasiatics in Ancient South China," p. 297.

[14] Pulleyblank, "Zou 鄒 and Lu 魯," pp. 44–5.

revealed a clear Indo-European presence reaching deep into the northwestern sector of China and put indigenous Indo-European speakers much farther east than anyone had previously imagined.[15] The language of these manuscripts was given the name "Tocharian" because of the appearance of the name *tuyry* in a Uighur colophon to one of them and the identification of this name with the Greek name *tócharoi* in Ptolemy.

Tocharian is known in two dialects, from two locales: Tocharian A, represented in manuscripts from the Turfan and Karashahr region, also known as Agnean; and Tocharian B, represented in manuscripts from Kucha, and therefore sometimes called Kuchean.[16] All three locales were major entrepôts on the "silk route" across Central Asia that went north of the Tarim Basin (see Map 2.1). The Tocharian manuscripts themselves date from no earlier than about A.D. 600, much too late to be directly relevant to our concern with the millennium from 1200 to 200 B.C. But the linguistic and archaeological circumstances surrounding Tocharian suggest that Tocharian-speaking people inhabited the region of China's far northwest from very early times.

The chief indication that Tocharian was not a latecomer to the linguistic environment of northwest China but had been there for a long time is the unexpected fact that Tocharian is a so-called *centum* language and thus shows linguistic affinities with the Celtic, Germanic, Greek, and Italic groups of Indo-European rather than with the geographically much closer *satem* languages of the Indic and Iranian groups.[17] This feature of Tocharian was first

[15] Manuscripts written in the Brahmi script, in the previously unknown language that, once deciphered, came to be known as Tocharian, were among those discovered in the last decade of the nineteenth century and in the early years of the twentieth by explorers, archaeologists, and naturalists crossing through Central Asia and into Chinese Turkestan, often under the auspices of one or another of the European imperial powers, in search of historical sites and antiquities. For a popular narrative account of these expeditionary enterprises, see Peter Hopkirk, *Foreign Devils on the Silk Road* (London: John Murray, 1980), esp. chapter 3, "The Great Manuscript Race." For a first-person commentary on the importance of the Tocharian manuscripts in particular, see Albert von Le Coq, *Buried Treasures of Chinese Turkestan* (1928; rpt. Oxford: Oxford University Press, 1985), p. 21: "We connect with these people [the Yuezhi] the European heads with blue eyes and red hair on the frescoes, as well as the European language which we found in great quantities of manuscripts in and near the respective temples and for which the name of the 'Tocharish' language is in itself a testimony."
The scholarly historical, archaeological, and linguistic literature in the early years of this century is replete with reports and studies of these finds. For a comprehensive bibliography, see Ernst Schwentner, *Tocharische Bibliographie, 1890–1958*, Deutsche Akademie der Wissenschaften zu Berlin, Institut für Orientforschung, Veröffentlichung, no. 47 (Berlin: Akademie, 1959).
The fullest and most recent account of both the discovery of Tocharian and its study is Ji Xianlin, *Dunhuang Tulufan Tuhuoluo yu yanjiu daolun*, Dunhuangxue daolun congkan, no. 6, ed. Lin Congming (Taibei: Xinwenfeng, 1993).
[16] See H. W. Bailey, "Recent Work in 'Tocharian,'" *Transactions of the Philological Society* (London, 1947): 126–53. Bailey prefers to see the two dialects as separate languages and to call them Agnean and Kuchean.
[17] In languages of the *centum* group, the Indo-European *k*- does not palatalize, as exemplified by Latin *centum* (orthographic *c*- = phonetic [k]) "hundred". In the Indic and Iranian languages, the Indo-European *k*- palatalizes, giving, for example, Avestan *satəm*, Sanskrit *sata*- "hundred", hence the name

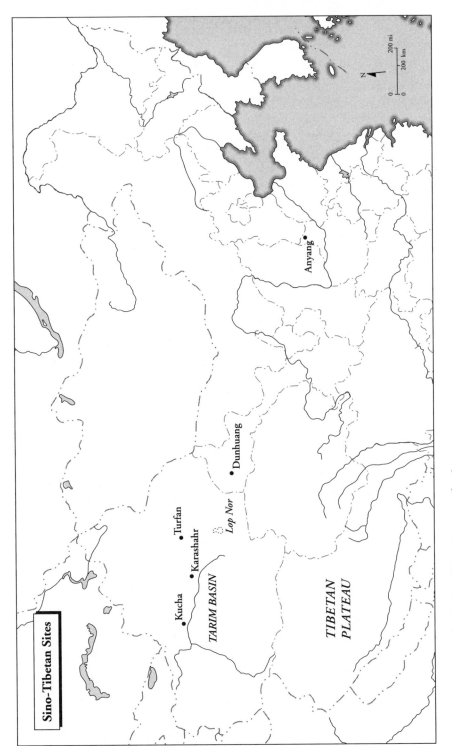

Map 2.1 Sites associated with Sino-Tibetan language family

interpreted to mean that the Tocharians must have migrated at some undetermined, but relatively recent time into Chinese Turkestan from an
unknown and very far-removed locale that was their original homeland in
western or southern Europe, that is, in the neighborhood of the majority of
centum languages. The unsatisfactory nature of such an explanation, pre-
supposing an otherwise traceless migration across all of Eurasia, soon became
apparent. At the same time it was realized that the distribution of *centum*
and *satem* languages favors a different explanation. The *centum* languages,
showing the original, nonpalatalized Indo-European velar stop, that is, the
more conservative phonological feature in comparison with the palatalized *s-*
of the *satem* languages (see footnote 17), appear at the periphery of the Indo-
European linguistic ecumene; the *satem* languages, showing phonological
innovation, arose in the central portion of the overall area and spread
outward. This pattern is both predicted and explained perfectly by a principal tenet of the "age and area hypothesis" developed by the Italian Neo-
linguistic school in the first decades of the twentieth century. The theory
maintains that, other things being equal, when related languages are spoken
over a wide territorial expanse, those on the periphery will conserve features
of earlier stages of the language, while those in the center will exhibit innovations first.[18] Phrased slightly differently, we can say that phonological
changes appear to spread gradually outward from the point of their first
occurrence in all directions (if no obstacle is encountered). Thus, the remoter
the language from the point of origin of the change, the longer it takes for
the change to reach it, irrespective of direction. Changes that arise in the
central area of a linguistic domain, as the *satem* change did, may never reach
languages on the periphery, again irrespective of direction; in that case, the
peripheral languages will show the same original feature, untouched by the
change.

The presence of Tocharian, a *centum* language, in the extreme northeastern portion of the Indo-European domain, matching the *centum* languages
at the other extremes (Celtic in the west and Italic and Greek in the southwest) gives exactly this pattern with respect to the particular change involved
in the *centum/satem* correspondence and, viewed in the light of this principle of linguistic geography, is entirely natural. It implies that Tocharian
speakers were present in the area of Chinese Turkestan from very early, certainly prehistoric, times.

---

satem for this group. Tocharian A has *känt* and Tocharian B has *kante* for "hundred", clearly placing
Tocharian with the *centum* group. Cf. English *hund(-red)* < Germanic *hundam*, where the [k] has
become a spirant, *h-*.

[18] See e.g., Matteo Bartoli, *Saggi di linguistica spaziale* (Turin: Rosenberg & Sellier, 1945), chapters 1–5;
and G. Bonfante and Thomas A. Sebeok, "Linguistics and the Age and Area Hypothesis," *American
Anthropologist* 46 (1944): 382–6.

There is a growing body of archaeological evidence for a manifestly non-Chinese people, quite possibly an Indo-European people, living in the Tarim Basin at least as early as the second millennium B.C. The most important part of this evidence is a large number of clearly Caucasoid corpses excavated over the last fifteen or more years from burial sites in the Tarim Basin dating from the second and first millennia B.C.[19] The corpses may well be the remains of the Tocharian speakers which the "age and area hypothesis" puts in the area of Chinese Turkestan as early as about 2000 B.C.[20]

J. P. Mallory has speculated that the early Tocharian speakers might be identified with the people of the so-called Afanasievo culture of the Upper Yenisei region, north of the Altai Mountains. The Afanasievo culture is typically associated with the culture of the Pontic-Caspian region, which is indisputably Indo-European. Mallory suggests that the Afanasievo-Tocharians moved south into the Tarim Basin at about the beginning of the second millennium B.C., and points to a number of similarities in the archaeological record between the fourth- and third-millennium Afanasievo culture in the Yenisei area and the second-millennium Tarim Basin finds.[21] Stuart Piggott has suggested that the Tocharians might have been the people responsible, at least as the easternmost agency of the transmission, for the introduction of the chariot from the Causcasus into north China, where it is first known about 1200 B.C.[22]

Beyond these linguistic and archaeological surmises there is tangible evidence of early Tocharian contact with Chinese speakers in the form of at least two Tocharian loanwords in pre-Han Chinese. The better known one is Chinese 蜜 *mi* < EMC *mjit* "honey" taken from Tocharian B *mit* "honey" (cognate with Skt. *madhu*, Eng. *mead*); the second and less widely recognized is 獅子 *shizi* < EMC *ṣi-tsɨ'* "lion", suggesting, in the opinion of E. G. Pulleyblank, a Western Han form like *ṣə̀j-cə̀ʔ* and identified by him as a virtually certain borrowing from Tocharian; the B dialect word for "lion" is *secake* and the A word is *śiśäk*.[23]

---

[19] See, for example, these recent reports in the popular press: Evan Hadingham, "The Mummies of Xinjiang," *Discovery*, April 1994, pp. 66–77; and Victor H. Mair, "Mummies of the Tarim Basin," in *Archaeology*, March–April 1995, pp. 28–35, both well illustrated with color photographs.

[20] See E. G. Pulleyblank, "Why Tocharians?" *Journal of Indo-European Studies* 23 (1995): 415–30.

[21] See J. P. Mallory, *In Search of the Indo-Europeans* (London: Thames & Hudson, 1989), pp. 223–6 and passim.

[22] See Stuart Piggott, "Chariots in the Caucasus and China," *Antiquity* 48 (1974): 16–24. For the chariot in ancient China and 1200 B.C. as the date of its earliest appearance, see Edward L. Shaughnessy, "Historical Perspectives on the Introduction of the Chariot into China," *HJAS* 48 (1988): 189–237. For a résumé of the archaeological history of the chariot in the ancient Near East and the Aegean, see Robert Drews, *The Coming of the Greeks* (Princeton, N. J.: Princeton University Press, 1988). See esp. chapter 5, "The New Warfare."

[23] See Pulleyblank, "Why Tocharians?" Chinese records of contact with non-Chinese peoples in the northwest as well as elsewhere become substantial with the Han. On the basis of both linguistic and historical evidence, Pulleyblank has identified the Yuezhi 月氏, the Wusun 烏孫, the Dayuan 大宛, the

Periodization

The evolution of the Chinese language over the millennium from 1200 to 200 B.C. can be known only from the evidence of written texts. On that evidence it can be divided into three distinct periods, the first of 200 years, the second and third of 400 years each. The language itself changed, as all languages do, seamlessly and unnoticeably. The three periods we suggest here are discernible only when the history of the language is scrutinized from a distance after the fact, and as reflected in written texts, and are therefore artificial to that extent.

THE ARCHAIC PERIOD. The first of the three periods comprises the two centuries from 1200 to 1000 B.C. This we will call the Archaic period. The texts from this period are all discovered, as opposed to being transmitted, and consist of the so-called oracle-bone inscriptions (*jia gu wen* 甲骨文) and very short inscriptions cast on bronze vessels (*jin wen* 金文). The term "oracle-bone inscriptions" is the English name commonly given to divinatory texts incised typically on ox scapulas or turtle plastrons and known only from the Shang and very early Zhou.[24] The few Zhou examples are the so-called Zhouyuan 周原 oracle-bone inscriptions, several of which include personal names associated with the early Western Zhou and a few of which mention Shang names, seeming to suggest that perhaps prior to their conquest of the Shang, the Zhou sacrificed to the Shang ancestors.[25]

In spite of our very imperfect knowledge of the script, lexicon, and grammar of these inscriptions, there is no question that the language written is Chinese. All the same, it is difficult to set out a general characterization of the language of this period because the content of the texts is limited almost exclusively to divinatory matters, giving us a very skewed picture of the language's use. The vocabulary, assumed to be equivalent to the number of different characters used, consists of a core of between 3,000 and 4,000 words, many of which are proper nouns and a small number of which are infrequently seen specialized words. Of the total of 4,000 or more characters that

---

Kangju 康居, and the people of Yanqi 焉耆, all names occurring in the Chinese historical sources for the Han dynasty, as Tocharian speakers. The name Dayuan itself is thought to be a Chinese transcription of whatever original ethnonym underlies the Greek name Tócharoi, Tácharoi. See E. G. Pulleyblank, "Chinese and Indo-Europeans," *Journal of the Royal Asiatic Society*, April 1966: 9–39.

On the original name of the "Tocharians," see W. B. Henning, "Argi and the 'Tocharians,'" *BSO(A)S* 9, 3 (1938): 545–64.

[24] The term "oracle bone," accurate only for the scapulas, is for convenience commonly extended to refer to turtle plastrons as well.

[25] The authorship and nature of the Zhouyuan inscriptions is uncertain and much disputed. See Edward L. Shaughnessy, "Zhouyuan Oracle-Bone Inscriptions: Entering the Research Stage?" *EC* 11–12 (1985–7): 146–63; and the responses from Wang Yuxin, Li Xueqin, and Fan Yuzhou, and the surrejoinder by Shaughnessy, in ibid., pp. 164–94.

appear in the texts of this period, identification of the word for which the character stands is certain for no more than half. The remainder fall into two groups, the uncertain and the unknown.

Grammatically the language of this period is far less characterized by overtly analyzable syntactic constructions, for example, for modification or nominalization, than standard Classical Chinese (the language of the third period), and has far fewer grammatical particles (*xu zi* 虛字). Much grammatical structure is apparently indicated by no more than juxtaposition of the words involved, and grammatical relation seems therefore to be implicit rather than explicit, at least from the perspective of later stages of the language. Overall there is much about the grammar, as there is about the identification of characters, that is uncertain or unknown.

THE PRE-CLASSICAL PERIOD. The period from 1000 B.C. to 600 B.C., corresponding very roughly to the Western Zhou, we can call the "Pre-Classical" period. It is distinguished from the Archaic period by a profusion of texts, both discovered and transmitted, by a markedly broader range of subject matter reflected in the texts, and by a noticeable development in the grammar and vocabulary of the language toward what we recognize as conventional in standard Classical Chinese.

Of transmitted texts, significant parts of the *Shu jing* 書經 (Classic of documents), the *Shi jing* 詩經 (Classic of poetry), and the *Yi jing* 易經 (Classic of changes) come from this period. In particular a number of sections of the *Shu jing* and some of the earliest odes of the *Shi jing* show marked grammatical, stylistic, and content similarities to bronze inscription texts from this period.[26] Bronze inscriptions themselves now become primary historical sources and are often of substantial length and great importance. The practice of inscribing texts on ox scapulas and turtle plastrons seems, based on present evidence, to have ended in the early Western Zhou, although the use of the bones and shells themselves in divination procedures did not.

The language is still clearly not that of standard Classical Chinese. It retains a succinctness of style and a spartan grammatical austerity, but it now shows occasional use of overt syntactic constructions for modification and some forms of nominalization. The vocabulary appears somewhat richer and much changed from that of the archaic period, though this is likely in part merely a consequence of the greatly expanded range of subject matter of the extant texts. The size of the core vocabulary remains about the same as for the language of the Archaic period, though the number of unknown characters is fewer than for the oracle-bone inscriptions.

[26] See, for example, the discussion in Edward L. Shaughnessy, *Sources of Western Zhou History: Inscribed Bronze Vessels* (Berkeley: University of California Press, 1991), section 3.2.1.

THE CLASSICAL PERIOD. The four centuries from 600 to 200 B.C. constitute what might be called the golden age of Classical Chinese literature
and philosophy. This is the classical period *sensu stricto*, where we find most
of the revered works of early Chinese literature, including the *Lun yu* 論語
(The Analects of Confucius), the *Xiao jing* 孝經 (Classic of filial piety), the
Mengzi 孟子 (Mencius), and the *Zuo zhuan* 左傳 (Zuo's tradition). The last
two, both substantial literary compositions from the latter part of the period,
have in particular been viewed from the Han period down to the present day
as models of correct and elegant Classical Chinese prose style, though at different levels of sophistication, to be sure.

Bronze inscriptions are numerous and remain important as primary historical sources, but in volume they are overwhelmed in this period by the
transmitted texts. Oracle-bone inscriptions are unknown in this period; on
the other hand we now find texts written on jade and numerous texts written
in ink, apparently with a brush, on bamboo or wood strips. Toward the end
of the period we also find texts written on silk.[27]

Archaeological finds show that when bamboo strips were used, the convention was to write a single column of characters on each strip. Chapter 30
of the *Han shu* 漢書 (History of the [Former] Han), titled "Yi wen zhi" 藝
文志 and based on Liu Xiang's 劉向 (79–8 B.C.) catalog of works in the imperial library, suggests that it was also conventional to use strips of uniform
length for a given text, varying between 0.8 and 2.4 Han feet (one Han foot
equals 23 cm) and to write the same number of characters on each strip of a
single text, at least for formal versions of certain kinds of texts. This number
was often either twenty-two or twenty-five (probably an error in the *Han shu*
for twenty-four) characters per strip.[28] These conventions are not generally
confirmed by discovered strips, and there is little archaeological evidence to
show a regular adherence to a particular number of characters per strip. All
the same, the discrepancy may not be significant since the *Han shu* passage
seems to say that the convention applies only to certain kinds of texts, for
example, the classics, and perhaps only to formal copies of them, though it
is not clear just what "formal" might mean in this context. Several structural
features of transmitted texts seem to confirm the existence of some such convention, in particular the observation that when a text is defective, a short
portion of it having been displaced to a spot before or after where it is known

[27] For full discussions of these various kinds of early written documents, see Edward L. Shaughnessy, ed.,
     New Sources of Early Chinese History: An Introduction to Reading Inscriptions and Manuscripts, Society
     for the Study of Early China monograph series, no. 3 (Berkeley: Institute for East Asian Studies and
     the Society for the Study of Early China, 1997).
[28] *Han shu*, 30, p. 1706. See also E. Chavannes, "Les livres chinois avant l'invention du papier," *JA*, series
     10, 5 (January–February 1905): 5–75, esp. 18–38; and P. A. Boodberg, "Marginalia to the Histories of
     the Northern Dynasties," *HJAS* 4 (1939): 230–83, esp. 246–9.

from other evidence to have been originally, the length in characters of the displaced portion is often a multiple of twenty-two (or twenty-four). This suggests that the defective part arose from misplacement of the corresponding number of bamboo strips, each with twenty-two (or twenty-four) characters.

Typology

Linguists usually describe Chinese as a "monosyllabic" and "isolating" language, by which they mean that its words are all of only one syllable and that they take the same invariable form irrespective of such features of usage as person, tense, number, and grammatical function. Whatever validity this claim may or may not have for modern Chinese, it appears at least superficially to be true for Classical Chinese. Classical Chinese words are typically thought of as isolated, that is, as being untouched and unaffected by affixes of any kind, or by vowel or consonant changes to any part of the word correlated with any change of meaning – in brief, the kinds of thing that are usually subsumed under the term "morphology." On first inspection it seems that at no stage of its observable history down to the beginning of the Chinese empire does Chinese show any overt signs of a productive morphology of the kind we are automatically predisposed to think of based on our familiarity with the morphological structure of Indo-European languages. There appear to be no declensions or conjugations and no stem changes that correspond to grammatical or semantic distinctions such as we see in, for example, English *sit* (verb, present tense) / *sat* (verb, past tense) / *seat* (noun); or Latin *leō* ("lion", nominative singular), / *leōnis* (genitive singular) / *leōni* (dative singular) / *leōnem* (accusative singular) / *leōne* (ablative singular).

The absence of any evidence of morphology may be as much a consequence of the camouflaging effect of the Chinese script, and of the unnoticed biases that the script imposes on our perspective, as it is an indication of the true nature of the Chinese language. Even today the script fails to register, for example, the distinction between the two clearly related words *cháng* "long" and *zhǎng* "to grow, become long" and writes them both with the character 長. On the other hand, the script distinguishes the two just as clearly related words *zhāng* "to stretch (as of, e.g., a bowstring)" and *zhàng* "stretched" > "inflated, expanded" by writing the first with the character 張 and the second with 脹. In the first case we are prone to think of the two vaguely as "variants" of a "single" word, because they are both written with the same character, whereas in the second case we think of them as two separate and distinct words because they are written with different characters. Objectively, there is little to justify thinking of the first pair as variants of the same word and the second as two different words; in both cases we are probably looking at evidence for some kind of earlier morphological processes. We just do not know yet exactly what the phonetic and semantic nature of those processes was.

As we scrutinize the language with a heightened awareness of the biases that its script imposes, we find accumulating evidence to suggest that the language may not have been as typologically isolating as it appears. It may well have had numerous productive morphological processes, vestiges of which still survive into later stages of the language, as the preceding examples of *cháng/zhǎng* 長 and *zhāng* 張/*zhàng* 脹 are intended to show.[29] The specific features of these processes are not easily discernible directly from the script, and instead have to be conjectured from the evidence of the reconstructed Old Chinese words.

Scholars, both Chinese and Western, have long noticed that there are numerous cases in which several Chinese words seem to form a set characterized by similar pronunciation and similar or related meanings, and are often written with characters that share a common "phonetic" element. The words in the set listed below, for example, all have pronunciations centered on the syllable *an*, have a meaning related to the sense of SIT/SET/SEAT, and, with one exception, are written with characters having the 安 element as phonetic.

1. 安 *ān* < EMC *ʔan* < *ʔ *án* "stability"
2. 按 *àn* < EMC *ʔanʰ* < *ʔ *áns* "to press or hold down, make stable"
3. 案 *àn* < EMC *ʔanʰ* < *ʔ *áns* "seat, stool"
4. 晏 *yàn* < EMC *ʔainʰ* < *ʔ *ráns* "at rest, settled"
5. 鞍 *ān* < EMC *ʔan* < *ʔ *án* "saddle"
6. 燕 *yàn* < EMC *ʔɛnʰ* < *ʔ^*j*ʔáns* "at rest", "banquet" < "seated".

Sets like this are often called "word families."[30] Until recently no one has been able to go beyond the grouping and the observations about similar pronunciation and meaning to say anything about the relation between the words in a family. Now, thanks to the work of E. G. Pulleyblank and others,[31]

---

[29] I owe these examples as they are used to make this point to E. G. Pulleyblank.

[30] We might also include the word 侒 *ān* < EMC *ʔan* < *ʔán "banquet" < "sitting mat", but for the fact that it is attested only lexicographically for the early period. All the same, it conforms perfectly to the phonetic and semantic (and, as it happens, graphic) criteria that define this word family.

[31] The classic work on this topic is Gordon B. Downer, "Derivation by Tone Change in Classical Chinese," *BSOAS* 22 (1959): 258–90. While Downer does not deal directly with what are usually called word families, he does try to show derivational processes that underlie related words that differ only in tone. This is an integral part of the effort to find derivational patterns to account for the members of a word family. For more recent work, see, e.g., E. G. Pulleyblank, "The Locative Particles *yü* 于, *yü* 於 and *hu* 乎," *JAOS* 106 (1986): 1–12, and idem, "Ablaut and Initial Voicing in Old Chinese Morphology: *a as an Infix and Prefix," *Proceedings of the Second International Conference on Sinology*, Section on Linguistics and Paleography (Taibei: Academia Sinica, 1989), pp. 1–21.

we can discern vestiges of morphological processes that might account for the relation among some of the members of the set. For example, the -*s* of *ʔáns "hold down" (按) and of *ʔáns "seat" (案) is likely to have been what we might call a "concretizing" suffix, a suffix that turns abstractions into concrete acts or objects, added to the word *ʔán "stability" (安).[32] In this word family the two words with the suffix -*s* would then bear a *derivational* relation to the word *ān* < *ʔán (安) "stability, settledness". The relation between other members of the set may be one of semantic specialization rather than morphological derivation, as, for example, between 鞍 *ān* "saddle" and 案 *àn* "seat" (with the alternation between the level tone and the falling tone unexplained). A word family as it is traditionally understood, in other words, includes words resulting from both morphological derivation and semantic specialization, and the distinction between the two will often appear blurred.

We can see another example of the concretizing suffix -*s* in 故 *gù* < EMC *kɔʰ* < *kʷáʔs "an old friend, home" and otherwise, including an "old and established way of doing something, or of thinking" > "reason, basis, cause", derived from 古 *gǔ* < EMC *kɔʼ* < *kʷáʔ "antiquity". The second word, 故 *gù*, with OC final -*s*, is not the abstract entity "antiquity", but refers to a concrete head (故人 "old friend", 故鄉 "old home town", even 故吾 "the former me", etc.).

Traces of the concretizing suffix -*s* can sometimes be seen in alternative readings for a single character when the change of reading is accompanied by a change of meaning; for example, 從 is commonly read *cóng* < EMC *dzuawŋ* < *ǎtsàŋᵠ "to follow", but with the -*s* suffix (becoming in modern Chinese a falling tone) is read *zòng* < EMC *dzuawŋʰ* < *ǎtsàŋᵠs "follower". Here the suffix -*s* is more easily described as a noun-forming suffix than a concretizing one. Similarly, we find 上 *shǎng* < EMC *dʑiaŋʼ* < *ǎtàŋʔ "to rise, raise" is also read *shàng* < EMC *dʑiaŋʰ* < *ǎtàŋs "top" with the addition of the -*s* suffix. We can preserve a unified description of the functioning of the -*s* suffix by saying that "the -*s* suffix makes abstract nouns

---

[32] It is tempting, of course, to treat *ān* 安 as a verb, meaning "stable, secure", and then to identify the -*s* of *àn* < *ʔáns 案 "seat" as a noun-forming suffix. This seems a priori and intuitively more natural than calling it a "concretizing" suffix. But the word *ān* 安 in standard Classical Chinese is clearly not a verb but an abstract noun, so one cannot meaningfully call the suffixed -*s* in derivatives a noun-forming suffix. It may be that at the productive period of this process, the word *ān* 安 was a verb and that in a way not clear to us it became an abstract noun by the Classical period. In this case, of course, the term "noun-forming suffix" would be consistent with the grammatical facts. Until we have some evidence for such a shift in word-class membership of *ān* 安, it seems to me preferable to make the description consistent with what we know of the grammar rather than with what we have to surmise about the grammar on the basis of the very description at issue. Identifying the -*s* as a concretizing suffix has the advantage of also explaining the concrete verb *àn* 按 "press or hold down", that is, "make secure". The alternative would be to identify this second -*s* as a "causative suffix" distinct from the noun-forming suffix -*s* in *àn* 案 with which it is formally identical.

concrete, otherwise derives nouns, i.e., the "concrete" thing itself, from verbs."[33]

As early as 1963, E. G. Pulleyblank proposed that the Old Chinese vowel system could be analyzed as a two-term close/open contrast between ə and a.[34] In 1965 he suggested that the vowel contrast ə/a could be identified as morphologically meaningful in a number of examples and that it carried with it a semantic sense of extrovert/introvert corresponding to a nearly identical contrast, both phonologically and semantically, in Indo-European languages.[35] In more recent formulations of this phenomenon, Pulleyblank has interpreted the ə/a contrast as a contrast between ə as a "minimal feature of syllabicity inserted . . . between consonants by rules of syllabification" and a as the consequence of morphological infixation.[36]

The word 古 *gǔ* < *kʷáʔ "antiquity", just given, can be analyzed phonetically, for example, as the word 久 *jiǔ* < EMC *kuwˀ* < **kʷə́ʔ* "to last a long time" modified by an infixed *-a-* and semantically as the introvert member of the extrovert/introvert pair 久 / 古, where 久 *jiǔ* with OC *-ə-*, meaning "to last a long time", is the extrovert sense; that is, the meaning is processive and verbal, acting on or characterizing some other thing, whereas 古 *gǔ* with OC *-a-* means "antiquity" as an abstract noun and is, hence, introvert, that is, semantically "self-contained."

The same *a-* element appears sometimes as a nonsyllabic prefix, transcribed *ă-*, rather than as an infix, and carries with it the same introvert sense. One of the clearest examples of this is the pair 見 *jiàn* "see" / 現 *xiàn* "appear, be seen" (typically written 見 in early texts, i.e., not orthographically distinct from *jiàn*). We can reconstruct *jiàn* < EMC *kɛnʰ* "see" as OC *kʷjáns and *xiàn* < EMC *ɣɛnʰ* "appear" as OC *ăkʷjáns, with the *ă-* prefix. The word *jiàn* "see" (no OC prefix) is the extrovert sense and *xiàn* "appear, be seen" (with the OC *ă-* prefix) the introvert.[37] Another example, which shows how apparently unrelated words may in fact be related phonetically and semantically, that is, morphologically, is 説 *shuō* < EMC *ɕwiat* "explain" (< "loosen") and 説 / 悦 *yuè* < EMC *jwiat* "pleased, relaxed" (< "loosened"; like the *jiàn* / *xiàn* pair, both words were also typically written in early texts

---

[33] Unfortunately the case for 下 *xià* is just the opposite of that for 上 *shàng* in that the noun "bottom" is read in Middle Chinese in the *rising* tone (上聲), implying an OC final *-ʔ*, and the verb "to go down" is read in the departing tone (去聲), which has devolved from an OC *-s*; 中 *zhōng* "center" is different yet again, the noun being the level tone (平聲) reading while the departing tone from OC *-s* gives the verb "to hit the center/bull's eye". These examples suffice to show that whatever morphological formatives we may think we have identified, the complete scheme is still very much shrouded in uncertainty.

[34] E. G. Pulleyblank, "An Interpretation of the Vowel Systems of Old Chinese and of Written Burmese," *AM*, n.s., 10, 2 (1963): 200–21.

[35] Pulleyblank, "Close/Open Ablaut in Sino-Tibetan," *Lingua* 14 (1965): pp. 230–40.

[36] Pulleyblank, "Ablaut and Initial Voicing in Old Chinese Morphology."

[37] When the *a-* prefix precedes a voiceless consonant, it typically has the effect of producing a voiced initial in EMC, as the example of 現 *xiàn* < EMC *ɣɛnʰ* given here shows.

with the same character, 説). Both words are semantic aspects of a root meaning of LOOSEN, 説 *shuō* < *ɬwàt* being the extrovert form, "to explain" (transitive) and 説 / 悦 *yuè* < *ăɬwàt* the introvert, "to be relaxed".[38]

To the extent that the vocabulary of Old Chinese can be convincingly analyzed as characterized by these sorts of morphological processes, Chinese will no longer be classifiable as an isolating language, but will assume a structure closer to its presumed Tibetan and Burman linguistic affines than is now apparent, and this will strengthen the case for a true cognate relation with those languages. The fact that such a "deep" structural feature of Old Chinese as the ə/a "extrovert / introvert" pattern is matched by a virtually identical feature of proto-Indo-European, coupled with the identification of numerous possible lexical cognates and of the outlines of a set of regular, if tentative, sound correspondences, has induced Pulleyblank to take the possibility of a cognate relation between Sino-Tibetan and Indo-European seriously.[39] While such a hypothesis remains at present highly speculative, it cannot be dismissed out of hand as untenable or unworthy of further exploration.

Linguistic Philosophy

Prior to political unification in the Qin (221–210 B.C.) and Han (206 B.C. – A.D. 220) dynasties, the Chinese seem not to have had any specific intellectual focus that matches what we would in modern terms call "linguistic knowledge" or "linguistic science." No notion corresponding to grammar, whether in the sense of "philology and criticism" of the late classical West or in the very limited sense of "naming and classifying letters" as it was used by the Greeks before the third century B.C., is apparent in extant pre-Han Chinese texts. What we find instead is an ill-defined but wide-ranging concern with words: with their meanings, their logical usage, and their relation to one another and to the outside world of real things.

This concern with words takes two separate but related forms in the received pre-Han textual tradition: (1) the "Rectification of Names" (*zheng ming* 正名) doctrine of the *Analects* and the *Xunzi* 荀子 (ca. late sixth century and mid-third century B.C., respectively), and (2) the Later Mohist "Canons" (*Jing* 經) and "Canon explanations" (*Jing shuo* 經説), and "Greater pick" (*Da*

---

[38] Notice also in this same series of words the word 蜕 *tuì* "exuviae (namely, of insects, snakes, etc.)" (<something peeled off < loosened) OC *ɬwáts and 税 *shuì* "taxes in kind" (<something "peeled off"), OC *ɬwàts, both with the concretizing -s suffix.

[39] For the fullest and most up-to-date discussion of this hypothesis, see E. G. Pulleyblank, "The Typology of Indo-European," *Journal of Indo-European Studies* 21 (1993): 63–118, with "Comments" by W. P. Lehmann and Karl Horst Schmidt, pp. 119–31, and a reply by Pulleyblank, pp. 135–41. See also Pulleyblank, "The Historical and Prehistorical Relationships of Chinese," in *The Ancestry of the Chinese Language*, ed. William S.-Y. Wang, pp. 145–94. The last-mentioned source includes a limited number of very detailed analyses of possible Sino-Tibetan/Indo-European cognate words.

qu 大取) and "Lesser pick" (*Xiao qu* 小取) treatises of the fourth century B.C. The first form tends to be political and social in its application, the second strictly logical, though A. C. Graham sees the *Xunzi* essay as very likely "a digest of the techniques of Mohist disputation adapted to Confucian purposes."[40] Neither becomes what we would properly call a fully developed philosophy or science of language, but both, while remaining firmly anchored to the overall Chinese worldview and intrinsically reflective of its ethical concomitants, reveal an intellectually sophisticated sense of the nature of words and language and of the relation of these to the world of real objects that they are used to describe.[41]

The better recognized of these two intellectual concerns with words and meanings is that doctrine usually known as the "Rectification of Names."[42] The *locus classicus* for the term *zheng ming* and its associated significance is *Analects* 13/3 (I italicize the lines and give the original text for those sentences in which the phrase *zheng ming*, or just the word *ming*, occurs):[43]

Zilu 子路 said: "Were you to undertake to bring about right government (*wei zheng* 為政), having been given such a charge by the Lord of the state of Wei, how would you proceed first?"

The Master [Confucius] said: "*What is necessary is to 'set names aright'!* (*bi ye zheng ming hu* 必也正名乎)."

Zilu said: "You say that?! Surely this means you have strayed far from the mark! Why that kind of 'setting aright'?"

The Master said: "What a yokel you are, You 由 [Zilu]! Ought not a junior lord (*junzi* 君子) [like you] keep his distance from things about which he knows nothing?!

"*If names are not set aright, then what one says will not follow properly* (*ming bu zheng ze yan bu shun* 名不正則言不順); if what one says does not follow properly, then one's affairs will not come to successful completion; if one's affairs do not come to successful completion, then the rites of ceremony and music will not provide the proper spiritual elation; if the rites of ceremony and music do not provide the proper spiritual elation, then punishments and penalties will not accord properly [with transgressions], if punishments and penalties do not accord properly, then the populace will have no basis for choosing how to behave.

---

[40] A. C. Graham, *Later Mohist Logic, Ethics, and Science* (Hong Kong: Chinese University; and London: University of London, School of Oriental and African Studies, 1978), p. 63; see also pp. 64, 233–5.

[41] For a full presentation of the way in which the Chinese worldview affected the traditional understanding of the nature and function of language, and of the way in which that understanding bears on the interpretation of the written texts of the linguistic tradition from the Han period on, see Roy A. Miller, "The Far East," in *Current Trends in Linguistics, Vol.* 13.2, "Historiography of Linguistics," ed. Thomas Sebeok (The Hague: Mouton, 1975), pp. 1213–64, esp. pp. 1213–25.

[42] The phrase *zhèng míng* is a verb–object construction and is thus more accurately translated as "setting names aright" or "rectifying names" than "rectification of names".

[43] *Lun yu*, 13/3.

"*When a junior lord gives a name to something, it cannot but be properly sayable* (*junzi ming zhi bi ke yan ye* 君子名之必可言也); when he says something, it cannot but be properly implementable. In relation to what he says a junior lord shall in no respect whatsoever appear slack."

Two generations ago, Arthur Waley, in the introduction to his translation, *The Analects of Confucius*, declared that this passage was a late interpolation and not representative of the thought of Confucius.[44] He came to this conclusion on two grounds: first, that the doctrinal content is unlike anything else in the *Analects* or otherwise associated with Confucius and is unknown, apart from this one ostensible instance, as early as the fifth century B.C., and second, that "chain-arguments" like this ("if not A, then not B; if not B, then not C; etc.") are characteristic of texts from the third, not the early fifth, century B.C. Irrespective of how much persuasive force we may accord to Waley's arguments, and apart from the question of whether the passage is original in the *Analects* or not, its association with Confucius in the third century B.C. is surely what motivates the "Zheng ming" 正名 chapter of the *Xunzi* (ch. 22), where the meaning of the term is developed well beyond the somewhat anecdotal quality it has in the *Analects*.[45]

While much of Xunzi's concern with "setting names aright" has to do with the prescriptive authority a ruler has to determine what names are proper and what ones are not, and how they are to be used, thereby exerting over his people a controlling force for good order, Xunzi is at the same time capable of expressing a significant conceptual understanding of the nature and function of words in and of themselves. This can be seen in passages such as:

名聞而實喻，名之用也。

When a name is heard, the [corresponding] reality is conveyed; such is the usefulness of a name.

and

名無固宜。約之以命。約定俗成。謂之宜。異於約則謂之不宜。
名無固實。約之以命實。約定俗成。謂之實名。

Names lack any intrinsic proper significance; they achieve their denominative power by virtue of users agreeing on it (i.e., on their significance or meaning). Once such an agreement has been established and a customary (meaning) has been achieved, we refer to that as (the name's) "proper significance". When (a usage) differs from the agreed upon (meaning), we refer to that as "an improper significance".

[44] Arthur Waley, *The Analects of Confucius* (London: Allen & Unwin, 1938), pp. 22, 172.
[45] For this chapter, translated as "On the Correct Use of Names," see John H. Knoblock, *Xunzi, A Translation and Study of the Complete Works* (Stanford, Calif.: Stanford University Press, 1994), Vol. 3, pp. 113–38.

Names also lack any intrinsic (association with) real things; they achieve their power to denominate real things by virtue of users agreeing on that (i.e., on the associations). Once such an agreement has been established, and a customary (association with real things) has been achieved, we refer to that as "(a) name and reality (pairing)".[46]

The especially curious feature of the second of these two passages is what Xunzi intends by the juxtaposition of *míng* 名 and *mìng* 命, two words that differ phonetically only in that the latter had a final *-s* in Old Chinese (giving a Middle Chinese *qù shēng* 去聲 "departing tone", modern Chinese fourth tone) where the former did not; namely, *míng* 名 < EMC *mjiajŋ* < **màŋ*ʲ and *mìng* 命 < EMC *mjiajŋs* < **màŋ*ʲ*s*. Makeham explains the sense of *mìng* 命 in the first line of this passage as "to cause to be brought about by naming", and translates the line as "[A] name has no intrinsic appropriateness; rather, the appropriateness of a particular name is demarcated by being ordained."[47]

That there was in Xunzi's understanding a semantic link between *míng* 名 and *mìng* 命 cannot be doubted; the question is what was the nature of that link, and how might it have been a part of the perception of the nature and function of words and language in general during the third century B.C. John Knoblock recognizes that Xunzi's insistence on the importance of determining suitable names, besides being a fundamental perquisite of the ruler, may also reflect a belief that to name an object is to create a reality, and that the very act of naming something can influence that thing's fate.[48] Given the sense of *mìng* 命 as "fate, destiny", this notion may be most directly represented by the perceived, and perhaps genuinely cognate, relation between the two words *míng* 名 and *mìng* 命 themselves.[49]

The texts of the Later Mohists on names and objects, often fragmentary and corrupt, are a part of the essays on knowledge, language usage, and dis-

---

[46] Wang Xianqian, *Xunzi jijie* (Rpt. Taipei: Lantai, 1972), 16, pp. 14, 11. Knoblock *Xunzi*, pp. 132, 130–1, translates as "The 'use' of a particular name consists in the object being clearly understood when the name is heard" and as "Names have no intrinsic appropriateness. They are bound to something by agreement in order to name it. ..." He translates the last phrase of the passage as "it is called the name of that object." John Makeham, similarly, translates as "it is called the object's name"; *Name and Actuality in Early Chinese Thought* (Albany: State University of New York Press, 1994), p. 58. Clearly, these are possible translations of Xunzi's phrase "*wei zhi shi ming*," but my own sense is that there is more to the statement than this and that Xunzi intends to designate the correlation between the name and the thing that has been established by conventional agreement.

[47] Makeham, *Name and Actuality*, p. 58.

[48] Knoblock, *Xunzi*, p. 117.

[49] It is likely that the appearance of the "mouth" classifier (no. 030) 口 in both *míng* 名 and *mìng* 命 is phonetically as well as semantically significant; compare also its presence in *míng* < **màŋ*ʲ 鳴 "the calling of a bird". In two of these three characters there is no apparent "phonetic" element at all; in *mìng* 命 one could argue that the *líng* 令 component serves that purpose, but the question of how to account for the initial *m-* would remain. My speculation is that the graph 口 was in origin a polyphone, standing either for the noun *kǒu* "mouth" or for the verb *míng* "to call out (with the mouth)", by extension "to name", and in this second reading it served as a phonetic and semantic (hence, etymonic) component in all three of these graphs. Cf. English "fate" < Latin FATUM "what is spoken".

putation in general that constitute chapters 40–5 of the traditional received text of the *Mozi* 墨子. These are the treatises titled *Jing* 經, *Jing shuo* 經說, *Da qu* 大取, and *Xiao qu* 小取.[50] Graham has said of these writings:

A general characteristic which distinguishes these writings from all others of the pre-Han philosophers which survive as wholes is their deliberately theoretical nature. They do not propagate Mohism, they codify the techniques for defending it in debate.[51]

The *Jing* and *Jing shuo* sections (chs. 40, 42), which, like the other four of these six chapters, appear to be corrupt in their transmitted form, include lines that Graham has excerpted and reconstructed into a single passage that he then reads as a part of the codification of the Later Mohist view of knowledge, its sources and its objects, with an explanation of each. Graham's reconstruction from diverse lines of the *Jing* and *Jing shuo* sections, and his translation, are as follows:

知：聞，説，親。名，實，合，為。
(知)　：傳受之，聞也。方不運，説也。身觀焉，親也。
所以謂，名也。所謂，實也。名實耦，合也。志行，為也。

Chih (know). By hearsay, by explanation, by personal experience. The name, the object, how to relate, how to act.

Having received it at second hand is knowing by "hearsay". Knowing that something square will not rotate is by "explanation". Having been a witness oneself is knowing by "personal experience".

What something is called by is its "name". What is so called is the "object". The mating of name and object is "relating". To intend and to perform are to "act".[52]

In his preliminary discussion Graham states the summary in a more straightforward way as, "there are three sources of knowledge, report, explanation, and observation, and four objects of knowledge, names, objects, how to relate them (*he* 合) and how to act (*wei* 為)."[53] He argues further that the "Canons" are designed as a survey of all four of the branches of knowledge together with their explanations.[54] This summary is the clearest indication I know of in any of the extant pre-Han texts of the central position of "name" and "object", and of the relation of the one to the other, and is as close as

<hr>

[50] These are the chapters translated and studied at length in Graham, *Later Mohist Logic*. Without Graham's pioneering work in these texts, little could be said with any confidence about the Later Mohist theories of words and language. His work is the basis of much of the present discussion.

[51] Ibid., p. 24.

[52] Ibid., p. 327, no. A80.

[53] Ibid., p. 30. I would slightly modify Graham's understanding of *wéi* 為 and his translation of the last line cited. The phrase *zhì xíng* 志行 is not, I think, coordinate "to intend and to perform," as Graham has it, but rather "when one's intentions are performed"; that is, when what is potential is made manifest, this is *wéi* 為 "acting". There is, I think, a subtle pairing of *míng/shí* 名/實 with *zhì/xíng* 志/行 that suggests "name is to referent" as "intention is to enaction."

[54] Ibid., pp. 30, 229–33.

the pre-Han intellectual world seems to have come to establishing a distinct and explicit science of language.

The Sound System of Old Chinese

In many respects the study of Classical Chinese texts, literary and historical alike, cannot proceed seriously without recourse to the pronunciation of the words, that is, of the language, in which those texts are written. Word studies, morphological and grammatical studies, identification of foreign words and names, not to mention investigation of the linguistic affinities of Chinese per se, all depend on a clear picture of the phonological structure of Old Chinese.

Numerous twentieth-century scholars, beginning with Bernhard Karlgren, trained in the methods of Western comparative and historical linguistics and dialectology, have devoted their energies for much of the twentieth century to the problem of reconstructing the sound systems of Middle and Old Chinese.[55] This has been, and continues to be, no small enterprise, and as important as it is for sinological research, close to a century of work has gained few results, especially for Old Chinese, that can be said to be free from controversy.

Attempts to reconstruct Old Chinese have nearly always proceeded from first reconstructing Middle Chinese, the language of the Sui–Tang–Song period, in particular as codified by the Sui period riming dictionary known as the *Qie yun* 切韻 (compiled in 601), its Song recension called *Guang yun* 廣韻 (completed in 1011), and by the slightly later rime tables (*dengyuntu* 等 韻圖), the best known of which is the *Yun jing* 韻鏡 (compiled mid-twelfth century), and then projecting this reconstruction backwards.[56] The riming dictionaries and the rime tables taken together give the underlying Middle

---

[55] Karlgren was not actually the first Western scholar to undertake the reconstruction of early stages of Chinese, but he is probably the best known of the "first generation" of such scholars. See E. G. Pulleyblank, "European Studies on Chinese Phonology, the First Phase," in *Europe Studies China: Papers from an International Conference on the History of European Sinology*, ed. Ming Wilson and John Cayley (London: Han-shan Tang, 1995), pp. 339–67.

Karlgren's first book-length contribution was his University of Uppsala doctoral dissertation of 1915, titled *Études sur la phonologie chinoise*. It was subsequently published in an expanded version in installments between 1915 and 1926. His best-known and most commonly used work is the revised version of his dictionary of early graphic forms accompanied by his reconstructions of both Middle and Old Chinese (which he calls Ancient and Archaic Chinese, respectively). This is the *Grammata Serica Recensa*, first published in *BMFEA* 29 (1957): 1–332, and frequently reprinted *separatim* thereafter. As the title suggests, this is a revised version of an earlier work that Karlgren published in *BMFEA* in 1940, called simply *Grammata Serica*. Both of these works are in dictionary format and give reconstructions for nearly every character included. For that reason alone they continue to be widely resorted to, even now, in spite of the fact that much of Karlgren's linguistic work, valuable as it was when it was first done, has been superseded.

[56] Pulleyblank distinguishes two varieties of Middle Chinese, Early and Late. The former is the language registered in the *Qie yun* 切韻, of about A.D. 600, representing in his view the literary standard of the Nan-Bei Chao period capitals of both the North and the South. The latter is the Tang standard lan-

Chinese language a formal phonological structure and provide it for the first time with a complete closed system of phonological distinctions that in turn can serve as a framework for its reconstruction. For Old Chinese there is no such convenient textual starting point and no obvious way to make its reconstruction conform to a formally closed system. The rime groups of the *Shi jing* 詩經 as they have been identified and analyzed by the Qing philologists are commonly taken as a substitute for such a framework in reconstructing the Old Chinese finals.[57] There is no obvious counterpart available to help with the initials.

Ideally we would like to be able to distinguish the language of the several periods of the pre-imperial historical era phonologically from one another and to see how the sounds of the language changed over time, but to do this systematically or comprehensively with any degree of accuracy is not possible at the present stage of research. In addition to the reconstructed form of Middle Chinese and the *Shi jing* rime groups, the reconstruction of Old Chinese also depends on, among other things, the evidence of *xie sheng* (諧 聲; for this term, see p. 120 below) characters and transcriptions of foreign words. These kinds of data tend to be of different types and to derive from different periods of time. For these reasons it is difficult to establish a single reconstruction that can be said to represent Old Chinese as a real language at a particular time. When one or another feature is reconstructed using only a limited and demonstrably homogeneous body of evidence, that feature can then be associated with the specific time represented by the evidence. But the evidence for one feature will not necessarily be contemporaneous with the evidence for another, precluding a simple amalgamation of the various reconstructed parts into a meaningful whole.[58] While some sense of

guage of Chang'an and is reflected in the rime tables, about three centuries later than Early Middle Chinese. See his *Middle Chinese*, p. 62 and passim. Most other scholars reconstruct only a single form of Middle Chinese, representing the Tang–Song *koine* generally. Middle Chinese is what Karlgren called Ancient Chinese.

For a succinct description of the nature and use of the *Qie yun* and the rime tables as sources for Middle Chinese phonology, see Norman, *Chinese*, pp. 24–42.

[57] There were, of course, Ming and even Song and Yuan predecessors to the Qing scholars who recognized that the sounds of the language had changed over time and that this was an important consideration in the study of early texts, but the philological enterprise came to fruition in an extended way only in the Qing. See Benjamin A. Elman, *From Philosophy to Philology* (Cambridge, Mass.: Council on East Asian Studies, Harvard University, 1984), for a complete study of how this scholarship arose from earlier intellectual and textual concerns and for a survey of the intellectual setting in which much of this work took place.

[58] Some of the most recent work of William H. Baxter and E. G. Pulleyblank has taken account of the temporal disparities in the nature of the evidence for Old Chinese and has included proposals for reconstructions associated with particular periods depending on the date of the evidence. See Baxter, "Zhou and Han Phonology in the *Shijing*," in *Studies in the Historical Phonology of Asian Languages*, ed. William G. Boltz and Michael C. Shapiro, Amsterdam Studies in the Theory and History of Linguistic Science, series 4: Current Issues in Linguistic Theory, no. 77 (Amsterdam: John Benjamins, 1991), pp. 1–34.

an overall phonological picture of Old Chinese and its phonetic evolution can be discerned from what is presently known, attempts to establish a single unified and comprehensive phonological description of Old Chinese are still premature.

The sketch presented here is based on the reconstructions and proposals most recently set out by E. G. Pulleyblank.[59] This is not because this reconstruction is definitive and answers all questions or solves all problems about the Old Chinese language; far from it. But it does seem to me to make fuller use of a greater variety of evidence than other research on this subject has achieved to date. For all of its speculative and sometimes controversial aspects, Pulleyblank's work promises to result in a reasonably complete picture of the phonological and morphological structures of Old Chinese, providing in turn a firm basis for pursuing the question of the language-family affinity of Chinese. His approach is also less constrained by traditional but questionable assumptions about Chinese linguistic history than most others.[60]

On the other hand, the sketch we give is prima facie a *mixtum compositum*. The phonetic values reconstructed for the Old Chinese finals are based on the set of distinctions defined by the *Shi jing* rime groups, and therefore reflect a date of about the sixth century B.C. The reconstruction of the initials, by contrast, is based on extrapolating from the consonants reconstructed for the finals coupled with Pulleyblank's hypothesis that the set of twenty-two signs know as the "Heavenly Stems and Earthly Branches" (*tian gan di zhi* 天干地支) represents an exhaustive and nonrepeating inventory of the consonants in the language.[61] This means that those reconstructed values reflect the language at the time when the *ganzhi* set was first established. Since the *ganzhi* signs occur already in the earliest known Shang inscriptions, the phonetic values that Pulleyblank reconstructs for them will, per force, have to be taken as reflecting that time of the language, ca. 1200 B.C., at the latest. This predates the time of the values he reconstructs for the finals, based as they are on the evidence of the *Shi jing*, by more than half a millennium. While some suggestions may be made to describe the phonetic evolution of

[59] The discussion given here is my responsibility, based on my own understanding of Pulleyblank. It is by no means a comprehensive presentation of Pulleyblank's views on Old Chinese, nor should it be assumed that Pulleyblank would endorse any particular part of it that either diverges from or extends beyond his own published remarks. The relevant recent publications are Pulleyblank, "The Ganzhi as Phonograms and Their Application to the Calendar," *EC* 16 (1991): 39–80; idem, "The Old Chinese Origin of Type A and B Syllables," *Journal of Chinese Linguistics* 22 (1994): 73–100; and idem, "The Historical and Prehistorical Relationships of Chinese."

[60] Apart from Pulleyblank's work, the most recent major contribution to the study of the Old Chinese sound system is William H. Baxter, *A Handbook of Old Chinese Phonology*, Trends in Linguistics: Studies and Monographs, no. 64 (Berlin: de Gruyter, 1992). For a review of this work, see William G. Boltz, "Notes on the Reconstruction of Old Chinese," *Oriens Extremus* 36, 2 (1993): 185–207.

[61] See Pulleyblank, "The Ganzhi as Phonograms."

the language over the course of this period, and also over the subsequent half a millennium down to the Han period, what is not known far exceeds what is known at present about the early history of the language. In sum, the reconstructions set out here, valid and useful as carefully considered postulates, should in every respect be recognized as provisional and do not in any case fit together to make a uniform or comprehensive description of the Old Chinese sound system.

FINALS. The term "final" is typically used in Chinese historical phonology to refer to all parts of the syllable, save the initial, as a unit, that is, the medial (if any), head vowel, final consonant (if any), and tone (or segmental feature that corresponds to what later became tone). Phrased another way, we may say that the final is that part of the syllable involved in riming. This would define every part of the syllable except the initial and, sometimes, the medial.[62] In most analyses of Chinese phonology, the medial is included as a part of the final, but for Old Chinese the best characterization of medials, especially as they are related to initial consonant clusters, is not entirely clear. It may be preferable to consider the medial separately from both initials and finals.

Column (c) of Table 2.2 is the set of finals corresponding to what in Middle Chinese is the *ru* (入 "entering") tone, distinguished by having a final voiceless stop. The other three Middle Chinese tones, *ping* (平 "level"), *shang* (上 "rising"), and *qu* (去 "departing"), are thought to have arisen at some point after the beginning of the imperial era from earlier types of syllables with finals of the (a) or (b) columns; in the cases of the *shang* and *qu* tones, when followed by an additional segmental feature. The *shang* tone arose from syllables with a glottal stop (ʔ) following any of those finals; the *qu* tone arose from an *š* following any of them; and the *ping* tone arose from any (a) or (b) column final that did not have either a ʔ or *š*.[63]

All Old Chinese syllables can be divided into two large classes, traditionally recognized as those that Karlgren reconstructed with and those that he reconstructed without a medial yod (his -*i̯*- semi-vowel, elsewhere often transcribed -*j*-) after the initial. The actual existence of this yod in Old Chinese, and for Pulleyblank in both Early and Late Middle Chinese as well, has recently come into serious doubt. Pulleyblank calls the two classes type A

---

[62] For a very clear description of how these parts of the syllable were conceptually recognized in the Chinese linguistic tradition, see Norman, *Chinese*, pp. 25–8. For Old Chinese specifically, Pulleyblank (private communication) has suggested that the concept of "medial" may be less useful than that of "initial cluster."

[63] See Baxter, *A Handbook of Old Chinese Phonology*, pp. 302–24. What is written here as *š* is more commonly identified as *s*, as in examples given elsewhere in this chapter. The proposition about the origin of the *qu* tone is not affected by the difference.

Table 2.2. *Old Chinese* Shi jing *finals*

	(a) *yin*	(b) *yang*	(c) *ru*
I		侵 -əm	緝 -əp
II		談 -am	盍 -ap
III	微 -əl	文 -ən	術 -ət
IV (i)	歌 -al	元 -an	月 -at
(ii)	祭 -atš		
V	脂 -əj	真 -əŋʲ	質 -əkʲ
VI	支 -aj	耕 -aŋʲ	錫 -akʲ
VII	之 -əɣ	蒸 -əŋ	職 -ək
VIII	魚 -aɣ, -a	陽 -aŋ	鐸 -ak
IX	幽 -əw	冬 -əŋʷ	毒 -əkʷ
X	侯 -aɥ	東 -aŋᵗ	屋 -akᵗ
XI	宵 -aw		藥 -akʷ

and type B and explains the distinction between them as "a prosodic difference in Old Chinese between syllables with prominence on the second mora
(type A) and syllables with prominence on the first mora (type B)."[64]

Jerry Norman also doubts the factual accuracy of the yod in Old Chinese
and attributes the difference between the two classes to the propensity of a
given Old Chinese syllable to palatalize at a later stage of the language or
not. Palatalization is the norm, and according to Norman a syllable's failure
to palatalize is the consequence of either retroflexion or pharyngealization at
the Old Chinese stage blocking that development. He sees nonpalatalizing
syllables therefore as the phonologically marked form. This is consistent with
the fact that the majority of Middle Chinese syllables have a palatal glide
(Karlgren's *yod*) after the initial consonant, which in Karlgren's view typically
led to palatalization of the initial or fronting of the vowel, or both.[65] Whether
one prefers Pulleyblank's or Norman's interpretation of the distinction
between the two types of syllables, the implication for Old Chinese is in one
fundamental respect the same, namely, that all of the Old Chinese syllables
that Karlgren and others following him have traditionally reconstructed with
a *yod* did not in fact have one.

---

[64] Pulleyblank, "The Old Chinese Origin of Type A and B Syllables," p. 79. Pulleyblank has in past work
marked type A syllables with an acute accent mark over the head vowel, and type B with a grave one,
for example, -*án* and -*àn*, respectively, for final -*an*, and so mutatis mutandis for other finals. Most
recently, he has suggested marking the distinction with the IPA symbol for stress, to avoid confusion
of the acute and grave accent marks with the tone marks of transcriptions of later stages of Chinese
(ibid., note 4).

[65] See Jerry Norman, "Pharyngealization in Early Chinese," *JAOS* 114, 3 (1994): 397–408.

Table 2.3. *Old Chinese* ganzhi *initials*

Voiceless stops	p	t	k	kʷ	kʲ	kꞯ
	丙	丁	庚	甲	子	癸
Voiceless spirants	ɬ	x	xʷ	xʲ	xꞯ	
	申	己	丑	辛	戌	
Nasals	m	n	ŋ	ŋʷ	ŋʲ	ŋꞯ
	戊	壬	午	未	寅	卯
Voiced spirants	l	ɣ	w	j	ɥ	
	辰	巳	亥	乙	酉	

INITIALS. In Pulleyblank's view the set of twenty-two *tian gan di zhi* signs is a complete and nonrepeating representation of the set of initial consonants in Old Chinese. These signs, therefore, provide the same kind of closed set of phonological distinctions for the initials that the *Shi jing* rime groups provide for the finals, except that they reflect the language at a much earlier time than do the latter. Since the *ganzhi* signs are known from the time of the earliest Shang period inscriptions, ca. 1200 B.C., the language they reflect must also be of that time.

While it is not generally considered obvious that the *ganzhi* signs constitute a closed set representative of the Old Chinese initials, Pulleyblank defends this claim in part by observing that rows one, three, and four of the table of *ganzhi* initials (Table 2.3) match the final consonants in columns (c), (b), and (a), respectively, that he reconstructs for the *Shi jing* finals (Table 2.2); only the 祭 *-atš* final is exceptional. By the time of the *Shi jing* the set of initial consonants would in all likelihood have included voiceless aspirated stops (p^h, t^h, k^h), dental or alveolar affricates (ts, ts^h), an *š* (or perhaps *s*), and a glottal stop (*ʔ*). Some of these might have arisen from the row two series of the *ganzhi* initials. The last two are the segmental features thought to be responsible for the later development of the *qu* and *shang* tones, respectively. By Han times the inventory of initials would have included voiced stops (*b*, *d*, perhaps *g*) and an *r* / *l* contrast.

There is little doubt that Old Chinese was replete with syllables that had initial consonant clusters. This has long been recognized and is apparent from abundant *xie sheng* evidence of the following kind, where the nonhomorganic initials in what otherwise appear to be typical *xie sheng* pairs suggest a complex initial of some kind:[66]

---

[66] For the meaning of the term *xie sheng*, see p. 120.

各 EMC *kak*	洛 EMC *lak*	(both < *-*ak*)
林 EMC *lim*	禁 EMC *kim*	(both < *-ə*m*)
魚 EMC ŋ*iǎ*	穌 EMC *sɔ*	(both < *-*a*)
今 EMC *kim*	貪 EMC *t'əm*	(both < *-ə*m*)
少 EMC ç*iaw'*	妙 EMC *mjiaw^h*	(both < *-*aw*)
朝 EMC *triaw*	廟 EMC *miaw^h*	(both < *-*aw*)

The list of pairs (and sometimes threes or fours) like these could be multi-plied many times over. As apparent as it is that at least some of these data are to be explained by initial consonant clusters, the precise phonetic nature of those clusters and their development in later stages of the language remain largely unclear.[67]

Problems associated with the reconstruction of clusters, and the related question of medials, which for Old Chinese probably includes -*r*- as well as the semi-vowels -*j*- and -*w*-, are more intractable than the problems presented by reconstructions of simple initials and finals because there is as yet no phonological framework within which to work such that we can know what clusters are possible and what ones are not. At the present stage we do not know enough to exclude any possibility, although no one presumes that all possibilities actually occurred.

THE CHINESE SCRIPT

Chinese writing is first known from the so-called oracle-bone inscriptions (often abbreviated OBI) found early in this century at Anyang 安陽, the site of the last Shang capital.[68] These inscriptions, incised on the scapulas of oxen or on the plastrons of turtles (both types typically subsumed under the general rubric "bone"), record the texts of divinations (whence the designa-tion "oracle-bone inscriptions") performed at the Shang court, often in con-junction with sacrifices to one or another of the royal ancestors. The content of the divinatory inscriptions in the aggregate allows for the identification of nine kings in particular during whose reigns divinations were performed and who are unambiguously identifiable with the last nine kings of the Shang

---

[67] For speculations on the nature of Old Chinese consonant clusters and how they may have devolved in later stages of the language, see Bernhard Karlgren, *Analytic Dictionary of Chinese and Sino-Japanese* (Paris: Librairie orientaliste Paul Geuthner, 1923), pp. 31–2; Peter A. Boodberg, "Some Pro-leptical Remarks on the Evolution of Archaic Chinese," *HJAS* 2 (1937): 329–72, especially section 4, "Archaic 'Anlaut' and Dimidiation of Graph and Phoneme," pp. 353–60; and Baxter, *A Handbook of Old Chinese Phonology*, pp. 218–34.

[68] See Chapters 3 and 4, this volume; and David N. Keightley, *Sources of Shang History: The Oracle-Bone Inscriptions of Bronze Age China* (Berkeley: University of California Press, 1978).

state given in Sima Qian's 司馬遷 (ca. 145–86 B.C.) *Shi ji* 史記 of the first century B.C. The first of the nine is King Wu Ding 武丁, dated to approximately 1200 B.C., and it is thus to this date that we must attribute the earliest evidence for Chinese writing. Short inscriptions cast in ceremonial bronze vessels are also known from the same period. At the present stage of our knowledge about these artifacts, it is impossible to say whether one is earlier than the other; we can only say that both bone and bronze inscriptions are known from about 1200 B.C., neither from any earlier time.

It remains an unanswered question whether texts at this early period were also written on other materials that were less durable than scapulas, shells, and bronzes. Are the texts we have from this period, exclusively ceremonial and religious as they appear to be, the only kind of written documents that there were, or were there other kinds of texts, perhaps more quotidian, which did not happen to survive because they were written on perishable materials such as bamboo or wooden strips, as in later periods? Phrased another way, and approached culturally rather than archaeologically, we can ask whether writing in the earliest period was used exclusively for religious and ceremonial purposes or whether it also had a more utilitarian use not documented in the archaeological record because the material on which those more utilitarian texts were written was perishable.[69]

The most suggestive indication that there were in fact texts written on bamboo or wooden strips contemporaneous with the Shang inscription texts is the appearance of the character 冊 in the inventory of recognized Shang characters, identified with modern 冊 *cè* "writing tablet(s)" (also written 策). The inscription form of the graph is usually understood as depicting several bamboo or wooden strips tied together with a thong, which we know from direct archaeological evidence is the form later texts take.

The interpretation of what any Chinese character depicts is always subjective and never the same thing as understanding what word the character writes, but if the interpretation is arrived at thoughtfully, and without recourse to unwarranted a priori assumptions, it can sometimes be legitimately suggestive all the same of specific aspects of material culture. If the interpretation of the graph 冊 as "writing tablets laced together with a thong" is correct, then the indisputable implication is that these kinds of texts existed in the archaic period and have simply not survived because of the perishable nature of the bamboo or wood on which they were written.

Beyond this, the presumption is that any writing on bamboo or wooden

---

[69] On the general question of the utilitarian versus ceremonial use of early writing, including a discussion of the Chinese case, see Nicholas Postgate, Tao Wang, and Toby Wilkinson, "The Evidence for Early Writing: Utilitarian or Ceremonial?" *Antiquity* 69 (1995): 459–80. I am grateful to Robert W. Bagley for drawing my attention to this article.

tablets would have been done with a brush. There is no later indication that bamboo or wood was ever incised with characters, and thus there is no reason to suppose that that was a practice of the Shang. Evidence of brush writing in the late Shang period, on the other hand, is known from characters that seem to have been written with a brush on the smooth surface of pottery or jade, and David Keightley has allowed for the possibility that the characters of some oracle-bone inscriptions were brush-written on the bone's surface prior to being incised.[70] This evidence also suggests that there were probably texts written on bamboo or wood, contemporaneous with the Shang inscription texts, so that we cannot assume writing to have arisen in an exclusively religious context.

There is at present no significant archaeological evidence to suggest that Chinese writing was in use in locales other than Anyang at this early time, but given the highly incomplete and accidental nature of the archaeological record of early China, it would be foolhardy to suggest that such evidence may not one day be found. Neolithic pottery fragments, some dating to the fifth millennium B.C., occasionally bear incised or painted marks of one kind or another that suggest, in an abstract sense, written characters. This has prompted the claim that Chinese writing has an origin much earlier than the middle or late Shang.[71] None of these marks can be successfully identified with the characters of the Shang inscriptions or in any other way as Chinese writing. Apart from the virtual impossibility of deciphering a few scattered graphs occurring outside of a known linguistic context, the sheer extent of time, anywhere from 1,000 to as much as 3,500 years in some cases, precludes the possibility that these marks could be direct forerunners of Shang characters.[72] Whether they are a form of writing at all must remain an open question; we can say with confidence that they are not related in any historical way to the Chinese writing system we know from the late Shang on. Neither is there any indication that writing was imported into China from any civilization in western Asia or from anywhere else. On present evidence the Chinese writing system seems to have been invented not much earlier than 1200 B.C. and to have been entirely sui generis.

---

[70] In Chapter 3, this volume, Robert W. Bagley refers to a jade *ge* 戈 on which brush-written characters appear. This *ge* is illustrated in *Kaogu xuebao* 1981.4: 504, as well as in the source Bagley cites. For Keightley's basis for recognizing brush-written characters on oracle-bone inscriptions, see Keightley, *Sources of Shang History*, pp. 46–7.

[71] There are many studies on these kinds of marks from various Neolithic sites. For the best summary and discussion of the extent to which these marks can be considered writing, see Qiu Xigui, "Hanzi xingcheng wenti de chubu tansuo," *Zhongguo yuwen* 1978.3: 162–71; and K. C. Chang's discussion in Chapter 1, this volume.

[72] For a discussion of this issue, see William G. Boltz, *The Origin and Early Development of the Chinese Writing System* (New Haven, Conn.: American Oriental Society, 1994), pp. 35–9.

In spite of the very different appearance that Chinese writing now has from Western alphabetic scripts, all indications are that in origin the Chinese script was invented and developed according to the same pattern that characterized the appearance and early development of all other writing of antiquity, namely, Egyptian hieroglyphic and Mesopotamian cuneiform writing, the former ultimately giving rise to all of the familiar (and unfamiliar) alphabets and syllabaries of the modern world, save those of East Asia. The same developmental pattern also characterizes Mayan hieroglyphic writing in Mesoamerica. In all four cases the pattern consists at the outset of three developmental stages: (1) the *zodiographic*, (2) the *multivalent*, and (3) the *determinative*. We must acknowledge that to describe the invention of a writing system as having these three developmental stages is an artificial way of identifying the principles on which the writing system was built. Except at the earliest moments when the possibility of using graphs phonetically was first realized, it is not likely that the actual operation of the principles entailed in these three stages was anything other than simultaneous.

The Zodiographic Stage

It is widely and correctly assumed that writing arose first largely through a process of realistically depicting actual things or easily portrayable actions or relations.[73] This seems to have been as true in China as it was wherever else writing was invented ex nihilo. But to draw a picture of a thing is not the same as to write the word for that thing, in China or anywhere else. Pictures of things, irrespective of how depictively realistic or conventionalized and stylized they may be, are just pictures of things, and not writing. To be writing, the picture must be conventionally and regularly associated with the *name* of the thing depicted, that is, with the *word* for the thing in question. Only then can the picture be considered writing. In other words, for a picture

---

[73] For an important apparent exception to this general rule, see Denise Schmandt-Besserat, *Before Writing*, Part I, "From Counting to Cuneiform" (Austin: University of Texas Press, 1992). Her thesis, in a nutshell, is that in parts of the ancient Near East prior to the advent of writing, small tokens of simple shapes, for example, round, rectangular, triangular, and ovoid, were used as "counters" or "tallies" to keep track of commodities such as livestock, oil, grain, and so forth, the arbitrary association of a particular shape with a particular commodity becoming over time conventional and regular. By impressing the tokens into soft clay one could make an accountancy record in which a particular shape represented a commodity according to the established conventional association between tokens of a given shape and that particular commodity. These impressed shapes eventually became phoneticized, transforming them into graphs standing for the words naming the commodities.

Although Schmandt-Besserat's proposal, strictly seen, is an exception to the rule that writing arose through the phoneticization of realistic pictographs, it is only in the matter of realistic depiction versus arbitrary representation, that is, icon versus token, that it differs; the more important feature of the phoneticization of a representative graph remains the same.

to be writing it must be associated with a *sound* or, in the case of whole words, a *sequence of sounds*. This constraint on what kind of pictures can constitute writing is implicit in the general definition of writing: writing is the graphic representation of speech.[74]

When a graph is primarily a depictive representation of a thing, it is a *pictograph* and is not writing. When the same graph, or a modified version of it, represents primarily the name of the thing, that is, the word for the thing, and stands for the thing itself only as information conveyed by the word, we call it a *zodiograph* and define it as writing. The difference between a pictograph and a zodiograph lies not in the graph itself, but in whether in its usage it carries a conventional phonetic association (a pronunciation) or not. The process of shifting from a pictograph to a zodiograph is the process of acquiring a pronunciation. This process we call "phoneticization," and it is at this point that pictographs, or any other kind of graphs, turn into writing. Whether the graphs, once they have become phoneticized, remain depictively realistic or not is largely irrelevant to their function as writing.

Zodiographs uniformly consist of a single constituent element and cannot be divided into smaller graphic components (except individual strokes, of course). These are the graphs that we presume to have had an origin principally in the phoneticization of earlier pictographs. Once writing had been invented and the concept of graphs standing for words was established, many zodiographs may have been created consciously standing for words, not things, in the first place, on the model of those that had arisen originally through the phoneticization of pictographs. Even though a graph may have been created with an associated pronunciation at the outset, its invention may still have been, and in many cases likely was, based on an appeal to pictographic representation.

We have no direct archaeological testimony of this stage in the origin of writing in China; the script we find in evidence in the Shang divinatory inscriptions is a complete, fully workable writing system, in which all three of the developmental stages identified above are represented. This is so for two clear reasons. First, a script that was restricted to one of graphs depicting only concrete things or easily portrayable actions would be a very limited script indeed and would have little potential for fully expressing connected speech. As a consequence, it is unlikely that such a script would have received much practical use. Second, as mentioned above, these developmental stages

---

[74] One could, of course, define writing differently, to allow for all kinds of graphic representations of meaning. But to do that is to shift the discussion away from what we typically and straightforwardly think of as writing and, more important, from the history of Chinese writing, into the realm of semasiography and allied conceptual domains. For a longer discussion of this definition of writing and its implications, see Boltz, *The Origin and Early Development of the Chinese Writing System*, pp. 16–22 and passim.

Table 2.4. *Chinese characters commonly viewed as pictographic*

	Shang character	Modern character	Modern reading	Meaning
1.		人	*rén*	person
2.		女	*nǚ*	woman
3.		子	*zǐ*	child
4.		又	*yòu*	(right) hand
5.		齒	*chǐ*	teeth
6.		口	*kǒu*	mouth
7.		目	*mù*	eye
8.		耳	*ěr*	ear
9.		首	*shǒu*	head
10.		鳥	*niǎo*	bird
11.		羊	*yáng*	sheep
12.		馬	*mǎ*	horse
13.		虎	*hǔ*	tiger
14.		犬	*quǎn*	dog
15.		豕	*shǐ*	pig
16.		月	*yuè*	moon
17.		日	*rì*	sun
18.		木	*mù*	tree
19.		舟	*zhōu*	boat
20.		立	*lì*	stand

are not to be equated with temporal stages; except at the initial moment, they are likely to have operated simultaneously until a fully workable writing system was achieved.

All the same, the earliest known form of the Chinese script includes characters that are often invoked as "pictographic," that is, as being realistic pictures of the things for which they stand. Examples of such allegedly pictographic characters typically include those in Table 2.4.

If by the term "pictograph" we mean a graph that is a realistic depiction of a thing, such that a viewer can identify the thing in question from the graph itself, none of the characters in Table 2.4 seems to qualify as a genuine pictograph. Most, perhaps all, of them might indeed have been pictographs in origin, but they do not function as pictographs in the Chinese writing system of the Shang, or any other, period. We may well be able to see a genuine pictographic representation of the thing in question for some of them when we know in advance what that thing is, that is, when we already know what *word* the graph stands for. But that is not the same thing as knowing *from the appearance of the graph itself* what the thing intended is. If we did not already know that 人 (no. 1 in Table 2.4), for example, stands for the word *rén* "person", would we really be able to say with any conviction that that Shang graph is an unambiguous depiction of a person, and therefore must be the graphic representation of the word *rén*? Or that 豕 (no. 15) is clearly a depiction of a pig, and therefore writes the word *shǐ* "pig"? The number of Shang characters that are truly unambiguous in their depictive quality, and that therefore can be reasonably said to convey their intended meaning through the power of their depictive realism itself, is extremely limited, perhaps to the point of nonexistence. The so-called pictographic Chinese characters convey meaning no differently from any other Chinese character; they stand for words. Words have meanings, and when a character writes a word it inherently conveys the meaning of that word. Chinese characters do not represent meanings except by representing words.

Both at the earliest stage and at later stages in their evolution, Chinese characters are *logographs*; that is, they are graphs that stand for words. Those that consist of a single constituent element, and that are often recognized as having pictographic origins, we have called "zodiographs" for the purpose of identifying them as characteristic of the earliest stage in the development of the script. Zodiographs are one type of logograph; they are not pictographs, nor are they ideographs, a term often seen used in this connection. Just as a pictograph ought to mean a graph that is a realistic picture, so an ideograph ought to mean a graph that writes an idea. But such a graph, whatever it may be, cannot be a kind of writing, Chinese or otherwise, since writing by definition must represent speech at some level, and an idea becomes speech only via the word.

We now have a good explanation for why so many, perhaps all, of the Shang graphs that we might have expected to function pictographically do not. Once a pictograph has become a logograph, standing for a word, not a thing, and conveying its meaning by virtue of the *word* it represents, not by a visually identifiable representation of the *thing* it depicts, it need not maintain its depictive realism any longer. This is indisputably a great advantage to the establishment and implementation of a workable writing system; the effort to render a graph depictively realistic must have been in many cases a formidable challenge. When that was no longer necessary, graphs could become stylized in ways that made them easy to write. A scribe then need not have been an artist as well; in fact for any true writing system, a scribe must not need also to be an artist. The bulk of the Shang graphs, including the ones exemplified in Table 2.4, are not depictively realistic precisely because they do not need to be so; they stand for words.

There is one category of graphs seen in Shang inscriptions that stands out as often undeniably realistic in depictive quality and that might at first glance be thought an exception to the foregoing analysis. These are the so-called clan-name insignias (*zuming* 族名 or *zuhui* 族徽) that occur on many Shang bronze vessels (see Fig. 2.1). They appear either alone, with no inscriptional context at all, or, less commonly, in very short inscriptions. In both cases they are thought to represent the clan commemorated or otherwise honored by the casting of the vessel. Many of the *zuming* include graphic elements that are obviously identifiable with forms known from everyday Shang characters, while others are very precisely executed realistic representations of humans or animals, real and fanciful, or ceremonial objects, and are sometimes more reminiscent of bronze vessel decor than of anything in the writing system.

Clearly these graphs are depictively very realistic, much more so than the average Shang graph seen in either bronze or bone inscription texts. It is their very pictographic distinctiveness, coupled with their very limited and contextually specific use, that suggests they do not function as normal graphs in the Chinese writing system and are probably not writing at all; certainly they are not a kind of writing that has any bearing on the ostensible pictographic nature of the Chinese script. They are instead iconic representations of aristocratic Shang period clans, more on the order of European coats of arms, or heraldic insignias, than writing, their particular graphic identity perhaps being influenced by the perceived meaning of the clan's surname. That their typological forebears may have played some role in the invention or development of Chinese writing cannot be ruled out, but the clan-name graphs themselves as they exist contemporaneously with the Shang script do nothing to support contentions of the pictographic or ideographic nature of Chinese characters.[75]

---

[75] See the discussion in Boltz, *The Origin and Early Development of the Chinese Writing System*, pp. 44–52.

Figure 2.1. Examples of clan-name insignia graphs. Graphs are reproduced from the catalog listing in Gao Ming, *Gu wenzi leibian* (Beijing: Zhonghua, 1982), pp. 557–658, where the vessel bearing each is identified.

The Multivalent Stage

As crucial as phoneticization was in marking the turning point between non-writing and writing, the resulting body of zodiographs, no matter how large, could never become rich enough or versatile enough to write all of the things that a language can say, but that do not lend themselves to direct depiction. Overcoming this limitation was the next step in the process of developing a writing system, and the way in which it was done was the same in China as it was in Egypt, in Mesopotamia, and among the Mayas. It consisted in the

Table 2.5. *Paronomastic (rebus) usages of Chinese zodiographs*

	Character	Zodiographic usage	Paronomastic usage
1.	足	*zú* "foot"	*zú* "sufficient"
2.	亦	*yì* "armpit"	*yì* "also"
3.	又	(*yòu*)[a] "hand"	*yòu* "again"
4.	自	(*zì*) "nose"	*zì* "start from"
5.	象	*xiàng* "elephant"	*xiàng* "image"
6.	云	*yún* "cloud"	*yún* "said"
7.	其	*jī* "osier basket"	*qí* "possessive pronoun"
8.	舟	*zhōu* "boat"	*zhōu* "encircle", "engird"
9.	莫	*mù* "dusk"	*mò* "no one"
10.	栗	*lì* "chestnut (tree)"	*lì* "shivering"

[a] The pronunciation of this example and the next are placed in parentheses because these are obsolete words even in Old Chinese for "hand" and "nose" and are known only through early lexicographical identification of their respective graphs. See *Shuowen jiezi gulin*, p. 1228, which has the entry *you shou ye* 又手也, and p. 1472, which has *zi bi ye* 自鼻也.

recognition that a zodiograph standing for a particular word could be used to stand for a homophonous or nearly homophonous, but otherwise entirely distinct, second word the direct depiction of which would have been difficult or impossible. This is commonly called the "rebus" use of graphs, less commonly, the "paronomastic" use. Examples of this usage for Chinese graphs are given in Table 2.5.

The first character of Table 2.5, 足, is still used even in the modern script to write either the (literary) word *zú* "foot" or the homophonous word *zú* "sufficient". As will be discussed in the next section on the determinative stage, most characters that might have once been used paronomastically were later orthographically modified in order to avoid or eliminate any ambiguity about what word the character was intended to write. The paronomastic use of any given character is, therefore, often known only inferentially; that is, an actual paronomastic use may not be attested in any extant text, but can reasonably, sometimes easily, be surmised on the basis of the modified forms of the character in evidence in transmitted texts, coupled with what we know of the principles informing the writing system and its overall evolution. All the same, we can find more than enough actual examples of paronomastic usages even in transmitted texts to leave no doubt that this was one of the three developmental stages that accounts for the structure of the script. The character 云, for example, appears in the following line in the received text of the *Zhanguo ce* 戰國策: "Chu Yan zhi bing yun xiang" 楚燕 之兵云翔 (The troops of Chu and Yan swirled around like clouds). The same phrase "swirled around like clouds," referring again to troops, appears in the *Shi ji* 史記 as 雲翔.[76]

The richest source of the paronomastic usage of characters is the corpus of late pre-Han and early Han manuscripts recently discovered in diverse archaeological sites in China. One of the best known of such finds is the group of manuscripts written on silk from the tombs at Mawangdui 馬王堆, in modern Hunan province, near Changsha.[77] Because these manuscripts were written largely prior to, and independent of, efforts to standardize the writing system emanating from the Qin capital in the north, they show literally hundreds of examples of paronomastic uses of characters that would be viewed as nonstandard and eccentric, or even wrong relative to what came later to be established as the precepts and conventions for a standard orthography.[78] We find, for example, in the Mawangdui manuscript that matches closely the received text of the *Zhanguo ce* the word *shì* "clan" written sometimes as 氏, just as we would expect based on the orthographic conventions of the script from Han times on, but sometimes written quite unexpectedly as 是. Similarly, in the same manuscript the clan name Zhao is sometimes written 趙, again as we would expect, but is just as often written 勺. The combination of these two unexpected uses of paronomasia leads to occasional appearances of the at first baffling two-character sequence 勺是, which we come to recognize as standing for the phrase *zhào shì* "the Zhao clan" once we have realized the orthographic idiosyncrasies of this manuscript. The same manuscript, within a few lines of these unexpected usages of 勺 and 是, will write the same words *zhào* and *shì* with 趙 and 氏, as we find normal from our later perspective.[79]

In the same way that the inventors of the script realized that graphs could be used paronomastically, they also realized that they could be used *polyphonically*, that is, standing for a *semantically* congruent but phonetically distinct second word. The polyphonic use of characters cannot be readily illustrated with actually occurring examples, but must for the most part be

[76] *Zhanguo ce*, 6/6a (Yao Hong text, Taipei: Yiwen, n.d., photo-rpt. of the 1803 Huang Peilie ed.); and *Shiji* 78, p. 2388 (Beijing: Zhonghua, 1959, rpt. 1973).

[77] See *Mawangdui Han mu boshu*, Vol. 1, ed. Guojia Wenwuju guwenxian yanjiushi (Beijing: Wenwu, 1980); and *Vol. 3*, ed. Mawangdui Han mu boshu zhengli xiaozu (Beijing: Wenwu, 1983).

[78] See, for example, the discussion in Boltz, *The Origin and Early Development of the Chinese Writing System*, chapter 5 (pp. 156–77).

[79] See *Mawangdui Han mu boshu*, Vol. 3, p. 37 and passim. The phonetic basis for the graphic alternatives 是 and 氏 for *shì* "clan" is straightforward: the two words *shì* "clan" and *shì* "this", the latter being the word that is "normally" written with the character 是, are homophonous in Old Chinese as far as can be determined. For 勺 and 趙, both standing for the clan name Zhao, the case is slightly less neat, because the graph 勺 is conventionally associated with the word *sháo* < EMC *dʑiak/dʑiaw* "ladle", which is not exactly the same pronunciation as *zhào* < EMC *driaw*. Our assumption must be that in whatever dialect underlies this manuscript, the pronunciations that we register here as EMC *dʑiaw* and *driaw* were close enough to allow this graphic interchange.

inferred from the evidence of compound characters produced at the third stage of the script. This is so because nearly all instances of this use have been effectively "camouflaged" by the introduction in the third stage of determinatives (see the next section). Nevertheless, there is no question but that this type of graphic multivalence was as fundamental to the development of the Chinese script as it was to that of the Mayan and Egyptian hieroglyphic and Mesopotamian cuneiform scripts.

The word *míng* "call out", for example, was written with the graph ㅂ (= 口, no. 6 in Table 2.4), in origin presumably depicting an opening of some kind and standing for the word *kǒu* "mouth". The pronunciation of the two words *míng* "call out" and *kǒu* "mouth" are clearly unrelated, but just as clearly the words are linked semantically, namely, as the noun "mouth" and the related verb "what one does with the mouth". To someone creating a script the former would appear to be easily depictable, the latter less so. As a practical way to write the nondepictable verb "call out", the graph ㅂ for "mouth" makes good sense. Similarly, the graph ☞ (= 目, no. 7 of Table 2.4), originally *mù* "eye", was used to write the verb *jiàn* "to see"; and ♪ (= 月, no. 16) standing originally for *yuè* "moon", was used to write the word *míng* "brighten", the semantic rationale in this last case apparently being that as a concrete reflection of the *process* of brightening (which is what *míng* really means), the crescent (lit. "growing") moon was the most obvious choice. The graph 禾 stood zodiographically for the word *hé* "growing grain", but was also used for the phonetically unrelated but semantically allied word *nián* "harvest" (>"year"; cf. German *Herbst*). This recourse produced a great many characters that ended up at this stage standing for more than one word, semantically akin but phonetically distinct and unrelated.

Both paronomasia and polyphony are innovations in the use of characters; neither involves graphic modification of the character itself. Nor does either involve using a character to stand for anything other than a word. Thus, at this point in their development, all Chinese characters, whether used in their original sense as zodiographs or used paronomastically or polyphonically, structurally represent the zodiographic stage of the script, and each still stands for a whole word; that is, each is a *logograph*. Because a word by definition has both a pronunciation and a meaning, the paronomastic and the polyphonic uses of characters are simply the complementary pair of multivalent uses whereby one either holds the pronunciation associated with the words written by that character constant and allows the meaning to vary (paronomasia), or holds the meaning constant and allows the pronunciation to vary (polyphony).[80] The realization that characters

---

[80] In both types the phrase "to hold constant" must be understood as "to hold within subjectively discernible bounds." Except for homophony proper, which of course is well-defined, objectively precise

could be used in such a versatile way was an intrinsic and essential step in the early development of all writing systems of antiquity, allowing the script to escape the limitation of being able to write only that which could be directly depicted.

The Determinative Stage

While the multivalent use of characters provided a way around one kind of limitation on what could be written, it introduced another: the potential for ambiguity in what word was intended. When the graph ㅂ (口) for example, was written, was it meant to stand for the word *kǒu* "mouth" or *míng* "call out"? When ⟩ (月 / 夕) was written, did it represent *yuè* "moon", *míng* "brighten", or *xì* "night", yet a third word written with the same graph?[81] The same potential for ambiguity attended the rebus, or paronomastic, use of graphs. Did the character 足 in a particular occurrence mean *zú* "foot" or *zú* "sufficient"? Did an occurrence of 象 stand for *xiàng* "image" or *xiàng* "elephant"?

The more recourse was had to the multivalent capacity of the early script, the more ambiguity was introduced into what was written. While context alone could be relied on to resolve many instances of ambiguity, as it does even now for some of those characters given in Table 2.5 that are still used paronomastically, it could not be counted on to resolve the growing impact of ambiguous usages in the majority of cases. To do that the Chinese took the same step in modifying the early writing system that the Egyptians, the Mesopotamians, and the Mayans took. They resorted to appending secondary graphs, drawn largely from the inventory of already existing zodiographs, to the ambiguous primary graph to specify either the intended pronunciation or the intended meaning, according to which aspect of the character was ambiguous. When a graph was used paronomastically, the meaning – not the pronunciation – was the source of any potential ambiguity, and so the secondary graph that was appended was chosen to determine meaning. Conversely, graphs used polyphonically were ambiguous principally as to pronunciation, so the appended graph was chosen to specify pronunciation. Secondary graphs that are appended to ambiguous primary graphs are typically called "determinatives" because they determine which

---

parameters for either phonetic constancy, that is, near-homophony, or semantic constancy, that is, semantic congruence have so far resisted identification. This may be due to our presently imperfect knowledge of the languages and scripts involved, or it may be that in principle such parameters, especially those pertinent to semantic congruence, are not amenable to explicit identification.

[81] The modern graphic distinction between 月 and 夕 does not reflect a consistent orthographic distinction in the early script. While the graph did indeed take forms antecedent to both 月 and 夕, this was a matter of free variation except perhaps in very limited contexts. In general, either form could stand for any of the three words mentioned.

one of two or more possible words is intended. Those that determine meaning are *semantic determinatives*; those that determine pronunciation are *phonetic determinatives*.

Several of the examples of paronomastic usages given in Table 2.5 came to be written in a way that distinguished the different meanings by simply appending to the graph a semantic determinative for one of the two possibilities, as illustrated in Table 2.6.

The characters in the right-hand column of Table 2.6 are typical of the great majority of Chinese characters in that they consist of two (or more) graphic components, one of which can be identified as a secondary element that has been added as a semantic determinative to an identifiable phonetic element. The rationale behind the particular semantic determinative used varies between obvious and inexplicable, with most cases falling close to the obvious end of the scale. In nos. 2, 3, 4, and 5 from Table 2.6, the choice of semantic determinatives 竹 "bamboo", 日 "sun", 心 "heart/emotions", and 雨 "rain", respectively, seems to be obvious. For no. 1, with 人 "person", it is less clearly motivated.

The process of adding semantic determinatives to primary characters came to be very productive and is responsible for the hundreds of sets of compound characters in the modern writing system where each set consists of characters that share a given phonetic element but have different semantic determinatives. Item no. 3 in Table 2.6, for example, is one member of the following sizable set of compound characters based on the 莫 *mù/mò* phonetic element:

1. 幕 *mù* "tent" (巾 "drape/cloth")
2. 慕 *mù* "long for" (心 "heart/emotions")
3. 墓 *mù* "grave" (土 "earth/dirt")
4. 募 *mù* "summon" (力 "strength")
5. 漠 *mò* "stilled" (as of water) (水 "water")

Table 2.6. *Examples of semantic determinative usages*

1.	象 *xiàng* "elephant"	像 *xiàng* "image"
		(Addition of 人 "person" semantic determinative)
2.	其 *qí* "possessive pronoun"	箕 *jī* "osier basket"
		(Addition of 竹 "bamboo" semantic determinative)
3.	莫 *mò* "no one"	暮 *mù* "dusk"
		(Addition of 日 "sun" semantic determinative)
4.	栗 *lì* "chestnut"	慄 *lì* "shivering" (from fear or cold)
		(Addition of 心 "heart/emotions" semantic determinative)
5.	云 *yún* "said"	雲 *yún* "cloud"
		(Addition of 雨 "rain" semantic determinative)

6. 膜 *mò* "kneel" (肉 "flesh/body part")
7. 寞 *mò* "silenced" (宀 "covering/roof")
8. 騔 *mò* "prance" (馬 "horse")
9. 模 *mú* "model, overlay" (木 "wood/tree")
10. 摹 *mó* "rub" (手 "hand")
11. 謨 *mó* "announce" (言 "speech")
12. 摸 *mō* "stroke" (手 "hand")
13. 嫫 *mó* "hag" (女 "woman")
14. 糢 *mó* "blurred" (米 "rice")

By Han times, characters consisting of two or more parts, one of which functioned clearly as a phonetic element, were called *xié shēng* 諧聲 characters, usually rendered in English as "phonetic compounds," and the series of characters built around a single phonetic is usually called a *xié shēng* series. These characters have the familiar structure of a radical and a phonetic, though both terms "radical" and "phonetic" are imprecise. What are typically called "radicals" are the secondary semantic determinatives that were added to already existing characters; they are therefore in no way radical, that is, they do not constitute the core or root of the character. What are called "phonetics" are the elements that bear the pronunciation, called technically "phonophorics."

The actual occurrence of paronomastic uses in extant texts is the exception rather than the rule. For most Chinese characters of this kind, as for example the dozen or more in the 莫 set, only uses of the compound form of the character are attested and we can only infer an original paronomastic use as the reason behind the appearance of the compound form. In fact it seems unlikely that there would have been actual paronomastic use of every graph that comes to serve as the phonophoric in a *xié shēng* series like that given here for every different word included. It is much more likely that once the step of using semantic determinatives was first taken and the principle of "phonophoric plus semantic determinative" as a basic character structure was clear, such characters could be created de novo "on the spot," so to speak, without actually having to have been used paronomastically first.

The use of phonetic determinatives is a more difficult process to document, though it must have originally been just as productive as the use of semantic determinatives. Consider, for example, the following set:

名 *míng* name, call
命 *mìng* fate
鳴 *míng* bird-call

Based strictly on these data, without recourse to any external knowledge, we would be justified in identifying this small set as a *xié shēng* series with the graphic component 口, read *ming*, (second or fourth tone, in modern pronunciation) as the phonophoric. But such an identification is rarely proposed because the graph 口 by itself is not known to be read as either *míng* or *mìng* in any documented stage of the language, and therefore does not look like a possible phonophoric in the set. When we consider the possibility suggested earlier that the graph 口 was polyphonic at the formative stage of the script, doing "double duty" so to speak, in that it stood in some cases for the noun *kǒu* "mouth" and in others for the verb *míng* "call out", we can then see that at that stage it may well have served as a phonophoric read *míng* in a set like the one just listed. Even more, the first of the three characters listed stands for none other than the very word *míng* "call out" (> "calling, name") that was probably originally written simply as 口. Here it has been augmented by the graph 夕, which is for its part a graphic variant of 月, read *míng* (standing for the word *míng* "brighten", not the word *yuè* "moon") and functioning as a phonetic determinative to specify the pronunciation (and meaning) *míng* "call" as opposed to the alternative *kǒu* "mouth". If, as seems likely, every case of the graph 口 that was to be read *míng* "call" was augmented by the phonetic determinative 夕, in an effort to render the writing system unambiguous, then we would naturally not find examples of 口 itself used to stand for the word *míng*, and our speculation that it was so used will have to remain inferential.

Similarly, the character 禾 (禾), which could stand equally well either for the word *hé* "growing grain" or for the semantically akin but phonetically distinct word *nián* "harvest" (> "year"), was written 秂 (年), consisting of the original 禾 with the graph 亻 (人 *rén*, Old Chinese *ɣnə̀n/ʲ) added underneath to specify the pronunciation *nián* (Old Chinese *ɣnə̀n/ʲ) unambiguously. In both this and the preceding example, the secondary graphs 夕 *míng* and 人 *rén* function as phonetic determinatives; their intrinsic meaning is irrelevant to these usages, and only their pronunciation is pertinent.

With this development, we find Chinese characters that are compound in their structure, consisting of a primary component that was originally deemed ambiguous either semantically or phonetically and was therefore augmented by a secondary element to determine the primary component's intended meaning or pronunciation. Like unit characters, compound characters could be used multivalently and thus were susceptible to receiving additional graphic elements appended to them as determinatives. The character 幕 *mù* (no. 1 of the set listed earlier), for example, already consisting of a phonophoric (莫 *mò* / *mù*) plus a semantic determinative (巾), occurs further augmented by 网, the semantic determinative for "net", giving 羃, and by the semantic determinative 冖 "cover", giving 冪, both characters read *mì* and standing for a word meaning "the cloth covering placed over a bowl of food". And also as with the creation of two-part compound characters out of unit characters augmented by a determinative, actual multivalent use was not essential once the structural principle had been established. It was necessary only to recognize the potential for multivalency and its attendant ambiguity to allow for the creation of a new character in which a semantic determinative was added to a preexisting character that already included one or more determinatives in its graphic structure. By the time the writing system and its operative rules were well established, even this recognition was probably superfluous, and in many cases no more than an aesthetic appeal underlies the use of semantic determinatives.

This, then, is the origin of compound (Chinese *he ti* 合體), or what we might call "multibodied," Chinese characters. This kind of character came to be called by the technical word *zì* 字 in the terminology of the Han lexicologists, as opposed to *wén* 文 , which by contrast designated "single-bodied," or "unit," characters (Chinese *du ti* 獨體), zodiographs in the terminology used here.[82]

The versatility that compound characters brought to the script invested the Chinese writing system with a capacity that allowed for full expression of the language while remaining in its fundamentally logographic guise. In a given written context, any character – compound or unit – stood for a single syllable, and as far as we know at the formative stages of the script, that syllable regularly corresponded to a word. There may have been a few words that were of more than one syllable, but there was no syllable that was not also a word (technically, at least a morpheme). All syllables, therefore, had meaning. This was the crucial feature as far as the writing system was concerned. If there was no syllable that did not have a meaning, then there was no possibility of writing a character (which per force had to stand for a syllable) that did not stand for a meaningful phonetic entity, in simple terms, for a word. For this reason the "one syllable – one word – one character" rule was orthographically inviolable. Some characters always stood for the same word; others, thanks to the multivalent feature of the script, could stand for one of several different words depending on context. No character ever stood for an "idea" independently of a word. Chinese characters stood, and continue to stand, either singly or in combination, for words, and only via that phonetic medium for the ideas that those words convey.

Both semantic and phonetic determinatives were used extensively in the early development of the Chinese script, ultimately becoming intrinsic, permanent parts of the characters to which they were appended. Later, once the

---

[82] The distinction given here between *wén* 文 and *zì* 字 is precisely the sense in which those two terms were used by Xu Shen 許慎 in the title of his work *Shuowen jiezi* 説文解字, which means "Explaining the *wén* and Analyzing the *zì*" and that forms the overall basis for his classification of characters.

formative principles of the script had had their effect and the writing system was completely evolved, the use of phonetic determinatives waned, ultimately leaving so few recognizable vestiges that even an understanding of it in principle was threatened. The use of semantic determinatives, by contrast, came to be not only an easily recognized feature of the script, but one deemed aesthetically so central that the semantic determinatives themselves were welded, so to speak, permanently to their host graph, such that the resultant compound character was felt intuitively to be a single unit in spite of its obviously analyzable and componential structure.

The practice in Egypt and Mesopotamia was significantly different from that for Chinese; in those cases, determinatives remained largely separable and removable. It is this feature, as much as anything else, that is responsible for the different evolutionary trajectories taken from this point on by the Near Eastern scripts on the one hand and the Chinese on the other. Mesopotamian cuneiform writing gradually became obsolete and has left no modern descendants. Egyptian, by contrast, ultimately gave rise to all historically known scripts of the modern world, save those of East Asia. The medieval and modern scripts of East Asia all owe their origin and development, one way or another, to Chinese.[83] China is, in other words, one of only two civilizations in the history of mankind to have invented ex nihilo a script that has endured down to the present day, and thus to have influenced the course of human history in regard to the most fundamental feature of historical civilization itself, the use of writing.

---

[83] See William G. Boltz, "East Asian Writing Systems (Introduction)," in *The World's Writing Systems*, ed. Peter T. Daniels and William Bright (Oxford: Oxford University Press, 1996), pp. 189–90, and the pertinent script-specific essays following.

CHAPTER THREE

SHANG ARCHAEOLOGY

Robert Bagley

When Shang 商 archaeology came into being seventy years ago it was the archaeology of one site, Anyang 安陽 in northern Henan province, a place firmly connected with the Shang dynasty of traditional history by the oracle-bone inscriptions unearthed there. Since 1950 its scope has widened steadily to take in new sites which, though they have not yielded inscriptions, are related to Anyang in material culture. The absence of inscriptions leaves the political status of these sites uncertain, but the practice of Chinese archaeologists has been to give them a place in history by assuming connections with the Shang royal house. New finds have been attached to traditional history on a model supplied by tradition: since the Shang dynasty was represented by later writers as the paramount cultural and political power of its time, sites and finds distant from the Shang court have been assigned either to political subordinates of the Shang king or to inferiors vaguely imagined as barbarians. No independent check of this model is supplied by the Anyang oracle inscriptions, for they too have been interpreted on the assumption of the Shang court's paramount status. Shang archaeology has operated on the premise that traditional history provides an adequate account of the past and that all archaeological discoveries should find a natural place within that account.

Yet as archaeological finds multiply, it becomes increasingly evident that the centrality and cultural unity which are the essence of the traditional model are nowhere to be seen in the archaeological record of the time of the Anyang kings. By that time, the last two or three centuries of the second millennium B.C., civilization had long since spread to a very large area, and the evidence for civilized societies geographically remote and culturally different from Anyang is now abundant. Rationalizations that would attach the whole of a large and diverse archaeological record to a royal house attested at one city in north China have come to look arbitrary and improbable.

124

This chapter therefore seeks to set out the archaeological evidence in a way that does not assume that the picture it paints is known in advance. The chapter begins with a brief history of the archaeology of the Shang dynasty, in other words, of archaeology conceived as an exploration of the textual record. This will serve to explain how the assumptions of traditional historiography have manifested themselves in archaeology. In subsequent parts of the chapter, terms that embody those assumptions will be used only in very strict senses. "Shang" and "Shang dynasty" will refer only to the family whose kings (real or mythical) are named in the Anyang oracle texts. "Anyang period" will refer to the time of the nine kings whose inscriptions have been found at Anyang, and it will be used only in reference to the Anyang site. Since no such archaeological definition can be given for the expression "Shang period," it will be avoided. The word "dynasty" calls for special caution, since in Chinese historiography its connotations extend dangerously beyond the dictionary meaning of a ruling family. The expression "Chinese civilization" is open to the similar objection that it represents a vague and anachronistic concept whose projection backward into the second millennium B.C. can only mislead.

Apart from two or three centuries in the life of one city, the second millennium belongs to prehistory. We cannot take later traditions as our guide to prehistory, for this is only to impose the beliefs and purposes of later times on the archaeological record. Awkwardly, however, our present knowledge of the archaeological record has itself been shaped by tradition. Fieldwork has been planned under the guidance of texts, and it has focused above all on the so-called Central Plain (Zhongyuan 中原) region of North China, in other words on the middle Yellow River valley and the Wei 渭 valley, because tradition locates the first dynasties there.

Fortunately a corrective to the geographical bias of text-based archaeology is available in the form of chance finds – the same finds, in fact, that have made the expression "Shang archaeology" problematic by persistently widening its application. Reliance on chance finds amounts in practice to reliance on a single category of artifact, cast bronzes, since no other is so widely known or so consistently reported in the archaeological literature, but the limitation to this one form of evidence is by no means fatal. Artifacts of cast bronze are technologically and typologically the most distinctive trait of material culture in second-millennium China. Moreover to a far greater degree than in other ancient civilizations, the metal industry in China is a revealing index of cultural development. The second part of the chapter therefore turns to the bronze industry for a purely archaeological definition of the chapter's scope and approach. Large-scale metallurgy supplies a workable criterion for identifying the earliest civilized societies in China, and by tracing its development we obtain a sensitive measure of relative chronology and cultural affiliations.

The development of the bronze industry sketched in the second part provides the scaffolding for the main part of the chapter, a survey of sites and finds whose relationships can be tentatively diagnosed on the evidence of bronzes. The principal features of Early Bronze Age material culture are introduced in the course of this survey. The survey has the further purpose, however, of reviewing the known archaeological record in a way that lends itself to inferences of a historical kind, against which the images of traditional history can be tested.

THE ARCHAEOLOGY OF THE SHANG DYNASTY

From the moment of its birth in the early decades of this century, Chinese archaeology was involved in controversies over the value and credibility of received accounts of Chinese antiquity. The crisis of traditional culture at the fall of the Qing dynasty in 1911 called into question cherished beliefs about the past, and there was little agreement as to what could or should be salvaged. For many intellectuals the ratification or revision of ancient history was an important part of the effort to fashion a Chinese identity that could survive confrontation with the forces of modernization. Some sought to preserve tradition unchanged, others to adapt it to serve present ends, still others to write an ancient history that met modern standards of proof. At such a time the oracle bones, which collectors had begun acquiring from antique dealers at the turn of the century, could not fail to command wide attention, for it had been recognized from the first that they were inscribed with names recorded in traditional history as kings of the Shang dynasty. Scholars who might well agree on nothing else agreed on the importance of the oracle inscriptions. To Luo Zhenyu 羅振玉 (1866–1940) and Wang Guowei 王國維 (1877–1927), who combined a deep interest in the inscriptions with an anxiety to defend received history and the values it sanctioned, they were a precious vindication of tradition. To the historian Gu Jiegang 顧頡剛 (1893–1980), whose work in the early 1920s showed that accounts of the Xia 夏 dynasty and of earlier sage-kings had the character of folklore, they were evidence that Shang had a different status from Xia, and they promised fresh source material for a newly rigorous study of history.[1]

---

[1] For Luo Zhenyu, Wang Guowei, and early oracle inscription studies, see Joey Bonner, *Wang Kuo-wei: An Intellectual Biography* (Cambridge, Mass.: Harvard University Press, 1986), chapters 12–14. For Gu Jiegang, see Arthur W. Hummel, *The Autobiography of a Chinese Historian* (Leiden: Brill, 1931); and Laurence A. Schneider, *Ku Chieh-kang and China's New History* (Berkeley: University of California Press, 1971). At least one prominent scholar, Zhang Binglin 章炳麟, denounced the oracle bones as forgeries; it was the Anyang excavations that supplied the final demonstration of their authenticity.

By 1915 Luo Zhenyu had established that antique dealers obtained their supplies of oracle bones from farmers near modern Anyang (see Map 3.1). Whether the place the bones came from was viewed as anything other than a source of more oracle bones, however, depended on ideas brought to China by field archaeology, a Western discipline that met a favorable reception in the westernizing climate of the May Fourth Movement. The new discipline's potential for illuminating the Chinese past was demonstrated in the early 1920s by the Swedish geologist J. G. Andersson (1874–1960), who discovered the first Neolithic sites known in China; in 1923 the thirty-year-old Gu Jiegang saw an exhibition of Andersson's finds and lamented that he was too old to become an archaeologist. When in 1928 a new research organization of the Republican state, the Academia Sinica, decided to undertake an archaeological excavation, Anyang was the obvious site to choose; Li Ji 李濟 (1896–1979), an anthropologist trained at Harvard, was the fortunate choice to direct the excavations. Thus at a time of unprecedented threat to traditional ideas and openness to foreign ones, Chinese archaeology was born from the application of a Western scientific discipline to an inquiry that had intense significance for traditional culture.[2]

Between 1928 and 1937, despite unsettled local conditions, fifteen seasons of excavation were carried out at Anyang.[3] After the first three, devoted to trial diggings north of the village of Xiaotun 小屯, the excavators moved briefly to the site of Chengziyai 城子崖 in Shandong, where a survey had found Neolithic pottery quite unlike the painted pottery discovered by Andersson in northwestern China. The painted pottery, which some scholars identified with the Xia dynasty, was generally agreed to represent an extension into China of the Neolithic of western Asia; Li Ji and his colleagues therefore hoped that a site in eastern China might reveal a local prehistory native to East Asia. Chengziyai obligingly yielded a distinctive black pottery, and it also taught the excavators to recognize pounded-earth (hangtu 夯土) construction, which they had encountered previously at Anyang in the form of large architectural foundations but had mistaken for an alluvial deposit. On their return to Anyang in 1931, they found at Hougang 後岡 a stratified

---

[2] Li Chi [Li Ji], *Anyang* (Seattle: University of Washington Press, 1977), chapters 1–3, describes the arrival of field archaeology in China. A few decades earlier archaeology had come into being in the Near East in a similar crisis of tradition, a challenge from geology and biology to views of the past derived from the Bible (P. R. S. Moorey, *A Century of Biblical Archaeology* [Louisville, Ky.: Westminster/John Knox Press, 1991; Cambridge: Lutterworth, 1991], pp. 2–3). The parallel is close enough for the history of attempts at accommodation between archaeology and biblical tradition traced by Moorey to be read as a commentary on Shang archaeology.

[3] Li Chi's *Anyang* provides a detailed history of the 1928–37 excavations and a bibliography of the Academia Sinica's research publications. For brief accounts that include later excavations, see *Yinxu de faxian yu yanjiu*, ed. Zhongguo Shehui kexueyuan Kaogu yanjiusuo (Beijing: Kexue, 1994), chapter 2; and Zheng Zhenxiang, "Yinxu fajue liushi nian gaishu," *Kaogu* 1988.10: 929–41.

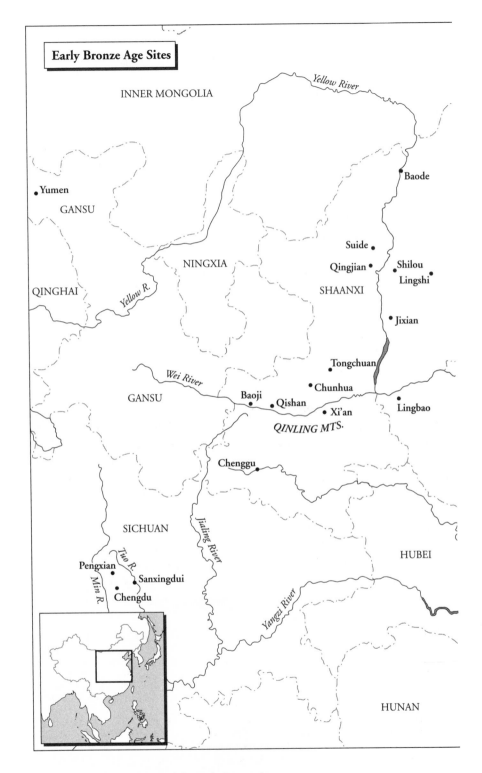

Map 3.1 Archaeological sites of the Early Bronze Age

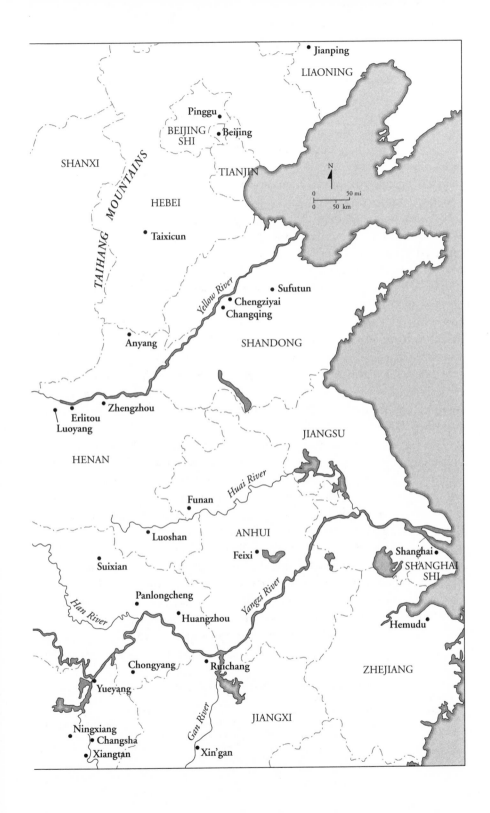

sequence with painted pottery in the lowest level, black pottery in the middle level, and Shang remains above. This they took to mean that a western-derived painted pottery culture had been succeeded by an indigenous black pottery culture and that the Shang culture, though indebted to both, owed the elements which marked it as East Asian, such as scapulimancy, to the latter. Understood as revealing the native component of East Asian prehistory, Chengziyai was judged an appropriate subject for the Academia Sinica's first excavation report.[4]

Between 1931 and 1934 the Anyang excavators worked mainly on large *hangtu* architectural foundations at Xiaotun. In 1934, however, a rumor that looters digging on the opposite side of the nearby Huan River 洹河 had discovered a set of spectacular bronze vessels (Fig. 3.10b) led them to Xibeigang 西北岡, where they found and excavated a cemetery of sacrificial burials and gigantic shaft tombs. In 1936 work shifted back to Xiaotun; the major discovery of the season was a pit containing more than 17,000 fragments of inscribed turtle plastrons. In 1937 the war with Japan halted the excavations, and the archaeologists were evacuated along with their collections to a series of wartime refuges in western China. Even in this difficult period study and publication of the finds were carried on, and work continued under the direction of Dong Zuobin 董作賓 (1895–1963) and Li Ji after the Academia Sinica moved to Taiwan in 1948.

The Anyang excavations began as an investigation of the source of the oracle bones, but they ended by unearthing a civilization. Chinese scholars were reassured that native traditions could be trusted; Western scholars were persuaded that China had an ancient past. This double triumph shaped the future of Chinese archaeology. Objectively considered, the Anyang excavations dealt only with a few centuries in the history of a single city. That city was connected with a textual tradition that spoke of a dynasty conceived as ruling the whole of civilized China, however, and the excavations inevitably were taken to ratify this vague larger conception. Thus, the entire time which later texts give as the duration of the Shang dynasty is often described as a fully historic period, though not even the Anyang period meets ordinary definitions of this term.[5] Indeed the Anyang excavations have been even more broadly construed as a comprehensive vindication of tradition and refutation

---

[4] Li Ji, Liang Siyong, and Dong Zuobin, eds., *Chengziyai* (Nanjing: Academia Sinica, 1934); see especially the prefaces by Fu Sinian and Li Ji.

[5] As noted by Gina L. Barnes, *China, Korea, and Japan* (London: Thames & Hudson, 1993), p. 19. The notion of archaeologically verified historicity, more problematic than Chinese archaeology has ever acknowledged, is usefully discussed in the literature of biblical and Homeric archaeology (see, e.g., Moorey, *A Century of Biblical Archaeology*, and M. I. Finley, "Schliemann's Troy: One Hundred Years After," *Proceedings of the British Academy* 60 [1974]: 393–412).

of skeptics. Although Xia inscriptions have never been found, so that the Xia dynasty is still the same purely textual phenomenon analyzed by Gu Jiegang, Chinese archaeologists today argue that since the recorded genealogy of the Shang kings has proved trustworthy, the Xia genealogy can probably be trusted too. Confidence borrowed from the Anyang excavations has made it possible to dismiss Gu's skepticism as unwarranted without addressing any of his arguments.

By demonstrating its power to sustain tradition, the Anyang excavations won for archaeology a secure foothold in China. A discipline which under less fortunate circumstances might have been rejected as foreign has received state support under both Republican and Communist governments (both of which have excluded foreigners from fieldwork). But archaeology gained its foothold at the price of becoming a tool for the vindication of tradition. The success in verifying texts which secured its future also defined its mission. The archaeology of the Early Bronze Age has remained the archaeology of the Shang dynasty; that is, it has been guided by and interpreted according to a mental image of the past which comes not from the archaeological record but from late Zhou 周 and Han 漢 texts. Archaeologists have been preoccupied with finding peoples and places named in texts, and this preoccupation has influenced the choice of regions for archaeological survey, the choice of sites to excavate, and the interpretation of what was found at those sites. The possibility that archaeology might encounter a past different from the past of tradition has not been consciously acknowledged.[6]

Li Ji and his colleagues were eager to find an indigenous component in Chinese civilization, but they were not dedicated to establishing Chinese isolation from the other civilizations of antiquity. The culture they had unearthed at Anyang was highly sophisticated. To explain its seemingly abrupt appearance, unheralded by more primitive stages, Li Ji suggested western Asia as the likely source for Chinese metallurgy, certain artifact types, and other features. The large tombs with human sacrifice at Xibeigang reminded him of Leonard Woolley's discoveries a few years earlier in Mesopotamia; the chariot was an obvious Western borrowing; and to explain the sudden advent of distinctive bronze vessels, he supposed that vessel shapes and decoration which had developed locally in pottery and carved wood were simply translated into bronze when metal technology arrived from outside. For an archaeologist of his generation, contact and diffusion were

---

[6] On the subordination of archaeology to written history in a climate of nationalism, see Lothar von Falkenhausen, "On the Historiographical Orientation of Chinese Archaeology," *Antiquity* 67 (1993): 839–49; Bruce Trigger, *A History of Archaeological Thought* (Cambridge University Press, 1989), pp. 174–7; and Barnes, *China, Korea, and Japan*, pp. 28–9, 40–1.

entirely natural explanations for culture change, and he never hesitated to invoke them.[7]

For a later generation, however, it was not enough to restore the credibility of tradition; the next task for a national archaeology was to free ancient China from the imputation of dependence on outside stimulus. Marxist ideas entered Chinese archaeology after 1949, but their influence was felt chiefly in Neolithic archaeology; in the archaeology of later periods the Marxist demand for a universal history was outweighed by the demand for a local history that could be a source of national pride.[8] Archaeology was required above all to feed an intense nationalism, and in this cause nothing was more timely than the discovery of local antecedents for the Anyang civilization. In 1949 Anyang was still the only excavated Shang site, and Shang archaeology was still Anyang archaeology. In 1952, however, excavations at Zhengzhou 鄭 州 began to disclose the remains of a large walled city demonstrably earlier than Anyang.[9] Although the Zhengzhou discoveries did not account for all the items Li Ji had explained as foreign, they did prove the existence of a pre-Anyang stage, and this was enough to end discussion of outside influence on the formation of the Anyang civilization. Soon afterward radiocarbon dates from the Banpo 半坡 site at Xi'an 西安 suggested that Andersson's painted pottery Neolithic was also a native development. Chinese archaeologists were thus encouraged to reject the possibility of outside influence at any stage and to concentrate on tracing a purely internal development.

This reorientation coincided with superficially similar changes in Western archaeological thinking. In his acceptance of diffusionist explanations, Li Ji had been at one with the international archaeological community of his time; that same community after 1950 abandoned diffusion for a variety of reasons, including dismay at the overthrow of trusted correlations by radiocarbon dating and sympathy with nationalistic demands for local prehistories. The rejection of outside influence that has prevailed since 1950 in Chinese archaeology has thus been warmly endorsed by Western archaeologists, who have

[7] See, e.g., Li Chi, *The Beginnings of Chinese Civilization: Three Lectures Illustrated with Finds at Anyang* (Seattle: University of Washington Press, 1957), p. 17; and idem, *Anyang*, p. 254.

[8] See Falkenhausen, "On the Historiographical Orientation of Chinese Archaeology"; Michèle Pirazzoli-t'Serstevens, "Pour une archéologie des échanges. Apports étrangers en Chine – Transmission, réception, assimilation," *Arts Asiatiques* 49 (1994): 21–33; and, on the role of Marxism, Albert Feuerwerker, ed., *History in Communist China* (Cambridge, Mass.: MIT Press, 1968), esp. pp. 27–31 (on Guo Moruo's Marxist periodization of ancient history). In suggesting that archaeology has been less subject to political pressures than historical research, Feuerwerker (p. 8) is clearly thinking only of Marxist pressures.

[9] Convincing arguments for the dating, based mainly on pottery typology, were advanced by An Zhimin ("1952 nian qiuji Zhengzhou Erligang fajue ji," *Kaogu xuebao* 8 [1954]: 65–108), and Zou Heng ("Shilun Zhengzhou xin faxian de Yin Shang wenhua yizhi," *Kaogu xuebao* 1956.3: 77–104). The same conclusion was implied by a seriation of bronzes proposed independently of archaeological evidence by Max Loehr, since graves at Zhengzhou were furnished with bronzes of his first two styles ("The Bronze Styles of the Anyang Period," *Archives of the Chinese Art Society of America* 7 [1953]: 42–53).

equated it with their own dogmatic rejection of diffusion as a mode of explanation.

But Chinese archaeologists rejected foreign influence, not diffusion; for them diffusion outward from the Yellow River valley has continued to be a natural assumption because it gives to this region the same civilizing role that traditional historiography ascribes to it. Hence, the search for remains connected with traditional dynasties and the search for evidence to support theories of indigenous development have continued since 1950 in the Central Plain, where the sites of Erlitou 二里頭, Zhengzhou, and Anyang are taken to provide a complete chronological sequence for the Early Bronze Age.[10] Excavation at Anyang resumed in 1950, under the auspices of a new Institute of Archaeology in Beijing, and a permanent Anyang field station was established in 1958. The site has now seen more than half a century of excavation, and the wealth of information it has yielded is unrivalled. At the earlier city of Zhengzhou, which seems to have been at least as large as Anyang, the remains of palatial buildings and a massive city wall have been found. Since the ancient city lies beneath the modern one, however, excavation is difficult, and current understanding of the Erligang 二里崗 culture, of which Zhengzhou is the type site, owes much to finds made at contemporary sites elsewhere. The still older site of Erlitou, near Luoyang 洛陽, was discovered in 1959 by a survey prospecting for Xia remains. It is at the moment the main representative of the stage immediately preceding Zhengzhou. Epigraphic evidence to identify the two cities has not been found, but their location in the Yellow River valley has made it easy to assume that they must in some way be connected with Xia and Shang.[11]

Archaeology has not been entirely monopolized by Xia and Shang, however, for a vast program of salvage archaeology has thrown light on regions far outside the Central Plain. Since 1950 the State Bureau of Cultural Relics has energetically fostered public alertness to finds made in the course of farming or construction work, and countless chance finds have been recorded.[12] These constitute a nationwide archaeological sample independent

---

[10] Until recently, Chinese archaeologists assumed that the occupations of Zhengzhou and Anyang formed a continuous sequence; some now speak of an intervening period, the so-called transition period, which coincides roughly with Style III in Loehr's bronze series. See below, note 38.

[11] The identification of Xia and Shang capitals is a central preoccupation of Chinese archaeologists on which a voluminous literature has accumulated. Outside observers unwilling to gloss over the problems of connecting material remains with texts find little of substance in this literature (see Barnes, *China, Korea, and Japan*, p. 130; and Robert L. Thorp, "Erlitou and the Search for the Xia," *EC* 16 [1991]: 1–38).

[12] The early encouragement given to salvage archaeology is indicated by two exhibitions held in Beijing, one in 1954 at the Historical Museum (*Cultural Relics Unearthed in the Course of Basic Construction*) and one in 1956 at the Palace Museum (*Important Cultural Relics Unearthed in Five Provinces*); see the preface to the catalog of the 1954 exhibition, Zheng Zhenduo, ed., *Quan guo jiben jianshe gongcheng zhong chutu wenwu zhanlan tulu* (Beijing: Guoji, 1955).

of textual bias, and it is a sample that has proved to differ importantly from that of text-based archaeology. A significant early achievement was the discovery of an Erligang-period city near the Yangzi River: at Panlongcheng 盤龍城 in Hubei province, repeated chance finds of bronzes led eventually to the excavation of a walled city culturally indistinguishable from Zhengzhou but 450 km south of it. The Panlongcheng discoveries were impressive enough to give new character to the Erligang culture, which began to attract interest in its own right rather than merely as a forerunner of the Anyang civilization. They also showed the geographic distribution of the Erligang culture to be unexpectedly wide, and this was taken to mean that the Shang empire was much larger than previously supposed.

Panlongcheng was easier to interpret than discoveries made further south. Bronzes somewhat later than the Erligang period have been unearthed at many places in the middle and lower Yangzi region, and unlike the bronzes from Panlongcheng, which are of perfect Erligang style, they are often highly idiosyncratic. But until recently these were isolated finds, with little or no archaeological context, and most observers were content with explanations that assimilated them to existing views. Connections with the Shang dynasty might simply be postulated: "Presumably the bronzes were buried there by Shang slaveowners fleeing from the north before the collapse of the Shang dynasty."[13] Alternatively, southern finds might be associated with names found in the oracle texts (drawing them into the world as viewed from the Anyang court), or labeled with later ethnonyms, or both.[14] The persistence of such explanations must be taken as a measure of the enormous difficulty of stepping outside a text-based image of the past. By about 1980, archaeologists in Jiangxi and Hunan were beginning to insist on the local character of finds in their part of the country, but this was distinctly a local and minority opinion.[15] Wide acknowledgment of a need to revise familiar assumptions

[13] Xia Nai writing in 1972 ("Wuchan jieji wenhua dageming zhong de kaogu xin faxian," *Kaogu* 1972.1: 30), apropos of bronzes unearthed at Ningxiang in Hunan, an explanation often quoted. A few scholars still defend similar views by contesting the dating of finds whose local character cannot be ignored.

[14] For instance, *Xin Zhongguo de kaogu faxian he yanjiu*, ed. Zhongguo Shehui kexueyuan Kaogu yanjiusuo (Beijing: Wenwu, 1984), p. 243, associates bronzes from the Yangzi region with Jing-Chu 荆楚, and Huai 淮 River bronzes with Huaiyi 淮夷. Similarly Li Xueqin assigns Yangzi bronzes to Jing-Chu and without further discussion takes them as an early manifestation of the Eastern Zhou Chu culture, showing how smoothly the habit of casual labeling leads to large and wholly unsubstantiated conclusions ("Chu Bronzes and Chu Culture," in *New Perspectives on Chu Culture in the Eastern Zhou Period*, ed. Thomas Lawton [Washington, D.C.: Smithsonian Institution, 1991], pp. 1–3).

[15] Peng Shifan, "Jiangxi diqu chutu Shang Zhou qingtongqi de fenxi yu fenqi," in *Zhongguo Kaogu xuehui di yi ci nianhui lunwen ji 1979*, ed. Zhongguo Kaogu xuehui (Beijing: Wenwu, 1980), pp. 181–94; and Gao Zhixi, "Shang wenhua bu guo Changjiang bian," *Qiusuo* 1981.2: 107–12. Japanese and Western scholars had begun to identify southern bronze-casting industries some years earlier, and the topic is still most fully treated in the Western literature. Early discussions include Virginia Kane, "The Independent Bronze Industries in the South of China Contemporary with the Shang and Western Zhou Dynasties," *Archives of Asian Art* 28 (1974–5): 77–107; Higuchi Takayasu, "Ka'nan shutsudo no Shô

has come only recently, following the discovery of spectacular sacrificial pits at Sanxingdui 三星堆 in Sichuan in 1986 and of a rich tomb at Xin'gan 新淦 in Jiangxi in 1989, both connected with nearby city sites.

The fact that two of the most extraordinary "Shang" discoveries ever made are in Jiangxi and Sichuan has put old explanations under heavy strain. As a first step toward a new interpretative framework, Chinese archaeologists have therefore begun to speak of "multiple centers of innovation jointly ancestral to Chinese civilization."[16] This vague formulation acknowledges that civilization was not limited to the Central Plain and thereby licenses the study of local developments in other regions, but it also assumes that the importance of those developments lies in their contribution to the "Chinese civilization" of some later time.[17] In fact the study of ancient China is perennially distorted by its concern not with the rise of civilization in China but with the rise of *Chinese* civilization, an entity never defined but always imagined in terms drawn from some later period. No student of fifth-century Athenian culture would be content to describe it as an early stage in the rise of Byzantine civilization, but this is exactly the sort of backward view that shapes the study of China before the Zhou period. Pride in the antiquity of Chinese civilization inspires a search for early precursors of familiar institutions. Late texts are trustingly quoted as sources of information about early times, a practice which naturally enhances the appearance of cultural continuity that is invoked to justify it. History takes on an air of inevitability, with evidence of cultural diversity shouldered aside by a traditional assumption of cultural unity.

Yet the archaeological record increasingly suggests that cultural diversity and historical contingency will be found if they are sought. It therefore seems worthwhile to strive for a fresh image of the second millennium B.C. undistorted by later concerns. To survey the material record evenhandedly requires finding a way to define the scope of the present chapter that does not depend

---

(In) shiki dôki no kenkyû," *Museum* 301 (April 1976): 4–16; Hayashi Minao, "In Seishû jidai no chihôkei seidôki," *Kôkogaku Memoir* (1980): 17–58; and Wen Fong, ed., *The Great Bronze Age of China: An Exhibition from the People's Republic of China* (New York: Metropolitan Museum, 1980), chapter 3. Some of these authors attempt to trace southern developments over time; in the Chinese literature the overriding concern is still to establish the dependence of local cultures on their Central Plain contemporaries.

[16] See Lothar von Falkenhausen, "The Regionalist Paradigm in Chinese Archaeology," in *Nationalism, Politics, and the Practice of Archaeology*, ed. P. Kohl and C. Fawcett (Cambridge University Press, 1995), pp. 198–217.

[17] The same assumption is contained in K. C. Chang's definition of a "Chinese interaction sphere," comprising all the Neolithic cultures that in his view contributed to the formation of Chinese civilization (*The Archaeology of Ancient China* [New Haven, Conn.: Yale University Press, 1986], pp. 234–42). Many scholars simply assume that everything within the present political boundaries of China contributed to form Chinese civilization. Thus, the most spectacular Neolithic cultures, Hongshan 紅山 and Liangzhu 良渚, are automatically regarded as ancestors of Chinese civilization, no matter how strange their character or tenuous their connection with later developments.

on the hypothetical geography of traditional dynasties, nor on notions of the "Chinese civilization" of some later time, but that is instead tied directly to the archaeological evidence of complex societies. The next section argues that on both practical and theoretical grounds, this is best done in terms of the characteristic bronze technology of the Erligang civilization. The remainder of the chapter then proposes that, even within the narrow limits set by a body of evidence that consists mainly of chance finds, it is possible to catch glimpses of a history significantly different from the one supplied by tradition. In the nature of the evidence, the history that can be inferred from archaeology is limited to large statements, devoid of personalities and particulars, and it is limited also by the bias and the perpetual incompleteness of the archaeological sample. Nevertheless for China in the second millennium B.C., archaeology is richly informative, and a comparison of the history deduced from archaeology with the history familiar from texts is illuminating, not least because it raises important questions about the texts.

THE ARCHAEOLOGY OF BRONZE METALLURGY

For a meaningful way to define the scope of the chapter we turn from traditional history to metallurgy. By its scale and character the bronze industry can identify the first civilized societies for us. Its development supplies the framework for a chronological survey of sites and material culture.

A Definition of the Bronze Age

The idea of an age of bronze entered archaeological thinking in the nineteenth century, when scholars hoped that artifacts of stone, bronze, and iron might serve to distinguish epochs of prehistory in the way that zone fossils served to identify geological strata. Later, when the transition from food gathering to food producing (the Neolithic revolution) and the rise of stratified societies (the urban revolution) came to be viewed as the major events of prehistory, it was tempting to seek some correlation with the older sequence of materials. Whether regarded as advances in knowledge or as advances in production technology, however, the materials showed no simple correlation with economic or social structures. In particular, the rise of civilization does not regularly coincide in the archaeological record with the first appearance of copper or bronze. Mesoamerican societies reached levels we would not hesitate to call civilized without metal. Bronze tools did not increase agricultural or craft production so dramatically as to be a major cause of social change, indeed bronze may always have been too costly to be much used for agricultural tools. The urban revolution was more social than technological, and when archaeologists today use the term "Bronze Age", in most parts of the world they use it only as a convenient label for some part of a local archaeological sequence, not as an acknowledgment of some special role played by metal.[18]

In China, however, the label is meaningful, for metal did play a special role, and the term "Bronze Age" can be defined in a way that firmly connects it with the rise of stratified societies. The Bronze Age of China is set apart from all others by the enormous quantities of metal it has left us. A single Anyang bronze vessel of about 1200 B.C., the *Si Mu Wu fangding* 司母戊方鼎, weighs 875 kg; an Anyang royal tomb of the same date contained 1,600 kg of bronze (a tomb of the fifth century B.C. contained ten metric tons of bronze). Nothing remotely comparable is known elsewhere in the ancient world.[19] Mining and casting on this scale presuppose an investment in labor and organization that makes them a clear symptom of the emergence of stratified societies. If the term "Bronze Age" is applied in China to the earliest societies that supported large metal industries, it labels exactly the stage of development that we would want to call civilized. In other words, whether or not it played any causal role, bronze in China supplies an unambiguous index of social complexity.

To make this index useful we must introduce a precise distinction between small-scale and large-scale metallurgy.[20] The distinction, visible in other metal-using traditions but particularly sharp in ancient China, separates two stages in the exploitation of metals that differ in scale and also in character. The first is a stage in which technical knowledge is acquired and applied to

---

[18] See Trigger, *A History of Archaeological Thought*, pp. 73–9; Bruce G. Trigger, *Gordon Childe: Revolutions in Archaeology* (London: Thames & Hudson; and New York: Holt, Rinehart, & Winston, 1980), pp. 144–8. E. N. Chernykh, who attributes a large causal role to metallurgy (*Ancient Metallurgy in the USSR* [Cambridge University Press, 1992], pp. 3–5, 10ff.), seems unaware of long-standing objections to his view. Cf. Theodore A. Wertime and James D. Muhly, eds., *The Coming of the Age of Iron* (New Haven, Conn.: Yale University Press, 1980), chapter 8.

[19] Compare the accounts of metalworking in Mesopotamia and Egypt in P. R. S. Moorey, *Ancient Mesopotamian Materials and Industries: The Archaeological Evidence* (Oxford: Clarendon Press, 1994), chapter 5; Moorey, "The Archaeological Evidence for Metallurgy and Related Technologies in Mesopotamia, c. 5500–2100 B.C.," *Iraq* 41, 1 (Spring 1982): 32; T. G. H. James, ed., *An Introduction to Ancient Egypt* (London: British Museum, 1979), pp. 218–28; and A. Lucas and J. R. Harris, *Ancient Egyptian Materials and Industries* (London: Edward Arnold, 1962), chapter 11.

[20] Ursula Martius Franklin, "On Bronze and Other Metals in Early China," in *The Origins of Chinese Civilization*, ed. David N. Keightley (Berkeley: University of California Press, 1983), pp. 285–9; cf. Wertime and Muhly, *The Coming of the Age of Iron*, p. 368. Periodizations based on the scale of metal production should be contrasted with periodizations based on narrowly metallurgical criteria. The latter regularly lead to debates about where the line should be drawn between Bronze Age and earlier metal-using phases (to which such terms as "aeneolithic" and "chalcolithic" are sometimes applied), yet neither in China nor elsewhere does the replacement of copper by copper alloys seem to be either a well-defined or an important event; it was an erratic and protracted process perhaps more dependent on fluctuating supplies of tin than anything else. Given that periodization in these terms would describe Egypt as a chalcolithic culture down to the time of the Middle Kingdom, alloying would seem to have no value as an index of cultural development.

the manufacture of simple tools and ornaments. It involves a knowledge of how to prospect, how to win metals from their ores, and how to hammer, cast, and alloy them. The second is a stage of production in large quantities, in which previously existing technical knowledge is exploited on a previously unknown scale. It depends on elite patronage and, if reached at all, is the stage at which a metal industry becomes the province of specialist metal-workers. Metalwork at this point loses its anonymity, becoming technologically and artistically sophisticated and distinctive.[21]

At present the earliest clear evidence for primitive, small-scale metallurgy in China dates from about 2000 B.C. The transition to large-scale production, which seems to have occurred at sites in the middle Yellow River valley about the middle of the second millennium, is indicated by several changes, all of which signify the work of specialists in the service of a powerful elite: a shift to an exclusive reliance on casting, a technique unsparing of metal; a dramatic increase in production, implying among other things large-scale mining; the elaboration of an efficient technical repertoire; and the formation of a distinctive artistic style. These changes are so decisively marked in the archaeological record as to be dependably meaningful outside the realm of metal technology. Reflecting new social organization rather than new technical knowledge, they mark the rise of civilization and identify for us the stage for which the term "Bronze Age" can most usefully be reserved.

Large-scale casting and the distinctive technical repertoire to be described below are therefore taken to identify the first civilized societies in China and to define the period and geographic region of concern to this chapter. The shared technical repertoire moreover implies historical connections between the societies so identified; in most of them the major product was cast bronze vessels, a further indication of common origin.[22] The term "Early Bronze Age" will be applied here to the period from the beginnings of large-scale production, on present evidence about the middle of the second millennium, down to, as a convenient endpoint, the founding of the Zhou dynasty (1045 B.C. on the chronology adopted in the present volume). Early Bronze Age

---

[21] See Bruce Trigger, *Beyond History: The Methods of Prehistory* (New York: Holt, Rinehart, & Winston, 1968), p. 54, and compare the application of similar ideas to Egypt in B. G. Trigger, B. J. Kemp, D. O'Connor, and A. B. Lloyd, *Ancient Egypt: A Social History* (Cambridge University Press, 1983), p. 67; and Barry J. Kemp, *Ancient Egypt, Anatomy of a Civilization* (London: Routledge, 1989), chapter 2.

[22] Bronze vessels have sometimes been proposed as the defining artifact of early Bronze Age civilization in China (see, e.g., Barnes, *China, Korea, and Japan*, pp. 18, 23, 118). The slightly different criterion proposed here, focusing on the Erligang bronze technology rather than on a particular artifact type, has the advantage of taking in cultures that used bronze less for vessels than for bells or other items. Both criteria exclude at least one pre-metal culture with evidence of social stratification, the Liangzhu culture of the Shanghai region, but the bearing of this third-millennium culture on second-millennium developments is very unclear, while the cultures that shared the Erligang technology must surely all be historically connected to a significant degree.

for the purposes of this chapter is therefore the second half of the second millennium B.C.

Bronze artifacts define the scope of the chapter. They are also one of its principal sources of information, for in the present state of archaeological knowledge many of the societies to which they draw our attention are known only from finds of bronzes. Fortunately much can be learned from objects which in their time were plainly of high importance – second only, perhaps, to architecture, of which scant trace survives. In second-millennium China the bronzes made for ritual or mortuary purposes were products of an extremely sophisticated technology on which immense resources were lavished. They have an individuality that sensitively registers differences of time and place; cultural differences and interactions can be read from their types, decoration, and assemblages. Because they served political or religious functions for elites, they reflect the activities of the highest strata of society; unlike the pottery on which archaeology normally depends, they supply information that can be interpreted in terms somewhat resembling those of narrative history. Moreover the value which has attached to ancient bronzes throughout Chinese history makes them today the most systematically reported of chance finds, with the result that the geographic distribution of published bronze finds is very wide.[23] No other sample of the archaeological record is equally comprehensive – no useful picture would emerge from a survey of architecture or lacquer or jade – and the study of bronzes is thus the best available corrective to the textual bias of Chinese archaeology.

Because firm understanding of the artifacts is the key to extracting information from their archaeological occurrence, the remainder of this section focuses narrowly on the bronze industry, tracing the unfolding of casting technology and bronze styles. The development of bronzes thus established is used in the next section as the organizing framework for a review of the archaeological record.

The Development of the Bronze Industry

SMALL-SCALE METALLURGY. The earliest metal industry known at present within the modern borders of China is that of the Qijia 齊家 culture of Gansu province.[24] Calibrated radiocarbon dates for Qijia fall in the neigh-

---

[23] On the place of ancient bronzes in Chinese culture since the Bronze Age, see Jessica Rawson, "The Ancestry of Chinese Bronze Vessels," in *History from Things: Essays on Material Culture*, ed. Steven Lubar and W. David Kingery (Washington, D.C.: Smithsonian Institution Press, 1993), pp. 51–73.

[24] A critical review of early metal finds by An Zhimin dismisses claims for earlier metalworking elsewhere ("Shilun Zhongguo de zaoqi tongqi," *Kaogu* 1993.12: 1110–19).

borhood of 2000 B.C.[25] Whether Qijia was ancestral to metallurgical developments in central North China remains uncertain.[26] It represents a stage more convincingly primitive than anything so far known there, however, and thus conveniently exemplifies the forerunners of large-scale metal industries. Some 350 Qijia sites are known in or near eastern Gansu, four of which have yielded altogether about fifty metal artifacts: mirrors, ornaments (finger rings, pendants), and tools (knives, awls, chisels, axes). Of these some were hammered and some cast in bivalve or slightly more complex molds. Twelve analyzed objects suggest that Qijia metalwork is mostly copper, occasionally alloyed with lead and/or tin. Arsenical copper has not been found, and this has sometimes been seen as a significant departure from the metallurgical sequence of the ancient Near East. Archaeometallurgists have recently begun to suspect that alloy sequences have more to do with the top-to-bottom geology of local ore deposits than with the laws of chemistry, however, and this view robs the sequence of larger implications for the history of metallurgy.[27]

A successor to Qijia still richer in metal, known from the Huoshaogou 火燒溝 site at Yumen 玉門 in Gansu, belongs apparently to the first half of the second millennium. Of 312 graves excavated at Huoshaogou, 106 yielded a total of more than 200 metal artifacts. Of 46 objects analyzed, 13 were copper and 33 were bronze containing tin or tin and lead.[28] The objects are axes, sickles, chisels, knives, daggers, spearheads, arrowheads, needles, bracelets, hammers, and mirrors. These are small and nondescript tools and ornaments, not distinctive items manufactured for the elite of a stratified society.

[25] *Zhongguo kaoguxue zhong tan shisi niandai shuju ji 1965–1991*, ed. Zhongguo Shehui kexueyuan Kaogu yanjiusuo (Beijing: Wenwu, 1991), pp. 274–86. The currently available dates, from seven sites, give little indication of the duration of the Qijia culture; it might have survived long after 2000 B.C. In general, radiocarbon dates are still too few to contribute importantly to the chronology of the period covered in this chapter; the statistical errors associated with calibrated dates in the second millennium are very large (for a clear discussion, see Sheridan Bowman, *Radiocarbon Dating* [London: British Museum, 1990]).

[26] An Zhimin ("Shilun Zhongguo de zaoqi tongqi") suggests that metallurgy could have come to Qijia from further west and inclines to see it as the source of later developments in central North China; Li Boqian ("Zhongguo qingtong wenhua de fazhan jieduan yu fenqu xitong," *Hua Xia kaogu* 1990.2: 82–91) dismisses it as one of several early traditions with minimal bearing on later developments.

[27] See, e.g., Wertime and Muhly, *The Coming of the Age of Iron*, chapter 9. The Western literature of archaeometallurgy has laid great stress on the intellectual achievement represented by metallurgical knowledge, and demonstrating that the achievement was indigenous has been correspondingly important to Chinese archaeologists. Archaeology has not supplied conclusive evidence one way or the other, however, and perhaps should not be expected to. The evidence for metallurgy in Precolumbian Peru is after all not now disputed, but whether it is interpreted as evidence for independent invention or for transpacific contact still depends on individual judgment as to which of those occurrences is less improbable.

[28] Analyses of Qijia, Huoshaogou, and Erlitou metal artifacts are reported in *Kaogu xuebao* 1981.3: 287–302; Zhang Zhongpei, "Qijia wenhua yanjiu (xia)," *Kaogu xuebao* 1987.2: 153–76, 173; and Zhang Zhongpei, *Zhongguo beifang kaogu wenji* (Beijing: Wenwu, 1986), chapter 20.

Since Qijia could have supplied all the technical knowledge that we find in use at the early-second-millennium Erlitou site, it is what we might expect a predecessor of Erlitou to look like. The contrast between its metal industry and that of Erlitou and the succeeding Erligang culture thus highlights for us the changes that took place in the middle Yellow River valley around the middle of the second millennium: first a shift to a seemingly total reliance on casting, and then an enormous increase in production. The difference between Qijia and Erlitou is not intellectual, not a matter of technical knowhow, but a matter of the purposes to which metal was put and the resources mobilized to achieve those purposes. The difference manifests itself both in volume of production and in technical and artistic quality. The metal artifacts of Erlitou and Erligang are material traces of the urban revolution.

ERLITOU: THE TRANSITION TO LARGE-SCALE METALLURGY. Several important developments are first in evidence at Erlitou. Graves in the upper two levels there have yielded metalwork more ambitious than anything yet found in Qijia, notably some two dozen bronze vessels and a few bells and weapons (Figs. 3.12–3.13), and the quantity of metal unearthed so far may be deceptively small, for foundry remains are said to cover 10,000 sq. m. The most important feature of the vessels is that they were made by casting. Elsewhere in the ancient world vessels and other simple metal shapes were invariably made by hammering, a technique far more economical of material. The cast vessels at Erlitou thus represent the first sign of a characteristically extravagant use of metal in China. The prerequisites for this extravagance were both geological and social: a geological abundance of metal ores, and the labor resources required for large-scale mining (which probably required coerced labor), fuel procurement, transport, and workshops. Geology must be the controlling factor which made metal scarce in the Near East and common in China, for the necessary labor was available in both places. But in other civilizations the labor was mobilized for other enterprises; in China it was invested in metalwork, and metalwork thus becomes a clear symptom of social changes.

Both technologically and artistically, the metalworking tradition that arose in China is unlike any other in the world. The features which set it apart reflect the profound difference between metal-conserving traditions and a tradition of abundant metal supplies. Metal abundance made possible an exclusive reliance on casting, and this had two important long-term consequences. First, casting more than hammering encourages division of labor and invites the organization of efficient workshops limited in size only by the resources and requirements of the patron. Industrial organization, which has some claim to be a distinguishing feature of later Chinese civilization, may well be a legacy of the bronze foundries.[29] Second, reliance on casting channeled subsequent technological choices because of the particular mold-making technique adopted by Erlitou casters. They constructed molds by applying clay to a model (made of any convenient material), removing the clay from the model in sections, and fitting the sections back together around a core (see Fig. 3.1, the mold assembly for an Erligang tripod). This proce-dure gave access to the interior of the mold, making it possible to carve dec-oration into the inner faces of the mold sections before casting. The few bronze vessels from Erlitou that have decoration accordingly bear simple pat-terns of lines and dots that were incised into mold sections and then trans-ferred to the bronze in the casting operation (Fig. 3.13c). These vessels represent the beginning of a long tradition in which decoration was not cut into cold bronze, routine practice in metalworking traditions that employed hammering, but cast. This seemingly minor detail of technical procedure shaped artistic developments for the next millennium.

ERLIGANG PERIOD: DEVELOPMENT OF FABRICATION METHODS AND FORMATION OF AN ARTISTIC TRADITION.

Bronze vessels are rare at Erlitou and all but unknown at other contemporary sites. By contrast they are abundant in the archaeological record of the next stage, the Erligang period, perhaps the fifteenth and fourteenth centuries B.C. The dramatically expanded Erligang bronze industry made technological and artistic advances that were of lasting importance.

The technological advances were simple but liberating extensions of the Erlitou mold-making procedure. The most ambitious products of the Erlitou casters had been tripod cups cast complete with strap handle in one pour of metal (Fig. 3.13a–b).[30] To cast such an object in one pour required a mold of half a dozen fitted sections; to cast a more complicated shape in one pour would have required more sections, and technical problems would multiply. Complicated shapes make it difficult to withdraw mold sections from the model; more important, they make it difficult to fill the mold without trap-ping pockets of air. The lost-wax process, invented in the Near East in the fourth millennium, solves the first problem but not the second; Erligang casters devised a stepwise procedure that solves both. Casting in a sequence of pours, the part cast in one pour being embedded in the mold for the next, opened the way to shapes of unlimited complexity. Thus, an elaborate handle

[29] See Robert Bagley, "Replication Techniques in Eastern Zhou Bronze Casting," in *History from Things*, ed. Lubar and Kingery, pp. 234–41; and idem, "What the Bronzes from Hunyuan Tell Us About the Foundry at Houma," *Orientations* 26, 1 (1995): 46–54; and compare the description of Egyptian mass production in Kemp, *Ancient Egypt*, pp. 289–91.

[30] Technical examination of Erlitou vessels has not found evidence of casting in more than one pour (Su Rongyu et al., *Zhongguo shanggu jinshu jishu* [Ji'nan: Shandong Kexue, 1995], pp. 96–9).

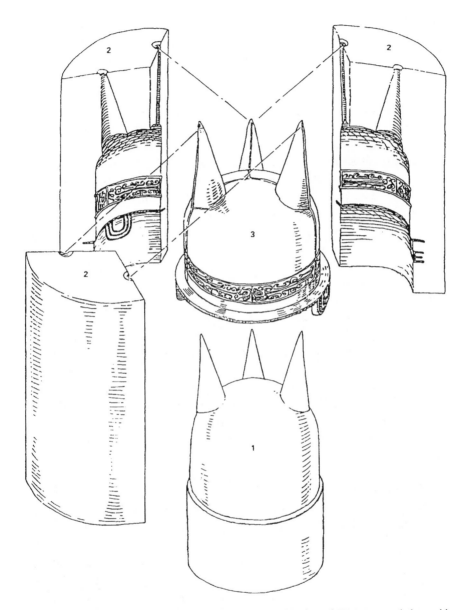

Figure 3.1. Diagram showing the relationship between the *ding* of Figure 3.2 and the mold used to cast it. 1, clay core; 2, clay mold sections (these were formed on an undecorated model, and the decoration was then carved into them); 3, finished bronze, showing mold marks along the lines where the mold sections met. After Wen Fong, ed., *The Great Bronze Age of China: An Exhibition from the People's Republic of China* (New York: Metropolitan Museum of Art, 1980), p. 72.

might be cast by itself, then embedded in the mold for the body of the vessel in such a way as to be mechanically locked in place when the body was cast. Alternatively, the body might be cast first and the mold for the handle built against it (though the same in principle, the two procedures are sometimes distinguished as precasting and casting on). Perhaps these methods were first devised for making repairs: defective or damaged castings were routinely repaired by casting patches onto them. The result was a technology which could make complicated shapes by making an object in pieces, but which had no need of joining techniques such as soldering and riveting because all joins were effected in the casting process. Outside China, joining techniques figure prominently in the metalworker's repertoire simply because outside China a large proportion of metalwork was not cast.

One further small but important technical device introduced by Erligang casters was the metal spacer. A chip of bronze wedged between the core and the outer part of a mold would serve to maintain the separation between the two during casting; by choosing a chip with the thickness desired for the object to be cast, the caster spared himself any finishing of the cast bronze, for the chip simply became part of the object. Spacers could be put wherever needed to stabilize the mold assembly, not only between core and outer mold, but also between independent cores, such as the core for the interior of a tripod bowl and separate cores for its legs. Along with precasting and casting on, therefore, the use of spacers assisted in the fabrication of complex shapes. Though simple to describe, these techniques were enormously versatile in application. Artistic developments for centuries to come unfolded within a technical repertoire that was complete before the end of the Erligang period.[31]

The artistic contribution of Erligang casters was a decorative system in which we must include not only the decoration itself, but also a remarkable relationship between the decoration and the shapes on which it appeared.[32] The character of this relationship suggests that Erligang casters did not

---

[31] For more detailed accounts of casting technology, see Robert Bagley, *Shang Ritual Bronzes in the Arthur M. Sackler Collections* (Cambridge, Mass.: Harvard University Press, 1987), pp. 37–45; and Su Rongyu et al., *Zhongguo shanggu jinshu jishu*, chapter 3 (which reconstructs mold assemblies and describes post-Erligang refinements such as inset molds and composite models). The demonstration that ancient Chinese foundry practice depended on section molds is owed to Orvar Karlbeck, "Anyang Moulds," *BMFEA* 7 (1935): 39–60; the basic techniques were elucidated by Rutherford John Gettens, *The Freer Chinese Bronzes, Vol. 2: Technical Studies* (Washington, D.C.: Smithsonian Institution, 1969). Further details have emerged from studies of bronzes from Fu Hao's tomb (Hua Jueming, Feng Fugen, Wang Zhenjiang, and Bai Rongjin, "Fu Hao mu qingtongqi qun zhuzao jishu de yanjiu," *Kaoguxue jikan* 1 [1981]: 244–72); and from Xin'gan (see note 69). Joining techniques somewhat more varied than those described here are seen in bronzes from Sanxingdui (see note 153), but all are straightforward extensions of section-mold casting.

[32] Bagley, *Shang Ritual Bronzes*, pp. 18–22; idem, "Shang Ritual Bronzes: Casting Technique and Vessel Design," *Archives of Asian Art* 43 (1990): 6–20.

borrow wholesale a decorative vocabulary already existing in some other medium but gradually elaborated patterns adapted to their mold-making procedure, a procedure that allowed them to open and carve the mold before casting.

Erlitou metalworkers had invented cast decoration by carving the mold in just this way. They could equally well have chosen to carve on the model, however, and much depended on the chance that they carved the mold sections instead. Decoration applied to the model would have had no reason to reflect the sectioning of the mold. But decoration applied to the mold was executed by a draftsman dealing one by one with individual mold sections, and he naturally enough improvised patterns that would be complete and self-contained on each section. As a result the decoration on the finished bronze had boundaries wherever the mold had divisions. In a subtle way, therefore, the subdivision of the mold was imprinted on the bronze, expressed in the layout of the decoration. Moreover that layout could hardly fail to suit the shape of the object, since the placement of the divisions had been decided by the practical need to remove the mold from the model in the smallest possible number of sections. In other words, the shape of the model determined the subdivision of the mold, and the subdivision of the mold presented the caster with fixed areas for which to design patterns. The major artistic development of the Erligang period was the elaboration of patterns within those fixed areas, and as the patterns became more elaborate, the subdivisions automatically became more prominent. The result was a tight relationship between decoration and shape that dominated bronze casting for centuries, disappearing gradually only in the latter part of Western Zhou.

The relationship is seen at an early stage in the tripod bowl of Figure 3.2. The shape of the vessel was inherited from Neolithic pottery, but the decoration, whatever inspiration it might owe to earlier motifs in jade or pottery, was in essential respects a bronze caster's invention. The mold was removed from the model in three sections, ease of removal dictating that the divisions between sections should be aligned with the legs (Fig. 3.1). Because the sections were equal arcs, the draftsman carved the same self-contained pattern into each. The result on the finished bronze was a pattern that repeats three times in the circumference, the boundaries between pattern units falling at the legs. In this early example the relationship between shape and decoration might seem too simple to deserve remark, but as the elaboration of shapes and patterns progressed the relationship became subtly compelling. Its effect must have been felt and valued already in the Erligang period, for Erligang casters continued to carve subdivided decoration even after they switched from carving on mold sections to carving on the model, a shift which removed any technical reason for subdivision. Transferring

Figure 3.2. Bronze *ding*, from Panlongcheng, Huangpi, Hubei (= Fig. 3.15, no. 36), fifteenth to fourteenth century B.C. Height 54cm. Loehr Style I. After *Chûka Jimmin Kyôwakoku kodai seidôki ten*, no. 4. Tokyo: Nihon Keizai, 1976.

the carver's activity from mold to model meant a change from thread-relief lines standing proud on the finished bronze to more varied forms of relief, but it did not change either the character of the motifs or their layout. If we think of the dissolution of subdivided designs as an adjustment to the decorated model, it is an adjustment that did not take place until late Western Zhou.

STYLISTIC DEVELOPMENT. The forms of pre-Zhou bronze decoration were arranged in a developmental sequence of five styles, each growing out of the last, in a closely reasoned argument published by Max Loehr (1903–1988) in 1953.[33] Having traced his sequence in unprovenanced bronzes, Loehr connected it with the Anyang site because at the time he wrote no pre-Anyang site had been excavated. Subsequent discoveries have shown that

[33] Loehr, "The Bronze Styles of the Anyang Period."

the development he charted took place somewhat earlier than he supposed, beginning with the first decorated bronzes at Erlitou and reaching his fifth style by about 1200 B.C. (the Anyang tomb of Fu Hao 婦好). Remarkably, however, the forms of decoration which archaeologists encountered at pre-Anyang sites proved to be exactly those that Loehr had singled out as early, and the line of reasoning that enabled him to anticipate archaeology continues to be instructive. Since a deposit that contained bronzes in several styles neatly stratified one above another would not explain why they occurred in that order rather than some other, while Loehr was able without the help of stratigraphy to order his styles and reason his way from one to the next, his analysis evidently went beyond description to detect an internal logic of development.[34] It strongly supports the still hesitant recognition by Chinese archaeologists of a so-called transition period intervening between the Zhengzhou and Anyang sites, and it can be extended beyond the body of material he studied to trace branching developments in different regions. Elaborated to incorporate new material, Loehr's sequence is taken to supply the chronological and geographical framework for the survey of finds presented in the next section. The sequence can only be sketched here, and since a brief description unavoidably gives it the look of a classification system, the point should be stressed that Loehr's styles are only conveniently described points in a continuous development. In particular, since each style survived after the invention of subsequent ones, they should be thought of not as mutually exclusive period styles, but as steps in the elaboration of a growing repertoire.[35]

Loehr's Style I is the thread relief seen in Figure 3.2. The pattern lines stand proud on the bronze because they were carved into the mold sections. Style I accounts for all the decorated bronzes so far found at Erlitou and many bronzes of the succeeding Erligang period. Loehr took it to begin his sequence because of the primitiveness of the vessel shapes on which it occurred. His choice is supported by the subdivided layout characteristic of the bronze designs; subdivision is characteristic of the bronze decoration in all five of Loehr's styles, but only in Style I, when the decoration was carved in the mold, was there any technical reason for it. It follows that the bronze decoration came into being at a time when Style I was the prevailing technique, acquiring from the technique a subdivided character that was preserved in later stages because its coordination with vessel shapes was admired.

---

[34] It should therefore be contrasted with purely descriptive typologies of shapes and motifs, which can give no indication of continuity or discontinuity and which can also mislead by encouraging essentialistic thinking about evolving motifs (see Ernst Mayr, *The Growth of Biological Thought* [Cambridge, Mass.: Harvard University Press, 1982], chapter 4, "Macrotaxonomy: The Science of Classifying").

[35] For a more detailed presentation, see Bagley, *Shang Ritual Bronzes*, pp. 19–36, which applies Loehr's analysis to forms of decoration unknown at the time Loehr wrote.

Figure 3.3. Bronze *jia*, from
Panlongcheng, Huangpi,
Hubei, fifteenth to four-
teenth century B.C. Height
30.1 cm. Loehr Style II. After
*Chûka Jimmin Kyôwakoku
kodai seidôki ten,* no. 2.
Tokyo: Nihon Keizai, 1976.

The principal motif of Style I is the two-eyed, animal-like pattern unit seen
in Figure 3.2, conventionally called *taotie* 饕餮.[36]

Style II differs from Style I in that the raised lines of the pattern are no
longer uniformly thin (Fig. 3.3). Modulated lines might have resulted from
drawing the patterns with brush and ink before carving them. The drawing

---

[36] The term comes from Eastern Zhou texts, but its application to bronze designs is purely conventional.
Some scholars prefer the term *shoumianwen* 獸面紋 (animal-face pattern) as avoiding irrelevant textual
associations, but *taotie* has the advantage of brevity and a more specific range of application. The motif
has sometimes been assumed to derive from the facelike motifs seen on jades of the Liangzhu culture
(see, e.g., Li Xueqin, "Liangzhu Culture and the Shang Dynasty *Taotie* Motif," in *The Problem of
Meaning in Early Chinese Ritual Bronzes,* ed. Roderick Whitfield [London: School of Oriental and
African Studies, 1993], pp. 56–66), but the occurrence of similar motifs in many parts of the world
suggests that the features which the *taotie* shares with Liangzhu motifs could have been independently
reinvented. On the origin of the bronze ornament, see Bagley, *Shang Ritual Bronzes,* pp. 19–24. On
efforts at iconographic interpretation, about which no consensus has been reached, see Roderick Whitfield, ed., *The Problem of Meaning in Early Chinese Ritual Bronzes.*

could have been done either in the mold (then excavating the ink-covered portions) or on the model (then excavating around the inked portions), yielding much the same result either way. At the stage of Style II, the *taotie* was joined in the bronze decoration by another motif, a one-eyed animal seen in profile. This can reasonably be called a dragon, since it is ancestral to at least some of the animals normally called dragons in the decoration of later bronzes.[37] The pattern unit visible in Figure 3.3 is a dragon; the adjacent pattern unit to the left, barely visible in Figure 3.3, is a *taotie*. The *taotie* and dragon, staple motifs of the bronze decoration until middle or late Western Zhou, were part of an enduring artistic tradition, all of whose essential features were established in the Erligang period. Styles I and II, along with early versions of Style III, were the characteristic forms of Erligang decoration, and by the end of the period, when about twenty distinct vessel types were in use, a high order of inventiveness had been achieved in shape and decoration alike. The *ding* 鼎 of Figure 3.2 is a clumsy caldron whose maker was evidently too preoccupied with the new decorative patterns to give much thought to the shape, but it was soon succeeded by more elegant versions. It was succeeded also by such mannered objects as the *jia* 斝 of Figure 3.3, which is not a familiar container translated into a new material but a shape consciously designed. Erligang bronzes are formidably accomplished objects. We cannot doubt that we are dealing with the potent visual style of a court, or perhaps of many courts.

Style III was an elaboration of Style II (there is no sharp dividing line between the two) in which the patterns became increasingly intricate and spread to cover more of the vessel surface (Figs. 3.4–3.6). At this stage a rapid diversification of designs and forms of relief took place. Since these developments accompanied a wide dispersal of the bronze industry and the first appearance of regional styles, tracing the variants of Style III is an important means of bringing order to an otherwise incoherent assortment of archaeological finds. Early versions (Fig. 3.4) are an easy step beyond Style II. From this stage onward the bronze decoration was executed on the model: in Figure 3.4 the raised surfaces vary in width but the sunken lines are uniform in width, arguing that the carver's tool cut into the model the sunken lines we see on the bronze. The same procedure must have been used for the looser Style III patterns seen in Figure 3.5, which here spread to cover the whole of a large bronze drum, one of the earliest known products of the bronze indus-

---

[37] The literature of Chinese archaeology commonly applies the label "dragon" to almost any imaginary animal and then takes it for granted that the animals so labeled, because they are all dragons, are all related (see, e.g., Sun Shoudao and Guo Dashun, *Wenming shuguangqi jisi yizhen: Liaoning Hongshan wenhua tanmiaozhong* [Beijing: Wenwu, 1994], pp. 140–1). The problem of actual relationships has therefore hardly been addressed.

Figure 3.4. Bronze *gui*, from Panlongcheng, Huangpi, Hubei, fifteenth to fourteenth century
B.C. Height 17.4 cm. Loehr Style III. Drawing by Li Xiating.

try of the middle Yangzi region. In Figure 3.6 the uniform mesh of ordinary
Style III patterns has been superimposed on undulating high relief (a form
of relief that would surely never have been invented by carvers working in
the mold). This undulating relief, which appeared late in the history of Style
III, restored emphasis to designs that had become less readable as the carvers
elaborated more intricate patterns: though still elusive, an animal face does
speak more forcibly in Figure 3.6 than in the almost featureless design of
Figure 3.5. Early versions of Style III are known from Zhengzhou,
Panlongcheng, and other Erligang sites, but its full development belongs to
the transition period (Figs. 3.5–3.6, 3.16–3.18).[38]

Style IV (Figs. 3.7–3.8) achieves more decisively the visual emphasis
sought, tentatively and incoherently, in Figure 3.6. It amounts to an abrupt
change in the nature of the bronze decoration, from patterns of uniformly
dense sunken lines to patterns in which the density of lines is varied so as to
distinguish an image (low density) from a ground (high density). On the *jia*

---

[38] Chinese archaeologists do not agree on the continuity or discontinuity of the Zhengzhou–Anyang
sequence (see Meng Xianwu, "Anyang Sanjiazhuang, Dongwangducun faxian de Shang dai qingtongqi
ji qi niandai tuiding," *Kaogu* 1991.10: 936–8). The present chapter assumes that the sequence is indeed
discontinuous and that it is necessary to assign some sites and finds to a "transition period" (this is a
literal translation of the rather unsatisfactory term used by Chinese archaeologists, *guodu shiqi* 過渡時
期). The difficulty of defining the period archaeologically and giving it absolute dates is, of course,
only a reflection of the difficulty of defining and dating the periods to be associated with Zhengzhou
and Anyang. For convenience it is here equated with the thirteenth century B.C.

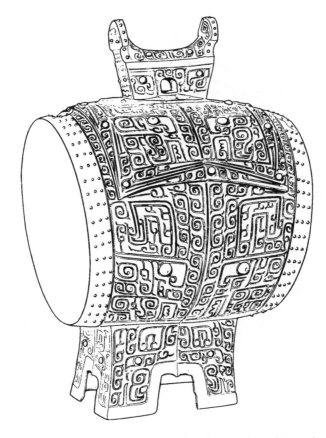

Figure 3.5. Bronze drum, from Chongyang, Hubei, fourteenth to thirteenth century B.C. Height 75.5 cm. Loehr Style III. Drawing by Li Xiating.

of Figure 3.7 the register at the neck still belongs to Style III, but the decoration lower down qualifies as Style IV, for the *taotie* faces are perfectly distinct from the nearly homogeneous ground patterns. The ground patterns derive from Style III embellishments. In Figure 3.7 they are still comparatively large in scale, and their origin in Style III is clear (compare Fig. 3.18). In Figure 3.8 a stronger contrast has been obtained by miniaturizing them, producing the fine spirals conventionally called *leiwen* 雷文, and only a few telltale remnants survive to betray the connection with Style III. The contrast between image and ground was sometimes further heightened, as in Figures 3.7–3.8, by filling the sunken lines with a black pigment.

Style IV gave the bronze decoration new impact. Emphasizing the motifs laid emphasis also on the subdivided framework in which they were arranged,

Figure 3.6. Bronze *zun*, from Funan, Anhui, fourteenth to thirteenth century B.C. Height 47 cm. Loehr Style III. After *Anhui Sheng Bowuguan cang qingtongqi* (Shanghai: Shanghai Renmin meishu, 1987), no. 2.

and this in turn reinforced the relationship between decoration and shape. The introduction of an image–ground distinction moreover converted the dragon and *taotie* from rectangular pattern units into animals of well-defined shape; these Style IV animal *images* thus differ essentially from the animal-inspired *patterns* of Styles I–III.[39] Converting dragon and *taotie* into concrete images opened the way to an enlargement of the decorator's vocabulary, for motifs drawn more directly from nature could now be set next to the imaginary animals without disharmony. The new borrowings from nature nevertheless remained within the animal kingdom. In the ancient Near East, Egypt, Crete, and the European tradition descended from them, the principal raw material of decoration has always been real or imaginary plant motifs. Decoration that incorporates staring animals differs crucially in having the power to focus the viewer's attention on particular points. Even a design as simple as that in Figure 3.2 draws the viewer's gaze to a single point, and at

[39] The common description of the early patterns as "abstract" or "stylized" should be avoided, since it assumes the existence of concrete versions that had not yet been invented.

Figure 3.7. Bronze *jia*, said to be from Anyang, thirteenth century B.C. Height 39.5 cm. Loehr Style IV. Museum für Ostasiatische Kunst, Köln (C76, 2). After Hans Juergen von Lochow, *Sammlung Lochow, Chinesische Bronzen II* (Beijing: [FuJen], 1944), no. 9.

the stage of Style IV the bronze decoration achieved an almost hypnotic effect. This psychological power has channeled the attention of modern scholars no less than that of Bronze Age patrons, with the result that study of the bronzes has concentrated overwhelmingly on motifs, but any analysis of effects shows that the motifs are not to be separated from a system in which motifs, layout, and vessel shape operate jointly. A *taotie* lifted out of context is much diminished.

Style V is dependent on Style IV in the sense that it employs the same contrast between motifs and *leiwen*, but the motifs are no longer flush with the *leiwen*, rising now in high relief (Fig. 3.9). The older form of high relief that appeared transiently in Style III (Fig. 3.6) differs from Style V high relief by the even density of the intaglio lines, a difference which signifies its independence of the Style IV image–ground distinction. (On certain bronzes with high-relief decoration from the Yangzi region, such as the bell of Figure 3.29c, the absence of *leiwen* and of variable density linear patterns

Figure 3.8. Bronze *hu*, said
to be from Anyang,
thirteenth century B.C.
Height 31 cm. Loehr Style
IV. Gugong Bowuyuan,
Beijing. After
*Kunstausstellung der
Volksrepublik China* (East
Berlin: Staatliche Museen
Berlin, 1951), p. 85.

is important evidence of local developments that originated in Style III
high relief rather than in the later high relief of northern Style V designs.)
The heavy emphasis supplied by Style V was given additional weight by
the vertical flanges marking subdivisions which became common at this
stage (Fig. 3.9). From this point on Style V was the usual form of decoration
on major bronzes (Fig. 3.10b), though varieties of low relief remained
common on lesser items, perhaps simply because easier execution made them
cheaper.

The evolution of decoration just sketched is one aspect of a complex development that involved interrelated changes in vessel shapes, motifs, forms of
relief, and decorative layouts. These changes cannot be described here, but
some sense of their cumulative effect can be suggested by juxtaposing versions of a single vessel type a few centuries apart. Figure 3.10 shows two *he*
盉, one of about 1200 B.C., the other perhaps two centuries earlier. The drawings cannot convey the delicate execution of the earlier vessel, but they

Figure 3.9. Bronze *fangyi*, provenance unknown, twelfth century B.C. Height 29.8 cm. Loehr Style V. Winthrop Collection, Harvard University Art Museums (1943.52.109).

convey clearly enough the theatricality of the later one. These two objects are not separated by aimless drift. They are landmarks in a sustained and intensely self-conscious artistic development. The bronzes owe their individuality to their designers' concern with visual effects, and it is this individuality which makes them promising sources for the following attempt to read historical information from material artifacts.

The Archaeological Record

The rise of civilization will always lie beyond the reach of narrative history. By the time written records become available, the first urban societies belong to the past, and such understanding as we can have of formative ages must come from material evidence alone. Later texts do speak of early times, but when they seem most credible they are also most vague, readily accommodating themselves to almost any reconstruction of the past we might wish to propose. If we are to come to grips with archaeological realities we must

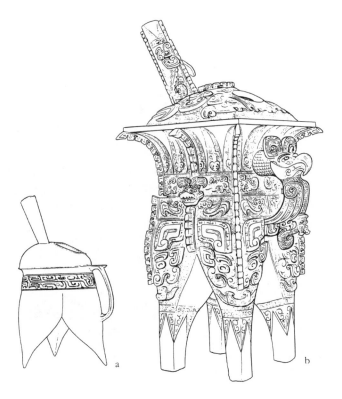

a   b

Figure 3.10. (a) Bronze *he*, from Panlongcheng (= Fig. 3.15, no. 20), fifteenth to fourteenth century B.C. Height 34.6 cm. (b) Bronze *he*, one of a set of three from Xibeigang M1001, ca. 1200 B.C. Height 71.2 cm. Nezu Bijutsukan, Tokyo. To the same scale. Drawings by Li Xiating.

forgo the names, personalities, and comforting particulars of written history and rest content to study the outlines of events large enough to have impressed themselves on the material record.

A first reading of that record suggests the following sequence of events in ancient China. Urban societies arose in the middle Yellow River region during the first half of the second millennium B.C.[40] About 1500 B.C. a major state formed there and expanded outward to rule, perhaps only briefly, large territories. By about 1300 B.C. that state had retreated, perhaps under pressure from newer powers that had formed on its borders. For the next few

---

[40] Here and throughout the chapter, calendar dates are only rough guesses used as a convenient way of indicating relative chronology.

centuries thereafter, civilized China was a network of interacting powers, among them the dynasty that ruled at Anyang. Most were culturally different from the Anyang civilization but some were not inferior. The following paragraphs elaborate this interpretation of the archaeological record; the record itself is surveyed in the remainder of the chapter.

Highly stratified societies seem to have appeared first in the Erlitou culture. Foundations of large buildings have been excavated at Erlitou, city walls are known at a few contemporary sites, and the extensive foundry remains and cast bronze vessels known from Erlitou indicate the employment of specialized workers. The rather wide distribution of the Erlitou culture (defined by its pottery assemblage) is hard to interpret in political terms, however, the more so as it is said to show regional variation.

The picture becomes clearer with the emergence of a spectacular civilization in the Erligang period, the fifteenth and fourteenth centuries B.C. In China as elsewhere, the importance which civilized rulers attached to a visually impressive setting for their public lives needs no demonstration beyond the evidence of the resources they dedicated to it. Nothing has survived so well or so abundantly as the bronze vessels, which must have functioned in ceremonies of great religious and political significance, but the visual culture of the Erligang elite certainly included silk clothing, jade ornaments, lacquers, and large buildings as well. The artistic sophistication of the bronzes and the large quantities in which they were produced speak unambiguously of a transformed society. They moreover have a wide geographic distribution, implying a wide dissemination of the Erligang technology, the artistic style, and whatever beliefs dictated the deposit of bronze vessels in graves. Since they are uniform in style throughout their geographic range, it seems reasonable to see in them the material record of the expansion of a state. Uniformity did not outlive the Erligang period, however, and the widely distributed, short-lived Erligang style fits the definition of a horizon style.

Expansion of an Erligang-period state out of the Yellow River valley must have brought civilization and bronze metallurgy to areas where they were previously unknown. Evidently the result was to stimulate the formation of secondary civilizations on the Erligang frontiers. This development coincides approximately with Loehr's Style III and with the time Chinese archaeologists call the transition period, which might be loosely equated with the thirteenth century B.C. Bronzes of unmistakable local style emerged at this time, but they developed from foundations in Erligang bronze casting, and they were made using its characteristic technology. The fact that most of these local castings were vessels argues that Erligang ceremony, or at least the Erligang ceremonial apparatus, was found seductive or useful. But new artifact types, such as large bells and drums in the Yangzi region, represent the adaptation of Erligang technology to local needs. Cultural and ethnic differences must lie behind these developments, and the expression of such differences may signify the end of whatever political unity had been imposed in the preceding period; perhaps an Erligang empire collapsed under pressure from frontier states that had formed in reaction to it. The new states evidently remained in contact, however, for the same finds that reveal emerging local styles also include items in styles that were widely shared. In all periods, bronzes were valuable enough to travel as gifts from one ruler to another. Outlying courts might employ imported artisans, and imported bronzes must have been coveted as luxuries and status symbols.

The city of Anyang, which became a major settlement about 1200 B.C., coexisted and interacted with a variety of culturally distinct neighbors. The horse-drawn chariot, a borrowing that implies contact with the Northern Zone, appeared at Anyang about 1200 B.C., and the tomb of Fu Hao, of about the same date, contained artifacts from many different sources. On the evidence of material culture, the most civilized neighbors of the Anyang kings were in the Yangzi region. When in the eleventh century the Anyang dynasty fell, however, it was to the Zhou, less civilized contemporaries from the Wei River valley. The transmitted texts which shaped all later views of ancient China originated in the Zhou period; since in those texts the Zhou chose to link themselves to Anyang and to ignore their neighbors, the neighbors faded from historical consciousness, to reemerge only now from the material record.

THE EARLY BRONZE AGE

Erlitou and the Erlitou Culture

On present evidence, monumental building and ambitious bronze casting appeared together, in the first half of the second millennium B.C., in the Erlitou 二里頭 culture, named after a type site discovered in 1959 at Yanshi 偃師 near Luoyang in western Henan. The complex of cultural traits encountered at Erlitou, partly Neolithic and partly new, was destined for long survival. It includes building types and techniques; a burial form; vessels and other objects of cast bronze, some inlaid with turquoise; vessels of pottery in shapes later to appear in bronze; jades; a standard Bronze Age weapon, the *ge* 戈, in both bronze and jade versions; lacquered wood, encountered in the

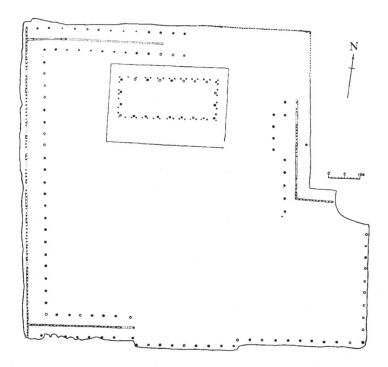

Figure 3.11. Palace foundation no. 1 at Erlitou, 3d stratum, ca. sixteenth century B.C. After *Kaogu* 1974.4: 235.

form of fragments of coffins and smaller articles; animal bones used for divination; and human sacrifice.[41]

The Erlitou site lies on the south bank of the Luo River 洛河, reaching 2 km south of the river and extending 1.5 km from east to west. In the center of this area, test probes have located a number of pounded-earth terraces and building foundations. The largest so far excavated is a square terrace more than 100 m on a side (Fig. 3.11). This was constructed by pounding thin layers of earth into an excavation up to 2 m deep and then continuing to add layers until a height of 80 cm above the surrounding ground was reached. Individual layers are about 4.5 cm thick; their upper surfaces carry the circular impressions of pounding tools 3–5 cm in diameter. The terrace was enclosed

[41] For general descriptions of the site, see *Henan kaogu sishi nian*, ed. Henan sheng Wenwu yanjiusuo (Zhengzhou: Henan Renmin, 1994), pp. 170–7; *Erlitou taoqi jicui*, ed. Zhongguo Shehui kexueyuan Kaogu yanjiusuo (Beijing: Zhongguo Shehui kexue, 1995) (endpapers provide a site map); Thorp, "Erlitou and the Search for the Xia"; Zhao Zhiquan, "Lun Erlitou yizhi wei Xia dai wanqi duyi," *Hua Xia kaogu* 1987.2: 196–204, 217; Chang, *The Archaeology of Ancient China*, pp. 307–16. Excavations are described in a series of preliminary reports, of which the latest is *Kaogu* 1992.4: 294–303; for references to earlier reports, see *Henan kaogu sishinian*, p. 220.

by an earthen wall with a gate in the south side; lines of post holes parallel
to the wall show that a roofed structure was built against it. Inside the enclosure was a pounded-earth building foundation that had been constructed
before the rest of the terrace. Judging from post holes, the building it carried
was a large rectangular wood-framed hall measuring 30 m east–west and 11 m
north–south. The post holes along the south side are set well back from the
edge of the foundation, so the hall must have had an unroofed porch. Just
outside the line of post holes is a line of smaller holes; if these were left by
eave supports, they imply a hipped roof, for they encircle the building. A few
traces of earth mixed with straw might be remains of the walls or the roof.
No other evidence of walls was found, but the hall of a similar compound
nearby was enclosed and divided into three rooms by walls of wattle and
daub. Pits dug into the terrace contained human skeletons, apparently sacrificial burials not connected with the construction of the compound but
perhaps with its later use. If the compound was a setting for ceremonies performed on the porch of the hall, an audience of several thousand could have
watched from within the enclosure.

The arrangement of a pillared hall in a walled compound, along with the
building technology employed for the hall itself, represents the beginning of
a long architectural tradition. The pounded-earth technique, known earlier
from Neolithic house floors, platforms, and walls, was used in preference to
stone or brick for major constructions throughout the Bronze Age. The technique was laborious but the resulting material, today called *hangtu* 夯土, was
extremely durable. The earth fill of tombs was sometimes pounded hard, and
with the help of wooden forms the technique could also be used to construct
walls. No city wall has been found at Erlitou, but *hangtu* city walls are known
from other sites of comparable date as well as from Neolithic sites such as
Chengziyai.

A second compound 150 m from the first differs by the addition of a large
tomb dug into the terrace between the hall and the north wall of the enclosure. Said to be contemporary with the hall, the tomb was a rectangular shaft
that had been filled with pounded earth. The shaft measured 5 by 4 m at the
mouth and 6 m deep; about a meter from the bottom its walls stepped inward
to form a shelf around the coffin called by archaeologists an *ercengtai* 二層
臺, a feature of grave construction known earlier from Neolithic burials. At
later sites the *ercengtai* was often made by pounding earth into the space
between the coffin and the walls of the shaft, but here it was earth left
untouched when the shaft was dug. The tomb had been plundered and contained little besides traces of cinnabar, fragments of a lacquer coffin, and the
skeleton of a dog that had evidently had a lacquer coffin of its own. Nevertheless the tomb's size (about the same size as the Anyang tomb of Fu Hao,

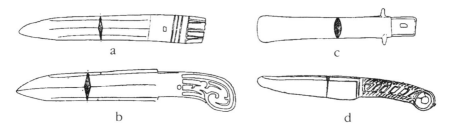

Figure 3.12. Bronze weapons, from Erlitou, ca. sixteenth century B.C. To the same scale. (a–b) Two *ge* blades, the larger one 32.5 cm long. After *Kaogu* 1976.4: 260, fig. 3. (c) Axe blade. Length 23.5 cm. After *Kaogu* 1976.4: 260, fig. 3. (d) Knife. Length 26.2 cm. After *Kaogu* 1983.3: 204, fig. 10.

discussed below) and its location in the compound argue that this was a burial of far higher status than any other yet known from the first half of the second millennium. The only other well-furnished burials thus far excavated at Erlitou are considerably smaller. They have *ercengtai*, traces of a lacquer coffin, a sacrificial pit beneath the coffin which archaeologists call a *yaokeng* 腰坑 (waist pit), cinnabar on the floor, and up to a dozen articles of bronze, jade, and pottery. Most were not found intact, and they may originally have been more richly furnished, but they are unlikely to be the graves of the most powerful members of Erlitou society.

The metal artifacts from these graves constitute our evidence for the most advanced bronze industry yet known from early-second-millennium China. The word "bronze" must be used provisionally, since analyses have been reported for only three items, but those three are said to be about 5 percent tin, a proportion high enough to suggest that the tin was a deliberate additive rather than a contaminant of the copper ore. The artifacts are vessels and an assortment of smaller items such as plaques, bells, knives, and *ge* blades (Figs. 3.12–3.13). One ring-handled knife with a decorated grip might be an import from the Northern Zone (Fig. 3.12d).[42] Two *ge* blades represent the first appearance of a standard Bronze Age weapon, a sort of battle-axe consisting of a dagger-shaped bronze blade mounted perpendicular to a wooden shaft (Fig. 3.12a–b). A third blade from Erlitou is unusual in having a rounded rather than pointed end (Fig. 3.12c); this perhaps copies a northern battle-axe but substitutes a flat tang for the characteristic northern shaft hole. The bells are small and probably had clappers. The total of six so far reported makes this one of the more common metal artifact types at Erlitou. At later sites bells of this type, called *ling* 鈴, have sometimes been found at the necks

[42] For the Northern Zone, see below, pp. 221–6.

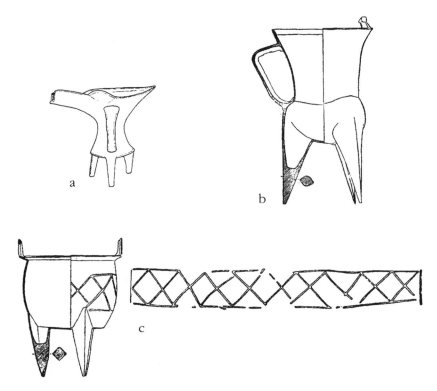

Figure 3.13. Bronze vessels, from Erlitou, ca. sixteenth century B.C. To the same scale. (a) *Jue*. Height 12 cm. Drawing by Li Xiating. (b) *Jia*. Height 26.8 cm. After *Kaogu* 1991.2: 1138. (c) *Ding*, with decoration unfolded. Height about 20 cm. After *Kaogu* 1991.2: 1138.

of dogs or horses. The most attractive of the bronzes are plaques of unknown purpose inlaid or covered with turquoise (turquoise is found also in the form of beads).

The metal inventory is dominated by cast vessels; in this respect Erlitou sets a precedent for the entire Bronze Age. Three *jia*, one *ding*, one *he*, and fragments of a *gu* 觚 are reported, but the most common shape by far is the *jue* 爵, of which about twenty examples have been found (Fig. 3.13).[43] Using a prestigious new material for a function previously served by pottery, the

---

[43] The names nowadays applied to bronze vessel types are for the most part conventions established in the Song period or more recently. What seem to be depictions of *jue*, *jia*, and *ding* occur as graphs in the Anyang oracle texts, in a few instances in contexts suggesting some connection with ritual, but early evidence bearing on the names and functions of the vessels is exceedingly slight. The fullest discussions of nomenclature and use, inevitably relying mainly on anachronistic Zhou and Han sources, are by Hayashi Minao ("In Shû seido iki no meishô to yôto," *Tôhô gakuhô* 34 [1964]: 199–298; and "In Seishû jidai reki no ruibetsu to yôhô," *Tôhô gakuhô* 53 [1981]: 1–108). On the ancestry of the shapes and on Erlitou casting in general, see Bagley, *Shang Ritual Bronzes*, pp. 15–18.

vessels put into graves probably contained food and drink offered to the deceased.[44] At least one *jue* is reported to have traces of soot on the underside, suggesting that it had been used for some time above ground before it was buried.[45] Only two vessels, a *jue* and a *ding*, have decoration, and it is very primitive, amounting only to simple patterns of dots and lines (Fig. 3.13c). What deserves note about these bronzes is their function as grave furnishings; their distinctive shapes, all of which survived for centuries; manufacture by casting; and finally decoration which, however crude, was made in the casting process, not by working on the already cast metal. In all these respects Erlitou set lasting precedents. With the single exception of the Northern Zone, which owed its metallurgy to Siberia, all the bronze industries surveyed in the remainder of this chapter descend from that of Erlitou.

The jades found in Erlitou burials present a more complex picture. Unlike bronze, which is easily melted down and recast, jade is not recycled without loss, and the intrinsic value of the material, along with the ornamental function of many items, must often have kept jades in circulation above ground long after their manufacture. The distribution pattern of archaeological finds is correspondingly chaotic. The inventory of types at Erlitou does not agree with that of any other Neolithic or Bronze Age culture, indeed probably no two of the shapes have the same pattern of occurrence. Only about forty items have so far been found, a meager quantity by the standards of the jade-rich Liangzhu 良渚 culture (a third-millennium Neolithic culture of the lower Yangzi region), but richer than many Bronze Age sites.[46] The most numerous types are trapezoidal knives, *ge* blades (Fig. 3.14a), axes, disk-axes (Fig. 3.14b–c), arc-ended blades (Fig. 3.14d), and handles. Each type has a different history.[47] The trapezoidal knives seem to be enlarged versions of an east coast Neolithic shape which itself copied a harvesting knife ordinarily made in pottery or stone. The jade *ge* blade is new, copying the new metal weapon. The axes have east coast Neolithic ancestors, but the sawcuts that decorate their sides are new. The disk-axe, which combines the serrated sides

---

[44] At later sites, traces of food have occasionally been found in bronze vessels, for example, animal bones in *ding* from M8 at Sufutun (*Hai Dai kaogu* 1 [1989]: 261; for the Sufutun site see below, pp. 219–21).

[45] Bronze vessels with coatings of soot are reported also from later sites, including Zhengzhou (*jue, ding, fangding* 方鼎, *li* 鬲), Panlongcheng, and Anyang, but the reports leave it unclear whether the coatings indicate any extended period of use. A study of several Erligang period bronzes in the Royal Ontario Museum concluded that they had been damaged in long use, then repaired so crudely that they could not have been used again except as grave furnishings (Barbara Stephen, "Shang Bronzes with Ancient Repairs," in *1961 Annual: Art and Archaeology Division, The Royal Ontario Museum, University of Toronto* [Toronto: Royal Ontario Museum, 1962], pp. 8–14).

[46] On Liangzhu jade, see *Liangzhu wenhua yuqi*.

[47] See Jessica Rawson, *Chinese Jade from the Neolithic to the Qing* (London: British Museum Press, 1995), pp. 167–78 (axes), 184–96 (blades), 233–6 (handles, an arbitrary name for a puzzling shape; notable are six examples from an Anyang tomb at Hougang inscribed in vermilion with dedications to ancestors: *Kaogu* 1993.10: 880–901).

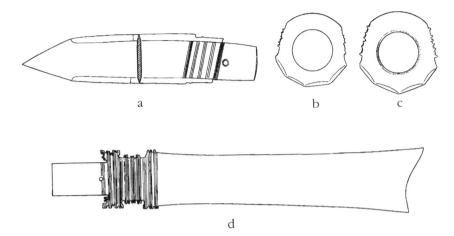

Figure 3.14. Jades, from Erlitou, ca. sixteenth century B.C. To the same scale. Drawings by Li Xiating. (a) *Ge* blade. Length 30.2 cm. (b–c) Disk-axes. Heights 9–10 cm. (d) Arc-ended blade. Length 48.1 cm.

and sharpened edge of an axe with the proportions and circular perforation of a disk, is also new at Erlitou, where plain jade disks have not been found. The origin of the arc-ended blade is unknown and its chronological and geographic distribution is curiously erratic.[48] The jade handles might derive from a type of Liangzhu pendant; the resemblance is not very close, but one example is decorated with faces in thread relief folded around its corners in a way that undoubtedly derives from Liangzhu jades.[49] Otherwise the jade inventories of Erlitou and Liangzhu barely overlap, giving no reason to suspect any particular connection between the two cultures. Of the three most common and characteristic Liangzhu jade shapes, the axe, the *cong*, and the disk, the first occurs at Erlitou in versions not particularly close to those of Liangzhu, the second barely occurs (one fragment of a *cong* is reported), and the third does not occur at all.

Erlitou is the largest and richest site of an archaeological culture whose distribution covers Henan and adjacent parts of Shaanxi, Shanxi, Hebei, and Hubei. The raw materials represented in Erlitou burials, including copper, tin, jade, turquoise, and cowry shells, cannot all have been locally available, and Erlitou must have traded widely. Whether it was part of any larger political unit seems impossible to decide. The building foundations required a considerable labor force, and social stratification is implied by the rich burials

---

[48] See below, under Sanxingdui (pp. 213–17 and Figure 3.35a–b).
[49] Yang Boda, *Zhongguo meishu quanji: Gongyi meishu bian 9, yuqi* (Beijing: Wenwu, 1986), pl. 49.

and by the use of casting to make bronze vessels, but archaeology is very far from being able to say what sort of polity these items presuppose. More certain is the continuity with later developments. The foundations, tombs, and artifacts just described all come from the third and fourth levels at the site. Radiocarbon determinations put those levels near the middle of the second millennium,[50] and their contents, the pottery vessels in particular, suggest a close relationship with the Erligang culture defined at the Zhengzhou site 85 km to the east.[51] On present evidence the Erlitou culture is the immediate ancestor of the Erligang culture, the first great civilization of East Asia.

Zhengzhou: Type Site of the Erligang Culture

The Erligang 二里崗 culture is named after a type site excavated in 1952 and 1953 at the modern city of Zhengzhou 鄭州 in Henan province.[52] Two levels were distinguished, Lower and Upper Erligang, and similar remains have since been found throughout Zhengzhou. The two levels are here assigned to the period 1500–1300 B.C., but this date is only a convenient approximation intended to fix the position of Erligang between the Erlitou culture (first half of the second millennium) and the transition period (thirteenth century B.C.).[53]

The Zhengzhou site is very large. Remains are spread over an area of 25 sq. km, and northwest of this area a palace or ritual complex has recently been discovered 20 km away.[54] Unfortunately the ancient city lies beneath the modern one and cannot be systematically explored. Nevertheless its main feature, a *hangtu* city wall nearly 7 km in circumference, is by itself enough to show that Zhengzhou was no ordinary place. Excavations carried out in 1955 and 1956 mapped the wall and established that it was built early in the Lower Erligang period.[55] The sides measure 1,690 m (north), 1,700 m (east),

---

[50] Qiu Shihua et al., "Youguan suowei Xia wenhua de tan shisi niandai ceding de chubu baogao," *Kaogu* 1983.10: 923–8.

[51] *Kaogu* 1984.7: 590. A walled city of the Erligang culture has been discovered about 5 km northeast of Erlitou at Shixianggou 尸鄉溝 (*Henan kaogu sishi nian*, pp. 177–81).

[52] For general surveys of Zhengzhou archaeology, see *Henan kaogu sishi nian*, pp. 181–204; and *Zhengzhou Shang cheng kaogu xin faxian yu yanjiu 1985–1992*, ed. Henan sheng Wenwu yanjiusuo (Zhengzhou: Zhongzhou Guji, 1993), which includes a comprehensive bibliography (pp. 272–7).

[53] Only two radiocarbon dates are reported from the Zhengzhou site, one from the city wall, a Lower Erligang construction, and one from an Upper Erligang accumulation overlying the wall's inner slope. Both dates calibrate to 1600–1400 B.C. The Erligang period site at Shixianggou supplies a larger number of radiocarbon dates, some in the same range and some as late as 1400–1100 B.C. See *Zhongguo kaoguxue zhong tan shisi niandai shuju ji 1965–1991*, pp. 157–8, 162.

[54] *Zhengzhou Shang cheng kaogu xin faxian yu yanjiu 1985–1992*, pp. 242–71; Chen Xu, "Zhengzhou Xiaoshuangqiao Shang dai yizhi de niandai he xingzhi," *Zhongyuan wenwu* 1995.1: 1–8.

[55] For the wall, see *Wenwu ziliao congkan* 1 (1977): 1–47; and *Wenwu* 1977.1: 21–31. It was renovated in the Warring States and later periods and is largely covered by earth added in those periods.

1,700 m (south), and 1,870 m (west); the northeast corner runs aslant to avoid
a natural ridge. The first step in the wall's construction was to level the
ground and dig a shallow trench into which the first layers of earth were
pounded. The *hangtu* courses, which average 8–10 cm thick, run horizontally
in the main thickness of the wall, but the inner and outer faces of the wall
are sloped, gently on the inside and steeply on the outside, and the *hangtu*
courses follow the slope. Traces of planks were found between the horizontal and sloping portions, suggesting that the horizontal courses were hammered within wooden forms which the slanting courses braced. The portion
of the wall where the courses run horizontally is about 10 m thick. The overall
thickness at the base is about 22 m, and the greatest surviving height is 9 m.
Another, perhaps earlier wall has recently been found a kilometer or so
outside the east, south, and west walls, roughly paralleling them for about
2,900 m.[56]

The Erligang type site is located outside the walled city, 500 m from the
southeast corner. Inside the city in the northeast quarter more than twenty
hangtu building foundations have been discovered, their pounded earth
exactly matching that of the city wall in such construction details as layer
thickness and tool impressions.[57] The buildings were very large: one measured 65 by 13.6 m, another 31 by 38 m. Building technology was the same as
at Erlitou, except that at Erlitou the bottoms of pillars were buried while at
Zhengzhou (as later at Anyang) they were sometimes set on stone footings
on top of the foundations, perhaps to protect them from rot. Other finds in
the northeast quarter of the city include a refuse deposit, perhaps from a
workshop, that contained more than a hundred human skulls, mostly of
young men, some of which had been sawn open at brow level.[58] A test trench
just inside the northeast corner of the city wall found a group of eight pits
with the remains of ninety-two sacrificed dogs, between six and twenty-three
to a pit, accompanied in one pit by ornaments of gold leaf and in another
by two human skeletons.

Workshops and graveyards have been found outside the walls, in some
cases as much as a kilometer away. The workshops include bronze foundries
to the north and south, a bone workshop to the north, and a pottery workshop to the west. Pollution and the danger of fire were no doubt sufficient
reasons for locating foundries and kilns outside the city. Judging from mold
fragments, the foundries produced vessels, craft tools, and a few weapons (*ge*
blades and arrowheads). The bone workshop, which used both animal and

[56] *Zhongyuan wenwu* 1991.1: 87–95.
[57] *Wenwu* 1983.4: 1–14, 28; for more recent excavations, see *Zhengzhou Shang cheng kaogu xin faxian yu
yanjiu 1985–1992*, pp. 98–143.
[58] *Wenwu* 1977.1: 21–31.

human bone, seems to have produced mainly arrowheads and hairpins, along with a few awls and needles. The pottery workshop was large, with fourteen kilns, but seems to have specialized in making only a few vessel types. A small amount of the pottery carried designs copied from bronzes; on pots these designs were applied using stamps, but on bronzes, more luxurious objects, they were carved in the clay of model or mold. In other respects as well the ceramic technology of the foundries, which had to meet requirements specific to mold-making, differed from that of the pottery workshops. By the Erligang period the bronze and pottery industries were distinctly separate.

Graveyards have been found on three sides of the city, but only a few modest burials have been excavated, only fifteen of them rich enough to contain bronze vessels. None of the fifteen was larger than about 2 by 3 m, though one contained a sacrificed human and five included a small pit (*yaokeng*) beneath the deceased containing a sacrificed dog. On grave floors a thin layer of powdered cinnabar was often found. Among the grave furnishings it was common to include a pottery disk painted red on one side, and sometimes a pot was broken and the shards scattered over the burial. Imprints in the corrosion on bronze vessels show that they were sometimes wrapped in linen. One grave contained hundreds of cowry-shell beads. The richest, Baijiazhuang 白家莊 M3, was furnished with nine bronze vessels, two jades, and half a dozen other artifacts. This is not the grave of a commoner, but it is a modest burial; the rulers of a city as large as Zhengzhou must have had vastly greater tombs. Two hoards or sacrificial deposits found outside the city, one at the southeast corner and one 300 m from the west wall, contained a few large bronzes more impressive than any yet found in graves.[59] Even taking these into account, however, the total inventory of finds does not much surpass what has been unearthed at other Erligang-period sites that are far smaller, suggesting that we will greatly underestimate the splendor of the city at Zhengzhou if we judge it by Zhengzhou finds alone. The safest conclusion to draw from the scarcity of jades, for instance, is simply that good jades were confined to burials of far higher status than any yet discovered.

Thus, to form an adequate image of the Erligang civilization we must combine the evidence of the Zhengzhou city wall with that of artifacts found elsewhere, at sites less important than Zhengzhou but more accessible to excavation. Though we may still fail to imagine what rich Zhengzhou tombs could show us, we see clearly enough a civilization of spectacular wealth and power, far removed from its timid forerunner at Erlitou. A single bronze vessel from one of the Zhengzhou hoards outweighs by a factor of ten all the metal yet found at Erlitou. As against the four or five bronze vessel shapes

[59] *Zhengzhou Shang cheng kaogu xin faxian yu yanjiu 1985–1992*, pp. 60–63; *Wenwu* 1975.6: 64–8; *Wenwu* 1983.3: 49–59.

known at Erlitou, twenty or more were in use by the end of the Erligang
period, and by that time an artistic style that would shape developments for
the next millennium had come into being. Moreover bronze vessels were by
then being cast in many places besides Zhengzhou. The geographic distribution of Erligang bronzes argues that the Erligang period was the time when
civilization expanded out of the Yellow River valley, laying the foundation
for subsequent developments over a wide area of north and central China.
The Panlongcheng site in Hubei is one witness to this expansion, and the
richest Erligang burials yet known have been found there.

Panlongcheng and the Erligang Horizon

The Erligang remains at Panlongcheng 盤龍城 are spread over an area of
about 1 sq. km on the north bank of a Yangzi tributary at Huangpi 黃陂 in
eastern Hubei. A small part of this area was enclosed by a rectangular *hangtu*
city wall that measured 260 m east–west and 290 m north–south (the
Zhengzhou city wall, with a perimeter of 6,960 m, enclosed an area forty
times greater). Excavations in 1963 and 1974 unearthed habitation remains
dating from Lower Erligang but established that large building foundations
inside the wall, rich graves outside, and the wall itself date from Upper
Erligang (the Zhengzhou wall is Lower Erligang).[60] The wall has the same
trapezoidal section as the Zhengzhou wall and was built in the same way.
Though it is not well preserved, a few sections survive to a height of 3 m
and measure 26 m thick at the base. A large *hangtu* terrace at the northeast
corner of the area inside the wall carried the foundations of three buildings,
one of them very well preserved. These showed the same construction techniques as foundations at Zhengzhou and even the same orientation, 20°
east of north. The city wall and the grave shown in Figure 3.15 also have this
orientation.

   Outside the wall, graves were found on all four sides of the city, the largest
ones in the east at Lijiazui 李家嘴. Lijiazui M1 and M2, the richest Erligang
tombs yet known, resemble Zhengzhou burials in form and furnishings but
greatly surpass them in wealth. M2 was a rectangular shaft provided with
yaokeng and *ercengtai* and measuring 3.8 by 3.4 m at the level of the *ercengtai*
(Fig. 3.15). Traces survived of a carved and painted wooden housing built
against the upper walls of the shaft and, lower down, of inner and outer
coffins, also carved and painted in red and black. The *yaokeng* contained a
jade *ge* blade broken into three pieces, and it may originally have contained

---

[60] The 1963 excavations are reported in *Wenwu* 1976.1: 49–59, the 1974 excavations in *Wenwu* 1976.2:
5–15. Both reports are summarized in Robert Bagley, "P'an-lung-ch'eng: A Shang City in Hupei,"
Artibus Asiae 39 (1977): 165–219. See also Fong, *Great Bronze Age of China*, nos. 4–10; and Chen
Shuxiang, "Shixi Panlongcheng de xingshuai," *Hubei sheng Kaogu xuehui lunwen xuanji* 2 (1991): 54–9.

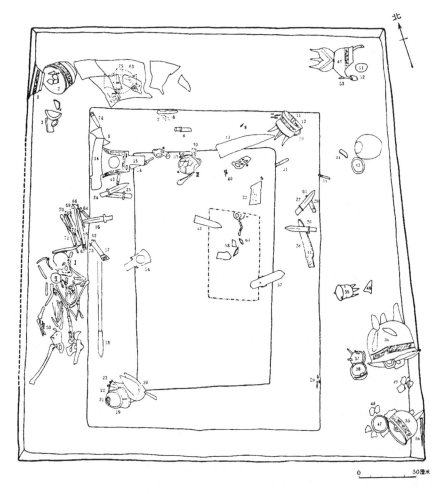

Figure 3.15. Plan of Lijiazui M2, Panlongcheng. Dimensions at mouth 3.7 by 3.4 m. After *Wenwu* 1976.2: 12, fig. 10.

I, II, III. human skeletal remains
1. bronze *pan*
2. bronze *yu*
3. bronze spade
4. pottery sherds
5. bronze *gu*
6, 65–8, 70, 71. bronze knives
7, 32, 34, 39, 40. turquoise
8, 29, 31, 33, 41. jade handles
9, 50, 59. bronze arrowheads
10, 19, 22. bronze *jia*
11, 12, 21, 23. bronze *jue*
13, 14, 28, 42, 57, 58. jade blades
15, 54. bronze axes
16, 24–7. bronze *ge* blades
17. bronze axe
18, 56. bronze spearheads
20. bronze *he*
30. jade hairpin

35, 36, 55. bronze *ding*
37. flat-legged *ding*
38. bronze *li*
43–4, 51–3. small bronze *pan*
45. bronze *yan*
46. bronze *ding* leg
47. pottery *guan*
48. pottery *li*
49. hard-pottery *weng*
60. pottery spouted *guan*
61–2. pottery disks
63. wood impressions
64. bronze adze
69. bronze saw
72. bronze chisel
73. bronze shaft foot
74. jade ornament
75. bronze *lei*

a sacrificial victim as well (the *yaokeng* of another grave contained the skeleton of a dog). The only skeletons that survived in recognizable condition were in the upper part of the tomb, three human victims laid on top of the outer coffin and on the *ercengtai*. Bronzes, jades, pottery, and objects of carved wood were set mainly on the *ercengtai* and on or inside the larger coffin. The bronzes were the major furnishings, a total of twenty-three vessels and forty weapons and tools (Figs. 3.2–3.4, 3.36a).[61] This tomb belongs to a well-defined burial tradition. The rectangular shaft tomb with one or more wooden coffins, a *yaokeng* containing a jade *ge* and a sacrificed dog or man, and an *ercengtai* with grave goods and human victims was a standard Early Bronze Age form with antecedents at Erlitou, close parallels at Zhengzhou, and hugely magnified descendants a century or two later in the Xibeigang cemetery at Anyang.

Crucibles and other casting debris were found at Panlongcheng, and there is no reason to doubt that the bronzes from the tombs were cast locally. In style, however, they are identical to bronzes from Zhengzhou, which has yielded larger castings but none finer. The bronzes thus agree with the city wall, the architectural remains, and the burials in testifying that despite its location in the Yangzi valley, 450 km south of Zhengzhou, Panlongcheng is a site of the Erligang civilization. The pottery, however, is said to show differences from Erligang, an observation for which the most obvious explanation would be an indigenous population ruled by an intrusive Erligang elite. Since ancient copper mines are known at places 100 km or so further south, Panlongcheng might have been a fortress securing trade routes that brought metal to the north. Even so it cannot have been entirely isolated, for other places in the middle Yangzi region have also yielded Erligang bronzes.[62]

Southern finds are not alone in suggesting that the Erligang culture was widespread. Although no city site comparable to Panlongcheng has been excavated elsewhere, typical Erligang bronzes have been found throughout a large part of North and Central China. Since the bronzes are indistinguishable from Zhengzhou counterparts no matter where they are found, they argue that the dispersion of the Erligang civilization was not a gradual process but a sharply defined event. It seems difficult to imagine any mechanism other than conquest that could spread a uniform inventory of bronze artifacts and a complex technology in a short space of time over so large an area, and the evidence of archaeology is thus that the Erligang period saw not only the formation of a civilization but also a sudden territorial expansion.

The expansion seems, however, to have been short-lived. After the

---

[61] The vessels were four *jue*, three *jia*, one *gu*, one *he*, five *ding*, one *lei* 罍, one *yan* 甗, one *yu* 盂, one *pan* 盤, and five "small *pan*."
[62] E.g., Suixian (*Wenwu* 1981.8: 46–8) and Huangzhou (*Wenwu* 1993.6: 56–60), both in Hubei.

Erligang period bronzes no longer exhibit any widespread stylistic uniformity; nothing comparable is seen again in the archaeological record before the Zhou period. The next few centuries instead witnessed the rise of local bronze-using cultures, and presumably of local powers, in regions which before the arrival of the Erligang civilization probably had no knowledge of metallurgy (and metallurgy may be only the visible part of a larger debt). The most impressive and at the moment best-known regional bronze culture of the time immediately following the Erligang period was centered in northern Jiangxi, some 300 km south of Panlongcheng, at modern Wucheng 吳城 and Xin'gan 新干 on the Gan River 贛江. Here, just beyond the reach of the Erligang expansion, we find a local culture pushed over the threshold of civilization by contact with the culture of the north.[63]

The Emergence of Regional Powers: Xin'gan and the Wucheng Culture

In 1973 an Early Bronze Age habitation site was excavated at Wucheng on the Gan River in Jiangxi province.[64] The middle level at the site gave evidence of writing, in the form of short unreadable inscriptions incised on a few pots, and also of bronze casting, in the form of a few bronze weapons and many molds of pottery and stone for casting tools and weapons. Pottery with impressed geometric designs was found in large quantities, along with a small amount of technically sophisticated glazed and high-fired ware which the excavators call "primitive porcelain."[65] The pottery was distinctive enough for the excavators to propose taking Wucheng as the type site of a new archaeological culture, but the Wucheng culture did not attract wide attention until 1989, when a rich tomb was discovered 20 km away at Xin'gan on the other side of the river.[66]

---

[63] The pattern of Erligang period expansion followed by the rise of local powers was first described in Bagley, "P'an-lung-ch'eng"; and Fong, *Great Bronze Age of China*, chapter 3. Events in the south are traced in more detail in Robert W. Bagley, "Changjiang Bronzes and Shang Archaeology" (in *Proceedings: International Colloquium on Chinese Art History, 1991, Antiquities, Part 1* [Taipei: National Palace Museum, 1992], pp. 209–55). A similar pattern of advance and retreat at the northern frontiers of the Erligang culture has been described by Lin Yun (pp. 238–41 in "A Reexamination of the Relationship Between Bronzes of the Shang Culture and of the Northern Zone," in *Studies of Shang Archaeology*, ed. K. C. Chang [New Haven, Conn.: Yale University Press, 1986], pp. 237–73).

[64] *Wenwu* 1975.7: 51–71. For later excavations, see *Wenwu* 1993.7: 1–9 and references cited there. The county, formerly Qingjiang 清江, has been renamed Zhangshu 樟樹.

[65] Similar glazed ware has been found at more northerly sites (Panlongcheng, Zhengzhou, Anyang, Taixicun, and Sufutun), but in much smaller quantities (*Xin Zhongguo de kaogu faxian he yanjiu*, pp. 328–32). It may have been a southern product traded to the north; recent technical studies favor southern manufacture (Liao Genshen, "Zhongyuan Shang dai yinwentao yuanshici shaozao diqu de tantao," *Kaogu* 1993.10: 936–41).

[66] See *Wenwu* 1991.10: 1–26 (the excavation report) and Robert Bagley, "An Early Bronze Age Tomb in Jiangxi Province," *Orientations*, July 1993, pp. 20–36. The Xin'gan find and the Wucheng culture have

The Xin'gan tomb could be firmly connected with the Wucheng site on the evidence of the pottery it contained, which exactly matched Wucheng pottery in shapes, clays, glazes, decoration, and incised marks. Nothing found at Wucheng prepared the excavators for the tomb's other contents, however. The Xin'gan tomb is the second richest Early Bronze Age burial known, surpassed only by the contemporary or slightly later Anyang tomb of Fu Hao (ca. 1200 B.C.). Besides 356 pieces of pottery it contained 50 bronze vessels, 4 bells, more than 400 bronze tools and weapons, and about 150 jades, not counting some hundreds of jade beads.[67]

The bronzes conveniently exhibit the history of the local bronze industry. The earliest items, about half a dozen standard Erligang types, leave no doubt that its starting point was Erligang bronze casting, which must have reached Jiangxi from southern outposts of the Erligang civilization such as Panlongcheng. Among the slightly later bronzes which account for the bulk of the assemblage, many show idiosyncratic features, representing the gradual emergence of a local tradition. Others are imports or copies of imports which show that contact with the north continued after the Erligang period. Since the latest of the bronzes are a few pieces roughly contemporary with Fu Hao's tomb, the assemblage neatly spans the so-called transition period, defined as the interval between the end of the Erligang period and the beginning of large-scale activity at Anyang about 1200 B.C. Only scanty remains dating from the transition period have been found at Zhengzhou and Anyang; the Xin'gan tomb supplies the largest assemblage of transition period bronzes known.

Local taste manifests itself in the bronzes in several different ways. Their decoration occasionally copies Wucheng pottery. Three peculiar tripods seem to have been converted from vessels that were originally ring-footed; these might be imported items radically remade to serve local purposes. A large *fangding* 方鼎, one of the earliest of the bronzes, is in most respects similar to *fangding* from Zhengzhou, but it differs by the startling addition of tigers standing on its handles. This is a local feature repeated on at least ten other bronzes from the tomb (Fig. 3.16). The four bells deserve special

been the subject of countless recent articles, many in the journal *Nanfang wenwu*. See, e.g., Peng Shifan and Yang Rixin, "Jiangxi Xin'gan Shang dai da mu wenhua xingzhi chuyi," *Wenwu* 1993.7: 10–18, and references cited there; Sun Hua, "Xin'gan Dayangzhou da mu niandai jianlun," *Nanfang wenwu* 1992.2: 35–40; and, for the best presentation of the contents of the tomb, Peng Shifan, Zhan Kaixun, and Liu Lin, *Changjiang zhongyou qingtong wangguo: Jiangxi Xin'gan chutu qingtong yishu* (Hong Kong: Liangmu, 1994). Some scholars have doubted that the Xin'gan find was a tomb, since shifting sands and decay had left little trace of skeletal remains or coffins, but the exact nature of the find does not affect the present discussion, and the excavators' description of it as a tomb is adopted without further comment. Whether a tomb or not, the assemblage is very different from any northern tomb or deposit.

[67] Few of the jades have been published, but those few include some remarkable items. See Peng Shifan, Zhan Kaixun, and Liu Lin, *Changjiang zhongyou qingtong wangguo*, for illustrations, and Rawson, *Chinese Jade*, for discussion of related examples.

Figure 3.16. Bronze *fangding*, from Xin'gan, Jiangxi, fourteenth to thirteenth century B.C. Height 29 cm. Loehr Style III. Drawing by Li Xiating.

note, for they connect Wucheng with a broad cultural province that seems to have embraced the lower Yangzi region and, perhaps somewhat later, the middle Yangzi region as well. Though Wucheng is so far the only city site known within this region, widely distributed bronzes of high quality and extraordinary character leave no doubt that it was the home of a distinct civilization, of which large bells are the defining artifact.[68] The four bells from Xin'gan are the earliest well-dated examples and the only ones yet found in company with bronze vessels. Three of them belong to the clapperless type called *nao* 鐃, which was mounted mouth-upward on a hollow stem and struck on the exterior; the fourth, a *bo* 鎛, has a loop for suspension. Averaging about 40 cm high, the Xin'gan bells are comparable in size and decoration to bells found elsewhere in the lower Yangzi region; they are larger than Anyang bells but not nearly as large as bells from the middle Yangzi region (Fig. 3.29).

Motifs, styles, and unusual artifact types all advertise the local character of the Xin'gan find, but perhaps the most revealing idiosyncrasy is the composition of the assemblage as a whole. The only tomb of comparable wealth yet discovered, the Anyang tomb of Fu Hao, cannot be much different in date, but its inventory is very different. It contained only 11 pieces of pottery; the Xin'gan tomb contained 356, perhaps because the high quality of the local ware gave it unusual prestige. Fu Hao's tomb had many more jades, 755 items as compared with 150 from Xin'gan, and more bronze vessels, 195 as against 50 from Xin'gan. Differences of quantity probably mean only that Fu Hao was richer than the occupant of the Xin'gan tomb; differences of type are more interesting. Of the 195 vessels in Fu Hao's tomb, 105 belong to the types *jia, jue,* and *gu.* These types are invariable features of northern burials, but they are missing entirely from the Xin'gan assemblage, where instead 37 of the 50 vessels were *ding* and *li.* The absence of the types most essential to northern funerary ritual, the predominance of *ding* and *li,* and the presence of four large bells can only mean that the occupant of the Xin'gan tomb was not a northerner.

It is a tradition of long standing in Chinese archaeology to explain bronzes found outside the North China Plain in ways that attach them to that region, for instance by describing them as imports from Anyang or as imitations of Anyang bronzes or as the property of Anyang fief holders. This has the effect of shifting attention away from the settings in which they are found and preserving the assumption that civilization was a monopoly of the Yellow River valley. But the Xin'gan find cannot be dismissed in this fashion, and it has prompted major shifts in archaeological interpretation. The bronzes show complete mastery of the Erligang technical repertoire;[69] they are of undeniable local character, making it impossible to explain them as imports from Anyang; and the finest of them yield nothing in design or execution to bronzes from any northern site, making it equally impossible to describe them as provincial imitations of Anyang castings (nor can they be dated by synchronizing them with supposed Anyang prototypes). Wucheng and Xin'gan are clearly the remains of a local power, a city and the cemetery of its rulers.

The Wucheng culture thus represents a notably vigorous response to contact with the expanding Erligang civilization. Clearly the society which here received the Erligang stimulus had a ruling class wealthy enough to supply a large-scale bronze industry with raw materials and to support specialized workers employing a complex foundry technology. Perhaps the more primitive metal-using Hushu 湖熟 culture of Anhui and Jiangsu exemplifies the response of a simpler society to the same stimulus.[70] A large copper mine at Ruichang 瑞昌 in northern Jiangxi seems to have been in use as early as

---

[69] Su Rongyu and Peng Shifan, "Xin'gan qingtongqi qun jishu wenhua shuxing yanjiu," *Nanfang wenwu* 1994.2: 30–6.

[70] Chang, *The Archaeology of Ancient China,* pp. 394–6.

the Erligang period,[71] and we might speculate that the Wucheng culture owed its wealth to the copper trade. For whatever reason, its contacts reached far. The bells in the Xin'gan tomb connect it with neighbors in the Yangzi region, and other items point to traffic with more distant places to be mentioned under the next heading, most notably with southern Shaanxi, at the far end of the Han River 漢水.

Sites of the Transition Period in Anhui, Hebei, and Shaanxi

For the century immediately following the Erligang period, Wucheng in Jiangxi and Taixicun 臺西村 in Hebei are the only sites that are archaeologically at all well known, and chance finds of bronzes therefore assume great importance as clues to events that would otherwise go unsuspected. These finds suggest that the development seen at Wucheng, where a distinctive local culture arose on a foundation supplied by the Erligang civilization, is an apt model for the emergence of bronze-using cultures in other regions as well. The transition period saw a breakdown of the cultural unity temporarily imposed in the Erligang period. It was not a time of isolation, however, for similar bronzes have sometimes turned up at widely scattered locations, and we must therefore imagine a network of interacting centers. In most cases it is chance finds which alert us to the existence of these centers, and when the finds have not been followed up by excavation or survey, we have no further information about them. The developments they allow us to glimpse are nevertheless so remarkable as to suggest a flowering of civilization at this stage. The following brief survey of a few particularly notable finds will suggest the wide distribution of civilized powers in the transition period, their variety, and their interconnections.

Two finds in Anhui province require mention, one made in 1957 at Funan 阜南 on the Huai River 淮河 and one made in 1965 at Feixi 肥西 between the Huai River and the Yangzi. Both were chance discoveries about which little is known, and their interest lies chiefly in the extraordinary quality of the bronzes. The Feixi find consisted of a pair of *jia* and a pair of *jue* (Fig. 3.17).[72] The *jia* are imposing and the *jue* are the largest examples on record. The Funan find consisted of pairs of *jue*, *jia*, and *gu*, along with two

---

[71] Lu Benshan and Liu Shizhong, "Tongling Shang Zhou tongkuang kaicai jishu chubu yanjiu," *Wenwu* 1993.7: 33–8. Ancient copper mines are now known in northern Jiangxi, southern Anhui, and southern Hubei (Liu Shizhong, Cao Keping, and Tang Shulong, "Changjiang zhongyou diqu de gu tongkuang," *Kaogu yu wenwu* 1994.1: 82–8). For a thorough survey of ancient mining and smelting, see Su Rongyu et al., *Zhongguo shanggu jinshu jishu*, chapter 2.

[72] No report was published, and no information is available beyond that included in the entries for two bronzes in Fong, *Great Bronze Age of China*, nos. 15–16.

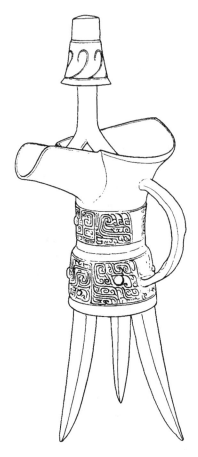

Figure 3.17. Bronze *jue*, from Feixi, Anhui, fourteenth to thirteenth century B.C. Height 38.4 cm. Loehr Style III. Drawing by Li Xiating.

unmatched and spectacular *zun* 尊 (Fig. 3.6 shows the smaller of the two).[73] The *zun* have immediate ancestors among Upper Erligang bronzes, but they are very large and finer in execution than any Erligang bronze. Their decoration, though unusual, is not a local development but belongs to a widespread transition period style; *zun* of similar design have been found as far away as Sichuan and Shaanxi.[74] Both assemblages have the composition of

[73] The one-page report in *Wenwu* 1959.1 contains the only published information about the find. The bronzes are best illustrated in *Anhui sheng bowuguan cang qingtongqi*, ed. Anhui sheng bowuguan (Shanghai: Shanghai Renmin Meishu, 1987), pls. 1, 2, 4, 5, 7; for discussion see Bagley, *Shang Ritual Bronzes*, pp. 22–3.

[74] See Bagley, "Sichuan Province," figs. 26–9, illustrating the Funan bronzes along with counterparts from Sanxingdui and Chenggu; and for the Sanxingdui *zun*, see *Zhongguo qingtongqi quanji, 13, Ba Shu* (Beijing: Wenwu, 1994), pls. 87–8. See also Bagley, "An Early Bronze Age Tomb in Jiangxi Province,"

standard northern burial sets, and bronzes of this size and quality can only have belonged to a very high stratum of society. Poorly documented as they are, they tell us something about the Huai region in the transition period.

A large grave discovered in 1977 at Pinggu 平谷 in Beijing is notable for an inventory that mixes familiar bronze vessels with objects that seem distinctly foreign.[75] The grave had been partly destroyed before it came to the attention of archaeologists, but it seems to have had an *ercengtai* and a sizable complement of at least sixteen bronze vessels.[76] It also contained a bronze axe with an iron blade, five small bronze disks decorated with human faces (items common in Shaanxi graves), and four gold ornaments, including a funnel-shaped earring of a type associated with the Lower Xiajiadian 夏家店 culture of western Liaoning.[77] The combination of foreign personal ornaments and an Erligang burial form leaves the ethnic identity of the occupant uncertain. Cultural differences between a northern border region and the civilization of the Yellow River valley are clearer at a slightly later stage, when similar ornaments occur at sites in Hebei, Shanxi, and northern Shaanxi, in company with exotic bronze tools, weapons, and sometimes vessels.[78]

Southwest of Pinggu is the Taixicun site at Gaocheng 藁城 in Hebei province, where many storage pits, 112 graves, and the remains of 14 houses were excavated in 1973 and 1974.[79] The graves sometimes had *yaokeng* and *ercengtai*, and the bronze vessels found in them are free of local peculiarities, but pottery from the site is said to show northern affiliations, and one burial contained a bronze spatula of northern type, while another contained a bronze axe with iron blade like the one from Pinggu.[80] The excavators divide the remains into an early phase contemporary with Upper Erligang and a later phase that corresponds to the transition period. Though 9 graves con-

---

figs. 44–5, suggesting a connection with Xin'gan. The larger of the two Funan *zun* is ancestral to a southern bronze of extravagantly local design, the famous four-ram *zun* from Ningxiang in northern Hunan; this may be a further indication that its design was widely known in the transition period (see Bagley, *Shang Ritual Bronzes*, p. 35 and figs. 171, 174).

[75] *Wenwu* 1977.11: 1–8.

[76] *Fangding, ding, li, yan, jue, jia, lei, he, pan, you* 卣, and *pou* 瓿, some of Upper Erligang type (Styles I and II) and some belonging to the transition period (several varieties of Style III).

[77] On Lower Xiajiadian, see Sarah Milledge Nelson, ed., *The Archaeology of Northeast China: Beyond the Great Wall* (London: Routledge, 1995), chapter 5. In the civilization of the Yellow River valley, gold was rarely used; personal ornaments were mostly jade, seldom or never bronze or precious metal (Franklin, "On Bronze and Other Metals in Early China," pp. 289–91). It is possible that occasional finds of gold leaf, for instance in some of the Xibeigang tombs, reflect northern contact.

[78] See below, "The Northern Zone," pp. 221–6.

[79] *Xin Zhongguo de kaogu faxian he yanjiu*, pp. 235–9; *Gaocheng Taixi Shang dai yizhi*, ed. Hebei sheng Wenwu yanjiusuo (Beijing: Wenwu, 1985).

[80] Technical study has established that the blade was meteoritic iron shaped by forging; see Li Chung, "Studies on the Iron Blade of a Shang Dynasty Bronze *Yüeh*-axe Unearthed at Kao-ch'eng, Hopei, China," *Ars Orientalis* 11 (1979): 259–89. Tang Yunming, following Zou Heng, connects both Taixicun and the Pinggu grave with Lower Xiajiadian; see Tang Yunming, "Taixi yizhi qiqi de yuanyuan ji yizhi wenhua xingzhi de tantao," *Hua Xia kaogu* 1988.2: 62–8.

tained human sacrifices and 38 contained sacrificed dogs, none could be considered richly furnished by the standard of Lijiazui M2 at Panlongcheng or the grave that yielded the Funan bronzes. Several had bundles of three divination scapulas (uninscribed) laid on the *ercengtai*; bones used for divination have not elsewhere been found in burials. Uninscribed scapulas and turtle shells were also found among the house remains. Bronze vessels from the graves belong to the types *jue, jia, gu, ding, lei,* and *dou* 豆. On some of them traces of silk cloth were found fused with corrosion, and in the remains of one house a roll of coarse linen cloth was discovered.[81] Another house yielded fragments of two wooden vessels carved and painted with red and black lacquer, one of them inlaid with turquoise.[82] Both human and animal victims appear to have been sacrificed in connection with the building of one of the larger houses at the site, an earth-walled structure measuring 3.6 by 10.35 m. Despite such evidence of social stratification, however, the Taixicun site is small, the burials are modest, and there seem to be no *hangtu* foundations, so that on present evidence other sites less well investigated seem more important.

Of these the most tantalizing is Chenggu 城固 at the confluence of the Han and Xushui 湑水河 Rivers in southern Shaanxi. Since 1955 more than a dozen accidental finds on both sides of the Xushui have yielded over 500 bronzes, mostly weapons but also a few chariot fittings and a good many vessels, ranging in date from Upper Erligang through the transition period and perhaps later.[83] The finds seem to be not graves but pit deposits of unknown purpose. The vessels are often of extremely high quality, finer than any from Taixicun and comparable to bronzes from Xin'gan (Fig. 3.18). One deposit, at Sucun 蘇村, attests to a remarkable range of contacts. It contained 95 *ge* blades; 34 small bronze faces or masks, 23 human and 11 animal; more

[81] Both silk and linen are known much earlier. The evidence for domesticated silk reaches back as far as the third millennium in the Liangzhu Neolithic of the Lower Yangzi region (Xia Nai, *Kaoguxue he kejishi* [Beijing: Kexue, 1979], p. 101; Zhou Kuangming, "Qianshanyang can juan pian chutu de qishi," *Wenwu* 1980.1: 74–7). Weaves have been studied from pseudomorphs preserved in bronze corrosion; see Vivi Sylwan, "Silk from the Yin Dynasty," *BMFEA* 9 (1937): 119–26; John Vollmer, "Textile Pseudo-morphs on Chinese Bronzes," in *Archaeological Textiles*, ed. Patricia L. Fiske (Washington, D.C.: Textile Museum, 1974), pp. 170–4.

[82] These fragments (shown in *Gaocheng Taixi Shang dai yizhi*, color pl. 2) are the only substantial remains of lacquer so far known from the second millennium. The use of lacquer (a natural varnish that can be colored with cinnabar, lampblack, and other pigments) to decorate and preserve articles of wood is believed to go back to the fifth millennium, on the evidence of a red wooden bowl unearthed at the Hemudu 河姆渡 site in Zhejiang. Coffins at many early Bronze Age sites seem to have been lacquered, and other articles of lacquered wood may also have been common (though expensive), but the earliest well-preserved examples of lacquer come from Eastern Zhou sites.

[83] Finds from 1955 to 1976 are surveyed in Tang Jinyu, Wang Shouzhi, and Guo Changjiang, "Shaanxi sheng Chenggu xian chutu Yin Shang tongqi zhengli jianbao," *Kaogu* 1980.3: 211–18, and illustrated in *Shaanxi chutu Shang Zhou qingtongqi* (Beijing: Wenwu, 1979), vol. 1, nos. 99–123. The most important find since then is reported in Wang Shouzhi, "Shaanxi Chenggu chutu de Shang dai qingtongqi," *Wenbo* 1988.6: 3–9.

Figure 3.18. Bronze *pou*, from Chenggu, Shaanxi, thirteenth century B.C. Height 32 cm, greatest diameter 38.7 cm. Loehr Style III. Photograph courtesy of the Shanghai Museum.

than 200 bronze disks or bosses; and a pair of *fanglei* 方罍. The *fanglei* are almost identical to a pair in Fu Hao's tomb,[84] but the closest relatives of the animal faces come from the Wei River valley, and the human faces have parallels there and at Xin'gan as well (Fig. 3.19). These and other links between Shaanxi sites and Xin'gan leave no doubt of traffic between the two places and indeed suggest that some Wei River valley weapon types derive from Jiangxi prototypes. Though excavations have never been undertaken at Chenggu, the repeated chance finds suggest that it was a place of importance with connections reaching north to the Wei River valley, south into Sichuan, eastward to Anyang, and southeast to Hunan and Jiangxi.[85] Our limited knowledge of the site is a pointed reminder of the unevenness of the presently known archaeological record.

The sites just reviewed do not exhaust the list of places where bronzes of the transition period have been unearthed. Finds in the Wei River valley,[86]

[84] Bagley, *Shang Ritual Bronzes*, figs. 123 (Fu Hao) and 124 (Chenggu).
[85] An animal-shaped *zun* unearthed a few kilometers from Chenggu, at Yangxian 洋縣, is likely to be an import from the middle Yangzi region; see Bagley, *Shang Ritual Bronzes*, pp. 11 (illustration) and 416–20.
[86] Bao Quan, "Xi'an Laoniupo chutu Shang dai zaoqi wenwu," *Kaogu yu wenwu* 1981.2: 17–18, and perhaps some of the graves at Laoniupo reported in *Wenwu* 1988.6: 1–22.

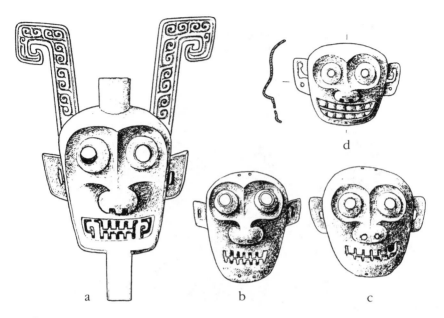

Figure 3.19. Human faces in bronze, all probably thirteenth century B.C. Not to scale. Drawings by Li Xiating. (a) From Xin'gan, Jiangxi. Height 53 cm. The object is hollow; front and back are identical. (b–c) From Sucun at Chenggu, Shaanxi. Height approx. 16 cm. (d) From Laoniupo at Xi'an, Shaanxi. Height 7.8 cm.

western Henan,[87] and Shanxi[88] are not so rich as the ones already discussed, but they clearly belong to the same period. Zhengzhou by contrast has yielded little to compare with the finds just reviewed, nor is there much sign that Anyang was a place of importance at this time; the transition period is even less well known in the Yellow River valley than in outlying areas. This is a considerable gap in our knowledge, since it leaves us unprepared for the upsurge of activity at Anyang about 1200 B.C. that is taken to mark the end of the period. The remainder of this chapter deals with developments following the transition period, first at Anyang, then in the middle Yangzi region, the Chengdu plain, Shandong, the Northern Zone, and the Wei River valley.

Anyang ca. 1200 B.C.

INTRODUCTION. The oracle inscriptions found at the Anyang 安陽, or Yinxu 殷墟, site record divinations performed on behalf of nine kings whose

---

[87] *Kaogu* 1979.1: 20–2 (Lingbao 靈寶, the 1974 find).
[88] *Wenwu* 1982.9: 49–52 (fig. 7 and pls. 7:2, 7:4); *Shanxi chutu wenwu*, ed. Shanxi sheng Wenwu gongzuo weiyuanhui (Taiyuan: Shanxi Renmin, 1980), nos. 48 and 51; and other scattered finds.

names appear in later texts as the last kings of a dynasty called Shang 商 or
Yin 殷.[89] The site is therefore identified as the last capital of the Shang
dynasty. The inscriptions sometimes inquire about sacrifices to earlier kings
of the dynasty, but it is not known where those earlier kings ruled, nor indeed
how many of them were real and how many were mythical. For the period
of the last kings, any close estimate of calendar dates depends on later texts;
the estimate used in the present volume puts the reign of Wu Ding 武丁,
first of the nine, around 1200 B.C.[90]

To assign relative dates to Anyang archaeological remains the excavators
rely chiefly on a seriation of Anyang pottery that divides the occupation of
the site into four stages, Yinxu 1–4. Connecting those remains with particular kings depends on finding inscribed materials whose place in the pottery
sequence can be established. The present consensus seems to be that Wu
Ding's reign corresponds to late Yinxu 1 and early Yinxu 2. Since the first
large building foundations at the site seem to belong to late Yinxu 1, while
remains antedating those foundations suggest only a modest settlement, it
may have been in Wu Ding's time that the foundations were constructed and
Anyang became an important city. In fact all the features that set Anyang
apart from other sites made their first appearance about this time: inscribed
oracle bones, enormous tombs, countless sacrificial burials, and chariot
burials. No earlier site approaches Anyang in the scale of human sacrifice; no
tomb is so rich as that of Wu Ding's consort Fu Hao; and the oracle bones
are the first clear evidence for writing in China. Anyang's prominence in the
archaeological record reflects not only second-millennium realities but also
decades of archaeological activity; if Zhengzhou or Sanxingdui or the Yangzi
region were better known, Anyang might seem less exceptional. For the
moment, however, it is a uniquely spectacular site, and it became so in Wu
Ding's reign, on which the present description focuses.[91]

WRITING. When documents become available to us, the way we visualize
the past changes dramatically. The Anyang oracle inscriptions inevitably
make Anyang seem very different from its undocumented neighbors and predecessors. Does the difference correspond to anything real in second-

---

[89] The literature of Anyang archaeology is enormous. The most comprehensive survey is *Yinxu de faxian yu yanjiu*. Other general treatments include Li Chi, *Anyang*, and K. C. Chang, *Shang Civilization* (New Haven, Conn.: Yale University Press, 1980).

[90] See Chapter 4. A few radiocarbon dates from relevant strata fall mainly in the thirteenth and twelfth centuries (after calibration), but they have very large error margins; see *Zhongguo kaoguxue zhong tan shisi niandai shuju ji 1965–1991*, pp. 171–2.

[91] On the periodization of the Anyang site, see *Yinxu de faxian yu yanjiu*, chapter 3 (by Zheng Zhen-xiang). On material remains assigned to Wu Ding's reign, see also Tang Jigen, "Yinxu yi qi wenhua ji qi xiangguan wenti," *Kaogu* 1993.10: 925–35; and Meng Xianwu, "Anyang Sanjiazhuang Dongwang-ducun faxian de Shang dai qingtongqi ji qi niandai tuiding." On the oracle inscriptions, see Chapters 2 and 4 of the present volume.

millennium China, or is it merely an illusion arising from the different nature of our sources? No sure answer can be given, but some notion of probabilities can be obtained by examining a related question: Is it merely an accident of preservation and discovery that writing first appears in the archaeological record at Anyang about 1200 B.C., or was writing in fact invented at that time and limited to that place?

Inscriptions first appear on bronzes at about the same time they appear on oracle bones, a coincidence which favors the possibility that this was the first appearance of writing itself.[92] But it is also possible that the only innovation of Wu Ding's time was the decision to carve divination records on the divination bones. Writing on perishable materials undoubtedly existed at Anyang; the evidence for brush writing and, less direct, for wood or bamboo writing surfaces is clear.[93] At Anyang, therefore, we have only a fraction of a larger corpus, limited to texts that were singled out for transcription onto bone. Perhaps we lack evidence of writing from other cities or earlier periods simply because it was confined to perishable materials that have perished. This possibility is not easily dismissed if we reflect on the archaeological evidence for literacy in the Western Zhou period. On the evidence of inscribed bronzes, literacy was geographically widespread in Western Zhou, yet were it not for the practice of casting inscriptions in durable bronze, we would have no indication that the Zhou were literate at all. We cannot suppose that Western Zhou writing was confined to bronzes, but the other documents that must have existed have left no trace.

Writing thus may not have been limited to Anyang, to carved bones used for royal divinations, or to the time of Wu Ding and his successors. Those are the limits of our epigraphic sample, however, and the bias of the sample clearly forbids certain inferences. First, since we cannot be confident that writing first appeared in Wu Ding's time, we should resist any temptation to connect its appearance with events that are more securely dated to his time (e.g., the advent of chariots). Second, since writing was not confined to divination bones, we cannot assume that it originated in a religious or royal context or that it was limited to religious uses. Anyang has left us nothing to compare with the wealth of literary, historical, and economic texts that survive from the ancient Near East, but this is not necessarily a sign that writing in China had different functions from writing in the Near East, much

---

[92] No scientifically excavated Erligang bronze is inscribed; the inscriptions on a few unprovenanced Erligang bronzes are likely to be modern additions.

[93] See, e.g., Liu Yiman, "Shilun Yinxu jiagu shuci," *Kaogu* 1991.6: 546–54, 572 (brush-written oracle inscriptions), *Yinxu yuqi*, nos. 21–2 (a jade *ge* with an inscription written in vermilion); and *Kaogu* 1989.10: 893–905 (fig. 6, a potsherd with vermilion inscription). Most of these date from Wu Ding's reign, but the last comes from a pit which the excavators assign to early Yinxu I, before his reign. On evidence for wood or bamboo writing surfaces, see Chapter 2, the present volume.

less a sign of some deeper cultural difference. It is far more likely to reflect the fact that no writing surface used at any time in the history of China was simultaneously as durable and as cheap as the clay tablets of the Near East, which, alongside peace treaties and epics, have preserved for us exercises written out by schoolboys. On the hypothesis that the major differences between the textual records of China and the Near East are owed to accidents of preservation rather than to differences of culture, the Near Eastern record can suggest how our mental picture of China might change if our documents were less restricted in subject matter and authorship.

Finally, whether or not Anyang had a monopoly on writing, it does have a monopoly on our written sources, and we must beware the distortion that this entails. If a substantial body of texts were discovered at some other site, our mental picture of the second millennium would change in ways we cannot hope to imagine. We can only remind ourselves that the view of outlying regions we glimpse in the oracle texts is that of the Anyang king, who may not have been well informed and who certainly was not concerned with objective reporting. Precious as it is, our earliest sample of writing is a narrowly focused collection of fragmentary, brief, and cryptic royal texts from two centuries in the history of one city.

THE ANYANG SITE. The main areas of activity at Anyang[94] just before Wu Ding's time seem to have been in the angle of the Huan River 洹河 northeast of the modern village of Xiaotun 小屯 and across the river at Sanjiazhuang 三家莊. In his time large buildings, tombs, and workshops appeared, and the settlement began to grow, covering perhaps 15 sq. km by the end of his reign and at least 24 sq. km by the end of the dynasty. Many cemeteries and dwelling areas are known, but the site has not been systematically explored and settlement patterns are not well understood.[95] No trace of a city wall has been found.[96] Along with graveyards and dwellings likely to be for the workers, many workshops have been excavated at Miaopu Beidi 苗圃北地 in the south, among them a bronze foundry which by the end of the dynasty covered 10,000 sq. m.[97] Building foundations near Xiaotun are

---

[94] For a comprehensive account of the layout and chronology of the site, see *Yinxu de faxian yu yanjiu*, chapters 4–6.

[95] For cemeteries, see ibid., chapter 6; *Xin Zhongguo de kaogu faxian he yanjiu*, pp. 232–5; Yang Hsi-chang, "The Shang Dynasty Cemetery System," in *Studies of Shang Archaeology*, ed. K. C. Chang, pp. 49–63.

[96] Ma Shizhi, "Shilun Shang dai de chengzhi," in *Zhongguo Kaogu xuehui di wu ci nianhui lunwen ji 1985*, ed. Zhongguo Kaogu xuehui (Beijing: Wenwu, 1988), pp. 24–30; Zhang Guoshuo, "Yinxu chengqiang shangque," *Yindu xuekan* 1989.2: 26–30. It is sometimes suggested that settlements with walls (Zhengzhou, Panlongcheng) differed in function from settlements without walls (Erlitou, Anyang), the latter being labeled "ceremonial centers," but what function required a city wall, or what function Zhengzhou had that Anyang lacked, is not clear.

[97] For bronze and bone workshops, see *Yinxu de faxian yu yanjiu*, pp. 83–96. Excavations at Miaopu Beidi are reported in *Yinxu fajue baogao 1958–1961*, ed. Zhongguo Shehui kexueyuan Kaogu yanjiusuo (Beijing: Wenwu, 1987).

large enough to be royal, as are the tombs in a cemetery across the Huan River at Xibeigang 西北岡.

The Xiaotun building foundations, which fall into three irregular groups, are taken to be the remains of palaces and temples because of their size, the sacrificial burials associated with some of them, and the deposits of inscribed oracle bones found in the central and southern groups.[98] All told more than fifty large *hangtu* foundations were excavated. The stratigraphy was difficult to interpret and the relative dating of the various buildings is uncertain, but it seems likely that the earliest belong to Wu Ding's reign and that the area was occupied continuously to the end of the dynasty. The foundations vary in depth according to the terrain and are sometimes as much as 3 m thick. Many are 20 to 50 m long; the longest was a building that measured 14.5 by 85 m. In the central and southern groups the excavators found burials of dogs, horses, oxen, sheep, chariots, and hundreds of human victims, at least some of them sacrifices associated with the construction of the buildings.[99] Interspersed with the foundations were pits interpreted as semisubterranean dwellings, pits for grain storage, and pits that stored oracle bones. H127, a deposit that contained more than 17,000 plastron fragments, was excavated in 1936 about 100 m northeast of modern Xiaotun. Some 5,000 inscribed bones were unearthed at the southern edge of Xiaotun in 1973, and at Huayuanzhuang 花園莊 nearby more than 500 inscribed plastrons, almost 300 of them complete, were found in 1991.[100]

The only intact royal burial yet discovered at Anyang, that of Wu Ding's consort Fu Hao, is located 100 m northwest of Xiaotun. Other large but plundered tombs have been found southeast of Xiaotun at Hougang 後岡.[101] By far the largest, however, are across the Huan River at Xibeigang, about a kilometer north of the villages of Houjiazhuang 侯家莊 and Wuguancun 武官村 (Fig. 3.20a).[102] Within an area that measures about 450 m east–west by 250 m north–south, 11 tombs were excavated in 1934–5, another in 1950, and 1 more in 1984. A modern road divides the area into a western part and an eastern part. The western part contains 8 tombs, the eastern part contains the other 5 and at least 1,400 pits for sacrificial burials. Apparently none of the tombs is earlier than Wu Ding's reign. All were looted in antiquity and

---

[98] The foundations are described briefly in Chang, *Shang Civilization*, pp. 90–9, and in more detail in *Yinxu de faxian yu yanjiu*, pp. 51–70.

[99] Huang Zhanyue, *Zhongguo gudai de rensheng renxun* (Beijing: Wenwu 1990), pp. 46–53.

[100] Xiaotun Nandi: *Kaogu* 1975.1: 27–46; Huayuanzhuang: *Kaogu* 1993.6: 488–99. A refuse deposit about 500 m from Xiaotun Nandi contained the bones of oxen in vast quantities (*Kaogu xuebao* 1992.1: 97–128). Oracle-bone finds are surveyed in detail in *Yinxu de faxian yu yanjiu*, chapter 7.

[101] Some in the 1930s, one in 1991 (*Yinxu de faxian yu yanjiu*, pp. 129–32; *Kaogu* 1993.10: 880–901).

[102] The first Anyang excavators referred to the area as Houjiazhuang Xibeigang, the excavators since 1950 have called it Wuguancun Beidi. The tombs are briefly described and their chronology is discussed in *Yinxu de faxian yu yanjiu*, pp. 101–12.

in modern times, but their great size makes it plausible to connect them with the Anyang royal house, and one contained a bronze inscribed with the name of a royal consort, possibly a consort of Wu Ding.[103] The find that led archaeologists to the Xibeigang cemetery, a set of 3 bronze *he* unearthed by looters in 1934 (Fig. 3.10b), came from M1001, which might be the tomb of Wu Ding.

All thirteen tombs are oriented a few degrees east of north. Except for one that was empty and unfinished (M1567), all had sloping or stepped ramps opening into a nearly vertical shaft, at the bottom of which was a wooden burial chamber. The ramps probably had less to do with the construction of the tomb than with the funeral ceremony during which it was filled with layers of pounded earth, grave goods, and sacrifices. Since in most cases the south ramp was the only one that descended all the way to the floor of the shaft, the wooden chamber may have been entered by a door in the south side. The other ramps usually entered the shaft higher up, sometimes higher than the ceiling of the chamber. The shafts ranged from 10 to 13 m deep, and since the water table in 1934–5 was about 10 m down, the excavators were not able to reach the bottoms of all of them, but whenever the bottom was reached, a small pit containing an armed man was found in the center of the shaft floor beneath the wooden chamber. The tomb furnishings had been deposited mainly in the chamber, but this had invariably been emptied by looters, and most of the artifacts recovered by the excavators came from the ramps or other nooks that had escaped looting. In the south ramp of M1004, for instance, the earth fill was found to contain four successive layers of grave goods, one above the other: at the bottom, chariot fittings and remains of leather armor and shields; in the next layer, more than 100 bronze helmets and about 360 bronze *ge* blades; in the next layer, 36 bronze spearheads; and in the top layer, a stone chime, a jade, and 2 large bronze *fangding*.

M1001. M1001 can be taken as typical of the large Xibeigang tombs.[104] One of the earliest tombs in the cemetery, perhaps that of Wu Ding, it yielded artifacts that have close parallels in the tomb of Wu Ding's consort Fu Hao.[105] It is vastly larger than Fu Hao's tomb and must have been richer in proportion, but looters had left very little in it, and the following description therefore focuses on its structure, leaving the description of Fu Hao's tomb, which was discovered intact, to suggest how it might have been furnished.

[103] The *Si Mu Wu fangding* was unearthed in 1946; the tomb from which it is believed to come, M260, was excavated in 1984 (*Kaogu xuebao* 1987.1: 99–117).

[104] The description here is based on the excavation report; Gao Quxun, *Houjiazhuang* (*Henan Anyang Houjiazhuang Yin dai mudi*) *di er ben, 1001 hao da mu* (Taipei: Academia Sinica, 1962).

[105] Cao Dingyun, "Lun Yinxu Houjiazhuang 1001 hao mu muzhu" (*Kaogu yu wenwu* 1986.2: 44–51), reviews the evidence for assigning M1001 to Wu Ding.

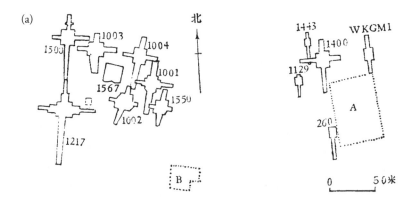

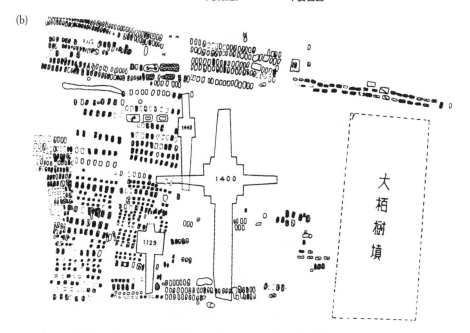

Figure 3.20. Plans of the Xibeigang cemetery. (a) Showing large tombs, including two excavated since 1950 (WKGMI, M260) and the locations of sacrificial burials excavated in 1976
(dotted area A) and 1978 (B). After *Kaogu* 1987.12: 1062. (b) Detail of eastern part, showing
large tombs and sacrificial burials excavated in 1934–5. After Yang Ximei, "Henan Anyang
Yinxu muzang zhong renti guge de zhengli he yanjiu," *BIHP* 42 (1970): pl. 13. (c) Detail of
eastern part, showing sacrificial burials excavated in 1976 (= dotted area A in Fig. 3.20a). After
Kaogu 1977.1: 21.

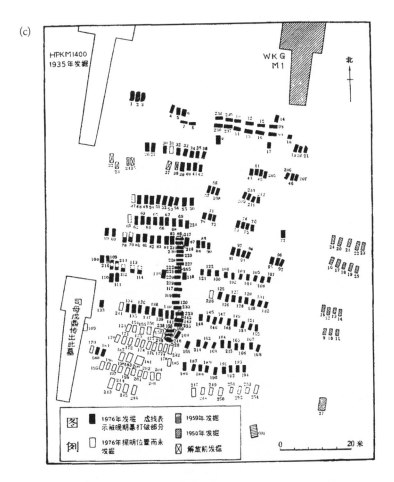

Figure 3.20. *(cont.)*

The basic features of M1001 have already been encountered on a modest scale in Lijiazui M2 at Panlongcheng: it was a vertical shaft containing a wooden chamber at the bottom, a sacrificial pit (*yaokeng*) beneath the chamber, and a shelf (*ercengtai*) formed by packing earth into the space between the chamber and the shaft walls; and it was supplied with bronze vessels, other grave goods, and sacrificial victims. It differs, however, by the addition of four entrance ramps and by its tremendous size (Fig. 3.21). Including the ramps it measured about 66 m north–south and 44 m east–west. The southern ramp, 30.7 m long, was the longest. It entered the shaft 2.3 m above the floor; perhaps a stairway connected it with a door in the wooden chamber. The other three ramps entered the shaft 5.5 m above the floor.

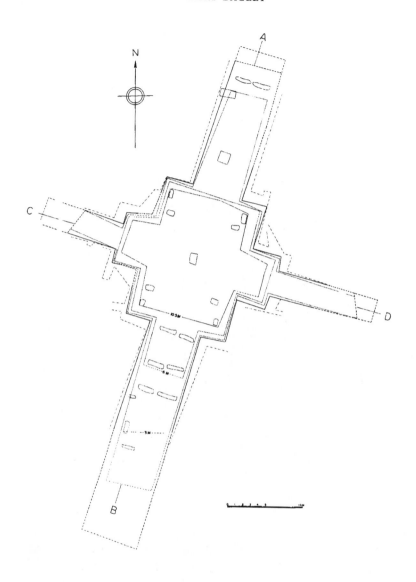

Figure 3.21. Xibeigang M1001, plan and north–south section. After Gao Quxun, *Houjia-zhuang, (Henan Anyang Houjiazhuang Yin dai mudi) di er ben, 1001 hao da mu*, vol. 2 (Taipei: Academia Sinica, 1962), pls. 1–2.

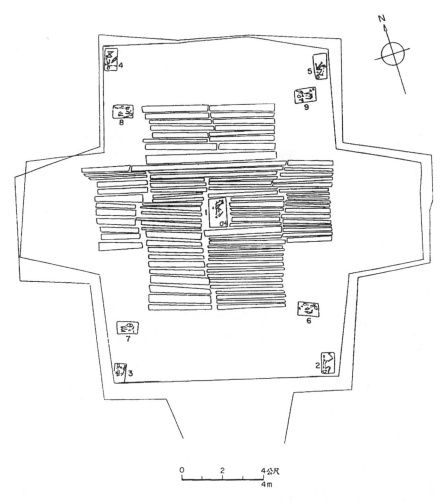

Figure 3.22. Xibeigang M1001, shaft floor, showing nine sacrificial burials and impressions of burial chamber floor timbers. After Gao Quxun, *Houjiazhuang (Henan Anyang Houjiazhuang Yin dai mudi) di er ben, 1001 hao da mu*, vol. 1 (Taipei: Academia Sinica, 1962), pp. 24, 29.

The shaft was 10.5 m deep. In plan it was cross-shaped; at floor level, including the arms of the cross, it measured 15.9 by 19.15 m (Figs. 3.22, 3.23). In its floor nine sacrificial pits were found, one in the center and two in each corner, each pit containing a man, a dog, and a *ge* blade. In the eight corner pits the *ge* blades were bronze, and they were of functional size, about 24 cm long; in the central pit the blade was jade, 43 cm long, and it was found in ten pieces, perhaps deliberately broken. No other Xibeigang tomb seems to have had more than one sacrificial pit, a *yaokeng* at the center of the shaft,

Figure 3.23. Xibeigang M1001, shaft floor during excavation, 1935. After Gao Quxun, *Houjia-zhuang (Henan Anyang Houjiazhuang Yin dai mudi) di er ben, 1001 hao da mu*, vol. 2 (Taipei: Academia Sinica, 1962), pl. 14.

but the man in the *yaokeng* was always armed with a jade *ge* blade. If the men are interpreted as guardians, then perhaps jade *ge* found by themselves in the *yaokeng* of lesser tombs, without human victims, should be understood as symbolic guardians. No evidence connects any other jade shape with so specific a ritual or magical function.

Like the shaft itself, the wooden chamber on the shaft floor was cross-shaped, but it was smaller, measuring about 12 m in each direction (arms of the cross included). The floor area was 78 sq. m and the ceiling height was about 3 m. No trace of the tomb's owner or of a coffin could be identified within the chamber. Sometime after the tomb was closed the ceiling collapsed under the weight of the *hangtu* fill, and further damage was caused by looters who dug vertically through the fill into the chamber. The wood itself eventually decayed away, but impressions of the floor timbers survived on the floor of the shaft, and the decoration of the inside walls was partly preserved in the form of earth impressions carrying pigments, inlays, and carved patterns transferred from the vanished wood.[106] The inlays were shell, bone, and ivory; red was the main pigment but black, white, and green also occur. The patterns were similar to those known from carved bone and bronzes. The bulk of the grave goods had been placed in the chamber, which we may imagine as a sumptuously decorated room 3 m high filled with a king's possessions.

Further offerings and sacrifices were made as the tomb was filled. Once the nine guardians had been buried in the floor of the shaft, the space between the shaft walls and the wooden chamber was filled with pounded earth. Perhaps when the funeral began the shaft had already been partly filled, leaving access to a door facing the south ramp but otherwise burying the chamber, so that the other three ramps opened directly onto a layer of earth over the chamber. At this level offerings were laid on the earth fill. Those placed directly above the chamber were taken or destroyed by looters, but near the shaft walls the excavators found traces of a chariot box, a shield, and painted and inlaid impressions left by objects of carved wood. Also at this level were the skeletons of eleven human victims. Six had been buried face up, apparently in coffins, and wore ornaments of turquoise and jade. The other five were prone and without coffins or grave goods. None was well enough preserved for sex to be determined.

The deposit of human victims continued as the ramps were filled. The west ramp contained the burial of an adolescent accompanied by five bronze vessels and other grave goods; the skeleton was complete. A headless skeleton was found in the east ramp and a total of thirty-one skulls in the east,

---

[106] Umehara Sueji, *In bo hakken mokki in'ei zuroku* (Kyoto: Benridô, 1959), publishes color photographs that were later issued also as a supplement to the excavation report.

north, and west ramps. Sacrifice was concentrated in the south ramp, however, where successive layers contained eight rows of headless skeletons and fourteen groups of skulls, a total of fifty-nine skeletons and forty-two skulls. Except for a few infants, all the victims were teenage males with their hands bound behind them who had been lined up five or ten at a time in rows facing the shaft and beheaded. The heads were collected for later deposit in a higher level, earth was poured over the bodies and pounded hard, and the process was repeated.

Additional burials were made outside the tomb. The excavators found thirty-one pits that were arranged neatly along the east perimeter of the tomb and must therefore have belonged to it. Twenty-two of them contained altogether sixty-eight humans, from one to seven in a pit, mostly prone with head to the north. Most of the pits contained a few grave goods and one was richly furnished, having inner and outer coffins, a *yaokeng* beneath the coffins, horse and chariot ornaments, a set of bronze vessels, and on the *ercengtai* two humans and two dogs. Among the other pits were seven containing horses. Four of the seven were intact at the time of excavation and contained twelve horses with decorated bridles, turquoise ornaments, and small bronze bells at their necks. These are likely to have been chariot horses. Perhaps the humans in the other pits were an escort or bodyguard for the tomb's owner. The human victims in and around M1001 seem to fall into two groups: those buried with care, with bodies intact, and those beheaded or otherwise mutilated and buried without grave goods. The former, of which the tomb contained at least ninety, must have been servants or familiars of the king. The latter, perhaps less familiar to the king than his chariot horses, numbered at least seventy-four.

The closing of such a tomb must have been a protracted ritual involving a great many people. Simply to fill the tomb with *hangtu* required a large labor force, and besides the laborers the ritual with its succession of sacrifices seems to presume an audience. Staging a lavish funeral is a way for a successor to assert his legitimacy, and excavation at Xibeigang has shown that the sacrifices made at the funeral were only the first of a series which the reigning king supplied to his deceased predecessors.

SACRIFICIAL BURIALS. More than 1,200 sacrificial pits, most containing human victims, were excavated at Xibeigang along with the large tombs in 1934 and 1935, most of them near M1400 in the eastern part of the cemetery (Fig. 3.20b).[107] Grave goods accompanied complete skeletons more often than

[107] Kao Ch'ü-hsün, "The Royal Cemetery of the Yin Dynasty at An-yang," *Bulletin of the Department of Archaeology and Anthropology, National Taiwan University* 13–14 (November 1959): 1–9; *Yinxu de faxian yu yanjiu*, pp. 112–21 (which describes also the sacrificial burials excavated in 1977 and 1978).

dismembered ones, but headless skeletons were often accompanied by knife, axe, and whetstone. One pit in which chariot fittings were found may have been a burial of dismantled chariots. Twenty pits contained horses, from one to thirty-seven horses in a pit. Birds, two monkeys, and a few other animals were found, most notably two elephants, each buried in its own pit with a human attendant. The pits with human victims were laid out in east–west rows in distinct groups, all the pits of a group containing only complete skeletons or skulls or beheaded skeletons, as though each group constituted a single sacrifice performed in a single way. The excavators assumed that these burials were laid down during funeral ceremonies connected with one or more of the large tombs, but more recent excavations suggest that they were sacrifices subsequent to funerals.

A group of 191 pits excavated southeast of M1400 in 1976 contained the remains of more than 1,200 victims (Fig. 3.20c).[108] Sex and age were determined for about a third of the skeletons; they were sometimes women or children but mostly young adult males. Beheading was the normal method of sacrifice but some victims were dismembered or cut in half and a few children seem to have been trussed up and buried alive. Skeletons were usually incomplete, heads normally buried separately from bodies. In most cases the bodies were neatly arranged, usually laid prone. Few were accompanied by any sort of grave good. The excavators took special care to establish relationships between pits; judging by spacing, size, depth, and burial style, they were able to distinguish 22 groups of pits, the smallest group consisting of a single pit, the largest consisting of 47 pits with more than 339 victims. Each of the 22 groups evidently represents a single occasion of sacrifice, the average sacrifice exceeding 50 victims. Stratigraphic relations suggest that most of the sacrifices were performed in the reigns of Wu Ding and his two immediate successors. Forty pits excavated in 1978, this time in the western part of the cemetery, seem to represent slightly later sacrifices (Fig. 3.20a).[109] The pits fell into 15 groups and contained mainly horses, a total of 117. Since test probes have located additional pits in the area between the eastern and western parts of the cemetery, the excavators speculate that all the pits found so far belong to a continuous sacrificial ground used for a considerable time and covering several hectares, a substantial part of the Xibeigang cemetery. Oracle inscriptions from Wu Ding's reign mention sacrifices of human victims (occasionally by the hundred) dedicated to royal ancestors, sometimes to several ancestors jointly. Xibeigang must have been the place where these sacrifices were performed, including perhaps sacrifices to ancestors who were not buried there.

[108] *Kaogu* 1977.1: 20–36.
[109] *Kaogu* 1987.12: 1062–70, 1145.

Human sacrifice seems to have served more than one purpose at Anyang. Foundation burials suggest that the construction of buildings sometimes required human victims, and sacrificial pits of unknown purpose have been found at many parts of the site. Nevertheless human sacrifice was dedicated above all to the mortuary cult of the Anyang kings. What this cult meant to the population at large is unknown. Among the Aztecs the terror inspired by public sacrifices, chillingly felt in Spanish accounts like that of Bernal Díaz, may have been an instrument of political policy. Certainly it was a reality ever present in the consciousness of both the Aztecs and their neighbors. But sacrifice in Mesoamerica was also sustained by religious beliefs which made the gods and therefore the welfare of human society dependent on it, and sacrifice on the scale seen at Anyang might not have been possible without the support of some similar belief. From the sacrifices that the royal ancestors commanded we can infer at least that they were believed to have great power. Though sacrifice at funerals and burial of retainers persisted to much later times, however, the recurrent slaughter of anonymous victims in rituals subsequent to funerals seems to have ended with the Anyang dynasty. Even the memory of Anyang sacrifices seems to have been lost. Western Zhou texts charge the Shang kings with drunkenness, not bloodiness. Eastern Zhou moralists and Han historians seem curiously unaware that the way of the former kings they so admired revolved around human sacrifice.

THE TOMB OF FU HAO. The tomb of Wu Ding's consort Fu Hao 婦好, excavated in 1976, is the only Anyang royal tomb discovered intact and also the only Anyang burial yet discovered whose occupant can be confidently identified with a person named in the oracle texts.[110] It is located 200 m west of the Xiaotun palace foundations, near several lesser burials of similar date.[111] Much smaller than the Xibeigang tombs, and without entrance ramps, it was a rectangular shaft only 4 by 5.6 m at the mouth and 7.5 m deep. Nevertheless it contained 1,600 kg of bronze and the largest assemblage of jades ever unearthed. The inventory includes 195 bronze vessels; 271 weapons, tools, and other small bronzes; 755 jades; 110 objects of marble, turquoise, and other

[110] The excavation report is *Yinxu Fu Hao mu*, 2d ed. (Beijing: Wenwu, 1984); the tomb furnishings are best illustrated in Zheng Zhenxiang and Chen Zhida, *Yinxu dixia guibao: Henan Anyang Fu Hao mu* (Beijing: Wenwu, 1994). Many of the bronzes and jades are published also in *Yinxu qingtongqi*, ed. Zhongguo Shehui kexueyuan Kaogu yanjiusuo (Beijing: Wenwu, 1985); and idem, *Yinxu yuqi* (Beijing: Wenwu, 1982). Fu Hao oracle inscriptions are discussed in the report (pp. 226–8) and in Wang Yuxin, Zhang Yongshan, and Yang Shengnan, "Shilun Yinxu wu hao mu de Fu Hao," *Kaogu xuebao* 1977.2: 1–22. Initial controversy over the identity of the tomb's occupant was inspired chiefly by a conviction that the bronzes were too advanced for Wu Ding's time (see *Kaogu* 1977.5: 341–50); the excavators' dating of the tomb is now generally accepted.
[111] *Kaogu xuebao* 1981.4: 491–518; Zheng Zhenxiang, "The Excavation of Tombs Number 17 and 18 and Their Significance," *EC* 7 (1981–2): 55–9.

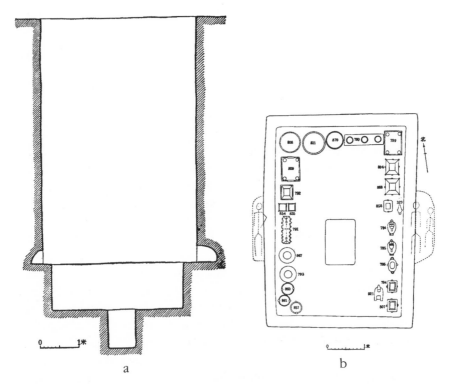

Figure 3.24. Fu Hao's tomb. Dimensions at mouth, 5.6 by 4 m; depth to shaft floor, 7.5 m. After *Yinxu Fu Hao mu* (Beijing: Wenwu, 1984), pp. 8, 14. (a) Vertical section. Niches for sacrificial victims are at the level of the *ercengtai*. (b) Plan, showing arrangement of major bronzes on floor.

stones; 564 objects of carved bone; 15 pieces of shell, probably inlays; 3 ivory cups, 2 inlaid with turquoise, of a kind previously known only from fragments found in M1001; and 11 pieces of pottery. If the Xibeigang tombs were richer than this, their contents are beyond imagining.[112]

The excavators believe that nested coffins of red and black lacquer nearly filled the bottom of the shaft, but this part of the tomb was under water and much damaged, and little survived of the coffins and their occupant. The shaft had only a very narrow *ercengtai* ledge (Fig. 3.24a), and most of the tomb furnishings had been placed inside the coffins. The largest bronzes were in the outer coffin, ranged along three sides of the inner one (Fig. 3.24b); the jades were in the inner coffin, along with nearly 7,000 cowry shells. Corrosion preserved textile imprints on more than fifty of the bronzes, suggesting

---

[112] The excavation report's rather mechanical classification of the tomb's contents is not followed in the present discussion. It produces misleading statistics, particularly in the case of the jades.

that they were put into the tomb wrapped in cloth. Eight human skeletons, some incomplete, were found in the outer coffin. Another was found with a dog in the *yaokeng*, four more were above the coffins, and three were in niches at the sides of the shaft.

Most of the bronze vessels and a few of the stone and jade items are inscribed. The tomb's occupant is assumed to be Fu Hao because more than a hundred bronzes carry this name. Another five, including two monumental *fangding*, are inscribed with the name Mu Xin 母辛, known from oracle texts as the posthumous name which Fu Hao's sons used in presenting sacrifices to her.[113] Since oracle texts are known in which Wu Ding asks about sacrifices to Fu Hao, she must have died before him; in these inquiries he addresses her as Fu Hao.[114] The excavation report, perhaps doubting that so many bronzes could have been cast for a funeral, suggests that the ones inscribed with Fu Hao's name were her possessions in life. This may underestimate the capacity of Anyang foundries, however, and it is worth considering the possibility that the vessels inscribed Fu Hao were made by Wu Ding. He must have contributed vessels to the tomb, and these are the only ones appropriately inscribed. Many of them are said to bear traces of soot, indicating use, but this is true also of the *fangding* inscribed to Mu Xin.

The assemblage of bronzes reflects Fu Hao's high status in at least three ways.[115] First, some of the vessels are of types that seldom or never occur in lesser tombs and that may therefore have been aristocratic luxuries rather than ritual necessities. Two *fanglei* and four *fangyi* 方彝, fairly rare types, fall into this category, along with a few unique items (e.g., a large casket called, for want of a better name, a double *fangyi*). A second category consists of vessels which, however common as types, are of uncommon size. Perhaps 56 of the vessels are distinctly above the sizes usual for their types. Thirty-four of these are inscribed to Fu Hao, but the 2 largest bronzes in the tomb, weighing 120 kg each, are the *fangding* dedicated to Mu Xin. Many of the large vessels are rectangular versions of normally round-bodied types; the tomb contained only 21 rectangular vessels, but they are so imposing that they dominate the assemblage. A third category consists of bronzes conspicuous not for size or shape but for sheer quantity. Most of Fu Hao's *jue* and *gu* are ordinary enough, but their numbers, 40 *jue* and 53 *gu*, are not. Where lesser aristocrats might have single items, Fu Hao had matched sets, sometimes with 5 or 10 items in a set. M18, a tomb near Fu Hao's and contemporary with it,

---

[113] On this and other Fu Hao inscriptions, see Li Xueqin, "Lun Fu Hao mu de niandai ji youguan wenti," *Wenwu* 1977.11: 32–7. The two *fangding* resemble the still larger *Si Mu Wu fangding* from Xibeigang M260, which has an inscription of similar form dedicated to another royal wife, possibly another of Wu Ding's consorts. See Bagley, *Shang Ritual Bronzes*, figs. 117, 133, and p. 55, n. 102.

[114] Wang Yuxin, Zhang Yongshan, and Yang Shengnan, "Shilun Yinxu wu hao mu de Fu Hao," pp. 18–20.

[115] Jessica Rawson, "Ancient Chinese Ritual Bronzes: The Evidence from Tombs and Hoards of the Shang and Western Zhou Periods," *Antiquity* 67 (1993): 805–23.

would be considered a rich burial if hers were not known, but it contained only 23 vessels, and they are mostly small and nondescript by comparison with hers. A functional classification of Fu Hao's vessels can only be tentative, since functions are by no means certain, but at a rough guess 144 of the 195 vessels are for wine. Only 6 of the 56 large bronzes are food vessels, but they include the 2 great *fangding* dedicated to Mu Xin. Almost all the major bronzes carry Style V decoration.[116]

Apart from vessels the bronzes are mostly tools and weapons, among them eighty-nine *ge* blades. Two large axe blades inscribed with Fu Hao's name might have been used to behead sacrificial victims at the funeral; at Anyang and elsewhere tombs with human sacrifice sometimes contain impressive axes (e.g., 3.36a from Lijiazui M2 at Panlongcheng). Twenty-three small bells are of two types, *nao* (3.29a–b) and *ling*. A few small ornaments and two cheek-pieces were the only objects of horse gear found in the tomb. Four bronze mirrors, a knife, and a pointed tool are imports or copies of imports from the Northern Zone, and six of the enigmatic artifacts called "bow-shaped objects," three with horsehead terminals, probably also belong in this category (Fig. 3.25).[117] These items reflect contact with the region from which, in Wu Ding's time, the chariot came to Anyang. Mirrors resembling the ones in Fu Hao's tomb have been found most often in northwestern China, sometimes in Qijia contexts; two from Qinghai were found with a shaft-hole axe of northern type.[118] Remembering also artifacts of Anyang type found in places remote from Anyang, such as the pair of *fanglei* resembling Fu Hao's found at Chenggu in Shaanxi, we must imagine Anyang as a partner in active exchange with neighbors in several directions.

Discussion of Fu Hao's jades requires first some consideration of the jade material itself.[119] Jade is an intractable mineral that can be worked only with

---

[116] Alloy analyses have been reported for sixty-four vessels and twelve weapons (*Kaoguxue jikan* 2 [1982]: 181–93). About three-quarters of the vessels are binary alloys, typically 15–20 percent tin; the remainder are ternary alloys with less tin and up to 6 percent lead. The weapons have little or no lead and a more variable tin content, with corresponding variation in hardness. A point of technical interest is that the members of matched sets are reported to be cast from models decorated independently (Hua Jueming et al., "Fu Hao mu qingtongqi qun zhuzao jishu de yanjiu"). Since reconstructions of casting technology suggest no obvious reason for not reusing a decorated model (see Bagley, *Shang Ritual Bronzes*, p. 60, n. 174), it seems possible that our reconstructions are somehow at fault.

[117] See below, under "The Northern Zone", (pp. 221–6), and see Lin Yun, "Northern Zone," pp. 250–4, 263–6.

[118] Li Hancai, "Qinghai Huangzhong xian faxian gudai shuangma tong yue he tong jing," *Wenwu* 1992.2: 16.

[119] Fu Hao's jades are reported to be mostly nephrite or nephrite-related minerals; trace-element analysis of five pieces suggests Khotan in Xinjiang province as a likely source (Shen Bin, "Fu Hao mu yuqi cailiao tan yuan," *Zhongyuan wenwu* 1991.1: 73–8). On provenance studies, see Rawson, *Chinese Jade*, pp. 413–23; Wen Guang and Jing Zhichun, "Fengxi Xi Zhou yuqi dizhi kaoguxue yanjiu," *Kaogu xuebao* 1993.2: 251–80. On jade-working technology, see *Yinxu de faxian yu yanjiu*, pp. 325–8. The jades from the Xin'gan tomb include one technical tour de force not seen among Fu Hao's jades, a figurine with a chain of freely moving links (Peng Shifan et al., *Changjiang zhongyou qingtong wangguo*, no. 86).

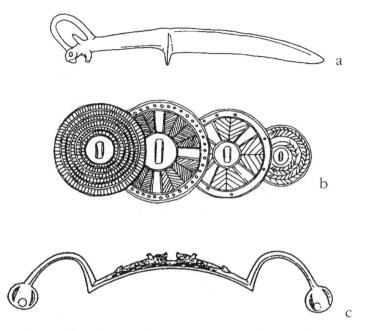

Figure 3.25. Bronzes of northern style, from Fu Hao's tomb. Not to scale. (a) Knife. Length 36.2 cm. After Lin Yun, "A Reexamination of the Relationship Between Bronzes of the Shang Culture and of the Northern Zone," in *Studies of Shang Archaeology: Selected Papers from the International Conference on Shang Civilization*, ed. K. C. Chang (New Haven, Conn.: Yale University Press, 1986), p. 252. (b) Mirrors. Diameters from 12.5 to 7.1 cm. After ibid. (c) Bow-shaped object. Length 40.4 cm. After *Yinxu qingtongqi* (Beijing: Wenwu, 1985), fig. 31:3.

abrasives. The effort required to shape it is clearly visible in the most unusual of Fu Hao's jades, two dozen stiff figurines whose finished forms are not far removed from the rectangular blocks with which the carver began (Fig. 3.26). Flat objects were more amenable to the jade worker's technique, and throughout the Bronze Age they were more common and more accomplished (Figs. 3.14, 3.27d, 3.35). The first step in manufacturing a plaque, disk, blade, or any other flat item was to saw the pebble of raw jade into slices. Designing an object consisted of drawing it on the surface of the slab in a way that took advantage of any attractive coloration, avoided any defects, and wasted as little of the stone as possible. The role of these constraints is best illustrated by the most obvious examples, such as two small turtles given dark shells and light bodies by exploiting the veining of the raw material,[120] but their effect was more telling when their operation was more subtle. The object drawn

---

[120] Found at Xiaotun in what is thought to have been a small jade workshop (*Yinxu yuqi*, pl. 67).

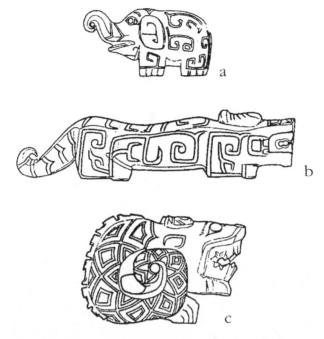

Figure 3.26. Three-dimensional jade animals, from Fu Hao's tomb. Anyang, ca. 1200 B.C. After *Yinxu Fu Hao mu* (Beijing: Wenwu, 1984), p. 157. To the same scale. (a) Elephant. Length 6.5 cm, height 3.3 cm. (b) Tiger(?). Length 14.1 cm, height 3.5 cm. (c) Dragon. Length 8.1 cm, height 5.6 cm.

on the slab was cut out jigsaw fashion, sometimes decorated with incised surface patterns, and polished. The tools which applied the abrasive were saws, drills, and probably a small rotating disk that sped up the incising of fine lines on surfaces. Many jades are obviously recut from other jades, perhaps in salvage of broken items, reminding us of the intrinsic value of the raw material and also of the extent to which designs were inspired by particular pieces of material. Many small fishes in Fu Hao's tomb were clearly recut from collared disks, and an openwork plaque in the shape of a bird and a dragon retains the median crest of a *ge* blade.[121] Paired items were often sliced from a single piece of jade,[122] and some jade types may have originated as pieces left over from the manufacture of others (tubular beads from the perforations of disks?). The combination of a narrow technical repertoire and a costly raw material each piece of which had its own character engendered

[121] Ibid., pl. 15, and cf. pl. 6; and Zheng Zhenxiang and Chen Zhida, *Yinxu dixia guibao*, p. 133.
[122] *Yinxu yuqi*, pl. 94.

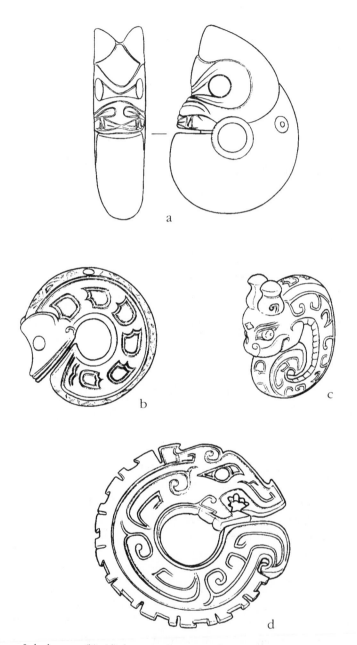

Figure 3.27. Jade dragons, (b)–(d) drawn to the same scale, (a) drawn at half that scale. Drawings by Li Xiating. (a) Neolithic, Hongshan culture, third to second millennium B.C., from Jianping, Liaoning. Height 15 cm. (b) From Fu Hao's tomb. Diameter 5.8 cm. (c) From Fu Hao's tomb. Height 5.2 cm. (d) From Fu Hao's tomb. Diameter 7.8 cm.

a two-dimensional art that put its emphasis on surface, silhouette, and the material itself.

Some of Fu Hao's jades are undecorated; *ge* blades, disks, rings, and bracelets often derive their interest from shape, material, and polish alone. The majority, however, have decoration of one kind or another. With flat slabs as the normal starting point and sawing the easiest technique, jaggedly sawn edges that concentrate attention on silhouettes were a natural embellishment used at least as early as the Erlitou period (Fig. 3.14d). More common on Fu Hao's jades are linear surface patterns less easy to execute (Figs. 3.26, 3.27d). The lines of such patterns appear to stand in relief, but as a rule the surface surrounding them was not uniformly ground down; instead the appearance of relief was given by grinding trenches on either side of the desired line. Painstakingly executed lines in true thread relief are seen on Neolithic jades of the Shijiahe 石家何 culture, including one that Fu Hao owned,[123] and the Anyang technique may have aimed to produce a similar effect by a shortcut. The lines on Fu Hao's jades have none of the fluency that suddenly appears, perhaps because of some improved technique or abrasive, on jades of the middle Western Zhou period.

The inventory of Fu Hao's jades contains several surprises. One is the conspicuous absence of large trapezoidal knives and arc-ended blades, types known first from Erlitou (Fig. 3.14d) and then in very large numbers from Sanxingdui in Sichuan (Fig. 3.35a–b), the latter examples roughly contemporary with Fu Hao's tomb.[124] Apart from a single knife that imitates a standard metal form, the only large blades in the tomb were *ge*; since there were thirty-nine of these, we may wonder whether Fu Hao sought them for their magical efficacy or from sheer acquisitiveness.[125] A few of the jades are recognizable as imports: tubular beads and a few other items are likely to be of southern manufacture,[126] and an isolated verbal record of traffic in luxuries is the inscription "X sent in five *ge*" incised on one jade *ge*, recalling notations sometimes found on oracle plastrons.[127] But the most startling feature

---

[123] Zheng Zhenxiang and Chen Zhida, *Yinxu dixia guibao*, pl. 56. On Shijiahe, see Rawson, *Chinese Jade*, pp. 199–204.

[124] For these two types, see Rawson, *Chinese Jade*, pp. 184–91. Apparently no arc-ended blade has ever been found at Anyang.

[125] One (no. 922, 43.5 cm long, *Yinxu Fu Hao mu*, color pl. 17:1) is almost identical to the *ge* found in the central guardian pit of M1001 (Gao Quxun, *Houjiazhuang*, vol. 2, pl. 108:1). Compare also the slightly larger *ge* from the *yaokeng* of M260 (*Kaogu xuebao* 1987.1 pl. 12:1).

[126] Compare jades from Xin'gan (Peng Shifan et al., *Changjiang zhongyou qingtong wangguo*, pls. 77–8, 87–8, 94–5) and jade beads found in a bronze vessel rumored to come from Anhui or Zhejiang (Bagley, *Shang Ritual Bronzes*, p. 373).

[127] *Yinxu Fu Hao mu*, p. 131; Zheng Zhenxiang and Chen Zhida, *Yinxu dixia guibao*, pl. 93. A similar inscription appears on a chime stone (*Yinxu Fu Hao mu*, pp. 198–9). A few bronzes in the tomb that bear names not obviously connected with Fu Hao have similarly been explained as imported items (ibid., pp. 96–9), but the names could be accounted for in many ways and the bronzes are not obviously exotic.

of the assemblage is a diverse group of Neolithic jades, some perhaps a thousand years old by Fu Hao's time. They include items from the Shijiahe culture of Hubei, the Liangzhu 良渚 culture of the lower Yangzi region, the Longshan 龍山 culture of Shandong, and the Hongshan 紅山 culture of the far northeast.[128] Hongshan jades were evidently well enough known at Anyang to inspire a variety of imitations: jade animals coiled into a ring in Fu Hao's tomb seem to represent stages in the naturalization of a foreign type, ending with flat dragon-shaped plaques decorated in standard Anyang fashion (Fig. 3.27).[129]

Imports and heirlooms, conspicuous among Fu Hao's jades, are less in evidence among her bronze vessels. The difference says something about the functions of jades and bronzes and their reasons for being in the tomb. The jades probably accompanied Fu Hao in death simply because they were prized possessions in life. Many are perforated for suspension, and it may be that the vast majority were ornaments or other cherished objects of high value. Certainly Neolithic jades that were already ancient when Fu Hao acquired them were not apparatus for Anyang rituals but valuables handed down from generation to generation or perhaps mined from ancient burials. Bronze vessels on the other hand must have had specific ritual functions to perform; the regular composition of funerary sets implies as much. No random collection of heirlooms and imports could be relied upon to serve these functions, and with few exceptions Fu Hao's bronzes look uniformly up to date.[130]

CHARIOTS. The horse-drawn chariot appeared at Anyang about the time of Wu Ding. The earliest archaeological traces date from his time, and since there is no sign of any other wheeled vehicle at Anyang, the vehicle depicted in a graph that occurs in the oracle inscriptions of his reign is almost certainly a chariot. In China the chariot appears in the archaeological record fully formed, unheralded by any previous use of animal traction or wheeled vehicles and identical in most respects to vehicles with a long history in

---

[128] Hayashi Minao, "Inkyo Fukô bo shutsudo no gyokki jakkan ni taisuru chûshaku," *Tôhô gakuhô* (Kyoto) 58 (1986): 1–70; Rawson, *Chinese Jade*, pp. 40–3 and passim.

[129] Rawson, *Chinese Jade*, pp. 209–12.

[130] For a review of archaeological evidence bearing on the functions of jades, see Rawson, *Chinese Jade*. As Rawson emphasizes, the uses and associations of jade types are so changeable that it is very unsafe to assume that a given type had at Anyang the same function it is recorded as having in some later period. In naming and sorting Fu Hao's jades according to criteria derived from traditional lore, the excavation report assumes functions for which there is no evidence and in the process obscures actual typological relationships; its classification was criticized by Xia Nai, who nevertheless based his own ideas on the same anachronistic lore (Hsia Nai, "The Classification, Nomenclature, and Usage of Shang Dynasty Jades," in *Studies of Shang Archaeology*, ed. K. C. Chang, pp. 207–36). In the absence of evidence that any jade shape other than the *ge* had a ritual function, even the vague term "ritual jade" seems risky.

western Asia. It represents a complex package of skills and technologies, and its advent therefore acquires special interest as a clue to the external relations of the Anyang civilization.

Chariots figure in the archaeological record in orderly burials, usually with horses and sometimes with charioteers, sometimes in or near tombs (traces of a chariot were found in the shaft of M1001 at Xibeigang) and sometimes as independent sacrifices (five chariot burials near the Xiaotun foundations are so interpreted). The number of such burials excavated at Anyang has now reached about twenty.[131] Most contained one or two chariots (though in one case an estimated twenty-five), two horses for each chariot, and in about half the known burials, from one to three human skeletons. The only contemporary chariot known elsewhere, from a burial at Laoniupo 老牛坡 near Xi'an 西安 in Shaanxi, is indistinguishable from chariots found at Anyang.[132] Although vehicle burial is widely encountered in the Near East, Egypt, and Europe, it does not seem necessary to assume some widely diffused idea to explain the practice. Chariot burial must have been a natural way of asserting the status of the deceased simply because chariots and their horse teams were luxuries of such high cost that they inevitably signaled rank.[133]

Buried chariots likely to be as early as Wu Ding's reign are not well preserved, little besides their bronze fittings having survived. In somewhat later burials excavators have managed to recover complete ghosts of chariots, that is, earth casts formed by fine soil that infiltrated the cavities left by the decay of wooden parts. A fairly complete and typical example is the pit M52, dated Yinxu 4, excavated at Guojiazhuang 郭家莊 in 1987 (Fig. 3.28).[134] M52 is one of a group of three pits, all perhaps connected with an unlocated tomb. One contained the skeletons of a man and two horses; another probably contained a chariot but had been destroyed by later digging; the third, M52, contained

---

[131] A useful inventory appears in Yang Baocheng, "Yin dai chezi de faxian yu fuyuan," *Kaogu* 1984.6: 546–55 (it is reproduced in Yang's discussion of chariots in *Yinxu de faxian yu yanjiu*, pp. 138–47); other writers give slightly different counts, and at least two burials have been reported since Yang's paper was published. See also Lu Liancheng, "Chariot and Horse Burials in Ancient China," *Antiquity* 67 (1993): 824–38; Edward L. Shaughnessy, "Historical Perspectives on the Introduction of the Chariot into China," *HJAS* 48 (1988): 189–237; and, for terminology, Sun Ji, "Zhongguo gu duzhou mache de jiegou," *Wenwu* 1985.8: 25–40.

[132] *Wenwu* 1988.6: 1–22; the excavators take the Laoniupo chariot to be roughly contemporary with Wu Ding's reign. A chariot burial is said to have been excavated in 1965–6 at Sufutun in Shandong, but no report has been published.

[133] In Egypt and the Near East, chariots were gifts exchanged by kings; in the Amarna letters "wishes for the welfare of a brother sovereign's chariot team are placed directly after those for himself and the royal family" (M. A. Littauer and J. H. Crouwel, *Chariots and Related Equipment from the Tomb of Tutankhamun* [Oxford: Griffith Institute, 1985], p. 97; in Egypt the vehicles were included in tombs, but not their horses or drivers). In Western Zhou bronze inscriptions, chariots and chariot fittings rank high in the bounty conferred by the king on subordinates (Shaughnessy, "Historical Perspectives on the Introduction of the Chariot into China," p. 222), and late Eastern Zhou texts such as the *Zuo zhuan* 左傳 attest to a similar valuation.

[134] *Kaogu* 1988.10: 882–93. Guojiazhuang is 300 m southwest of Gaolouzhuang 高樓莊.

Figure 3.28. Chariot burial, Guojiazhuang M52, Anyang. Yinxu 4, eleventh century B.C. After *Kaogu* 1988.10: pl. 4.

a chariot, the skeletons of two men about twenty-five to thirty years old, and the skeletons of two horses. This third pit was square, about 3.5 m on a side and 1.8 m deep. The horses and men had been killed and laid in the pit before the chariot was lowered into place. The wheels, axle, and draft pole fitted into trenches that allowed the chariot box to rest on the bottom of the pit, taking the weight off the wheels and saving them from deformation; perhaps this imitated the normal way of parking a chariot (otherwise the wheels of a parked vehicle probably had to be removed). In M52, however, the wheels had been deformed by the pounded-earth fill of the pit, which bent the draft pole as well. The man beside the horses lay prone on matting with his head turned to the side and his hands tied behind him. A piece of patterned red cloth covered his lower body. The second man lay prone behind the chariot and was sprinkled with cinnabar. Cinnabar was also found beneath the horses. M52 contained no weapons; weapons have been found in only about half of the Anyang chariot burials so far excavated (bronze knives, arrowheads, and *ge* blades, not in any regular combination).

The M52 chariot was unusually large but standard in construction. It had two spoked wheels which rotated on a fixed axle. The axle was located halfway between the front and back edges of the chariot box. The draft pole, a square timber 268 cm long, rested on top of the axle and curved upward from the underside of the box to the height of the yoke. The yoke, 235 cm long, carried inverted-V-shaped yoke saddles which rested on the horses' necks forward of the withers. The yoke was curved; though the graph for chariot in the oracle-bone and bronze scripts depicts a curved yoke, all examples previously excavated at Anyang were straight. The wheels had eighteen spokes and were about 140 cm in diameter. The construction of the felloes (wheel rims) was not clear, but in other Anyang chariots they were made from as few as two pieces of bent wood into which the spokes were mortised. Bronze axle caps with wood linchpins kept the wheels in place on the axle, but the wheels themselves had no metal parts (the felloes and hubs of Zhou chariots were sometimes reinforced with metal fittings). The axle had an overall length of 308 cm and the distance between the wheels was 230 cm.

The chariot box sat on top of the draft pole and axle. It measured a meter and a half from side to side and nearly a meter from front to back, easily large enough for three kneeling passengers. The sides of the box were formed by a lattice of wooden bars about 50 cm high; the entrance, 40 cm wide, was at the back. Traces of red and black lacquer were found on the floor and sides, and it may be that all the wood parts of the chariot were lacquered, for protective as well as decorative reasons. Yoke saddles, axle caps, a mechanism for joining the draft pole to the box, and a few small ornaments were made of bronze. The horses wore bronze frontlets, headstalls ornamented with cowry shells, and perhaps red cloth, and one had a bronze bell of the type *ling* at its neck. No bits or cheekpieces were found, but both are known from other Anyang chariot burials.[135]

---

[135] Yinxu Xiqu 西區 M1613 contained both, the bits formed of two linked pieces (*Kaogu* 1984.6: 505–9). A pair of cheekpieces was found in Fu Hao's tomb (*Yinxu Fu Hao mu*, p. 110 and pl. 74:5). Since Anyang chariot burials supply little evidence of harnessing systems, reconstructions of harnessing must depend on much later evidence, notably two bronze carts found at the tomb of Qin Shihuangdi 秦 始皇帝; see Lu Liancheng, "Chariot and Horse Burials in Ancient China," pp. 831–3; Barbara Stephen,

The absence of weapons from the burial and the decoration of the chariot were taken by the excavators to indicate that it was a passenger vehicle rather than a war chariot. It is not structurally different from chariots found in burials that do contain weapons, however, nor is there any reason to suppose that chariots taken to battle were plain (no matter how richly decorated the chariot might be, the team of horses that drew it was more precious). No chariot box with higher sides has been found at Anyang, and since the sides of the M52 chariot box would come only to the knees of a standing passenger, it seems unlikely that Anyang chariots were ridden standing. The use of such chariots in battle is uncertain. They could have served as showy vehicles for commanders or as transport for shifting special troops rapidly from one part of the field to another; kneeling archers could perhaps have fought from them. Though the chariot's passengers were sometimes armed, it does not follow that the weapons they carried were intended for use from moving chariots; in a society of warrior aristocrats, weapons are articles of apparel.[136]

By Near Eastern standards Anyang chariots are unusually large. Six chariots preserved in the fourteenth-century tomb of Tutankhamun, intended for one or two standing passengers and thus with railings reaching to hip height, had floor dimensions averaging 103 cm wide and 47 cm front to back; the wheels averaged 93 cm in diameter, and the distance between them (wheel track) averaged 170 cm.[137] The same measurements are available for six Anyang chariots, and for this sample the corresponding averages are: floor dimensions 134 by 85 cm, wheel diameter 137 cm, wheel track 227 cm.[138] Evidently Anyang chariots carried more passengers, less swiftly. The floor of the chariot in M52 was wood, but some Anyang chariots, like some Egyptian ones, had floors of plaited leather, meant no doubt to soften a jolting mode of transport. Two unusual features of Anyang chariots are the large number of wheel spokes (anywhere from eighteen to twenty-six, as compared with

---

"Formal Variation in Shang Dynasty Vehicles," in *Proceedings: International Colloquium on Chinese Art History, 1991, Antiquities, Part 1* (Taipei: National Palace Museum, 1992), pp. 119–21; Sun Ji, "Zhongguo gudai mache de jijia fa," *Ziran kexue shi yanjiu* 3, 2 (1984): 169–76. On disputed details of chariot reconstruction, see Shi Zhangru, "Yin che fuyuan shuoming," *BIHP* 58 (1987): 253–80 and references cited there.

[136] Shaughnessy suggests that the active functions chariots later had in warfare only gradually accrued to vehicles that served first for elegant transport ("Historical Perspectives on the Introduction of the Chariot into China"), but the function of chariots even in later periods is by no means clear. The literature discussing the battlefield uses of Near Eastern chariots is instructive, though it concerns vehicles ridden standing (P. R. S. Moorey, "The Emergence of the Light, Horse-Drawn Chariot in the Near East c. 2000–1500 B.C.," *World Archaeology* 18 [1986]: 203–4; M. A. Littauer and J. H. Crouwel, *Wheeled Vehicles and Ridden Animals in the Ancient Near East* [Leiden: Brill, 1979], pp. 90–4 and passim).

[137] Littauer and Crouwel, *Chariots and Related Equipment from the Tomb of Tutankhamun*, p. 91.

[138] Excavations at Anyang in 1986–7, south of Xiaotun at Huayuanzhuang 花園莊, came upon parallel ruts left by a two-wheeled vehicle with a wheel track of about 1.5 m (*Kaogu xuebao* 1992.1: 124). Whether the vehicle was a chariot or some other conveyance could not be determined.

four, six, or eight in the Near East) and the mounting of the axle not at the rear edge of the box but midway between front and back. In western Asia both features are known only from mid-second-millennium chariots buried at Lchashen in the Caucasus, and for the moment these are the closest relatives of Anyang chariots.[139]

The horse-drawn chariot is a technically sophisticated artifact requiring special skills and resources for its construction, use, and maintenance.[140] To form some notion of the interaction that brought it to China it is helpful to review these novelties briefly. Horses were not native to China but probably existed in Mongolia. Although domestication of the horse goes back at least to the fourth millennium B.C. in the steppes of western Asia, horses were not used there as draft animals until after long experience with oxen, donkeys, and other equids. On present archaeological evidence, animal traction, whether with vehicles or for plowing, whether with horses or with less high-strung animals, had no history in China prior to the appearance of horse-drawn chariots at Anyang. Training horses to work in pairs is a job for experienced handlers who must have come from a region where domesticated horses were already familiar, and maintaining a supply of horses required horse traders and breeders, horse breakers, and ostlers. Even limited use of chariots thus seems to imply a trade with regions to the north which not only procured horses, but also, at least at first, brought experts to Anyang.

Speed, the chariot's raison d'être, depended on horse traction and on light construction, above all on spoked wheels.[141] In western Asia and Europe chariots were preceded by heavy ox-drawn conveyances with one-part or three-part solid disk wheels, attested as early as the fourth millennium B.C. The weight of a third-millennium European wagon, the product of stone-tool carpentry, might be 600 or 700 kg. By Tutankhamun's time sophisticated joinery, carefully chosen woods, and spoked wheels had achieved vehicles as light as 35 kg. In China no wheels of any kind earlier than the spoked wheels of Anyang chariots have been found.[142] In some cases these wheels have two-piece felloes that must have been shaped by heat bending, a technique that

[139] Stuart Piggott, *The Earliest Wheeled Transport* (Ithaca, N.Y.: Cornell University Press, 1983), pp. 95–7; Stuart Piggott, *Wagon, Chariot and Carriage* (London: Thames & Hudson, 1992), pp. 63–6; and Shaughnessy, "Historical Perspectives on the Introduction of the Chariot into China," pp. 200–201, 206–7.

[140] On chariotry as a technological complex, see Piggott, *Wagon, Chariot and Carriage*, pp. 45–8. On its arrival in Egypt, perhaps in the wake of the Hyksos occupation, as a package that included the horse and possibly also the composite bow, see Littauer and Crouwel, *Wheeled Vehicles and Ridden Animals in the Ancient Near East*, p. 76.

[141] On carpentry, wood-bending techniques, and wheel construction, see Piggott, *The Earliest Wheeled Transport*, pp. 27–9; and Piggott, *Wagon, Chariot and Carriage*, pp. 17, 44–6.

[142] Piggott (*Wagon, Chariot and Carriage*, p. 14) rejects any connection between wheeled transport and spindle whorls or potter's wheels; in the abstract, all qualify as rotary motion, but nowhere in the world do they appear together in the archaeological record.

might also have been employed in the manufacture of composite bows (known at Anyang from epigraphic evidence). Skilled carpenters were needed not only to build chariots, but also to keep them in running order. Harness making was another essential specialty.

The management of a two-horse chariot in parade, not to mention whatever maneuvering and tactics were required for hunting and war, was the business of a skilled charioteer. The driver on whom a high-ranking warrior depended is likely to have been of higher status than an ordinary soldier, and at the beginning he might have been a foreigner (in some Near Eastern societies charioteers were an elite class of foreigners). Like handlers and wheelwrights, charioteers had skills that could be passed on only at first hand, requiring demonstration and practice. Although the association of knives and chariots is not very consistent, bronze knives of northern type found in Anyang chariot burials have sometimes been taken to indicate that the charioteers included in the burials were northerners.

Anyang chariot burials thus seem to indicate a substantial interaction with northern neighbors beginning about 1200 B.C.: not an invasion, but not a border incident either. The mere capture of enemy chariots and horses would not have brought the skills required to use, maintain, and reproduce them. Northern bronzes, including knives and bow-shaped objects, appear in the Anyang archaeological record at the same time as chariots and, whether or not they had any functional connection with chariots, might have arrived with them.[143] The clearly marked advent of the chariot is a clue to an episode of cultural contact that deserves more attention than it has received.

The Middle Yangzi Region: Southern Hubei, Northern Hunan

During the Erligang period, bronzes were cast in one unvarying style throughout their range of distribution, making it appropriate to speak of an Erligang horizon. This uniformity broke down during the transition period. In the time of the Anyang kings the manufacture of bronze vessels was spread over a wider region than ever before, but nowhere within that region was there any very large area of uniform style. There was no Anyang horizon; on the contrary, this was a time of flourishing local industries.

On the evidence of material culture the most sophisticated contemporaries of the Anyang civilization were located in the middle and lower Yangzi region. Despite variation within it, this region had an overarching cultural

---

[143] Knives appear in only four of the burials listed by Yang Baocheng ("Yin dai chezi de faxian yu fuyuan"); bow-shaped objects are slightly more common, but they are not associated exclusively with chariot burials (Fu Hao's tomb contained six: see Fig. 3.25c).

unity that manifests itself in the archaeological record in finds of large bells.[144] The most common type is the *nao*, a clapperless bell mounted mouth-upward and sounded by striking the outside wall near the mouth. Bells of this type are found at Anyang, but at Anyang they are minor artifacts, small and scantily decorated, and so rare that they cannot have been essential to ritual. Examples from the south are large and lavishly decorated. Though no bell of any kind has yet been found at an Erligang site, it seems likely that both Anyang and southern *nao* derive from an Erligang prototype which in the north had only modest progeny but which in the south inspired monumental artifacts. In the lower Yangzi region the type was well established by the transition period; the Xin'gan tomb, which represents the southern bronze industry at a formative stage, contained three examples. *Nao* from the middle Yangzi region are later and larger. Typical of Anyang *nao* are the five found in Fu Hao's tomb, the largest of which is 14 cm high and weighs 600 grams. Bells from the south belong to another world (Fig. 3.29). The largest so far reported, from Ningxiang 寧鄉 in northern Hunan, weighs 220 kg.[145]

The middle Yangzi region of southern Hubei and northern Hunan has yielded the largest number of southern bronze finds, not only bells but also vessels. Few objects here are as early as the transition period; a remarkable exception is a large drum from Hubei decorated in Style III (Fig. 3.5). The finds seem often to be deposits unconnected with burials, sometimes a deposit of only a single item. Occasionally a vessel was buried filled with jades. Ningxiang has repeatedly been the scene of spectacular discoveries, including at least ten large bells, five found together in one pit.[146] In technical quality southern castings yield nothing to bronzes from Anyang, and they are often significantly larger than their Anyang counterparts. The repertoire of types is limited: bells are the most common items, followed by large *zun* and *lei* (Fig. 3.34a),[147] and then by vessels in animal shape (elephants, buf-

[144] Large bells were first suggested as the defining artifact of a distinctive Yangzi bronze industry by Virginia Kane in her 1974–5 article "The Independent Bronze Industries in the South of China Contemporary with the Shang and Western Zhou Dynasties." See also Fong, *Great Bronze Age of China*, no. 19; Bagley, "Changjiang Bronzes and Shang Archaeology," pp. 216–18; and, for a detailed survey, Bagley, *Shang Ritual Bronzes*, pp. 32–6. Apart from studies of bells by Gao Zhixi ("Shang and Zhou Period Bronze Musical Instruments from South China," *BSOAS* 55 [1992]: 262–71, and others cited there), the Chinese archaeological literature has generally ignored the local character of southern bronzes.

[145] Anyang *nao* were sometimes made in graduated sets of three with matching decoration, but the sets have randomly assorted pitches; southern *nao* have not been found in matched sets. For tone measurements of Anyang *nao*, see Lothar von Falkenhausen, *Suspended Music: Chime-Bells in the Culture of Bronze Age China* (Berkeley: University of California Press, 1993), pp. 228–9.

[146] For bronzes from Ningxiang, see Bagley, *Shang Ritual Bronzes*, figs. 163–5, 167, 174 (four-ram *zun* now in the Historical Museum, Beijing), 187 (*fangding* decorated with human faces), 57.4, 64.2, and 64.4–5 (*you* vessels filled with jades), and 93.3.

[147] See Bagley, *Shang Ritual Bronzes*, no. 43; and, for a Zhengzhou ancestor of Hubei/Hunan *lei*, *Wenwu* 1983.3: 49–59, pl. 4:2.

Figure 3.29. Bronze bells of the type *nao*. To the same scale. Drawings by Li Xiating. (a–b) The smallest (height 7.7 cm) and largest (height 14.4 cm) of five from the tomb of Fu Hao, ca. 1200 B.C. (c) From Ningxiang, Hunan, twelfth to eleventh century B.C. Height 71 cm, weight 67.25 kg.

faloes, even a boar; Fig. 3.30). Animals were favorite motifs in the south, not the formalized imaginary animals of Anyang bronzes but real animals treated with affectionate naturalism. A few vessels unearthed in Hunan are likely to have been imported from Anyang, and local casters occasionally made use of Anyang ideas, but these were small perturbations in a self-assured local industry. Find contexts, the repertoire of types, extravagant size, eccentricities of shape and decoration – in all these features southern bronzes advertise a civilization sharply different from that of Anyang. The narrow range of types, dominated by large bells, must signify important differences of ritual. The knowledge of bronze casting that had been transmitted to the south in the Erligang period was put to local purposes by a local culture.

Castings that weigh 200 kg are not the products of simple villages; only

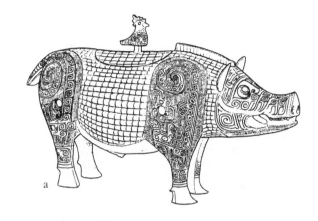

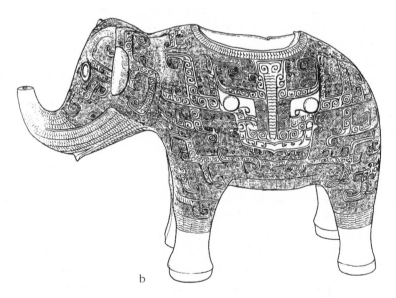

Figure 3.30. (a) Bronze boar, from Xiangtan, Hunan. Height 40 cm, length 72 cm. (b) Bronze elephant, said to be from Changsha. Height 64 cm, length 96 cm. Musée Guimet, Paris (EO1545). Both thirteenth to twelfth century B.C. To the same scale. Drawings by Li Xiating.

one Anyang bronze, the *Si Mu Wu fangding*, is larger than this, and it is not flawless. If our knowledge of civilization in the Yangzi region rests on bronzes rather than cities, if we have no city site in Hunan to compare with Anyang, this is because Anyang has been a focus of archaeological investigation for decades and Hunan has not. Even the haphazard evidence of chance finds is sufficient to establish the presence in the south of civilized centers with far-flung connections, and it seems likely that developments in the north, the rise of the Zhou in particular, will not be properly understood until the Yangzi region has been better explored.

The Chengdu Plain: Sanxingdui

In 1980 Sichuan archaeologists began excavating the site of a walled city at a place called Sanxingdui 三星堆 in Guanghan 廣漢 county, 40 km north of Chengdu 成都. They established that the city wall was a *hangtu* construction and estimated that it was built at about the same time as the Zhengzhou city wall or perhaps even earlier. Surviving parts measure up to 6 m high and 40 m thick at the base. Though most of the wall is destroyed, it seems to have enclosed an area of 2.6 sq. km, almost as large as the area within the walls at Zhengzhou. Building foundations were excavated inside the wall, and outside it settlement debris has been found over an area of about 12 sq. km (as compared with 25 sq. km at Zhengzhou). Sanxingdui was clearly a major city, a point dramatically underscored in 1986 when two remarkable sacrificial deposits were found at the site. Judging from their contents, the two pits differ slightly in date, representing sacrifices performed perhaps a few decades apart. A convenient rough approximation for their dates might be just before and just after the tomb of Fu Hao, here dated ca. 1200 B.C.[148]

Pit 1, the earlier of the two, was a rectangular pit measuring 4.6 by 3.5 m at the top and 1.6 m deep. It contained more than 300 artifacts of bronze, jade, and gold, along with cowry shells, thirteen elephant tusks, and more than three cubic meters of burnt animal bones (no trace of human skeletons was found). Since the artifacts showed signs of burning while the pit itself did not, the excavators concluded that the deposit was the result of an offering ceremony in which animals were killed and burned, artifacts were burned and in some cases broken, and the remains of both were pushed into the pit and covered with pounded earth. No similar ritual is known from any other site (sacrificial pits at Anyang typically contain human victims and few if any

---

[148] For the city and the pits, see Robert W. Bagley, "A Shang City in Sichuan Province," *Orientations*, November 1990, pp. 52–67, and idem, "Sacrificial Pits of the Shang Period at Sanxingdui in Guanghan County, Sichuan Province," *Arts Asiatiques* 43 (1988): 78–86; Roger Goepper et al., *Das Alte China, Menschen und Götter im Reich der Mitte* (Essen: Kulturstiftung Ruhr, 1995), pp. 115–29 and 248–77 (the map on p. 118, which in some respects contradicts other descriptions, represents the excavators' latest thinking as to the layout of the site). Preliminary excavation reports are published in *Wenwu* 1987.10: 1–15 (pit 1) and *Wenwu* 1989.5: 1–20 (pit 2). Many articles on the site have appeared in *Sichuan wenwu* and other journals; some are collected in Li Shaoming, Lin Xiang, and Zhao Dianzeng, eds. *Sanxingdui yu Ba Shu wenhua* (Chengdu: Ba Shu, 1993). The artifacts are best illustrated in Chen De'an, *Shang dai Shu ren mibao: Sichuan Guanghan Sanxingdui yiji* (Beijing: Wenwu, 1994); and *Zhongguo qingtongqi quanji, 13, Ba Shu*.

bronzes or jades), but the objects in the pit were so strange that it is hardly surprising that the ceremony in which they were used was also strange. Many of the jades were unusual, and life-sized bronze heads were artifacts of a kind never seen before.

The second pit was similar but richer. The contents were more neatly disposed, in three layers, with small items (including more than a hundred jades) at the bottom, large bronzes in the middle layer (Fig. 3.31), and more than sixty elephant tusks in the top layer. The bronzes included a life-size statue on a pedestal (Fig. 3.32); forty-one heads, some masked with gold leaf, their eyes and mouths sometimes painted with vermilion (Fig. 3.33a); about twenty masklike items varying in size and also in character, some comparatively human but others like monstrous animals (Fig. 3.33b); three astonishing bronze trees, the largest over 4 m tall, found in fragments;[149] and a dozen large vessels – the most ordinary and familiar of the artifacts, and for that reason reassuring guides to the dating of an otherwise bewildering find. The vessels are all of the types *zun* and *lei*; they match examples from the middle Yangzi region and may well have been imported from there (Fig. 3.34). Trade along the Yangzi is suggested by metal provenance studies also: some of the Sanxingdui bronzes, not only vessels but items of undoubted local manufacture such as heads, monstrous faces, trees, and the statue, are reported to contain lead of an unusual isotopic composition that matches lead in bronzes from the Xin'gan tomb, implying a common ore source.[150] Clearly the civilizations of the Chengdu Plain and the middle Yangzi region were in contact. Equally clearly, they were distinct, for the bronze heads and masks from Sanxingdui have no parallel in Hubei or Hunan, and the large *nao* bells of the middle Yangzi region have not been found in Sichuan. The only bells at Sanxingdui are two clappered bells of bizarre shape and several *ling*, some with decoration.[151]

Neither the bronzes nor anything else in the Sanxingdui pits shows much sign of contact with Anyang. The inventory of jades, notably unlike Fu Hao's, is dominated by disks and large blades – arc-ended blades, trapezoidal knives, and *ge* blades (some resembling Fu Hao's), all exceedingly varied in design. Some of the arc-ended blades are reasonably close to examples from Erlitou,

[149] The largest tree, carrying peachlike fruits and inhabited by birds and a dragon, is shown reassembled in Goepper, *Das Alte China*, p. 125; for a detail of the lower part, see Chen De'an, *Shang dai Shu ren mibao*, pl. 37.

[150] Jin Zhengyao et al., "Guanghan Sanxingdui yiwu keng qingtongqi de qian tongweisu bizhi yanjiu," *Wenwu* 1995.2: 80–5. Connections between Sanxingdui and the middle Yangzi region are discussed in Bagley, "Changjiang Bronzes and Shang Archaeology," "Sichuan Province," and "Sacrificial Pits of the Shang Period"; and in Zheng Zhenxiang, "Zao qi Shu wenhua yu Shang wenhua de guanxi," *Zhongyuan wenwu* 1993.1: 6–11, 46.

[151] *Zhongguo qingtongqi quanji, 13, Ba Shu*, pls. 59–62; Chen De'an, *Shang dai Shu ren mibao*, pls. 47–52 and p. 110.

Figure 3.31. Sanxingdui Pit 2 under excavation. Length 5.3 m, width 2.2 m. The bronze statue shown in Figure 3.32 is visible here, but it is in two pieces, broken near the bottom of the robe. The upper half is at the center of the pit, its head pointing toward the upper left corner. The lower half, near the right wall of the pit, is turned upside down; the base of a bronze tree lies across it. Thirteenth to twelfth century B.C. After *Wenwu* 1989.5: pl. 1.

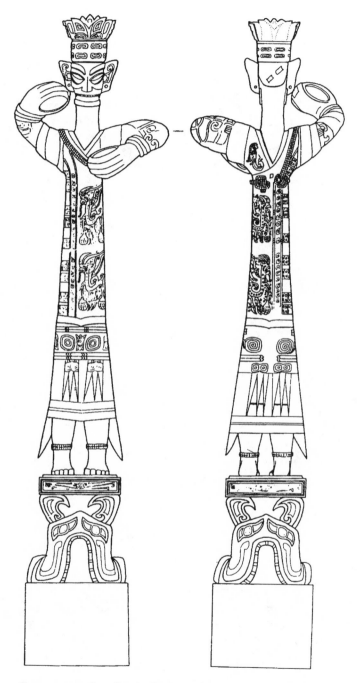

Figure 3.32. Bronze statue, from Sanxingdui Pit 2, thirteenth to twelfth century B.C. Height of base 80 cm, height of figure 182 cm, overall height 262 cm. After *Wenwu* 1989.5: 4.

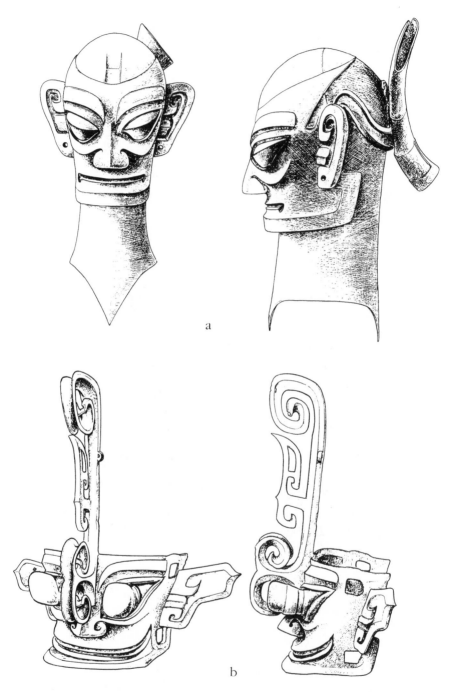

Figure 3.33. Bronzes, from Sanxingdui Pit 2, thirteenth to twelfth century B.C. Not to scale.
Drawings by Li Xiating. (a) Bronze head. Height 46.6 cm. (b) Bronze mask. Height 82.6 cm,
width 77 cm.

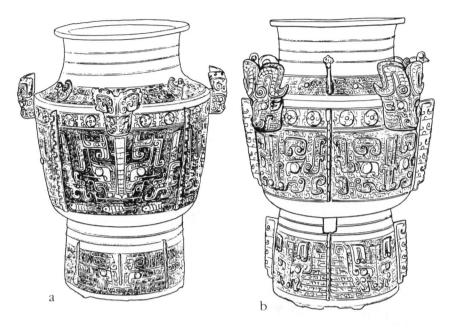

Figure 3.34. (a) *Lei*, from Yueyang, Hunan. Height 50 cm. (b) *Lei*, from Sanxingdui Pit 2. Height 54 cm. Both thirteenth to twelfth century B.C. To the same scale. Drawings by Li Xiating.

some are more wayward, and some are hitherto unknown hybrids with the *ge* shape (Fig. 3.35).[152] Forty-one jade chisels were found in Pit 2, most of them inside a *zun*. Ornaments, which account for the bulk of Fu Hao's jades, are absent, perhaps because they were not appropriate to the sacrifice.

Pottery from the Sanxingdui site points to contact with the Erlitou culture, a connection which the arc-ended blades might be taken to confirm, and the *hangtu* city wall might reflect contact with Erlitou or Erligang. On the other hand the bronzes show no obvious Erligang influence, though their technology does belong to the Erligang tradition.[153] Of those that are conventional enough to be easily dated, the earliest is a *zun* of the transition period; the decoration of the statue might be related to Style III. Perhaps Sanxing-

---

[152] The arc-ended blade is discussed in Rawson, *Chinese Jade*, pp. 188–91 (its puzzling geographic distribution is clearly shown by the map in Rawson, p. 190); in Deng Cong, ed., *Nan Zhongguo ji linjin diqu gu wenhua yanjiu* (Hong Kong: Xianggang Zhongwen daxue, 1994), and in Wang Yongbo, "Si xing duan ren qi de fenlei yu fenqi," *Kaogu xuebao* 1996.1: 1–61.

[153] Chen Xiandan, "Guanghan Sanxingdui qingtongqi yanjiu," *Sichuan wenwu* 1990.6: 22–30; Zeng Zhongmao, "Sanxingdui chutu tongqi de zhuzao jishu," *Sichuan wenwu* 1994.6: 68–9, 77. Some items show unusually heavy use of joining methods such as running on, perhaps because of their odd shapes or large sizes. The smallest branches of the bronze trees are said to have been made by hammering, which is also unusual. On the use of gold at Sanxingdui, see Zheng Zhenxiang, "Zao qi Shu wenhua yu Shang wenhua de guanxi," pp. 8–9.

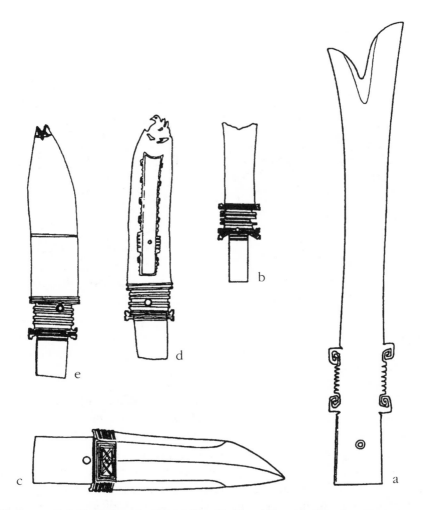

Figure 3.35. Jade blades from Sanxingdui Pit 1 (b)–(e) and Pit 2 (a), Guanghan. To the same scale. (a–b) Arc-ended blades. Lengths 68 cm, 24.8 cm. (c) *Ge* blade. Length 40.9 cm. (d–e) Hybrids. (d) has a drawing of an arc-ended blade on one side. Lengths 38 cm, 39.2 cm. After Deng Cong, *Nan Zhongguo ji linjin diqu gu wenhua yanjiu* (Hong Kong: Xianggang Zhongwen daxue, 1994), p. 93 (a); *Wenwu* 1987.10: 8 (b)–(e).

dui had a history significantly different from other regional cultures, acquiring its bronze technology not directly from the Erligang civilization but later, during the transition period. Contacts with Hunan and Shaanxi might also have played a role in forming its peculiar character. Yet present information does not go very far toward explaining this exotic culture, nor is its bearing on later developments in the Chengdu Plain at all clear. Though some observers have called it an ancestor of the Eastern Zhou culture of Shu 蜀,

continuity between the two has been assumed rather than demonstrated. Remarkable deposits of early Western Zhou bronzes found only 10 km away from the Sanxingdui site seem untouched by its culture.[154]

Sufutun

In 1931 farmers at Yidu 益都 in Shandong province came upon two deposits of bronzes in a small hill at the edge of the village of Sufutun 蘇埠屯. In 1936 an observer sent by the Academia Sinica concluded that the bronzes had come from tombs. Later excavations confirmed the presence of a cemetery, but no dwelling remains were ever found in the vicinity, and below plow level the archaeologists report virgin soil. A chariot burial and four tombs were excavated in 1965–6, six more tombs in 1986. By that time the hill was much damaged by road building and earth removal, and the excavators seem to have decided that little more was to be found there. Since most of the tombs had been robbed before excavation, only three have been described in any detail: M7 and M8, which were small but intact, and the very large tomb M1, which was of great interest despite looting. All are dated by the excavators to Yinxu 3 or 4, that is, contemporary with the latter part of the Anyang occupation.[155]

M7 was a rectangular shaft 2.9 m deep and 3.65 by 2.6 m at the top. It had a *yaokeng* containing a dog skeleton and an *ercengtai* on which were the remains of three sacrificed humans, one a child. The grave goods, chief among which were 8 bronze vessels and 7 weapons, were located mainly between inner and outer wood coffins. They include a *gu* and a *jue* inscribed with an emblem conventionally transcribed Ya Chou 亞醜. M8 contained no sacrificed humans but was a little larger than M7, with a sloping ramp 10 m long that entered the shaft from the south. Animal bones in the *yaokeng* could not be identified, but the skeletons of 2 dogs were found in the upper part of the tomb. Again the grave goods were between the inner and outer coffins, among them 17 bronze vessels, 3 small bells of the type *nao* and 8 of the type *ling*, a stone chime, 202 arrowheads, 2 axes, and 30 bronze weapons (the weapons are flimsy and are interpreted by the excavators as cheap substitutes made strictly for burial). The Ya Chou emblem does not occur on bronzes from M8; 15 of them bear a different emblem.

[154] For Western Zhou hoards at Pengxian 彭縣, see Jessica Rawson, *Western Zhou Ritual Bronzes from the Arthur M. Sackler Collections* (Cambridge, Mass: Harvard University Press, 1990), p. 136; and *Zhongguo qingtongqi quanji 13, Ba Shu*, pls. 70–81, 92.

[155] The report on M1, excavated in 1965–6, is *Wenwu* 1972.8: 17–30. The only other information reported from the 1965–6 excavations is the mention of a chariot burial (never published) and a few sentences about M2 (which contained a set of bronze horse and chariot gear) in Qi Wentao, "Gaishu jinnianlai Shandong chutu de Shang Zhou qingtongqi," *Wenwu* 1972.5: 3–18. The report on M7 and M8, excavated in 1986, comments briefly on other tombs examined that year and on the condition of the site (*Hai Dai kaogu* 1 [1989]: 254–74). Yidu xian has been renamed Qingzhou 青州 shi.

M1, the largest tomb, was a rectangular shaft with four ramps and a cross-shaped wooden burial chamber. It is the only tomb of this description known outside the Xibeigang cemetery at Anyang. The southern ramp, 26 m long, descended to the floor of the shaft; the others, two of which were stepped, gave onto the *ercengtai*. The shaft was 8 m deep and had sloping walls, so that it measured 15 by 11 m at the top but only 10 by 6 m at the bottom. Though the floor area was thus only about a fifth that of Xibeigang M1001, this is the largest tomb yet known outside Anyang. It is also the one most abundantly supplied with human sacrifices. Of the total of forty-eight victims, mostly teenaged or younger, two were buried in two distinct pits in the floor of the burial chamber, one accompanied by a dog; seven more were on the *ercengtai*, apparently in coffins (two in one coffin, four in another, and one in a third); and the remainder, either complete bodies or heads alone, were in three layers in the south ramp, along with five dogs. Although the tomb had been stripped by looters, two large bronze axes were found near the north wall of the shaft, one inscribed with the Ya Chou emblem, and fragments of a *jue* and an adze carried the same emblem. Fourteen pieces of gold foil, a few jades, and 3,790 cowries were also found.

Three of the ten tombs excavated at Sufutun are said to have had ramps, a feature otherwise known only in the great tombs at Xibeigang, and two were very large. All were filled with *hangtu* and most had an *ercengtai*, an outer coffin or burial chamber containing most of the grave goods, an inner coffin, and a *yaokeng* with sacrificed dogs. Along with these familiar features were a few details that seem odd. Under the wooden outer coffin of M1 a large area of the floor was covered with a layer of charcoal 5 cm thick. In M8 the lower walls of the shaft were lined with bundles of reeds. And in M2, a large tomb excavated in 1965–6, a *ge*, a shield, and a human head were found in each corner of the shaft. On the whole, however, the Sufutun tombs seem free of local idiosyncrasy. Perhaps if tombs belonging to a comparable stratum of society were known elsewhere, the features that Sufutun shares with Xibeigang would prove widespread and seem less significant, but at the moment they suggest an unusually close relationship with Anyang 400 km to the west. A cemetery about the same distance to the south of Anyang, at Luoshan 羅山 on the Huai River in Henan province, offers some measure of contrast. The Luoshan tombs were smaller (the largest about half the size of Sufutun M1) but well furnished with bronzes, and both the burial form and the bronzes depart noticeably from Anyang norms.[156]

The Ya Chou emblem, seen on three bronzes from M1 and two from M7,

---

[156] *Henan kaogu sishi nian*, pp. 219–20; *Kaogu xuebao* 1986.2: 153–97; and *Zhongyuan wenwu* 1988.1: 14–20. The Luoshan cemetery includes burials contemporary with the Sufutun cemetery, as well as somewhat earlier and perhaps later ones.

occurs also on one of the bronzes found at Sufutun in 1931, on six spearheads said to be from Sufutun, and on a large number of unprovenanced bronzes. Since it does not seem to occur on objects reliably reported to come from other sites, we might tentatively connect the unprovenanced Ya Chou bronzes with Sufutun: among them, perhaps, are vessels looted from M1. A survey of published Ya Chou bronzes counts fifty-six items (forty-five vessels, two *nao*, eight spearheads, one axe).[157] Half the vessels are rectangular, a proportion considerably larger than in the tomb of Fu Hao; they include four square-bodied *jue*, grotesque objects representing the high-water mark of the vogue for rectangular vessels that began around Fu Hao's time. Many of the bronzes are large and flamboyant castings that until recently had no parallel at Anyang. In 1990, however, very similar items were found in a small Anyang tomb assigned by the excavators to Yinxu 3.[158] The Ya Chou bronzes thus seem to be within the stylistic range of Anyang bronze casting, and they might be taken as a further hint of close connections between Anyang and Sufutun during the last few Anyang reigns. The only other substantial find of bronzes in Shandong, a deposit of sixteen vessels, fifty-eight weapons, eleven tools, and fourteen items of horse and chariot gear unearthed in Changqing 長清, may be roughly contemporary with Sufutun.[159] On present evidence, therefore, this region looks more like a late colony of the Anyang civilization than a local descendant of the Erligang culture.

The Northern Zone

Part forest, part desert, mostly grassland, the Northern Zone lies along the northern borders of modern China, stretching from Xinjiang and Gansu in the west to Jilin in the east and including parts of Inner Mongolia and Liaoning, along with much of Hebei, Shanxi, and northern Shaanxi. In the first millennium B.C. increased dependence on animal herding gave rise to societies of pastoral nomads in this region.[160] Already in the last few centuries of the second millennium, however, the Northern Zone was home to cultures recognizably distinct from the civilization of the middle Yellow River valley. In the material record this distinctiveness takes the form of an inven-

[157] Yin Zhiyi, "Shandong Yidu Sufutun mudi he Ya Chou tongqi," *Kaogu xuebao* 1977.2: 23–34.

[158] *Kaogu* 1991.5: 390–1 (the tomb is Guojiazhuang M160). Compare pl. 1:2 in this report with the Ya Chou vessel shown in Wan-go Weng and Yang Boda, *The Palace Museum: Peking* (New York: Abrams, 1982), p. 125. Nothing else of this date found at Anyang can compare in size and quality with the Ya Chou bronzes.

[159] *Wenwu* 1964.4: 41–7, reporting a find made in 1957; three of the bronzes are illustrated in Li Xueqin, *Zhongguo meishu quanji: Gongyi meishu bian 4, qingtongqi (Shang)* (Beijing: Wenwu, 1985), pls. 82–5. Changqing is 160 km west of Yidu. A smaller find from Shouguang 壽光, 30 km northeast of Yidu, is reported in *Wenwu* 1985.3: 1–11.

[160] See Chapter 13.

tory of weapons and other small bronzes sometimes collectively referred to as the Northern Complex.

The bronzes of the Northern Complex are interesting for several reasons. First, although the various types cannot be traced to origins at any single place or date (some probably arose in the Northern Zone itself, others in Siberia), their affiliations far to the north and west establish the Northern Zone as the home of a metal industry that originated outside China, independent of the Erligang tradition.[161] Second, the widespread appearance of this inventory on the northern frontier of China seems to coincide with a southward retreat of the Erligang culture. In other words, at the northern limit of its distribution the Erligang culture is succeeded in the archaeological record by the Northern Complex. Lin Yun takes this to signify the arrival of new people and points to the gold ornaments in northern finds as markers of a distinct ethnic group.[162] No doubt the proximity of these people has something to do with the appearance at Anyang around 1200 B.C. of the chariot and other northern artifacts, including knives, mirrors, and bow-shaped objects like those found in Fu Hao's tomb (Fig. 3.25).[163] Borrowing in the opposite direction is attested by bronze vessels found in the Northern Zone, most often in Shaanxi and Shanxi.

The bronzes of the Northern Complex are distinctive as types and distinctive also in decoration. Characteristic features are simple decorative patterns of striae and zigzags, loops or buttons for suspension, and terminals in the form of rattles or naturalistic animal heads. The types include weapons, mirrors (Fig. 3.25b), bow-shaped objects (Fig. 3.25c), and a variety of wands, spatulas, spoons, and ladles (Fig. 3.39d–e). Mirrors have been found most often in Gansu and Qinghai, at the far western end of the Northern Zone, but occasionally also in Inner Mongolia and Liaoning. Weapons form the largest category and the one whose affiliations reach farthest into Siberia. Typical items are battle-axes with tubular sockets (Figs. 3.36, 3.39c), knives with integrally cast handles (Fig. 3.37b), and daggers, that is, double-edged stabbing blades (Fig. 3.37c). Related knives and daggers occur in the late-

---

[161] Chernykh (*Ancient Metallurgy in the USSR*, chapter 9) treats the Northern Zone as the southeastern edge of his "Central Asian Metalworking Province," an archaeological entity defined by an assemblage whose distribution extends from Sayano–Altai and the Minusinsk Basin of the middle Yenisei to the northern and northwestern frontiers of China.

[162] Lin Yun, "Northern Zone," pp. 238–41.

[163] No chariot burial has yet been reported from the Northern Zone, but a pair of bronze axle caps has been found at Baode 保德 in northern Shanxi accompanied by typical northern artifacts, including the axe and dagger of Figures 3.36c, 3.37c (Wu Zhenlu, "Baode xian xin faxian de Yindai qingtong qi," *Wenwu* 1972.4: 62–6). For the northern bronzes in Fu Hao's tomb, see Lin Yun, "Northern Zone," pp. 250–4 and (on the bow-shaped object) 263–6.

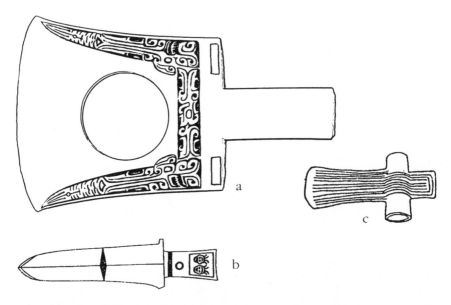

Figure 3.36. Axes. To the same scale. (a) Axe of the type *yue*, from Panlongcheng (= Fig. 3.15, no. 15). Length 40.8 cm. Drawing by Li Xiating. (b) Axe of the type *ge*, from Xin'gan, Jiangxi. Length 26.1 cm. After *Wenwu* 1991.10: 11, fig. 12:2. (c) Axe with tubular socket, from Baode, Shanxi. Length 17.1 cm. After Lin Yun, "A Reexamination of the Relationship Between Bronzes of the Shang Culture and of the Northern Zone," in *Studies of Shang Archaeology: Selected Papers from the International Conference on Shang Civilization* (New Haven, Conn.: Yale University Press, 1986), fig. 52:9 (provenance given there is incorrect).

second-millennium Karasuk culture of the Minusinsk Basin, and the battle-axes have a long history in Siberia, south Russia, and beyond.[164]

When these weapons occur at Anyang they are instantly recognizable as intrusive, for the native tradition had no daggers, and its knives and axes were quite different. Anyang knives have broad curved blades with short stems for mounting in a separate handle (Fig. 3.37a); northern knives have blades cast in one piece with their handles (Fig. 3.37b). The axes native to China have flat tangs for hafting, whether the blade is broad (Fig. 3.36a) or pointed (Fig. 3.36b: the *ge* is an axe with a pointed blade); northern axes, made in great variety, were hafted through shaft rings or tubular shaft holes (Figs. 3.36c, 3.39c). The two hafting methods are so different as to make it tempting to suppose that all shaft-hole tools and weapons in China depend ultimately on northern prototypes. Loehr long ago advanced typological arguments in favor of a Siberian origin, pointing out that shaft holes,

---

[164] Chernykh believes that socketed axes were invented in the fourth millennium in eastern Europe or the Caucasus (*Ancient Metallurgy in the USSR*, pp. 300–301).

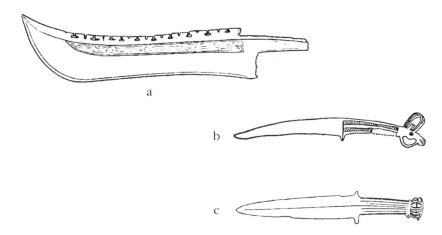

Figure 3.37. Knives and daggers. To the same scale. (a) Knife, from Fu Hao's tomb. Length 45.7 cm. Drawing by Li Xiating. (b) Knife, from Yantoucun, Suide, Shaanxi. Length 32 cm. After Lin Yun, "A Reexamination of the Relationship Between Bronzes of the Shang Culture and of the Northern Zone," in *Studies of Shang Archaeology: Selected Papers from the International Conference on Shang Civilization* (New Haven, Conn.: Yale University Press, 1986), fig. 51:7. (c) Dagger with rattle pommel, from Linzheyu, Baode, Shanxi. Length 32 cm. After Tao Zhenggang, "Shanxi chutu de Shang dai tongqi," in *Zhongguo Kaogu xuehui di si ci nianhui lunwenji 1983* (Beijing: Wenwu, 1985), fig. 5:1.

ubiquitous in western Siberia, are a metalworker's invention, while all the blade types indisputably native to China (because their distribution coincides with that of bronze vessels) have flat tangs for hafting and thus are allied in principle with older stone tools.[165] His argument applied to socketed implements as well, but socketed spearheads and celts occur in considerable variety at Panlongcheng and Xin'gan; if these were northern imports, they were naturalized early. Some northern borrowings had only a short life in China: *ge* blades made with shaft rings rather than flat tangs must have been inspired by the hafting method preferred in the Northern Zone, but they were an experiment that had lost favor by early Zhou. By contrast ring-handled knives like the one unearthed at Erlitou (Fig. 3.12d) were a permanent acquisition. Fu Hao's tomb contained ten examples, and in the Zhou period this standard northern type completely superseded the native stemmed type.

Distributed over a vast area, the bronzes of the Northern Complex were the common property of otherwise diverse societies that ranged from forest dwellers heavily dependent on hunting in the east to societies more depen-

---

[165] Max Loehr, "Weapons and Tools from Anyang, and Siberian Analogies," *American Journal of Archaeology* 53 (1949): 135; and idem, *Chinese Bronze Age Weapons* (Ann Arbor: University of Michigan Press, 1956), pp. 25–7.

dent on farming in the west. Slight differences in the metal inventory suggest a broad division along the line of the Taihang Mountains 太行山 (the Shanxi–Hebei border).[166] The division is clearest in the forms of certain ornaments. East of the mountains these include gold armlets and funnel-shaped earrings.[167] West of the mountains, on the loess plateau of northern Shanxi and Shaanxi, gold earrings take the form of flat spirals, often combined with turquoise beads, and they are sometimes found with gold or bronze arcs, perhaps ornaments for the head (Fig. 3.39a–b). The region west of the mountains has yielded a particular abundance of finds. Bronze vessels are more common here than elsewhere in the Northern Zone, and it therefore seems likely that this was the region most intimately in contact with Anyang and the Wei valley (the closest parallels to the vessels come from the Wei valley). But bronze finds in the Northern Zone have seldom been accompanied by any indication of context beyond occasional skeletal remains, and presently available information gives no clear picture of the inhabitants.

Graves at three places in Shanxi will suggest the complexity of the archaeological picture. A small grave at Jixian 吉縣 contained four bronzes: a battle-axe and a rattle-pommel dagger on either side of the occupant's head and two large spoons next to the left hand (Fig. 3.38).[168] There is no sign here of contact with the Anyang culture. By contrast two large graves farther north at Lingshi 靈石 contained a very few northern items alongside a rich array of Anyang-style vessels, and the graves themselves had such familiar features as yaokeng with sacrificed dogs.[169] Here the northern items look like intrusions in burials no more exotic than Fu Hao's. At Shilou 石樓, however, 85 km west of Lingshi, small bronzes of northern type have repeatedly been found together with vessels so eccentric that they must be local castings.[170] Here, it seems, northerners adopted into their own culture the manufacture and use of bronze vessels. Figure 3.39 shows objects from several different Shilou finds: gold earrings with turquoise beads, a bronze arc-shaped ornament, a battle-axe, a spatula or wand, a ladle, a bell-shaped rattle with noise-making attachments on its exterior (spoons like the pair in the Jixian grave often have similar attachments), and a strange boat-shaped vessel (one of half a dozen unusual vessels from a tomb reported to have a yaokeng).[171] Jixian,

[166] Lin Yun, "Northern Zone," pp. 247–8.
[167] For the bronze culture of this region, see Nelson, ed., *The Archaeology of Northeast China*, chapters 5–6.
[168] *Kaogu* 1985.9: 848–9.   [169] *Wenwu* 1986.11: 1–18.
[170] For finds at Shilou and neighboring sites, see Zou Heng, *Xia Shang Zhou kaoguxue lunwenji* (Beijing: Wenwu, 1980), pp. 274–8; Tao Zhenggang, "Shanxi chutu de Shang dai tongqi," *Zhongguo Kaogu xuehui di si ci nianhui lunwen ji 1983* (Beijing: Wenwu, 1985), pp. 57–64; *Shanxi chutu wenwu*, nos. 36, 41, 44, 47, 57; and *Wenwu* 1981.8: 49–53. Similar sites across the river in Shaanxi include Qingjian and Suide (see note 176).
[171] Fong, *Great Bronze Age of China*, pp. 127–8.

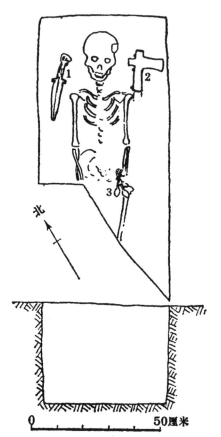

Figure 3.38. Grave excavated in Jixian, Shanxi, thirteenth to eleventh century B.C. After *Kaogu* 1985.9: 848.

Lingshi, and Shilou are not far apart, nor can they be very different in date. So much variety in the burial assemblages of a comparatively small region is not easy to interpret, nor is it clear how the graves and hoards from which the bronzes come relate to habitation sites and ceramic assemblages in the same region. It is possible, as Lin Yun suggests, that parts of the Northern Zone were shared by coexisting societies with different economies.[172] There must at least have been many different groups or tribes.

The Wei River Valley

The Wei 渭 River valley, homeland of the Zhou both before and after their conquest of Shang, has been the focus of intensive archaeological explo-

---

[172] Lin Yun, "Northern Zone," pp. 272–3; cf. Zou Heng, *Xia Shang Zhou kaoguxue lunwenji*, pp. 274–8.

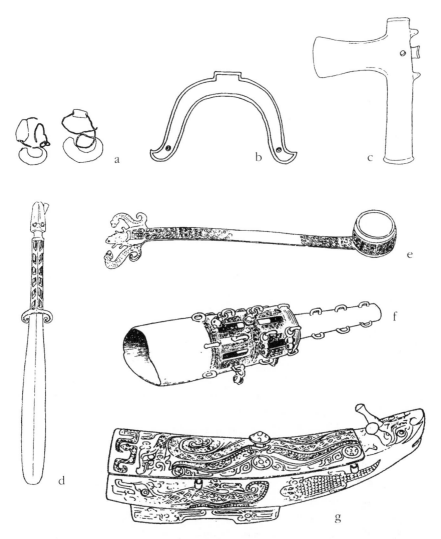

Figure 3.39. Objects from various finds at Shilou, Shanxi. Not to scale. (a) Gold earrings with turquoise beads, from Taohuazhuang. (b) Bronze arc (head ornament?), from Chujiayu. Height 14.5 cm, distance between tips 24.8 cm. (c) Battle-axe with tubular shaft hole, from Caojiayuan. Length along tube 18.7 cm. (d) Wand or spatula, from Houlanjiagou. Length 35 cm. (e) Ladle, from Houlanjiagou. Length 37 cm. (f) Bell-shaped rattle, from Caojiayuan. Length 29 cm. (g) Boat-shaped vessel, from Taohuazhuang. Length 41.5 cm. After Tao Zheng-gang, "Shanxi chutu de Shang dai tongqi," figs. 3 and 5 (a, d–g); Lin Yun, "A Reexamination of the Relationship Between Bronzes of the Shang Culture and of the Northern Zone," in *Studies of Shang Archaeology: Selected Papers from the International Conference on Shang Civilization* (New Haven, Conn.: Yale University Press, 1986), figs. 49:10 and 50:3 (b–c).

ration.[173] For the period before the conquest the main concern of Shaanxi archaeologists has been to find remains that could be assigned to a Zhou people, in other words, to find an archaeological culture – a pottery type – that could be labeled "proto-Zhou." In the absence of inscribed artifacts the only way to show even tentatively that a particular pottery type might correspond to the Zhou people is to show that the area of its distribution coincides with the area they inhabited; the only clues to the area they inhabited are references in later texts, which are ambiguous and contradictory, and the known locations of major Zhou settlements at the time of the conquest and after. The latter evidence favors the western end of the Wei valley, but there is no agreement as to which of the many archaeological cultures found there should be identified with the Zhou, nor for that matter is there any good reason to expect pottery types to correlate with peoples mentioned in texts.[174] The eastern end of the valley, represented for instance by the site of Laoniupo near Xi'an, is said to be archaeologically distinct; it is described as an extension of the Anyang civilization, though it was clearly in contact with the Northern Zone as well.

Attempts to find a Zhou people in the pottery assemblages of the Wei Valley rest on the doubtful premise that the Zhou dynasty was founded by an archaeologically distinguishable group. It seems more important to observe that the founders of the dynasty emerged from a region of cultural mixing that drew contributions from many sources and sometimes from great distances. Erligang bronzes have been found as far west as Qishan 岐山, suggesting that the Erligang civilization penetrated deep into the Wei Valley, though it may only have been a transient presence there.[175] Influence from the Northern Zone, by contrast, was sustained and pervasive, indeed no sharp archaeological boundary separates the Wei Valley from the Northern Zone: proceeding northward to Chunhua 淳化 and Tongchuan 銅川, and then to such sites as Suide 綏德 and Qingjian 清澗 in northern Shaanxi, we encounter archaeological assemblages in which a growing number of northern bronzes accompanies a fairly consistent selection of bronze vessel types.[176]

Artifacts that connect the Wei Valley with the south are found at the same

---

[173] For a general survey, see Li Zizhi, "Jianguo yilai Shaanxi Shang Zhou kaogu shuyao," *Kaogu yu wenwu* 1988.5–6: 60–70; and Chapter 6, this volume.

[174] Zou Heng (*Xia Shang Zhou kaoguxue lunwenji*, chapter 7) nevertheless goes so far as to distinguish the pottery of different Zhou clans. On his and other arguments, see Chapter 6, this volume.

[175] *Wenwu* 1977.12: 86–7.

[176] Tongchuan: *Kaogu* 1982.1: 107, 102; Chunhua: Yao Shengmin, "Shaanxi Chunhua xian chutu de Shang Zhou qingtongqi," *Kaogu yu wenwu* 1986.5: 12–22; Qingjian and Suide: *Shaanxi chutu Shang Zhou qingtongqi*, vol. 1, nos. 61–98 (similar sites across the Yellow River in Shanxi include Shilou, Baode, and Liulin 柳林).

sites as northern items, sometimes in the same graves.[177] Contact reaching as far as the Yangzi region is suggested by a face-shaped ornament from Laoniupo that has parallels not only at Chenggu in southern Shaanxi but even at Xin'gan in Jiangxi (Fig. 3.19).[178] Chenggu may have been some sort of intermediary between the Yangzi region and the Wei valley. Traffic moving north probably entered the Wei Valley at its western end, skirting the Qinling 秦岭 Mountains and passing through Baoji 寶雞; moving southward from Chenggu, tributaries of the Yangzi led to Sichuan and areas downstream. After the Zhou conquest southern influence in the Wei Valley was even stronger than before, accounting for many of the most striking features of early Zhou bronzes, and communications must have stayed open for some time, for large bells of southern type did not appear in the north until several generations after the conquest.[179] Of traffic in the other direction there is no trace. Perhaps in the realm of material culture the Wei Valley had little to offer the sophisticated societies of the south. Certainly preconquest bronzes do not suggest a particularly high level of material culture: they present a rude contrast to the finely cast bronzes made in the Wei Valley immediately after the conquest, which are conspicuous for their large numbers, their imposing sizes, and above all for their magnificent inscriptions. The Anyang dynasty was not overthrown by the most civilized of its contemporaries, but perhaps by the one most eager to acquire civilization.[180]

Archaeology and Traditional History

The archaeological evidence that has been surveyed in this chapter allows us glimpses of complex societies scattered over a large part of north and central China. All belong to the latter part of the second millennium, though in the present state of archaeological knowledge we cannot be sure that all survived as late as the Zhou conquest. The civilization of the middle Yangzi region clearly did, since its influence is apparent in the Wei Valley both before and after the conquest. On the other hand we do not know whether the city that

[177] For example, at Chunhua; see Jessica Rawson, "Statesmen or Barbarians? The Western Zhou as Seen Through Their Bronzes," *Proceedings of the British Academy* 75 (1989): 81–4.

[178] A small bronze plaque from another Laoniupo grave matches items found at Chenggu (compare *Wenwu* 1988.6: 13, fig. 21:2, with Tang Jinyu et al., "Shaanxi sheng Chenggu Xian chutu Yin Shang tongqi zhengli jianbao," pl. 5:1). See also note 85.

[179] Kane, "The Independent Bronze Industries in the South of China Contemporary with the Shang and Western Zhou Dynasties," p. 92; Rawson, "Statesmen or Barbarians?" pp. 90–3; Falkenhausen, *Suspended Music*, pp. 154–5 and 159–62. The earliest known Zhou bells of southern type are from Baoji; on these and other southern elements in Western Zhou bronzes, see Chapter 6, this volume. Spectacular early Western Zhou castings unearthed at Pengxian in Sichuan supply further evidence of early Zhou contact with the south (see note 154).

[180] See Chapter 6, this volume, and see Rawson, "Statesmen or Barbarians?"

left sacrificial deposits at Sanxingdui around 1200 B.C. was still in existence two centuries later. But whatever the fortunes of particular cities, at the time of the conquest civilized communities must have existed at many places in the Yangzi valley, from Sichuan to the sea, while simpler bronze-using societies occupied the Wei River valley and the vast expanses of the Northern Zone. The Anyang kings had dealings with many of these areas, and they had powerful neighbors in Shandong as well. The civilized world on the eve of the Zhou conquest was large, diverse, and intricately interconnected.

In the light of archaeology, therefore, the most striking feature of traditional history is the absence from it of any such world. Transmitted texts present us instead with an ancient China in which the only civilized powers were Zhou and Shang, and with an ancient history in which the principal event was the transfer of rule from one to the other. Ever since the Eastern Zhou period the Zhou conquest has been viewed as an event of towering significance, not because of anything tangible connected with it, such as a building project or a reform of script or a standardization of weights and measures, but because it provided a model for the morally correct transfer of power and for the maintenance of power through dynastic virtue. In that model a unified political order coextensive with civilization was ruled by the Shang until their rule grew oppressive, whereupon the Shang were replaced by the Zhou.

This is a distinctly schematic account of the past, one that left us quite unprepared for archaeology's discovery of a wider civilized world, and if we are to understand its emphases and omissions, we must begin by reminding ourselves that the tradition in which the Zhou figure so centrally is a Zhou creation. The oldest surviving statements about pre-Zhou history, including the first mentions of a dynasty earlier than Shang, occur in Western Zhou texts enunciating the doctrine of the Mandate of Heaven, in other words in texts concerned with political legitimation.[181] Though long accepted at face value, these statements about the past form part of an account of the Zhou conquest that seems more expedient than factual. Depicting a momentous struggle between the Zhou and a single opponent to whom the Zhou attributed what they themselves wished to claim – universal rule, divinely sanctioned – it bears the stamp of symbolic history. Attributing universal rule to the Anyang kings required assigning them a unique status which on the evidence of archaeology they did not possess. Legalizing the transfer of rule was achieved by inventing a precedent, an earlier dynasty whose equally universal rule had been lawfully transferred to Shang. The Zhou claim to legiti-

---

[181] That is, parts of *Shang shu* 尚書 and *Shi jing* 詩經 that are likely to be of Western Zhou composition, though not necessarily as early as the events they describe.

macy took the form of a claim to preserve an existing political order, and this depended on an account of the past significantly at variance with reality.[182]

The question arises, of course, why the Zhou singled out Shang rather than some other contemporary to be the source of their legitimacy. To explain the choice by supposing that the Anyang kings did in fact claim some sort of universal kingship or some sort of divine mandate, and that they alone in second-millennium China made such a claim, is merely to adopt the self-serving explanation offered to us by the Zhou. Did the Zhou perhaps choose to link themselves with a culture which had high prestige in their eyes because they had borrowed its writing system? To answer such questions we need to know more than we do about the second millennium. To discover how the Zhou remade history, we must explore the discrepancy between history as the Zhou reported it and history as recovered by archaeology.

For Chinese archaeologists, unfortunately, it has been difficult to admit that any such discrepancy might exist. The always thorny problem of interpreting mute archaeological evidence has been complicated by national pride, which insists that tradition is reliable and that the task of archaeology is to vindicate it. Searching always for correspondence with the written record, inclined to overlook or explain away evidence that conflicts with it, archaeology sadly misses its chance of giving us an independent view of the second millennium. In the process it deprives us also of an independent view of the Zhou, who might seem more interestingly creative if their efforts at rewriting history had not been quite so successful. When archaeology someday frees itself from politics to take a more detached view of tradition, the time before Zhou will become an archaeological reality, and the Zhou period itself will take on new interest.

---

[182] Compare the role played by symbolic history in the ideology of Egyptian kingship (Kemp, *Ancient Egypt*, pp. 31–53 passim, discussing the story of the first dynasty's unification of Upper and Lower Egypt; see also Trigger et al., *Ancient Egypt*, pp. 44–6). On the elaborated moralizing accounts of the Zhou conquest that were accepted as history in the late Eastern Zhou period, see John Knoblock, *Xunzi*, vol. 2 (Stanford, Calif.: Stanford University Press, 1990), introduction. Typical is the story that 800 states shifted their allegiance from Shang to assist the first Zhou king, a story less likely to preserve a memory of eleventh-century events and powers than to be an invention illustrating the magic charisma of a leader who possessed the Mandate of Heaven.

CHAPTER FOUR

THE SHANG: CHINA'S FIRST HISTORICAL DYNASTY

David N. Keightley

The Shang 商 (ca. 1570–1045 B.C.) is the first Chinese dynasty to have left written sources. Because those sources – primarily the oracle-bone inscriptions – have been found only for the reigns of the last nine Shang kings, true history, that of the "late Shang," can be said to cover only the period from the reign of Wu Ding 武丁, the twenty-first king of the line, to the reign of Di Xin 帝辛 (d. ca. 1045), the twenty-ninth and last king (Fig. 4.1). Many features of Shang culture emerged from the Henan Longshan 龍山 or from other late Neolithic cultures to the east or northeast.[1] It is only with the late Shang and its written records, however, that one can, for the first time begin to speak with confidence of a civilization that was incipiently Chinese in its values and institutions, a civilization characterized by its political and religious hierarchies, centralized management of resources, and complex, deeply rooted art forms.

The traditional view (first recorded in the third century A.D.), that the dynasty's name was Shang prior to Pan Geng's 盤庚 removal of the capital to Yin 殷 and was Yin after it, is supported by neither contemporary evidence nor later use. The divinations of the last two Shang kings, for example, refer only to the *da (tian) yi Shang* 大（天）邑商 – which may be translated either as "the great (or heavenly) settlement, Shang" or, taking Shang as the name of a core region, as "Shang of the great (or heavenly) settlements" – but make no reference to any settlement or region named Yin. Rather than being the Shang name for their last dynastic stage, Yin appears, in later texts that sometimes use Shang or Yin interchangeably, to have been a Zhou 周 term for the dynasty they had replaced.[2]

---

[1] K. C. Chang, *Shang Civilization* (New Haven, Conn.: Yale University Press, 1980), pp. 335–48; Huang Zhongye, "Cong kaogu faxian kan Shang wenhua qiyuan yu woguo beifang," *Beifang wenwu* 1990.1: 14–19; Zhongguo Shehui kexueyuan Kaogu yanjiusuo, *Yinxu de faxian yu yanjiu* (Beijing: Kexue, 1994), pp. 465–9.

[2] Chen Mengjia, *Yinxu buci zongshu* (Beijing: Kexue, 1956), p. 262; Zhou Hongxiang, *Shang Yin diwang benji* (Hong Kong: Wanyou tushu, 1958), pp. 1–3. See the "Shang settlement" inscriptions transcribed

The origins and meaning, if any, of the dynastic name itself are unclear. The Shang may, like the Zhou, Han 漢, and many subsequent dynasties, originally have taken their name from a place. Sima Qian 司馬遷 (ca. 145–86 B.C.) recorded the tradition that Xie 契, the predynastic founder of the lineage, was enfeoffed at Shang.[3] Some scholars have linked the dynasty name to the Shang 滴 River and its River Power, a name that appears in the bone inscriptions (Y782.1–2).[4]

SOURCES

Traditional Accounts

The chroniclers and philosophers of the Eastern Zhou knew few details about the Shang dynasty. Confucius, for example, is supposed to have lamented that records from the Shang successor state of Song 宋 did not permit a full reconstruction of Shang ceremonial practice.[5] In his "Yin benji" 殷本紀 (Basic annals of the Yin), the Han historian, Sima Qian, starts with the miraculous conception of Xie, whose mother conceived when she swallowed an egg dropped by a black bird. He then records anecdotes, events, character analyses, and moral judgments regarding fourteen predynastic ancestors and thirty dynastic kings, from Cheng Tang 成湯, the dynasty's founder, down to Di Xin, the depraved last ruler, whom the Zhou king Wu 武 overthrew at the battle of Muye 牧野. Sima Qian ends his account with a brief reference to the abortive rebellion that Di Xin's son, Wu Geng 武庚, led against the Zhou. The Han historian provides great narrative detail in some cases, little more than a royal name in others. He also refers to five removals of the Shang capital, the last being the move to Yin, under Pan Geng.[6]

in Yao Xiaosui and Xiao Ding, eds., *Yinxu jiagu keci leizuan* (Beijing: Zhonghua, 1989), p. 778.1. This concordance, hereafter abbreviated as Y, conveniently transcribes the corpus of inscriptions in both oracle-bone and modern Chinese script. For Zhou use of the name Yin, see, below note 121.

[3] *Shi ji*, 3, p. 91 (William H. Nienhauser, Jr., et al., eds., *The Grand Scribe's Records*, vol. 1 [Bloomington: Indiana University Press, 1994], p. 41). This Shang was traditionally located in the area of Shangxian 商縣 county in southeast Shaanxi; modern scholarship, however, now places it near Shangqiu 商丘 in eastern Henan (Chang, *Shang Civilization*, p. 5).

[4] The modern term "power" is used to refer to all the forces that, conceived animistically, affected the Shang world. Kaizuka Shigeki (*Kyôto daigaku jimbun kagaku kenkyûjo zô kôkotsu moji. Hombun hen* [Kyoto: Kyôto daigaku jimbun kagaku kenkyûjo, 1960], p. 534, no. 2139); Qu Wanli (*Xiaotun dier ben: Yinxu wenzi – Jiabian kaoshi* [Taipei: Academia Sinica, 1961], p. 98, no. 623), and Wang Yuzhe ("Shangzu de laiyuan diwang shitan," *Lishi yanjiu* 1984.1: 61–77) summarize the scholarship about the possible locations of the Shang River and other place-names associated with the Shang homeland.

[5] *Analects*, 3/9. See also David N. Keightley, "The *Bamboo Annals* and Shang–Chou Chronology," *HJAS* 38 (1978): 426 n. 14, p. 427 n. 18.

[6] For Western-language translations of the "Yin benji," see Édouard Chavannes, tr., *Les mémoires historiques de Se-Ma Ts'ien* (Paris: Ernest Leroux, 1895–1905; rpt., Paris: Adrien Maisonneuve, 1967), pp. 173–208; Nienhauser et al., eds., *The Grand Scribe's Records*, pp. 41–54.

Temple Name   Generation

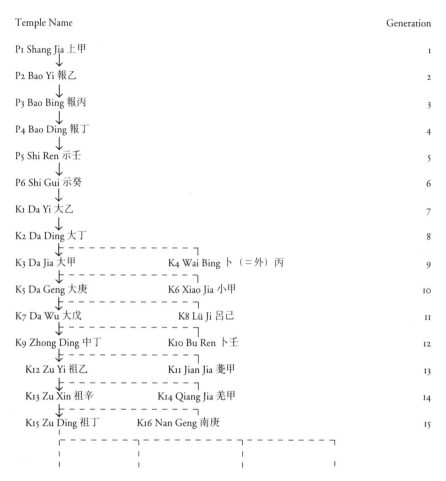

Figure 4.1. The royal genealogy as recorded in late Shang sacrifice inscriptions. For particular problems involving the reconstruction of the Shang king list see David N. Keightley, *Sources of Shang History: The Oracle-Bone Inscriptions of Bronze Age China* (Berkeley, Calif.: University of California Press, 1978), pp. 185–7, 204–9; K. C. Chang, *Shang Civilization* (New Haven, Conn.: Yale University Press, 1980) pp. 6–7, 165–8. P = predynastic ancestor; K = king. The ↓ indicates the main line of father-to-son descent known traditionally as the *dazong* 大宗 (see note 45).

Sima Qian acknowledges that he drew much of his information from the *Shi jing* 詩經 (Classic of poetry) and the *Shang shu* (Venerated documents; also known as *Shu jing* 書經, Classic of documents); modern scholars have also traced his debt to a number of other Zhou and Han sources, such as the *Zuo zhuan* 左傳 (Zuo's tradition), *Guo yu* 國語 (Sayings of the states), and *Da Dai Li ji* 大戴禮記 (Dai the Elder's record of ritual). The historicity of many of these accounts is uncertain, and modern scholars have devoted much

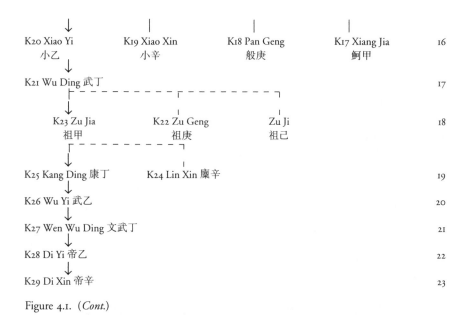

Figure 4.1. (*Cont.*)

energy to comparing the "Yin benji" accounts with the information in the oracle-bone inscriptions.[7] It is true that the Han historian, and the Zhou accounts upon which he must have relied, generally possessed reliable knowledge of the posthumous temple names of the Shang kings and the order in which the kings came to power. On the other hand, he and later historians were ignorant of many salient events and persons recorded in the divination inscriptions.[8]

Bronze Inscriptions

As detailed in Chapter 3, thousands of ritual Shang bronzes have been excavated for the late Shang period, and their provenance and decor frequently provide archaeologists and art historians with valuable information about the extent of Shang culture, its regional variations, and rival states. Although the temple name of the ancestor or ancestress to whom the vessel was dedicated was, on occasion, cast into the vessel, the number of lengthier Shang bronze inscriptions that provide material for the writing of Shang history is relatively small.[9]

[7] Zhou Hongxiang, *Shang Yin diwang benji*; Chang, *Shang Civilization*, p. 3; Yan Yiping, *Yin Shang shiji* 3 vols. (Taibei: Yiwen, 1989); Nienhauser et al., eds., *The Grand Scribe's Records*, p. 52.

[8] Keightley, "The *Bamboo Annals* and Shang–Chou Chronology," pp. 429–34.

[9] Akatsuka Kiyoshi, *Chûgoku kodai no shûkyô to bunka: In ôchô no saishi* (Tokyo: Kadokawa, 1977), pp. 611–859, presents a corpus of 102 Shang bronze inscriptions that he found worth translating and dis-

Oracle-Bone Inscriptions

The Shang foretold the future and tested the Powers' approval of their plans by applying an intense heat source to hollows bored into the back of a cattle scapula or turtle shell (Fig. 4.2) and then interpreting the resultant stress cracks as auspicious or inauspicious. That the divination records, which the Shang diviners then incised into the bone, were unknown to later Chinese historians until late Qing scholars – working from about 1898 onwards – recognized their true nature, is another sobering reminder of what the Zhou texts have not transmitted to posterity. Private collectors and archaeologists eventually collected over 200,000 oracle-bone fragments from the Xiaotun 小屯 site (the name dates only to the Ming dynasty) 3 km northwest of Anyang 安陽, in the northern Henan panhandle (see Fig. 3.23). The inscriptions, together with the complex of temple palaces, workshops, and elite burials, reveal the Xiaotun area to have been the Late Shang's major sacro-administrative center. If tradition, as recorded in such texts as the "Pan Geng" 盤庚 chapter of the *Shang shu* and Sima Qian's "Yin benji," is correct, the site – which modern scholars have come to associate with the traditional name of Yinxu 殷墟 (The Wastes of Yin) – was the Shang capital for the last twelve kings, starting with Pan Geng. Archaeological confirmation of a pre–Wu Ding (d. ca. 1189 B.C.) dynastic Shang presence at Xiaotun has not yet, however, been provided.[10]

The gathering of the cattle scapulas and turtle shells, some of which were presented as tribute – frequently in their hundreds – by neighboring countries, the killing of the donor cattle (sometimes offered to the ancestors in cult) and turtles, the cleaning of the scapulas and plastrons, the ritual consecration of scapulas, the preparation of the hollows,[11] the time spent in the ritual cracking of the bones, the labor invested in carving the record, and the eventual disposal of the used oracle bones – all this specialized activity indicates the degree to which royal divination was one of the central dynastic

---

cussing. Robert W. Bagley (*Shang Ritual Bronzes in the Arthur M. Sackler Collections*) [Cambridge, Mass.: Harvard University Press, 1987], pp. 582–7; see too, pp. 521–33) reproduces 82 insignia and inscriptions on Shang bronzes. See too Matsumaru Michio, "In Shû kokka no kôzô," *Iwanami kôza: sekai rekishi* 4 (1970): 65–71; David N. Keightley, *Sources of Shang History: The Oracle-Bone Inscriptions of Bronze Age China* (Berkeley: University of California Press, 1978), p. 134, n. 5; and Chang, *Shang Civilization*, pp. 21–3.

[10] David N. Keightley, "Religion and the Rise of Urbanism," *JAOS* 93, 4 (1973): 527–38; J. A. Lefeuvre, "Les inscriptions des Shang sur carapaces de tortue et sur os; aperçu historique et bibliographique de la découverte et des premières études," *TP* 61 (1975): 1–82; Wang Yuxin, *Jiaguxue tonglun* (Beijing: Zhongguo Shehui kexue 1989), pp. 23–42; Liu Qiyu, "Chonglun Pan Geng qian Yin ji qian Yin de yuanyin," *Shixue yuekan* 1990.4: 1–5. For the pre-Shang cultural remains at the site, see Zhongguo Shehui kexueyuan Kaogu yanjiusuo, *Yinxu de faxian yu yanjiu*, pp. 49 and 419–34.

[11] For the preparation of the scapulas and plastrons and the drilling and chiseling of the hollows, see Keightley, *Sources of Shang History*, pp. 12–21.

Figure 4.3, on page 239. Wu Ding harvest divination. The positive charge, 我受黍年 (We will receive millet harvest), was divined on the right side of the turtle plastron, with each crack numbered from "1" to "5" (the numbers are recorded in the upper quadrant of each of the T-shaped cracks). The negative charge, 我弗其受黍年 (We may not "receive millet harvest"), was divined on the left side, with its cracks numbered in the same way. An auspicious crack notation, 二告 "*er gao*" (two reports; the precise meaning is uncertain), was also inscribed in the lower quadrant of crack number 4 on the left. Both the positive and negative charges shared the identical preface, 丙辰卜殼貞, (Crack-making on *bingchen* [day 53], [the diviner] Que divined: . . .). The date, 四月 (fourth moon), was recorded at the end of the negative charge on the left (*Heji*, 9950f).

---

institutions. Over 48,000 of the total excavated corpus of 200,000 oracle-bone fragments have been thought worth reproducing in the form of modern rubbings, recently assembled in one comprehensive collection of Shang inscriptions.[12]

SHANG DIVINATION: PROCEDURES. After the diviners had produced and interpreted the cracks and the king had pronounced his forecast, the number of each crack (1, 2, 3, etc.), together with the occasional "crack notation" about the good fortune of a particular crack, was incised beside it (Fig. 4.3). Thereafter, specialists carved a record of the entire divination, probably copied from a preliminary account written on perishable material, into the bone. The engraved characters and the cracks too were sometimes filled with colored pigments. After a certain interval, the oracle bones, their usefulness now ended, were buried in storage pits in the temple palace area.[13] Figure 4.4 provides an excellent example of a full divination record.

DIVINERS, DIVINATION TOPICS, AND DIVINATION FORMS. The last nine Shang kings were served by over 120 diviners whose names are known. That some, like Gu 古, Xuan 宣, or Xi 喜, bore the names of communities or countries whose leaders and activities also formed part of the divination record suggests that the diviners, as members of named lineages, were not of low status. Modern scholars have identified some ten major diviner groups on the basis of their periods of activity, writing styles, divination forms, and divination topics. They have also conveniently, if sometimes imperfectly, divided these groups chronologically into five periods (see Table 4.1). By the

---

[12] Guo Moruo, ed., Hu Houxuan, ed. in chief, *Jiaguwen heji*, 13 vols. (N.p.: Zhonghua, 1978–82); hereafter cited as *HJ*. For an introduction to this *corpus inscriptionum*, see David N. Keightley, "Sources of Shang History: Two Major Oracle-Bone Collections Published in the People's Republic of China," *JAOS* 110, 1 (1990): 39–51. An *HJ* number followed by an "f" or "b" refers to the front or back of the bone or shell.

[13] Keightley, *Sources of Shang History*, pp. 12–56.

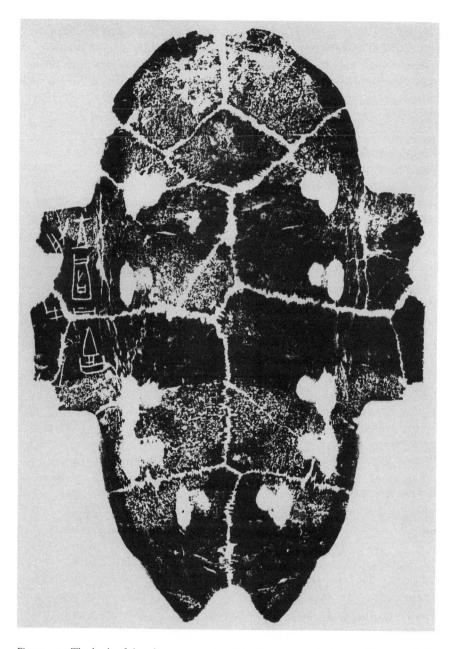

Figure 4.2. The back of the plastron reproduced in Fig. 4.3 records the royal forecast: "The king read the cracks and said: 'Auspicious. We will receive this harvest.'" The diviner had applied his heat source to the ten hollows that had earlier been bored into the shell, five on the right and five on the left; their location determined the position and direction of the T-shaped cracks that formed on the front (*HJ* 9950b).

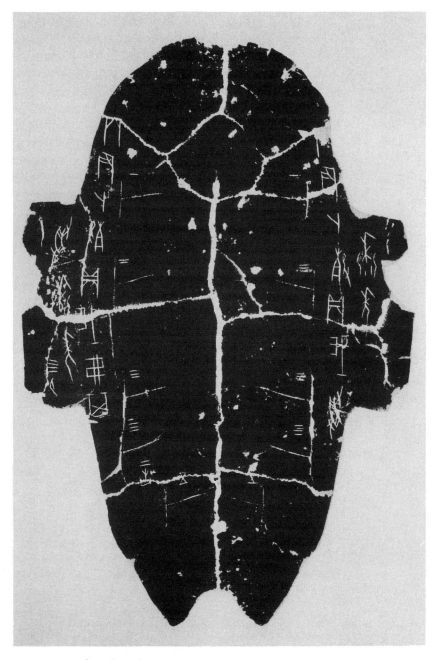

Figure 4.3. See figure legend on p. 237.

Table 4.1. *Diviner groups: Periodization and chronology*

Approximate B.C. dates[a]	King reigns	Dong Zuobin periods[b]	Major diviner groups
—	Pan Geng[c]	I	—
—	Xiao Xin	I	—
—	Xiao Yi	I	—
		Ib[d]	Shi 白 group (large graphs)
		Ib[d]	Shi group (small graphs)
		Ib[d]	—
–1189[e]	Wu Ding (K21)	I	Shi–Bin 賓 Transitional group (Early Bin group)
		I	Shi–Li 歷 Transitional group
		I	Li group, Type 1 (Li group, Father Yi category); Standard Bin group (Middle Bin group)
1188–1178	Zu Geng (K22)	IIa	Late Bin group; Li group, Type 2 (Li group, Father Ding category)
1177–1158	Zu Jia (K23)	IIb	Chu 出 group; Nameless 無名 diviner group
1157–1149[f]	Lin Xin (K24)	IIIa	Nameless 無名 diviner group, He 何 group
1148–1132	Kang Ding (K25)	IIIb	—
1131–1117	Wu Yi (K26)	IVa	—
1116–1106	Wen Ding (K27)	IVb	Late Nameless diviner group; Huang 黃 group
1105–1087	Di Yi (K28)	Va	Huang group
1086–1045[g]	Di Xin (K29)	Vb	Huang group

Notes to Table 4.1

Sources: David N. Keightley, *Sources of Shang History: The Oracle-Bone Inscriptions of Bronze Age China* (Berkeley: University of California Press, 1978), pp. 203, 228; Edward L. Shaughnessy, "Recent Approaches to Oracle-Bone Periodization," *EC* 8 (1982–3): p. 8 (based on an earlier version of the next item); Lin Yun, "Xiaotun nandi fajue yu Yinxu jiagu duandai," *Guwenzi yanjiu*, 9 (1984): 142. For a more finely divided periodization, see Huang Tianshu, *Yinxu wang buci de fenlei yu duandai* (Taibei: Wenjing, 1991), p. 3.

[a] Many of these dates, which follow what may be called the "revised short chronology," are at best approximations; those from Wu Ding to Wu Yi derive from calculations based upon average reign lengths, counting back from the end of the Eastern Zhou, and upon lunar eclipse inscriptions (as in *HJ* 40610fb and 40204b) from the reign of Wu Ding (whose reign, if longer than the average, could have started well before 1200 B.C.). For an introduction to these issues, see Keightley, *Sources of Shang History*, pp. 171–6. For the dates of the kings from Wen Ding to Di Xin, see David S. Nivison, "The Dates of Western Chou," *HJAS* 43, 2 (1983): 500–501; Edward L. Shaughnessy, "The 'Current' Bamboo Annals and the Date of the Zhou Conquest of Shang," *EC* 11–12 (1985–7): 48.

[b] Subperiodizations like "IIa" and "IIb" were added by later scholars (see Keightley, *Sources of Shang History*, p. 93); they were not present in Dong Zuobin's original periodization as it is seen, for example, in his monumental *Yinli pu* (Nanqi: Academia Sinica, 1945).

[c] There is no firm evidence that divination inscriptions were recorded on bone and shell prior to the reign of Wu Ding.

[d] The designation "Ib" was devised by Japanese scholars to refer to what they identified as the inscriptions of the "Royal Family Group" (王族 卜辭); these were essentially inscriptions that Dong Zuobin and his supporters had dated to the reign of Wen Ding (Period IVb), seeing them as restoring the "Old School" divinatory practices of Wu Ding. The "Ib" date shifted the inscriptions to the reign of Wu Ding, thus removing much of the evidence for a IVb Old School restoration. On these issues, see Keightley, *Sources of Shang History*, p. 32, n. 18. The "Royal Family Group" has now generally been superseded, through the research of scholars such as Li Xueqin (e.g., "Yinxu jiagu fenqi xinlun," *Zhongyuan wenwu* 1990.3: 37–44), Lin Yun ("Xiaotun nandi fajue"), and Qiu Xigui ("Lun 'Lizu buci' de shidai," *Guwenzi yanjiu* 6 [1981]: 263–321), who have established the existence of the Shi 自 and Li 歷 diviner groups, who operated in Periods I and II.

[e] See the argument of Shaughnessy ("The Last Years of Shang King Wu Ding: An Experiment in Reconstructing the Chronology of Ancient China," Unpublished manuscript [7 May 1990], p. 22), that, on the basis of the stylistic analysis proposed by Qiu Xigui ("Lun 'Lizu buci' de shidai," pp. 304–16), the lunar eclipse recorded on *Heji* 11482b, which may be dated to October 25, 1189, should be classified as a late Bin-group inscription, probably datable to the reign of Zu Geng. This suggests that Wu Ding had died before that date.

[f] In order to reach the conquest date of 1045, a reign of only nine years is arbitrarily assigned to the reign of Lin Xin. This is partly justified by the consideration that he did not receive cult in the Period V ritual cycle, an indication that, for whatever reason, his reign, by that point, was regarded as unimportant. On the issues involved, see Keightley, *Sources of Shang History*, p. 187, n. h; p. 209, n. a; Chang Yuzhi, *Shangdai zhouji zhidu* (N. p.: Zhongguo Shehui Kexueyuan, 1987), p. 183. The reign lengths assigned to Kang Ding, Wu Yi, and Wen Wu Ding are also arbitrary. For Di Xin's dates, see Nivison, "The Dates of Western Chou," p. 501; Shaughnessy, "The 'Current' Bamboo Annals," p. 174, n. 20.

[g] For Di Yi and Di Xin, see Keightley, *Sources of Shang History*, p. 174, n. 20. For earlier scholarship on the reign lengths of Di Yi and Di Xin.

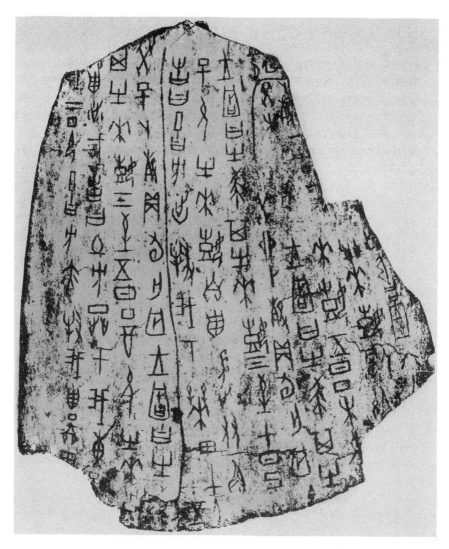

Figure 4.4. A full divination record. The front (and back; not shown) of this large scapula, from the reign of Wu Ding, records several divinations that were performed over a period of at least thirty days in the fifth and sixth moons. In each case, the record of the results confirmed the king's initial forecast of disaster. Thus, the inscription on the left (which starts at the top of the column on the left of the vertical boundary line and is read down and to the left), records: "癸巳卜㲉貞旬亡禍王固曰有咎／其有來嬉乞至五日丁酉允有來嬉／自西沚馘告曰土方征于我東鄙／𤞤二邑𢀛方亦侵我西鄙田" "[Preface:] Crack-making on *guisi* (day 40), Que divined: "In the next ten days there will be no disasters." [*Prognostication:*] "There will be calamities; there may be someone bringing alarming news." [*Verification:*] When it came to the fifth day, *dingyou* [day 34], there really was someone bringing alarming news from the west. Guo of Zhi [a Shang general] reported and said: "The Tufang [an enemy country] have attacked in our eastern borders and have seized two settlements." The Gongfang (another enemy country) likewise invaded the fields of our western borders)." The large, bold graphs were typical of the reign of Wu Ding; they had also been filled with bright red pigment (*Heji*, 6057f).

end of the dynasty, however, the king himself had become virtually the only diviner recorded in the inscriptions, monopolizing the mantic role that Wu Ding had earlier shared with other notables.

The diviners from the Bin 賓 group (Period I), in particular, favored a form of divination in which they treated the topic at issue in complementary fashion. Rather than offer a direct question to the Powers, they formulated a pair of "charges" (the modern term is *mingci* 命辭), one positive and one negative, the "charge" being best understood as the statement of a prediction, a hope, or a fear.[14] These paired formulations of the issue were generally cracked and inscribed on the right and left sides of a turtle shell, as in Figure 4.3. Wu Ding's diviners treated charges about a large variety of topics in this dualistic way: harvests, bad omens, the capture of prisoners, childbearing (Fig. 4.5), the activities of Di 帝 (the high God) and other Powers, dreams, floods, military strategy, the issuing of orders, rain and sunshine, royal tours of inspection, sickness, sending men on a mission, settlement building, sorties and other trips, spiritual approval, assistance, harm, tribute payments, and so on. That much Shang art was also characterized by the symmetrical opposition of images (Figs. 3.8 and 3.9) further suggests the value that the Shang elites attached to such binary oppositions.[15]

As divinatory practice and its underlying religious assumptions evolved, the content and form of Shang divination changed considerably.[16] Not only did diviners use complementary, positive and negative charge pairs increasingly rarely, but they reduced the whole scope of the enterprise. Most Period V divinations focused on the performance, according to strict schedule, of ancestral cult, apotropaic wishes for "no harm" in the next ten-day week, and queries about the royal hunts, which were now divined on the same five days – the second, fourth, fifth, eighth, and ninth – in every ten-day week.[17] Charges about what the Powers might do to the Shang, about receiving or not receiving millet harvest (Figs. 4.2, 4.3), and many of the other topics that Wu Ding's diviners had addressed – such as the hopes for the birth of a male child (Fig. 4.5), the meaning of dreams, the cause of and ritual cure for sickness, the choice of allies in war and of officers to carry out the king's affairs, the mobilization of conscripts, the building of settlements, and the will of Di – had vanished from the record.[18]

---

[14] See Qiu Xigui, "An Examination of Whether the Charges in Shang Oracle-Bone Inscriptions Are Questions," *EC* 14 (1989): 77–114, 165–72, and the attendant discussion.

[15] K. C. Chang, "Some Dualistic Phenomena in Shang Society," in idem, *Early Chinese Civilization: Anthropological Perspectives* (Cambridge, Mass.: Harvard University Press, 1976), pp. 93–114; David N. Keightley, "Shang Divination and Metaphysics," *Philosophy East and West* 38 (1988): 367–97.

[16] Keightley, "Shang Divination and Metaphysics," pp. 378–83.

[17] Matsumaru Michio, "Inkyo bokujichū no denryōchi ni tsuite: Indai kokka kôzô kenkyû no tame ni," *Tôyô bunka kenkyûjo kiyô* 31 (1963): 70.

[18] These will be taken up below, pp. 282–4.

Figure 4.5. Childbirth oracle-bone inscriptions. The inscription on the right, reads down-wards, in columns that move from right to left: 甲申卜殻貞：婦好娩嘉。王固曰：其佳丁娩嘉其佳庚娩引吉。三旬又一日甲寅娩允不嘉佳女 (Crack-making on *jiashen* [day 21], Que divined: [*Charge:*] "Lady Hao's childbearing will be good." [*Prognostication:*] The king read the cracks and said: "If it be a *ding*-day childbearing, it will be good; if it be a *geng*-[day] child-bearing, there will be prolonged luck." [*Verification:*] [After] thirty-one days, on *jiayin* [day 51], she gave birth; it was not good; it was a girl). The paired charge on the left, couched in the negative, undesired mode, reads downwards, in columns that move from left to right: 甲申卜殻貞：婦好娩不其嘉。三旬又一日甲寅娩允不嘉佳女 [*Preface:*] Crack-making on *jiashen* [day 21], Que divined: [*Charge:*] "Lady Hao's childbearing may not be good." [*Verification:*] [After] thirty-one days, on *jiayin* [day 51], she gave birth; it really was not good; it was a girl) (*HJ* 14002f).

Calligraphy, moreover, once large and bold in Period I (Figs. 4.2, 4.3, 4.4, and 4.5) had become minuscule (Fig. 4.6). Crack notations that, in Period I, had identified the auspiciousness of particular cracks (Fig. 4.3), were almost completely discarded. The number of cracks per charge, which might, under Wu Ding, have involved up to twenty for a charge pair (see the ten numbered cracks in Fig. 4.3), had generally been reduced to no more than three cracks per unpaired charge (Fig. 4.6).[19] Royal prognostications, which under Wu Ding had forecast both good fortune (Fig. 4.2) and bad (Fig. 4.4), and could on occasion be lengthy (Fig. 4.5), were now uniformly auspicious and brief (Fig. 4.6).

Shang divination, in short, had, during the century and half from the reign of Wu Ding to that of Di Xin (1086–1045 B.C.), become more systematic, less spontaneous, and less comprehensive; it had also become routinely optimistic. These changes in form and scope, however, may be related to a variety of other cultural developments: to the systematization of the five-ritual cycle of ancestral cult (for this system of rites and ceremonies, see p. 260 below); to the triumph of filial over fraternal succession, which regularized as it simplified both political and cultic practice; to the increasing power and confidence of the kings as they came to head a more routinized administration; and to the replacement of pyromancy by the simpler form of divination, involving the manipulation of numbers, that was to produce the hexagram-based system of the *Yi jing* 易經 (Classic of changes).[20] Given the reduction in the scope of Period V divination, however, modern scholars are, in many areas, less informed about the activities, hopes, and fears of Di Yi and Di Xin than they are about those of Wu Ding.

SHANG DIVINATION AND ITS RELIGIOUS ASSUMPTIONS. Although the Shang inscriptions suggest that some turtle shells had numinous value, the bulk of the evidence indicates that the oracle bones served as a divination medium because the diviners sanctified and employed them in rituals performed in the presence of the ancestors.[21] It may be assumed that the ancestor in whose temple a divination was performed acted as an ancestral "saint" who mediated between the divinatory supplicants below and other ancestral Powers above.

---

[19] Keightley, *Sources of Shang History*, pp. 38–40.

[20] Guan Xiechu, "Shang Zhou jiagu he qingtongqi shang de guayao bianshi," *Guwenzi yanjiu* 6 (1981): 141–9; Zhang Yachu and Liu Yu, "Some Observations About Milfoil Divination Based on Shang and Zhou *bagua* Numerical Symbols," trans. Edward L. Shaughnessy *EC* 7 (1981–2): 46–55.

[21] The Shang diviners may also have attributed special powers to the vaulted carapace and *ya* 亞-shaped plastron of the turtle, whose shapes would have symbolized Heaven above and Earth below (Sarah Allan, *The Shape of the Turtle: Myth, Art, and Cosmos in Early China* [Albany: State University of New York Press, 1991], pp. 104–11); it is difficult, however, to demonstrate such analogies, known only from later texts, in the oracle-bone record itself.

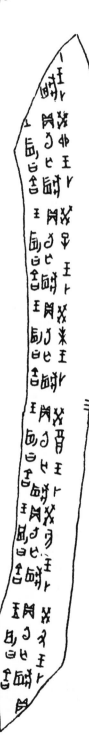

Figure 4.6. Late oracle-bone inscriptions. This series of seven inscriptions on the remaining edge of a scapula (the bone would have fragmented along the line of the vertical T-shaped cracks whose crack numbers, all "3," are visible on the right) typify the inscriptional style of the last two kings, Di Yi and Di Xin. The inscriptions were unpaired, the king was the diviner of record, the calligraphy was small, the results were uniformly auspicious. Each divination was performed on the *gui*-day, the last day of the Shang ten-day week, and was concerned to determine the good fortune of the week to come. The first inscription (at the bottom of the fragment) reads 癸丑王卜貞旬亡禍王固曰吉 (On the day *guichou* [day 50], the king made cracks and divined: "In the next ten days there will be no disasters." The king read the cracks and said: "Auspicious"). The subsequent and identical charges and forecasts moved up the bone, being divined on *guihai* (day 60), *guiyou* (day 10), and so on (*Heji* 39393).

Ancestral responsibility for the cracks is also suggested by a significant number of charges that specifically appealed to the ancestors for aid. Here, as everywhere in Shang divination, there is evidence of a hierarchy based on seniority. Where, for example, the good fortune of particular individuals or of the king's hunts was involved, the ancestor to whom appeal was made might be relatively junior (*HJ* 10608f, 32680). Where larger, dynastic topics, like harvest, enemy invasions, or victory in battle were concerned, the pyromantic appeal for religious action was frequently to the senior ancestors, dynastic and predynastic (*HJ* 6204f, 6316). The pattern of the divination charges reveals the hierarchy of jurisdictions that the Shang conferred upon the dead.

The diviners might formulate the charges and preside over the divinatory rituals, but with few exceptions, only the king – who is occasionally referred to in the bones as "I, the one man" (*yu yi ren* 余一人)[22] – had the ability to read the cracks (as in Figs. 4.2, 4.4, 4.5, and 4.6). His monopoly of the crucial interpretive act may plausibly be explained in terms of his kin relationship to the ancestors.

CHRONOLOGY

Absolute Dating

Modern attempts to date the Shang employ some combination of evidence drawn from the oracle-bone inscriptions, from Western Zhou bronze inscriptions, and from Zhou accounts of varying date and reliability. Carbon-14 dating can provide parameters within which the various stages of the Shang dynasty must fall, but it is not sufficiently precise to resolve the disputes of the text-based chronologists.[23]

Various attempts have been made to assign absolute dates to events recorded in the oracle-bone inscriptions.[24] The lunar eclipse inscriptions, for example, suggest that Wu Ding was on the throne in the period from at least 1198 to 1189 B.C., but more work is needed before we can specify precise reign dates.[25] Until that work is done, it seems preferable to anchor the late Shang

---

[22] Hu Houxuan, "Chonglun Yu yi ren wenti," *Guwenzi yanjiu* 6 (1981): 15–33.

[23] Keightley, *Sources of Shang History*, pp. 172–3 and 188; Chang, *Shang Civilization*, pp. 322–4. Additional carbon 14 dates are published each year in the seventh issue of *Kaogu*.

[24] The most heroic of these has been Dong Zuobin, *Yinli pu* (Nanqi, Sichuan: Academia Sinica, 1945); see, however, the issues raised throughout Zhang Peiyu's summary, "Yinxu buci lifa yanjiu zongshu," *Xian Qin shi yanjiu* 12, 3 (1986): 1–14. For the reign dates offered by Dong Zuobin, Chen Mengjia, and Liu Xin 劉歆 (ca. 46 B.C. – A.D. 23), see Keightley, *Sources of Shang History*, pp. 226–7, table 37.

[25] On late Shang dates, see Table 4.3, note a. On the lunar eclipse inscriptions, see Keightley, *Sources of Shang History*, p. 174; and idem, "Shang China Is Coming of Age: A Review Article," *JAS* 41 (1982): 550–2. For a promising new methodology, see Edward L. Shaughnessy, "Micro-Periodization and the

chronology in the lunar eclipse inscriptions of Wu Ding, the reign dates of the last king, Di Xin (Table 4.1), and a Zhou conquest date of ca. 1045 B.C. (see below). Absolute dates have been assigned to a few other events, such as the campaign against the Renfang 人方 that Di Xin conducted in his tenth ritual cycle,[26] but, at present, scholars have a firmer sense of the relative, rather than absolute, dates of the bone inscriptions.

The attempt to establish the first year of the Shang has benefited from new initiatives in archaeo-astronomy. Entries in Zhou texts have been taken as mythologized memories of the five-planet conjunction that occurred in Sagittarius in 1576. Other records of what appear to be similar conjunctions, understood as symbolizing Heaven's transferral of the Mandate, at the time of the founding of the Xia and the overthrow of the Shang, support this view. Using the absolute date of such astronomical events it is possible to conclude that the first year of Cheng Tang would have been 1554.[27]

As to the end of the dynasty, Sima Qian was unable to date the year when the Zhou swept out of the Wei 渭 River valley in the west and overthrew Di Xin. The Han scholar Liu Xin 劉歆 (46 B.C.–A.D. 23) had calculated a conquest date of 1122 B.C. (with the dynasty starting in 1766), while an entry in what has been regarded as the so-called ancient *Bamboo Annals* (*Guben Zhushu jinian* 古本竹書紀年) – a record of events down to 299 B.C. that was discovered by grave robbers, probably in A.D. 279 – has suggested a date of 1027 B.C. (with the dynasty starting in 1523). The argument that the dates given in the so-called modern, or current, *Bamboo Annals* (*Jinben Zhushu jinian* 今本竹書紀年) – traditionally regarded as a Ming 明 dynasty fake – may, with proper compensation for the manipulations of later numerologists, be used to deduce the Shang dates has led to a proposed conquest date of 1045 B.C. or years close to it.[28]

Calendar of a Shang Military Campaign," in *Chinese Language, Thought and Culture: Essays Dedicated to David S. Nivison*, ed. P. J. Ivanhoe (La Salle, Ill.: Open Court, 1996), pp. 58–93.

[26] David S. Nivison ("The Dates of Western Zhou," *HJAS* 43, 2 [1983]: 501) and Shaughnessy ("The 'Current' Bamboo Annals and the Date of the Zhou Conquest of Shang," *EC* 11–12 (1985–7): 48–9) date the campaign to 1077–1076 B.C.; He Youqi ("Di Yi Di Xin jinian he zheng Yi fang de niandai," *Yindu xuekan* 1990.3: 1–9) dates it to 1072. On the numbered ritual cycles, see below under "Time and the Calendar."

[27] David W. Pankenier, "Astronomical Dates in Shang and Western Zhou," *EC* 7 (1981–2): 17–19, 23, 24; and idem, "*Mozi* and the Dates of Xia, Shang, and Zhou: A Research Note," *EC* 9–10 (1983–5): 177. This may be compared with the estimate of Itô Michiharu ("Part One: Religion and Society," in *Studies in Early Chinese Civilization: Religion, Society, Language, and Palaeography*, ed. Itô Michiharu and Ken-ichi Takashima [Hirakata: Kansai Gaidai University Press, 1996], vol. 2, p. 43, n. 29) that the dynasty started ca. 1600.

[28] Shaughnessy (*Sources of Western Zhou History: Inscribed Bronze Vessels* [Berkeley: University of California Press, 1991], pp. 217–21) reviews the difficulties involved with the *Guben Zhushu jinian* dates. David S. Nivison ("The Dates of Western Chou," pp. 481–580) concluded that the battle of Muye took place on January 15, 1045; he subsequently revised that conclusion in, "1040 as the Date of the Chou Conquest" (*EC* 8 [1982–3]: 76–8). Pankenier, employing some of Nivison's methodology, proposed a conquest date of 1046; see Pankenier, "Astronomical Dates," pp. 2–37; idem, "The *Bamboo*

Relative Dating

Scholars have determined the relative date of many of the divination inscriptions by calling on various types of evidence. Ancestral titles permit a temple name like Father Ding to be taken as a reference to Wu Ding, made in the generation of his sons, Zu Geng 祖庚 and Zu Jia 祖甲. Other clues are found in archaeological provenance, shapes and placement of the hollows, diviners' names and diviner groups, writing style, "same-bone" relationships, and the presence or absence of particular divinatory conventions and topics. Changes in style and content did not necessarily coincide with a change of rulers – indeed, technical studies now classify inscriptions by diviner groups rather than reigns – but, for broad analyses, the five periods by which Dong Zuobin and later scholars correlated the inscriptions with the royal reigns (as shown in Table 4.1), may still be used.[29]

TIME AND THE CALENDAR

To the Shang diviner, human time was concerned with the hours of the day, the seasons of the year, the birth of royal sons, the timing of royal hunts, the mobilization of conscripts for fighting, agriculture, or other public work. It was also inextricably linked to, and conceived in terms of, religious time, which was concerned with the schedule of rituals and sacrifices, the luck of a particular day or week, the portentous significance of events occurring at one time rather than another.

In the reign of Wu Ding, the diviners referred to the periods within a day and night by at least eight different terms, such as: *ming* 明, the time of "brightening"; *xiaoshi* 小食, the time of the "small meal"; and *zhongri* 中日, "midday."[30] The nature of the terms, some of which were related to the sun's motion (dawn, midday, afternoon), and others to social events (small and great meals), suggests no consistent or punctual system of "hours."

The Shang named their days by combining the ten "heavenly stems" (*tian gan* 天干, a later term) – *jia* 甲, *yi* 乙, *bing* 丙, *ding* 丁, etc., ending with *gui* 癸 – and the twelve "earthly branches" (*di zhi* 地支, also a later term) – *zi* 子, *chou* 丑, *yin* 寅, etc., ending with *hai* 亥. These combined

Annals Revisited: Problems of Method in Using the Chronicle as a Source for the Chronology of Early Zhou, Part 1," *BSOAS* 55 (1992): 272–97; "Part 2: The Congruent Mandate Chronology in *Yi Zhou shu*," pp. 498–510. Shaughnessy (*Sources of Western Zhou History*, pp. 217–36) concludes that a conquest date of 1045 is "thoroughly supported" by numerous pieces of evidence.

29 Keightley, *Sources of Shang History*, pp. 91–133; Edward L. Shaughnessy, "Recent Approaches to Oracle-Bone Periodization," *EC* 8 (1982–3): 1–13.

30 Chen Mengjia, *Yinxu buci zongshu*, pp. 229–33; Yao Xiaosui, "Du 'Xiaotun nandi jiagu' zhaji," *Guwenzi yanjiu* 12 (1985): 116–24.

terms created a repeating six-week cycle of sixty days, with each week being ten days long, as stem 1 was linked with branch 1 (*jiazi* 甲子, day 1), stem 2 with branch 2 (*yichou* 乙丑, day 2), down to stem 10, which was linked with branch 12 (*guihai* 癸亥, day 60). That living Shang kings employed these "heavenly stems" to confer posthumous temple names upon their royal ancestors and ancestresses – such as Da Jia 大甲 (the third king), Da Yi 大乙 (the first), and Wai Bing 卜 (= 外) 丙 (the fourth) – and increasingly structured the ancestral cult so that the ancestors and ancestresses received cult on the day of their temple names, demonstrates the religious significance of the day names. These offerings were sometimes divined in advance, but increasingly by Period II and invariably in Period V, the charge about the offering was divined on the name day of the ancestral recipient, as in:

Crack-making on *jiayin* (day 51), Yin divined: "The king hosts (*bin* 賓) Da Jia (the third king), performs the *yong* 彡 ritual, no fault. . . ."

Crack-making on *gengshen* (day 57), Yin divined: "The king hosts Da Geng (the fifth king; next on the main line of descent), performs the *yong*-ritual, no fault. . . ." (*HJ* 22723)

Da Jia was hosted on a *jia*-day, Da Geng on a *geng*-day. References to "the Ding temple" (*ding zong* 丁宗) and "the temple of Da Yi" (*Da Yi zong* 大乙宗) document the existence of ritual structures dedicated to particular *gan*-named ancestors.[31]

Ten stem-named days formed the Shang week, known as the *xun* 旬, which started on the *jia* 甲 day and ended on the *gui* 癸 day, and the common incantatory charge, *xun wang huo* 旬亡禍 (In the [next] ten days there will be no disasters; Y444.2–46.1, 447.1–2), appears to have been divined on the last *gui*-day of every ten-day week for at least the 150 or more years of the Shang historical period. The regularity of these divinations suggests a hallowed and traditional unit, the basic sequence of ten days and ten suns. It was only by the end of the dynasty that a few postfaces provide an unequivocal date and suggest the development of a more linear view of time, counted by ritual cycles (*si* 祀), as in:

"It was in the sixth moon, on the *jiawu* (day 31) when we performed the *yong*-ritual to Qiang Jia (the fourteenth Shang king); it was in the king's third ritual-cycle" (*wei wang san si* 隹王三祀).[32]

---

[31] Chen Mengjia, *Yinxu buci zongshu*, pp. 468–9, 472–3, 478. For an introduction to the associations between sun, day, and ancestor, see Allan, *Shape of the Turtle*, pp. 19–56. For how the temple names were assigned, see below under "Royal Succession and Temple Names."

[32] *HJ* 37838; Keightley, *Sources of Shang History*, pp. 115–16. See, too, Itô Michiharu, "Part One: Religion

By Period V, in fact, the growing number of ancestors whose sequential cult constituted the ritual cycle permitted that cycle to serve as a counter for periods that were 360 or, more commonly, 370 days long; this "ritual year," however, did not, apparently, start at a fixed point in the solar year.[33]

The late Shang synchronized the lunar months with the solar year by the addition of intercalary months. Following Zhou and Han accounts, and in accordance with the practice of Chinese calendars that have traditionally started with or near the winter solstice, it is generally, though not universally, thought that the first Shang moon started with the new moon after the winter solstice, and that the calendrical Shang day started at midnight (rather than at dawn). Although numerous uncertainties remain, the general picture that emerges is of a calendrical system that was evolving from observation and description toward one that was increasingly mathematical and pre-scriptive. That some variability may still be observed in the calendars of Eastern Zhou supports the view that Shang calendrical methods were still relatively inexact.[34] Zhou accounts of Shang (and earlier) astrological events, strongly suggest that the Shang would have been observing and recording the rising and setting of certain stars, such as Da Huo 大火 (Great Fire, i.e., Antares), and major planetary conjunctions, but the degree to which they divined such matters or put their astronomical knowledge to calendrical use is uncertain.[35]

ROYAL SHANG RELIGION

Starting with the reign of Wu Ding, the cult center at Xiaotun (Fig. 4.7) was the site of numerous activities that expressed and reinforced royal claims to knowledge and authority. Here were the burials of royal ancestors, whose powerful assistance the living king and his dependents solicited with cult and whose spirits offered pyromantic guidance about the conduct of the dynasty's affairs. Here was the impressive bronze-founding industry of the royal Shang, which produced the shining, ritual vessels that the kings on earth employed in their communications with the ancestors and other Powers who received cult at the site. Here labored the kings' diviners, engravers, and record keepers. And here were the surrounding settlements, workshops, and ceme-

---

and Society," vol. 1, pp. 49–53. Bagley (*Shang Ritual Bronzes*, pp. 521–31) discusses twelve such ritual-date inscriptions on bronzes.

[33] Chang Yuzhi (*Shangdai zhouji zhidu* [N.p.: Zhongguo Shehui kexueyuan, 1987], pp. 221–5, 234, 249, 260, 290) provides detailed calendrical reconstructions.

[34] For a judicious summary of the technical issues, see Zhang Peiyu, "Yinxu buci lifa."

[35] For examples of the claims made, see Wen Shaofeng and Yuan Tingdong, *Yinxu buci yanjiu: Kexue jishu pian* (Chengdu: Sichuan renmin, 1983), pp. 1–121; and Feng Shi, "Yinli suishou yanjiu," *Kaogu xuebao* 1990.1: 19–42.

teries of lineages that were closely allied to the dynasty. That the oracle bones were consistently stored at Xiaotun, and were returned there for burial even though they had been used on the king's hunts and travels, reveals that the king regarded the site as the dynasty's paramount sacro-administrative center.

The Upper Pantheon

DI, THE HIGH GOD. The original meaning of the word *di* 帝, the name or title by which the Shang kings addressed their High God (and their royal ancestors on the main line of descent) remains hard to determine. Some scholars, for example, have argued that the oracle-bone graph (帝 in Period I) depicted a celestial, vegetative, anthropomorphic, or ritual object. Others, relying upon the etymology of the term, have suggested that *di* meant "tightly tied" (締) and that the name Di may thus have identified a corporate group of spirits, like the royal ancestors, or a higher Power that unified the various cultures of the North China Plain, much as the Shang themselves may have been seeking to do politically.[36]

The Late Shang kings and their supporters believed that Di presided over a hierarchy of ancestral and other Powers that were capable of influencing the success or failure of most aspects of Shang life. That Di was conceived as being "above" is indicated by his ability to "send down" (*jiang* 降) disasters and approval on men below (Y480.1).[37] That Di was virtually the only Power who could directly order (*ling* 令) the Rain, or the Thunder, as well as the only Power who had the Wind Powers under his control, set him apart from all the other Powers, natural, predynastic, or ancestral. Where weather was concerned, Di's most important function was his control of the rain. Typical charges are: "From today, *gengzi* (day 37), down to *jiachen* (day 41), Di will order rain" (*HJ* 900f), and "Di, when it comes to the fourth moon, will order rain" (*HJ* 14138). One may note the parallels between the worlds of religion and politics; just as no other Power but Di ever issued orders in the world of the inscriptions, neither did any other person but the king.

[36] For the scholarship on Di, see Matsumaru Michio and Takashima Ken-ichi, *Kôkotsumoji jishaku sôran* (Tokyo: Tokyo University Press, 1994), no. 0006. For Western-language studies, see, e.g., Herrlee Glessner Creel, *The Birth of China: A Study of the Formative Period of Chinese Civilization* (New York: Reynal & Hitchcock, 1937), pp. 182–4; and Robert Eno, "Was There a High God *Ti* in Shang Religion?," *EC* 15 (1990): 18–20. See too Tôdô Akiyasu, *Kanji gogen jiten* (Tokyo: Gakutôsha, 1969), p. 471.

[37] The title Shang Di 上帝 (Upper Di, or Di on High) found in later texts, also indicates that Di resided above; it rarely if ever occurs, however, in the oracle-bone inscriptions (Y396.2 cites only three instances; see too Shima Kunio, *Inkyo bokuji kenkyû* [Hirosaki: Hirosaki daigaku Chûgoku kenkyûkai, 1958], p. 197). It is uncertain if Shang Di appears in any Shang bronze inscription (Bagley, *Shang Ritual Bronzes*, pp. 526–8, 535, nn. 29–31).

It has frequently been suggested that Di was the first Shang ancestor,[38] but the evidence is problematic. Di might, on rare occasions, share certain functions with the ancestors, being able, for example, to cause sickness (*HJ* 14222Cf). Such instances suggest that the Shang, living in a world dominated by kin relations, tended to conceive all great power in quasi-kin terms. The living Shang kings divined about Di infrequently, however, and they offered him little or no sacrificial wealth. The contrast with the generous and importuning way in which the kings treated their ancestors implies that Di was regarded quite differently.

This conclusion is supported by the consideration that, on rare occasions, Di might order enemy attacks, as in "... the ... fang 方 [an enemy country] is harming and attacking [us]; it is Di who orders it to make disasters for us" (*Yingcang* 1133f), and "It is not Di who orders [an enemy country] to make disasters for us" (*HJ* 6746). That Di could order the dynasty to suffer harm in this way, or could cause unspecified disasters to descend on the Shang cult center or other settlements (*HJ* 14176, 14178; see also Y420.1), further implies that Di's role was nonancestral. The Shang ancestors never struck at the dynasty in such vital spots, presumably because they lacked the power and the motivation. These few "Di makes disaster" cases are significant, for they suggest that Di was potentially a Tian 天 ("Heaven")-like figure capable, like the Zhou deity, of harming and destroying the dynasty. The Zhou claim that Di (or Tian) had ordered their rulers to conquer the Shang (see Chapter 5) would thus not have been a Zhou invention, but a logical extension of Shang religious concepts.

THE HIGH POWERS. The Powers of the Shang pantheon may be divided into six groups: (1) Di, the High God; (2) Nature Powers, like Tu 土, the Earth Power or Altar of the Soil (the *she* 社 of later texts), He 河, the (Yellow) River Power, Yang 羊 (Xiang?; sometimes given in modern transcription as Yue 岳), the Mountain Power (which modern scholars have identified with Mount Song 嵩, the sacred peak some 50 km southwest of modern Zhengzhou 鄭州), and Ri 日, the sun;[39] (3) Former Lords (*Xian Gong* 先公, a modern term) such as Nao 夒 and Wang Hai 王亥, whom the Shang wor-

---

[38] For example, Guo Moruo (*Qingtong shidai* [Shanghai: Qunyi, 1946], pp. 21–4) argued that Di was equivalent to the divine progenitor, Di Ku 帝嚳, and thus, through Di Ku's union with his secondary consort, Jian Di 簡狄, the founder of the Shang lineage. Eno has proposed "a root meaning of 'father' for the word *di*" ("Was There a High God?" p. 19); see too Qiu Xigui, "Guanyu Shangdai de zongzu zuzhi yu guizu he pingmin liangge jieji de chubu yanjiu," *Wenshi* 17 (1983): 2–3.

[39] Itô Michiharu, "Part One: Religion and Society," pp. 63 and 73–5. Zhang Bingquan, *Xiaotun di er ben: Yinxu wenzi – Bingbian* (Taipei: Academia Sinica, 1955–1972), commentary to no. 124, finds that *he* 河 had four uses in the inscriptions: as the name of a Shang ancestor, place, river, or diviner. Yang Shengnan ("Yinxu jiaguwen zhong de he," *Yinxu bowu yuan yuankan* 1 [1989]: 54–63) argues that the Shang treated the He as an actual ancestor rather than a Nature Power.

shippers treated differently from their ancestors; (4) predynastic ancestors, such as Shang Jia and the three Bao 報 (see Fig. 4.1); (5) the dynastic ancestors, starting with Da Yi (the first king); and (6) the dynastic ancestresses, the consorts of the kings on the main line of descent.[40]

The distinctions between these groups, especially the distinctions between Nature Powers, Former Lords, and predynastic ancestors, who may be called, collectively, the High Powers, were by no means rigid; the Shang conceived of the High Powers as sharing many essential functions. Furthermore, they referred to some of the High Powers as "Ancestor" (*zu* 祖) or "High Ancestor" (*gao zu* 高祖), thus incorporating them into their ancestral pantheon.[41] The Nature Powers, such as Di and a few of the Former Lords, like Huang Yin 黃尹 (Y977.1–78.2), tended to affect the dynasty or the country as a whole, influencing the weather, the crops, and warfare. Unlike the ancestors, they were not directly concerned with the king's personal activities: his well-being, his illnesses, the childbearing of his consorts, the fault-free management of his rituals, and the oracular cracking of bone and shell. The High Powers occupied a middle ground, unable to emulate Di by commanding (*ling*) natural phenomena, but, above the ancestors, still having a large impact on the weather and the crops.

The Former Lords were apparently powerful figures, not of royal origin, to whom the Shang offered cult outside the system of ancestral worship. In the case of Former Lords like Wang Hai and Yi Yin, legends about their activities as rulers or ministers appear in texts of far later date; it is possible that the Shang shared such a legendary view of their persons and histories.[42] The Former Lords were apparently regarded as early progenitors of the Shang elite, but they were not accorded temple names or a scheduled place in the regular ritual cycle. The Shang kings' worship of these figures laid the seeds of a practice maintained throughout China's imperial history. The canoniza-

---

[40] Other divisions are possible. Itô Michiharu ("Yindai shi de yanjiu," in *Riben kaoguxue yanjiuzhe: Zhong-guo kaoguxue yanjiu lunwenji*, ed. Higuchi Takayasu, tr. Cai Fengshu [Hong Kong: Dongfang shudian, 1990], pp. 205–60), for example, proposes that the Shang employed two sacrificial systems: one was external, centered on the Nature Powers, the other was internal, centered, through the five-ritual cycle, on the ancestors. For the Former Lords and predynastic ancestors recorded in traditional texts, see Chang, *Shang Civilization*, pp. 4–5.

[41] The Former Lords, Nao (*HJ* 30398, 30399, and 33227) and Wang Hai (*HJ* 30447), were called High Ancestor; He, the River Power, was also so honored (*HJ* 32028). Later legends about, for example, He Bo 河伯, Lord of the Yellow River (see, e.g., Anne Birrell, *Chinese Mythology: An Introduction* [Baltimore: Johns Hopkins University Press, 1993], pp. 88, 101–2, 140–1, 263), confirm this tendency to anthropomorphize Nature Powers.

[42] The way in which late Shang worshippers associated Yi Yin 伊尹 (Y980.1–2) with groups of dead kings on the main line of descent, generally starting with the dynasty founder, suggests both that Yi Yin was an important, if nondynastic figure and that his importance started with the reign of the founder; see Chang, *Shang Civilization*, p. 177; Cai Zhemao, "Yin buci Yi Yin jiu shi kao: Jianlun ta shi," *BIHP* 58, 4 (1987): 755–808. The Zhou accounts that present him as an important minister of Da Yi are thus tacitly supported by the Shang evidence.

tion of dead officers, who, like the royal ancestors, were capable of cursing the living and of receiving sacrifices, demonstrated that high status in this life, conferred by the king, could be maintained, with the help of the king's descendants, in the next. Views of the afterlife thus served to validate status relations among the living.

That the Shang distinguished the Predynastic Ancestors from the dynastic kings is suggested by the artificial regularity of their temple names, which followed, in sequence, the first four days of the Shang week, Shang Jia, Bao Yi 報乙, Bao Bing 報丙, Bao Ding 報丁, and the last two days, Shi Ren 示壬, Shi Gui 示癸 (P1–6 in Fig. 4.1). That the consorts of the first four figures were not offered cult is a further reason for thinking that their nature differed from that of the dynastic ancestors.[43]

The higher reaches of the Shang pantheon were thus occupied by a loose cluster of High Powers whose jurisdictions were wide and nonexclusive and whose qualities were partly, though not wholly, conceived in ancestral terms. The divinations that sought to determine their influence and the cult that sought to win their favors suggest that such religious negotiations were conceived in ad hoc and expedient terms. At this level of the pantheon, responsibility for such large topics as the weather, harvest, and insect plagues could not be strictly assigned to one Power.

The Ancestors

Since the royal lineage served as the core of the dynastic state in which religious and social idioms and institutions, still largely undifferentiated, were given political expression, the commemoration of the names of ancestors, singly or in groups, in divination and in cult, served to reaffirm the genealogical charter by which the Shang kings ruled. It likewise reminded the participants, in a sacred context, of the accumulated generations of Shang rulers and of the king's unique relationship to a fundamental source of ultrahuman power. The king stood at the center of his own kinship community, known, at least to later ages, as the Zi 子 lineage.[44] The kings themselves, particu-

---

[43] Zhu Fenghan ("Lun Yinxu buci zhong de dashi ji qi xiangguan wenti," *Guwenzi yanjiu* 16 [1989]: 39–41) provides additional reasons for distinguishing the predynastic from the dynastic ancestors. Additional predynastic ancestors may perhaps be discerned in the bone record. According to later texts, thirteen such figures spanned thirteen generations prior to the reign of Da Yi; see Chang, *Shang Civilization*, pp. 4–5.

[44] The traditional genealogies are given in Chang, *Shang Civilization*, pp. 3–5. For the view that such lineage names appeared only at the start of Western Zhou, with the Zi name deriving from the corporate group represented by the Zi (princes) of Shang, see Léon Vandermeersch, *Wangdao ou la voie royale: Recherches sur l'esprit des institutions de la Chine archaïque. Tome 1: Structures culturelles et structures familiales* (Paris: École française d'Extrême Orient, 1977), pp. 301–2. For Zi as a status term, see Lin Yun, "Cong Wu Ding shidai de jizhong Zi buci shilun Shangdai de jiazu xingtai," *Guwenzi yanjiu*

larly those on the main line of descent whose fathers and sons were both kings,[45] formed an unbroken lineage whose members were continually sustained and refreshed by the offering of regularly scheduled sacrifices in which the living king "hosted" his ancestors in sequence, according to their seniority. Shang dynastic identity was above all that of lineage descendants whose primary obligation was to strengthen and continue the lineage just as they drew strength from it.

Affinal ties were believed to persist after death, the consorts of the kings who constituted the main line of descent being worshipped jointly with their royal spouses. This suggests the importance of the marriage ties that linked the sublineages to the royal dynasty. Further, as in later times, there is evidence that shifts in political power among the living were reflected in shifts in sacrificial practice.[46] Death provided no alternative vision of how society might be structured; status relations between the rulers and the ruled, between older and younger generations, remained unchanged. The ancestors were still conceived of as having human concerns rather than being transcendentally different entities. This may help to account for the characteristic this-worldliness, not only of Shang religion itself, but also of subsequent Chinese philosophy. It is worth stressing, however, that the ancestors were not simply the commemorated dead. Ancestor worship, in the words of one anthropologist, "is a representation or extension of the authority component in jural relations of successive generations."[47] The Shang ancestors had jobs to do, and it was the role of their living descendants both to sustain the ancestors with cult and to provide the hierarchical, jurisdictional, and functional structures that enabled the ancestors to exert their continuing and orderly influence in the world.

MAIN-LINE AND COLLATERAL DESCENT. The distinction between the main-line and collateral kings was critically important to the Shang ritual-

---

1 (1979): 320–4: Chang Cheng-lang, "A Brief Discussion of Fu Tzu," in *Studies of Shang Archaeology: Selected Papers from the International Conference on Shang Civilization*, ed. K. C. Chang (New Haven, Conn.: Yale University Press, 1986), pp. 107–8.

[45] This line is known in later texts as the *dazong* 大宗. *Dazong* in the Shang inscriptions (Y753.2) evidently referred to the Great Temple itself, where cult was offered to the great ancestors, but the term had not yet assumed its later meaning; see Yang Shengnan, "Cong Yinxu buci zhong de shi zong shuo dao Shangdai de zongfa zhidu," *Zhongguo shi yanjiu* 1985.3: 3–16; Zhu Fenghan, "Yinxu buci suo jian Shang wangshi zongmiao zhidu," *Lishi yanjiu* 1990.6: 5–6.

[46] Under Wu Ding, Qiang Jia 羌甲 (K14), for example, was not treated as a main-line king but as a member of a collateral line that produced no kings; during the reign of the next six kings he was treated as a member of the main line of descent; but in the reigns of the last two kings, Di Yi and Di Xin, he was again relegated to collateral status (see Keightley, *Sources of Shang History*, p. 187, n. f). These shifts presumably reflected changes in the value of collateral and main-line descent and in the status of Qiang Jia's descendants.

[47] Meyer Fortes, "Some Reflections on Ancestor Worship in Africa," in *African Systems of Thought*, ed. M. Fortes and G. Dieterlen (London: Oxford University Press, 1965), p. 133.

ists. The inclusion of a royal ancestor in the schedule of sacrifices addressed to the main-line kings, and the exclusion of the collateral kings (see note 46) served to strengthen not only the power of those royal progenitors and their descendants, but also the principle of father-to-son descent itself, thus legitimizing the political status of the incumbent king and his sons at the expense of those who were descended from the collateral kings.

The title Di 帝 was only attached to the temple names of kings on the direct line of descent. Thus, in Period II, Wu Ding might be referred to as Di Ding 帝丁 (*HJ* 24982), and, in Period III, Zu Jia as Di Jia 帝甲 (*HJ* 27439). This confirms the importance attached to these distinctions,[48] as does the treatment of the royal consorts. Only the consorts of the main-line kings received cult in the five-ritual cycle. Whether these consorts were honored because they were the mothers of kings, so that they received status from their sons, or whether the sons became kings because their mothers were the official consorts (so that the sons received status from their mothers) cannot be determined from the oracle-bone record, which focuses almost exclusively on the post-mortem, ritual treatment of these figures. Lineages whose daughters were taken in marriage by the royal sons would have understood, from these ritual arrangements, that the greater religious power was reserved for women whose husbands and sons were both kings.[49]

ANCESTRAL TABLETS AND TEMPLES. The Shang symbolized and commemorated each royal ancestor by a spirit tablet (or its Shang precursor) to which the ancestor returned when receiving cult. Few if any archaeological remains of such tablets have been found,[50] but it is generally agreed that the oracle-bone graph 示 (Y398.2–403.2), read as *shi* 示, could refer to both the altar stands or tablets (known as *zhu* 主 in later texts) and to the ancestors themselves. The tablets were housed in temples (Fig. 4.7) – the bone

---

[48] Shima Kunio, *Inkyo bokuji kenkyû*, p. 186; Qiu Xigui, "Guanyu Shangdai de zongzu zuzhi," p. 2; Itô Michiharu, "Part One: Religion and Society," pp. 45–6. Qiu notes that the "Yin benji" erroneously assigns the title of Di to all, rather than just the main-line Shang kings, and suggests that the word *di* was related to *di* 嫡, "son of the chief or legal consort."

[49] That "Yin benji" (e.g., *Shi ji*, 3, p. 105; Nienhauser et al., *The Grand Scribe's Records*, p. 49) records distinctions between the sons of primary and secondary Shang consorts has encouraged some scholars to argue that Shang power struggles led to shifts in the rules of succession (see the later section "Royal Succession and Temple Names"); see, e.g., Ping-ti Ho, *The Cradle of the East: An Inquiry into the Indigenous Origins of Techniques and Ideas of Neolithic and Early Historic China, 5000–1000 B.C.* (Hong Kong: Chinese University of Hong Kong Press; and Chicago: University of Chicago Press, 1975), pp. 289–91; Yang Shengnan, "Cong Yinxu buci zhong de shi," pp. 14–15.

[50] Liu Zhao ("Anyang Hougang Yin mu suochu 'bing xing shi' yongtu kao," *Kaogu* 1995.7: 623–5, 605) has proposed that a small number of stone and jade "plumb-bob" shapes, 7 cm long, excavated from two graves at Hougang 後岡 (see Figure 3.23, this volume), some of them engraved with the temple names of ancestors, such as Zu Geng and Fu Ding 父丁 ("Father Ding"), were Shang ancestral tablets. It is thought, however, that most ancestral tablets would have been made of wood.

graph 宀 (modern zong 宗) depicted a roof over a tablet (Y753.1–57.2) – where cult offerings and divinations were performed. There were temples to the Former Lords, like Nao, and to Nature Powers, like the River and the Mountain. There were temples named for individual kings, starting with Da Yi. Only kings on the main line of descent, however, whose fathers and sons had also both been kings, were so honored, with their temples being maintained over generations; temples named for collateral kings were rarely recorded and were evidently dismantled after a certain period. There were also temples for royal consorts, although only two or three such temples actually appear in the record, for example, for Mother Xin (Mu Xin 母辛), the consort of Wu Ding (*HJ* 27566). And there were joint temples, described as "The Great Temple," (see note 45), "The Small Temple," and so on, in which groups of ancestors, sometimes starting with Shang Jia, sometimes with Di Yi, received cult.[51]

THE CHARACTER OF THE CULT. Millet ale (usually rendered as "wine"), cattle, dogs, sheep, grains, and human victims were among the items offered to the ancestors, in a regular series of rituals and offerings: in prayers for rain, good harvests, good births, and assistance (in battle or other enterprises); in exorcisms to ward off hostile spirits or appease their malevolence; and in ritual announcements about the king's plans, his health, the activities of his enemies, natural disasters, and so on. Many animals were burned, buried whole in pits, or drowned in rivers, but much attention was also paid to the shedding of blood and to the dismembering of the animal and human victims, for reasons, perhaps, of both display and allocation.[52] Several considerations indicate that the offering of wine, whose fragrance and taste, like the smoke from the roasting meat, was pleasing to the Powers, would have been a routine part of Shang cult. This conclusion is based on the large number of Shang ritual bronzes, such as *he* 盉, *jia* 斝, *jue* 爵, and *gu* 觚, for heating and pouring wine; the evidence that a Shang industry existed for brewing alcoholic beverages; and the Duke of Zhou's (Zhou Gong 周公) command that the Shang elites (and other lords) should desist, upon pain of death, from wine drinking.[53]

[51] Keightley, *Sources of Shang History*, 17, n. 71; Yang Shengnan, "Cong Yinxu buci zhong de shi," pp. 3–9; Chao Fulin, "Guanyu Yinxu buci zong de shi he zong de tantao," *Shehui kexue zhanxian* 1989.3: 158–9; Zhu Fenghan, "Lun Yinxu buci zhong de dashi," pp. 40, 42, 45; Zhu Fenghan, "Yinxu buci suo jian Shang wangshi zongmiao zhidu," pp. 10–19.

[52] Itô Michiharu, "Part One: Religion and Society," pp. 71–3; K. C. Chang, "Shang Shamans," in *The Power of Culture: Studies in Chinese Cultural History*, ed. Willard J. Peterson (Hong Kong: Chinese University Press, 1994), pp. 31–2.

[53] See e.g., Elizabeth Childs-Johnson, "The *Jue* and Its Ceremonial Use in the Ancestor Cult of China," *Artibus Asiae* 48, 3–4 (1987): 171–96; Robert L. Thorp, "The Archaeology of Style at Anyang: Tomb 5 in Context," *Archives of Asian Art* 41 (1988): 50 and 62, who remarks on the notable increase in the

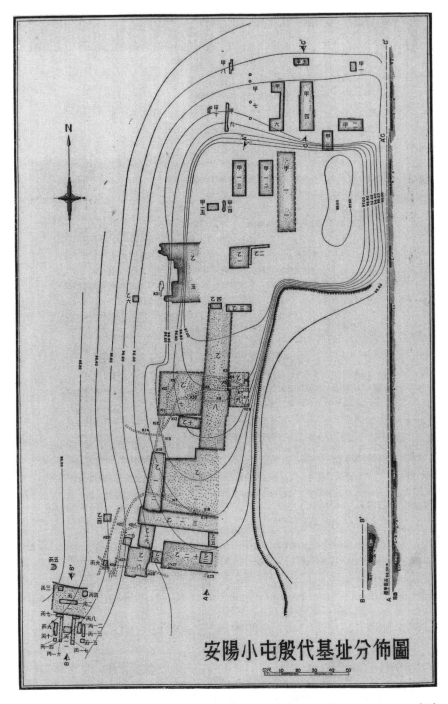

Figure 4.7. Plan of the late Shang temple-palace foundations at Xiaotun, Anyang, which archaeologists have divided into the Jia 甲, Yi 乙, and Bing 丙 sectors. The "K" numbers refer to water ditches (see note 102). The modern bank of the Huan River is shown at the right (*Yinxu de faxian yu yanjiu*, p. 52).

The social nature of Shang sacrifice is suggested by the *bin* 賓 ritual in which the king "hosted" one of his ancestors or ancestresses. Another Shang ritual, *xiang* 饗 (Y139.1–40.2), the bone graph for which, 𝕬, depicts two men facing a vessel, appears to have involved the offering of a feast or banquet to a spirit. The same word was used when the king entertained his supporters with banquets that, either by analogy, or by direct involvement with the sacrifice, shared the religious blessings of the lineage.[54] It is not likely that the cattle, sometimes several hundred head, that were slaughtered in offerings would have gone uneaten. That the king virtually ceased to divine about feasting his supporters in Period V suggests a change in the political (and thus the religious) situations in which the increasing power and confidence of the king (or perhaps the decreasing number of his supporters) removed the need to determine or to validate which groups should be invited. Participation in the cult of the descent group was apparently reserved for close lineage members, royal consorts, sons, and affines. To participate in these rituals was to draw close to the source of dynastic power, that of the royal ancestors.[55]

THE FIVE-RITUAL CYCLE. Cult to the Shang ancestors was centered on a cycle of five rituals whose repeated performance, routinely divined in Periods II and V (less frequently in III and IV), permits us to reconstruct the Shang calendar and the Shang king list. A typical series of Period II inscriptions on a scapula fragment begins,

Crack-making on *guiyou* [day 10], the king divined: "On the next day, *jiaxu* [day 11], when the king hosts Da Jia [K3] and performs the *zai* 𝕬 [sometimes transcribed 𝕬] ritual, there will be no harm"; Crack-making on *dinghai* [day 24], the king divined: "On the next day, *wuzi* [day 25], when the king hosts Da Wu [K7] and performs the *zai* ritual, there will be no harm." (*HJ* 22779).

with the divining of the rituals continuing to move down the ranks of the ancestors and the days of the sixty-day cycle.

The divinatory formulas and the scope of the recipients changed with time, but the basic sequence in which the five rituals were performed to the

number and variety of bronze vessels for containing alcohol in the period from late Wu Ding to Zu Jia; Guo Shengqiang, "Lüelun Yindai de zhijiu ye," *Zhongyuan wenwu* 1986.3: 94–5; Chang, "Shang Shamans," pp. 33–4; and *Shang shu zhengyi*, "Jiu gao," 14, pp. 20b–24a (James Legge, tr., *The Chinese Classics, Vol. 3: The Shoo King, or the Book of Historical Documents* [London: Henry Frowde, 1865], pp. 408–11).

[54] On the nature of these feasts, see Yang Shengnan, "Shangdai de caizheng zhidu," *Lishi yanjiu* 1992.5: 92–3.

[55] Whether the participation of outsiders involved the establishment of fictive kinship ties – as Matsumaru Michio has suggested – is not certain. He has also suggested that the true rulers of the dynasty, in the mind of the royal court, were the former kings rather than the living one ("In Shū kokka no kōzō," *Iwanami kōza, sekai rekishi* 4 [1970]: 60–70, 85).

individual ancestors was *yi* 翌 (or *yi ri* 翌日, "*yi* day"), *ji* 祭, *zai* 歆, *xie* 脅 (or *xie ri* 脅日, "*xie* day"), and *yong* 肜. Once the cycle to a particular ancestor was completed, ending with the *yong*, it started again with the *yi*. Although many of the five rituals might be performed to various ancestors or ancestresses in the course of any one ten-day week, it appears that a particular recipient received only one of the five rituals in any one week.[56]

A shorter cycle of four of the five rituals (excluding the *ji*) was also offered to the consorts of the main-line kings, but only in association with the "hosting" ritual: "When the king hosts Wu Ding's consort, Ancestral Mother Xin (Bi Xin 妣辛), and performs the *zai* ritual, there will be no fault" (*HJ* 36268). As in the case of the kings, the rituals were offered to the consorts on the *gan* days of their temple names (thus, the charge just cited had been divined on *xinsi*), but their cycle lagged behind that of the kings by one week.[57]

By Period V, and even earlier, the five-ritual divinations had become so well ordered that each oracle bone was reserved for charges about only one of the five rituals, even though various ancestral recipients, kings, or consorts, were specified; divinations about any of the other four rituals were divined on other bones. And the cult was so regular that particular rituals could be recorded in the postfaces to charges as a way of identifying the particular week.

EVOLVING RELIGIOUS CONCEPTIONS. After the reign of Wu Ding, the kings no longer divined about Di ordering the rain or thunder or about seeking his approval or assistance. Di's virtual disappearance from the record suggests either the increasing confidence with which the Shang kings relied on the power of their ancestors, their increasing indifference to Di's existence, or their increasing realization that Di's will was so inscrutable that it was fruitless to divine about his intentions. That the ancestral main-line kings were given temple names that included the title of Di (see note 48) may indicate an increasing Shang belief in the majesty of their ancestors. The growing power of the ancestral spirits after Period II, together with the regularization

---

[56] The relevant inscriptions are listed at Y705.2–706.2, 350.1–352.2, 1068.1–1070.1, 264.1–266.2, 1286.2–1290.2. For an introduction to the cycle, see Itô Michiharu, "Part One: Religion and Society," pp. 92–102. For the order of the rituals adopted here, see Xu Jinxiong, *Yin buci zhong wuzhong jisi de yanjiu* (Taipei: Guoli Taiwan daxue wenxueyuan, 1968); and Chang Yuzhi, *Shangdai zhouji zhidu*. For a calendar of the five rituals and their recipients over a ten-week period, see, e.g., ibid., pp. 109–10; for a reconstruction of the full ritual calendar, see Y1474. There is no certainty about the five rituals' content; Dong Zuobin, for example – who placed the rituals in a different sequence – proposed that *yong* involved drum music, *yi* a feather dance, *ji* a meat offering, *zai* a grain offering, and that *xie* was a combined offering to conclude the cycle (*Yinli pu*, pt. 1, *j.* 1, p. 3a).

[57] See note 56. For the consort cycle, see Ge Yinghui, "Zhou ji buci zhong de zhixi xian bi ji xiangguan wenti," *Beijing daxue xuebao: Zheshe ban* 1990.1: 121–8.

of the ancestral sacrifices, appears to reflect both a more precise definition of the ancestors and an increase in the authority of the kings themselves.[58] These conclusions accord with the way in which the later kings discarded the balanced, positive–negative charge pairs of Wu Ding's time (Figs. 4.3 and 4.5) and simply proposed one unequivocal charge for the approval of the Powers (Fig. 4.6). They also accord with the king's monopoly of the diviner's role. These shifts in divinatory practice indicate the degree to which religious conceptions were evolving during the century and a half of the late Shang historical period. The culture was not unchanging.

THE KING AS ROYAL SHAMAN. The view that the Shang kings were shamans has frequently been advanced. It has been argued, for example, on philological grounds that the word *wang* 王 (king), was related to words like *wang* 尪 (emaciated, crippled) and *kuang* 狂 (mad), with both of these states thought to be characteristic of shamans. The motifs on the Shang ritual bronzes have been understood as depictions of the shaman's animal familiars; and much stress has been placed on Eastern Zhou references to the role played by shamans in the courts of early rulers, some of whom were said to have visited Di or Tian.[59] The issues are complex and depend to a significant degree upon matters of definition. The good, bureaucratic order of the divination inscriptions, like the "plain Chinese" in which they were written, does not suggest the ecstatic possession or trance voyages that anthropologists normally associate with the shamanic experience. As Robert Bagley notes in Chapter 3, the iconographic significance of the Shang ritual bronzes is also open to interpretation. The Shang kings were undoubtedly heirs to Neolithic and early Bronze Age traditions of religious communication that involved the early iconography of animal masks and the use of ritual jade objects, such as *cong* 琮 tubes. By late Shang, they had so routinized and ordered their mediations with the Powers that they would have found the impromptu qualities of shamanic ecstasy and inspiration inimical to their religious and political authority.

---

[58] Itô Michiharu, "Bokuji ni mieru sorei kannen ni tsuite," *Tôhô gakuhô* 26 (1956): 25–6 and 31; idem, "Part One: Religion and Society," vol. 1, pp. 38, 42–5, 49, 53–5, 86, 100.

[59] Chen Mengjia, "Shangdai de shenhua yu wushu," *Yanjing xuebao* 20 (1936): 485–576; Edward H. Schafer, "Ritual Exposure in Ancient China," *HJAS* 14 (1951): 130–3, 160–2; K. C. Chang, *Art, Myth, and Ritual: The Path to Political Authority in Ancient China* (Cambridge, Mass.: Harvard University Press, 1983), pp. 45, 56–80; idem, "Shang Shamans," pp. 10–36. Akatsuka (*Chûgoku kodai no shûkyô to bunka*) advanced at least fourteen arguments to show that shamanism flourished in Shang times; see David N. Keightley, "Akatsuka Kiyoshi and the Culture of Early China: A Study in Historical Method," *HJAS* 42 (1982): 299–301.

Treatment of the Dead

The assiduous attention paid to their dead both reflected early Chinese social patterns and influenced their development. This was partly because experiencing the death of others would have been a more frequent occurrence for the Shang than it is for modern populations; the average age at death of the over 5,300 skeletons excavated from the cemeteries in and around Xiaotun has been estimated at 34.5 years.[60]

The ritual treatment required to transform a newly deceased person into a living ancestor or ancestress involved appropriate burial. Throughout the late Neolithic, distinctions of wealth and status among the living had been increasingly applied to the dead, and by the late Shang, such distinctions, mirroring the secular world and its ideals, had become central to the Bronze Age mortuary system. The segregation of the late Shang kings, for example, buried across the Huan 洹 River, at Xibeigang 西北岡 (the Northwestern High Ground, a site name that is frequently used to include the sites of Houjiazhuang 侯家莊 and Wuguancun 武官村; Map. 4.1), some 2.5 km northwest of the temple-palace complex at Xiaotun, symbolized their special status, as did the great wealth of the grave goods.

Shang mortuary customs also reflected the elite culture's general concern with orientation and placement. The cardinal orientation of the great royal tombs at Xibeigang was notable (see Figs. 3.20a and 3.20b), the longer ramps generally being oriented on an axis north-by-east/south-by-west. The so-called commoner, or, more appropriately, petty elite, burials at Yinxu West (ca. 2.5 km west of Xiaotun; see Fig. 3.20c) were also oriented to the cardinal directions. So were the burials of Shang sacrificial victims.[61]

The posture of the dead was equally significant. The supine, extended position was preferred, as it had been in Neolithic burials. In the numerous sacrificial burials around the temple-palace foundations of Xiaotun area C, for example, there was a clear distinction between supine and prone victims. All had been decapitated, but most of the supine victims appear to have had only the top halves of their heads hacked off; the jawbones or lower halves of the skulls were still connected to the neck. Prone victims, by contrast, had

---

[60] Song Zhenhao, "Xia Shang renkou chutan," *Lishi yanjiu* 1991.4: 104–106. Since, as in Neolithic practice, the occupants of these cemeteries were, by a ratio of two to one, men rather than women, men received far greater ritual attention than women.

[61] *Kaogu xuebao* 1979.1: 35 and 121–46; *Kaogu* 1977.1: 22 and 27; Chang, *Shang Civilization*, p. 121. For the characterization of the Yinxu West cemetery as "petty elite," see Thorp, "The Archaeology of Style at Anyang," p. 62.

Figure 4.8. Beheaded victims, buried prone, in the south ramp of M1001 at Xibeigang (Liang Siyong and Gao Quxun, *Houjia zhuang 1001 hao damu*, pl. 28.1).

generally lost their heads entirely (Fig. 4.8).[62] The occupants of elite burials, by contrast, were generally buried in the supine, extended position, their bodies not being dismembered in any way.

GRAVE GOODS. Because the royal tombs at Xibeigang were repeatedly looted, we can only guess at the opulence of their furnishings. The relatively modest tomb of Wu Ding's consort, Lady Hao (Fu Hao 婦好; posthumously known as Mu Xin 母辛, Mother Xin), which was situated in the temple-palace complex at Xiaotun itself (some 200 m west of the Bing sector) had been furnished with 468 bronzes weighing over 1.5 metric tons, 755 jades, and over 6,880 cowrie shells. Of the bronzes, 44.8 percent were ritual vessels, 28.6 percent were weapons, and 8.8 percent were tools.[63] Being veritable under-

---

[62] Shi Zhangru, *Xiaotun diyiben: Yizhi de faxian yu fajue: Yibian: Jianzhu yicun* (Nangang: Zhongyang yanjiuyuan, 1959), p. 304.

[63] The remaining bronzes consisted of miscellaneous vessels, musical instruments, and art objects. See *Yinxu Fu Hao mu*, Zhongguo Shehui kexueyuan Kaogu yanjiusuo (Beijing: Wenwu, 1980), pp. 15, 114, 220; see too Chang, *Shang Civilization*, pp. 87–8. The pit measured 5.6 by 4 m and was 7.5 m deep. For the argument that the name Fu Hao 婦好 should be read as Fu Zi 婦子, see Chang Cheng-lang, "A Brief Discussion of Fu Tzu," pp. 103–4. Since most modern scholars refer to her as Fu Hao, however, that romanization is used here. For one hypothesis that attempts to demonstrate her lineage affiliation

Figure 4.9. Model showing the victims who accompanied the grave lord in death in the great tomb at Wuguancun (*Yinxu de faxian yu yanjiu*, pl. 12).

to a Zi country (rather than to the Zi lineage [on which see note 44], see Cao Dingyun, "Fu Hao nai Zi Fang zhi nü," in *Qingzhu Su Bingqi kaogu wushiwu nian lunwenji bianjizu* (Beijing: Wenwu, 1989), pp. 381–5. Cao Dingyun ("Yinxu Fuhao mu mingwen zhong renwu guanxi zongkao," *Kaogu yu wenwu* 1995.5: 44–54) has also attempted to identify the status and wide geographic distribution of the other Shang individuals whose inscribed bronzes were included in the grave goods buried with Lady Hao. Yan Yiping ("Fu Hao liezhuan," *Zhongguo wenzi* 3 [1981]: 1–104) has provided an account, based on the inscriptions, of Fu Hao's life.

ground storehouses of the finest products that Shang civilization could create, late Shang burial tombs testify to (1) the belief that the dead were thought to employ these objects in the afterlife, (2) the emotional dominion that dead parents exercised over living descendants, and (3) the intensity with which mortuary worship both exploited and stimulated the labors of the community.

Shang petty elites were also provided with grave goods. A total of close to 10,000 items was found in 800 of the 939 tombs in the Yinxu West cemetery, the individual burials usually containing from 3 to 8 items; for example, 2,014 ceramic vessels have been found in 719 graves, 175 bronze vessels in 61 graves. As with elite burials, a certain logic appears to have governed the choice of objects, but ceramic *jue* and *gu* wine-pouring vessels were commonly provided as substitutes for the bronze vessels found in elite tombs. Dagger-axes, spears, and other weapons, generally made of bronze, were found in 160 burials, all male; these weapons constituted one-sixth of the grave goods found. Fifty-six of the smaller graves were equipped with craft or agricultural tools such as adzes, chisels, awls, stone axes, and spinning whorls.[64] The service and work one had performed in life was, as in the Neolithic, frequently provided for in death.

Although the finest objects, particularly those made of ceramic, jade, and bronze, were buried with the elite dead, cruder facsimiles, known in Zhou and Han texts as "spirit objects" (*mingqi* 明器) might also be present. A small number of light, thin bronze dagger-axes found in the tomb of Lady Hao, for example, made with a low proportion of tin, may have been designed for mortuary use. Pottery replicas of bronzes appear in late Shang tombs, and some of the mortuary bronze vessels themselves were less well made. Large numbers of *mingqi*, including weapons made of lead, were found in the petty elite cemetery at Yinxu West.[65]

FOLLOWING-IN-DEATH AND HUMAN SACRIFICE. The preservation of both status and kin, or kinlike, relations in a postmortem existence was powerfully expressed by the sacrifice of family members, elites, or other dependents who were buried with a grave lord in death. The Shang had institutionalized the custom to such a remarkable degree that it serves as one of the characteristic features of their emerging dynastic institution.

---

[64] *Kaogu xuebao* 1979.1: 49, 61, 80; Yang Baocheng and Yang Xizhang, "Cong Yinxu xiaoxing muzang kan Yindai shehui de pingmin," *Zhongyuan wenwu* 1983.1: 30, 31, 50.

[65] *Yinxu Fu Hao mu*, pp. 16, 239–40. For the pottery replicas in Dasikong cun 大司空村 M21 and M53 (M stands for *mu* 墓, "grave, burial," in the reports), see *Kaogu* 1964.8: 383–4. Thirty-seven ritual vessels made of lead (as opposed to 175 made of bronze) were excavated at Yinxu West; other bronzes appear to have been crudely made (*Kaogu xuebao* 1979.1: 61, 80, 83, 98; Robert L. Thorp, "The Growth of Early Shang Civilization: New Data from Ritual Vessels," *HJAS* 45 [1985]: 35).

The hierarchy of mortuary victims in late Shang royal burials at Xibeigang may be classified, moving from the bottom of the grave pit towards the top, as follows: (1) those buried, mainly with their bodies whole and equipped with a bronze or jade dagger-axe, in the "waist pit" (yaokeng 腰坑; below the burial chamber, where dogs were frequently buried) or in the burial chamber's four corners; they presumably were to guard the deceased, and (2) those buried whole, with their own coffins, grave goods, bronzes, and even with their own followers-in-death or an attendant dog (see Fig. 4.9). Generally placed on the ledge (ercengtai 二層臺) or on the roof of the coffin chamber, and showing no evidence of having been bound or having struggled, these presumably were high-status relatives, close dependents, or personal attendants of the deceased. Evidence of this sort suggests that the royal tombs may be regarded as inverted representations of the sociologist's conical clan, with those retainers close to the king in life being buried close to him in death and enjoying the highest post-mortem status. (3) The most numerous group of victims consisted mainly of young males, between fifteen to thirty-five years of age, and a few children. Generally decapitated or dismembered, they were frequently buried in the fill, in the ramps, or in rows of sacrificial pits in the vicinity of the tomb, mainly with ten pits to a row and 5 to 10 victims to a pit (see Fig. 4.8). Their heads were frequently buried in the pits, with their bodies in the ramps, and their hands appear to have been tied.[66] These, presumably, were prisoners from enemy states. Often referred to in the divination inscriptions as Qiang 羌, they were frequently sacrificed to the Shang ancestors, with the numbers offered at one time varying from 3 to 400, but usually being about 10.[67] In general, human sacrifice has not been reported in association with any of the small-scale burials in the Xiaotun area; at most 1 or 2 followers-in-death might have been present.[68]

HIERARCHY OF THE DEAD. As with the mortuary victims, the graves in the Xiaotun core area reflected the marked stratification of political and social life. At least five categories of burial can be identified: (1) tombs with ramps, mainly at Xibeigang and at Hougang, south of the Huan River and ca. 1.3

---

[66] Huang Zhanyue, "Wo guo gudai de renxun he rensheng – Cong renxun rensheng Kan Kong Qiu keji fuli de fandongxing," *Kaogu* 1974.3: 159–60; idem, "Yin Shang muxang zhong renxu rensheng de zaikaocha – Fulun xunsheng jisheng," *Kaogu* 1983.10: 937–8, 941; Yu Weichao, "Gushi fenqi wenti de kaoguxue guancha (yi)," *Wenwu* 1981.5: 50–1.

[67] According to Hu Housuan ("Zhongguo nuli shehui de renxun he renji (xia pian)," *Wenwu* 1974.8: 57), the inscriptions record 7,426 Qiang victims. For Wu Ding's continual wars with the Qiangfang, see Wang Yuxin, "Wuding qi zhanzheng buci fenqi de changshi," in *Jiaguwen yu Yin Shang shi: Di san ji,* ed. Wang Yuxin (Shanghai: Shanghai Guji, 1991), pp. 170–1, 174.

[68] Yang Baocheng and Yang Xizhang, "Cong Yinxu xiaoxing muzang," p. 30. Only 18 of the 939 burials at Yinxu West, for example, contained victims, 38 in all, who had followed a master in death (*Kaogu xuebao* 1979.1: 45; Huang Zhanyue ["Yin Shang muzang," p. 936] gives slightly different figures, but of the same order of magnitude).

km east of Xiaotun; (2) burials of those who followed their lords in death, some buried in the grave lord's tomb, some in its vicinity; (3) medium-size pits, some 4 to 6 m deep, mainly at Hougang, Wuguancun, and Dasikong-cun, northeast of Xiaotun, across the Huan River (see Fig. 3.23); (4) shallow pits, like those used at Dasikongcun and Yinxu West; and (5) burials in refuse pits and disused wells.[69]

Much labor was invested in the construction of the tomb ramps and the massive burial chambers of elite graves. These latter were built in cruciform shape with heavy wooden beams; measuring approximately 3 m in height, they formed true rooms in which the mourners could have performed their final rituals. The four-ramp tombs (whose shape, also cruciform, probably had cosmological significance) were those of kings, while those with two ramps (to the north and south) or one ramp (to the south) were for lesser elites.[70] Even the lesser tombs would have been costly to construct. The two-ramp tomb M1 at Wuguancun would have required the preparation of a hundred wooden beams for the inner and outer coffins and the raising of a substantial workforce.[71] By contrast, of the 710 burials at Yinxu West that still preserve traces of burial furnishings, no more than 47 had been provided with a burial chamber; the other 663 had only wooden coffins. Coffinless burials occasionally show traces of rudimentary planking, a mat, or a piece of hemp cloth laid over the corpse, but generally the lower classes of the Early Bronze Age were buried with no containers or protection at all.[72]

By late Shang, the care of the royal and elite dead had become one of the great Bronze Age enterprises. The constant investment of wealth – labor, tools, weapons, bronzes, ceramics, jades, ornaments, food, drink, and animal and human victims – to provide for the dead, to say nothing of the wealth and lives consumed in the subsequent ancestral sacrifices, cannot have failed to demonstrate the high status of the survivors who provided the wealth. Such lavish use of grave goods, moreover, would have stimulated the productive powers of craftsmen and laborers, who presumably believed that the sustained consumption of wealth by the ancestors would bring blessings to the survivors, to their dependents, and to the community they ruled.

---

[69] Huang Zhanyue, "Wo guo gudai de renxu he rensheng," p. 159. Huang combines the preceding categories (4) and (5).

[70] Yang Xizhang, "Anyang Yinxu Xibeigang damu de fenqi ji Youguan de wenti," *Zhongyuan wenwu* 1981.3: 50.

[71] Guo Baojun, "Yijiuwuling nian chun Yinxu fajue baogao," *Kaogu xuebao* 1951.5: 59. Li Ji (preface to Shi Zhangru, *Xiaotun diyiben*: p. 3) estimated that each of the large graves would have required about 7,000 man-workdays for the earth moving alone.

[72] *Kaogu xuebao* 1979.1: 39; Yang Baocheng and Yang Xizhang, "Cong Yinxu xiaoxing muzang," p. 30.

THE DYNASTIC STATE

The Political and Cultural Landscape

Many of the communities recorded in the oracle-bone inscriptions were focused on a sacred place where the genius loci, which had either given the place its name or taken its name from it, was worshipped, where the lineage leader of the same name derived his authority from that of his mythical progenitor, and where the population of the community also bore the same appellation.[73]

In cosmological terms the Shang conceived of a square world, oriented to the cardinal points, surrounding the core area known as Zhong Shang 中商, literally, "center Shang."[74] Beyond the core area, the Shang domain was divided, ideally, into four areas, known as "the Four Lands" (si tu 四土)" or "the Lands" (tu) named for the cardinal directions. Thus, a series of Period V charges on a single scapula fragment (HJ 36975) starts with the general charge, 〔今〕歲商受〔年〕 "[This] year Shang will receive [harvest]," followed by four subcharges about the East, South, West, and North Lands receiving harvest. Similarly, prayers for harvest were directed to the Powers of "the Four Regions" (si fang 四方) (HJ 14295).

Fang 方, in fact, was a word of broad scope that may be translated as "side, border, country, or region." Local, usually hostile, rulers with the title of Bo 伯 sallied forth from the Fang (Y1205.2). The king divined about patrolling and attacking these border areas (Y1208.1–2). Fang was also used as a suffix to refer to non-Shang or enemy countries that existed in and beyond the borders of the Shang polity.[75]

That the divinations refer to numerous lineage groups and to various single zu 族 lineages (Y986.1–87.1), with many of the lineage names also appearing as insignia at the end of Shang bronze inscriptions,[76] indicates that

[73] Zhang Bingquan, "Jiaguwen zhong suo jian ren di tongming kao," in *Qingzhu Li Ji xiansheng qishi sui lunwenji* (Taipei: Qinghua xuebaoshe, 1967), pp. 687–776; Keightley, "Akatsuka Kiyoshi and the Culture of Early China," pp. 139–92. On the nature and agricultural activities of local Shang "communes" (identified in the inscriptions as *dan* 單 [Y1172.1]) around Xiaotun, see Yu Weichao, *Zhongguo gudai gongshe zuzhi de kaocha – Lun Xian Qin Liang Han de dan dan dan*" (Beijing: Wenwu, 1988), pp. 21–42; Zhu Fenghan, *Shang Zhou jiazu xingtai yanjiu* (Tianjin: Tianjin guji, 1990), p. 41; Lian Shaoming, "Yinxu buci suojian shang dai de wangji," and *Kaogu yu wenwu* 1995.5: 39.

[74] Four Wu Ding inscriptions at Y1123.1. On this term, see J. A. Lefeuvre, "An Oracle Bone in the Hong Kong Museum of History and the Shang Standard of the Center," *Journal of the Hong Kong Archaeological Society* 7 (1976–8): 51; David N. Keightley, "The Late Shang State: When, Where, and What?" in *The Origins of Chinese Civilization*, ed. David N. Keightley (Berkeley: University of California Press, 1983), pp. 533, 548–51.

[75] Chang, *Shang Civilization*, pp. 216–20, 248–59.

[76] Hayashi Minao ("In Shû jidai no zuzô kigô," *Tôhô gakuhô* (Kyoto) 39 [1968]: 34–43) identified 217 oracle-bone names – Fang countries, Hou 侯 and Bo 伯 rulers, and places and persons – that appear as lineage insignia on Shang and Western Zhou bronzes. See also note 82.

the Shang king presided over a confederation of patrilineal descent groups. Composite names, moreover, reveal the fission and union of lineages. The name of the Ge 戈 lineage, for example, whose leaders and members appear in the Shang divinations (e.g., *HJ* 775f, 8398f, 8401), is also combined in various sublineage insignia on forty-four bronzes, thirty of which were excavated in or near the Xiaotun core.[77]

The existence of lineage groups may also be discerned in the cemeteries excavated in the Xiaotun area. The graves in the Yinxu West cemetery, for example, may be separated into eight sectors, distinguished by both their pottery assemblages and the lineage insignia cast into the buried ritual bronzes, showing that the lineage associations of the living were preserved among the dead.[78] These *zu* functioned as social and political entities whose members were linked to the king by a differential hierarchy of kinship ties, benefits, privileges, and obligations; led by their lineage heads, they served the king in warfare, in hunting, and in the providing of tribute, and they received, in return, his spiritual and military assistance.

The Royal Lineage

The "Royal Lineage" (Wang Zu 王族; Y986.1–2),[79] which formed the core of the dynasty, included both the ruling king and his sons, who, as adult Princes (Zi 子), and as heads of their own minor lineages, served in the royal entourage, accompanied their father on his hunts and travels, and participated in his ancestral sacrifices. The inscriptions generally link the title of Prince to a lineage and place-name. Wu Ding, for example, ordered Prince Hua, Zi Hua 子畫 (or, sometimes, Hua alone, without the title of Prince; Y1189.2–91.2), to undertake various tasks; he divined about his sickness and hunts and about reporting his activities to the ancestors. The domain of Hua, presumably through its leader, sent men, turtle shells as tribute, and reports to the King. Brief references to "the men of Hua" (*Hua ren* 畫人) further confirm that Prince Hua administered an eponymous domain. And the king occasionally hunted at Hua, which was probably not far from Xiaotun.

Because some of these lineage heads, such as Prince Yu (Zi Yu 子漁), worshipped main-line kings no more distant than those of the previous

---

[77] Zhu Fenghan, *Shang Zhou jiazu*, pp. 94–104, 143–218; Cao Dingyun, "Yinxu Fuhao mu mingwen zhong renwu guanxi zongkao," pp. 48–9.

[78] Yang Hsi-chang, "The Shang Dynasty Cemetery System," in *Studies of Shang Archaeology: Selected Papers from the International Conference on Shang Civilization*, ed. K. C. Chang (New Haven, Conn.: Yale University Press, 1986), pp. 56–7; Zhu Fenghan, *Shang Zhou jiazu*, pp. 106–23.

[79] The following discussion is largely based, with revisions, on Zhu Fenghan, *Shang Zhou jiazu*, pp. 35–90. For further discussion of the Shang lineages, see Cao Dingyun, "Yinxu Fuhao mu mingwen zhong renwu guanxi zongkao," pp. 44–54.

two generations, they may be identified as the king's sons. That, moreover, only 30 of the 116 or more Princes appear in divination charges with any frequency, and the place or lineage names of only about half of those 30 were recorded as providing service to the king, is further indication that some Princes were more important than others. The king's special authority over the Princes is also indicated by his ability, when directing campaigns, to command (*ling*) the Princes, a verb that was not used, for example, in his divinations about the Hou 侯 lords with whom he could only ally (*bi* 比) himself.[80]

The next level in the dynastic hierarchy, which was more distant in terms of kin ties and privileges, was that of the "Lineages of the Princes" (Zi Zu 子族; Y986.2), composed of all those royal descendants who had established their own collateral minor lineages, and about whose health and childbearing the king still divined. The title of the "Many Princes" (Duo Zi 多子; Y198.2–99.2) or the "Many Princely Lineages" (Duo Zi Zu 多子族; Y986.2) referred to these royal cousins. That the Lineages of the Princes frequently served on the battlefield indicates that the royal armies were, to a significant degree, composed of lineage groups and their leaders.

Other powerful figures were capable of leading their own dependents (the *zhong* 眾) in battle and casting their insignia into ritual bronzes; for example, Qin 卓 (sometimes read Bi), Bing 竝, Cha 甶, Gu 壹, Qiao 雀 (sometimes read Que), Yue 戉, ⽊, and 彳 (the pronunciation of the last two is unknown) were never styled "Prince." These magnates did not offer cult to Wu Ding's "Father Yi" (i.e., the twentieth king, Xiao Yi), but indeed did so to the more distant ancestors on the main-line of descent. In addition, the king sought spiritual assistance on their behalf from the earlier kings (those before Zu Ding, the fifteenth king) and from collateral kings. Such evidence suggests that these were leaders whose localized lineages had segmented from the royal, main-line lineage more than two generations earlier, but were still members of the royal clan whose claims of descent from more distant ancestors were evidently accepted, and even perhaps encouraged, by the king. While Princes who were active in the royal service appear to have been situated relatively close to the Xiaotun core area, some of these non-princely leaders formed a line of defense further to the west. Thus, it has been suggested that Qiao 雀 and 彳 were located in western Henan, overlooking the Yellow River; Cha was in southeast Shanxi; Bing was close to Cha; and Yue was probably in southern Shanxi.[81]

---

[80] On these distinctions, see too Lin Yun, "Jiaguwen zhong de Shangdai fangguo lianmeng," *Guwenzi yanjiu* 6 (1981), p. 77.

[81] Zhu Fenghan, *Shang Zhou jiazu*, p. 74, nn. 42–4. For the possible location of Bing, in Shilou 石樓 county, in western Shanxi, however, see Keightley, "The Late Shang State," pp. 535–6.

Non-Royal Lineages

Approximately half of the roughly 120 diviners known to us, such as Fu 般,
Que 㱿, Yong 永 (all Period I), Xing 行 (Period II), and He 何 (Periods I–III),
were members of lineages whose names appear as pictorial insignia on Shang
or early Zhou bronzes.[82] Xi 喜 appears as a Period II diviner for over seventy
oracle bones (Y1494); he was presumably connected by blood, social ties, or
political service to the Lady Xi (Fu Xi 婦喜) who had prepared scapulas and
plastrons in Period I and was linked to Wu Ding by marriage; and both the
diviner and the lady would have come from the region of Xi, which is
recorded as having sent in five turtle shells (*HJ* 900b). The diviners, and
other officers like them, represent yet another level of the patrimonial, dynastic hierarchy, tied to the royal house by marriage or other alliances, but not
privileged to offer the ancestral rituals themselves.

Local Officers, Chiefs, and Rulers

Beyond the core area, the king concerned himself with the activities of
various officers or chiefs, such as the "Field Officers" (*Tian* 田 [= *Dian* 甸],
involved in agriculture), "Pastors" (*Mu* 牧), "Guards" (*Wei* 衛), and "Dog
Officers" (*Quan* 犬, involved in hunting). They were generally identified as
being at a specified place, as in, "If the king joins with Qin, the Dog Officer
at Cheng (*zai Cheng Quan Qin* 在成犬卑), there will be no regrets and he
will have no disasters" (*HJ* 27925). These local chiefs were evidently capable
of leading their own dependents in the king's service; whether they were
doing so as his deputies (as the king may have thought) or in terms of their
own independent self-interest (as they may have thought) is not easy to
determine. Greater distance from the Shang core and the passage of time, in
fact, encouraged many of these local officers' or chiefs' descendants to become
more independent so that they appear in the later inscriptions as rulers in
their own right.[83]

The more distant zones were ruled by leaders identified in the inscriptions as Hou 侯 and Bo 伯. The Hou were more likely than the Bo to
appear as allies of the Shang, sending in tribute and assisting the king's
affairs; they received in return military assistance from the king and benefited from his divinations about their harvest.[84] Numerous divinations

---

[82] Hayashi Minao ("In Shû jidai no zuzô kigô," pp. 43–6, figs. 21, 22) documents sixty-two cases.

[83] Qiu Xigui, "Jiagu buci zhong suo jian de tian mu wei deng zhiguan de yanjiu – Jianlun Hou Dian
Nan Wei deng jizhong zhuhou de qiyuan," *Wenshi* 19 (1983): 1–13.

[84] David N. Keightley, "The Shang State as Seen in the Oracle-Bone Inscriptions," *EC* 5 (1979–80): 28.

about whether the king should ally with various leaders (Y61.1–64.1, 106.1–08.1, 911.2–14.1) suggest the problematic and changeable nature of these alliances.

King List and Polity

The Shang recorded no actual king list or genealogy of the "A begat B, B begat C" variety on the oracle bones; scholars must derive such a list from the schedule of ancestral sacrifices divined by the late Shang kings. Such a schedule, moreover, presents only one possible view of the past, designed to validate, through the order and majesty of the sacrifices, the lines of descent so sanctified (see note 46). It may also be noted that some of the collateral kings' temple names may have represented a place name or tribe name combined with the heavenly stem (*gan*) that formed part of the temple name, so that names such as Jian Jia 戔甲 (K11), Qiang Jia 羌甲 (K14), Xiang Jia 象甲 (K17), and Pan Geng 般庚 (K18) may have represented the dynastic incorporation of different ethnic groups, polities, or lineages such as the Qiang.[85] That for the pre-Wu Ding period, none of these anomalous names belongs to the kings on the main line of descent, the first part of whose names was always Da 大 (great), Zhong 中 (middle), Xiao 小 (small), or Zu 祖 (ancestor), further suggests the peripheral nature of these collateral ancestors and the groups from which they may have come.

Royal Succession and Temple Names

The Shang ritualists emphasized the distinction between main-line and collateral kings. It appears from both contemporary and traditional records that the later Shang kings increasingly relied upon father-to-son descent, so that there were no cases of fraternal succession after Kang Ding (K25) succeeded Lin Xin (K24) (Fig. 4.1). The precise nature of the kin relationship involved in each succession, however, is often uncertain. Not only does the order and nature of the succession, as gleaned from the bone inscriptions, differ on occasion from the account provided by the "Yin benji" or other Zhou and Han texts, but the inscriptions, which only indicate the order of succession, provide no information about the relative ages of brothers. It may only be concluded, accordingly, that the *Shi ji*'s

---

[85] Zhang Bingquan: "Jiaguwen zhong suo jian ren di tongming kao," pp. 773–4. The Qiang of Qiang Jia, for example, appears as the name of a tribe or place (Y41.1–42.1, 47.1); so does the Pan of Pan Geng (e.g., *HJ* 152f, 4259f, 9504b). For other examples of such religious incorporation, see Itô Michiharu, "Part One: Religion and Society," pp. 38, 49, 62, 70, 75, 85, 86, 126.

statement – "After Zhong Ding [中丁; K9], they neglected the eldest son and once again set up the sons of younger brothers. Among the younger brothers and their sons, some competed with each other for the succession. This chaos lasted for nine generations" – perhaps reflected Shang concerns about the instability that descent through the junior brother engendered.[86]

The ten *gan* stems in the posthumous names of the Shang kings, such as Wu Ding (K21) and Zu Jia (K23), appear to follow a principle of alternation in which, to put it simply, generations of kings whose temple name was *ding* 丁, on the one hand, frequently alternated with generations of kings whose temple name was *jia* 甲 or *yi* 乙, on the other. Thus, there were Yi or Jia kings in generations 7, 9, 10, 13, 14, 16, 18, 20, and 22; there were Ding kings in generations 8, 12, 15, 17 19, and 21 (see Fig. 4.1). The alternation of Jia and Yi with Ding kings is by no means perfect, but it had become so regular by generations 14 through 22 that K. C. Chang has proposed a system of circulating succession in which the kingship alternated between two major ritual, political, or lineage groups that were identified by their *gan*.[87] It is also possible, however, that temple names were chosen both to suit Shang conceptions of hemerology (the names of the auspicious days [like *jia, yi, ding, geng,* and *xin*] were chosen as kings' temple names over inauspicious ones [like *bing, wu, ren,* and *gui*]) and to provide for a workable ritual calendar, in which the ancestors receiving cult were suitably spaced. In this view, the temple names would have been assigned, after death, among the auspicious days of the week.[88]

The Royal Women

The way in which certain royal ancestresses were incorporated into the five-ritual cycle has already been described. The situation of the royal

---

[86] *Shi ji*, 3, p. 101; the span proposed, however, covers only nine kings (K9–K17; see Table 4.1, this chapter) rather than nine generations (Chavannes, *Les mémoires historiques*, p. 193, n. 3; Yan Yiping, *Yin Shang shiji*, vol. 2, p. 140). Itô Michiharu suggests that the transfers of capital may have been related to succession disputes as various clans struggled for control ("Part One: Religion and Society," pp. 103–4, 125, 128).

[87] One group would have consisted of the Yi, Jia, Wu 戊, and Ji 己 units; the other group would have consisted of the Ding, Bing 丙, and Ren 壬; the Geng 庚 and Xin 辛 units could affiliate with both groups. See Zhang Guangzhi, "Shang wang miaohao xin kao," *Zhongyang yanjiuyuan minzuxue yanjiusuo jikan* 15 (1963): 65–95. Chang (*Shang Civilization*, pp. 165–89) suggests that the *gan* names reflected a system of patrilateral cross-cousin marriage.

[88] Ji Dewei, "Zhongguo gudai de jiri yu miaohao," *Yinxu bowuyuan yuankan* 1 (1989): 20–32. See too Inoue Satoshi ("Shangdai miaohao xinlun," *Zhongyuan wenwu* 1990.2: 54–60), who, after summarizing seven theories about temple-name distribution, applies a classical distinction between the performance of rituals on "soft" (*rou* 柔) and "hard" (*gang* 剛) days to the Shang evidence.

women, while alive, however, provides further illustration of the way in which the dynasty commingled personal and political ties. The names of the consorts, referred to in death, as the "Many Mothers" (Duo Mu 多母; Y172.1), frequently indicate their social origins in another community or country.[89] These royal women, some of whose communities also supplied diviners who served the king, took part in consecrating the plastrons and scapulas used in divinations.[90] The ability of these women to produce sons, a topic frequently divined (see Fig. 4.5; Y783.1–85.2), would have influenced the endurance of such ties. The case of Lady Hao serves as an example. Buried in splendor in M5, she became the recipient of considerable cultic attention, both as Lady Hao (or Lady Zi; see note 63) and, provided with a temple name, as Mother Xin. Her prominence, which derived primarily from her role as Wu Ding's consort, is also reflected in the status of her son, known variously in the inscriptions as Prince Jie (Zi Jie 子卩), the Royal Jie (Wang Jie, 王卩), and the Young King (Xiao Wang 小王) – as heir apparent. Although he died prematurely, Wu Ding's descendants worshipped him by such titles as, in Period II, Elder Brother Ji (Xiong Ji 兄己), and, in Period III, Father Ji (Fu Ji 父己); post-Shang texts knew him as Xiao Ji 孝己.[91]

Political Geography

The royal lineage and its collateral kinship units, such as the Many Princely Lineages, were clustered in and around the cult center at Xiaotun (Map 4.1), whose remains cover an area of some 30 sq. km. Other elites also resided in a series of settlements that, like Xiaotun itself, lay near the foothills of the Taihang 太行 Mountains to the west, running from approximately Xingtai 邢台 in the north to Xinxiang 新鄉 in the south. These settlements constituted a core area of the Shang state.[92]

---

[89] These women provided services, both personal and official, at the court. See Chang Cheng-lang, "A Brief Discussion of Fu Tzu," pp. 109–10; Cao Dingyun, "Fu Hao nai Zi Fang zhi nü," p. 381; and Cao Dingyun, "Yinxu Fuhao mu mingwen zhong renwu guanxi zongkao," p. 45.

[90] For the case of the diviner Xi, see the discussion above under "Non-Royal Lineages." For other combinations of diviners' names with consort (and other) titles of status, see Rao Zongyi, *Yindai zhenbu renwu tongkao* (Hong Kong: Xianggang daxue, 1959), pp. 1195–8; Zhang Bingquan, "Jiaguwen zhong suo jian ren di tongming kao," p. 858.

[91] Keightley, *Sources of Shang History*, p. 206; Cao Dingyun, "Fu Hao Xiao Ji guanxi kaozheng – cong Fu Hao mu Simu Xin mingwen tanqi," *Zhongyuan wenwu* 1993.3: 70–9; idem, "Yinxu Fuhao mu mingwen zhong renwu guanxi zongkao," p. 46.

[92] Chang, *Shang Civilization*, pp. 9, 10, 130. On the nature of this "royal domain" as it appears in the bone inscriptions, see Lian Shaoming, "Yinxu buci suojian shang dai de wangji," pp. 38–43, 66. Zheng Ruokui ("Yinxu Dayi shang zuyi buju chutan," *Zhongyuan wenwu* 1995.3: 84–93, 83) identifies various lineage settlements, handicraft industries, and cemeteries at sites, such as Beixinzhuang 北辛莊 and

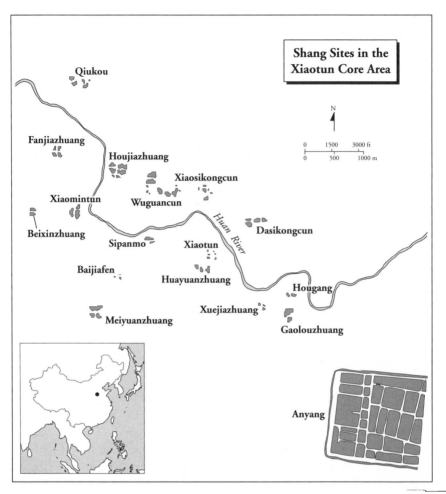

Map 4.1 Shang sites in the Xiaotun core area.

The well over 500 Shang sites that have been identified in Henan, Hebei,
Shanxi, Shaanxi, Anhui, Shandong, Jiangsu, Zhejiang, Hubei, Jiangxi,
Hunan, Sichuan, Inner Mongolia, Liaoning, and other provinces help to
explain the traditional view that the Shang state was extensive. Sites that were
culturally Shang, however, were not necessarily politically Shang. The area,
in fact, within which the late Shang king and his entourage could move with
safety, and which, through his allies and dependents, he could make some

Baijiafen 白家墳 (*see* Map 4.1), that were scattered in and around the royal settlement at Xiaotun;
Zheng links these sites to the names of particular lineages that appear in the bone and bronze
inscriptions.

claims to control, was not particularly large. It is generally concluded that after a significant expansion of Shang culture during the middle Shang or Zhengzhou period, which stimulated the rise of a number of bronze-working countries on the periphery that may be associated with many of the sites just referred to, the late Shang dynastic core, despite some military successes under Wu Ding, was increasingly on the defensive, being forced back into its heartland in northern and eastern Henan and western Shandong.[93]

The Shang state and its frontiers, which were undoubtedly porous and fluid, can be located by matching place-name and travel information from the inscriptions with archaeological sites and traditional accounts, but it is not yet possible to delineate the political geography of late Shang China with great precision. Study of the lineage names seen in both bone and bronze inscriptions suggests, however, that the descent groups which supported the Shang state tended to concentrate in northern and northwestern Henan, the core of the dynastic state, and in southeastern Shanxi along the courses of the Yellow and Qin 沁 Rivers.[94] Insufficient evidence is available to estimate the size of the Shang population with any confidence.[95]

Agriculture

Studies of the paleoflora and paleofauna and of the divination inscriptions indicate that in the twelfth and eleventh centuries B.C., the climate of North China and the Anyang region was wetter and warmer, by some 2 °C, than it is today, with rain likely to have been more prolonged and heavier in months that are now virtually rain-free.[96] For the late Shang, which was primarily an agricultural society, the more equable distribution of rainfall would have been especially beneficial during the months of spring planting.

The population of the various communities and countries within the Shang sphere of influence lived in small settlements (yi 邑; Y119.1) surrounded by cultivated fields (tian 田). Wu Ding's central religious role in their food production is indicated by the consideration that his numerous

[93] Song Zhenhao, "Xia Shang renkou chutan," pp. 96–7; Keightley, "The Late Shang State," pp. 546, 548; Itô Michiharu, "Part One: Religion and Society," p. 88.

[94] Keightley, "The Late Shang State," pp. 532–48; Edward L. Shaughnessy, "Historical Geography and the Extent of the Earliest Chinese Kingdoms," AM, 3d series, 2, 2 (1989): 1–13; Xia Hanyi, "Zaoqi Shang Zhou guanxi ji qi dui Wu Ding yihou Yin Shang wangshi shili fanwei de yiyi," Jiuzhou xuekan 2, 1 (1987): 20–32; Zhu Fenghan, Shang Zhou jiazu, pp. 83–4.

[95] For the conclusion that, by Period V, approximately 230,000 people lived in the Xiaotun area, see Song Zhenhao, "Xia Shang renkou chutan," pp. 101–5.

[96] Hu Houxuan, "Qihou bianqian yu Yindai qihou zhi jiantao," Zhongguo wenhua yanjiu huikan 4 (1944): 1–84, 289–90; Zhang Bingquan, "Yindai de nongye yu qixiang," BIHP 42 (1970): 267–336; Chang, Shang Civilization, pp. 136–41, 145; Zhongguo Shehui kexueyuan Kaogu yanjiusuo, Yinxu de faxian yu yanjiu, pp. 435–6.

divinations about the harvest (Figs 4.2 and 4.3; Y531.2–35.2) were not limited to enquiries about his own crops, but extended to every place within the Four Lands that comprised the Shang domains.[97] Questions about his own crops were prefixed with qualifiers such as "the king's" (*wang* 王), "Shang's," "the great settlement's" (*da yi* 大邑), or "our" (*wo* 我).

The king, furthermore, controlled a significant number of farms, cleared and worked by royal labor gangs and under the control of various officers, like the Xiao Chen 小臣 (Junior Servitors; *HJ* 12). These farms were sufficiently fruitful and efficiently organized to support the royal house, a privileged ruling elite, a considerable handicraft industry, and a formidable army. Numerous charges demonstrate the king's enduring pyromantic attention to rainfall, the opening up of new fields, inspections, planting, harvest, and the agricultural activities of the royal labor gangs. Many charges involve the king's personal leadership in these matters or his administrative decisions: "The king should not go to inspect the millet planting" (*HJ* 9612); "… if [we] greatly order the laborers [*zhongren* 眾人], saying 'Work together in the fields,' [we] will receive harvest" (*HJ* 1).[98] The king was also concerned about the agriculture of particular officers and locations, as in charges like: "We will receive the harvest that Fu 甫 cultivates at Zi 姑" (*HJ* 900f). The discovery, in the Xiaotun area, of large numbers of stone sickles, some still in the process of manufacture – with up to a thousand stored in one pit – is further evidence of labor organization that was devoted to bringing in the harvest.[99]

CROPS. The Shang staple was millet, recorded in the oracle-bone inscriptions as *shu* 黍 (Y536.1–38.2) or *he* 禾 (Y523.1–26.2). The variety of millets mentioned in the *Shi jing* (ca. 1000–600 B.C.), together with the difficulty involved in distinguishing the threshed grain of *Setaria Italica* from that of *Panicum miliaceum*, suggests both that a similar variety would have existed in the twelfth century B.C. and that the diviners, whose concerns, as ritual technicians rather than farmers, were presumably with harvests as a whole rather than with particular crop varieties, in referring to *shu* or *he*, did not necessarily distinguish between the two major species.[100]

---

[97] Chen Mengjia, *Yinxu buci zongshu*, pp. 313–16, 322, 639; see *HJ* 9741f, 21091, 24429, 33272, 36975.

[98] Amano Motonosuke, "Indai no nôgyô to sono shakai kôzô," *Shigaku kenkyû* 62 (1956): 1–16; Chen Mengjia, *Yinxu buci zongshu*, pp. 523–52; David N. Keightley, "Pubic Work in Ancient China: A Study of Forced Labor in the Shang and Western Chou" (Ph.D. dissertation, Columbia University, 1969), pp. 74–5, 98–125; Sun Miao, *Xia Shang shigao* (Beijing: Wenwu, 1987), pp. 385–429.

[99] Keightley, "Public Work," pp. 99–100, 110–11; Chang, *Shang Civilization*, p. 223; Yang Shengnan, "Shangdai de caizheng zhidu," pp. 81–2.

[100] Te-tzu Chang, "The Origins and Early Cultures of the Cereal Grains and Food Legumes," in *The Origins of Chinese Civilization*, ed. David N. Keightley (Berkeley: University of California Press, 1983),

Millets in the modern Anyang area have been subject to the ravages of pest and disease.[101] There is no reason to think that the Shang crops were spared similar visitations. To the Shang farmers and diviners such blights would have been a sign that some Power was harming their crops: "Yang [the Mountain Power] is harming the harvest' (*HJ* 34229); "It is Di [the High God] who is harming our harvest" (*HJ* 10124f) ; "It is He 河 [the River Power] who is harming our harvest" (*HJ* 33337). Every successful harvest would have produced a profound sense not just of economic security but of spiritual vindication.

OPENING UP NEW LAND. The inscriptions suggest that the Shang may have engaged in the drainage of low-lying fields, but no archaeological evidence indicates that they constructed large-scale irrigation works.[102] The development of new fields, however, which involved clearing land and raising field boundaries, was an important part of "the king's affairs" (*wang shi* 王 事; Y256.2–58.1). Various Shang officers were in charge of these tasks, which were initiated by royal command:

If the king orders the Many Yin [*Duo Yin* 多尹 officers] to open up fields in the West, [we] will receive crops. (*HJ* 33209)

"The king orders the Many Qiang [officers] [Duo Qiang 多羌] to open up fields." (*HJ* 33213)

There was an intimate connection between hunting, also used for military training, and agricultural development, with the burning of brush to drive the game leading to the clearing and fertilization of new fields (the word *tian* 田 meant both fields [Y465.1–2] and hunting [Y803.2–10.2]); hunting areas, in fact, were frequently major farming areas, with the hunts also pro-

---

pp. 65–70; Wayne H. Fogg, "Swidden Cultivation of Foxtail Millet by Taiwan Aborigines: A Cultural Analogue of the Domestication of *Setaria italica* in China," in *The Origins of Chinese Civilization*, ed. David N. Keightley (Berkeley: University of California Press, 1983), pp. 109–10; Chang, *Shang Civilization*, p. 146; Qiu Xigui, "Jiaguwen zhong suo jian de Shangdai nongye," *Nongshi yanjiu* 8 (1985): 12–15.

[101] John Lossing Buck (*Land Utilization in China* [Nanking: University of Nanking, 1937], pp. 4, 32) lists black smut, leaf curl, yellow rust, aphis, locusts, scales, army worm, mole cricket, and kernel smut for the Anyang area.

[102] Qiu Xigui, "Jiaguwen zhong suo jian de Shangdai nongye," pp. 32, 38. This conclusion, which accords with a Shang climate that was wetter than today's, contradicts Karl A. Wittfogel's view that "a hydraulic way of life" had arisen "long before the Shang dynasty" (*Oriental Despotism: A Comparative Study of Total Power* [New Haven, Conn.: Yale University Press, 1963], p. 33, n. b). The water ditches excavated at the Xiaotun site (Fig. 4.7) may have been for drainage or to provide water levels for surveying purposes; see Keightley, "Public Work," pp. 134–8; Chang, *Shang Civilization*, pp. 76–8; Wen Shaofeng and Yuan Tingdong, *Yinxu buci yanjiu*, pp. 25–6.

tecting the crops from predators.[103] The quasi-military nature of some of the
expeditions to open up new land is suggested by the leadership of officers
who, in other contexts, were employed on military expeditions, by the use
of the *zhongren* 眾人 laborers, who also served as soldiers in war, and by the
occasional reference to expeditions in enemy territory: "Should [we] order
the *zhongren* … to enter the Qiang Country … open up fields" (*HJ* 6). Such
royal agriculture was part of a functionally diffuse system of dependent labor,
in which both officers and conscripts might serve in warfare, construction,
or agriculture.

These agricultural expeditions were probably related to Shang conceptions
of territoriality. Since labor was more scarce than land, the ability to exploit
the land must have been more important than outright ownership. Divinations about "our northern fields" (*wo bei tian* 我北田) and "southern fields"
(*nan tian* 南田) receiving harvest were presumably about lands that had been
cleared for agriculture, sometimes by the king's labor gangs. Shang territory
would have been partly conceived in terms of areas where the king could
hunt, partly in terms of land that the Shang had rendered arable.[104]

ANIMAL HUSBANDRY. The rulers evidently controlled large herds of livestock. The raw materials used in the bone workshops of Xiaotun were primarily the leg bones of cattle, sheep, pigs, deer, dogs, and horses. Some of
these animals may have been captured in the hunt or war, but others would
have been bred and domesticated by the Shang.[105] Titles such as the Many
Dog (Duo Quan 多犬) and Many Horse (Duo Ma 多馬) officers (Y606.2,
624.1–2; see also note 115) suggest that, in origin at least, these officers had
been involved in animal management.

The variety and number of animals offered in sacrifice also indicates the
existence of considerable animal husbandry. Ten head of cattle were frequently offered at one time, and divinations proposed the sacrifice of 100,
300, or 500 cattle, 100 sheep, 200 pigs, 100 dogs, and so on. Royal pasture
lands (*mu* 牧) were located in various places or referred to as Northern or
Southern (*HJ* 28351) and the king or his officers inspected the cattle (*HJ*
11177). On the assumption, furthermore, that the ritual feasts offered to his
ancestors involved the offering of cattle or sheep (as in *HJ* 27321) and were

---

[103] Keightley, "Public Work," pp. 102–8; Zhang Zhenglang, "Buci poutian ji qi xiangguan zhu wenti,"
Kaogu xuebao 1973.1: 93–120; Chang, *Shang Civilization*, p. 223; Qiu Xigui, "Jiaguwen zhong suo jian
de Shangdai nongye," pp. 22–3, 30–2.
[104] Keightley, "The Late Shang State," pp. 526–7; Chang, *Shang Civilization*, pp. 220, 223.
[105] Li Chi, *The Beginnings of Chinese Civilization: Three Lectures Illustrated with Finds at Anyang* (Seattle:
University of Washington Press, 1957), p. 22; Cheng Te-k'un, *Archaeology in China. Vol. 2: Shang China*
(Cambridge: Heffer, 1960), pp. 88–91; Chang, *Shang Civilization*, p. 143.

shared by the officiants, the Shang elites would have consumed large quantities of meat, thus anticipating the characterization of the Eastern Zhou ruling class as "meat eaters."[106]

Tribute Offerings and Service

Part of the dynasty's economic strength depended on tribute offered by Shang dependents and allies. Various states and leaders sent in human beings (frequently Qiang prisoners), primarily for sacrifice in the ancestral cult. Similarly, the use of their own laborers (*zhong* 眾) in the service of the king by leaders like Qin 卓 or Bing 竝 constituted another form of service to the king. The Shang also received tribute in the form of animals, as in "Xi 奚 will bring white horses" (*HJ* 9177f) and "This season, Xi will bring cattle" (*HJ* 9178A), but the general economic impact of such offerings was probably not large and the value of such tribute would primarily have been symbolic.[107]

The major tribute items recorded in the inscriptions, in fact, were the turtle shells and cattle scapulas sent in for pyromancy. A large number of shells, up to 1,000, were received at one time, with shipments of 100 and 250 being the most common; scapulas, by contrast, were supplied in smaller quantity, the largest number being 50 pairs. The importance that the Shang diviners attached to these offerings is indicated by the care with which they recorded such information on the Period I bones, either in the sockets of scapulas or on the bridges of plastrons, as in, "Wo 我 brought in 1,000 (shells); Lady Jing (Fu Jing 婦井) ritually prepared 30. (Recorded by) Que 殼 (the diviner)" (*HJ* 116b).[108]

The Shang kings, in short, stood at the center of a network of symbolic exchanges in which, with the exception of the bones and shells, their supporters provided various tribute items and services on an irregular basis and the king conferred (the verb was written *yi* 易, read as *ci* 賜) occasional gifts such as cowries, cattle, sheep, and weapons in return.[109] The contemporary evidence, however, does not permit the conclusion that a "tribute system"

---

[106] Shima Kunio, *Inkyo bokuji kenkyū*, p. 502; Yang Shengnan, "Shangdai de caizheng zhidu," pp. 83–4. For "meat eaters," see *Zuo zhuan*, 9 (Ai 13), p. 8b (James Legge, trans., *The Chinese Classics: Vol. 5: The Ch'un Ts'ew with the Tso Chuen* [London: Trübner, 1872], p. 832).

[107] Yang Shengnan, "Shangdai de caizheng zhidu," pp. 87, 89. The king divined some twenty charges about the loss of *zhong* by other leaders or places (Y520.1).

[108] Keightley, *Sources of Shang History*, pp. 15–17; Yang Shengnan, "Shangdai de caizheng zhidu," pp. 89–90.

[109] For gifts, mainly of cowries, recorded on Shang bronzes, see, e.g., the thirty-seven inscriptions listed at Akatsuka *Chūgoku kodai no shūkyō to bunka*, p. 856; for gifts divined in a small number of oracle-bone charges, see Yang Shengnan, "Shangdai de caizheng zhidu," p. 93.

existed; the donations recorded probably provided the dynasty with support that was psychological as much as economic.

Dependent Labor

The royal house directed a significant proportion of the agriculture and manufacturing in the Xiaotun core area. Considerable evidence of handicraft industries, more extensive than those of the Erligang period, and revealing much evidence of craft specialization, have been found there. The bronze casters of Miaopu 苗圃 North, for example, who worked in an area that covered over 10,000 sq. m, mainly produced ritual vessels; those at Xiaomintun 孝民屯 mainly produced tools and weapons. The bone workers at Dasikongcun, where more than 35,000 pieces of bone have been found, mainly produced hairpins, with a small quantity of arrowheads, awls, and ladles (for these sites, see Map 4.1).[110]

Labor conscripts were the fundamental source of state power in ancient China. They served in armies, built temple-palaces, excavated tombs, hauled supplies, cleared the land and farmed it, and worked at the sundry tasks of production and manufacture required by the elites. Efficient labor conscription was both a sign of, and a precondition for, a strong state; it made power both possible and desirable. Early evidence of communal labor mobilization can be discerned in the pounded-earth walls that surrounded Late Neolithic and Early Bronze Age fortifications such as those at Pingliangtai 平粮台, Wangchenggang 王城崗, and Shixianggou 尸鄉溝. By the late Shang, the oracle-bone inscriptions permit us to delineate the existence of an extensive system of dependent labor that primarily involved service in "the king's affairs" (*wang shi* 王事), "Our affairs" (*zhen shi* 朕事; Y256.2–58.1), and, by extension, the affairs of the king's elite supporters.

The laborers of late Shang were the *zhong* 眾 (literally, "the many") or *ren* 人 ("the men"). Their status has been much disputed. The character for **tśjuŋ* / *zhong*, as it appears on the Shang bones, 眾 (Y69.1–71.1), depicted three (rarely, two) *ren*, "men," under the sun. Some scholars have seen the *zhong* fundamentally as slaves, but have also argued that given their membership in the Shang clan and their long tradition of service, *zhong* status was higher than that of captives and criminals. Others have argued that the *zhong* were free men, members of the Shang aristocracy, belonging to localized Shang lineages. Still others, avoiding anachronistic terms like "slave" and "free," have seen the *zhong* as collective laborers of low, commoner status,

[110] Yang Shengnan, "Shangdai de caizheng zhidu," pp. 84–6; Zhongguo Shehui kexueyuan Kaogu yanjiusuo, *Yinxu de faxian yu yanjiu*, pp. 83–96, 439–41.

organized as lineage members, who, serving in the palace guard, enjoyed a certain personal freedom.[111] The inscriptional evidence suggests that the *zhong* (the standard abbreviation for *zhongren*) should be regarded as the "many," petty elite dependents located at the social and economic base of the royal and localized lineages; they may be distinguished from the *ren* by their relatively small numbers and by their state of permanent attachment and proximity to their lord.[112]

Ren, "man" or "person," was a status-neutral term. The king might use *ren* of himself, as in "I the one man"; *ren* might be applied to the *zhong*, as in the term *zhongren*; *ren* was also used of men serving in the royal armies, of enemy peoples on the borders, of captives taken in battle, and of human victims offered in sacrifice. The Shang king's frequent use of *zhong* and *ren*, either together or separately, in both warfare and agriculture, suggests that their roles may on occasion have merged. That the *zhong*, like the "Archers" (*She* 射) and "Horse officers" (*Ma* 馬) were rarely mobilized (*HJ* 698f, 5760f), suggests that they were available to serve the king on a semipermanent basis. The king mobilized the *ren*, by contrast, with much greater frequency. The fundamental distinction between the two groups, accordingly, probably did not involve the function but rather the degree of dependency, servitude, and reward. The possible loss in battle of *zhong* and *ren* was a divinatory concern, as in "Qin will not lose *zhongren*" (*bu sang zhongren* 不喪眾人) (*HJ* 57) and "Bing will not have disasters and he will not lose *zhong*. . . ." (*HJ* 52). Since, when the *zhong* were numbered at all, the count never exceeded 100 (*HJ* 26906), one senses that their total numbers were not large; the *ren*, by contrast, were counted in their thousands (as in *HJ* 6168, 6169, 6409, 6177). Although the king divined about mobilizing the *ren* for battle, he divined their loss far less frequently; the *ren* were, evidently, more expendable.

The *zhong*, or *zhongren*, were frequently led by a named retainer or ally of the king; they might also be led by some of the king's officers, like the "Many Archers" (*Duo She* 多射; *HJ* 69). Command over the *zhong* might be further delegated: "If Qin orders Guo 郭 to take the *zhong* and penetrate [the

[111] Raimund Theodor Kolb (*Die Infanterie im Alten China: Ein Beitrag zur Militärgeschichte der Vor-Zhan-Guo-Zeit* [Mainz: Philipp von Zabern, 1991], pp. 27–8) summarizes the various opinions. For the *zhong* as slaves, see, e.g., Sun Miao, *Xia Shang shigao*, p. 526. For their status as free men, see, e.g., Chao Lin, *The Socio-Political Systems of the Shang Dynasty* (Nankang, Taipei: Institute of the Three Principles of the People, 1982), p. 117. For the *zhong* as low-status lineage members, see Chang, *Shang Civilization*, p. 227; Zhang Yongshang, "Lun Shangdai de zhong ren," in *Jiagu tan shilu*, ed. Hu Houxuan et al. (Beijing: Sanlian, 1982), pp. 261–4; Peng Bangjiong, "Shangdai zhongren de lishi kaocha – Guanyu zhongren de xin tansu," *Tianfu xinlun* 1990.3: 77–85. Yang Baocheng and Yang Xizhang ("Cong Yinxu xiaoxing muzang," pp. 32–3) argue that most of the burials found in the "commoner" cemetery at Yinxu West were those of *zhong* and *zhongren*.
[112] Keightley, "Public Work," pp. 66–144. Li Xiaoding (*Jiagu wenzi jishi* [Nangang: Zhongyang yanjiuyuan lishi yuyan yanjiusuo zhuankan zhi wushi, 1965], p. 1262) likened the *wang zhong* 王眾 (royal multitude) of Shang to the *buqu* 部曲 (personal retainers) of early medieval China.

enemy], [we] will receive assistance" (*HJ* 31981). And it seems likely that in some cases the *zhong* were not attached to the king but were members of the same localized lineage as the officer who led them; they were his *zhong*, not the king's: "If the king orders Qin's *zhong* to penetrate and attack the Shao-fang 召方, [we] will receive assistance" (*HJ* 31974); "Order Bing's *zhong* to guard" (*HJ* 40911).[113]

Mobilization and Warfare

The royal workshops produced a variety of bronze armaments, including dagger-axes, arrowheads, spearheads, helmets, shields, and chariot fittings.[114] Faced with reports of enemy invasions, Wu Ding led his forces in person, allied himself with other leaders, or dispatched his generals, men like Qin (Y1091.1–93.1), Qiao (Y667.2–69.2), Cheng of Wang (Wang Cheng 望乘; Y106.2–08.2), and Guo of Zhi (Zhi Guo 沚馘; Y911.2–14.1). And he mobilized his troops. That the charges often link the mobilizations to particular campaigns suggests the ad hoc nature of these levies and the need to have them validated by divine sanction:

In the present period, if the king raises men, 5,000 [of them], and campaigns against the Tufang 土方, (some Power) will confer assistance in this case. (*HJ* 6409)

If [we] raise *ren*, 3,000 [of them], and call upon them to attack the Gongfang 舌方, [some Power] will confer assistance in this case. (*HJ* 6168)

The Shang usually raised their troops in numbers of 3,000 to 5,000, but on one occasion reference was made to 10,000, who were called upon to attack an enemy country (*Yingcang* 150f).

The soldiers were probably raised by, and served in, the lineages (*zu*) that served as both social and military organizations. That, moreover, in Period V, the Yufang 盂方, an enemy state, was reported as having "raised" its own men (*HJ* 36518), suggests that the Shang were not the only state that was able to mobilize its population in this way. That another period V inscription (*HJ* 36481f) refers to the capture of two chariots from a Bo ruler is further indication that the last Shang kings enjoyed no absolute social or technological advantages.[115]

---

[113] Zhu Fenghan, *Shang Zhou jiazu*, pp. 40–1.

[114] See, e.g., Hayashi Minao, *Chûgoku In Shû jidai no buki* (Kyoto: Kyôto daigaku jimbun kagaku kenkyûjo, 1972); Chen Zhida, "Yinxu wuqi gaishu," in *Qingzhu Su Bingqi kaogu wushiwu nian lunwenji* (Beijing: Wenwu, 1989), pp. 326–37.

[115] For Shang chariot warfare, see Edward L. Shaughnessy, "Historical Perspectives on the Introduction of the Chariot into China," *HJAS* 48 (1988): 213–21, 232–4. Specific references to chariots are not frequent in the divination inscriptions, but if Wang Guimin ("Jiu Yinxu jiaguwen suojian shishuo Sima zhiming de qiyuan," in *Jiaguwen yu Yin Shang shi*, ed. Hu Houxuan [Shanghai: Shanghai guji, 1983], pp. 173–90) is correct in understanding oracle-bone *ma* not simply as "horse" but as "horse-chariot,"

The *zhong* and the *ren* were organized into left, right, and center units, probably in multiples of one hundred men. The Archers (She) and Horse officers (Ma) were similarly organized by units of one hundred, as were, possibly, the Artisans (Gong 工). These numbers suggest that the Shang military would have employed a system of record keeping, for if the king assigned 100 *zhong* to an officer or mobilized 5,000 *ren*, there would probably have been rolls to specify which *zhong* were assigned, which *ren* were mobilized.[116] The officers and men of the Shang army, in fact, appear to have been organized by numerical units that were divided into three large divisions: "The king will form the three armies [*zuo shi* 作師], right, center, and left" (*HJ* 33006). And when the king mobilized 100 or 300 Archers or 100 or 300 Horse officers, they were probably assigned in units of 100 each to these larger divisions. It is not yet clear whether the larger numbers of *ren*, who, in the case of the 3,000-man mobilizations could have been assigned in the same tripartite way, were organized primarily as infantry, or were grouped around large chariot units (see note 115), but there is little doubt that the majority of the Shang king's soldiers fought on foot. The lightly constructed chariots, glistening with bronze, and raised high on their large, multispoked wheels (up to 1.46 m in diameter), provided effective mobile platforms for command, observation, and archery, and were presumably supported by units of foot.

Although the large-scale conscriptions provided the main fighting power of the Shang army, there is little doubt that a core, standing army existed, and there are intimations that with titles like Guard of the Many Horse (*Duo Ma Wei* 多馬衛) and Junior Servitor of Horse (*Ma Xiao Chen* 馬小臣), the Shang army was organized on command lines and in numerical units that may have benefited from, as they may have stimulated, the genesis of Shang bureaucracy in general.[117]

Slave Society

Terms like "slave" or "freeman" do not appear in the Shang (or Zhou) records; nor are there records, or even traditions, of any person being bought or sold.

---

then the (Duo) Ma officers, for example, become the "(Many) Horse-Chariot" officers. Not only would this provide many more divinations about the use of chariots in hunt and warfare, but their being numbered in units of 30, 100, and 300 would be well suited to a situation in which the archers, also numbered in units of 30, 100, 300 (Y1010.1–2), would have served 1 to a chariot, and the *zhong* or *ren*, the latter mobilized in groups of 1,000 and 3,000, would have been attached in units of 10 to each chariot.

[116] Keightley, "Public Work," pp. 140–1.
[117] Chang, *Shang Civilization*, p. 196; Kolb, *Die Infanterie im alten China*, pp. 24–6; Lin Yun, "Shangdai bingzhi guankui," *Jilin daxue shehui kexue xuebao* 1990.1: 11–17; Yang Shengnan, "Lüelun Shang dai de jundui," in *Jiagu tanshi lu*, ed. Hu Houxuan (Beijing: Sanlian, 1982), pp. 367–99.

Where no legal concept of individual rights existed, it is more useful to characterize Shang society in terms of degrees of dependency and privilege, rather
than slavery and freedom. Attempts to assign slave status to particular groups
recorded in the inscriptions, or to read a particular oracle-bone graph as *nu*
奴 (slave), have generally involved more theoretical assertion than paleographic demonstration.[118]

The argument that the large numbers of human victims associated with
some of the larger tombs were slaves, as opposed to ritual victims, is also hard
to accept. There is little evidence that these victims were routinely employed
in productive labor prior to their execution and considerable support for the
argument that late Shang society was not yet able to absorb a large number
of slave laborers.[119] The human victims were, rather, one expression of the
belief, both religious and political, that those related to a lord by blood or
service in life were expected to continue that relationship in death. The grave
victims, accordingly, should be understood as a cross-section of a grave lord's
dependents: his relatives, women, guards, menials, and prisoners.

Personnel Decisions and Incipient Bureaucracy

The king's success depended, in Shang as in later times, upon selecting the
right officers for particular tasks. These selections were frequently the subject
of divination, especially in Period I, where we find numerous charges of the
form: "If Qiao 雀 pursues Xuan 旦, there will be occasion for capture" (*HJ*
6947); "It should be Ya Qin 亞 卓 who takes the *ren* to penetrate [the enemy]"
(*HJ* 32272). In a culture and state system that was heavily dependent upon
familial connections, such personnel decisions would frequently have been
personal decisions. At the same time, however, the king's issuing orders to
such groups as the Many Horse officers (see note 115), the Many Dog officers (Y606.2), the Many Artisans (Y1118.1–2), and the Many Archers
(Y1010.2) suggests the rudimentary beginnings of a more impersonal form of
administrative organization. The royal court was also manned with numbers
of Junior Servitors, some of whom, on the basis of titles like the Junior
Servitor for the *Zhongren* (*Xiao Zhongren Chen* 小眾人臣) or the Junior Servi-

---

[118] The work of Guo Moruo is representative; see, e.g., his *Nuli zhi shidai* (Beijing: Renmin, 1954) and
the summary of his early views offered by Arif Dirlik, *Revolution and History: Origins of Marxist Historiography in China, 1919–1937* (Berkeley: University of California Press, 1978), pp. 150–8, 168–9. Yao
Xiaosui and Xiao Ding provide only two graphs, each occurring once in unhelpful contexts, of a word
that they read as *nu* (Y195.1, 359.2); on such identifications, see Keightley, "Public Work," pp. 360–9;
and Matsumaru and Takashima, *Kôkotsumoji jishaku sôran*, nos. 1098, 1447, 1610, 4286, 8092.

[119] Keightley, "Public Work," pp. 370–2; Yang Hsi-chang, "The Shang Dynasty Cemetery System," p. 62.
It may be noted, however, that the deformities and illnesses revealed by a good number of the male
skeletons found in the sacrificial burials M26–36 near Wuguancun suggest lives of considerable hard-
ship (*Kaogu* 1977.1: 30; cf. Chang, *Shang Civilization*, p. 121).

tor for Cultivation (?) (*Xiao Ji Chen* 小耤臣), may have been charged with particular duties.[120] The extent to which such titles involved specialized jurisdictions and regulatory capacity rather than being ceremonial or customary in nature is hard to specify. By the time of Di Yi and Di Xin, the situation is still harder to assess. The administrative jurisdictions of Shang officialdom, however, appear to have been flexible and relatively unspecialized.

At the same time, the divinatory process itself reveals the existence of bureaucratic routines. A number of clues suggest the existence of a storage system, a meticulous attention to good order, and routinized record keeping. These include the notations, inscribed on plastrons or scapula sockets, which recorded what group had sent in so many cattle scapulas or turtle shells, who had consecrated them, and the date when they had been delivered (Y718.1–19.1); the assiduous recording of diviners' names, dates of divination, positive and negative versions of charges and, on occasion, the results that followed; the use of sets of five (sometimes three) bones, each crack being appropriately numbered with totals of up to a hundred cracks per set; the way in which certain bones were reused, in sequence, after an interval of nonuse; the reserving of particular bones for particular rituals; and the return of oracle bones, divined on the king's hunts, to the Xiaotun cult center.

The content of the divination inscriptions also demonstrates the existence of a proto-bureaucracy. The records of enemy slain and prisoners and booty taken, as well as the numerous and detailed head counts of animals captured in the hunt, confirm the interest of the Shang kings in recording manpower and other types of figures. The *dian* 典 (tablets), which were involved at certain points in the five-ritual cycle (Y1136.1–2), and *ce* 冊 (or 𠕋; wooden strips), which appear in charges about the offering of registers at times of military alliance and mobilization (Y1130.2–31.1) and, as a verb, in charges about the offering of written promises to the ancestors (Y1133.1–35.1), provide further evidence that written documents played a significant role in the operations of the dynasty.[121]

Finally, some simple hierarchy of control must have existed in the Shang mobilization of armies that were several thousand strong; in the direction of the ore-mining, bronze-casting, and other dependent labor; and in the collection of whatever levies were extracted from the peasantry. The possession of a written script would have assisted the ability of the Shang elites to organize their subjects in this way. And a general belief in the power of the royal

---

[120] Zhang Yachu ("Shangdai zhiguan yanjiu," *Guwwenzi yanjiu* 13 [1986]: 82–116) discusses and tabulates sixty-five Shang officials, comparing them with their putative Western Zhou successors.

[121] The "Duo shi" 多士, an early Western Zhou chapter of the *Shang shu*, employs the same words: "You know that your Yin forebears had tablets and written strips (*you ce you dian* 有冊有典) about the Yin changing the mandate of Xia" (*Shang shu zhengyi*, 16, p. 6a; Legge, trans., *The Shoo King*, p. 460).

ancestors and in the king's ability to understand and to intercede with all the spiritual forces that dominated the Shang world would have legitimated the exploitation of his subjects' labors.[122]

POLITICAL AND MILITARY DEVELOPMENTS

The apparent absence of defensive walls at late Shang settlements, together with the fact that the moat, which ran to the west and south of the Xiaotun settlement, joining the Huan River at both ends, appears to have become choked by the end of the dynasty, suggests that the Shang core area enjoyed considerable security against external invasion.[123] No Period V divinations, for example, record that enemy states were "going out" (*chu* 出) against the Shang (see Y273.2–74.2, 1207.2–08.1); there are no Period V divinations about the loss of *zhong* (Y520.1); there are no Period V charges that hope for divine assistance in battle (Y1218.1). These silences may reflect a change in the divination record rather than a change in reality, but the general situation toward the end of the dynasty, as the kings chose to divine it, was of the Shang as the raiders rather than the raided.

In the reign of Wu Ding, the Shang had engaged in a series of major wars against the Tufang and Gongfang. They had been involved in frequent struggles with the Qiangfang, and had obtained a series of military victories in Shanxi, west of the Taihang range, often under the command of Qiao. Under the next king, Zu Geng, the Shang armies, led by Qin, proved less successful in their battles with the Shaofang (Y958.1–2) and Gongfang (Y269.2–72.2), and the Shang's western alliances began to crumble. In the reigns that followed, the Zhou – an embattled Shang ally under Wu Ding who may originally have been located along the Fen 汾 River – together with other allies in western Shanxi, such as Gu 壴 (or 鼓), Yue 岳, Xuan 亘, Yue 戉, and Sui 繐, were lost to the diminishing Shang sphere of influence as the power of the Gongfang grew in the northwest. Thus, we find post–Wu Ding references to the Suifang 繐方, Yuefang 戉方, Xuanfang 亘方, and Zhoufang 周方 – the suffix "-*fang*" indicating that they had become enemies. Other

---

[122] Keightley, "Public Work," pp. 1–144, 346–55. On the complex and large-scale organization of labor required in the bronze-casting industry, see Ursula Martius Franklin, "On Bronze and Other Metals in Early China," in *The Origins of Chinese Civilization*, ed. David N. Keightley (Berkeley: University of California Press, 1983), pp. 285–9; idem, "The Beginnings of Metallurgy in China: A Comparative Approach," in *The Great Bronze Age of China: A Symposium*, ed. George Kuwayama (Los Angeles: Los Angeles County Museum of Art, 1983), p. 97.

[123] An Zhimin, Jiang Bingxin, and Chen Zhida, "1958–1959 nian Yinxu fajue jianbao," *Kaogu* 1961.2: 66; Keightley, "Religion and the Rise of Urbanism," p. 530; Yang Xizhang, "Yinren zun dongbei fangwei," in *Qingzhu Su Bingqi kaogu wushiwu nian lunwenji* (Beijing: Wenwu, 1989), p. 307. Zheng Ruokui ("Yinxu Dayi Shang zuyi buju chutan," pp. 89, 93) argues that a wall would not have been needed at Xiaotun because, until the arrival of the Zhou armies under Wu Wang, the outlying lineage settlements provided adequate defense.

Shang supporters simply vanished from the record. In the later periods, the kings do not appear to have relied upon magnates analogous to Qin, Qiao, Cheng of Wang, and Guo of Zhi who could lead their armies. The divination record, in which the king had become virtually the sole diviner, represents him as the major military leader, powerful but more isolated than his predecessors.[124] The virtual disappearance of many "personnel" divinations by the reigns of Di Yi and Di Xin, is striking.[125]

The Shang were able to stabilize the situation closer to home, but the size of the state had grown considerably smaller; it has even been proposed that, by Period V, the kings' hunts ventured no further than 15 to 20 k from his Xiaotun base, with only occasional expeditions to more distant quarters.[126] The most notable of these forays involved a lengthy campaign against the Renfang 人方 to the east in Period V, which show that the last kings were still able to mount impressive expeditions when the occasion warranted. By one estimate, the king spent up to 106 days on his outbound march, 99 days on his return;[127] evidently the king did not need to be in a capital to function effectively. Indeed, throughout the late Shang period, it was presumably the king's presence, as chief diviner and chief ritualist, that energized the Xiaotun core. And it was the king's presence, on his travels, that intermittently brought the full authority of the dynasty to the various settlements that served as the nodes of the early state. The last kings may have perfected the arts of Shang rulership as they buried their predecessors with splendor, maintained the cycle of the complex ancestral cult, and hunted according to a fixed weekly schedule, but they appear to have acted within a smaller compass, now hemmed in by former dependencies and allies. It was to one of these states, the Zhou, now turned enemy, that the Shang succumbed in the middle of the eleventh century.

THE LEGACY OF SHANG

The Shang polity was a patrimonial theocracy ruled by a lineage head, the king, "I, the one man," whose authority derived from his unique relation-

---

[124] Edward L. Shaughnessy, "Extra-Lineage Cult in the Shang Dynasty: A Surrejoinder," *EC*, 11–12 (1985–7): 187–90; Xia Hanyi, "Zaoqi Shang Zhou guanxi," pp. 20–32. See also Wang Yuxin, "Wuding qi zhanzheng buci," especially table 1, p. 174; Fan Yuzhou, "Yin dai Wuding shiqi de zhanzheng," in *Jiaguwen yu Yin Shang shi: Di san ji*, ed. Wang Yuxin (Shanghai: Shanghai guji, 1991), pp. 175–239.

[125] For example, of approximately 640 divinations about the king allying (*bi* 比) with other leaders (Y59.1–64.1, 106.1–08.2, 911.2–14.1), only 7 (Y63.2) are from Period V. Of some 60 divinations about the king ordering (*ling* 令) officers, generals, and other groups (Y127.2–28.1), none are from Period V. See also Keightley, "The Late Shang State," pp. 551–4.

[126] Matsumaru, "Inkyo bokujichū no denryôchi ni tsuite," pp. 127–62.

[127] Chen Mengjia, *Yinxu buci zongshu*, pp. 301–9. The scholarship on the dating and geography of the Renfang campaign is extensive; see, e.g., Yan Yiping, "Jiao Zheng Renfang ripu," *Zhongguo wenzi* 11 (1986): 173–7; Chang Yuzhi, *Shangdai zhouji zhidu*, pp. 277–8. See note 26 above.

ship to the ancestors, and who relied on the socioreligious ties of patriarchal authority and filiality to bind his dependents to the dynastic enterprise. The degree to which lineages were key elements in the state, so that political status was frequently based on kin status rather than assigned title, suggests that the Shang polity still shared some of the features of the complex chiefdoms that had appeared in the Late Neolithic. The large numbers of princes and other leaders about whose activities a king like Wu Ding divined suggests both a lack of routine administrative delegation and the great importance attached to such quasi-personal attention on the part of the king, who, in this regard, was still functioning like the "big man" of a prestate chiefdom. In social terms, the "conical clan" provides an appropriate model to describe the Shang evidence. This was a kinship unit that used familial ties to bind its members, but that allocated wealth, social standing, and power unequally among those members, favoring the lineal descendants, in this case the kings on the main line of descent, over the collateral lines.[128]

Late Shang elites took a profound psychological and spiritual satisfaction in the ritual acknowledgment of the dead and in the ritualized hope for obtaining their post-mortem assistance. The economic, emotional, and political impact of such belief was deep and enduring. At the same time, the generational, hierarchical, and jurisdictional logic of Shang ancestor worship shaped and reinforced political and administrative expectations and practices.[129] Hierarchy is, in fact, one of the key terms that appears in many modern definitions of the "state."

The ritual taking of human life in mortuary contexts, as revealed by the burials of the late Shang kings, who took a large number of dependents with them into death, represented the ultimate expression of the belief that the hierarchy of status and service obligations should continue after death. Such sacrifices indicate that similar demands for service and obedience must surely have been part of the idealized, and in all likelihood actual, political culture of the living.

The Shang legacy to the dynasties that followed is seen in the continuing role of ancestor worship; the significant, even extravagant, wealth spent on ritual bronzes, burial rites, and grave goods; the patrimonial nature of the politico-religious state and administration in which political process and religious process frequently overlapped; the increasing role of bureaucracy; the

---

[128] Paul Wheatley, *The Pivot of the Four Quarters: A Preliminary Enquiry into the Origins and Character of the Ancient Chinese City* (Edinburgh: Edinburgh University Press, 1971), pp. 53–5; for an account that confirms the existence of such conical clans in both Shang and Zhou, see Zhu Fenghan, *Shang Zhou jiazu*, pp. 17, 163–86, 219. For the argument that *wang* 王 (oracle-bone forms 示 and 大) meant "big man," see Qi Wenxin, "Wang zi benyi shitan," *Lishi yanjiu* 1991.4: 141–5.

[129] David N. Keightley, "The Religious Commitment: Shang Theology and the Genesis of Chinese Political Culture," *History of Religions* 17 (1978): 220–4.

large-scale mobilization of labor by a central elite; the use of a calendar built on the sixty-day *ganzhi* cycle; the importance of a logographic script to both the functioning of the state and the status of its officers; and, last but not least, the role of divination in the running of the state and the selection of auspicious moments. Truly, despite their overthrow at Muye, the Shang kings and their officers were not without descendants.

CHAPTER FIVE

WESTERN ZHOU HISTORY

Edward L. Shaughnessy

Throughout China's long history, the Western Zhou dynasty has served as its guiding paradigm for governmental, intellectual, and social developments. The Zhou conquest of Shang at the battle of Muye in 1045 B.C. represented at the time perhaps only the replacement – through force of arms – of one local power by another, but for later Chinese it came to illustrate the irrepressible will of Heaven turning its mandate from one state, the rulers of which had grown distant from the people, to another state blessed with virtuous rulers. In the case of the Western Zhou, these virtuous rulers were, at least in the legends of the dynasty's founding, King Wen (r. 1099–1050 B.C.), who died before the final conquest; his son King Wu (r. 1049/45–1043 B.C.), who led the conquest army; and another son, Zhou Gong 周公 (often referred to as the Duke of Zhou), who is credited with ensuring that the dynasty would outlive its founders. Some of Zhou Gong's thoughts on government were put into writing: these documents, preserved in the *Shang shu* 尚書 (Venerated documents; also known as the *Shu jing* 書經, Classic of documents), are probably the earliest writings in China's traditional literature. Other texts probably written toward the end of the dynasty, some 250 years later, were also attributed to Zhou Gong and to his father King Wen; these include the *Zhou yi* 周易 (Zhou changes; the earliest stratum of the work better known in the West as the *Yi jing* 易經, Classic of changes) and much of the *Shi jing* 詩經 (Classic of Poetry), the other two of China's three most important classics. It is in large part as the context for the creation of these classics that the history of the Western Zhou has had such a unique significance in Chinese historiography.

The current study of Western Zhou history, however, does not stop with just the examples of kings Wen and Wu and Zhou Gong, the formulation of the Mandate of Heaven, or the creation of the classics. New sources from the period, including thousands of bronze inscriptions and other archaeological artifacts, now provide numerous details about lesser figures and also about the long period in the middle of the dynasty not represented by the classics or the histories they inspired. Perhaps of greatest importance, these new sources suggest another extremely important cultural legacy bequeathed to later ages by the Western Zhou: bureaucratic government. Originally organized on the basis of close kinship relationships in which brothers and cousins of the king were deputed to rule colonized territories formerly dominated by the Shang and its allies, midway through the dynasty there seems to have been a restructuring of the royal government and the way it related to the society's leading families. Beginning about the reign of King Mu (r. 956–918 B.C.), a reign ushered in by a disastrous defeat in which the preceding king (King Zhao, r. 977–957 B.C.) was killed and the royal army was decimated, there emerge signs of an incipient bureaucracy: bronze inscriptions commemorate the appointment of individuals – often without any apparent relationship to the king – to court positions with specific responsibilities and powers. This restructuring of the court eventually extended to new social and even intellectual developments. These reforms, which are only now beginning to be perceived in the historiography of the period, will be a major concern in the second half of this chapter.

In the chapter, I will attempt to blend narrative and analysis, while giving more or less equal weight to all of the written evidence for Western Zhou history – both traditional and paleographic. I will begin with an evaluation of the sources; treat briefly the legendary and preconquest history of the Zhou people; provide a narrative of the conquest and immediate postconquest years, with an extended consideration of the most important political-philosophical debate of the time; examine bronze inscriptions and especially what they tell us about the reforms developing in the middle of the dynasty; propose how some of these reforms may have influenced the composition of the *Shi jing* and *Yi jing*; and conclude with a narrative of the dynasty's last generations and a consideration of how they form a transition to the following Eastern Zhou period. The story is an old one; the analysis may be rather new.

SOURCES

Unlike the Shang dynasty, which, as the preceding chapter has shown, is known almost entirely from the oracle-bone inscriptions – known now for less than one hundred years – the Western Zhou offers a variety of textual sources. It is traditionally regarded as the period during which the *Yi jing*, *Shang shu*, and *Shi jing* were composed, three texts that during the Han dynasty (206 B.C.–A.D. 220) came to be canonized as the first of the Chinese classics.[1] Because it was regarded as a golden age of history, however, the Western Zhou also served as the context for other works, including some that were also included in the classical canon; other texts of the Warring States (481–221 B.C.), Qin (221–207 B.C.), and Han periods frequently refer to events of the Western Zhou, usually revealing more about the concerns of their own times than about the Western Zhou itself. On the other hand, inscriptions from the Western Zhou have been discovered in ever increasing numbers, and these do give us an undoubted Western Zhou perspective, though one that is also not without its own biases. All of these sources bring advantages and disadvantages, which historians must weigh for themselves.

Shang shu

Certain chapters of the *Shang shu* traditionally dated to the beginning years of the Western Zhou are in fact written in the archaic language of the period as exemplified in contemporary bronze inscriptions, and do seem therefore to provide invaluable information about the history of the period. Among the chapters of the *Shang shu* generally regarded as dating to the Western Zhou,[2] I believe that the following can be used with considerable confidence: the five *gao* 誥 (Pronouncement) chapters (i.e., "Da gao" 大誥, "Kang gao" 康誥, "Jiu gao" 酒誥, "Shao gao" 召誥 and "Luo gao" 洛誥), two of which ("Da gao" and "Jiu gao") probably record speeches of King Wu's son and successor, King Cheng (r. 1042/35–1006 B.C.), two speeches of Zhou Gong ("Kang gao" and "Luo gao"), and one ("Shao gao") a speech by Shao Gong Shi 召公奭, Zhou Gong's half-brother and the other most important figure of the founding years. Another chapter, the "Jun Shi" 君奭, links Zhou Gong and Shao Gong, being a statement of political philosophy made by the former to the latter (perhaps in response to the latter's "Shao gao"); it too is an important source for early Western Zhou conceptions of government. Shao Gong Shi also figures importantly in the "Gu ming" 顧命 chapter, which records King Cheng's final testament and the installation of his son, King Kang (r. 1005–978 B.C.), as third king of the dynasty. In addition to these chapters, the "Shi fu" 世俘 chapter of the *Yi Zhou shu* 逸周書 (Remainder of Zhou documents) provides a detailed account of the Zhou conquest

---

[1] For critical introductions to these three texts, see Michael Loewe, ed. *Early Chinese Texts: A Bibliographical Guide* (Berkeley: Society for the Study of Early China and the Institute of East Asian Studies, University of California, 1993), pp. 216–28 (*Yi jing*), 376–89 (*Shang shu*), and 415–23 (*Shi jing*).

[2] The standard source in Western languages for the date and authenticity of the various chapters of the *Shang shu* is Herrlee G. Creel, *The Origins of Statecraft in China: The Western Chou Empire* (Chicago: University of Chicago Press, 1970), pp. 447–63. For a more detailed comparison of the language of the *Shang shu* and Western Zhou bronze inscriptions, arriving at much the same conclusions as those of Creel, see W. A. C. H. Dobson, *Early Archaic Chinese: A Descriptive Grammar* (Toronto: University of Toronto Press, 1962).

of Shang; it also certainly dates to the early Western Zhou.[3] These are the most important documents for the establishment of the dynasty and the only ones that will be used for the historical narrative given in this chapter. Other chapters of the *Shang shu*, though also ostensibly dating to the Western Zhou, contain linguistic and intellectual features that show them probably to have been written during the subsequent Eastern Zhou period;[4] while these chapters can still be used as important sources for that later period, they are not reliable for the Western Zhou.

Shi jing

Of the 305 poems of the *Shi jing*, most of which are traditionally dated to the early Western Zhou, only some of the poems of the *Zhou song* 周頌 (Zhou liturgies) were written at such an early date; other poems of this earliest section of the anthology probably date to after the middle of the dynasty.[5] These poems, which are almost all liturgical hymns that were originally sung in the ancestral temples, reflect some of the reforms that were taking place during the middle Western Zhou. The poems of the *Da ya* 大雅 (Greater encomia) and *Xiao ya* 小雅 (Lesser encomia) generally date to the late Western Zhou and very early Eastern Zhou; while their topics often concern heros of earlier periods, they are best used as sources for the periods when they were composed.[6] The 160 poems of the *Guo feng* 國風 (Airs of the states) almost all date to the first century of the Spring and Autumn period. Many of these poems also refer to – or, as is more often the case, are interpreted as referring to – earlier events, or, since many of them display elements of folk songs, preserve seemingly timeless accounts of the people's lives; nevertheless, they too are best understood within the context of the Eastern Zhou period.

Zhou yi

The hexagram and line statements of the *Zhou yi* are supposed to have been written by King Wen and Zhou Gong; it is much more likely that they

---

[3] See Edward L. Shaughnessy, " 'New' Evidence on the Zhou Conquest," *EC* 6 (1980–1): 55–81.

[4] Chapters such as the "Hong fan" 洪範 and "Jin teng" 金縢 betray both linguistic and conceptual traits for which there is no other evidence before the late Spring and Autumn period at the earliest. Two other speeches purported to have been made by Zhou Gong, the "Duo shi" 多士 and "Duo fang" 多方, are more problematic; although they are often regarded as being of Western Zhou date, there is some evidence to suggest that they were written after this time, and so will not be used in this chapter.

[5] For a full discussion of the date of the *Zhou song* poems, see Edward L. Shaughnessy, "From Liturgy to Literature: The Ritual Contexts of the Earliest Poems in the *Book of Poetry*," *Hanxue yanjiu* 13, 1 (1994): 133–64.

[6] For the date of the *Da ya* and *Xiao ya*, and indeed all of the *Shi jing* poems, see W. A. C. H. Dobson, "Linguistic Evidence and the Dating of the Book of Songs," *TP* 51 (1964): 322–34.

achieved something resembling their current form in the transitional period at the end of Western Zhou and beginning of Eastern Zhou.[7] This book derived from a type of divination employing the counting of stalks, and the text does indeed reflect this divinatory origin. However, much of the omen imagery that served as the basis for the divinations is similar in form to the poetry of the *Xiao ya* and *Guo feng* sections of the *Shi jing*; in this chapter the *Zhou yi* will be treated together with these poems to illustrate the first formulations of correlative thought in China.

Later Histories

Because of the Western Zhou's prominent place in Chinese historiography, numerous traditions regarding it are recorded in the philosophical texts of the Warring States period (481–222 B.C.) and especially in the *Shi ji* 史記 (Records of the historian), the great synthetic history written in the first century B.C.[8] Another text from this later period, the *Zhushu jinian* 竹書紀年 (Bamboo annals), completed ca. 298 B.C., then buried and rediscovered in A.D. 279, provides an annalistic history of the entire ancient period, including the Western Zhou.[9] Much of the information that it contains about the Western Zhou is more detailed than, and often more or less at variance from, that of the other traditional sources. Some of this information has now been corroborated by bronze inscriptions.[10] While the transmission history of the *Zhushu jinian* remains too problematic to place too much faith in it, by the same token it has proved to be too reliable on too many points to disregard it.

Bronze Inscriptions

In addition to all of these traditional literary sources, historians of the Western Zhou now have available to them thousands of inscriptions originally cast into ritual bronze vessels. These vessels were generally intended to commemorate some achievement of the person for whom they were cast; the inscriptions run the gamut from the briefest mention that "So-and-so makes

---

[7] For the date of the *Zhou yi*'s composition, see Edward L. Shaughnessy, "The Composition of the *Zhouyi*" (Ph.D. dissertation, Stanford University, 1983), chapter 1.

[8] For the view of ancient history held by the Warring States philosophers, see D. C. Lau, *Mencius* (Harmondsworth: Penguin, 1970), pp. 223–34; John Knoblock, *Xunzi*, vol. 2 (Stanford: Stanford University Press, 1990), pp. 3–27. The best account of the *Shi ji*'s view of history is still that of Édouard Chavannes, *Les mémoires historiques de Se-Ma Ts'ien*, vol. 1 (Paris: Ernest Leroux, 1895), pp. cix–clxxi.

[9] For the *Zhushu jinian*, including discussion of its discovery and transmission, as well as of the doubts often expressed about the authenticity of the received text, see Loewe, ed., *Early Chinese Texts*, pp. 39–47.

[10] See Edward L. Shaughnessy, "On the Authenticity of the *Bamboo Annals*," *HJAS* 46, 1 (1986): 149–80.

the vessel" to narratives of several hundred characters, recounting such events as appointments at court, victories in battle, and successful legal suits.[11] Because the inscriptions appear to us virtually as they did to their Western Zhou makers, we can be confident – as we cannot be with received texts, which have been copied and recopied over the centuries – that they preserve aspects of the period's language and script. Moreover, because the vessels were cast by a broad range of people within Western Zhou society, and in all periods of the dynasty, their inscriptions fill significant gaps in the traditional record. Important though the inscriptions thus are as historical sources, however, we must also admit that they are not the one key to unlocking the door of Western Zhou history: there is much that they do not tell us about the period, and there is also much that they do tell us that represents a bias of the person for whom the vessel was cast. Nevertheless, with them Western Zhou history is now much richer than hitherto and, thanks to the ongoing efforts of China's archaeologists, is becoming ever richer.[12]

The Extent of Writing During the Western Zhou

The bronze inscriptions are supremely valuable too for providing a standard against which to evaluate the traditional literary record of the Western Zhou. The iconoclastic *Gu shi bian* 古史辨 (Discriminations of ancient history) movement of the 1920s and 1930s declared much of the *Shang shu* and the *Zhou yi* to be late retrospective creations,[13] valuable perhaps for the study of how the Eastern Zhou viewed its heritage but not as primary documents for Western Zhou history. This iconoclasm regarding the traditional literary record remains influential among Western sinologists, many of whom regard the evidence turned up by archaeology as being "hard" and, thus, of greater authority than these texts that have been transmitted through the centuries.[14] However, the bronze inscriptions have tended to corroborate the authentic-

[11] See Edward L. Shaughnessy, *Sources of Western Zhou History: Inscribed Bronze Vessels* (Berkeley: University of California Press, 1991).

[12] In addition to these bronze inscriptions, there is also a corpus of about 300 fragments of inscribed turtle shell that had been used – like the Shang oracle bones – in divinations. Although uninscribed turtle shells showing signs of having been used in divination appear in most archaeological sites of the Western Zhou period, the inscribed pieces found to date are almost all from the Plain of Zhou (Zhouyuan 周原) area of Fufeng 扶風 and Qishan 岐山 counties, Shaanxi, and all of these seem to date to the first generations of the dynasty. For scholarship on these inscriptions, see Wang Yuxin, *Xi Zhou jiagu tanlun* (Beijing: Zhongguo shehui kexue, 1984); Xu Xitai, *Zhouyuan jiaguwen zongshu* (Xi'an: San Qin, 1987); Edward L. Shaughnessy, "Zhouyuan Oracle-Bone Inscriptions: Entering the Research Stage?" *EC* 11–12 (1985–7): 146–63.

[13] For the *Yijing*, see Gu Jiegang, ed., *Gu shi bian*, vol. 3 (Shanghai: Pushe, 1931). For the *Shang shu*, see ibid., vol. 2 (1930), esp. pp. 43–81.

[14] For perhaps the most important statement of this viewpoint, see Noel Barnard, "Chou China: A Review of the Third Volume of Cheng Te-k'un's *Archaeology in China*," *MS* 24 (1965): 307–442. Similar sentiments are also evident in Chapter 3, the present volume.

ity of much of the received literature of the period. For instance, the chapters of the *Shang shu* discussed above share to a great extent the same grammatical structures as the bronze inscriptions. Since these structures had changed by the Eastern Zhou period (as seen by bronze inscriptions of that period), it is hard to imagine how a putative Eastern Zhou author could have consciously used anachronistic language to create these chapters.

What is more, the bronze inscriptions suggest that the Western Zhou was an extremely literate culture. They do this not only by their very number – and we should probably assume that the many thousands of inscribed vessels now known were but a fraction of the total number cast at the time – but also by the insight they give into their own creation. As mentioned above, many, indeed most, Western Zhou bronze vessels were cast by individuals who had been recognized at the royal court for their accomplishments. The inscriptions on these vessels often describe the court audience in step-by-step detail, as in the case of that on the *Song gui* 頌簋, a vessel cast for a man named Song 頌 probably in 825 B.C. during the reign of King Xuan (r. 827–782 B.C.).[15] The inscription begins with notations of the date and place where the king received Song in audience;[16] proceeds through a narration of the audience, including the text of the king's command to Song and a listing of the gifts the king gave to him; and concludes with a dedication in which Song extols the king's beneficence and entreats the blessings of his own deceased father and mother, for sacrifices to whom the vessel was intended:

It was the third year, fifth month, after the dying brightness, *jiaxu* [day 11]; the king was at the Zhao [Temple] of the Kang Palace. At dawn the king entered the Great Chamber and assumed position. Intendant [*zai* 宰] Yin to the right of Song entered the gate and stood in the center of the court. Yinshi received the king's command document. The king called out to Scribe [*shi* 史] Guo Sheng to record the command to Song.

The king said: "Song, [I] command you to officiate over and to supervise the Chengzhou warehouses, and to oversee and supervise the newly constructed warehouses, using palace attendants. [I] award you a black jacket with embroidered hem,

---

[15] *Shang Zhou qingtongqi mingwen xuan*, ed. Ma Chengyuan (Beijing: Wenwu, 1988), no. 435; Shirakawa Shizuka, *Kinbun tsûshaku* (Kobe: Hakutsuru bijutsukan, 1962–84), 24, no. 153. Bronze vessels are routinely referred to by the name of the person identified in the inscription as the patron for whom the vessel was cast, in this case Song, and by the type of vessel, in this case a *gui* tureen.

[16] The date here is a "full" date, indicating the year of the king's reign (which, as is usual, is unspecified, but in this case is discernible on the basis of other evidence in the inscription and from the shape and decor of the vessel), the lunar month, the phase of the moon (indicated with one of four terms [*chuji* 初吉, "first auspiciousness"; *jishengpo* 既生霸, "after the growing brightness"; *jiwang* 既望, "after the full moon"; and *jisipo* 既死霸, "after the dying brightness], each apparently of seven or eight days duration), and the day in the sixty-day *ganzhi* 干支 cycle. For a full discussion of these dates and the use to which they can be put in reconstructing the chronology of the Western Zhou, see Shaughnessy, *Sources of Western Zhou History*, pp. 134–55.

red kneepads, a scarlet demi-circlet, a chime pennant, and a bridle with bit and cheekpieces; use [them] to serve."

Song bowed and touched his head to the ground, received the command, and suspended the strips from his sash in order to go out. He returned and brought in a jade tablet. Song dares in response to extol the Son of Heaven's illustriously fine beneficence, herewith making [for] my august deceased-father Gongshu and august mother Gongsi [this] treasured offertory *gui*-tureen, to use to send back filial piety and to beseech vigor, pure aid, thorough riches, and an eternal mandate. May Song for ten-thousand years be long-lived, truly ministering to the Son of Heaven [until] a numinous end, and [have] sons' sons and grandsons' grandsons eternally to treasure and use [it].

This inscription shows that prior to the audience, the court scribes had prepared Song's appointment in writing – written on bamboo or wooden strips. During the audience, the Intendant read this document on behalf of the king; at the same time, a royal scribe made a copy of it. At the end of the ceremony, the written command (whether the original or just the written copy is not clear) was handed over to Song, and he exited the court with the actual strips suspended from his sash. Song then presumably copied the text of the command into the inscription that he then produced in bronze. The inscription on this vessel is thus but a tertiary record of Song's appointment, the other copies doubtless being kept in the archives of the royal court and of his own family.

It is perhaps to be expected that a culture so concerned with the written record that even lower-level appointments were recorded in triplicate would also have kept copies of royal speeches and discussions at court, or of the liturgical hymns and poems of the dynastic founders sung in the ancestral temple and in the royal banquet hall, such as those preserved in the *Shang shu* and in the *Shi jing*. A history of the period that disregarded these sources would be very much impoverished.

LEGENDARY EVIDENCE FOR ZHOU BEFORE THE CONQUEST OF SHANG

The Zhou people traced their ancestry to a woman named Jiang Yuan 姜嫄, which means "The Jiang (People's) Progenitress." According to the poem "Sheng min" 生民 (Giving birth to the people) of the *Da ya* section of the *Shi jing* (Mao 245),[17] probably written toward the end of the Western Zhou, Jiang Yuan became pregnant by stepping in the footprint of Di 帝, the high

---

[17] *Maoshi zhengyi* ("Sheng min"), 17/1, 1a–20b (Arthur Waley, *The Book of Songs: The Ancient Chinese Classic of Poetry* [1936; rpt. New York: Grove, 1960], pp. 241–3).

Power of the Shang pantheon (for which, see Chapter 4, p. 252). Although the birth of her son, whom she named Qi 棄 (Abandoned), but who would come to be better known as Hou Ji 后稷, or the Lord of Millet, was auspiciously easy, Jiang Yuan believed that Di disapproved of the infant. She thereupon abandoned him (whence his name Qi), first placing him in a country lane; there the oxen and sheep far from trampling him lay beside him to keep him warm. Jiang Yuan then placed him in the middle of the forest, where he was found by woodcutters. She then placed him on ice, but birds covered him with their wings. When the birds flew off, Hou Ji cried out in a loud voice, and then began, step by step, to make his way in the world. Learning to nurture the plants that he found, he handed down to the people both the crops that he grew and the way of growing them; in this way he became the progenitor of the Zhou people and of their agricultural way of life.

According to the "Zhou benji" 周本紀 (Basic annals of Zhou) of the *Shi ji*, these events took place during the time of the legendary emperor Yao 堯. Hearing of Hou Ji's accomplishments, Yao is said to have granted him the surname Ji 姬, which has connotations of both "footprint" and "foundation."[18] As might be expected of such legends, both the chronology and the exact genealogy are confused. The "Zhou benji" says that Hou Ji's son Buku 不窋 lived during the declining years of the Xia 夏 dynasty, at which time the Zhou people were living "among the Rong 戎 and Di 狄" barbarians, understood by most later commentators to mean that they had given up their settled agricultural life. Two generations later, Buku's grandson Gong Liu 公劉, though still living among the Rong and Di, is said to have returned the Zhou to the ways of agriculture. "Gong Liu" (Mao 250), another poem in the *Da ya* section of the *Shi jing* sings his praises, beginning:

> Staunch Gong Liu,
> Neither dwelling nor relaxing,
> Then cleared, then bordered,
> Then piled up, then stored,
> Then enclosed cereals
> In bags, in sacks.
> Through collecting he became radiant,
> And bows and arrows were then drawn,
> The awe of shields and dagger-axes raised;
> And with that he opened the path.[19]

After Gong Liu, the "begats" of another eight generations are listed in the *Shi ji* without further comment, until we come to the time of Gu Gong

---

[18] *Shi ji*, 4, p. 111 (William H. Nienhauser, Jr., et al., eds., *The Grand Scribe's Records*, vol. 1 [Bloomington: Indiana University Press, 1994], p. 55).

[19] *Maoshi zhengyi* ("Gong Liu"), 17/3, 5a–b (Waley, *The Book of Songs*, p. 244).

Danfu 古公亶父. This leader is said there to have led the Zhou people on a great migration out from among the Rong and Di, settling finally at the base of Mount Qi (Qishan 岐山), in the central Wei 渭 River valley of present-day Shaanxi province. Another *Shi jing* poem, "Mian" 綿 (Extended; Mao 237), also of the *Da ya* section, describes the building of a city there, ono-matopoeia adding to the vividness of the description:

> Then summoning the Supervisor of Works,
> Then summoning the Supervisor of Lands,
> He caused them to erect houses.
> Their lines then were straight,
> Lashed planks were used to carry,
> Making temples all in line.
> They mounded them *rengreng*,
> They pounded them *honghong*,
> They raised them *dengdeng*,
> They scraped and chiseled them *pingping*;
> A hundred measures all about arose;
> The chimes and drums could not keep up with the beat.
>
> Then they erected the Citadel Gate;
> The Citadel Gate was lofty.
> Then they erected the Response Gate;
> The Response Gate was so commanding.
> Then they erected the Mound Altar,
> Whence war campaigns would proceed.[20]

With Gu Gong Danfu's building of this city at Qishan, we come to a time and place for which there is some, albeit tenuous, archaeological evidence for the Zhou people.[21] The historical narrative also begins to take shape, though there is still no contemporary written evidence for it. Gu Gong Danfu, also referred to as Taiwang 太王 (the Great King), is supposed to have sired three sons, the youngest of whom, Jili 季歷, in turn sired a son named Chang 昌 (who would eventually come to be known as King Wen). Traditions hold that because Chang was the favorite grandson of Gu Gong Danfu (some of those traditions saying that he bore auspicious markings on his body),[22] Gu Gong Danfu indicated that he wished to have Jili as his successor; his two eldest sons thereupon voluntarily removed themselves from the scene. The *Shi ji* says little

[20] *Maoshi zhengyi* ("Mian"), 16/2, 18a–20a (Waley, *The Book of Songs*, pp. 248–9).
[21] For an overview of the archaeological excavations carried out in Qishan and Fufeng counties, which lie at the base of Qishan, see Chen Quanfang, *Zhouyuan yu Zhou wenhua* (Shanghai: Shanghai Renmin, 1988). See also Chapter 6, "The Zhouyuan."
[22] *Taiping yulan* 太平御覽 (984; rpt. Beijing: Zhonghua, 1960), vol. 2, p. 1708 (371, p. 2b), quoting the Tang period *Chunqiu yuan ming bao* 春秋元命保, describes Chang as having had four nipples on his chest, a trait often featured in later illustrations of him.

about Jili except that he was staunch in his conduct and that the many lords complied with him.[23] The *Zhushu jinian* records numerous Zhou attacks under the leadership of Jili against peoples in the Wei and Fen 汾 River valleys (the latter of which is in present-day Shanxi).[24] It also records in its account for the eleventh year of Shang king Wen Ding's reign (r. ca. 1116–1107 B.C.) that Jili was eventually killed at the Shang capital. Jili's death brought his son Chang, long since marked for rule, to the leadership of the Zhou people. Jili's death also apparently initiated the adversarial relations between the Zhou and Shang that would assume such a special importance in the Zhou people's own view of their history, as well as in that of subsequent ages.

As we draw nearer in time to the Zhou conquest of Shang, the traditional histories of both of these peoples tend to focus just on their relations with each other. The Shang seem to have perceived the Zhou as a threat and, in about the twentieth year of the reign of Di Xin (r. 1086–1045 B.C.), arrested Chang, imprisoning him at Youli 羑里, not far from Di Xin's palace at Zhaoge 朝歌, just south of present-day Anyang 安陽. There Chang is said to have been held for seven years before the Zhou people ransomed him. The year after his release, which evidence in the *Zhushu jinian* suggests came in 1059 B.C., the year of a momentous conjunction of the five visible planets,[25] Chang was granted by the Shang king the exclusive privilege to conduct military campaigns in the areas to the west of Shang.[26] Shortly thereafter he assumed the title Wen Wang 文王 (the Cultured King), by which he was known throughout the Western Zhou and to later history.

INSCRIPTIONAL AND ARCHAEOLOGICAL EVIDENCE FOR ZHOU BEFORE THE CONQUEST OF SHANG

Before going on to consider Western Zhou history itself, it is well first to return to Gu Gong Danfu's settlement at Qishan, and to consider – this time not on the basis of legend but rather on the basis of textual, inscriptional, and archaeological evidence – the location, or at least direction, from which the Zhou people came to that place. Over the past fifteen years, this has been one of the most hotly contested issues in studies of Zhou history.

[23] *Shi ji*, 4, p. 116 (Nienhauser, ed., *The Grand Scribe's Records*, vol. 1, p. 57).

[24] *Zhushu jinian* (Sibu beiyao ed.), 1, pp. 17b–18a (James Legge, *The Chinese Classics, Vol. 3: The Shoo King, or The Book of Historical Documents* [1865; rpt. Hong Kong: Hong Kong University Press, 1960], Prolegomena, pp. 137–8).

[25] *Zhushu jinian*, 1.19b (Legge, *The Shoo King*, Prolegomena, p. 140). For this planetary conjunction and its possible importance for early Zhou history, see David W. Pankenier, "Astronomical Dates in Shang and Western Zhou," *EC* 7 (1981–2): 2–37.

[26] *Shi ji*, 4, p. 116 (Nienhauser, ed., *The Grand Scribe's Records*, vol. 1, p. 58).

Traditional Accounts

Traditional accounts of the Zhou people prior to their migration under Gu Gong Danfu locate them at a place called Bin 豳 (or 邠), before they crossed over the Liang 梁 Mountains to settle at the base of Qishan.[27] Most geographical works have routinely identified this Bin as the Bin 豳 of present-day Binxian 豳縣 in Shaanxi, about 75 km due north of Qishan, between which two places there runs a low mountain range called the Liang Mountains.[28] Thus, the Zhou have been seen as native to present-day Shaanxi province and, consequently, at least in comparison with the Shang and other states of the Central Plain (Zhongyuan 中原), as being of western, and perhaps therefore semibarbaric, origin.[29]

On the other hand, there is some evidence in traditional sources linking the early history of the Zhou people with areas further east, particularly in the Fen River valley of present-day Shanxi province. This evidence was first collected and discussed by Qian Mu 錢穆 in 1931; the "eastern origin" thesis for the Zhou people that he based on it has since come to be identified with him.[30] Among the items of evidence adduced by Qian, three points in particular are deserving of mention. First, the Bin from which the Zhou people migrated is also written in early texts as 邠 or 汾, both of which variants employ as phonetic the *fen* 分 of the Fen 汾 River,[31] presumably indicating some relationship between the two names. Second, in Linfen 臨汾 county of Shanxi province there is a tributary of the Fen River that was anciently called the Gu 古 River, from which the name Gu Gong 古公 (Duke of Gu) of Gu Gong Danfu could conceivably have derived. Third, the major north–south mountain range running just east of and parallel to the Yellow River, which forms the border between present-day Shaanxi and Shanxi provinces, has long been known as the Lüliang 呂梁 Mountains, perhaps to be identified with the Liang Mountains over which the Zhou people are said to have crossed (see Map 5.1). Each of these pieces of evidence linking the origins of the Zhou people with the more eastern area of Shanxi province is consistent with one of the basic tenets of historical geography – that while the names

[27] The earliest such account is found in *Mencius*, 1B/14, 1B/15; see, too, *Shi ji*, 4, pp. 113–14 (Nienhauser, ed., *The Grand Scribe's Records*, vol. 1, pp. 56–7).

[28] For a comprehensive review of this traditional evidence, see Qi Sihe, "Xi Zhou dili kao," *Yanjing xuebao* 30 (1936): 63–106.

[29] This view has been incorporated in the major modern general histories of China; see Guo Moruo, *Zhongguo shi gao* (Beijing: Renmin, 1964), vol. 1, pp. 117–18; Fan Wenlan, *Zhongguo tongshi* (Beijing: Renmin, 1978), vol. 1, pp. 65–6; Jian Bozan, *Zhongguo shi gangyao* (Beijing: Renmin, 1983), vol. 1, pp. 31–2. In Western sinology, this view is perhaps best exemplified in the argument by Wolfram Eberhard that the Zhou were a proto-Turkic people; *A History of China: From the Earliest Times to the Present Day* (London: Routledge & Kegan Paul, 1950), p. 25.

[30] Qian Mu, "Zhou chu dili kao," *Yanjing xuebao* 10 (1931): 1955–2008.

[31] *Mencius* 1B/14, 15; *Yi Zhou shu* 逸周書 ("Di yi"; Sibu beiyao ed.), 5.3a.

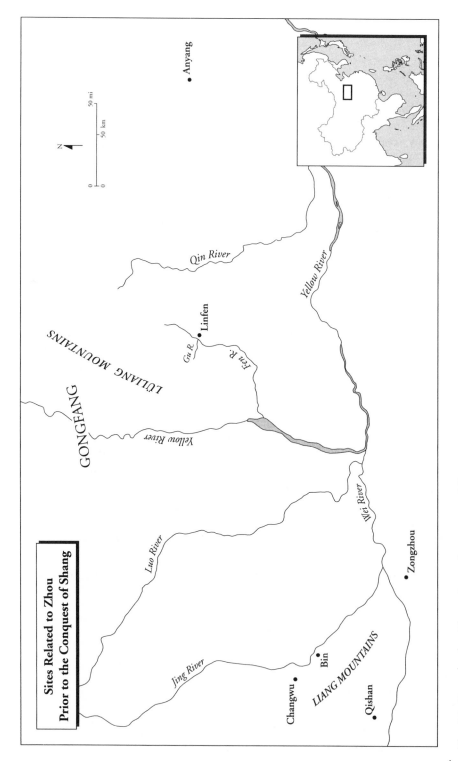

Map 5.1 Sites related to Zhou prior to the conquest of Shang

of cities and states frequently change, those of rivers and mountains tend to remain the same.

Shang Oracle-Bone Evidence

Two and a half decades after its publication, Qian Mu's "eastern origin" thesis received important support with the publication of Chen Mengjia's 陳蒙家 study of the geography of the late Shang state, which was based almost entirely on Shang oracle-bone inscriptions.[32] In this study, Chen examined the relations between Shang names and place-names mentioned in the inscriptions, often as enemies or allies of Shang in military campaigns. By assuming that places mentioned together in the same context must have been located in close proximity to each other, he was able to describe networks of states within limited geographic regions. The most important of these was centered in the southern part of present-day Shanxi province, more or less along the Fen River. Among the states in this network was one called Zhou, which almost all historians have assumed was antecedent to the Zhou that later overthrew the Shang. In Shang oracle-bone inscriptions dating to the reigns of King Wu Ding (d. ca. 1189 B.C.) and his son Zu Geng (ca. 1188–1178 B.C.), Zhou appears first as an enemy of Shang, then as an ally, and then, apparently at the time of or just after the Shang war against the Gongfang 舌方 (for which, see Chapter 4, p. 284), again as an enemy. It is important to note that these inscriptions would correspond to the time just before Zhou migrated to Qishan.[33] After this early flurry of contact between Shang and Zhou, Zhou is never again mentioned in the Shang inscriptions. One plausible explanation for such a lack of mention might be that a Zhou migration out of the Fen River valley westward to the middle Wei River valley took them outside the reach of Shang political influence. Conversely, that they were previously within such reach might support Qian Mu's suggestion that they were originally located east of the Wei River valley, as, for instance, in the Fen River valley.

Archaeological Evidence

After another two and a half decades, the archaeologist Zou Heng 鄒衡 added the third leg to Qian Mu's "eastern origin" thesis. Arguing that Proto-Zhou Culture (Xian Zhou wenhua 先周文化) appears suddenly in the Wei

---

[32] Chen Mengjia, *Yinxu buci zongshu* (Beijing: Kexue, 1956), esp. pp. 249–312.

[33] This would be true whether or not we give any credence to the *Zhushu jinian* record that Zhou migrated in the first year of the reign of King Wu Yi (r. ca. 1131–1117 B.C.); *Zhushu jinian*, 1.17b (Legge, *The Shoo King*, Prolegomena, p. 137).

River valley without any apparent cultural precedents, Zou traced one of its most notable features – the "linked-crotch *li*" (*liandang li* 連襠鬲, the *li* being a lobed tripod with hollow legs) – to the Guangshe 光社 culture that extended across the northern parts of present-day Shaanxi and Shanxi, and concluded that this must represent the distinctively "Zhou" (or Ji 姬, the surname of the Zhou people) contribution to Proto-Zhou Culture.[34] According to Zou, the reason that Proto-Zhou culture also appears to be very different from Guangshe culture is because when the Zhou people reached Qishan, their culture was thoroughly merged with that of people living farther to the west, which he referred to as the Jiang Yan 姜炎 culture, the name referring to the Jiang 姜 people with whom historical texts say the Zhou regularly intermarried.

The publication of Zou Heng's study touched off a heated debate between archaeologists and historians from the two provinces of Shaanxi and Shanxi, each claiming to be the native place of the Zhou people. It will not be possible here to give anything approaching a complete bibliographic survey of this debate, which still continues.[35] The dramatically differing interpretations notwithstanding, however, there does seem to be a consistent body of evidence on which both parties draw. First and perhaps most important, what can be identified as Proto-Zhou culture, that is a culture that displays important features in common with the later Zhou culture located in the same area, begins to appear in the Wei River valley archaeological inventory only toward the end of Yinxu Phase II or even into Yinxu Phase III, which is to say toward the middle of the twelfth century B.C. Wherever the Zhou originated, there is no trace of them in the Wei River valley before that time – which is just about the time that their own legends say they moved there. Second, the counties of Changwu 長武 and Binxian, the area in Shaanxi traditionally identified with the Bin from which the Zhou people are supposed to have migrated, have to date produced no cultural remains prior to the middle period of the Proto-Zhou culture (i.e., into the eleventh century B.C.).[36] Third, Proto-Zhou culture is an amalgamation of at least two distinct subtypes, one of which is usually referred to as the Zhengjiapo Beilü 鄭家坡 北呂 type and the other as the Liujia Doujitai 劉家斗雞臺 type. Sites of the

---

[34] Zou Heng, *Xia Shang Zhou kaoguxue lunwenji* (Beijing: Wenwu, 1980), pp. 279–355.

[35] A partial listing of recent scholars supporting the "eastern origin" thesis would include: Wang Yuzhe, "Xian Zhou zu zui zao laiyuan yu Shanxi," *Zhonghua wenshi luncong* 1982.3: 1–24; Li Min, "Shi Shang shu Zhou ren zun Xia shuo," *Zhongguo shi yanjiu* 1982.2: 128–34; Yang Shengnan, "Zhou zu de qiyuan ji qi boqian," *Renwen zazhi* 1984.6: 75–80; Wang Kelin, *Xia shi luncong* (Jinan: Qi Lu, 1985), pp. 79–80; Xu Chuan, "Jin zhong diqu Xi Zhou yiqian gu yicun de biannian yu puxi," *Wenwu* 1989.4: 40–50; Ye Wenxian, "Xian Zhou shi yu Xian Zhou wenhua yuanyuan bianxi," in *Xi Zhou shi lunwenji* (Xi'an: Shaanxi Renmin jiaoyu, 1993), pp. 376–86. Among those upholding the Shaanxi origin are: Xu Xitai, "Zao Zhou wenhua de tedian ji qi yuanyuan de tansuo," *Wenwu* 1979.10: 50–9; Yin Shengping, "Cong Xian Zhou wenhua kan Zhou zu de qiyuan," in *Xi Zhou shi yanjiu, Renwen zazhi congkan* 2 (Xi'an, 1984), pp. 221–31; Lin Xiaoan, "Cong jiagu keci lun Xian Zhou qiyuan," *Kaogu yu wenwu* 1991.2: 66–9.

[36] See Ye Wenxian, "Xian Zhou shi yu Xian Zhou wenhua yuanyuan bianxi," p. 381.

Zhengjiapo Beilü type are found to the east of Qishan and are characterized by the "linked-crotch *li*" noted before by Zou Heng. Sites of the Liujia Doujitai type, on the other hand, are all found to the west of Qishan and feature a distinctly different type of *li*, usually referred to as a "high-necked pocket-footed *li*" (*gaoling daizu li* 高領袋足鬲). That these two types of *li*, as well as many other heterogeneous cultural artifacts, occur together at Qishan does suggest a cultural mixing that would be consistent with the movement of a new people into the area.

None of these points of archaeological evidence proves that the Zhou people migrated to Qishan from the Fen River valley of Shanxi. However, combined with the evidence from Shang oracle-bone inscriptions, such a migration would seem to make better sense of the dynamics behind the development of the Zhou state than does the assumption of an indigenous Shaanxi origin. It might also explain two close relationships that the Zhou people maintained throughout the Western Zhou dynasty proper: first, with the Jiang people, who continued to provide spouses for, and thus to bear, most of the Zhou kings, just as legend has it that Jiang Yuan bore Hou Ji; and second, with the Fen River valley, to which they returned at several different important moments in their history.

THE ZHOU CONQUEST OF SHANG

Campaigns Under King Wen

According to both the *Shi ji* and the *Zhushu jinian*, by the time the Zhou ruler Chang assumed the title of king – King Wen – the Zhou were attempting to return to the Fen River valley, or at least to bring it under their military control. About 1053 B.C., King Wen led a Zhou army through southern Shanxi attacking and defeating the state of Li 黎 (also known as Qi 耆), located just south of present-day Changzhi 長治 at the Huguan 壺關 Pass through the southern tip of the Taihang 太行 Mountains; this lay along the major natural defense perimeter to the west of the Shang capital region. When shortly thereafter the Zhou also defeated Yu 盂, located at Qinyang 沁陽, on the Qin 沁 River, southeastern Shanxi's major tributary to the Yellow River,[37] this brought the Shang capital region and the capital of Anyang itself, just 100 km due east, under immediate threat (see Map 5.2).

After yet one further attack, against the citadel of Chong 崇, probably located at the site of modern Luoyang 洛陽 just south of the major ford across the Yellow River at Mengjin 盟津, King Wen died, according to tra-

---

[37] For these locations and an analysis of this campaign, see Gu Jiegang and Liu Qiyu, "Shangshu Xibo kan Li jiaoshi yilun," *Zhongguo lishi wenxian yanjiu jikan* 1 (1980): 46–59.

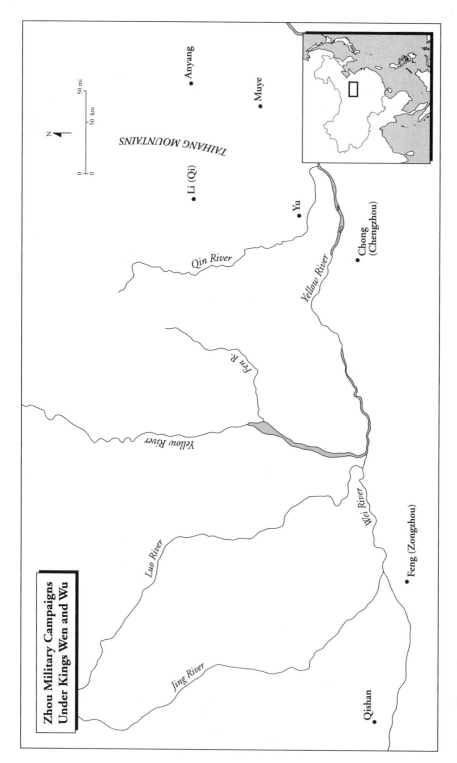

Map 5.2 Zhou military campaigns under Kings Wen and Wu

dition in the fiftieth year of his rule. He was survived by eight direct-line sons.[38] The eldest of these, named Fa 發, succeeded to the Zhou kingship, being known as King Wu (the Martial King). King Wu continued to press the Zhou campaign, now clearly directed against the Shang state itself. Two years after King Wen's death, King Wu brought the Zhou army back to the ford at Mengjin, where tradition says he was met by 800 local lords. Although he apparently did cross to the north of the Yellow River at this time, he aborted the campaign before approaching the Shang capital area. This campaign may well have been a practice run designed to demonstrate his strength, thereby attracting further allies, and also to secure a forward base at the all important Yellow River crossing point.

The Conquest Campaign

Two years later, early in 1045 B.C., King Wu again led the Zhou army and its allies – a force said in the *Shi ji* to have numbered 45,000 troops and 300 chariots – across the Yellow River, but this time he did not turn back.[39] Entering the Shang capital region from the south in this way would have allowed the Zhou army to bypass the Shang western defense perimeter anchored in the Taihang Mountains. After a short march (said to have taken five days)[40] through the flat terrain of this area, the Zhou army reached a place called Muye 牧野 (Shepherd's Wild), just outside of Shang king Di Xin's capital at Zhaoge (about 50 km due south of Anyang). On a *jiazi* 甲子 morning (*jiazi* was the first day in the cycle of sixty days by which both the Shang and Zhou designated days), the Shang army assembled to face the Zhou. The poem "Da ming" 大明 (Great brightness; Mao 236) of the *Shi jing* describes the scene from the Zhou perspective:

> The Yin-Shang legions,
> Their battle flags like a forest,
> Were arrayed on the field of Muye.
>
> "Arise, my lords,
> The Lord on High looks down on you;
> Have no second thoughts."
>
> The field of Muye was so broad.
> The sandalwood chariots were so gleaming.
> The teams of four were so pounding.

[38] By "direct-line sons," I mean sons born of his principal wife; there were other sons as well, some of them – Shao Gong Shi, for instance – very important figures in the early Western Zhou state. In addition to the eight direct-line sons who survived King Wen, there was also another son, Boyi Kao 伯邑考, the eldest, who predeceased him.

[39] *Shi ji* 4, p. 121 (Nienhauser et al., eds., *The Grand Scribe's Records*, vol. 1 p. 60).

[40] For a calendar of events associated with the Zhou conquest, see Shaughnessy, "'New' Evidence on the Zhou Conquest," pp. 68–9.

> There was the general Shangfu.
> He rose as an eagle,
> Aiding that King Wu,
> And attacked the great Shang,
> Meeting in the morning, clear and bright.

It seems that the Zhou chariots quickly routed the Shang army.[41] Although later Confucian moralists refused to concede that a confrontation between the "extreme virtue" of King Wu of Zhou and the "extreme vice" of King Di Xin of Shang could possibly have resulted in any bloodshed at all,[42] there is little doubt that the Zhou did win a decisive military victory. Tradition holds that although Di Xin retreated to his Deer Terrace (*Lu tai* 鹿台) pavilion, set it on fire and committed suicide, he did not escape having his corpse mutilated when it was found by King Wu. Some of the captured Shang elite survived only until they were taken back to Zhou a few months later; others were eventually relocated to assist in the building of the Zhou state.

According to the "Shifu" (Great capture) chapter of the *Yi Zhou shu*,[43] the Zhou army remained in the vicinity of the Shang capital for about two months, mopping up remaining resistance in the area and securing the allegiance of local lords. Returning west to their capital Feng 酆, which had been established by King Wen about one hundred kilometers east of Qishan (in the outskirts of present-day Xi'an 西安), apparently subduing remaining resistance in Shanxi along the way, the Zhou celebrated their victory by executing 100 of the captured Shang officials. At this time, or shortly thereafter, King Wu deputed two or three of his younger brothers, Guanshu Xian 管叔鮮, Caishu Du 蔡叔度, and perhaps Huoshu Chu 霍叔處, to oversee governance of the former Shang domain, which had been put under the nominal rule of Di Xin's son Wu Geng 武庚. At the same time, King Wu retained another brother, Zhou Gong Dan 周公旦, next senior after Guanshu Xian, in the Zhou capital to serve as his chief advisor. This seems to have been the extent of his governmental structure. It went unchallenged while he was alive. He did not live for long.

The Death of King Wu and the Succession Crisis

Two years after the conquest of Shang, King Wu died. There then ensued a succession crisis that has come to be seen as a defining moment not only for

---

[41] For the role chariots may have played in this battle, see Edward L. Shaughnessy, "Historical Perspectives on the Introduction of the Chariot into China," *HJAS* 48.1 (1988): 230–1.

[42] For the classic enunciation of this view of history, see *Mencius*, 7B/3.

[43] *Yi Zhou shu* ("Shi fu") (Sibu beiyao ed.), 4.9a–12a (Shaughnessy, "'New' Evidence on the Zhou Conquest," pp. 57–61).

the Western Zhou dynasty but for the entire history of Chinese statecraft. According to the precedent of at least the preceding two generations, King Wu was to be succeeded by his eldest son, named Song 誦. However, it would seem that King Wu's younger brother Zhou Gong Dan stepped in, declaring Song, subsequently to be known as King Cheng (r. 1042/35–1006 B.C.), too young to rule and declaring himself regent. Not only is there real doubt whether King Cheng was indeed too young to rule,[44] but even if he were it is obvious that Dan's right to rule in his place was questioned by King Wu's other brothers, including especially Guanshu Xian, next in line of seniority after King Wu himself. Guanshu Xian together with his two brothers Caishu Du and Huoshu Chu, who were with him in the east governing the former Shang territory, thereupon joined together with the nominal ruler of the Shang people, Wu Geng, and rebelled against Zhou Gong Dan's apparent usurpation. This resulted in a civil war, with brothers literally fighting brothers.

Zhou Gong Dan, joined by King Cheng and yet another elder royal sibling, his half-brother Shao Gong Shi, launched the second "eastern campaign." In two years, they not only suppressed by force of arms the eastern rebellion, killing Guanshu Xian and Wu Geng and forcing Caishu Du to flee into exile, but they pressed the attack into areas yet farther east, now bringing the various peoples of the eastern seaboard under Zhou rule.

Colonization of the East

To control this dramatically enlarged state, the victorious triumvirate initiated a program of rapid colonization, with members of the royal family sent out to defend strategic points all along the two main geographic axes of north China, the Yellow River and the Taihang Mountains. Zhou Gong Dan himself seems to have taken responsibility for establishing a stronghold, usually referred to as Chengzhou 成周, at the site of present-day Luoyang; not only did this control the ford across the Yellow River at Mengjin, the crucial significance of which we have already seen, but it also blocked entrance to the Wei River valley through the Tongguan 潼關 Pass, the principal eastern entrance to the Zhou capital region. In fact, so important was

---

[44] Several Han dynasty sources describe Song as being "in swaddling clothes" (see, e.g., *Huainanzi* 淮南子 [Sibu beiyao ed.], 21.6b, and *Shi ji* 33, p. 1518), but this description seems clearly designed to justify the action of Zhou Gong Dan, who by then was regarded as one of the sages of antiquity. Other Han sources give Song's age as thirteen *sui* 歲; see, e.g., Zheng Xuan, *Shangshu zhu* 尚書注 (Zhengshi yishu ed.), 7.5a; Xu Shen, *Wujing yiyi* 五經異義 (Han Wei yishu chao ed.), 2.3b–4a. A recent article by Wang Hui, "Zhou chu Tangshu shou feng shiji san kao," in *Xi Zhou shi lunwenji* (Xi'an: Shaanxi Renmin jiaoyu, 1993), pp. 933–43, esp. pp. 940–3, argues cogently that Song must have been about twenty-three *sui* at the time of his father's death.

this location that Zhou Gong Dan, King Cheng, and Shao Gong Shi seem all to have agreed that it should serve as an eastern capital, claiming that its establishment had been King Wu's dream.[45] King Cheng's two younger brothers were appointed to rule critical points farther north and south of the Yellow River that guarded the northeastern and southeastern approaches to the main Zhou capital area: Tangshu Yu 唐叔虞 established the state of Jin 晉, at Qucun 曲村 near Houma 侯馬 in the Fen River valley of present-day Shanxi, perhaps, as suggested earlier, the original homeland of the Zhou people;[46] Ying Hou 應侯 established the state of Ying 應 near Pingdingshan 平頂山 in central Henan province, probably intended to protect the southern approach along the Han 漢 River valley.[47] Kangshu Feng 康叔封, another brother of King Wu, was given the area of Wey 衛 in the northeastern part of Henan province, once again along the Yellow River and, not coincidentally, in the heart of the former Shang capital area.[48] Farther east, Zhou Gong Dan's eldest son Bo Qin 伯禽 went to rule Lu 魯, at Qufu 曲阜 just south of present-day Ji'nan 濟南 in Shandong province,[49] then the location of the state of Pugu 蒲姑, one of the Zhou's major eastern adversaries in the just concluded civil war. Meanwhile, Tai Gong Wang 太公望, the commander of the Zhou army in the first conquest of Shang, had colonized Qi 齊, at present-day Zibo 淄博, also in Shandong.[50] Finally, at least insofar as the major colonies are concerned (there were also scores of minor colonies), Shao Gong Shi was given responsibility for the area near modern Beijing, the state being known as Yan 燕, which controls the northern entrance to North China's Central Plain between the Taihang Mountains and the sea.[51] Situated as they were at strate-

---

[45] For the attribution of the plan to build an eastern capital at Luo, see *Yi Zhou shu* ("Du yi"), 5.4a, which seems to be confirmed by the inscription on the *He zun* 何尊; see *Shang Zhou qingtongqi mingwen xuan*, no. 32; Shirakawa, *Kinbun hoshaku*, 48, no. 1.

[46] For the enfeoffment of Tangshu Yu, see *Shi ji*, 39, p. 1635. For reports on excavations carried out at Qucun, see *Wenwu* 1982.7: 1–16; 1993.3: 11–30; 1994.1: 4–32; 1995.7: 4–39. See too Chapter 6, "The States of Northern Central China," p. 404.

[47] For the enfeoffment of Ying Hou, see *Yi Zhou shu* ("Wang hui"), 7, p. 7a, and especially Kong Zhao's 孔晁 comment thereto; for excavations at Pingdingshan, see *Wenwu* 1984.12: 29–32; *Hua Xia kaogu* 1988.1: 30–44; 1992.3: 92–103.

[48] For the establishment of the state of Wey, see *Shi ji*, 37, p. 1589, and probably the "Kang gao" 康誥 (Announcement to [the lord of] Kang) chapter of the *Shangshu*; *Shangshu zhengyi*, 14, 1a–14a (Legge, *The Shoo King*, pp. 381–98). It is perhaps also recorded in the *Mei Situ Yi gui* 沬司土𢀷簋 (better known as the *Kanghou gui* 康侯簋); see *Shang Zhou qingtongqi mingwen xuan*, no. 31; Shirakawa, *Kinbun tsūshaku*, 4, no. 14. For excavations at Xunxian 濬縣, Henan, see Guo Baojun, *Xunxian Xincun* (Beijing: Kexue, 1964).

[49] For the establishment of Lu, see *Shi ji* 33, p. 1515. For excavations at Qufu, see *Qufu Lu guo gucheng* (Ji'nan: Qi Lu, 1982). See too Chapter 7, "The Cemeteries at Qufu, pp. 497–501."

[50] See *Shi ji*, 31, p. 1480. For Western Zhou archaeological discoveries at the site, see Shandong sheng Wenwu Kaogu yanjiusuo and Qichang yizhi bowuguan, "Linzi Liangchun mudi fajue jianbao," in *Haidai kaogu*, ed. Zhang Xuehai (Ji'nan: Shandong daxue, 1989), pp. 274–82.

[51] For the establishment of the state of Yan, see *Shi ji*, 34, p. 1549, and perhaps also the inscriptions on the *Ke he* 克盉 and *Ke lei* 克罍, for which see Yin Weizhang, "Xin chutu de Taibao tongqi ji qi xiang-guan wenti," *Kaogu* 1990.1: 66–77. For archaeological discoveries at the site, Liulihe 琉璃河, see Beijing

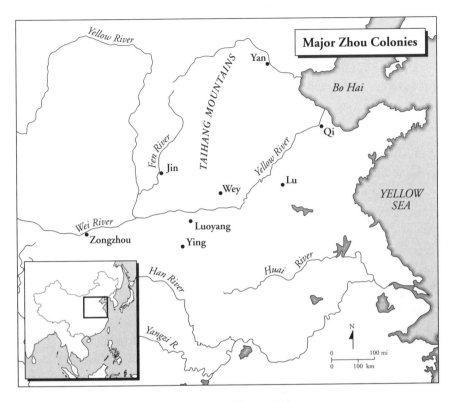

Map 5.3 Major Zhou colonies.

gic points along the principal routes of transportation in North China (see Map 5.3), all of these colonies were destined to thrive; indeed, after the fall of Western Zhou, they grew into the major independent states of the Spring and Autumn and Warring States periods.

THE PHILOSOPHICAL FOUNDATION OF ZHOU RULE

With the initial succession crisis now resolved, the Zhou leadership triumvirate of Zhou Gong Dan, King Cheng, and Shao Gong Shi faced another, in some ways more vexing problem: how to establish a lasting form of government. It seems that Zhou Gong Dan had one understanding of how a ruler derived and maintained his right to govern, while Shao Gong Shi had another; King Cheng would tilt the balance. The completion of the eastern capital Chengzhou was the catalyst that caused their disagreement to

shi Wenwu yanjiusuo, ed., *Liulihe Xi Zhou Yan guo mudi, 1973–1977* (Beijing: Wenwu, 1995); and *Kaogu* 1990.1: 20–31. See too Chapter 6, "The States of Northern Central China."

break into the open. The debate is preserved for us in several chapters of the *Shang shu*. The documents are subtly argued, in an extremely difficult archaic language; nevertheless, throughout traditional Chinese history they were regarded as foundational texts. There is some reason to think that they were preserved as such, even in Western Zhou times.

The Role of Heaven in Royal Authority

As just described, King Wu's death had been followed by a civil war. It is possible that this war was precipitated by nothing more than naked ambition and sibling rivalry. However, there is evidence in the *Shang shu* that radically different understandings of the relationship between Heaven's agency and royal authority were also involved. Glimmers of this disagreement are to be seen in the "Da gao" (Great proclamation), now a chapter in the *Shang shu*. The "Da gao" describes King Cheng performing turtle shell divination in an attempt to determine whether or not to attack his uncles. Although the oracles regarding such an attack were auspicious, the king's advisors all urged him to disregard them in the face of the difficulty of the task and the disquietude of the people. The king acknowledged this difficulty and disquietude, but refused to go against the apparent will of Heaven:

Stop! I the young son do not dare to disregard the command of the Lord on High. Heaven was beneficent to King Wen, raising up our little country of Zhou, and it was turtle-shell divination that King Wen used, succeeding to receive this mandate. Now Heaven will be helping the people; how much more so should it be turtle-shell divination that I too use. *Wuhu!* Heaven is brightly awesome – it helps our grand foundation.[52]

King Cheng concluded this proclamation to his advisors by asserting that Heaven had given the Zhou a mandate to rule; this is the earliest reference we have to the notion of the Mandate of Heaven (*Tian ming* 天命), which would continue to loom large in discussions of statecraft throughout Chinese history:

How is it that I go to the limits with divination and dare not to follow you? It is that I will proceed through the borders and lands pointed out by our ancestors; how much more so now that the divination is also auspicious. And so, expansively I will take you east to campaign. Heaven's mandate is not to be presumed upon; the divination is aligned like this.[53]

Although Zhou Gong Dan is not here mentioned among the advisors attempting to dissuade the king from embarking on the second eastern cam-

---

[52] *Shangshu zhengyi* ("Da gao"), 13, 20b (Legge, *The Shoo King*, pp. 369–70).
[53] *Shangshu zhengyi* ("Da gao"), 13, 24a (Legge, *The Shoo King*, p. 374).

paign (indeed, no names are recorded), and given his prominent role in the campaign it would seem unlikely that he was not always a supporter of it, he did subsequently become identified as the leader of the faction that questioned Heaven. A believer that "Heaven helps those who help themselves," in virtually all of the *Shang shu* texts attributed to him, Zhou Gong Dan would come to argue for a meritocracy, government by those who have demonstrated their practical ability and moral virtue.

The Debate Between Zhou Gong and Shao Gong

As reasonable as a meritocracy may sound to us today, it is not hard to see that it might be construed as a threat to King Cheng's royal prerogatives, especially considering the circumstances under which Zhou Gong Dan had installed himself as nominal regent but de facto head of state after King Wu's death, a role that he was still playing seven years later. The completion of the eastern capital Chengzhou seems to have precipitated a showdown, not between Zhou Gong and King Cheng, but between Zhou Gong and Shao Gong Shi, Zhou Gong's half-brother. We find in yet two other chapters of the *Shang shu*, the "Shao gao" (Proclamation of Shao Gong) and "Jun Shi" (Lord Shi), what seems to be a debate between these two figures, initiated by Shao Gong's threat to withdraw from the government because of his displeasure with Zhougong.[54] Zhou Gong begins the debate by referring again to Heaven's mandate, but significantly in this case, it is portrayed as a mandate given to the Zhou people (*wo you Zhou* 我有周). "Unpitying Heaven sent down destruction on Yin. Yin having dropped its mandate, we Zhou have received it."[55] After asserting that "Heaven cannot be trusted," Zhou Gong reverts to a favorite argumentative tactic of his: historical precedent. All of the great kings of the Shang dynasty relied on virtuous ministers for their greatness. Even kings Wen and Wu of Zhou relied on their ministers; indeed, Zhou Gong goes so far as to claim that it was these ministers "who enlightened King Wen" and also they who "received the Yin's mandate":

[Zhou] Gong said: "Lord Shi, in antiquity Di on High observed King Wen's virtue (in) the fields of Zhou. His settling the great mandate on his person was because King Wen was richly capable of cultivating and harmonizing us, the Xia (i.e., Chinese people), but also was because there were [men] such as Hong Yao, such as San Yisheng, such as Tai Dian, and such as Nangong Kuo." He also said: "If there were

---

[54] For a revisionist study of these texts and the dispute between Zhou Gong Dan and Shao Gong Shi, see Edward L. Shaughnessy, "The Duke of Zhou's Retirement in the East and the Beginnings of the Minister–Monarch Debate in Chinese Political Philosophy," *EC* 18 (1993): 41–72.

[55] *Shangshu zhengyi* ("Jun Shi"), 16, 18a (Legge, *The Shoo King*, p. 474).

not these [men] able to go and come to conduct the fine teaching, King Wen would have had no virtue to send down upon the men of the state. These [men] also purely had and held fast to virtue. By acting to make known Heaven's awesomeness, it was these [men] who made King Wen enlightened; by acting to make [him] visible and striving to make (him) audible to Di on High, it was also these [men] who had received the mandate of the Yin. Later, together with King Wu, they extended and directed Heaven's awesomeness to cut off their enemies. It was these four men who made King Wu enlightened; it was [they] who strove illustriously to uphold virtue."[56]

Shao Gong Shi countered these arguments directly. Whereas Zhou Gong saw Heaven giving its mandate to all of the Zhou people, Shao Going begins his speech by stating that it was the king alone, the "eldest son," who had received the mandate. "August Heaven, Di on High, has changed its eldest son and the mandate of that great state of Yin. It is the king who has received the mandate."[57] Shao Gong also meets Zhougong's argument by historical precedent. Not only can all rest assured that King Cheng will duly consult the able men of state, but more important, the king has the unique virtue of being able to consult the designs of Heaven itself, which is, after all, his "father":

Examining the ancient prior people, the Xia, Heaven led [them] to follow and protected [them], and they faced and fathomed Heaven's approval; [yet], now they have already lost their mandate. Now examining the Yin, Heaven led [them] to approach and protected [them], and they faced and fathomed Heaven's approval; [yet], now they have already lost their mandate. Now if the young son succeeds, there will be no neglect of the elders. If it be said, "May he fathom the virtue of our ancient men," how much more so should it be said, "May he be able to fathom plans from Heaven!"[58]

Finally, after granting Zhou Gong's belief that men have a hand in their own fate, Shao Gong argues that still they are endowed from birth with unique virtues. And unique among men is the king; indeed, in some sense, only the king is capable of virtue:

Wuhu! It is like giving birth to a son: there is nothing that is not in his initial birth; he himself is bequeathed his wisdom and his mandate. Now Heaven will command wisdom, command fortune, and command a set number of years. Knowing that now we have for the first time undertaken to inhabit this new city, may it be that the king quickly respects his virtue.[59]

This debate was destined to be rejoined over and over again throughout Chinese history. In fact, it is in essence the same debate that has appeared in

[56] *Shangshu zhengyi* ("Jun Shi"), 16, 23a–24b (Legge, *The Shoo King*, pp. 480–2).
[57] *Shangshu zhengyi* ("Shao gao"), 15, 15b–16a (Legge, *The Shoo King*, p. 425).
[58] *Shangshu zhengyi* ("Shao gao"), 15, 7a–b (Legge, *The Shoo King*, p. 427).
[59] *Shangshu zhengyi* ("Shao gao"), 15, 11a (Legge, *The Shoo King*, pp. 430–1).

so many different guises throughout world history: in government, between the ruler and his ministers; in religion, between faith and works; in social status, between birth and merit; in human potential, between nature and nurture. Although it has never been satisfactorily resolved (and doubtless never will be), it is easy to understand that within the early Zhou ruling triumvirate, Shao Gong's position would be supported by King Cheng (who, after all, stood to gain the most from it). There is evidence, oblique, to be sure, that the combined weight of King Cheng and Shao Gong sufficed first to force Zhou Gong to relinquish his leading role and then, eventually, to retire from government entirely.

The Retirement of Zhou Gong

Zhou Gong's decision to retire is preserved for us in yet another chapter of the *Shang shu*, the "Luo gao" (Proclamation at Luo). As a dialogue between Zhou Gong and King Cheng that took place in the recently completed eastern capital of Chengzhou just months after Shao Gong's proclamation of the "Shao gao," the "Luo gao" records Zhou Gong as saying that he would be "remaining" (*hou* 後) there rather than returning with King Cheng to the Zhou capital in the Wei River valley. Zhou Gong does not miss the opportunity to advise the king one final time to issue a command to "record merits in the ancestral temple, that those with merit should be first in sacrifice,"[60] but it seems that this was his last contribution to the contemporary political discourse; after this time, the name of Zhou Gong figures only very sporadically in Western Zhou sources (though one should hasten to add that beginning no later than the time of Confucius (551–479 B.C.), his legacy as a political hero grew to the point of matching, and in some cases surpassing, even that of King Wen).

CONSOLIDATION OF ZHOU RULE

So concludes the major chapter of Zhou political theorizing, at least as represented in the *Shang shu*. Indeed, only one other chapter in the *Shang shu* purports to date to the early Western Zhou from after this time, the "Gu ming" (Retrospective command). It describes the death of King Cheng, thirty years after his de facto assumption of the kingship, and the installation of his eldest son Zhao 釗, to be known as King Kang (r. 1005/03–978 B.C.). Overseeing this transition in the critical third generation of the dynasty was Shao Gong Shi, by then certainly quite aged; he ensured that the Zhou would

---

[60] *Shangshu zhengyi* ("Luo gao"), 15, 17b (Legge, *The Shoo King*, p. 439).

continue thereafter to follow a succession policy of primogeniture. The "Gu ming" chapter also records what amounts to King Cheng's last will and testament, advice that has since become proverbial for good government: "Make pliable those distant and make capable those near. Pacify and encourage the many countries, small and large."[61]

There is some evidence that both King Cheng and King Kang were able at least to approach this ideal. The later general history *Shi ji* describes their reigns as constituting "more than forty years during which punishments were not applied."[62] Even the more detailed annals of the *Zhushu jinian* show no evidence of any military activity from the midpoint of King Cheng's reign until the end of King Kang's. Instead, the period seems to have been one during which the gains of the conquest and immediate postconquest years were consolidated, with only some adjustments made to fill in the defensive "fence" of eastern colonies.

Appointments to Rule Lands as Seen in Bronze Inscriptions

Some of the appointments made at this time have been preserved for us in the form of inscriptions on bronze vessels cast to commemorate them. One of the most detailed describes King Cheng's appointment of one of Zhou Gong's sons, known as Xinghou Zhi 邢侯旨, to move, probably from near the eastern capital Chengzhou, to establish a new colony at Xing 邢, present-day Xingtai 邢臺 in southern Hebei province (about 100 km due north of the former Shang capital at Anyang). It was commissioned by one of Xinghou Zhi's adjutants, named Mai 麥, and thus is now known as the *Mai zun* 麥尊.

The king commanded the ruler, Lord of Xing, to depart Bu and be lord at Xing. In the second month, the lord appeared [in audience] at Zhongzhou 宗周 [i.e., the Zhou capital] and was without impropriety. [He] joined the king and approached Pangjing 旁京 [a detached palace area] and performed a libation ritual. On the next day, at Biyong 辟雍 Lake, the king rode in a boat and performed the Dafeng 大封-rite. The king shot at a large goose, bagging [it]. The lord rode in a red-pennanted boat following and arrayed [it]. That day the king together with the lord entered into the apartments. The lord was awarded a black, carved dagger-axe. When the king was at An, in the evening, the lord was awarded many axe-men vassals, two hundred families, and was offered use of the chariot team in which the king rode; bronze harness-trappings, a dustcoat, a robe, cloth and slippers. When [the lord] returned, [he] extolled the Son of Heaven's grace, reporting that

---

[61] *Shangshu zhengyi* ("Gu ming"), 18, 16a (Legge, *The Shoo King*, p. 548).
[62] *Shi ji*, 4, p. 134 (Nienhauser et al., eds., *The Grand Scribe's Records*, vol. 1, p. 66).

there was no error. Using a ritual, he [gave] repose to the lord's brilliant deceased-father at Xing. The lord's Recorder Mai was awarded metal by the ruling lord. Mai extolled [the lord's grace], herewith making [this] treasured, precious vessel, to use to perform libations for the lord's return and to extol the bright command. It was in the year that the Son of Heaven was beneficent to Mai's ruling lord. Together with grandsons and sons, may [he] eternally be without end, and use [the vessel] to visit virtue [upon us] and send down many blessings, and receive the command to move [to Xing].[63]

A similar appointment by King Kang to a local lord, known first as Yu Hou Ze 虞侯矢 and then, after his appointment to be lord at a new site called Yi 宜, as Yi Hou Ze 宜侯矢, was recorded on a bronze *gui* 簋 tureen that was discovered in 1954. This vessel has taken on great importance in modern studies of the Western Zhou state because of the place where it was discovered: Dantu 丹徒 in Jiangsu province, about 100 km east of present-day Nanjing 南京 on the south bank of the Yangzi River.[64] Every general history of Western Zhou, including the two major English-language general histories of the period, has relied on the place of this discovery to describe a geographically extensive, even "gigantic," state.[65] There can be no denying that Zhou influence extended widely in the early decades of the Western Zhou; early Zhou culture sites have been excavated from present-day Gansu in the west and throughout almost all of Shaanxi, Shanxi, Henan, Hebei, and Shandong provinces, which is to say virtually all of North China. However, there is little or no evidence of any sustained Zhou occupation in the Yangzi River valley.[66] What seems to have happened in the case of this *Yi Hou Ze gui* is that the vessel was cast for the lord of Yi, a place located along the Yi 宜 River just to the southwest of the eastern capital Chengzhou,[67] and then was taken later (and probably as late as the early Eastern Zhou period) to the far southeast where it was eventually unearthed.

[63] *Shang Zhou qingtongqi mingwen xuan*, no. 67; Shirakawa, *Kinbun tsûshaku*, 11, no. 60.

[64] For the inscription, see *Shang Zhou qingtongqi mingwen xuan*, no. 57; Shirakawa, *Kinbun tsûshaku*, 10, no. 52. For translations, see Noel Barnard, "A Recently Excavated Inscribed Bronze of Western Chou Date," *MS* 17 (1958): 12–46; Edward L. Shaughnessy, "Historical Geography and the Extent of the Earliest Chinese Kingdoms," *AM*, 3d series, 2, 2 (1989): 14–15.

[65] See, e.g., Guo Moruo, *Zhongguo shi gao*, vol. 1, p. 229; Creel, *The Origins of Statecraft in China*, p. 405; Cho-yun Hsu and Katheryn M. Linduff, *Western Chou Civilization* (New Haven, Conn.: Yale University Press, 1988), p. 143.

[66] For a convenient geographical survey of Western Zhou archaeological sites, see Jessica Rawson, *Western Zhou Ritual Bronzes from the Arthur M. Sackler Collections* (Cambridge, Mass.: Harvard University Press, 1990), vol. IIA, pp. 136–43: Appendix I: Archaeological Excavations.

[67] For this geography, see Huang Shengzhang, "Tongqi mingwen Yi Yu Ze de diwang ji qi yu Wuguo de guanxi," *Kaogu xuebao* 1983.3: 295–305; see too, Shaughnessy, "Historical Geography and the Extent of the Earliest Chinese Kingdoms," pp. 13–17.

Military Expansion

Nevertheless, the *Yi Hou Ze gui* inscription, like that of the *Mai zun*, reflects the impressive control that kings Cheng and Kang could command at least over their capital areas and the strategic Yellow River and Taihang Mountain corridors. By the end of King Kang's reign, there is evidence that the Zhou did attempt to expand beyond these areas, at least to the north. In the twenty-third year of his reign (i.e., 981 B.C.), he appointed a man named Yu 盂, who was the grandson of Nangong Kuo 南宮括, one of the high ministers mentioned by Zhou Gong Dan as serving both kings Wen and Wu, to act as an overseer of the Supervisors of the Military (*si rong* 司戎). Yu commemorated this appointment by casting a great *ding* 鼎 cauldron, now referred to as the *Da Yu ding* 大盂鼎, one of the most impressive bronze vessels of the entire period (see Fig. 5.1).[68]

Two years later Yu cast another bronze cauldron, the inscription on which describes in grand detail the ceremony held to celebrate a decisive military victory won by Yu over a people known as the Guifang 鬼方, probably living in the Ordos area of northern Shaanxi and Shanxi. Only portions of the lengthy inscription of this vessel still survive (the vessel itself, probably discovered in the 1840s, was lost shortly thereafter in the course of the Taiping Rebellion), but it deserves extensive quotation both for the light it sheds on the Zhou expansion late in King Kang's reign and also as an excellent example of the sort of military and court ceremonial narrative found in some bronze inscriptions:

> It was the eighth month, after the full moon, the day was on *jiashen* [day 21]; in the morning dusk, the three [officials of the] left and the three [officials of the] right and the many rulers entered to serve the wine. When it became light the king approached the Zhou temple and performed the *guo*-libation rite. The king's state guests attended. The state guests offered their travel garments and faced east.
>
> Yu with many flags with suspended Guifang . . . entered the Southern Gate, and reported saying: "The king commanded Yu to take .. .. to attack the Guifang [and shackle chiefs and take] trophies. [I] shackled two chiefs, took 4,8-2 trophies, captured 13,081 men, captured .. horses, captured 30 chariots, captured 355 oxen and 38 sheep."
> . . .
>
> The king called out to .. .. to command Yu with his trophies to enter the gate and present [them in] the Western Passageway . .. .. entered and performed a burnt offering [in] the Zhou temple. ... entered the Third Gate, assumed position in the central court, facing north. Yu reported. ...

[68] For the inscription on the *Da Yu ding*, see *Shang Zhou qingtongqi mingwen xuan*, no. 62; Shirakawa, *Kinbun tsûshaku*, 12, no. 61; for a translation, see Dobson, *Early Archaic Chinese*, pp. 221–6.

Figure 5.1. *Da Yu ding* inscription and vessel, reportedly found at Fufeng, Shaanxi (early Western Zhou). Vessel after Li Xueqin ed., *Zhongguo meishu quanji: Gongyi meishu bian 4, Qingtongqi (shang)* (Beijing: Wenwu, 1985), no. 148; inscription after Ma Chengyuan, ed., *Shang Zhou qingtongqi mingwen xuan* (Beijing: Wenwu, 1988), no. 62.

The guests assumed position. [He] served the guests. The king called out: "Serve." Yu in their . . . presented guests .. .. . At mid-morning, three Zhou .. entered to serve wine. The king entered the temple. The invocator . . . the state guests grandly toasted . .. .. used a victim in ancestral sacrifice to the king of Zhou [i.e., King Wen], to King [Wu] and to King Cheng. ... divination cracks have pattern. The king toasted. Toast followed toast: the king and state guests. The king called out to .. .. to command Yu with the booty to enter. All of the booty was registered.[69]

King Zhao's Southern Campaign

Successful as this northern campaign obviously was, an attempt made shortly thereafter by King Kang's son and successor, King Zhao (r. 977/75–957 B.C.), to expand Zhou control southwards resulted in the Zhou court's first military setback. It was a crushing defeat, and one that was to have lasting and far-reaching repercussions. Only hinted at in the traditional historical record, a campaign or campaigns led by King Zhao against the southern state of Chu 楚 is commemorated by so many inscribed bronze vessels that we may be justified in assuming that it began with high hopes.[70] The *Zhushu jinian* is again our best source for what happened, even if part of its annal is phrased in fantastic images:

Nineteenth year [i.e., of King Zhao's reign; 957 B.C.]: There was a comet in [the lunar lodge] Ziwei. She Gong 葉公 and Xinbo 辛伯 followed the king to attack Chu. The heavens were greatly obscured, and pheasants and hares were all shaken. They lost the six armies in the Han River; the king died.[71]

The "six armies" are often referred to in bronze inscriptions as the "Western six armies" (*Xi liu shi* 西六師), as opposed to the "Yin eight armies" (*Yin ba shi* 殷八師) stationed in the eastern territories.[72] Thus, according to this

[69] *Shang Zhou qingtongqi mingwen xuan*, no. 63; Shirakawa, *Kinbun tsûshaku*, 12, no. 62; for another translation, see Dobson, *Early Archaic Chinese*, pp. 226–32. As is conventional in paleographic studies, two dots (..) here indicate one missing graph in the original inscription, while three dots (. . .) indicate an indeterminate number of missing graphs.

[70] See, for instance, the *Ling gui* 令簋 (*Shang Zhou qingtongqi mingwen xuan*, no. 94; Shirakawa, *Kinbun tsûshaku*, 6, no. 24; Dobson, *Early Archaic Chinese*, pp. 187–90); *Yiyu gui* 釱馭簋 (*Shang Zhou qingtongqi mingwen xuan*, no. 106; Shirakawa, *Kinbun tsûshaku*, 14, no. 70; Shaughnessy, *Sources of Western Zhou History*, p. 205); *Hui gui* 誨簋 (*Wenwu* 1986.1: 12; Shaughnessy, *Sources of Western Zhou History*, p. 207).

[71] *Zhushu jinian*, 2, p. 4a (Legge, *The Shoo King*, Prolegomena, p. 149). For oblique references to this event elsewhere in the traditional historical record, see *Chunqiu Zuo zhuan zhengyi* (Xi 4), 12, p. 91 (James Legge, *The Chinese Classics. Vol. 5: The Ch'un Ts'ew with the Tso Chuen* [1872; rpt. Hong Kong: Hong Kong University Press, 1960], pp. 139–40); *Chuci buzhu* 楚辭補注 (Sibu beiyao ed.), 3.19b–20a; *Lüshi chunqiu* 呂氏春秋 ("Yin chu"; Sibu beiyao ed.), 6.5b.

[72] Regarding the "Western six armies" and "Yin eight armies," see Yu Xingwu, "Lüelun Xi Zhou jinwen zhong de liu shi he ba shi ji qi tuntian zhi," *Kaogu* 1964.3: 152–5; Yang Kuan, "Lun Xi Zhou jinwen zhong liu shi ba shi he xiangsui zhidu de guanxi," *Kaogu* 1964.8: 414–19.

record, not only did King Zhao lose his own life in this campaign, but the main force of the royal army was also destroyed. As we will see, the Zhou state never really recovered from this loss.

THE MIDDLE WESTERN ZHOU REFORMS

The reign of King Mu of Zhou (r. 956–918 B.C.) is one that traditional historians have viewed with ambivalence. On the one hand, the king is storied in legend for his long-distance romance with the Queen Mother of the West (*Xiwangmu* 西王母);[73] on the other hand, he is criticized for being too much out of the capital. On the one hand, he is said to have defeated the Quan Rong 犬戎, a people living to the north and west of Zhou; on the other hand, from this time forth border states no longer entered into relations with the Zhou court.[74] On the one hand, the *Shang shu* credits him with establishing the first systematic legal code; on the other hand, if he had been a virtuous king there would have been no need for laws.[75] There is reason to continue to view this reign with ambivalence.

Even without the disaster that brought him to power, King Mu's reign probably would not have been easy. He came to power, exactly 100 years after the Zhou "receipt of the mandate," at a time when the natural demographic dynamic was beginning to cause the Zhou state to fragment. The colonies established by King Cheng's uncles and brothers were now governed by cousins twice or even thrice removed, men whose identification with the Wei River capital region was doubtless diminishing. To govern, the king would no longer be able to call on personal ties, but would have to create a "faceless" bureaucracy. At the same time, it had also been three generations since the subject populations of the eastern territories had been defeated in battle. Even if the royal Zhou army had not just been decimated, it might well have been time for the eastern peoples to test the Zhou will. As it was, they did not wait long to do so.

War with the Xu Rong

The *Zhushu jinian* records King Mu's campaign against the northeastern Quan Rong as taking place in the twelfth and thirteenth years of his reign. In the annal for the thirteenth year, there is also a record that the Xu Rong

---

[73] The locus classicus for this romance is the fourth century B.C. historical novel *Mu tianzi zhuan* 穆天子傳 (Biography of the Son of Heaven Mu); for the affair with the Queen Mother of the West, see *Mu tianzi zhuan* (Sibu beiyao ed.), 3.1a–b (Rémi Mathieu, *Le Mu Tianzi Zhuan: Traduction annotée–Étude Critique* [Paris: Collège de France, 1978], pp. 44–54).

[74] *Guo yu* 國語 ("Zhou yu, shang"; Sibu beiyao ed.), 1.1a.

[75] *Shangshu zhengyi* ("Lü xing"), 19, pp. 16a–34b (Legge, *The Shoo King*, pp. 588–612).

徐戎 invaded the eastern capital Chengzhou.[76] Xu Rong (*rong* 戎, often translated as "barbarian," refers generally, as in the case of Quan Rong as well, to enemy "belligerents") here seems to be a general reference to eastern peoples usually referred to in Zhou bronzes inscriptions as the Eastern Yi (*Dong Yi* 東夷) and/or Southern Yi (*Nan Yi* 南夷). Xu 徐 itself was a state probably located in the northwestern part of present-day Jiangsu province on the north shore of Lake Hongze 洪澤湖. There is a record in the *Hou Han shu* 後漢書 (History of Later Han), probably based on an early text of the *Zhushu jinian*, that the ruler of Xu, King Yan of Xu 徐偃王, forged a confederation of thirty-six different eastern states stretching from Hubei in the south, through eastern Henan, northern Anhui and Jiangsu, as far north as southern Shandong, that was responsible for this invasion of the Zhou eastern capital.

> Later the Xu Yi arrogated a title and then led the nine Yi to attack Zongzhou, reaching the bank of the Yellow River to the west. King Mu, fearing that they were about to wax strong, then divided the many lords of the east, commanding King Yan of Xu to rule them.[77]

This record, obviously representing a Zhou perspective, seems to be an oblique recognition of the eastern states' independence.

Several bronze inscriptions cast at this time suggest that these traditional records are credible. One of these, the *Dong gui* 彧簋 commemorates a Zhou victory over these Eastern Yi.[78] But it is important to note first that the inscription makes explicit that this victory was defensive in nature, the battle having been precipitated by a Yi attack on a Zhou position. Second, the battle was fought at a place called Yu Woods 膩林, located at present-day Yexian 葉縣 in central Henan. This is right next to Pingdingshan, the site of the colony Ying that was established by one of King Cheng's younger brothers to guard the southern approaches to the eastern capital Chengzhou, just about 125 km to the northwest along a direct communication route (the Nanyang 南陽 to Luoyang rail line runs through it today; see Map 5.3). Other inscribed vessels cast by Dong and other military officers seem to suggest that sometime after this battle, the Zhou commander Captain Yongfu 師雍父, traveled to a Yi stronghold, Hu 麸, and negotiated an armistice.[79]

[76] *Zhushu jinian*, 2, p. 5a (Legge, *The Shoo King*, Prolegomena, p. 150).

[77] *Hou Han shu*, 85, p. 2808.

[78] For the *Dong gui* inscription, see *Shang Zhou qingtongqi mingwen xuan*, no. 176; Shirakawa, *Kinbun hoshaku*, 49, no. 12; Shaughnessy, *Sources of Western Zhou History*, pp. 179–80.

[79] These inscriptions include, most prominently, those on the *Lu gui* 彔簋 (*Shang Zhou qinqtongqi mingwen xuan*, no. 175; Shirakawa, *Kinbun tsûshaku*, 17, no. 91), the *Yu yan* 遇甗 (*Shang Zhou qing-tongqi mingwen xuan*, no. 183; Shirakawa, *Kinbun tsûshaku*, 17, no. 89), and *Yu ding* 寏鼎 (*Shang Zhou qingtongqi mingwen xuan*, no. 184; Shirakawa, *Kinbun tsûshaku*, 17, no. 89). For a full discussion of these inscriptions and their historical background, see Xia Hanyi, "Xi Zhou zhi shuaiwei," in Xia Hanyi, *Wen gu zhi xin lu* (Taipei: Daohe, 1997), pp. 149–56.

Whether or not this interpretation of these particular bronze inscriptions, and indeed the interpretation of the Zhou war with Xu and the Eastern Yi on which it is based, is valid in all particulars, it does seem clear that beginning with the reign of King Mu, the Zhou court was no longer able to rule the eastern lands formerly under its control. One concrete manifestation of this geopolitical contraction of the Zhou state is that whereas early Western Zhou bronze vessels with inscriptions recognizing royal Zhou rule have been unearthed throughout these eastern areas, inscribed vessels from the middle and late Western Zhou have been found almost exclusively in the western Wei River capital region.[80]

Reform of the Zhou Military

Bronze inscriptions of about the time of King Mu's reign found in that capital region provide evidence of some of the changes that were overtaking Zhou institutions. After the debacle that had befallen King Zhao and the war with the Xu Rong, the military required restructuring. The command to do so may well be commemorated in a bronze vessel of King Mu's reign cast for a man named Li 盠 upon his appointment to command all of the Zhou military forces, the *Li fangyi* 盠方彝.

It was the eighth month, first auspiciousness; the king entered into the Zhou Temple; Duke Mu to the right of Li stood in the center of the court, facing north. The king in writing commanded Yin to award Li red kneepads, a black girdle-pendant, and bridle, saying: "Herewith supervise the six armies and the royally empowered Three Supervisors: the Supervisor of Lands, Supervisor of the Horse and Supervisor of Work."

The king commanded Li, saying: "Concurrently supervise the six armies and the eight armies' registers." Li bowed and touched his head to the ground, daring in response to extol the king's beneficence, herewith making [for] my cultured grandfather Yi Gong [this] treasured offertory vessel.

Li said: "The Son of Heaven is unspoiled and unlimited; for ten-thousand years [may] he protect our 10,000 states." Li dares to bow and touch his head to the ground, saying: "Valorous is my person; [may I] continue my predecessors' treasured service."[81]

This inscription is illustrative of a type of bronze inscription that would become all but ubiquitous throughout the remainder of the dynasty: the investiture inscription (though this one differs from other investiture inscriptions in portraying Li as responding orally to the king, virtually the only inscription from the Western Zhou that does so).

---

[80] For the first developed statement of this thesis, see Itô Michiharu, *Chûgoku kodai ôcho no keisei* (Tokyo: Sôbunsha, 1975), p. 307.

[81] *Shang Zhou qingtongqi mingwen xuan*, no. 314; Shirakawa, *Kinbun tsûshaku*, 19, no. 101.

Reform of Court Offices

The most frequent recipients of these investitures or appointments were other, lesser, military officers with the rank of *shi* 師, probably best rendered functionally as "captain."[82] This perhaps also indicates a restructuring of the military and perhaps more important a growing professionalization within it. The vogue in investiture inscriptions extended also to nonmilitary court officials, perhaps suggesting a similar bureaucratization of the royal government. In place of the generic early Western Zhou *hou* 侯, or regional "lords," the most powerful figures came to be the Three Supervisors (*can you si* 參有司), the Supervisor of the Horse (*sima* 司馬), Supervisor of Lands (*situ* 司土), and Supervisor of Works (*si gong* 司工), mentioned already above in the *Li fangzun* inscription. At court affairs *zai* 宰 (intendants), and *shanfu* 膳夫 (provisioners), "took out and brought in" (*chu na* 出納) the king's commands. The court scribes (*shi* 史) also now became all but ubiquitous; everything done at court was now put in writing: the investitures themselves, of course (copies of which were both given to the investee and also apparently stored in the royal archives),[83] but also verdicts in legal cases,[84] maps,[85] and so forth. This apparatus, combined with the need for those appearing at court to be introduced to the king (by a person that bronze inscriptions describe as "standing at his right hand"), suggests perhaps a distancing of the king from his people. Once ruling by virtue of his unique charisma, the king now had his power mediated – and probably restrained – by this royal bureaucracy.

Land Reforms

In addition to the investiture inscriptions, another important type of bronze inscription that begins to appear, albeit in lesser numbers, at about this time

[82] For statistics regarding bronze vessels cast by these *shi* (captains) and some discussion of their significance, see Shaughnessy, *Sources of Western Zhou History*, p. 169.

[83] For an example in which a previous investiture command was quoted in a subsequent investiture, suggesting that a copy had been consulted in its preparation, see the *Third Year Shi Dui gui* 師兌簋 (*Shang Zhou qingtongqi mingwen xuan*, no. 278; Shirakawa, *Kinbun tsûshaku*, 31, no. 188; Shaughnessy, *Sources of Western Zhou History*, p. 282).

[84] For a case, admittedly earlier than the period presently under discussion, in which, after a verdict had been reached, the defendant is described as taking it (i.e., the verdict) to the central scribe to document, see the *Shi Qi ding* 師旂鼎 (*Shang Zhou qingtongqi mingwen xuan*, no. 84; Shirakawa, *Kinbun tsûshaku*, 13, no. 67).

[85] One of the rooms in the royal palace was called the Map Chamber (*Tushi* 圖室); see, for instance, the inscriptions on the *Shanfu Shan ding* 膳父山鼎 (*Shang Zhou qingtongqi mingwen xuan*, no. 445; Shirakawa, *Kinbun tsûshaku*, 26, no. 154; Edward L. Shaughnessy, "Western Zhou Bronze Inscriptions," in *New Sources of Early Chinese History: An Introduction to Reading Inscriptions and Manuscripts*, ed. Edward L. Shaughnessy (Berkeley: Society for the Study of Early China and the Institute of East Asian Studies, University of California, 1997), Chapter 2; and *Wuhui ding* 無惠鼎 (*Shang Zhou qingtongqi mingwen xuan*, no. 444; Shirakawa, *Kinbun tsûshaku*, 26, no. 153).

commemorates decisions made in legal cases, particularly those involving disputes over land tenure and ownership.[86] Probably the earliest such inscription yet known, cast in the fifth year of the reign of King Gong (r. 917/15–900 B.C.; i.e., 913 B.C.), the son and successor of King Mu, is found on a *ding*-cauldron cast by a man named Qiu Wei 裘衛, the *Fifth Year Qiu Wei ding* 裘衛鼎. In it he recounts his lawsuit against one States-lord Li 厲, who had promised to relinquish to him five fields but, apparently despite having taken payment for them, did not in fact give the fields over to Qiu Wei. The narrative recounts his interrogation by a panel of judges, their verdict (in Qiu Wei's favor, of course), and the steps that they took to have the fields properly surveyed and turned over to Qiu Wei:

It was the first month, first auspiciousness, *gengxu* [day 47]; [Qiu] Wei took the States-lord Li to report to Jingbo, Bo Yisu, Dingbo, Liangbo and Bo Sufu, saying: "Li said, 'I hold King Gong's irrigation works at the two Rong rivers northeast of the Zhao Great Chamber,' [and also] said: 'I relinquish to you five fields.'"

The officials then interrogated Li, saying: "Did you sell the fields or not?" Li then acceded, saying: "I sold all five fields." Jingbo, Bo Yifu, Dingbo, Liangbo and Bo Sufu then reached a verdict, making Li swear an oath. Then [they] commanded the Three Supervisors, Supervisor of Land Yiren Fu, Supervisor of Horse Shanren Bang and Supervisor of Work Fu Ju, and Interior Scribe's friend Si Zou to lead and pace off Qiu Wei's four Li fields, and then to relinquish domicile at his city: his northern boundary [extending] as far as Li fields; his eastern boundary as far as San fields; his southern boundary as far as San fields and Zhengfu fields, and his western boundary as far as Li fields.

States-lord Li went to give Qiu Wei the fields. Li's younger son Su, Li's supervisors Shen Ji, Qing Gui, Bin Biao, Xingren Gan, Jingren Chang Yi and Wei's young son Zhu Qi feasted me. Wei herewith makes [for] my cultured deceased-father [this] treasured *ding*-cauldron; may Wei for 10,000 years eternally treasure and use (it).

It is the king's fifth ritual-cycle.[87]

If this were an isolated case, one would not want to infer from it much about the contemporary socioeconomic condition. However, since several similar inscriptions appear over the course of the next generation or two,[88] it is

---

[86] For studies of these inscriptions, see Lutz Schunk, *Dokumente zur Rechtsgeschichte des alten China: Übersetzung und historisch-philologische Kommentierung juristischer Bronzeinschriften der West-Zhou-Zeit (1045–771 v.Chr.)*, Doctoral dissertation, Westfalischen Wilhelms-Üniversitat zu Münster, 1994; Laura A. Skosey, "The Legal System and Legal Tradition of the Western Zhou (1045 B.C.E.–771 B.C.E.)," Ph.D. dissertation, University of Chicago, 1996.

[87] *Shang Zhou qingtonqi mingwen xuan*, no. 198; Shirakawa, *Kinbun hoshaku*, 49, no. 11.

[88] The most important such inscriptions are on the *Hu ding* 智鼎 (*Shang Zhou qingtongqi mingwen xuan*, no. 242; Shirakawa, *Kinbun tsûshaku*, 23, no. 135), the *Ge You Cong ding* 誦攸從鼎 (*Shang Zhou qingtongqi mingwen xuan*, no. 426; Shirakawa, *Kinbun tsûshaku*, 29, no. 180), and the *Sanshi pan* 散氏盤 (*Shang Zhou qingtongqi mingwen xuan*, no. 428; Shirakawa, *Kinbun tsûshaku*, 24, no. 139). The social reforms of this period, and especially changes in land tenure, are thoroughly explored in Itô Michiharu, *Chûgoku kodai kokka no shihai kôzô* (Tokyo: Chûô, 1987), pp. 154–230.

perhaps reasonable to see in them important new social pressures due to the combination of a contraction in the supply of land available with increased demand for it from the splitting of families into branch lineages.

There seems to be other evidence that at about this same time estates of old families were being broken up and parceled out to new families. The inscription on the *Da Ke ding* 大克鼎, for instance, records a royal award to Ke 克 of "the Jing 井 family's attached fields at Yun, with their retainers and women" and "the registers of men raised by and attached to Jing," and the "Jing men who had fled to Dong."[89] It is likely that this Jing property had belonged to the family of Jingbo 井伯, seen above in the inscription on the *Fifth Year Qiu Wei ding* as the first of the panel of judges who decided Qiu Wei's lawsuit against States-lord Li, and seen also in numerous other inscriptions serving similarly important functions at court.[90] The dissolution of such a family's estate and, especially, the redistribution of it on the part of the king might suggest one of two possibilities: either the king was attempting to assert his title to all landholdings, and was not compelled to recognize any hereditary rights of families, even one as important as Jing's; or else the Jing family, perhaps like that of States-lord Li and other families as well, was overwhelmed by new social developments. In the latter case, the Zhou king's "award" of Jing's land to Ke may have been little more than a ratification of these developments. The political history of this period suggests that this latter possibility may indeed have been the case.

THE DECLINE OF THE ZHOU ROYAL HOUSE

The latter half of the middle Western Zhou period, roughly the reigns of King Gong, his son King Yih (r. 899/97–873 B.C.) and his brother King Xiao (r. 872–866 B.C.), and, perhaps, King Yih's son King Yi (r. 865–858 B.C), is a frustrating period for historians. While the new vogue in investiture inscriptions makes available a wealth of information about the social structure and governmental bureaucracy, there is little in the traditional historical record about the political history of the period to which to tie this information. Moreover, although many of these inscriptions are dated to the reigns of these three or four kings, the dates seem to be contradictory; it is this period upon which almost all attempts to reconstruct the absolute chronology of the

---

[89] *Shang Zhou qingtongqi mingwen xuan*, no. 297; Shirakawa, *Kinbun tsûshaku*, 28, no. 167.

[90] Among the many inscriptions in which Jingbo features prominently are those on the *Chang Xin he* 長甶盉 (*Shang Zhou qingtongqi mingwen xuan*, no. 163; Shirakawa, *Kinbun tsûshaku*, 19, no. 103), *Yong yu* 永盂 (*Shang Zhou qingtongqi mingwen xuan*, no. 207; Shirakawa, *Kinbun hoshaku*, 48, no. 3), and *Fifteenth Year Jue Cao ding* 趞曹鼎 (*Shang Zhou qingtongqi mingwen xuan*, no. 209; Shirakawa, *Kinbun tsûshaku*, 20, no. 107). For the possibility that Jingbo's tomb has been discovered recently, see *Wenwu* 1986.1: 1–31.

Western Zhou have floundered. The apparent contradictions of these dates may reflect, although not very clearly, real contradictions in the life of the court.

After the ambivalent account of King Mu's achievements, the *Shi ji* provides almost no information regarding these next four successors. For instance, about King Yih, it says only that during his time "the royal house thereupon declined and poets composed satires." Then, without any explanation for why King Yih should have been succeeded by his uncle, King Xiao, the *Shi ji* remarks that "the many lords restored" King Yi.[91]

The *Zhushu jinian* provides little more specific information. For King Yih's reign, other than the record of a dawn solar eclipse in the first year of his reign, which almost surely corresponds to an eclipse on April 21, 899 B.C.,[92] there are annalistic entries in the seventh and thirteenth years for attacks by *rong* and *di* "barbarians" on the Zhou capital region, and another in the twenty-first year for a failed Zhou counterattack. The most intriguing entry is recorded under the fifteenth year; it says simply that "the king moved from Zongzhou to Huaili 槐里."[93] It may be that this move implies King Yih's exile from the capital, probably forced out by his uncle, who then declared himself king.[94] This not only would provide a single plausible explanation for King Yih's move from the capital, for the irregularity of King Xiao's succession, and for the need for the many lords "to restore" King Yi to the kingship, but it also explains why the dated bronze inscriptions of this period seem to reflect two different royal calendars in use simultaneously.[95]

The restoration of King Yi provided only a temporary resolution of these intracourt conflicts. They were to break to the surface again, violently, just twenty years later. Before this, however, two new conflicts would pose perhaps even greater threats to the Zhou court. The first, recorded in the *Zhushu jinian* under King Yi's third year and also in the *Shi ji*'s "Genealogy of the House of Tai Gong of Qi" (*Qi Tai Gong shijia* 齊太公世家), states that King Yi boiled the leader of the state of Qi, Ai Gong 齊哀公, in a cauldron.[96] These records are substantiated by a bronze inscription, on the *Fifth Year Shi Shi gui* 師旋簋, which also almost certainly dates to this same year and which does indeed record that a Zhou army attacked Qi.[97] Qi was one of the most important of the original Zhou eastern colonies, established by Tai Gong

[91] *Shi ji*, 4, pp. 140–1 (Nienhauser et al., eds., *The Grand Scribe's Records*, vol. 1, p. 70).

[92] For this eclipse, see Fang Shanzhu, "Xi Zhou niandai xue shang de jige wenti," *Dalu zazhi* 51, 1 (1975): 15–23; for its implications for the chronology for the period, see too Shaughnessy, *Sources of Western Zhou History*, pp. 256–7.

[93] *Zhushu jinian*, 2.6b (Legge, *The Shoo King*, Prolegomena, p. 152).

[94] This explanation was first proposed in David S. Nivison, "Western Chou History Reconstructed from Bronze Inscriptions," in *The Great Bronze Age of China: A Symposium*, ed. George Kuwayama (Los Angeles: Los Angeles County Museum of Art, 1983), pp. 49–50.

[95] For a discussion of this evidence, see Shaughnessy, *Sources of Western Zhou History*, pp. 259–65.

[96] *Zhushu jinian*, 2, p. 7b (Legge, *The Shoo King*, Prolegomena, p. 153); *Shi ji*, 31, p. 1481.

[97] *Shang Zhou qingtongqi mingwen xuan*, no. 259; Shirakawa, *Kinbun tsûshaku*, 25, no. 141.

Wang, the commander of the Zhou army at the battle of Muye. That a royal Zhou army should have invaded it, even if it were responding to an internal succession struggle within the state (as the *Shi ji* account suggests), is surely further evidence of the diminishing authority of the Zhou king.

Shortly after this royal intervention in Qi, the southern state of Chu, which would grow to be one of the two or three most powerful states of the Eastern Zhou period, apparently took advantage of the weakened Zhou court to make its first incursion into North China. Again, there are records of this in both the *Zhushu jinian* and the *Shi ji* and also in bronze inscriptions contemporary with the events. The *Shi ji* account sets the scene:

Xiong Qu sired three sons. At the time of King Yi of Zhou, the royal house weakened, and some of the many lords did not come to court but attacked each other. Xiong Qu greatly obtained the harmony of the peoples living between the Han and Yangzi rivers, and then raised troops to attack Yong and Yang Yue, and reached as far as E.[98]

E 噩, the last of the place-names mentioned by the *Shi ji* here, is located at the site of Nanyang 南陽 in present-day Henan province, an extremely important strategic location defending both the major southeastern approach, through the Wuguan 武關 (Military pass), to the Wei River valley, and also the southern approaches to the Zhou eastern capital at Luo. Its loss to the Zhou would have posed an immediate external threat to both capitals.

Bronze inscriptions show that the Zhou were again able to repulse this threat but, as the inscription of the *Yu gui* 敔簋 shows, apparently not before it reached the banks of the Luo 洛 River, easily within striking distance of the Zhou eastern capital. This inscription refers to the enemy generically as the "Southern Huai Yi" (*Nan Huai Yi* 南淮夷):

It was the king's tenth month; the king was at Chengzhou. The Southern Huai Yi had moved reaching to the interior, attacking Jiu, Mao, Can Springs, and Sumin, on the south and the north banks of the Luo [River]. The king commanded Yu to pursue and drive off [the Yi] at the Upper Luo's Xi Valley as far as the Yi [River].

He returned, long side-poles carting 100 heads and 40 manacled prisoners. [He] retook 400 captured men and located [them] at Rongbo's place. At Xi they were clothed and registered, and returned and given to their lords.

It was the king's eleventh month; the king entered into the Chengzhou Grand Temple. Wu Gong entered at the right of Yu to report the catch: 100 heads and 40 prisoners. The king praised Yu's accomplishments and caused Yinshi to give in reward to Yu a *gui*-tessera and *li*-tripod, and 50 strands of cowries, and to award him 50 fields at Han and 50 fields at Zao.

Yu dares in response to extol the Son of Heaven's beneficence, herewith making

---

[98] *Shi ji*, 40, p. 1692.

this offertory tureen; may Yu for 10,000 years have sons' sons and grandsons' grandsons eternally to treasure and use it.[99]

Another inscription, on the *Yu ding* 禹鼎,[100] indicates that when, sometime thereafter, the Zhou counterattacked E, even the combined might of their Western Six Armies and Yin Eight Armies failed to retake the area. It was only when Wu Gong 武公, who is mentioned as well in the *Yu gui* inscription, provided 100 of his own chariots, 200 charioteers, and 1,000 infantrymen that the Zhou were able to resecure the strategic area of Nanyang.

According to the *Zhushu jinian*, King Yi died the year after the Chu attack on E, in only the eighth year of his reign. He left a son, named Hu 胡, to be known as King Li (r. 857/53–842 B.C.), who was apparently quite young at the time of his succession.[101] He would prove to be no better equipped than his father to resolve the problems facing the Zhou royal house. Indeed, he is viewed in traditional Chinese histories as one of the major causes of its ultimate downfall. Before examining the events of his reign, together with the downfall following it, it would be well to return to the beginning of the middle Western Zhou, the reigns of Kings Mu and Gong, to consider one other important restructuring of Zhou society, one that produced an intellectual florescence, which was probably at least in part a response to these crises.

THE DEVELOPMENT OF THE LATE WESTERN ZHOU WORLDVIEW

Beginning about the time of King Mu, a dramatic change took place in Zhou bronze casting. Not only were the vessels themselves given new shapes and ornamentation, but even the types of vessels cast and especially the way they were grouped into ritual sets were completely different from all earlier precedents. This change has been noted before. Bernhard Karlgren, writing in 1936, called it a

> sudden, complete and fundamental change . . . characterized on the one hand by a ruthless abolition of the whole array of Yin elements . . . on the other hand by the introduction of a series of new elements, most of which were entirely unknown in China before that time.[102]

A generation later, Max Loehr said of the reign of King Mu that "the Western Chou [Zhou] style moved rapidly, for better or worse, away from lingering

[99] *Shang Zhou qingtongqi mingwen xuan*, no. 411; Shirakawa, *Kinbun tsûshaku*, 27, no. 164.
[100] *Shang Zhou qingtongqi mingwen xuan*, no. 407; Shirakawa, *Kinbun tsûshaku*, 27, no. 162; Shaughnessy, "Western Zhou Bronze Inscriptions."
[101] For a discussion of his dates of reign, including the suggestion that he reached the age of majority only in the fifth year of his de facto reign, see Shaughnessy, *Sources of Western Zhou History*, pp. 272–86.
[102] Bernhard Karlgren, "Yin and Chou in Chinese Bronzes," *BMFEA* 8 (1936): 116.

Shang reminiscences."[103] In the following chapter (Chapter 6), Jessica Rawson explores this change, which she attributes to a Ritual Revolution. She suggests that the move from small sets of ritual vessels, which characterized the early Western Zhou, to the very large sets that began to appear about the time of King Mu and reached a high degree of elaboration by the middle of the ninth century B.C. (about the time of King Li), would have had the effect of distancing the participants in the rituals from the vessels. Indeed, whereas rituals in the early Western Zhou may have been private matters, with only the family members participating, the ritual reform may have entailed performance of the rituals by appointed specialists in front of a large audience of invited guests.[104]

Changes in Ritual and the Development of Poetry

This change in the performance of ritual seems to be reflected as well in changes in Zhou poetry. The earliest poems in the *Shi jing*, poems in the *Zhou Song* section dating to the first century of the dynasty, reflect a close-knit human community celebrating (or, better, concelebrating) the foundation of the Zhou state. These were liturgical hymns meant to be sung and danced by the temple congregation while they were performing rituals addressed to their ancestors, as for example, in the hymn "Wei tian zhi ming" 維天之命 (It is Heaven's mandate; Mao 267):

> It is Heaven's mandate;
> Oh, stately, is it unending!
> *Wuhu*, illustrious!
> The purity of King Wen's virtue
> Approaches to shower down upon us.
> May we receive it;
> Quickly help us, King Wen's great grandsons, to make it steadfast.[105]

Several features mark this poem as a communal hymn; among these features, perhaps the most important is the use of the modal auxiliary *qi* 其 (may) to introduce the concelebrants' prayer in line 6.[106]

Formal and linguistic features mark other poems about sacrifices to the ancestors as having been composed somewhat later, about or just after the time of King Mu. But by that time poetry had become a more individual

---

[103] Max Loehr, *Ritual Vessels of Bronze Age China* (New York: Asia House Gallery, 1968), pp. 14–15.

[104] For an early statement of this insight, see Jessica Rawson, "Statesmen or Barbarians? The Western Zhou as Seen Through Their Bronzes," *Proceedings of the British Academy* 75 (1989): 71–95.

[105] *Maoshi zhengyi* ("Wei tian zhi ming"), 19/1, 12a–13a (Waley, *The Book of Songs*, p. 226).

[106] For a full discussion of these and other poems in the *Zhou Song* section of the *Shi jing*, see Shaughnessy, "From Liturgy to Literature."

production. Now a single poet, standing at a distance, describes the ritual that he is observing. The poem, "You gu" 有瞽 (There are blind drummers; Mao 280), is a good example of this type of descriptive poem:

> There are blind drummers, there are blind drummers
> In the court of Zhou.
> Erecting stands, erecting racks
> With high flanges and mounted wings.
> The echo-drums, kettle-drums, suspended drums,
> Little-drums, chimes, rattles, and clappers
> Being ready then are played.
> The pan-pipes and flutes are all raised:
> *Huang-huang*, their sound.
> Solemn and harmonizing the concordant sound.
> The prior ancestors hear this.
> Our guests arrive and stop,
> Long viewing their performance.[107]

Just as Rawson surmises from the evidence of the ritual implements themselves, the poems after the Ritual Revolution also imply that the rituals were observed by an audience, perhaps standing at some distance from the altar. And just as ritual specialists probably came to enact the ritual at the altar, so too does it seem that there developed poetic specialists who reenacted the rituals for other audiences.

These poets must have come from the corps of scribes (*shi* 史) that became so prominent at the Zhou court during the middle Western Zhou. It was probably not long before they moved from singing about the rituals to the ancestors to singing about the deeds of the ancestors themselves. Thus, the poems quoted at the beginning of this chapter, "Sheng min," "Gong Liu," and "Mian," describe the achievements of Jiang Yuan, the Lord of Millet, Gong Liu, and Gu Gong Danfu. Of course, King Wen, the nominal first king of the dynasty, would find his place among this pantheon, as in the following poem (only the first three and final one of seven stanzas of which are quoted) entitled, fittingly, "Wen wang" 文王 (King Wen; Mao 235):

> King Wen is on high;
> Oh, radiant in Heaven.
> Though Zhou is an old country,
> Its mandate is new.
> Zhou is illustrious,
> Di's mandate is grandly timely.
> King Wen ascends and descends,
> At Di's left and right.

---

[107] *Mao Shi zhengyi* ("You gu"), 19/3, 4b–7a (Waley, *The Book of Songs*, p. 218).

So energetic was King Wen!
His commanding renown is endless.
Arrayed and awarded, indeed, is Zhou,
Making lords of King Wen's descendants.
Trunk and branches for a hundred generations:
All of the sires of Zhou,
Illustrious also for generations.

The generations' illustriousness,
Their plans are so displayed.
Consider the august many sires
Who have given life to this royal state.
That the royal state can live
Is because of the upright pole of Zhou.
So dignified are the many sires;
King Wen through them is tranquil.
. . .
The mandate is unchangeable,
And not to stop with your person.
Broadcast and radiate proper renown;
Take the measure of what Yin got from heaven.
High Heaven's communication
Is without sound, without smell.
Properly emulate King Wen
And the 10,000 countries will be trusting.[108]

Contemporary heroes, particularly those who won victories in battle, would also have their praises sung, in encomia that often sound very much like the wording of bronze inscriptions. Thus, Shao Gong Hu 召公胡, a descendant of the Zhou founding father Shao Gong Shi and a leading figure during the reign of King Xuan (r. 827/25–782 B.C.), was praised for victories won over the Eastern Yi:

The king commanded Hu of Shao:
So widespread, so broadcast!
"Wen and Wu received the mandate,
Shao Gong was the support.
Don't say "I am a young son."
You are just like Shao Gong.
You have initiated and persevered in martial accomplishments,
And therefore I award you blessings.

"I grant you a tessera and a ladle,
And a bucket of black-millet fragrant-wine.

---

[108] *Mao Shi zhengyi* ("Wen wang"), 16/1, 6a–14a (Waley, *The Book of Songs*, pp. 250–1).

Report it to the cultured men.
I award you mountains and lands and fields.
The mandate received at Zhou
Is commanded from the Shao ancestor."
Hu bowed and touched his head to the ground:
"Ten-thousand years to the Son of Heaven."[109]

However, the poets' comments on contemporary affairs were not always laudatory. As noted above, in one of its few substantive comments about the middle Western Zhou period, the *Shi ji* says that during King Yih's reign, when the authority of the Zhou royal house reached a low ebb, the poets began to compose satires. Some of these satirical poems, probably dating from the somewhat later reign of King Li, are also preserved for us in the *Shi jing*. One, "Ban" 板 (Contrary; Mao 254), is quite astounding in the directness with which it criticizes the government (criticism is explicitly directed against an official in the government, but implicitly surely meant as a criticism of the king):

> Di on High is so contrary;
> The people below are all exhausted.
> You utter talk that is not true,
> And make plans that are not far-reaching.
> There are no sages so reliable,
> And no substance at the altar.
> That the plans are not far-reaching
> Is why I greatly remonstrate.
>
> Heaven's current difficulty
> Is nothing to be so complacent about.
> Heaven's current commotion
> Is nothing to be so indifferent about.
> If your words are pliant,
> The people will be concordant;
> If your words are relaxed,
> The people will be settled.
>
> Although I have a different service,
> I am in the same office as you.
> When I approach you to consult,
> You listen to me so arrogantly.
> My words are of service;
> Don't take them to be a laughing matter.

---

[109] *Mao Shi zhengyi* ("Jiang Han"), 18/4, 15a–18b (Waley, *The Book of Songs*, pp. 131–2).

> The former people had a saying:
> "Inquire of the fuel gatherers."[110]

Other poets at about this time devised a more subtle technique to present their criticisms: descriptions of natural dislocations, suggesting (again either implicitly or explicitly) that the state of man was analogous. A prolonged drought in the middle of the ninth century provided one of these poets with just such a natural manifestation of the troubles besetting the royal government. One stanza of the poem "Yun Han" 雲漢 (The Milky Way; Mao 258), will suffice to illustrate the correlation:

> The drought has become so severe,
> That it cannot be stopped.
> Glowing and burning,
> We have no place.
> The great mandate is about at an end,
> Nothing to look ahead to or back upon.
> The host of dukes and past rulers
> Does not help us;
> As for father and mother and the ancestors,
> How can they bear to treat us so?[111]

This is one of the first examples of what would come to characterize traditional Chinese thinking: correlative thought. In the later sections of the *Shi jing*, the *Xiao Ya* and *Guo Feng*, most of the poems of which date to the eighth and seventh centuries B.C., that is, after the end of Western Zhou, this correlative thought came to be expressed in a unique poetic form called *xing* 興 (evocation). The form generally consists of a pair of parallel rhyming couplets, the first of which describes an event in the natural world and the second an event in the human realm. Events in the natural world need not be so momentous as the long drought described in "Yun Han." Even the chirping of a bird could reverberate into the human realm. In "Fa mu" 伐木 (Chopping wood; Mao 165), the poet dwells at some length on the chirping of a bird, surmising that it must be calling to its mate, before coming finally to the conclusion (more explicitly than is usual with "evocations") that humans too should seek a mate in order to be happy:

> Chopping wood, *ding-ding*;
> A bird chirps, *ying-ying*.
> Coming out of that dark valley,
> Moving to that high tree;

---

[110] *Mao Shi zhengyi* ("Ban"), 17/4, 14b–16b (Bernhard Karlgren, *The Book of Odes* [Stockholm: Museum of Far Eastern Antiquities, 1950], pp. 212–14).

[111] *Mao Shi zhengyi* ("Yun Han"), 18/2, 17b–18a (Karlgren, *The Book of Odes*, pp. 223–6).

> *Ying*, its chirp,
> Seeking the sound of its friend.
> Examine that bird;
> Just as it seeks the sound of a friend,
> How much more so should people
> Seek the sound of a friend.
> Take spirit from it; listen to it;
> In the end, it will be harmonious and peaceful.[112]

By the time this technique of evocation reached its mature form in the *Guo Feng* section of the *Shi jing*, poets seem to have recognized that drawing explicit associations limited the possible range of evocations. No longer was it necessary to tell the listener to "examine that bird"; simply imitating its sound would suffice to stir him or her. Thus, the first and most famous poem in the collection, "Guan ju" 關雎 (*Guan* cries the osprey; Mao 1), begins with an "evocation" pregnant with correlations:

> *Guan, guan* cries the osprey
> On the river's isle.
> Delicate is the young girl:
> A fine match for the lord.

Strange though it may seem that the crying of an osprey could evoke the image of a nubile girl, we can begin to see in it something of the intellectual consciousness of the time. Elsewhere in the *Shi jing*, as in later Chinese culture and in many other cultures as well, the image of the fish signifies sexual fertility.[113] Knowing that the osprey is a fish-eating bird, it is not hard to see that this is a poem concerned with the hunt for a sexual partner. Indeed, the sound of the osprey's cry, as written onomatopoeically by the poet, confirms this: *guan* 關 means "to join; to bring together." The poet heard the osprey calling out: "Join, join."

When Confucius later advised his students to study the *Shi jing* because it can be used "to recognize the names of birds and animals, plants and trees,"[114] this was for him no pedantic exercise. Some animals are crafty, while others can be tamed; some plants are bitter, while others can bring about a smile and even more. Because Confucius, like the poets of the time, regarded these actions of nature as partaking of the same world order as did the affairs of men, he saw them as invaluable signs for understanding human society as well. Confucius knew that the better able his students were to understand

---

[112] *Mao Shi zhengyi* ("Fa mu"), 9/3, 16b–2a (Waley, *The Book of Songs*, pp. 204–5).
[113] For the classic study of this image with regard to the *Shi jing*, see Wen Yiduo, "Shuo yu," in *Wen Yiduo quanji* 4 vols. (1948; rpt. Beijing: Sanlian, 1982), vol. 1, pp. 117–38.
[114] *Analects*, 17/9.

the natures and effects of these things, the better able they would be to divine
their own circumstances.

Poetic Evocations and the Origin of the Zhou Yi

Using "birds and animals, plants and trees" to divine one's own circumstances
lies at the heart of the third of the great literary legacies usually dated to the
Western Zhou: the *Zhou yi* (Zhou changes); better known in the West as the
Yi jing [Classic of changes]. Tradition has it that the *Zhou yi* was composed
by King Wen while he was imprisoned at Youli, and perhaps was completed
by Zhou Gong. In fact, formal and linguistic comparisons between the text
and both the *Shi jing* and bronze inscriptions shows the *Zhou yi* to have
achieved its present form no earlier than the late Western Zhou.[115]

Many individual lines of the *Zhou yi* resemble the evocation form of the
Shi jing, relating an image in the natural world (though the *Zhou yi* also uses
in this regard historical vignettes and aspects of human society) to one in the
human realm. An almost perfect comparison is found in the second line statement of "Zhong fu" 中孚 (Centered sincerity; no. 61) hexagram:[116]

> A calling crane is in the shadows;
> Its young harmonize with it.
> We have a fine chalice;
> I will share it with you.

Other line statements are less developed; for instance, they are not usually
composed of two full couplets. Nevertheless, many of them are also unmistakably poetic and evocative. The second and fifth line statements of "Da
guo" 大過 (Great surpassing; no. 28) read respectively (though without trying
to reproduce the rhyme of the original):

> The withered willow bears shoots:
> The old man gets his wife.

and

> The withered willow bears flowers:
> The old maid gets her man.

---

[115] Li Jingchi, *Zhouyi tanyuan* (Beijing: Zhonghua, 1978), pp. 130–50; Shaughnessy, "The Composition of
the *Zhouyi*," pp. 16–49.
[116] The *Zhou yi* is organized around sixty-four combinations of six lines that are either solid (—) or broken
(- -). Each one of these graphs (known in the West as hexagrams) is named and has a statement
attached to it (known as the hexagram statement). Each line also has a statement attached to it (the
line statement), in most cases the line statements of a single hexagram all being related to a single
image.

The *Zhou yi* differs from the *Shi jing* in having served as a manual of divination. Technical divination terminology (whether representing a prognostication, verification, or some other feature of divination) was often added to its poetic images. Thus, after "The withered willow bears shoots: The old man gets his wife," we find the formulaic phrase "There is nothing not beneficial," and after "The withered willow bears flowers: The old maid gets her man," we read "There is no trouble, there is no praise." This terminology is of at least two different types, one advisory (usually beginning with the word *li* 利 [it is beneficial]) and one determinative (words such as *ji* 吉 [auspicious], *xiong* 凶 [inauspicious], *li* 厲 [danger], and *lin* 吝 [distress], which seem to have served as prognostications, and phrases such as *wu you li* 无有利 [There is nothing beneficial] or *wu bu li* 無不利 [There is nothing not beneficial], *hui* 悔 [regret] or *hui wang* 悔亡 [regret is gone], and *wu jiu* 無咎 [There is no trouble], which may have derived originally from verifications. Sometimes these divinatory terms can be strung together and are occasionally apparently contradictory. The top line statement of "Jin" 晉 (Advancing; no. 35) hexagram provides one such example:

> Advancing its horns: It means to use it to attack the city; danger;
> auspicious; there is no trouble; divining: distress.

But usually the divinatory determinations are both simple and reasonably straightforward; that is, they accord with what we know, or can reasonably conjecture, about the meaning of the image, as in the top line of "Gui mei" 歸妹 (Returning maiden; no. 54) hexagram:

> The girl raises the basket but there is no fruit,
> The sire stabs the sheep but there is no blood;
> there is nothing beneficial.

A fruitless basket and a bloodless stabbing, whatever they might portend, could almost surely not be a desirable image, and the determination "There is nothing beneficial" is thus consistent with the image.

This line of "Gui mei" is typical of *Zhou yi* line statements in another way as well. Although it presents an image taken from human society rather than from nature, it should probably be understood as representing only the initial or "evocation" image couplet; the rejoinder couplet – which would relate the image to the human realm – is here unstated. In fact, this is true of the great majority of line statements in the *Zhou yi*. To give several examples (together with their divinatory determinations), almost at random:

> Flying dragon in the skies; beneficial to see the great man.
> "Qian" 乾 (Vigor; no. 1), Nine in the Fifth line

Yellow skirts; auspicious.
> "Kun" 坤 (Compliance; 2), Six in the Fifth line

The troops now carting corpses; inauspicious.
> "Shi" 師 (Troops; no. 7), Six in the Third line

Beneficent return; auspicious.
> "Fu" 復 (Return; no. 24), Six in the Second line

The ridgepole sags; inauspicious.
> "Da guo" 大過 (Great surpassing; no. 28), Nine in the Third line

The well is lined with brick; there is no trouble.
> "Jing" 井 (The well; 48), Six in the Fourth line

Wets his tail; distress.
> "Weiji" 未濟 (Not yet completed; no. 64), Initial Six line

To understand these images, it is necessary to consider the relatively few (though by no means rare) examples where the rejoinder couplet relating the image to the human realm is present. One of the best such examples is the third line of "Jian" 漸 (Advance; no. 53) hexagram:

The wild goose advances to the land: the husband campaigns but does not return, the wife is pregnant but does not give birth; inauspicious; beneficial to drive off robbers.

The wild goose's advances to various points (the bank of a stream, a large rock, land, a tree, a ridge, and a hill) constitute the nature image of the six line statements of "Jian" hexagram. In the case of this third line, the wild goose's advance to the land evokes the rhyming rejoinder that "the husband campaigns but does not return, the wife is pregnant but does not give birth." Although the association between a wild goose and marital problems is not intuitively apparent, it is the case that throughout the *Shi jing* whenever a wild goose serves as the image it invariably evokes a separation between man and woman. This was perhaps because military campaigns in ancient China were typically launched at the onset of winter, thus avoiding the summer monsoon rains and coming after the autumn harvests had been collected. The seasonal coincidence of soldiers marching off in formation with wild geese flying off – also in formation – might well have suggested that the flight of geese was invariably associated with the march of soldiers. For wives, in particular, this could not have been an auspicious omen.[117]

This line statement of "Jian" hexagram can also be used to show how a

---

[117] For further discussions of the image of the wild goose in the *Zhou yi*, see Edward L. Shaughnessy, "Marriage, Divorce and Revolution: Reading Between the Lines of the *Book of Changes*," *JAS* 51, 1 (1992): 587–99; Edward L. Shaughnessy, "The Origin of an *Yijing* Line Statement," *EC* 20 (1995): 223–40.

Zhou yi line statement may have been composed, or at least how it was used in divination. Compare it with an account of a turtle-shell divination recorded in the *Zuo zhuan* 左傳 (Zuo's tradition) under the tenth year of Lu Xiang Gong 魯襄公 (i.e., 563 B.C.). This divination was performed on behalf of Sun Wenzi 孫文子, Lord of Wey 衛, as he contemplated whether or not to counter an attack on his state made by Huang'er 皇耳 of Zheng 鄭:

Sun Wenzi divined by turtle-shell about pursuing them. He presented the crack to Ding Jiang. Madame Jiang asked the omen-verse. They said:

The crack is like a mountain peak: there is a fellow who goes out to campaign, but loses his leader.

Madame Jiang said: "The campaigner loses his leader; this means the benefit of driving off robbers." The great ministers planned it, and the men of Wey pursued (Zheng). Sun Peng captured Huang'er of Zheng at Quanqiu.[118]

The "omen-verse" (*yao* 繇) here, "The crack is like a mountain peak: there is a fellow who goes out to campaign, but loses his leader," is formally exactly like the line statement of "Jian": "The wild goose advances to the land: the husband campaigns but does not return, the wife is pregnant but does not give birth." It is clear that its first phrase, "The crack is like a mountain peak," which corresponds to the nature image in the "evocations" of the *Shi jing* and *Zhou yi*, is a description of the crack caused to appear in the turtle shell. That it was in the shape of a "mountain peak" must have suggested danger to the diviner (an association that is perhaps intuitive even today), so that when he composed the rhyming rejoinder couplet, which presumably had to be related to the topic of the divination – a military campaign, he related it to the loss of a leader. This response in itself was doubtless ambiguous to Sun Wenzi (after all, which leader was to be lost?), and thus he enlisted another prognosticator, Madame Jiang, to provide a further interpretation and advice. It is interesting that her prognostication, that this indicated the "benefit of driving off robbers," is almost exactly the one found in the line statement of "Jian" under consideration.

From this, it would appear that the *Zhou yi* does indeed derive from divinations, and that the images in it (such as the wild goose, the dragon, "yellow skirts," and so on) evoked associations in the mind of the diviner. It remains unclear how these images may have been seen – and thus written into the text – in the first place. But what is clear is that by emphasizing different aspects of the images (such as the six different positions to which the wild goose advances in the line statements of "Jian" hexagram) the *Zhou yi* shows that they were by no means constant, but were subject to constant

---

[118] *Zuo zhuan* 31 (Xiang 10), 8a (Legge, *The Ch'un Ts'ew with the Tso Chuen*, pp. 443, 447).

change. Indeed, traditional Chinese exegetes have viewed this changeability as the fundamental notion of the *Zhou yi*: just as the world is in constant flux, so too is the *Zhou yi* when it is used in divination, producing different views of the image or even of different images.[119] In place of the *Shi jing's* poetic descriptions, which might be likened to individual snapshots, the *Zhou yi* presents, and invites the reader/diviner to re-present, an ever changing scene, even more than a moving picture, a kaleidoscopic interactive vision as splendidly various as life itself.

THE DECLINE AND FALL OF WESTERN ZHOU

The story of late Western Zhou political history, which we left with the Chu attack on E and the succession to power of the young King Li (857 B.C.), is no less interesting for being more or less predictable. King Li has gone down in history as one of the paradigmatic evil last rulers. According to the *Shi ji*, his major failings were a refusal to listen to criticism from either the people or the many lords, and an excessive reliance on one minister, Rong Yi Gong 榮夷公 (probably the Rongbo 榮伯 mentioned in the *Yu gui* inscription translated above), who, for profit (*li* 利), pandered to the king's personal predilection.[120]

As is often the case, the *Zhushu jinian* adds certain important details. It indicates that although in the king's first year, Chu came to court to present gifts of turtle shell and cowries, presumably as a peace offering, just two years later the Southern Yi again invaded the Luo River valley. The text states that King Li commanded "Guo Gong Changfu 虢公長父 to attack them, but that he did not succeed."[121] This command is probably corroborated by the inscription of the *Guozhong xu gai* 虢仲盨蓋; of an original set of twelve oblong tureens, only a single cover is now extant: "Guozhong took the king to campaign to the south, attacking the Southern Huai Yi. At Chengzhou (he) makes these set *xu*-tureens. There are twelve of these *xu*-tureens."[122] Again according to the *Zhushu jinian*, in King Li's eighth year of reign, Ruibo Liangfu 芮伯良父, a prominent lord, remonstrated with the "hundred officers" (*bai guan* 百官) at court, though the target of his criticism was probably the king, as it was in the poem "Ban" translated above.[123] The *Zhushu*

---

[119] For an analysis of divination with the *Zhou yi*, albeit based on Eastern Zhou sources, see Kidder Smith, "*Zhou yi* Interpretation from Accounts in the *Zuozhuan*," *HJAS* 49 (1989): 421–63.

[120] *Shi ji*, 4, p. 141 (Nienhauser et al., eds., *The Grand Scribe's Records*, vol. 1, p. 70).

[121] *Zhushu jinian*, 2, p. 7b (Legge, *The Shoo King*, Prolegomena, p. 153).

[122] *Shang Zhou qingtongqi mingwen xuan*, no. 418; Shirakawa, *Kinbun tsûshaku*, 25, no. 144.

[123] Ruibo's remonstration is given at length in the *Shi ji*, 4, p. 141 (Nienhauser et al., eds., *The Grand Scribe's Records*, vol. 1, pp. 70–1), quoting *Guo yu* ("Zhou yu 1"), 1.5b–6a; for another version of Ruibo's remonstration, see *Yi Zhou shu* ("Rui Liangfu"), 9.1a–2b.

jinian account continues with a record that in the king's eleventh year (843 B.C.), "western belligerents entered into Quanqiu 犬丘," within the Wei River valley itself.

We are fortunate in the case of King Li in having three inscribed bronze vessels that the king commissioned in his personal name, Hu 胡 (written in the inscriptions as 鈇). Perhaps we should not expect otherwise,[124] but these inscriptions give no hint of the manifest threats, both internal and external, to the very existence of the house of Zhou. The most imposing of these vessels is a gigantic *gui*-tureen (weighing 60 kg), the *Hu gui* 鈇簋, with an inscription of 124 characters (see Fig. 5.2).

The king said: "Although I am but a young boy, I have no leisure day or night. I always support the former kings, in order to match august Heaven; I broadly embroider my heart, so that it descends to the four quarters. And so I take the eminent warriors and presented people and elevate them in line with the former kings and ancestral house.

I, Hu, make this giant offertory treasured *gui*-tureen, with which vigorously to aid my august and cultured and valorous ancestors and deceased father; may they approach the prior cultured men, may they constantly be in the court of Di on High, ascending and descending, continuously visited with the august Di on High's great and felicitous mandate, with which commandingly to protect our family, my position, and Hu's person. Cascadingly send down upon me much good fortune and model assistance, comprehensive counsels and far-reaching plans. May I, Hu, for 10,000 years bring to fruition my many sacrifices, with which to seek long life and entreat an eternal mandate, to rule in position and to make roots in the lower realm."
It is the king's twelfth ritual cycle.[125]

It is likely that the "twelfth ritual cycle (*si* 祀)" in which this tureen was cast corresponds to 842 B.C., the year of the earliest generally accepted dated event in Chinese history: in this year King Li was driven out of the capital and forced to go into exile at a place called Zhi 彘, near present-day Linfen in the Fen River valley of Shanxi province (perhaps the area in which the Zhou had once lived). Interpretations vary as to whether this was the first "peasant uprising" in Chinese history[126] or, as is more likely, a conspiracy on the part of the "many lords."[127] But our sources are in agreement that the king's eldest son, Jing 靖, who was but a toddler at this time, was saved from a mob surrounding the royal palace only through the sacrifice by Shao Gong Hu, mentioned above in the poem "Jiang Han," of his own young son.

---

[124] See Lothar von Falkenhausen, "Issues in Western Zhou Studies: A Review Article," *EC* 18 (1993): 170, for the suggestion that the content of inscriptions was formulaically circumscribed.

[125] *Shang Zhou qingtongqi mingwen xuan*, no. 404; Shaughnessy, *Sources of Western Zhou History*, pp. 171–2.

[126] For a more nuanced exposition of this view than is typical, see Sun Zuoyun, *Shijing yu Zhoudai shehui yanjiu* (Beijing: Zhonghua, 1966), pp. 204–38.

[127] See, e.g., He Fan, "Guoren baodong xingzhi bianxi," *Renwen zazhi* 1983.5: 76–7, with citations to traditional sources.

Figure 5.2. *Hu gui* inscription and vessel, found at Fufeng, Shaanxi (late Western Zhou). Vessel after Li Xueqin ed., *Zongguo meishu quanji: Gongyi meishu bian 4, Qingtongqi (shang)* (Beijing: Wenwu, 1985), no. 225; inscription after Ma Chengyuan, ed., *Shang Zhou qingtongqi mingwen xuan* (Beijing: Wenwu, 1988), no. 404.

Interpretations have varied too as to the nature of government put in place at this time. The *Shi ji*, construing references to *gong he* 共和 (Joint harmony) as the sort of reign-era name used in the Han dynasty, states that Shao Gong and Zhou Gong, descendants of the two famous founding fathers, ruled

Figure 5.2. *(cont.)*

together in place of the exiled King Li.[128] The *Zhushu jinian*, on the other hand, records that it was one of the many lords, Lord He 和 of the state of Gong 共 (and thus known as Gong He), who stepped in as regent. This latter record has now almost certainly been corroborated by bronze inscriptions.[129] This Gong He ruled for fourteen years. The few records we have of these years, primarily the *Zhushu jinian*, show them to have been relatively uneventful except for a continuing drought, mentioned in the annals for each of his last five years. When, in 828 B.C., King Li died in exile at Zhi, Shao Gong and Zhou Gong apparently did join forces to persuade Gong He to retire, installing the heir apparent Jing as King Xuan (r. 827/25–782 B.C.).

King Xuan's lengthy reign of forty-six years is traditionally regarded as something of a restoration. There is evidence, both in traditional sources such as the *Shi ji* and *Zhushu jinian* and also in bronze inscriptions, that he did move quickly in the early years of his reign to reassert royal authority. One of the most pressing continuing threats came from the "western barbarians,"

---

[128] *Shi ji*, 4, p. 144 (Nienhauser et al., eds., *The Grand Scribe's Records*, vol. 1, p. 72).

[129] *Zhushu jinian*, 2, p. 8a (Legge, *The Shoo King*, Prolegomena, p. 154). For a bronze inscription that mentions Lord He acting as de facto king, see *Shi X gui* 師㝅簋 (*Shang Zhou qingtongqi mingwen xuan*, no. 84; Shirakawa, *Kinbun tsûshaku*, 31, no. 186; Shaughnessy, *Sources of Western Zhou History*, p. 272).

now usually referred to as the Xianyun 玁狁, who are first mentioned by name as invading the Zhou capital itself in the second year of the Gong He interregnum (i.e., 840 B.C.). In his fifth year of reign (i.e., 823 B.C.), King Xuan commanded a leading figure at court, known variously as Yin Jifu 殷吉甫 or as Xi Jia 兮甲,[130] to lead a counterattack against the Xianyun. Yin Jifu is well known from the *Shi jing*, two poems of which are signed by him as their composer, while another poem celebrates his military accomplishments.[131] He also commissioned a bronze vessel, the *Xi Jia pan* 兮甲盤, with an inscription commemorating the success of this campaign and his subsequent appointment to govern the old eastern territories:

It was the fifth year, third month, after the dying brightness, *gengyin* [day 27]; the king for the first time went and attacked the Xianyun at Tuyu. Xi Jia followed the king, cutting off heads and manacling prisoners; the victory was without defect. The king awarded Xi Jia four horses and a colt chariot.

The king commanded Jia to regulate the taxes of the four regions of Chengzhou as far as the Southern Huai Yi. "The Huai Yi of old were our tribute money men; they ought not dare not to produce their tribute, their taxes, their presented men, and their trade-goods. They ought not dare not to come to the encampments and come to the markets. If they dare not to obey the command, then according to precedent strike and attack them. If it be the trade-goods of our many lords and hundred families, none ought not be brought to market, and they ought not dare then to send in illicit trade-goods, for then they will also be [held to] precedent."

Xibo Jifu makes this basin; may he have long life for 10,000 years without limit, and sons' sons and grandsons' grandsons eternally to treasure and use it.[132]

In addition to the evidence that it contains regarding Yin Jifu, or Xi Jia's, attack on the Xianyun in the fifth year of King Xuan's reign, the *Xi Jia pan* inscription is also of great interest for the light it sheds on the king's perception of his sovereignty over the Huai Yi. Despite the claims here that the "Huai Yi of old were our tribute money men," there is no evidence that such a dependent relationship had obtained at least since the war between King Yan of Xu and King Mu's army well over 100 years earlier.[133] Nevertheless, it is of interest that King Xuan hoped to be able to regulate trade between the eastern capital and areas farther east.

[130] For the equation of the names Yin Jifu and Xi Jia, see Wang Guowei, *Guan tang ji lin* (1923; rpt. Beijing: Zhonghua, 1959), p. 1206.

[131] For the two *Shi jing* poems explicitly signed as having been composed by Jifu, see "Song gao" 嵩高 (Mount Song is High; Mao 259); *Mao Shi zhengyi*, 18/3, 1a–11a (Waley, *The Book of Songs*, pp. 133–5); and "Cheng min" 丞民 (The Multitude of People; Mao 260); *Mao Shi zhengyi*, 18/3, 11a–17b (Waley, *The Book of Songs*, pp. 141–3). For the poem praising Yin Jifu, see "Liu yue" 六月 (The Sixth Month; Mao 177); *Mao Shi zhengyi*, 10/2, 1a–8a (Waley, *The Book of Songs*, pp. 126–7).

[132] *Shang Zhou qingtongqi mingwen xuan*, no. 437; Shirakawa, *Kinbun tsûshaku*, 33, no. 191; Shaughnessy, *Sources of Western Zhou History*, p. 141.

[133] For one study of Zhou–Huai Yi relations during the reign of King Xuan, see Xia Hanyi, "Cong Jufu xu gai mingwen tan Zhou wangchao yu Nan Huai Yi de guanxi," *Hanxue yanjiu* 5, 2 (1987): 567–73.

According to the *Zhushu jinian*, in the year after Yin Jifu was commanded to regulate the trade relations with the Huai Yi, Shao Gong Hu led an army as far as the Huai River to reestablish by force of arms Zhou control over the area.[134] The poem "Jiang Han," translated in part above, describes the success of this campaign and the awards made to Shao Gong to celebrate it. Three years later (i.e., in King Xuan's ninth year of reign, 819 B.C.), the king is said to have convened a convocation of the lords in the eastern capital at Luo.[135] Bronze inscriptions show that further victories over the Xianyun were won in the king's twelfth and thirteenth years (i.e., 816–815 B.C.).[136] But this was the high-water mark of King Xuan's reign; indeed, for the dynasty itself, it was the final brief flash before the light was to go out entirely.

At the same time that he was pressing campaigns against the Xianyun and Eastern Yi, King Xuan was also moving to reestablish royal authority within the old Zhou states. Succession struggles broke out in Wey 衛, Lu, and Qi.[137] The longest lasting of these was in Lu, the important eastern state that had been ruled hereditarily by descendants of Zhou Gong Dan. According to the "Genealogy of the House of Zhou Gong of Lu" in the *Shi ji*, upon a visit to court by Lu Wu Gong 武公 (r. 825–816 B.C.) and his sons, King Xuan became enamored of the younger of the two sons, Xi 戲, and commanded Wu Gong to name him (i.e., Xi) rather than the elder son Kuo 括 as heir apparent. About ten years later, in 807 B.C., after Xi had indeed been installed as Yi Gong 懿公 (r. 815–807 B.C.), the people of Lu rose up and deposed him, installing Kuo's son Bo Yu 伯御 as the ruler of Lu (r. 806–796 B.C.). Eleven years later, a royal army attacked Lu; Bo Yu was killed, and King Xuan installed Yi Gong's younger brother, Cheng 稱, to be the new lord. The *Shi ji* genealogy concludes its account of these machinations and wars laconically: "From this time on, the many lords mostly rebelled against royal commands."

King Xuan's final intercession in the affairs of a Zhou state is clouded in the sort of euphemism traditional Chinese history often uses to report disasters. For the forty-third year of his reign (i.e., 785 B.C.), the *Zhushu jinian* records directly enough that "the king killed the great man Dubo 杜伯, his

---

[134] *Zhushu jinian*, 2.9b (Legge, *The Shoo King*, Prolegomena, p. 155).

[135] For a *Shi jing* poem said to celebrate this convocation at the eastern capital, see "Che gong" 車攻 (The Chariots' Attack; Mao 179); *Mao Shi zhengyi*, 10/3, 1a–7b (Waley, *The Books of Songs*, pp. 287–8).

[136] These victories are commemorated by three important bronze vessels: the *Guoji Zi Bo pan* 虢季子伯盤 (*Shang Zhou qingtongqi mingwen xuan*, no. 440; Shirakawa, *Kinbun tsûshaku*, 32, no. 192), the *Buqi gui* 不嬰簋 (*Shang Zhou qingtongqi mingwen xuan*, no. 441; Shirakawa, *Kinbun tsûshaku*, 32, no. 193), and the *Duo You ding* 多友鼎 (*Shang Zhou qingtongqi mingwen xuan*, no. 408). For a study of these inscriptions and this campaign, see Edward L. Shaughnessy, "The Date of the 'Duo You *Ding*' and Its Significance," *EC* 9–10 (1983–5): 55–69.

[137] *Shi ji* ("Wei Kangshu shijia"), 37, p. 1591; ("Lu Zhougong shijia"), 33, p. 1528; ("Qi Taigong shijia"), 32, p. 1482.

son Xishu 隰叔 going off into exile at Jin."[138] Although the *Zhushu jinian* says nothing more about this event (indeed, it records nothing more concerning King Xuan except that "the king died" in the forty-sixth year of his reign [i.e., 782 B.C.]) and the *Shi ji* does not mention it at all, a sort of ghost story found in the *Guo yu* 國語 (Sayings of the states) completes the story. It quotes a "Zhou Spring and Autumn Annals" (*Zhou Chunqiu* 周春秋; now lost) as saying:

King Xuan killed Dubo, but he was guiltless. Three years later King Xuan gathered the many lords to hunt in the royal game preserve. At mid-day, Dubo arose by the side of the road, and wearing a scarlet jacket and hat and wielding a scarlet bow and arrow, shot King Xuan, hitting him in the heart and splitting his sternum, so that he died.[139]

Whatever the circumstances surrounding his death, King Xuan did die in 782 B.C., and with his death so too died his great restoration. If any credence is to be given to the *Guo yu's* account of his assassination, it is ironic that Dubo's home was located at the site where the Great Goose Pagoda (Da Yan ta 大雁塔) now stands in Xi'an,[140] just a few minutes walk from either the Shaanxi Historical Museum or the Shaanxi Provincial Institute of Archaeology, the two institutions most responsible for preserving the material heritage of the Western Zhou.

King Xuan was succeeded by his son, King You (r. 781–771 B.C.). King You's reign began no more auspiciously than the way in which that of his father seems to have ended. In the second year of his reign, all of our sources report that an earthquake struck the Zhou capital region, causing the region's three rivers (i.e., the Wei, Luo 洛, and Jing 涇) "all to dry up and Mount Qi to crumble."[141] To make matters worse, in the same year there were eclipses of both the sun and the moon.[142] A poem in the *Shi jing* entitled "Shiyue zhi jiao" 十月之交 (The conjunction of the tenth month; Mao 193) describes the scene as follows:

---

[138] *Zhushu jinian*, 2.10a (Legge, *The Shoo King*, Prolegomena, p. 156).

[139] *Guo yu* ("Zhou yu 1"), 1.11b. For a study of this legend, see Li Xixing, "Guanyu Zhou Xuanwang zhi si de kaozheng," in *Xi Zhou shi lunwenji*, 2 vols. (Xi'an: Shaanxi Renmin jiaoyu, 1983), vol. 2, pp. 966–76.

[140] Wu Zhenfeng, "Zhou wangchao jiena yi zu rencai chutan," in *Xi Zhou shi lunwenji*, 2 vols. (Xi'an: Shaanxi Renmin jiaoyu, 1983), vol. 2, p. 817, reports that five vessels cast for Dubo were found at this site in 1899.

[141] *Shi ji*, 4, p. 145 (Nienhauser et al., eds., *The Grand Scribe's Records*, p. 73); *Zhushu jinian*, 2.10b (Legge, trans., *The Shoo King*, Prolegomena, p. 157); *Guo yu* ("Zhou yu 1"), 1.10a. Note that the Luo River here is to be distinguished from that in western Henan on which the city of Luoyang is located.

[142] These eclipses are usually dated to King You's sixth year (i.e., 776 B.C.), however the solar eclipse of that year would not have been visible in the Xi'an area. Fang Shanzhu, "Xi Zhou niandai xue shang de jige wenti," pp. 15–23, has shown that there was in fact an eclipse visible there in 780 B.C.

At the conjunction of the tenth month
On the first day *xinmao*,
The sun was eclipsed;
The enormity of the malevolence!
That moon being diminished,
This sun being diminished;
Now these people below;
How vast the woe!

The sun and moon report the balefulness
And do not use their paths.
The four states are without government
And do not use their worthies.
For that moon to be eclipsed
Is something common;
For this sun to be eclipsed,
Wherein lies the evil?

So violent are the thunder and lightning,
Not tranquil, not good.
The hundred rivers bubble and jump,
The mountains and mounds crumble and fall,
The high banks become valleys,
And the deep valleys become ridges.
Woeful are the men of today!
How is it that the grief does not punish this.[143]

As discussed above in the section on the late Western Zhou worldview, it was just at this time that correlative thought, the notion that natural and human events are correlated, each exerting an irresistible influence over the other, was achieving its first elaboration. To the people of the time, an earthquake or a solar eclipse alone would have been enough to portend difficult times. The combination of both, and with a lunar eclipse thrown in for good measure, could only have been seen as a sign of imminent disaster.

An important aspect of correlative thought is that natural events not only serve to predict the future, but since they are correlated in the first place with human events, they also serve to exhibit the present state of those events. Especially influential were events at the royal court, and these events, at least as related in the traditional histories, were indeed rotten enough to cause earthquakes and eclipses. According to the *Shi ji*, at this time King You had become so infatuated with one of his consorts, Bao Si 褒姒, that he divorced his queen, a daughter of the lord of the state of Shen 申, deposed the legitimate heir apparent, Yi Jiu 宜臼, and forced him into

---

[143] *Mao Shi zhengyi*, 12/2, 2a–5b (Karlgren, *The Book of Odes*, pp. 138–40).

exile, and established another son – borne to him by Bao Si – as the new heir apparent.[144] This story, obviously intent on finding both a moral imperative and internal causes to explain the downfall of the Zhou dynasty, goes on to relate that the lord of Shen, who had been instrumental in helping King Xuan reestablish control in the eastern territories, joined forces with the "western barbarians," now called the Quan Rong (Dog barbarians) but almost certainly the same people as the Xianyun who had been threatening the Zhou capital region for more than half a century, and invited them to attack again.

The story – obviously fanciful but too important in the Chinese historiographical tradition not to retell – goes that, on one occasion, a nervous sentinel manning the defense lines thought that the Quan Rong were attacking and lit a warning beacon that communicated this news back to the capital. Those lords who were still loyal to the Zhou court came rushing to defend the capital only to find that this was a false alarm; Bao Si, usually of quite dour demeanor, is supposed to have burst out laughing. King You was so pleased with this result that he had the warning beacons lit repeatedly. Needless to say, even those few lords still loyal to the king soon tired of this game, and quit coming to the rescue. When, in King You's eleventh year of reign, 771 B.C., the Quan Rong really did attack, there was no one to defend against them. They sacked the capital, killed King You, captured Bao Si, and brought the great Western Zhou dynasty to an all too human end.

As the remaining chapters of this book will show, the end of the Western Zhou period was by no means the end of the Zhou dynasty. Although the "many lords" did not come to the defense of the western capital, two states that would prove to be the most powerful states of the Eastern Zhou (at least for a time), Jin 晉 and Qin 秦, were instrumental in securing the evacuation of the Zhou elite from their Wei River homeland (to which they never returned)[145] to the eastern capital. They there installed King You's original heir apparent, Yi Jiu, as King Ping (r. 770–720 B.C.). Zhou kings would continue to occupy (and, nominally, to rule) this capital for more than 500 more years; this was the Eastern Zhou period.

While the year 771 B.C. has always provided a convenient and definitive cleavage between the two periods, it is perhaps an artificial divide. In many ways, this moment marks the culmination of tendencies that first appeared a century before. When the traditional histories note, however laconically, that during the reigns of Kings Yih, Xiao, Yi, and, especially,

---

[144] This account, obviously fictionalized but doubtless based on a core of historical fact, is found in *Shi ji* 4, p. 147 (Nienhauser et al., eds., *The Grand Scribe's Records*, pp. 73–4).

[145] Chen Quanfang, *Zhouyuan yu Zhou wenhua*, p. 18, notes that not a single Eastern Zhou artifact has ever been found at the Plain of Zhou (Zhouyuan) site straddling present-day Qishan and Fufeng counties, Shaanxi.

Li, "the many lords did not come to court," they are really telling us that the eastern colonies established at the very beginning of the dynasty were growing away from the king and moving toward independence. The philosophical argument for "honoring the worthy" (*gui xian* 貴賢) found in the writings of Confucius, Mozi, and many other Eastern Zhou thinkers had its roots in the bureaucracy that first emerged in the middle Western Zhou. And the individual consciousness so prominent in the *Airs of the States* poems of the *Shi jing* can probably also be traced back to the poetic specialists celebrating the new style of ritual, which in its own right would also become ever more systematized throughout the next two centuries. Whether in terms of politics, government, social order, literature, or worldview, the Zhou state of 850 B.C. probably had more in common with that of 650 B.C. than with that of 1050 B.C.; as for 771 B.C., in some ways it was just another year.

THE LEGACY OF WESTERN ZHOU

Much of the preceding narrative has read like an unremitting series of crises. This probably represents more the concerns of the modern historian than it does the general dynamic of Western Zhou historical development. To be sure, the civil war after the death of King Wu, the disagreement between Zhou Gong Dan and Shao Gong Shi over the nature of government, the disastrous southern campaign of King Zhao and its geopolitical implications for succeeding reigns, the irregular successions of King Xiao and Gong He, the wars in the eastern states in the decades 800 and 790, and the Xianyun invasions and sacking of the capital Zongzhou were perhaps the most critical moments within that historical development, but they were not by any means the sum total of the dynasty. For 275 years the Zhou royal court was able to sustain itself at a single capital, longer than any other dynasty would be able to do for the rest of Chinese history. But it did more than just sustain itself. During those 275 years, the Zhou court and people established canons of governmental propriety, poetic expression, and an understanding of the changes of the world that would undergird all subsequent Chinese intellectual discourse. It is true that some, perhaps many, of the notions in these canons were anticipated already in the Shang dynasty, or even in the Xia and Neolithic periods. Nevertheless, if those earlier periods can be said to be the foundation of Chinese history, necessary, to be sure, but underground and all but invisible throughout most of that history, then surely the Western Zhou would have to be called its cornerstone, the highly visible symbol that the architects of traditional China returned to again and again to assure themselves that its edifice was secure and well founded.

CHAPTER SIX

WESTERN ZHOU ARCHAEOLOGY

Jessica Rawson

Inscribed ritual bronzes feature in the legacy of the Western Zhou and have been revered throughout Chinese history. For traditional scholars these have appeared to complement the famous texts of the *Shang shu* 尚書 (Venerated documents) and the *Shi jing* 詩經 (Classic of poetry) that have been discussed in Chapter 5. The inscriptions are indeed fundamental to all Western Zhou studies, as they are the only surviving contemporary texts. They are especially important as a means of establishing the date of transmitted documents such as the *Shang shu*. Here these bronzes will be the principal benchmark by which material remains of the Zhou period will be identified, and against which other materials will be assessed. Chronological sequences of bronzes can be suggested by means of an analysis of the shapes and ornament of the inscribed vessels and pieces that resemble them.

The bronze vessels allow us to identify a whole spectrum of Zhou sites, houses, and larger buildings, workshops and city walls, but above all tombs and chariot burials. The objects and the sites they come from are closely interrelated. One of the most striking features of such Zhou sites is the way in which they are concentrated in Shaanxi (see Map 6.1). Indeed the Western Zhou period is the time when the principal centers of power were situated along the Wei River. This power is evident in the large number of sites, their proximity to one another, and the large number of objects of high quality that they have revealed.

But this very abundance raises several questions, for as we shall see below, it remains something of a mystery as to how this material culture came into being. It may be asked how the peoples who made the bronzes and dug the tombs emerged; whether they were always in Shaanxi or came from beyond the borders of the present province; how much they themselves contributed, and what did they borrow from the Shang and others? These are important questions to answer, for the single simple reason that before the time when we can place the Zhou conquest, there were no large centers of occupation along the Wei River.

Sites at the metropolitan capital at present-day Xi'an 西安 and at the ritual center in the counties of Fufeng 扶風 and Qishan 岐山, known as the Zhouyuan 周原, indicate that large and rich populations were living there from the time of the conquest. Further, much of central Shaanxi along the Wei River and its tributaries was occupied by elite bronze-using families. Similarities of vessels in ceramics and bronze and of chariot parts and weaponry also suggest that the Zhou, or their dependents, spread out and established centers near Houma 侯馬, Shanxi, identified as the heart of the state of Jin 晉; at Luoyang 洛陽, identified as the secondary Zhou capital Chengzhou 成周; at Xunxian 濬縣 and Huixian 輝縣, Henan, the center of Wey 衛, and at Fangshan 房山 near Beijing, the center of a small state called Yan 匽 (i.e., 燕). Other sites have produced less distinguished remains. A shared material culture seems to have permeated and influenced an immense area: from Baoji 寶雞, Shaanxi in the west to Beijing in the northeast is a distance of about 1,250 km; the region is approximately 800 km north to south in some places. Obviously it would be unrealistic to claim that the Zhou controlled this whole area in detail. However, it is evident that the lengths of their lines of communication were exceptionally impressive. Moreover, similarity of material implies centralized direction not only of political relations, seen in royal gifts and the implements of war, but also of practical matters, such as the organization of foundries, and of ideological ones, such as ritual and belief. The Zhou achievement thus lay in creating a large unified state, unified at least in terms of an elite culture, where none had existed on this scale before. Not until the Qin 秦 dynasty was such extensive control and such relative homogeneity achieved again.

In 771 B.C., the Zhou capital near Xi'an was devastated. The Zhou elite either fled or were extinguished. The control of much of northern Central China from a major western center was over. Thereafter, separate states ruled Central China. The period to be described does not display an unchanging culture, as it indeed witnessed significant developments, but it does have two clear temporal boundaries, and it is the time when the center of activity was in present-day Shaanxi.

THE MATERIAL RECORD

Western Zhou finds of all categories are widely distributed, ranging from Gansu and western Shaanxi, to Liaoning in the north and Shandong in the east. A Zhou elite was probably surrounded by local populations, whose languages and cultures are largely unknown. Although this account will not examine these populations, in theory excavations could make it possible to illustrate the material possessions of a wide-ranging society.

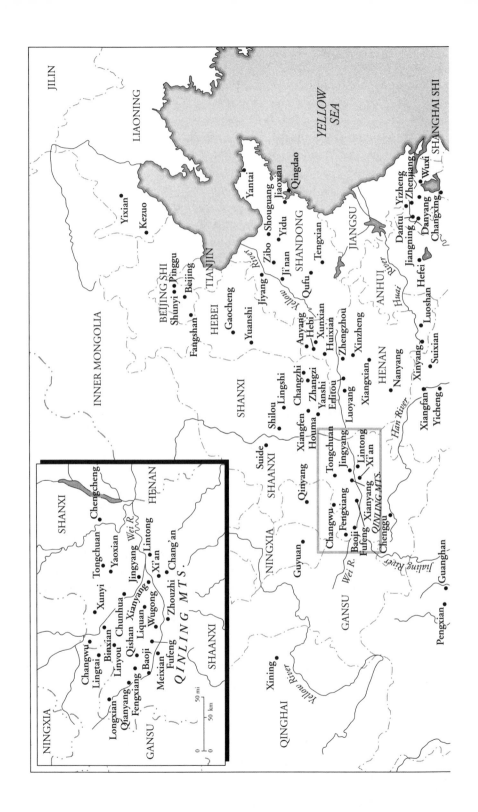

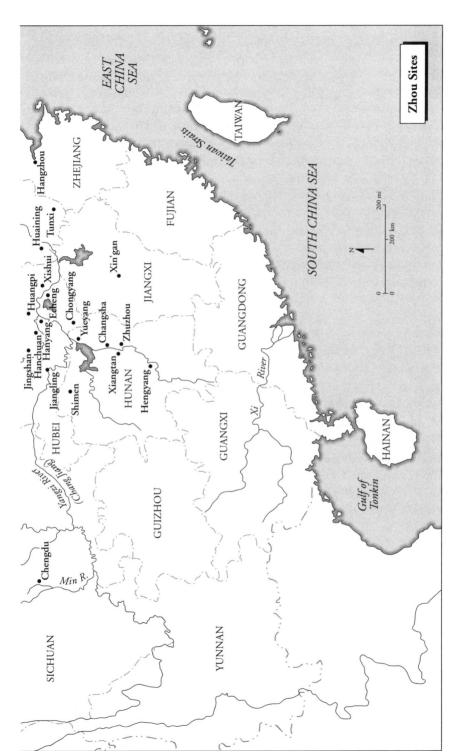

Map 6.1. Archaeological sites of the Western Zhou period.

Chinese archaeologists have in part investigated Zhou sites in order to complement the textual record. But the progress of modernization, which has spurred the construction of buildings of all types within archaeological sites, has been of equal importance. Chance finds have then stimulated sustained excavation campaigns, often lasting more than a decade, and impressive sequences of excavations have been carried on in many areas.[1] One of the major objectives has been to elucidate the origins of the Zhou. Any remaining sites that might be preconquest Zhou have been unusually thoroughly investigated. Indeed, the whole of northern Central China has received considerable attention. It is, therefore, reasonably clear that representative major Western Zhou centers have been discovered. The south, as we shall see, is a very different matter.

The capital near Xi'an, particularly Chang'an 長安 county, has been investigated over more than thirty years.[2] The Zhouyuan, where a ritual center seems to have been sited, has brought hoards to light for more than 100 years, often as chance finds (see Map 6.2). This area was also systematically investigated during the 1970s and early 1980s.[3] A third area of concentrated work has been at Baoji, where tombs of the state of Yu 強 have been found and described in detail.[4] The quantity of archaeological work throughout Shaanxi is impressive. Few buildings have come to light, but hundreds of tombs have been found at each of the major centers, such as those at Chang'an, at Fufeng, and, further west, at Fengxiang 鳳翔. Several thousand tombs have been investigated in all. A smaller number of sites has revealed hoards of bronzes, numbering in the hundreds, and chariot burials numbering in the tens. Various articles by Chinese scholars survey these finds and some of the categories of artifacts, especially ceramics, ritual vessels, and chariots.[5] The ceramics in particular have been employed to produce chronological sequences against which to measure new finds as they appear.

---

[1] Site reports will be cited in the discussion of the sites themselves later in the chapter. At this point survey articles only will be mentioned.

[2] See the section entitled "The Capitals Feng and Hao." The principal site report on the excavation of the cemetery at Fengxi still awaits publication.

[3] For summaries of hoards see Chen Quanfang, "Zao Zhou ducheng Qi yi chutan," *Wenwu* (1979).10: 47–8; Ding Yi, "Zhouyuan jianzhu yicun he tongqi jiaocang," *Kaogu* 1982.4: 398–401, 424; Luo Xizhang et al., eds., *Fufeng xian wenwuzhi* (Xi'an: Shaanxi renmin jiaoyu, 1993), pp. 57–93; Wu Zhenfeng, "Shaanxi Shang Zhou qingtongqi de chutu yu yanjiu," *Kaogu yu wenwu* 1988.5/6: 73–5, table 1.

[4] Lu Liancheng and Hu Zhisheng, *Baoji Yu guo mudi* (Beijing: Wenwu, 1988).

[5] Site reports published to date do not record all the tombs excavated. However, surveys of artifacts, especially ceramics, give some impression of the size of the venture; see Teng Mingyu, "Feng Hao diqu Xi Zhou muzang ruogan wenti," *Kaoguxue wenhua lunji* 3 (1993): 201–29, esp. p. 229, n. 34; Jiang Zudi, "Lun Feng Hao Zhou wenhua yizhi taoqi fenqi," *Kaoguxue yanjiu* 1 (1992): 256–86. For a survey of bronzes excavated in Shaanxi, see Wu Zhenfeng, "Shaanxi Shang Zhou qingtongqi de chutu yu yanjiu." For bronzes from Fufeng county, see Luo Xizhang et al., eds., *Fufeng xian wenwuzhi*, pp. 57–127; for a survey of chariot burials, see Li Zizhi, "Yin Shang liang Zhou de chema xunzang," in *Zhou wenhua lunji*, ed. Shaanxi Lishi bowuguan (Xi'an: San Qin, 1993), pp. 168–86. For a survey in English of archaeological finds up to 1986, see Jessica Rawson, *Western Zhou Ritual Bronzes from the Arthur M. Sackler*

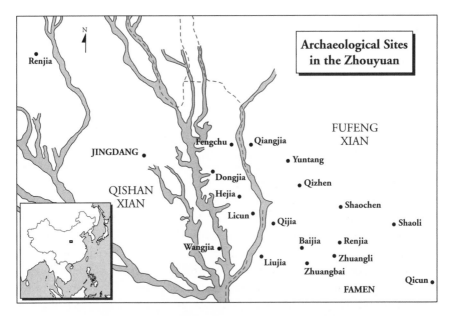

Map 6.2. Archaeological sites in the Zhouyuan.

Outside of Shaanxi, the principal areas of protracted excavation campaigns are the cemetery of the Jin state at Tianma-Qucun 天馬曲村 near Houma; the city and cemetery of the Yan state at Liulihe 琉璃河, near Fangshan to the south of Beijing; and the city and cemetery sites of Lu 魯 at Qufu 曲阜 in Shandong. Excavation has, however, been carried out throughout Shanxi, Henan, Hebei, and Shandong, and Western Zhou levels, represented primarily by ceramics, are known in many more areas than those mentioned.[6] Traces of city foundations have been found near Luoyang, Beijing, and Qufu in Shandong. Chinese archaeological excavation is comparatively well recorded in numerous reports. Moreover, fruits of surveys have informed maps of all the counties in a growing number of provinces, indicating not only where excavated but also where unexcavated sites are to be found.[7]

Southern China is much less well understood than the provinces just named, systematic survey and excavation being undertaken less frequently.

Collections (Cambridge, Mass.: Harvard University Press, 1990), vol. 1, pp. 136–43. Sites in areas outside Shaanxi will be cited in the appropriate section.

[6] For Shanxi, see *Kaoguxue yanjiu* 1 (1992): 124–228; Shanxi sheng Kaogu yanjiusuo, ed., *Shanxi kaogu sishi nian* (Taiyuan: Shanxi Renmin, 1994), pp. 115–51; for Henan, see Henan sheng Wenwu yanjiusuo, ed., *Henan kaogu sishi nian (1952–1992)* (Zhengzhou: Henan Renmin, 1994), pp. 225–76.

[7] A series of volumes of maps of archaeological sites, county by county within provinces, is under preparation. Three volumes have been published. The volume on Henan is to date the only one relevant to the present discussion; see *Zhongguo wenwu dituji: Henan fence*, ed. Guojia wenwuju (Beijing: Zhongguo ditu, 1991).

However, both Hunan and Hubei, as well as the more easterly provinces of Jiangxi, Anhui, Jiangsu, and Zhejiang, have revealed finds that will form part of the later discussion.[8] Unlike conditions of the central northern areas, it is difficult to be sure that a reasonably representative range of sites is known. Surprises are likely to turn up and these surprises may well change our view of the history of the period.

Criteria for Dating

While a large body of material that is of the approximate period under discussion exists, detailed dating is a more complex matter. Fundamental to all discussion is pottery typology, which has been studied for more than forty years and is well established for both the Shang and the Zhou periods in the main central northern provinces, especially Henan and Shaanxi. Within overall sequences, the development of three vessels is especially significant, the lobed tripod (li 鬲), the basin (gui 簋), and the jar (guan 罐). Such ceramics are useful not only for defining chronological phases of development, but also for separating subregions within the Zhou complex. Weapons, likewise, have some of this interest. At the start of the Zhou period, interactions with the peoples of the western, northern, and eastern peripheries are especially relevant, and the impact of these peoples on the centers of late Shang and early Zhou rule is evident in the sharing of particular weapon types.

While ceramics and weapons are in part interesting for their local varieties, the apparatus of elite culture is remarkable for a large degree of uniformity at any one period. The main features that will preoccupy us are the structures of cemeteries and tombs and their contents. Following the metropolitan Shang pattern, Western Zhou tombs are of the form of rectangular pits with a stepped platform, known as an *ercengtai* 二層台. Below the body was a subsidiary pit known as a waist pit (*yaokeng* 腰坑). Especially large tombs had long access ramps. In addition, tombs were arranged in family groups, aligned adjacent to one another, with chariot burials positioned near the most significant male burials.

Few buildings will be described, as few large buildings have been excavated and recorded. The most completely examined are those in the Zhouyuan and follow a tradition seen as early as the Erlitou 二里頭 period, with a walled enclosure surrounding small rooms. They, like Shang buildings, were founded on *hangtu* 夯土 (pounded-earth) platforms. *Hangtu* was also extensively used in the construction of city walls, such as those excavated at Fangshan near Beijing. As striking as the uniformity of building and burial

---

[8] For a discussion of developments in the south, which builds upon both textual and archaeological evidence, see Xu Shaohua, *Zhoudai nantu lishi dili yu wenhua* (Wuhan: Wuhan daxue, 1994).

structures across the Zhou territory is the use of standard types of ritual vessels and chariot fittings. From the conquest, and perhaps earlier, the Zhou offered sacrifices to their ancestors. Their sets of ritual bronzes are major components of the burial goods. Considerable conformity in both individual vessel types and in the components of vessel sets is visible at all periods of the Western Zhou. The conformity in chariot parts is equally striking.

Bronze weapons were essential to the management of the state, and we can imagine that the Zhou royal house and its officials were concerned with the foundries and their direction. Some remains of foundries have been recognized from remains of mold and model fragments and other casting debris. A question relevant to all aspects of casting is whether the majority of fittings, weapons, and vessels were cast at only one or two foundries under direct supervision by the Zhou royal house, or whether significant foundries worked beyond its reach. In the latter case, some system of disseminating shapes and ornaments of all categories must have been in place. By whatever means it was achieved, an extraordinary uniformity of bronze work spread across the whole of the Zhou territory throughout most of the period. As already noted, such uniformity was achieved again only in the Qin period, and then never as completely.

Similarity of elite bronze objects makes it possible to use a single line of typological development as a chronological measure. Ritual vessels belonged to well-established categories, developed by the Zhou on the basis of a series of shapes and ornamental styles available to them as already executed in Shang period casting. A very large number, probably exceeding 10,000, of Zhou period bronzes is known, both from excavations and in collections assembled over the last 500 years. Over several generations, scholars have worked on a convincing sequence of development, which stands on several types of evidence: typological and stylistic evolution; interrelated tombs of several generations of a single family, such as those of the Yu state to be discussed below; and hoards containing bronzes whose inscriptions name several different generations, as well as other inscriptional evidence, also to be discussed below.

The following general sequence of bronze vessel evolution is widely accepted.[9] As a first step, Zhou casters employed various Shang vessel types

[9] Hayashi Minao, *In Shū seidōki sōran* (Tokyo: Yoshikawa Kōbunkan, 1984–8) is a pioneering work in this area, linking epigraphic, stylistic, and archaeological work. Fundamental studies are to be found in Shirakawa Shizuka, *Kinbun tsūshaku* (Kobe: Hakutsuru bijutsukan, 1962–84); Tang Lan, *Xi Zhou qingtongqi mingwen fendai shizheng* (Beijing: Zhonghua, 1986). Rawson, *Western Zhou Bronzes in the Arthur M. Sackler Collection*, vol. 1, pp. 144–54, provides a survey in English of the principal criteria adopted by Japanese and Chinese scholars in assigning inscribed bronzes to particular periods. The catalog as a whole uses scholarship based on such inscriptions and stylistic similarities to group vessel types and designs by broad period, recognizing that such broad periods imply dating to king's reigns.

and decorative styles, including angular and flanged forms carrying *taotie* 饕
餮 designs and rounded vessels with narrow borders of what is known in the
West as triple bands.[10] During the same period, some very flamboyant
bronzes, which seem to have been essentially Zhou variations on Shang prototypes, were employed in western and central Shaanxi. As the first century
of Zhou rule advanced, the vessels became progressively more conventional.
The vessel in Figure 6.1a–b represents early Zhou versions of Shang bronze
design and belongs to the last part of the first phase, which spans the reigns
of Kings Wu (1049/45–1043 B.C.), Cheng (1042/35–1006), and Kang
(1005/03–978), and perhaps the beginning of King Zhao's (977/75–957).

During the reign of King Zhao or perhaps King Mu (956–918 B.C.) the
degree of variety declined, and flanged and angular vessels all but disappeared; the principal vessels were now smooth and rounded in form, their
decoration comprising birds or dragons, either in large panels of ornament
or confined to narrow bands (Fig. 6.1c–d). This new style clearly differs
visibly from the bronzes of the early Zhou. But the principal shapes remained
the same. The rituals practiced with them may therefore have been very
similar to those of the early Zhou. Bronzes of this type will be described as
belonging to the middle Western Zhou. A further and even more major
change took place when these vessel shapes were abandoned and new types
took their place after the reign of King Gong (917/15–900). This change
started gradually in the extreme west of Shaanxi, but in the center of Shaanxi
it seems to have taken place rather suddenly, with new shapes and motifs
ousting the previous ones. New vessel shapes imply new ways of offering food
and wine, indeed a new form of ritual, a change that might be described as
a Ritual Revolution. Methods of decoration also changed dramatically, and
almost all zoomorphic designs disappeared. In their place repetitive designs,
including ridges, horizontal grooves and ribbon bands in waves came to dominate (Fig. 6.1e–f). Bronzes of this category belong to the late Western Zhou,
namely the period from the early or middle ninth century to the fall of the
Zhou house in 771 B.C. This relatively simple account does not depend solely
on an analysis of single vessel categories or single stylistic groups.

Divisions in the three-part scheme are primarily related to typological
changes and stylistic features of bronze ritual vessels; the chronological
sequence could in theory, therefore, be stretched or compressed. However,
as we shall see, this sequence is held at certain fixed points by information

---

[10] The term "triple band" was developed to describe such bronze design by Bernhard Karlgren, "Yin and
Chou in Chinese Bronzes," *BMFEA* 8 (1936): 96. However, Karlgren did not refine the dating of stylistically interrelated pieces, which come from a wide period, ranging from Erligang, ca. 1500 B.C., to
middle Western Zhou, ca. 900 B.C.

(a)

(b)

Figure 6.1. Vessels from the
Zhuangbai hoard, Fufeng,
Shaanxi; (a)–(b): *Zhe fangyi*
vessel and inscription;

(c)

(d)

Figure 6.1. (c)–(d): *Feng zun* vessel and inscription;

(e)

(f)

Figure 6.1. (e)–(f): *Xing gui* vessel and
inscription. After *Shaanxi chutu Shang
Zhou qingtongqi*, vol. 2 (Beijing:
Wenwu, 1980), pp. 16, 18, 33.

from hoards, tombs, and inscriptions. Indeed, long inscriptions on a few bronzes have made it possible to link the vessel sequence to a skeletal historical account given in the whole corpus of inscriptions and in transmitted texts that correlate with them, and to set the sequence alongside the list of kings. The inscriptions largely validate the list of kings given in the *Shi ji* 史記 (Records of the historian). Such work thus raises the possibility of aligning evidence from archaeology and stylistic analysis with epigraphic and textual studies. Indeed the inscriptions are of exceptional interest and importance in dating the bronzes and in illuminating their role in their own day and now in the study of the Western Zhou. But while the chronological sequence of ritual bronzes in the Western Zhou is possibly more fully studied and better understood than for any other period, inevitable lacunae remain. We do not know, for example, at what period, whether before or after the conquest, the Zhou started to cast vessels, weapons, and chariot parts.

Inscriptions

Inscriptions were probably cast on the bronzes that were used in sacrifices to the ancestors in order to facilitate communication between the living and the dead. The vessels held food and wine of which the ancestors were believed to partake. These vessels were used repeatedly at the formal banquets that were held at a royal or ducal court. As a consequence those who attended these banquets would have become well familiar with the contents of the inscriptions, and the events and the people named therein would have been commemorated in the ceremonies.

Although inscriptions had been cast on Shang vessels, those on Western Zhou vessels are much more frequent and in general longer (short ones are also very common). They have several features – some internal, some external – that enable them to be dated. The external ones are references to the names of kings, which suggest that they can be linked with specific reigns, and very occasionally to events known from early Zhou texts. The internal evidence is provided by calligraphy, grammatical structure, formal contents, and the names and activities mentioned. For all periods calligraphic conventions are evident, the characters almost invariably being written with care and style. Early characters are large and in some cases almost florid, with their rows drawn tightly together, one against the other. These inscriptions are found on the varied bronzes assigned to the early Zhou in the typological and stylistic sequence just outlined (Fig. 6.1b). Inscriptions found on the smooth shaped and bird decorated bronzes are written in much smaller characters, well spaced horizontally and vertically (Fig. 6.1d). In the last period the script seems to have been reformed, with much larger characters reappearing (Fig. 6.1f). It would seem that this late script is modeled on that of the early period and was in effect a revival.

Inscribed vessels assigned to the early period on the basis of their calligraphy and references to the early kings, Wen and Wu, also mention the founding of a new city, Xin Yi 新邑, and attacks on the Shang. The few inscriptions mentioning such key events refer to other less certainly identifiable figures, such as Yan Hou 匽侯 or Tai Bao 太保 (these titles name a rank rather than a particular individual), enabling other vessels also naming such titles to be linked to them. Vessels with bird ornaments, described above as belonging to the second stage, have inscriptions in neat characters that mention southern and eastern campaigns and individuals who are linked by the inscriptions to the campaigns. These campaigns have been generally identified as belonging to the period of Kings Zhao and Mu. Dating of the vessels to this period depends as much on stylistic features, such as the calligraphy of the inscriptions and shapes and ornament of the bronzes, as on historical references. Although vessels of the late Western Zhou do not generally carry inscriptions with historical data that can be correlated with the transmitted texts, the internal consistency of such inscriptions in calligraphy, content, and shared names makes it possible to build up arguments for their dating. Epigraphical and art historical studies have acted as complementary tools in describing the development of the bronzes.[11] Although much effort has gone into establishing links between the reigns of specific kings and individual inscribed bronzes, and many of these arguments lie behind the chronological account given in the preceding chapter, this chapter will rather use the general divisions of the period mentioned above.

It may be surmised that a well-developed organization of bronze casting must have existed in the early Zhou period. The inscriptions underline this need. Whether bronzes were transported from centralized foundries, for example, at Feng, Hao, or Chengzhou, or whether foundries capable of highly sophisticated casting were located in several areas, close contact between the royal household and the owner of the bronzes is implied. For not only must the ceremony have taken place in which an honor was granted

---

[11] A number of major studies have discussed inscription contents; see especially Shirakawa, *Kinbun tsûshaku*; Guo Moruo, *Liang Zhou jinwenci daxi tulu kaoshi* (Tokyo: Bunkyôdô, 1935; 2nd rev. ed., Beijing: Kexue, 1958); Chen Mengjia, "Xi Zhou tongqi duandai" (*Kaogu xuebao* 1955.9: 137–75; 1955.10: 69–142; 1956.1: 65–114; 1956.2: 85–94; 1956.3: 105–27; and 1956.4: 85–122. In these studies, a very large number of inscribed bronzes is assigned to the reign of King Cheng. With the discovery of further groups of bronzes, both inscribed and not inscribed, these assignments have been radically revised. See especially Tang Lan, *Xi Zhou qingtongqi mingwen fendai shizheng*.

by a king to a particular noble, but there would have had to be a system for ensuring a proper record in words and a full and correct transfer of that record to the foundry for casting. Thereafter, the cast bronze would have been transmitted to the noble concerned. In both the situations suggested, trained scribes in close contact with foundries would have been essential. If all such casting was centralized, then close communication would have been necessary between the centers in Xi'an and Luoyang and the more distant cities in Yan near Beijing, or Yu near Baoji. If casting of inscribed bronzes was not centralized, then close communication between different centers would have been needed to ensure the adoption of standard language and calligraphy.[12] In either case, a formidable unity of purpose and practice seems to have linked the diverse parts of the Zhou realm in its early phases.

The inscriptions reveal some part of the political will that held this large polity together. They record events and honors that link the royal house with the Zhou elite through the offering of rewards that enhanced the status of the recipients. In their own day such inscribed bronzes were memorials of political events and social relationships essential to the structure of Zhou government and society. Thus, the bronzes articulated both by their very physical existence and in their inscriptions the ways in which these bonds were formed and commemorated.

The inscriptions often describe in narrative scenes and reported speech the occasions at which honors were conferred on subjects. Sometimes they include an account of the events that gave rise to the honors, and they often give a context in place and time, with the names of the persons present (i.e., witnesses) and the gifts made to cement the bond; they announce the new status acquired and the rituals and sacrifices that gave weight to the events. In addition, some early inscriptions recount aspects of the major political tenets of the Zhou. Inscriptions were thus ways of presenting to the Zhou themselves their own society, as well as its changes, practices, and beliefs.

Many inscriptions have been considered in the preceding chapter. Here a relatively early example, the inscription on the *Tian Wang gui* 天亡簋 in the Historical Museum in Beijing (Fig. 6.2), can serve as an example of the ways in which such inscriptions voiced current aspirations:

On the day *yihai*, the King [i.e., King Wu] held the Great Feng ceremony. The King rode in a boat on all three sides [of the moat]. The King sacrificed in the Hall of Heaven. He ordered me, Tian Wang, to assist him in the service of sacrificing the

---

[12] For various aspects of bronzes cast for or by Zhou lords, see Matsumaru Michio, "Sei Shû seidôki chû no shokô seisaku ki ni tsuite," in Matsumaru Michio, *Sei Shû seidôki to sono kokka* (Tokyo: Tokyo daigaku, 1980), pp. 137–84.

a

Figure 6.2. *Tian Wang gui* vessel and inscription. Early Western Zhou. Vessel after Li Xueqin, *Zhongguo meishu quanji, Gongyi meishu bian 4: Qingtongqi (shang)* (Beijing: Wenwu, 1985), no. 147; inscription after Ma Chengyuan, ed., *Shang Zhou qingtongqi mingwen xuan* (Beijing: Wenwu, 1988), no. 23.

b

Yi sacrifice to his glorious father, King Wen, and in the *Xi* sacrifice to the God Most High. King Wen is watching over us from above. Our glorious King [i.e., King Wu, the King who performed the sacrifice above] is his exemplar [here below]. Our majestic King is his successor. He most assuredly can continue the sacrifices of the Yi [i.e., the Yin] Kings.

On the day *dingchou* [i.e., two days later], the King entertained [with the offerings made] at the Great *Yi* ceremony. The King decreed that I, [Tian] Wang ... In order to record my good fortune, I have set forth each of the King's favors [to me] on this honored [vessel].[13]

Possibly the most striking feature of this and many other inscriptions is the immediate, dramatic form in which a concrete situation is presented.[14] It almost seems as if the texts were meant to be read aloud, repeating as a story or drama in such detail that the events and the accompanying words might be seen and heard. Possibly such a presentation, employing recorded speech and describing specific actions and places, reflected quite closely the actual ceremony in which the honor took place. Or possibly preservation of this initial record validated the honor. Even if both of these suppositions are weak, what the inscription seems to have made possible was a re-creation of the occasion and the marking of an honor.

The inscription on the *Tian Wang gui* illustrates some of the major preoccupations of the Zhou. Status, and especially a change in status, was a central concern and was kept alive by the detailed description of the conferment of an honor. Relationships between peers and between high and low are illustrated in accounts of how the king received and honored a Zhou noble and of how the noble interacted with others. The past was seen to be of intense importance as well as to reinforce and, as it would indeed, legitimate the present. Finally, all activity took place in a ritual context. The ancestors' interest was implied by the record of status and relationships and of the history of the Zhou on a bronze vessel. In addition, ceremonies and sacrifices were also recorded in the inscription, with the cumulative effect that the reader, that is, the audience, would recognize and respect the grip that the other world held over this one.

Tombs, Hoards, and Archaeological Finds as Sources of Information

The ways in which inscriptions recount some of the principal preoccupations of the Zhou suggest that it might be possible to identify similar perspectives

---

[13] W. A. C. H. Dobson, *Early Archaic Chinese: A Descriptive Grammar* (Toronto: University of Toronto Press, 1962), pp. 175–9 (romanization modified).

[14] For a theoretical discussion of self-presentation, see Erving Goffman, *The Presentation of Self in Everyday Life* (1959; rpt., Harmondsworth: Allen Lane and Penguin, 1990).

from the material remains.[15] In pursuit of a wider understanding, it seems unlikely that single objects, even the most elaborate of ritual bronzes, will be particularly helpful. Indeed, it was groups or sets of ritual vessels that were important to the practices of the society. While the distribution of any particular type of wine cup or food tripod might seem random, once we look at recurring groups of ten or even twenty vessel types, the patterns become much more informative, because they seem to be more obviously calculated.

For example, Figure 6.3 illustrates three vessel sets from times near the conquest. An early set, from what was possibly a preconquest tomb at Fengxi (83 Fengmao 灃毛 M1), comprises only two bronzes (Fig. 6.3a). The rituals practiced with that set would have been very different from those practiced with an early Zhou set from the Ge 戈 clan tombs at Gaojiabao 高家堡, Jingyang 涇陽, which comprises many more individual pieces (Fig. 6.3b). A second set from Gaojiabao (Fig. 6.3c) is visually different from the first, but contains very similar vessel types. Here the emphasis is to be placed not simply on the differences in range of shapes, or expenditure of bronze; it is just as important to note that differences of vessel sets argue for differences in practice, while similarity argues for similar or identical practice.

Ritual vessel sets did not occur in tombs without other objects. Burials were equipped with many necessities, including pottery containers for food and some fine high-fired ceramics and lacquerwares to supplement the bronzes for feasting and ritual. A male lord might be interred with a woman and her possessions, including her own ritual set for offerings to her own ancestors, as in the case of tomb 7 at Zhuyuangou 竹園溝, Baoji, a tomb of the westerly Yu state (Figs. 6.4, 6.5).[16] In such cases, vessel sets might be of completely different ranges, that of the man being much larger and allowing therefore a more complex ritual than that of the woman. Both man and woman had antiquities among their bronzes, presumably inherited from earlier members of their families. Such antiquities often carry inscriptions, naming different owners or ancestors. Sometimes these owners were of markedly different families. Thus, the Yu state tombs include vessels formerly belonging to the Ge family, apparently acquired by gift, marriage, looting, or conquest.

The structure of tombs recurs: they generally have an *ercengtai* and *yaokeng*. Both features were borrowed from the Shang. So too was the practice of burying whole chariots. Thus, not only is the individual vessel embed-

---

[15] For a discussion of the information provided by objects both to their original users and to posterity, see Jessica Rawson, "Ancient Chinese Ritual as Seen in the Material Record," in *Court and State Ritual in China*, ed. Joseph McDermott (Cambridge University Press, forthcoming).
[16] Lu Liancheng and Hu Zhisheng, *Baoji Yu guo mudi*, vol. 1, pp. 92–128.

(a)

(b)

(c)

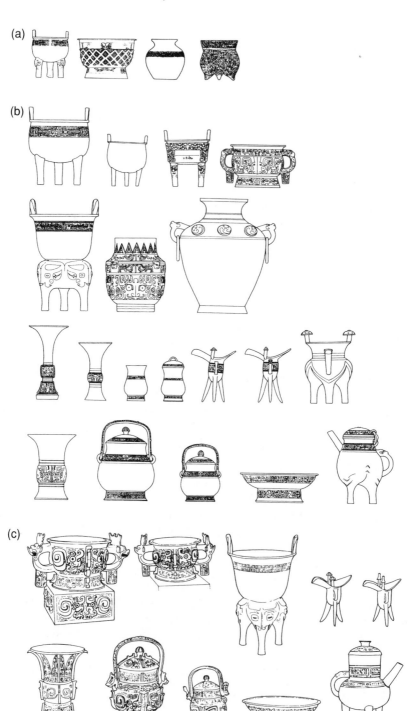

Figure 6.3, on opposite page. Comparison of vessels from 83 Fengmao M1, Fengxi, Chang'an, Shaanxi, and from M4 and M1, Gaojiabao, Jingyang, Shaanxi; (a) (top row): bronze *ding* and *gui* with ceramic *li* and *guan* from Fengmao (after *Kaogu* 1984.9: 782, figs. 8, 10.2, 10.4); (b) (second through fifth rows): vessels from M4, Gaojiabao (after *Gaojiabao Ge guo mu* [Xi'an: San Qin, 1995], pp. 70–102); (c) (bottom two rows): vessels from M1, Gaojiabao (after *Shaanxi chutu Shang Zhou qingtongqi*, vol. 4 [Beijing: Wenwu, 1984], nos. 136–45). Drawing by Ann Searight.

---

ded within a specific set, but also the vessel set is embedded in a complex of groups of objects, each relating to different functions, and all assembled in tombs.

The rich tomb contents suggest that the Zhou believed that such pieces would have a use in a future life. But although the objects obviously relate very closely to the lives of the owners, it is unlikely that they represent the full range of their worldly possessions. These objects are likely to have been the essentials to provide for the ideal needs of the dead. They give us an idealized picture of their lives and may represent as much their hopes as a realistic picture of actual practice. In using these objects to look at the past we must be conscious of the reasons why they were buried, and read therein not a simple factual account of daily life but, what is of greater importance, an idealized account of life, ritual, status, relationships, and history. Indeed, the ideal plan and ideal contents of a tomb tell us about the ideology of the society. As Barry Kemp has suggested with respect to village plans of ancient Egypt, they are

testimony of one particular facet of the creative element in society: its capacity to structure its own environment and beyond this to create visions of how human society should look. . . . If . . . we admit that the evidence in a particular case points to a clear and consistent underlying human ideal, we are tacitly admitting to the existence of an ideology. Not necessarily a formally conceived and expressed ideology such as that which portrayed Egyptian kingship, but an implicit ideology of social ordering.[17]

While tombs were put together at particular moments in time, hoards are very different. These hoards comprise vessels and bells assembled over centuries and owned by elite families at the moment when they had to flee Shaanxi in 771 B.C. They seem to have consisted of the principal bronzes employed in the late Western Zhou and various heirlooms from previous generations. Many of these bronzes in hoards are inscribed, and these inscriptions have been described in Chapter 5. The largest number of hoards have come from the area of the Zhouyuan to the west of Xi'an, but others have

---

[17] Barry J. Kemp, *Ancient Egypt: Anatomy of a Civilization* (London: Routledge, 1989), pp. 137–8.

Figure 6.4. Drawing of tomb plan from tomb M7, Zhuyuangou, Baoji, Shaanxi. Early
Western Zhou. After Lu Liancheng and Hu Zhisheng, *Baoji Yu guo mudi* (Beijing: Wenwu,
1988), vol. 1, fig. 73.

Figure 6.5. Principal vessels from tomb M7, Zhuyuangou, Baoji, Shaanxi. Early Western Zhou. After Lu Liancheng and Hu Zhisheng, *Baoji Yu guo mudi* (Beijing: Wenwu, 1988), vol. 1, figs. 77–9, 80, 82, 84. Drawing by Ann Searight.

been found near Xi'an or in other parts of Shaanxi.[18] Very few have come from anywhere outside Shaanxi. It seems that, fleeing before the invaders, the Zhou buried their bronzes near their ancestral temples. Such bronzes were carefully placed in pits, often with one bronze inside another.

[18] Wu Zhenfeng, "Shaanxi Shang Zhou qingtongqi de chutu yu yanjiu."

The most illuminating hoard found in recent years comprised 103 vessels and bells from Zhuangbai 莊白, Fufeng county, Shaanxi, in the Zhouyuan.[19] Four large flasks (*hu* 壺) in the hoard stood at the corners of the pit, and other bronzes were carefully placed in three layers, one above the other (Fig. 6.6). The bells were laid in rows, small ones fitting inside larger ones. The vessels are interesting both for specific information in a long inscription on one of them, the *Shi Qiang pan* 史墙盤, and for the interrelationships between members of the family and their bronzes disclosed by the inscriptions on the other bronzes.[20]

Vessels belonging to a man named Zhe 折 are among the earliest bronzes in the hoard. The Zhe bronzes comprise three vessels with angular shapes, hooked flanges, and full *taotie* motifs (Fig. 6.1a). A *jia* 斝 belonging to Zhe had, by contrast, a smooth rounded form and a narrow band of ornament. These pieces are characteristic of the first bronze-casting stage outlined earlier. Bronzes belonging to the next generation, those of a man named Feng 豐, were made at the time when bronzes had smooth rounded shapes and carried decoration of plumed birds (Fig. 6.1c), designated here as the first part of middle Western Zhou. The *Shi Qiang pan* itself is a later version of such bird-decorated bronzes. Its long inscription names the Western Zhou kings up to and including King Mu, and such evidence is used to date the *pan* to the reign of King Gong or later. After this stage, vessel shapes and decoration changed yet more dramatically. A new type of vessel belonged to one Wei Bo Xing 微伯瘋 (Fig. 6.1e). Although the date of this man is not certain, he probably lived one generation after Shi Qiang. This type of bronze defines, as set out above, late Western Zhou bronzes and their decoration, and dates from the time of the Ritual Revolution that will be discussed later.

When the family fled, the bronzes belonging to Wei Bo Xing were probably still in use (although they may have been made a considerable time before). These bronzes, which included a set of basins on square stands and large wine flasks and bells, was kept, it would appear, with bronzes of earlier generations. They were buried together and had probably stood together on an altar or in a treasury. The inscriptions on these bronzes concern the status of the family and record its honors and relationships. Together the assembled inscriptions form an archive. The forms and decorations of the bronzes themselves, representing different fashions and interests, are a record of the

---

[19] There is an extensive literature on the discovery and dating of this hoard; see especially Yin Shengping, ed., *Xi Zhou Wei shi jiazu qingtongqi qun yanjiu* (Beijing: Wenwu, 1992). This edited volume includes papers also listed by Edward L. Shaughnessy, *Sources of Western Zhou History: Inscribed Bronze Vessels* (Berkeley: University of California Press, 1991), pp. 1–4, nn. 1–2, pp. 183–92, where an annotated translation of the inscription on the *Shi Qiang pan* 史墙盤 is given.

[20] Discussed in Rawson, *Western Zhou Ritual Bronzes from the Arthur M. Sackler Collections*, vol. 1, pp. 19–21.

passing of the generations, as much as the inscriptions are records of family members' ranks, deeds, and connections with the king, other nobles, and officials. If they were used together at one time, the vessels and their inscriptions would have constituted both a visual and a verbal record. If they were not used, but simply retained on an altar temple, they would have still embodied the long history of the family.

Contents of both tombs and hoards illustrate the interests already observed in the inscriptions. Ritual life was of overwhelming importance; rites and sacrifices are recorded in inscriptions, and the ritual bronzes are the objects preserved above all others for their owners and posterity, in tombs or on altars and in hoards. The ancestors were, it would appear, an all-embracing force, and all action was taken with them in mind. Among those aspects of life with which they were deemed concerned were status and the standing of their descendants. Thus, the inscriptions report changes in status, and the tombs and hoards record status in several different ways, such as the multitude, types, or antiquity of possessions. This interest in the past is seen in the hoarding of bronzes, in the preservation of records of earlier generations, and in the burying of ancient objects in tombs. In all these activities the past gave weight to the present. In addition these objects, whether bronzes that record the achievements of their owners in the past or those that belonged to different families, indicate a network of family and other relationships that made the Zhou a strong and tightly knit society, a series of bonds that perhaps allowed unity of practice and belief, ranging from Yu in the west to Yan in the northeast.

In sum, the Zhou interest in highly articulated presentations of their worldview is apparent from inscriptions and the contents of tombs and hoards. These reveal a concern with ancestors, status, relationships with others, and the legitimating force of the past. As will be seen, the archaeological record shows the impact of parallel processes over the whole of the Western Zhou period.

PRE-CONQUEST SHAANXI PROVINCE AND THE ZHOU CONQUEST

Pre-Conquest Shaanxi

The origins of the Zhou are a mystery. At present, archaeological evidence has yet to establish the place of origin of this formidable people, who dominated northern central China for nearly 300 years. The post-conquest impact of their rule in the material record and in the texts, especially the bronze inscriptions, is so impressive that it is hard not to believe that equally impres-

Figure 6.6. The Zhuangbai hoard, Fufeng, Shaanxi; (a) (top row): the Zhe vessels; (b) (second row): the Feng vessels; (c) (third row): the Shi Qiang vessels; (d–i) (fourth through ninth rows): the Xing vessels. After *Shaanxi chutu Shang Zhou qingtongqi*, vol. 2 (Beijing: Wenwu, 1980), nos. 14–24, 27–74. Drawing by Ann Searight.

sive remains must survive from the period before the conquest. But to date such remains have been elusive. Use of bronze was not well developed in Shaanxi province as a whole before the conquest, although, as we shall see, pockets of bronze-using peoples go back to at least Erligang 二里崗 times. From about the time of the conquest, which may be dated at ca. 1045 B.C., the Zhou appear in Shaanxi using bronzes in the form of ritual vessel sets, weapons, and chariot fittings.

Archaeologists turned first to Shaanxi in their search for the Zhou ancestors because poems in the *Shi jing* mention Qishan.[21] Spectacular Western Zhou bronzes found in the Zhouyuan have reinforced the assumption that this was the homeland of a powerful bronze-using people contemporary with the Shang. Shang period bronzes, which might have been used by the Zhou, have indeed been found at Qishan. Among the many Zhou tombs from

[21] *Mao shi Zheng jian*, 16 (20 ("Mian"), 16a (Arthur Waley, *The Book of Songs: The Ancient Chinese Classic of Poetry* [London: Allen & Unwin, 1937]), p. 248).

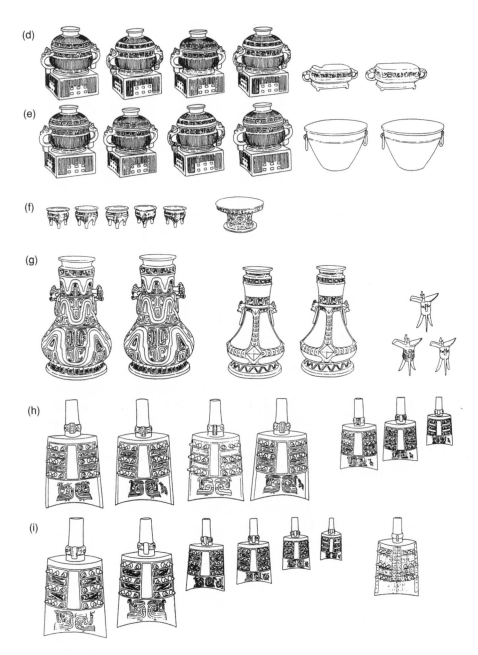

Figure 6.6. *(cont.)*

Qishan are some that include objects identified as pre-conquest ceramics. In addition, remains of a tomb containing a number of varied bronze pieces is possibly of the pre-conquest period. The contents comprise a motley group of standard Anyang types, local Shaanxi bronzes, and exotica from the south: a fitting decorated with a human face and a wine vessel carrying finely cast birds in three dimensions. As suggested in Chapter 3, such finds show that the inhabitants of Shaanxi, whether they were the pre-conquest Zhou or not, had a wide range of geographical contacts; as will be seen, such contacts were maintained in Shaanxi after the conquest.[22]

In the search for full arrays of Shang ritual vessels in Shaanxi, a site at Lao-niupo 老牛坡 near Xi'an was excavated and described in reports in the 1980s. During the principal archaeological campaigns by North Western University (Xibei daxue) at Xi'an in 1986, forty-five tombs and a chariot burial were uncovered. The majority of tombs are typically Shang in form; most of them have a *yaokeng* and an *ercengtai*. The *yaokeng* in particular is a feature of Shang tombs not generally found in other pre-conquest burials in Shaanxi. Because the shapes of the tombs and their contents of bronzes and ceramic wares are typical of Anyang, the archaeologists identified these tombs as being of individuals who belonged to some sort of Shang outpost and not to the Zhou or their ancestors.[23] The date of the site is relatively early, with the objects belonging to Yinxu 殷墟 1 and Yinxu 2. Indeed many of the Shang finds in Shaanxi date to this stage.[24] But according to the terms whereby Zhou has been defined above, and in the light of developments subsequent to the conquest, it is particularly noteworthy that adjacent peoples inhabiting Shaanxi did not adopt wholesale the ritual practices of the Shang, even though it would seem that peoples practicing Shang-type rituals were quite close.[25] This situation seems to indicate some sort of discontinuity between the situations in Shaanxi before and after the conquest.

A search for the antecedents of the Zhou has taken place over the last twenty years, in the course of extensive investigations in Shaanxi. Most of the recent work has concentrated on sites at which ceramics have been identified that just predate the conquest. What has emerged is a description of a mosaic of cultural groups using a variety of tripods and jars. Before describ-

[22] *Kaogu* 1976.1: 31–48, fig. 2, pl. 1:3–6; pl. 2:2–3; pl. 3:2; see Chapter 3, the present volume; for an early tomb at Qishan, see Xu Xitai, "Qishan Hejiacun Zhou mu fajue jianbao," *Kaogu yu wenwu* 1980.1: 7–12.

[23] For excavations at Laoniupo, see *Wenwu* 1988.6: 1–22; Bao Quan, "Xi'an Laoniupo chutu Shang dai zaoqi wenwu," *Kaogu yu wenwu* 1981.2: 17–18. See also finds from Weinan 渭南; Zuo Zhongcheng, "Weinan shi you chu yipi Shangdai qingtongqi," *Kaogu yu wenwu* 1987.4: 111.

[24] A recent reassessment of Shang-type remains in Shaanxi is given in Sun Hua, "Guanzhong Shangdai zhu yizhi de xin renzhi: Yijiabao yizhi fajue de yiyi," *Kaogu* 1993.5: 426–43. See, too, p. 181 above.

[25] Xu Tianjin, "Shilun guanzhong diqu de Shang wenhua," in *Jinian Beijing daxue kaogu zhuanye sanshi zhounian lunwenji (1952–1982)*, ed. Beijing daxue kaoguxi (Beijing: Wenwu, 1990), pp. 211–42.

ing the different pottery types in any detail, it is necessary to reflect upon what a discussion based upon pottery types can be expected to reveal. The particular vessels concerned are the cooking pot with three lobes, known in later writing as a *li*, and a jar or container, known as a *guan*.

Ceramic cooking pots and ritual bronzes occupy rather different places in the hierarchy of possessions. In particular, because ceramic clay is relatively easy to find and the kiln need be no more than a small stove, ceramic cooking pots can be made almost anywhere by almost anyone. Thus, regional variety is relatively common. Shaanxi shows just such regional variety before the conquest, but much greater homogeneity after it. Such an observation suggests that before the conquest Shaanxi was inhabited by a number of loosely related groups of people, who had their own slightly different skills and customs.

The two cooking pot types just mentioned are found in most areas in a variety of forms. The relative paucity of bronzes west of the Xi'an area seems to indicate that the inhabitants there had not yet reached the level of economic prosperity or complex organization achieved by the Shang. The existence of some bronzes in the area indicates that some high-ranking individuals had access either to bronzes from elsewhere or to products of small-scale local foundries.[26] That the ritual vessels were not more widely employed may perhaps suggest that the peoples of the area did not at this date aspire to the customs of the Shang. Thus, the groups that archaeologists have identified were very different in manner and attitude from their successors, the Zhou.[27] This difference may have been of an economic nature; it was also one of ideology.

The predecessors of the Zhou in Shaanxi may be defined here in terms of the ceramic *li* that they produced, and that may be broadly divided into two main types: those with separate gourd-shaped lobes joined to a high neck (*fendang li* 分襠鬲) and the type in which the separation of the lobes is less pronounced (*liandang li* 聯襠鬲; Fig. 6.7).[28] Chinese archaeologists hold three different views regarding these *li*. The first is that the *li* type with joined

---

[26] A number of discussions of the preconquest culture of Shaanxi illustrate Shang-type bronzes found with the ceramic types discussed in this section; see especially Xu Xitai, "Zao Zhou wenhua de tezheng ji qi yuanyuan de zai tansuo: Jian lun Wen Wu shiqi qingtongqi de tezheng," in *Kaoguxue yanjiu* ed. Shi Xingbang et al. (Xi'an: San Qin, 1993), pp. 280–320. See also Gao Xisheng, "Shaanxi Fufeng xian Yijiabao Shangdai yizhi de diaocha," *Kaogu yu wenwu* 1989.5: 5–8.

[27] Contrast the use of the handleless *gui* decorated with diamond and bosses (as seen in Figure 6.3a and discussed by Robert W. Bagley, *Shang Ritual Bronzes in the Arthur M. Sackler Collections* [Cambridge, Mass.: Harvard University Press, 1987], pp. 505–7, and found at Fengxiang; see Cao Mingtan and Shang Zhiru. "Shaanxi Fengxiang chutu de Xi Zhou qingtongqi," *Kaogu yu wenwu* 1984.1: 53–65, fig. 18:2–4) and the later standard *gui* with handles as in Figure 6.1e. See also bronzes from Chunhua 淳化; Yao Shengmin, "Shaanxi Chunhua xian chutu de Shang Zhou qingtongqi," *Kaogu yu wenwu* 1986.5: 12–22.

[28] For a definition of the two different *li* types, see Li Feng, "Xian Zhou wenhua de neihan ji qi yuanyuan tantao," *Kaogu xuebao* 1991.3: 265–84, esp. p. 270, fig. 1.

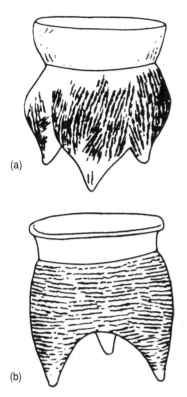

(a)

(b)

Figure 6.7. Comparison of a *li* with divided lobes (a) (*fendang li*) with one with joined lobes (b) (*liandang li*), both from Hejiacun, Fufeng, Shaanxi. After Hu Qianying, "Lun Nianzipo yu Qi yi Feng yi Xian Zhou wenhua yizhi muzang de niandai fenqi," in *Kaoguxue yanjiu: Jinian Shaanxi sheng Kaogu yanjiusuo chengli sanshi zhounian,* ed. Shi Xingbang et al. (Xi'an: San Qin, 1993), p. 348, fig. 19.

lobes, the *liandang li*, represents the pre-conquest Zhou culture. This type of *li* is found in its early stages at Nianzipo 碾子坡 and in its later stages at Zhengjiapo 鄭家坡. This *li* type occurs in the Zhouyuan and also as far east as Zhangjiapo 張家坡; on these grounds, such sites are often taken as representing the major ancestral culture of the Zhou. Indeed, after the conquest, this *li* type became universal in Shaanxi.

The second, opposing, view is to regard the occupants of sites that have yielded *li* whose lobes are firmly subdivided as the ancestors of the Zhou. Such *li* were first identified in the extreme west at Doujitai 斗雞台 (Baoji) by Su Bingqi in the 1930s. Other sites in that area have produced *li* of both this type and others. Such *li* are deemed to belong to the cultures known as Chaoyu 晁峪 and Shizuitou 石嘴頭. According to a third view, such sites belonged not to the Zhou but to the Jiang 姜, who are said to have intermarried with the Zhou.

However, the divided-lobed *li* is most abundantly found in the so-called

Liujia 劉家 culture, named after a site in the Zhouyuan, and this culture is not easily related to the pre-conquest Zhou. The burial of a mass of pottery in the Liujia tombs is at variance with the practice of burial at other sites, including early Western Zhou tombs; thus, the Liujia practices show no continuity with the later identifiable Zhou burial customs. Further, water-washed stones are used in some number in these tombs, and the tombs are constructed as hollow cave tombs (that is with the corpse and burial goods in a hollow excavated to one side of the main pit). In these two features also, they thus differ from the vertical shaft tombs adopted as the main form for Western Zhou burials.[29]

The antecedents of these different pottery types in the ceramics of Neolithic cultures in western Shaanxi and Gansu have been considered by archaeologists in order to seek the geographic origins of the peoples who made the vessel categories found in Shaanxi. However, although some clear typological links have been suggested, the findings do not resolve the question of the origins of the Zhou.[30]

The variety of views and uncertainty about date and sequence suggest that the investigations are far from conclusive. It seems unlikely on present evidence that the peoples who overthrew the Shang did so entirely on the basis of the resources hitherto revealed in Shaanxi. None of the sites just named has produced more than an occasional bronze ritual vessel or some bronze weapons. There are several quite separate problems or issues embedded in this examination of sites in Shaanxi. The first question is whether it is possible to use these distinctions between ceramic types to identify a people who in recorded history are described as defeating the Shang. Second, is it possible to go on to say that these ceramic types define peoples who were the ancestors of those who are seen in the archaeological record to set up substantial settlements in Shaanxi and to bury their dead in Shang style with numerous bronze ritual vessels, weapons, and chariot burials? If one of these

---

[29] There is a considerable body of discussion on the varieties of peoples and their artifacts in Shaanxi before the conquest. See, especially, Li Feng, "Xian Zhou wenhua de neihan ji qi yuanyuan tantao"; Zhang Changshou and Liang Xingpeng, "Guanzhong Xian Zhou qingtongqi wenhua de leixing yu Zhou wenhua de yuanyuan," *Kaogu xuebao* 1989.1: 1–23; see also collected articles in Shaanxi Lishi bowuguan, ed., *Zhou wenhua lunji* (Xi'an: San Qin, 1993), pp. 1–83; Iijima Taketsugu, "Xian Zhou wenhua taoqi yanjiu," *Kaoguxue yanjiu* 1 (1992): 229–55. See also Hu Qianying, "Lun Nianzipo yu Qi yi Feng yi Xian Zhou wenhua yizhi (muzang) de niandai fenqi," in *Kaoguxue yanjiu: Jinian Shaanxi sheng Kaogu yanjiusuo chengli sanshi zhounian*, ed. Shi Xingbang et al. (Xi'an: San Qin, 1993), pp. 332–55; Hu Qianying, "Tai Wang yiqian de Zhoushi guankui," *Kaogu yu wenwu* 1987.1: 70–81; Liu Qiyi, "Wen Wang qian Feng Wu Wang mie Shang qianhou tongqi lizheng," in Shi Xingbang et al. eds., *Kaoguxue yanjiu* (Xi'an: San Qin, 1993), pp. 376–97, 218.

[30] Qin Xiaoli, "Shilun Kexingzhuang wenhua de fenqi," *Kaogu* 1995.3: 238–55; Lu Liancheng, "Xian Zhou wenhua yu zhoubian diqu de qingtong wenhua," in *Kaoguxue yanjiu*, ed. Shi Xingbang et al. (Xi'an: San Qin, 1993), pp. 243–79. See also Li Feng, "Xian Zhou wenhua de neihan ji qi yuanyuan tantao."

groups embarked on the conquest of the Shang and, moreover, having defeated the Shang, adopted many aspects of their ritual and burial practices, it may be asked why they apparently showed no inclination to do so earlier.

It is more likely that the forces who defeated the Shang comprised a variety of groups, local and from afar, who banded together to overthrow the Shang. They may or may not have been led by peoples who were living at Qishan, calling themselves the Zhou, as the later poetry suggests. The peoples who then settled in Shaanxi and developed a highly elaborate Shang-type culture, may or may not have been coextensive with the groups who defeated the Shang. They may have been only one component of that force, and one that may or may not have embarked on the conquest from Shaanxi. In the light of these questions, the bronze-using peoples in adjacent areas are probably of some interest.

Adjacent Areas

One obvious possible location of the pre-conquest Zhou could be among the bronze-using peoples in areas adjacent to Shaanxi. For example, concurrently with Shang occupation of Anyang, small groups lived in other parts of northern central China employing ritual bronzes in some of the Shang ways: that is to say, offering meals in a relatively large number of bronze food containers and wine cups – rather than just in one or two, – and burying them in tombs. Sites such as Laoniupo near Xi'an, as well as Jingjiecun 旌介村 at Lingshi 靈石 in Shanxi, Sufutun 蘇埠屯 at Yidu 益都 in Shandong, and Mangzhang 蟒張 at Luoshan 羅山 near Xinyang 信陽 in southern Henan are just such areas.[31] Many of the vessels from these sites carry single graphs that may be names of the families or groups who lived in these regions. Although some of these sites seem to span the Shang–Zhou transition, especially the cemeteries at Sufutun and Mangzhang, none of them seems, on present evidence, to have been established by the Zhou themselves.

There are no traces of a large-scale bronze-using power in other adjacent areas, such as Gansu or Shanxi. In central and southern Shanxi, on the Fen River, few remains have been found, or at least reported. Tombs at Jingjiecun have *yaokeng*, and their contents derive from those of the Shang at Anyang.[32] Ritual vessels in the *gu* 觚 and *jue* 爵 shapes suggest that Shang-style rituals had been practiced. Although they also used vessels of types that were later

[31] *Wenwu* 1988.6: 1–22; *Wenwu* 1986.11: 1–18; *Wenwu* 1972.8: 17–30; see also Chapter 3, this volume; *Kaogu* 1981.2: 111–18; *Kaogu xuebao* 1986.2: 153–97.

[32] *Wenwu* 1986.11: 1–18; for a continuation at Hongtong (to the south of Lingshi, but still on the Fen River) into the post-conquest period, see *Wenwu* 1987.2: 1–16; see also a survey of late Neolithic finds that predate the founding of the Jin state; Zhang Wenjun and Gao Qingshan, "Jin xinan san xian shi guwenhua yizhi diaocha," *Kaogu yu wenwu* 1987.4: 3–18.

found in Shaanxi, and the tomb contents come quite close to those employed at tomb M4, Gaojiabao, Jingyang, various other details emphasize the local character of this find. In the first place the tomb contains northern weapon types that are not characteristic of the principal dynastic Zhou tombs. Second, bronzes inscribed with the symbol ⊓ suggest that these tombs belonged to a particular clan. In the past, individual, isolated examples of vessels carrying this inscription have been found in a number of different provinces. This find is thought to locate the clan in this area. It is possible that this group joined with the Zhou in their attacks on the Shang.

There remain two possible solutions to the conundrum as to who the Zhou were and how they conquered the Shang. One is that somewhere in the area ranging from Gansu or Sichuan in the west to Henan and Hebei in the east and the north, the remains of a pre-conquest Zhou capital are to be found, which would reveal a people with bronze armory, bronze-decorated chariots, and bronze ritual vessels equivalent to those of the Shang, and who might at the same time be the predecessors of the peoples whose culture was established in Shaanxi after the conquest. If this culture was highly unusual and different from anything we have seen before, there follows the next question: Why did the Zhou abandon it in favor of a style of weaponry, chariots, and, above all, ritual vessels and inscriptions of Shang type? It is rather surprising that their post-conquest bronzes do not show more of an amalgam of Shang and non-Shang traits. The only area where there is such an amalgam is in the extreme west near Baoji and continuing into Sichuan. It may be asked whether this western amalgam indicates the shadowy presence of a lost Zhou bronze-using culture. Alternatively, it may be asked whether this local amalgam suggests a quite different attribute of the Zhou, the ability to draw together peoples of differing cultures in a broad spectrum of alliance.

A second possibility is that a previously materially insignificant people, known as the Zhou, drew together a mass of loosely connected clans and tribes across the whole of northwestern Shaanxi and Shanxi, as well as possibly further east, and exploited all available resources, even including defectors from the Shang, in the contest for control. Some of the peoples in Shaanxi, such as those that occupied Chunhua 淳化, obviously owned weapons and chariots. While they are unlikely to have been the sole ancestors of the Zhou, they might have contributed to their military strength.[33]

Archaeological evidence from around the time of the conquest and afterwards, in the form of shared weapon types and ritual vessels, indicates that

---

[33] Yao Shengmin, "Shaanxi Chunhua xian chutu de Shang Zhou qingtongqi," pp. 12–22. This site contained many weapons of the type found in the Northern Zone and a few chariot fittings.

a string of peoples were in touch with one another from Gansu and western Shaanxi in the west as far as Beijing and Liaoning in the east. There seems to have been a long-standing link across the whole western area ranging from Sichuan through western Shaanxi to Inner Mongolia, Shanxi, Hebei, and Liaoning from at least the late Neolithic period. Certain pottery and burial types occur along this line that are not typical of the central northern Chinese culture.[34] Shared weapon types in particular indicate continuing contacts in the late Shang period, suggesting that this line of communication was continually reinforced. Moreover, ritual vessels found in this area show these peripheral peoples to have had contacts with the Zhongyuan. Along the Yellow River, dividing northern Shaanxi from northern Shanxi, there have been found a number of sites that display ritual vessels.[35] But this is an area with unusual versions of relatively early Shang bronzes, employed concurrently with non-Shang weapon types and gold ornaments, alien to the Shang. Peoples who used short, often curved knives and axes with tubular hafts were clearly bound into this network. In the early Zhou period, such weapons, with features also typical of Inner Mongolia, Mongolia, and South Siberia, emerge in tombs as far apart as Gansu and Beijing, combined with bronze ritual vessels and chariot parts, both typical of metropolitan Zhou centers. These weapon types later also penetrated Henan.[36] In addition, the military character of early Zhou rule and rituals, with an emphasis on archery and chariots, suggests that the Zhou origins lay in the northwest rather than in Central China. Thus, although the ways in which the Zhou drew on other peoples around the time of the conquest is not clear, there are signs that these peripheral peoples were in touch with one another and with the Zhou, especially from the time of the conquest.

Despite evidence of alien features in parts of the Zhou world, once the Zhou were in power they demonstrated an unusual facility for borrowing many aspects of Shang culture, while at the same time articulating concerns with their position or status; they were much dedicated to using the past as a means to legitimate the present, and they were concerned with relation-

[34] Tong Enzheng, "Shi lun wo guo cong dongbei zhi xinan de biandi banyuexing wenhua zhuanbodai," in Wenwu chubanshe bianjibu ed., *Wenwu chubanshe chengli sanshi zhounian jinian: Wenwu yu kaogu lunji* (Beijing: Wenwu, 1986), pp. 17–43.

[35] See Chapter 3, this volume; Lu Zhirong, "Shilun Shaan-Jin beibu Huang he liang'yan diqu chutu de Shangdai qingtongqi ji youguan wenti," in *Zhongguo kaoguxue yanjiu lunji: Jinian Xia Nai xiansheng kaogu wushi zhounian* (Xi'an: San Qin, 1987), pp. 214–25; Dai Yingxin, "Shaanbei he Jin xibei Huang he liang'an chutu de Yin Shang tongqi ji youguan wenti de tansuo," in *Kaoguxue yanjiu: Jinian Shaanxi sheng Kaogu yanjiusuo chengli sanshi zhounian*, ed. Shi Xingbang et al. (Xi'an: San Qin, 1993), pp. 219–35.

[36] Lu Liancheng, "Xian Zhou wenhua yu zhoubian diqu de qingtongqi wenhua," pp. 272–4, fig. 11. See also Jessica Rawson, "Statesmen or Barbarians? The Western Zhou as Seen Through Their Bronzes," *Proceedings of the British Academy* 75 (1989): 71–95.

ships and contracts. Perhaps these three interests expressed essential aspects of their political strengths: an ability to muster power and to express it in material form, a mission to assume control by adopting the attributes of their predecessors, and an ability to exploit some of the peoples around them for support.

The Conquest

Evidence of the conquest appears in material form in Shaanxi, somewhat dramatically, in a great increase in the use of bronze, especially for items other than weaponry; in the burial of bronzes of all sorts in tombs; in the appearance of types of ritual vessel that were new to the area and the use of a large number of bronzes by individuals; in burials of antiquities, that is, inherited vessels among these bronzes; and in the use of inscriptions, both long and short, on vessels. The geographic extent of the change is also dramatic. As we shall see, the Zhou elite seem to have spread out across the whole width of the present-day province, on either side of the Wei River. High-quality bronze ritual vessels have come to light from Baoji in the west to Xianyang 咸陽 in the east. If Shaanxi before the conquest is remarkable for the paucity of burial goods that measure up to those of the Shang, the post-conquest period displays abundant remains.

Numerous bronze vessels and substantial buildings and tombs suggest a sudden increase in wealth, the result of an influx of a new people or the enrichment of the existing ones. The direction of the change is also significant, as it made both the ritual bronzes and the tombs of the Shaanxi area much more like those of the Shang than like those of the predynastic inhabitants of Shaanxi. The Zhou had evidently acquired skilled labor and the patterns of vessel shapes for the craftsmen to copy and develop. They had also acquired abundant material resources, enabling them to make a large number of ritual vessels, in addition to the weaponry that they required. They were also rich enough to bury the bronzes in tombs.

Changes in bronzes and ceramics buried in tombs seem to have taken place at the time of the conquest. Burials equipped with basins that were decorated with pointed bosses are among those generally assigned to the pre-conquest period. Tomb 83 SCM1 at Kexingzhuang in Fengxi near Xi'an contained typical pre-conquest bronze weapons and ceramics.[37] The weapons in

---

[37] *Kaogu* 1984.9: 779–83. Liu Qiyi dates this tomb to the preconquest period with reference to pits found at Fengxi, Chang'an; see Liu Qiyi, "Wen Wang qian zhi Feng Wu Wang mie Shang qianhou tongqi lizheng," p. 377, referring to *Kaogu* 1959.11: 588–91; Liang Xingpeng and Feng Xiaotang, "Shaanxi Chang'an Fufeng chutu Xi Zhou tongqi," *Kaogu* 1963.8: 413–15.

this tomb, halberd blades with openwork tangs in the shapes of birds, can be compared with weapons in late Anyang tombs and support a pre-conquest date for the Fengxi burial.[38] Slightly later in date is 83 Fengmao 灃毛 M1, a tomb in the same area that contained typical bronze *gui* and *ding* 鼎, borrowed from Shang-style bronze design (Fig. 6.3a). From soon after the conquest, tombs held full complements of ritual vessels (Fig. 6.3b).[39] Tomb M4 at Gaojiabao contained seventeen conventional vessels of types that can be paralleled throughout Shaanxi; in addition they come close in shape and decoration to bronzes of the Shang. Between the dates of the two tombs, that is, at some point in the eleventh century, some momentous change had taken place. In the material record the conquest is plain.

Gaojiabao also shows the rapid development of ritual bronzes for use in sets. Tomb M1 may have held the body of the son of the deceased in M4, both being members of the Ge clan (Fig. 6.3c). The bronzes in M1 are much more advanced than those in M4, some displaying a vigorous coiled dragon design of a type never seen on Shang bronzes. This bold three-dimensional motif occurs on four of the vessels. The coiled dragon is specific to the Zhou and is found on various inscribed bronzes, including the *Tian Wang gui* (Fig. 6.2), the inscriptions of which date them to the first part of early Western Zhou.[40] Not only can these vessels in tomb M1 be dated by reference to inscribed bronzes, so too can those of tomb M4.[41]

Vessel sets found at Gaojiabao suggest that by the early Western Zhou, the Shang forms of ritual offering were standard. The simple shapes seen in the earlier tomb 83 Fengmao M1 at Fengxi had come to be superseded by ritual sets very like those of the Shang. The manufacture and burial of a large number of ritual bronzes have several implications. They suggest that the Zhou had become richer in resources and that they chose to use these resources to make a spectacular show in banquets for the ancestors. These banquets were arranged in Shang style, but with emphasis on Zhou tastes. Moreover, the bronzes required for banquets were buried in tombs.

---

[38] *Kaogu* 1984.9: 779–83.

[39] For the archaeological report, see Shaanxi sheng kaogu yanjiusuo, ed., *Gaojiabao Ge guo mu* (Xi'an: San Qin, 1995), esp. pp. 67–107.

[40] For a discussion of the sources of the coiled dragon design, see Rawson, *Western Zhou Bronzes in the Arthur M. Sackler Collection*, vol. 1, pp. 55–7. For another *gui* on a square base decorated with coiled dragons, see the *Shu De gui* in the Arthur M. Sackler Museum, Harvard University Museums (Chen Mengjia, *Yin Zhou qingtongqi fenlei tulu* [Tokyo: Kyūko, 1977], A219, R 321).

[41] Among the vessels from tomb M4 there are several that inscriptional evidence dates to before and after the conquest. For example, a rectangular *ding* decorated with snakes and roundels may be compared with a Shang period *ding* in the British Museum, London, and a Western Zhou *ding* in the Arthur M. Sackler Gallery, Washington, D.C.; a *you* from tomb M4 can be compared with one of the Shang period in the Hakutsuru Museum, Kobe, and a Western Zhou example in the Victoria and Albert Museum, London (Rawson, *Western Zhou Ritual Bronzes from the Arthur M. Sackler Collections*, vol. 2, p. 237, fig. 6.5; p. 235, no. 6; p. 497, fig. 68.4; p. 498, fig. 68.5).

As Zhou rule developed, other features were added to burials, including separate pits containing chariots and horses. In some cemeteries, separate horse pits were also constructed. Such advances continued to be made in the direction of the Shang style of burial. Indeed, even small detailed features of Zhou tombs illustrate Zhou concern with Shang practice. While pre-conquest tombs in most parts of Shaanxi do not have *yaokeng*, once the conquest had taken place this feature became almost universal.[42] Such careful attention to the Shang pattern shows both that the Zhou had access to correct information about Shang tomb construction and that they valued this form of tomb as being the valid way in which to provide for the dead.

Their aspirations were also articulated in words. Inscribed bronzes, so abundant after the conquest, were not, it seems, used in the area before it. However, lengthy early inscriptions refer to events and individuals probably associated with the conquest. The *Li gui* 利簋, unearthed at Lintong 臨潼 near Xi'an, mentions events at the time of the conquest (Fig. 6.8), and the inscription on the *Kang Hou gui* 康侯簋 in the British Museum refers to a later expedition against the remnants of the Shang. The *Ming Shi Qing zun* 鳴士卿尊 in the National Palace Museum, Taipei, refers to the foundation of the city at Chengzhou.[43]

Use of written Chinese in inscriptions on the ritual vessels indicates another facet of Zhou emulation of the Shang; that is, texts employed as communication, including reports to the ancestors and spirits. We do not know whether the Zhou used writing before the conquest, and whether indeed they inscribed the oracle bones discovered in the Zhouyuan (discussed earlier), but after the conquest they seem to have extended the Shang practice of casting long texts on bronze vessels. The content was intended to announce the achievements of the owners of the bronzes and their relationships to the activities of the king. By such proclamations of status, the Zhou were directing their claims to the ancestors in a manner that they had not done earlier. In the ways in which the Zhou thus presented themselves, we see a definite change from the pre-conquest culture of Shaanxi to the Zhou style of warfare, ritual, and burial from the time of the conquest. The idealized picture presented by new object types, new words, and a new underlying message suggests that the Zhou were using the weight of Shang precedent to legitimate their own rule. Even if they did not share Shang beliefs and ideas in their entirety, they had taken on and wished to display an ideology whose primary message was that they, the Zhou, were like, or indeed better than the Shang.

[42] Teng Mingyu, "Feng Hao diqu Xi Zhou muzang de ruogan wenti," p. 229, n. 34.
[43] For a note in English on vessels whose inscriptions mention names or facts that can be dated to the early Western Zhou, see Jessica Rawson, *Western Zhou Ritual Bronzes from the Arthur M. Sackler Collections*, part I, pp. 145–6.

(a)

Figure 6.8. *Li gui* vessel and inscription, from Lintong, Shaanxi. Early Western Zhou. Vessel after Wen Fong, ed., *The Great Bronze Age of China* (New York: Metropolitan Museum of Art, 1980), no. 41; inscription after *Wenwu* 1977.8: 2, fig. 2.

A claim to legitimate power both in words and objects had an enormous force. What is more, the extent of the territory over which such claims were manifested obscured and obliterated most traces of the earlier mosaic of competing states that had coexisted with the Shang. The Zhou achievement was truly remarkable. Indeed the Zhou contribution has been too little considered, and the extent to which they rose from obscurity to overarching influence is too often ignored. The Zhou sites now to be described belonged to a power that imprinted itself indelibly, not only on its own day, but on all succeeding generations.

(b)

Figure 6.8. *(cont.)*

EARLY WESTERN ZHOU

The Zhouyuan

It might seem logical to start the discussion of the main area of the Wei River valley with an account of the finds at Feng 豐 and Hao 鎬, the capitals created near the present-day city of Xi'an. However, the remains discovered there so far do not do justice to the might of the Zhou. A much more remarkable picture is presented by the sites revealed in the area known as the Zhouyuan, straddling the counties of Qishan and Fufeng. This area has revealed such a large range of finds over the last century or more that it must rank as one of China's most important ancient centers (Map 6.2).

Although situated more than 100 km from the capitals at Feng and Hao, the finds from the Zhouyuan clearly belong to a center of immense importance. The area has revealed foundations of substantial buildings, a deposit of oracle bones and a large number of hoards of bronze ritual vessels that were probably buried when the Zhou were forced to flee before the invading Quan Rong 犬戎 in 771 B.C. The hoards each belonged to a different family and thus suggest that the Zhou elite maintained family altars here. The presence of early bronzes in the hoards indicates continuous family traditions, starting in the early Western Zhou.

One of these remarkable hoards, that found at Zhuangbai, has already been described (Figs. 6.1 and 6.6). Although this hoard is perhaps the single richest one ever excavated, it is only one of dozens of such deposits.[44] The majority were found in the Zhouyuan, but as we shall see there are abundant examples elsewhere in Shaanxi. These deposits illuminate the ritual lives of the Zhou and are not matched in any other period of pre-Han history.

Hoards usually included highly prized bronzes, valued in terms of their fine workmanship and long inscriptions recording family honors; these bronzes were usually more sumptuous than those buried in tombs. Since early and middle Western Zhou inscribed bronzes have been found with late ones in use in the eighth century, it would appear that the elite families consciously preserved early pieces. As did the hoard of 103 vessels from Zhuangbai, a hoard from Dongjiacun 董家村 in Qishan contained part of a set of late Western Zhou vessels together with several middle Western Zhou vessels car-

---

[44] Chen Quanfang, "Zao Zhou ducheng Qi yi chutan," pp. 44–9; Wu Zhenfeng, "Shaanxi Shang Zhou qingtongqi de chutu yu yanjiu;" Luo Xizhang et al., eds., *Fufeng xian wenwuzhi*, pp. 57–110; Luo Xizhang, "Zhouyuan qingtongqi jiaocang ji youguan wenti de tantao," *Kaogu yu wenwu* 1988.2: 40–7; Luo Xizhang, "Fufeng chutu de Shang Zhou qingtongqi," *Kaogu yu wenwu* 1980.4: 6–22, 53; Zhongguo Kexueyuan Kaogu yanjiusuo ed., *Fengxi fajue baogao: 1955–1957 nian Shaanxi Chang'an xian Fengxi xiang kaogu fajue ziliao* (Beijing: Wenwu, 1962); *Wenwu* 1976.5: 26–44; *Kaogu yu wenwu* 1985.1: 12–18.

rying highly significant inscriptions, suggesting that vessels had been retained in the family from the early and middle Zhou.[45]

The buildings, the oracle bones, and the ritual bronzes suggest that the Zhouyuan was of ritual importance and was occupied for a long period. As the site is placed some distance from the capital, it probably had to be supported by representatives of the noble families living there. It seems to have been provided with a city wall and workshops. Tombs are, however, not especially sumptuous. Several large cemeteries have been discovered, but the contents of the tombs do not seem to match those at Fengxi, and it seems possible that only limited representatives of families lived and died in the Zhouyuan. The majority of the excavated tombs seem to belong either to the pre-conquest period or to the middle Western Zhou.[46]

Two complex building structures have been unearthed in the Zhouyuan. One, at Fengchu 鳳雛, which may be the earlier of the two (Fig. 6.9),[47] was founded on a *hangtu* platform and was supported by wooden pillars. Carbon-14 dating has given dates in the Western Zhou period. The buildings covered 1,469 sq. m and were constructed on a typical northern Chinese plan; that is, their structure comprised a central hall surrounded by narrow buildings, forming an enclosure. It can be assumed that there was a gateway in front, possibly with a screen before it. A cache of inscribed oracle bones was found beneath the foundations. Their date and origin are subject to debate.[48] Another group of buildings stood to the east of this courtyard. Various assumptions have been made about the relationship between the two groups, but as yet there is no way to determine their relative dates or functions. The buildings were made with mud and brick walls and some use of plaster. Traces of mother-of-pearl decoration have been found. Roofs were probably covered with bundles of thatch.

A second group of buildings, at Shaochen 召陳, is possibly later in date (Fig. 6.10).[49] The most conspicuous surviving features are clusters of large water-washed stones acting as foundations for columns. However, it is not clear from these column bases how the buildings were planned and constructed. Roof tiles and tile fragments have been found at this site, as well as

[45] For a study of vessel shape and decoration of bronzes found in the Zhouyuan, see Cao Wei, "Zhouyuan Xi Zhou tongqi fenqi," *Kaoguxue yanjiu* 2 (1994): 144–65.

[46] Luo Xizhang et al., eds., *Fufeng xian wenwuzhi*, pp. 23–31; *Wenwu ziliao congkan* 8 (1983): 77–94; *Wenwu* 1980.4: 39–55.

[47] Yang Hongxun, "Xi Zhou Qi yi jianzhu yizhi chubu kaocha," *Wenwu* 1981.3: 23–33.

[48] For a discussion in English on the subject, see Edward L. Shaughnessy, "Zhouyuan Oracle-Bone Inscriptions: Entering the Research Stage?" *EC* 11–12 (1985–7): 146–90. For references to the Zhou in Shang oracle bones from Anyang, see Zhu Fenghan, "Guanyu Yinxu buci zhong de Zhou hou," *Kaogu yu wenwu* 1986.4: 68–9.

[49] *Wenwu* 1981.3: 10–22; Fu Xinian, "Shaanxi Fufeng Shaochencun Xi Zhou jianzhu yizhi chutan," *Wenwu* 1981.3: 34–45.

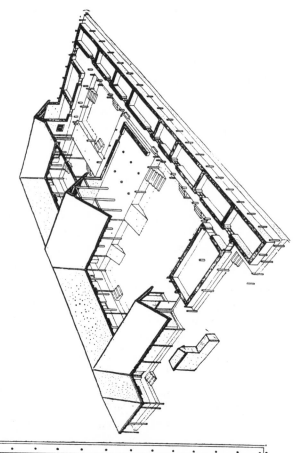

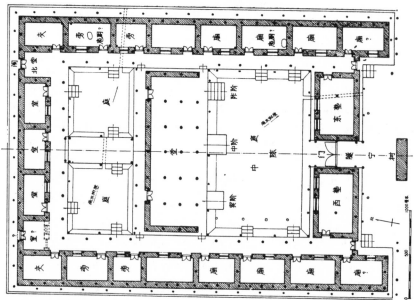

Figure 6.9, on opposite page. Plan and reconstruction of building complex at Fengchu, Qishan, Shaanxi. After Yang Hongxun, "Xi Zhou Qi yi jianzhu yizhi chubu kaocha," *Wenwu* 1981.3: figs. 2, 3.

at others; these seem to have been an innovation of the Zhou. The tiles are large, long, and arc-shaped in cross-section, with knobs that made it possible to interlock them. From these early beginnings arose one of the most characteristic and enduring elements of the Chinese ceramics industry.

Some potting shops have been excavated, and ceramic workshops must have been essential, not just for everyday utensils, but particularly for production of the tiles just mentioned.[50] Bronze casting sites have also been reported. A large bone workshop is the most spectacular find among these workshops. The area has revealed tens of thousands of unworked bones, presumably abandoned in the late Western Zhou when the Zhou fled from the area.[51]

The Capitals Feng and Hao

Before the conquest the Zhou are said to have established a capital at Feng, and thereafter at Hao, the first to the east and the second to the west of the Feng River.[52] Excavation here has so far failed to reveal structures or objects connected with the Zhou royal family. Neither royal tombs, nor palaces, nor administrative buildings have been found. Layers of occupation of the Xi'an area over the intervening millennia may have covered up or obliterated the majority of ancient Zhou buildings and tombs.

The principal excavations have taken place in Chang'an, south of the present city, on both sides of the Feng River. The main sites to the west of the river, that is Fengxi 灃西,[53] include Zhangjiapo, Dayuancun 大原村, Mawangzhen 馬王鎮, and Kexingzhuang 客省莊. On the other side of the river, in Fengdong 灃東, are Huayuancun 花園村, with a large number of tombs, and Puducun 普渡村.

[50] Luo Xizhang et al., eds., *Fufeng xian wenwuzhi*, pp. 162–5; Luo Xizhang, "Zhouyuan chutu taozhi jianzhu cailiao," *Kaogu yu wenwu* 1987.2: 9–17, 65.

[51] *Wenwu* 1980.4: 27–38.

[52] Bao Quan, "Xi Zhou ducheng Feng Hao yizhi," in *Zhou wenhua lunji*, ed. Shaanxi Lishi bowuguan (Xi'an: San Qin, 1993), pp. 321–3; Lu Liancheng, "Xi Zhou Feng Hao liang jing kao," *Zhongguo dili luncong* 1988.3: 115–52; idem, "Lun Shangdai Xi Zhou ducheng xingtai," *Zhongguo dili luncong* 1990.3: 143–60.

[53] For an early, fairly comprehensive report, see Zhongguo Kexueyuan Kaogu yanjiusuo, *Fengxi fajue baogao: 1955–1957 nian Shaanxi Chang'an xian Fengxi xiang kaogu fajue ziliao*. For a chronology based on ceramic typology, see Teng Mingyu, "Feng Hao diqu Xi Zhou muzang de ruogan wenti"; for ceramics from the Feng Hao area, see Jiang Zudi, "Lun Feng Hao Zhou wenhua yizhi taoqi fenqi," *Kaoguxue yanjiu* 1 (1992): 256–86.

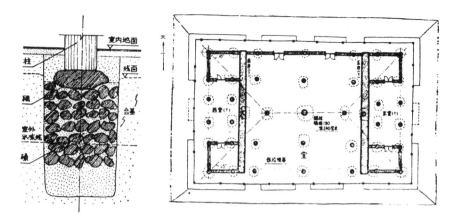

Figure 6.10. Plan of building and post holes at Shaochen, Fufeng, Shaanxi. After Yang Hongxun, "Xi Zhou Qi yi jianzhu yizhi chubu kaocha," *Wenwu* 1981.3: figs. 12, 13.

The excavated areas to the south of Xi'an, in Chang'an county, seem to have been the sites of cemeteries and perhaps also of the abodes of high- and middle-level Zhou families. Striking features include the number of chariot burials and the relatively large number of good, but nonetheless rather modest, bronze vessels found in the tombs. From the period of the conquest or slightly before, the area seems to have been inhabited by people of sufficient wealth to bury bronzes with their dead.

Two or three decades of work have shown a more or less chronologically continuous sequence of burials at Fengxi, from the period during which the diamond and boss decorated *gui* and the segmented ceramic *li* of tomb 83 Fengmao M1 were in general use (Fig. 6.3a), down to the second half of the middle Western Zhou.[54] However, very few tombs containing bronzes of the late Western Zhou have been found. Late tombs have been identified on the basis of ceramic types.

Apart from a group of burials of the Jingshu 井叔 clan (discussed below), none of the tombs is as complex or as richly equipped as are the tombs of the Yu state at Baoji, to be further considered in the next section. The burials generally occupy rather confined spaces and few subordinate individuals are buried with the main occupant, quite unlike the case in Yu, where the Yu

[54] *Kaogu* 1962.1: 20–2; *Kaogu* 1964.9: 441–7, 474; *Kaogu* 1965.9: 447–50; *Kaogu xuebao* 1980.4: 457–502; *Kaogu* 1981.1: 13–18; Zhao Yongfu, "1961–62 nian Fengxi fajue jianbao," *Kaogu* 1984.9: 784–9; *Kaogu* 1986.3: 197–209; *Kaogu* 1986.11: 977–81; *Kaogu* 1987.1: 15–32; *Kaogu* 1988.9: 769–77, 799; Zheng Hongchun and Jiang Zudi, "Chang'an Fengdong Xi Zhou yicunde kaogu diaocha," *Kaogu yu wenwu* 1986.2: 1–6.

lords were accompanied by their wives or concubines. There are also relatively few weapons and almost no evidence of the exotica seen in the far west.

The cemetery at Zhangjiapo is especially interesting for the chariot burials that are placed in separate pits (Fig. 6.11).[55] This was indubitably a Shang practice, and the chariot used by the Zhou was very similar to that of the Shang.[56] Shang-type chariots were known in Shaanxi at the time of the Laoniupo occupation, but then became too much prized or too scarce to bury. Traces of chariots, in the form of parts but no complete burials, have been found at Chunhua, dating perhaps to before the conquest.[57] If indeed the Zhou had chariots at the moment when they defeated the Shang, they would appear not to have been interested in burying them, as significant chariot remains from the time of the conquest have so far eluded archaeologists. Occasional chariot parts have also been found in the Zhouyuan. These observations throw into relief difficulties that arise when archaeological evidence and later textual traditions do not coincide. It is possible that the Zhou had some sort of cart or chariot, which they were not accustomed to bury, or that they seized Shang chariots and charioteers.

Chariot burials with the complete vehicle – its bronze parts, horses, and driver – seem to have been more common at the capital than elsewhere in Shaanxi. From the types of chariot parts found in these burials, the majority appear to belong to the second half of the early Western Zhou or later. While most of the chariots were drawn by two horses, a few drawn by four have also been found. Burial grounds with chariot pits have also been found at Fengxi and Huayuancun.[58] Such pits displayed the chariots, horses, and drivers in approximately the manner and disposition whereby they had been used in life. As in the Shang period, the bodies of the horses and drivers are neatly placed, with no signs of struggle.[59]

Display of chariots was perhaps essential to the definition of status or even to a formal Zhou ranking system. Chariots would appear to have been more widely distributed than in the Shang, although for both periods we lack sufficient information to give a coherent account of how the use of chariots and the ranking of the burials fit together. That chariots were particularly prized is also evident from bronze inscriptions, many of which list gifts from the

[55] For surveys of chariot burials, see Lu Liancheng, "Chariot and Horse Burials in Ancient China," *Antiquity* 67: 257 (1993): 824–38; Li Zizhi, "Yin Shang liang Zhou de chema xunzang," pp. 168–86; Zhang Changshou and Zhang Xiaoguang, "Yin Zhou chezhi lüeshuo," in *Zhongguo kaoguxue yanjiu: Xia Nai xiansheng kaogu wushi nian jinian lunwenji* (Beijing: Wenwu, 1986), pp. 139–62.

[56] Cf. *Kaogu* 1988.10: 882–93 (and fig. 3.28, this volume), for an excavated chariot from Anyang.

[57] Yao Shengmin, "Shaanxi Chunhua xian chutu de Shang Zhou qingtongqi," *Kaogu yu wenwu* 1986.5: 12–22.

[58] *Wenwu* 1986.1: 1–31.

[59] See Lu Liancheng, "Chariot and Horse Burials in Ancient China," p. 831, fig. 6.

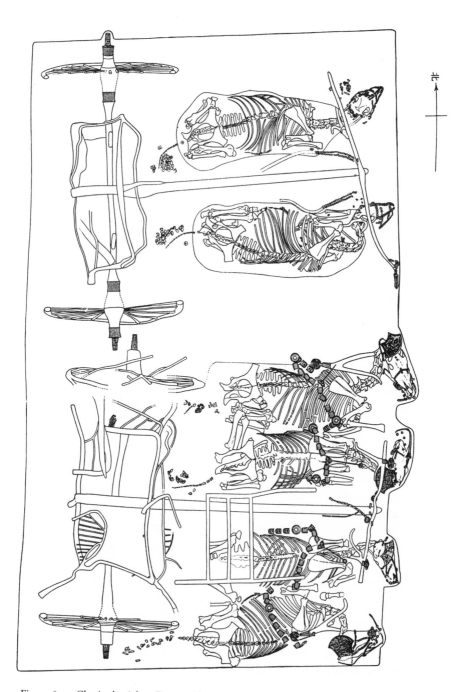

Figure 6.11. Chariot burials at Fengxi, Chang'an, Shaanxi. Middle Western Zhou. After *Fengxi fajue baogao* (Beijing: Wenwu, 1962), fig. 94.

Zhou king to his subjects that include ornaments or other parts for chariots.[60] This evidence indicates a concern with warfare or at least military display as part of transactions between the king and his nobles. As already mentioned, Zhou emphasis on both archery and chariots, including bronze inscription records of suitable equipment for these activities, may have stemmed from Zhou origins in lands to the northwest of central China. At this period, the conduct of war seems to have been important to the Zhou, not surprisingly in view of the large territory they sought to control.[61]

Small States and Outposts in Other Parts of Shaanxi

Zhou activity in Shaanxi can also be plotted westward from Xi'an and the Zhouyuan along the Wei River and its main tributaries. Both tombs and hoards have come to light containing ritual bronzes, often of the same high quality as those from the major centers just described. These deposits are widely scattered and indicate an area inhabited by the elite that was far more diffuse than the city of the Shang at Anyang.

The area around Baoji has been investigated since the 1930s. A notable set of bronze *you* 卣 with a bronze *zun* 尊, formerly in the collection of Duanfang 端方, and now in the Metropolitan Museum of Art, is reputed to have come from the area. Most important of all is a group of tombs belonging to lords of the Yu state, excavated in the 1970s and already mentioned earlier.[62]

Although Yu is not mentioned in extant texts, the tomb contents indicate that their owners were powerful and wealthy. Tomb 7 at Zhuyuangou near Baoji has already been illustrated (Figs. 6.4 and 6.5). Twenty-one other tombs and three chariot burials were excavated in the same area. A later, large tomb of a man accompanied by two women, together with a chariot pit, was found at Rujiazhuang 茹家莊; it will be included in the discussion of middle Western Zhou remains. A third site at Zhifangtou 紙坊頭 revealed an early but partially robbed tomb. The bronzes that escaped looting are strangely idiosyncratic (Fig. 6.12). The *ding* and *gui* from Zhifangtou are particularly interesting for their variety; all items are different from one another, the differences among the *gui* being especially striking, and the collection being quite unlike the matched sets of later times. Their owner may have valued the variety. Three *gui* are on rectangular bases. One has a lid and four handles; another has no lid and two handles, its ornament comprising large *taotie* faces

---

[60] Huang Ranwei, *Yin Zhou qingtongqi shangci mingwen yanjiu* (Hong Kong: Longmen, 1978), pp. 166–206; Chen Hanping, *Xi Zhou ceming zhidu yanjiu* (Shanghai: Xuelin, 1986), pp. 239–51.

[61] A suit of armor found in a tomb at Puducun also indicates concern with warfare; see Bai Rongjin, "Xi Zhou tongjia zuhe fuyuan," *Kaogu* 1988.9: 849–51, 857.

[62] Lu Liancheng and Hu Zhisheng, *Baoji Yu guo mudi.*

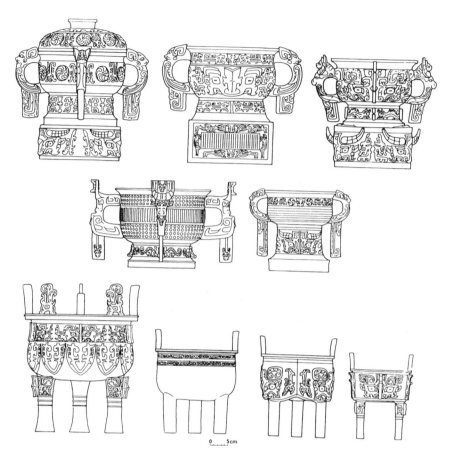

Figure 6.12. Drawings of five *gui* and four *ding*, from a partially destroyed tomb at Zhifangtou, Baoji, Shaanxi. Early Western Zhou. After Lu Liancheng and Hu Zhisheng, *Baoji Yu guo mudi* (Beijing: Wenwu, 1988), vol. 1, figs. 11, 13, 14, 17, 19, 22, 24, 26. Drawing by Ann Searight.

with projecting horns. This last detail was perhaps introduced from the south, as the small figures of a tiger grasping a buffalo head on the handles and flanges in the shape of birds also found on this *gui* are features of bronzes from Hunan. The third *gui* on a base has a man-like *taotie* face on the body. A four-handled *gui*, without a base, is also adorned with buffalo heads. A fifth *gui* has a tubular foot and seems to be a modified form of a quite different vessel type, a *dou*. This unusual vessel type, square bases, four-handled *gui*, and animal-face motifs with projecting buffalo horns are all features that either are never seen on Shang bronzes or are very rare.[63]

[63] For the tomb at Zhifangtou, see ibid., vol. 1, pp. 17–42.

Figure 6.13. *Lei* from Zhuwajie, Pengxian, Sichuan. Early Western Zhou. After Li Xueqin, *Zhongguo meishu quanji, Gongyi meishu bian 4: Qingtongqi (shang)* (Beijing: Wenwu, 1985), no. 195.

They are, however, shared with other bronzes that have come from western China. Among such bronzes is a group of large *lei* 罍 found in two hoards at Pengxian 彭縣, in Sichuan province, interred within pottery vessels (Fig. 6.13).[64] They do not seem likely to have belonged to a burial and do not include the range of bronze vessel types normally associated with ritual offerings and with burials of Shang or early Western Zhou type. However, their shapes and above all their surface ornament are similar to those of some Zhou bronzes, especially pieces from western sites. For instance, they carry small buffalo motifs and buffalo heads on the handles, like the Baoji bronzes. They also share coiled dragon designs with several notable excavated bronzes,

[64] Wang Jiayou, "Ji Sichuan Peng xian Zhuwajie chutu de tongqi," *Wenwu* 1961.11: 28–31; Feng Hanji, "Sichuan Peng xian chutu de tongqi," *Wenwu* 1980.12: 38–47; *Kaogu* 1981.6: 496–9, 555; Liu Ying, "Ba Shu tongqi wenshi tulu," *Wenwu ziliao congkan* 7 (1983): 1–12; *Zhongguo qingtongqi quanji: 13, Ba Shu* (Beijing: Wenwu, 1994), nos. 70–80.

including the vessels from Gaojiabao (Fig. 6.3c), the *Tian Wang gui* (Fig. 6.2) and other inscribed pieces.

Some weapons and small bronzes are likewise common to western Shaanxi and Sichuan provinces.[65] Broad *ge* 戈 blades, axes with rounded cutting edges, and small pointed bronze jars are found in both of these areas. In addition to links between Baoji and Sichuan, contacts with Gansu further north are indicated by inscriptions. Thus, the robbed tomb at Zhifangtou contained two *li* with inscriptions naming Ze 矢, a small state in western Shaanxi.[66]

Indeed, Yu seems to have been only one of several small lordships in the west and center of Shaanxi, all of which followed Zhou practices in the forms of ritual vessels they employed and the types of burial they adopted. Just as the Zhou followed Shang practices, these dependents of the Zhou followed Zhou ritual and burial customs. Like the Yu tombs, those of the lords of Hei 潶 and Luan 灋 at Lingtai 靈臺 in eastern Gansu have some Shang features, including the use of *yaokeng* and *ercengtai*. Both tombs also had loose chariot fittings within them, while tomb 2, belonging to the Luan lord, was accompanied by a chariot burial with four horses. The vessels included some specifically non-Shang types, that is, western types, including a pair of tubular wine vessels or *you* (Fig. 6.14) and a *gui* decorated with coiled dragons. In addition, the weapons were markedly western in character; they included a small knife with an openwork scabbard of the type found in several western and northern areas and various substantial blades with decorated fittings. As discussed below in the section on the state of Yan, many of the weapon types in Gansu are related to those employed in Hebei.[67]

Among these is a curved weapon of a type that is also known with an iron blade. Iron is not a material the Chinese had themselves exploited by this date, and such combinations suggest contact with Central Asia, where iron was perhaps employed at the time of the Western Zhou.[68] The Yu tombs contain faience beads, which also indicate such contact and which will be

[65] Lu Liancheng and Hu Zhisheng, "Baoji Rujiazhuang Zhuyuangou mudi youguan wenti de tantao," *Wenwu* 1983.2: 12–20.

[66] Lu Liancheng and Hu Zhisheng, *Baoji Yu guo mudi*, p. 24; for further Ze state vessels, see Lu Liancheng and Yin Shengping, "Gu Ze guo yizhi mudi diaochaji," *Wenwu* 1982.2: 48–57; Tang Aihua, "Xinxiang bowuguan cang Xi Zhou Ze Bo yan," *Wenwu* 1986.3: 93; *Shaanxi chutu Shang Zhou qingtongqi (3)* (Beijing: Wenwu, 1980), nos. 148–53.

[67] *Kaogu xuebao* 1977.2: 99–130; for the small openwork scabbard, see ibid., fig. 12. This scabbard is compared with a piece from the Beijing area in Fig. 6.17, this volume. Other weapon types from these tombs resemble those from Beijing. See *Kaogu xuebao* 1977.2: 99–130, figs. 11:10, 13:3, and cf. *Kaogu* 1976.4: 246–58. 228, fig. 7:4, 8.

[68] The weapon is in the Idemitsu Museum, Tokyo (unpublished, but seen by the author in 1995). It resembles the curved bronze weapon from the Lingtai tombs (*Kaogu xuebao* 1977.2: 2, fig. 12:3). For iron pieces from Xinjiang province, see *Kaogu* 1991.8: 684–703, 736. The dating of these tombs relative to Western Zhou finds is not secure. However this evidence, combined with the information about the

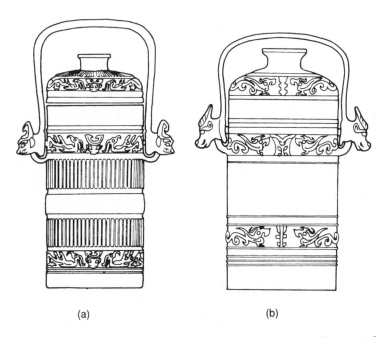

(a)   (b)

Figure 6.14. Tubular *you* (a), from tomb M13, Zhuyuangou, Baoji, Shaanxi (after Lu Liancheng and Hu Zhisheng, *Baoji Yu guo mudi* [Beijing: Wenwu, 1988], vol. 1, fig. 49), compared with a tubular *you* (b) from tomb M2, Baicaopo, Lingtai, Gansu (after *Kaogu xuebao* 1977.2: 107, fig. 7). Both early Western Zhou.

mentioned again below in connection with the tomb of a later Yu lord buried at Rujiazhuang.[69]

The bronze industry flowered here in western Shaanxi early in the Zhou period and was clearly less dependent on Henan precedent than the bronze industry further east. This wealth was probably founded on an early, possibly pre-conquest industry.[70] Although ritual vessel shapes and decoration were related to Shang models, the bronzes were often highly individual. Contacts both with the west and with southern China, discussed below in connection with the introduction of bells, were perhaps responsible for the innovations. But if the lords of the region were thus both wealthy and independent, they did not remain so. From the middle Western Zhou, bronzes

Idemitsu blade is suggestive of a date in the middle Western Zhou for the use of iron on the western periphery of the main Chinese area. This view is at variance with arguments put forward by Donald Wagner in *Iron and Steel in Ancient China* (Leiden: Brill, 1993), pp. 97–146.

[69] Lu Liancheng and Hu Zhisheng, *Baoji Yu guo mudi*, vol. 2, color pl. 25.

[70] See *Kaogu yu wenwu* 1986.1: 1–7, for tombs and a horse burial at Yujiawan 于家灣 in Chongxin 崇信 county, Gansu. The bronze *gui* illustrated seems a very inferior example of typical Shaanxi type and may be later than the pieces used further south.

of higher quality were employed further east in the Zhouyuan, at Xi'an, and in centers in Henan province. Moreover, these later bronzes carried long inscriptions detailing the kings' gifts to the lords of these areas. Such later bronzes and the inscriptions that accompany them are missing from the western area. It would seem that the initial wealth and power of the area, perhaps owing to some form of military or natural advantage, were dissipated and disappeared by the middle Western Zhou.

Many other tombs and hoards have come to light. If we start in the west of the province and look at the area of the Qian 汧 River, we find some very early Western Zhou pieces at Longxian 隴縣, where the Ze state bronzes already mentioned were found; we can also note early Western Zhou or even pre-conquest pieces, including *gui* with diamond and boss pattern, at Qianyang 汧陽. Fengxiang, yet further south and east, has revealed several different deposits, hoards, and many tombs ranging in date from the pre-conquest period to late Western Zhou.[71] Along the Jing 涇 River are finds at Changwu 長武, which include items that are probably pre-conquest in date.[72] Lingtai in southeastern Gansu is nearby. Further deposits have come from Binxian 彬縣, Xunyi 旬邑, Linyou 麟游 and Qianxian 乾縣.[73]

Hoards in particular have been found at sites on the southern side of the Wei River at Meixian 眉縣.[74] Among the items found there are a magnificent large inscribed *ding* and a set of bells, bronzes that may quite often have been deemed too valuable to bury in standard tombs, but were hidden underground when the Zhou had to flee. This site, Meixian, and Wugong 武功 and Zhouzhi 周至 somewhat further east are probably best understood as a southern extension of the Zhouyuan.[75] In the same way a number of further sites cluster around the Xi'an area, especially at Xianyang and Lintong.[76]

---

[71] For Longxian and Qianyang, see *Shaanxi chutu Shang Zhou qingtongqi*, vol. 3, nos. 148–68, 169–74; for Fengxiang, see Han Wei and Wu Zhenfeng, "Fengxiang nan Zhihui Xicun Zhou mu de fajue," *Kaogu yu wenwu* 1982.4: 15–38; Cao Mingtan and Shang Zhiru, "Shaanxi Fengxiang chutu de Xi Zhou qingtongqi," pp. 53–65; *Kaogu yu wenwu* 1987.4: 17–18.

[72] *Wenwu* 1975.5: 89–90.

[73] *Shaanxi Chutu Shang Zhou qingtongqi*, vol. 3, nos. 141–7, 175–9.

[74] Li Changqing and Tian Ye, "Zuguo lishi wenwu de you yici zhongyao faxian," *Wenwu* 1957.4: 5–9; Shi Yan, "Meixian Yangjiacun da ding," *Wenwu* 1972.7: 3–4; Liu Huaijun and Ren Zhoufang, "Mei xian chutu Wang zuo Zhong Jiang bao ding," *Kaogu yu wenwu* 1982.2: 5–6, 13; Liu Huaijun and Ren Zhoufang, "Mei xian chutu yipi Xi Zhou jiaocang qingtong yueqi," *Wenbo* 1987.2: 17–25.

[75] For Zhouzhi county, see Liu Hexin, "Shaanxi sheng Zhouzhi xian faxian Xi Zhou wang qi yijian," *Wenwu* 1975.7: 91; idem, "Shaanxi sheng Zhouzhi xian jinnian zhengji de jijian Xi Zhou qingtongqi," *Wenwu* 1983.7: 93; idem, "Shaanxi Zhouzhi chutu Xi Zhou Tai Shi gui," *Kaogu yu wenwu* 1981.1: 128; *Shaanxi chutu Shang Zhou qingtongqi*, vol. 4, nos. 164–74; for Wugong county, see *Kaogu* 1983.5: 394–7; *Wenwu* 1964.7: 20–7; Lu Liancheng and Luo Yingjie, "Shaanxi Wugong xian chutu Chu gui zhuqi," *Kaogu* 1981.2: 128–33; *Kaogu* 1988.7: 601–15; *Shaanxi chutu Shang Zhou qingtongqi*, vol. 4 nos. 108–35.

[76] For Xianyang, see Cao Fazhan and Chen Guoying, "Xianyang diqu chutu Xi Zhou qingtongqi," *Kaogu yu wenwu* 1981.1: 8–11; for Lintong, see *Wenwu* 1977.8: 1–7; Han Mingxiang et al., "Lintong Nanluo Xi Zhou mu chutu qingtongqi," *Wenwu* 1982.1: 87–9; for Lantian, see Tang Lan, "Yong yu mingwen jieshi," *Wenwu* 1972.1: 58–62; Duan Jiexi, "Shaanxi Lantian xian chutu Er Shu deng yiqi jianjie," *Wenwu*

Bronzes from counties somewhat further north, in Yaoxian 耀縣, Chunhua 淳化, Tongchuan 銅川, and Chengcheng 澄城, belong to yet another region, ranging in date from the late Shang period to the Western Zhou. They include weapons that can be linked with the Northern Zone and vessels and fittings that have affinities with the south. In addition, the standard *gui* with bosses appears, as does one remarkable large *ding* that has unusual ornament and handles like a *gui* and is a highly unconventional bronze by the standards of the principal Shang and early Western Zhou ritual tradition.[77] This last area is not so very far from the Jin state in Shanxi, to which attention will be directed in the next section.

Precise conclusions from this wide distribution of bronzes, not all of which date to the early Western Zhou, are difficult to formulate. Many were buried in hoards at the end of the Western Zhou. But these deposits are also accompanied by tombs in these areas. Thus, it seems likely that they are not simply the deposits of the elite fleeing to safe and remote areas from the attack of outsiders. The finds suggest that the Zhou elite occupied the fertile regions on both sides of the Wei River and its tributaries. Further, the early finds in the western area indicate that that region was particularly important in the early Western Zhou and declined in later periods. The large number of finds and their wide distribution are features of Zhou life quite different from the circumstances of the Shang, insofar as we can read them from excavations. This manner of occupation of Shaanxi is only one of the many distinctive features of Zhou elite life, to which little attention has been paid hitherto.

The States of Northern Central China

A number of centers that may be treated as states in their own right, including especially Yu, have already been identified in Shaanxi. When we come to consider the archaeology of the area outside present-day Shaanxi, particularly the part stretching eastward north of the Huai 淮 River, we find that activity was concentrated in relatively fewer and generally larger centers than those of the groups just mentioned.

Traces of large cities, tombs of conventional Zhou form, and chariot burials – all containing bronzes whose inscriptions name individuals recog-

---

1960.2: 9–10; Ren Song and Fan Weiyue, "Ji Shaanxi Lantian xian xin chutu de Ying Hou zhong," *Wenwu* 1975.10: 68–9; Fan Weiyue, "Lantian chutu yizu Xi Zhou zaoqi tongqi taoqi," *Kaogu yu wenwu* 1987.5: 12–13.

77 For Tongchuan, see *Kaogu* 1982.1: 107, 102; *Kaogu yu wenwu* 1987.2: 1–8; for Chunhua, see Yao Sheng-min, "Shaanxi Chunhua xian chutu de Shang Zhou qingtongqi"; *Chunhua xian wenwuzhi* (Xi'an: Shaanxi Renmin jiaoyu, 1991), pp. 11–12; for Yaoxian, see Hu Lingui and Xue Dongxing, "Yaoxian Dingjiagou chutu Xi Zhou jiaocang qingtongqi," *Kaogu yu wenwu* 1986.4: 4–5; much further north in Yanchang 延長, a group of late Western Zhou bronzes have been found with part of an early *gong* and *he*; see Ji Naijun and Chen Mingde, "Shaanxi Yanchang chutu yipi Xi Zhou qingtongqi," *Kaogu yu wenwu* 1993.5: 8–12.

nizable as members of the Zhou elite – indicate that these centers were in close contact with metropolitan Zhou areas. Outside the principal centers, Zhou culture was absent, it would seem.

The Zhou centers form a network different from the areas of high Shang activity. As described in Chapter 3, the archaeological remains of the Shang period indicate two widely differing conditions. During the Erligang and the early Yinxu phases, similarities between objects and tomb plans used at Zhengzhou 鄭州 and Anyang and those employed at some of the outlying centers suggest that the peoples shared religious rites and beliefs as well as technologies. It seems likely that the lords of Panlongcheng 盤龍城 were closely linked with the Shang elite at Zhengzhou, those at Sufutun or at Laoniupo with Anyang. Furthermore, these centers diverged as the Anyang period progressed. On present evidence, many fewer centers were dominated by the Shang elite than were ruled by Zhou nobility. Moreover, in both the Erligang and the Anyang periods, strong bronze-casting competitors flourished in southern regions. Bronzes from Xin'gan 新干 in Jiangxi and Guanghan 廣漢 in Sichuan amply demonstrate that in both the early and the late Yinxu periods, some of the inhabitants practiced rites and held religious beliefs that were very different from those of the Shang. The possessions and the functions these possessions made possible, as well as the ideologies they represented, were quite unlike those displayed in the tombs at Anyang.

For the Zhou period, there is plenty of evidence that large tracts of southern and eastern China were beyond Zhou control, with few if any metropolitan Zhou artifacts being found in these areas. But by the same token, these areas have as yet revealed few competing powers on the scale of those demonstrated by the finds of the Shang period in the south and southwest. This difference, indeed, will probably be shown to be false. While the Zhou did not control the whole of the Chinese landmass, we as yet know nothing about their bronze-casting competitors in the east and the south.

THE STATE OF JIN. Nearest of all to the sites occupied by the Zhou nobility in Shaanxi was the state of Jin, with its center near Houma at Tianma-Qucun. As described in the preceding chapter, traditional accounts indicate that the state was established by Tangshu Yu 唐叔虞, one of the brothers of King Cheng. The area has been the center of recent archaeological activity, and it is likely that further surveys and excavations will reveal more extensive remains yet. The most spectacular finds are of the late Western Zhou and will be described in detail in the section "Late Western Zhou."

First discovered in the early 1960s, the site has been extensively investigated by archaeological teams from Peking University. Measuring approximately 3,800 by 2,800 m, it has a cemetery located on its western edge. More than 600 Jin burials have been excavated here, as well as 5 horse and chariot pits.[78] The burials are of the same type as those found in Shaanxi, especially at Xi'an, and those at Luoyang. For the early Western Zhou period, the bronze types resemble those employed both in Shaanxi and in Henan, with the usual types, especially *ding, gui, you,* and *zun* predominating. The decorative schemes of the early pieces are highly traditional, comprising narrow borders of simplified *taotie* face and dragon patterns and some larger *taotie* schemes. Such bronzes might almost have come from the foundries that supplied the Zhou families in Shaanxi. The more exaggerated sculptural designs of buffalo horns or coiled dragons seen on early Zhou bronzes, especially in western Shaanxi, have not, to date, been found here. The earliest inscription that names the state of Jin may perhaps be dated to the middle Western Zhou. At this early stage, the Jin state seems to have been in close contact with Zhou practices in Shaanxi. The area seems to have grown in wealth, in contrast to the Zhou homeland in the latter part of the Western Zhou. As we shall see, very rich burials of that later period would seem to indicate a powerful and confident polity, willing to consign its resources to the ground.

CHENGZHOU. The area of present-day Luoyang, the site of the secondary capital of the Western Zhou, is mentioned several times in bronze inscriptions and in the transmitted texts of the *Shang shu*, but has less of a presence in the reported archaeological record. Indeed, in the present state of knowledge, finds from the area are much less spectacular than those from other regions, and the range of excavations to be considered is small.[79] Tombs and workshops excavated in the 1960s and 1970s are more modest than those discovered in Shaanxi or at the capital of Yan near Beijing. Nevertheless, on the evidence of early finds of inscribed bronzes, the Luoyang area was inhabited by eminent members of the Zhou elite. Specialized scribes and artisans must presumably have been involved in writing and casting inscriptions that describe their activities. We know that scribes were using brush and ink because of some weapons and a vessel that have ink inscriptions upon them (the inscriptions are of names).[80] Foundry remains excavated at Luoyang indi-

---

[78] Only a limited number of these tombs have been published. The excavators have concentrated on a group that they identify as belonging to the lords of Jin and their relatives. For the principal reports, see *Wenwu* 1994.1: 4–28; *Wenwu* 1994.8: 1–33, 68; *Wenwu* 1995.7: 4–39. This last report gives a chronological ordering of the tombs reported in the four articles. However, the absolute dating is far from certain. Very few of the pieces that might be dated to the early and middle Western Zhou are illustrated in these reports. A few are shown in Zhang Xishun, *Shanxi wenwuguan zang zhenpin* (Taiyuan: Shanxi renmin, n.d.), nos. 51, 53–9.

[79] Guo Moruo and Lin Shoujin, "1952 nian qiuji Luoyang dongjiao fajue baogao," *Kaogu xuebao* 9 (1955): 91–116; *Wenwu* 1972.10: 20–37; *Wenwu* 1981.7: 52–64.

[80] Cai Yunzhang, "Luoyang Beiyao Xi Zhou mu moshu wenzi lüelun," *Wenwu* 1994.7: 64–9, 79.

cate that, here at least, casting was undertaken locally. Molds and model fragments were found at a foundry site or sites in Beiyao 北窯.[81] Chariot burials and fittings interred in tombs suggest that chariot warfare and military display were significant in the lives of the elite in this area.[82]

The best-known inscribed vessel from the area, noteworthy for its long and indeed dramatic inscription, is probably the *Ling fangyi* 令方彝 in the Freer Gallery, Washington, D.C. It records administrative changes and a commission granted to a man named Ze 矢. This account is followed by a record of a particular sacrifice and then by a royal decree. The long inscription is very carefully written, and it is repeated in the lid and the body. Both contents and calligraphic style suggest a close dependence on metropolitan Zhou conventions.[83] Moreover, the shape of the bronze and its decoration are very like those of bronzes from Shaanxi, most especially the *Zhe fang yi* (Fig. 6.1a) from the Zhuangbai hoard described earlier. Perhaps the Zhou elite at Chengzhou saw themselves in exactly the same light as did their contemporaries at the Zhouyuan and at the capitals near Xi'an.[84] Other vessels with significant inscriptions include pieces of early to middle Western Zhou, several being inscribed with the name Bo Maofu 伯懋父.[85] Such inscriptions are associated with the southern campaigns of the period (see Chapter 5).

Like the inscribed bronzes and the molds, the surviving tombs also suggest that the area was prosperous in the second half of the early and the beginning of the middle Western Zhou. Vessels of this date are found in tombs that are noteworthy for their high-fired pottery. Although the source of this high-fired pottery is by no means certain, it is likely to have come from the south, from Jiangxi or Anhui provinces.[86] Moreover, it would appear that this commodity was most abundant in the early to middle Western Zhou. The absence of high-fired pottery from later sites does, indeed, suggest that it was an import rather than a local product.

[81] *Kaogu* 1983.5: 430–41, 388.

[82] *Kaogu* 1988.1: 15–23.

[83] For an illustration of the *Ling fangyi* and its inscriptions, see Rawson, *Western Zhou Ritual Bronzes from the Arthur M. Sackler Collections*, fig. 80. The inscription is discussed in Shaughnessy, *Sources of Western Zhou History*, pp. 193–216.

[84] Another similar *fangyi*, now in the Luoyang City Museum, and probably retrieved in the area, is the *Shu X fangyi*; see Zhang Jian, "Luoyang bowuguan cang de jijian qingtongqi," *Wenwu ziliao congkan* 3 (1980): pp. 41–5.

[85] For a list of such pieces and references to discussion and illustrations, see Rawson, *Western Zhou Ritual Bronzes from the Arthur M. Sackler Collections*, p. 148.

[86] *Wenwu* 1972.10: 20–37, pl. 3. I am grateful to Rose Kerr for drawing my attention to recent scientific analysis that suggests that high-fired ceramics found at Shang sites originate in Jiangxi province. It is likely that Western Zhou period finds were similar imports: Chen Tiemei, George Rapp, Jr., Jing Zhicun, and He Nu, "Provenance Study on the First Chinese Porcelain Wares Using Neutron Activation Analysis Technique," a paper presented to the 1995 *International Symposium on Ancient Ceramics: Its Scientific and Technological Insights*, Shanghai, November 1995.

THE STATE OF YING. As in the state of Jin, many of the most interesting finds from the area of the state of Ying 應 in central Henan are of the late Western or even early Eastern Zhou, and these finds will be discussed in a later section. However, it is also evident that the area was already under control of the Zhou elite from at least the early Western Zhou. A tomb at Pingdingshan 平頂山, Xiangxian 襄縣, Henan, belongs to this period. It contained the standard ritual vessels of the sort seen all over Shaanxi province and also in the Jin state, at Luoyang, and in the state of Wey 衛.[87] This homogeneity is impressive and suggests that the bronzes may have been made centrally and then been distributed to many areas. On the other hand, since the bronzes are often inscribed, if there was a central foundry it must presumably have been able to receive orders from areas as distant as southern Henan and Shandong. Among such inscribed bronzes there is a group of pieces that have been retained in collections, some of which are simply recorded in ancient woodblock printed catalogs, including the catalog of the former Imperial Collections by the Qianlong emperor of the Qing dynasty (Fig. 6.15).[88] Most of these pieces have rounded forms and carry narrow borders of decoration that we shall identify, by comparison with sequences of pieces in tombs and hoards, as belonging to the period of King Zhao or King Mu.

THE STATE OF WEY. Wey 衛 is another state for which there is archaeological as well as textual evidence. Inscribed bronzes have been excavated from Xunxian in Henan province, and in the 1930s a number of well-known pieces, including the *Kang Hou gui*, came from Huixian. The inscription in the *Kang Hou gui* describes the appointment of Kang Hou 康侯 in Wey. The bronze was cast by a man named Mei 沬, with the title of Situ 司土 (Supervisor of Lands). The vessels from the Zhuangbai hoard belonged to a family that had moved to the metropolitan Zhou area from the Shang state of Wey, presumably also in Henan, where the late Zhou state was established.

The majority of over eighty Wey state tombs of the Western Zhou period, which had been excavated during four campaigns in the period 1932–3, had been robbed, at least in part.[89] The cemetery was evidently highly important, with eight tombs with two large access ramps. These structures are more complex than the tombs reported from the Zhouyuan and from Fengxi, although they probably match the status of the Jin state tombs (in the Jin state one rather than two access ramps seems to have been the norm). Indeed,

---

[87] *Wenwu* 1977.8: 13–16. See also Zhang Zhaowu, "Henan Pingdingshan shi chutu Xi Zhou Ying guo qingtongqi," *Wenwu* 1984.12: 29–32.

[88] For an account of these items, see Zhou Yongzhen, "Liang Zhou shiqi de Ying guo Deng guo tongqi ji dili weizhi," *Kaogu* 1982.1: 48–53, esp. fig. 1.

[89] Guo Baojun, *Xunxian Xincun* (Beijing: Kexue, 1964).

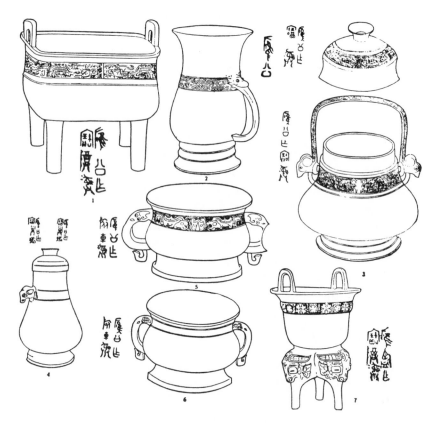

Figure 6.15. Drawings of vessels from the state of Ying. Mainly early to middle Western Zhou. After Zhou Yongzhen, "Liang Zhou shiqi de Ying guo Deng guo tongqi ji dili weizhi," *Kaogu* 1982.1: fig. 1.

the cemetery is assigned to the Wey state on account of the grandeur of the tombs, as well as its geographical location. Furthermore, although the majority of bronzes had been looted from the tombs, weapons and other fittings carry inscriptions that incorporate titles such as *hou* 侯, *gong* 公, and *bo* 伯. Archaeologists have assigned the eight tombs to dates across the whole of the Western Zhou period; smaller tombs and chariot burials likewise cover the whole period. It is, however, difficult to get a full picture of the cemetery owing to the damage done to the site by tomb robbers.

THE STATES OF LU, QI, JI, AND TENG. As the preceding chapter has indicated, named members of the Zhou elite have been described in the much later history, the *Shi ji*, as setting up states in Shandong: Lu 魯 at Qufu

曲阜 and Qi at Zibo 淄博. Archaeological evidence does indeed show traces of Western Zhou occupation in these areas. However, equally strong evidence of early and early-middle Western Zhou centers survives at many other sites. The earliest finds seem to be the Shang tombs at Yidu, discussed in Chapter 3, and tombs of the Ji 紀 state at Shouguang 壽光, where a group of Shang bronzes was found.[90] Shang-type chariots have come from further east at Jiaoxian 膠縣,[91] while early and middle Western Zhou tombs have been found at Tengxian 滕縣.[92] The early Western Zhou bronzes from Tengxian are of high quality and share some decorative features with the bronzes from the Yan state to be described below. Further early and middle Western Zhou tombs have come from Jiyang 濟陽.[93] These Zhou tombs contained, in addition to bronzes, a few fine jades and indicate a growing interest in this material in the reigns of King Zhao and King Mu. It would seem that the area was first occupied perhaps by remnants of Shang forces and that only in the period of King Kang and King Zhao was Zhou occupation evident.

THE STATE OF YAN. Much more remote than Shanxi or Henan is a Zhou outpost at Fangshan near Beijing. A large pounded-earth platform that is probably the remains of the city of Yan still survives. In two different campaigns of excavations, 61 tombs and 5 chariot burials were first uncovered (in the 1970s);[94] 121 tombs and 21 chariot burials were excavated later (in the early 1980s).[95] Large tombs with highly decorated and inscribed bronzes indicate that Zhou elite lived here. Tombs accompanied by massive burials of chariots and horses further suggest that this city near Fangshan was some sort of stronghold.

The excavations have attracted considerable interest among Chinese scholars because some of the bronzes name individuals made famous from accounts in the *Shang shu*, principally Tai Bao 太保, and record the title Yan Hou 燕侯 as ruler of the state. Tai Bao is the title given in texts to Shao Gong 召公, a half-brother of King Wu. Fangshan was evidently the site of a cemetery for rulers and their associates in the Yan state. The discovery of bronzes cast by a man named Ke 克 in tomb M1193 at Liulihe in Fangshan caused considerable excitement, as their inscriptions name Tai Bao.[96] The title Yan

90 *Wenwu* 1985.3: 1–11.
91 *Wenwu* 1977.4: 63–71.
92 *Kaogu* 1984.4: 333–7; *Kaogu xuebao* 1992.3: 365–92.
93 *Wenwu* 1981.9: 18–24; *Wenwu* 1985.12: 15–20.
94 The excavations undertaken between 1973 and 1977 are described in *Liulihe Xi Zhou Yan guo mudi, 1973–1977* (Beijing: Wenwu, 1995).
95 *Kaogu* 1984.5: 405–16, 404.
96 Other references to the Tai Bao are found in a group of vessels found in Shandong; see Thomas Lawton, "A Group of Early Western Chou Period Bronze Vessels," *Ars Orientalis* 10 (1975): 111–21; Chen Shou, "Tai Bao gui de fuchu he Tai Bao zhuqi," *Kaogu yu wenwu* 1980.4: 23–30.

Hou appears in several bronzes from the cemetery at Fangshan, including the *Fu zun* 复尊, the *Jin ding* 堇鼎, the *Yu fangding* 圉方鼎, and the *Bo Ju li* 伯矩鬲. An inscription naming Yan Hou also appears on an exceptionally fine basin, the *Yan Hou yu* 匽侯盂, found in Liaoning province. The large florid dragons on this basin are seen in a miniature form on the Zhe vessels from the Zhuangbai hoard (Fig. 6.6). In this case the motif is so rare and so specific that a direct connection between the foundries that made the pieces used in Shaanxi and those that made the Yan Hou bronzes is likely.[97] It is interesting that the name of Bo Ju is also found again on a vessel from Liaoning.[98] This connection suggests either that the influence of Yan extended northward into Liaoning or that bronzes from near Beijing were captured and taken to Liaoning.[99]

All the bronzes mentioned are exceptionally fine castings, often being inventively decorated, their quality matching the high rank of their owners. The *Bo Ju li*, for example, is a superb piece (Fig. 6.16), with *taotie* carrying projecting buffalo horns that stand away from the body of the vessel and curve upwards from the vessel lid.[100] As with the *Yan Hou yu*, this decoration is much more closely connected with bronzes from sites in the extreme west at Baoji, including tomb M7 of the Yu state (Fig. 6.5), than with vessels from other areas occupied by the Zhou. The similarity suggests some direct communication between Yan and Shaanxi: either Bo Ju was dispatched there from Shaanxi, bringing his bronzes with him, or the bronzes were commissioned on his behalf from workshops in the Shaanxi region, indeed even western Shaanxi. The *Bo Ju li* and other bronzes from the tombs at Fangshan are more impressive than the early Western Zhou bronzes from the Jin state or from Ying, and even few bronzes from Chengzhou itself can match the variety and quantity of those from Yan.

A number of minor bronzes and jade ornaments also indicate some sort of contact with the extreme west and north (Fig. 6.17). Two small openwork scabbards from tombs M52 and M253 are almost identical with openwork scabbards of a pair of small daggers from the early to middle Western Zhou tombs at Baicaopo 白草坡, Lingtai, Gansu, mentioned above, and they

---

[97] The Yan Hou bronzes are listed in Rawson, *Western Zhou Ritual Bronzes from the Arthur M. Sackler Collections*, Vol. 1, p. 147. For the *Yan Hou yu*, see Wen Fong, ed., *The Great Bronze Age of China: An Exhibition from the People's Republic of China* (New York: Metropolitan Museum of Art, 1980), no. 53.

[98] For a listing of the Bo Ju bronzes, see Rawson, *Western Zhou Ritual Bronzes from the Arthur M. Sackler Collections*, Vol. 1, pp. 147–8.

[99] *Wenwu* 1977.12: 23–33, fig. 52. As noticed in connection with the Zhou conquest and the finds from Gaojiabao (Fig. 6.3b–c), Liaoning is one of the areas where bronzes similar to the pre-conquest and early Zhou bronze types typical of Shaanxi are found. For Western Zhou bronzes that seem to have been seized and carried off to Liaoning, see Xiang Chunsong and Li Yi, "Ningcheng Xiaohe shigou shigou mu diaocha qingli baogao," *Wenwu* 1995.5: 4–22.

[100] See Wen Fong, ed., *The Great Bronze Age of China*, no. 56.

Figure 6.16. *Bo Ju li*, from tomb M251, Liulihe, Fangshan, Beijing. Early Western Zhou. After Wen Fong, ed., *The Great Bronze Age of China* (New York: Metropolitan Museum of Art, 1980), no. 56.

resemble a type from the Yu state near Baoji, as in an example from tomb 19 at Zhuyuangou. Sets of agate and jade beads also have closer parallels in the Yu state than in the intervening regions of eastern Shaanxi and Henan. Other bronzes suggest contacts with the south, but these too may often have passed through western Shaanxi; they include circular bronze ornaments (*pao* 泡) decorated with faces, and *ge* blades with upstanding projections. Both such *pao* and *ge* are found at a much earlier period at Chenggu 城固 in southern Shaanxi and even have connections with the Shang period site at Xin'gan in Jiangxi province (Fig. 3.19). It seems likely that pieces with a southern pedigree reached the Yan state not directly from the south by way of Henan, but rather from the connections that the elite of Yan had with the west. On the other hand, like the tombs in Henan, the Yan state burials were supplied

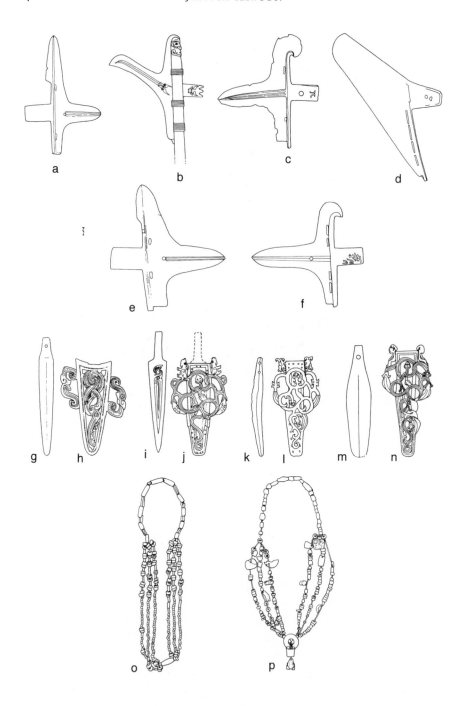

a b c d

e f

g h i j k l m n

o p

Figure 6.17, on opposite page. Comparison of weapons and strings of beads from sites in the west and from Yan; (a)–(b) two halberds from Lingtai, Gansu (after *Kaogu xuebao* 1977.2: 115, fig. 13:1, 13:3); (c)–(d) two halberds from Changping, Beijing (after *Kaogu* 1976.4: 252, fig. 7:6, 7:8); (e) halberd from tomb M4, Gaojiabao, Jingyang, Shaanxi (after *Gaojiabao Ge guo mu* [Xi'an: San Qin, 1995], p. 105, fig. 88:3); (f) halberd from Liulihe, Fangshan, Beijing (after *Liulihe Xi Zhou Yan guo mudi* [Beijing: Wenwu, 1995], p. 203, fig. 119:1); (g)–(j) short dagger blades with bronze scabbards from Zhuyuangou, Baoji, Shaanxi, and Lingtai, Gansu (after Lu Liancheng and Hu Zhisheng, *Baoji Yu guo mudi* [Beijing: Wenwu, 1988], color pl. 14:1); (k)–(n) short dagger blades with bronze scabbards from Liulihe, Fangshan, Beijing (after *Liulihe Xi Zhou Yan guo mudi* [Beijing: Wenwu, 1995], p. 201, fig. 117:1, 3, p. 202, fig. 118:1, 3); (o) beads from tomb M1, Rujiazhuang, Baoji, Shaanxi (after Lu Liancheng and Hu Zhisheng, *Baoji Yu guo mudi*, color pl. 25:2); (p): beads from Liulihe, Fangshan, Beijing (after *Liulihe Xi Zhou Yan guo mudi*, color pl. 48:2). Drawing by Ann Searight.

---

with very fine high-fired ceramics that may indeed have come all the way from Jiangxi.[101]

In addition to tombs, a number of large chariot burials have come to light. While in other parts of the Zhou domain chariots were buried one by one or else in small numbers in neat rows, here in Yan, chariot burials have been found in a much more chaotic state. In pit 202, burials of four chariots with twelve horses were laid out in dense array. This exceptionally large pit had two access ramps and the remains of substantial coffins in the main chamber. Pit 1100 also contained a large number of vehicles and animals. By contrast M52 contained one four-horse chariot and a second one drawn by a pair of horses. Pits containing horses without chariots were also found. The importance of chariots probably lay as much in the display of might as for actual warfare; extravagant burial suggests a wish to parade power at funerals, in death as in life.[102]

---

[101] For the scabbards, see *Liulihe Xi Zhou Yan guo mudi, 1973–1977*, pl. 46; *Kaogu xuebao* 1977.2: pl. 14:3, 4; Lu Liancheng and Hu Zhisheng, *Baoji Yu guo mudi*, pl. 14:1. Comments on this scabbard type are made in Jenny F. So and Emma C. Bunker, *Traders and Raiders on China's Northern Frontier* (Washington, D.C.: Arthur M. Sackler Gallery, Smithsonian Institution; and Seattle: University of Washington Press, 1995), no. 41. For the beads, see *Liulihe Xi Zhou Yan guo mudi*, pl. 48; and Lu Liancheng and Hu Zhisheng, *Baoji Yu guo mudi*, pl. 25. For bronze *pao* decorated with human faces and *ge* with upstanding projections, see *Kaogu* 1990.1: 20–31, and cf. Robert W. Bagley, "An Early Bronze Age Tomb in Jiangxi Province," *Orientations*, July 1993, figs. 42, 43; for *ge*, see *Kaogu* 1974.5: 309–21, pl. 10:3, and *Wenwu ziliao congkan* 8 (1983): 77–94, fig. 14:5. As discussed earlier in connection with preconquest Zhou and Western Shaanxi, contacts between the extreme north and the western part of Shaanxi are considered in Tong Enzheng, "Shi lun wo guo cong dongbei zhi xinan de biandi banyuexing wenhua zhuanbodai," in Wenwu chubanshe bianjibu, ed., *Wenwu chubanshe chengli sanshi zhounian jinian: Wenwu yu kaogu lunji* (Beijing: Wenwu, 1986), pp. 17–43.

[102] *Liulihe Xi Zhou Yan guo mudi*, pp. 214–30; *Kaogu* 1976.4: 246–58, 228; *Kaogu* 1974.5: 309–21; *Kaogu* 1984.5: 405–16, 404; *Kaogu* 1990.1: 20–31.

MIDDLE WESTERN ZHOU

Sites and Their Bronzes

As mentioned above (p. 360), the middle Western Zhou can be defined as the time when new types and styles of bronze ritual vessel were in vogue. The reigns of kings Zhao and Mu witnessed the introduction of this new style. In the Zhuangbai hoard, the *Feng you* 豐卣 and *zun* survive from what was presumably a much larger series. They have rounded smooth shapes, without flanges, emphasized by elaborate bird patterns. These birds have long tails, which are combined with plumage on the wings to make ribbons. Bird designs and the smooth vessel shapes on which they appear are the defining characteristics of bronzes in the first part of the middle Western Zhou. The small widely spaced characters employed in the inscriptions of the Feng bronzes are a further feature of bronzes of this date.[103]

The middle Western Zhou is interesting for changes not only in these details of vessel shape and ornament, but also for more far-ranging developments, including a very conspicuous standardization in vessel shape and ornament, which we shall examine in more detail shortly. These developments were accompanied by changes in burial patterns, particularly insofar as they affected chariots. More than a change in material culture is at stake. The bronzes and burials to be described suggest that wide-ranging changes were taking place in society.

In order to understand a little more about the stylistic change and its implications, it is useful to consider sets of bronzes more complete than those of Feng. The contents of a tomb at Fufeng provide just such a group.[104] The tomb, which was excavated in 1975, was located not far from where the Zhuangbai hoard was found. It contained a set of vessels with bird motifs of the kinds just mentioned. The vessels were interrelated not just by their shapes and decorative motifs, but also by their inscriptions, which name an individual as Dong 𣪘, or Bo Dong 伯𣪘 (Fig. 6.18).[105] The excavation report describes a set of thirteen vessels: three *ding*, two *gui*, one *yan* 甗, two tall *hu* 壺, two *jue* 爵, one *gu* 觚, one *he* 盉, one *pan* 盤. Although the vessel shapes and ornament had evolved, the components of this set are very similar to a

---

[103] For illustrations of bronzes with smooth shapes decorated with bird patterns, see Hayashi, *In Shû jidai seidôki no kenkyû*, vol. 1 (text), pls. 38–54. See also Rawson, *Western Zhou Ritual Bronzes from the Arthur M. Sackler Collections*, vol. 2, nos. 53–5.

[104] Luo Xizhang, Wu Zhenfeng, and Luo Zhongru, "Shaanxi Fufeng Chutu Xi Zhou Bo Dong zhuqi," *Wenwu* 1976.6: 51–60.

[105] The set is dated by Hayashi to the second half of middle Western Zhou; see Hayashi, *In Shû jidai seidôki no kenkyû*, vol. 1 (text), pp. 53–4. See also Shaughnessy, *Sources of Western Zhou History*, pp. 249–50.

typical early Western Zhou ritual set, such as that from tomb M1 at Gaojiabao (Fig. 6.3c). The principal differences are that the Dong bronzes include three *ding* instead of two in the early group, as well as a pair of *hu* instead of two *you* and a *zun*.[106] These two changes suggest a significant alteration in the ritual procedure, which we will see much further elaborated with the ritual changes of the late Western Zhou. But the *jue* and *gu* indicate the continued survival of Shang traits.

The decoration on this set comes in three categories (Fig. 6.18): motifs that cover the whole vessel (one *gui* carries plumed birds, while a tall *hu* has a stylized feather pattern); motifs that fill narrow borders, which can be either bird or dragon design motifs (they appear on a number of the vessels, notably the *ding* and the small *hu*); and pairs of thread relief lines defining an undecorated band that might on some bronzes display a narrow border of birds of some such motif, or be left vacant (as on the *jue* and the *yan*). Such examples form three possible categories, or variations, which must have had different costs in terms of craftsmanship and may, therefore, have indicated differing degrees of value accorded to the vessels.

Of this group the *gui* is the most elaborately decorated. Indeed, consistently in both early and middle Western Zhou periods, *gui* seem to have been the most highly decorated vessel type. Almost equal in popularity were the *you* and *zun*, as seen for example in the Feng vessels mentioned earlier. These three vessel types are the ones that are most likely to carry elaborate plumed bird patterns. *Ding*, although obviously essential, were fully decorated much less frequently. Yet it is the *ding* and the *gui* that in all periods of the Western Zhou carry long inscriptions, as indeed in the Dong group.

While decoration seems to have been used to rank vessels in the Dong set, it could also, it would appear, be used to rank sets one with another. A set of middle Western Zhou bronzes in tomb 19 at Qijia carries narrow borders of bird and dragon motifs (Fig. 6.19). The entire set is similarly decorated, and all elements are less elaborate than the bird-decorated *Dong gui* or the two Feng bronzes.[107] Other tombs contain vessels that are predominantly plainer still, carrying the pairs of thread relief lines mentioned as the lowest level in the hierarchy. For instance, a *gui* on a square pedestal from tomb M20 at Yuntang 雲塘, Fufeng, a vessel type that would normally be very fully decorated, carries only pairs of relief lines, as do vessels from tombs at Liutaizi 劉台子 in Jiyang 濟陽, Shandong.[108] It is possible to make this comparison among tombs in widely scattered areas because vessel shapes

[106] A tomb of the same date, M19 at Qijia, Fufeng, retains *ding* and *gui* in pairs and keeps the old-fashioned *you* and *zun*; see *Wenwu* 1979.11: 1–11.

[107] *Wenwu* 1979.11: 1–11.

[108] *Wenwu* 1980.4: 39–55; *Wenwu* 1981.9: 18–29; *Wenwu* 1985.12: 15–20.

(c)

Figure 6.18 (opposite page and left). Bo Dong bronzes from Zhuangbai, Fufeng, Shaanxi; (a) *Dong gui*; (b) *Dong fangdong*; (c) *Dong yan*. After *Shaanxi chutu Shang Zhou qingtongqi*, vol. 2 (Beijing: Wenwu: 1980), nos. 104, 99, 102.

and a hierarchy of designs seem to have become fairly standardized. Such a uniform system, in which the shapes of the vessels conformed to a single standard and the decoration seems to have been graded to some degree, may suggest that vessel casting was under some sort of centralized control or direction and that it supplied an appropriately ordered elite society. Since it seems unlikely that all vessels were made in a single foundry, it would appear that a system of propagating the standardized shapes and designs had been in force. In addition, the owners of such bronzes were evidently willing to accept the standardized picture that such bronzes enabled them to present at ritual banquets.

These standardized vessels, conforming still to early Western Zhou ritual practice, can be dated to the time of some sort of military instability, for a number of the inscriptions on the bronzes mention conflicts with southern or eastern peoples. The *Dong gui* and one of the *Dong ding* belong to this category. Several other vessels with campaign inscriptions also carry

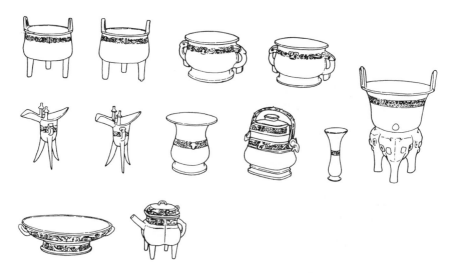

Figure 6.19. Drawings of bronzes from tomb M19, Qijia, Fufeng, Shaanxi. Middle Western Zhou. After *Shaanxi chutu Shang Zhou qingtongqi*, vol. 3 (Beijing: Wenwu: 1980), nos. 15–26. Drawing by Ann Searight.

bird designs, including the *Meng gui* 孟簋 from a hoard at Zhangjiapo near Xi'an and the *Lu Dong you* 录戜卣 in the Princeton University Art Museum.[109] It is possible that these campaigns placed the Zhou on the defensive and led to economic difficulties, which had an impact on ritual life, leading in turn to standardization. Such bronzes were also considerably smaller on average than the bronzes of the preceding and succeeding periods. Beautifully cast though the best bronzes are, there is certainly a sense that the glories of inventive bronze casting were over. A reduction in size seems to confirm that social and economic changes dictated a need to control expenditure.

A second phase of middle Western Zhou bronzes indicates that troubles continued over the succeeding decades. A general decline is in evidence among bronzes that would, on stylistic and epigraphic grounds, appear to succeed the Feng and Bo Dong vessels. Many continued to be small, as in the case of the *Li* 盠 vessels mentioned in Chapter 5. Others had gauche shapes and simplified ribbon patterns, a decline from the standards set by the earlier bird bronzes. To this category belong the *Qiu Wei ding* 裘衛鼎, also discussed in Chapter 5 for their important inscriptions detailing

[109] For a note on vessels that carry inscriptions that refer to campaigns, see Rawson, *Western Zhou Ritual Bronzes from the Arthur M. Sackler Collections*, vol. 1, pp. 150–51; see also Shaughnessy, *Sources of Western Zhou History*, pp. 177–82.

legal cases. These rare inscriptions suggest that there was some sort of change in landholding and in the legal system that was part of a social change, if not a social upheaval.[110] At the same time, standardized inscriptions, known as investiture inscriptions, came into being and are found on many bronzes of this period and later. Standardized bronzes of the early middle Western Zhou were followed by a growing uniformity in the way inscriptions were executed during the subsequent decades. Ritual bronzes both individually and in sets thus point to the pressures on the Zhou and their search for and achievement of some sort of control of bronze production for ritual purposes. On present evidence also, there seem to have been only small differences between the owners of bronzes. The large contrasts evident in the early period had disappeared. Presumably such leveling of social groups was a cause rather than a consequence of the changes in bronze vessel size and decoration.

Early-middle Western Zhou bronzes from the Yu state confirm that a decline in casting had taken place throughout Zhou territory (Fig. 6.20). However, at the same time changes in burial patterns indicate developments that were to have a significant effect in the latter part of the Western Zhou. It is, therefore, worth looking at the tomb of a middle Western Zhou lord of Yu buried with two consorts at Rujiazhuang near Baoji (Fig. 6.21).[111] In both form and contents, this tomb group anticipates developments further east. The burial is complex, with the lord interred as usual with a wife or concubine in the same pit. Alongside the main pit is a secondary tomb, presumably also of another woman. The three burials form a distinct group, which is more extensive than the earlier burials, suggesting a wish to cluster close relatives together. Moreover, although there is also a separate chariot pit, chariot parts were also placed inside the man's tomb. As we shall see below, burials at this time frequently included chariot parts, a departure from previous practice.

Vessel types in all three tombs belong to the middle Western Zhou categories. They have predominantly smooth shapes, although they are far from being standard examples. Several vessel types, especially *jue* and *zhi* 觶, descend from Shang vessel types that were soon to become obsolete. The tomb group is particularly important for some exotic features that foreshadow later trends. First, bells, probably copied from the south (see below), appear in a set of three. This is not the earliest such set, but follows a similar

---

[110] *Wenwu* 1976.5: 26–44; Tang Lan, "Shaanxi sheng Qishan xian Dongjiacun xin chu Xi Zhou zhongyao tongqi mingci de yiwen he zhushi," *Wenwu* 1976.5: 55–9, 63; Shaughnessy, *Sources of Western Zhou History*, pp. 85–7, 153–5.

[111] Lu Liancheng and Hu Zhisheng, *Baoji Yu guo mudi*, vol. 1, pp. 270–412.

Figure 6.20. Selected vessels from tomb of a Yu Bo and accompanying burials at Rujiazhuang, Baoji, Shaanxi. Middle Western Zhou. After *Shaanxi chutu Shang Zhou qingtongqi*, vol. 4 (Beijing: Wenwu: 1984), nos. 61, 63, 65, 68, 73, 74. Drawing by Ann Searight.

one in tomb M7 at Zhuyuangou (Fig. 6.5) and seems to precede one found further east in a tomb at Puducun in Chang'an county.[112] Bells seem to have become established as part of the ritual paraphernalia in the extreme west in advance of their full use at the major centers in the Zhouyuan and at the capital. In addition, vessels in the shapes of animals appear, another southern bronze type originating in the Shang period.

The lord of Yu and his consorts owned a number of other unusual and perhaps exotic pieces. Two small bronze figures with large grasping

[112] For the tomb at Puducun, see Shi Xingbang, "Chang'an Puducun Xi Zhou muzang fajueji," *Kaogu xuebao* 8 (1954): 109–26.

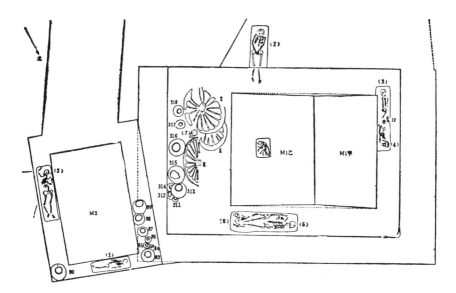

Figure 6.21. Plan of the tomb of a Yu Bo and two accompanying burials at Rujiazhuang, Baoji, Shaanxi. Middle Western Zhou. After Lu Liancheng and Hu Zhisheng, *Baoji Yu guo mudi* (Beijing: Wenwu, 1988), p. 272, fig. 187.

hands follow in stance and style the great figure from Sanxingdui 三星堆, Guanghan 廣漢, Sichuan (cf. Fig. 3.32).[113] The reference to a much earlier type of bronze from a completely different area is very clear. These are not isolated bronzes, but examples of a steady stream of pieces in the Baoji area that copy vessels, weapons, and ornaments of the southwest. References to the northwest can also be discerned. Knives held in openwork scabbards resemble those even from as far afield as Yan (Fig. 6.17). In addition, a chariot fitting depicting a man with a jacket that carries designs of antlered deer presumably also refers to the traditions of the northern zone.

Matching groups of *ding* and *gui*, found in the tomb of the secondary woman, are also foreign to the Yu state and indeed to other parts of Shaanxi. It is possible that the tomb occupant came from a neighboring area to the west, where simplified groups of identical ceramics were customarily buried. In Baoji, ceramic shapes were then perhaps copied in bronze. These simplified identical vessels presage the kinds of food vessel sets that were to become common throughout the Zhou area with the Ritual Revolution. The Rujiazhuang tombs, again anticipating trends further east, illustrate an interest in bronze copies of pottery vessels. A bronze version of a pottery *li* appears

---

[113] For bells, animal-shaped bronzes, and the small figures with large hands from Rujiazhuang, see Lu Liancheng and Hu Zhisheng, *Baoji Yu guo mudi*, vol. 2, pls. 155, 162–3, 169, 202–3.

in tomb M1. It would appear that a cluster of features, which we will later come to associate with the Ritual Revolution, were already crystallizing in western Shaanxi.[114]

Both the man and the women were clearly adorned in burial with a multitude of plaques and beads. This proliferation goes against the trend of the early Western Zhou, when there had been a diminishing interest in jades. The jade-working industry must have expanded greatly at this time to carve so many new pieces.[115] In addition, and of equal importance, persons here in Yu and later further east must apparently have had new views about the propriety of wearing such jades, presumably in life as in death, and of the benefits of burying them. Multitudes of jades were later buried in tombs at the capitals in Chang'an county and in the Jin state. That the Yu state seems to have taken the initiative in this practice, perhaps supports the suggestions made earlier, that other major developments – the use of bells and the manufacture of sets of identical and rather restrained food vessels – were practices that spread from this area eastward. The priority of the western regions in these changes in ritual and burial practice suggests that, within the Zhou sphere, the west had a special role. While we cannot now work out what that role was or how these western areas were viewed from the Zhou court, taken together with the earlier observations of the role of the peripheral areas in contributing some aspects of early Zhou material culture, this western priority suggests a pervasive feature of Zhou elite life that is generally little considered.

The changes in burial pattern seen at Rujiazhuang in the west are also found, somewhat later, near the capital in the region of Xi'an. The cemetery at Fengxi, already mentioned, has revealed a number of tombs of the latter part of the middle Western Zhou. Those belonging to the Jingshu family have attracted particular attention; like the tombs at Rujiazhuang, the burials are arranged in consciously planned groups. The main Jingshu tomb, M157 is surrounded by other tombs belonging to the same family, M161 and M163 on either side, as well as by other smaller burials. Like the tomb at Rujiazhuang, a large number of chariot parts, especially chariot wheels, was placed within the tomb, in the case of tomb 157 on the access ramp. But, as at Rujiazhuang, separate chariot and horse pits were also used.[116]

In the middle Western Zhou, chariots were treated in new ways in burial.

---

[114] For sets of identical vessels, and vessels in ceramic forms, see ibid., vol. 2, pls. 153–4, 158.
[115] Ibid., vol. 1, pp. 275, 279, 363.
[116] For the Jingshu tombs, see *Kaogu* 1986.1: 22–7, 11; *Kaogu* 1990.6: 504–10; Zhang Changshou, "Guanyu Jingshu jiazu mu di 1983 nian–1986 nian Fengxi fajue ziliao zhi yi," in Shi Xingbang et al. eds., *Kaoguxue yanjiu* 398–401; Zhang Changshou, "Lun Jingshu tongqi: 1983–1986 nian Fengxi fajue ziliao zhi er," *Wenwu* 1990.7: 32–5.

In the Zhouyuan, there are instances of chariot wheels disposed within the tomb, as though the chariot had been placed in the burial either under or on top of the corpse.[117] This arrangement may imply that in life the person and the vehicle were equally closely associated. The change in the way in which the presentation of the individual was made must reflect both a change of fact and a change in the way that fact was part of a general understanding of the world. The fact must have been the perceived, if not the actual, role of the elite in relation to ceremonial display or to actual warfare. Like the bronzes already described and the jades to be further discussed later, a number of chariot fittings display bird motifs, a hallmark of the period.[118]

The Jingshu tombs, like those from Rujiazhuang, contained many more jades than earlier tombs had done. These jades have two salient characteristics. Some were obviously designed especially to cover the face, being shaped, for example, in the forms of eyes, mouths, and noses. These shapes and general arrangement anticipate the jades employed in the Jin state tombs to be described later (Fig. 6.22). Furthermore, plaques joined to long strings of beads, especially beads in agate, proliferated.[119]

The Jingshu tombs were extensively robbed. However, again like the Rujiazhuang tombs, they may have contained bronzes that belonged to a new style of ritual. A large animal-shaped bronze of the kind associated with southern China was found in tomb 163. It is clearly an early Western Zhou bronze that had survived into later periods as a piece to be treasured. In addition, a bell has come from the same tomb; others have been transmitted to posterity in collections. These bells are later than those seen in the Rujiazhuang tomb and are clearly local Shaanxi versions of what was originally a southern bronze type.

Southern Connections

Several points in the preceding section suggest that the middle Western Zhou is the time when the relations of the Zhou state with the southern regions of China that were outside their direct control became noteworthy. The south has been much less thoroughly investigated than Shaanxi and the other provinces of northern Central China. It is, therefore, very difficult indeed to have any idea of how the southern provinces were inhabited and how this

---

[117] *Wenwu* 1986.8: 56–68.

[118] For a horse bit from the Ying state, see Zhang Zhaowu, "Henan Pingdingshan shi chutu Xi Zhou Ying guo qingtongqi," *Wenwu* 1984.12: 32, fig. 12.

[119] Zhang Changshou, "Xi Zhou de zang yu: 1983–1986 nian Fengxi fajue ziliao zhi ba," *Wenwu* 1993.9: 55–9.

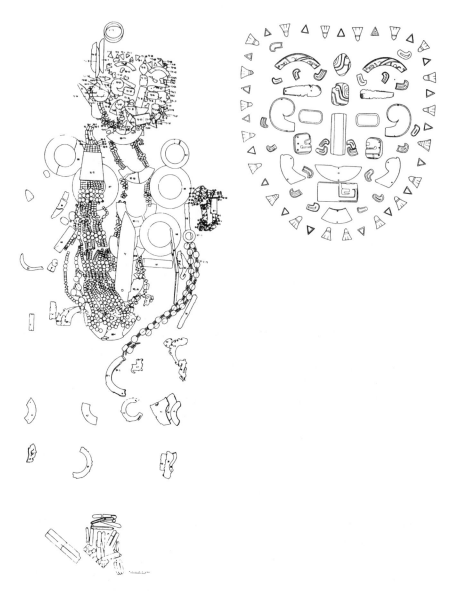

Figure 6.22. Drawings of jades found on the head and body in tomb M31, Tianma-Qucun, Houma, Shanxi, with detail of the jades on the face. Late Western Zhou to early Eastern Zhou. After *Wenwu* 1994.8: 24, fig. 3; 27, fig. 7.

occupation differed from that of the areas under Zhou control. The southern areas of Jiangxi, Hunan, and Sichuan, which have yielded the extraordinary finds described in Chapter 3, made by strong groups of peoples who had little or nothing to do with the Shang, have as yet revealed few comparable finds. On the other hand, bells and jades copied from southern prototypes indicate Zhou contact with peoples as yet unidentified.

Eastern China

Military campaigns mentioned earlier may have been caused by incursions from the peoples of the south and east. There is evidence of the impact of such upheavals on the Zhou nobility from bronzes unearthed in Anhui and Jiangsu provinces. A number of fine middle Western Zhou bronzes have come from early Eastern Zhou *dun* 墩 (mound) burials in the southeast. The vessel that has excited the most attention is the *Yi Hou Ze gui* 宜侯矢簋 from Yandunshan 煙墩山, Dantu 丹徒, Jiangsu. Interest has been aroused because its inscription, which refers to the enfeoffment of the Yu Hou 虞侯 at Yi 宜, seems at first reading to suggest that Yu was in the southern area where the bronze was found. However, such a presumption is unwise. The *gui* seems simply to be one of several bronzes that were seized in the middle Western Zhou by invading tribes and carried off to that area.[120]

Almost as well known is a *you* from Tunxi 屯溪 decorated with long plumed birds. Also carrying birds is a *gui* from Muzidun 母子墩, Dagang 大港, Dantu, Jiangsu.[121] While these three bronzes recovered from mounds are all likely to have been made in the metropolitan area, mounds also contained local bronzes that copy the middle Western Zhou bronze tradition to which these three bronzes belong. Indeed, the tomb at Muzidun brought to light quite a large group of vessels all dependent on metropolitan vessels of the middle Western Zhou. A spectacular large *zun* from Danyang, decorated with birds, shows the degree of accuracy achieved (Fig. 6.23), for while this *zun* is much larger than the originals (Fig. 6.1c), it retains the same profile and the same distribution of bird motifs.[122]

The relatively late date of these sites supports the view that the peoples who came to inhabit the southeast, perhaps during early Eastern Zhou, had at some earlier stage looted or seized a significant number of middle Western Zhou bronzes. Had the people of the area lived there over a considerable

[120] *Wenwu* 1955.5: 58–69. See Shaughnessy, *Sources of Western Zhou History*, p. 164, n. 4.

[121] For the *you* from Tunxi, which is decorated with birds with interlaced plumes, see *Anhui sheng bowuguan cang qingtongqi* (Shanghai: Renmin Meishu, 1987), pl. 24. For the vessels from Dagang in Dantu county, see *Wenwu* 1984.5: 1–10.

[122] Li Xueqin, *Zhongguo meishu quanji: Gongyi meishu bian 4, Qingtongqi, (shang)* (Beijing: Wenwu, 1985), no. 191.

Figure 6.23. *Zun* from Situ, Danyang, Jiangsu. In middle Western Zhou style but probably created later. After Li Xueqin, *Zhongguo meishu quanji, Gongyi meishu bian 4: Qingtongqi (shang)* (Beijing: Wenwu, 1985), no. 192.

period of time and had intermittent contact with the Zhou state, they would have had a greater exposure to Western Zhou bronzes of all periods. In that situation we might imagine or expect considerable variety in the models that they chose to follow in making their own bronzes. Instead almost all the bronzes from the southeast copied metropolitan bronzes of a single period, the early part of the middle Western Zhou. Thus, it is likely that the metropolitan bronzes were all acquired during a relatively confined period of time. Considerable variety appears among the copies to be sure, suggesting that they were made over some decades or more. They range from the convincing accuracy of the *zun* from Tunxi, to *gui* and *zun* that carry tiny spikes and filigree flanges, which are obviously local interpretations of forms first developed by the Western Zhou in Shaanxi.[123] As the tombs in which these bronzes are found generally date to the early Eastern Zhou, it is possible that the peoples had at the date moved into the area fairly recently and that at an earlier stage they had lived nearer to and preyed on the Zhou elites.

[123] *Anhui Sheng bowuguan cang qintongqi*, pls. 32, 35.

The Han and the Huai Rivers

While the Zhou and their immediate followers established fortified cities in Shanxi, Henan, and Hebei, there is less evidence of Zhou settlement in the regions of the Han 漢 and Huai 淮 Rivers. There are few finds in these areas. The only settlement that can be said to be of state level is north of the Huai River, at Pingdingshan in central Henan. Here the first stages of the Ying state have produced some early Western Zhou period bronzes.

Western Zhou ceramics have been found at various sites in Henan, such as Xinzheng 新鄭, but there is little evidence of higher levels of the nobility inhabiting the area. A group of fine bronzes from a chance find during construction of the Nanwan 南灣 Reservoir at Shihegang 泗河港, Xinyang, is something of an oddity. The vessels, some complete and some in fragments, are of exceptional quality. They are very unlikely to have been products of the Huai area and would seem to have come from the metropolitan areas further north and west. The vessels carry similar inscriptions, but have different dedications to at least two ancestors. Thus, while it is possible that these bronzes came from a contemporary tomb in the Huai region, it is more likely that they were brought to the area at some later time during the upheavals of the middle and later Zhou. The presence among the group of fragments of several large *zun*, more than would have been usual in a single tomb, suggests that we are dealing here with bronzes that had been amassed rather than with a discrete set for single burial. In fact the bronzes are much more sumptuous than those generally revealed by excavations of tombs in Shaanxi itself.[124]

There seems to have been little in the way of local bronze manufacture in central southern China to match the considerable ebullience documented in Chapter 3. A single large find at Lutaishan 魯臺山, Huangpi 黃陂 on the Yangzi River suggests that a group of Zhou people was located there, far removed from the major centers in Shaanxi and northern Henan. It is not clear whether the bronzes of metropolitan appearance were made locally or had been brought from Shaanxi.[125]

Bells

The single most pervasive feature of the southern bronze industry in the Shang period was the bells produced there.[126] This industry seems to have

---

[124] *Kaogu* 1989.1: 10–19.

[125] *Jiang Han kaogu* 1982.2: 37–61. For Western Zhou period ceramics typical of Hubei, see Zhou Houqiang, "Hubei Xi Zhou taoqi de fenqi," *Kaogu* 1992.3: 236–44. It is likely that the bronzes were introduced to an area where utensils were generally of ceramic.

[126] A pioneering discussion of the southern contribution to bell casting is to be found in Virginia Kane, "The Independent Bronze Industries in the South of China Contemporary with the Shang and

survived and flourished in the south during the Zhou period, though without the artistic flair or technological conviction so evident at earlier times. Technical changes in the ways in which the sounds were produced are, however, very much apparent in changes to bell design, and such developments suggest that bell casting continued to be vigorous. There are three changes to the bells themselves that are generally explained as having been directed to improving the sound. In the first place, where bells had formerly been decorated with pairs of knobs that had derived from the eyes of the *taotie*, now the numbers of knobs were increased to fill three rows on each face (Fig. 6.24a).[127] Over a century perhaps, the sides of the bells were lengthened, so that they became longer in proportion to their widths.[128] Third, loops were added to the shanks, so that the bells hung with their mouths downwards.[123]

For such changes to have been made and to have been introduced consistently across a relatively large area, ranging from Guangxi in the southwest to Jiangxi in the southeast, with considerable numbers found in Hunan, bell music must have been common to all these regions. Similar bells imply similar sounds and perhaps, though not necessarily, related forms of music. Similar casting technologies were also required to produce these bells in widely separated regions. It is rather surprising that there is little sign of other bronze use at this time in these areas. However, it is highly likely that weapons were made, even though few were buried in such a way as to come to light in later times.

So lively was bell casting, and so distinctly southern, that when bells appear in Shaanxi, they can be recognized as imports. Bells from the Yu state are decorated with small thread-relief circles around tiny pointed bosses that frame the main panels of large bosses, a feature of southern bronze casting (Fig. 6.24b). Bells of this type were introduced to the north, probably from the lower Han River by way of the tributaries of the Yangzi and the passes over the Qinling 秦嶺 Mountains to Baoji. When bells came to Shaanxi, new types of music as well as new casting technologies came with them. Although the essentials of bell casting are the same as for vessel manufacture, special expertise and experience must have been required to achieve musically tuned

Western Zhou Dynasties," *Archives of Asian Art* 28 (1974–5): 77–107. Important research on southern bells has been carried forward by Gao Zhixi and is reported in English in Kao Chih-hsi, "An Introduction to Shang and Chou Bronze *Nao* Excavated in Southern China," in *Studies of Shang Archaeology: Selected Papers from the International Conference on Shang Civilization*, ed. Chang Kwang-chih (New Haven: Yale University Press, 1986), pp. 275–99. The most comprehensive discussion, introducing the most up-to-date research, is to be found in Lothar von Falkenhausen, *Suspended Music: Chime-Bells in the Culture of Bronze Age China* (Berkeley: University of California Press, 1993). Additional points to those made there follow.

[127] *Wenwu* 1984.7: 49; Gao Zhixi, "Hunan sheng bowuguan cang Xi Zhou qingtong yueqi," *Hunan kaogu jikan* 2 (1984): 29–34; *Hunan kaogu jikan* 3 (1986): 27–35.

[128] Xiong Chuanxin, "Hunan faxian de qingtongqi," *Wenwu ziliao congkan* 5 (1981): 103–5.

[129] Xue Yao, "Jiangxi chutu de jijian qingtongqi," *Kaogu* 1963.8: 416–18.

Figure 6.24a. *Nao* from southern China. Early Western Zhou. Arthur M. Sackler Museum, Washington D.C. (S-87.0278).

(a)

(b)

Figure 6.24b. Set of three bells from tomb M1, Rujiazhuang, Baoji, Shaanxi. Early Western Zhou. After *Shaanxi chutu Shang Zhong qingtongqi*, vol. 4 (Beijing: Wenwu, 1984), no. 68.

bells that could be used together. If the first bells were imports, it seems likely
that the Zhou copied these by taking molds from the imported pieces themselves. In fact, one of the bells in the set belonging to Wei Bo Xing might
be just such a copy. It carries a cast-in dedication and is thus likely to have
been made in Shaanxi. However, it retains the small circles and spikes that
are features of the southern tradition.

It was a major change thus to introduce a southern custom of such complexity and prominence to an existing elite activity, the offering of sacrifices
to the ancestors. At first, perhaps, the bells were a small adjunct to a major
ceremony, as in the case of the sets of three in tombs mentioned above. But
by the time of Wei Bo Xing, the bells had gained a central position, both in
terms of use within the ritual itself and in terms of the resources dedicated
to them (Fig. 6.6). This remarkable borrowing of an alien bronze type was
consolidated during the ritual changes. Just as surprising as the casting of
such bells is the way in which the Zhou court must have developed music
that was appropriate to such bells and to the occasions when they were
played.

The Use of Jade

At about the same time that bells began to be used in western Shaanxi, contacts with the south seem to have been responsible for a new use of jade.
Jades were used as scepters, as pendants, and in burials during the late
Western Zhou, and from these uses sprang the jade types current in the
Eastern Zhou period. The conditions that made possible this use of jade are
thus of immense importance for the history of the material and for its central
position in Chinese ceremonial and intellectual life. To examine further the
southern and essentially foreign sources from which jade forms and motifs
were introduced to the heart of Zhou ceremonial life, it is necessary to review
the use of jade at earlier stages in the Western Zhou.

Early Western Zhou burials contain far fewer jades than do the tombs of
their Shang predecessors. This is a significant distinction between the practices of the two dynasties. Whether we look at tombs at the principal centers
is Shaanxi, such as Fengxi, or at the more widely scattered tombs in places
like the capital of the Yan state at Fangshan, we find that they contain only
a very few pieces or none at all. The majority are animal-shaped amulets, primarily in the forms of fish or birds.[130] A few other types were used quite regularly, and the tombs of the Yu state, for example, routinely held sets of three

---

[130] For early to middle Western Zhou burials with the characteristically limited repertory, see *Kaogu xuebao*
1980.4: 457–502, esp. the table at pp. 495–501; *Wenwu* 1986.1: 1–31, figs, 50–1; for some unusual jades
of the Yan state, see *Kaogu* 1984.5: 405–16, 404, fig. 12.

arcs (*huang* 璜) cut from a single block or ring. Jades in the shapes of handles were used. These tombs contained a number of stone and jade axes also. The jade pieces may have been antiquities, inherited from or, rather, looted from the Shang; the stone items may have been local pieces.[131] As already mentioned, the states of Yu and Yan are interesting for the use of strings of agate and other bead types including faience, a western Asian material.[132] Other major jades, including discs, *cong* 琮, and pointed blades deriving from the Shang style of ceremonial *ge*, were rare. Where these do occur, it seems likely that they are older pieces handed down over many generations. While such jades appear in the Yu tombs, they are much less common in the cemeteries of the Zhouyuan or the capitals at Xi'an. Very few have been found at Zhangjiapo, rather more at Huayuancun. But in all these instances the repertory of shapes is limited and the quality of the craftsmanship is also rather inferior. Jade carving was far less advanced than bronze casting.

In the middle Western Zhou several changes seem to have come together. Many more jades were carved; arc-shaped pendants were strung with beads; small animal-shaped carvings appeared in the west; ornament on the surface of many jade types was reintroduced; bird motifs on such jades were very popular, and composite figures of human heads and dragons, as well as of dragons and birds, were worked into this surface ornament. These changes appear most clearly in western Shaanxi at the tombs of the Yu state at Rujiazhuang, but they also affected the burials at the capitals and spread as far east as Shandong.[133]

In part what seems to have happened is that practices local to the Yu state, such as wearing strings of beads or combinations of them with arc-shaped plaques, appear to have spread slowly eastward; in addition, new categories of jade surface ornament seem to have been introduced from the south. Once again the route may have been through the passes over the Qinling to Baoji. Bird patterns on the jades seem to be related to motifs of strange human-like creatures with large heads shown in profile, with long very fine incised lines suggesting hair and legs bent under the body. Such a design appears, for example, on a handle in the Erickson collection. These handles are often

[131] For jades in the state of Yu, see Lu Liancheng and Hu Zhisheng, *Baoji Yu guo mudi*, vol. 2, pl. 39–40, 87–90, 137–41, 173–93, 205–208.

[132] Tombs of the state of Yu at Baoji, namely Zhuyuangou M9 and Ruijiazhuang M1 and M2, contain strings of beads, in which beads identified as being of *liao* were threaded with beads of agate and jade (Lu Liancheng and Hu Zhisheng, *Baoji Yu guo mudi*, vol. 2, color pl. 25). *Liao* 料 is the name given to a material derived from a silica, such as sand, which in English usage is often termed "faience," a substance related to glass. Faience may have been developed in China. However, like the glass used for beads buried in Eastern Zhou tombs, it may have been introduced to China from further west; ibid., vol. 1, pp. 646–50.

[133] For an arc-shaped pendant strung with beads, later a very popular ornament type, see ibid., vol. 2, pl. 69.

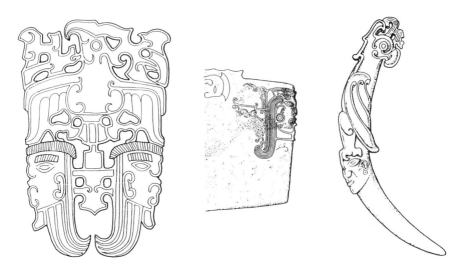

Figure 6.25. Neolithic jades showing either human-like faces in combination with birds or a human face in profile. After Jessica Rawson, ed., *Mysteries of Ancient China: New Discoveries from the Early Dynasties* (London: British Museum, 1996), p. 260, fig. 12. Drawing by Ann Searight.

decorated with the birds on their own. On other jades, including a fine *huang* in the Institute of Arts, Minneapolis, figures appear without the birds. Characteristic of such jade carving is the combination of thick and thin intaglio lines and extensive beveling. Such variety called for great jade-carving skills, indeed a variety that had not been seen in the jade work of Shang times.[134]

Motifs in which figures are combined with birds seem to refer to much earlier jades of the Neolithic period, found in the Shijiahe 石家河 culture of Hubei and perhaps also shared with east coast peoples (Fig 6.25). It seems likely, however, that Zhou interest in these jade motifs came not by way of the Shang but from the south. We know that such interchanges took place because a Shijiahe-type jade showing a face with fangs has come from a middle Western Zhou tomb at Fengxi. This jade displays exceptional skills in carving, with fine relief lines and carefully modulated surfaces. It is thus possible that this jade type provided the models that stimulated the new kinds of jade carving.[135]

[134] See Jessica Rawson, "Shang and Western Zhou Designs in Jade and Bronze," in *International Colloquium on Chinese Art History, 1991: Proceedings, Antiquities, Part 1* (Taipei: National Palace Museum, 1992), pp. 73–105; Jessica Rawson, *Chinese Jade from the Neolithic to the Qing* (London: British Museum Press, 1995), pp. 45–7.

[135] Rawson, *Chinese Jade*, p. 37, fig. 22; pp. 199–201.

Very interesting jades, including the earliest sets of jades for covering the faces of the dead, have come from Fengxi.[136] Such jades often take the forms of the features they were intended to cover, including for example the eyes. From this tradition arose the elaborate jade plaques used in the Jin state tombs to be discussed below (Fig. 6.22). Their number, types, and decoration are all notable innovations. New crafts had sprung up, stimulated, as with bells, by some sort of southern connection. But then the jades were developed, as were the bells, in response to new Zhou uses. These jades reached their full development with the Ritual Revolution. Derived ultimately from the south or southeast, carvings that display crouching figures are seen among the post–ritual Revolution tombs of Qiangjia 強家 at Fufeng (Fig. 6.26c) and in the Jin state tombs at Tianma-Qucun. Human faces and figures and interlaced dragon patterns are among the recurring features of these jades. Further jades then came to be made in standardized shapes and designs, implying a highly organized series of workshops. While it seems likely that we should see the changes in both vessels and jades as resulting in part from contact with the south, the fact that these new bronze and jade types became so well integrated into the ritual and burial practices of the Zhou indicates a significant change in these practices made in response to social and political conditions that fostered and advanced an overall ritual change.

LATE WESTERN ZHOU

The Ritual Revolution

The previous section has indicated that the middle Western Zhou (tenth century B.C.) witnessed significant change in bronze and jade types that had implications both for ritual and burial practice, and by extension for belief. Tombs at Rujiazhuang, Huangdui in Fufeng, and Fengxi all illustrate a range of far-reaching developments: some new bronze ritual vessel types, bronze bells introduced from the south, burial of whole or parts of chariots within tombs rather than in separate pits, and an increase in the range of burial jades and in their ornament. The discussion of the preceding section indicates that many of these developments took place over 50 or 100 years. However, at the capitals near Xi'an there seems to have been a moment when the changes, especially in ritual vessel type, became a standard from which few deviations were made. This relatively complete change from one series of vessels to a

---

[136] Zhang Changshou, "Xi Zhou de zang yu: 1983–1986 nian Fengxi fajue ziliao zhi ba," pls. 8:1, 8:3.

very different series prompts the suggestion that this might be described as a Ritual Revolution. The date of this change is in the reigns of Kings Yih, Xiao, and Yi, from 899/97 to 858 B.C.

As yet no tombs show an even mixture of the two types, that is middle Western Zhou bronzes of the kinds described in the preceding section with smooth rounded forms and bird decoration or the rather less sophisticated Qiu Wei bronzes, and solid and boldly decorated late Western Zhou bronzes illustrated at the beginning of the chapter with the Wei Bo Xing vessels (Fig. 6.6). The tombs at Rujiazhuang, the nearest that we come to such a transition, include the middle Western Zhou ritual vessel repertory mixed in with simplified vessel groups and exotic pieces. The mixture seems to be the result of local happenstance rather than of any central change.

A tomb at Qiangjia 強家 in Fufeng county in the Zhouyuan illustrates a completely different situation (Fig. 6.26). The tomb structure is characteristic of the whole of the Western Zhou, including a stepped pit, with a coffin at the center and a group of ritual vessels on the *ercengtai*. But the vessel set and the jade ornaments of this tomb are quite different from those of earlier burials, even those of the Yu state and certainly those of the early-middle Western Zhou at Zhouyuan, such as the tomb that held the Bo Dong bronzes.[137] The ritual vessels from Qiangjia include several subgroups: four *ding* in descending size, four identical *li*, and four identical *gui*. Both the *li* and the *gui* are of new types, based upon ceramic forms, a development whose beginning appears in the Rujiazhuang tombs. Another innovation is a pair of large wine flasks (*hu*). Like the *gui*, these are very substantial pieces, much heavier than their predecessors in this category. Their weight must have demanded many people to lift them onto substantial altars used to present them. In the Qiangjia tomb are a number of older vessels, including a small two-handled *gui*. But the piece looks insignificant, and it is difficult to imagine it being used with the new *gui* type. Its place in this tomb may have been little more than a remnant of the past, a reminder of a former owner, in just the same way as antiquities were buried in many other tombs. With this tomb a change in ritual practice seems fairly complete.[138] The tomb also includes a complex string of beads and jade plaques, also unparalleled in earlier tombs.[139] At the date of this burial, probably at the transition from middle to late Western Zhou as defined in this chapter, a very significant

[137] *Wenbo* 1987.4: 5–20.

[138] For further comments see Rawson, "Tombs and Hoards."

[139] The Qiangjia jades have been exhibited at Shaochen village in the Zhouyuan but are not fully published. A comparable but less elaborate group from the Jingshu tombs are included in Zhongguo Shehui Kexueyuan Kaogu Yanjiusuo, ed., *Kaoguxue zhuankan, yi zhong di ershi jiu hao, Kaogu jinghua: Zhongguo Shehui kexueyuan Kaogu yanjiusuo jiansuo sishi nian jinian* (Beijing: Kexue, 1993), p. 188, no. 155.

change had taken place in burial, in ritual practice, and in the manufacture of bronzes and jades for these uses.

Such changes appear yet more marked in the bronze ritual vessel hoards excavated at Zhuangbai, Fufeng. This hoard shows a radical realignment of vessel types in the generation of Wei Bo Xing (Fig. 6.6). Most of the earlier Shang wine vessels (i.e., the *jue, gu, jia, fangyi* 方彝, and *gong* 觥) had declined in use and, by this date, had virtually disappeared. This family seems to have piously retained some Shang-type vessels long after most of their Zhou contemporaries had abandoned them. But even they gave them up in the generation of Wei Bo Xing. Meanwhile, the wine vessels that had been generally popular with the Zhou (the *you* and the *zun*), were changed radically to make various very large wine flasks, principally the *hu*. Wine rituals were now limited to those that could be performed using the *hu* vessels.

The roles of the food vessels, *ding* and *gui*, were also transformed. Where earlier food containers of different shapes and decoration might be used together, identical tripods and basins were now favored. These could be seen as subgroups. When such pieces were inscribed, as were the *gui* belonging to Wei Bo Xing, they all carried identical inscriptions. Extensive repetition of shape and inscription was very different from the variety seen on earlier bronzes. In the first two periods discussed, the same inscription might be used on matching pieces, such as the *Feng you* and *zun* (Fig. 6.1c–d), but such pieces were generally of different functional types. The new designs were often very simple. Although they might appear rather coarse alongside the detailed workmanship of the Shang or early Western Zhou, such rows of *ding* or *gui* were probably very imposing in the flickering half-light of a temple. Later texts assert that such subgroups indicated specific rank.[140] Whether they did so already in the late Western Zhou is not clear. Yet the strong, simple shapes and surface decoration repeated many times may well have been intended to convey the importance of their owners. Moreover, with absolutely identical pieces it would have been relatively easy to assess how many an individual owned. Thus, one effect of the change in the designs of *ding* and *gui* was to make them readily recognized as increments of the wealth and, thus, status of their owners.

The *li*, the *dou*, and the *xu* – types that had often been made of ceramic, lacquer, or bamboo – were now also routinely cast in bronze. The motives for this change are not clear. One possibility was that the officiants and their

---

[140] Yu Weichao and Gao Ming, "Zhou dai yong ding zhidu yanjiu," *Beijing daxue xuebao* 1978.1: 84–98 (part 1); 84–97 (part 2); 1979.1: 83–96 (part 3). See also Li Xueqin, *Eastern Zhou and Qin Civilizations*, trans. K. C. Chang (New Haven, Conn.: Yale University Press, 1985), pp. 461–2, for a general discussion, including reference to the comments by He Xiu (A.D. 129–82) to a passage in *Gongyang zhuan* 4 (Huan 2), 7a.

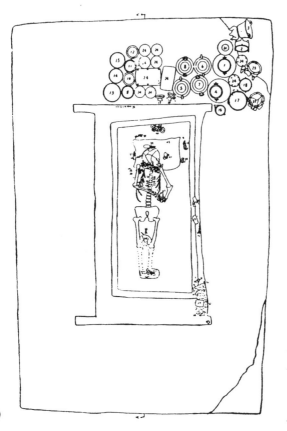

Figure 6.26. Plan of tomb M1
Qiangjia, Fufeng, Shaanxi; (a),
vessel set from the tomb (b),
and rubbings of some of the
jades (c), Qiangjia, Fufeng,
Shaanxi. Middle to late
Western Zhou. After *Wenbo*
1987.4: 5–20, figs. 4, 5, 6, and
rubbing 6. Drawing of (b) by
Ann Searight.

(a)

patrons wished to reinforce the bronze ritual set with vessels that had a long
history, especially among the Zhou, but a history that was outside the range
of the earlier use of bronze.[141]

The final component to be mentioned is the bell set. As already described,
bells probably came into Shaanxi from the south by way of western Shaanxi.
Over fifty years or more, a foreign bronze type was introduced and adapted
in the period of Wei Bo Xing. In other words, exotic variety was tamed by
this date. But the bells added a completely new element to the rituals, that
of resonant music. While bells occur occasionally in Anyang tombs, there is
little evidence of their use in the period before the late-middle Western Zhou

[141] The sources of some shapes in materials other than bronze is discussed in Rawson, *Western Zhou Ritual
Bronzes from the Arthur M. Sackler Collections*, vol. 1, pp. 105–13.

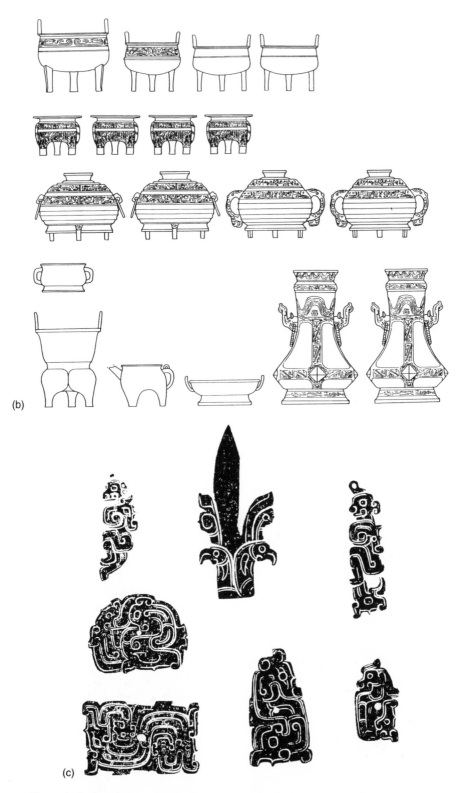

(b)

(c)

Figure 6.26. *(cont.)*

in metropolitan Shaanxi. They were not, it seems, available or perhaps not required. Their introduction, with many large pieces forming sets to produce music, would have made the rituals quite different from those held at earlier times.[142]

These bronze vessels and bells were simply not equivalent to the range of vessels of the early part of the middle Western Zhou, as seen in the Dong tomb or in tomb 19 at Qijia in Fufeng county. The rituals practiced by the owners of those bronzes were different from those now practiced with this new vessel set. Just the weight of the new bronzes would have made them difficult to lift. Indeed, the visual effects of the rites were also likely to have been transformed. Solid heavy *ding* and *gui* in the Wei Bo Xing group (Fig. 6.6) had a different impact from the highly varied vessels in tomb 13 at Zhifangtou, Baoji (Fig. 6.12). In addition, the uniform and repetitive *li, dou,* and *xu* 盨 must have looked and felt very different from the vessels of the same shapes previously made in other materials. The picture presented by the new vessels and bells, the movements required for their use, and the accompanying music had all changed. Some new interpretation of the ritual seems likely. Such changes were probably not simply a matter of fashion.

The new ritual set is likely to have been embedded within a worldview rather different from that in which the earlier sets were located. For instance, the much larger sizes of the ritual vessels, their comparative uniformity, and the use of bell music presuppose a need to impress by weight and by sound, be the audience the living world or that of the ancestors and spirits. The very regularity of the bronzes in number and design suggests a need for some sort of visible ordering, one much more explicit than that of the earlier ritual system. The presentation of status had changed from a concern with high quality and variety in ritual vessels to an exposure of mass and uniformity. If the visual order was now explicit, so perhaps was Zhou aspiration to social order through ritual. That order was relatively unchanging. While early Western Zhou bronzes seem to have varied from decade to decade and those of middle Western Zhou at least by quality of surface design, the late Western Zhou period bronzes are rigidly uniform. There seems to have been little variety either from owner to owner or from place to place over the hundred years of their use. A strong centralized control of ritual seems to have been in place.

In the same way, inscriptions seem unvarying, as though a single model for the range of expression, for the contents, and for the shapes of the char-acters was in force. As already mentioned these characters seem closely depen-

---

[142] For a discussion of the sources of late Western Zhou bells in the south and their possible transmis-sion by way of Shaanxi, see Rawson, *Western Zhou Ritual Bronzes from the Arthur M. Sackler Collec-tions,* vol. 2, nos. 123–9.

dent on early written forms and thus suggest an element of deliberate archaism. Other suggestions of archaism are seen in some vessel shapes, such as the *gui* on a square base. It would appear that this interest in the past was twofold, first in the reproduction of ancient shapes of vessel and character type, and second in the collection of older bronzes. Inscribed bronzes are characteristic of almost all hoards. Where the vessels are late and fall into the sets just mentioned, the inscriptions are beautifully written but stereotyped in content. The hoards also include inscribed vessels important for their individually specific content, as with the *Shi Qiang pan* in the Zhuangbai hoard or the Qiu Wei vessels in the Dongjiacun hoard.

The sense of order and organization that derives from these hoards is first and foremost visible in Shaanxi. It is here that the majority of finds have been made, and as mentioned at the beginning of the chapter, most of the hoards have come from the Zhouyuan. The principal features of the hoards are that they regularly include the sets of *ding* and *gui* necessary for any ritual practice. Thus, large groups have come from the hoards at Dongjiacun in Qishan county and at Zhangjiapo near Xi'an.[143] Hoards of bronzes similar to those already mentioned in connection with the Zhouyuan are much more scarce in the Feng area of the capitals and in Hao. Perhaps ancestral temples were less common in this area than they were in the Zhouyuan. It is also possible that at the capital the Zhou had more warning than their relatives further west and were able to flee with their bronzes, but this seems unlikely; there is very little evidence that any significant number of early Western Zhou bronzes were taken eastward. For instance, eighth-century tombs at Sanmenxia 三門峽, Henan, belonging to the Guo 虢 state, contained many ancient jades but only replica bronzes.[144] It would appear that the principal ritual vessels had been left behind.

As the Zhou fled, they probably buried these hoards of bronzes first of all because they represented real wealth. The bronze of which they were cast was intrinsically valuable. The Zhou obviously had no wish to see such a resource fall into the hands of the enemy. But the very large number of inscriptions on the buried pieces suggest that these were particularly valuable. Pieces carrying inscriptions earlier than the date of the main bronzes in the hoards also confirm this view. Indeed, hoards were archives preserved precisely because the records were important. Later burials in other parts of China do

---

[143] For the hoard at Dongjiacun, see *Wenwu* 1976.5: 26–44. For the hoard from Zhangjiapo, see Zhongguo Kexueyuan Kaogu yanjiusuo, ed., *Chang'an Zhangjiapo Xi Zhou tongqi qun* (Beijing: Wenwu, 1965).

[144] "Replica bronzes" denotes vessels made in forms that had long been obsolete, in such sizes that they could not have been used for the same purposes as those of the original models that they copied. It would appear that such replicas were made purposefully for inclusion in tombs, in order to convey a link with earlier or ancestral practice.

not reveal many examples of inscribed bronzes. They were thus not carried eastward, or if similar bronzes were taken with the fleeing Zhou, they were later lost or recast. In later centuries inscribed bronzes were relatively rare.

Late Zhou bronzes are often very large, suggesting that there was sufficient wealth to enable large pieces to be cast. Outstanding in this category are several very large *ding* tripods. Among these is the *Shi Zai ding* 師𩛥鼎 from a pit at Qiangjiacun 強家村, Fufeng, the *Da Yu ding* 大盂鼎, the *Da Ke ding* 大克鼎, and a *ding* from Meixian.[145] However, such items were rarely buried in tombs. Late Western Zhou tombs have, for example, been identified at Fengxi, but they do not seem to have included bronzes. Further, relatively few large groups of late Western Zhou bronzes have been found outside Shaanxi. The major exceptions to this observation are the bronzes in the Jin state tombs near Houma in southern Shanxi. Other Western Zhou bronzes have come from Henan and Shandong. But in all likelihood the majority of what have been identified as late Western Zhou burials probably date to early Eastern Zhou, with some late Western Zhou pieces.

The State of Jin and Other Late Western Zhou Finds Outside Shaanxi

Late Western Zhou burials are also very scarce in other areas already discussed. The northern state of Yan would appear to have been without members of the Zhou elite who wished to be buried there with their ritual furnishings. In the same way, there do not seem to be significant late Western Zhou burials at Luoyang. In this regard, the recent finds of late Western Zhou tombs at the cemetery of the Jin state are highly unusual. A series of magnificent burials has been unearthed.[146] A cemetery with seventeen tombs, the majority with a single access ramp (two with two such ramps), and six chariot pits was excavated between 1992 and 1995. A number of bronzes from this area, together with a number of looted pieces, some later purchased by the Shanghai Museum, record the names of Jin lords in their inscriptions. The burials are of the typical Zhou pattern, with coffins laid within rectangular pits. Bronze ritual vessels were placed upon the *erengtai*. The burials are particularly remarkable for their exceptional jade ornaments that cover the bodies of the dead. These indicate the wealth of the tomb occupants, and the access ramps also suggest that these tombs rank well above most of those discovered in Shaanxi and are of equivalent status to that of the large tombs discovered in Wey and at Yan.

---

[145] Wu Zhenfeng and Luo Zhongru, "Shaanxi sheng Fufeng xian Qiangjiacun chutu de Xi Zhou tongqi," *Wenwu* 1975.8: 57–62; Shi Yan, "Meixian Yangjiacun da ding," *Wenwu* 1972.7: 3–4.

[146] *Wenwu* 1994.1: 4–28; *Wenwu* 1994.8: 1–21, 22–33, 68; *Wenwu* 1995.7: 4–39.

Early tombs excavated among this group have not been reported fully. The only bronzes so far reported are standard early to middle Western Zhou pieces. The tombs and contents that have been described are dated to the second half of late Western Zhou; on the evidence of the ritual vessels, several clearly belong to the early Eastern Zhou, matching in shape and design those of categories known from other sites, especially in Henan and Hubei. Tombs M8 and M31 are thought to belong to the late Western Zhou, while tombs M93 and M102 are deemed by the excavators to belong to the early Eastern Zhou. In addition tombs M62 and M64 may also be of late Western Zhou or Eastern Zhou.[147] These late tombs contain up to five *ding* and four *gui*; thus, their owners claimed status substantially lower than that of Wei Bo Xing, who had owned eight *gui* (and presumably nine *ding*). In addition, the tombs routinely hold large *hu* (see Fig. 6.27) which are characteristic of the Western Zhou ritual vessel set, and also sets of bells. These highly conventional items are similar to pieces from Shaanxi. Indeed, the *gui* from tomb M64, a relatively late tomb, are almost identical with the Wei Bo Xing *gui*, confirming the very static nature of bronze design at this period.[148] Some unusual pieces have been found; for example, tomb M8, a late Western Zhou tomb, contained vessels in the shape of hares. These animal-shaped containers appear to have developed from the middle Western Zhou animal-shaped vessels, such as those seen in the Yu state.

While tombs M8 and M31 seem to contain generally conventional bronzes, bells, and chariot parts, they introduce, and the later tombs contain more of, a number of striking categories of vessels that raise certain basic questions. The first of the three principal categories to be considered is use of neat but rather poorly cast standard ritual vessels, especially sets of *ding*, *gui* and *yi* (Fig. 6.28a). While most of these match their Shaanxi counterparts, they are often inferior in design and casting. Simple rounded *ding*, *gui* on square bases, and bells from tomb M8 are such pieces.

The second category comprises vessels that can perhaps be described as sculptural (Fig. 6.28b). Among the earliest in date is a disc-shaped *he* from tomb M31. It has a bird on the lid, a dragon spout, and small human figures as feet. In a later tomb, M63, a square boxlike creation has human feet and animal handles; it is accompanied by a cylindrical example, also with a bird on the lid, and human-like feet.[149] These pieces seem to be a later development of a phenomenon, seen rather fleetingly in Shaanxi, where disc-shaped

---

[147] The excavators date tombs M93, M102, and M63 to Eastern Zhou (*Wenwu* 1995.7: 4–39). Tomb M63 holds a rounded *hu* of a type seen in Eastern Zhou tombs in Henan and Hubei; see *Wenwu* 1980.1: 51–3, fig. 7; *Kaogu* 1984.6: 510–14, pl. 4:5.

[148] *Wenwu* 1994.8: 7, fig. 8:2.

[149] *Wenwu* 1994.8: 12, 13, 14, 66, figs. 22, 23, 24: 2, 4.

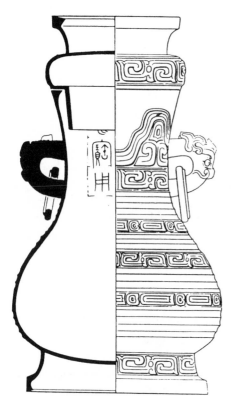

Figure 6.27. Drawing of a *hu* from tomb
M63, Tianma-Qucun, Houma, Shanxi.
Probably early Eastern Zhou. After
Wenwu 1994.8: 14, fig. 24:3.

he were also employed, as was an unusual form of cooking vessel with a lower
section in which hot charcoal could be placed. This vessel type appears in
the Zhuangbai hoard and has a human figure acting as door guardian. While
the pieces may ultimately have had an exotic origin, their most striking features are the use of shapes derived from materials such as wood and sculptural figural appendages.[150]

The third category, perhaps the most remarkable feature of the Jin tombs,
is replica bronzes, that is, bronzes that cannot be viewed as fully functional.
They are small, often roughly cast, and manifestly unusable because in some
cases the bodies and lids were cast as a single piece or because the ceramic

[150] For a *he* from Qijiacun in Shaanxi, see Liang Xingpeng and Feng Xiaotang, "Shaanxi Chang'an Fufeng
   chutu Xi Zhou tongqi," pl. 2:6. This *he* was accompanied by a *pan* in the same find; it has feet in
   the shape of human figures and thus belongs to the same category as the vessels from Shanxi. Both
   the animals of the *he* and the human figures on the *pan* suggest contacts with border areas that
   may include the western periphery of the Zhou territory as well as the south. For the vessel from
   Zhuangbai, see *Shaanxi chutu Shang Zhou qingtongqi*, vol. 2, pls. 77, 78.

core was left solid inside them (Fig. 6.28c). These vessels were made primarily in the shapes of ancient pieces. While tomb M8 holds actual ancient pieces in the form of a middle Western Zhou *he* and an even earlier *jue* (Fig. 6.29), the later tombs contain copies of several vessel types, among which rectangular vessels, known as *fang yi*, as well as *jue*, stand out.[151] In Shaanxi ancient versions of these out-of-date bronzes were retained in hoards.

The replicas discovered in late Jin tombs were accompanied by another equally remarkable phenomenon, the burial of a large number of antique jades (Fig. 6.30). As we have seen, the number of jades buried increased dramatically from the time of the Ritual Revolution. Both a change in practice and a change in manufacturing is implied by such developments. But the burial of ancient pieces in large numbers was yet another phenomenon. The most prized ancient jades seem to have been small animal-shaped amulets dating from the Shang and perhaps the early Western Zhou. Occasionally a great rarity was included in this group, as for example when a dragon of the Hongshan 紅山 type was found in a Guo state tomb.[152] Other early jades include *ge* scepters of the Shang period, found in quite a number of tombs; they formed the basis for the development of copies, presumably as scepters, that were signs of rank. Occasional oddities include a *cong* 琮 (a Neolithic jade of square cross-section, with a circular base) of the southeastern Neolithic Liangzhu 良渚 culture (or a copy of a Liangzhu piece) in tomb M8 at Tianma-Qucun and a fine disc with a Shang inscription from tomb M31.[153]

Two other areas, or small states, share with Jin this interest in reproducing much earlier bronze types and the burial of ancient jades, the state of Ying in southern Henan and the state of Guo at Sanmenxia on the Yellow River.[154] At both Ying and Guo there have been found simple, standardized bronzes of a quality lower than the castings in Shaanxi. However, both areas made vessels that could not be employed in practice; that is to say, they were replicas made for burial, especially *gui* that were cast with lids fixed to the body. Reproductions that copy forms that were otherwise long obsolete, especially the *fang yi*, also appear in Ying and Guo.[155]

---

[151] For a replica *fang yi* from Tianma-Qucun tomb M63, see *Wenwu* 1994.8: 14, fig. 24:1; and M93, *Wenwu* 1995.7: 4–39, fig. 43:7; and for *jue*, see ibid., fig. 43:5.

[152] For tomb M63 at Tianma-Qucun, see *Wenwu* 1994.8: 16, fig. 26; and for M2006 at Shangcunling, Sanmenxia, Henan, see *Wenwu* 1995.1: 4–31. The latter burial is dated by the archaeologists to the late Western Zhou, but the *hu* type in the tomb suggests a later dating.

[153] *Wenwu* 1994.1: 4–28, figs. 35, 36; *Wenwu* 1994.8: 30, fig. 14.

[154] Closely related bronzes are found in early Eastern Zhou sites in Shandong; see *Wenwu* 1983.12: 1–6.

[155] For bronzes from the Guo state, see *Wenwu* 1995.1: 4–31. This tomb includes bronzes that reproduce the kind of *zun* with extension seen among the Bo Dong vessels (Fig. 6.18), as well as *jue* and *fang yi*. The *hu* from this tomb dates to the Eastern Zhou. For a replica *fang yi* from Pindingshan in the Ying state, see *Hua Xia kaogu* 1988.1: 30–44, pl. 8:6.

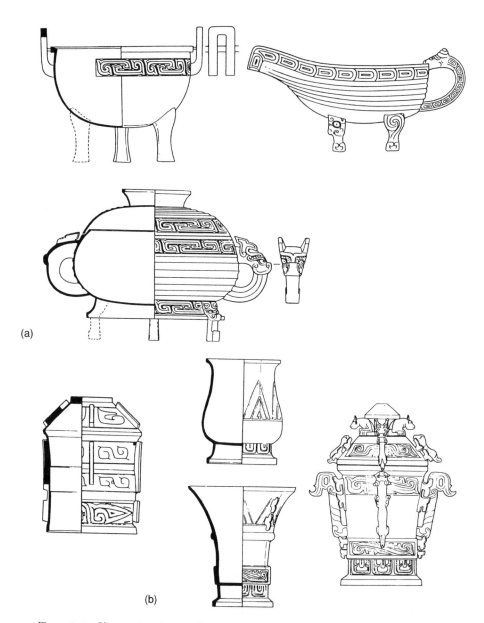

Figure 6.28. Characteristic bronzes from Tianma-Qucun, Houma, Shanxi; (a) standard ritual vessels from tomb M62 (after *Wenwu* 1994.8: 10, fig. 16:1–3); (b) replica bronzes in ancient shapes (after *Wenwu* 1995.7: 30, fig. 43:4, 5, 7); (c) exotic bronzes with sculptural appendages from tombs M63 and M31 (after *Wenwu* 1994.8: 14, figs. 24:4, 2; 25, fig. 4:4).

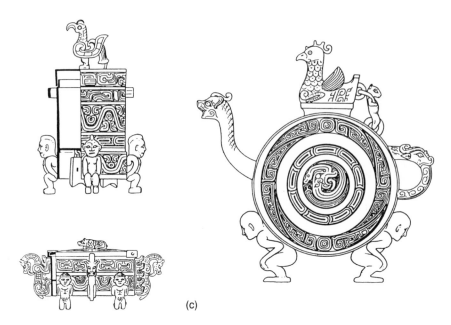

(c)

Figure 6.28. (cont.)

For a short time after the fall of the Zhou, these replicas were occasionally copied to provide forms for usable vessels in the shapes of ancient *fangyi*. Such pieces were especially popular in southern Henan and northern Hubei, and one piece has come from Anhui. But once bronze casting was well established in these areas, these antiquated forms were abandoned. Indeed, the states of the Eastern Zhou period seem to have been much less concerned with keeping and treasuring ancient obsolete vessels than were the Western Zhou.[156] Bronze replicas were deviations from what had been and what was to continue to be the norm for Henan and Hubei. These areas did not develop replicas progressively for burial; once Henan became wealthy enough, great quantities of innovative bronzes were buried. These innovations perhaps suggest that all these trends indicate a dissolution of previous practices, a dissolution that certainly took place after 771 B.C. but that may have already been under way a couple of decades earlier. Replicas or *ming qi* 明器 (spirit vessels) seem to indicate that real bronzes were not available,

---

[156] For an early Eastern Zhou *fangyi* from Suixian 隨縣, Hubei, see E Bing, "Hubei Suixian faxian Zeng guo tongqi," *Wenwu* 1973.5: 21–5, pl. 4:1. For a *fangyi* from Anhui, see Fang Guoxiang, "Anhui Congyang chutu yijian qingtong fangyi," *Wenwu* 1991.6: 94. This bronze seems to be based upon early Western Zhou models and may indeed have been copied from a bronze of this date much earlier than the replicas that are the subject of the present discussion.

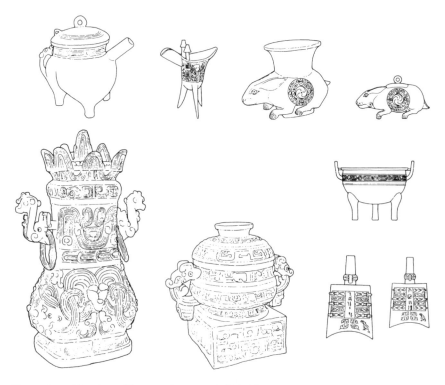

Figure 6.29. Drawing of bronzes from tomb M8, Tianma-Qucun, Houma, Shanxi. After *Wenwu* 1994.1: 4–12, figs. 21, 22, 23, 25, 28 and color plate. Drawing by Ann Searight.

either because they had been left behind in Shaanxi or because they were too precious to bury.

The burial practices of Shanxi and Henan seem to have been distinct from those of Shaanxi. Moreover, they differ from the principal Eastern Zhou developments. We might see the period as a moment when the traditions of Shaanxi were for the last time rehearsed in the lands beyond the pass before they were changed out of all recognition by the demands of display and competition between the states. As such competition developed, the homogeneity that the Zhou seem to have prized above much else was exchanged for a stimulating variety, defying once more the difficulties of technology and the bonds of tradition.

CONCLUSION

During the Western Zhou, the principal seat of political power was in Shaanxi, unlike the periods before and after, when more important centers

Figure 6.30. Early jades from tomb M63, Tianma-Qucun, Houma, Shaanxi. After *Wenwu* 1994.8: 16, fig. 26; 17, fig. 27.

were located in Henan, Hubei, and Shanxi. This political power was represented materially in buildings, tombs, and their contents. As we have seen, major questions that remain unanswered concern the origin of the Zhou and their reasons for and manner of establishing their base in Shaanxi. This chapter has emphasized the contribution of disparate forces, including the influence of peoples of the periphery, to what we call Zhou culture. Relatively obscure origins seem to have been rapidly overshadowed by the skill with which the Zhou adopted Shang practices. The material culture of Shaanxi was transformed. Furthermore, Zhou command of their territory was great enough to achieve a series of links, or lines of communication, across a broad area.

In northern Central China, Zhou material culture shows a very pronounced degree of uniformity, even though there are three quite distinct stages visible in ritual bronzes. In addition to unity in burial practice and ritual bronze manufacture, these items also show a Zhou interest in status and in the commemoration of links between members of the same and different social levels, as well as a preoccupation with the past. These concerns are enshrined in rituals that embraced a link with the ancestors and drew them into the lives of their descendants, just as the descendants saw their own lives absorbed by those of their ancestors.

When the Zhou and their contemporary lords and officials left their homeland, a very significant physical change was effected. Whatever else remained the same, a major void appeared in the previous fabric of political and social relations. The life of the small states perhaps continued as it had in the decades before 771 B.C. But life in Shaanxi did not. Furthermore, from the perspective of the states in Henan, Shandong, and Hubei, relationships between the princes and lords and the Zhou royal house, and the significance of that royal house, were also irrevocably changed. As a result, the rites and ceremonies of these states were cut loose from those of the Zhou royal house in a way that would have been inconceivable earlier. We can literally see, as the people of the day surely also saw, that the rites now enacted and the ideology that was purveyed with bronzes, jades, and chariots deployed in burial, as in life, no longer presented the power and achievements of the Zhou polity as a whole.

Certainly for later periods, we do not have any similar assemblages of bronzes of such a wide range of date or of such legal or political value. The centuries of the Spring and Autumn period provide many examples of princely tombs, but there is no evidence of the kind of family networks seen in Shaanxi, with their scions ruling in other parts of the territory. The Zhouyuan was the unique center of ritual for the Zhou elite. It had a unique practical function and also a unique representational role.

Another major change followed from the first. As this chapter has explained, Zhou material culture had a major characteristic: the Zhou employed inscribed bronzes to record in words and preserve in physical form the achievements of a succession of generations within a family. In addition, the record of the family's achievements and relationships, both with their peers and with the royal household, remained embodied in these inscribed bronzes. As they were used and preserved, they kept this verbal and visual record intact. Numerous sites in Shaanxi emphasize how particular this practice was to Zhou life in that area. Even in Zhou times these large assemblages were less frequent beyond the passes that led to the east. Once the Zhou lost their western capital, the custom seems to have fallen into disuse. The replicas in the Jin, Ying, and Guo tombs are evidence of its decline. Inscribed bronzes held together in an archive that records the honors of a family for posterity are the ideal possessions of a particular ideology. The Eastern Zhou states seem to have given up the use of bronzes in this way and thus probably espoused a very different ideology. The fall of Western Zhou brought to an end not only the use of Shaanxi as a royal center, but also its use in a very particular way. When the Qin in turn came to build up its power base in the same region, the objects it chose to use were different. The Western Zhou was a special moment in the history of China, when a special message about the role of a ruling house was formulated and when the portable objects of society were enlisted to propagate that view.

Zhou rule across a large area, reinforced by a strongly articulated message in words and material objects, became and remained a model for all later rulers. Moreover, rulers, their officials, and later historians took the Zhou model at its face value. They believed what the Zhou said: namely that the Zhou were the true successors of a single earlier state, the Shang, and that the natural condition of China was such a single state. Yet we know that before the Zhou conquest, the Chinese landmass was occupied by many different competing people who created diverse states and cultures, some of the most remarkable of which are described in Chapter 3. Furthermore, not only in the subsequent period of the Eastern Zhou, but throughout all later history, regional cultures and political differences pulled against the efforts to create and maintain a single state. Thus, the most salient Zhou contribution lies in the tenacity of the political model they proclaimed and the tensions their aspirations generated within the more naturally fragmented Chinese region.

CHAPTER SEVEN

THE WANING OF THE BRONZE AGE: MATERIAL CULTURE AND SOCIAL DEVELOPMENTS, 770–481 B.C.

Lothar von Falkenhausen

The period under discussion, from the abandonment, in 771 B.C., of the Zhou royal capitals in present-day Shaanxi to the usurpation of power in Qi 齊 by the Chen 陳 lineage in 481 B.C., is defined by the concerns of political history;[1] in the evolution of material culture, it does not constitute a self-contained unit. Ample archaeological discoveries nevertheless allow one to trace some important cultural and social transitions over the course of these three centuries. Briefly stated, the ritual system established in the course of the Late Western Zhou Ritual Reform, described in the preceding chapter, was implemented in large portions of the Zhou culture area, leading to a homogenization of Zhou civilization at the elite level and to ever more salient contrasts with the lifeways of the "Barbarians" in the surrounding areas. In spite of some important technological innovations that occurred after ca. 600 B.C., especially in the area of metallurgy (mass production of bronzes and incipient iron manufacture), this period is characterized, for the most part, by the consolidation of earlier trends. Fundamental social transformations, accompanied by the rise of new religious ideologies, did not occur until the mid-fifth century B.C.

Textual records dating mostly to the fourth to second centuries B.C., sup-

---

[1] This time span partly corresponds to the time covered by the *Chunqiu* 春秋 (Spring and Autumn), the official chronicle of the polity of Lu 魯 as edited (allegedly) by Confucius, which covers the years 722–481 B.C. A supplement to the *Zuo zhuan* 左傳 (Zuo's tradition; originally a separate historical work, recast into a running commentary on the *Chunqiu*) extends coverage through 468 B.C. Even though the Eastern Zhou period, so called because the royal Zhou then resided at their Eastern capital of Luoyang 洛陽, begins as early as 770 B.C. (almost half a century before the *Chunqiu*), its first three centuries or so are conventionally referred to as the "Spring and Autumn period" (more correctly, in this writer's opinion, "Springs and Autumns period"), a term also used, albeit reluctantly, in this chapter. There is little agreement among traditional historians as to when this period ends; as alternatives to 481 B.C., commonly suggested cutoff dates include 479, 475, and 403 B.C. For an archaeological study, a date of ca. 450 B.C. would work better than 481, adopted in this volume.

plemented by a relatively small corpus of authentic epigraphic material,[2] convey a fairly detailed picture of political events and processes during this period (to be described in the following chapter), as well as of the mores, rites, and diplomatic customs of the Zhou aristocracy. Historical narratives commonly emphasize three broad social and political developments during this period: the rise of territorial polities during the early part in the face of weakening royal Zhou government (a process already well under way during the final century of the Western Zhou); the subsequent devolution of political power within polities to competing lineages or branch lineages interlinked by kinship ties; and incipient attempts, after the mid-sixth century B.C., to replace the old aristocratic order by more rationalized and centralized political structures (attempts that would come to fruition during the following centuries).

Eastern Zhou material culture is often assumed to reflect the political fragmentation of the age (see Map 7.1). Historians and archaeologists in the People's Republic of China – particularly, and perhaps not fortuitously, since the recent loosening of the central government's grip on the provinces – have been much preoccupied with the definition of separate "cultures" for each of the different polities mentioned in the historical sources. Such efforts have imposed simplistic and often dubious interpretations on the diverse archaeologically defined regional traditions that had simultaneously evolved in various parts of China over several millennia. Actually, compared with the extent of material diversity observable in earlier times, Eastern Zhou archaeological remains on the whole suggest increasing cultural convergence; salient regional peculiarities persist only in the border areas of the Zhou realm, that is, the lower Yangzi area, the area south of the Yangzi, the Sichuan Basin, the northern steppe zone, the Manchurian plains, and the tip of the Shandong Peninsula. Over time, some of these outlying areas, especially in the southeast and east, were drawn into the Zhou culture sphere; along the northern peripheries, on the other hand, differences vis-à-vis the Zhou realm grew ever more pronounced, apparently mirroring an increasingly hermetic distinction between Chinese versus Barbarian lifeways in the minds of Eastern Zhou

---

[2] Besides bronze inscriptions (on which, see Gilbert L. Mattos, "Eastern Zhou Bronze Inscriptions," in Society for the Study of Early China, and *New Sources of Early Chinese History*, ed. Edward L. Shaughnessy [Berkeley: Institute of Asian Studies, University of California, Berkeley, 1997]), surviving epigraphic materials from this period comprise the Qin stone drums (*shigu* 石鼓), inscribed with hunting poems and datable to the sixth or fifth century B.C. (see Gilbert L. Mattos, *The Stone Drums of Ch'in* [Nettetal: Steyler Verlag Wort und Werk, 1988]), and the Houma covenant strips (*mengshu* 盟書), which record the texts of sworn alliances between lineages and were ritually buried with an animal sacrifice, and which probably date to the first decades or so of the fifth centuy B.C. (*Houma mengshu*) [Beijing: Wenwu, 1976]; for discussion and further references, see Susan R. Weld, "Covenant in Jin's Walled Cities: The Discoveries at Houma and Wenxian" [Ph. D. dissertation, Harvard University, 1990]).

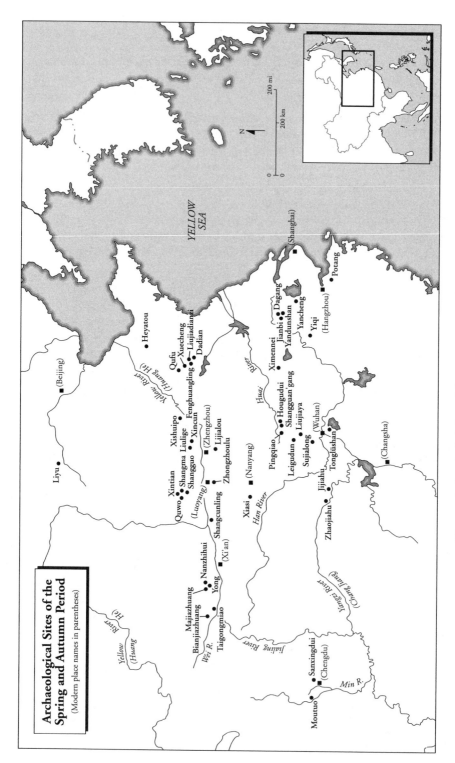

Map 7.1 Archaeological sites of the Spring and Autumn period.

writers. Viewed in hindsight, this situation presages the eventual unification of the Zhou realm at the end of the third century B.C. and the concomitant rise of powerful empires on the northern steppes.

Serious research into the archaeology of the Spring and Autumn period began in 1923 with the discovery of the large tomb of a ruler of Zheng 鄭, at Lijialou 李家樓, Xinzheng 新鄭, Henan. Ever since then, excavations have focused on tombs and cemeteries, though a small number of Eastern Zhou settlement sites has also been investigated. Like the historical texts, the available archaeological record is strongly biased in favor of remains pertaining to the aristocratic segment of the population; even mines and workshop sites had their raisons d'être in providing luxury items to the elite. Some excavated evidence from settlements pertains to ordinary urban dwellers, but as yet archaeology provides no direct information about the life of the rural population. Such a lopsided perspective is a fundamental problem in research on the Chinese Bronze Age, severely curtailing archaeology's potential contribution as an independent source of evidence that may complement as well as modify the conclusions of text-based historiography.

In spite of such shortcomings, archaeological finds have added much to our knowledge of the Spring and Autumn period. Archaeological chronologies have been worked out for most subareas of the Zhou culture, as well as for some peripheral regions; the study of cemeteries and constellations of burial goods in tombs has opened new perspectives on social organization; by tracing stylistic developments regionally, it has become possible to define distinct workshop traditions in different parts of China; and much has been learned regarding the history of technology, especially in the realm of metallurgy. New evidence continues to emerge.

SETTLEMENT SITES AND ACTIVITY AREAS

Early Eastern Zhou society was kinship-based and dominated by aristocratic lineages that resided at walled settlements, often problematically referred to as "cities" (cheng 城). The distribution and hierarchy of such settlements, which were political as well as ritual centers, mirrors political configurations. The territorial structure of the Zhou realm during most of this period is best conceptualized as a network of such centers, each sustained by its surrounding rural periphery; the notion of a bounded territory only arose gradually after the sixth century B.C.[3]

[3] See K. C. Chang, *Early Chinese Civilization: Anthropological Perspectives* (Cambridge, Mass.: Harvard University Press, 1976), pp. 47–92; Paul Wheatley, *The Pivot of the Four Quarters: A Preliminary Enquiry into the Origins and Character of the Ancient Chinese City* (Edinburgh: Edinburgh University Press, 1971); Hans Stumpfeldt, *Staatsverfassung und Territorium im antiken China: Über die Ausbildung einer territorialen Staatsverfassung* (Düsseldorf: Bertelsmann Universitätsverlag, 1970).

Figure 7.1. Bronze stove, from a cache at Rujiazhuang, Baoji, Shaanxi. Eighth century B.C. From Gao Ciruo and Liu Mingke, "Baoji Rujiazhuang xin faxian tongqi jiaocang," *Kaogu yu wenwu* 1990.4: inside front cover, fig. 2.

Major architecture was limited to the walled settlements of the aristocracy. It consisted of rectangular buildings with stamped-earth foundations and, sometimes, tiled roofs. Construction principles differed little from those of "palace" buildings seen since the Early Bronze Age. Only coffins and burial chambers now attest to the dexterity of carpenters of the Spring and Autumn period, who undoubtedly put the same skills to use in architecture.[4] Some details, such as latched double-pane doors and lattice windows, are rendered on some late Western Zhou and early Spring and Autumn period bronze stoves (Fig. 7.1); but it remains unclear how the weight of the roof was transferred onto vertical supports. The only known representation of an entire building from the Spring and Autumn period, a bronze house model with performing musicians and dancers from tomb 306 at Potang 坡塘, Shaoxing 紹興, Zhejiang,[5] is uninformative on this point (Fig. 7.2); and coming from

---

[4] Eastern Zhou wood joinery techniques are systematically discussed in Lin Shoujin, *Zhanguo ximugong sunjiehe gongyi yanjiu* (Hong Kong: Zhongwen daxue, 1981). For an especially good example from the Spring and Autumn period, see tomb 5 at Caojiagang 曹家崗, Dangyang 當陽, Hubei (*Kaogu xuebao* 1988. 4: 455–500).

[5] *Wenwu* 1984. 1: 10–37.

the non-Zhou periphery, it may not, in any case, be representative. Throughout the period, the vast majority of the population, including, in all probability, large portions of the ranked elite, still dwelled in thatched rectangular or oval huts, often semisubterranean, that were little different from Neolithic houses. Only during the Warring States did above-ground houses become the normal type of residence in most parts of China.[6]

So far, survey and excavation of settlements has been far from sufficient to allow reconstruction of the social landscape of Late Bronze Age China in any detail. Remains datable specifically to the Spring and Autumn period have been identified at some urban enclosures, but in most cases they have been overbuilt by later construction. While conveying some general ideas on urban layout, large-scale ceremonial architecture, and workshop sites, the material is insufficient to allow insights into regional varieties of urban layout or architectural style.

At Luoyang 洛陽, Henan, the sole royal Zhou capital after 770 B.C., no urban remains have yet been found from the first two centuries of the Spring and Autumn period.[7] On the banks of the Jian 澗 River in the western part of the Luoyang plain, a settlement known as Wangcheng 王城 (Royal city) arose gradually after the middle Spring and Autumn. Of approximately square shape, it was surrounded by stamped-earth walls some 3 km on each side; remains of gates have not been found. Stratigraphic evidence underneath a large architectural compound of Warring States date in the southwest corner of the walled area hints at the possible presence of earlier palace buildings from the late Spring and Autumn, grouped around courtyards and axially aligned.[8] Extensive Eastern Zhou cemeteries were found inside as well as outside of Wangcheng, some predating the walled settlement. Wangcheng continued to flourish as a manufacturing center during the Warring States.

The much-repaired walls of Confucius's hometown, the capital of Lu 魯

---

[6] Excavated Spring and Autumn period dwellings of nonelites are extremely scarce; instances have been reported from Beiwu 北塢, Houma 侯馬, Shanxi (*San Jin kaogu* 1 [1994]: 154–84); the Houma foundry (*Houma zhutong yizhi* [Beijing: Wenwu, 1993], vol. 1, pp. 43–55); and Xiwusi 西吳寺, Yanzhou 兗州, Shandong (*Yanzhou Xiwusi* [Beijing: Wenwu, 1990], pp. 126–9).

[7] Possibly, the Zhou capital during that period was located east of modern Luoyang and has been obliterated by the capital of the Han and Northern Wei dynasties (see Li Xueqin, *Eastern Zhou and Qin Civilizations*, trans. K. C. Chang [New Haven, Conn.: Yale University Press, 1985], pp. 16–18). For a speculative discussion of Zhou period sites at Luoyang in the light of textual evidence, see Qu Yingjie, *Xian Qin ducheng fuyuan yanjiu* (Ha'erbin: Heilongjiang Renmin, 1991), pp. 126–58.

[8] On Wangcheng, see *Xin Zhongguo de kaogu faxian he yanjiu* (Beijing: Wenwu, 1984), pp. 270–1, and its references to early excavation reports; Zhongguo Shehui kexueyuan Kaogu yanjiusuo, *Luoyang fajue baogao: 1955–1960 nian Luoyang Jianbin kaogu fajue ziliao* (Beijing: Yanshan, 1989), pp. 107–65; newer discoveries, not yet comprehensively reported, are discussed by Ye Wansong, "Jin shinian Luoyang shi Wenwu gongzuodui kaogu gongzuo gaishu," *Wenwu* 1992. 3: 40–5, 54.

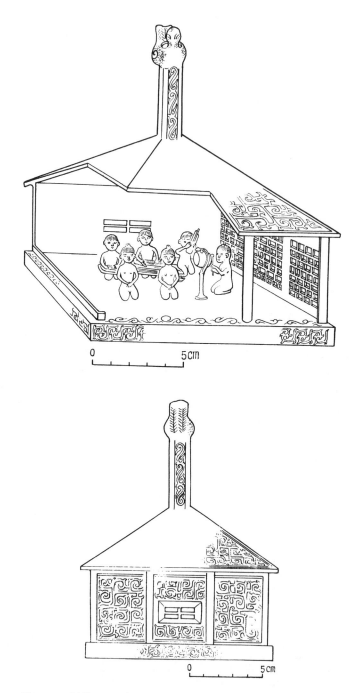

Figure 7.2. House model from tomb no. 306 at Potang, Shaoxing, Zhejiang, *ca.* 500 B.C. After *Wenwu* 1994.1: 24, figs. 38, 39:3. Drawings by Li Xiating.

at Qufu 曲阜, Shandong, are partly preserved to this day.[9] The settlement was probably founded sometime during the Western Zhou and continued to be occupied through Han times. The rectangular enclosure is comparable to Wangcheng in size. Surveys have ascertained the location of eleven gates, three on each side, except for the north side, which has two gates. Even though the gates on opposite sides of the settlement are not in alignment and arteries of traffic inside the walled area do not appear to be laid out exactly according to the cardinal directions, the overall layout of Qufu is, among all known Zhou settlements, closest to the idealized plan of the *Kaogongji* 考工記 (Records for examining the artisans).[10] This text, albeit of much later date, purports to describe conditions under the Zhou dynasty; it stipulates that a capital should be square, with three gates on each side, connected by streets crossing at right angles.

According to this idealized plan, one would expect to find the rulers' residences and temples at the center of the settlement; but that area was overbuilt in the Han dynasty, obliterating all traces of earlier construction. Spring and Autumn period bronze-casting, bone-carving, and pottery-making workshops were found in various locations within the walled area. Zhou period Qufu differed from Han and later cities in that a large part of the walled area was filled with cemeteries for the aristocracy. A rectangular earthen platform some 1.7 km to the southeast of the settlement is thought to be the site of a Zhou dynasty altar for rain-making dances (*wuyutai* 舞雩臺).

The remains of the Jin 晉 capital of Xintian 新田 at Houma 侯馬, Shanxi, exemplify a more complex pattern of urban layout, which may prefigure that of the large Warring States period capitals.[11] Founded in 589 or 585 and abandoned in 376 B.C., the settlement is strategically placed on high ground overlooking the Fen 汾 and Kuai 澮 Rivers near their confluence. The original walled enclosure, known as the Pingwang City 平望城 was a rectangle of approximately 1 sq. km, in the center of which the ruler's palace stood on a slightly elevated platform. During the following century or so, two slightly larger rectangular enclosures were added at the south side, perhaps as residences for branches of the ruling lineage.[12] Several much smaller satellite set-

[9] *Qufu Lu guo gucheng* (Ji'nan: Qilu, 1982); see also Komai Katsuchika, *Kyokufu Rojô-no iseki*, Kôkogaku Kenkyû 2 (1950). For the identification of sites mentioned in textual sources, see Qu Yingjie, *Xian Qin ducheng fuyuan yanjiu*, pp. 260–84.

[10] Sun Yirang, *Zhou li zhengyi* (Beijing: Zhonghua, 1987), vol. 14, pp. 3415–3507. The *Kaogongji*, now attached to the *Zhou li* 周禮 (Rites of Zhou), probably dates no earlier than the third century B.C., though it possibly incorporates earlier lore. For diagrams and further discussion, see Nancy Shatzman Steinhardt, *Chinese Imperial City Planning* (Honolulu: University of Hawaii Press, 1990), pp. 29–36.

[11] See Yu Weichao, "Zhongguo gudai ducheng guihua de fazhan jieduanxing: Wei Zhongguo Kaoguxuehui diwuci nianhui er zuo," *Wenwu* 1985.2: 54–7.

[12] Stratigraphic relationships in the area are still not certain; only Niucun 牛村, the easterly of the two added enclosures, is relatively well known and is datable to the period between the latter half of the

tlements in the immediate surroundings of this triple palace-city are thought to have been the seats of lineages of ministerial rank. Sacrificial caches of covenant strips (*mengshu* 盟書), discovered nearby, document alliances among such groups.[13] The mass of the population apparently dwelled outside the walled enclosures, in areas that developed into the "outer enclosures" (*guo* 郭) of Warring States period capitals.

Towering stamped-earth building platforms in and just outside the major enclosures at Xintian may well be the earliest examples of a new, vertical approach to palace construction, which was to become common during the Warring States period. While little is known about the urban layout of the three larger enclosures, large portions of two of the satellite settlements have been excavated.[14] Each consisted of several smaller walled units, each of which contained extensive complexes of regularly aligned stamped-earth platforms for buildings. The eastern enclosure of the Beiwu 北塢 settlement, for instance, featured twenty-three large buildings grouped around one central structure. Some of these were individually surrounded by stamped-earth walls. Their function, whether for elite residence, ritual, military purposes, or some combination thereof, remains to be elucidated. To the west of these buildings stood three gigantic granaries (each measuring 57 by 15.4 m) in regular alignment. Only one of the ordinary dwellings filling the northern portion of Beiwu has been reported; it is described as an above-ground building of rounded rectangular shape with an associated subterranean storage pit containing remains of sorghum, apricots, and jujubes. Other habitation remains included refuse pits, ovens, drainage ditches, and wells.

Cemeteries for aristocrats and substantial temple building compounds were spread over large areas outside the walled portions of Xintian. The presumed ancestral temple of the Jin rulers, dated to ca. 550–480 B.C., extends over a crescent-shaped area 1 km long, the largest known architectural ensemble from its period.[15] The largest foundation measures 77 by 55 m; its religious function is made plain by the countless sacrificial pits that were dug in the adjacent courtyard and into the foundations of the building after it had been abandoned. In order of frequency, victims include sheep, cattle, horses, and dogs. (Elsewhere at Houma, human sacrifices occur in sacrificial pits, though rarely.) Numerous additional pits, some containing inscribed covenant strips, were found near other ritual structures further afield. Some altar platforms on the south bank of the Kuai River are thought, somewhat

---

sixth to the latter half of the fifth century B.C.; see *Kaogu* 1988.10: 894–909; *Kaogu yu wenwu* 1988.1: 57–60; and Shanxi sheng Kaogu yanjiusuo, *Shanxi kaogu sishinian* (Taiyuan: Shanxi Renmin, 1994), p. 154, where further references may be found.

[13] See note 2.

[14] These are Chengwang 呈王 (*Wenwu* 1983.3: 28–34) and Beiwu (*San Jin kaogu* 1 [1994]: 154–84).

[15] *Kaogu* 1987.12: 1071–85.

unconvincingly, to be the sites of the Suburban Sacrifice (*jiao* 郊) offered to Heaven.[16]

The best-preserved ensembles of Spring and Autumn ceremonial architecture have been reported from Majiazhuang 馬家莊, Fengxiang 鳳翔, Shaanxi, in the walled enclosure of Yong 雍, the capital of Qin 秦 from 677 to 383 B.C.[17] The late Spring and Autumn complex no. 1 constitutes a wall-enclosed compound (Fig. 7.3). Three of the four principal buildings face into a central courtyard, the one on the south side serving as an entrance building; a screen wall blocks the view into the courtyard. An additional small building is located behind the central building. Wood-constructed porticoes surround each building, and each is subdivided symmetrically by stamped-earth walls. Rows of sacrificial pits are aligned in the courtyard. These contain cattle (87, one also containing a sheep), sheep (55), chariots (2), and human victims (9, one also containing a sheep); 28 "empty" pits may have been used for blood sacrifice. The ensemble has been interpreted as an ancestral temple of the Qin rulers. The nearby, approximately contemporaneous complex no. 2 features a succession of five wall-enclosed courtyards (some containing symmetrically aligned buildings), with a screen wall outside the principal entrance; it has been taken as the Qin rulers' palace. Spatial arrangements such as these are directly ancestral to later Chinese architecture.

Qin buildings at Fengxiang are remarkable for their ornate bronze fittings, which were inserted into the timbering of the walls (Fig. 7.4). Another testimony to luxurious elite living, indicating an incipient penchant for chilled beverages, is a Late Spring and Autumn period icehouse (*lingyin* 凌陰) near the palace compounds.[18]

The best evidence for Spring and Autumn period workshop remains comes from Houma. Between the principal walled settlements and the Kuai River, archaeologists uncovered a large-scale bronze foundry, ceramic kilns (some of them specialized in the manufacture of one particular product),

---

[16] Wang Kelin, "Houma Dong Zhou shesi yiji de tantao," *Shanxi wenwu* 1983.1: 8–14. See also *San Jin kaogu* 1 (1994): 208–12.

[17] *Kaogu yu wenwu* 1982.5: 12–20; *Wenwu* 1985.2: 1–29; Shang Zhiru and Zhao Congcang, "Fengxiang Majiazhuang yihao jianzhu yizhi fajue jianbao buzheng," *Wenbo* 1986.1: 11–13. Han Wei has speculatively identified the main buildings as the *zumiao* 祖廟 (temple of the lineage founder), flanked by *mumiao* 穆廟 and *zhaomiao* 昭廟 (temples of descendants in alternating generations), and the small building in the back of the *zumiao* as the Earth Altar of the Vanquished Polities (*wangguo zhi she* 亡國之社); "Majiazhuang Qin zongmiao jianzhu zhidu yanjiu," *Wenwu* 1985.2: 30–8; he has also proposed an elaborate explanation of the "palace" buildings of Complex 2 at Majiazhuang, for which no report has been published as yet; "Qin gong miaoqin zuantantu kaoshi," *Kaogu yu wenwu* 1985.2: 53–6.

[18] Three hoards of bronze fittings for timbered walls were found near the remains of a "palace" at Yaojiagang (*Kaogu* 1976.2: 121–8; Yang Hongxun, "Fengxiang chutu Chunqiu Qin'gong tonggou Jingang," *Kaogu* 1976.2: 103–8); some round metal bosses with animal designs reported by Zhao Congcang ("Shaanxi Fengxiang faxian Chunqiu Zhanguo de qingtongqi jiaocang," *Kaogu* 1986.4: 337–43) may also have served as architectural ornaments. On the *lingyin*, see *Wenwu* 1978.3: 43–5.

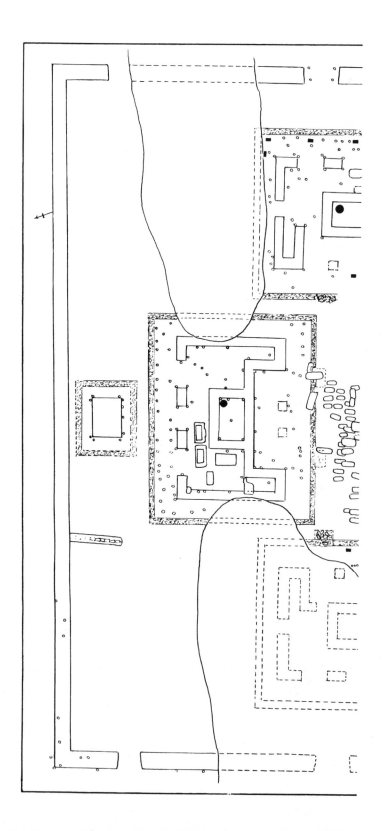

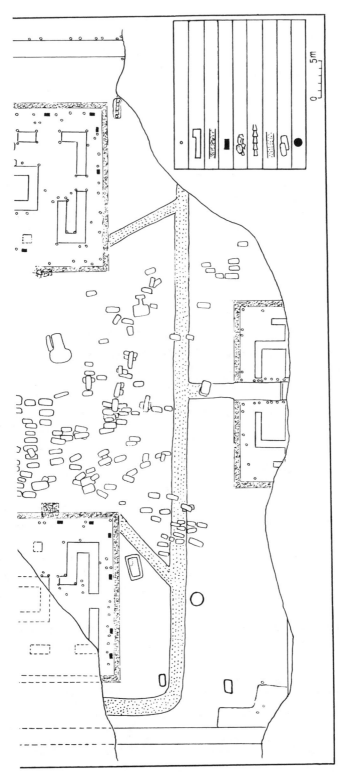

Figure 7.3. Plan of architectural complex I at Majiazhuang, Fengxiang, Shaanxi. Second half of sixth century B.C. After *Wenwu* 1985.2: 4–5, fig. 6. Drawing by Li Xiating.

Figure 7.4. Bronze fitting from a Qin palace building, found in a cache at Yaojiawan, Fengxiang, Shaanxi. Middle to late sixth century B.C. After *Kaogu* 1976.2: 123, fig. 5. Drawing by Li Xiating.

bone-carving workshops, and a workshop that produced stone or jade tablets for use in funerals and for covenant inscriptions.[19] Little planning seems to have gone into their spatial arrangments; constituent structures were not aligned with the cardinal directions and were modified as demanded by the needs of the moment. It appears that workers and their families lived within workshop areas; some were also buried there, especially children, who, throughout Eastern Zhou China, were habitually buried in pots (*wengguan-zang* 瓮棺葬) within the settlements.

The best known of the Houma workshops is the bronze foundry, two sectors of which have been reported:[20] locus 2, which produced ritual vessels

[19] On the kilns, see *Wenwu* 1959.6: 45–6; *Kaogu yu wenwu* 1989.3: 13–19; and *Houma zhutong yizhi*, vol. 1, pp. 59–61; on the stone-tablet-manufacturing workshop at Houma, see *Wenwu* 1987.6: 73–81. Spring and Autumn period kilns in the Yellow River basin generally adhere to the "bun-shaped" type in use since the Neolithic, though kilns of larger firing chambers more rectangular in shape arose during the Eastern Zhou, and there were improvements in ventilation. On the much more sophisticated "dragon kilns" in the Yangzi River system, see below, "The Southeastern Regional Cultures."

[20] *Houma zhutong yizhi*; Li Xiating et al., *Art of the Houma Foundry* (Princeton, N.J.: Princeton University Press, 1996).

as well as other decorated objects destined for high-ranking patrons, and the much more extensive locus 22, mainly specialized in the production of bronze tools. The site is a maze of interpenetrating building remains, activity floors, and refuse pits; their stratigraphic relationships afford some chronological control. At locus 22, a roughly T-shaped activity floor was surrounded by fifty buildings, five of which were entirely subterranean, the rest semisubterranean. Some served as dwellings, others as workshops or storage facilities. Although most of the metal processed was in all probability transported to Houma in the form of ingots, the ores having been smelted near the mines, a certain amount of smelting did go on at the site. Mostly, however, the workshops were devoted to casting, as attested by plentiful raw materials, implements, fragments of crucibles and bellows, and core remains, as well as high-quality ceramic models, pattern blocks (Fig. 7.5), and molds for manufacturing ornamented bronzes. Nonworker officials must have exerted close supervision; little is known about the social and legal status of the artisans.

BRONZES: GENERAL STYLISTIC AND
TECHNOLOGICAL TRENDS

Ritual bronze vessels and bells lend themselves as guideposts in tracing the cultural history of the Spring and Autumn period because they constitute a relatively extensive body of material. They occur at most if not all important archaeological sites, tend to be relatively well preserved, and have been studied extensively over the centuries. Like ceramics (which are difficult to study from publications without access to original specimens) and to a far higher degree than jades or other commonly encountered artifacts, bronzes can be discriminated chronologically, and their shape and ornamentation often allow one to infer their place of manufacture. Since many bronzes bear inscriptions,[21] they are located at the interstice of material- and text-based history. Moreover, they constituted a universally recognized indicator of social status; and their manufacture encapsulates the major developments in technological and economic history.

Overall stylistic trends during the three centuries under consideration require brief summary before considering the archaeological contexts in which bronzes occur.[22] From ca. 770 B.C. through the middle of the seventh

---

[21] See note 2.

[22] See Jenny So, *Eastern Zhou Ritual Bronzes from the Arthur M. Sackler Collection* (New York: Adams, 1995), pp. 10–45. On the pattern-block technique, see also: Robert W. Bagley, "Replication Techniques in Eastern Zhou Bronze Casting," in *History from Things: Essays on Material Culture*, ed. Steven Lubar and W. David Kingery (Washington, D.C.: Smithsonian Institution Press, 1993), pp. 231–41; idem, "What the Bronzes from Hunyuan Tell Us About the Foundry at Houma," *Orientations* 26, 1 (1995): 46–54; and Barbara Keyser, "Decor Replication in Two Late Chou Bronze Chien," *Ars Orientalis* 11 (1979): 127–62.

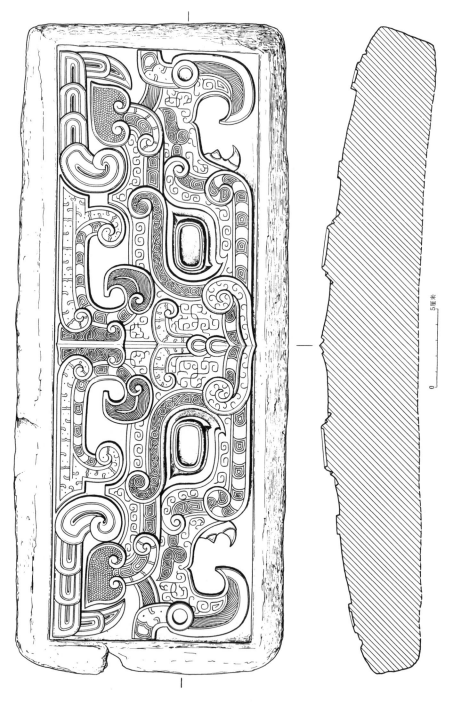

Figure 7.5. Pattern block from the Houma foundry. Late sixth to early fifth century B.C. After *Houma zhutong yizhi* (Beijing: Wenwu, 1993), vol. 1, p. 231, fig. 121. Drawing by Li Xiating.

Figure 7.6. *Zeng Zhong Youfu hu* from Sujialong, Jingshan, Hubei. Eighth century B.C. From Wen Fong, ed., *The Great Bronze Age of China* (New York: Metropolitan Museum of Art, 1980), no. 62.

century, shapes and ornamentation followed late Western Zhou models (Fig. 7.6). On occasion, artisans would indulge in playful variations on these models – compressing or exaggerating their shapes; twisting, turning, and interlacing the ornamentation motifs; filling ever-larger areas on the vessels with ornament; and making increasing use of relieved detail, for example, in accentuating the eyes of dragons or in outfitting vessels with fully sculptural appendages. Such efforts resulted in ever more complex visual effects (Fig. 7.7). From the mid-seventh century B.C. onward, one observes the multiplication of ornamentation bands. They featured extremely miniaturized versions of the earlier decorative motifs, which became ever more intricately interlaced and abstracted. In time, large parts of vessel surfaces thus came to be filled with a monotonous maze of ornamentation, mostly dragon-derived (Fig. 7.8).

Sometime after ca. 600 B.C., these endlessly repeated units of decor came to be produced in the newly invented pattern-block technique, which in time

Figure 7.7. *Huang Zi hu* from tomb 2 at Shangguan'gang, Guangshan, Henan. Mid-seventh century B.C. After *Kaogu* 1984.4: 317, fig. 18:4. Drawing by Li Xiating.

revolutionized both their production process and their visual appearance. Master versions of the decoration units were sculpted in baked clay, from which the manufacturers could obtain a virtually unlimited number of neg-ative impressions; clay strips impressed on these pattern blocks were fitted into the molds, which were then fired. This resulted in a significant economy of labor over traditional procedures practiced at least since Shang times, in which artisans had to carve the decoration individually for each object. Although the casting continued to proceed according to the time-honored piece-mold process, the use of pattern blocks enabled workshops to make do with but a small number of the skilled artisans who designed and carved bronze decoration. By assigning different steps in manufacturing to special-

Figure 7.8. *Song Gong Luan hu* from tomb 1 at Hougudui, Gushi, Henan. *Ca.* 500 B.C. From Li Xueqin, ed., *Zhongguo meishu quanji, gongyi meishu bian 5, qingtongqi (xia)* (Beijing: Wenwu, 1986), no. 29.

ized workers, production was rationalized, facilitating large-scale production of high-quality vessels. This opened the way for commercialization and trade.

The earliest vessels that were apparently produced by the pattern-block technique date to around 600 B.C., but the geographical origins of the technique remain unclear.[23] Though by no means used for every object, it was quickly adopted by workshops throughout the Zhou culture sphere. The stylistic transformations enabled by the use of pattern blocks are best documented by the Houma foundry. During the late Spring and Autumn, the Houma casters abandoned what remained of the late Western Zhou–derived decorative motifs and explored new visual territory with their boldly imaginative banded zoomorphic decor (Fig. 7.9), sometimes referring archaistically to much earlier Shang and early Western Zhou precursors (see Fig. 7.5). But simultaneously with these innovative styles, more generic modes of decora-

---

[23] Efforts at rationalizing bronze production by using uniform units of ornamentation, which may have prefigured certain aspects of the pattern-block technique, may be observed on late Western Zhou and early Spring and Autumn period bronzes; this issue needs further study.

Figure 7.9. *Hu* excavated at Liyu, Hunyuan, Shanxi. Early fifth century B.C. From Wen Fong, ed., *The Great Bronze Age of China* (New York: Metropolitan Museum of Art, 1980), no. 69.

tion with endlessly repeated interlaced dragon motifs continued to be produced. Technological innovations of the late Spring and Autumn period include metal inlay (Fig. 7.10) and the (very infrequent) use of the lost-wax process for casting objects of complex shapes (Fig. 7.11). This was a technique of West Asian derivation that may first have been used in China by artisans working with precious metals.

While motifs and stylistic tendencies had been essentially uniform throughout the first two centuries of the Spring and Autumn period, several geographically distinct workshop traditions emerged during the final century of the period, continuing during the Warring States. In tandem with the sty-

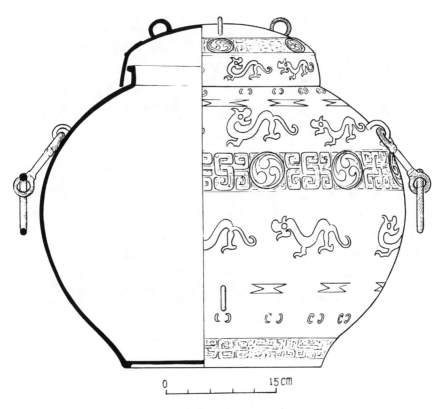

Figure 7.10. Copper-inlaid *Wei Zi Peng yufou* from tomb 2 at Xiasi, Xichuan, Henan. Second half of sixth century B.C. After *Xichuan Xiasi Chunqiu mu* (Beijing: Wenwu, 1991), p. 130, fig. 106. Drawing by Li Xiating.

listic changes, vessel shapes were altered, and vessel assemblages changed slightly as certain old classes of vessels were discarded and new ones were adopted. Of particular significance are the adoption of covered *ding* 鼎 in the place of, or sometimes in addition to, coverless tripod types, and, apparently simultaneously, the pervasive replacement of *gui* 簋 by functionally equivalent kinds of grain-offering vessels.[24] These innovations, which

---

[24] As *gui* equivalents, patrons in the Yellow River basin used, in turn, sets of *cheng* 盛, *zhan* 盏 (or *dui* 敦), and *dou* 豆 (some of these classes of vessels had antecedents during Western Zhou times, others were new); see Gao Ming, "Zhongyuan diqu Dong Zhou shidai qingtong liqi yanjiu," *Kaogu yu wenwu* 1981.2: 68–82; 1981.3: 84–103; and 1981.4: 82–91. Their southerly contemporaries preferred sets of *hú* 匡, complemented by single *cheng* or *dui*; see Li Ling, "On the Typology of Chu Bronzes," trans. Lothar von Falkenhausen, *Beiträge zur Allgemeinen und Vergleichenden Archäologie* 11 (1991): 57–113. Other new classes of vessels in the middle Spring and Autumn period include the oval *hé* 鋓, more rarely seen in its three-legged, covered manifestation (*xing* 鉶) and different kinds of water basins, such as *pen* 盆 (also known as *dian* 奠) and *jian* 鑑. Due to inconsistencies in the epigraphic records, the nomenclature of these vessel types is still under dispute.

Figure 7.11. Altar stand from tomb 2 at Xiasi, Xichuan, Henan. Mid-sixth century B.C. From Li Xueqin, ed., *Zhongguo meishu quanji, gongyi meishu bian 5, qingtongqi (xia)* (Beijing: Wenwu, 1986), no. 17.

occurred at about the same time throughout the Zhou realm, may indicate shifts in ritual practices, although it is difficult to know what they signify.

Aristocratic tombs regularly feature a core set comprising *ding, gui* (or their equivalents), *hú* 壺 (seen only in tombs of those with relatively high status), and a *pan* 盤 and *yi* 匜 combination; beyond this, preferences differed somewhat from area to area. In time, one observes emerging differences between the typological preferences in assemblages associated with individuals of different ranks, with curious archaized types surviving at the highest levels. Overall, however, the vessel constellations established through the Late Western Zhou Ritual Reform remained remarkably stable throughout the three centuries under discussion.

CEMETERIES AND TOMBS IN NORTHERN AND CENTRAL HENAN

Spring and Autumn archaeology is largely tantamount to the investigation of the period's burial customs; archaeologists assume that these reflect, albeit perhaps not always directly, real-life activities, beliefs, and social divisions.

While this is a somewhat risky assumption, it seems to be backed up to some extent by textual evidence.

Over a thousand Eastern Zhou tombs have been excavated around Luoyang, the vast majority dating to the Warring States period. Finds from this area have long been looked to as a standard by archaeologists all over China.[25] Over the years, however, the accuracy of the model chronology promulgated in the 1959 report on 260 tombs at Zhongzhoulu 中州路 has been called into question: while the proposed seriation is approximately correct, the sequence probably does not start right at the beginning of the Eastern Zhou, but only around the mid-seventh century B.C.[26] Distributed in a corridor 2 km long and 30 m wide (cutting through the center of the Wangcheng enclosure and continuing further eastward), the Zhongzhoulu tombs constitute disjointed portions of larger cemeteries that remain largely unknown. Seventy-three of these tombs have been dated to before 450 B.C. The universally modest nature of their funerary assemblages and the absence of relieved decor on the few bronzes they contained suggest that none of these tombs belonged to members of major lineages surrounding the royal house.[27]

A better point of departure for a comprehensive survey of early Eastern Zhou funerary customs is the cemetery of the Guo 虢 lineage at Shangcunling 上村嶺, Sanmenxia 三門峽, Henan. Two hundred and thirty-four tombs were excavated here in 1956–7, followed by nine additional tombs in the early 1990s.[28] Parts of the cemetery remain unexplored. Tombs are laid out in an

[25] *Luoyang Zhongzhoulu* (Beijing: Kexue, 1959). Additional tombs have been found over the years; see *Henan kaogu sishinian (1952–1992)* (Zhengzhou: Henan Renmin, 1994), pp. 252–60, for further references. See also Ye Wansong, "Jin shinian Luoyang shi Wenwu gongzuodui kaogu gongzuo gaishu."

[26] Hayashi Minao, *Chûgoku In Shû jidai-no buki* (Kyoto: Kyôto Daigaku Jinbun Kagaku Kenkyûjo, 1982), p. 482; idem, *Shunjû Sengoku jidai seidôki-no kenkyû* (Tokyo: Yoshikawa Kôbunkan, 1988), pp. 7–8 and passim; Gao Ming, "Zhongyuan diqu Dong Zhou shidai qingtong liqi yanjiu"; Li Xueqin, *Eastern Zhou and Qin Civilizations*, pp. 23–9. Some Western Zhou tombs have been found at Zhongzhoulu, but their chronology is not continuous with that of the Eastern Zhou tombs.

[27] From the Spring and Autumn period, only eight bronze-yielding tombs (plus one containing a set of lead *mingqi* 明器 [spirit vessels; for this term, see note 30] ritual vessels) have been reported at Luoyang; the richest is tomb 4 at Zhongzhoulu, with three *ding* and a total of eleven bronzes. Stylistically, typologically, and in their constellations, bronzes from this area mirror the same developments as are observable in other areas of the Zhou realm.

[28] *Shangcunling Guo guo mudi* (Beijing: Kexue, 1959). Lin Shoujin's important studies on this material have been republished in his *Xian Qin kaoguxue* (Hong Kong: Chinese University Press, 1991), pp. 23–57; see also Wang Shimin in *Xin Zhongguo de kaogu faxian he yanjin* (Beijing: Wenwu, 1984), pp. 285; Li Xueqin, *Eastern Zhou and Qin Civilizations*, pp. 80–4; and Li Feng, "Guo guo mudi tongqiqun de fenqi ji qi xiangguan wenti, *Kaogu* 1988.11: 1035–43. On the more recent discoveries, see *Henan kaogu sishinian (1952–1992)*, pp. 245–9; *Hua Xia Kaogu* 1992.3: 104–13; *Wenwu* 1995.1: 4–31; and Hu Xiaolong, "Qiantan Sanmenxia Shangcunling Guo guo mudi chemakeng," *Hua Xia Kaogu* 1993.4: 96–7, 86. Preliminary historical studies include Xu Yongsheng, "Cong Guo guo mudi kaogu xin faxian tan Guo guo lishi gaikuang," *Hua Xia Kaogu* 1993.4: 92–5; Cai Yunzhang, "Lun Guozhong qi ren: Sanmenxia Guo guo mudi yanjiu zhi yi," *Zhongyuan wenwu* 1994.2: 86–9, 100; and idem, "Guo Wen gong mukao: Sanmenxia Guo guo mudi yanjiu zhi er," *Zhongyuan wenwu* 1994.3: 42–5, 94.

orderly fashion, with clusters of small tombs grouped around pairs of larger ones; each such pair may have contained the founder of a lineage segment and his principal wife. The largest and richest tombs are positioned somewhat apart from these clusters, but they are apparently not placed in a separate sector of the cemetery, as is the case at some other rulers' cemeteries from the Zhou dynasty. The funerary assemblages are strictly graded according to sumptuary rules (see Table 7.1). They document a wide spectrum of ranks, ranging from rulers down to fairly low-ranking kinsmen, thus attesting to considerable social stratification within the lineage.

Chinese archaeologists habitually draw distinctions of rank among Zhou tombs based on the number of *ding* tripods.[29] The Guo cemetery lends itself to this type of analysis, though one should not overlook the considerable differences in wealth within *ding*-determined rank categories. The largest tomb so far found is tomb 2009, which contained multiple sets of *ding*, including one status-defining set of nine specimens; several chimes of bells; and full sets of all the major classes of ritual bronzes. Among the more than 800 jade objects found in that tomb were face and body coverings comparable to those from the Jin rulers' tombs at Qucun 曲村, Quwo 曲沃, Shanxi, described in Chapter 6, as well as miniature sculptures, for example, of animals, some of which may be Shang heirlooms. The principal tomb occupant was buried in two nested coffins (*chongguan* 重棺) with rich lacquer and bronze ornamentation. Inscriptions identify him as a member (probably the head) of the Guozhong 虢仲 branch lineage; the name indicates that this branch lineage occupied the "second-born" position within the overall lineage structure, perhaps because its members were descended from the second son of the lineage founder.

Of the two tombs with seven-part sets of *ding* so far reported, one (tomb 2001), though containing only about half the number of burial goods found in tomb 2009, is considerably richer than the other (tomb 1052). The two tombs nevertheless share certain crucial elements of their assemblage besides their sets of seven *ding*: a single chime of bells, a full set of ritual vessels, and rich constellations of ornamented jades. Inscriptions indicate that the principal occupant of tomb 2001 was a leading member of the "last-born" branch

---

[29] On this topic, see Guo Baojun, *Shanbiaozhen yu Liulige* (Beijing: Kexue, 1959), pp. 11–13 and passim; and idem, *Shang Zhou tongqiqun zonghe yanjiu* (Beijing: Wenwu, 1981), pp. 57–69 and passim; Shi Ming, "Xi Zhou Chunqiu shidai lizhi de yanbian he Kong Qiu 'keji fuli' de fandong shizhi," *Kaogu* 1974.2: 81–8; Du Naisong, "Cong lieding zhidu kan keji fuli de fandongxing," *Kaogu* 1976.1: 17–21; Yu Weichao and Gao Ming, "Zhou dai yong *ding* zhidu yanjiu," *Beijing Daxue xuebao* 1978.1: 84–98, 1978.2: 84–97, and 1979.1: 83–96; Li Xueqin, *Eastern Zhou and Qin Civilizations*, pp. 460–4; Wang Shimin, "Guanyu Xi Zhou Chunqiu gaoji guizu liqi zhidu de yixie kanfa," *Wenwu yu kaogu lunji* (Beijing: Wenwu, 1986), pp. 158–66; Wang Fei, "Yongding zhidu xingshuai yiyi," *Wenbo* 1986.6: 29–33; Li Ling, "On the Typology of Chu Bronzes," pp. 68–71; and Lin Yun, "Zhou dai yongding zhidu shangque," *Shixue jikan* 1990.3: 12–23.

Table 7.1. *Bronze assemblages excavated at the Guo cemetery at Shangcunling, Sanmenxia, Henan*

Tomb no.	2001	1052	1810	1706	1689	2006	1820	1602	1705	1712	1711	1777	1640	1704	1761	1701	1702	1714
Condition	intact	intact	intact	intact	looted	intact	intact	looted	intact	intact	intact	looted	looted	intact	intact	intact	intact	intact
Period	II	II	I	II	II		I	I	III	III	II		II		II	II	III	
guo/guan	1 + 2	1 + 2	1 + 2	1 + 2	1 + 2	1 + 1	1 + 2?	1 + 2	1 + 1	1 + 1	1 + 2	1 + 1	1 + 2	1 + 1	1 + 2	1 + 2	1 + 2	1 + 1
Occupant's sex	M	M	M?	M?	F?	F	F	M?	M?	M?	M?	F?	F?	F?	F?	F?	F?	F?
ding	7 + 3m	7	5	5	4	3	3	3	3	3	2	1	1		1	1	1	1
yiding														1M				
li	8	6	4	4		4	2	2				1		1				
yan	1	1	1	1		1	1					1						
gui	6 + 3m	6	4	4	5		4	4	4									
xu	4					2												
hu	2	1				1	2											
fu	2	1	1	1			1											
"shouxingdou"														1				
fanghu	2	2	2	2			2	2	2									
yuanhu	2	2	2	2		2			2				2					
guan							1											
"xiaoguan"	1	1					1		1									
jue	1 + 2m					1m												
zhi	2m					1m												
zun	3m					1m												
fangyi	2m					1m												
pan	1 + 3m	1	1	1	2	1	1	1	1	1	1				1	1	1	1
he	1 + 2m	1	1m		1	1m			1	1								
yi				1	1		1	1			1				1	1	1	1
yongzhong	1/8	1/9																
niuzhong																		
zheng	1	1																
chimestones	1/10																	
Totals	**57** (20m)	**28**	**19**	**18**	**13**	**19** (3m)	**19**	**11**	**12**	**5**	**4**	**3**	**3**	**3** (1M)	**3**	**3**	**3**	**3**

Note: This enumeration includes only tombs with three and more bronzes. The periodization follows Li Feng ("Guo guo mudi tongqiqun de fenqi ji qi xiangguan wenti," *Kaogu* 1988.11: 1035–43). Occupants' sex determined on the basis of inscribed bronzes (no question mark), or on presence/absence of weapons (instances with question mark). For bells and chimestones, the number before the slash indicates the number of chimed sets, the number following the slash the number of individual items. Chimestones are not included in totals figures; in the case of bells, it is the number of sets that counts.

"m" indicates *mingqi* vessels; "M" indicates non-*mingqi* miniatures.

lineage of Guo (Guoji 虢季), while that of tomb 1052 was Yuan, the heir apparent of Guo 虢太子元.

The next lower-ranked category, characterized by sets of five *ding*, is also represented by several instances at Shangcunling (tombs 1810, 1705, 2010, and 2012); these tombs feature full sets of ritual bronzes, but lack bells. Each tomb of five or more *ding* had a horse and chariot pit (*chemakeng* 車馬坑), their contents likewise graded according to rank: the one associated with the tomb of Yuan, the heir apparent (seven *ding*) had ten chariots and twenty horses, exactly twice the amounts found in tomb 1810 (five *ding*). The horse and chariot pit of tomb 2009 (nine *ding*) was much larger, half of the space being filled with an as yet undetermined number of horses and chariots, the other half with horses only. Such constellations may indicate subdivisions in military organization.

Of the four tombs with sets of three *ding*, two are in all likelihood those of females who had married into the Guo lineage: inscriptions seem to identify the occupants of tombs 1820 and 2006 as princesses from the otherwise little-known polities of Su 穌 and Shou (?) 獸. In analogy with similar gender-based differentiation observed at Qucun, it appears likely that their respective husbands occupied positions above the three-*ding* rank. That such females outrank male occupants of tombs featuring sets of three *ding* (such as tombs 1602 and 1705) is also suggested by the considerably greater number of bronzes in their tombs. One gender-differentiating criterion is the absence from the princesses' tombs of weapons, prominent in the assemblages of tombs 1602 and 1705. Three-*ding* tombs of both sexes contain horse and chariot fittings, but they lack horse and chariot pits and bells.

Tombs 2009 (nine *ding*), 2001 (seven *ding*), and 2006 (female; three *ding*) are remarkable in that besides having sets of fully functional ritual vessels, they contain additional sets of unornamented miniature vessels reproducing (albeit in curiously distorted shapes) the major types of wine-offering vessels that had been abolished in the Late Western Zhou Ritual Reform. Similar *mingqi* 明器 have also been found at Qucun;[30] their main role must have been to symbolize the memory of earlier, already obsolete ritual customs. Such items appear to have been restricted to the highest elite and to have been abandoned shortly after the beginning of the Eastern Zhou.

Another important class of status symbols, new at the time, are iron objects, including a bronze *ge* 戈 (dagger-axe) with an iron blade and three iron "production tools" from tomb 2009, and a jade-handled dagger with a

---

[30] *Mingqi* (spirit vessels) are low-quality and/or reduced-scale reproductions, made for funerary purposes, of the objects that were used in temples. The function and significance of such objects appears to have changed significantly over the course of the Bronze Age; a comprehensive study is needed. For *mingqi* vessels from Qucun, see *Wenwu* 1994.8: 14, 11, fig. 24.1; and *Wenwu* 1995.7: 26–7, 30–1, figs. 43–7.

turquoise-inlaid iron blade from tomb 2001. They were carefully wrapped in silk-lined leather sheaths. The iron blades were cast from smelted iron, not forged from meteoritic iron as was the case with the iron-bladed bronze weapons of the Shang dynasty; they may have been imported from areas further west.[31]

Below the three-*ding* level, the Shangcunling cemetery yielded 5 tombs with two *ding* and 22 tombs with one *ding*, 3 tombs with other kinds of bronze vessels but no tripods, and 2 tombs that had obviously once contained ritual bronzes but had been looted. The bulk of the tombs excavated, however, did not contain any bronze vessels; more than half of the total (120 tombs) featured pottery vessels, including cooking vessels (*li* 鬲) and container vessels (mostly *dou* 豆, *pen* 盆, and *guan* 罐), all *mingqi* imitations at reduced scale; another 64 tombs featured no vessels but did contain sundry articles such as jade ornaments or weapons; while 10 tombs had no funerary goods at all.[32] Remains of lacquered wooden vessels with shell inlay were found in 7 tombs, complementing either bronze or ceramic vessel assemblages.

Another way of looking at status distinctions at Zhou cemeteries is through the constellations of burial chambers (*guo* 椁) and coffins (*guan* 棺). According to late Warring States period textual records, a burial chamber was the mark of aristocratic rank, and the number of nested coffins within them could further mark sumptuary distinctions.[33] Of the 234 tombs excavated at Shangcunling in 1956–7, 139 (59.4 percent) have a burial chamber; 26 of these (6.8 percent of the total) have two nested coffins; the rest have single coffins. Of the 95 tombs lacking a burial chamber, 89 (38.0 percent) have single coffins, and 6 have neither burial chamber nor coffins. It would appear, thus, that the lineage that buried its members at Shangcunling comprised both aristocratic and nonaristocratic components. Although the percentages are misleading because the excavated sample of tombs is not representative, it is noteworthy that all 38 bronze-yielding tombs without exception had burial chambers, demonstrating that ownership of ritual bronzes was contingent on membership in the ranked elite. Moreover, the fact that bronzes were found

---

[31] On the possible western origin of the Eastern Zhou iron technology, as well as for further references, see Tang Jigen, "Zhongguo yetieshu de qiyuan wenti," *Kaogu* 1993.6: 556–65, 553. Donald B. Wagner's alternative theory (proposed in his *Iron and Steel in Ancient China*, [Leiden: Brill, 1993]), that the Chinese iron-making tradition has autochthonous origins in the southeast, is not supported by present evidence. Large-scale iron industries, in any case, only arose during the Warring States period.

[32] It should be noted that these ratios in all likelihood do not reflect the social composition of the population, since the excavated sample of tombs is not statistically representative. This is a problem with virtually all cemetery data from the Chinese Bronze Age; comparison with the data from Shangma, the only cemetery so far to have been completely excavated, suggests that excavators are invariably guided by a significant bias for tombs promising to yield rich finds.

[33] On this point, see Mu-chou Poo, "Ideas Concerning Death and Burial in Pre-Han China," *Asia Major*, 3d series, 3, 2 (1990): 25–62.

in more than two-thirds of burial chamber tombs with double coffins, but only in about one-sixth of the burial chamber tombs with single coffins, hints at significant stratification within the aristocratic component of the Guo ruling lineage. At the same time, if the presence of a burial chamber is indeed a reliable indicator of aristocratic rank, it is noteworthy that by no means all of the cemetery's aristocratic tombs contained sacrificial bronzes. Such apparent parsimony may show that the genealogically based claim to a certain sumptuary status was not always correlated with sufficient wealth to afford the trappings allowed to that status.

Since the stylistic and typological features of the Shangcunling bronzes adhere very closely to the canon of vessel shapes and ornamentation instituted by the Late Western Zhou Ritual Reform, the establishment of a stylistic sequence still poses some problems. Curiously, even though the main vessels and bells from the major tombs, 2009, 2001, and 2006, are very large and represent a tremendous investment of raw material, their casting quality is low – far lower than in most metropolitan Western Zhou castings. Jessica Rawson ascribes this to the political turmoils of the mid-eighth century b.c. and dates the tombs accordingly.[34] As to the bronzes from lower-ranking tombs at Shangcunling, it is difficult to decide whether the fact that some of them are thinner, smaller, and somewhat deformed when compared with late Western Zhou specimens from Shaanxi and Shanxi reflects a difference in date, workshop tradition, or social status. Many of them appear to be *mingqi*.

Some scholars believe that the absolute chronology of the Shangcunling tombs straddles the transition from Western to Eastern Zhou; the alternative view, that they are all Eastern Zhou in date, reflects the traditional opinion that Guo was moved to the Sanmenxia area (modern western Henan) in the course of the removal of the Zhou dynastic centers from Shaanxi in 771 b.c. The actual situation may, however, have been more complex. Bronze inscriptions from Shangcunling and elsewhere mention individuals who appear to have belonged to different branches of the Guo lineage; lands held by these Guo branch lineages seem to have been scattered over different parts of the Zhou realm, including both banks of the Yellow River in the Sanmenxia area; a tract of land near present-day Baoji 寶雞 (Shaanxi), which, known by then as Little Guo (Xiaoguo 小虢), was annexed by Qin in 687 b.c.; and an Eastern Guo (Dongguo 東虢) in the area of Zhengzhou 鄭州, Henan. Rather than as a "state" with a circumscribed territory, Guo is more appropriately viewed as, primarily, a widely distributed

---

[34] Jessica Rawson, "Die rituellen Bronzegefäße der Shang- und Zhou-Perioden," in *Das alte China: Menschen und Götter im Reich der Mitte*, ed. Roger Goepper (Essen: Kulturstiftung Ruhr, 1995), p. 89.

kin group, which shifted its main base of operations between Shaanxi and Henan as called for by the political situation. The details of how such a scattered polity may have been administered have not yet been unraveled; it remains enigmatic, for instance, why members of several Guo branch lineages appear prominently at the Shangcunling cemetery.

During the late Western Zhou period, and also probably during the first century of Eastern Zhou, the rulers of Guo and Zheng occupied key positions in the entourage of the Zhou kings. Rather than being seen as independent (or semi-independent) polities governed by recognized rulers (*zhuhou* 諸侯) these strategically positioned territories should perhaps be considered as extensions of the royal domain. Their closeness to the royal person might account for the differences in status between the occupants of the largest tombs at Shangcunling and Jin rulers' tombs at Qucun, which contain only five-part sets of *ding*, even though their owners had become, by Spring and Autumn times, politically and territorially far more powerful than the lineage heads of Guo. (Jin, in fact, conquered the Guo territories around Sanmenxia in 655 B.C., which forms the *terminus ante quem* for the Shangcunling necropolis.)

However, the Guo tombs lack sloping passageways into the tombs (*mudao* 墓道), a sumptuary feature that is observed in Western and Eastern Zhou tombs of *zhuhou* rulers. Most of the Qucun tombs, for instance, had single *mudao*; the tombs of the rulers of Wey 衛 at Xincun 辛村, Xunxian 濬縣, Henan,[35] each had two. Like Guo and Jin, Wey was governed by a junior branch of the Zhou royal house (Ji 姬 clan); although the Xincun tombs had been severely looted before excavation, the style of sundry objects found in them suggests that their chronology (like that of Qucun and, probably, Shangcunling) spans the transition from Western to Eastern Zhou. Like Shangcunling, and unlike Qucun, the cemetery also comprised a large number of regularly aligned medium- and small-size tombs. As we go on exploring Spring and Autumn period funerary remains in other areas of the Zhou realm, we shall observe numerous other differences of detail within a generally unified pattern of ritual behavior. Local custom appears to have subtly modified particular applications of the Zhou sumptuary system, resulting in distinguishable family traditions.

The further development of funerary customs at the highest level of society in the central part of the Zhou realm is exemplified by another necropolis of Wey rulers, located at Liulige 琉璃閣, Huixian 輝縣, Henan, and the already-mentioned tomb of a Zheng ruler at Lijialou, Xinzheng, Henan. Dating from the mid-sixth century B.C. down into the middle

[35] Guo Baojun, *Xunxian Xincun* (Beijing: Kexue, 1964).

Warring States, Liulige comprised seven large tombs, each containing between thirty-five and sixty bronze vessels, plus up to four chimes of bells. There were also hundreds of minor tombs, about a dozen of which also yielded bronzes.[36] Due to incomplete reporting, tomb shape and structure remain for the most part unclear, but the large tombs were apparently grouped in pairs, and they lacked *mudao*. Some of them had pits lined with layers of accumulated stones and charcoal, as seen earlier at Qucun. Their bronzes present a puzzling stylistic mix: some feature conservative forms of decoration modeled upon those of late Western Zhou bronzes, while others are characterized by more "contemporary" modes of ornamentation in bands of tiny, endlessly repeated units of intertwined dragon bodies or with broad bands of intertwined abstracted dragon bodies similar to those seen at Houma. The first group comprises sets of coverless *ding* with matching sets of *gui* (not seen ordinarily after ca. 650) and paired rectangular *hú* with interlaced-dragon ornamentation that is virtually indistinguishable from that of some late Western Zhou specimens. The second group, which constitutes a majority of the assemblage, includes most other kinds of vessels current during the late Spring and Autumn period, such as covered *ding*, *hú* 匜, *hé* 鉌, and *jian* 鑑. Bells sometimes feature ornaments of the one, sometimes of the other type. The typological and stylistic dualism seems to indicate the practice, by rulers and their entourage, of special types of rites of ancient origin alongside the more contemporary rituals performed by the rest of the aristocracy; unfortunately, none of the preserved textual sources throws any light on this phenomenon.

Increasing complexity of ritual activities is intimated also by the grouping of tripods in late Spring and Autumn period rulers' tombs. Tomb 60 at Liulige, for instance, comprised twenty-nine *ding* of four different types: a single large *ding*, a set of nine coverless *ding*, fourteen covered *ding* (forming two sets), and seven miniature *ding* (probably *mingqi*). It is likely that these served different functions, though the number of pieces to the set does not correspond exactly with the specifications in later ritual texts. The nine-part set of coverless *ding* was probably the principal, status-defining set; significantly, in tomb 55, which was paired with tomb 60, the status-defining set of similar *ding* numbered only seven, thus showing the continued expression of gender differences comparable to practices at Qucun and Shangcunling.

---

[36] Guo Baojun, *Shanbiaozhen yu Liulige*, pp. 53–76. Twenty-seven Warring States tombs excavated in the early fifties are published in *Huixian fajue baogao* (Beijing: Kexue, 1956), pp. 32–52. Hayashi (*Shunjû Sengoku jidai seidôki-no kenkyû*, p. 6) dates the bronze assemblage from the small tomb 130 to the late part of middle Spring and Autumn, perhaps indicating the initial occupation of the cemetery.

Very little is known about the construction of the Zheng tomb at Lijialou,[37] but its approximately forty-six bronze vessels and twenty-three bells constitute one of the most splendid assemblages of Spring and Autumn period bronzes found so far. Dating probably to around 575 B.C., they are among the latest specimens that were not made by the pattern-block technique. As at Liulige, two main stylistic groups of vessels may be distinguished. The first group mostly comprises vessels with typological precedents in late Western Zhou ritual assemblages and decorated with archaic motifs resembling those of late Western Zhou bronzes, though slightly modified and thus recognizable as "quotations" in a new stylistic milieu. Some of the members of this group are vessels with exuberant, high-relief decoration that is based on archaic patterns (Fig. 7.12). The second, larger group comprises vessels that are either undecorated or feature decoration in endlessly repeated small units of dragon-derived decor, sometimes with additional fully sculptural appendages. These are vessels that are also seen in contemporaneous tombs of the lower aristocracy, reflecting the stylistic and typological changes that had occurred after the middle of the Spring and Autumn period.[38] Interestingly, the two groups do not comprise exactly the same object classes as those at Liulige.

A dozen or so cemeteries with several hundred Spring and Autumn period tombs of Zheng, mostly postdating the mid-sixth century B.C., have been excavated around Xinzheng.[39] In this area, waist pits (*yaokeng* 腰坑) with dog burials underneath the tomb owners' coffins remain common during the Zhou period; the larger tombs are habitually accompanied by horse and chariot pits. The bronzes from these tombs closely resemble those from the second group of bronzes in the Lijialou tomb. Their distinctive shapes and ornaments probably testify to an independent workshop tradition at Xinzheng, where extensive foundry remains have been found, but so far only dating from the Warring States period. Typological preferences indicate some parallels with developments in the Chu 楚 area, which may not be an accident given the geographical situation of Zheng at the interstice of the northern and southern alliances. For instance, *gui* are replaced preferentially by *zhan* 盞 and *hú* in combination, as is the case in Chu, rather than by sets of

---

[37] The finds are published in: Jiang Hongyuan et al., *Xinzheng chutu guqi tuzhi*, 3 vols. (n.p., 1923); Wang Youqiao, *Xinzheng guqi fajianji* (Kaifeng: Henan Sheng Jiaoyuting, 1924); Sun Haibo, *Xinzheng yiqi*, 2 vols. (Kaifeng: Henan Sheng Tongzhiguan, 1937); Guan Baiyi, *Xinzheng guqi tulu*, 2 vols. (Shanghai: Shangwu, 1929); and Guan Baiyi, *Zhengzhong guqi tukao*, 4 vols. (Shanghai: Zhonghua, 1940). See also Li Xueqin, *Eastern Zhou and Qin Civilizations*, pp. 85–7.

[38] The only item falling outside these two groups is the *Wangzi Yingci lu* 王子嬰次鑪, a brazier pan on a stand shaped like a bizarre demon with snakes coming from its head; it is identified by its inscription as a Chu import.

[39] See *Henan kaogu sishinian (1952–1992)*, pp. 26–63, where further references may be found.

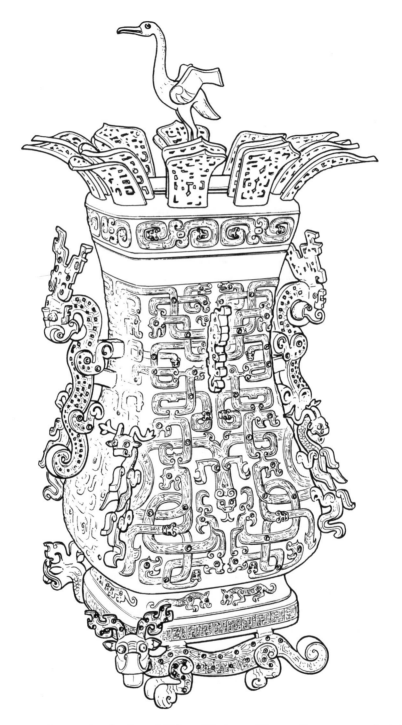

Figure 7.12. Rectangular *hu* from Lijialou, Xinzheng, Henan. First quarter of sixth century B.C. Traditional style woodblock drawing. After Guan Baiyi, *Zhengzhong guqi tukao* (Shanghai: Zhonghua, 1940), *juan* 5:26a. Drawing by Li Xiating.

cheng 盛, later replaced by *zhan* 盞 (or *dui* 敦), then by *dou* 豆, as observed in northerly contexts.[40] Another possible Chu parallel is the relatively early onset of the use of sets of ceramic *mingqi* ritual vessels (imitating the stylistic features of Zheng bronzes) in tombs of the lower aristocracy. Whether such similarities hint at Chu "influence" on Zheng or vice versa, or reflect more general trends, remains open.

FINDS FROM JIN CEMETERIES

Excavated Jin tombs from the Spring and Autumn period currently total some 2,000 tombs at more than two dozen cemeteries.[41] Linked to walled settlements inhabited by aristocratic lineages, the geographic spread of these cemeteries widened significantly over the course of the period, documenting the gradual penetration, by Jin and its subordinate lineages, of the valleys of the Fen River and other tributaries of the Yellow River, and of the western foothills of the Taihang 太行 Mountains. This expansion was paralleled, from the sixth century B.C., by a dramatic increase in bronze manufacture, probably reflecting the activity of the Houma foundry. Zhou-type tombs and/or funerary paraphernalia spread along the northern borders of Jin during the late Spring and Autumn period. For instance, the early fifth century B.C. tombs at Liyu 李峪, Hunyuan 渾源, Shanxi, which probably belonged to leaders of unassimilated (and possibly nonsedentary) non-Zhou populations, yielded some of the most dazzling Houma bronzes, including some types produced specifically for the northern steppe markets.[42]

Important data pertinent to the analysis of Zhou aristocratic society have been recovered from two Jin cemeteries in southern Shanxi: Shangguo 上郭, in Wenxi 聞喜 county, and Shangma 上馬, in Houma city. The chronology of both cemeteries reaches from the late Western Zhou to the fifth century B.C. – the time during which Jin rose to become for a time the most powerful of the northern polities. The cemeteries document aristocratic lineages of quite unequal rank. Whereas Shangguo, located next to the site of ancient Quwo, belonged to the ambitious junior branch of the ruling house that

---

[40] Such preferences are also apparent in the bronze assemblages from the Eastern Zhou tombs at the Ying lineage cemetery at Beizhicun 北滍村, Pingdingshan 平頂山, Henan, and from the important early Spring and Autumn period tomb at Taipuxiang 太僕鄉, Jiaxian 郟縣, Henan (*Wenwu cankao ziliao* 1954.3: 60–2).

[41] See Shanxi sheng Kaogu yanjiusuo, *Shanxi kaogu sishinian* (1952–1992), pp. 169–89, where further references may be found.

[42] Finds recovered in 1923 were published in Umenara Sueji, *Sengokushiki dôki-no kenkyû* (Kyoto: Tôhô bunka gakuin Kyôto kenkyûjo, 1936); and Shang Chengzuo, *Hunyuan yiqitu* (Nanjing: Jinling daxue Zhongguo wenhua yanjiusuo, 1936); the results of recent investigations are summarized in Li Xiating, "Hunyuan yiqi yanjiu," *Wenwu* 1992.10: 61–75, where further references may be found. See also Bagley, "What the Bronzes from Hunyuan Tell Us About the Foundry at Houma."

usurped power in Jin in 679 B.C., Shangma represents the lower aristocracy. At Shangguo, the larger tombs (all looted recently) feature ash- or stone-lined pits similar to those of contemporaneous rulers' tombs. Inscribed bronzes document marital connections between the lords of Quwo and the ruling families of neighboring polities. The fact that at Shangguo bronzes some- times occur even in tombs without a wooden burial chamber, a unique finding in Zhou archaeology, may further attest to the high rank, or rank aspiration, of that cemetery's patrons.

Only small portions of the Shangguo cemetery have been scientifically excavated,[43] yielding mostly small tombs with incomplete assemblages of bronzes, often *mingqi*. A group of bronzes conspicuous for their especially ornate, sometimes three-dimensionally sculpted decoration may be products of an eighth to seventh century B.C. local foundry. Many of them are of miniature format, but they must be distinguished from lower-quality *mingqi*; their significance remains enigmatic. To this stylistic group belong several rectangular bronze boxes with hinged door openings and playful, exuberant decor, such as the "chariot box" from tomb 89M7, which has an attached pair of wheeled tigers, dragons, birds, a monkey, and a door guardian with his left foot amputated (a custom documented in Eastern Zhou texts) (Fig. 7.13). How such items could have served in rituals is unclear.

Though located near the last Jin capital of Xintian, the Shangma ceme- tery goes back to an earlier period and must have belonged to another nearby settlement.[44] As at Shangcunling, burials are clustered around the paired tombs of important ancestors, who may be the founders of branch lineages. Shangma is of great importance because it is so far the only cemetery from the Chinese Bronze Age to have been excavated virtually in its entirety, yield- ing evidence that is representative (at least for this site) and hence amenable to statistical analysis. Fortunately, the 1,387 excavated tombs had been virtu- ally unlooted, and many of the skeletons were sufficiently well preserved to permit determination of age and sex. A fine-tuned pottery sequence provides chronological control. One can thus tentatively reconstruct the demographic development as well as the social composition of the Shangma "cemetery- using group," which comprised the adult members of the patron lineage.[45]

From what seems to have been a single nuclear family in late Western Zhou times, the Shangma cemetery-using group grew rapidly until the

[43] Zhu Hua, "Wenxi Shangguocun gumuqun shijue," *San Jin kaogu* 1 (1994): 95–122; *San Jin Kaogu* 1 (1994): 123–38; and *San Jin kaogu* 1 (1994): 139–53. The northernmost and most recent part of the same necropolis is known as Qiujiazhuang 邱家莊 (*Kaogu yu wenwu* 1983.1: 5–11).

[44] *Shangma mudi* (Beijing: Wenwu, 1994). Lothar von Falkenhausen, "Shangma: Demography and Social Differentiation in a Late Bronze Age Community in North China," forthcoming.

[45] Since most children were buried within settlements, the nineteen child burials from Shangma do not reflect the probable extent of infant mortality.

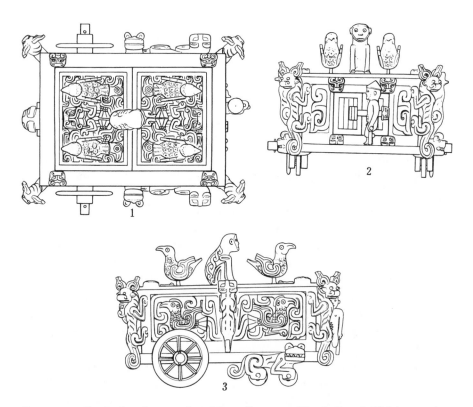

Figure 7.13. Chariot box from tomb 89M7 at Shangguo, Wenxi, Shanxi. Eighth to early seventh century B.C. After *San Jin kaogu*, 1994.146, fig. 8.1–3. Drawing by Li Xiating.

second half of the seventh century B.C., when it reached a size of somewhere between 250 and 310 persons. After that time, the numbers decline, probably because the patron lineage became absorbed into the newly founded Xintian capital; burial activity appears to have virtually stopped by the end of the fifth century B.C. To judge from the construction and furnishings of the tombs, the Shangma patron lineage encompassed a fairly wide spectrum of social ranks; and the concentration of larger and wealthier tombs in certain sectors of the cemetery seems to indicate the early separation of unequal segments. Tombs with burial chamber and funerary bronzes appeared from the early part of early Spring and Autumn onward, tombs with burial chamber and double nested coffins not until about half a century later; this may reflect either general developments in elite burial customs or a gradual rise in status of some members of the lineage.

Although the percentages of tombs with trappings of aristocratic status increased slightly over time, they remained very low overall. One hundred and eighty-seven (13.5 percent) of the tombs at Shangma had burial chambers, nineteen of which (1.4 percent of the total) featured double nested coffins. At the opposite end of the social spectrum, forty-nine tombs (3.5 percent) were earthen pits without coffins or other tomb furniture. Fully 83 percent of the tombs belonged to the single-coffin/no burial chamber category. These percentages contrast sharply with those from other cemeteries, including Shangcunling, where in each case the credibility of the data is marred by the fact that samples are not representative. As at Shangcunling, however, the distribution of funerary goods only partly coincides with these divisions. Tombs without burial chambers, it is true, never contained bronzes but were limited to, at most, *mingqi* versions of utilitarian pottery vessels.[46] The nineteen bronze-yielding tombs (1.4 percent) all had burial chambers; but by no means all tombs with burial chambers contained ritual bronzes: the probability amounts to 26.3 percent in tombs with burial chambers and double nested coffins, and a mere 8.8 percent in tombs with burial chambers and single coffins.

The vast majority of tombs with burial chamber at Shangma thus had either only low-level funerary goods such as ceramics and sundry polished-stone ornaments (76.5 percent) or no funerary goods at all (7.0 percent). As at Shangcunling, divergences between status and wealth seem evident. The numbers of bronze-yielding tombs per generation are far too low to allow the hypothesis that the presence of bronzes indicates a particular, privileged social stratum within the lineage; if aristocratic rank was hereditary, and if Shangma does indeed represent the cemetery-using lineage in its entirety, one must conclude that the vast majority of persons who had a right to ritual vessels were buried without them. The motivations underlying such apparent parsimony, and the reasons why other individuals were in fact buried with sets of bronzes, in varying degrees of richness, are probably now beyond the reach of archaeological reconstruction.

The Shangma bronze vessel assemblages document basic adherence to Zhou-style sumptuary divisions, indicating significant rank differences within the aristocratic segment of the cemetery-using lineage. The richest tomb (61M13) featured seven *ding* (two more than the rulers of Jin at Qucun, thereby indicating either a change over time or, perhaps, differences in family tradition), and chimed musical instruments; two tombs (1004 and 5218) had five *ding* and bell chimes (a difference vis-à-vis Shangcunling, where chimes were limited to tombs with seven *ding* or more). One of the five-*ding* tombs had a horse and chariot pit associated with it. The two other horse and

---

[46] Tombs rarely contained more than a single *li* vessel, with the ocasional addition of a piece of polished stone or a bone implement. Of tombs without bronzes, 16.9 percent yielded only such minor items, lacking ceramics; and 16.8 percent had no funerary items at all.

chariot pits at Shangma belonged to two relatively early tombs that contained sets of three *ding* (another difference with regard to Shangcunling, where horse and chariot pits are seen only with five *ding* or more). All other bronze-containing tombs had from one to three *ding* and relatively few other bronzes. When correlating the constellations of tomb furniture and the distribution of funerary goods with the age and sex of tomb occupants, one finds relatively little correlation between age and indicators of wealth or status. This suggests that aristocratic rank per se was hereditary within lineage segments, though perhaps an individual's specific sumptuary privileges could be augmented according to personal merit. Moreover, one finds evidence for a systematically different treatment of women, who on average had fewer grave goods than men and were less likely to be buried with the trappings of high status.

Although they follow the same stylistic and typological developments as do those found at Shangguo, the Shangma bronzes are generally of lesser quality. Vessels are thin-walled and their decoration is poorly executed. Since Shangma is located within 5 km of the Houma foundry, all post–585 B.C. bronzes were probably made there; curiously, their ornamentation, though produced by the pattern-block method, is defined by sunken-line contours and hatching with almost no surface relief. In this they differ strikingly from the kinds of vessels that would have been produced with the gorgeous pattern blocks from the excavated portions of the foundry.[47] That a correlation existed between a person's status and the execution of that person's bronzes, including the degree of relief allowable on bronzes, is evident also from contemporaneous finds elsewhere. The Shangma finds indirectly show that the excavated portions of the Houma foundry must have specialized in the manufacture of ornate bronzes for the higher ranks of the aristocracy.

Lack of space forbids more extensive coverage of pertinent finds in the territories along the middle reaches of the Yellow River. While the available materials convey a general idea of funerary customs and bronze sequences, one should not underestimate the lacunae still glaring in the archaeological record from this part of China. Some polities that figure prominently in the *Chunqiu* chronicle and the *Zuo zhuan*, such as Cao 曹 (Ji 姬 clan), Song 宋 (Zi 子 clan), Chen 陳 (Gui 嬀 clan), and Xuu 許 (Jiang 姜 clan), are undocumented except by sundry inscribed bronzes that are either of unknown provenance or were found out of area.[48] We shall now branch out to areas in

---

[47] Such bronzes were excavated, for example, from the late fifth century B.C. tomb 251 at Jinshengcun 金勝村, Taiyuan 太原, Shanxi; *Wenwu* 1989.9: 59–86; Tao Zhenggang and Hou Yi, *Jin guo qingtong kuibao* (Taipei: Guangfu, 1994), and at Liyu (see note 42).

[48] These finds are comprehensively discussed in their historical context in Li Xueqin, *Eastern Zhou and Qin Civilizations*.

the western, eastern, and southern parts of the Zhou realm, where regional characteristics may be observed alongside evidence of adherence to the Zhou ritual system.[49]

FINDS FROM QIN CEMETERIES

After 770 B.C., the ancient cradle of the Zhou kingdom in central Shaanxi became the territory of Qin. The 21 sq. km necropolis of the Qin ruling lineage at Nanzhihui 南指挥, Fengxiang, Shaanxi, in the southern suburb of the capital Yong, encompassed thirteen enclosed burial compounds with a total of forty-four tombs.[50] The scale of these tombs surpasses anything seen elsewhere in the Spring and Autumn period and may well constitute an infraction, in spirit if not in letter, of the sumptuary privileges due to the rulers of a polity (*zhuhou*) nominally subordinate to the Zhou kings. Unfortunately, the absence of archaeological information on the Zhou royal tombs renders direct comparison impossible. Tomb 1, measuring 300 m in length and 24 m in depth, is the only one excavated to date; it is thought to be the tomb of Jing Gong 景公 (r. 576–537). Although it had been exhaustively plundered, the ruler's sumptuary ambitions are powerfully expressed in its two tomb passages (*mudao*), the triple layers of wooden beams used in the construction of its enormous burial chamber, the use of precious kinds of wood that were probably forbidden to the ordinary population, and the presence of as many as 166 human victims. The similarity in scale to the tombs of Shang kings at Anyang has been taken as confirming the eastern descent of the Qin ruling house (Ying 嬴 clan);[51] but it seems more appropriate to interpret such phenomena in terms of contemporaneous political priorities.

---

[49] The northeastern part of the Zhou culture sphere, the area of Yan and neighboring polities, is not covered because archaeological discoveries from the period under analysis are too fragmented so far to convey any sense of local developments. Late Spring and Autumn period bronze assemblages from this area are conveniently depicted in Hayashi, In *Shû seidôki sôran*, pt. 3: *Shunjû Sengoku jidai seidôki-no kenkyû*, pp. 25–7, where further references may be found. On their stylistic characteristics, see Li Xiating, "Hunyuan yiqi yanjiu."

[50] Han Wei, "Fengxiang Qin gong lingyuan zuantan yu shijue jianbao," *Wenwu* 1983.7: 30–7; see also Wang Xueli, Shang Zhiru, and Hu Lingui, eds., *Qin wuzhi wenhua shi* (Xi'an: San Qin, 1994), pp. 256–73, where further references may be found.

[51] Han Wei, "Guanyu Qin ren zushu wenhua yuanyuan guanjian," *Wenwu* 1986.4: 23–8; see also Li Ling, "Shi Ji zhong suojian Qin zaoqi duyi zangdi," *Wenshi* 20 (1982): 15–23. Caution is warranted with unverifiable mythological accounts of this sort. Han's alleged Shang parallels can also be observed piecemeal in non-Qin areas of early Eastern Zhou China; after all, Zhou culture had absorbed many features from the Shang. Even if the aristocrats of the Ying clan were indeed of eastern origin, most salient features in the cultural inventory of early Eastern Zhou Qin are squarely of west Chinese origin; and the *Qin Gong gui* 秦公簋 inscription (see note 53) tells that the polity of Qin was established "within the footsteps of Yu (of Xia)," that is, within the Chinese culture sphere, possibly implying that the earliest rulers came from outside. One should consider the possibility that the Qin rulers were originally a non-Zhou lineage that took on a Zhou-style clan name, as was certainly the case in Wu and, possibly, in Qi.

The Qin rulers' intention to usurp Zhou royal privileges is evident from bronze inscriptions. Rhetorical formulas derived from Western Zhou royal inscriptions abound, for instance, in the text inscribed on eight enormous bells excavated at Taigongmiao 太公廟, Baoji, Shaanxi.[52] Here a ruler of Qin, probably Wu Gong 武公 (r. 697–678 B.C.), touts his own pedigree and his royal Zhou bride, who is unknown from transmitted historical sources; he uses the royal Zhou formula of self-address "I, the little child" (referring to the king's position vis-à-vis his ancestors in Heaven); he announces that his ancestors obtained the Mandate of Heaven (*Tian ming* 天命); and he claims the right to govern the inhabitable world of the Four Quarters (*si fang* 四方) and to subdue the Barbarians (*man* 蠻). Similar formulations appear in inscriptions on two bronzes of unknown provenance dating to the end of the seventh century B.C.,[53] where the Qin ruler menaces "those who will not come to court" (i.e., submit to his authority), be they "Barbarians" or Xia-Chinese. A desire to emulate and, in doing so, to challenge the Zhou kings may also be inherent in the extreme stylistic conservatism of early Qin bronzes, as well as that of the written characters of their inscriptions (Fig. 7.14); this, however, may also reflect the continuing operation of the former Western Zhou palace workshops under Qin rule.

The Qin rulers' assertive, yet subtle manipulations of their sumptuary and political privileges implicitly acknowledged the validity of the Zhou ritual system, outside of which their assumptions of grandeur would have been meaningless. Their verbal and material statements could impress only those who were conversant with the discourse of Zhou ritual and who had to awaken to the fact that the actual distribution of political power no longer corresponded to the status differences as defined during the Western Zhou dynasty.

With respect to structure, size, and quantity of furnishings, tombs of Spring and Autumn Qin aristocrats ranking below the ruler are roughly comparable to those of equivalent status from other parts of the Zhou realm.[54]

[52] Lu Liancheng and Yang Mancang, "Shaanxi Baoji xian Taigongmiao faxian Qin Gong zhong, Qin Gong bo," *Wenwu* 1978.11: 1–5; Zhongguo Shehui kexueyuan Kaogu yanjiusuo, *Yin Zhou jinwen jicheng*, vol. 1, nos. 262–9. For full translations of the texts, and for further references, see Mattos, "Eastern Zhou Bronze Inscriptions," pp. 111–14. All translations in this chapter are the author's own.

[53] These are the *Qin Gong gui* (Zhongguo Shehui kexueyuan Kaogu yanjiusuo, *Yin Zhou jinwen jicheng*, vol. 1, no. 270) and the *Qin Gong bo* 秦公鎛 (*Yin Zhou jinwen jicheng*, vol. 8, no. 4315). For translations and further references see Mattos, "Eastern Zhou Bronze Inscriptions," pp. 114–21; I accept the dates proposed by Li Ling, "Chunqiu Qin qi shitan: Xinchu Qin Gong zhong boming yu guoqu zhulu Qin zhong guiming de duidu," *Kaogu* 1979.6: 515–21. For the political interpretation here proposed, see also Lothar von Falkenhausen, "Ahnenkult und Grabkult im Staat Qin: Der religiöse Hintergrund der Terrakotta-Armee," in *Jenseits der Großen Mauer: Der Erste Kaiser von China und seine Terrakotta-Armee*, ed. Lothar Ledderose and Adele Schlombs (Munich: Bertelsmann, 1990), pp. 35–48.

[54] For synthetic treatments (where references to reports may be found), see Han Wei, "Lüelun Shaanxi Chunqiu Zhanguo Qin mu," *Kaogu yu wenwu* 1981.1: 83–93; Ye Xiaoyan, "Qin mu chutan," *Kaogu*

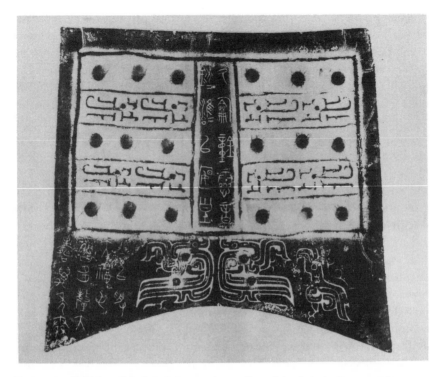

Figure 7.14. Rubbing of the inscription on the smallest of the five *qin Gong yongzhong*, excavated at Taigongmiao, Baoji, Shaanxi. From Zhongguo Shehui kexueyuan Kaogu yanjiusuo, *Yin Zhou jinwen jicheng* (Beijing: Zhonghua, 1984), vol. 1, no. 266.

Data from more than 500 tombs at a dozen or so cemeteries distributed throughout the Wei 渭 River system can be distilled into a continuous chronological sequence spanning virtually the entire Eastern Zhou period. In the adjacent loess plateau of northern Shaanxi, extensive Zhou-type cemeteries began to appear sometime after 550 B.C., possibly testifying to increased Qin settlement of those areas, which had formerly been inhabited by non-Zhou populations.

The Qin cemeteries are regularly laid out and were undoubtedly occupied by lineages over successive generations.[55] The presence of a burial chamber is

1982.1: 65–73; Shang Zhiru, "Qin guo xiaoxingmu de fenxi yu fenqi"; *Shaanxi sheng Kaogu xuehui di yi jue nianhui lunwenji* (i.e., *Kaogu yu wenwu congkan* 3 [1983]), pp. 58–67; Chen Ping, "Shilun Guanzhong Qin mu qingtong rongqi de fenqi wenti," *Kaogu yu wenwu* 1984.3: 58–73, 4: 63–73; Okamura Hidenori, "Shin bunka-no hennen," *Koshi shunjû* 2 (1985): 53–74; and Teng Mingyu, "Guanzhong Qin mu yanjiu," *Kaogu xuebao* 1992.3: 281–300.
[55] Han Wei (in "Lüelun Shaanxi Chunqiu Zhanguo Qin mu") takes the presence of tombs of different sumptuary ranks at the same cemeteries as indicating the rapid decline of aristocratic society in Qin, but as has been shown above, this is actually a common phenomenon throughout the Zhou cultural sphere, reflecting the nature of lineages in Zhou aristocratic society during the Eastern Zhou period.

a probable indicator of aristocratic status, and further social subdivisions are indicated by double nested coffins, seen occasionally after about the middle of the seventh century B.C. Since excavated samples of tombs are not statistically representative, the relative percentages of social strata within each lineage remain unknown. Perhaps reflecting the exhaustion of timber resources, burial chambers are sometimes not entirely constructed in wood; instead, the floors and walls of the burial chamber are executed in stamped earth with only the ceiling fashioned from wooden planks. Likewise, a relatively large percentage of tombs without burial chambers lacks wooden coffins, some of them featuring jar burial, a funerary custom not usually seen in lineage cemeteries elsewhere in the Zhou culture sphere.

Funerary assemblages document pervasive adherence to the norms of the Zhou sumptuary system (see Table 7.2). Status privilege was expressed through odd-numbered sets of *lieding* 列鼎, paired with *gui* of the next-lower even number. Tombs containing high-ranking individuals and possessing bells and chimestones have so far not been found, but there are three bronze-yielding tombs representing the five-*ding* rank (in one case with a supernumerary, larger *ding* of different type) and several of three-*ding* rank, as well as numerous instances of tombs with a smaller number of bronzes. Vessel assemblages remained remarkably constant over the course of the Spring and Autumn period; besides *lieding* and *gui*, they always comprise a pair of rectangular *hú*, a *pan* and *yi* set (with a *he* 盉 taking the place of the *yi* in some early assemblages), and a four-legged *yan* steamer. Sometimes additional kinds of vessels occur. After the middle of the seventh century B.C., *gui* were sometimes replaced by other, functionally equivalent vessels such as *chang*, *dui*, and *dou*; but *mingqi* versions of *gui* (and of coverless *ding*) continue to be seen down into the Warring States period. Apparently, lower-ranking Qin aristocrats, at least in funerary situations, did not adopt some or any of the new rituals that caused changes in vessel assemblages in other parts of the Zhou realm during the Middle Spring and Autumn period.

The ritual vessels from Qin aristocratic tombs show some idiosyncrasies. To start with, all bronzes found in tombs are *mingqi*. They are notable for their enduring conservatism of shape: late Western Zhou types are maintained with little modification all the way into the fourth century B.C. As they were progressively reduced to miniature versions over time, vessel proportions became awkwardly distorted, and the decoration was simplified (see Fig. 7.15). Often, a vessel and its cover were cast as one piece, without a bottom, precluding any usage except for display. The trend toward increased use of *mingqi* in funerary contexts was accompanied by the rise of high-quality pottery imitations of the standard late Western Zhou ritual vessels.

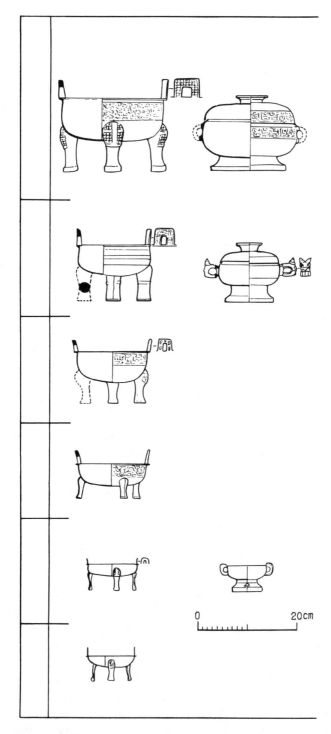

Figure 7.15. Typological development of funerary bronzes from Eastern Zhou Qin tombs. After Okamura Hidenori, "Shin bunka no hennen," *Koshi shunjû* 2 (1985): 56, fig. 1. Drawing by Li Xiating.

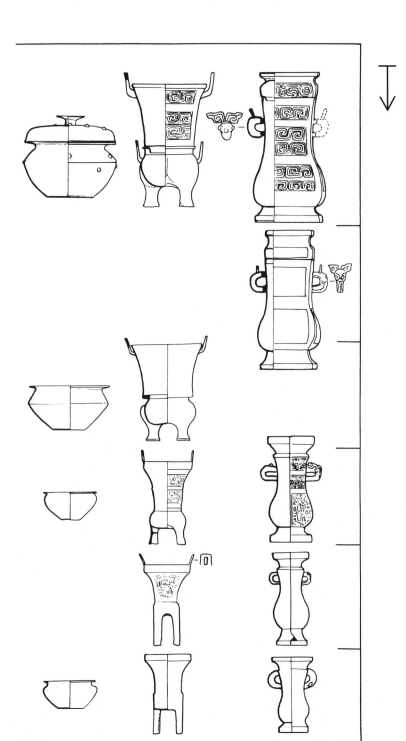

Table 7.2. Bronze assemblages excavated from Spring and Autumn period Qin aristocratic tombs

Locality	JBC	JJZ	BJZ	BJZ	SC	FLB	QJG	QJG	BQT	BQT	BQT	BQT	BQT	BQT	GZ	GZ	GZ	SMC	KSZ	BQT	RJZ
Tomb no.	?	1	5	1	3	1	1	2	C2	B27	A9	B31	14	26	10	49	48	27	202	C9	
Condition									intact	intact	looted	intact		intact						looted	
guo/guan	?	1+1	1+1	1+1	1+1	1+1	1+1	1+1	1+2	1+2	1+2	1+1	1+1	1+1	1+2	1+1	1+1	1+1	1+1	1+0(?)	1+1
ding	3	3	5	6	5	3	3	3	3	3	1(2)	(2)	1?	3	3	2	1(2)	1(2)	2	3	3
liandangding																			1	1	1
yan		1	1	1	1	1			1	1	1	1	1	1			1(1)	1	1	1	2
gui	2		4	4	4	2	4	4	1		1				(2)	(2)	(2)		2	1	
penyulcheng						1				1				2	1(1)	1(1)	(1)				
dui										(1)					1	1(1)	1			2	
dou													2		2						
hé	2		2	2	2	2	2	2			(3)			2	2(1)	2(2)	(2)	(1)	2	2(2)	2
hú										1		1	1	1	2					2	2
gaobinghú	1		1	1	1	1	1	1	1		(1)	1	1	3		1(1)	1(2)		1	1	1
fou	1		1	1																	
pan			1	1	1	1	1	1	1	(1)	(1)	1	1	1	(1)	1(1)	1(1)		1		
he																		1	1		
yi																					
jian																					
Total	9	4	14	15	14	11	11	11	7	5	3	3	5	13	9	8	5	2	10	10	11

Note: The tombs are listed in approximately chronological order, ranging from the late eighth to the early fourth century. Unbracketed numbers indicate bronzes, numbers in brackets ceramic vessels. Most of the bronzes are *mingqi*. Nothing is known about the occupants' sex.

JCB = Jiangchengbao, Baoji
FLB = Fulinbao, Baoji
QJG = Qinjiagou, Baoji
SMC = Shangmengcun, Changwu
KSZ = Keshengzhuang, Chang'an

JJZ = Jingjiazhuang, Lingtai
SC = Songcun, Hu Xian
BQT = Baqitun, Fengxiang
GZ = Gaozhuang, Fengxiang
RJZ = Renjiazui, Xianyang

Source: Partly based on Okamura Hidenori ("Shin bunka no hennen," *Koshi Shunjū* 2 [1985]: 55).

Made of a clayey grey earthenware, they translate the often angular bronze prototypes into shapes that could be produced on the potter's wheel. Specimens from the seventh through the end of the sixth century B.C. are often painted with abstract red and white spiral designs that imitate, albeit very roughly, the interlaced dragons of contemporary bronze decoration. In tombs, such ceramics may occur either instead of bronzes or in combination with them.

Both miniature bronzes and ceramic equivalents had already been manufactured in Shaanxi during the late Western Zhou period,[56] and workshops may have operated continuously under Qin rule. It should be stressed that Spring and Autumn period Qin *mingqi* were, at least at the beginning, quite different in appearance, quality, context, and probably significance from the kinds of *mingqi* that came into fashion throughout the Zhou culture sphere during the fifth century B.C.; during the Spring and Autumn period, the only other known place where bronzes were similarly de-emphasized and, for a time, replaced by pottery imitations was in west-central Hubei during the late seventh and early sixth century B.C.

The absolute dating of Qin bronze-yielding tombs still presents some difficulties. It is clear enough that the stylistic sequence ends in the early fourth century B.C., after which time no ritual vessels occur in Qin tombs. As to its starting point, some scholars have fixed it at the very beginning of the Spring and Autumn period, cross-dating the bronzes from Bianjiazhuang 邊家莊, Longxian 隴縣, Shaanxi,[57] with an early capital on the Qian 汧 River (762–715 B.C.), the cemeteries in the Baoji area with the Pingyang 平陽 capital (714–678 B.C.), and the Fengxiang cemeteries as contemporary with Yong (677–383 B.C.), but this conclusion is quite unwarranted as the Qin continued to hold the Qian and Pingyang areas after the move to Yong. Comparisons with other areas suggest that the earliest known assemblages may date no earlier than the first half of the seventh century B.C.

The often abysmal quality of Qin funerary bronzes does not justify the conclusion that metalworking in the Shaanxi area generally went into a decline after the abandonment of the Zhou capitals. Qin artisans continued to cast bronze objects of excellent quality for use by the living, and possibly for interment with the very highest-ranking individuals; a small number of

---

[56] See, for example, those unearthed from tomb 222 at Fengxi; *Fengxi fajue baogao* (Beijing: Wenwu, 1962), pl. 73.

[57] See Yin Shengping and Zhang Tian'en, "Shaanxi Long Xian Bianjiazhuang yihao Chunqiu Qin mu," *Kaogu yu wenwu* 1986.6: 15–22; *Wenwu* 1988.11: 14–23, 54; Xiao Qi, "Shaanxi Long Xian Bianjiazhuang chutu Chunqiu tongqi," *Wenbo* 1989.3: 79–81; Zhang Tian'en, "Bianjiazhuang Chunqiu Qin mudi yu Qian yi de diwang," *Wenbo* 1990.5: 227–31, 251; and Liu Junshe, "Bianjiazhuang Qin guo mudi fajue de zhuyao shouhuo ji qi yiyi," *Baoji wenbo* 1 (1991): 12–18.

them survive, including the inscribed items already discussed.[58] To a larger extent than is the case with funerary vessels, their shapes and ornaments follow the general stylistic trends of the time when they were produced. The seventh century B.C. bronze architectural fittings from the Yong palaces (see Fig. 7.4) exhibit the dissolution of dragon motifs into a nearly abstract, banded pattern. Later vessels feature ornamentation bands of dragon bodies reduced to small-scale interlacery, with no animal likeness discernible; some late sixth to early fifth century B.C. items are virtually indistinguishable from Houma products. Besides vessels, Qin workshops produced high-quality weapons and accessories, such as some of the earliest bronze mirrors of Eastern Zhou China.[59] At least two tombs have yielded display weapons with iron blades comparable to those from Shangcunling, notable for their highly ornate inlaid bronze or gold handles.[60] Like the Houma foundry, Qin work-shops appear to have supplied the markets of the northern steppes.[61]

Despite the long-standing text-based prejudice that Qin practiced human sacrifice with particular severity, the frequency of tombs of non-*zhuhou* aris-tocrats with human victims and the number of victims per tomb (up to five) do not seem to differ much from contemporaneous finds of comparable rank in the east and south of the Zhou culture sphere. Differences in the place-ment of victims suggest a hierarchy among them: relatives, minor consorts, or other close associates of the principal occupants were deposited in the burial chamber, while lower-ranking servants or guardians were placed on a "second-level ledge" (*ercengtai* 二層臺) or in niches carved into the tomb walls. Many tombs also contain sacrificed dogs, sometimes placed in waist pits underneath the principal tomb occupant's coffin. Horse and chariot pits containing from one to three two-horse chariots and sometimes also a human charioteer accompany many tombs of five-*ding* and three-*ding* rank; a most unusual find is the human-drawn chariot (*nian* 輦) from the early Spring and

---

[58] Among such objects, one should also consider a hoard of stylistically and typologically idiosyncratic bronzes excavated at Rujiazhuang 茹家莊, Baoji, Shaanxi (Gao Ciruo and Liu Mingke, "Baoji Rujiazhuang xin faxian tongqi jiaocang," *Kaogu yu wenwu* 1990.4: 11–16), including four animal-shaped bronzes (a tiger holding its cub, a stag, a dog, and a fish-shaped *zun*), and a rectangular bronze stove featuring a gatekeeper with his left foot amputated, standing on gazelle-head-shaped feet (Fig. 7.1). Though originally assigned to late Western Zhou, the similarity to the box-shaped vessels from Shang-guo suggests an early Spring and Autumn period date.

[59] See Diane N. O'Donoghue, "Reflection and Reception: The Origins of the Mirror in Bronze Age China," *BMFEA* 62 (1990): 5–183.

[60] Such weapons have been found in the late-seventh century B.C. tomb at Jingjiazhuang 景家莊, Lingtai 靈臺, Gansu (Liu Dezhen and Zhu Jiantang, "Gansu Lingtai xian Jingjiazhuang Chunqiu mu," *Kaogu* 1981.4: 298–301); and in the late sixth century B.C. tomb at Yimencun 益門村, Baoji, Shaanxi (*Wenwu* 1993.10: 1–27).

[61] Evidence for this is a bronze bucket of a type widespread across the Eurasian steppes, but with Qin-style ornamentation, from Fengxiang (Zhao Congcang, "Fengxiang chutu yipi Chunqiu Zhanguo wenwu," *Kaogu yu wenwu* 1991.2: 2–13). Similar objects were also made at the Houma foundry and have been found at Liyu, as well as in various sixth century B.C. tombs in the Jin area.

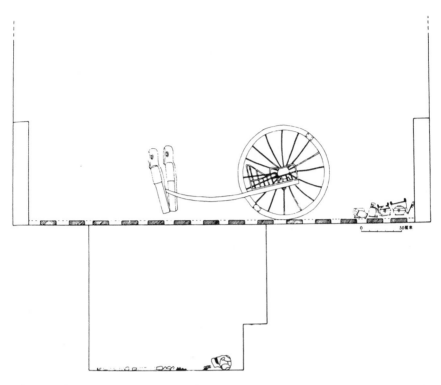

Figure 7.16. Tomb 5 at Bianjiazhuang, Longxian, Shaanxi, containing a chariot pulled by human figurines. Late eighth to early seventh century B.C. From *Wenwu* 1988.11: 15, fig. 2.

Autumn period tomb 5 at Bianjiazhuang.[62] To the yokebar were attached two crudely hewn, partly painted wooden figurines, too small to be realistic in proportion to the chariot. This is the earliest known instance of figurine use in a Zhou mortuary context; their "high noses" led the excavators to propose that they depict (dwarf-size?) individuals with alien racial features (Fig. 7.16). Human figurines are not seen again in Qin tombs until the latter part of the Warring States period, but incipient use of models depicting aspects of everyday life, so common later on, is exemplified during the last century or so of the Spring and Autumn period by pottery vessels in the shape of granaries.

Qin tombs are predominantly laid out in an east–west direction with the occupant's head pointing west, and the bodies of the deceased are deposited lying on the side and with the knees drawn toward the body (flexed burial); this contrasts with pervasive north–south orientation and stretched supine burial in tombs of the earlier Chinese Bronze Age, as well as in contempo-

[62] *Wenwu* 1988.11: 14–23, 54.

raneous contexts east of Shaanxi.[63] It should be noted that orientation with respect to the cardinal directions is principally a feature of larger tombs; little attention appears to have been paid, in Qin or elsewhere, to the uniform alignment of smaller tombs. As to the flexed mode of burial, it does not appear to have become current in Qin all at once: during the first century or so of the Eastern Zhou, stretched burial still occurs in some relatively high-ranking aristocratic tombs. Some instances where human victims were buried in the flexed position, whereas the principal tomb occupant were not, have given rise to the theory that flexed burial was originally meted out to the "enslaved" lower classes, a practice to be later adopted throughout the society as a consequence of the collapse of the old aristocratic order.[64] But flexed burial had been practiced since Neolithic times in areas west of the Zhou culture area, from Gansu and Qinghai through much of Central Eurasia; the possibility that it was a Qin ethnic custom seems supported by the discovery of a continuous sequence of tombs with flexed burials, with dates ranging from the late Western Zhou through the middle of Eastern Zhou, in what is thought to have been the Qin homeland before their move into Shaanxi.[65] It is unclear whether the early instances of stretched burial in Eastern Zhou Qin represented a remnant Zhou population or constituted initial attempts by the Qin aristocracy to accommodate itself to locally entrenched Zhou ritual traditions. From the mid-seventh century B.C. onward, in any case, flexed burial was pervasively practiced in the Qin area down to around the time of the founding of the Qin empire, when it once again gradually gave way to stretched burial.

These Qin practices may well reflect conceptualizations of death and the afterlife that differed from those of their neighbors within the Zhou culture sphere.[66] Details remain elusive, however, as ethnographic comparison suggests a number of divergent explanations.[67] At the basis of the differences from more easterly areas may be an emphasis placed on the discontinuity between the spheres of the living and the dead, evident from the peculiari-

---

[63] Gao Quxun ("Huanghe xiayou de quzhizang wenti: *Di er ci tanjue Anyang Dasikongcun nandi jianbao fulun zhi yi," Zhongguo kaogu xuebao* 2 [1947]: 121–66) already noticed instances of flexed burial in easterly areas of China, dating both to Eastern Zhou and to earlier times; they are especially frequent in the Luoyang area during the Warring States; but in these areas, flexed burials always seem to have been somewhat exceptional; Ye Xiaoyan (in "Qin mu chutan") has observed that the degree of flexing of the skeletons is less extreme than what is normally observed in Qin tombs. In some areas, the incidence of this feature may be indicative of Qin impact.

[64] Han Wei, "Lüelun Shaanxi Chunqiu Zhanguo Qin mu."

[65] See *Kaogu xuebao* 1987.3: 359–96.

[66] Catacomb tombs (in which the coffin is placed in an enclosed chamber laterally adjacent to a vertical shaft) are sometimes stated to be another Qin ethnic characteristic. But although such tombs are common in antecedent Neolithic cultures and occasionally seen during the Western Zhou, they appear in Qin contexts only during the second half of the fourth century B.C., when they seem to be a new phenomenon, undoubtedly linked to changes in the mortuary ideology that occurred during that period.

[67] Gao Quxun, "Huanghe xiayou de quzhizang wenti."

ties of Qin funerary vessel manufacture. In a somewhat uneasy fusion with the material manifestations of the Zhou ritual system, the Qin tombs seem to evince religious concepts, possibly of westerly origin, that were novel to this area during the Spring and Autumn period, but were to hold sway over all of the Zhou culture sphere after the fifth century B.C.[68]

THE CEMETERIES AT QUFU

Though they were all drawn into the overarching political framework of the Zhou league, the approximately twenty polities that existed in the Shandong Peninsula during the Spring and Autumn period had quite different historical origins. Qi, the largest, had apparently been among the constituent polities of the Shang realm; Confucius's home polity of Lu, ruled by a lineage of the royal Ji clan, had been founded at the beginning of the Western Zhou dynasty as a local bastion of Zhou rule; others, such as Zhu 邾, Ju 莒, and Lai 萊, were considered as Barbarian (Eastern Yi 東夷) polities not fully on a par with the others. The *Chunqiu* chronicle and the *Zuo zhuan*, based on the court annals of Lu, are full of interesting detail about the varying relationships between these polities and their neighbors – a history punctuated by marriage alliances (also documented in bronze inscriptions), court visits, assassinations, usurpations, war campaigns, grand funerals, and endless debates about what constituted ritually correct political behavior.

Among various attempts to distinguish the different "cultures" of these polities on archaeological grounds, the most influential has been proposed in connection with the analysis of finds from six aristocratic cemeteries at Qufu.[69] The report on a decade of excavations by the Shandong Institute of Archaeology and Cultural Relics proposes a distinction between two groups of tombs, which are assigned, respectively, to the descendants of the pre-Zhou inhabitants of the area (Group A), and to the members of Ji-clan lineages who originally immigrated there from Shaanxi (Group B).[70] This analysis

---

[68] See Falkenhausen, "Ahnenkult und Grabkult"; and Lothar von Falkenhausen, "Sources of Taoism: Reflections on Archaeological Indicators of Religious Change in Eastern Zhou China," *Taoist Resources* 5, 2 (1994): 1–12.

[69] *Qufu Lu guo gucheng*; English translations of the preliminary reports and of the conclusions of the final report are provided in David D. Buck, ed. and trans. "Archeological Explorations at the Ancient Capital of Lu at Qufu in Shandong Province," *Chinese Sociology and Anthropology* 19, 1 (1986): 3–76.

[70] Group A comprises seventy-eight tombs at five cemeteries: Yaopu 藥圃 (thirty-four tombs, datable from Western Zhou through Spring and Autumn); Doujitai 鬥雞臺 (not to be confused with the early Bronze Age cemetery of the same name at Baoji; twenty-seven tombs, datable from Western Zhou through Spring and Autumn); the northwest corner of the Ming dynasty county seat (fourteen Spring and Autumn period tombs), Beiguan 北關 (two Warring States period tombs), Huayuan 花園 (one Warring States period tomb). As described in the archaeological report, Group A includes only the fifty-one tombs at the cemetery of Wangfutai 望父臺, dated to Western Zhou and from Late Spring and Autumn through Warring States; the gap in the sequence is bridged by recently excavated thirty Spring and Autumn period tombs at Linqiancun 林前村 (Wenwu Bianji weiyuanhui, *Wenwu kaogu gongzuo shinian*

purports to reveal that these two ethnic groups, while living side by side with one another at the same settlement, maintained their distinct traditions without merging throughout the Western and Eastern Zhou dynasty. Intriguing though it is, this idea seems problematic in a variety of ways.

The main differences that have been isolated are as follows.

(1) TOMB CONSTRUCTION. About one-third of Group A tombs feature a waist pit (*yaokeng*) under the principal occupant's coffin, usually containing the remains of a dog sacrifice; by contrast, no waist pits occur in tombs of Group B. Long known as a common feature of Shang aristocratic tombs at Anyang, waist pits in Western Zhou tombs, when first discovered at Luoyang in the 1950s,[71] were interpreted as representing the "Shang remnants" who had been transferred to Luoyang after the destruction of the Shang capital. Although tombs with waist pits no longer occur in the Luoyang area after middle Western Zhou, later instances, some as late as the Warring States period, have been found in various places, especially in the eastern parts of the Zhou realm.

(2) MODE OF BURIAL. Occupants of Group A tombs at Qufu are predominantly buried with the head pointing south, whereas Group B tomb occupants are buried with the head pointing north. Bones of sacrificial animals are seen in many Group A tombs, and one tomb contained a human victim, placed on top of the principal occupant's coffin. By contrast, Group B tombs contain no animal bones; in the sole instance of a human sacrifice the remains were placed in a separate coffin within the burial chamber.[72]

(3) BURIAL GOODS. Six horse and chariot pits were found in connection with Group B tombs, but none with Group A. Funerary ceramics in both groups are almost entirely *mingqi*, though early Group B tombs contain *li* of Zhou type with lateral flanges, whereas Group A tombs feature *li* of an "eastern" (Shang-derived) type without flanges. In the later Group B tombs, *li* are transformed into *fu* 釜, a class of vessels absent from Group A tombs. Other differences between the ceramic assemblages of Groups A and B seem minor.

(1979–1989) [Beijing: Wenwu, 1990], pp. 170–2), a location where inscribed Lu bronzes had been found before 1937.

[71] To this writer's knowledge, this idea was first promulgated by Guo Baojun and Lin Shoujin in their report on their 1952 excavations in the eastern suburbs of Luoyang (Guo Baojun and Lin Shoujin, "Yijiuwu'ernian qiuji Luoyang dongjiao fajue baogao," *Kaogu xuebao* 9 [1955]: 93 and passim).

[72] The original report on this tomb (Wangfutai M4) interprets it as a joint husband and wife burial, but couples were virtually never buried in the same tomb during the Chinese Bronze Age; this situation probably reflects basic conceptions of lineage and kinship that should be addressed in future specialized research.

Skepticism is in order with regard to this bicultural vision because many of the features contrasted do not coexist in the same periods and because the cemeteries under comparison represent populations of different social ranks. A recent study of Zhou ceramics from Shandong intimates that many of the features adduced to differentiate Group A and Group B tombs actually reflect changes over time;[73] the absence of *li* with flanges and of *fu* in Group A tombs, for instance, may be explained by the fact that the Group A cemeteries comprise no ceramic-yielding tombs from the periods when those vessel types were current.

Moreover, the main reason why Group A exhibits greater ceramic variety than Group B is that its tombs yielded ceramic *mingqi*, whereas contemporaneous Group B tombs featured bronze vessels. In spite of extensive looting, the Group B tombs strike one as being far richer on average than their counterparts at the Group A cemeteries. For instance, 50 percent of Group A tombs contained no burial goods whatsoever; by contrast, every Group B tomb had something, and the proportion of tombs with bronze vessels is 32.5 percent, as opposed to 10.3 percent in Group A. The bronze-yielding tombs in Group B, moreover, far exceed those in Group A in the number of bronzes per tomb, typological diversity, and incidence of inscribed vessels. Certain kinds of elite objects, weapons, horse and chariot gear, personal ornaments, funerary jades adorning the deceased person's body, lacquer vessels, and glass frit beads, are altogether limited to Group B. Although the two groups comprise approximately the same percentages of tombs with burial chambers, only Group B features some (relatively late) tombs with burial chamber and double nested coffins. Status differences among aristocratic lineages therefore probably constitute the primary explanation for most of the differences observed. Withal it remains enigmatic why *li* of eastern regional type and (possibly) waist pits, though far from ubiquitous at the cemeteries of lower-elites, are completely absent from those of higher-ranking elites. The notion of different "family traditions" may lead to a less sweeping explanation, and be less prone to anachronistic misinterpretation, than that of ethnic affiliation.

As at Zhongzhoulu, it appears that the ceramic-based sequences established in the report on the Qufu cemeteries are by and large tenable, but the absolute datings are not. Rather than in early Western Zhou, the chronology of the cemeteries starts in the time after the Late Western Zhou Ritual Reform, probably not before ca. 800 B.C.; it extends down into the fourth century B.C.[74] The Qufu bronzes reflect stylistic developments analogous to

---

[73] Cui Lequan, "Shandong diqu Dong Zhou kaoguxue wenhua de xulie," *Hua Xia kaogu* 1992.4: 72–97.

[74] Even though Qufu is said to have been settled throughout the Western Zhou period, virtually no mortuary finds from the first two and a half centuries of that period have so far come to light, in spite of a fair amount of archaeological investigation.

Figure 7.17. *Houmu hu* from tomb 48 at Wangfutai, Qufu, Shandong. Eighth to early seventh century B.C. From Li Xueqin, *Zhongguo meishu quanji, gongyi meishu bian 5, qingtongqi* (*xia*) (Beijing: Wenwu, 1986), no. 6.

those observed in the north-central area. From orthodox versions of the standard late Western Zhou vessel types, the fashion progresses to vessels with ever more playful elaborations of the same motifs. Some of the early tombs additionally yielded bronzes representing an idiosyncratic regional workshop tradition that flourished between ca. 800 and 600 B.C.; they are characterized by simple, rounded shapes reminiscent of ceramic prototypes and by hatched geometric designs that are sometimes juxtaposed awkwardly with the dragon-derived decor typical of "mainstream" late Western Zhou and incipient Eastern Zhou bronzes (Fig. 7.17).[75]

As elsewhere, the sixth century B.C. brought about significant typological changes. Late Spring and Autumn period vessels from the Qufu cemeteries

---

[75] Similar pieces have been found elsewhere in Shandong, especially in the southeastern and eastern parts of the province, long the domain of non-Zhou polities, for example, at Guheya 崮河崖, Rizhao 日照 (Yang Shenfu, "Shandong Rizhao Guheya chutu yipi qingtongqi," *Kaogu* 1984.7: 594–7, 606) and Shangkuangcun 上夼材, Yantai 煙臺 (*Kaogu* 1983.4: 289–92).

display an almost industrial character: relatively thin-walled, they are characterized by multiple ring-shaped appendages, as well as by a fascination with movable fixtures such as chain links. Unlike contemporaneous products of the Houma foundry, for example, they feature little or no surface ornamentation, their aesthetic appeal relying mainly on elegance of shape and, in their own time, metallic sheen. Ceramics and bronzes broadly similar to those from Qufu occur throughout Shandong, with few stylistic variations that would correlate with the political boundaries within this area.[76]

TOMBS OF THE HIGH ELITE IN THE EASTERN PART OF THE ZHOU REALM

Aside from Qufu, data from multiperiod lineage cemeteries with tombs representing occupants of different ranks are not yet available from Shandong.[77] A number of tombs of high-ranking individuals dating from the seventh to the fifth century B.C. have, however, been excavated on the Shandong peninsula and in the Huai River basin further to the south, yielding significant bronze assemblages. In spite of their relatively wide geographical spread and some stylistic variety, these tombs share some features in common. While their burial chambers (*guo*) contained for the most part items for the principal occupant's personal usage, ritual paraphernalia were displayed on wide second-level ledges (*ercengtai*), for the most part in separate storage chambers. Many of these tombs contain a relatively large number of human victims, who were buried in separate graves dug into the second-level ledges, often with their own coffins and burial goods; those victims who were buried in the principal tomb occupant's burial chambers probably differed in status from those buried on the second-level ledges.

The most important discoveries in Shandong are the following.

(1) TOMB 5 AT HEYATOU 河崖頭, LINZI 監淄, SHANDONG.[78] Part of the exhaustively looted necropolis of the rulers of Qi in the northern part of their capital, this is believed to be the tomb of Jing Gong 景公 (r. 547–490

---

[76] In spite of the area's political fragmentation, it is with good reason that Hayashi Minao (in *Shunjū Sengoku seidōki-no kenkyū*), designates Shandong as one of his regional units of analysis. Even Zhang Xuehai ("Lun sishinianlai Shandong xian-Qin kaogu de jiben shouhuo," *Hai Dai kaogu* 1 [1989]: 325–343), in arguing, unconvincingly, for a fundamental cultural difference, throughout the Bronze Age, between a "Qi–Ji–Lai" league in the north and a "Lu–Teng–Xue" league in the south of the province, admits that differences between sites within one area are sometimes as pronounced as inter-area differences, if not more so. See also Cui Lequan, "Shandong diqu Dong Zhou kaoguxue wenhua de xulie."

[77] Such data have been recovered in the environs of the Qi capital of Linzi, but have not yet been published in usable form; for preliminary reports, see *Hai Dai kaogu* 1 (1989): 274–82, 283–91.

[78] *Wenwu* 1984.9: 14–19. For other finds from the necropolis, see *Xin Zhongguo de kaogu faxian he yanjiu*, 286; Qi Wentao, "Gaishu jinnianlai Shandong chutu de Shang Zhou qingtongqi," *Wenwu* 1972.5: 8, 18, fig. 36; and Li Jian and Zhang Longhai, "Linzi chutu de jijian qingtongqi," *Kaogu* 1985.4: 380–1.

B.C.). In a case that is parallel with the Jin tombs at Qucun (described in Chapter 6), the tomb features a single sloping tomb passage (*mudao*) and was lined with charcoal and pebble masonry; its most impressive feature is the ensemble of horse pits surrounding it on all four sides, in which the carcasses of at least 600 immolated horses are aligned in orderly double rows – an extraordinary feat of conspicuous consumption.

(2) THE TOMB OF AN AS YET UNIDENTIFIED MIDDLE SEVENTH CENTURY B.C. RULER OF JU AT LIUJIADIANZI 劉家店子, YISHUI 沂水, SHANDONG.[79]

The tomb contained at least thirty-five human victims; a sacrificed charioteer was buried with his own bronze assemblage in the nearby chariot pit. While the ruler's triple nested coffin chamber yielded only funerary jades and some weapons, the two wooden storage chambers contained one of the richest assemblages of Eastern Zhou bronzes known, including sixteen *ding*, eleven of which form a set (perhaps of status-defining *lieding*),[80] as well as thirty-eight bells of different types. Inscriptions show that these bronzes had originally been made for donors from various neighboring polities; on some objects, inscriptions had been deliberately erased, suggesting that they had been obtained as war booty. Not surprisingly, the assemblage is somewhat heterogeneous stylistically. Some vessels are typologically conservative though enhanced by idiosyncratic local features, such as the sets of *lieding* and *li*, all of which feature flat covers; yet instead of *gui*, the tomb contained a set of seven covered *dou* (self-named in their inscriptions as *gui*) on elaborate openwork stems.

(3) THE LATE SIXTH CENTURY B.C. TOMB AT FENGHUANGLING 鳳凰嶺, LINYI 臨沂, SHANDONG,[81] WHICH MAY HAVE BELONGED TO A MEMBER OF THE RULING FAMILY OF THE SMALL POLITY OF YU 郚.

In this tomb, the wooden storage compartment for ritual paraphernalia apparently constituted the "front" or "outer" portion, with the tomb chamber proper, beside or behind it, suggesting patterns of access that are comparable to those of palace architecture. The excavators noted an evident hierarchy among the fourteen human victims, definable in terms of spatial proximity to their master. Although the tomb had been severely looted, an unlooted storage pit was found a short distance away, containing bronze vessels (including a status-defining set of seven *ding*), weapons, and

---

[79] *Wenwu* 1984.9: 1–10.

[80] The number eleven is of course unorthodox in terms of the Zhou sumptuary rules as they appear in the light of current research (see note 29); such a set might reflect the uneasy accommodation into the Zhou system of the Ju ruler, who, while yielding to the Zhou king (twelve *ding*), yet placed himself above rulers of other territorial polities (nine *ding* or less).

[81] *Linyi Fenghuangling Dong Zhou mu* (Ji'nan: Qilu, 1987).

musical instruments (all rather thin-walled); there was also a horse and chariot pit.

(4) TWO LARGE MOUNDED TOMBS AT DADIAN 大店, JUNAN 莒南, SHANDONG,[82] ONE OF WHICH IS LINKED BY INSCRIPTION TO A SCION OF THE RULING HOUSE OF JU. Their spatial layout is similar to that of the Fenghuangling tomb, but the storage chamber was a separate pit separated from the tomb chamber by a block of earth, with a narrow sloped passageway (*mudao*) leading into it. In each of the two tombs, looters had left behind bronze vessels and bells, as well as pottery vessels. Each tomb had ten victims, all placed in their own coffins, some with simple gravegoods. The style of the bronze vessels, for the most part unadorned and with prominent ring-shaped appendages, as well as the presence of ceramic *mingqi* ritual vessels and of mounds atop the tomb chambers, suggests an early fifth century B.C. date.

Tombs of lower-ranking aristocrats of Ju have also been discovered in an increasing number;[83] their assemblages are all remarkable for their relatively strict adherence to Zhou sumptuary distinctions.

(5) NINE TOMBS INSIDE THE WALLED CAPITAL OF THE XUE 薛 POLITY AT XUECHENG 薛城, TENGZHOU 滕州, SHANDONG.[84] Part of a larger, regularly aligned cemetery, four of these tombs (1–4) are of late eighth to seventh century B.C. date, whereas the others (5–9) date to the fifth to early fourth century. All nine tombs had burial chambers, and the four earlier ones had wooden storage compartments; the presence of triple nested coffins in tombs 1 and 2 indicates an occupant of considerable prominence. Human victims were found in all but one of the tombs, in one case placed in a waist pit underneath the principal occupant's coffin. Except for tomb 3, which had been looted, the earlier tombs each yielded spectacular funerary jades adorning the deceased person's body, as well as rich assemblages of ritual bronzes, whereas in the later, smaller tombs, bronzes have been predomi-

---

[82] *Kaogu xuebao* 1978.3: 317–36.

[83] The earliest bronze-yielding Ju tombs so far known, dating to the eighth century B.C., are those at Zhongqiagou 中洽溝, Linyi (*Kaogu* 1987.8: 701–706, 762) and Lijiazhuang 李家莊, Yishui (*Shandong wenwu xuanji (pucha bufen)* [Beijing: Wenwu, 1959], pp. 44–6). Seventh century B.C. Ju tombs have been found, inter alia, at Donghebeicun 東河北村, Yishui (Ma Xilun, "Shandong Yishui faxian yizuo Xi Zhou muzang," *Kaogu* 1986.8: 756–8) and at Tianjingwang 天井汪, Juxian 莒縣 (Qi Wentao, "Gaishu jinnianlai Shandong chutu de Shang Zhou qingtongqi," pp. 11–12). Several other interesting assemblages have been reported from southeastern and eastern Shandong; a synthetic treatment is needed.

[84] *Kaogu xuebao* 1991.4: 449–95. More excavations have taken place at the site since; see Wenwu bianji weiyuanhui, *Wenwu kaogu gongzuo shinian (1979–1989)*, pp. 170–2. Previous finds of inscribed Xue bronzes from the site were reported by Wan Shuying and Yang Xiaoyi, "Tengxian chutu Qi Xue tongqi," *Wenwu* 1978.4: 94–6.

Table 7.3. *Bronze assemblages excavated at the Xue cemetery at Xuecheng, Tengzhou, Shandong*

Tomb no.	1	2	3	4	5	6	7	8	9
Condition	intact	intact	looted	damaged	intact	intact	intact	intact	intact
guo/guan	2 + 2	1 + 3	1 + 2	?	1 + 2	1 + 2	1 + 1	1 + 1	1 + 2
Date	E/MCQ	E/MCQ	E/MCQ	E/MCQ	ZG	LCQ	LCQ	ZG	LCQ
ding	7	7		7	(4)	1		(4)	1
peiding		1		3					
fangding	1								
li	6	6		6	(2)	(6)	(4)	(2)	(3)
yan					(2)				
gui	6	6		6					
gaidou	(6)				(8)	1			2
gaobingdou					(5)	(4)	(4)	(2)	(2)
hú	2	2		2					
hé		1		1		1	1		
bei				3	(1)				
yuanhú	2	2		2	(4)			(2)	
bianhú	1	1		1					
tilianghú			1						
fang					(2)				
guan/lei	6	1(4)	(4)	1(6)		(5)	(4)	(2)	(3)
xiaoguan		1							
pan	1	1			(2)				1
yi	1	1			(2)				1
he				1					
jian				1					
Totals	32	30	1	34	—	3	1	—	5
	(6)	(4)	(4)	(6)	(32)	(15)	(12)	(12)	(8)

Note: Unbracketed numbers indicate bronzes, numbers in brackets ceramic vessels. Most of the bronzes are *mingqi*. Nothing is known about the occupants' sex.
CQ = Spring and Autumn period
ZG = Warring States period
E = Early, M = Middle, L = Late

nantly or entirely replaced by ceramic *mingqi*. The bronze assemblages from the earlier tombs (Table 7.3) each contain sets of seven *lieding* paired with sets of six *li* and six *gui*, as well as pairs of *hú*, as in tombs 2001 and 1052 at Shangcunling, Sanmenxia, Henan. Also similar to conditions elsewhere is the fact that supernumerary *ding* of other types (in one case, a *fangding*) are added to the status-defining *lieding*. Bronze inscriptions identify the tomb occupants as members of the ruling lineage of Xue; that they were the rulers themselves seems doubtful in view of the absence of horse and chariot pits and of bells, which, to judge by other finds from the area, seem to have been de rigueur even in the tombs of rather minor rulers during this period.

Major discoveries in the Huai River basin (except for late Spring and Autumn period Chu finds) include the following.

(6) THE MID-SEVENTH CENTURY B.C. TOMBS OF HUANG JUN MENG 黃君孟 AND HIS CONSORT MENG JI 孟姬 AT SHANGGUAN'GANG 上官崗, GUANGSHAN 光山, HENAN.[85] They were originally reported as two

separate tomb chambers located in one tomb pit, but the published section drawing strongly suggests that tomb 2, the tomb of Meng Ji, precedes that of her husband. In each tomb, burial and storage chambers are encompassed within a larger chamber. The situation of joint burial has been interpreted as an unorthodox variation of Zhou standards,[86] but the custom of pairing important tombs is actually well-attested at northern cemeteries (e.g., at Qucun, Shangcunling, Shangma, and Xincun). What is curious here is that the female partner has far more plentiful burial goods: Meng Ji's tomb contained 18 bronzes and 131 funerary jades, as opposed to her husband's 10 bronzes and 54 jades (see Fig. 7.7). The tombs are also remarkable for their rich textile and lacquer finds. To judge from her skeletal remains, Meng Ji died in her forties. Inscriptions identify her as a princess from an unnamed polity with a ruling lineage related to the Zhou royal house.

(7) FOUR MID-SEVENTH CENTURY B.C. TOMBS AT PINGQIAO 平橋, XINYANG 信陽, HENAN.[87] From inscribed bronzes found in tomb 5 and

other tombs in the area, it seems likely that this was a cemetery of the Fân 番 polity. Most prominent are the tombs of Lady Long Ying of Fán 樊夫人 龍嬴 (a lineage of the royal Zhou Ji clan, not to be confused with Fân) and her unnamed husband (who may have been of Fân lineage), which are paired in an arrangement similar to that observed at Shangguan'gang. Funerary assemblages are also similar to those at Shangguan'gang, though somewhat less rich. Different opinions have been voiced about the identity of Fân. Li Xueqin reads the character as Shen 瀋, a lineage of the Ji 姬 clan that became subordinate to Chu early in the Spring and Autumn period and was assigned to govern its northern border territories; against this, others have argued that Shen was located elsewhere, and that Fân was a polity of the Jí 姞 clan, an early Chu ally in this area.[88]

---

[85] *Kaogu* 1984.4: 302–32, 348.

[86] See Li Xueqin, "Guangshan Huang guo mu de jige wenti," *Kaogu yu wenwu* 1985.2: 49–52.

[87] *Wenwu* 1981.1: 9–14; *Zhongyuan wenwu* 1981.4: 14–15; and *Kaogu* 1989.1: 20–5, 9.

[88] Li Xueqin, "Lun Han Huai jian de Chunqiu tongqi," *Wenwu* 1980.1: 54–8. Against this, see Wang Entian, "Henan Gushi Gouwu furen mu: Jiantan Fan guo dili weizhi ji Wu fa Chu luxian," *Zhongyuan wenwu* 1985.2: 59–62, 64; and Ou Tansheng, "Gushi Hougudui Wu Taizi Fuchai furen mu de Wu wenhua yinsu," *Zhongyuan wenwu* 1991.4: 33–8.

(8) TOMB I AT HOUGUDUI 侯古堆, GUSHI 固始, HENAN. This sizable tomb may testify to the continued existence of Fân in the first quarter of the fifth century B.C.[89] Here the storage chamber is placed in a separate pit a short distance from the tomb proper, which featured a single tomb passage (*mudao*), a burial pit lined with layers of stone boulders and charcoal, and apparently, a mound. The principal tomb occupant, a woman about thirty years old, was buried in a single coffin placed in double nested wooden burial chambers. There were seventeen human victims (nine female, five male, three of indeterminate sex, ranging from twenty to forty years of age), each in their own coffins. Funerary items include a plethora of bronzes, jades, pottery, lacquered wooden musical instruments, chariot items, and several sedan chairs. They present an interesting stylistic mix. Among the ritual bronzes, many, including the principal set of nine covered *ding* and a pair of square covered *dou* with inlaid decoration, are executed in the late Spring and Autumn period Chu style; others, however, are apparently of Lower Yangzi derivation. Ou Tansheng has noted, furthermore, that of thirty-one ceramic items, only six can be related to Chu prototypes, the others, some of them made of glazed, hard-fired ware, evincing southeasterly connections.

The historical interpretation of the Hougudui tomb hinges on the interpretation of two controversial inscriptions. One of them is on a *hû* 匜 (see Fig. 7.8) and states: "I, Luan 欒, ruler of Song 宋, descendant of Heavenly Yi 天乙, Tang 唐, the Possessor of Yin 有殷, make this *hû* vessel for the marriage of my younger sister Ji Zi 季子, Lady of Gouyu 句敔 [= Wu 吳]."[90] Luan of Song can be identified with Jing Gong 景公 (r. 516–469).[91] On the basis of this inscription, it has been hypothesized that Hougudui was a Wu 吳 tomb, but this seems to be difficult to reconcile with historical geography. Others have taken their clue from a set of *niuzhong* bells, the original inscriptions on which had been erased and replaced with the name Chengzhou, Prince of Fan 鄱子成周, identifying the tomb occupant as Chengzhou's wife, who might have obtained the *hû* as a gift, heirloom, or booty. Fan 鄱 is probably equivalent to Fân 番.

The Huai River basin finds have connections in various directions. With their ornamentation mostly of elaborate geometricized dragon bodies, often interlaced and of considerable complexity, the bronzes from Shanguan'gang

---

[89] *Wenwu* 1981.1: 1–8. There is still a certain amount of controversy over the dating of this tomb, ranging from the early part of late Spring and Autumn (Hayashi, *Shunjû Sengoku seidôki-no kenkyû*, p. 33) until after the middle of the fifth century B.C. (Li Xueqin, *Eastern Zhou and Qin Civilizations*, pp. 158–60); on balance, a date around 500 seems plausible. In any case, the accession of Jing Gong of Song gives a *terminus post quem*. For further discussion, see Wang Entian, "Henan Gushi Gouwu furen mu: Jiantan Fan guo dili weizhi ji Wu fa Chu luxian," and Ou Tansheng, "Gushi Hougudui Wu Taizi Fuchai furen mu de Wu wenhua yinsu."

[90] Zhongguo Shehui kexueyuan Kaogu yanjiusuo, *Yin Zhou jinwen jicheng*, vol. 9, nos. 4589–90.

[91] These dates follow the *Zuo zhuan*; note that the *Shiji* dates for this ruler are incorrect.

Figure 7.18. *Xu* with star-band pattern from Huyao, Taihe, Anhui. Middle to late sixth century B.C. From Anhui sheng bowuguan, *Anhui Sheng Bowuguan cang qingtongqi* (Shanghai: Shanghai Renmin meishu, 1987), no. 50.

and Pingqiao are stylistically typical for the mid-seventh century B.C. Zhou mainstream; on later bronzes from the same area, these ornaments evolve into "star-band pattern" (*xingdaiwen* 星帶文) ornamentation (an ornament in which dragon bodies are reduced to relieved lines, with joins and bends accentuated by circlets), which seems to be an eastern specialty; the size of the units of decoration decreases steadily with time (Fig. 7.18).[92] Certain idiosyncrasies, such as flat covers on vessels of various kinds and the presence of bronze *li* with sharply broken profile and high pointed legs, recall contemporary assemblages from Shandong.

Considerable typological affinities also exist with areas further to the southeast. Tomb 2 at Shangguan'gang, for instance, yielded a bronze stand for a "tomb-protecting animal" (*zhenmushou* 鎮墓獸). Although such creatures, the religious significance of which remains a subject of speculation, are usually associated with Chu, where they are plentiful in Warring States period

---

[92] The *xu* 盨 in Fig. 7.18, undoubtedly the most excellent example of *xingdaiwen* decoration on record, represents a class of grain-offering vessels that had become virtually extinct since late Western Zhou times; the same pattern also appears on functionally equivalent *cheng* (e.g., at Liujiadianzi), as well as on other types of bronzes.

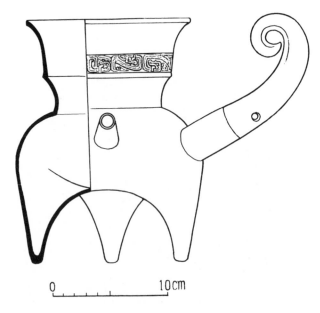

Figure 7.19. *Yanxinghe* from Yanshancun, Lu'an, Anhui. Seventh century B.C. After *Kaogu* 1993.7: 656, fig. 1:5. Drawing by Li Xiating.

tombs, the earliest evidence for them actually comes from the Jiangnan 江 南 area. Vessels of archaic types clearly made in non-Zhou regional work-shops south of the Yangzi have also been found in seventh century B.C. con-texts in this area.[93] Moreover, the Shangguan'gang and Pingqiao tombs contained specimens, either in bronze or ceramic, of the highly distinctive "steamer-shaped pouring vessels" (*yanxinghe* 甗形盉), in which a funnel-shaped container is joined to a *li*-shaped bottom that has a tubular spout and a horn-shaped (sometimes elaborately sculpted) handle (some specimens, referred to as *lixinghe* 鬲形盉, lack the upper portion). This kind of vessel, which is clearly not part of the Zhou mainstream assemblage, is a leading indicator for middle to late seventh century B.C. bronze assemblages in the area south of the Huai; specimens have been found in southern Henan, Anhui, Hubei, as well as (intrusively) in areas south of the Yangzi (Fig. 7.19).[94]

[93] See, for example, an unusual coverless *fanghú* from Liuzhai 劉砦, Huangchuan 潢川 Henan (Zheng Jiexiang and Zhang Yafu, "Henan Huangchuan xian faxian yipi qingtongqi," *Wenwu* 1979.9: 91–3).

[94] Discoveries in Anhui include Fenghuangzui 鳳凰嘴, Shucheng 舒城 (*Kaogu* 1964.10: 498–503); Renxing 人形, Huaining 懷寧 (*Wenwu* 1983.11: 68–71); Xiaobali 小八里, Feixi 肥西 (Wenwu bianji weiyuanhui, *Wenwu kaogu gongzuo sanshinian (1949–1979)* [Beijing: Wenwu, 1979], pp. 230–2; *Wenhua Dageming qijian chutu wenwu* 1 [Beijing: Wenwu, 1972], p. 98); Zhaozhuang 趙莊, Lujiang 盧江 (Anhui sheng bowuguan, ed., *Auhui sheng bowuguan cang qingtongqi* [Shanghai: Shanghai Renmin meishu, 1987],

From historical records, it is well known that the Huai River area gradually came under the political sway of Chu during the seventh century B.C. According to Li Xueqin, the occupants of the tombs at Pingqiao were local rulers invested by Chu, whereas the individuals buried at Shangguan'gang were the last independent (Ying 嬴 clan) rulers of Huang 黃 before their polity was conquered by Chu in 648 B.C.[95] Nevertheless, one cannot help noticing that the splendor of the Shangguan'gang tombs pales before such contemporaneous rulers' tombs as Liujiadianzi; it therefore seems possible that they, too, represent local lords under Chu suzerainty.[96] In any case, it is interesting that there is virtually no material or stylistic distinction that would set the Shangguan'gang and Pingqiao tombs apart, either from one another or from contemporaneous non-Chu remains in the surrounding area. Likewise, the mixture of Chu and non-Chu stylistic traits in the considerably later tomb I at Hougudui would seem to indicate that its occupants, although almost certainly dependent on Chu, still enjoyed a certain amount of ritual autonomy. In this respect, the Hougudui assemblage differs strikingly from contemporaneous tombs of the nearby polity of Cai 蔡, remarkable for their almost purely Chu-style bronzes. Such observations may be relevant in assessing the character of Chu's early conquests.

The panorama presented here could be complemented by other examples; but it is sufficiently clear that elite ritual display all over the eastern portion of the Zhou culture sphere followed the general tendencies observed elsewhere. Such essential uniformity, regardless of the clan, or "ethnic," affiliation of tomb occupants, is highly significant. In Shandong, for instance, although the ruling families of Ju and Yu were considered to be Eastern Yi (Barbarian) in origin, and although the ruling lineage of Xue was marginal to the Ji-centered clan structure of the Zhou kingdom, their respective tombs are almost indistinguishable from those of contemporaneous individuals of

nos. 18–19); Mozhuang 莫莊, Lujiang (Ma Daokuo, "Anhui sheng Lujiang xian chutu Chunqiu qingtongqi: Jiantan Nan Huaiyi wenhua," *Dongnan wenhua* 1990.1/2: 74–8); and Yanshancun 燕山村, Lu'an 六安 (*Kaogu* 1993.7: 656–7, 670). At Xizhengjiewei 西正街尾, Hanchuan 漢川, Hubei, such a vessel occurs in association with a lower Yangzi-type *gui* (Shen Yinhua, "Hubei sheng Hanchuan xian faxian yipi Chunqiu shiqi qingtongqi," *Wenwu* 1974.6: 85); specimens were also found in a tomb of non-Zhou character at Baoheyu 保和圩, Hengnan 衡南, Hunan (*Kaogu* 1978.5: 297–300), and in the important tomb 306 at Potang, Shaoxing, Zhejiang (*Wenwu* 1984.1: 10–37).

95 Li Xueqin ("Guangshan Huang guo mu de jige wenti") thinks that Pingqiao tombs 1 and 2 belonged to lords of Fán 樊, even though he admits that Fán could not have been located in that area; he thinks that they must have been "posted" away from their area of origin, an infelicitous ad hoc solution. It seems preferable to suppose that the Fán female buried in tomb 1 had been obtained as a bride from a neighboring polity, according to Zhou custom. On the other hand, Fán was, in all likelihood, governed by a Ji 姬 lineage (see Chen Pan, *"Chunqiu dashibiao: Lieguo juexing ji cunmiebiao" zhuanyi* [new edition, Taipei: Academia Sinica, 1988], vol. 2, pp. 274b–278a), whereas the female in question was of Ying clan affiliation.

96 Such a view seems to be implied by Hayashi's dating of the assemblage to the latter part of middle Spring and Autumn (*Shunjû Sengoku seidôki-no kenkyû*, p. 16).

comparable rank in adjacent non-Barbarian polities. Observable idiosyncrasies consist merely in subtle modifications that self-consciously refer to the Zhou sumptuary system, thereby acknowledging its validity; other differences, for example those between the Lu aristocratic cemeteries at Qufu and such rulers' tombs as Fenghuangling or Liujiadianzi, are more likely to reflect disparities in rank and sumptuary status than cultural or ethnic ones. The political and ritual integration of originally non-Zhou polities into the Zhou league is also documented in written sources, which record their participation in rulers' meetings, war campaigns, and intermarriage networks.

THE MIDDLE HAN RIVER BASIN

As in Shandong and the nearby Huai River basin, a number of different polities coexisted in the middle Han 漢 River basin during much of the Zhou period. Since this is, geographically, an important transitional zone between northern and southern China, it is noteworthy that, throughout the Bronze Age, bronzes and other finds from elite burials show extremely close adherence to metropolitan prototypes – even closer than finds from further east. Three main centers of archaeological discovery include the area around Nanyang 南陽 in southwestern Henan; the stretch of the Han River valley between Gucheng 谷城 and Xiangfan 襄樊 (Hubei); and the valley of the Yun 溳 River, a tributary of the Han in north-central Hubei.

Nanyang, on the Bai 白 River, was the seat of the ancient polity of Shen 申 (or Southern Shen 南申). Bronzes from Eastern Zhou aristocratic cemeteries show the same stylistic transitions as contemporary specimens from the Yellow River valley. No stylistic break seems to have occurred after the area was conquered by Chu in the 680s B.C.; a *hú* inscribed on behalf of one Pengyu, ruler of Shen 申公彭宇,[97] appears to date from the late seventh century B.C., possibly showing that the former ruling lineage was left in place under Chu suzerainty. Late Spring and Autumn period tombs at the same cemetery, on the other hand, yielded vessels indistinguishable from contemporaneous Chu products.

Xiangfan was the center of Deng 鄧, conquered by Chu in 678 B.C. Extensive aristocratic cemeteries have been excavated here and at nearby Gucheng, but most finds date to the late Spring and Autumn period and correspond exactly to contemporaneous Chu assemblages elsewhere.[98] Curiously,

---

[97] Wang Rulin and Cui Qingming, "Nanyang shi Xiguan chutu yipi Chunqiu qingtongqi," *Zhongyuan wenwu* 1982.1: 39–41; see also Li Xueqin, "Lun Zhong Chengfu gui yu Shen guo," *Zhongyuan wenwu* 1984.4: 31–2, 39.

[98] For finds from Xiangfan, see *Jianghan kaogu* 1983.2: 1–35; *Kaogu* 1991.9: 781–802; Wang Shaoquan, "Xiangfan shi Bowuguan shoucang de Xiangyang Shanwan tongqi," *Jiang Han kaogu* 1988.3: 96–7, 62; Chen Zhenyu and Yang Quanxi, "Xiangyang Shanwan wuzuo Chu mu de niandai ji qi xiangguan

however, several bronzes from this period bear inscriptions on behalf of rulers of Deng,[99] postdating the alleged Chu "annihilation" (*mie* 滅) of the Deng polity by more than a century. While it is possible that scions of the former Ying-clan ruling house continued to administer their territory under Chu auspices, one cannot exclude the possibility that Chu-appointed governors of nonlocal origin assumed the old title.

The Yun River valley was anciently the seat of the Zeng 曾 polity. Though unmentioned in historical texts, Zeng has become famous in archaeological circles worldwide on account of the extraordinary early Warring States period tomb of Zeng Hou Yi 曾侯乙 (d. ca. 433 B.C.) at Leigudun 擂鼓墩, Suizhou 隨州, Hubei, which will be fully described in Chapter 10.[100] Li Xueqin's widely embraced theory that Zeng was identical with the important local polity of Sui 隨, which, like Zeng, was governed by a lineage of the royal Zhou Ji clan, while not implausible (there were many polities in ancient China with more than one name), is mainly supported by negative evidence: the historical texts do not record that Sui was "annihilated" by Chu, and bronze inscriptions mentioning Sui do not seem to exist.[101] The earliest bronzes of known provenance that bear Zeng-related inscriptions date to the late Western Zhou to early Spring and Autumn continuum; it remains under dispute whether Zeng had been located in Hubei since the early part of Western Zhou, acting as a royal Zhou representative among the local polities, or whether it was moved there from the Zhou metropolitan area at the end of Western Zhou.[102] To judge by its inscribed bronzes, Zeng existed as a separate entity well into the fourth century B.C., its ruling family intermarrying with families of non-Ji neighbor polities such as Huang and Chu; although by the late Spring and Autumn period, it had already become, like its neighbors, part of the Chu-dominated network of polities.

wenti," *Jiang Han kaogu* 1983.1: 19–24, 71. For the Gucheng finds, see Chen Qianwan, "Zhong Zi Bin-fou chutan," *Jiang Han kaogu* 1985.3: 56–61; *Kaogu* 1987.5: 410–13, 430; and Chen Qianwan, "Gucheng Xindian chutu de Chunqiu tongqi," *Jiang Han kaogu* 1986.3: 13–16.

[99] Yang Quanxi, "Xiangyang Shanwan chutu de Ruo guo he Deng guo tongqi," *Jiang Han kaogu* 1983.1: 51–3.

[100] Archaeologically based studies on Zeng include: Zhou Yongzhen, "Zengguo yu Zengguo tongqi," *Kaogu* 1980.5: 436–43; Yang Baocheng, "Shilun Zeng guo tongqi de fenqi," *Zhongyuan wenwu* 1991.4: 14–20; and Zhang Changping, "Zeng guo tongqi de fenqi ji qi xiangguan wenti," *Jiang Han kaogu* 1992.3: 60–6.

[101] Li Xueqin, "Zeng guo zhi mi," in his *Xinchu qingtongqi yanjiu* (Beijing: Wenwu, 1990), pp. 146–50 (first published in 1978). Opposition to this idea has been repeatedly voiced, most recently by Zhang Changping, "Zeng guo tongqi de fenqi ji qi xiangguan wenti." One ought perhaps not to insist too strongly on the identification, which is based on nothing but plausibility, that is, the similar location and the same governing clan; but there are many examples to show that political entities in China could have more than one name.

[102] The former point of view is taken by Zhou Yongzhen ("Zeng guo yu Zeng guo tongqi") and what seems to be the majority of scholars; Hu Dianxian ("Zeng guo de laiyuan," *Wenwu yanjiu* 3 [1988], pp. 53–6) argues the opposite.

About a dozen Zeng-related bronze assemblages from the time preceding Zeng Hou Yi have been reported. Most of them are chance discoveries; the shape and furnishings of a tomb have been recorded in only a few cases. Socially, the sample is not representative. At the top of the rank order, the tomb of a junior prince of Zeng at Sujialong 蘇家壟, Jingshan 京山, Hubei, comprises a set of nine *ding* and an assemblage of twenty-seven bronzes total, including some of the best-quality bronzes from the late Western Zhou to early Spring and Autumn period found anywhere (see Fig. 7.6); the unnumbered tomb at Liujiaya 劉家崖, Suizhou,[103] has thirty bronze vessels including twelve tripods, dating from the later part of the Spring and Autumn period. The extraordinary wealth of Zeng Hou Yi's tomb can hardly serve as a measuring rod for Zeng rulers' tombs of the Spring and Autumn period, since it is later in date and different in religious significance, and since its principal vessels and bells had been donated by the king of Chu. It nevertheless appears probable that rulers' tombs contemporary with Sujialong and Liujiaya considerably surpassed these two tombs in the extravagance of their furnishings. Most other known Zeng bronze assemblages, on the other hand, come from tombs of lower-ranking aristocrats with one to three *ding* and comprising four to fifteen bronzes. This leaves major lacunae in the middle ranges of the spectrum.

Chronologically, as well, the sample is unbalanced. The shapes and ornaments of a majority of known Zeng bronzes conform exactly to the usage known after the Late Western Zhou Ritual Reform; they might date anywhere between the mid-ninth and the late eighth century B.C.[104] Bronzes of the middle to late Spring and Autumn period date, by contrast, are relatively rare; they too exhibit the typological and stylistic tendencies observable in contemporaneous Yellow Valley basin contexts. As in contemporaneous contexts in the Huai River basin, some assemblages contain individual intrusive vessels of extraneous style, which must have been obtained from southerly workshops where casters still followed earlier, pre-Reform models and traditions diffused from the Yellow River basin during the Early Bronze Age.[105]

---

[103] For Sujialong, see *Wenwu* 1972.2: 47–53. For Liujiaya, see *Kaogu* 1982.2: 142–6.

[104] Zhang Changping ("Zeng guo tongqi de fenqi ji qi xiangguan wenti") boldly distinguishes a late Western Zhou group, a transitional Western Zhou to early Spring and Autumn group, and an early Spring and Autumn group of bronzes, but his stylistic criteria seem arbitrary. At the opposite extreme, Hayashi Minao (in *Shunjū Sengoku jidai seidōki-no kenkyū*) dates all Zeng-related finds from the Han River area to the Spring and Autumn period, implying discontinuity with earlier bronze finds in the area. This ultimately brings one back to the controversial question of whether Zeng existed in the Han River valley before 770 or not.

[105] Examples include the *fangyou* 方卣 from tomb at Xiongjialaowan 熊家老灣, Suizhou (E Bing, "Hubei Suixian faxian Zeng guo tongqi," *Wenwu* 1973.5: 21–3), and the *pan* from Wangcheng 王城, Zaoyang 棗陽 (Xu Zhengguo, "Zaoyang Dongzhaohu zaici chutu qingtongqi," *Jiang Han kaogu* 1984.1: 106).

Regional modifications of the Zhou assemblage during the seventh century B.C. include the use of *hú* 匜 as a major replacement for the obsolete *gui* vessels, prefiguring later Chu preference. Another novelty in this period is the *sheng* 鼎 : a flat-bottomed coverless tripod with strongly angular, flaring profile and rim-attached handles, derived from a prominent late Western Zhou *ding* type.[106] The decoration of *sheng* is often deliberately archaistic, harking back to Western Zhou models. Sets of such tripods were to serve as the prime status indicators in very high-status tombs of Chu and its allied polities from the late Spring and Autumn period onward; in their earlier Zeng contexts, they likewise seem to be associated with individuals of high rank. The donor of the two earliest *sheng* known to date was a junior member of the Zeng ruling family, who may have served as Taibao 太保 (Grand Protector), a high administrative position.[107] In the two early sixth century B.C. tombs at Liujiaya, *sheng* appear as part of a group of bronzes notable for their persistent typological and stylistic allusions to late Western Zhou models, coexisting (and contrasting) with other vessels that are decorated in a more contemporary style. These differences correspond with the dichotomies observed in contemporary rulers' tombs in the Yellow River basin (e.g., at Liulige and Lijialou).

In the later sixth and fifth centuries B.C., the Zeng area, like most of the middle and lower Yangzi Basin, was swept up in the spread of Chu-style bronzes; this is especially evident in the bronzes from Zeng Hou Yi's tomb. On the other hand, it would appear that any impact that Chu might have made on this area during the seventh and early sixth centuries B.C. was diffuse and indirect. Both inscriptions and bronze vessel style suggest that, in many places, previously established lineages remained in control throughout most of the Spring and Autumn period, even in supposedly conquered areas. To assume that large-scale political and cultural transformation ensued as soon as Chu had won the allegiance of another polity may amount to an all too ready generalization based on Warring States period patterns of events. Conversely, Chu influence became widespread after the mid-sixth century B.C., regardless of whether or not an area had been "conquered."

---

[106] This type of *ding* (for which the *Wuhui ding* 無惠鼎 and the *Ke ding* 克鼎 are prominent inscribed late Western Zhou examples [see Hayashi Minao, *In Shû jidai seidôki-no kenkyû* (Tôkyô: Yoshikawa Kôbunkan, 1984–8), vol. 2, pp. 24.260, 28.298–99], and which is also documented by several early Spring and Autumn specimens [ibid., p. 33.356]) is characterized by a shallow-rounded bottom, a slightly sagging lateral profile, and rim-attached, slightly outward-bent handles; all these features were exaggerated by the Spring and Autumn period bronze casters in the Han-Huai region who invented the *sheng*.

[107] *Kaogu* 1984.6: 510–14. For Liujiaya, see note 103.

EARLY CHU FINDS

The expansionist southern power of Chu has hovered like a specter over much of the preceding discussion. But there are still no archaeological finds that are unquestionably Chu from before approximately 600 B.C. By this time, we find Chu established in the water-rich area along the middle Yangzi in west-central Hubei. To date, however, it remains unclear whether the Chu polity was indigenous to that area or whether (and if so, when) it was moved there from further north.

The *Shi ji* states that King Cheng of Zhou invested Xiong Yi 熊繹 of Chu with a title and a territory in the south of the Zhou realm;[108] bronze inscriptions attest to the existence of a polity named Chu during Western Zhou times. But the only inscribed Chu bronzes from this period with secure provenance come from a northern (Jin) archaeological context.[109] The stylistic similarity of all early Chu bronzes to middle and late Western Zhou products of metropolitan workshops would suggest that the Chu ruling lineage at this time resided in a location fairly close to the Zhou heartland. So far, however, all efforts to locate Danyang 丹陽, the earliest Chu capital mentioned in the *Shi ji*, have been inconclusive.[110]

After a long hiatus, provenanced Chu-related bronze inscriptions occur again from about 600 B.C. onward, notably in west-central Hubei, which by then was unquestionably part of Chu territory. It would of course be most convenient to assume that Chu was always located in that area.[111] Archaeologists have endeavored for some time to isolate "proto-Chu" characteristics, mostly in the realm of utilitarian ceramic typology, that were present continually from late prehistoric times into the historically documented period. One often-adduced example is the ubiquitous "Chu-style *li*," characterized by high, columnar feet and an almost bowl-shaped bottom, and usually made of cord-marked red-fired, sand-tempered pottery.[112] But whether or not the

---

[108] *Shi ji* 40, pp. 1691–2.

[109] This is the late Western Zhou *Chu Gong Ni yongzhong* 楚公逆甬鐘 chime recently found at Qucun (see *Wenwu* 1994.8: 22–33, 68); an earlier *Chu Gong Ni bo* 鎛 has been lost since the Song period; for this and all other early Chu inscriptions, see Li Ling, "Chu guo tongqi mingwen biannian huishi," *Guwenzi yanjiu* 13 (1986): 353–97, and Liu Binhui, "Chu guo youming tongqi biannian gaishu," *Guwenzi yanjiu* 8 (1984): 331–72.

[110] The best monograph on the topic is Shi Quan, *Gudai Jing-Chu dili xintan* (Wuhan: Wuhan daxue, 1988). In English, see the articles by Barry B. Blakeley ("In Search of Danyang I: Historical Geography and Archaeological Sites," *EC* 13 [1988]: 116–52; and "On the Location of the Chu Capital in Early Chunqiu Times in Light of the Handong Incident of 701 B.C.," *EC* 15 [1990]: 49–70), which provide further references.

[111] Such a view has indeed been widely embraced; see, e.g., Yu Weichao, *Xian Qin liang Han kaoguxue lunji* (Beijing: Wenwu 1985), pp. 211–69.

[112] Liu Jianguo, "Lun Chu li wenhuatezheng de liangzhongxing: Jianji Chu wenhua yu Zhongyuan wenhua de guanxi," *Zhongyuan wenwu* 1989.4: 4–13.

late prehistoric populations of the later Chu core area were already organized in a polity comparable to those elsewhere in the Zhou culture sphere, and ruled by the Mi 芈 clan ancestors of the later Chu royal lineage, cannot be resolved by such analysis. On this point, historical, epigraphic, and archaeological evidence are all ambiguous.

The area around Zhijiang 枝江 and Dangyang 當陽, near the sizable, but incompletely explored Eastern Zhou walled settlement at Jijiahu 季家湖, Dangyang 當陽 Hubei,[113] has yielded considerable remains of the Spring and Autumn period; yet it is not altogether certain that these all pertain to Chu, as traditional texts mention the existence of other polities in that area during the early part of Eastern Zhou. For instance, the mid-seventh century B.C. bronzes from Bailizhou 百里洲, Zhijiang, Hubei,[114] the earliest full set found in this area, may have belonged to the otherwise little-known polity of Luo 羅.[115]

The report on six partially excavated lineage cemeteries in the area around Zhaojiahu 趙家湖, also in Dangyang,[116] establishes a continuous sequence of lower-aristocratic and commoner tombs ranging from late Western Zhou down through the end of the Warring States period. One comparatively high-ranking group of early to middle Spring and Autumn period tombs features pottery *mingqi* of a high-quality polished ware, somewhat resembling those pieces known from contemporaneous Qin contexts; additionally, these tombs, like almost all others, contained sets of utilitarian vessels. Some tombs also yielded a few bronzes, but none had a complete set. Such combinations are very unusual when compared with finds in the Yellow River region, where far fewer ceramics are seen in tombs and *mingqi* and bronzes are virtually never found in combination during the Spring and Autumn period (except for Qin). Whether or not these finds belonged to lineages of the Chu polity is as unclear as in the case of the Bailizhou bronzes.

Significantly, a sharp break in the Zhaojiahu archaeological sequence occurs around 600 B.C., when the high-quality *mingqi* ceramics all but disappear from the inventory. It seems as though the social group represented by the tombs with mixed assemblages of bronze and ceramic vessels suddenly went out of existence. Following this watershed, assemblages of *mingqi* ceramic vessels that are generally considered to be characteristic for Chu tombs became established at Zhaojiahu. Later middle to late Spring and Autumn period bronze-yielding tombs in the same region contain virtually

[113] Yang Quanxi, "Dangyang Jijiahu kaogu shijue de zhuyao shouhuo," *Jiang Han kaogu* 1980.2: 27–30.
[114] *Wenwu* 1972.3: 65–8.
[115] See Chen Pan, *"Chunqiu dashibiao: Lieguo juexing ji cunmiebiao" zhuanyi*, vol. 2, p. 486.
[116] *Dangyang Zhaojiahu Chu mu* (Beijing: Wenwu, 1992).

no ceramics. The bronzes from those tombs manifest thoroughgoing stylistic changes in bronze decoration, signaling the adoption of the pattern-block technique; although they are stylistically similar to contemporaneous products of the Houma foundry, subtle details of typology and in the composition of assemblages mark them as ancestral to Warring States period Chu types.

At present, we cannot exclude that this impression of significant change, based on very incomplete evidence, is no more than a construct of archaeological discovery; it is also risky to claim that the observable innovations reflect a change of political regimes. Nevertheless, three considerations suggest that this might have been the case: the stylistic transition coincides with initial urban construction at what was to become the Warring States period Chu capital of Ying 郢 (Jinancheng 紀南城), near Jiangling 江陵, Hubei; all Chu-related bronze inscriptions found in Hubei postdate the transition; and it is after this time that a Chu impact on the material culture of neighboring areas becomes palpable. Just possibly, therefore, the evidence may indicate a transformation in the nature of the Chu polity sometime around 600 B.C.; a transformation that may have included its physical removal to west-central Hubei.

A comparison of Chu bronze inscriptions from before and after the ca. 600 B.C. watershed reveals major differences in the self-conception of the Chu rulers and of the Chu polity vis-à-vis its neighbors. Whereas in early inscriptions, the ruler of Chu refers to himself by the generic title of Chu Gong 楚公 (Ruler of Chu), he always appears as King of Chu (Chu Wang 楚王) after the middle Spring and Autumn period. This recalls a *Shi ji* account according to which, after an abortive early attempt to assume the royal title during the reign of King Yi of Zhou (r. 865–858 B.C.), Xiong Tong 熊通 (r. 740–690 B.C.) actually did so in 703 B.C., after having unsuccessfully petitioned the Zhou king, through the good offices of the ruler of Sui, to grant him a new title.[117] Since chiefs of unassimilated non-Zhou populations such as Lü 呂, Xu 徐, Wu 吳, and Yue 越, as well as the Rong 戎 (Barbarians), commonly bore the title of *wang* 王 (king), the Chu rulers may have long referred to themselves by that title when interacting with their southern neighbors. That they requested permission to do so from the Zhou royal house (assuming the much later *Shi ji* account is historically reliable) may indicate that they were transplants from the north who felt troubled by the dichotomy between regional custom and Zhou ritual convention. The initial Chu use of *wang* in inscriptions on vessels used in performing Zhou-style rituals therefore may not have implied quite as radical a defiance as did

[117] *Shi ji* 40, pp. 1692, 1695.

the arrogation of the royal title by Warring States rulers (for which see Chapter 9).

In bronze inscriptions from the mid-sixth century B.C. onward, however, the use of the royal title by the Chu ruler does seem to connote a claim to exclusive, quasi-numinous authority, both over his own subjects and over the rulers of allied polities. Even bronzes inscribed by members of branch lineages of the Chu ruling house bear obsequious declarations of loyalty to the king, unparalleled in non-Chu inscriptions.[118] Similar pronouncements were expected of allied rulers; in the inscriptions on his chime bells, Cai Hou Shen 蔡侯申 (r. 519–491 B.C.) proclaims: "Possessed of reverence, ever-unflagging, I am in the entourage of the king of Chu," and later on he makes it explicit that in serving the king of Chu, he is "implementing the Mandate of Heaven."[119] The point of such language lies in asserting Chu's supremacy over its allies (who were not free to conclude alliances outside the Chu network of polities)[120] and in claiming equality with, if not superiority to, the Zhou royal house in the north. Many bronzes bearing such inscriptions appear to have been manufactured at Chu court workshops and given to Chu aristocrats and allied rulers as legitimizing presents, affirming that they held their position by the grace of the Chu king. The spread of Chu-style ritual bronzes throughout the southern part of the Zhou culture sphere during the late Spring and Autumn period may encapsulate political events of high significance.

The Chu ruler had in this way become the pinnacle of a league of polities analogous to the Zhou network of polities in the Yellow River basin. Some inscriptions refer to the King of Chu conspicuously using traditional royal Zhou phraseology familiar from Western Zhou bronze inscriptions (for Qin parallels, see "Finds from Qin Cemeteries"). For instance, the inscription on the mid-sixth century B.C. *Yuan (Wei) Zi Peng ge* 薳 (爲) 子佣戈 dagger-axe from tomb 2 at Xiasi reads in part: "Fan 馭, the newly mandated

---

[118] For instance, the *Wangsun Gao yongzhong* 王孫誥甬鐘 inscription from tomb 2 at Xiasi 下寺, Xichuan 淅川, Henan (*Xichuan Xiasi Chunqiu Chu mu* [Beijing: Wenwu, 1991], pp. 140–78), made on behalf of a prince of the Chu royal house, emphasizes that these bells were made foremost for the purpose of "reverently serving the king of Chu," mentioning the king in a part of the text where the divinized lineage forebears in Heaven would have appeared in earlier times. In the mid-sixth century B.C. *Lü Wangzhisun Gan bo* and *niuzhong* 呂王之孫斷鐸、鈕鐘 from tomb 10 at Xiasi, the donor boasts of his ancestors' relationship as "servants by ritual alliance" (*mengpu* 盟僕) to Cheng Wang 成王 of Chu (r. 671–626 B.C.) and proclaims himself to be "a subordinate of rare virtue" (*Xichuan Xiasi Chunqiu Chu mu*, pp. 257–88).

[119] Zhongguo Shehui kexueyuan Kaogu yanjiusuo, *Yin Zhou jinwen jicheng*, vol. 1, nos. 210–22.

[120] Sixth century B.C. members of the ruling family of Xu, another client polity of Chu, bore such personal names as Yichu 義楚 (Serve Chu with Righteous Demeanor; see Li Xueqin, *Eastern Zhou and Qin Civilizations*, pp. 190–1) and Xunchuhu 尋楚乎 (loosely: Have Thine Eyes upon Chu; see Shang Zhitan and Tang Yuming, "Jiangsu Dantu Beishanding Chunqiu mu chutu zhongding mingwen shizheng," *Wenwu* 1989.4: 51–9).

King of Chu, accepted the Mandate of Heaven. I, Peng 倗, on this account brought to obedience those who did not appear in audience."[121] It is this assertive, self-confident Chu polity that manifests itself fully formed around 600 B.C. Its earlier development remains shrouded in mystery.

According to a decade-old estimate, Chu tombs constitute some 70 percent of known Eastern Zhou tombs.[122] Only about 150 of these can, however, be assigned to the Spring and Autumn period. They are distributed in a fairly narrow north–south corridor that stretches from southwestern Henan through west-central Hubei into northernmost Hunan.[123] In addition, a small number of Late Spring and Autumn tombs with Chu-related material have been found in the areas of neighboring polities such as Huang, Shen, Cai, Zeng, and Wu. The great eastward and southward expansion of Chu, as a result of which it became for a time the largest polity in the Zhou culture sphere, did not occur until the Warring States period.

Whereas tombs of the Spring and Autumn period that are known in the environs of the Warring States period capital near Jiangling are mostly quite small and poor,[124] those at the Zhaojiahu cemeteries slightly further west show considerable social variety. As elsewhere in the Zhou culture sphere, ritual vessels (whether usable or *mingqi*) are never seen in tombs without burial chamber from this period. Although ritual vessels by no means occur in all tombs that have a burial chamber (38.2 percent of the nonrepresentative sample), this seems to reflect one basic social dividing line. The Zhaojiahu archaeological report distinguishes four size classes, which the authors make bold to identify with social groups mentioned in Warring States period texts,[125] as follows:

I.   Tombs with burial chambers featuring partial sets of bronze vessels, high-quality ceramic *mingqi*, and utilitarian ceramics; assigned to Upper *shi* (*shangshi* 上士), the lowest tier of the landholding aristocracy.[126]

II. Tombs with burial chambers that contain for the most part sets of utilitarian

---

[121] See Zhao Shigang in *Xichuan Xiasi Chunqiu Chu mu*, 374–5. The remainder of the inscription is illegible except for some individual characters; which king of Chu is referred to is unclear.

[122] Wang Shimin in *Xin Zhongguo de kaogu faxian he yanjiu*, p. 304.

[123] On Chu finds in Hunan, see pp. 539–40, below.

[124] *Jiangling Yutaishan Chu mu* (Beijing: Wenwu, 1984).

[125] *Dangyang Zhaojiahu Chu mu*, pp. 216–19 and passim. Slightly divergent interpretations have been proposed by Gao Yingqin and Wang Guanghao, "Dangyang Zhaojiahu Chu mu de fenlei yu fenqi," *Zhongguo Kaoguxuehui de er ci (1980) nianhui lunwenji* (Beijing: Wenwu, 1982), pp. 41–50; and Gao Yingqin, "Zhaojiahu Chu mu xingzhi yu leibie zongshu," *Jiang Han kaogu* 1991.1: 29–39, 56.

[126] Although the Zhaojiahu report, elaborating on systematizations found in much later texts, constructs the *shi* 士 as a rank in a "feudal" system, this is certainly a misconception. Still undocumented in Western Zhou sources, the social label *shi* seems to have designated the lower-ranking members of the Eastern Zhou aristocratic lineages; they somewhat resemble the samurai of medieval Japan in that they originally seem to have been warriors, but later (after the middle of the Spring and Autumn period) came to be viewed as possessing intellectual and social skills.

ceramics, augmented sometimes by a small number of ritual vessels made of pottery or bronze (these tombs are, on average, about half the size of those in Class I); assigned to Middle and Lower *shi* (*zhongshi* 中士 and *xiashi* 下士), who did not possess landed estates or official positions.

III. Tombs without burial chamber, but featuring a coffin and burial goods (mostly ceramics); assigned to Commoners (*shumin* 庶民).

IV. Tombs without either burial chamber or burial goods; assigned to Paupers (*pinmin* 貧民) (most, but not all of these had coffins).

Even though tomb contents changed considerably during the Warring States period, the hierarchical structure appears to have endured: each of the four categories has its own trajectory of development into the Warring States, during which period the funerary record reflects rank distinctions with great precision by means of graded assemblages of low-quality ceramic *mingqi*. Consequently, if the rank divisions proposed are valid for Chu society during the Warring States period, it may be legitimate to project them back into the late and middle Spring and Autumn period; caution is necessary, however, in view of the considerable social changes that occurred during this crucial timespan. The data from the Shangma cemetery near the Jin capital also urge some skepticism toward any too easy equation of wealth and rank.

The middle ranks of late Spring and Autumn period Chu aristocratic society are documented by a dozen or so tombs with full assemblages of ritual bronzes, from various locations.[127] Among these, tombs with single and double nested coffins form two clearly distinct size classes, a dichotomy that is far more palpable in Chu than in the Yellow River basin cemeteries. Instances of the former category typically feature a single set of bronzes, usually between five and ten vessels, including covered *ding*, two kinds of *gui* equivalents (single *zhan* or *dui* and single or paired *hû*), a *pan* and *yi* set, and often a liquid container vessel (*fou* 缶). All known tombs with double nested coffins have been looted; considerably larger than tombs with single coffins, such tombs feature from one to four human victims, and they seem to have contained several sets of the kinds of bronzes just enumerated. Moreover, they yielded the earliest Chu instances of tomb-protecting animals (*zhen-mushou*), made of lacquered wood. One mid-sixth century B.C. tomb in this category yielded a set of lacquered wooden vessels,[128] remarkable for their archaistic shapes and ornaments (Fig. 7.20), which are reminiscent of Qin *mingqi* bronzes.

[127] *Kaogu xuebao* 1988.4: 455–500; *Wenwu* 1990.10: 25–32; Yu Xiucui, "Dangyang faxian yizu Chunqiu tongqi," *Jiang Han kaogu* 1983.1: 81–2, 73; *Wenwu* 1989.3: 57–62; *Wenwu* 1982.10: 16–17; *Zhongyuan wenwu* 1982.1: 42–6. The only place where such tombs may be seen embedded within a larger ceme-tery context is the Yugang–Tuanshan 余崗團山 necropolis near Xiangyang 襄陽, Hubei, in the erst-while Deng territory; see note 98.

[128] This is tomb 4 at Zhaoxiang 趙巷, Dangyang, Hubei; see *Wenwu* 1990.10: 25–32.

Figure 7.20. Lacquered wooden *gui* from tomb 4 at Zhaoxiang, Dangyang, Hubei. Mid-sixth century B.C. From *Wenwu* 1990.10: pl. 6.4.

The necropolis of the Yuan 薳 (or Wei 蒍, or Hua華) lineage extends on the slopes of the now-submerged Danjiang 丹江 River valley at Xiasi 下寺 and neighboring sites in Xichuan 淅川, Henan. It was apparently reserved for the highest-ranking members of that lineage. Of interest to this chapter are the nine principal tombs at Xiasi, which range in date from the second quarter of the sixth to the first quarter of the fifth century B.C.;[129] the nearby tombs at Heshangling 何尚嶺 and Xujialing 許家嶺 are slightly later in date.

By far the largest tomb at Xiasi is the partly looted tomb 2. Its principal occupant, named in inscriptions as Chu Shuzhisun Peng 楚叔之孫倗 (Peng, descendant in a junior line of Chu), is in all likelihood identical with Yuan Zi Feng 薳子馮, a distant relative of the Chu royal house who served as Chief Minister (*lingyin* 令尹) from 551 B.C. until his death in 548 B.C. This

[129] *Xichuan Xiasi Chunqiu Chu mu.* The historical interpretations offered in this report, which attempt to connect tomb 2 with the Chu chief minister, Wangzi Wu (see below), are strongly biased and for the most part spurious. Most scholars now accept Li Ling's identification of the principal occupant of tomb 2 (Chu Shuzhisun Peng jiujing shi shui?" *zhongyuan wenwu* 1981.4: 36–7). For preliminary reports on other tombs in the area, see *Hua Xia kaogu* 1992.3: 114–30; and Cao Guicen, "Henan Xichuan Heshangling Xujialing Chu mu fajueji," *Wenwu tiandi* 1992.6: 10–12.

tomb is surrounded by fifteen small tombs containing human victims, as well as three large, unlooted tombs containing Peng's female consorts and the largest of five horse and chariot pits in the necropolis. The enormous wealth of these tombs (see Table 7.4), far surpassing that of the other tombs in the necropolis, plausibly represents a one-time ad personam emolument stemming from Peng's tenure as Chief Minister, an emolument that did not, however, entail a rise in the hereditary status of his lineage.

The remaining five tombs at Xiasi had been sequentially constructed in a single row, three of them predating and two postdating tomb 2. Although the wooden tomb furniture had largely disintegrated, their assemblages were roughly comparable to those of contemporaneous Chu aristocratic tombs with double nested coffins. That the Yuan lineage heads enjoyed high status may be gleaned from inscribed bronzes attesting that they intermarried with the ruling families of various neighboring polities allied with Chu. This probably constituted a deliberate parallel to the Zhou system, where junior members of the royal lineage and officeholders in the service of the royal court were considered equivalent in sumptuary rank to *zhuhou* rulers.

The Xiasi bronzes have attracted attention for their number, quality, typological variety, technical versatility, and the frequency and length of their inscriptions. Those from the tombs that date before and after Peng's generation are relatively unexceptional in assemblage and shape. This is true also of their flat, monotonous ornamentation, which consists for the most part of tiny rectangular units of interlaced dragons. By contrast, the bronzes from Peng's tomb and those of his two principal consorts excel in all conceivable respects. Some can be identified by their inscriptions as Chu princely bronzes, which Peng must have obtained in the course of his activities at the Chu court; the most important of these is the status-defining set of seven *sheng* inscribed on behalf of Peng's predecessor as Chief Minister, the Chu royal prince Wangzi Wu 王子午 (also known as Zi Geng 子庚; served 558–552 B.C.). As on their earlier counterparts in Zeng tombs, the ornate decoration on these *sheng* self-consciously refers to that of late Western Zhou period models. The same is true of the ornamentation on Peng's *gui*, a class of vessel not normally seen in this period, and on several other vessels.[130] As in several roughly contemporaneous contexts (e.g., Liulige, Lijialou, Liujiaya), a separate group of vessels, possibly used for special kinds of more archaic rituals reserved for the highest elite, stands out from the funerary ensemble. Tombs containing such "special assemblage" vessels also yielded all the sorts of vessels seen in connection with lower ranks, albeit in larger numbers.

---

[130] Peng's two *gui* were probably part of a larger set, now incomplete due to looting. Similarly elaborate and at the same time archaistic vessels were found in tomb 1: two *sheng*, two *gui*, and a pair of rectangular *hú* (the absence of such *hú* from Peng's tomb is also probably due to looting).

Table 7.4. *Bronze assemblages excavated at the Yuan lineage cemetery at Xiasi, Xichuan, Henan*

Tomb no.	8	7	36	1	2	3	4	10	11
Condition	looted	intact	intact	intact	looted	intact	intact	intact	intact
Sex	M	F	M	M	M	F	F	M	M
Sheng+			2	7					
Other *ding*	1	2	2	10	11	5	1	4	2
li				2	2				
gui				1	2				
zhan		1		1	1	1			
dui								1	1
dou					1				
hú	4	2	2	2	1	4	1	2	2
Rectangular *hú*				2					
Round *hú*					1	1			
zunfou		2	2	2	1	2		2	
hé					1				
yufou	1	2	2	2	2	2		2	2
yuding		1		1	1				
pan		1	1	1	1	1	1	1	1
yi	1	1	1	1	1	1	1	1	1
he	1			1					
shuiyu				1					
jian					1				
pen					1				
Rectangular footed box						1			
zhenmushou socle				1				*(1)	*(1)
Altar table					2				
Coal shovel				2				1	
yongzhong					1/26				
niuzhong				1/9				1/9	
bo							1/8		
Chimestones				1/13	1/13			1/13	
Total	**8**	**10**	**8**	**39**	**55**	**23**	**5**	**20**	**13**

Note: The tombs are listed in approximately chronological order, ranging from the second quarter of the sixth through the first quarter of the fifth century. The number and constellation of burial chambers (*guo*) and coffins (*guan*) are unclear. For bells and chimestones, the number before the slash indicates the number of chimed sets, the number following the slash the number of individual items. Chimestones are not included in totals figures; in the case of bells, it is the number of sets that counts.

As elsewhere, access to vessels reflecting the full technical versatility of Chu bronze casters appears to have been directly dependent on sumptuary rank. Bronzes from the higher-ranking tombs at Xiasi (especially specimens of the special assemblage) are decorated in a far more elaborate manner and in higher relief than bronzes from more ordinary assemblages. Objects executed in new and unusual techniques are likewise limited to these tombs, as, for example, the extraordinary bronze altar from tomb 2 (see Fig. 7.11), the only intact Spring and Autumn period lost-wax cast bronze known to date, as well as bronzes featuring metal inlay (see Fig. 7.10), which is sometimes combined with the more traditional relieved decor.

The Xiasi finds show many parallels to those from the two known tombs of rulers allied with Chu: those of Cai Hou Shen (r. 519–491 B.C.) at Ximennei 西門內, Shouxian 壽縣, Anhui,[131] and of Zeng Hou Yi. Cai Hou Shen's tomb may have been a multichambered tomb, prefiguring Warring States Chu instances. Again, vessels of a special assemblage with telltale features harking back to late Western Zhou models coexist with others of more contemporary style. The former include a status-defining set of seven *sheng* (Fig. 7.21), a set of eight socled *gui*, and a pair of rectangular *hú*. Double-bottomed wine-cooling vessels and a variety of washing vessels attest to the increased use of bronze vessels in banquets rather than sacrifices, which is also evident from contemporaneous bronze inscriptions. In all probability, most of Cai Hou Shen's bronzes were manufactured at a Chu court work-shop. Some of them are unornamented and a few feature metal inlay, but the vast majority feature decoration in the relieved style characteristic of late Spring and Autumn period high-status Chu bronzes, the jagged, knobbly relief of which may have intended to imitate the surface effect of elaborate lost-wax cast objects such as the altar from tomb 2 at Xiasi. Several vessels found in his tomb, moreover, testify to the occupant's marriage alliance with the newcomer polity of Wu in the southeast; interestingly, their decoration closely imitates the Chu style.

Archaeological finds show that the burial customs of the Chu elite during the Spring and Autumn period conformed in most if not all essential respects to those observed elsewhere in the Zhou cultural sphere. As in more northerly polities, the sumptuary rules originating in the Late Western Zhou Ritual Reform were implemented in different ways at different levels of society. Much has been made of the notion that the grouping of round-bottomed, covered *ding* in Chu aristocratic tombs, which tend to come in even-numbered sets, might indicate indigenous Chu ritual traditions. This cannot,

---

[131] *Shouxian Cai Hou mu chutu yiwu* (Beijing: Kexue, 1956). For historical discussion, see Chen Mengjia, "Shouxian Cai Hou mu tongqi," *Kaogu xuebao* 1956.2: 95–123.

Figure 7.21. *Cai Hou sheng* from the tomb of Cai Hou Shen at Ximennei, Shou Xian, Anhui. Ca. 500 B.C. From Li Xueqin, ed. *Zhongguo meishu quanji. Gongyi meishu bian 5: Qingtonggi (xia)* (Beijing: Wenwu, 1986), no. 35.

however, be substantiated through assemblages datable to the Spring and Autumn period, where *ding* are not numerous enough to allow generalization.[132] In the highest-ranking Chu-related tombs, the principal, status-indicating class of tripods was, in any case, not the round-bottomed, covered ones, but the flat-bottomed, conservatively ornamented *sheng*, and their numbers are in close conformity with the Zhou sumptuary system. The set of seven from tomb 2 at Xiasi, for instance, reflects Peng's position as a royal Chief Minister (here again, it is implied that the king of Chu is equal to the Zhou king: the Chief Minister of a *zhuhou* polity would have ranked one notch lower on the sumptuary scale); the set of two found in tomb 1 appear to constitute the female complement to such a set. Cai Hou Shen's set of seven *sheng*, in turn, defined him as the ruler of a subordinate polity of the

---

[132] See Guo Dewei, "Chu mu fenlei wenti tantao," *Kaogu* 1983.3: 249–59; Li Ling, "On the Typology of Chu Bronzes," pp. 68–71; Liu Binhui, "Lun Dong Zhou shiqi yongding zhiduzhong Chu zhi yu Zhou zhi de guanxi," *Zhongyuan wenwu* 1991.2: 50–8; and Li Anmin, "Chu wenhua de li yu dengji yanjiu," *Dongnan wenhua* 1991.6: 198–206, 72.

Chu league – the sumptuary equal of Peng of Yuan. As Cai Hou Shen vacillated between the Chu and Zhou alliances, it is possible that he simultaneously used his set of nine covered *ding* to express his claim to the status of *zhuhou* ruler in terms of the Zhou league. Zeng Hou Yi, as a full-fledged *zhuhou* ruler, possessed a set of nine *sheng*.

Interpreting such findings in conjunction with the eloquent bronze inscriptions, we arrive at a picture of Chu during the Spring and Autumn period as a polity very much in the Zhou mold. As in the case of Qin, the choice of Zhou royal rhetoric to assert for Chu rulers the privileges of kingship presupposes the universal recognition of the Zhou system. This would tend to negate strongly the currently fashionable image of a "Chu civilization" that was radically different from that of the Zhou;[133] such a distinction was certainly not operative at the ritual and the political level during the middle to late Spring and Autumn period. Of course, the possibility remains that the folk culture of the Chu region differed from that of northern areas, but this is impossible to verify at present through textual or archaeological materials. The situation may have changed somewhat during Warring States times, when Chu, like other polities, tried its utmost to distinguish itself from rival contenders for supreme power; but even then, its deliberate emphasis on regionally specific trappings of rulership was pursued with the Zhou system as an implicit point of reference.

That Spring and Autumn period Chu was unambiguously part of the Zhou realm is further corroborated when comparing its remains with those from adjacent non-Zhou areas, to which we shall now turn.

THE SOUTHEASTERN REGIONAL CULTURES

Throughout the Bronze Age, indigenous regional cultures flourished in the vast region to the south of the Yangzi River – areas inhabited by non-Zhou populations whose ethnic and linguistic diversity may have resembled that of continental Southeast Asia in the ethnographic present. During the three centuries under discussion, both the Zhou league and its Chu clone were beginning to extend their reach into this part of China. Archaeological remains in areas directly bordering on the Zhou realm, that is, the lower Yangzi region and the northern parts of Jiangxi and Hunan, testify to significant exchange in both directions; even so, those areas' material culture and ritual customs remained, for the most part, fundamentally distinctive. An even lesser awareness of Zhou elite culture is evident from contempora-

---

[133] On the essentially political character of this concept, see Lothar von Falkenhausen, "The Regionalist Paradigm in Chinese Archaeology," in *Nationalism, Politics, and the Practice of Archaeology*, ed. Philip Kohl and Clare Fawcett (Cambridge University Press, 1995), pp. 198–217.

neous archaeological remains from the second tier of the Zhou southern periphery, encompassing southern Zhejiang, northern Fujian, the southern parts of Jiangxi and Hunan, central Guangdong, northern Guangxi, and parts of Sichuan.

In historical geography, the area along the lower reaches of the Yangzi that includes southern Jiangsu, northern Zhejiang, southern Anhui, and parts of northeastern Jiangxi, is known as the territory of the Wu and Yue polities. The *Chunqiu* chronicle records the first of Wu's diplomatic overtures to the Zhou league under the year 576 B.C.; the outlines of Wu political history until its conquest by the more southerly Yue in 473 B.C. are known from that time onward. Yue, by contrast, is an almost unknown entity during the Spring and Autumn period. Its name, which means "The Beyond," is used in two distinct meanings: as a collective designation for a variety of groups spread over a wide terrain, and as the name of a polity centered upon the Shaoxing area in central Zhejiang. The rulers of both Wu and Yue referred to themselves as kings (*wang*). Although they have been traditionally regarded as Barbarian, sixth and fifth century B.C. bronze inscriptions of Wu and Yue are remarkable for their ornate writing style and often archaic formulations, closely adhering to late Western Zhou conventions.[134] They may reflect the impact of official contact with the Zhou league, which also affected late Spring and Autumn period archaeological remains in the area.

Until the mid-sixth century B.C., however, archaeological finds from the Lower Yangzi area show pervasive idiosyncrasies; major distinctive features include mounded tombs (*tudunmu* 土墩墓), high-quality hard-fired and sometimes glazed stoneware (sometimes inaccurately referred to as "proto-porcelain"), and bronzes of regional styles. Eastern Zhou walled enclosures in the lower Yangzi area, likewise, differ remarkably from contemporary urban remains within the Zhou realm. The best known, Yancheng 淹城, in Wujin 武進, Jiangsu, is an irregularly shaped site some 850 m in diameter, surrounded by three roughly concentric tiers of walls and moats and accessible only by boat.[135] Conspicuous features are three enormous burial(?) tumuli aligned in the outer enclosure, one of which was excavated and found to contain a large amount of ceramics. Neither the inner nor the outer enclosure was found to contain any remains of habitation whatsoever; the middle-

---

[134] See, for example, the inscriptions on the *Zhejian yongzhong* 者减甬鐘 from Wu (Zhongguo Shehui Kexueyuan Kaogu Yanjiusuo, *Yin Zhou jinwen jicheng*, vol. 1, nos. 193–202) and the *Zhediao niuzhong* 者刀 鈕鐘 (ibid., nos. 120–32) from Yue.

[135] See Che Guangjin, "Fajue Yancheng yizhi de zhuyao shouhuo," in *Nanjing Bowuyuan jianyuan 60 zhounian jinian wenji*, ed. Nanjing Bowuyuan (Nanjing: n.p., 1992), pp. 178–80, where further references may be found. A similarly irregular site with concentric double enclosures at Huzhou 湖州, Zhejiang, has been reported by Lao Bomin ("Huzhou Xiagucheng chutan," in *Zhongguo Kaoguxuehui di wu ci nianhui (1985) lunwenji* [Beijing: Wenwu, 1988], pp. 31–9).

tier enclosure did yield some ceramic sherds, but since no architectural remains were identified, dwellings, if present, must have been of flimsy construction. Rather than an urban site, Yancheng might have been either a ritual center or an emergency military stronghold.

Mounded tombs, though differing somewhat according to period and region, stand out saliently from the vertical-pit tombs of the Zhou realm. They seem to have spread northward from an area of origin somewhere to the south of the Lower Yangzi area; the earliest known instances (in southwestern Zhejiang) seem to date to the second half of the second millennium B.C.[136] The two principal types are simple earthen mounds and mounds containing chambers constructed in stone masonry. Simple earthen mounds are distributed all over the Lower Yangzi area, whereas stone-chamber mounds, which apparently evolved from simple earthen mounds during the first half of the first millennium B.C., are seen only in the area around Lake Tai 太湖 and in Zhejiang.[137] They never came into fashion in southwestern Jiangsu and southern Anhui, where simple earthen mounds were gradually displaced by pit tombs of Zhou type during the late Spring and Autumn period.[138] Other highly distinctive types of burial in the area south of the Yangzi include megalithic chamber tombs in the coastal areas of southern Zhejiang,[139] and cliff-cave tombs in the Wuyishan 武夷山 Mountains of eastern Jiangxi and northern Fujian, notable for their boat-shaped wooden coffins.[140] Their funerary assemblages are broadly similar to those from mounded tombs. The

---

[136] Mou Yongkang and Mao Zhaoting, "Jiangshan xian Nanqu gu yizhi muzang diaocha shijue," *Zhejiang sheng Wenwu kaogu yanjiusuo xuekan* 1 (1981): 57–84.

[137] Chen Yuanfu, "Jiangzhe diqu shishi tudun yicun xingzhi xinzheng," *Dongnan wenhua* 1988.1: 20–3 (this article contains further references); see also Tan Sanping and Liu Shuren, "Taihu diqu shishi tudun fenbu guilü yaogan chubu yanjiu," *Dongnan wenhua* 1990.4: 100–103. The placement of these tombs on hillcrests gave rise to the fanciful interpretation, still encountered occasionally in the archaeological literature, that their function was primarily a military one, as fortifications (zhanbao 戰堡); recent excavations have, however, demonstrated beyond doubt that they are indeed tombs.

[138] For comprehensive treatments, where further references may be found, see Liu Jianguo, "Lun tudunmu de fenqi," *Dongnan wenhua* 1989.4–5: 96–115; Liu Xing, "Tantan Zhenjiang diqu tudunmu de fenqi," *Wenwu ziliao congkan* 6 (1982): 79–85; Zou Houben, "Jiangsu nanbu tudunmu," *Wenwu ziliao congkan* 6 (1982): 66–72; and Yang Debiao, "Shilun Wannan tudunmu," *Wenwu yanjiu* 4 (1988): 81–8. See also *Kaogu xuebao* 1993.2: 207–37. Important studies of mounded tombs in their cultural contexts include: Zou Heng, "Jiangnan diqu zhu yinwentao yizhi yu Xia Shang Zhou wenhua de guanxi," *Wenwu jikan* 3 (1981): 46–51; Li Boqian, "Shilun Wu Yue wenhua," *Wenwu jikan* 3 (1981): 133–43; Xiao Menglong, "Chulun Wu wenhua," *Kaogu yu wenwu* 1985.4: 61–72; Okamura Hidenori, "Go Etsu izen-no seidôki," *Koshi shunjû* 3 (1986): 63–89; Zhou Daming, "Lun Ningzhen diqu gudai wenhua yu qita wenhua de guanxi," *Nanfang wenwu* 1992.1: 30–5; Chen Yuanfu, "Tudunmu yu Wu Yue wenhua," *Dongnan wenhua* 1992.6: 11–21; Liu Jianguo, "Jiangnan Zhou dai qingtongwenhua," *Dongnan wenhua* 1994.3: 20–41; and Zhang Min, "Ningzhen diqu qingtongwenhua puxi yu zushu yanjiu," in *Nanjing Bowuyuan jianyuan 60 zhounian jinian wenji*, ed. Nanjing Bowuyuan (N.p.: 1992), pp. 119–77.

[139] An Zhimin, "Zhejiang Rui'an, Dongyang zhishimu de diaocha," *Kaogu* 1995.7: 585–8.

[140] *Wenwu* 1980.6: 12–20; *Wenwu* 1980.11: 1–25. These discoveries have spawned a sizable secondary literature; see, e.g., Liu Dashen, Gao Shenlan, and Pu Haiying, "Zhongguo xuanguan dili fenbu yu xianzhuang," *Jiangxi wenwu* 1991.1: 8–14, where further references may be found.

relationships of these different types of tomb with similar ones in other areas of East Asia, as well as possible ethnic ramifications, remain a highly controversial topic.

Cemeteries comprising, in some cases, hundreds of mounded tombs have been surveyed at a number of places, but the number of properly excavated tombs is still small, and the evidence does not yet allow one to draw firm conclusions about social organization. It stands to reason that the spatial distribution of mounds in a cemetery reflects degrees of closeness in kinship terms; and when a mound contains more than one burial (as is almost always the case in stone-chamber mounded tombs), all occupants presumably were members of the same family. Rank and wealth are not correlated in an immediately obvious way; large mounds and/or single rather than multiple burials in a mound may indicate high rank, but sometimes reflect interregional differences instead. Little regularity is evident from the composition of funerary assemblages, where the presence or absence of bronze objects sometimes but not always indicates rank distinctions.

An impressive agglomeration of simple earthen mounds with bronze-yielding tombs extends over approximately 8 km between Jianbi 諫壁 and Dagang 大港 in Dantu 丹徒, Jiangsu, on the hilly south bank of the Yangzi just east of where the Grand Canal now intersects the river.[141] Each of the eight large mounds so far reported contains a single burial, and some are surrounded by smaller, subsidiary mounds. These do not represent a full sample, as a number of mounds are known to have been destroyed, and others remain unexcavated; but the finds intimate a continuous chronological sequence from about the ninth through the early fifth century B.C. In the earlier mounds, the body of the deceased was deposited on leveled ground, either on a layer of rocks (*shichuang* 石床) or in a shallow pit; funerary goods were grouped around it, and earth was piled up subsequently. No traces of wooden coffins or any other sort of tomb furniture have been identified. The later mounds, in what appears to have been a selective adoption of features of the Zhou ritual system, had been erected on top of pit chambers dug into the bedrock; these tombs had wooden tomb furniture, and one of them featured a sloping tomb passage (*mudao*) and a pit lined with layers of rocks and charcoal. Some contained human victims (no more than two per tomb) and horse and chariot pits. Curiously, the two largest among these later tombs, Qinglongshan 青龍山 and Beishanding 北山頂, had been dug up and their contents deliberately destroyed shortly after burial, in one case apparently even before the mound was erected. This may reflect enemy action in wartime or internal unrest.

---

[141] Xiao Menglong, "Wu guo wanglingqu chutan," *Dongnan wenhua* 1990.4: 95–9, 55. This article provides further references.

In all likelihood, the Jianbi–Dagang necropolis represents a lineage of regional power holders. The consensus of local archaeologists assigns them to the kings of Wu,[142] conflicting with the received view that locates the political center of that polity in the Suzhou 蘇州 area 150 km further to the east. No incontrovertible Wu-related epigraphic material has been recovered from the Jianbi–Dagang tombs; and the pre-550 B.C. tombs at the necropolis are equalled if not exceeded in wealth and size by contemporaneous finds, for example, the mounded tombs at Yiqi 弈旗, Tunxi 屯溪, Anhui, with their extraordinarily rich bronze and ceramic assemblages.[143] If the Jianbi–Dagang tombs were indeed those of the Wu royal house, it would appear that during most of the first half of the first millennium B.C., Wu was merely one of several regional polities of comparable rank. Qinglongshan and Beishanding, by contrast, are the largest and richest known late Spring and Autumn period tombs in the lower Yangzi region. Their size and richness are a clear order of magnitude above all others in the surrounding region. This and their self-conscious integration of features of the Zhou burial system into the mounded tombs of regional type may reflect new patterns of social and political organization, corresponding to the efforts, documented in written sources, at building a Zhou-style polity. Due to these later developments, even the names of Wu's earlier peer polities have been lost to history, like those of the southern contemporaries of the Shang dynasty described in Chapter 3. Future systematic study of archaeological assemblages throughout the lower Yangzi may help elucidate how Wu rose to become the leading power in the region.

Local developments toward greater social complexity in the lower Yangzi region, unequalled elsewhere in the Zhou southern peripheries, must have capitalized on indigenous economic factors, such as ceramic and metal production. The flourishing Bronze Age ceramic industry of the Lower Yangzi region is the fountainhead of the outstanding porcelain-manufacturing traditions in this part of China, which continue to the present day. The two

---

[142] The following identifications, all somewhat dubious, have been proposed. Tomb 1 at Yandunshan 煙墩山, famous for having yielded the *Yi Hou Ze gui* 宜侯矢 𣪘, has been associated with Zhouzhang 周章, the fourth king in the semilegendary royal genealogy preserved in the *Shi ji* (Tang Lan, "Yi Hou Ze gui kaoshi," *Kaogu xuebao* 1956.2: 79–83); the Qinglongshan tomb has been designated as that of Shoumeng 壽夢, the first fully historical king of Wu (r. 585–561) (Xiao Menglong, "Wu guo wanglingqu chutan"); and the tomb at Beishanding, on the basis of the controversial, virtually illegible inscription on a bronze spearhead found there, has been assigned to King Yumei 餘眛 (r. 530–527) (Zhou Xiaolu and Zhang Min, "Beishan siqi ming kao," *Dongnan wenhua* 1988.3–4: 73–82; against this, see Wu Yuming, "Beishanding siqi ming shikao cunyi," *Dongnan wenhua* 1990.1–2: 68–70).

[143] *Kaogu Xuebao* 1959.4: 59–90; Anhui Sheng Bowuguan, ed., *Anhui Sheng Bowuguan cang qingtongqi*, nos. 22, 23, 25–8, 32, 40, 44 (tomb 1), and nos. 21, 24, 29–31, 33–9, 41–3 (tomb 3); Yin Difei, "Anhui Tunxi Zhou mu di er ci fajue," *Kaogu* 1990.3: 210–13, 288. For discussion, see Li Guoliang, "Wannan chutu de qingtongqi," *Wenwu yanjiu* 4 (1988): 161–6; and Zhou Ya, "Wu Yue diqu tudunmu qingtongqi yanjiuzhong de jige wenti: Cong Anhui Tunxi tudunmu bufen qingtongqi tanqi," paper presented at the International Symposium on Wu–Yue Bronzes, Shanghai, August 1992.

principal kinds of ceramics seen are stoneware, fired at a temperature of
1,200–1,300 degrees C and produced industrially, and low-fired earthenware,
which may have been produced by village artisans or even at the household
level. Within the stoneware category, one may distinguish roughly between
unglazed "impressed-pattern hard-fired ceramics" (*yinwen yingtao* 印紋硬陶)
and glazed stoneware.[144] The potters' principal repertoire comprised but a few
types of storage and serving vessels, which changed very little over time. Stylistic chronologies therefore rely heavily on changes in the impressed geometric patterns, which develop from being haphazard and coarse to evenly
distributed and fine.[145] Stoneware ornamentation greatly influenced local
bronze decoration styles, but the elaborate "double *f*" motif seen on glazed
wares contemporary with the Zhou dynasty may in fact have been derived
from abstracted dragon bodies on Western Zhou bronzes. Some glazed
stoneware vessels even imitate bronze shapes, the greenish, shiny glaze
perhaps enhancing an intended resemblance.

Glazed stoneware vessels appear to have been exported as luxury items
into northern China throughout the Bronze Age.[146] The superiority of the
southern products in terms of appearance, hardness, and porosity over the
grey earthenware found throughout the Zhou culture sphere results from differences in manufacturing technology. Rather than using the round or oval
single-chamber kilns of their northern peers, stoneware makers south of the
Yangzi early on invented the dragon-kiln (*longyao* 龍窰), a multichamber kiln
built on a slope, designed to optimize heat flow and economize on fuel. The
plentiful output of the southern kilns is evident from the ubiquitousness of
their products south of the Yangzi. That local consumers did not consider
them especially precious is clear from the large quantities of vessels in tombs
of all ranks.

The hilly areas of southern Anhui and Jiangsu were rich in mineral
deposits. Survey and excavation of ancient copper-mining sites have revealed
indications of metal extraction on a large scale, beginning in the first quarter
of the first millennium B.C. and increasing during the following centuries.[147]

[144] Unglazed stoneware is commonly referred to as "proto-porcelain" (*yuanshici* 原始瓷), although neither
its clay composition nor its physical properties conform to the definition of porcelain.

[145] Liu Xing, "Zhenjiang diqu chutu de yuanshiqingci," *Wenwu* 1979.3: 56–7; and Mou Yongkang,
"Zhejiang yinwentao: Shitan yinwentao de tezheng yiji yu ciqi de guanxi," *Wenwu jikan* 3 (1981):
261–9. See also the studies cited in note 138, esp. Okamura Hidenori, "Go Etsu izen-no seidôki," pp.
80–3.

[146] The current debate on whether or not stoneware-manufacturing workshops existed in the north during
the Bronze Age will, one hopes, soon be resolved by chemical analysis and clay sourcing.

[147] Yang Lixin, "Wannan gudai tongkuang de faxian ji qi lishi jiazhi," *Dongnan wenhua* 1991.2: 131–7;
Kaogu 1993.6: 507–17; Lu Benshan and Liu Shizhong, "Tongling Shang Zhou tongkuang kaicai jishu
chubu yanjiu," *Wenwu* 1993.7: 33–8; Ni Jinbin, "Tongling gudai gongye wenxue chutan," *Dongnan
wenhua* 1991.2: 104–105; Zou Youkuan, Lu Benshan, Liu Shizhong, and Xia Zongjing, "Tongling Xi
Zhou liuzao xuankuangfa moni shiyan yanjiu," *Dongnan wenhua* 1993.1: 244–8.

The ore was smelted close to the mines, and the raw metal was cast into ingots of portable size, which could be traded.[148] By the Spring and Autumn period, such activities must have played an important role in the economy of the area and should not be underestimated as possible factors in the rise of the Wu and Yue kingdoms.

Local bronze-casting industries, established already in the Erligang period, appear to have expanded in tandem with the increased intensity of mining.[149] Approximately three dozen pre-450 B.C. bronze assemblages have been reported from the lower Yangzi area. Vessels of local manufacture are recognizable as such by their alloy composition, in which a dearth of tin is often compensated for by large proportions (up to 30 percent) of lead; moreover, the high iron content of local copper ores accounts for a percentage of sometimes up to 40 percent of iron.[150] Local bronzes, especially early ones, tend to be thinner and duller than contemporaneous specimens from the Zhou realm, and they are often covered with blowholes resulting from imperfect venting of the core-mold unit during casting. Over time, however, local casters' technical versatility improved to a point at which extremely fine casting was possible.[151]

While the possession of bronzes was probably restricted to high-ranking individuals, archaeological contexts in the lower Yangzi region give no indications of a clearly defined graded hierarchy of ranks; nor do standard sets for specific rituals appear to exist. The choice of classes in individual assemblages seems haphazard; one possible criterion of preference may have been whether an object's function was equivalent to or complementary with that of locally established pottery types. Tripods play a minor role in the assemblages; the so-called Yue-style tripods (*Yueshi ding* 越式鼎), the type most

[148] On some hoards of objects, possibly intended to be melted down for reuse, see Li Xueqin, "Cong xinchu qingtongqi kan Changjiang xiayou wenhua fazhan," *Wenwu* 1980.8: 35–40, 84; and Liu Xing, "Zhenjiang diqu jinnian chutu de qingtongqi," *Wenwu ziliao congkan* 5 (1981): 106–11.

[149] General studies on bronzes from this area include: Liu Xing, "Zhenjiang diqu jinnian chutu de qingtongqi"; idem, "Tan Zhenjiang diqu chutu qingtongqi de tese," *Wenwu ziliao congkan* 5 (1981): 112–16; idem, "Dongnan diqu qingtongqi fenqi," *Kaogu yu wenwu* 1985.5: 90–101; Okamura, "Go Etsu izen-no seidôki"; Ma Chengyuan, "Changjiang xiayou tudunmu chutu qingtongqi de yanjiu," *Shanghai bowuguan jikan* 4 (1987): 198–220; Chen Peifen, "Ji shanghai bowuguan suocang Yue zu qingtongqi: Jianlun Yue zu qingtongqi de wenshi," *Shanghai bowuguan jikan* 4 (1987): 221–32; Cao Jinyan, "Zhejiang chutu Shang Zhou qingtongqi chulun," *Dongnan wenhua* 1989.6: 104–12; Du Naisong, "Tan Jiangsu diqu Shang Zhou qingtongqi de fengge yu tezheng," *Kaogu* 1987.2: 169–74; and Li Guoliang, "Wannan chutu de qingtongqi."

[150] Zeng Lin, Xia Feng, Xiao Menglong, and Shang Zhitan, "Sunan diqu qingtongqi hejin chengfen de ceding," *Wenwu* 1990.9: 37–47; and Shang Zhitan, "Sunan diqu qingtongqi hejin chengfen de tese ji xiangguan wenti," *Wenwu* 1990.9: 48–55.

[151] Tan Derui et al., "Wu Yue lingxing wenshi tongbingqi jishu chutan," *Nanfang wenwu* 1994.2: 120–6. A late Spring and Autumn period *zun* excavated at Songjiang 松江, Shanghai, now in the Shanghai Museum, features ornamentation of thin ridges spaced less than 1 mm apart (see Tan Derui and Huang Long, "Wu Yue wenhuaxi qingtong jishu diaocha baogao," paper presented at the International Symposium on Wu–Yue Bronzes, Shanghai, August 1992).

Figure 7.22. Typologically indeterminate vessel (*zun* or *gui*) from Miaoqian, Qingyang, Anhui. Seventh century B.C. From Anhui sheng bowuguan, *Anhui sheng bowuguan cang qingtongqi* (Shanghai: Shanghai Renmin meishu, 1987), no. 47.

widespread in the area, are thin walled and coverless, with small, rim-attached handles and spindly legs, and are usually unornamented. Soot traces show that they were used as kitchen vessels; whether they also served sacrificial purposes is uncertain.[152] The Late Western Zhou Ritual Reform does not seem to have affected bronze production in this area; *you* 卣 and *zun* 尊, for instance, obsolete in the Zhou realm since that time, continued to be made south of the Yangzi throughout the Spring and Autumn period; *gui*, as well, are seen long after they went out of fashion elsewhere in the Zhou realm.

Locally manufactured bronzes, though in most cases derived from Shang or Western Zhou prototypes, are easily recognizable on account of their distinctive shapes and decorations, which, as mentioned, show similarity to local ceramics. Shapes such as that of a typologically indeterminate container (midway between *zun* and *gui*) ornamented with horizontal ribbing and enormous dragon-shaped handles (Fig. 7.22) have no equivalent in the Zhou repertoire; others were playful adaptations, such as three-wheeled *pan* from Yancheng (Fig. 7.23), where figurative appendages are soldered on to a *pan*

---

[152] Peng Hao, "Woguo Liang Zhou shiqi de Yue shi ding," *Hunan kaogu jikan* 2 (1984): 136–41, 119.

Figure 7.23. Three-wheeled *pan* from a cache at Yancheng, Wujin, Jiangsu. Late sixth century B.C. From Wen Fong, ed., *The Great Bronze Age of China* (New York: Metropolitan Museum of Art, 1980), no. 65.

vessel of local style;[153] and the bird-topped house model from tomb 306 at Potang (see Fig. 7.2) evinces an unusual interest in narrative representation. Non-Zhou religious customs are intimated by the earliest known bronze *zhenmushou* stands (Fig. 7.24), which come from tomb 3 at the above-mentioned cemetery at Yiqi, Tunxi, in southern Anhui, which is rich in bronze vessels of unusual types.[154] Casters attempted to transform local signal-giving bells made for use in warfare into visual and functional equivalents of Zhou-type chime bells.[155] Such idiosyncratic objects were apparently produced mostly for local consumption.

The court bronze casters of Wu and Yue enjoyed legendary renown for their weapons. Swords and spears of exceptional quality, razor-sharp even today, and with dazzlingly patterned surfaces, appear from the late sixth century B.C. onward (Fig. 7.25). They are descended from the well-made and

[153] Ni Zhenkui, "Yancheng chutu de tongqi," *Wenwu* 1959.4: 3–5.
[154] See note 143.
[155] Sets of *chunyu* 錞于 were found within the Jianbi–Dagang necropolis at Wangjiashan 王家山 and at Beishanding, Dantu, Jiangsu (*Dongnan Wenhua* 1988.3–4: 13–50; and *Wenwu* 1987.12: 24–37); sets of *goudiao* 句鑃 (chimed *zheng* 鉦, another signal-giving bell) were found at Yancheng (Ni Zhenkui, "Yancheng chutu de tongqi") and elsewhere. For more discussion, see Lothar von Falkenhausen, "Shikin-no onsei: Tô Shû jidai-no shun taku dô taku-ni tsuite," *Sen'oku hakkokan kiyô* 6 (1989): 3–26.

Figure 7.24. Bronze stand for a "tomb-protecting animal" (*zhenmushou*) from tomb 3 at Lianqi, Tunxi, Anhui. Probably no earlier than 650 B.C. From Anhui sheng bowugan, *Anhui sheng bowuguan cang qingtongqi* (Shanghai: Shanghai Renmin meishu, 1987), no. 43.

often ornate local weapon types developed during the preceding centuries. Many bear "bird script" inscriptions (Fig. 7.26), sometimes gold-inlaid, mentioning kings or other aristocrats of Wu and Yue. Such items were traded far and wide, even into remote areas.[156] Bronze tools are also found with some frequency. A recent theory holds that Wu and Yue, with their abundant mineral resources, their advanced metal-casting industry, and presumably lacking the Zhou prejudice that reserved bronze for objects belonging to the elite, were the birthplace of the large-scale iron industries of the Warring States period, which for the first time supplied the laboring masses with metal tools.[157]

---

[156] See Li Xueqin, *Eastern Zhou and Qin Civilizations*, pp. 271–2.

[157] Wagner, *Iron and Steel in Ancient China*. Evidence for this theory is so far mostly indirect; very few actual iron objects have been found in the lower Yangzi area, none predating the end (*cont. on p. 537*)

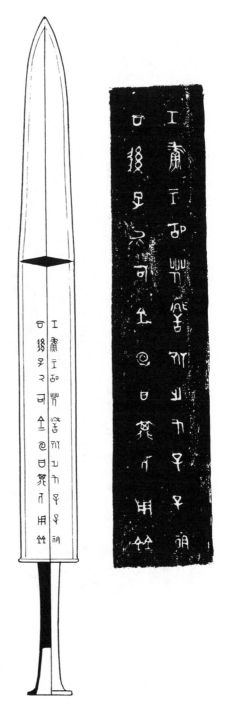

Figure 7.25. *Wu Wang Gufa jian* from San-
jiaoping, Yushe, Shanxi. First quarter of fifth
century B.C. After *Wenwu* 1990.2: 78, fig. 2.
Drawing by Li Xiating.

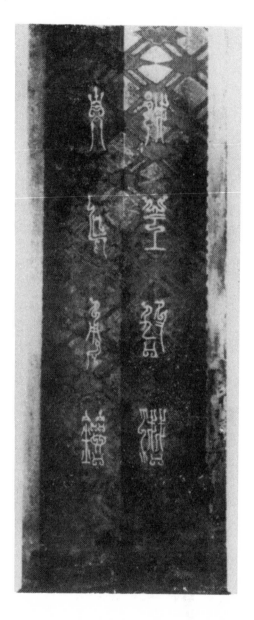

Figure 7.26. Inscription of the *Yue Wang Fuchai jian* from tomb 1 at Wangshan, Jiangling, Hubei. First quarter of fifth century B.C. From *Wenwu* 1966.5: pl. 1.

Within the Zhou realm, the assumption that objects found in a tomb were interred a relatively short time after manufacture is probably correct most of the time; this is not so in the cultures of the lower Yangzi area, where mounded tombs routinely yield bronzes of vastly different dates and workshop origins. In particular, a small number of inscribed vessels of Western

Zhou metropolitan manufacture, for example, the early western Zhou *Yi Hou Ze gui* 宜侯夨殷 from tomb 1 at Yandunshan 煙墩山, Dantu, Jiangsu, discussed in Chapters 5 and 6, and in note 142, this chapter were found in association with locally manufactured objects of clearly later, in some cases much later, date.[158] Their stylistic traits were creatively incorporated into the very different aesthetics of the local workshops.[159] Various proposed chronologies of mounded tombs, their ceramics, and regional-style bronzes use these early imports as reference points in establishing absolute dates, fallaciously placing the bulk of known finds into Western Zhou.[160] Some scholars have long questioned such early dates for the finds from the Jianbi–Dagang necropolis, Yiqi, and other sites,[161] and in fact the sequence of bronzes from mounded tombs probably starts sometime in the ninth century B.C., with the bulk of finds falling into the second quarter of the first millennium B.C.

Okamura Hidenori has pointed out that even though idiosyncratic regional bronze styles continued to prevail in the eastern portions of the lower Yangzi area until the middle of the first millennium B.C., a new wave of northern influence hit the western portions of the lower Yangzi area during the early (or rather, in the light of more recent discoveries, middle) Spring and Autumn period, resulting in the spread of vertical-pit tombs and of bronze assemblages similar to those in the Huai River basin.[162] Toward the end of the Spring and Autumn period, vertical-pit tombs richly furnished with Chu-style bronzes testify to an ongoing reorientation of elite burial preferences even at the Jianbi–Dagang necropolis; similar tombs at other cemeteries have yielded the only provenanced Wu-related bronze inscriptions

of the sixth century B.C. Whatever its later course of development, it would seem that siderurgy did not originate independently in this part of east Asia (see note 31, this chapter).

[158] Besides the *Yi Hou Ze gui*, instances include the middle Western Zhou *Bo gui* 伯殷 from Muzidun 母子墩, Dantu, Jiangsu (*Wenwu* 1984.5: 1–10), as well as an inscribed *zun* from tomb 1 and two inscribed *you* from tomb 3 at Yiqi, Tunxi, Anhui (Anhui sheng bowuguan, ed., *Anhui sheng bowuguan cang qingtongi*, nos. 24 and 27; Yin Difei, "Anhui Tunxi Zhou mu di er ci fajue."

[159] The finds from Yiqi furnish a rare case where both a locally made object and its imported model have been recovered: the *Gong you* 公卣 from tomb 3 (Anhui sheng bowuguan, ed., *Anhui sheng bowuguan cang qingtongi*, no. 24) features the typical middle Western Zhou decoration of phoenixes with interlacing head plumes, which was taken up on a *you* discovered in tomb 1 (ibid., no. 26). The local artisan took considerable liberties with the original decor, duplicating it on each vessel face (perhaps because the interlaced original did not appear symmetrical to local modes of seeing) and surrounding it with geometric background patterns.

[160] See the works cited in notes 138 and 149.

[161] Ma Chengyuan, "Changjiang xiayou tudunmu chutu qingtongqi de yanjiu;" Li Guoliang, "Wannan chutu de qingtongqi." Ma is somewhat extreme in arguing that all regional bronzes from the middle and lower Yangzi (including such finds as Dayangzhou, discussed in Chapter 3) cannot date any earlier than Eastern Zhou. This writer would largely accept Okamura's well-argued stylistic sequence ("Go Etsu izen-no seidôki"), though recent finds suggest that the absolute dates might have to be adjusted later.

[162] Okamura, "Go Etsu izen-no seidôki"; that article provides further references.

found in Wu territory.[163] Okamura believes that these vertical-pit tombs with their northern connections represent the establishment of the Wu polity, which he views as a new, intrusive element in the lower Yangzi region, replacing the mound-building culture. Actually, however, the vertical-pit tombs in the lower Yangzi area are quite mixed in character, containing ceramics, bronze weapons, and bronze vessels of regional derivation alongside Chu-style bronzes. Moreover, recent excavations in the Jianbi–Dagang area have revealed that mounded as well as unmounded bronze-yielding tombs were constructed approximately contemporaneously during the late Spring and Autumn period.

Tombs throughout the area south of the Yangzi, including the Jianbi–Dagang necropolis, have yielded a number of sixth century B.C. bronze objects inscribed on behalf of aristocrats from Xu 徐, an ancient semi-Barbarian polity in the Lower Huai area that was annihilated by Wu in 512 B.C. These are probably Chu products, bestowed on Xu aristocrats to underscore their polity's client relationship with Chu; they may have reached Wu as war booty, through trade, or as tokens of political or marriage alliance. That Xu might have played a role in the mediation of Zhou elements to the Lower Yangzi region even before is suggested by the similarity of some of the bronzes in local middle Spring and Autumn vertical-pit tombs, which Okamura ascribes to "northern" influence, to specimens found in the Xu core area.[164] By the same token, Xu may have been the conduit for such southeastern features as *zhenmushou* into the Chu area.

Instead of attempting to explain the highly distinctive, non-Zhou Bronze Age cultures of southeastern China during the first half of the first millennium B.C. principally in terms of outside stimuli, the time may have come to put primary emphasis on local continuities and to explore this region's impact on surrounding areas. The picture that now emerges is one of a gradual convergence of local traditions with the ritual institutions of the Zhou, essentially confirming the textually documented interest shown by

---

[163] Moundless vertical-pit tombs at the Jianbi–Dagang necropolis include Wangjiashan (*Wenwu* 1987.12: 24–37) and tomb 2 at Liangshan 糧山 (Liu Jianguo, "Jiangsu Dantu Liangshan Chunqiu shixuemu," *Kaogu yu wenwu* 1987.4: 29–38). Wu-related inscribed bronzes were unearthed from the vertical-pit tombs 1 and 2 at Chengqiao 程橋, Luhe 六合, Jiangsu (*Kaogu* 1965.3: 105–15 and *Kaogu* 1974.2: 116–20); a similar tomb at Heshan 何山, Wuxian 吳縣, Jiangsu, yielded one bronze tripod inscribed by a Chu donor (*Wenwu* 1984.5: 16–20). Much further to the south, the vertical-pit tomb 306 at Potang, Shaoxing, Zhejiang, yielded Chu-style bronzes inscribed by Xu donors as part of an interestingly mixed assemblage (*Wenwu* 1984.1: 10–37).

[164] Spring and Autumn period bronzes inscribed by Xu donors were excavated at Beishanding (*Dongnan Wenhua* 1988.3–4: 13–50) and tomb 306 at Potang (*Wenwu* 1984.1: 10–37), as well as at Shuikou 水口, Jing'an 靖安, Jiangxi (*Wenwu* 1980.8: 13–15). In terms of traditional historical geography, the first of these three sites is located in Wu, the second in Yue, and the third in virtual no-man's land inhabited by unassimilated populations. Ironically, no Xu-related inscribed objects have so far come to light in the purported Xu territory.

indigenous Wu aristocrats in making themselves compatible with their new northern allies. However, the area's incorporation into the Zhou political sphere was not yet complete at the end of the Spring and Autumn period.

OTHER SOUTHERN REGIONAL CULTURES

Since Erligang times, indigenous non-Zhou populations had exploited the rich copper deposits of the middle Yangzi River basin. Distinctive bronze-manufacturing cultures continued to flourish in this area during the Spring and Autumn period. At the well-preserved Spring and Autumn period mining site of Tonglüshan 銅綠山, Daye 大冶, Hubei,[165] access to copper-ore deposits was achieved by means of a maze of vertical pits and horizontal galleries reinforced with timber; the construction principles are astonishingly advanced by comparison with ancient mines in other parts of the world. While it seems reasonable to assume that the mines supplied the markets of nearby Chu, there is no indication of a Chu presence in the area before the Warring States period.

The presence of such resources notwithstanding, no local developments toward greater sociopolitical complexity are observable in this part of China. Jiangxi is still a virtual blank spot in Spring and Autumn period archaeology. In the Xiang 湘 River valley and around Lake Dongting 洞庭 in Hunan, likewise, remains from this period are paltry by comparison to earlier stages. Finds include some vertical-pit tombs of elongated shape in the Changsha 長沙 area, as well as numerous bronze vessels and bells found with virtually no context.[166] Bronze objects comprise for the most part weapons and Yue-style tripods of a variety of subtypes.[167] Some regional-style *you* and *zun*, all from poorly documented contexts, feature unusual raised-line decor of inter-laced snakes (or worms) as well as frogs or toads in conjunction with geometric patterns (Fig. 7.27).[168] Late Spring and Autumn period Chu remains

[165] Xia Nai and Yin Weizhang, "Hubei Tonglüshan gu tongkuang," *Kaogu xuebao* 1982.1: 1–14.
[166] The most important discoveries are reported in: *Hunan kaogu jikan* 1 (1982): 25–31; *Hunan kaogu jikan* 2 (1984): 35–7; *Wenwu* 1985.6: 1–15; Song Shaohua, "Changsha chutu Shang, Chunqiu qingtongqi," *Hunan bowuguan wenji* 1 (1991): 133–6. See also Gao Zhixi, "Hunan faxian de jijian Yuezu fengge de wenwu," *Wenwu* 1980.12: 48–51; He Jiejun, "Hunan Shang Zhou Shiqi gu wenhua de fenqu tansuo," *Hunan kaogu jikan* 2 (1984): 120–7; Wu Mingsheng, "Hunan Dong Zhou shiqi Yueren muzang de yanjiu," *Hunan kaogu jikan* 5 (1989): 161–4; and Xiong Chuanxin and Wu Mingsheng, "Hunan gu Yuezu qingtongqi gailun," *Zhongguo Kaoguxuehui di si ci nianhui (1983) lunwenji* (Beijing: Wenwu, 1985), pp. 152–66.
[167] Only the tomb at Baoheyu, Hengnan, Hunan (*Kaogu* 1978.5: 297–300) yielded a complete set of seventh century B.C. bronze vessels, probably imports from the eastern part of the Han–Huai region.
[168] Zhou Shirong, "Cansangwen zun yu wushi xiexingyue," *Kaogu* 1979.6: 566–7, 563; Xiong Jianhua, "Xiangtan xian chutu Zhou dai qingtong tiliangyou," *Hunan kaogu jikan* 4 (1987): 19–21; *Zhongguo wenwu jinghua 1990* (Beijing: Wenwu, 1990), no. 63; and *Hunan bowuguan wenji* 1 (1991): 142–51. Similar objects, probably made at the same workshops, have also been unearthed at Yangjia 秧家, Gong cheng 恭城, Guangxi (*Kaogu* 1973.1: 30–4, 41).

Figure 7.27. *You* excavated at
Yingkou, Yueyang, Hunan.
Seventh century B.C. After
Hunan bowuguan wenji 1
(1991): 146, fig. 4. Drawing by
Li Xiating.

have been reported only from the extreme north of Hunan; recent research
has shown that the chronological sequence of Chu tombs in the Changsha
長沙 area, formerly thought to have started in the middle Spring and Autumn
period, does not actually begin until Warring States times.[169] The historical
texts tell us little about the indigenous inhabitants, who are conventionally
identified as one or another variety of "Yue"; use of this ethnic label should
not, however, be construed as implying political control by the Yue kingdom.

The regional Bronze Age culture of the Lingnan 嶺南 region, centered on
northern Guangxi and central Guangdong,[170] shares a number of features

---

[169] The chronology promulgated in the much-quoted report on Chu tombs at Changsha (*Changsha fajue baogao* [Beijing: Kexue, 1957]) is thus in need of revision.

[170] Important synthetic treatments, where further references can be found, include the following. For Lingnan as a whole: Huang Zhanyue, "Lun Liang Guang chutu de xian Qin qingtongqi," *Kaogu xuebao* 1986.4: 409–34; Li Longzhang, "Hunan Liang Guang qingtongshidai Yue mu yanjiu," *Kaogu xuebao* 1995.3: 275–312; and Francis Allard, "Interaction and Social Complexity in Lingnan During the First Millennium B.C.," *Asian Perspectives* 33, 2 (1994): 309–26. For Guangdong: He Jisheng, "Lüelun Guangdong Dong Zhou shiqi de qingtongwenhua ji qi yu jiheyinwentao de guanxi," *Wenwu jikan* 3 (1981): 212–24; Xu Hengbin, "Guangdong qingtongqishidai gailun," in *Guangdong chutu xian Qin wenwu*, ed. Guangdong sheng bowuguan and Xianggang Zhongwen daxue wenwuguan (Hong Kong: Art Gallery, Chinese University of Hong Kong, 1984), pp. 45–63, English translation ibid., pp. 64–85. For Guangxi: Jiang Tingyu and Lan Riyong, "Guangxi xian-Qin qingtongwenhua chulun," *Zhongguo Kaoguxuehui di si ci nianhui (1983) lunwenji* (Beijing: Wenwu, 1985), pp. 252–63.

with Spring and Autumn period phenomena in the middle Yangzi basin. Although a few bronze vessels and bells had been introduced into Lingnan from the Yangzi and Yellow River basins as early as the late Shang period, and there may have been early efforts to cast simple weapons and implements, indigenous bronze workshops capable of manufacturing Yue-style tripods and local types of bells did not arise until the fifth century B.C. A number of fairly large tombs dating from the late Spring and Autumn to the Warring States period have been reported; unlike contemporary tombs in the middle Yangzi region, they are for the most part square and far richer in bronzes. Bronzes imported from the Zhou culture sphere (including but not limited to Chu items) occur side by side with objects resembling specimens from workshops in the Xiang River system. It has been suggested that the latter represent the leaders of "Yue" groups formerly resident in Hunan, who had moved south under the pressure of Chu encroachment. However, the significance of indigenous components in the Lingnan Bronze Age culture should not be underestimated. It seems very unlikely that social complexity at any time before the Qin unification exceeded the chiefdom level, though the area gradually became linked to northerly areas through networks of economic and possibly low-level diplomatic exchange.

Further up the Yangzi, a plethora of vigorous independent bronze-manufacturing cultures flourished during the Eastern Zhou period in the vast and fertile Sichuan basin. As described in Chapter 3, the splendid Early Bronze Age culture at Sanxingdui 三星堆, in the Chengdu Plain, the traditional nucleus of the Shu 蜀 polity, stands out in isolation even more than do the cultures of the lower and middle Yangzi regions. Some continuity with the well-documented later stages conventionally referred to as the "Ba-Shu 巴蜀 culture" is, however, undoubtable, since the distinctive Ba-Shu weapons preserve significant similarities to Erligang period weapon types from the Yellow River basin. Currently, scholars invariably relegate all Ba-Shu finds to the Warring States period, leaving the Spring and Autumn period completely blank.[171] In fact, however, bronze vessels of undisputably Spring and Autumn period manufacture (including both products of the Zhou realm and objects imported from the middle Yangzi area) have been discovered variously in Ba-Shu contexts. Local archaeologists, failing to distinguish between date of deposition and date of manufacture, have routinely reported them as Warring States period objects because some of them occur in tombs of such date. A restudy of the material may well succeed in identifying bronze-yielding tombs and caches that are contemporary with the Spring and Autumn period.

Imported bronzes unquestionably of Spring and Autumn period date have

---

[171] Sichuan sheng bowuguan, *Ba Shu qingtongqi* (Chengdu: Ziyunzhai, 1991).

also been found among the remains of an as yet scarcely known stone-cist building culture in the mountains of west-central Sichuan. The rich bronze assemblages from one tomb and three funerary pits at Moutuo 牟托, Maoxian 茂縣, Sichuan,[172] deposited not long after 500 B.C., strike one as being easily the most heterogeneous of those known from the entire East Asian Bronze Age. Finds include a vessel from a Western Zhou metropolitan workshop, as well as Spring and Autumn period vessels, bells, ornaments, and weapons produced in Chu, along the middle Yangzi, in the Huai River basin, the Sichuan plain, Yunnan or Southeast Asia, and on the Central Eurasian steppes. All these appear in combination with pottery that derives directly from Gansu and Qinghai chalcolithic precedents of the third millennium. Two iron swords were found, which, in spite of their marginal location, may be earlier in date than most early iron finds within the Zhou culture area. How such wealth could have been concentrated in the hands of seminomadic chieftains in this remote area remains to be elucidated.

THE NORTHERN AND NORTHEASTERN REGIONS

Throughout the later part of the Bronze Age, nomadic tribes interacted with settled agricultural and livestock-raising populations along the northern and northeastern peripheries of the Zhou culture sphere. Here, the cultural divide between Zhou and non-Zhou populations appears to have been far more pronounced than was the case in the south; this continued to be true during the imperial period. Due in part to the unstratified nature of sites and deposits, the definition of clearly dated chronologies for the vast area from Xinjiang in the west to Liaoning in the east has proven extremely difficult. So far, archaeological finds from the second quarter of the first millennium B.C. cannot be distinguished with confidence from those that are assigned a Warring States date; the time does not seem ripe for a comprehensive assessment.[173] Cultural developments in that part of China, which form part of greater Eurasian developments, are treated in Chapter 13.

CONCLUSION

Recent work on earlier chronological segments of the Chinese Bronze Age suggests that the extent of centralized political control exercised by the early royal dynasties in the Yellow River valley may have been greatly exaggerated

---

[172] *Wenwu* 1994.3: 4–40. See also Lothar von Falkenhausen, "The Moutuo Bronzes: New Perspectives on the Late Bronze Age in Sichuan," *Arts Asiatiques*, 51 (1996): 29–59.

[173] Recently, the whole chronology proposed over decades of research has been challenged by Sophia-Karin Psarras ("Exploring the North: Non-Chinese Cultures of the Late Warring States and Han," *Monumenta Serica* 42 [1994]: 1–125); a restudy is urgently needed.

in traditional historiography. Evidence presented in this chapter shows that, conversely, the often vaunted fragmentation of the Zhou political structure after 770 B.C. should not be overemphasized. Western Zhou and Spring and Autumn period cultural patterns are but reverse sides of the same coin – the outcome of enduring trends that had evolved over many centuries and that had found their culminating systemic expression in the Late Western Zhou Ritual Reform. As established structures underwent increasing stress, piecemeal modifications occurred; but even the thoroughgoing cultural transformation of the Warring States period left crucial parts of the Bronze Age heritage intact.

The avenues of diffusion and modalities of exchange underlying the homogenization processes traced in this chapter remain very incompletely known. Ritual and religious dimensions may have been stressed at the expense of the military. As will be discussed in Chapter 8, warfare, conquest, and the threat thereof were an inseparable part of the same system of activities that embraced the carefully staged ritual celebration with which so much of the surviving material evidence is associated. Developments in military technology, so far traceable mainly through weapon typology, but which must also have involved such matters as fortification design, constitute fertile topics for future study of this violent aspect of Spring and Autumn civilization. One pertinent archaeological discovery is seen in the mass graves at Xishuipo 西水坡, Puyang 濮陽, Henan,[174] where excavations brought to light thirty-two regularly aligned pits, each containing the skeletons of 18 males aged twenty to twenty-five who had suffered violent deaths; in addition, a varying number of severed heads was found in each pit. Buried individuals total more than 600. Such an arrangement bespeaks military-style labor organization. The site is close to the ancient battlefield of Chengpu 城濮, where, in 632 B.C., a northern alliance led by Jin decisively defeated Chu; however, a connection to that event cannot be proven in the absence of chronologically sensitive burial goods. It remains unclear on which side the dead soldiers had fought and why they had been buried in groups of 18, a number that, to judge from textual evidence, does not seem to have been important in military organization.

In the background of the phenomena here presented, the Late Western Zhou Ritual Reform emerges as a key event in Chinese history. Still largely elusive, it succeeded in establishing social and religious structures of tremendous clarity, flexibility, and universality that were to endure throughout the history of imperial China. The encompassing trends toward homogenization we have observed in archaeological materials of the Spring and Autumn

---

[174] *Kaogu* 1989.12: 1057–66.

period undoubtedly manifest the implementation, throughout the Zhou realm, of the new standards. Such a trend very probably reflects an even more self-conscious awareness of the defining criteria of Zhou civilization on the part of its elite participants, as is also evinced by the early Confucian texts. In a milieu where adherence to codified rules of ritual consumption and behavior was central to political and religious activity at any level, it is legitimate to argue that such archaeologically observable phenomena as the use of more or less uniform sets of ritual paraphernalia, and the adoption of largely comparable burial customs throughout a wide area, may reflect an underlying shared system of politicoreligious values, as well as homologies in the social organization of elites.

Unlike the stylistic changes accompanying the late Western Zhou Ritual Reform, the innovations in bronze ornamentation around the end of the seventh century B.C. appear not to have been forced by changes in ideology, but rather to reflect a belated technological response to this reformed social and ritual system. Significantly, these innovations are seen more or less simultaneously in all parts of the Zhou realm. The greater availability of mass-produced ritual bronzes may account in part for the rise, during the sixth century B.C., of new types of bronze assemblages in tombs of lower elites. The manifest contrasts between these and the more conservative and complex constellations encountered in middle to late Spring and Autumn period tombs of high elites may bespeak increasing social differentiation within the ranked elite. The historical background and significance of this development still demand closer study.

Archaeological materials document, furthermore, the piecemeal adaptation of the reformed Zhou system to regional Bronze Age traditions within the Zhou culture sphere, as well as the integration of originally non-Zhou border regions, especially in the east and southeast. As adherence to Zhou ritual conventions became increasingly a recognized barometer of civilization, the contrast between Chinese (self-designated as Zhou, Xia 夏, or Hua Xia 華夏) and Barbarians became ever more accentuated over the course of the Eastern Zhou period.[175] The establishment and ever-renewed enactment of Zhou-derived ritual structures continued to be fundamental to the later expansion of the Chinese culture sphere under the imperial dynasties.

---

[175] Okura Yoshihiko, "I-i no toriko: *Saden*-no Ka-I kannen," *Chûgoku kodaishi kenkyû* 2 (1965): 153–88.

CHAPTER EIGHT

THE SPRING AND AUTUMN PERIOD

Cho-yun Hsu

This chapter is an account of various transformations that took place during the Spring and Autumn period (770–481 B.C.). It covers the transition from a Zhou feudal system to a multistate system; from the expansion of the Zhou into the Yellow River drainage to the ancient China that spanned the Yellow and Yangzi Rivers and the highlands in the north and the west; from an economy based on manorial management to a market economy; and from a family-based society to one based upon great social mobility. The most significant development in this period was a major breakthrough in the intellectual sphere, in which the moral values of Confucius provided an innovative reinterpretation of feudal ethics. This breakthrough brought Chinese culture into a Jaspersian "Axial Age" of civilization.[1] Thereafter, intellectuals served not only as officials in government but, of more profound impact, also as cultural carriers who interpreted the meaning of life and ideals of society. This new condition in the intellectual sphere continued beyond the Spring and Autumn period, remaining characteristic throughout Chinese history. In other words, this breakthrough initiated in the Spring and Autumn period would eventually lead China to develop a persistent, collective identity – Chinese civilization.

THE FALL OF THE WESTERN ZHOU

After nearly three centuries of reign, the Western Zhou collapsed. King You (r. 781–771 B.C.) was killed by a joint force led by the vassal states Shen 申 and its ally, the non-Zhou tribe Quan Rong 犬戎. The fall of the royal house was not a simple matter, its problems having been accumulating for several

[1] Karl Jaspers, *The Origin and Goal of History*, trans. Michael Bullock (New Haven, Conn.: Yale University Press, 1953).

generations. As early as the mid-ninth century B.C., King Li (r. 857–842 B.C.) was overthrown and exiled by nobles who then installed a regent to lead the government for fourteen years until King Li's son King Xuan (r. 827–782 B.C.) was installed in power. This in itself suggests that royal authority was no longer strong.

Several factors had developed in the Western Zhou that probably resulted in its final downfall. First, the numerous garrison states established by children of the royal house in the eastern part of the kingdom had gradually become localized and were no longer eager to support the court in the west. Meanwhile, the western domain, with its limited size and resources, had to bear the burden of maintaining that court and its continually expanding household. There also seems to have been some degree of social mobility, with nobles becoming impoverished and commoners becoming wealthy; this state of affairs took place outside of the Zhou feudal structure, which it was eventually to undermine.

In addition, the encroachment of foreign invaders from the north and the west not only required the Zhou often to pay dearly in fending off intruders, but also the infiltration of foreign populations into the royal domain increased demographic pressure on its already limited land resources. Finally, natural disasters, including a massive earthquake, delivered heavy blows to the economy, as well as to the people's morale. Several treasure pits of late Western Zhou bronze vessels discovered in recent years show that the Zhou nobles hastily left their households to flee the various turmoils on the eve of the final collapse.[2] The fall of the Western Zhou, just like the fall of other great kingdoms in history, was due to the combination of a number of causes; factors internal to its institutions as well as blows originating from outside brought down this previously well-functioning political entity.

After the death of King You, two royal sons, each supported by a faction of lords from vassal states, contended for the throne. The son who prevailed, installed as King Ping (r. 770–720 B.C.), had been the original heir apparent, but had been replaced in that status by a half-brother, named Bofu 伯服, born to a favored consort. King Ping moved the court to the eastern capital at Chengzhou 成周 (at present-day Luoyang 洛陽, Henan), which had been a Zhou stronghold in the east providing the eastern states with logistical support. This decision was reached for two compelling reasons. First, the western royal domain of Zongzhou 宗周 (in present-day Shaanxi) had been desolated by wars and natural disasters. Second, King Ping preferred to be close to his principal supporters in the east. At this capital, the dynasty

[2] Cho-yun Hsu and Kathryn Linduff, *Western Chou Civilization* (New Haven, Conn.: Yale University Press, 1988), pp. 258–87.

nominally survived until 256 B.C., though the Eastern Zhou was only a pale shadow of the preceding Western Zhou period.

THE BEGINNING OF THE SPRING AND AUTUMN PERIOD

The first two and a half centuries of the Eastern Zhou are known as the Spring and Autumn period, taking this name from the title of the chronicles of the state of Lu 魯, the *Chun qiu* 春秋 (Spring and Autumn [annals]), which cover the years 722–481 B.C. (from the first year of the reign of Lu Yin Gong 魯隱公 to the fourteenth year of Lu Ai Gong 魯哀公). The most important source for this period, however, is not the *Chun qiu* itself, but rather the *Zuo zhuan* 左傳 (Zuo's tradition), which provides much more detailed information than the brief entries of the chronicles. The main body of the *Zuo zhuan* was compiled – possibly by more than one author – in the Warring States period (481–221 B.C.), the second half of the Eastern Zhou. Despite a lack of corroborating evidence from other sources, there is no reason to doubt the details of political and military activities given in the *Zuo zhuan* or the roles played by prominent figures in it, such as Guan Zhong 管仲. One supplementary source is the *Guo yu* 國語 (Sayings of the states), which also contains considerable information.[3]

The main arena of activities in the Spring and Autumn period was the alluvial plain of the Yellow River and the Shandong Peninsula, as well as the Huai 淮 and Han 漢 River valleys. It eventually expanded to include much of present-day Shaanxi, Shanxi, and Hebei in the north and the Yangzi River valley in the south. For areas beyond, there is only fragmentary information.

The Zhou States

The people who inhabited these areas belonged to both Zhou and non-Zhou groups, the latter often labeled "barbarians." The states in the east had been established by scions and relatives of the Zhou royal family. The *Zuo zhuan* mentions 148 such states.[4] However, most of these were small in size and came to be annexed by larger neighbors over the course of the Spring and Autumn period. There were 15 major states: Qi 齊, Jin 晉, Qin 秦, Chu 楚, Lu 魯, Cao 曹, Zheng 鄭, Song 宋, Xu 許, Chen 陳, Wey 衛, Yan 燕, Cai 蔡, Wu 吳, and Yue 越 (see Map 8.1). All of these claimed to be members of

[3] Cho-yun Hsu, *Ancient China in Transition* (Stanford, Calif.: Stanford University Press, 1965), pp. 184–6; Michael Loewe, ed., *Early Chinese Texts: A Bibliographical Guide* (Berkeley: Society for the Study of Early China and the Institute of East Asian Studies, University of California, 1993), pp. 67–76, 263–8.
[4] Gu Donggao, *Chunqiu da shi biao*, vol. 5 (Huang Qing jingjie xubian), ed. Wang Xianqian (Jiangyin: Nanjing Academy, 1888), chart 5. Chen Pan identified even more states than did Gu; see Chen Pan, "*Chunqiu da shi biao: Lieguo juexing ji cunmiebiao*" *zhuanyi* (Taipei: Academia Sinica, 1969).

Map 8.1 Major states of the Spring and Autumn period.

the Zhou feudal system, even though a few of them – such as Chu, Wu, and Yue – definitely derived from non-Zhou backgrounds.

The Non-Zhou Peoples

Intermingled among the Zhou states were numerous non-Zhou peoples who appear not to have formed complicated statehood structures. When the Zhou conquered the eastern territory, their vassal states were mainly garrison stations at strategic spots, many of them already inhabited. The troops led by Zhou nobles normally included the king's men, detachments of allied forces, and some of the Shang people who surrendered to the Zhou. Meanwhile, the native populations in these states, some of whom may have been members of old eastern states while others were probably tribal peoples – referred to in Chinese sources as Man 蠻, Yi 夷, Rong 戎, and Di 狄, the barbarians, were ruled as subjects, but without membership in the state of a type that could be compared to citizenship in the Greek city-states. However, the Zhou garrison states were by no means independent polities as were the Greek city-states, being instead a part of the Zhou feudal network.[5]

Early texts refer to these natives as "people of the field" (*ye ren* 野人) in contrast to "people in the state" (*guo ren* 國人), which refers to the Zhou colonizers who lived in the garrisons. In short, a Zhou vassal state normally consisted of a mixture of several ethnic and cultural groups. The Man, Yi, Rong, and Di peoples were scattered throughout the open spaces that were not effectively controlled by the Zhou vassal states. They were regarded as aliens probably because they held distinctive cultural identities.

The Yi groups perhaps were very ancient inhabitants of the east, some of them having been formidable enemies of the Zhou order during the Western Zhou period. It was only with great effort that the Zhou had established vassal states in their lands after conquering the Shang. By the Eastern Zhou, the Yi groups appearing in our sources most frequently are the Xu 徐, Shu 舒, Huai 淮, and Lai 萊. The Xu and Shu were active in present-day Anhui and Jiangxi; the Huai were in the Huai River valley, while the Lai were long-time natives of the Shandong Peninsula. The Xu had once assumed leadership among the various Yi groups, though others seem to have been loosely affiliated tribes.

The category of Man is hard to define. It appears to have been a generic term to refer to southern peoples. Chu was regarded as a Man state, for instance. On the other hand, some of the Man peoples mentioned in early sources were located very near the Zhou core area of the east.

Rong seems to refer to the several groups of non-Zhou peoples scattered in the northern highlands, especially in the mountains of today's Shaanxi, Shanxi, Hebei, and Shandong provinces. The Bei Rong 北戎 lived in the uplands near the states of Jin, Zheng, Qi, and Xu. The Shan Rong 山戎 were active in Shandong and Hebei, near the states of Yan and Qi. Interspersed among the states were the Li Rong 驪戎, Quan Rong, Luhun Rong 陸渾戎, Yiluo Rong 伊洛戎, and others. The Quan Rong were the group that had invaded the western capital and killed King You. The Yiluo Rong dwelt very close to the Zhou capital of Chengzhou. The names of these Rong peoples might have differed over time and place, as well as in different sources, so that it is impossible to define their ethnic or cultural origins with any clarity.

[5] Hsu and Linduff, *Western Chou Civilization*, pp. 147–85.

The Di groups were also scattered throughout the northern states. Three rather strong groups, the Bai Di 白狄, Chi Di 赤狄, and Chang Di 長狄 are frequently mentioned as intruders in Shanxi, Hebei, Shandong, and Henan. The states of Qi, Lu, Wey, and Song were all disturbed by the Di, who seem to have been the most militant of the groups. Whether the Rong and Di were related or of totally different ethnic stock cannot be decided without further archaeological data.[6] Although there is still no way to establish their ethnic identities, these various non-Chinese groups appear to have been culturally distinct. During the Spring and Autumn period, they were gradually absorbed into the Zhou states, which had the common identity of being regarded as Hua Xia 華夏.

By the fall of the Western Zhou, even though a number of Zhou states had been located in the east for centuries, the area was still not densely populated, and there were unclaimed lands scattered about. The history of the state of Zheng reveals that a major state could find plenty of open space among the existing states. It was founded in the western domain in 806 B.C. During the reign of King You, one of his high ministers, to be known as Zheng Huan Gong 鄭桓公, decided to move to the east. He selected and moved to a new site in the vicinity of the eastern capital. Our sources describe the new land as "full of thorns and bushes," and the settlers had to make considerable effort in its reclamation.[7]

Thus was the stage set for the Spring and Autumn period. With the fall of the Western Zhou, there had disappeared the system that had held the Zhou together, whereby the Zhou king served simultaneously as the patriarch of the royal lineage and as supreme lord of the nobility. This status, regarded as having been conferred by the Mandate of Heaven, was confirmed periodically by rituals and ceremonies performed in conferences, court visits, and ancestor worship.[8] With the royal court's move to the east, there was a realignment of power and resources among all of the Hua Xia as well as the Man, Yi, Rong, and Di. The history of the Spring and Autumn period thus marks the first phase in a transition from the Western Zhou feudalism toward the unified empires of the Qin and Han dynasties. The changes that took place in this and the subsequent Warring States period constitute one of the most exciting episodes in history, when the Chinese defined for themselves a culture as well as a world.

[6] Gu Donggao, *Chunqiu dashi biao*, 39; also, E. G. Pulleyblank, "The Chinese and Their Neighbors in Pre-Historic and Early Historic Times," in *The Origins of Chinese Civilization*, ed. David N. Keightley (Berkeley: University of California Press, 1983), pp. 411–66.

[7] *Guo yu* 國語 (*Sibu beiyao* ed.), 16 ("Zheng yu"), 1a–b, 6b; *Zuo zhuan*, 47 (Zhao 16), 18b (James Legge, *The Chinese Classics*, 5 vols., 2d ed. rev. [Oxford: Clarendon Press, 1893–4; rpt. Hong Kong: University of Hong Kong Press, 1960], vol. 5: *The Ch'un Ts'ew with the Tso Chuen*, p. 664).

[8] Hsu and Linduff, *Western Chou Civilization*, pp. 177–85.

THE FORMATION OF THE *BA* SYSTEM

The Eastern Zhou court, as reorganized by King Ping, was virtually a government in exile. King Ping defeated his rival for power with support from the states of Jin and Zheng, whose troops escorted him as he resettled at Chengzhou. The leadership of these two states, together with that of Lu, a state that had been founded at the beginning of the Western Zhou, was crucial for the survival of the new court.

The Leadership of Zheng

As mentioned in the preceding section, Zheng was a relatively new member of the eastern states. Its first ruler, Zheng Huan Gong (r. 806–771 B.C.), was a younger brother of King Xuan (r. 827–782 B.C.). Enfeoffed in 806 B.C., he established a state within the royal domain, near Huaxian 華縣, Shaanxi. While serving King You as a high minister at the royal court, he moved the state to a new eastern location, at present-day Zhengzhou 鄭州, Henan, also near the eastern capital. Thus, the house of Zheng, close cousins to the royal court, served as a vanguard for its move to the east. The intimate relationship between Zheng and the royal court is shown by the fact that for three generations Zheng rulers continuously served the court as *qingshi* 卿士, one of the two top-ranking ministers.

The strength of Zheng was due not only to its intimacy with the royal court, but also to the way in which its leaders had reclaimed a piece of territory in swampland surrounded by few existing states. It is recorded in the *Zuo zhuan* that the founders of Zheng arrived at this new site with a group of people who were itinerant merchants known as Shang 商 (probably descendants of the Shang people). Assisted by these Shang people, Zheng began to cultivate the reclaimed land.[9] There were also non-Zhou people, the Man, Rong, and Di, living in the vicinity. Probably because of these adverse conditions, during the founders' reigns the Zheng people developed a pioneering spirit that the older eastern states lacked. In addition, as a relatively young state Zheng had not experienced the sort of continuous segmentation that was intrinsic to the process of feudalism, and so could mobilize its resources more easily than could the older states. In any event, Zheng was soon reckoned as one of the major powers supporting the Zhou court. Zheng Zhuang Gong 鄭莊公 (r. 743–701 B.C.), the third ruler of the state, was especially active in royal politics. He defeated Rong intruders and,

---

[9] *Zuo zhuan*, 47 (Zhao 16), 19a (Legge, *The Chinese Classics*, vol. 5, p. 664).

in the name of the royal court, led an allied force against states that refused
to submit.[10]

Although Zhuang Gong successfully defended the royal court, his forceful assaults against other Zhou states and Rong people constituted unprecedented behavior toward fellow members of the Zhou polity. The arrogance
of Zhuang Gong seems to have caused King Ping to feel threatened. The
king appointed a noble of the state of Guo 虢, also located near the Zhou
capital, at present-day Sanmenxia 三門峽, Henan, to be another high
minister to balance Zheng's dominance. When an enraged Zhuang Gong
demanded an explanation, to mollify him the king sent one of his own sons
as hostage to Zheng in exchange for Zhuang Gong's heir apparent. For the
king and a vassal to exchange hostages in this way was again an unprecedented breach of feudal ethics.[11]

The relationship between Zheng and the royal court worsened after
King Ping's death. When King Huan (r. 719–697 B.C.) appointed another
lord of Guo as chief minister, Zheng Zhuang Gong raided crops in the
fields of the royal domain. In 707 B.C., King Huan mobilized troops of
Chen, Wey, and Cai to attack Zheng. The result of this armed encounter
proved to be an embarrassment to the royal court, its army suffering defeat
and the king himself being wounded in the shoulder by an arrow. This represented more than just a physical wound; it meant that the Zhou king's
status as Son of Heaven was now discredited. The court continued to exist
for several more centuries; however, after this conflict between Zhou and
Zheng, the authority of the Zhou king was no longer taken seriously; thereafter, the Zhou king merely served as nominal head of the Zhou feudal
system.[12]

Zheng thus assumed leadership among the Zhou states. Although the
title of Ba 霸 (lit. the senior one) had not yet been established, Zheng
Zhuang Gong was the first to obtain the status of leader of the interstate
community. In this role, Zheng led allied states in attacking other states
that challenged Zheng's leadership, which after a number of victories,
was recognized by virtually all the Zhou states in the north, including
Qi, Lu, Song, and Wey. The death of Zhuang Gong in 701 B.C. triggered
a succession struggle between his two sons. Other states, especially Song,
also became involved in the struggle between these two sons – a civil
war that lasted for two decades and resulted in the end of Zheng's
leadership.[13]

---

[10] E.g., *Zuo zhuan*, 4 (Yin 10), 16b–17a (Legge, *The Chinese Classics*, vol. 5, pp. 29–30).
[11] *Zuo zhuan*, 3 (Yin 3), 5a–6a (Legge, *The Chinese Classics*, vol. 5, p. 13).
[12] *Zuo zhuan*, 6 (Huan 5), 9b (Legge, *The Chinese Classics*, vol. 5, pp. 45–6).
[13] *Zuo Zhuan*, 9 (Zhuang 14), 8a–9b (Legge, *The Chinese Classics*, vol. 5, p. 92).

The Leadership of Qi

Zhuang Gong's leadership was too short-lived to give any real structure to the *ba* system. It was in the later hands of Qi Huan Gong 齊桓公 (r. 685–643 B.C.) and Jin Wen Gong 晉文公 (r. 636–628 B.C.) that this system was gradually institutionalized. For decades, there had been no obvious leadership among the Zhou states. The royal court had little authority, while states, both large and small, faced turmoil. Taking advantage of the disunity of the Zhou states, the non-Zhou groups, various kinds of Rong and Di people, intruded on the weaker Zhou states. Meanwhile, the state of Chu, a new power in the south, rose to pose an even greater threat to the Zhou world in the Yellow River valley.[14]

Subsequently, Qi Huan Gong developed a new kind of hegemony in answer to the need for leadership. Qi had an important background. When the Zhou had risen to power in the Wei 渭 River valley, their closest alliance was with the Jiang 姜 people, probably natives of the loess highland in the present provinces of Shaanxi and Gansu, frequently intermarrying with them. At the time of the Zhou conquest of Shang, Jiang Shang 姜尚, leader of the Jiang, led the Zhou army. After Zhou successfully conquered the east, the Jiang people shared in the victory by being able to establish several vassal states. Qi was one of these states, established by Jiang Shang himself.

Qi was located on the Shandong peninsula at a strategic spot controlling the non-Zhou groups in the eastern coastal region as well as all north–south communication. It was a neighbor of Lu, which had been established by a son of Zhou Gong, one of the founding fathers of the Zhou dynasty. Support from Qi and Lu was always crucial for the Zhou feudal order in the east. This was especially so during the Eastern Zhou, when Qi became an even more important polity. Even during the early reigns of the Eastern Zhou, when Zheng dominated the scene, Qi was regarded as being too powerful for Zheng to offend. Qi took an active role in campaigns organized, or at least nominally led, by the royal court. However, it was not until the influence of Zheng began to decline that Qi became the primary leader in the politics of the Zhou states.

Qi's ascendance to the *Ba* overlordship was due to a combination of several factors. Its territory was extensive as a result of having annexed a number of lesser neighboring states. Its location at a major trade route junction gave it the opportunity to profit from interstate trade. Its Shandong coastal salt flats provided it with a very important resource, and it also gathered wealth from

---

[14] E.g., *Zuo zhuan*, 8 (Zhuang 10), 24a, b (Legge, *The Chinese Classics*, vol. 5, pp. 86–7); 11 (Min 1) 1b (ibid., p. 124).

fishing and textile production.[15] Being located on the eastern frontier also
gave Qi ample space to expand beyond the Zhou world. Various kinds of
Rong, Di, and Yi peoples that had long maintained cultural and political
independence were absorbed by Qi. This potential for growth did not exist
for such states of the Central Plain as Cai, Wey, Song, and Zheng. As a result,
Qi became the first power to become *Ba*.

Qi Huan Gong and his advisor Guan Zhong 管仲 (ca. 730–645 B.C.)
jointly brought Qi to an unprecedented status of leadership in the entire
Zhou world.[16] What they managed to achieve was not necessarily due to the
above mentioned favorable conditions; it was due more to their success in
reorganizing the state of Qi and in their clear definition of the mission of
the *Ba*.

Reorganization of the state of Qi was probably the first of numerous
reform efforts that occurred in the Spring and Autumn and in the Warring
States periods. Vassal states of Zhou feudalism had been organized hierarchically in a social pyramid, in which each level represented a member of the
nobility who managed his own inherited fief. A ruler of the state could call
on subordinates to contribute a certain portion of the resources that they
controlled. In addition, aristocrats were related to each other by a kinship
network, the ruling house representing the stem of this network and exercising patriarchal authority. Theoretically, all noblemen were vassals of
the king. The reform led by Guan Zhong changed this feudal structure
drastically.

The state of Qi was divided into fifteen units termed *xiang* 鄉,[17] the lord
of the state and his two senior ministers, each commanding five units. Traders
and artisans in the state capital who were not required to render military
service were divided into six units. In the capital region, the *guo ren* (people
of the state) and *ye ren* (people in the field) were each divided into four levels
of administration. In both cases, civil and military functions were united in
one level, the administrators of which reported to their direct superiors and
eventually to the ruler. The performance of officers at all levels was judged,
as well as rewarded or punished accordingly.[18] If our sources are dependable,
this administrative structure should have provided Qi with the capability to
mobilize human and material resources more effectively than other Zhou
states, which remained loosely structured.

The mission of the *ba* system came to be defined by historical events. For

[15] Wang Gesen and Tang Zhiqing, *Qi guo shi* (Ji'nan: Shandong Renmin, 1992), pp. 174–8; also, *Shi ji*
32, pp. 1477–94.
[16] For the question of Guan Zhong's role, see Sydney Rosen, "In Search of the Historical Kuan Chung,"
JAS 35, 3 (1975): 431–40.
[17] *Xiang* demarcated territorial jurisdictions without reference to ownership or hereditary tenure.
[18] Wang Geshen and Tang Zhiqing, *Qi guo shi*, pp. 182–4; *Guo yu*, 6 ("Qi yu"), 4a–6b.

various reasons, the Zhou states were either indebted to Qi for its assistance or were subjugated by it in military engagements. One state after another fell into line, becoming followers of Qi. In 667 B.C., Huan Gong convened the rulers of Lu, Song, Chen, and Zheng for a conference in which he was elected leader of these Zhou states. Subsequently, King Hui of Zhou (r. 676–652 B.C.), who had recently put down a challenge to his rule by his own brother, dispatched a high-ranking minister to Qi to confer on Huan Gong the title of *Ba* and the privilege of undertaking military actions on behalf of the royal court. The very first assignment was to launch a campaign in 671 B.C. against Wey, which had assisted King Hui's brother in his challenge to the king. This marked the official recognition of Qi's status as *Ba*.[19] Subsequently, Qi intervened in a power struggle in Lu, effectively establishing its leadership credibility. In a series of actions, Huan Gong seems to have clarified the mission of the *Ba*; it was by no means intended to be sheer hegemony through military might, but rather to restore the authority of the Son of Heaven. In other words, the *Ba* was supposed to serve the function of guardian of the Zhou feudal system.

Meanwhile, the non-Zhou peoples posed a serious threat to the security of the Zhou world. In the north, several confrontations occurred almost at the same time. The Rong tribes in the highland regions of northern and eastern Hebei attacked the state of Yan (located near present-day Beijing). In 664 B.C., Qi and Lu planned to help Yan. However, afraid of the strength of the Rong, Lu backed out. Huan Gong nevertheless sent troops deep into the mountains to launch attacks on the Rong, and Yan was saved.[20]

Among the Di in the north, the Chi Di were the strongest. In 662 B.C., they invaded the state of Xing 邢, located in the central part of Hebei. Guan Zhong insisted that Qi should give military aid to Xing for the sake of solidarity among the Hua Xia world. In 659 B.C., Xing collapsed under an assault by the Di. Huan Gong led Qi troops, as well as troops from Song and Cao, to the rescue, driving the Di away. No sooner was victory declared than Huan Gong escorted the Xing people to a safe area where a new city was built for them with provisions supplied by Qi. A Qi garrison unit was stationed in Xing to protect it from further Di intrusions.

When in 660 B.C. the Chi Di also attacked Wey, killing the Wey ruler and occupying the capital city, Huan Gong again led Qi troops to reestablish Wey, bringing a few thousand of the Wey refugees to settle at a new site. One of the sons of the deceased ruler of Wey was then authorized to rule the

---

[19] *Zuo zhuan*, 10 (Zhuang 27), 11b (Legge, *The Chinese Classics*, vol. 5, p. 112).

[20] *Zuo zhuan*, 10 (Zhuang 30), 18b–19a (Legge, *The Chinese Classics*, vol. 5, pp. 117–18); *Shi ji* 32, p. 1488.

restored state, while a Qi detachment was stationed there to provide protection until it regained the capacity for self-defense.[21]

The successful rescue and restoration of these three Zhou states established Huan Gong's credibility as leader of the Zhou world. Huan Gong next needed to stop the expansion of Chu. Chu was a giant state in the Yangzi valley where over a few centuries numerous southern non-Zhou people had gradually formed political entities. The Zhou court had tried to stretch its influence into the south without any sustained success. Near the end of the Western Zhou, Chu emerged as a significant power. In 706 B.C., a Chu leader attacked Sui 隨 (in the northern part of Hubei) and adopted the title of king, which was supposedly a perquisite of the Zhou royal house. This is the first time that Chu showed such ambitions.[22]

Within two generations, Chu expanded northward by annexing territories of the non-Zhou peoples in the Huai River valley, as well as several minor Zhou states in the Han River valley. Chu's threat to the Zhou world appeared serious, as the states in the southern part of the Central Plain, such as Zheng, often fell victim to its northward movement. Qi therefore had to take action to curb Chu's expansion. In 656 B.C., Huan Gong led an allied force of eight states on campaign against Cai, which had been forced by Chu to become its satellite. Cai fell and Chu was compelled to attend an interstate conference at Shaoling 召陵 called by Huan Gong. This was the first such compulsory meeting attended by heads of state or their most prominent nobles at which the presiding state was the *Ba*, de facto leader of the interstate community. Huan Gong had set a precedent for *Ba* politics.[23]

Interstate Meetings

The Shaoling conference was followed by several other interstate meetings convened by Huan Gong, some of which were for military actions, while others were for reconfirming the existence of the interstate order. Nominally, the Zhou royal court sent a high-ranking official to supervise these conferences, and both Huan Gong and Guan Zhong paid due respect to the royal envoys, as well as to the royal decrees. By such means, Qi demonstrated its determination to restore royal authority. Moreover, at these conferences the attending delegates usually swore their support for the Zhou feudal structure

[21] *Zuo zhuan*, 11 (Min 1), 9a–11a (Legge, *The Chinese Classics*, vol. 5, pp. 129–30).
[22] *Zuo zhuan*, 6 (Huan 6), 16b–20b (Legge, *The Chinese Classics*, vol. 5, pp. 48–9). For recent scholarship on Chu studies, see Barry B. Blakeley, "Recent Developments in Chu Studies: A Bibliographical and Institutional Overview," *EC* 11–12 (1985–7): 371–87, 446; and for the early development of Chu, Barry B. Blakeley, "In Search of Danyang I: Historical Geography and Archaeological Sites," *EC* 13 (1988): 116–52.
[23] *Zuo zhuan*, 12 (Xi 4), 10b–13a (Legge, *The Chinese Classics*, vol. 5, pp. 140–2).

as spelled out in formal agreements. In an agreement signed in 657 B.C., Huan Gong had urged the allies: "Let there be no damming of irrigation water, no withholding sales of grain, no changes of heir apparents, no promoting of concubines to replace wives, and no involvement of women in state affairs."[24]

An agreement adopted at Kuiqiu 葵丘 in 651 B.C., recorded in the *Mencius*, stipulates five items:

First, slay the unfilial; change not the one who has been appointed heir; exalt not a concubine to be the wife. Second, honor the worthy and maintain the talented to give distinction to the virtuous. Third, respect the old, and be kind to the young; be not forgetful of strangers and travelers. Fourth, let not office be hereditary, nor let officers simultaneously hold more than one office, and in the selection of officers let the object be to get the proper men, and let not a ruler take onto himself to put to death a great officer. Fifth, make no crooked embankments, and impose no restriction on the sale of grain, and let no boundary markers [be] set without announcement.[25]

Three of these items seem to concern household affairs and the general principle of appointment of worthy and capable people. However, in Zhou feudalism patriarchy was an integral element of the state's structure; for this reason, it appeared relevant to maintain order within the households of the various ruling states. Two items related to the role of officials and to the prevention of hereditary tenure of positions; these should be regarded as a new trend breaking away from the feudal tradition of hereditary government positions. The restrictions against irrigation, hoarding grain, and establishing new borders were measures that guaranteed interstate cooperation and mutual respect of boundaries. In short, Huan Gong used his *Ba* leadership to set up a new order for an interstate community that was to be guarded by consensus rather than authority. As for actual deeds, Huan Gong repeatedly fended off invasions of non-Zhou peoples against Zhou states and settled succession disputes in the royal house, as well as in the important Zhou states of Jin and Wey.[26] For more than forty years, he brought order to the Zhou world and halted the expansion of the non-Zhou peoples, both the Rong and Di in the north and the newly emerging Chu in the south. This was a new kind of political unification, a system of interstate community.

In 645 B.C., Guan Zhong died. An ageing Huan Gong, having lost his major advisor, failed to keep his own state in order. In 643 B.C., he died. Five of his sons contended to succeed him; Qi's status as *Ba* thus came to an end.[27]

---

[24] *Chunqiu Guliang zhuan*, 8 (Xi 9), 8.5b–6a.

[25] *Mencius*, 6/2 (Legge, *The Chinese Classics, Vol. 2: The Works of Mencius*, p. 437); see also, Hsu, *Ancient China in Transition*, p. 54.

[26] Wang Geshen and Tang Zhiqing, *Qi guo shi*, pp. 215–18.

[27] *Zuo zhuan*, 14 (Xi 17), 18a (Legge, *The Chinese Classics*, vol. 5, p. 173).

The Leadership of Jin

After the death of Qi Huan Gong, his son Qi Xiao Gong 孝公 (r. 642–633
B.C.) and Song Xiang Gong 宋襄公 (r. 650–637 B.C.) attempted to claim the
Ba leadership. Both failed. The new leadership was soon established by Jin
Wen Gong (r. 636–628 B.C.); Jin leadership was to last for three generations.
Under the leadership of Jin the stage of interstate activities extended beyond
the Central Plain to include peripheral areas such as Qin and Chu. This was
a continuation of the earlier extensions, Zheng's domination of the heartland
of the Central Plain, and then Qi's even wider influence. It is yet another
step in the process by which individual ethnic and cultural entities joined to
form a common Chinese community.

Jin was founded by Tangshu Yu 唐叔虞, a son of King Wu of Zhou (r.
1049/45–1043 B.C.), at the beginning of the dynasty. Jin was originally located
in the southern part of Shanxi, on the north side of the Yellow River from
the Zhou eastern capital of Chengzhou. It was included among the Zhou
vassal states in order to shield the Zhou eastern capital from northern threats.
Indeed, Tangshu Yu brought Zhou troops and several lineages of surrendered
Shang people to Jin, while the native populations were mainly the remains
of the old nations of Xia, which according to tradition was the first of the
Three Dynasties. Jin also had within its territory some Rong peoples related
to other Rong active in the mountain areas to the north. Therefore, when
Jin was established, instructions were given to Tangshu Yu to use Jin's laws
and administrative regulations to integrate the customs of the Xia and the
Rong.[28]

The state of Jin fulfilled its function quite well. With the collapse of
Western Zhou, Jin joined Zheng and other states to help King Ping in the
succession crisis and to set up the new court in the east. Ironically, Jin itself
soon suffered from succession struggles. In 746 B.C., Jin, needing to guard
against possible disturbances from the Rong people, established a subsidiary
state at Quwo 曲沃, a strategic spot north of the Jin capital. This Quwo
branch rapidly developed into a power center that challenged Jin's own
authority. After prolonged struggles, the Quwo branch replaced the original
house of Jin, with Wu Gong 武公 of Quwo (r. 715–677 B.C.) being recognized by the royal court as duke of Jin in 678 B.C.[29]

This change in the Jin ruling house coincided with a more profound
change in its state structure. During the reign of Jin Xian Gong 晉獻公

---

[28] *Zuo zhuan*, 54 (Ding 4), 19a (Legge, *The Chinese Classics*, vol. 5, pp. 754–5).
[29] *Shi ji*, 39, pp. 1635–9; Li Mengcun and Chang Jincang, *Jin guo shi gangyao* (Taiyuan: Shanxi Renmin,
  1988), pp. 17–19. For archaeological excavations of early Jin sites, see Zou Heng, "Lun zaoqi Jin du,"
  Wenwu 1994.1: 29–34.

(r. 676–651 B.C.), the lord plotted to extinguish all powerful scions of the former rulers. This meant that Jin would not need to bear the burden of distributing its resources among members of the ruling house, an unprecedented break from the Zhou feudalism that required overlapping lineage segmentation.[30]

Served by capable assistants who were not members of the ruling house, Xian Gong gathered unchallenged power with which he conquered no fewer than sixteen small states located in present-day Shanxi. A number of Rong and Di peoples were also absorbed by Jin. Jin's territory and population expanded to such an extent that it became many times more powerful than it had been formerly.[31]

The death of Xian Gong triggered a succession struggle among his sons. Jin's western neighbor Qin was deeply involved in similar struggles. Within a century of the departure of the Western Zhou court from the Wei River valley, Qin had gradually taken control of it and organized a state with a multiethnic, multicultural population. However, at this time Qin did not participate in interstate activities. Like Jin, Qin was also located in a peripheral area with ample space to expand, and perhaps even more so than Jin, was unrestricted by a traditional background. As such, it constituted an inhibiting factor against the rise of Jin. Conflicts between the two created two highly militarized states. They both emerged as formidable powers in the Zhou world.[32]

By the mid-seventh century B.C., the Zhou world was dominated by four powers: Qi, Jin, Qin, and Chu. All four of these powers were located in the peripheries, while those states in the Central Plain, such as Zheng, Song, Lu, and Wey, were becoming ever less important in interstate politics. Among the four major players, Jin and Chu played the central roles on this historical state for the next two centuries.

The *ba* system organized by Jin Wen Gong 晉文公 (r. 636–628 B.C.) was an important milestone in the history of that period. Wen Gong was a son of Xian Gong, who had already consolidated Jin into a strong state. As already mentioned, after Xian Gong's death Jin was once again faced with a succession struggle. Wen Gong was in exile while his rivals ruled in his absence. After nineteen years of drifting from state to state, Wen Gong returned home to take over the then exhausted state of Jin.

Assisted by a group of extraordinarily capable followers, Wen Gong almost

---

[30] *Zuo zhuan*, 10 (Zhuang 23), 2b (Legge, *The Chinese Classics*, vol. 5, p. 106); 10 (Zhuang 24), 5b (Legge, *The Chinese Classics*, vol. 5, p. 108); 10 (Zhuang 25), 8b (Legge, *The Chinese Classics*, vol. 5, p. 110); 21 (Xuan 2), 12b–13a (Legge, *The Chinese Classics*, vol. 5, p. 291).

[31] Li Mengcun and Chang Jincang, *Jin guo shi gangyao*, pp. 23–5.

[32] Ibid., pp. 26–33.

immediately brought stability to Jin. In 635 B.C., King Xiang of Zhou (r. 651–619 B.C.) was challenged by his brother Zhao 朝 and fled from the capital. The exiled king requested help from Jin and Qin. Jin Wen Gong promptly responded to the royal call. Having declined assistance offered by Qin, he sent troops to escort the king back to the capital. To mark his gratitude, King Xiang bestowed upon Jin several territories in the vicinity of the royal capital. Thus, Jin gained not only prestige but also a foothold in the core of the Central Plain.[33]

The Emergence of Chu

For almost a decade after the death of Qi Huan Gong (643 B.C.), there was no recognized leader among the Zhou states. Not checked by effective resistance that any such leader might offer, Chu moved farther north. Its immediate targets were Song and Zheng, whose exposure on the southern edge of the Central Plain made them easy prey for Chu encroachment.

The first confrontation between Jin and Chu took place in 633 B.C., when Song was besieged by a Chu army. Jin took immediate action, expanding the number of its armies to three. Instead of sending reinforcements directly to relieve Song from its siege, Jin's forces went to attack Cao and Wei, both of which by then were satellite states of Chu. In 632 B.C., Jin led 700 of its own war chariots and was joined by troops from Qi, Qin, and Song, confronting Chu at Chengpu 城濮, where it won a decisive victory.[34]

Not only did Jin's victory in this battle curb Chu's northward expansion, but its contribution to the protection of the Zhou world was duly recognized. Shortly after the battle was won, Wen Gong presided at an interstate conference at Jiantu 踐土. Rulers of seven states as well as King Xiang of Zhou himself attended the meeting. Jin led the lords in affirming their loyalty to the royal authority; in turn, the king conferred on Wen Gong the status of *Ba*.[35]

Although Chu was defeated at the battle of Chengpu, it did not lose its formidable strength, nor did it give up efforts to invade the north. The pattern of Jin–Chu confrontation was one of precarious balance. Those Zhou states located along the southern front of the Central Plain were constantly under pressure from both Jin and Chu, turning the area into a battleground.

[33] *Zuo zhuan*, 15 (Xi 23–4), 8a–24b (Legge, *The Chinese Classics*, vol. 5, pp. 1186–7, 190–3); 16 (Xi 25), 1b–6a (Legge, *The Chinese Classics*, vol. 5, pp. 195–6).
[34] *Zuo zhuan*, 15 (Xi 23), 7b (Legge, *The Chinese Classics*, vol. 5, p. 187); 15 (Xi 24), 23b (Legge, *The Chinese Classics*, vol. 5, p. 193); 16 (Xi 26), 8a, b (Legge, *The Chinese Classics*, vol. 5, p. 199).
[35] *Zuo zhuan*, 16 (Xi 27), 10a (Legge, *The Chinese Classics*, vol. 5, pp. 201–202); 16 (Xi 28), 19a–27a (Legge, *The Chinese Classics*, vol. 5, pp. 207–11).

After Wen Gong died in 628 B.C., Chu once again gained the upper hand, defeating Jin at Mi 邲 in 598 B.C.[36]

To maintain its status as *ba*, Jin needed to keep the northern states in line, but Qin and Qi, both being strong powers, sometimes challenged Jin's leadership. By this point the interstate power struggle had become a four-sided affair. Immediately after the death of Jin Wen Gong, Qin attacked Zheng, a close ally of Jin. Qin's army was ambushed and defeated by Jin forces in 627 B.C., and then Qin was invaded by Jin in 625 B.C. In 624, Qin sought revenge, forcing Jin to retreat.[37]

For some time thereafter, a stalemate ensued on Jin's western front. In the east, Qi was also trying to regain its influence. In 589 B.C., Jin defeated Qi, which had invaded Lu and Wey.[38] Since Chu was too strong to be defeated outright, Jin adopted a new strategy, grooming the southern state of Wu, located in the lower reaches of the Yangzi River, to be an ally in Chu's rear. Chu subsequently had to fight simultaneously on two fronts.[39]

Caught in this struggle among the four states, in 580 B.C. Jin Li Gong 晉厲公 (r. 580–573 B.C.) restored good relations with Qi and Qin, so that the northern states were temporarily united to face the Chu threat. The state of Song, however, long exhausted by the constant conflicts between Jin and Chu, sought peace among the contending powers. In 579 B.C., a minister of Song arranged a conference for Jin, Chu, Qi, Qin, and others to declare a truce. The four powers also agreed to limit their military strength, thus providing one of the earliest records in history of interstate disarmament.[40]

Just as with other disarmaments in history, peace did not last long. Skirmishes between Chu and the northern states in 575 B.C. escalated into another large-scale confrontation, with Jin and its allies defeating Chu at Yanling 鄢陵 in 574 B.C.[41] An arrogant and over-confident Li Gong attempted to get rid of some of his powerful ministers. However, he was killed in a coup d'état in 574 B.C., being succeeded by Dao Gong 悼公 (r. 572–558 B.C.). During Dao Gong's reign, not only did Jin restore internal peace, but it also managed to regain the respect of the other states. This was due both to political reforms that enlisted the services of the best talents of Jin and especially to his policy

[36] *Zuo zhuan*, 23 (Xuan 1), 15a (Legge, *The Chinese Classics*, vol. 5, p. 310); 23 (Xuan 12) 3b–22a (Legge, *The Chinese Classics*, vol. 5, pp. 316–21).

[37] *Zuo zhuan*, 17 (Xi 32, 33), 10b–16b (Legge, *The Chinese Classics*, vol. 5, pp. 221, 224–5); 18 (Wen 2, 3), 10a (ibid., p. 233), 18.19a (Legge, *The Chinese Classics*, vol. 5, pp. 236–7).

[38] *Zuo zhuan*, 25 (Wen 2), 8b–16b (Legge, *The Chinese Classics*, vol. 5, pp. 344–6).

[39] *Zuo zhuan*, 26 (Cheng 7), 16a–17b (Legge, *The Chinese Classics*, vol. 5, pp. 363–4).

[40] *Zuo zhuan*, 27 (Cheng 12), 5a (Legge, *The Chinese Classics*, vol. 5, pp. 378–9).

[41] *Zuo zhuan*, 28 (Cheng 16, 17), 3b–14a (Legge, *The Chinese Classics*, vol. 5, pp. 395–8).

of pacifying the Rong people, through which Jin gained both internal stability and also the Rong land and population.[42] With this, Dao Gong was recognized as *Ba*.

A MULTISTATE SYSTEM

By the sixth century B.C., ancient China had gradually developed a multistate system. The four major powers, Jin, Chu, Qi, and Qin, had each acquired a sphere of domination, while the status of the Zhou royal house had become even further reduced. Both Jin and Chu realized that they had to coexist with the other powers, especially Qi and Qin in the east and west, respectively. Thus, the claim of dependence on a *Ba* to hold the Zhou states together was no longer meaningful. Even the cultural identity claimed by the Zhou against the non-Zhou was no longer convincing, since the process of assimilation had blurred such distinctions; each of the contending states had incorporated among its population various ethnic and cultural groups; for example, Jin had expanded to include Rong and Di lands, while Chu gained several satellites that were former Zhou states, such as Cai and Sui.

A Balance of Power

These developments had a profound impact on the last century of the Spring and Autumn period. Once again it was the states of Zheng and Song in the Central Plain that initiated a new type of interstate alignment. The ministers of these two states lamented that their locations made them vulnerable, caught in the midst of the seesaw struggles between Jin and Chu. Zheng especially suffered from the repeated wars.[43]

Song Xu 宋戌, a minister of Song, persuaded the prime ministers of Jin and Chu to hold an interstate peace conference. With their consent, Song Xu invited them, as well as ministers of Qi, Qin, and other states, to meet at Shangqiu 商丘 in 546 B.C. The peace agreement they reached provided that the various satellite states of Jin and Chu should pay court visits to these two powers; Qi and Qin were not to be held to this obligation because they were independent powers. In fact, Qi and Qin each claimed a few neighboring states as being within their own spheres of influence. For each of these major powers, there was to be a limit on the number of their war chariots.

---

[42] *Zuo zhuan*, 28 (Cheng 17), 23b–26b (Legge, *The Chinese Classics*, vol. 5, pp. 404–406); 29 (Xiang 3), 29.12a–14b (Legge, *The Chinese Classics*, vol. 5, p. 420).

[43] *Zuo zhuan*, 22 (Xuan 11), 115b–16b (Legge, *The Chinese Classics*, vol. 5, p. 310); 30 (Xiang 9), 28a–33a (Legge, *The Chinese Classics*, vol. 5, pp. 440–1).

The satellite states were clearly informed of the extent of the contributions they were to present to the major powers.[44]

For forty years thereafter there was no military conflict between Jin and Chu. Nevertheless, while the states in the north were temporarily spared the calamity of frequent wars, a new round of struggles began in the south. Among the lands in the lower reaches of the Yangzi valley, Wu 吳 and Yue 越 arose to challenge Chu, and also engaged in struggles for supremacy in their own regions.

The Rise of Wu and Yue

The state of Wu had allegedly been established by an uncle of King Wen of Zhou (r. 1099–1050 B.C.). But even if its ruling house was in fact related to Zhou, which seems doubtful, the population of Wu was still made up of native peoples of the southern region. Wu had not been at all active in the first part of the Spring and Autumn period, but by 583 B.C., when Jin and Chu were engaged in a series of wars, a former Chu minister who had sought refuge in Jin suggested that Jin should send aid to Wu in order to have an ally to the south of Chu. This strategy seems to have been very effective; after exchanges with Jin advisors, Wu annexed the land of several of Chu's former subordinates and began to take part in the interstate meetings in the north.[45] Wu's strategy was to maintain pressure on Chu by periodically sending one-third of its standing army to attack different areas of Chu. Chu had to keep fully alert at all times, while Wu only needed to use a portion of its capacity. Chu therefore became exhausted. In 506 B.C., Wu launched a full-scale invasion of Chu, defeating it in five consecutive battles and bringing it to the edge of total collapse.[46]

Chu had now lost its unchallenged leadership of the south. Wu's position, however, was by no means unchallenged, since Yue, another southern power located next to it, also claimed to be related to another of the Three Dynasties in the north, in this case Xia. Like Wu's claim to have been related to the Zhou royal house, this claim is also doubtful. Indeed, Yue never concealed the fact that its cultural background was that of coastal dwellers, a background shared by numerous subgroups of people referred to as the various Yue (Bai Yue 百越). The early history of this state is by no means clear. It seems that Wu and Yue were recognized in literary sources as appear-

---

[44] *Zuo zhuan*, 38 (Xiang 27), 6a–8b (Legge, *The Chinese Classics*, vol. 5, pp. 533–5); 39 (Xiang 29), 7b (Legge, *The Chinese Classics*, vol. 5, p. 549); 46 (Zhao 13), 16b–18b (Legge, *The Chinese Classics*, vol. 5, pp. 651–3).

[45] *Zuo zhuan*, 26 (Cheng 7), 16a–17b (Legge, *The Chinese Classics*, vol. 5, pp. 363–4).

[46] *Zuo zhuan*, 53 (Zhao 30), 15b–17a (Legge, *The Chinese Classics*, vol. 5, pp. 734–5); 54 (Ding 4), 22a–27b (Legge, *The Chinese Classics*, vol. 5, pp. 755–7).

ing almost simultaneously as a "contending pair" in the south. Beginning in
510 B.C., when Wu invaded Yue, they battled with each other constantly to
control the fertile rice-growing land of the Yangzi delta.

In 496 B.C., the king of Wu died of wounds suffered in an invasion of
Yue. Three years later, King Fuchai 夫差 (r. 495–474 B.C.), avenging the death
of his father, defeated Yue decisively, forcing its king, Goujian 勾踐 (r.
496–465 B.C.), to surrender to Wu.[47] After his victory, an over-confident King
Fuchai had ambitions to become *Ba*. In 486 B.C., Wu began to dig a canal
to link the Central Plain with the south. This was to be the first of several
such efforts, which did not finally succeed until the completion of the Grand
Canal more than a thousand years later during the Sui dynasty (A.D. 589–618).
In the next year, Wu defeated Qi. Extending the canal westward as far as
present-day Henan, Wu challenged Jin for the status as *Ba*. Confronted with
the best army of the time, Jin yielded, allowing Wu to preside at an interstate conference held at Huangchi 黃池 in 482 B.C. This marked the zenith
of Wu's leadership.[48]

King Fuchai's moment of glory did not last long. King Goujian of
Yue was anxious for revenge. With the remnants of his army consisting of
only 5,000 men, he attempted in every way possible to increase Yue's manpower and to store up food and wealth. He vowed that he would devote
one decade to the task of regaining Yue's strength and another decade to
training his people. Taking advantage of King Fuchai's maneuvers in the
north, with the main body of the Wu army away, King Goujian attacked
Wu. Wu's capital, named Wu, fell and Fuchai's heir apparent was killed.
Fuchai rushed back from Huangchi to negotiate a temporary peace with Yue,
but Goujian refused to give Fuchai the sort of opportunity to regain strength
of which he had availed himself earlier. Instead, Yue launched another full-
scale invasion in 473 B.C. Besieged for three years, Wu finally fell and Fuchai
hanged himself. These events took place just two decades after Yue had fallen
to Wu, thus fulfilling the previously humiliated Goujian's timetable for
revenge.[49]

Yue temporarily became the strongest power of the time. Even before Wu
had been completely defeated, the northern states had already looked to Yue
as a potential *Ba*. For instance, Lu Ai Gong 魯哀公 sought Yue's intervention in a power struggle in Lu.[50] After Wu fell, Goujian led his triumphant
army to a conference of rulers and delegates of the northern states at Xuzhou

[47] *Zuo zhuan*, 53 (Zhao 32), 22b (Legge, *The Chinese Classics*, vol. 5, p. 740); 56 (Ding 14), 16b (Legge,
     The Chinese Classics, vol. 5, p. 788); 57 (Ai 1), 2b–5a (Legge, *The Chinese Classics*, vol. 5, p. 794).
[48] *Zuo zhuan*, 59 (Ai 13), 7a–10b (Legge, *The Chinese Classics*, vol. 5, pp. 832–3).
[49] *Zuo zhuan*, 60 (Ai 20), 15a–16a (Legge, *The Chinese Classics*, vol. 5, pp. 853–4).
[50] *Zuo zhuan*, 60 (Ai 24), 19b (Legge, *The Chinese Classics*, vol. 5, p. 855).

徐州. From there, Yue sent tribute to the Zhou royal court, a gesture signifying its status as *Ba*. This conference was the last at which a *Ba* was recognized. The end of the struggle between Wu and Yue probably marks the end of the *ba* system. Indeed, Sima Qian 司馬遷 (ca. 145–86 B.C.), the grand historian of the Han dynasty, assigned the first year of his Table of the Six States (*Liu guo nianbiao* 六國年表) to 475 B.C.; this symbolized the beginning of a new era.[51]

The Transformation of the Ba System

To sum up the development of the *ba* system, it was initiated by Qi; fully realized by Jin, which held it continuously for more than eighty years; and ended with the short periods during which Wu and Yue claimed that status. In the meantime, however, Qin had gained control of the western region, establishing itself as a regional power. Chu, once the target of campaigns to expel it, not only evolved into another regional power, but once shared joint *ba* status with Jin. Indeed, the entire history of the *ba* system was a process of realigning states, both Zhou and non-Zhou, for the sake of establishing a new multistate order. The purpose of this system was originally supposed to be to restore royal authority; however, rather than restoring it, the *ba* replaced it.

In conventional Chinese historiography, the *Ba* was supposed to be the protector of the Hua Xia states in the Central Plain; that is, the defender of Chinese culture against foreign or barbarian cultural influence. In reality, ever since the state of Zheng faded out of the struggle for leadership, all of the states that held the *ba* status arose outside of the Central Plain. Several of them (i.e., Chu, Wu, and Yue) were decidedly of non-Hua Xia ethnic and cultural origin. Even Qi and Jin, though being old Zhou states, had also absorbed numerous non-Zhou (Yi, Rong, and Di) elements, thus becoming ethnically and culturally mixed entities themselves. Despite the bias that views the Yellow River valley as the heartland of Chinese civilization, the archaeological sources discussed in the preceding chapter have made abundantly clear that these peripheral areas around the Central Plain were not at all underdeveloped by comparison with the Zhou states.

The history of the Spring and Autumn period not only witnessed an expansion of the Zhou world toward its peripheries; it perhaps also testifies to an aggregation of several independently developed regional ethnic and cultural clusters into a large, multistate, multicultural system setting the stage for the further interaction and integration that took place in the subsequent

---

[51] *Shi ji*, 15, p. 687.

Warring States period. Though ostensibly an effort to preserve the Zhou cultural and political order, the *ba* system actually served to transform this order, laying the foundation for the eventual empire of the Qin and Han periods. This transformation was not just political in nature, but also extended into social, economic, and intellectual spheres. The tremendous changes in these spheres will be outlined in the following sections.

SOCIAL DEVELOPMENTS

During the heyday of Zhou feudalism, there were hundreds of small states. The feudal structure depended on the relationship between the lord and these vassal states, and on a kinship system known as *zongfa* 宗法. The supreme lord was the Zhou king, upon whom the Mandate of Heaven or rule was considered to have been bestowed on a hereditary basis. As the Son of Heaven, the king enfeoffed relatives to be rulers of vassal states. Since the king and these rulers were members of the same royal house, their descendants were also related (though, it should be added, there were also rulers of vassal states who were not Zhou kinsmen but were related to the Zhou royal house by matrimonial ties). In the respective states, the rulers were served by ministers (*qing* 卿) and high officers (*dafu* 大夫) who were again kinsmen. Each of these kinsmen had his own household, fief, and domain. The lowest ranking Zhou aristocrats were the *shi* 士, also related to their lords by blood or by marriage. The *shi* was a class of men similar to the *samurai* of medieval Japan. Originally serving as soldiers, often itinerant, by the end of the Spring and Autumn period they would develop into a distinct social and cultural elite.

Kinship Structure

In theory, the *zongfa* system provided for the succession of the Zhou kings and the rulers of the various states by primogeniture. In each generation, the eldest son took his place in the "principal lineage" (*da zong* 大宗). Within the various states, the feudal lineages were the principal lineages of all Zhou nobles, though these were of lesser status than the royal lineage, while the lineages of *qing* or *dafu* were similarly of still lesser status. In short, the Zhou feudal network was organized along patriarchal lines and in hierarchical order; political authority depended on hierarchy within the kinship group.

Any idealized framework exists only in theory. So too was the Zhou *zongfa* system little more than a principle of organization. In the Western Zhou period, the system was sustained by the maintenance of mutual relations between lord and vassals, mediated through elaborate rituals such as court visits, renewals of oaths and vows, reconfirmations of appointments, and so on. Many bronze inscriptions testify to these practices.[52]

Zhou feudalism served the pragmatic function of ruling an extensive territory by delegating authority to lords who in turn led detachments of troops, both Zhou and non-Zhou, to garrison strategic locations. These lords, especially those in the eastern territories, supported each other and were supported by the resources of the Zhou eastern capital. In turn, tribute sent to the royal house enriched all of the ruling houses who participated in this network. For all of the Zhou elite, it was to their common advantage that the ruling machinery should be sustained. This is probably one reason why the Western Zhou lasted for almost three centuries.[53]

After Zhou royal authority collapsed, cohesion among the members of the feudal structure dissolved. As mentioned above the wounding of the Zhou king by an army led by Zheng Zhuang Gong while he held a high ministerial position in the royal court symbolized much more than a physical injury to the king's body; it signified the bankruptcy of the Zhou feudal order.

An expansion of territory is a characteristic of all major states, and the four most powerful states of the Spring and Autumn period – Qi, Jin, Chu, and Qin – all expanded dramatically. Qi Huan Gong annexed 35 neighboring states to become the first *ba*. Jin Xian Gong took 17 states and subjugated 38, paving the way for Jin to lead the Zhou world for generations. Qin Mu Gong 秦穆公 (659–621 B.C.) combined 12 other states to extend its territory in the west. During the reign of King Zhuang 莊王 of Chu (613–591 B.C.), Chu annexed no fewer than 26 states, many of which were former important Zhou states, and thus became the main threat to the Zhou world.[54] Of 148 states that appear in the chronicles of the Spring and Autumn period,[55] the number extinguished by these four major powers adds up to 128.

Even Jin's *ba* status was achieved on the basis of expansion. When Jin annexed other states there was little concern as to whether they were of the same family, that is, having the surname Ji 姬, which was the surname of the Zhou royal household. A Jin minister is quoted as saying in 544 B.C.:

Yu 虞, Guo 虢, Jiao 焦, Hua 滑, He 霍, Yang 揚, Hann 韓, and Wei 魏 were all states of the surname Ji. This is how Jin grew to be a large state. If we had not taken

[52] Hsu and Linduff, *Western Chou Civilization*, pp. 177–85.
[53] Ibid., pp. 123–6, 183–8.
[54] *Xunzi* (*Sibu beiyao*, ed.), 3.13b (Zhongni 7); *Han Feizi* (*Sibu beiyao*, ed.), 2.1a (Youdu 6), 3.7a–b (Shiguo 10), 15.13a (Naner 37).
[55] Gu Donggao, *Chunqiu dashi biao*, chart 5.

over the smaller states, where would be the gain? Ever since the reigns of Wu Gong and Xiang Gong, Jin annexed many states. Who bothered to investigate?[56]

When Wen Gong received several cities bestowed upon him as royal gifts, he subjugated the populations within them, despite the fact that all of these people were related to the royal family.[57] The previously treasured kinship bonds were totally ignored. Family sentiments did not count any more.

Within the states as well, old kinship structures were also drastically weakened. It is especially ironic, however, that Zhou feudalism, which was explicitly built upon kinship relations, was undermined by internal power struggles. This phenomenon became noticeable as early as late Western Zhou, even before the final collapse of the dynasty.

For over a century (751–636 B.C.), Jin had been haunted by a series of succession crises. As already recounted, the minor Quwo branch took power after a long civil war. Generation after generation of brethren killed each other. Every ruler came to power through military action, often aided by other states. The most brutal episode was Xian Gong's murder of all of the descendants of the preceding rulers. In time, Xian Gong's own sons proceeded to kill each other until the last one, Wen Gong, finally came to power in 636 B.C. Wen Gong established a standing policy whereby not a single member of the ruling house should be given a position at the Jin court. In 606 B.C. even the name Gongzu 公族, literally "of the house of the *gong*, or lord," was assigned to children of ministers rather than to the true members of the Jin ruling house.[58]

In Zheng, a civil war between Zhuang Gong and his brother Gongshu 共叔 was the first such conflict in the Spring and Autumn period. Thereafter, succession crises occurred in Zheng for three generations.[59] In Qi, Huan Gong, who was to become the first *ba* of the new interstate order, also suffered the effects of a civil war, and after his death, his own funeral was delayed because of a power struggle among his own sons.[60]

Similar stories of conflict and fighting took place in virtually every state during this period. The ethics of Zhou feudalism were abused and ignored. Gone with the feudal system was the spirit of solidarity among members of the Zhou world. Indeed, the collapse of Zhou feudalism should be interpreted as the dissolution of an imagined community, a community built around the concept of the Zhou world.

---

[56]   *Zuo zhuan*, 39 (Xiang 29), 8a (Legge, *The Chinese Classics*, vol. 5, p. 549).
[57]   *Guo yu*, 2 ("Zhou yu B"), 4b.
[58]   *Zuo zhuan*, 21 (Xuan 2), 12b–14a (Legge, *The Chinese Classics*, vol. 5, p. 291).
[59]   *Zuo zhuan*, 2 (Yin 1), 15a (Legge, *The Chinese Classics*, vol. 5, pp. 5–6).
[60]   *Zuo zhuan*, 8 (Zhuang 8), 18b–19a (Legge, *The Chinese Classics*, vol. 5, pp. 82–4); 14 (Xi 17), 18a (Legge, *The Chinese Classics*, vol. 5, p. 172).

A comment made by Zhao Yang 趙鞅 at an interstate conference in 541 B.C. testifies to the end of this Zhou order. Zhao Yang was the chief minister of Jin, then still regarded as the *ba*. When, in the middle of the meeting, news reached the conference that Lu had invaded the small state of Ju 莒, the envoy of Chu suggested that the delegate from Lu be punished. Zhao Yang stated simply:

Territory is defined by battle. It belongs to one state at one time, to another state at another time. Where is the constancy? . . . Ever since the time when there has not been a true king, rulers of states have competed to preside at the inter-state conferences, which therefore rotate among the rulers. Is there a constant leader? Supporting large states at the expense of the small ones is the way a leading state has acquired its leading status. What else is useful? Which state has not lost some land? Which presiding power can pass judgment?[61]

Zhao Yang caught the mood of his time. Nevertheless, it is ironic that a leader responsible for securing the Zhou feudal order should be the one to declare such a mission absurd.

Inclusion of Non-Zhou Elements

On the other hand, it was probably just because of this loss of solidarity and identity in a Zhou order that the non-Zhou peoples had the opportunity to take part in the development of a more inclusive world. The very fact that Qin, Chu, Wu, and Yue emerged as powerful members of the interstate community has been mentioned in the preceding section. Archaeological evidence abundantly illustrates the degree to which cultural exchanges took place among the Zhou and many non-Zhou peoples in this period, even though this is hardly mentioned in ancient literary sources.

Various groups of Rong and Di did in fact actively participate in the interstate community. For example, Jin often enlisted some of the Rong and Di peoples to act as allies in its military actions against its neighbor state of Qin. Some of these Rong and Di leaders seem also to have been well versed in Chinese literature.[62] Moreover, intermarriage between Zhou and Rong and Di peoples no doubt also helped to bring the sides together. Jin Xian Gong, for instance, married four different Rong women, each of them giving birth to one of his four sons. Jin Wen Gong was one of them; he himself married a Di woman, and her sister married the important Jin officer Zhao Shuai 趙衰.[63] Likewise, the sister of Jing Gong became the wife of a Rong

[61] *Zuo zhuan*, 41 (Zhao 1), 8a–10a (Legge, *The Chinese Classics*, vol. 5, pp. 576–7).
[62] *Zuo zhuan*, 32 (Xiang 14), 8b–11a (Legge, *The Chinese Classics*, vol. 5, pp. 463–4).
[63] *Zuo zhuan*, 10 (Zhuang 28), 13a (Legge, *The Chinese Classics*, vol. 5, p. 114); 15 (Xi 23), 8b–9a (Legge, *The Chinese Classics*, vol. 5, p. 186).

leader.[64] Matrimonial ties that had once bound the Zhou feudal community together also facilitated the fusion of the Zhou and the non-Zhou into a more inclusive "nation," later to be known as China. Other elements, such as the northern peoples of the states of Yan 燕 and Dai 代, as well as the southwestern Ba 巴 and Shu 蜀 peoples of the Sichuan basin, also came to be incorporated during the subsequent Warring States period and later, but their stories are not properly part of this chapter. In short, the dissolution of the Zhou feudal world actually opened opportunities for the emergence of the ancient Chinese world.

CHANGES IN STATE STRUCTURE

Owing to ruthless competition among the contending states, as well as power struggles within their ruling elements, the Zhou feudal structure changed drastically. The impact of these changes was as great on the political structures of the time as it was on the social structures. As mentioned in previous sections, after numerous internecine struggles among the branches of the ruling houses, Jin Xian Gong systematically eliminated all of his cousins so as to prevent threats to his authority. Thereafter, power at the Jin court was concentrated in the hands of one ruler. This was indeed an extreme measure, one of complete denial of the Zhou ethics of *zongfa* kinship relations, a cornerstone of Zhou feudalism. Similar cases occurred in other states during the Spring and Autumn period, though probably less dramatically than in Jin. Nonetheless, struggles for power and authority broke out frequently among brothers and kinsmen. In short, the *zongfa* system had been discounted. Increasingly few of those who held power at the courts were direct descendants of the lineages. As rulers seized more power, the political structure changed considerably. Of course, the extent of such changes varied from case to case; in general, changes in the states of the old Zhou core, that is, those in the Central Plain, were less extensive than what took place in Qi and Jin.

As indicated in the preceding section, a few major states expanded at the expense of their neighbors. These new territories that they acquired needed to be governed, but before a new type of administration could be developed, they were incorporated into a sort of "secondary feudalization," in which authority derived from the various states rather than from the Zhou royal court.

Secondary Feudalization

The most obvious case of secondary feudalization was Jin's establishment of a few states during the early Spring and Autumn period. Jin's expansion

[64] *Zuo zhuan*, 24 (Xuan 15), 9b (Legge, *The Chinese Classics*, vol. 5, p. 328).

toward land of the Rong and the Di probably led to the establishment of the Quwo branch. Similarly, when, in 661 B.C., Jin Xian Gong conquered the two small states Geng 耿 and Wei 魏, he bestowed them on two meritorious generals, Zhao Shuo 趙朔 and Bi Wan 畢萬. Wen Gong also bestowed fiefs on several figures who had followed him into exile and subsequently helped him reclaim power. Without exception, these new aristocrats were not kinsmen of the Jin ruling house. Their receipt of domains was due to their personal merits and loyalty.[65]

Secondary feudalization also took place in several other states during the early Spring and Autumn period. For instance, in 626 B.C. in the state of Lu, which preserved much of the Zhou *zongfa* system, three sons of Huan Gong 桓公 (711–694 B.C.), each having been involved in succession struggles for the throne, received sizable domains that remained for generations as the most influential households of the state.[66]

At a later period, the *Qianfu lun* 潛夫論 of Wang Fu 王符 (ca. A.D. 90–165) traced the origins of surnames that had survived into the Han dynasty. A great many of these names had appeared in the Spring and Autumn period as surnames of aristocratic houses established by ministers of the various states. Typical examples are the three houses established by sons of Lu Huan Gong, the seven houses of descendants of Zheng Mu Gong 穆公, and six of Jin ministers. The fifty-one houses in the state of Song seem to represent a strong tradition of the *zongfa* system, indicating that kinsmen of the Song ruling house fared well throughout the period. Indeed, in Song, a large number of aristocratic houses, descended from various rulers, among whom the strongest were descendants of Dai Gong 戴公 (r. 799–766 B.C.) and Huan Gong 桓公 (r. 681–651 B.C.), were constantly engaged in power struggles.[67]

It appears that the high tide of this secondary feudalization was the last quarter of the seventh century B.C. After that time, few new households of any noticeable status were founded. From then on rulers were often overshadowed by high ministers. Indeed, ministers soon began to dominate state affairs. The end of secondary feudalization after about one century was probably determined by the exhaustion of available land for further distribution.

A statistical study of the extent of activities of persons of various status

[65] *Shi ji*, 39, pp. 1638, 1641–2, 1662.
[66] *Shi ji*, 33, pp. 1533–5.
[67] *Qianfu lun* 潛夫論 (Sibu beiyao, ed.), 9.1–28. For bibliographic information about the *Qianfu lun*, see Loewe, ed., *Early Chinese Texts*, pp. 12–15; for conditions in the individual states, see Barry Blakeley, *Annotated Genealogy of Spring and Autumn Period Clans. Vol. 1: Seven Ruling Clans* (Taipei: Chinese Materials Center, 1983); idem, "Functional Disparities in the Socio-Political Traditions of Spring and Autumn China, Parts I, II, III," *JESHO* 20, 2 (1977): 108–43; 20, 3 (1977): 307–43; 22, 1 (1979): 81–118; and Hsu, *Ancient China in Transition*, pp. 31–7.

mentioned in the *Zuo zhuan* shows that in the first three decades of the Spring and Autumn period, 722–693 B.C., the most active figures were sons of rulers. In the middle period, especially between 632 and 513 B.C., ministers played the most active roles. The *shi* gained significance during the last five decades (512–464 B.C.). Indeed, from the mid-seventh to the mid-sixth century B.C., state and interstate activities were dominated by ministerial houses. The last part of the sixth century B.C., however, witnessed a decline in their influence, internal struggles actually causing the extinction of many of them.[68]

While these noble houses might well have lost their political power and even their wealth, they still maintained to a certain extent their kinship organization. A number of recently excavated tablets of the late Spring and Autumn period yield interesting information about one Jin noble house, Xian 先, which had long since lost political influence but which still claimed to be loyal to the house of Zhao 趙, one of the ruling houses of Jin that was then engaged in a power struggle. This incident reveals two points of importance. First, Xian maintained solidarity as a kinship group. Second, Xian and Zhao needed each other. This was more a collaborative than a standing relationship between master and subordinates.[69]

State Administration

The state structure also drastically changed with increased population. The old Zhou states had essentially been garrison stations, each of which mainly consisted of a capital city and a number of fortified towns. The term *guo* 國 (state) normally referred to the state capital, while its surrounding countryside was called the *ye* 野. The population in a Zhou state was divided into two categories, the *guo ren* (people of the state; i.e., of the city) and the *ye ren* (people in the field). The *guo ren* probably included the Zhou garrison soldiers and their descendants, led by the ruler and the elite. These were roughly counterparts to the citizens of an ancient Greek city-state. They had civil and military obligations, as well as the privilege of consulting on state affairs and emergencies as they arose. On the other hand, the *ye ren* were probably natives dwelling in the region long before the Zhou garrison state was established. They lived in their own villages and maintained a certain degree of autonomy, while paying taxes in kind and rendering corvée duties if called upon to do so.[70]

The rather loose control that Zhou vassal states had over resources appears

---

[68] Hsu, *Ancient China in Transition*, Tables 1, 2, 3, 8, and 9.
[69] *Houma mengshu* (Beijing: Wenwu, 1976), p. 156.
[70] Du Zhengsheng, *Zhou du chengbang* (Taipei: Lianjin, 1979), pp. 48–55, 78–92.

to have been insufficient for them to face new situations arising from the intense competition after feudalism collapsed. Changes taking place in a number of states show that adjustment of the state structure was necessary in order to integrate resources that formerly had been differentiated into *guo* and *ye* sectors. The first such attempt at restructuring was carried out by Guan Zhong when he served Qi Huan Gong as his principal advisor. If the account given in the *Guo yu* is reliable, Guan Zhong thoroughly reintegrated the state into hierarchical units that had simultaneous administrative and military functions. This allowed Qi to mobilize its combat forces readily. Guan Zhong's reform seems to have reached beyond just the *guo ren*, since the traditional feudal boundaries were not taken into account. Meanwhile, satellite cities were also organized in this manner so as to establish a large number of standing troops.[71]

In the state of Jin, Xian Gong expanded the standing military strength from one army to two armies in 661 B.C. Then in 645 B.C. during the reign of Hui Gong 惠公 (r. 650–637 B.C.), Jin was defeated by Qin, with Hui Gong being captured. Qin was aided in this victory by a *ye ren* troop. Probably inspired by the performance of the *ye ren*, Jin reorganized its military to include people of the *ye* regions.[72] After Wen Gong came to power, Jin expanded its military into three armies in 633 B.C., and then again to five armies in 629 B.C. After temporarily reducing its military strength to three armies in 621 B.C., Jin finally set its standing strength at six armies in 588 B.C., which remained in effect until the end of the Spring and Autumn period.[73] A logical conclusion is that Jin was enabled to expand its military strength by drafting the services of the *ye ren*, who had not previously taken part in the armies.

In Lu in 594 B.C., a new system was adopted to levy taxes according to the acreage of arable land, while in 590 B.C. military duties were imposed on residents of the countryside. Both of these changes took place at a time when Lu faced both internal power struggles and outside threats.[74] Similar efforts to levy military taxes on people who resided outside of the cities were adopted fifty years later (538 B.C.) in Zheng, proposed by the chief minister Zi Chan 子產 (served 543–522 B.C.).[75] This might suggest that this sort of reorganization had become common practice.

---

[71] *Guo yu*, 6 ("Qi yu"), 1a–8a.

[72] *Zuo zhuan*, 14 (Xi 15), 13b (Legge, *The Chinese Classics*, vol. 5, p. 168).

[73] *Zuo zhuan*, 11 (Min 1), 3a (Legge, *The Chinese Classics*, vol. 5, p. 125); 16 (Xi 27), 16.11b (Legge, *The Chinese Classics*, vol. 5, p. 201); 17 (Xi 31), 9a (Legge, *The Chinese Classics*, vol. 5, p. 219); 19A (Wen 6), 5a (Legge, *The Chinese Classics*, vol. 5, p. 243); 26 (Cheng 3), 5a (Legge, *The Chinese Classics*, vol. 5, p. 353).

[74] *Zuo zhuan*, 24 (Xuan 15), 13a (Legge, *The Chinese Classics*, vol. 5, p. 329); 25 (Cheng 1), 1b (Legge, *The Chinese Classics*, vol. 5, p. 337).

[75] *Zuo zhuan*, 42 (Zhao 4), 30a (Legge, *The Chinese Classics*, vol. 5, p. 598).

Local Administration

In Chu, which perhaps never had the same feudal background as the northern states, political reorganization faced less resistance. In 548 B.C., a thorough statewide survey was conducted to prepare for registering the population; this was intended to regulate tax and military duties. It seems that Chu had firm control of its human and financial resources.[76] Indeed, there is some evidence that as early as the seventh century B.C., Chu had instituted administrative units called *xian* 縣. These were newly annexed lands administered by a governor who reported directly to the king. There is indirect evidence that the first such *xian* was established at Quan 權 in 690 B.C.[77] Throughout the Spring and Autumn period, the *Zuo zhuan* mentions at least thirty different *xian*, with more than forty *yin* 尹 (governors). These governors were appointed from among trusted courtiers rather than hereditary nobles. However, the *xian*, in most cases former Zhou states conquered by Chu, retained a great deal of autonomy, the governor having a free hand to enlist some of the inhabitants for military service and to levy taxes.[78]

The Chu *xian* administrative unit established a precedent for other states to follow. Jin soon had its own *xian*, though they were assigned to ministerial houses to govern as their own domains. By 537 B.C., Jin had at least forty-nine such *xian* belonging to several ministerial houses, among which Hann 韓 controlled nine and Yang 揚 ten.[79] Qin probably also used *xian* to organize newly conquered territories, the earliest evidence for which is Qin *xian* established on land taken from the Rong people in 688 B.C.[80] However, details of the Qin organization are not clear.

As mentioned above, the core of a state was originally its fortified capital, which controlled a number of satellite garrisons. As the *ye* territories were gradually incorporated into the state structure, the larger, more populous peripheries began to outweigh the center. Expansion meant that the ministers and governors controlling the new land had the resources to dominate state politics. This too contributed to the emergence of ministerial houses by

[76] *Zuo zhuan*, 36 (Zhao 25), 14a–16b (Legge, *The Chinese Classics*, vol. 5, p. 517).

[77] For the mention of the establishment of a *yin* (governor) at Quan, see *Zuo zhuan*, 9 (Zhuang 18), 16a (Legge, *The Chinese Classics*, vol. 5, p. 97). See also H. G. Creel, "The Beginning of Bureaucracy in China: The Origin of the *Hsien*," *JAS* 23 (1964): 155–84; Du Zhengsheng, *Zhoudai chengbang*, pp. 143–7.

[78] Yang Kuan, "Chunqiu shidai Chu guo xianzhi de xingzhi wenti," *Zhongguo shi yanjiu* 1981.4: 19–30; Xu Shaohua, *Zhoudai nantu lishi dili yu wenhua* (Wuhan: Wuhan daxue, 1994), pp. 275–98.

[79] *Zuo zhuan*, 43 (Zao 5), 11b (Legge, *The Chinese Classics*, vol. 5, p. 605). For the government structure of Qi, Chu, and Jin, see Melvin P. Thatcher, "A Structural Comparison of the Central Government of Ch'i, Ch'u and Chin," *MS* 33 (1977–8): 140–61.

[80] *Shi ji*, 5, p. 182. The Qin institution of *xian* is somewhat ambiguous; see Du Zhengsheng, *Zhou du chengbang*, p. 143, n. 19; also Melvin P. Thatcher, "Central Government of the State of Chin in the Spring and Autumn Period," *Journal of Oriental Studies* 23, 1 (1985): 29–53.

the end of the Spring and Autumn period. In fact, the seven powers of the Warring States period came about in just this way, Jin being divided into Hann 韓, Zhao 趙, and Wei 魏, while in Qi the Tian 田 family replaced the old ruling house of Jiang.

Parallel to the appearance of local administrative units, there emerged a category of local administrative staff, with positions such as *zai* 宰 (steward) and *shou* 守 (sheriff). A few disciples of Confucius, such as Zilu 子路 and Ranyou 冉有, served in functions such as these.[81]

Serving as local administrators, ambitious *shi* were sometimes able to influence state politics. One such powerful *shi* was Yang Huo 陽貨, a contemporary of Confucius who initially seized power to become the strongman of Lu for four years. Many of these *shi* rose from the rank and file of the old feudal structure, their activities becoming very conspicuous in the last decades of the Spring and Autumn period.[82]

Indeed, it was a long metamorphosis that these ancient states underwent in order to transform from garrison stations to incipient territorial states. From the days of secondary feudalization, smaller states kept being absorbed into larger ones, the organization and administration of which became increasingly complex. Within them the ruling houses, again through a process of concentration of authority, eliminated each other. The seemingly strong new ruling houses who entrusted new territories to the governance of their loyal followers found in later generations that the descendants of these followers acquired too great resources to remain subordinate. The same process permeated all levels, such that ministers were overshadowed by their stewards and sheriffs. Thus, the seemingly opposed processes of absorption and dispersion of power proceeded simultaneously. The final consequence was not just a reshuffling of power, but rather the complete disintegration of the Zhou feudal system, eventually totally transforming both state and society. Of course, this process was no more than half completed by the end of the Spring and Autumn period. Its completion is the history of the following Warring States period.

ECONOMIC DEVELOPMENTS

In the days when Zhou feudalism prevailed, land and labor were the only resources that yielded wealth. Sending the Zhou people out to establish vassal states was a simple way to reach sources of wealth seized by military occupation. Along with this feudal structure, exchange of materials during court

---

[81] *Shi ji*, 67, pp. 2185, 2190, 2193–5, 2201, 2207, 2212; see also Legge, *The Chinese Classics. Vol. 1: Confucian Analects, The Great Learning, and the Doctrine of the Mean*, pp. 112–27.
[82] Hsu, *Ancient China in Transition*, table 4 and pp. 34–8.

visits and interstate conferences, as well as by marriage dowries, gifts, or tribute, linked the lords and vassals and served to redistribute the wealth.

Land Tenure and Production

Ideally, such control should have been conducted through the feudal framework. In a hierarchy of authority and status, the lord would bestow on a subordinate land and the population who lived there. Part of the wealth produced by these people was then given to the lord for support. At the base of this economic pyramid were the peasants, who were assigned to work the farms, in return for which they were fed and clothed. The poem "Seventh Month" (Qi yue 七月) of the *Shi jing* 詩經 (Classic of poetry) is a vivid description of life in a manorial environment, as may be seen in the opening lines:

> In the seventh month the Fire Star passes the meridian:
> In the ninth month clothes are given out.
> In the days of [our] first month, the wind blows cold;
> In the days of [our] second, the air is cold.
> Without coats, without garments of hair,
> How could we get to the end of the year?
> In the days of [our] third month we take our plows in hand;
> In the days of [our] fourth month we make our way to the fields.
> Along with wives and children,
> We eat in those south-lying acres.
> The surveyor of the fields comes and is glad.

The peasant was in a state of servitude, rendering productive labor in exchange for basic subsistence.[83]

A so-called well-field system, first described in the *Mencius*, was an idealized land tenure system, of the Zhou period. This system, the name of which derives from the Chinese character for "well" (*jing* 井) organized individual lots for each of eight peasant houses around one central lot that they were to work jointly for the benefit of their lord.[84] In this system, the peasant paid the lord in services rather than rent. However, the peasants were not slaves; they probably had a degree of discretion with respect to their productive activities. In other words, the relationship seems to have been a close tenancy rather than contractual servitude. In theory, the entire Zhou kingdom belonged to the royal house; no one other than the king could have full claim to their land.[85]

---

[83] *Shi jing*, 8 (1), 9a–22a, *trs. auct.*; see also Arthur Waley, *The Book of Songs: The Ancient Chinese Classic of Poetry* (London: Allen & Unwin, 1937; rpt. New York: Grove, 1960), pp. 164–7; and Hsu, *Ancient China in Transition*, pp. 9–10.

[84] *Mencius*, 3/1 (Legge, *The Chinese Classics*, vol. 2, pp. 242–5).

[85] Hsu, *Ancient China in Transition*, pp. 108–12, 196–98.

After the deterioration of the Zhou feudal system, the vassal states initially proclaimed sovereignty, conquering and annexing other states without consideration of royal authority. Coincident with these political changes, there were also changes in the notion of land tenure. As discussed above, there is mention in early texts of land taxation. However, details are lacking. According to the earliest report, land taxation based on crop yield was instituted in the state of Lu in 594 B.C. It seems that the peasants' obligations of rendering labor services on a lot reserved for their lord was changed to an obligation to pay tax in kind from their production. The rate of tax was supposed to be one-tenth of the crop. In reality, at the time of Confucius it might have been as high as 20 percent.[86]

Adoption of taxes in kind fundamentally changed the well-field system, which, in any event, had probably only applied to the *guo ren* sectors of the garrison state. According to Mencius's account, the people in the *guo* had different obligations from those in the *ye*. Integration of *guo* and *ye* made it necessary to make taxation uniform.

A tax based on production from land held by the peasant was tacit recognition that the farmer was entitled to use the particular piece of land. In other words, it entailed ownership, or at least tenure of land. Parallel with the transformation from feudal structure to sovereign states, the status of the people likewise gradually changed to that of subjects of the state. The full process of this change was completed only in the Warring States period.[87]

Once released from manorial restrictions, the peasants had more incentive to increase productivity. In the Spring and Autumn period in both North and South China there were at least two major cereal crops, millet and wheat in the north, and rice and millet in the south. Legumes, originally grown in the Shanxi highland, had spread widely. It should be noted that broad beans were originally a common plant in the area of the Rong people in the northern mountains.[88] Differentiation of millet into subspecies, *shu* 黍 and *ji* 稷, and an increased significance of wheat as one of the main crops made it possible for farmers to rotate their crops, a strategy that also enhanced productivity. For instance, wheat could be planted in winter for summer harvest, while millet was planted in the spring for autumn harvest. Thus, the farmer could manage to grow three crops in two years. The rotation of crops also helped to preserve the fertility of the fields. This was the first step toward intensive farming.[89]

---

[86] *Analects*, 12/9 (Legge, *The Chinese Classics*, vol. 1, p. 255); *Zuo zhuan*, 24 (Xuan 15), 24.13a (Legge, *The Chinese Classics*, vol. 5, p. 329); *Guo yu*, 5 ("Lu yu"), 12b–13a.

[87] Hsu, *Ancient China in Transition*, pp. 108–9.

[88] Hu Daojing, "Shi Shu pian," *Zhonghua wenshi luncong* 1963: 111–19.

[89] Cho-yun Hsu, *Han Agriculture* (Seattle: University of Washington Press, 1980), pp. 81–8.

The use of iron implements, especially iron plowshares, could also have substantially contributed to efficient farming. It has always been disputed whether or not bronze tools were used in agriculture. In the past decades, however, no fewer than 300 bronze implements of various kinds have been found in archaeological excavations, distributed widely across many provinces. It seems that bronze was used for these implements until replaced by the less expensive and sturdier iron. Iron was then used to cast spades, hoes, and sickles, as well as plowshares.[90]

Related to the use of the plow was the harnessing of oxen to pull it. Ox-draft allowed for deeper cuts into the soil than was possible with hand-pulled plows. Plowing and oxen became so much a pair that they even appeared together in people's names; Confucius's disciple Ran Geng 冉耕, whose name Geng means "to till," was also called by the alternative name Niu 牛 (oxen). Moreover, the use of oxen as sacrificial offerings on ceremonial occasions began to decline as the productive capacity of the animal came to be more effectively exploited.[91]

Metallurgy

Two issues regarding the development of metallurgy need to be addressed here. They are the level of bronze-casting techniques and iron technology. Bronze casting had a long history in ancient China. As seen in the preceding chapters, Shang and Zhou bronze vessels were cast in a great variety of sizes and shapes, decorated with many kinds of ornamental designs, and inscribed with lengthy texts. By the Spring and Autumn period, the technique of bronze casting advanced in several ways, including the use of the lost-wax technique to produce different shapes.[92] These skills made it possible to produce bronze works of great artistic merit.

Bronze weapons were also of significant value, since the most powerful states of the time were blessed with rich copper deposits within easy reach. Jin had copper mines in the Zhongtiao 中條 Mountains, while Chu had numerous copper mines along the Huai 淮 and Han 漢 Rivers. Having such deposits of copper gave these two states strategic resources to develop their interstate leadership. The site of the Tonglüshan 銅綠山 copper mine in present-day Hubei and the bronze foundry at Houma 侯馬 in Shanxi both testify to the level of the bronze industries in Chu and Jin.[93]

---

[90] Li Xueqin, *Eastern Zhou and Qin Civilizations*, trans. K. C. Chang (New Haven, Conn.: Yale University Press, 1985), pp. 284–90, 323.
[91] *Guo yu*, 15 ("Jin yu"), 6b.
[92] Li Xueqin, *Eastern Zhou and Qin Civilizations*, pp. 272–6.
[93] For descriptions of these sites, see pp. 462, 539.

At the Tonglüshan mine, excavations have unearthed an upright furnace designed to draw off molten metal at the bottom while fired from the upper part of the furnace. This particular device suggests that bronze casting might have inspired the development of iron casting by a similar method.

Although iron appears at a Shang site at Gaocheng 藁城 in Hebei, this is meteoritic iron. The earliest man-made iron pieces discovered to date are iron parts of bronze swords, iron handles of some bronze materials, parts of iron in spades and knives, chunks of iron slats, and some pieces of cast iron, none of which dates before the late Spring and Autumn period.[94] The most interesting pieces are a good sword with an iron stem in a bronze body, and a *ding* 鼎 cauldron of cast iron. It seems that wrought iron and cast iron developed simultaneously, whereas in the Western world wrought iron predated cast iron. As mentioned above, this was probably influenced by the skill in bronze casting obtained over the centuries.[95]

Literary records and archaeological data seem to be consistent with respect to iron. In the state of Jin, in 536 B.C., an iron cauldron was cast on which was inscribed a law code. This event is frequently cited by historians to establish the early rise of casting iron.[96] This has now been substantiated by the discovery of an iron cauldron from the late Spring and Autumn period at a Changsha site in 1978.[97]

According to Chinese literary records, bronze was called a "fine metal" (*ji jin* 吉金) and was used for weapons, while iron, regarded as an inferior metal, was used to cast tools.[98] This classification shows that both metals were regarded as being closely related. The peak of bronze-making technology is well demonstrated in the fine quality of the bronze swords produced in the states of Wu and Yue.[99] Literary sources provide legends of how such marvelous weapons were cast in blast furnaces by repeatedly working the bronze. Wu and Yue bronze swords discovered in recent years confirm that they were made by this legendary method; still sharp and bright after thousands of years, one such sword was made of an iron blade on a bronze hilt, while another, dating from the late Spring and Autumn period, was made with a steel stem and bronze guard. This latter sword is the earliest example in China of steel with a certain amount of carbon (0.5–0.6 percent) that had been worked repeatedly.[100]

---

[94] Li Xueqin, *Eastern Zhou and Qin Civilizations*, pp. 315–23.
[95] Hua Jueming, *Shijie yejin fuzhan shi* (Beijing: Kexue jishu wenxian, 1985), pp. 104, 469–516; Joseph Needham, *The Development of Iron and Steel Technology in China* (Cambridge: Heffer, 1964), pp. 9–10.
[96] *Zuo zhuan*, 53 (Zhao 29), 11b (Legge, *The Chinese Classics*, vol. 5, p. 732).
[97] Li Xueqin, *Eastern Zhou and Qin Civilizations*, p. 322.
[98] *Guo yu*, 6 ("Qi yu"), 8b.
[99] Li Xueqin, *Eastern Zhou and Qin Civilizations*, pp. 276–80.
[100] Ibid., pp. 318, 322.

The advances in bronze- and iron-casting techniques seem to have taken place quite rapidly in the south, especially in the area of Wu and Yue, in the late Spring and Autumn period. It was also in this region and at this time that a type of glazed pottery reached a level of quality that could be called ceramic. Ruins of ancient kilns have been discovered in several locations in Zhejiang; they are linear in structure and could produce temperatures as high as 1,300 °C.[101]

The appearance of iron and ceramic industries, both of which required very high temperatures, in the same time and place does not appear to be sheer coincidence. It is likely that the early development of bronze casting in China was derived from the Neolithic pottery industry, while the southern technique of iron casting was developed on the foundation of bronze casting. It seems too that the skill needed to produce heat at such high temperatures was associated with both metallurgical and ceramic industries. The words *tao* 陶 (pottery) and *ye* 冶 (metallurgy) have always been linked in the compound *taoye*, which is still used to mean "transformation of character." Virtually all ancient cities of the pre-Qin period contain ruins of pottery and bronze-making workshops.[102]

Commerce

Advances in agriculture and basic industries were associated with the rise of an active market economy. In Zhou feudalism, distribution of wealth was conducted through channels dictated by political authority. Gift giving, rationing, tributes, and corvée labor formed a network for the collection and redistribution of resources. With the collapse of this network during the Spring and Autumn period, a new economic exchange system gradually emerged.

Frequent wars among the states, as well as equally frequent court visits and/or conferences, made interregional transportation commonplace. Gift exchanges also familiarized the elite with products from other places. Thus, trading developed in order to secure materials from far away. In the days of garrison states, there were checkpoints on the borders. In the state of Lu, there was a heated debate over whether to abolish six such border checkpoints. In 625 B.C., Zang Wenzhong 臧文仲, a somewhat liberal-minded minister, ruled to abolish them, while conservatives were against this.[103]

The road system had already been well developed in the Western Zhou

---

[101] Dong Chuping, *Wu Yue wenhua xintan* (Hangzhou: Zhejiang Renmin, 1988), pp. 244–50.
[102] Li Xueqin, *Eastern Zhou and Qin Civilizations*, p. 41.
[103] *Zuo zhuan*, 18 (Wen 2), 14b (Legge, *The Chinese Classics*, vol. 5, p. 234).

period. The vassal states were expected to maintain highways, as well as to provide security for them. One of the items in an interstate agreement of 579 B.C. was a promise not to block travelers. Water transportation was also good, enabling large shipments of grain to be transported on the rivers.[104] In addition, it seems that there was a network of roads between the capitals of the four major states, with the royal capital region and Jin at the center.

The Appearance of Currency

An important economic indicator is the appearance of minted coins. In Western Zhou bronze inscriptions, gifts in terms of *bei* 貝 (cowries), representing units of wealth, are often mentioned. The worth of real estate and valuable items could be valued in numbers of strings of cowries. Precious metals, gold, and copper also could be used for exchange purposes. Yet in the daily life of the ordinary people, bartering of materials in kind was commonplace.[105]

Bronze money began to circulate in the late Spring and Autumn period, the archaeological evidence for which is *bu* 布 (spade-coins). These spade-coins are bronze miniatures of a two-pronged digging implement with a socket for a handle. Archaeologists classify these early coins into two groups. One group has been excavated mainly near Luoyang, the area of the Eastern Zhou court. The other group has been excavated mainly in Shanxi, the area of Jin. That these *kong shou bu* 空首布 spade-coins retain a hollow socket for a handle, while similar examples from the Warring States period display a solid handle, suggests that the coins of the Spring and Autumn period represent an early stage of development in which the actual implement was imitated. Their distribution around the Zhou capital and Jin seems to reflect that these areas must have been busy centers for a brisk exchange of goods.

The state of Jin had been at the center of interstate politics for such a long time throughout the Spring and Autumn period that it would be natural for its money to have been widely circulated. The number of spade-coins in circulation must have been very large, as is shown by the discovery at a single site of a hoard of more than a thousand.[106] Nevertheless, discoveries of spade-coins of the Zhou type have been even more numerous than the Jin pieces.[107]

---

[104] Hsu, *Ancient China in Transition*, pp. 117–18; *Guo yu*, 2 ("Zhou yu"), 10a–b; *Zuo zhuan*, 13 (Xi 13), 13.21a (Legge, *The Chinese Classics*, vol. 5, p. 161), 27 (Cheng 12), 5a (Legge, *The Chinese Classics*, vol. 5, p. 378).
[105] Hsu, *Ancient China in Transition*, pp. 122–4.
[106] Li Xueqin, *Eastern Zhou and Qin Civilizations*, pp. 372–3.
[107] Ibid., pp. 373–7.

The appearance of minted coins reflects an active exchange of material wealth that the old feudal economy could not have accommodated. A related phenomenon that also helps to substantiate the prevalence of a market economy is the rise in status of merchants and the increase of their activities. In the state of Zheng, in particular, merchants enjoyed a special relationship. The state provided them with protection, while they informed the state court of any unusual conditions in their profession. In one instance, a Zheng jade trader reported to the court that a delegate from Jin was trying to purchase some valuable jade pieces. In another instance, a Zheng livestock dealer reported to the court that he saw an army of Qin on its way to invade Zheng. This dealer is said to have then given some cattle to the Qin army as a gift from the Zheng ruler, thereby indicating to the Qin general that the secret invasion had been noticed. In the state of Wey, as well, artisans and merchants often were consulted in state politics.[108] What is more, by the late part of the Spring and Autumn period, some merchants in the capital of Jin had become very powerful elements of society, living luxuriously and exercising political influence.[109] One of the most prominent businessmen of the period was Duanmu Si 端木賜 (also known as Zi Gong 子貢), a disciple of Confucius. He not only made a great fortune but also acquired a great reputation in interstate politics.[110]

The emergence of private traders as a phenomenon seems to be due to several factors. One is a better road system that connected all regions, perhaps resulting from the frequent interstate contacts necessitated by the *ba* system. Another is a layered economy owing to better productivity in agriculture and more demand for goods. Advances in various kinds of industries must also be associated with business prosperity. However, this prosperity brought a disparity in the distribution of wealth. By the late part of the Spring and Autumn period, a portion of the population appears to have been impoverished, needing to live on loans and aid from the wealthy.[111]

Economic growth in ancient China picked up momentum in the Warring States period, with private ownership of land and new manufacturing and commercial activities. When coupled with demographic growth, all of this culminated in urbanization and commercialization.[112] But the initial stage marking a tremendous transformation took place in the Spring and Autumn period.

[108] *Zuo zhuan*, 17 (Xi 33), 14a (Legge, *The Chinese Classics*, vol. 5, p. 224); 47 (Zhao 16), 18b (Legge, *The Chinese Classics*, vol. 5, p. 664); 55 (Ding 8), 115b–16a (Legge, *The Chinese Classics*, vol. 5, p. 770).
[109] *Guo yu*, 14 ("Jin yu"), 11a.
[110] *Shi ji*, 67, p. 2201.
[111] *Zuo zhuan*, 42 (Zhao 3), 9b–12a (Legge, *The Chinese Classics*, vol. 5, p. 589).
[112] Hsu, *Ancient China in Transition*, pp. 107–39.

INTELLECTUAL DEVELOPMENTS

In addition to the profound transformations in political, social, and economic spheres already discussed, the Spring and Autumn period also witnessed a major intellectual breakthrough, one that would influence all future courses of thought in China. This was the emergence of Confucianism and the transformation of the class of men known as *shi* from soldiers into intellectuals. While the content of this intellectual breakthrough will be the topic of Chapter 11, it is perhaps not out of place here to discuss some of its social background and implications.

The Shi

In Zhou feudalism, members of the elite class were more than just aristocratic warriors. A *shi* having the status of a common gentleman in the Zhou aristocracy nominally received an education in six fields: ritual, music, archery, charioteering, writing, and mathematics. In principle, *shi* were prepared to serve the state in both military and civil capacities. They were expected to be not just robust warriors, but also gentlemen with good manners and minds.[113]

Throughout the *Zuo zhuan*, there are numerous cases of learned ministers eloquently quoting history and poetry at the state courts or at interstate conferences. From this background came the *shi*, among whom was Confucius (551–479 B.C.). It was he who spearheaded the major intellectual breakthrough.

The first step in transforming the role and status of the *shi* was the appearance of functionaries who served their lords in various capacities, such as sheriffs, stewards, judges, and advisors. As Zhou feudalism underwent tremendous changes after the collapse of Western Zhou, competition both among and within states made it necessary for leaders to gather the best and the most capable persons as assistants. The term *xian* 賢 (worthy; i.e., one combining intellectual ability and moral integrity), was introduced as a criterion in selecting these functionaries. The pool of talent from which such worthy persons was chosen was swelled by former noblemen who had lost their status as their states and families fell in the severe competition of the time. Some of these noblemen also brought education to members of the lower social strata who previously had no access to literacy and learning.

Early examples of those selected as worthy are Guan Zhong, a man of

---

[113] It is interesting to note that this transformation of the *shi* parallels a similar transformation in the meaning of the term *junzi* 君子, which originally meant "son of the lord," but which gradually came to refer to any person of moral refinement.

obscure origin who helped Qi Huan Gong to become *Ba*, and many advisors of Jin Wen Gong, who were also drawn from a variety of social backgrounds. Later generations of Jin rulers continued the tradition of advancing worthy and capable persons to serve in important positions of the Jin state government, without regard for the status and seniority of the candidates.[114] This shift from consideration of status to that of competence eventually ushered in a new criterion of social preference. The term *shi* thus acquired a new definition, now referring to a person of excellence, one with high capabilities as well as character; it came to refer to a cultural status rather than social grouping. This new cultural elite brought a new consciousness of their responsibility to serve the world. It was a mentality that nurtured many of the best minds of the time to devote themselves to the task of defining and disseminating ideas. The Golden Age of Chinese civilization therefore was introduced during the Spring and Autumn period. It is this background that prepared Confucius to initiate the most important school of thought in Chinese history.

A Weakening Tradition

The intellectual changes of this time can perhaps be illustrated by events of three different types. In 625 B.C., the newly deceased Lu Xi Gong 魯僖公 was placed in an honored position in the ancestral temple, above that of his predecessor. In this instance, the old rule of respect for lineage rank was deliberately ignored by the presiding elder. Since the state of Lu was regarded as a bastion of the Old Zhou *zongfa* kinship system, this obvious violation of ritual became a topic of debate among the ministers. However, the decision to alter seniority prevailed. Thus, the *zongfa* system lost even more of its relevance.[115]

In 639 B.C., Zang Wenzhong, chief minister of Lu, abolished the practice of punishing a shaman who had failed to provoke rain in time of drought. Instead, he insisted that the more effective measure was to provide people with adequate relief and to enhance farming conditions.[116]

This same rational attitude toward ritual was also held by Zi Chan of Zheng. He gave rational explanations of death and sickness that rejected old superstitions of ghosts, curses, and destiny.[117] In 536 B.C., Zichan announced a law code, inscribing it in metal. Twenty-three years later, Jin also cast a

---

[114] Hsu, *Ancient China in Transition*, pp. 88–9.
[115] *Zuo zhuan*, 18 (Wen 2), 12b–15b (Legge, *The Chinese Classics*, vol. 5, p. 234).
[116] *Zuo zhuan*, 14 (Xi 21), 26b (Legge, *The Chinese Classics*, vol. 5, p. 180).
[117] *Zuo zhuan*, 41 (Zhao 1), 20a–29a (Legge, *The Chinese Classics*, vol. 5, pp. 580–1); 44 (Zhao 7), 12b–14b (Legge, *The Chinese Classics*, vol. 5, p. 618); 47 (Zhao 16), 21b (Legge, *The Chinese Classics*, vol. 5, p. 665).

legal code on an iron cauldron. Both of these events aroused debates between pragmatic statesmen and their conservative colleagues, among whom was Shu Xiang 叔向, a Jin minister and Zi Chan's friend. The conservatives argued that if the commoners knew the legal statutes, they would no longer obey the state authority nor respect its traditions.[118]

All of these events signal the changes that were clearly taking place. Indeed, in 539 B.C. Shu Xiang of Jin and Yan Ying 晏嬰 of Qi, both highly respected men of their time, exchanged observations about their respective states being on the eve of great changes:

Shu Xiang asked about the state of affairs in Qi and Yanzi replied: "This is the late age. I know nothing but this . . . the Qi will become the possession of the Chen family. The duke is throwing away his people, and they are turning to the Chen. . . ." Shu Xiang said, "Yes, and even with our ducal house, this also is the late age. The war horses are not yoked; the ministers never take the field. (Members of old established houses) are reduced to menials. The government is ordered by the heads of the clans. . . . No future day needs be waited for the humiliation of the ducal house. . . ." Yanzi then asked him what would become of himself, and Shu Xiang replied, "The ducal clans of Jin are at an end, . . . of the same ducal ancestry with me were eleven clans, and only the Yangshe 羊舌 remains."[119]

What their time needed was a set of ideas that would help with these changes. Confucius provided just such a new ideal world order.

Confucius

Confucius, or Kong Qiu 孔丘, was the son of Shu Liangge 叔梁紇, a warrior and local administrator of Lu. The Kong house was originally one of high-ranking aristocrats in Song, from which they had fled into exile at Lu after a power struggle there. At the time his father died, Confucius was still young; he was probably brought up by his mother. The young Confucius held various humble jobs, such as keeper of the grain and bookkeeper, to support himself. Therefore, Confucius had a family history that reflected the downward social mobility of many noble houses of the Spring and Autumn period. He retained a memory of the past glory, but had the experience of leading a life of service.[120] It was a condition that made Confucius a marginal person in both the upper and lower classes of the postfeudal society. The former status gave him knowledge of the roles, rituals, etiquette, and code of conduct of the old aristocrats, while the latter inspired him to envision a world where

[118] *Zuo zhuan*, 43 (Zhao 6), 16a–20a (Legge, *The Chinese Classics*, vol. 5, pp. 609–10); 53 (Zhao 29), 11a–12b (Legge, *The Chinese Classics*, vol. 5, p. 732).

[119] *Zuo zhuan*, 42 (Zhao 3), 9b–12a (Legge, *The Chinese Classics*, vol. 5, p. 589).

[120] *Shi ji*, 47, pp. 1905–40.

humans could transcend class background. Confucius was a conservative with respect to current politics, severely criticizing Zang Wenzhong for his liberal policies. In this regard, he claimed to be an interpreter rather than an innovator. Yet he did innovate, universalizing the code of conduct of the feudal society so that it would apply to all of humanity in general.

CONCLUSION

The Spring and Autumn period witnessed transformations in all aspects of the Zhou world. No sooner had King Ping of Zhou established a court in the eastern portions of the Zhou kingdom than the feudal structure started to disintegrate. The former vassal states took their futures in their own hands, initiating wars with cutthroat competition. Contentious rulers expanded their territory, extinguishing neighboring states. There were power struggles within states among branches of the ruling houses. These wars eventually reduced the number of states from several hundred to less than a few tens. Likewise, even in these states, there were only a few noble houses that survived the repeated power struggles. The number of fallen nobles must have been many times that of those who thrived. Some of the former elite, however, became responsible for the dissemination of knowledge and the establishment of a code of conduct that became adopted by the courtiers.

Among the many developments that mark the Spring and Autumn period, the following are perhaps the most important: the establishment of the *ba* system of recognized leadership among the states; the assimilation of the southern state of Chu (and, later, the states of Wu and Yue) into the political order, such that an unprecedented degree of cultural pluralism was achieved; the concentration of authority in the states, both through the recruitment of capable ministers and also through new governing structures such as the *xian* county organization; the gradual emergence of private land ownership; the beginning of iron casting; far-flung commercial activities; and, perhaps most important of all, the rise of the *shi* class and, with it, the dramatic intellectual breakthrough brought about by Confucius.

In all of these aspects, the two and a half centuries of the Spring and Autumn period brought changes with profound effects both for the following Warring States period and, indeed, for all subsequent Chinese civilization.

CHAPTER NINE

WARRING STATES POLITICAL HISTORY

Mark Edward Lewis

The two and a half centuries commonly known as the age of the Warring States (481–221 B.C.) witnessed the creation of the major political institutions that defined early imperial China. The old league of cities ruled by the Zhou nobility was replaced by a system of territorial states built around unchallenged monarchs who commanded a large number of dependent officials. These in turn were employed to register and mobilize the individual peasant households, primarily for the sake of imposing universal military service. The mass peasant armies of the period entailed the emergence of military specialists who were masters of the theories and techniques of warfare. At the same time, the needs of diplomatic maneuver produced theorists of stratagem and persuasion who formulated new models of interstate relations. The Zhou world was also reinvented as a geographic entity, both through expansion to the south and the southwest and through new patterns of physical mobility that marked differences of status.

However, the writings of this period present no tidy portrait of politics or institutions. Since written materials were still rare, difficult to produce, and not widely diffused, "books" tended to emerge, evolve, and survive as the legacy of groups who defined themselves through loyalty to a common master. Members of these groups sought patrons who took an interest in the wisdom or expertise that they claimed to offer. As a consequence, the writings that preserve information about the political history of the period are pragmatic and factional. They are devoted to the policies, philosophies, and actions of those who actively participated in creating the new states, and they defend these actions or philosophies as uniquely efficacious. Thus, the texts define a set of idealized roles that constitute the Warring States polity: the monarch, the reforming minister, the military commander, the persuader/diplomat, and the scholar. Each of these roles generated its own characteristic texts, and the remnants of these writings and associated archae-

ological finds provide our evidence regarding the political and social world
of the Warring States.

SOURCES

Chronicles

The first type of source, produced in the emergent royal courts and centered
on the ruler, was the chronicle. Chronicles dated major events – battles, institutional reforms, appointments or dismissals, and interstate meetings – and
are the only sources that provide a chronological framework for the sequence
of events. However, they do not allow us to reconstruct a sequential, narrative history of the period for two reasons. First, each state employed its own
calendar and hence no comprehensive time scheme existed. Second, since
chronicles were signs of royal power and invariably reflected badly on rival
states, the destruction of any kingdom entailed the elimination of its chronicles. Thus, following its successful wars of conquest, the Qin 秦 state
destroyed the historical chronicles of its defeated foes. Its own archives in
turn suffered substantial losses during the burning of the capital Xianyang
咸陽 by Xiang Yu 項羽 (d. 202 B.C.). As the political records of the various
Warring States had been destroyed, and following the civil war no groups
had a vital interest in recovering surviving fragments, the chronicles of the
period were largely lost.

What survived were some of the records of Qin that were removed from
their archives by Xiao He 蕭何 (d. 193 B.C.) and thus preserved from the
sacking of Xianyang. These formed the basis for the treatment of the
Warring States period in Sima Qian's 司馬遷 (ca. 145–86 B.C.) *Shi ji* 史記
(Records of the historian). The "Basic Annals of Qin" (Qin ben ji 秦本紀)
and the "Hereditary Household" (*Shi jia* 世家) chapters provide our sequential history of the period, and these can be supplemented by materials from
biographies of Warring States officials, philosophers, and writers, as well as
evidence scattered through the "monographs" (*shu* 書). Some dated events
within the *Shi ji* can also be compared with those in the surviving versions
of the *Zhushu jinian* 竹書紀年 (Bamboo annals), a chronicle that ends in the
year 299 B.C. that was composed in the state of Wei 魏 and discovered in a
tomb in the third century A.D. The *Bian nian ji* 編年紀 (Chronicle of years)
discovered in a Qin tomb at Yunmeng 雲夢 also provides dated events from
the late Warring States, and the surviving fragments of the *Shi ben* 世本 (Root
of the generations) offer another source for supplementing Sima Qian's
chronicles. Ban Gu's 班固 (A.D. 32–92) *Han shu* 漢書 (History of [former]
Han), particularly in its tables (*biao* 表) and monographs (*zhi* 志), also pro-

vides information on the period.[1] Several post-Han histories, most notably the fourth-century A.D. *Huayang guo zhi* 華陽國志 (Record of Huayang state) with its accounts of the history of the southwest, offer additional evidence. The Song dynasty *Zi zhi tong jian* 資治通鑒 (Comprehensive mirror for aid in government) of Sima Guang 司馬光 (A.D. 1019–86), the *Gu shi* 古史 (Ancient history) of Su Che 蘇轍 (A.D. 1039–1112), and the *Lu shi* 路史 (Great history) of Luo Bi 羅泌 (d. ca. A.D. 1176) also contain evidence that appears to be based on earlier texts that have since disappeared. Finally, the chronicles and anecdotes in the *Zuo zhuan* 左傳 (Zuo's tradition), though set in the pre–Warring States world, help us to understand the period.[2]

Works on Political Methods

The second new political role of the period was that played by the reforming ministers, to whom were attributed the new governmental institutions and practices. Several of these figures initiated or served as eponyms for books devoted to theories of government based on their reforms. The only book of this nature that has survived in anything other than fragments is the *Shang jun shu* 商君書 (Book of Lord Shang), compiled in the late Warring States by scholars committed to the reforms carried out in mid-fourth century B.C. Qin by Shang Yang 商鞅 (d. 338 B.C.). The *Han Feizi* 韓非子, begun in the third century B.C., attempts a synthesis of the teachings of traditions associated with such political figures as Li Kui 李悝 (fl. late fifth century B.C.), Shen Buhai 申不害 (d. 337 B.C.), Shang Yang, and Shen Dao 慎到 (fl. 310 B.C.), so it can serve as a source for such works. The *Guanzi* 管子 also contains much material on political institutions, and these essays, though attributed to an earlier figure, are of Warring States or Han origin. These diverse political reformers were grouped together in Han bibliographies under the rubric of "Legalist" (*Fajia* 法家), but there is no reference to such a school in the Warring States texts themselves.

Government Documents

These are closely linked to the above texts, because they are tied to actual government institutions. The large cache of strips found at Yunmeng in a

---

[1] For details on the texts, consult Michael Loewe, ed., *Early Chinese Texts: A Bibliographical Guide* (Berkeley: Society for the Study of Early China and the Institute of East Asian Studies, University of California, 1993); Edward L. Shaughnessy, ed., *New Sources of Early Chinese History: An Introduction to Reading Inscriptions and Manuscripts* (Berkeley: Society for the Study of Early China and the Institute of East Asian Studies, University of California, 1997); Yang Kuan, *Zhanguo shi*, 2d rev. ed. (Shanghai: Shanghai Renmin, 1980), pp. 5–19.

[2] The chronology employed in this chapter, as in the table of Warring States rules (Table 1, pp. 28–29), follows that reconstructed by Yang Kuan in his *Zhanguo shi*.

tomb dating to 217 B.C. includes a substantial portion of the Qin code, two fragments of the Wei 魏 code, and other documents instructing officials in the application of the laws. There is also a moralizing exhortation to officials on the proper execution of their duties. Bamboo strips found in Baoshan 包山 tomb 2, dating to 316 B.C., provide some late fourth century B.C. legal documents from the southern state of Chu 楚. Whereas the deceased at Yunmeng was a local official, and the documents are prescriptive texts to guide his conduct in office, the deceased at Baoshan was the highest administrator of law in the Chu court, and the legal documents consist primarily of actual case reports and decisions. These records complement one another to provide valuable evidence on details of administrative practices at the different levels of government in the late Warring States period.

Military Treatises

A third political role that developed during the Warring States and produced associated writings was that of the military officer. The texts, named after famous commanders of antiquity, the late Spring and Autumn period, or the Warring States period, deal with aspects of warfare and their relation to statecraft. They provide information about the organization and conduct of armies, as well as the political role of combat. The major works are the *Sunzi* 孫子, the *Sun Bin* 孫臏, the *Wuzi* 吳子, the *Yu Liaozi* 尉繚子 (also called *Wei Liaozi*), the *Sima fa* 司馬法, and the *Tai Gong liu tao* 太公六韜. Archaeological finds have confirmed that all these works existed in the era of the Warring States, though not necessarily identical in form or content to the received versions.

Persuasions

A fourth new political role was that of the persuader/diplomats, the engineers of the systems of alliances that dominated politics from the middle of the fourth century B.C. Many such men rose to high ministerial rank, and their followers produced collections of fictional political "persuasions" attributed to the leading diplomats of the period. The most notable of these are the *Zhanguo ce* 戰國策 (Stratagems of the Warring States), the *Zhanguo zong heng jia shu* 戰國縱橫家書 (Documents of the Warring States strategists of alliances) discovered at Mawangdui 馬王堆, and the *Yanzi chunqiu* 晏子春秋 (Master Yan's Spring and Autumn [annals]).[3] Not strictly historical in char-

---

[3] For a brief introduction to the *Documents of the Warring States strategists of alliances*, see Yumiko F. Blanford, "A Textual Approach to 'Zhanguo Zonghengjia Shu': Method of Determining the Proximate Original Word Among Variants," *EC* 16 (1991): 187–207. This article is adapted from Blanford, "Studies of the 'Zhanguo Zonghengjia Shu' Silk Manuscript," Ph.D. dissertation, University of Washington, 1989.

acter, they must be used with caution as sources for reconstructing sequences of events. However, they offer a vivid portrait of the ruthless amorality and the "byzantine" maneuverings that characterized the court life and interstate relations of the period.

Texts of the Schools

By far the most abundant documents from the period, texts of the schools offer some insights into political history. First, they contain references to institutions, practices, and events. Second, certain scholars sought office at court, and some of their texts thus dealt with political affairs. This category includes the so-called Confucian writings: the *Analects* 論語 (begun in the Spring and Autumn period and continued into the Warring States), the *Mencius* 孟子 (fourth century), and the *Xunzi* 荀子 (third century). Although not strictly a philosophical work, the *Zuo zhuan* was completed in the Warring States period, and many of its explicit judgments and extended speeches clearly express the ideas of the Warring States "Confucians." Even some of the historical anecdotes reflect, if not actually derive from, the pedagogy of the Confucian schools. The *Mozi* 墨子 (fourth and third centuries) likewise contains many useful anecdotes, as well as discussions of Warring States institutions and practices, and the later chapters contain a detailed account of military procedures.

The Confucians and the Mohists are the only two Warring States scholarly traditions maintained through the protracted interaction of masters with groups of disciples. All other traditions were based entirely on textual transmissions grouped under the name of a single, founding master. Among these the most important are the works brought together during the Han under the name Daoism (*daojia* 道家) – *Laozi* 老子 and *Zhuangzi* 莊子. Also valuable is the great Qin syncretic work, the *Lü shi chunqiu* 呂氏春秋 (Mr. Lü's Spring and Autumn [annals]), which attempted a synthesis of various scholarly traditions at the end of the Warring States. Finally, there are several late Warring States texts now grouped under the ill-defined rubric Huang Lao 黃老. These include the *Heguanzi* 鶡冠子, *Jing fa* 經法 (Classical model), and *Shiliu jing* 十六經 (Sixteen classics), the latter two texts having been discovered only recently at Mawangdui.

Ritual Texts

These can be used only with the greatest caution because of problems of dating. However, much of the *Yi li* 儀禮 (Etiquette and rites), which describes family rites for the lowest stratum of nobility, and the *Zhou li* 周禮 (Rites of

Zhou) probably date from the Warring States period, and they can be used in conjunction with other materials.

Geographic Works

The "Yu gong" chapter of the *Shang shu* 尚書 (Venerated documents) is almost certainly a Warring States composition, as is probably the "Zang shan jing" 藏山經 section of the *Shan hai jing* 山海經 (Classic of mountains and seas), an early account of magical plants and animals encountered in the wilds. These are extremely valuable for insights into contemporary under-standing of geography. Li Daoyuan's 酈道元 (d. 527 A.D.) *Shui jing zhu* 水經注 (Commentary on the classic of rivers), a sixth century A.D. compendium, contains much material culled from Warring States works, as well as discus-sions of the various walls and canals constructed in the period. Finally, several chapters of the *Yi Zhou shu* 逸周書 (Remainder of Zhou documents) appear to be Warring States compositions that contain material on geography.

Poetry

The only poetry datable to the period appears in the earlier chapters of the *Chu ci* 楚辭 (Verses of Chu), two chapters of verse in the *Xunzi*, and rhymed passages scattered through the texts of the schools. These provide material dealing with the political and religious thought of the period.

Han Anecdotal Collections

The *Han shi wai zhuan* 韓詩外傳 (Outer tradition of Master Han [Ying's version of the Classic of] Poetry) by Han Ying 韓嬰 (fl. 150 B.C.), *Shuo yuan* 説苑 (Garden of expositions), and *Xin xu* 新序 (New preface), both by Liu Xiang 劉向 (79–8 B.C.), contain anecdotes set in the Warring States period. Many of these can still be found in texts datable to the Warring States, so one might cautiously employ the rest as supplementary material.

The total amount of material is not inconsiderable, and texts discovered in tombs have increased it dramatically in recent decades. However, major prob-lems exist in its use. First, as noted earlier we lack a reliable chronological frame. As a result, many events cannot be dated. Second, most of our sources are rhetorical set pieces or philosophical arguments. They often invoke sup-posed historical events, but their polemical character and the contradictions between accounts call into question their reliability. Finally, most of these sources are difficult to date with any precision. This reflects both the physical and the social nature of written works in the period. As collections of wooden or bamboo strips, or rolls of silk, they were liable to deliberate or accidental alteration over time. Such texts were the legacy of a tradition, rather than the work of an "author," so it was conventional to add or modify materials in order to meet the needs of each new generation. Thus, the lack of firm dates is not a result of missing evidence but is inherent in the fluidity of the works themselves. As a result, much of our data can be applied only to the broad outline of the whole period, while the details remain open to doubt.

This chapter will focus on the creation of the new political order, as defined by the political roles enunciated in our sources. The collective creation and transmission of texts means that the writings that survived represent the intellectual interests or commitments of certain groups of people, rather than isolated individuals. Consequently, one can reconstitute a composite image of the political life of the period through the programs or ideals transmitted in the surviving texts. Seen in the light of this composite image, the uneven narrative of the period may gain a certain historical value.

THE STATES

The classic Warring States world was dominated by seven major states, though several minor ones also survived throughout much of the period.[4] In order to follow the history of the period, it is necessary to be familiar with the locations of the states and their physical characteristics. Precise borders are difficult to establish, except where walls were built, and they shifted considerably over the course of the period. Consequently, only the proximate location of the core areas of the states will be discussed.

Before describing the individual states, it is important to note two general features of the period. First, although the central and lower Yangzi regions had become important in the Spring and Autumn period, the Warring States world was still primarily defined by the drainage basin of the Yellow River. Second, the old states in what had been the geographic center (most notably the Zhou capital region, Zheng 鄭, Wey 衛, Song 宋, and Lu 魯, that is, modern northern Henan province and southern Shandong province) had no avenues for expansion and were reduced to buffer zones between the larger states that surrounded them. For the purposes of exposition, I will start in the northeast, proceed west up the drainage basin of the Yellow River, and finish in the southern regions (see Map 9.1).

---

[4] Li Xueqin, *Eastern Zhou and Qin Civilizations*, trans. K. C. Chang (New Haven, Conn.: Yale University Press, 1985), part 1; Yang Kuan, *Zhanguo shi*, pp. 261–8.

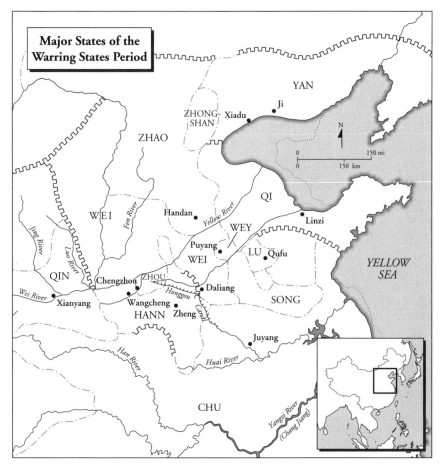

Map 9.1. Major states of the Warring States period.

Yan 燕

The smallest of the major Warring States and the last to emerge as a power, Yan was located in the far northeast. Its territory included the northern part of modern Hebei province, southwestern Liaoning province, and the northeast corner of Shanxi province. Its capital was just southwest of modern Beijing. Because the mouth of what we now call the Yellow River at this time lay inside Yan's borders, the region was probably damper and more fertile than it is today. It was certainly more forested. To the north it bordered on regions populated by nomads who were non-Hua 華 (that is, not part of Zhou civilization), to the west on Zhao 趙 and Zhongshan 中山, and to the south on Qi 齊 and the Bohai 渤海 Gulf. Although not one of the most powerful states, it achieved security through its remoteness and the absence of major threats from the north and the east.

Qi 齊

Qi's territory comprised the central and northern part of modern Shandong and the southern part of modern Hebei. It occupied a large alluvial flood plain centered on the Ji 濟 River, though the main course of the Yellow River shifted it to the north. It was rich in agriculture, minerals, and the resources of the sea. Qi was the demographic and economic center of the empire in the subsequent Han period and seems to have been likewise in the Warring States period.[5] At any rate, its capital Linzi 臨淄 seems to have been the largest metropolis of the era. Its eastern edge was delimited by the sea. To the south lay a cluster of small states, the most important of which were Lu 魯 and Song 宋, but also including some that were simply small cities: Zou 鄒, Xue 薛, Teng 滕, Tan 郯, and Ju 莒. To the west it bordered on Wey 衛, Zhao 昭, and Wei 魏. It also enjoyed a good strategic position, in that it faced danger only from the west, so long as its alliance to the north with Yan endured.

Wei 魏

Throughout most of the Warring States period, Wei was the strongest of the three states created by the partition of Jin 晉, which had been the most influential state during the preceding centuries. It also initiated the most significant institutional reforms. Its core straddled two areas: the region east of the bend of the Yellow River and valley of the Fen 汾 River, that is, the southwest of modern Shanxi province and the region of modern Henan province that is now north of the Yellow River, but at that time lay south of the Yellow River and north of the Ji River. At its peak, in the first half of the fourth century B.C., Wei expanded westward to the Luo 洛 River and pushed south of the Ji River in the east. It included rich agricultural land in its river valleys, and it was a pioneer in the use of large-scale irrigation. Wei also held some of the major trade centers, which provided an additional source of wealth. It suffered, however, from two linked strategic weaknesses. First, it confronted potentially hostile states on all sides: Qi to the east, Zhao to the north, Qin 秦 to the west, and Hann 韓 and Chu 楚 to the south. Consequently it often found itself fighting wars on several fronts or being forced to abandon a campaign because it was attacked from a different direction. This problem was

---

[5] Shi Nianhai, *He shan ji*, vol. 3 (Beijing: Renmin, 1988), pp. 117–30.

exacerbated by the geographic structure of Wei described above. Possessing two major centers linked only by the narrow territory of Shangdang 上黨, it was pulled in two directions. This often led to difficulties in the formulation of any grand strategy.

Zhao 趙

Second of the Jin successor states, Zhao lay to the north of Wei. Its territory covered the northern half of modern Shanxi and the south of Hebei, extending down into modern Henan. Like Yan it was a northern frontier state that was less developed and populous than its southern neighbors, but it enjoyed the strategic luxury of confronting enemies in only two directions: Qi and Yan from the east, and Wei and Qin from the south or southwest. In close contact with nomadic peoples to the north, Zhao pioneered the use of cavalry.

Hann 韓

Last and smallest of the Jin successor states, Hann was located in the southeast of modern Shanxi and central Henan. In the early Warring States period it acted as a junior partner of Wei and reached its peak in the year 375, when it occupied most of the old state of Zheng and moved its capital there. Like Wei it faced potential enemies on all sides: Wei to the north, Qin to the west, and Chu to the south. Since it was weaker than these three states, Hann often played the role of a buffer zone. It survived largely by shifting its alliance from one state to another as the balance of power changed.

Qin 秦

As Qin's center lay in the valley of the Wei 渭 River, the old capital region of the Western Zhou, it was the furthest west of the Warring States. Located in a fertile valley ringed by hills, Qin enjoyed a splendid geographic situation that combined productivity and security. It was accessible from the east only through the Hangu 函谷 Pass and from the southeast through the Wu 武 Pass. Therefore, the Qin core region was known as Guanzhong 關中, the area "within the pass." To the north the only threat was the Rong 戎 tribes. They occasionally pillaged Qin cities but posed no sustained menace and were conquered in the second half of the fifth century B.C. To the south lay Shu 蜀 and Ba 巴, in what is now Sichuan province. The conquest of this region between 441 and 316 B.C. provided Qin with a new, highly productive "grain basket" that supplied its wars of conquest in the third century.

Chu 楚

Southernmost of the major Warring States, Chu spread across the valley of the Han 漢 River, the middle of the Yangzi River (*Changjiang* 長江), and the valley of the Huai 淮 River. In 334 it conquered the state of Yue 越, thus also gaining control of the lower Yangzi. This region is much wetter than the valley of the Yellow River, but only with the development of superior techniques for drainage would the abundance of water be transformed from a problem into a blessing. In the Warring States period it was still not as productive as the irrigated zones of the north. Despite its great size, Chu suffered from a relatively weak monarchy, which led to several civil wars. This inhibited the full-scale development of the institutions that defined the Warring States polity, and consequently Chu's actual power never matched its geographic potential.

In addition to the seven great states, a number of minor states figure in Warring States history. First, the Zhou royal house lived on as a small state within the borders of Hann. Lu, birthplace of Confucius, and neighboring Zou, birthplace of Mencius, lay just to the south of Qi. To their south in turn lay Song, a state founded to preserve the Shang royal line at the time of the Zhou conquest (1045 B.C.). This state included the city of Dingtao 定陶, perhaps the greatest commercial center of the period and the target of campaigns by several great powers. Surrounded by Qi, Wei, and Zhao, the state of Wey played a role in several wars. Zheng, which had been a major power at the beginning of the Eastern Zhou and acted as a buffer state between Jin and Chu during the Spring and Autumn period, was still a focus of warfare and diplomacy in the first half of the Warring States. Finally, the state of Zhongshan 中山, which lay between Zhao and Yan in the north, also figured in the political history of the period.

THE RULER-CENTERED STATE

The new style of polity that appeared in the Warring States period was both an expansion and a contraction of the old Zhou model. It was an expansion in that it developed a full-blown territorial state in place of the city-based state of the Zhou world, but it was a contraction in that it concentrated all power in the court of the single monarch. In place of the hereditary nobility who had been scattered across the state in numerous local replicas of the king's court, the new state was centered on the unique person of the ruler and his single capital. The foundations of these changes were laid in the Spring and Autumn period, when the pressures of war had led both rulers and ministerial households to increase their armies through the recruitment of the rural populace. These new forces were controlled by recruited officials who had played no role in the earlier kin-based polity. The peasant-based armies and retinues of personal retainers expanded the scale of warfare, and the large-scale participation of men who had no place in the old networks of ritual performance and blood ties heightened its savagery. However, whereas in the Spring and Autumn period these changes had taken place largely within the framework of the old ruling lines and their sublineages, in the Warring States many of these lineages were swept away by new men who concentrated power in their own hands. These victors of the states' internal struggles emerged as the absolute monarchs of large territorial states.[6]

The earliest case of ministerial lineages supplanting the ruler of a state was the de facto usurpation by the Three Huan 三桓 lineages in Lu 魯 in 562 B.C. At this time the ministerial lineages partitioned control of the state's armies and tax revenues among themselves. In 537 B.C. the senior Jisun 季孫 lineage took the dominant position, and the power of the ruling line was further reduced. Attempts by rulers in 517 and 468 to form military alliances, first with lesser Lu lineages and then with the southern state of Wu 吳, in order to defeat the Three Huan were both defeated. However, the continuation of a divided sovereignty due to the entente of the three lines meant that Lu did not attain the new concentration of power that characterized subsequent cases.[7]

The first state in which a single ministerial line annihilated all of its rivals and assumed power was Qi 齊. Here the Tian 田 lineage came to dominate the state, destroyed several rival lineages in 532, and expanded Qi's power against rival states. In 485 B.C. the head of the Tian clan murdered the heir chosen by the recently deceased lord of Qi and put another child in his place. Soon a civil war broke out when several rival lineages joined together to install yet another puppet ruler. In 481 the new head of the Tian clan murdered the rival puppet, placed the victim's younger brother on the throne, and then killed all his adversaries and most of the ruler's family. He took personal control of virtually all of Qi, leaving only the capital Linzi and the western plain between Mount Tai 泰山 and the Yellow River in the nominal control of the ruler.[8] Since the *Chunqiu* 春秋 ends in 481 B.C., one could well adopt this seizure of power in Qi as the symbolic commencement of the Warring States period, though the old ducal line was not formally supplanted until 386 B.C.

---

[6] Mark Edward Lewis, *Sanctioned Violence in Early China* (Albany: State University of New York Press, 1990), chapters 1–2.

[7] *Chunqiu Zuo zhuan zhu*, ed. Yang Bojun (Beijing: Zhonghua, 1981) (Xiang 11), pp. 986–8; (Zhao 3), pp. 1234–6; (Zhao 5), p. 1261; (Zhao 25), pp. 1456–7; *Shi ji*, 33, p. 1545.

[8] *Zuo zhuan zhu* (Zhao 10), pp. 1315–18; (Ai 10), p. 1656; (Ai 14), pp. 1683–6, 1689; *Shi ji*, 32, p. 1508; 46, pp. 1883–4.

The methods of usurpation employed by the Tian are also significant, for they indicate the pattern by which the new rulers ensured the centralization of power in their persons. The accounts in the *Zuo zhuan* and the *Shi ji* both emphasize that the Tian clan surrounded itself with fugitives or refugees in order to expand its immediate entourage and that it secured the support of the populace of Qi's capital through conspicuous philanthropic activities. This support from outsiders and the lower elements of society proved decisive in its victories over rival noble lines. This drawing into service of new social elements, along with new methods to secure their loyalty, defined the Warring States polity.

These new methods appear most clearly in the state of Jin 晉, which had dominated the Spring and Autumn period and pioneered many of the reforms that created territorial states. Even as the Tian clan was rising to dominance in Qi, ongoing low-level warfare took place between Jin's noble lineages. In the course of these struggles the more powerful lineages employed a variety of new methods to eliminate their rivals. One method was the transformation of the fiefs of defeated lineages into directly administered districts (*xian* 縣) in 550 and 514 B.C., though these *xian* were still inherited as private possessions by loyal sublineages and not yet governed by appointed officials. Another innovation was the casting of laws on a bronze vessel in 513 B.C. in order to enforce the destruction of the Qi 祁 and Yangshe 羊舌 lineages.[9] In 497 these struggles erupted into a full-scale civil war between the Zhao 趙, Wei 魏, Hann 韓, and Zhi 智 lineages on one side and the Fan 范 and Zhonghang 中行 lineages on the other. Archaeological evidence from Houma 侯馬 and Wenxian 溫縣 has provided us with dramatic evidence of one of the major practices employed in Jin at this time to forge new states, the collective sacrificial oath.

The blood oath had an ancient pedigree, dating back at least to the late Western Zhou. It had come to the fore as the primary mechanism for establishing links between states or lineages in the age of the *ba* 霸, the seventh century B.C. However, while earlier oaths took place in interstate gatherings, the oaths discovered at Houma and Wenxian record attempts by the Zhao (Houma) and the Hann (Wenxian) lineages to impose their authority on the lesser lineages and perhaps the urban populace (*guo ren* 國人). In these oaths participants swore loyalty to the dominant lineage, and they called down a curse upon any who violated the oath. In the case of the

[9] *Zuo zhuan zhu* (Xiang 10), pp. 1073–6, 1078, 1084; (Zhao 3), pp. 1236–40; (Zhao 28), pp. 1491–2, 1493–4; (Zhao 29), p. 1504; (Ding 13), pp. 1589–1; *Shi ji*, 39, pp. 1683–6; Masubuchi Tatsuo, *Chûgoku kodai no shakai to kokka* (Tokyo: Kôbundô, 1962), pp. 328–450, esp. 444–50; Gosei Tadako, "Shunjû jidai no Shin no daifu Ki shi Yôzetsu shi no ôzato ni tsuite," *Chûgoku kodaishi kenkyû* 3 (Tokyo: Chûgoku kodaishi kenkyûkai, 1968), pp. 183–209.

Houma oaths, they placed a curse on named rival lineages and individuals who had been driven out of the fief, while the Wenxian texts simply anathematize unnamed "brigands." In these covenants we see how the cultic practices that had defined the Zhou state, at least in its decline, were adapted to lend religious sanction and majesty to the powers of rising territorial lords. The texts also suggest how the dispersed pattern of fiefs that had characterized the earlier state was turned into an integrated, territorial unit.[10]

The civil war ended in 490 with the destruction of the Fan and the Zhonghang lineages. It resumed in 458 with partition of the former fiefs of the Fan and Zhonghang lines among the four dominant lineages. These renewed hostilities lasted until 453, when the Zhi lineage was destroyed by the other three. Each being afraid to attract hostility by assuming the office of chief minister, the three surviving lines abandoned the Jin court as an arena of competition and contented themselves with developing their own states. About 424 they recognized their mutual independence, and this partition was officially recognized by the Zhou king in 403 B.C.[11]

In addition to the aforementioned use of centralizing administration, legal codes, and collective oaths, another aspect of the new polity that emerges from accounts of the civil war in Jin was the policy of granting or recognizing the private ownership of land in exchange for taxes. This element of state formation appears in a previously lost chapter of the *Sunzi* military treatise that was discovered in a Han tomb at Yinqueshan 銀雀山. This chapter describes how each of the six Jin lineages had abolished the old unit of land (*mu* 畝) and imposed new *mu* of varying dimensions. Since the account suggests that those with the larger units of land were more generous to their people, it clearly implies some form of allocation. In addition, it states that all except the Zhao lineage had imposed a 20 percent tax on harvest. Since this passage correctly "prophesies" the destruction of the Fan and Zhonghang lines, but incorrectly predicts the ultimate triumph of Zhao, it presumably was written between 490 and 403 B.C. and hence is virtually a contemporary account.[12]

In the Yangzi River valley the centralization of power emerged not through the internecine warfare of sublineages, but rather by means of a triangular struggle between the states of Chu, Wu 吳 (located in the plains south of the lower reaches of the Yangzi) and Yue. During the sixth century, the

[10] Lewis, *Sanctioned Violence*, pp. 43–9, 67–79; Susan Weld, "Covenant in Jin's Walled Cities: The Discoveries at Houma and Wenxian," Ph.D. dissertation, Harvard University, 1990.
[11] *Zuo zhuan zhu* (Ai 2), pp. 1613–14; (Ai 5), pp. 1629–30; *Shi ji*, 39, pp. 1685–7.
[12] *Shi yi jia zhu Sunzi* (Shanghai: Guji, 1978), pp. 494–5 (Ralph Sawyer, trans., *Sun Tzu: Art of War* [Boulder: Westview, 1994], pp. 246–8).

state of Wu had developed its power through recruiting nobles and officials who fled from Jin and Chu. Using their skills to introduce military and land reforms patterned on those of Jin, Wu had steadily expanded into Chu territory. In 506 Chu had been exhausted by the numerous wars of King Ling 靈 (r. 540–529) and its court divided by a recent coup d'état. King Helü 闔閭 (r. 514–496 B.C.) of Wu took advantage of this situation to launch an invasion that destroyed the Chu armies and occupied its capital. Chu was saved only through the intervention of Qin and an insurrection in Wu. In 494 the successor of Helü, Fuchai 夫差 (r. 496–473 B.C.), crushed the armies of Yue and reduced the latter to a tributary. Wu thus established itself briefly with *ba* status in 482 B.C. at the interstate conference at Huangji 黃棘.

Following the disaster of 494, King Goujian 勾踐 (r. 496–465 B.C.) of Yue prepared for revenge with a set of policy reforms. He granted remission from taxes for those who had lost sons in battle, recruited officials and commanders from neighboring states, and enticed additional population with tax remissions in order to open up new land. In 482 he took advantage of Fuchai's attendance at the Huangji assembly to crush Wu's army, occupy its capital, and capture the heir apparent. Fuchai was forced to negotiate a peace, but the war soon resumed and in 473 B.C. Yue destroyed Wu.[13] At this point, however, rather than resuming the rivalry with Chu to the west, the kings of Yue turned their attention northward and devoted their energies to wars of expansion against the lesser states in the south of what is now Shandong.

The consequences of these wars for Chu in terms of institutional reforms and the consolidation of royal power are not clear. It appears that under the pressure of the wars with Wu and Yue, power in the Chu court shifted from the collateral lineages to the royal line, though Kings Zhao 昭 (r. 516–489 B.C.) and Hui 惠 (r. 488–432 B.C.) were still dominated by their uncles.[14] Freed from the assaults of Wu and Yue, Chu expanded gradually throughout the fifth century by annexing small states along its northern frontier and on the upper Huai River. Wu Qi's 吳起 (ca. 440–361 B.C.) biography in the *Shi ji* asserts that he totally reformed the fiscal and military structure of Chu under King Dao 悼 (r. 401–381), but the account may be fictionalized, and it is likely that Wu Qi was given credit for reforms instituted over the course of the century.[15] However, it remains true that Chu was characterized

[13] *Zuo zhuan zhu* (Ding 4), pp. 1542–8; (Ding 5); pp. 1550–3; (Ai 1), pp. 1604–609; (Ai 13), pp. 1676–7; *Shi ji*, 31, pp. 1465–75; 40, pp. 1714–19; 41, pp. 1739–56; *Guo yu*, "Wu yu" and "Yue yu." See also the dramatized accounts in the *Wu Yue chunqiu* 吳越春秋 (Springs and Autumns of Wu and Yue) and the *Yue jue shu* 越絕書 (Documents on the destruction of Yue).
[14] Barry B. Blakeley, "King, Clan, and Courtier in Ancient Ch'u," *AM*, 3d series, 5, 2 (1992): 1–39.
[15] *Shi ji*, 65, pp. 2167–8 (Ralph Sawyer, trans., *The Seven Military Classics of Ancient China* [Boulder: Westview, 1993], pp. 191–202).

throughout the Warring States period by the relative weakness of the royal office.

Institutional reforms in the state of Qin came late (a land tax paid in grain was not introduced until 408 B.C.), and they emerged not from foreign or civil wars, but rather from a struggle between the rulers and their ministers for control of the state. Throughout most of the fifth century the rulers of Qin had been young, and power at court lay in the hands of the ministers. In 425 Huai Gong 懷公 (r. 428–425 B.C.), who had been established in power by the dominant ministers, was forced to commit suicide by his own officials, and for the next four decades Qin was ruled by a succession of youths. This state of affairs ended in 385 when the future Xian Gong 獻公 (r. 384–362 B.C.), who had spent his life in Wei, was able to return with the support of the Rong 戎 and Di 狄 tribes and a faction at court that murdered the infant ruler and his mother. Xian Gong ruled for twenty-two years during which he introduced many of the governmental institutions that he had observed in Wei. His reforms included the abolition of the human sacrifices that had accompanied the funerals of major nobles (384 B.C.), the registration of households in units of five (375 B.C.), and the establishment of directly administered districts (*xian*).[16] These began the transformation of Qin into a classic Warring States polity, a process that would be completed under his son Xiao Gong 孝公 (r. 361–338 B.C.) in the reforms of Shang Yang.

The last major state where a single ruler gained dominion was Yan 燕. In 316 B.C. the dying King Kuai 噲 (r. 320–312 B.C.) attempted to name his chief minister as successor. The heir apparent led a coalition of noble lineages against the arriviste, but they were decisively defeated in 314 B.C. At this point King Xuan 宣 (r. 319–301 B.C.) of Qi took advantage of the civil war to invade and conquer Yan. However, the cruelty of the invaders provoked a rebellion, and the Qi forces withdrew. King Wuling 武靈 (r. 325–229 B.C.) of Zhao then established a younger son of King Kuai as king of Yan, and the latter was able to take advantage of the political vacuum left by the defeat of the noble lineages to impose a full-scale land and military reform.[17] Similar struggles leading to the triumph of centralizing power also took place in several of the smaller states, but these were ultimately conquered by larger neighbors.

This concentration of power in the person of the ruler, achieved throughout the Warring States by the middle of the fourth century, found a clear expression in changing nomenclature. In 344 B.C. when Wei Hui Hou 魏惠侯 (r. 369–335 B.C.) was at the peak of his powers and compelling several small states to attend his court, he adopted the title of "king" (*wang* 王) that

[16] *Shi ji*, 5, pp. 199–205; 6, p. 289 (Burton Watson, trans., *Records of the Grand Historian. Vol. 3: Qin Dynasty* [Hong Kong: Columbia University Press, 1993], pp. 22–5).

[17] *Shi ji*, 34, pp. 1555–8.

had previously been reserved for the Zhou Son of Heaven. He also assumed the use of royal regalia and chariots patterned on those ascribed to the Xia 夏 dynasty, whose supposed ancient capital had been his own. This act of hubris was followed by a disastrous military defeat in 341 B.C. Rather than retract the title, which corresponded to the new political realities, at a meeting of the two rulers in 334 King Hui persuaded the victorious Qi Wei Hou 齊威侯 (r. 356–320 B.C.) also to take the title of "king." Following a series of military victories, Qin Huiwen Hou 秦惠文侯 (r. 337–325 B.C.) also adopted the title in 325 B.C. That same year, the ruler of Hann also took the royal title, and two years later Zhao, Yan, and Zhongshan all followed suit.[18] Since the Chu ruler had always held the title of "king" as a sign of the rejection of Zhou suzerainty, by 323 all the rulers of the major states had assumed the royal title. This marked, in name at least, the culmination of the process of centralizing state power.

INSTITUTIONS OF THE WARRING STATES

The correlate of the concentration of power in the ruler and the central court was the extension of state control into the rural hinterlands. This extension was based on the development of a new political role, that of the dependent official who was the creature of the ruler. The ability to appoint officials, dispatch them to remote cities, maintain control over them at a distance, and remove them when necessary was essential to the creation of a territorial state. Only with such powers could the ruler impose his writ across an extended realm. The institutional history of the Warring States thus consists of the development of the practices and values which underlay these powers.

In reality, the Warring States have no histories of institutions, but rather biographies of individuals. Laws and administrative procedures are mentioned in scholarly works, and they appear as a reality in the legal documents, but in the historical sources they figure only as pendants to accounts of the officials to whom they are attributed. The propensity to attribute all reforms to individuals was such that collective or gradual developments would be assigned to a single, nameable individual, such as Wu Qi 吳起 in Chu or Sun Wu 孫武 in Yue. Consequently the institutional history of the Warring States appears as a series of heroic innovations by daring reformers – each one lionized by the tradition which carried on "his" book – who were able to gain the attention of the monarch and persuade him to introduce some

---

[18] *Shi ji*, 5, pp. 206–207 (Watson, *Records of the Grand Historian*, vol. 3, p. 26); 15, p. 727; 40, p. 1722; 44, p. 1844; 45, p. 1869; 46, p. 1892; 70, p. 2284; *Zhanguo ce* (Shanghai: Guji, 1978) "Qin 4," p. 259; "Qi 5," p. 442; "Wei 1," pp. 804, 812; "Wei 2," pp. 835–7; "Zhongshan," pp. 1170–4 (J. I. Crump, trans., *Chan-Kuo Ts'e* [Oxford: Clarendon, 1970], pp. 143, 203, 385, 381–2, 574–6).

new practice. From such evidence the modern scholar can often only deduce general tendencies and common developments. Nevertheless, the tales of the individual reformers provide a rough chronological sequence as well as a genealogy of developing institutions. Consequently a complete account of Warring States politics cannot omit them.

As royal power increased, the character of office holding changed completely. From being a hereditary element of a government in which power was distributed among the nobility, office became an extension of royal power. Since officeholders were drawn from a much wider geographic and social range than their predecessors, and since the extension of government meant a larger number of offices, an expanding group of political "cadres" was the beneficiary of the new state. The career pattern of these cadres entailed a new ideal type, the "man of service" (*shi* 士), who through powers of mind and tongue won for himself the position of guide to the ruler. We have already seen one example of this in the figure of Wu Qi, the reformer to whom was attributed the strengthening of Chu in the fifth century.

Such figures became models for aspiring courtiers. Some wrote – or gathered disciples who wrote – texts laying out the principles underlying their policies. Their achievements formed the stuff of romance and fable. At the same time or shortly afterward, men discovered model political advisers in earlier history – Guan Zhong 管仲 (fl. seventh century B.C.), Zhou Gong 周公 (eleventh century B.C.), Lü Shang 呂尚 (eleventh century B.C.), and Yi Yin 伊尹 (Shang foundation) – and texts were attributed to these archetypes of ministerial success. Much of the surviving writing from the Warring States thus emerges directly from the context of pursuing or holding office. The tendency to treat institutional history as biography derives from these social origins of "authorship."

The earliest book attributed to a politically active author is the *Sunzi*, ascribed to the general who supposedly led the victorious armies of Yue at the end of the sixth century. However, the book probably originated a century after the putative author, whose very existence is questionable, and no institutional reforms are credited to him.[19] The first clear linkage of minister, reform, and book is the case of Li Kui 李悝. Appointed chief minister in Wei some time after 445 B.C., he was the eponym of a lengthy work, now lost, that appears in the *Han shu* bibliographic chapter as the first of the Legalist school. He is remembered for two achievements: the elaboration of a theory on the optimal use of land and the writing of the *Fa jing* 法經 (Classic of

---

[19] Lewis, *Sanctioned Violence*, p. 68, p. 285, n. 5; Jens Østergård Petersen, "What's in a Name? On the Sources Concerning Sun Wu," *AM* 3d series, 5, 1 (1992): 1–32. For a different position, see Sawyer, trans., *Sun Tzu*, pp. 151–7.

law).[20] The former became the basis for discussions of the political economy of the peasantry in the Warring States and the Han empire, while the latter is the earliest known administrative law code.

Although the books written in Li Kui's name have all been lost, their theory of agriculture is cited frequently enough to describe them as the fountainhead of Chinese rural political economy. The key feature of his work is that he takes the small-scale peasant freehold worked by a single family to be the basic unit of production, posits a standard size of landholding, and then offers advice on how to maximize production for the purpose of generating the highest possible revenue for the state without destroying the people's livelihood. While the peasant freehold had been evolving for some centuries, it is with Li Kui that we first find articulated a theory of the state based on revenue from small-scale farming. This was the economic foundation of the Warring States polity. Li Kui's writings were later classified as Legalist, and he is recognized as the inspiration for the agricultural theories of Shang Yang, but it is worth noting that the surviving fragments of his work could also have been the source for Mencius's accounts of self-sustaining peasant households under the imaginary "well-field" (jing tian 井田) system.

Closely linked to this theory of a state based on the landowning peasant household is the earliest record of a large-scale, state-controlled irrigation project that opened up new land for cultivation. This is attributed to Ximen Bao 西門豹, who served as magistrate of Ye 鄴 district in Wei during the 430s and built a system of canals to provide water for irrigation. Han dynasty records note that an expanded version of this system was still in use, and various sources attribute the rise of Wei to predominance at this time to the increased yields in the Henei 河內 region (centered on modern Cixian 磁縣 in Hebei province) made possible by the introduction of water control. Stories of initial peasant resistance to this development also suggest that some loss or redistribution of land was entailed. Li Kui's model of the individual household with its 100 mu of land might not have been merely theoretical, but may have been adopted as a government policy in certain regions.[21]

The Fa jing attributed to Li Kui is another key step in the emergence of the Warring States polity. We noted above the evolving use of laws in the internecine wars of the Jin nobility, but it is in the accounts of the Fa jing that we find the first discussion of Warring States law in its classic form as

[20] Han shu (Beijing: Zhonghua, 1962), 30, p. 1735; 24A, pp. 1124–5. Fragments of the work on land use are preserved in Taiping yulan, comp. Li Fang (925–66 A.D.) et al. (Beijing: Zhonghua, 1960) ("Tian"), 821.3b; Tong dian, comp. Du You (745–812 A.D.) (Taipei: Xinxing, 1963) ("Shui li tian"), 2.16c.

[21] Shi ji, 29, p. 1408; 44, p. 1839; 126, pp. 3211–13; Chen Qiyou, ed., Lü shi chunqiu jiao shi (Shanghai: Xuelin, 1984) (16 "Yue cheng"), pp. 990–1.

an extended code devoted to penal measures to control the people. These accounts, written much later than the supposed code, tell us that it was divided into six sections: bandits, brigands, prisons, arrests, miscellaneous punishments, and special circumstances.[22] This use of laws to control the actions of the populace at large was carried forward in the Qin legal code fashioned by Shang Yang, who had served in Wei, and thereafter into the Han dynasty.

Another of the Jin successor states, Hann, also produced a reformer of note in the person of Shen Buhai, chief minister appointed in 355 B.C. Like Li Kui, Shen Buhai served as the eponym of a work on political principles that was classified as Legalist. It survives only in scattered quotations. This work was identified in later writings as the first to articulate techniques (*shu* 術) by which the ruler could control his ministers, keep them from growing too powerful, and maintain his absolute authority.[23]

The theories of Shen Buhai highlight the pivotal role in the Warring States polity of dependent officials employed by the ruler to execute his decrees. The importance of this innovation has been sketched above, but to carry it out required a range of new practices that redefined the nature of political ties. These innovations included salaries measured, and partially paid, in grain; special payments of gold and silver to reward meritorious service; seals and tallies to bestow and withdraw authority; numerical accounting procedures to examine officials; regular methods of making appointments; and the transformation of fiefs into nonhereditary units which were bestowed by the ruler and served only to provide income.

Traditionally offices in the Zhou state had been associated with fiefs or held by nobles who drew their income from their estates rather than their offices. There are hints that already in the late Spring and Autumn period some officials were paid a salary in grain. However, it is in the Warring States that salaries became the norm, and the amount of grain supposedly paid as salary became the measure of rank. Different states employed different measures of volume, but the practice of rewarding officials with salaries graded in quantities of grain was universal.[24] Some of the grain received in salaries could have been converted into cash through sale, but it

[22] *Jin shu* 晉書 (Beijing: Zhonghua, 1974), 30, p. 922.

[23] Chen Qiyou, ed., *Han Feizi ji shi* (Shanghai: Renmin, 1974) (43 "Ding fa"), 17, pp. 906–908 and passim (W. K. Liao, trans., *The Complete Works of Han Fei Tzu*, 2 vols. [London: Arthur Probsthain, 1939, 1959], vol. 2, pp. 211–16); Herrlee G. Creel, *Shen Pu-hai: A Chinese Political Philosopher of the Fourth Century B.C.* (Chicago: University of Chicago Press, 1974).

[24] *Lun yu zhu shu* (Shisan jing zhu shu, ed.) ("Yong ye"), 6.2b–3a (James Legge, trans., *The Chinese Classics. Vol 1: Confucian Analects, The Great Learning, and the Doctrine of the Mean* [Oxford: Clarendon, 1893], p. 186); *Mengzi zhu shu* (Shisan jing zhu shu ed.) ("Gongsun Chou B"), 4B.6b–7a (James Legge, trans., *The Chinese Classics. Vol. 2: The Works of Mencius* [Oxford: Clarendon, 1895], pp. 226, 227); *Mozi jian gu*, ed. Sun Yirang (Zhu zi ji cheng ed.) (Taipei: Shijie, 1974), 47 "Gui yi," 12, pp. 269–70 (Yi-

is more likely that officials used it to support larger households or more numerous retainers.

While grain was the measure, and perhaps the content, of salaries, Warring States rulers also encouraged devoted service through occasional gifts in gold and silver. In the early Warring States such gifts were also made in land, for example, awards of land to Wu Qi, Ba Ning 巴寧, and Cuan Xiang 爨襄 in mid-fifth-century Wei, but these increasingly took the form of precious metals.[25] This shift from land, which was permanent and closely tied to political authority, toward "money," which was fluid, a mark of exchange, and easily withdrawn, was indicative of broader shifts in society. They are linked to the increased use of money in society, but it would be easy to exaggerate the role of cash in what was still primarily a barter economy. As Anna Seidel has noted, cash in the early periods was largely used within the sphere of government. Coins, which in this period took the form of miniature copies of agricultural implements and weapons, and precious metals seem to have served primarily as a store of value and a means of paying capitation taxes. They also began to figure in grave offerings, where precious metals or common metals labeled as "gold" were buried in tombs to be carried into the next world, just as gold and silver inlay became a major feature of bronze vessels.[26] The interplay between government, religion, and economy in defining the role of cash and metal in the Warring States has yet to be worked out. However, it seems that precious metals were more a matter of status than of disposable wealth and that rulers bestowed them to mark out those whom they favored.

Beyond the payment of salaries in grain and gifts in precious metals, the rulers of the Warring States preserved the name of the old Zhou institution of the "fief" (*feng* 封), but they transformed its character. Whereas the Zhou had awarded actual control over an area and its population, allowing the holder of the fief to act as a lesser replica of the central Zhou court, the fief-holders of the Warring States played no administrative or judicial role in their fiefs, but were simply granted the right to the tax income from a specific city or a specified number of households. Thus, Tian Wen 田文, the Lord of Mengchang 孟嘗君 (d. 279 B.C.), who served as chief minister in Qi in the late fourth century, held a fief of 10,000 households in Xue 薛, to which were

Pao Mei, trans., *The Ethical and Political Works of Motse* [London: Arthur Probsthain, 1929], p. 227); *Shi ji*, 6, p. 231 (Watson, *Records of the Grand Historian*, vol. 3, p. 39); 44, p. 1840; 47, p. 1919; *Zhanguo ce* ("Qi 4"), p. 420; ("Yan 1"), p. 1059 (Crump, *Chan-Kuo Ts'e*, pp. 166, 519); *Han Feizi ji shi* (35 "Wai chu shuo you B"), 14, p. 776; (43 "Ding fa"), 17, p. 907 (Liao, *Han Fei Tzu*, vol. 2, pp. 131, 215).

[25] *Shi ji*, 43, p. 1797; *Zhanguo ce* ("Wei 1"), pp. 784–5 (Crump, *Chan-Kuo Ts'e*, p. 375).

[26] Li Xueqin, *Eastern Zhou and Qin Civilizations*, pp. 371–98; Hou Ching-lang, *Monnaies d'offrandes et la notion de trésorerie dans la religion chinoise* (Paris: Collège de France Institut des Hautes Études Chinoises, 1975), pp. 3–4; Anna Seidel, "Buying One's Way to Heaven: The Celestial Treasury in Chinese Religions," *History of Religions* 17, 3–4 (1978): 419–31.

later added another thousand; the reforming minister Shang Yang of Qin
was enfeoffed in the mid-fourth century with fifteen towns in the vicinity of
Shang 商; and in mid-third-century Qin, Lü Buwei 呂不韋 (d. 235 B.C.)
received the income from 15,000 households in Luoyang 洛陽 and twelve
districts at Lantian 藍田. These were strictly units of income, and in most
cases officials were appointed by the ruler to handle administration. There
are records of certain individuals such as the Lord of Mengchang and Shang
Yang appointing local officials or mobilizing troops, but the scope for such
actions was clearly limited.[27] Fiefs were also generally small in size in order
to minimize the possibility of independent action.

Another major new feature of Warring States fiefs was that, with a few
exceptions, they were not hereditary. As a consequence, many holders of fiefs
made efforts to convert their temporary wealth into more permanent forms.
They did this through four primary methods. First, they used the income
from their fiefs to buy private estates. Second, some holders of fiefs were
granted special exemption from paying transit taxes on goods shipped
through government customs stations. Third, there is evidence of enfeoffed
individuals engaging in large-scale money lending. Finally, although there is
no direct evidence, stories suggest that some men obtained the right to collect
market taxes in urban fiefs.[28]

Although not hereditary in nature, fiefs were often awarded to members
of the royal houses, except in Qin. Thus, the famous Four Lords of the late
fourth century were members of the ruling lineages of their respective states
and also holders of large and valuable fiefs. This meant that in most of the
Warring States the practice of granting fiefs was devoted to securing the
power of the royal line. The exceptional character of Qin probably stems
from the fourth-century reforms of Shang Yang, which stipulated that
members of the royal lineage had to earn position and status through service
to the state.

Along with salaries, gifts, and titles, another element of the new polity was
new forms of insignia. Gifts accompanying appointments to office form a
major topic of Western Zhou bronze inscriptions, and these physical insignia
of nobility included chariots, bows, horses, and metals for casting vessels. In

[27] *Shi ji*, 6, p. 227 (Watson, trans., *Records of the Grand Historian*, vol. 3, p. 37); 43, p. 1826; 68, p. 2237
(Watson, *Records of the Grand Historian: Qin*, p. 99); 75, pp. 2359, 2362; 76, p. 2365; 77, pp. 2377, 2382;
78, p. 2394; 79, pp. 2412, 2414, 2416 (Watson, *Records of the Grand Historian: Qin*, pp. 142, 144, 145);
80, p. 2427; 85, p. 2509 (Watson, *Records of the Grand Historian: Qin*, p. 162); *Zhanguo ce*, ("Qin 5"),
p. 281; ("Qi 6"), p. 465; ("Zhao 1"), pp. 627–8 (Crump, *Chan-Kuo Ts'e*, pp. 139, 213, 315); *Zhanguo zong
heng jia shu* (Beijing: Wenwu, 1976), p. 112.

[28] On hereditary fiefs, see *Shi ji*, 43, p. 1826; 75, pp. 1351–3; 76; p. 2370; 77, p. 2377; 79, p. 2424 (Watson,
trans., *Records of the Grand Historian*, vol. 3, p. 155). On business activities and market taxes, see *Shi
ji*, 75, pp. 2359–61; *Han Feizi ji shi* (4 "Ai chen"), 1, p. 60 (Liao, *Han Fei Tzu*, vol. 1, p. 30); studies of
the "E Jun qi jie" 鄂君啟節 are listed in Li Xueqin, *Eastern Zhou and Qin Civilizations*, p. 167, n. 42.

the Warring States such military and religious paraphernalia were replaced by the seal of office for civil officials and the tally for military command. Seals, which were used to validate official commands, were worn at the waist as a sign of power, but it was a power that was visibly removable. Indeed the surrender of seals recurs throughout the biographies of the period. The tiger-shaped tally of military command was likewise a sign of delegated authority, for the commander retained only one-half, while the other was held by the ruler. Only if the ruler's half was obtained could the full army be called out. From excavated tallies we know that in some cases local military officials were empowered to levy small forces of up to fifty men on their own authority, but any larger mission required the ruler's half of the seal. Ceremonies for sending out the central army also included the bestowal of axes as a sign of the general's right to execute men on his own authority, but such delegation of power to commanders in the field was carefully circumscribed.[29]

Another form of "tally" used to control local officials was the "contract" (*quan* 券) employed in annual statistical assessments. Patterned on, or offering the pattern for, contracts used in land purchase agreements and presumably other commercial arrangements, such contracts consisted of budget projections written on a single roll of silk, which was then torn in half. One-half was kept by the ruler and one by the local official. Each year the latter was obliged to come to court in a distant echo of Zhou vassals who had shown submission by such journeys. The official presented a statistical report on stocks of grain, registered population, land opened to cultivation, tax and labor services collected, and public security. Through matching reported figures with projections, the ruler evaluated performance. Such procedures fit closely with Han Fei's account of *xing ming* 形名 (form and name), a practice which he attributes to Shen Buhai's theories of controlling officials. Like the use of cash rewards, this practice had religious overtones, for sage-kings were said to "match tallies" with spirits as a sign of world dominion.[30]

Such statistical accounting and transfer of records between localities and

[29] *Zuo zhuan zhu* (Xiang 29), p. 1155; *Shi ji*, 6, p. 227 (Watson, trans., *Records of the Grand Historian*, vol. 3, p. 37); 79, pp. 2412, 2416 (Watson, *Records of the Grand Historian: Qin*, pp. 142, 146; 80, p. 2428; *Zhanguo ce* ("Qin 3"), p. 220; ("Zhao 3"), p. 699; ("Hann 2"), p. 972 (Crump, *Chan-Kuo Ts'e*, pp. 136, 348, 487); *Han Feizi ji shi* (22 "Shuo lin A"), 7, p. 419; (33 "Wai chu shuo zuo B"), 12, pp. 694, 709 (Liao, *Han Fei Tzu*, vol. 1, p. 228; vol. 2, pp. 76–7, 84); *Lü shi chunqiu jiao shi* (17 "Zhi yi"), p. 1133; Wang Guowei, *Guan tang ji lin*, 2d rev. ed. (Beijing: Zhonghua, 1959) ("Qin Xinqi hu fu ba"), 18.11a; Li Xueqin, *Eastern Zhou and Qin Civilizations*, pp. 235–37; Lewis, *Sanctioned Violence*, pp. 23, 126.

[30] Liang Qixiong ed., *Xunzi jian shi* (Beijing: Guji, 1956) (11 "Wang ba") p. 154 (John Knoblock, *Xunzi: A Translation and Study of the Complete Works*, 3 vols. [Stanford: Stanford University Press, 1988–94], vol. 2, p. 166); *Shang jun shu* 商君書 (Si bu cong kan ed.) ("Qu qiang"), 1.7b; 5 ("Jin shi"), 5.30b; 5 ("Ding fen"), 5.32b (J. J. L. Duyvendak, trans., *The Book of Lord Shang* [London: Arthur Probsthain, 1928], pp. 205, 320, 328–9); *Zhou li zhu shu* (Shisan jing zhu shu ed.) ("Da zai"), 2.24a–b; ("Xiao zai"), 3.10a; ("Si shu"), 7.2a; *Mozi jian gu* (70 "Hao ling"), 15, p. 363; *Han Feizi ji shi* (35 "Wai chu shuo you

the central court, as well as the measuring of official salaries in kind, required the creation of fixed units of measure in each state. The importance of such policies is shown in the Qin legal documents found at Yunmeng, wherein the use of nonstandard weights, volumes, or measures by an official is to be punished by the payment of substantial fines. The various units of measure employed in different states are mentioned in several literary sources, and archaeological finds of actual standard measures have allowed modern scholars to establish the exact amounts of the units employed in several states.[31]

The Yunmeng documents also demonstrate that the legal codes themselves were intended as much to constrain the actions of officials as to regulate the common people. This can be demonstrated by a survey of their contents. The first and longest section, the "Eighteen Statues," deals almost entirely with rules for official conduct, guidelines for keeping accounts, and procedures for the inspection of officials. The second section, the "Rules for Checking," is concerned entirely with the maintenance of official stores and the records thereof. The content of the third section, "Miscellaneous Statutes," is the same as that of the first two. The fourth section, "Answers to Questions Concerning Qin Statutes," defines terms and stipulates procedures in order to ensure that officials interpret and execute items of the code in the manner intended by the Qin royal court. The fifth section, "Models for Sealing and Investigating," instructs officials how to conduct investigations and interrogations so as to secure and transmit accurate results. Thus, the primary focus of these actual Warring States legal documents was the rigorous control of the actions of those local officials charged with overseeing the people. This emphasis is reinforced in the text "On the Way of Being an Official" that was buried in the same tomb. This proclaims the new ideal of the official as a conduit who transmits the facts of his locality to the court and the decisions of the court to the countryside without interposing his own will or ideas.

A final and crucial element in the new type of official was the introduction of set procedures for making appointments. Warring States texts provide evidence of five major forms: (1) high officials making recommendations to

B"), 14, p. 784; (37 "Nan er") 15, p. 835 (Liao, *Han Fei Tzu*, vol. 2, pp. 134, 167–8). On *xing ming*, see *Han Feizi ji shi* (5 "Zhu dao"), 1, pp. 67–9; (7 "Er bing"), 2, pp. 111–12; (8 "Yang quan"), 2, pp. 121–4; (25 "An wei"), 8, p. 484; (32 "Wai chu shuo zuo A"), 11, p. 663; (37 "Nan er"), 15, p. 830; (45 "Gui shi"), 17, pp. 934–6, 939–40 (Liao, *Han Fei Tzu*, vol. 1, pp. 30–5, 48–9, 53–8, 264; vol. 2, pp. 59, 164, 230–1, 232–3). On matching tallies with spirits, see *Shi ji*, 1, p. 6.

[31] Yang Kuan, *Zhanguo shi*, pp. 225–9; idem, *Zhongguo lidai chi du kao* (Shanghai: Shangwu, 1955); A. F. P. Hulsewé, "Weights and Measures in Ch'in Law," in *State and Law in East Asia: Festschrift Karl Bünger*, ed. D. Eikemeier (Wiesbaden: Harrassowitz, 1981), pp. 25–39; *Shuihudi Qin mu zhujian* (Beijing: Wenwu, 1978), pp. 44–46, 56, 69–70, 113–14, 114–15 (A. F. P. Hulsewé, *Remnants of Ch'in Law* [Leiden: Brill, 1985], pp. 42 (A29), 52 (A43), 57 (A52–4), 93 (B3), 94 (B4).

the ruler; (2) wandering scholars attracting the attention of the ruler with a written policy proposal or an oral persuasion at court; (3) lower officials or commoners gaining office through meritorious service, especially in combat; (4) attendants of the ruler or a high minister gaining an administrative post; and (5)chief ministers or heads of local districts appointing a limited number of subordinates on their own authority. These last were legally liable for the malfeasance or incompetence of their appointees.[32]

All the reforms and institutions discussed thus far were devoted to securing the loyalty and reducing the scope for independent action of the king's servants. Other institutions were devoted to the control and mobilization of the rural populace. The transformation of the Zhou world into a group of competing territorial states was achieved through the extension of military service and tax liability into the countryside and the linked recognition of the property held and worked by the individual peasant households. Such reforms demanded the maintaining of population registers. Keeping these records of the rural population, their taxes, and services, along with wielding the power of punishment to enforce obedience, were the primary duties of the local officials.[33]

The linked institutions of universal military service, individual households as the unit of landholding and production, systematic registration and ranking of the population, and the rigorous use of punishments to secure obedience are inextricably linked to the name of the greatest of Warring States reformers, Shang Yang of Qin. While all these institutions had begun centuries prior to his reforms of 356 and 350 B.C., he put them into practice more systematically than had any of his precursors. The extent to which Shang Yang's achievements absorbed those of all his predecessors is shown in Dong Zhongshu's 董仲舒 (ca. 179–104 B.C.) attribution of the abolition of the Zhou well-field system and the appearance of private property in land to Shang Yang's reforms, as though the entire economic history of five centuries was the work of a single evil genius. Shang Yang is also the only Warring States reformer to be given a biography in the *Shi ji* and the only one whose eponymous book survived the Han.[34] Thus, by the middle of the Former Han dynasty his reforms already

---

[32] On recommendations, see *Shi ji*, 79, pp. 2405, 2415, 2425 (Watson, trans., *Records of the Grand Historian*, vol. 3, pp. 134–5, 145, 156); *Zhanguo ce* ("Qi 1"), p. 323; ("Qi 3"), p. 388; ("Qi 4"), p. 417. Examples of gaining posts through written or oral persuasions appear in the careers of Mencius, Shang Yang, Xun Kuang, Li Si, Zhang Yi, Su Qin, Fan Sui, and others. On gaining posts through service, see the discussion of the reforms of Shang Yang below. On attendants gaining posts, see *Shi ji*, 87, pp. 2540–1. (Watson, trans., *Records of the Grand Historian*, vol. 3, p. 180). On ministers making appointments and being liable, see *Shi ji*, 79, p. 2417 (ibid., p. 147).

[33] Lewis, *Sanctioned Violence*, chapter 2; Du Zhengsheng, *Bian hu qi min: Chuantong zhengzhi shehui jiegou zhi xingcheng* (Taipei: Lianjiang, 1991).

[34] *Han shu*, 24a, pp. 1126, 1137; *Shi ji*, chapter 68; *Shang jun shu*.

served as a synecdoche for the whole of Warring States institutional history.

Born in the state of Wey in a collateral line of the ruling house, Shang Yang had studied "forms and names" and obtained a position as a household official for the chief minister of Wei, home of the agricultural and legal reforms of Li Kui. Seeking advancement, he traveled to Qin and gained the support of Xiao Gong for a thoroughgoing implementation of the institutions for control and mobilization of the population that had been pioneered in the successor states of Jin. These reforms were initiated in 356 B.C.

His first policy was the introduction of a detailed legal code directing the conduct of Qin government and the behavior of the peasantry. Punishments were inflicted for a whole range of activities, ranging from violence and theft to use of nonstandard weights and measures – since Shang Yang had imposed official standards – or malfeasance in office. The code imposed severe punishments for minor crimes, in the expectation that such punishments would prevent disobedience. The entire population was divided into units of five and ten households for purposes of mutual responsibility and surveillance. Those who reported their neighbors' crimes were rewarded in the same manner as those who obtained the heads of enemy soldiers in battle, while those who failed to report crimes were punished along with the malefactor. Hiding a culprit was to be punished in the same manner as surrendering to the enemy.[35]

Shang Yang also set up a hierarchy of titles to reward meritorious service to the state, particularly military success. Originally seventeen ranks (*jue* 爵) were established, derived ultimately from subdividing the earlier rankings of the feudal nobility. Military success measured by the number of heads of slain enemies was rewarded with promotion in rank. For individual squad members or the chiefs of a squad of five, rewards were given for heads of enemies actually killed by the individual. For the commander of a unit of a hundred men or more, rewards were given for the total number of enemy killed by his troops. Those killed in battle could have their merits transferred to their descendants. Reaching certain ranks entitled the bearer to the possession of specified quantities of land, houses, and slaves. Those of the eighth rank or above also obtained the tax income of a specified number of villages, like the nobles of other states, and the highest four ranks in Qin's hierarchy of military merit were the equivalents of the lords (*jun* 君) and *hou* 侯 found elsewhere. Lower titles matched with ranks in the army and government

---

[35] *Shi ji*, 68, pp. 2230, 2232 (Watson, trans., *Records of the Grand Historian*, vol. 3, pp. 92–3, 94). Scattered references appear in *Shi ji*, 5, p. 203 (ibid., p. 24); 83, p. 2461; *Han Feizi ji shi* (43 "Ding fa"), 17, p. 907 (Liao, *Han Fei Tzu*, p. 213); *Xunzi jian shi* (10 "Yi bing"), pp. 194–5 (Knoblock, *Xunzi*, vol. 2, p. 223). Certain chapters of the *Shang jun shu* and the Yunmeng legal documents ultimately derive from these reforms.

administration, with the lowest four ranks corresponding to the soldiery, and ranks five and above serving as officers in the army and officials in the administration.

The ranks likewise entailed certain legal and religious privileges. In the legal realm, the surrender of titles could be used to remit certain punishments, so they provided a degree of protection against severe penalties. In the religious realm, they entitled the holder to privileges in burial, including the right to a higher tomb mound and the planting of more trees on the tomb.[36]

Shang Yang also initiated a series of reforms to encourage agriculture, which provisioned the army and provided the economic foundations of the state, and to discourage trade, which proved less amenable to taxation. The policy of encouraging agriculture reflected the status of Qin as a frontier state with considerable amounts of undeveloped land and a relatively sparse population. Numerous methods to attract rural population to settle in Qin and open up new land are recorded in the second chapter of the *Shang jun shu*. This chapter also records antimerchant measures, including registration of merchants' servants for corvée labor, high market taxes and taxes on goods in transit, and the registration of merchant households as "inferior people." As such they were not permitted to wear silk or ride horses, and were subject to extended terms of garrison duty at the frontier.[37]

Another measure Shang Yang initiated to encourage agriculture and the opening of land was to impose a grid of pathways across the fields in 350 B.C. These divided the land into blocks measured according to the expanded *mu* of 240 paces. The size of a block seems to have accorded roughly with the labor capacity of a household with one adult male. Since Qin law also increased capitation taxes on families where fathers and adult sons lived together, there was considerable pressure for households to divide and for each male to take charge of a single block. In this way, Qin sought to put under cultivation the maximum amount of land that could be worked by its population. The uniform blocks of land also provided standardized units for rewarding military service, and land thus received would have been worked by the slaves – probably recruited from convicts or prisoners – that accompanied the land.[38]

Another reform begun in 350 was the introduction of directly administered districts (*xian* 縣) throughout the state of Qin. All the towns and vil-

---

[36] Du Zhengsheng, *Bian hu qi min*, pp. 317–71; Lewis, *Sanctioned Violence*, pp. 61–4; Michael Loewe, "The Orders of Aristocratic Rank in Han China," *TP* 48 (1960): 97–174; Nishijima Sadao, *Chūgoku kodai teikoku no keisei to kōzō Nijū tō shakusei no kenkyū* (Tokyo: Tokyo daigaku, 1961).
[37] *Shang jun shu* ("Ken ling"), 1.2a–3a (Duyvendak, trans., *Lord Shang*, pp. 175–84).
[38] Lewis, *Sanctioned Violence*, pp. 63–4.

lages in Qin were administratively aggregated into forty-one *xian*, each of which had a magistrate (*ling* 令), a vice-magistrate (*cheng* 丞), a military commandant (*wei* 尉), and an unspecified number of subordinate officials, such as the "overseers" (*sefu* 嗇夫) in the villages. This new institution extended the king's writ into local communities, but it was also linked with the extension of universal military service, because the *xian* was used in military recruitment.

The *xian* had first appeared as administrative units in the Spring and Autumn period, when they were established in conquered frontier districts as administrative units directly controlled by officers of the ruler. Such units were primarily military in character, and if the area ceased to be of strategic concern the *xian* were often bestowed on noble lineages as hereditary fiefs. In the late Spring and Autumn period, Jin introduced another form of directly administered district, the *jun* 郡, in newly conquered, relatively underpopulated, frontier regions. These districts were physically larger than the *xian* but lower in rank because they were in areas of low population and little strategic value. As these *jun* were gradually filled in during the Warring States period through resettlement and the opening of new land, they were often subdivided into *xian*, thus creating a two-tiered system of administration. This first appeared in the successor states of Jin during the fourth century, but it was imitated in Qin, Chu, and Yan and then inherited by the Han dynasty.[39]

Because the *xian* and *jun* were established by conquest and located at frontiers or in the zones between states, they were closely tied to military functions and became the basic units of recruitment. Records attributed to the sixth century in the *Zuo zhuan* identify Jin armies in terms of the *xian* from which the troops were mobilized. Fuchai's army in 483 was mobilized from nine *jun*. Many discussions in the *Zhangguo ce* of the relative military power of states describe the number of soldiers available in terms of the number of *xian* or *jun*.[40] Thus, the establishment of *xian* throughout Qin was a necessary corollary of its universal extension of military service.

This identity of the units of civil administration and military recruitment was also linked to the extension of units of mutual responsibility into the army. As was noted above, the laws of Qin systematically equated the penalties for legal violations with those for failure in battle, and rewards for upholding penal law with those for success in battle. Members of units of mutual responsibility were neighbors in times of peace and fought side by

---

[39] Du Zhengsheng, *Bian hu qi min*, chapter 3; Masubuchi, *Chûgoku kodai no shakai*, pp. 328–450; Nishijima, *Chûgoku kodai teikoku*, pp. 503–74; Yang Kuan, *Zhanguo shi*, pp. 209–13.

[40] *Zuo zhuan zhu*, (Zhao 22), p. 1438; (Cheng 6), p. 830; *Shi ji*, 15, p. 753; 43, p. 1831; 67, p. 2200; *Zhanguo ce* ("Dong Zhou"), p. 5; ("Wei 3"), p. 857 (Crump, *Chan-Kuo Ts'e*, pp. 39, 429).

side in combat. Their collective responsibilities operated equally in both spheres. Thus, if one member of a squad of five fled in battle, the other four members would also be punished, unless they captured their fleeing comrade or were able to offer the head of an enemy to redeem their guilt. In addition, if any squad of five killed no enemy, its chief was liable for execution. Thus, the creation of a uniform territorial administration answerable to the ruler was tied to the identification of the civil order with the army.

In 348 B.C. Shang Yang introduced another reform, the capitation tax (*fu* 賦, identified in the Qin legal documents as "household tax" or "head tax"). This institution presupposed the practice, imported from the Jin successor states, of registering the population. By law all males were required to register upon reaching maturity, and the government would keep records of the number of men in a household and their ages. Tax was calculated on a per head basis, with a higher rate per individual imposed in households with several adult males. Any household that wanted to split up or move had to report to the local officials. From the chronicle of the man buried in the tomb at Yunmeng, it appears that registration as an adult took place at the age of fifteen, though this figure varied from state to state and across time. Several Warring States texts indicate that these registers also listed the amount of land held by each household.[41]

The reforms attributed to Shang Yang provide a complete inventory of the basic institutions of the Warring States. Records of the period show that the promulgation of detailed legal codes, the awarding of titles for service to the state, universal military service, civil administration and military recruitment through units administered by royal appointees, registration of population, and capitation taxes existed in most, if not all, of the Warring States to a greater or lesser degree. Even as Shang Yang was reforming Qin, Wei and Qi both undertook substantial reforms involving opening up and distributing new land through improved irrigation, as well as the rigorous selection and honoring of crack troops. Other significant military reforms, associated with the increased use of cavalry, took place in Zhao under King Wuling in the late fourth century. However, we have much less detail regarding states other than Qin. Evidence indicates that other states had fewer ranks than Qin, and they do not seem to have been so widely distributed throughout the population. This, however, may be a result of destruction of records. There is evidence that Zhao had introduced universal rankings by the third century. In addition, certain states had minor variations on certain institutions. Qi, for example, had no *jun*, but instead established five *du* 都 (major

---

[41] *Shuihudi Qin mu*, pp. 6, 129–30, 130–1, 242, 250–1, 292–3 (Hulsewé, *Remnants of Ch'in Law*, pp. 104 [C3], 104–105 [C4], 177 [D175], 181 [D189], 187 [E5], 208 [F1]); *Lü shi chunqiu jiao shi* (12 "Ji dong"), p. 616; *Guanzi* (Si bu cong kan ed.), 53 "Jin zang," 17.104b.

cities). Each *du* had a standing force of crack troops.[42] These served as the core of the Qi army, though supplemented by peasant levies in the event of major campaigns. However, despite such local variations, the major elements of Shang Yang's reforms existed to a greater or lesser degree in the other states.

THE FORMATION OF A MULTISTATE WORLD

The political history of the Warring States consisted not only of the development of a new form of state, but also the emergence of new patterns of interaction. While the earlier Zhou world had been composed of a multitude of cities and hinterlands linked by kin ties, religious rites, and continuous, low-intensity warfare, the Warring States period was characterized by a small number of territorial states involved in constant diplomatic maneuvering and intermittent but frequent large-scale military conflagrations. The century and a half from 481 to the middle of the fourth century was the formative period of this pattern of interstate relations, a pattern that was forged in warfare. These wars had two major consequences: the absorption of small states and non-Hua peoples into the expanding territorial powers, and the formation of a balance of power in which each state acted independently to further its own interests through the selective application of combat and diplomacy.

The wars of the first century and a half of the Warring States period can be divided into those that preceded the official division of Jin (403 B.C.) and those that followed. Prior to its partition Jin was involved in civil wars, while the peripheral states Chu, Yue, Qi, and Qin expanded through the conquest of smaller states. The first two pressed north toward the Yellow River, swallowing several lesser states, while the third pushed into the southern Shandong Peninsula. Qin expanded primarily at the expense of non-Hua peoples. To the north it engaged in a series of wars against the Rong, whom it gradually subjugated. More significant was the beginning in 441 B.C. of Qin's southwestward expansion into Shu and Ba, in modern Sichuan. This fertile region ringed with mountains became a major source of Qin economic and military power, and it proved a crucial base for launching expeditions against

---

[42] On variants of ranks in different states, see *Shi ji*, 74, p. 2347; 76, p. 2370; 79, p. 2401 (Watson, trans., *Records of the Grand Historian*, vol. 3, p. 131); 80, p. 2427; 81, pp. 1441, 1443; *Lü shi chunqiu jiao shi*, (10 "Yi bao"), p. 551; (15 "Xia xian"), p. 880; (22 "Wu yi"), p. 1492; (25 "Shen xiao"), p. 1681; *Han Feizi ji shi* (30 "Nei chu shuo A"), 9, p. 551 (Liao, *Han Fei Tzu*, vol. 1, p. 301); *Zhanguo ce* ("Dong zhou"), p. 5; ("Qi 2"), p. 355; ("Chu 1"), pp. 507, 519; ("Chu 4"), p. 561; ("Zhao 3"), p. 721; ("Wei 4"), p. 913; ("Yan 3") p. 1132 (Crump, *Chan-Kuo Ts'e*, pp. 39, 167, 235, 246, 357, 447, 556); *Mengzi zhu shu* ("Gongsun Chou A"), 3A.6B (Legge, *Mencius*, p. 185); ("Gongsun Chou B") 4A.11b (ibid., p. 220); *Chu ci bu zhu* 楚辭補注 (Si bu cong kan ed.) ("Yu fu") 7.1b (David Hawkes, trans., *The Songs of the South: An Anthology of Ancient Chinese Poems by Qu Yuan and Other Poets* [Harmondsworth: Penguin, 1985], p. 206).

Chu.[43] The conquest, however, was to require most of a century, and Qin played no major role in interstate politics until the 360s.

The wars of the second period, from the division of Jin in 403 until the middle of the fourth century, can be divided into three distinct stages of two decades each: (1) that of the alliance of the Jin successor states under Wei, (2) that of the conflict between the successor states and the reemergence of Chu, and (3) that of the appearance of Qin on the international stage and the career of Wei Hui Hou from 344 B.C. In the first period, from 403 to 383, the three Jin successor states pursued a foreign policy in common and expanded in all directions: eastward against Qi, southward against Chu, and westward against Qin. They also destroyed the small state of Zhongshan to the northeast. This coalition of the successor states was dominated by Wei, under the leadership of Wen Hou 文侯 (r. 445–396) and Li Kui. Under the celebrated general Wu Qi, Wei's armies pushed Qin back to a defensive line on the Luo 洛 River and occupied the Xihe 西河 region to the west of the great bend of the Yellow River.

The facts of geography and resentment of the rising power of Wei, however, ended the decades of concerted action by the Jin successor states. Fearful of Wei's increasing power and having gained little in the years of territorial expansion, Zhao established a new walled capital at Handan 邯鄲 and launched an offensive war in 383 against Wey to its southeast. Wey sought help from Wei, which attacked Zhao's western frontier. In desperate straits, Zhao sought aid from its old enemy Chu, which in 380 took advantage of Wei's military incursion into Zhao to reoccupy its territories up to the Yellow River. Zhao used the diversion provided by Chu to counterattack and occupy much Wei territory. This conflict was a major event in Warring States history not only in its scale and the fact of its being fought on several fronts, but also because it marked the definitive break with the old pattern of wars based on the dominance of Jin and its successors. Instead there emerged the interplay of alliances in which each state sided with whatever ally proved useful and changed allies as soon as the balance of power shifted.[44]

The war was also significant for the reemergence of Chu as a major power. This expansion of Chu after 400 is attributed to Wu Qi, the general administrator who had defeated Qin and occupied Xihe for Wei. Having fallen under suspicion and been expelled from Wei, he was appointed minister in Chu in 401 by the newly installed King Dao and then is said to have launched a series of reforms to strengthen the ruling house and the state along the lines pioneered in Jin. As argued in the preceding section, this account may attribute a series of incremental reforms to a single "hero," but the resurgence of Chu does indicate its adoption of Warring States institutions. Its new power also reflects expansion in the south. In various sources Wu Qi is credited with the conquest of Yangyue 揚越 and the founding of cities at Dongting 洞庭 and Cangwu 蒼梧 (in southern Jiangxi and Hunan, and northern Guangxi). These newly opened regions are cited in the *Zhanguo ce* as major bases of Chu power. A Warring States graveyard excavated in the region has a set of tombs containing numerous weapons in Chu style, several of which are inscribed with the place-names of Chu cities. This archaeological evidence confirms the literary tradition of Chu military expansion into this region.[45]

The decade following 380 witnessed an increase in the pace and scale of warfare among the now hostile Jin successor states and the resurgent Chu. The international scene was significantly altered, however, only in 366, when Qin reemerged from centuries of decline with a victory over the combined armies of Hann and Wei. Up to this time Qin had been a minor factor in interstate wars, suffering repeated defeats at the hands of Wei and losing its territory along the Yellow River. It had compensated for this in part by occupying non-Hua territory, but even its frontier wars had been less than completely successful. The fighting with Shu dragged on, and various Rong coalitions were still able to make major incursions into Qin territory. However, the reforms initiated by Xian Gong in 384 had begun to bear fruit, and the victory in 366 was followed by a decisive defeat of Wei in 364 at the battle of Shimen 石門. The Qin armies were said to have collected over 60,000 heads, and Wei was saved only by the intervention of Zhao. In 362, Qin again defeated the Wei armies, captured Wei's chief minister, and returned in force to the region east of the bend of the Yellow River. These victories presaged Qin's later rise, but the scene continued for some decades to be dominated by the three successor states of Jin, under the leadership of Wei Hui Hou.[46]

Wei Hui Hou was notable for four policies. First, in response to Qin expansion in the west he abandoned his capital Anyi 安邑, which was located toward the western edge of the Wei realm between the bend of the Yellow River and the valley of the Fen River. He shifted his capital in 361 B.C. to the city of Daliang 大梁, south of the Yellow River and out of reach of enemy

[45] *Shi ji*, 43, p. 1798; 65, p. 2168; *Lü shi chunqiu jiao shi* (14 "Yi shang"), p. 779; (21 "Gui zu"), p. 1473; *Han Feizi ji shi* (13 "He shi"), 4, pp. 238–9 (Liao, *Han Fei Tzu*, vol. 1, pp. 114–15); *Zhanguo ce* ("Qin 3"), pp. 212, 215, 216; ("Qin 5"), p. 428; ("Chu 1"), p. 500 (Crump, *Chan-Kuo Ts'e*, pp. 132, 133, 135, 195–6, 230); *Hou Han shu*, 86, p. 2831; *Kaogu xuebao* 1978.2: 211–58, esp. p. 251.

[46] *Shi ji*, 5, p. 201 (Watson, trans., *Records of the Grand Historian*, vol. 3, p. 22).

forces. At this time he also temporarily adopted Liang as the name of his state.

Second, between 362 and 359 B.C. he initiated a series of exchanges in which he occupied territory from Hann and Zhao, but then traded several of his own cities and districts for others held by the rival states. These transactions created a more integrated state in the center of the Yellow River valley, with a secure capital at Daliang and control of many of the most important transit points in the Warring States world. Hann and Zhao also achieved a higher degree of territorial integrity.

Third, this movement for territorial rationalization was accompanied by a series of interstate assemblies in which rulers met face to face in an attempt to secure alliances and stabilize the relations between the states. In 361 B.C. Hui Hou met with the ruler of Hann; in 358 and again in 357 he met with the ruler of Zhao. In the same year the ruler of Zhao traveled to Qi to meet with Wei Hou. In 356 Hui Hou compelled the rulers of Hann, Song, Lu, and Wey to attend court at his new capital of Daliang, marking the peak of his power. Also in 356, the year that Shang Yang began his reforms in Qin, Zhao Cheng Hou 趙成侯 (r. 374–350 B.C.) had meetings with the rulers of Qi and Song, and later in the year with the ruler of Yan. In 355 B.C. Wei Hui Hou visited Qi Wei Hou, and in the same year met with Qin Xiao Gong. This emergence of regular meetings and diplomatic exchanges foreshadowed the preeminent role of diplomacy and alliance in the next period of Warring States history.[47]

The final major change initiated by Hui Hou was the adoption of the royal title, by which he became the celebrated King Hui of Liang. This reform was discussed in the preceding section.

Thus, by the middle of the fourth century B.C., all of the leading states had carried out, or were in the midst of introducing, their most important reforms, and all but a handful of lesser states had been destroyed. This process culminated in the assumption of the royal title by the rulers of all the remaining states. Stretched along the Yellow River valley, Qi, Zhao, Hann, Wei, and Qin dominated the political scene, with Chu in the south still a threat and Yan emerging as a minor power in the northeast. Regular meetings of rulers and visits by embassies were beginning to establish a routine of diplomatic exchange between these seven leading states that divided the Zhou world between them. At what is almost exactly the midpoint of Warring States history, a system based on territorial polities in a perpetual state of regulated conflict had taken on its classic form. And the chief activity of these states was combat.

[47] Yang Kuan, *Zhanguo shi*, pp. 276–8.

THE MILITARY ARTS

The polities of this period were "states organized for warfare." Population registration, universal military service, and ranks of military merit were adapted to enable each state to expand at the expense of its neighbors. These new governmental institutions were paralleled by the transformation of warfare. However, just as the history of institutions comes to us as accounts of the careers of reformers, so changes in warfare emerge largely from the biographies of generals and in military treatises that grew up around the names of celebrated commanders. Thus, the military history of the period must be reconstructed from accounts of the lives of generals that are often little more than legends; discussions of strategy, tactics, and organization must be culled from the military treatises; and evidence about weapons and organization must be derived from archaeological finds.

The earlier armies of the Spring and Autumn period had combined chariots with infantry, the former being the primary weapon of the warrior aristocracy and the weapon of choice in pitched battles staged on flat terrain. Infantry, composed of lower members of the capital populace and peasants who accompanied their noble masters, served for skirmishes, storming cities, night battles, or battles against non-Hua peoples who often fought on foot in mountainous or watery terrain. The most important weapons were the convex bows for nobles on chariots and the lance for infantry. Armies were relatively small, no more than 30,000 men and usually much smaller. Maneuvers were simple, involving some variation of the head-on collision of two masses of men, and battles seldom lasted more than a single day, never more than two. As a consequence, there was little need for military expertise, and command was distributed among the various leading lineages. Individual nobles commanded men mobilized from their own fiefs, and these operated as independent units on campaign and even on the field of battle.[48]

The defining change in the Warring States army was the shift toward reliance on massed infantry. The rise of the infantry army was a gradual change that emerged during the Spring and Autumn period in the internecine struggles for power between states and, more important, among lineages within a state. As peasants from the rural hinterland were drawn into military service, the command of these new-style warriors became the key to political power. Their large-scale use underlay the decline of the nobility and the concentration of power in the royal lineage.[49] However, the creation of

---

[48] Lewis, *Sanctioned Violence*, pp. 36–43; Raimund Theodor Kolb, *Die Infanterie im alten China: Ein Beitrag zur Militärgeschichte der Vor-Zhan-Guo-Zeit* (Mainz: Phillip von Zabern, 1991), pp. 195–9, 252–8.

[49] Lewis, *Sanctioned Violence*, chapter 2.

infantry armies also entailed a comprehensive ensemble of changes in the conduct of war. This included modifications in composition, armaments, scale, and patterns of control.

Composition

As for the composition of armies, the infantry army marked the end of the dominance of the warrior nobility and the shift to a state based on the service of the peasant household. Indeed, the supplanting of the nobility in the army resulted in their ultimate disappearance, though it took many centuries for the process to be completed. However, the new pattern of service generated its own forms of social ranking, a hierarchy based on military service. One element of this pattern, the rankings of Qin and related systems in Zhao and Wei, has already been discussed. Another feature, however, was the distinction between the peasant levy based on the *xian* and *jun*, and the standing elite commands that developed in most states and were granted a variety of legal privileges.

The practice of selecting and training crack troops distinct from peasant conscripts emerged in the late Spring and Autumn period through the formation of bodyguards or retinues to accompany leading nobles. Thus, King Helü of Yue had a personal retinue of 500 crack soldiers and also a special corps of 3,000 runners who could continue 300 *li* without respite. Warring States texts attribute to various reformers such as Wu Qi and Shang Yang maxims on the necessity of selecting and training warriors, and a passage in the *Lü shi chunqiu* is interpreted as implying higher salaries for specially trained soldiers. Although we lack details for most states, the *Xunzi* describes the elite troops instituted by Wei Hui Hou. They were trained to wear heavy armor, shoulder a large crossbow and fifty arrows, strap their halberds to their backs, buckle helmets to their heads and swords at their sides, carry three days' supply of food, and quick march 100 *li* in a single day. Those who could meet these standards earned exemption from corvée labor and taxes for their entire household.[50] The aforementioned "five city" troops of Qi were also an elite standing force, as were the soldiery depicted in the terra cotta army of the First Emperor of Qin 秦始皇 (king of Qin 246–221, emperor 221–210 B.C.).

---

[50] *Mozi jian gu* (16 "Jian ai C"), 4, p. 79; (18 "Fei gong B"), 5, p. 85 (Yi-Pao Mei, trans., *Ethical and Political Works of Motse*, pp. 96, 105); *Lü shi chunqiu jiao shi* (8 "Jian xuan"), pp. 441–2; *Han Feizi ji shi* (13 "He shi"), 4, p. 239 (Liao, *Han Fei Tzu*, vol. 1, p. 115); *Zhanguo ce* ("Qi 1"), pp. 331, 334 (Crump, *Chan-Kuo Ts'e*, p. 150); *Xunzi jian shi* (15 "Yi bing"), pp. 193–5, 96 (Knoblock, *Xunzi*, vol. 2, pp. 222–3).

Armaments

The description of Wei's crack troops just cited introduces the second great change in military practice, the development of new military technology. Traditional weapons such as the lance (*mao* 矛) and dagger-axe (*ge* 戈) were lengthened, produced in greater quantities, and ultimately forged in the newly developed material of iron. The hybrid combination of lance and hook, the *ji* 戟 (halberd), also became a common weapon. Another style of long lance or grappling hook, the *gou ju* 鈎拒, was developed in Chu for combat on boats. It allowed soldiers to "hook" (*gou*) enemy boats as they tried to flee and to "block" (*ju*) them as they attacked. The use of this lance figures prominently in the scene of water combat depicted on a Warring States basin. The old-style "winged" arrowhead was replaced by the sturdier triangular form. For close combat the most crucial development was the large-scale use of the bronze sword, which is found in many tombs of the period. While excavated examples of iron swords remain relatively rare, they were widespread to the extent that texts of the period already speak of certain regions, notably those in the south, distinguished for the excellence of their iron blades.[51]

The single most important technological development, however, was the crossbow. It seems to have been of southern origin, as were perhaps the sword and even the large-scale infantry army. Their use is already attested in the *Sunzi*, where they also figure as a source of metaphor. This would suggest that they were in common use by the fourth century, that is, in the early Warring States period. The *Sun Bin* military treatise, probably originating in the late fourth century, treats them as the most important form of weapon and the decisive element in combat. The power and range of these bows depended on the strength of the bow string, so they were effective only if wielded by powerful and well-trained warriors. One contemporary account states that a single crack soldier of Hann with his powerful crossbow and sharp sword could match a hundred ordinary men. This text states that soldiers loaded the bows by applying both feet against the arc, probably while lying on their backs, and pulling the bowstring upward. This technique is still depicted in Han art from the second century A.D.

The technology of the crossbow, particularly the trigger mechanism, continued to develop throughout the period. The *Lü shi chunqiu* describes both

[51] *Xunzi jian shi* (15 "Yi bing"), p. 202 (Knoblock, *Xunzi*, vol. 2, p. 229); *Shi ji*, 79, p. 2418 (Watson, trans., *Records of the Grand Historian*, vol. 3, p. 147); *Lü shi chunqiu jiao shi* (21 "Gui zu"), p. 1473; Yang Hong, *Zhongguo gu bingqi luncong* (Beijing; Wenwu, 1980), chapters 4–5; Hayashi Minao *Chûgoku In Shū jidai-no bukki* (Kyoto: Kyôto daigaku Jimbun kagaku kenkyûjo, 1972), pp. 66–96, 117–30, 230–5, 365–74.

Figure 9.1. Depictions of the "cloud ladder" for scaling walls, from the Shanbiaozhen Basin. From Li Xueqin, *Eastern Zhou and Qin Civilizations*, trans. K. C. Chang (New Haven, Conn.: Yale University Press, 1985), p. 70.

the extraordinary accuracy of the bows and the great precision of the trigger mechanism. Another technological development was "linked crossbows" that could be fired mechanically in unison, sometimes mounted on carriages. These are described in detail in the military chapters of the Mohist canon.[52]

Other major developments took place in the realm of siege warfare. The *Mozi* briefly describes the invention of "cloud ladders" used to scale city walls, and these are depicted in the battle scenes shown on a bronze basin (Fig. 9.1). Perhaps more important was the use of mining technology in attacks on city walls. Armies dug tunnels under the walls of besieged towns in order to enter the city or bring the walls down. Defenders used large bellows employed in iron smelting to pump smoke into these tunnels and suffocate the attackers. This increasing reliance on technology in siege warfare figures prominently in the military chapters of the *Mozi*.[53] It is likely that the unusual interest in physical phenomena and technology evinced in the later chapters of the *Mozi*

[52] *Sunzi*, pp. 39, 104 (Sawyer, trans., *Sun Tzu*, pp. 174, 187); *Sun Bin bing fa* (Beijing: Wenwu, 1975), pp. 43, 64, 65 (Ralph Sawyer, trans., *Sun Pin: Military Methods* [Boulder: Westview, 1995], pp. 92, 116, 117); *Lü shi chunqiu jiao shi* (16 "Cha Wei"), p. 1004; *Shi ji*, 6, p. 263 (Watson, trans., *Records of the Grand Historian*, vol. 3, pp. 61–2); *Mozi jian gu* (53 "Bei gao lin"), 14, p. 320; *Zhanguo ce* ("Qin 2"), p. 165; ("Zhao 1") p. 608; ("Hann 1"), p. 930 (Crump, *Chan-Kuo Ts'e*, pp. 93, 324, 460); Noel Barnard and Sato Tamotsu, *Metallurgical Remains of Ancient China* (Tokyo: Nichiosha, 1975), pp. 116–17; Hayashi, *Chûgoku In Shû jidai-no, buki*, pp. 301–20; Jerry Norman and Mei Tsu-lin, "The Austroasiatics in Ancient South China: Some Lexical Evidence," *MS* 32 (1976): 293–4; Gao Zhixi, "Ji Changsha Changde chutu nuji de Zhanguo mu: Jian tan youguan nuji gongshi de jige wenti," *Wenwu* 1964.6: 33–45; Yang Hong, *Zhongguo gu bingqi luncong*, pp. 135–9; Robin Yates, "Siege Engines and Late Zhou Military Technology," in *Explorations in the History of Science and Technology in China*, ed. Hu Daojing, Li Guohao, Zhang Mengwen, and Cao Tianqin (Shanghai: Shanghai Chinese Classics, 1982), pp. 438–40.
[53] Yates, "Siege Engines and Late Zhou Military Technology."

derive from the military activities of the Mohist school, rather than from the school's links to merchants and craftsmen.

Another change, in both composition and technology, was the increasing use of cavalry. It is still impossible to date the introduction of soldiers mounted on horseback. (For the earlier role of horses in chariot warfare, see p. 284 n. 115.) There is one story in the *Zuo zhuan* for the year 517 B.C. that may refer to riding on horseback, but not for military purposes. The *Han Feizi* mentions combined chariot and cavalry forces in the Jin civil wars of the late sixth century, but the text was written three centuries after the events it narrates. Certainly by the middle or late fourth century independent cavalry forces accompanied infantry armies, but whereas infantry armies may have numbered one or two hundred thousand, cavalry forces apparently numbered no more than five or six thousand. Even in the army of King Wuling of Zhao, celebrated for adopting nomadic dress and the use of mounted bowmen in the late fourth century, it seems that the cavalry played only a supporting role. This is also indicated by the lengthy discussion of the uses of cavalry in a fragment of the *Sun Bin* military treatise. This lists ten benefits of cavalry, but these consist of reaching strategic points before the enemy, attacking undefended spots, pursuing fleeing soldiers, cutting supply lines, destroying bridges or ferries, ambushing unprepared troops, taking the enemy by surprise, burning stores and pillaging markets, and disturbing agriculture or kidnapping peasants.[54] In short, cavalry were employed in skirmish, reconnaissance, ambush, and pillage, but they were of no use in pitched battles against a prepared enemy force or defensive position.

A final important field of technological development lay in the manufacture of armor and helmets. Most of the armor of the period was made of rectangular leather strips tied together with cords (Fig. 9.2). This produced a flexible body armor providing some degree of security. Several late Warring States texts refer to iron armor and helmets, and some examples of these, most notably the oft-reproduced iron helmet found at Yan's secondary capital Xiadu 下都, have been excavated (Fig. 9.3). This helmet is composed of numerous plates sewn together, as are the few examples of iron armor. The armor depicted on the Qin terra cotta army is similar to the Yan examples in terms of the form of plates and the techniques of tying them together, but there are several distinct styles corresponding to different ranks and functions.[55]

---

[54] *Zuo zhuan zhu* (Zhao 25), p. 1466; *Han Feizi ji shi* (10 "Shi guo"), 3, p. 178 (Liao, *Han Fei Tzu*, vol. 1, p. 80); *Shi ji*, 43, pp. 1805–11; 110, p. 2885; *Zhanguo ce* ("Zhao 2"), pp. 653–63 (Crump, *Chan-Kuo Ts'e*, pp. 296–303); *Tong dian* ("Bing 2"), 149.779c.

[55] Yang Hong, *Zhongguo gu bingqi luncong*, pp. 1–29, 32–6; Hayashi, *Chûgoku In Shû jidai-no*, pp. 408–15.

Figure 9.2. Depictions of Warring States armor. From Yang Hong, *Zhongguo gu bingqi luncong* (Beijing: Wenwu, 1980), pp. 6 and 7.

Size of Armies

Closely related to these innovations in the composition and technology of armies was the change in scale. As noted above, the largest Spring and Autumn army would have numbered no more than 30,000 men, but Warring States armies were considerably larger. This expansion was made possible by the switch from chariot armies of nobles to infantry armies composed of peasants, for the latter required far less training and expense, and they were much more numerous and expendable. Although the numbers are not reliable, there are many descriptions in Warring States texts of the size of armies, as well as the number of enemy casualties in the victories of Qin. These latter statistics were collected by Qin for the awarding of titles and may have been transmitted to the Han imperial library when Xiao He collected material from the Qin imperial library during the civil war. Since rewards were based on these figures, they were doubtless inflated by officers in the field through the collection of additional ears from Qin dead or peasants who strayed too close to the Qin army. The figures can only be treated as orders of magni-

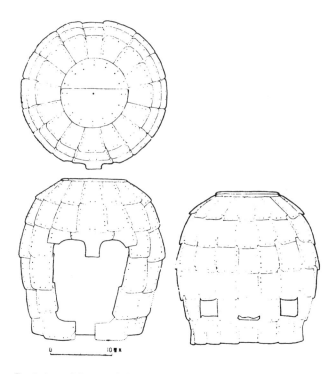

Figure 9.3. Depiction of the iron helmet from Yan Xiadu. From Yang Hong, *Zhongguo gu bingqi luncong* (Beijing: Wenwu, 1980), p. 14.

tude, but they are internally consistent and suggest general trends. Moreover, they clearly distinguish the total number of men at the disposal of the state from the actual numbers of men on individual campaigns, and the latter are not wholly out of line with what we know of the size of armies that primarily live off the land.

Thus, various accounts of Qin's total military capacity list 1,000,000 armored infantry, 1,000 chariots, and 10,000 horses. These round figures are clearly purely notional and serve only as rhetorical terms to suggest great size. For Wei one account says 360,000 infantry, while another says 200,000 crack troops, 200,000 spearmen, 100,000 menials, 600 chariots, and 5,000 cavalry. Zhao supposedly had several hundred thousand armored men, 1,000 chariots, and 10,000 cavalry. Hann had only 300,000, including menials and garrison troops. Qi had several hundred thousand or 1,000,000. Chu had 1,000,000 infantry, 1,000 chariots, and 10,000 cavalry. These figures are exactly the same as those for Qin and thus again appear to be notional figures suggesting a great power. Yan, a weaker state, is credited with only 100,000 infantry, 700 chariots, and 6,000 cavalry.[56] These figures would indicate that each of the leading states might have had a few hundred thousand men available for military service, and one passage makes it clear that these figures include porters, conscript laborers, and garrison troops. The figure of 1,000,000 is probably pure exaggeration intended to suggest the greater resources of Qin, Qi, and Chu, and in one passage it is clearly used to mean only "the largest possible army." The relative figures for the other states fit with what we know of their size and military importance.

Accounts of campaigns, however, suggest smaller numbers for actual forces in the field. This is quite plausible, since no state could put its entire force into action simultaneously, and limitations on logistics would restrict the size of armies that could go out on extended campaigns. The *Sunzi* military treatise, reflecting conditions in the first centuries of the Warring States period, several times uses the round figure of an "army of 100,000" men as a typical force. The *Mozi* also suggests this as a typical figure. The *Lü shi chunqiu*, written a century and a half after the events, states that the armies of Wu Qi never exceeded 50,000. At its defeat at Maling 馬陵 in 341 B.C., the forces of Wei are also supposed to have numbered 100,000. According to one speaker, Bo Qi 白起 (d. 257 B.C.) conquered the Chu capital region in 278 with an army of only "a few tens of thousands of men."[57] Clearly these are approximate figures, but it seems to have been a consensus that armies never exceeded 100,000 during the first centuries of the Warring States period and were generally much smaller.

This seems to have changed in the third century. The size of armies in the field appears to have increased once again, whether because of population growth, more effective registration, higher yields in crops or taxes, or – the most likely explanation – the shift from wars seeking advantage in a balance

---

[56] On Qin, see *Zhanguo ce* ("Qin 1"), p. 78; ("Hann 1"), p. 934; ("Chu 1"), p. 504. On Wei, see *Zhanguo ce* ("Qi 5"), p. 442; ("Wei 1"), pp. 790, 792; ("Wei 3"), p. 857. On Zhao, see *Zhanguo ce* ("Zhao 2"), p. 638. On Hann, see *Zhanguo ce* ("Hann 1"), pp. 930, 934. On Qi, see *Zhanguo ce* ("Qi"), p. 337; ("Qi 6"), p. 474. On Chu, see *Zhanguo ce* ("Chu 1"), pp. 482, 500; ("Qin 3"), p. 216 (Crump, *Chan-Kuo Ts'e*, pp. 55, 244, 466, 202, 386, 400, 429, 289, 460, 466, 157, 221, 225, 230, 134); *Shi ji*, 40, p. 1731. On Yan, see *Zhanguo ce* ("Yan 1"), p. 1039. *Zhanguo ce* ("Qi 5"), p. 441, uses the phrase "an army of 1,000,000 men" in a context which shows that it means "the largest possible army" (Crump, *Chan-Kuo Ts'e*, p. 201).
Some scholars have argued that the character 萬 is used rhetorically to mean "a large number." This may be true in such figures as 1,000,000 or 100,000, but the speakers indicate something more specific when they employ such figures as 70–80,000, 200,000, 300,000, or 600,000. Moreover, in several persuasions Zhang Yi uses the figures 200,000 or 300,000 to suggest how *small* are the forces available to a state, so the argument that the character 萬 is a rhetorical trope for "large number" ignores its actual use in the passages in question.
[57] *Sunzi*, pp. 31 (twice), 329 (Sawyer, trans., *Sun Tzu*, pp. 173, 231); *Mozi jian gu* (19 "Fei gong C"), 5, p. 91 (Mei Tsu-lin, *Ethical and Political Works of Motse*, pp. 109–10); *Lü shi chunqiu jiao shi* (19 "Yong min"), p. 1270; *Shi ji*, 79, p. 2422 (Watson, trans., *Records of the Grand Historian*, vol. 3, p. 154); *Zhanguo ce* ("Qin 3"), p. 216; ("Wei 2"), p. 835 (Crump, *Chan-Kuo Ts'e*, pp. 134, 382).

of power to the campaigns of all-out conquest launched by Qin. The Qin armies supposedly killed 240,000 men in their victory over the combined forces of Hann and Wei in 293; 150,000 soldiers of Wei in 273; and 400,000 Zhao soldiers in the cataclysm of Changping 長平 in 260. Even Yan, traditionally the weakest of the states, was said to have put 600,000 men, divided into two separate armies, into the field in 251 B.C.[58] While these have little value as absolute figures, and casualties of 20,000 to 40,000 men remain more common, they suggest a story stretching across four centuries of ever greater mobilization of forces in the name of ever more deadly wars of conquest. Drawn from a variety of sources of different origins, interests, and philosophical persuasions, they present a consistent picture of an expanding scale of military actions that fits well with what we know of the evolving institutions and practices of the period.

Scale

The growth in the size of armies was matched by significant increases in the scale of combat, in terms both of time and space. Whereas a campaign in the Spring and Autumn period lasted at most a season, and a battle no more than two days, Warring States campaigns often lasted for more than a year. Thus, forces of King Hui of Wei besieged the city of Handan for three years; King Wuling of Zhao waged a five-year campaign against Zhongshan; the combined armies of Qi, Hann, and Wei carried on a five-year campaign against Chu; the same allies battled Qin at the Hangu 函谷 Pass for three years; and the Qin army that won at Changping spent three years in the field.[59] Our sources do not provide sufficient detail to know whether some rotation of troops took place during these campaigns, but at any rate the old seasonal limits to campaigns were clearly no longer constraining.

The increase in warfare, both in terms of number of participants and duration of campaigns, was matched in the geographic sphere. Whereas the Spring and Autumn armies had fought as united bodies, with the full forces of both sides assembled opposite each other on a single field of battle, Warring States armies were regularly divided into several forces that operated independently and were separated by great distances. Thus, the campaign that culminated in Qi's defeat of Wei at Guiling 桂陵 in 353 B.C. entailed maneuvers by four distinct armies moving across much of modern Shanxi. The general war of 312 between the coalition of Qin, Wei, and Hann against

[58] *Shi ji*, 5, pp. 212–13 (Watson, trans., *Records of the Grand Historian*, vol. 3, pp. 29–31); 73, p. 2331 (Watson, *Records of the Grand Historian: Qin*, pp. 121–2).

[59] *Lü shi chunqiu jiao shi* (18 "Bu qu"), p. 1197; (18 "Ying yan"), p. 1212; *Zhanguo ce* ("Zhao 3"), p. 678 (twice); ("Yan 1"), p. 1056 (Crump, *Chan-Kuo Ts'e*, pp. 330–1, 512–13).

the forces of Chu and Qi involved simultaneous offensives on four separate fronts stretching across the loess highlands and the flood plain of the Yellow River. The great battle of Changping, though more geographically concentrated than the preceding campaigns, involved two armies deadlocked across a front that stretched for hundreds of *li*.

Defensive Walls

This geographic redefinition of warfare was even more striking in routine defensive procedures than in campaigns. The military aspect of the formation of territorial states was marked by the building of chains of watch stations and forts at strategic points, and ultimately the creation of large defensive walls along the boundaries of the various states. Even in the late Spring and Autumn period, states had already set up barriers and forts at strategic passes or narrows, but these were not routinely garrisoned. Such essential transit points became the keys to success in the extended territorial campaigns of the Warring States period, and most of the major battles of the period took place around passes, narrow defiles, and other points whose control was crucial to the passage of armies. As a result, each state built barriers and fortifications at its own strategic points and kept permanent garrisons stationed there. In hilly terrain the regions around such forts would also have towers to keep watch and send signals. These barriers also allowed states to check those who entered and exited their borders and to collect transit taxes from merchants who carried goods from state to state.[60]

More substantial than these systems of barriers, forts, and watch towers at strategic passes were the walls erected along state frontiers, as well as the boundaries between the northern nomads and the states of Qin, Zhao, and Yan. The latter are better known, for they were connected by the First Emperor to form the earliest version of the "Great Wall," but the interior walls were more significant in the Warring States period. These walls usually

---

[60] On the absence of permanent garrisons in the Spring and Autumn period, see Gu Donggao, *Chunqiu dashi biao*, in *Huang Qing jingjie xuebian*, ed. Wang Xianqin, 1748 (Beijing: Zhonghua, punctuated reprint ed., 1993) (8B "Chunqiu lie guo bu shou guan yi lun"), pp. 995–6. On major battles at passes and defiles, see *Shi ji*, 44, p. 1857; 65, p. 2164; 81, p. 2445; *Lü shi chunqiu jiao shi* (13 "You shi"), p. 658. On forts, see *Shi ji*, 73, p. 2333 (Watson, trans., *Records of the Grand Historian*, vol. 3, p. 122); *Zhan guo ce* ("Zhao 1"), pp. 617, 618; ("Wei 1"), p. 792; ("Han 1"), p. 934 (Crump, *Chan-Kuo Ts'e*, pp. 335 (twice), 400, 466); *Han Feizi ji shi* (30 "Nei chu shuo A"), 9, p. 551 (Liao, *Han Fei Tzu*, vol. 1, p. 300). On signal towers, see *Shi ji*, 77, p. 2377; 81, p. 2449; *Mozi jian gu* (70 "Hao ling"), 15, p. 361; (71 "Za shou"), 15, p. 367; Wang Guowei, *Guan tang ji lin* ("Qin Xinqi hu fu ba"), 18.11a. On border controls, see *Shi ji*, 44, p. 1862; 75, p. 2355; 79, p. 2412 (Watson, trans., *Records of the Grand Historian*, vol. 3, p. 142); *Lü shi chunqiu jiao shi* (24 "Dang shang"), p. 1611; *Han Feizi ji shi* (32 "Wai chu shuo zuo A"), 11, p. 629 (Liao, *Han Fei Tzu*, vol. 2, pp. 37–8); *Zhou li zhu shu* ("Zhang jie"), 15.10b–13b; "E Jun qi jie ming wen."

followed rivers, being placed behind the dikes that lined the banks, and were made of stamped earth. Thus, the earliest historical record of such a wall relates that in 461 B.C. Qin "walled the banks of the Yellow River," and later accounts note that this wall was extended in 417. When this defensive line did not hold and its armies were pushed back to the Luo River, Qin also began to wall the banks of that river. The building of similar defensive walls along rivers and mountainsides was undertaken by the other six states. Wei built two separate wall systems, one along the Luo River to contain Qin and one to the west of Daliang that was begun in 358, three years after the capital was moved there.[61] Although not particularly high and built largely of stamped earth, several of these walls stretched across whole modern provinces, and they were sufficiently sturdy for substantial foundations to survive to be excavated.

The Arts of War

The last great change in warfare during the Warring States period was the creation of a specialized, intellectual discipline devoted to the conduct and principles of combat. Just as the figure of the reforming minister defined an ideal type for a career in the court of a territorial lord, so the all-conquering commander became the emblematic figure for military specialists. And just as several of the leading reformers became authors or eponyms for texts on statecraft, so such celebrated commanders as Sun Wu, Wu Qi, and Sun Bin 孫臏 became the initiators or namesakes of treatises on the art of war. These texts developed along with the changes in warfare sketched above. Supplemented by discussions of the institutional bases of war in the Legalist texts, they are the chief written sources for the study of warfare in the Warring States.

In the Spring and Autumn period there was no military specialization. Those nobles who dominated the state also led its armies, and each head of a fief commanded its levies in the field. With the rise of mass infantry armies, which required elaborate administration and organization, and the development of new weapons, which had to be conjoined in order to be effective, a

---

[61] *Zuo zhuan zhu* (Xiang 18), p. 1037; (Zhao 13), p. 1351; *Shi ji*, 5, pp. 199, 200 (Watson, trans., *Records of the Grand Historian*, vol. 3, pp. 21–22); 15, p. 721; 40, p. 1730; 41, p. 1740, n. 12; 43, pp. 1799 (twice), 1802, 1806; 69, p. 2267; 110, p. 2885); *Zhu shu ji nian* 竹書紀年, quoted in the *zheng yi* commentary of *Shi ji*, 69, p. 2268, n. 6; *Lü shi chunqiu jiao shi* (15 "Xia xian"), p. 880; *Zhanguo ce* ("Qin 1"), p. 99; ("Yan 1"), pp. 1053, 1057; Shi Nianhai, "Huang He zhong you Zhanguo ji Qin shi zhu changcheng yiji de tansuo," in *He shan ji*, vol. 2, pp. 435–70; Zhang Weihua, "Zhao changcheng kao," *Yu gong* 7. 8–9 (1937): 40–68 (maps on unnumbered pages preceding the article); Gu Jiegang, "Gansu changcheng yiji," in *Shi lin za zhi* (Beijing: Zhonghua, 1963), pp. 77–8 (separate map included); Luo Zhewen, "Lintao Qin Changcheng Dunhuang Yumen guan Jiuquan kancha jian ji," *Wenwu* 1964.6: 46–57.

specialized officer corps based on expertise and education became essential. All the military treatises of the period insist on the need for absolute discipline and coordinated action, and they routinely employ the metaphor of the army as a single body with the commander as its mind. In such a context, the emphasis in military thought was placed on the actions of the officers responsible for bringing intelligibility and order to the collective behavior of the massed soldiery. Thus, the specialist commander, an idealized figure of supernatural intelligence, became emblematic of theories of combat in the period. The combined evidence of the biographies of major commanders and the development of military treatises both suggest that some degree of specialization for military officers first appeared in the late sixth century and that by the end of the fourth century, there were both officers who were exclusively commanders of armies and technical military treatises intended for a specialist audience.[62]

The figure of the general (*jiang* or *jiang jun* 將軍, i.e., "leader of an army") in biography appears with the legendary Sun Wu and Sima Rangju 司馬穰苴. Both these commanders are assigned to the late sixth century B.C., that is, the end of the Spring and Autumn period, and have early treatises associated with their names. However, each of their biographies consists of a single story, and in structure and message the two stories are identical. These tales are parables on the essential principles of military command – the need for fixed rules, the role of the general as master of life and death, the autonomy of the general in the field – and are totally detached from any actual careers. While there may have been historical figures at the origins of the books, they are lost beyond recovery.[63]

Only in the late fifth century do we find commanders, most notably Wu Qi, with sufficiently detailed records of their careers to be treated as historical, but many of the events in these narratives still belong to the realm of romance or later invention. Moreover, in the fifth century and the first half of the fourth century, commanders were still not exclusively military specialists. Wu Qi also acted as an administrator, perhaps even a local potentate, in Xihe, and supposedly as a reforming minister in Chu. Shang Yang, the great reformer of the mid-fourth century, also commanded armies in the field, as did such noted diplomat/persuaders as Zhang Yi 張儀 (d. 309 B.C.) and Gan Mao 甘茂 (fl. 310–305 B.C.). In the second half of the fourth century we first find military specialists who play no role in civil government, most notably Sun Bin, who never actually commanded an army but only served as adviser, and his arch-rival Pang Juan 龐涓 (d. 341 B.C.). By the third century

---

[62] Robin Yates, "New Light on Ancient Chinese Military Texts: Notes on Their Nature and Evolution, and the Development of Military Specialization in Warring States China," *TP*, 74, 4–5 (1988): 212–48.
[63] *Shi ji*, 64, 65, pp. 2161–2; Petersen, "What's in a Name?"

the historical records include many specialist military commanders, most notably the chief generals of the Qin conquest, Bo Qi and Wang Jian 王翦 (fl. 236–221 B.C.), and their rivals such as Zhao She 趙奢 (d. ca. 270 B.C.) and Lian Po 廉頗 (fl. 283–245 B.C.). Generalship became virtually a hereditary occupation, with the Meng 蒙 lineage in Qin, the Xiang 項 lineage in Chu, and – abortively – the generals Zhao *père* and *fils* all handing down the title of commander from father to son.

This specialization of careers was accompanied by a shift in military literature from discussions of the relation of the army to the state and the first principles of combat, in early texts, to detailed accounts of technology, placement of troops, and terrain. Later discussions of warfare also included elaborate accounts of waging war according to the principles of *yin–yang* 陰 陽 or the Five Phases (*wu xing* 五行).

The commander also figured, along with the "persuader," as one of the archetypal figures of the realm of stratagem and cunning. The military treatises describe the ideal commander as a potent figure who could penetrate the flux of appearance, perceive underlying order, recognize decisive moments of change, and then strike. He was able to disguise his intentions while penetrating the schemes of his adversary, and to manipulate appearances so that the enemy would march to its doom. A master of maneuver, illusion, and deception, he waged war in the realm of the mind and directly translated his stratagems into victory in the field. These arts of stratagem and manipulation, and the master of cunning wisdom who embodied them, figured prominently in Warring States literature and in later Chinese culture, and they derive from the military treatises and the handbooks of persuader/diplomats, to whom we will now turn our attention.

ALLIANCES AND PERSUADERS

By the mid-fourth century the Warring States world was dominated by seven great powers pursuing independent foreign policies and maintaining an approximate balance of power. The most powerful and ambitious state was Wei, whose King Hui had forged a unified territorial state controlling the central Yellow River valley and several of the chief transit points in the Warring States world. However, a series of military defeats soon eclipsed the power of Wei, and the political history of the next century was defined by the steady rise to dominance of the western state of Qin. Qin's ascent was opposed successively by Wei, Qi, and Zhao, each of which succumbed to military disasters. This left Qin totally dominant by the middle of the third century B.C. This century (350–250) figures in the sources as the age of the "horizontal," that is, pro-Qin, and "vertical," that is, anti-Qin, alliances. The horizontal alliances were so called because they formed along an east–west axis, with Qin in the far west. The vertical alliances, in contrast, linked states from north to south. The political world appears as a chaos of ever-changing coalitions, but in which each new combination could ultimately be defined by its relation to Qin: either forced alliances of subservient states (horizontal) or hostile alliances under the leadership of whichever rival was then most powerful (vertical).

The central figures of this era were the persuader/diplomats who moved from state to state promising a ruler to secure his interests through alliances that they would obtain through their persuasive skills. Through their mastery of stratagem and language, these courtiers offered the ruler a safe path through the shifting constellations of warfare and alliance that defined the interstate order, and they proved the power of their arts through their ability to manipulate the rulers themselves. Awarded the office of minister by one ruler, they proceeded to other states to secure alliances that would be sealed by the granting of another ministerial seal. Thus, several independent states came to share a single minister, whose primary loyalty to any state remained questionable. The fluidity of loyalties was intensified as persuaders dismissed from one state sought office in another, only to return to the state that had expelled them with offers of new alliances that they would secure if restored to their former position.[64] Like reforming ministers and the military commanders, the most successful masters of persuasion became centers of a body of literature devoted to their arts and accomplishments.

The archetype of the rhetorician, though a figure whose historicity is lost in later fictionalizing narratives, was Su Qin 蘇秦. According to the biography eventually constructed for him, he came from a humble background and after early years of failure finally obtained service with the King of Yan. Through the brilliance of his persuasions he was able to dismantle a horizontal alliance formed by Qin and create a vertical alliance of opposition led by Qi. He was said to have simultaneously held the ministerial seals of six states. While actually working for Yan, he became the closest adviser of the King of Qi, the ultimate target of Yan's ambitions, and distracted Qi by leading it into war with Qin. Assassinated by a coterie of jealous nobles of Qi, with his dying breath Su Qin instructed the King of Qi in a stratagem to trap the assassins. Following the instructions, the king denounced the deceased Su Qin as a spy in the pay of Yan and offered a reward to his killers. When the nobles admitted their deed in order to claim the reward, they were executed. Thus, Su Qin, by making a true confession of his treason disguised

---

[64] Jean Levi, "Ma-Chine à trahir: Sophistes et délateurs dans la Chine ancienne," *La genre humaine* 16–17 (1988): 355–73. Reprinted in *Les fonctionnaires divins: Politique, despotisme et mystique en Chine ancienne* (Paris: Seuil, 1989), chapter 2.

as a clever lie, manipulated his mortal enemy into avenging his death.[65] Such was the world of the alliances.

Before analyzing the century of the alliances, it is important to note one essential feature. The symmetry suggested by the terms "horizontal" and "vertical" alliances is illusory. While the vertical alliances were formed between independent states, though generally with one preeminent power, the horizontal versions were relations of dominance. To be in a horizontal alliance meant to be under the sway, if only temporarily, of Qin. This asymmetry meant that while success increased the stability of a horizontal alliance, because it enhanced Qin's power, success for a vertical alliance invariably led to its breakup, because it strengthened the preeminent ally and led the others to turn against it. The logic of the practitioners of alliance sketched above made any protracted coalition against Qin impossible. The empirical result of this principle was that Wei, the first leading opponent of Qin, was broken by Qi, while Qi in turn was toppled by an alliance led by Yan. Only at the end of the age of alliances, in its confrontation with Zhao, did Qin finally have to defeat its primary adversary in battle.

The century of alliances can be divided into three stages, corresponding to the three chief adversaries of Qin: (1) the last half of the fourth century, (2) the period of Qi, 301–284 B.C., and (3) the period of Zhao, 284–260 B.C. The first period in turn witnessed two major developments: the decline of Wei, and the territorial consolidation of Qin.

The Decline of Wei, 353–322 B.C.

The primary factors in the decline of Wei were the two crushing defeats, celebrated as marvels of strategy in later Chinese literature, suffered in 353 B.C. at Guiling and 341 B.C. at Maling. These were inflicted by Qi forces commanded by Tian Ji 田忌 and Sun Bin. Whereas Wei recovered from the first defeat sufficiently to allow Hui Hou to adopt the royal title, the second disaster led to a defeat at the hands of a Qin army under Shang Yang, and Wei was forced to accept a position as a subordinate ally of Qi. However, Wei's new alliance did it little good. In the next decade Qin armies led first by Gongsun Yan 公孫衍 (fl. 333–315 B.C.) and then by Zhang Yi – the first of the persuaders to appear in the historical record – inflicted virtually annual defeats on Wei. Qin not only reoccupied all the territory lost to Wei in the late fifth century, but also made major inroads into the Wei heartland. In 322 Wei accepted the first horizontal "alliance," by appointing Qin's chief minister Zhang Yi to be simultaneously minister of Wei. In response to

---

[65] *Shi ji*, 69, pp. 2265–6.

this, Gongsun Yan was able to form the first vertical alliance of the five remaining states against Qin. At this time the idea of horizontal and vertical alliances first came into common usage, and Zhang Yi and Gongsun Yan became the most celebrated politicians in the Warring States.[66]

Qin's Territorial Consolidation

Even as Qin began to project its power into the Central Plain, it also completed its conquests of its non-Hua neighbors and thereby created the integral state ringed by mountains that gave it a major geopolitical advantage over its allies (see Map 9.2). In 316 B.C., Qin finished the conquest, begun 130 years earlier, of the southwestern states Shu and Ba. Although it recognized a series of local chieftains as feudatory lords of Shu, actual administration was taken into Qin hands. Qin law, landholding patterns, and military service were imposed. In 314 Qin also defeated the last hostile Rong tribe, and thus brought an end to the last threat to its frontiers in the west. Through these conquests and the occupation of the Hangu Pass and other key points in the Yellow River valley, Qin had made itself virtually impervious to attack. The process was completed in 312 when Qin forces defeated Chu at Danyang 丹陽 and thus secured the Hanzhong 漢中 region. This conquest linked the Qin heartland to Ba and Shu as a single territorial block. In addition, Chu was gravely weakened, and it ceased to play any significant role in the balance of power.

Qin's expansion to the southwest was important not only from a strategic point of view, but also as a new source of economic wealth that gradually made Qin predominant among the Warring States. In 310, Zhang Yi initiated the construction of a new local capital for Shu at Chengdu 成都, where he built a city modeled on the Qin capital Xianyang. From this base Qin proceeded to develop the Sichuan Basin as a major agricultural center, most notably through Li Bing's 李冰 (fl. 300 B.C.) famous irrigation project at the modern Dujiangyan 都江堰.[67]

The Period of Qi, 301–284 B.C.

The second period of the age of alliances centered on the rise and fall of Qi. Politics during this period was dominated by the figure of Tian Wen 田文, the Lord of Mengchang 孟嘗君. A notorious figure in the period, Tian Wen accumulated considerable wealth from his fief and related business activities,

---

[66] Yang Kuan, *Zhanguo shi*, pp. 315–23.
[67] Sage, *Ancient Sichuan*, chapters 4–5; Joseph Needham, *Science and Civilisation in China. Vol. 4:3, Civil Engineering and Nautics* (Cambridge University Press, 1971), pp. 288–96.

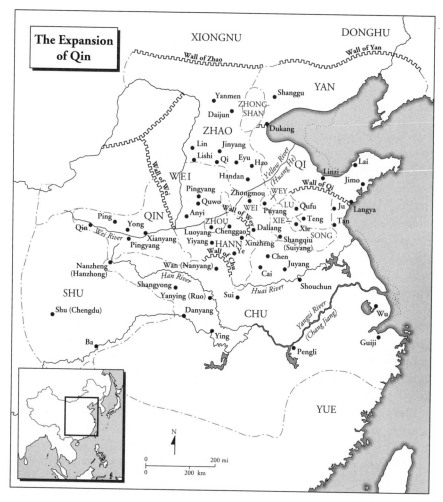

Map 9.2. The expansion of Qin ca. 350–249 B.C.

and he used his money to surround himself with thousands of retainers. In doing so he set the pattern for the competition among the leading enfeoffed ministers of his day, the so-called Four Lords, to assemble large personal followings of persuaders, assassins, and others of diverse talents. He was also emblematic of the tendency for enfeoffed relatives of the royal line to dominate most courts during this period.

With the accession of King Min 湣 (r. 300–284 B.C.), Tian Wen secured effective control of the government of Qi, which established a revived alliance with Hann and Wei. Since Qin had been seriously weakened by a succession struggle in 307, it temporarily yielded to this new coalition by appointing Tian Wen as chief minister. No sooner was this general peace secured, however, than a jealous Zhao offered Qin an allegiance against Qi. Tian Wen was dismissed as minister, and the struggle between the two great powers resumed. In 298 the Qi-led alliance attacked Qin, and their combined armies reached the Hangu Pass. After three years of warfare, the allied armies forced their way into the pass and compelled Qin to sue for peace. Substantial territories that had been lost were thus returned to Hann and Wei. The three allies then inflicted a crushing defeat on Yan. During the five years of its alliance with Hann and Wei, Qi had inflicted major defeats on Chu, Qin, and Yan, and thus secured a temporary dominance among the Warring States.

In 294, Tian Wen fled to Wei after being implicated in a coup d'état, and his carefully constructed alliance collapsed. Qin and Qi then agreed on a temporary truce in order to pursue their own interests. Qin's armies, now under their great general Bo Qi, resumed their eastward expansion against Hann and Wei. It is in these campaigns between 294 and 290 that we find the sudden rise in casualty figures that signals the escalation of warfare as Qin began its drive for absolute power. Qi, for its part, set out to conquer Song. This minor state was particularly desirable for its city Dingtao, perhaps the wealthiest commercial center in the Warring States.[68] The alliance of Qin and Qi culminated in 288, when the two rulers declared themselves to be the western and eastern di 帝, the first application of this divine title to human rulers. They swore a covenant cast in bronze and agreed to begin an attack on Zhao.

At this point a radical transformation of the political scene was supposedly engineered by the newly prominent Su Qin. If we accept the evidence of the newly discovered *Zong heng jia shu* from Mawangdui, Su Qin, acting in the service of the King of Yan, persuaded the king of Qi that his state's interests lay in the occupation of Song and the weakening of Qin, and that the proposed war with Zhao would benefit Qin at Qi's expense.[69] The king of Qi accepted the argument, and he formed an alliance with the other states in the name of compelling Qin to abandon the presumptuous title of *di*. A chastened Qin abandoned the contested title and restored recently conquered territory to Wei and Zhao. In the next year Qi completed the second element of its scheme by finally occupying Song.

Qi's success, however, immediately made it the target of collective fear and suspicion – all according to the scheme of Su Qin, if we trust our sources –

[68] Shi Nianhai, *He shan ji*, vol. 1 (Beijing: Sanlian, 1963), pp. 110–30.
[69] *Zhanguo zong heng jia shu* (Beijing: Wenwu, 1976), pp. 1–2, 3, 5–6, 9–11, 35; Levi, *Les Fonctionnaires divins*, pp. 73–80.

and a hostile coalition of all the states rapidly formed under the leadership
of the exiled Tian Wen in Wei, Wei Ran 魏冉 (fl. 307–266 B.C.) in Qin, and
King Zhao 昭 (r. 311–279 B.C.) of Yan. Yan had traditionally been a steadfast
ally of Qi, so that the latter's northern defenses were relatively weak. In 284,
the Yan armies, which had been intensively developed for three decades, were
led by general Yue Yi 樂毅 (fl. 300–279 B.C.) in a massed onslaught from the
north that caught Qi completely by surprise. At the same time the armies of
Qi, Zhao, Hann, and Wei attacked from the west. Chu declared itself an ally
of Qi and marched north, but it contented itself with reoccupying land it
had lost north of the Huai River. In the following campaign Qi's armies were
annihilated, its king slain, and the entire state occupied with the exception
of the cities of Ju 莒 and Jimo 即墨. Although a relative of Qi's royal line,
Tian Dan 田單, who had risen to command in Ju and Jimo, succeeded in
recovering Qi's territory in 279, the state never again attained the level of its
former influence and power. Like Wei it could no longer challenge Qin,
which in 278 captured Chu's capital and expelled Chu from the Han River
valley and the central Yangzi.[70]

The Period of Zhao, 284–260 B.C.

These developments mark the beginning of the third stage of the century of
alliances. It was the transitional period between the age of diplomatic maneuver in a multistate world based on a balance of power to the time of "total
war" aimed at conquest of all the other states. This shift was prefigured by
the increasing scale of combat noted earlier, and it was encouraged by the
weakening of Qin's major rivals. The disasters that had befallen Qi and Chu
left Zhao alone in opposition to Qin, so the importance of diplomatic
maneuvers was eclipsed by that of military prowess. As will be discussed
below, this new age found its theoretician in the last of the persuaders, Fan
Sui 范睢 (d. 255 B.C.).[71]

Zhao, strengthened by King Wuling's military reforms and the conquest
of Zhongshan in 300, had flourished by alternately supporting Qin and
Qi. It had been further strengthened through the policies of King Huiwen
惠文 (r. 298–266 B.C.), who had surrounded himself with able generals and
ministers, such as Yue Yi, Lin Xiangru 藺相如, Lian Po, and Zhao She. In
the decade between 285 and 275, Zhao expanded its territories at the expense
of the declining Wei and Qi, and texts make generalized statements
about the prosperity of his state in this period. The rise of Zhao reached its

---

[70] Yang Kuan, *Zhanguo shi*, pp. 340–51.

[71] There is disagreement as to the character for his personal name. Some scholars, such as Crump in his
translation of the *Zhanguo ce* and Watson in his translation of the *Shi ji*, read the character as 睢 *ju*.

climax in 269 B.C., when forces under Lian Po decisively defeated two Qin armies.[72]

This defeat led to the rise of Fan Sui and a shift in Qin policy. One reason for Qin's defeat was that even while part of the Qin forces fought against Zhao, other armies had been dispatched to Qi, where Qin's chief minister Wei Ran was seeking to expand the enclave around his recently acquired fief of Dingtao. Fan Sui, who had previously served in Wei, traveled to the Qin court, where he attacked the failings of Wei Ran and propounded the doctrine of "allying oneself with those who are distant [i.e., Qi] in order to attack those nearby [originally Hann, ultimately Zhao]." King Zhao 昭 (r. 306–251 B.C.) of Qin accepted these arguments and gave Fan Sui a ministerial appointment. From this position Fan Sui persuaded King Zhao of the virtues of direct royal rule, indirectly attacking the Queen Dowager and Wei Ran who had controlled the court since 307. In 266 the king dismissed the Dowager and banished Wei Ran. Fan Sui was appointed chief minister.

Fan Sui's appointment marked a significant moment in Warring States history, for he was the first politician to articulate a goal of irrevocable expansion for Qin. Abandoning the old policy of making and unmaking alliances to suit the needs of the moment and seizing territories scattered across the Warring States (e.g., Dingtao), he asserted "alliance with the distant and war with neighbors" as a basic principle allowing for the irreversible expansion of the state as an integrated territorial unit. To reinforce this policy of a unitary state, he insisted that "each inch or foot gained was the king's inch or foot."[73] This denounced not only Wei Ran, who had used the conquests of Qin's armies to expand his personal fiefs and those of his followers, but also the general trend of the late fourth and early third centuries for leading courtiers to receive noble titles and ever larger fiefs. In addition to Wei Ran and four of his allies who had been enfeoffed as lords, the other figures attacked included Tian Wen, Lord of Mengchang; Zhao Sheng 趙勝, Lord of Pingyuan 平原君 (d. 251 B.C.); Gongzi Wuji 公子無忌 of Wei, Lord of Xinling 信陵君 (d. 242 B.C.); Huang Xie 黃歇 of Chu, Lord of Chunshen 春申君 (d. 237 B.C.); and Qin's great commander Bo Qi, Lord of Wuan 武安君, a rival to Fan Sui's ascent. These men dominated the governments of their states, accumulated large fortunes, assembled armies of personal followers, and rivaled the monarch's authority. Fan Sui strengthened Qin by bringing this to a temporary halt.

A final maxim of Fan Sui that articulated recent political developments and defined the new ambitions of Qin was "attack not only their territory but also their people." This meant to aim not only at territorial expansion,

---

[72] *Shi ji*, 43, pp. 1818–22; 81, pp. 2439–45.
[73] *Shi ji*, 79, p. 2409 (Watson, trans., *Records of the Grand Historian*, vol. 3, p. 139).

but also at the destruction of armies on such a scale that rival states would lose the capacity to fight.[74] Here we find enunciated as policy the mass slaughters of the third century.

The first tangible expression of these policies was the abandonment of the war with Qi and the concentration of Qin's power on the destruction of Hann, the weakest surviving state and one that bordered directly on Qin. In 265 Qin began an offensive that cut off the seventeen districts of Shangdang 上黨 from the rest of Hann. The king of Hann agreed to cede these, but the local governor refused to comply and instead presented the territory to Zhao. Lian Po, the hero of Zhao's victories over Qin, took responsibility for the defense of the territory and based his army at Changping. Qin sent out its armies under Bo Qi, and thus began the greatest campaign of the Warring States period.

The two armies remained locked in a standoff for three years. Finally King Xiaocheng 孝成 of Zhao (r. 265–245 B.C.) was persuaded that Lian Po was avoiding combat and that he should entrust the command to Zhao Kuo 趙括 (d. 260 B.C.), son of the successful general Zhao She. The new commander threw his troops into the decisive battle that he had promised the king. Bo Qi allowed Zhao's forces to advance in the center, encircled them on the flanks, cut their supply lines, and seized the fortifications they had left behind. When their advance in the center was finally blocked by Qin's fortifications, the Zhao army found itself entirely surrounded. Failing to break through, they dug in and awaited relief. Both states mobilized all the troops at their disposal, with the king of Qin making a special visit to Henei, mobilizing all males over fifteen years of age, and granting them all one rank in the state hierarchy. After forty-six days Zhao had failed to relieve the encircled troops, who were now on the brink of starvation. Zhao Kuo launched a last, desperate attempt to break out, but he himself was killed in the final assault. The starving army surrendered. According to the sources all of its soldiers were buried alive by Bo Qi. Zhao's losses supposedly totaled more than 400,000, and though this figure is certainly exaggerated, Zhao never entirely recovered from the defeat.[75] Like Wei and Qi, it was no longer able to match Qin in the field.

Due to the exhaustion of its own forces and the growing rivalry between Fan Sui and Bo Qi, Qin was unable to follow up the victory immediately. When the policy he advocated was rejected, Bo Qi retired to his fief and was forced to commit suicide. The general who replaced him lost his entire command when attacked from the rear while besieging the Zhao capital, and

---

[74] *Shi ji* 79, pp. 2409–12 (ibid., pp. 138–42); *Zhanguo ce* ("Qin 3"), p. 200 (Crump, *Chan-Kuo Ts'e*, p. 112).

[75] *Shi ji* 73, pp. 2333–5 (Watson, trans., *Records of the Grand Historian*, vol. 3, pp. 122–4); 81, pp. 2446–7.

Fan Sui was stripped of office for his role in the debacle. Two years later he was executed for involvement in a case of colluding with foreign monarchs. The catastrophe of Changping, followed shortly by the deaths of Bo Qi and Fan Sui, marked the end of another period of Warring States history. Qin now dominated the world of the Warring States. No single state could match it, and there was no mechanism to hold together a multistate alliance against it for any period of time. Although the Warring States period would last three more decades, the issue was no longer in doubt. All that remained was a chronicle of steady Qin expansion and the sequential destruction between 230 and 221 B.C. of the remaining states.[76]

SCHOLARS AND THE STATE

Unlike kings, reforming ministers, commanders, and persuader/diplomats, the scholars were neither an indispensable element of the new state structure nor active participants in the political world, but they evolved in close relation with the states of the period. The teacher–disciple relationship as a social form first appears in the careers of Confucius and his followers, as reflected in the *Analects*. While this text and later traditions tell of Confucius's attempts to find a ruler who would employ him, he held only low office and played no role in the politics of the period. However, several of his disciples attained high office in minor states, and others found patrons who supported their cultural activities as teachers and masters of ritual. These men in turn attracted students, so the "school" (*jia* 家), defined by links between successive teachers and disciples and the texts that they transmitted and reworked, became a distinctive social form.

Apart from those that emerged from Confucius's disciples, the only full-blown school attested to in the records is the Mohist tradition. Otherwise, each intellectual tradition is identified by the name of its putative founder and is defined entirely by a book or books that bore his name.[77] The sociology of these intellectual traditions remains obscure, for we cannot be certain in many cases of their composition or of their economic bases. Clearly the holding of office was one means of turning scholarship into wealth, but those few scholars whose names and careers are preserved seem not to have had successful political careers. Whereas successful officials such as Li Kui, Shen

---

[76] Hann fell in 230 B.C., Zhao in 228, Wei in 225, Chu in 223, Yan in 222, and Qi in 221. See Chapter 14, this volume.

[77] *Xunzi jian shi* (6 "Fei shier zi"); (21 "Jie bi"), pp. 290–2 (Knoblock, *Xunzi*, vol. 1, pp. 222–9; vol. 3, pp. 102–103); *Zhuangzi ji shi* (Zhuzi jicheng ed.) (33 "Tian xia"), pp. 461–81 (Burton Watson, trans., *The Complete Works of Chuang Tzu* [New York: Columbia University Press, 1968], pp. 361–77); *Han Feizi ji shi* (50 "Xian xue"), 19, pp. 1080–104 (Liao, *Han Fei Tzu*, vol. 2, pp. 298–310).

Buhai, Shang Yang, several generals, and leading persuaders attracted disciples and formed textual traditions, the process does not seem to have gone in the opposite direction. Rarely were the proponents of scholarly textual traditions able to obtain high office. This asymmetry could explain why the Confucians and Mohists were the only known "schools" of the Warring States. By contrast the traditions of the actual politicians – institutional reformers, military men, or adepts of persuasion and alliance – were transformed into categories such as the "Legalists," "School of names," and "Military schools" only by Han bibliographers, who, from the time of Liu Xiang (79–8 B.C.), reinvented the past in the image of a triumphant state scholasticism defined by the Confucian inheritance.[78]

If scholarship was not the road to high office, then we must seek its economic bases elsewhere. Confucius was known to charge his disciples a fee, if only a token one from the poorest, so teaching may in some cases have been a source of income.[79] Those trained in the schools could sell their services as clerks and ritual specialists, occasionally to royal courts but more often to great families, the courts of lesser states, or the households of newly enfeoffed nobles. Funerals were central to religious cult, and the *Xunzi* speaks contemptuously of "petty antiquarians" who hired themselves out as funerary experts, and the *Mozi* contains similar denunciations of Ru 儒 (used here to indicate followers of the Confucian tradition) who made money through selling their ritual expertise.[80] The later Mohists offered their talents to various towns and courts as experts in siege warfare. In addition, the theory of *yin–yang* and the Five Phases may have emerged from meteorological and divinatory traditions that lay outside literary circles but still perpetuated themselves through master–disciple transmission and patronage from both court and noncourt levels.[81] Thus, some types of scholarship could provide a means of earning a living in various spheres of society. While the expertise of politicians in government, warfare, or diplomacy was only of value in the royal courts, textual scholars could maintain themselves apart from the world of politics. This "bipolar" social character of scholarship, whereby scholars were able to move between the courts and local society, between public

[78] *Han shu*, 30.
[79] *Lun yu zhu shu* ("Shu er"), 7.2b (Legge, *Analects*, p. 197). *Zhuangzi ji shi* (28 "Rang wang"), p. 420, describes the elaborate clothing, the ornate chariots, and the fine horses that Zi Gong earned through teaching (Watson, trans., *Complete Works of Chuang Tzu*, p. 316). Another account of gaining wealth and honor through teaching appears in *Han Feizi ji shi* (49 "Wu du"), 19, p. 1058 (Liao, *Han Fei Tzu*, vol. 2, p. 287).
[80] *Xunzi jian shi* (8 "Ru xiao"), pp. 92–3. See also (1 "Quan xue"), pp. 10–11; (6 "Fei shier zi"), p. 70 (Knoblock, *Xunzi*, vol. 1, pp. 140–1, 229; vol. 2, pp. 79–80); *Mozi jian gu* (15 "Fei ru xia"), 9, pp. 180–1 (Yi-Pao Mei, *The Ethical and Political Works of Motse*, pp. 202–3).
[81] A. C. Graham, *Disputers of the Tao: Philosophical Argument in Ancient China* (La Salle, Ill.: Open Court, 1989), pp. 313–70.

service and private retirement, is one reason why, unlike the intellectual products of the courts, it was able to survive and flourish after the unification under Qin rendered the skills of the Warring States courtiers and generals obsolete.

Although organized scholarship originated outside the courts of the new territorial states and preserved its bases in social and geographic hinterlands, elements of it were gradually drawn into the state sphere. Both the state and the scholarly traditions were thereby altered. From the late Spring and Autumn period, masters of religious and historical traditions occasionally found service as functionaries or policy advisers. However, the first signs of scholarly traditions becoming a significant element in the territorial states appear in the mid-fourth century. From that time the rulers of Wei and above all Qi began to gather scholars who were granted stipends and sometimes titles solely so that they might pursue their intellectual labors. In Qi, chosen scholars carried out their activities outside the Ji 稷 gate of the capital Linzi and hence came to be called "the scholars [or 'men of broad learning' *boshi* 博士] beneath the Ji [gate] 稷下."[82] The exact nature of this "institution" is not clear, its scale should not be exaggerated, and it is only one element of the broader social practice of collecting a large number of clients. Nevertheless, it marks a significant development. For the first time on record a state began to act as patron of scholarship out of the apparent conviction that this was a proper function of the state or a means of increasing its prestige.

The history of state patronage of scholastics elsewhere in the Warring States could charitably be described as sketchy. The *Shi ji* states that when Lü Buwei, chief minister of Qin from 250 to 238 B.C., began to assemble the retainers who composed the *Lü shi chunqiu,* he was inspired by his jealousy of the Four Lords. He felt that the dominant state, Qin, should not be surpassed in any field. This suggests that the practice of attracting scholars that began in Qi had since spread to the other states, though the royal courts were often surpassed as patrons of scholars by the great officers in their fiefs. It is significant that having previously been a Jixia scholar, Xun Kuang 荀況 (ca. 310–213 B.C.) was given an official post through the patronage of one of the Four Lords, Huang Xie in Chu.[83] This suggests that the "collecting" of scholars was part of the broader phenomenon of building extensive personal retinues of dependents with a wide variety of skills. In this way the scholars assembled in the courts of kings and their officers were the literary equivalents of the assassins and bravos (*you xia* 游俠) who attached themselves to leading politicians, while the schools that held themselves apart from state

[82] *Shi ji,* 74, pp. 2346, 2347–8.
[83] *Shi ji,* 74, p. 2348; 85, p. 2510 (Watson, trans., *Records of the Grand Historian,* vol. 3, pp. 162–3).

service in the lower reaches of society were the counterparts of the independent *you xia* syndicates. This linkage is directly articulated in the work attributed to Han Fei in its lists of those who challenge the legal order imposed by the ruler.[84]

While in some cases these official scholars might have acted as adornments to the life and prestige of a ruler or minister, or proofs of his power and prestige, they also played a distinctive role in the governments of the period. Specifically, they acted as experts on ritual performances in the court, the ancestral temple, and the sacred sites of the realm. In the sphere of religion and received practices, the ritual expertise preserved in certain scholarly traditions such as those derived from Confucius or the arts of "masters of techniques" (*fangshi* 方士) gave men of letters a claim to a role in the state. Religious cults, both ancestral and those devoted to nature deities, had been central to political power in the Shang 商, Western Zhou, and Spring and Autumn periods, and there is much evidence that this continued into the Warring States period. Finds in Warring States tombs increasingly reveal that members of the Warring States elite held elaborate beliefs about and a deep concern for the world of the spirits and the afterlife.[85] Received texts such as the *Chu ci* and the *Shan hai jing,* as well as anecdotes scattered throughout other works, point in the same direction.

However, due to the destruction of state records we lack detailed evidence about state cults and what could be called political religion. Our only literary evidence comes from accounts of the Qin state cult and the career of Qin Shihuang 秦始皇 (the First Emperor) preserved in the *Shi ji,* but this record is sufficient to confirm both the extent of state cults in the period and the role of scholars in their performance. The *Monograph on the Feng and Shan Sacrifices* (*Feng shan shu* 封禪書) describes the establishment of the cults of the Lord on High (*Shang Di* 上帝) and those of the four directional gods (*di* 帝) in Qin during the fifth and fourth centuries B.C., but its discussion of Qin deals primarily with the reign of the First Emperor.[86]

The adoption of the theory of the Five Phases as a model of history and guide for colors and numbers in court ritual by the First Emperor was a major modification of policy brought about by the influence of one scholarly tradition. The importance of state ritual at the end of the Warring States is also indicated by the First Emperor's program of progresses through his newly conquered realm during which he made repeated sacrifices at sacred moun-

[84] *Han Feizi ji shi* (49 "Wu du"), 19, pp. 1057, 1058; (50 "Xian xue"), 19, pp. 1091, 1095 (twice) (Liao, *Han Fei Tzu,* vol. 2, pp. 285, 287, 302, 305); *Shi ji,* 124, pp. 3181, 3184 (Burton Watson, trans., *Records of the Grand Historian of China,* vol. 2, pp. 452, 455).
[85] On this, see Chapter 12, this volume.
[86] *Shi ji,* 28, pp. 1358–77 (Watson, trans., *Records of the Grand Historian,* vol. 2, pp. 17–30).

tains and commemorated these acts with inscriptions in praise of his own achievements. The First Emperor also adopted the cults of conquered states. The monograph narrates his performance of sacrifices to the Eight Spirits, sacrifices instituted by the first lord of Qi, Tai Gong 太公, shortly after the Zhou conquest. His ritual program culminated in the performance of the feng 封 and shan 禪 rites. In preparation for these he consulted numerous scholars from Qi and Lu, both followers of Confucius and adepts of immortality, though he seems to have ultimately designed much of the ritual himself. Apart from these ritual performances, the First Emperor kept a large number of "broadly learned" official scholars (boshi) at his court, and from accounts of their later careers we know that many of them were devoted to the Zhou classics and the Confucian tradition.[87] Thus, by the end of the Warring States period the prestige of scholarship and state-sponsored ritual had become so great that the supposed arch-enemy of the Confucian scholars still employed them at his court, along with exponents of other scholastic traditions, and consulted them on ritual matters. Even the infamous burning of the books was not an attempt to destroy the scholarly traditions, since copies were to be preserved in the imperial collection. Instead, it sought only to bring these scholars under state control and thereby create the identity of political and intellectual authority that was a shared postulate or ambition of most scholars in the third century.[88]

HUMAN GEOGRAPHY

The preceding typology of texts and political roles omits one element of the new polity: the people. Producing no texts themselves, they appear in the writings of institutional reformers, military men, persuaders, and scholars as objects of control or manipulation. Sometimes threatening, sometimes docile, sometimes savages to be tamed, sometimes children to be protected, they appear only through the eyes of others who demonstrate their right to rule through inscribing commoners in their political theories and on population registers. It was through registration and mapping that the ordinary people were written into the political order, so population registers and the maps routinely associated with them became metonyms for authority and the hallmark of a ruler.[89] However, neither maps nor registers from the period

[87] Kanaya Osamu, Shin Kan shisô shi kenkyû, 2d rev. ed. (Kyoto: Heiraku, 1981), pp. 230–57.

[88] Xunzi jian shi (21 "Jie bi"), pp. 304–305 (Knoblock, Xunzi, vol. 3, p. 110); Zhuangzi ji shi (33 "Tian xia"); Shi ji, 6, pp. 254–5; 87, pp. 2546–7 (Watson, trans., Records of the Grand Historian, vol. 3, pp. 54–5, 185).

[89] On maps and population registers as metonyms of authority, see Zhanguo ce ("Qin 1"), p. 115; ("Qi 2"), pp. 350, 351; ("Yan 3"), pp. 1134, 1138 (Crump, Chan-Kuo Ts'e, pp. 66, 176, 177, 557, 559); Shi ji, 53, p. 2014; 86, pp. 2532, 2534; Han Feizi ji shi (49 "Wu du"), 19, p. 1067 (Liao, Han Fei Tzu, p. 292);

have come down to us, and we can see them only secondhand in the legal documents from Yunmeng and Baoshan.

The common people are inscribed in these texts as objects of registration, surveillance, and punishment. As was noted earlier, the Yunmeng documents are primarily guides to official action, so registration figures as an invariable element in identifying individuals brought within the ambit of the legal system. Presenting a detailed hierarchy of punishments according to the type of crime and the status of the convicted party, the texts also suggest the realities underlying the linked institutions of extracting service from the population and then ranking them by their achievements. These same fundamental concerns appear in the Baoshan materials as actual cases, in which the Chu officials tracked down attempts to avoid registration, examined the conduct of criminal investigations, and reviewed punishments imposed.[90] Population registers even became attributes of divine power, for a text excavated from a tomb shows that by the third century B.C., some Chinese believed in a spirit bureaucracy that used written registers to control human life spans.[91]

In addition to these indications in the legal documents, references scattered throughout the sources permit us to situate the people within the spatial reworking of the state. This geographic redefinition had two basic aspects, which correspond to the "expansion" and "contraction" metaphors discussed earlier. As a process of expansion, the Warring States polity was created through the extension of administration into significant elements of the countryside by the increased use of irrigation, land allocation, and registration of population. The states actively reshaped the countryside by introducing large-scale water-control projects, building roads, constructing forts and towers, and erecting walls. They also changed the relation of the population to the countryside through encouraging the ownership of land by individual households, furthering grain production through systems of rewards and penalties, and legally binding people to their places of residence through registration.

As a process of contraction, the Warring States tended to reduce the number of politically significant central places through the destruction first of noble sublineages, then of lesser states, and finally of all states save Qin. This contraction forced politically active elements of the population to pursue careers within a geographically narrowed ambit, for anyone aspiring

---

Xunzi jian shi (4 "Rong ru"), p. 38; (8 "Ru xiao"), pp. 78 (twice), 79; (9 "Wang zhi"), p. 117; (18 "Zheng lun"), p. 234 (Knoblock, *Xunzi*, vol. 1, p. 189; vol. 2, pp. 68, 69; vol. 3, p. 34).

[90] Hubei sheng Jingsha tielu kaogudui, ed., *Baoshan Chu jian* (Beijing: Wenwu, 1991), pp. 9–12.

[91] Li Xueqin, "Fangmatan jianzhong de zhiguai gushi," *Wenwu* 1990.4: 43–7; Donald Harper, "Resurrection in Warring States Popular Religion," *Taoist Resources* 5, 2 (1994): 13–28. See also Jeffrey K. Riegel, "Kou-mang and Ju-shou," *Cahiers d'extrême-Asie: Special Issue, Taoist Studies II* 5 (1989–90): 57–66.

to political eminence had to seek his fortune in a shrinking number of capitals. It also potentially reduced the number of sacred sites that dotted the landscape, though local cults could be absorbed by a conqueror or preserved by elements of the population that did not seek their fortunes in a distant court.

The extent of physical reconstruction of the countryside cannot be established from the records, which give only samplings of the relevant activities. In the course of this chapter we have noted such celebrated achievements of water control as the "twelve canals" of Ye built by Ximen Bao, Shang Yang's grid of pathways in the Wei River valley, and Li Bing's opening of the Sichuan Basin through the construction at Dujiangyan. Another major project undertaken in the third century B.C. was the canal constructed by Zheng Guo 鄭 國 that linked the Jing 涇 and Luo 洛 Rivers to the north of the Wei 渭 River and thereby dramatically increased the usable acreage in the Guanzhong region.[92] The extent of these projects in the Wei River valley and the loess highlands along the Yellow River is suggested by the grid patterns of roads and canals that have survived to the present day in these regions.[93] Dikes were also built by Wei, Zhao, and Qi along the lower course of the Yellow River, though the diking of the river was not completed until Han times. As walls between states tended to follow river valleys and often were built on top of dikes, this other great form of rebuilding the landscape appeared in the same regions as the water control projects.

However, in spite of the appreciable scale of some of these water-control projects and their importance to the rise of states like Wei and Qin, the majority of the peasantry lived in regions where agriculture had developed prior to irrigation or where no large-scale water control was necessary. These regions included mountain valleys in the upper reaches of tributaries and the hills of the loess highlands, as well as such regions as the oasis towns of the Gansu corridor or the settled parts of the middle Yangzi valley. In still other regions, notably the Huai and the Han River valleys, the recorded cases of dikes and irrigation systems are usually attributed to wealthy local families. In such places the state did not play a crucial role in developing agricultural production, but simply acted as administrator and regulator, usually in alliance with powerful local families.[94]

As regulator and registrar, the state paid no heed to "natural" units of geography, such as the village, in order to establish a direct administration

---

[92] *Shi ji*, 29, p. 1408 (Watson, trans., *Records of the Grand Historian*, vol. 2, pp. 71–2).

[93] Frank Leeming, "Official Landscapes in Traditional China," *JESHO* 23 (1980): 153–204. For suggested modifications of Leeming's conclusions, see Lewis, *Sanctioned Violence*, pp. 63, 273, n. 40.

[94] Kimura Masao, *Chûgoku kodai teikoku no keisei: Toku ni sono seiritsu no kiso jôken* (Tokyo: Fumeitô, 1967).

of the individual household. In addition to population registers, which have not survived, this attempt to create a state-based social order is reflected in the systems of hierarchical rankings based on military service and in a variety of theoretical systems based on hierarchies of ever more encompassing administrative units that ascend in diverse mathematical ratios. These theoretical systems found a real-life expression in the patterns of military organization that were extended into civil society, as was discussed above. They also figured in the ward organization of some capital cities.[95]

Conceiving the landscape in the image of the army also developed into the Warring States geographic models of the world, the "nine provinces" of the "Yu gong" 禹貢 chapter of the *Shang shu* and beyond that the multiple continents theory of Zou Yan 騶衍 (ca. 305–240 B.C.). The number "nine" had from ancient times been used to suggest an undefined large number, and in this sense the world was divided into nine "provinces" (*zhou* 州) according to an eastern Zhou bronze from the state of Qi and into nine units with various names in poems in the *Shi jing* 詩經. However, it is in the "Yu gong" that for the first time the number "nine" is taken at face value and the regions are geographically delimited.[96] This transformation of the old "nine" in the sense of "many" into a literal "nine" may have been tied to the rise of interest in magic squares.[97] We see hints of this in the *Mencius*'s "well-field" system, a grid derived from contemporary practice, but one with precisely nine squares, and it is interesting that the *Mencius* also speaks of nine large states that make up the area within the seas. Many scholars have suggested a Warring States date of composition for the "Yu gong," and it is possible that the nine provinces in the book can be identified with specific states.[98] The two changes in the listing of the nine provinces in the *Lü shi chunqiu* (239 B.C.) might then reflect changes in the political map by the end of the Warring States period. Whatever the case, in the theories of Zou Yan the number "nine" had come to have only an arithmetic sense, with nine provinces forming a small continent, nine small continents forming a great

[95] Koga Noboru, *Kan Chôanjô to senpaku kenkyôteiri seido* (Tokyo: Yûsankaku, 1980).

[96] *Mao shi zheng yi* (Shisan jing zhu shu ed.) (20.3 "Xuan niao"), p. 15a; (20.4 "Chang fa"), 4b; Guo Moruo, ed., *Liang Zhou jinwenci daxi tulu kaoshi* (Tokyo: Bunkyûdo, 1935) "(Qi) Shu Yi zhong," p. 245; *Yi Zhou shu* (Sibu beiyao ed.) (56" Chang mai"), 6.26b, 27a; *Shang shu zhu shu*, 6 "Yu gong."

[97] On magic squares and their significance in the thought of the period, see John S. Major, "The Five Phases, Magic Squares, and Schematic Cosmography," in *Explorations in Early Chinese Cosmology*, ed. Henry Rosemont, Jr. (JAAR Thematic Issue 50/2, Chico, Calif.: Scholar's Press, 1984), pp. 133–66; Schuyler Cammann, "The Evolution of Magic Squares in China," *JAOS* 80 (1960): 116–24; idem, "The Magic Square of Three in Old Chinese Philosophy and Religion," *History of Religions* 1 (1961): 37–80; idem, "Old Chinese Magic Squares," *Sinologica* 7 (1963): 14–53; Marcel Granet, *La pensée chinoise*, 1934 (Paris: Albin Michel, 1968), pp. 145–74.

[98] Shi Nianhai, *He shan ji*, vol. 2, pp. 400–404.

continent, and so on.[99] Here the mathematical modeling of administrative hierarchies and the grids of irrigation networks combined to form a geometric schema for the entire earth.

If the Warring States world was to be defined through grids, with the common people fixed in their individual squares, then the ability to move marked political power. Most of the peasantry was to be granted land and then legally rooted in place, even if the texts of the period are full of advice on how to lure away the peasants of alien states. With peasants defined by immobility, the elite was distinguished by constantly moving. Since political success could only be found at the capital, aspiring ministers, persuaders, and generals moved to the center of their states. If advancement was blocked in one state they would shift to a second, just as Wu Qi moved to Chu or Shang Yang to Qin. In the case of the persuader/diplomats who dominated the political scene between 350 and 250 B.C., these movements became a perpetual round of journeys between courts. They moved to seek employment, then went on missions for their new masters, and if they succeeded in forming an alliance they would move between the allied states as ministers of both.

Just as moving toward the center was the hallmark of those participating in the new state order, to draw men in was the hallmark of the ruler. The courts were in competition to employ the most skillful ministers or generals, so a successful ruler would be known by the quality and number of the men he brought into his service. Thus, Wei Wen Hou was noted for employing Li Kui, Wu Qi, Ximen Bao, Tian Zifang 田子方, Duan Ganmu 段干木, and other outstanding figures. This pattern was echoed in the courts of the great enfeoffed ministers who dominated the late fourth and early third centuries and competed with one another to attract talented followers. It is also the organizing principle of the "Yu gong," where the regions are defined not only through their topographic features, but more importantly through the goods that they send into the center and the riverine routes along which these goods pass. The finest goods, like the finest men, must flow to the center, and the ability to attract them is proof of the ruler's potent virtue. Thus, *de* 德 (virtue) was glossed as *de* 得 (obtain).

A final geographic transformation of the period was a new sacred geography. As lordship of territory became the hallmark of political authority, territorial cults supplanted the ancestral cult as the most important religious performances. The most important sacrifices were offered on open altars, either in the outskirts of the capital, at some spot sacred to the state such as

[99] *Mengzi zhu shu* ("Liang Huiwang A") 1B.6a; ("Liang Huiwang B") 2A.14a; ("Ten Wengong A") 5A.8b, 9a–b (Legge, *Mencius*, pp. 146, 162, 244, 245 (twice); *Shi ji*, 74, p. 2344; *Lü shi chunqiu jiao shi* (13 "You shi"), p. 685; Shi Nianhai, *He shan ji*, vol. 2, pp. 391–434.

Qin's cultic center at Yong 雍, or at the major mountains. Lordship over the earth was marked by the making of sacrifice at the numinous sites of the realm, and the conquest of a state was ritualized through the conquering ruler's performance of sacrifice at the spiritual centers of his new territory.[100]

Such mountain sacrifices entailed royal progresses to various spots of the realm, and these too formed part of the new sacred geography. Ancient traditions of royal processions, probably based on the frequent hunts and expeditions of Shang and Zhou kings, were presented as models of sage kingship within certain scholarly traditions. In the same period the spirit flights of mediums and holy men were imaginatively transformed into a sacred mandala of the four directions traced by the conquering ruler who thereby claimed possession of the world.[101]

These various elements of spatial redefinition were drawn together in the rituals and policies by which the First Emperor marked the completion of his conquest. By establishing *jun* and *xian* throughout his realm, he declared the uniform regulation of the people in the countryside. By building models of the palaces of the conquered states in his own capital, he completed the process of drawing all power into the capital. By casting statues from the metal of captured weapons and setting them up in the pattern of the Dipper, he declared the cosmic bases of the centrality of the capital. By forcibly moving the great families and nobility of the conquered states to the capital region, he reenacted the centripetal flow of talent and tribute. Finally, in his processions through his new provinces in the east, his sacrifices at their sacred peaks and places of cult, his repeated inscriptions to commemorate these deeds, and his performance of the Feng and Shan sacrifices he instituted the sacred geography of the newly united empire. In his inscriptions, the *res gestae* of his reign, he repeatedly insisted on the geographic character of his accomplishments. He asserted that all men came to his court, that the common people were at peace in their places, that he himself had inspected his new realm and marched to the edges of the earth, that he had reached the eastern edge and gazed across the sea to the place where the sun rose.[102] Thus, in proclaiming the end of the Warring States period, he summarized the processes by which the men of that time had redefined their world, and he claimed their achievements as his own.

---

[100] Lester Bilsky, *The State Religion of Ancient China* (Taipei: Chinese Association for Folklore, 1975), vol. 2.

[101] Ogura Yoshihiko, *Chûgoku kodai seiji shisô kenkyû* (Tokyo: Aoki, 1970), pp. 62–73; David Hawkes, "The Quest of the Goddess," in *Studies in Chinese Literary Genres*, ed. Cyril Birch (Berkeley: University of California, 1974), pp. 42–68.

[102] *Shi ji*, 6, pp. 242–6, 249–50, 261–2 (Watson, trans., *Records of the Grand Historian*, vol. 3, pp. 46–48, 50–2, 60–1.

CHAPTER TEN

THE ART AND ARCHITECTURE OF THE WARRING STATES PERIOD

Wu Hung

The Warring States period was an era of magnificent artistic creation and renewal in Chinese history. By the end of the Spring and Autumn period, changes within traditional ritual art and architecture had reached a critical point. Many new artistic and architectural forms, styles, and genres appeared during the following centuries and redefined the whole visual vista. In architecture, the city was reshaped and its internal structure reconfigured. Tall platforms and terrace pavilions won great favor from political patrons, replacing the deep, enclosed compound of a traditional temple or palace to determine the center of a city or palace town. With their monumental appearance and dazzling ornamentation, these architectural forms supplied powerful visual symbols much needed by the new elite. In art also, the reaction against ritual bronzes – the dominant artistic genre during the Shang and Western Zhou – continued. Although vessels and other equipment made for ceremonial usage never disappeared, the ritual occasions that they served had gone through fundamental transformations, becoming increasingly mundane. The commemorative inscription declined further. Ornate interlacing patterns or depictions of human events transformed a bronze vessel into a carrier of geometric decoration or pictorial representation. Monochrome vessels had gone out of fashion; lacquers and inlaid objects, both reflecting a fascination with fluent imagery and coloristic effects, enjoyed great popularity. Beautifully decorated mirrors, belt hooks, and other types of personal belongings became major showpieces. Lamps, screens, tables, and other objects of daily use were created as serious works of art; combining expensive materials, exquisite workmanship, and exotic images, these objects best documented the desire for material possession and the taste for extravagance. The interest in images also stimulated the development of sculpture and painting, two art forms that had languished with the dominance of ritual vessels.

While the palace provided one focus for the creation and consumption of art, the graveyard provided another. The growing importance of the tomb was closely related to the period's social and political transformation. During this period, the Zhou royal house further declined, so that society was no longer united in a hierarchical genealogical structure, even in theory. Political struggles were waged by families and individuals who gained power from the control of economic resources and military forces. The old religious institutions and symbols could no longer convey political messages and were consequently replaced or complemented by new ones. The lineage-temple system declined, and tombs belonging to families and individuals came to symbolize the strength and status of the new social elite.[1] Two important manifestations of this transformation in art and architecture were the increasing grandeur of funerary structures and the development of an art tradition called *mingqi* 明器 (spirit articles) made specifically for tomb furnishing. The earliest known architectural design was commissioned for a royal "funerary park." That part of a tomb that was above ground attracted considerable attention; a huge tumulus or a multileveled terrace pavilion standing above the grave pit enhanced its conspicuous position. The underground chamber was correspondingly enlarged and designed as a series of rooms with different functions. Numerous grave goods, sometimes registered on bamboo strips buried with them, included many imitations of real vessels and objects, as well as wood and clay figurines, and portraits of the deceased painted on silk banners.

This chapter synthesizes and analyzes these and other visual phenomena. In order to reconstruct a general visual context, I will depart from two familiar formats used to introduce Warring States art and architecture: the first inventories archaeological finds and extant objects according to the political divisions of the states, while the second organizes art objects into individual genres such as bronzes, jades, lacquerwares, and paintings.[2] The two sections of the chapter, "Art and Architecture of the Living" and "Art and Architecture for the Dead," correspond to the two main fields of artistic production during the Warring States period. Within this basic functional and contextual framework, visual materials will be discussed in interrelated categories such as architecture and portable objects, bronze and lacquer, sculpture and

---

[1] For the change in the center of ancestral worship from temple to tomb, see Wu Hung, *Monumentality in Early Chinese Art and Architecture* (Stanford, Calif.: Stanford University Press, 1995), pp. 110–17. For a discussion of the clan and lineage system of ancient China, see K. C. Chang, *Art, Myth, and Ritual: The Path to Political Authority in Ancient China* (Cambridge, Mass.: Harvard University Press, 1983), pp. 9–32.

[2] A representative of the first format is to be found in Li Xueqin's *Eastern Zhou and Qin Civilizations*, trans. K. C. Chang (New Haven, Conn.: Yale University Press, 1985), pp. 3–262. The second format is exemplified by Thomas Lawton's *Chinese Art of the Warring States Period: Change and Continuity, 480–222 B.C.* (Washington D.C.: Freer Gallery of Art, 1982).

painting, and others. It is hoped that this structure, as well as the selection of examples, will highlight the major tendencies and characteristics of Warring States art and will link the art of this period to its social, political, and religious environment. However, owing to its contextual nature, this discussion will focus on the general development, essential characteristics, and regional variations of a homogeneous artistic and architectural tradition in China proper and will not address art and architectural forms that are found in border areas and often indicate alien cultural identities.

ART AND ARCHITECTURE OF THE LIVING

Architecture: Cities and Palaces

Many of the cities and towns of the Warring States period had long functioned as political and economic centers, many of them having existed before the fifth century B.C. Even with those said to have been founded thereafter, archaeological excavations often uncover traces of earlier habitation. In either case, the physical forms of the city were subject to constant change. A rigid typology of ancient cities is therefore misleading because it classifies cities into standard and essentially static designs and because it often lends undue importance to a two-dimensional floor plan over any real visual appearance. Such a typology especially distorts the architectural history of the Warring States period, during which China experienced one of the most intensive stages of city construction in its history and during which many new architectural forms and concepts were invented. Several new types of palace structures, the *tai* 台 platform, the *ge* 閣 terrace pavilion, the *que* 闕 gate, and the *guan* 觀 tower came into prominence. With their shared emphasis on the third dimension and monumental images, these structures dramatically altered the appearance of a Warring States city.

THE CITY IN TRANSITION.   The rapid growth of cities, both in number and size, was intimately related to the political and economic conditions of the time. Textual and archaeological data suggest that starting from the middle Spring and Autumn period, rulers of various states engaged in feverish construction to enhance existing city walls, multiply enclosures and barricades, and establish satellite towns. The most frequent reason for such activities given in historical writings was military defense.[3] Indeed, in an age when a large number of small states were rapidly reduced to a handful of kingdoms, any ambition for political dominance had first to rely on the

---

[3] Gu Donggao (1679–1759) summarized records on the construction of cities during the Spring and Autumn period in "Chengzhu biao" (*Chunqiu dashi biao* 38).

ability to survive; it was only natural that great attention should be paid to consolidating one's home base. Consequently, the city gained a new definition as "[the means for] self-defense" (*zishou* 自守).[4] Writings of the strategists of the period often contain detailed instructions about how to strengthen a city that was open to invasion.[5]

The frequent relocation of state capitals contributed another reason for constant urban construction. Although this type of move had been a general feature throughout ancient Chinese history, this tradition was intensified during the fourth and third centuries B.C., when the struggle between the remaining kingdoms became severe. The move of the Qin 秦 capital to Xianyang 咸陽 in 350 B.C., for example, largely served Shang Yang's 商鞅 political reforms, which finally led to Qin's unification of China. Chu 楚, on the other hand, was forced to relocate its capital five times in some fifty years after Ying 郢, its traditional capital since the seventh century, was captured by a Qin army in 278 B.C. Among other states, Hann 韓 moved its capital from Yangdi 陽翟 to Zheng 鄭 in 375 B.C.; Wei 魏 relocated its royal house from Anyi 安邑 to Daliang 大梁 in 361 B.C.; and Zhao 趙, after moving from Jinyang 晉陽 to Zhongmou 中牟 in 425, founded its last capital in Handan 邯鄲 in 386 B.C. In most cases, the founding of a new capital was followed by the construction or reconstruction of city walls and palaces. The old capital was not abandoned, however. For example, after Yan 燕 moved the court to Wuyang 武陽 near Yixian 易縣, Hebei, its old capital of Jicheng 薊城 continued to provide a stage for important political events. The two cities were known as the state's Lower and Upper Capitals.[6]

The most important reason for the large-scale construction of Warring States cities, however, must perhaps be found in economic growth and technological innovations, which reached a new height during the fourth and third centuries B.C. The wide use of iron tools, the advanced irrigation operations, and the new techniques of husbandry may all have contributed to a rapid increase in population and to the accumulation of great wealth. Commercial and craft activities were in full swing, giving rise to a new class of merchants. Consequently, the capitals of the states no longer were just the seats of political power, but also integrated important economic functions to become commercial and manufacturing centers. As political reforms were carried out in various kingdoms, walls were built in an increasing number in

---

[4] *Mozi* 墨子, 5 ("Qihuan") (Sibu beiyao ed.), 1. 10a.

[5] See, e.g., *Mozi*, 52–71 (from "Bei chengmen" to "Jishou"); *Sun Bin bingfa* 孫臏兵法, 27 ("Xiong-pincheng"), Xu Peigen and Wei Rulin, *Sun Bin bingfa zhushi* (Taipei: Liming wenhua shiye, 1967), pp. 195–8; *Yu Liaozi* 尉繚子, 8 ("Wuyi") (Congshu jicheng ed.), pp. 19–24.

[6] It is also possible that Yan never moved its capital to Wuyang, but only established Wuyang as its second capital; see Ou Yan, "Shilun Yan Xiadu de niandai," *Kaogu* 1988.7: 648–9.

the new administrative units of *jun* 郡 and *xian* 縣; some of these also developed into famous commercial cities.

To writers of the Warring States period, who often contrasted cities of antiquity with those of their own times, the latter were much more impressive in physical scale, as well as in their concentration of people and wealth. In one instance, a minister of Zhao stated that ancient cities were never larger than 300 *zhang* 丈 (approx. 690 m) in circumference and never housed a population greater than 300 households, but, he continued, it was not rare for his contemporaries to find "cities of a thousand *zhang* and towns of ten thousand households within sight of one another."[7] Although such statements should not be taken literally, they do reflect the general phenomenon that a Warring States city was no longer restricted by traditional building codes that had regulated the size according to rank in the Zhou social and political system.[8] We know perhaps of a trace of one such code from a statement made by Ji Zhong 祭仲, an official of Zheng, in 722 B.C.:

According to the rule of the former [Zhou] kings, the larger capital [of a lord?] does not exceed one-third the size of the national capital; the middle capital [of a minister?] does not exceed one-fifth the size of the national capital; and the smaller capital [of an officer?] does not exceed one-ninth the size of the national capital.[9]

In the fourth and third century B.C., however, such a rigid hierarchy in city planning had become a matter of remote memory. The most active and glamorous city at the time was not to be seen in the Royal City (Wangcheng 王城) of Zhou, but in prosperous regional urban centers such as Linzi 臨淄 of Qi 齊 or Ying of Chu. In a somewhat rhetorical statement it was said that Linzi had 70,000 households and at least 210,000 adult males. It was said that the roads

are so crowded that "cart hubs bang each other and people rub shoulders; their garments form an [endless] curtain. When people raise their sleeves, it looks as if there is a tent; when they shake off sweat, it feels like rain. Families are rich, individuals are well off. Aspirations are high and spirits soar.[10]

Archaeological discoveries of more than fifty Warring States cities, ranging from a major metropolis to a small county town, have proven that such records are not just some ancient authors' fantasy.[11] Most significantly, none

---

[7] *Zhanguo ce* 戰國策, 20 ("Zhao ce," 3) (Congshu jicheng ed.), p. 68.
[8] For Western Zhou regulations of city planning, see He Yeju, "Shilun Zhoudai liangci chengshi jianshe gaochao," in *Zhongguo jianzhushi lunwen xuanji*, ed. Li Runhai (Taipei: Mingwen, 1983), pp. 200–201.
[9] *Zuo zhuan* 2 (Yin 1), 16b–17a, (James Legge, *The Chinese Classics. Vol. 5: The Ch'un Ts'ew with the Tso Chuen* (London: Trübner, 1872; rpt. Hong Kong: Hong Kong University Press, 1960), pp. 4–5).
[10] *Shi ji*, 69, p. 2257 (William H. Nienhauser, Jr., *The Grand Scribe's Records. Vol. 7: "The Memoirs of Pre-Han China"* [Bloomington: Indiana University Press, 1994], p. 106).
[11] For a summary of these excavations, see Nancy S. Steinhardt, *Chinese Imperial City Planning* (Honolulu: University of Hawaii Press, 1990), pp. 46–53.

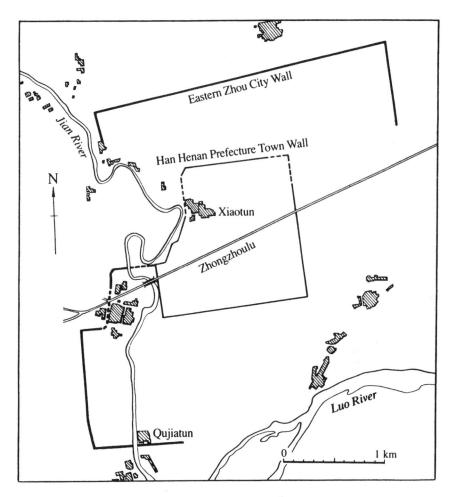

Figure 10.1. Plan of the royal city of the Eastern Zhou at Luoyang. From Li Xueqin, *Eastern Zhou and Qin Civilizations*, trans. by K. C. Chang (New Haven, Conn.: Yale University Press, 1985), fig. 3.

of these cities and towns followed the Zhou regulations cited by Ji Zhong; some of them even surpassed the Eastern Zhou capital in both size and grandeur. According to archaeological surveys, the Zhou Royal City at Luoyang 洛陽 was roughly square in shape with a north wall 2,890 m long; the length of the entire city wall, running round all sides, was thus about 12,500 m (Fig. 10.1). By contrast the walls of Linzi stretched over 15,000 m (Fig. 10.2), the outer city walls of Xinzheng 新鄭 were about 16,000 m in circumference (Fig. 10.3), and the walls of Wuyang were over 27,000 m (Fig.

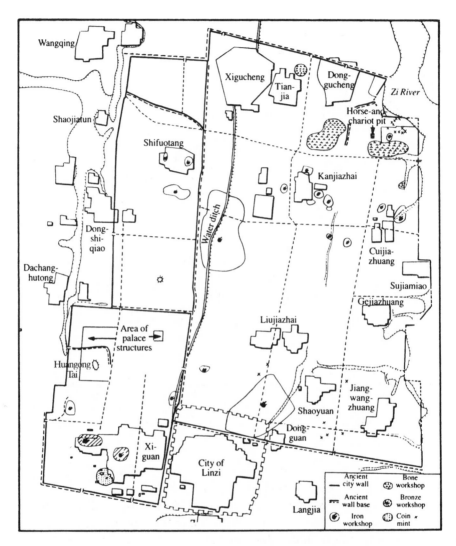

Figure 10.2. Plan of Linzi of Qi. From Li Xueqin, *Eastern Zhou and Qin Civilizations*, trans. by K. C. Chang (New Haven, Conn.: Yale University Press, 1985), fig. 55.

10.4).[12] However, it was only after long periods of expansion that these and other Warring States cities attained such a size; to reconstruct their history we need to explore the cumulative process of their construction.

Xue 薛, the capital of the state of Xue at present-day Tengzhou 滕州 in Shandong, provides perhaps the most illuminating example for the contin-

---

[12] See Ye Xiaojun, *Zhongguo ducheng fazhan shi* (Xi'an: Shaanxi Renmin, 1988), pp. 61–76.

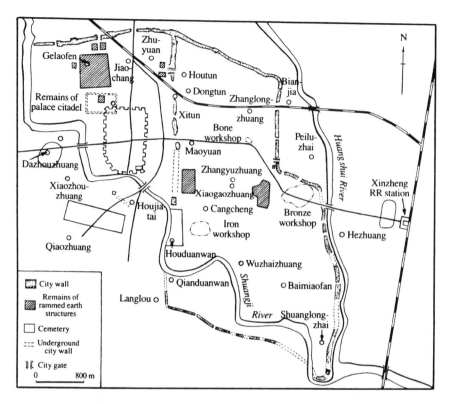

Figure 10.3. Plan of Xinzheng of Zheng and Hann. From Li Xueqin, *Eastern Zhou and Qin Civilizations*, trans. by K. C. Chang (New Haven, Conn.: Yale University Press, 1985), fig. 22.

uous construction and transformation of an ancient Chinese city. Archaeological surveys and excavations were conducted here from 1964 to 1993; they unearthed four towns, built over a period of close to two millennia, being superimposed on to one another.[13] The oldest of the four was a Longshan 龍山 town with walls built of solid rammed earth 170 m east to west and 150 m north to south. At the same time that this ancient town was rebuilt toward the end of the Shang dynasty, another town of similar size and shape was constructed to the east. The result was a dualistic complex similar to the paired structures found at the Shang capital at Anyang 安陽.[14] During the Western Zhou, a larger wall enclosure, about 900 m east to west and 700 m north to south, was constructed to encircle both of these towns, with the

[13] For reports on this site, see *Kaogu* 1965.12: 622–35; *Kaogu xuebao* 1991.4: 449–96; *Zhongguo wenwu bao* 389 (June 26, 1994), front page.

[14] For palace structures at Anyang, see K. C. Chang, *Shang Civilization* (New Haven, Conn.: Yale University Press, 1980), pp. 90–5.

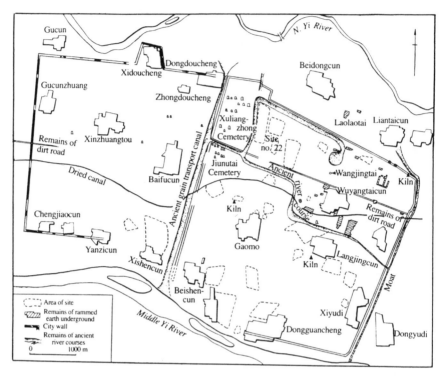

Figure 10.4. Plan of Wuyang of Yan. From Li Xueqin, *Eastern Zhou and Qin Civilizations*, trans. by K. C. Chang (New Haven, Conn.: Yale University Press, 1985), fig. 31.

first town being placed at its exact center. It is thus possible, as the excavators have suggested, that this old town, inherited from pre-Shang and Shang times, now functioned as a "palace-town" inside the Zhou city. Tombs and inscribed bronzes found outside the city help to identify it as the capital of Xue during the Western Zhou and the Spring and Autumn period. Finally, a much larger city was built during the Warring States period. Extending about 5,000 m from east to west and 3,500 m from north to south, it integrated the earlier city into a walled space twenty-eight times larger. This Warring States city continued to exist into the Han.

Early texts add more information to the archaeological evidence. The *Zuo zhuan* 左傳 (Zuo's tradition) records that an official of the Xia dynasty named Xizhong 奚仲 first had a town built in Xue. After the Shang conquered the Xia, Zhonghui 仲虺, King Tang's 湯 Minister of the Left, took it over as his home.[15] Xue subsequently became one of the many states of the Zhou, its

---

[15] *Zuo zhuan*, 54 (Ding 1), 3b (Legge, *The Ch'un Ts'ew with the Tso Chuen*, pp. 744–5).

lords paying regular audience to the Zhou kings.[16] After Xue was finally swallowed up by its powerful neighbor Qi during the Warring States period, one of its new masters, none other than the illustrious Lord Mengchang 孟嘗, "rebuilt the city, the strength of its walls being unsurpassable."[17] Supported by this textual evidence, the excavation of Xue highlights two important aspects of an ancient Chinese city. First, it demonstrates that a city constantly altered its shape and function in the course of its expansion. Therefore, a single Longshan town (built by Xizhong?) was absorbed into the Shang "twin cities" (built by Zhonghui?) and was then turned into the palace-town of Xue of Western Zhou. Likewise, Xue's outer walls (*guo* 郭) of the Western Zhou and Spring and Autumn periods became its inner walls (*cheng* 城) during the Warring States period. Second, the excavation of Xue suggests that the "concentric city" and the "double city," previously thought to be two distinctive types of Warring States cities, were invented in different periods.[18] The concentric city with an integral enclosure and an internal palace district was the main form of Western Zhou and early Eastern Zhou cities, while the double city consisting of two separate or attached enclosures resulted from Warring States modifications of earlier cities.

Not all concentric cities grew into double cities. Several major Warring States cities, such as Qufu 曲阜 in Lu 魯, Ji'nan cheng 紀南城 in Chu, and probably also Yong 雍 in Qin,[19] were old cities that survived without alteration of their overall shape. They were all defined by a continuous wall. Although the locations of the palace and ceremonial buildings may have varied, they were mainly located inside the city, sometimes surrounded by an inner wall and therefore forming a nested "palace city" (*gongcheng* 宮城). Of greatest importance, these cities were constructed during the Spring and Autumn period or even earlier, and the basic principles of their design had been established by Shang precedents.[20]

Among these cities, Qufu, the capital of Lu founded by the Zhou Gong 周公 at the beginning of the Western Zhou, has been most thoroughly investigated. Excavations at Qufu have continued since the early 1940s; archaeol-

---

[16] *Zuo zhuan 4* (Yin 11), 19a (Legge, *The Chinese Classics*, vol. 5, *The Ch'un Ts'ew with the Tso Chuen*, p. 32).

[17] *Kuadi zhi* 括地志, cited in Gu Zuyu (1631–92), *Dushi fangyu jiyao*, 6 vols. (Shanghai: Shangwu, 1936), vol. 2, p. 1418. For a different record, see Sima Zhen 司馬貞 (early eighth century), *Shi ji suoyin* 史記索引, in *Shi ji*, 75, p. 2352.

[18] Steinhardt classifies Eastern Zhou cities into three types, but her third type, that of a city with an internal palace town attached to the north wall, is only represented by a Spring and Autumn town found in Xiangfen 襄汾 in Shanxi, probably Ju or Jiang of the state of Jin. *Chinese Imperial City Planning*, p. 47.

[19] For reports on Jinancheng and Yong, see *Kaogu xuebao* 1982.3–4: 325–50, 477–508; 1982.4: 477–508; *Kaogu yu wenwu* 1985.2: 7–20.

[20] For the plans of three excavated Shang towns at Erlitou 二里頭, Zhengzhou 鄭州, and Panlongcheng 盤龍城, see Wu Hung, *Monumentality in Early Chinese Art and Architecture*, pp. 83–4.

ogists have concluded that although the city was built and rebuilt many times from the Zhou to the Han, its layout remained basically unaltered.[21] Very few remains of early Zhou date have been found; the wall, defining a roughly rectangular city of about 14 km in circumference, was probably built in the late Western Zhou and continuously strengthened throughout the Eastern Zhou. Eleven city gates have been located, two on the southern wall and three on each of the three other sides. These gates led to broad avenues that ran across the city. A coherent city plan is also indicated by the location of temples and palaces. The center of the city was marked by the expanse of a rammed-earth platform about 1,000 m east to west, probably the base of a large palace district. The northeast portion of this area was occupied by a well-defined compound, the foundation of which still rises 10 m above the ground. At the site, archaeologists have discovered Eastern Zhou foundations, on top of which were Han buildings including the famous Hall of Spiritual Light (Lingguang dian 靈光殿). The palace district at the center of Qufu was surrounded by residential areas, as well as workshops manufacturing bronze, iron, pottery, and bone artifacts. The location of these workshops next to the palaces suggests that they were probably under direct government control. Eastern Zhou tombs, including some very large Warring States burials, have been found in the western and northwestern parts of the city.

The second group of Warring States cities, the "double cities," includes Linzi in Qi, Wuyang in Yan, Xinzheng in Zheng (and later Hann), Handan in Zhao, and Anyi in Wei.[22] Most of these consisted of two walled enclosures, either divided by a shared wall or completely detached from each other. In most cases (e.g., Linzi, Handan, Anyi, and Xinzheng), the smaller enclosure containing the palace district was located to the west or southwest of the larger enclosure. Although some scholars believe that this type of city represented an orthodox Western Zhou urban form,[23] new archaeological information shows that the bipartite structure resulted from gradual expansion. In other words, before the Warring States period, most of these double cities had only a single enclosure and therefore resembled a concentric city like Qufu; they became double cities only later, when a new walled section was added to the existing city.

[21] For reports on Qufu, see Komai Kazuchika, *Kyokufu Rojô no iseki* (Tokyo: Tôkyô daigaku Bungakubu Kôkogaku kenkyûshitsu, 1950); *Kaogu* 1965.12: 599–613; D. Buck, ed. and trans. "Archaeological Explorations at the Ancient Capital of Lu at Qufu in Shandong Province," *Chinese Sociology and Anthropology* 19, 1 (1986): 1–76.

[22] For reports on Handan, see Komai Kazuchika and Sekino Takeshi, *Han-tan, Archaeologia Orientalis*, series B, 7 (1954); *Kaogu* 1959.10: 531–6; 1980.2: 142–6. For reports on Anyi, see *Wenwu* 1962.4–5: 59–64; *Kaogu* 1963.9: 474–9.

[23] See Yang Kuan, *Zhongguo gudai ducheng zhidu shi yanjiu* (Shanghai: Guji, 1993), pp. 66–7, 88–91.

Sometimes, the old town in a double city retained its role as an administrative center; the new town was built next to it to serve certain economic
or military functions. At other times, the new addition was the palace-city
and its construction reflected a major change in power structure. Xinzheng,
the capital of Zheng prior to 375 B.C. and the capital of Hann thereafter, is
an example of the first case (Fig. 10.3).[24] As in the case of Xue, this city had
come into existence long before the Warring States period. When the rulers
of Zheng moved there from Shaanxi in the eighth century B.C., they built
Xinzheng as a city with a single enclosure. Roughly rectangular and rather
large, the northern side measured about 2,400 m long and the eastern side
about 4,300 m. More than a thousand rammed-earth foundations, some as
large as 6,000 sq. m, covered the northern and middle sections. An underground structure found in this area yielded pottery vessels that belonged to
a palace kitchen. This rammed-earth area, therefore, must have been part of
the palace district, even though it was outside the walled compound in the
center of the city. It is possible that this walled compound, about 500 m long
east to west and 320 m north to south, housed the most important structures
and/or the ruler's residence.

Xinzheng was expanded into a double city during the Eastern Zhou, when
walls were added to the east to enclose an area even larger than the original
city. The relatively later date of this eastern section is indicated by the lack
of palace, residential, and burial sites. In their place, archaeologists
have found remains of many Eastern Zhou workshops, including an enormous bronze foundry, as well as a site of an ironworks. It is possible that
Xinzheng's eastern city was constructed to protect these workshops, which
not only supplied luxury goods, but, of greater importance, produced
weapons and agricultural tools. As evidence of its role, the irregular shape of
the eastern wall seems to have been intended to accommodate the existing
bronze foundry.

Linzi in Qi exemplified the second sort of double city, in which a palace-
city was built and later became the locus of political power (Fig. 10.2). One
of the most famous cities in Chinese history, Linzi has been under archaeological investigation since the 1930s. Sekino Takeshi identified its basic layout
in 1940 and 1941; subsequent excavations by Chinese scholars have yielded
considerable information about both its various components and the process
whereby the city was constructed.[25] The larger enclosure of this double city,
about 3,300 m from east to west and 5,200 m from north to south, was built
much earlier than the smaller enclosure attached to its southwest corner.

---

[24] *Wenwu ziliao congkan* 3 (1980): 56–66.
[25] Wang Xiantang, *Linzi fengni wenzi xumu* (Jinan: Shandong shengli tushuguan, 1936); Sekino Takeshi,
   Chûgoku kôkogaku kenkyû (Tokyo: Tokyo University Press, 1963), pp. 241–94; *Kaogu* 1961.6: 289–97.

Although archaeologists have not located a palace district within the larger enclosure, sufficient finds indicate its grandeur during the Western Zhou and the Spring and Autumn periods. Seven broad avenues, some 20 m wide and over 4,000 m long, ran north–south and east–west, roughly forming a grid pattern. Four major avenues met in the northeast section of the city. It is no coincidence that this area yielded the richest cultural remains from the Western Zhou to the Han.[26] In 1965, a horde of bronze artifacts, including some ritual vessels, was discovered there, suggesting nearby residences or temples of noble families.[27] It is also in this area that some thirty large Western Zhou and early Eastern Zhou burials are located. Among them, an enormous tomb excavated in 1972 and 1973 had unfortunately been previously looted; but the unusual status of the deceased is revealed by his stone burial chamber and the sacrificial pits surrounding the tomb, which contained the astonishing number of 600 horses. These and other factors have led the excavators to attribute this tomb to Qi Jing Gong 齊景公 (r. 547–490 B.C.).[28]

Archaeological evidence indicates that the smaller enclosure at the southwestern corner was not constructed until the Warring States period. Similarly, the Huan Gong Tai 桓公台 (Platform of Duke Huan), the most important palace building that was within, was also built no earlier than the middle Warring States period. This evidence suggests a possible relationship between the construction of this small city and an important political event: in 386 B.C., the Tian 田 family, the most powerful ministerial family in the state, took over power from the Jiang 姜 family, which had ruled Qi since the beginning of the Western Zhou, an event that divided the history of Qi into two phases, known as Jiang Qi and Tian Qi. It is possible that when the reign of Tian Qi began, the family's old quarter was enlarged into a palace-city, with commanding platforms and elaborate halls designed to demonstrate their rulership.[29] But the significance of this new town was not purely symbolic. Its thick walls (28–38 m across at the base) and the surrounding ditches reveal an intense concern with security. It is of interest that the ditches outside the north and east walls, where it joined with the old town, were much wider than those outside the south and west sides, being 25 m instead of 13 m in width. It seems that to the master of this new city, the main threat came not from outside but from Linzi's old quarter. The new city was also strengthened by the facilities that it possessed for the production of goods and by the presence of an intellectual community. Among other items, the workshops produced iron implements and bronze coins, and the city housed the famous Jixia 稷下 Academy. Sponsored by various Tian Qi

[26] *Wenwu* 1972.5: 50.   [27] *Wenwu* 1972.5: 8.   [28] *Wenwu* 1984.9: 14–19.
[29] See Qu Yingjie, *Xian Qin ducheng fuyuan yanjiu* (Ha'erbin: Heilongjiang Renmin, 1991), p. 236.

rulers from Huan Gong 桓公 (r. 374–355) to Kings Wei 威 (r. 356–317 B.C.) and Xuan 宣 (r. 319–301 B.C.), this academy attracted influential thinkers such as Zou Yan 騶衍, Chunyu Kun 淳于髡, and Shen Dao 慎到.[30]

The construction of the Yan capital of Wuyang presents a more complex case. Although it was traditionally believed that this city was walled by King Zhao 昭 in the late fourth century B.C.,[31] archaeological excavations have proven that at least part of the city had existed long before this date: bronze weapons from earlier reigns, residential and burial sites of the Spring and Autumn period, and even a thick layer of Western Zhou cultural deposit have all been found here.[32] The view that the city consisted of an eastern town and a western town is also erroneous. It actually had three walled sections, a partition wall dividing the so-called eastern town into two sections north and south. These two revisions provide a new basis for reconstructing the city's history. All of the archaeological evidence suggests that Wuyang's lower eastern section had existed long before King Zhao's time. In addition to the Spring and Autumn and early Warring States sites found there, the most convincing evidence is a group of ten large tombs located in the northwest corner.[33] The extraordinary size and unusual construction technique of tomb 16, which has been excavated, proves that it belonged to a person of high social status. A set of 135 *mingqi* ritual vessels found in this tomb date to the early Warring States period.[34]

The graveyard in the southern section of the eastern town was separated from another cemetery in the northern section by the partition wall. The thirteen tombs in this second cemetery, which are also enormous mausoleums with huge tumuli, date to the middle to late Warring States period.[35] Other sites in this section, including palace structures and weaponry workshops, have also been dated to this period.[36] These excavations suggest that what King Zhao walled was this single section, which was to serve as his new palace town. This is perhaps why Wuyang Tai, the most important structure in the city, stood next to the partition wall linking the two sections of the city. But this was not the end of the city's expansion, since toward the end of the Warring States period an enormous western section was added onto the eastern section. In sharp contrast to the old town, which was filled with palace foundations, tombs, workshops, and residential sites, very few remains

[30] *Shi ji*, 46, p. 1895. For the location of the Jixia school, see Qu Yingjie, *Xian Qin ducheng fuyuan yanjiu*, p. 250.
[31] Li Daoyuan (d. 527), *Shuijing zhu* 11 ("Yi shui") (Shanghai: Shangwu, 1936), vol. 2, p. 104.
[32] *Kaogu* 1987.5: 414–28.
[33] *Kaogu xuebao* 1965.1: 79–102.
[34] *Kaogu xuebao* 1965.2: 79–102.
[35] Qu Yingjie, *Xian Qin ducheng fuyuan yanjiu*, p. 310.
[36] *Kaoguxue jikan* 2 (1982): 69–82; *Kaogu* 1965.11: 562–70; *Wenwu* 1982.8: 42–50.

have been found inside this enclosure. It is possible that it was not long after its construction that Yan perished.

The double cities of the Warring States, therefore, clearly reflected the tendency toward fortification: what we find in Linzi, Handan, and Wuyang is the increasing independence and detachment of the administrative center from the rest of the city. It is questionable whether the Royal City at Luoyang could have escaped this trend. As shown in Fig. 10.1, its remaining walls seem to have belonged to two interconnected rectangles: a small enclosure with relatively precise cardinal orientations was constructed over the top of the southwest corner of the main enclosure. The similarity between this plan and other double cities such as Linzi may not be without significance: according to the excavation report, the southwestern walls were built during the Warring States period, later than other walls.[37]

MONUMENTAL PALACE STRUCTURES. The increasing independence of the palace provided the historic basis for an idealized city plan, which emerged during the Warring States period (Fig. 10.5). Recorded in the *Kaogong ji* 考工記, this plan placed the palace in the center of the state capital (*guo* 國), flanked by the ancestral temple and the Altar to the Soil, two prominent components of a traditional capital that became secondary elements of the new city.[38] This plan, however, can do no more than illustrate the ideal capital in two dimensions and does not show an extremely important development of Warring States cities, which is seen in their rapid growth toward the third dimension. At Linzi for example, the Huan Gong Tai, a large mound approached by flights of stairs, was constructed near the center of its palace town. Even after more than 2,000 years, its oval-shaped foundation is still 86 m long and 14 m high. Numerous architectural remains surround this platform, suggesting that it was not an isolated tower, but the commanding focus of the palace complex. In Wuyang, many large earthen foundations, some still rising 20 m above ground, were located both inside and outside the city's eastern section (Fig. 10.6). Exquisite bronze accessories and ornate roof tiles found near Laomu Tai 姥姆台 suggest the splendor of vanished palace halls and pavilions built on the building's tall foundation (Fig. 10.7).[39] Significantly, the *tai* platforms in Wuyang formed a straight line as the city's

---

[37] *Kaogu xuebao* 1959.2: 29, 34.

[38] *Zhou li* 周禮, 41 ("Jiang ren"), 24b–25a. For an illustration, see Dai Zhen, *Kaogongji tu* (Shanghai: Shangwu, 1955), p. 102; Steinhardt, *Chinese Imperial City Planning*, p. 33.

[39] For the remains of the *tai* platforms in Wuyang, see *Kaogu xuebao* 1965.1: 88–95. For bronze door rings and other architectural remains from Laomu Tai, see *Hebei sheng chutu wenwu xuanji* (Beijing: Wenwu, 1980), no. 115; Umehara Sueji, *Sengokushiki dôki no kenkyû* (Kyoto: Tôhô bunka gakuin Kyoto kenkyûjo, 1936), pl. 7a; Komai Kazuchika, "En koku no sôryûmon gatô," in *Chûgoku kôkogaku ronsô* (Tokyo: Keiyûsha, 1974), pp. 323–7.

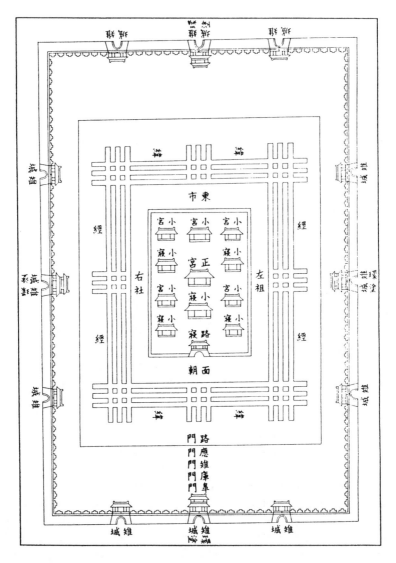

Figure 10.5. Idealized plan of the "state capital" as described in the *Kaogong ji*. From *Yongle dadian*, by Xie Jin et al. (Rpt. Shanghai: Zhonghua, 1960), p. 9591.

north–south axis: Wuyang Tai 武陽台, the city's symbolic center, was in the middle; to its north were Wangjing Tai 望景台 (Platform for Enjoying the Scenery), Zhang Gong Tai 張公台, and Laomu Tai, while to its south stood Laoyemiao Tai 老爺廟台 and Yangjia Tai 楊家台. Other rammed-earth foundations have been found in this area, sometimes flanking a tall platform.

Figure 10.6. The remaining foundation of Laomu Tai in Wuyang. After Chinese Academy of Architecture, *Ancient Chinese Architecture* (Beijing: China Building Industry Press, 1982), fig. 31. Drawing by Li Xiating.

Figure 10.7. Bronze door ring, from Laomu Tai in Wuyang. From Li Xueqin, *Zhongguo meishu quanji: Gongyi meishu bian 4, Qingtongqi* (Beijing: Wenwu, 1985), fig. 112.

Taken together, these remains indicate a systematically designed architectural complex centered on a series of *tai* buildings.

Handan provides another illuminating example for understanding this architectural system. The southwestern town in this double city consisted of three walled enclosures, often known collectively as the palace district of Zhao. The center of the palace is indicated by the ruins of Long Tai 龍台 (Dragon Platform) in the southern part of the western enclosure. Once occupying an area of about 80,000 sq. m, this earthen platform is still 16.3 m tall, formed by at least eight layers of rammed earth. Starting from this structure, a series of platforms, built some 200 m apart from one another, extended the town's axis northward. Large groups of palace buildings also existed in the adjacent eastern enclosure, where two principal architectural complexes, each centered on an enormous *tai*, constituted a north–south axis, parallel to the axis of the western enclosure.

Although our received texts mention some *tai* in the Shang and Western Zhou periods,[40] this architectural type began to be fashionable only in the sixth century B.C. and was adopted thereafter by rulers of almost every major state. The construction of *tai* platforms was frequently mentioned in historical texts, not for their architectural merit but for their waste of economic resources and manpower. The *Zuo zhuan* records, for example, that in 556 B.C., Song Ping Gong 宋平公 insisted on building a tall platform, regardless of the project's interference with the work of the agricultural season.[41] Another instance took place in the state of Jin: it took six years to build Chiqi Tai 虒祁台, a project initiated by Ping Gong 平公 in 534 B.C. Both projects provoked strong opposition from workers as well as from ministers, who wished to promote the practice of thrift. It is said that Chiqi Tai, an extremely "lofty and extravagant palace," "took the strength of the people to an exhausting degree." As a result, its construction stirred "discontent and complaints everywhere."[42] Such criticism, however, had little effect either on the feverish construction of *tai* platforms or on the increasing height and elaboration of these structures.

Imposing in appearance, a *tai* best represents the architectural difference between an Eastern Zhou and a Western Zhou palace. A Western Zhou royal compound, as demonstrated by a well-known example excavated at Fengchu 鳳雛 in Shaanxi, consisted of alternating halls and courtyards within a walled enclosure. This compound concealed its architectural components, as well as the ritual activities taking place inside it. Its design emphasized symmetry, depth, and movement in terms of time, but it did not constitute an abrupt monumental image.[43] A later site, probably a Qin palace complex of the Spring and Autumn period, signifies the further development of this traditional architectural form toward horizontal expansion. Found in the Qin capital of Yong, it had a chain of five courtyards built along the central axis, with a total length of 326.5 m.[44] This much enlarged palace complex, however, remained two-dimensional and self-contained; even the front gate was

---

[40] These include, for example, Lu Tai (Deer Platform) of King Zhou of Shang and Ling Tai (Spirit Terrace) of King Wen of Zhou. The former is mentioned in Han texts, while the latter is said to have been completed in a few days. See *Shi ji*, 3, p. 105; *Shi jing* ("Ling Tai"), 1a–7b (Arthur Waley, *The Book of Songs: The Ancient Chinese Classic of Poetry* [1936; rpt. New York: Grove, 1960], p. 259).

[41] *Zuo zhuan* 33 (Xiang 17), 7b–8a (Legge, *The Ch'un Ts'ew with the Tso Chuen*, pp. 474–5).

[42] *Zuo zhuan* 44 (Zhao 8), 23b (Legge, *The Ch'un Ts'ew with the Tso Chuen*, p. 622).

[43] For the social and ritual symbolism of this design, see Wu Hung, *Monumentality in Early Chinese Art and Architecture*, pp. 85–92.

[44] *Kaogu yu wenwu* 1985.2: 14–17.

blocked by an earthen screen to make the enclosure complete. Such an architectural structure was conceived as "closed," "vast," "hallowed," "solemn," and "mysterious," as we read in Zhou temple hymns.[45] A Warring States palace, on the other hand, was centered on tall platforms that stressed a powerful three-dimensional image and an immediate visual effect. Among excavated platforms, the one in Houma 侯馬, the Jin capital, preserves a standard design of this type of structure.[46] A road, 6 m wide, let to a rectangular ground in front of a series of ascending terraces. The top level of these terraces, 35 m north to south and 45 m east to west, originally served as the foundation for a wood-framed pavilion. Images of such structures decorate Eastern Zhou "pictorial bronzes." Often, the artist depicts activities inside buildings on top of a raised platform, with steps leading to the top (Fig. 10.8). Instead of stressing the depth of a palace hall, the emphasis lies here in its vertical elevation.

We find the same emphasis in literary references to *tai*, whose height both fascinated a writer and tempted him to exaggerate. In one instance, a platform in Chu is said to have measured a hundred *ren* 仞 (approx. 160 m) high and reached the floating clouds.[47] Although unrealistic, such descriptions clearly reveal the symbolism of a Warring States platform: the higher a *tai* would be, the stronger would its patron feel in the contemporary political arena. In the eastern state of Qi, when Jing Gong 景公 climbed onto Boqin Tai 柏寢台 and surveyed his capital, he sighed with satisfaction: "Wonderful! Who in the future will be able to possess a platform like this!"[48] In the north, King Wuling of Zhao 趙武靈 built an extremely tall *tai* that allowed him to overlook the neighboring states of Qi and Zhongshan; this structure thus demonstrated his strength and intimidated his enemy.[49] In the south, a Chu king constructed an imposing platform as the site of his meeting with other lords. Struck with awe, his guests agreed to join the Chu alliance and made a vow: "How tall is this platform! How deep the mind it shows! If I betray my words, let me be punished by other states in this alliance."[50] In the west, Qin Mu Gong 秦繆公 tried to intimidate foreign envoys by showing them his palaces, which "even spirits could not build without exhausting their strength."[51] In the state of Wei in central China, a terrace was so tall that it was named Platform Reaching Midway to Heaven (Zhongtian Tai 中天台).[52] The same political symbolism also underlay the popularity of other types

---

[45] *Shi jing*, 20.2 ("Bi gong"), 1a; 19.1 ("Qingmiao"), 9b, (Waley, *The Book of Songs*, pp. 269, 226).

[46] *Wenwu* 1958.12: 32–3.

[47] Lu Jia 陸賈, *Xin yu* 新語 (Wang Liqi, *Xin yu jiaozhu* [Beijing: Zhonghua, 1986]), p. 134.

[48] Hanzi (untraced), as cited in *Taiping yulan*, 177, 4a.

[49] *Shi ji*, 43, p. 1805.

[50] Liu Xiang 劉向 (79–8 B.C.), *Shuo yuan* 說苑 13 ("Quanmou"), 15a (Sibu congkan ed.).

[51] *Shi ji*, 5, p. 192.   [52] Liu Xiang 劉向, *Xin xu* 新序, 6 ("Cishe"), 1b (Sibu congkan ed.).

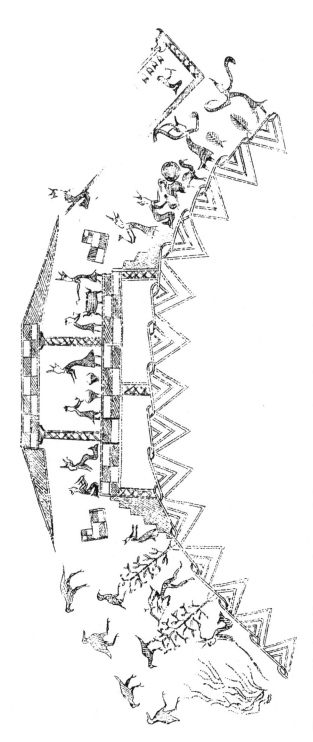

Figure 10.8. Ritual activities centered on a *tai* platform, a scene on a bronze bowl in Shanghai Museum. Ca. fifth century B.C. After Charles D. Weber, *Chinese Pictorial Bronze Vessels of the Late Chou Period* (Ascona: Artibus Asiae, 1968), fig. 25. Drawing by Li Xiating.

of tall buildings. One such type was the pillar gate called *que* 闕, which by the Warring States period had become detached from its architectural context to become a self-contained status symbol.[53] Some writers claimed that only the Son of Heaven could enjoy a *que* gate with a pair of flanking *guan* 觀 towers.[54] Others considered the height of the *guan* towers as well as the number of their "wings" (*yi* 翼) to be measures of social privilege.[55] Situated in front of a palace, a multistoried *guan* invited its owner to climb thereon and look out; it thus raised the viewing point, empowering a lord to over-look his kingdom and subjects.[56] But as a concrete symbol of authority, a *guan* was also an object to be looked at, its imposing appearance and intri-cate design inspiring public awe.[57] Following the lead of palace architecture, gates also appeared in a mausoleum to mark the entrance.[58]

Another type of tall building, which developed rapidly during the Warring States period, is the terrace pavilion: a series of rooms and corridors were built on top of one another around an earthen core, giving the impression of a multi-leveled structure of amazing volume and height. Compared with the low foundations of Shang and Western Zhou palace compounds (which rarely exceeded 1 m in height),[59] the earthen core employed by Warring States architects no longer functioned as the flat base of an entire courtyard struc-ture, but only served to raise a palace hall. Its role was mainly visual and sym-bolic: in an age when techniques for true multilayered structures had not yet been fully developed, this device made it possible to make a building more easily visible and to enhance its value as a monument, although the actual living area remained the same as or even smaller than that of a single-level structure. Although in technical terms the rammed-earth foundation of a Shang and Western Zhou building anticipated the later earthen core, this

---

[53] For differences between a Western Zhou gate and an Eastern Zhou gate, see Wu Hung, *Monumental-ity in Early Chinese Art and Architecture*, p. 277.

[54] *Chunqiu Gongyang zhuan* 春秋公羊傳, 24 (Zhao 25), 7a.

[55] *Li ji* 禮記, 23 ("Liqi"), 13b; 25 ("Jiaotesheng"), 15a (James Legge, trans., *Li Chi, Book of Rites*, 2 vols. [New York: University Books, 1967], vol. 1, pp. 399, 422).

[56] Liu Xi 劉熙 (second to third century A.D.), *Shi ming* 釋名, 5 ("Shi qiu"). Wang Xianqian, *Shi ming shuzheng bu* (1896; rpt. Shanghai: Shanghai guji, 1984), 5.18: "Guan means 'to see.' On top of it one observes." For the date and authorship of the *Shi ming*, see Michael Loewe, ed., *Early Chinese Texts: A Bibliographical Guide* (Berkeley: Society for the Study of Early China and the Institute of East Asian Studies, University of California, 1993), pp. 424–8. See also *Li ji*, 21 ("Li yun"), 1a (Legge, trans., *Li Chi*, vol. 1, p. 364): "In the past, Confucius attended a *la*-ritual. Upon the completion of the ceremony he came out, strolled on top of a *guan* terrace, and sighed. What he sighed for was the state of Lu." Zheng Xuan 鄭玄 explained that "*guan* means *que*."

[57] See the commentary of Kong Yingda 孔穎達 (574–648) to *Li ji*, 21 ("Li yun"), 2a–b.

[58] *Zuo zhuan* (Zhuang (Zhuang 19)), p. 1773; (Xuan 14), p. 1886 (Legge, *The Ch'un Ts'ew with the Tso Chuen*, pp. 98–9, 324).

[59] According to Yang Hongxun's reconstruction, both the Shang temple at Erlitou and the Western Zhou temple at Fengchu had a foundation about 1 m high. Yang Hongxun, *Jianzhu kaoguxue lunwen ji* (Beijing: Wenwu, 1987), pp. 72, 100.

new architectural device was used for entirely different purposes and made it possible to break away from the norms of the ritual architecture of those times. Like a *tai* platform, a terrace pavilion conveyed the double significance of a Warring States monument: it stood as a protest against tradition and symbolized political domination. Such symbolism was manifested most clearly in the Jique 冀闕 palace in Xianyang 咸陽.

From the middle Warring States period, Qin was becoming the most aggressive of all the contending kingdoms. Chief credit for its rapid rise to power belongs to Shang Yang, who instituted a series of political reforms from 356 to 338 B.C. As discussed in Chapter 9, Shang Yang dedicated his life to transforming an old feudal principality into a "modern" political state. One of his crucial decisions, which also provided an institutional framework for his other new policies, was to move Qin's capital to Xianyang. The strategic position of the city, placed as it was at the intersection of major rivers and traffic roads, allowed Qin to exercise a strong influence on the political moves of the kingdoms.[60] It was no mere coincidence that when Shang Yang began to construct the new capital, he completely ignored the fundamental precept in traditional architecture, that a noble man had first to build an ancestral temple in his city.[61] His first buildings were a pair of palace halls, which Sima Qian 司馬遷 called Jique 冀闕, or the Ji Gate Towers.[62] Shang Yang may have given priority to this type of building not just because of its imposing appearance, but also because of its political symbolism; the *que* gates in front of a palace were the place where the government posted legal documents and official pronouncements. The gatelike Qin palace can thus be viewed as an architectural manifestation of Shang Yang's new laws and the imperial authority that he hoped to forge.[63] This interpretation is supported by the palace's name. Ji means "to record official orders on a *que*-tower" and, alternatively, "tall and imposing."[64]

After years of work, in 1976 Chinese archaeologists published their report on the excavation of a building at the center of the enormous palace complex of the First Qin Emperor.[65] Located north of the Wei 渭 River near present-day Xianyang, the remaining foundations of the palace are 60 m long east to west, 45 m wide north to south, and about 6 m high. According to the report and reconstruction plans (Fig. 10.9), the palace originally consisted of two wings with a symmetrical layout. The foundation of the western wing is

[60] *Shi ji*, 68, p. 2232.
[61] *Li ji*, 2 ("Quli 2"), 4, 11a (Legge, *Li Chi*, vol. 1, pp. 103–104).
[62] *Shi ji*, 68, p. 2232.
[63] See Wang Xueli, *Qin du Xianyang* (Xi'an: Shaanxi Renmin, 1985), pp. 18–20.
[64] Sima Zhen's commentary in *Shi ji*, 68, p. 2232; Sun Yirang's commentary in *Zhou li*, 2 ("Tianguan Zhongzai"), 16a.
[65] *Wenwu* 1976.11: 12–24.

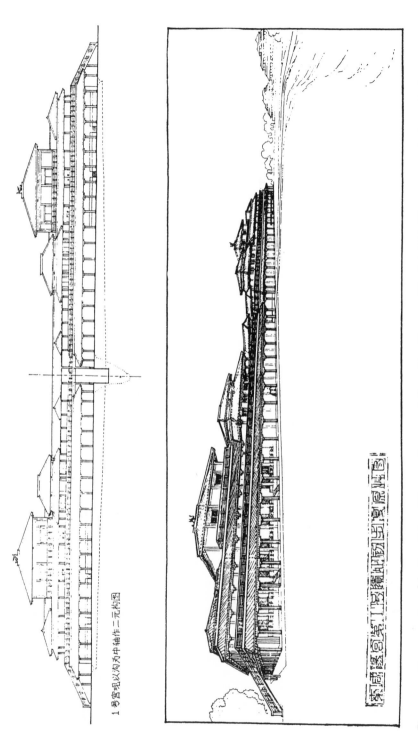

1 号宫观以沟为中轴作二元构图

秦咸阳宫第1号遗址复原鸟瞰图

Figure 10.9. Reconstruction of the Jique Palace (Xianyang Gong no. 1). From Yang Hongxun (Tao Fu). "Qin Xianyang gong diyihao yizhi fuyuan wenti de chubu tantao," *Wenwu* 1976.11: 31–41, fig. 6.

better preserved, showing clearly the structure and technique of a terrace pavilion. Its earthen core was covered by bays on all sides, creating the image of a three-story building of considerable size. A drainage system guided water into underground pipes. The chambers were connected by intricate passages and balconies and were decorated with elaborate bronze accessories and colorful murals. Patterned eave tiles accentuated the outline of each level, while a row of columns surrounding the first level gave the whole structure a stable appearance. This building was initially identified as the Xianyang Palace of the First Qin Emperor, but the traces of repeated repair and reconstruction strongly suggest that it was first built during the Warring States period and was only subsequently integrated into the First Emperor's palace complex. Its peculiar architectural form, resembling a *que* gate with two *guan* towers, has led some scholars to argue further that it was originally the Jique Palace constructed by Shang Yang in the fourth century B.C.[66]

Art: Vessels, Ornaments, Painting, and Sculpture

As with the development of the city and palaces, major changes in Eastern Zhou art first appeared within the traditional genre of ritual objects (*liqi* 禮器). The continuous transformation of old zoomorphic motifs into abstract decorative patterns – a phenomenon that has long been recognized by art historians – was only one of several interrelated changes in bronze art. Other important developments from the middle and late Spring and Autumn period onward include the further decline of inscriptions, the appearance of realistic animal motifs, the employment of the lost-wax casting technique and inlaid decoration, and the emergence of pictorial images. A traditional Chinese concept, *wen sheng yu zhi* 文勝於質 (decoration overpowering the substance), best summarizes these changes and signifies that bronze art was rapidly losing its traditional political and religious significance, which had relied on either symbolic imagery or commemorative inscriptions.[67]

The conflict between tradition and innovation reached a new stage as the second half of the Eastern Zhou began. Among artworks dated to the early Warring States period, those from the tomb of Zeng Hou Yi 曾侯乙 include an astonishing assemblage of some 10,000 objects of various shapes, materials, and functions, and provide an invaluable group of materials for study-

---

[66] See Wang Xueli et al., "Qin du Xianyang fajue baodao de ruogan buchong yijian," *Wenwu* 1979.2: 85–6; Wang Xueli, "Qin du Xianyang yu Xianyang gong bianzheng," *Kaogu yu wenwu* 1982.2: 67–71; Yang Hongxun (Tao Fu), "Qin Xianyang gong di yi hao yizhi fuyuan wenti de chubu tantao," *Wenwu* 1976.11: 31–41.

[67] For the role of symbolic imagery and commemorative inscriptions in Shang and Western Zhou ritual art, see Wu Hung, *Monumentality in Early Chinese Art and Architecture*, pp. 48–61.

ing many facets of the artistic development during this period. The following discussion of several major components of Warring States art – namely
bronze vessels, sculpture and ornaments, lacquerwares and pictorial images
– will therefore begin with a survey of examples from this great tomb.

BRONZE ART. Located at Leigudun 擂鼓墩 in Suixian 隨縣, Hubei
province, Leigudun tomb 1 of Zeng Hou Yi has been dated to 433 B.C. or
slightly later,[68] but its 114 bronze vessels, including an amazing set of 64
bronze bells, and many other bronze objects must have been made prior to
Yi's death. One striking feature of these objects is their uniform inscription,
"Hou Yi makes and holds onto the bronze, using it forever." This is a straightforward declaration of ownership. Unlike many earlier ritual bronzes, including some examples from Zeng that date from the Spring and Autumn
period,[69] these vessels neither commemorated important historical events nor
facilitated routine ancestral sacrifices. Most likely they were made to fulfill
the needs of the extravagant court life as well as new kinds of rituals that
prevailed during the Eastern Zhou.[70] Conducted at various social occasions
that ranged from court audiences and archery contests to weddings and the
welcome of guests, these new rituals were designed to maintain social relations rather than to venerate ancestral deities. Pictorial bronzes of the sixth
and fifth centuries B.C. correspondingly depicted such rituals and other social
activities. The focal image is often a multileveled palace hall in which noblemen handle ritual vessels while dancers and musicians stage a performance
(Fig. 10.8). These scenes most vividly illustrate the uses of ritual vessels and
musical instruments, and also link architecture and portable objects, two
principal topics of this chapter, into a single context.

Nonetheless, these scenes cannot capture the physical appearance and
artistic styles of the vessels. Bronzes from Leigudun tomb 1 amaze us, first of
all, for their sheer weight and volume, which seem disproportionate to the
small state that produced them. In addition to the sixty-four bells that transformed 2,500 kg of raw copper and tin into the most exquisite set of musical
instruments that we know from ancient China, there are two wine containers, each 1.3 m high and 1.1 m wide, that are so enormous that they had to be
made in separate upper and lower halves. But from an art historical point of

---

[68] The uncertainty is caused by different interpretations of the date (corresponding with 433 B.C.),
inscribed on a large bronze bell from the tomb, which was a gift from King Hui of Chu. Some scholars believe that Hou Yi died in this year and that the bell was a mortuary present from the ruler of a
neighboring state. Other scholars consider the bell to have been made when he was still alive, so that
his death must have occurred afterwards. See Qiu Xigui, "Tantan Suixian Zeng Hou Yi mu de wenzi
ziliao," *Wenwu* 1979.7: 25–31; *Zeng Hou Yi mu*, 2 vols. (Beijing: Wenwu, 1989), vol. 1, p. 461.

[69] For Zeng bronzes, see Zhou Yongzhen, "Zengguo yu Zengguo tongqi," *Kaogu* 1980.5: 436–43; Zeng
Zhaoming and Li Jin, "Zengguo he Zengguo tongqi zongkao," *Jiang Han kaogu* 1980.1: 69–84.

[70] For a discussion of these rituals, see Yang Kuan, *Gushi xintan* (Beijing: Zhonghua, 1965), pp. 218–370.

view, the chief value of the Suixian bronze vessels and musical instruments lies in their extreme exaggeration of decorative details. It is here that we may observe a culmination of the tendency toward patterns. Tight and dense interlace motifs, which already dominated bronze art during the preceding century, now developed into many variations including sculpted, three-dimensional forms. Sometimes, as in the case of the bronze base for a drum, the traditional piece-mold casting method was employed with amazing perfection to produce the complex configuration of bold, writhing serpents. In other cases, such as that of the bronze bells, numerous curled elements form a dense, almost prickly texture. But the most astonishing achievement of Suixian bronze art, both in aesthetic and technical terms, is demonstrated by a *zun* 尊 vase that was placed inside a matching basin (Fig. 10.10). Its rim is formed by hundreds of tiny, wormlike dragons, which twist, intertwine, and overlap. Serpentine forms also decorate the vessel's neck, belly, and base, but in these positions they increase in size, gain more organic features, and are detached from the surface to become projecting sculptures. These relief and three-dimensional images are further combined with openwork designs on the neck and handles.

Technically, this *zun* demonstrates the maturity of the lost-wax casting method, which began to be used in China at least from the early sixth century B.C.[71] This new technique was employed because it served an artistic aim of the time.[72] What we find on the *zun*, as well as on many other Suixian bronzes, is the autonomy of decoration. Their relief and openwork designs are no longer surface patterns in a traditional sense. Decoration has become so crowded, deep-cut, and overwhelming that it literally buries a vessel. In other words, the shape of a vessel is obscured and transformed into patterns, and solid bronze is modified into a honeycomb that is intricate and unreal. With such features, these objects represent an extravagant art style characterized by physical intensification, discernible in the depth of cutting, degree of curvature, and multiplicity of forms.[73] However astonishing the appear-

---

[71] For the casting technique of the *zun*, see Hua Jueming and Guo Dewei, "Zeng Hou Yi mu qingtong qiqun de zhuhan jishu he shilafa," *Wenwu* 1979.7: 46–8. For earlier use of the lost-wax technique, see *Wenwu* 1980.10: 13–20; Tan Derui, *The Splendid Craft of Lost Wax Casting in Ancient China* (in Chinese and English) (Shanghai: Shanghai Scientific and Technological Literature Publishing House, 1989).

[72] As Jenny So has pointed out, throughout the Warring States period and the Han, the lost-wax technique remained an ancillary technique, used primarily to produce openwork designs and sculpted forms; *Eastern Zhou Ritual Bronzes from the Arthur M. Sackler Collection* (Washington, D.C.: Arthur M. Sackler Foundation, 1995), pp. 54–5.

[73] For a definition of the "extravagant art style," see Martin Powers, "Artistic Taste, the Economy and the Social Order in Former Han China," *Art History* 9, 3 (1986): 285–9. See too E. T. Cook and A. Wedderburn, eds. *The Works of John Ruskin*, 39 vols. (London, 1904), vol. 6, pp. 6–7; E. H. Gombrich, *The Sense of Order: A Study in the Psychology of Decorative Art* (Ithaca, N.Y.: Cornell University Press, 1979), pp. 42–6.

Figure 10.10. A set of bronze *zun* and *pan* vessels, from tomb 1 at Leigudun, Suixian, Hubei. Second half of the fifth century B.C. Height 33.1 cm (*zun*); 24 cm (*pan*). From Li Xueqin, *Zhongguo meishu quanji: Gongyi meishu bian 4, Qingtongqi* (Beijing: Wenwu, 1985), fig. 76.

ance of these bronzes might have appeared to be, it required little sophistication to understand their message, since their extremely ornate decoration resulted from the intense development of pattern making and motif distortion; in E. H. Gombrich's words, "They are the consequence of situations in which outbidding has become necessary."[74] In traditional Chinese terms, it meant the final conquest of substance (*zhi*) by decoration (*wen*).

[74] Gombrich, *The Sense of Order*, p. 44.

LACQUERWARES AND THE ART OF INLAY. If the Suixian *zun* exhausted the means of pursuing this extravagant art style with pure bronze material,[75] other objects from the same tomb indicate a new departure toward an art of mixed media. A second style in Suixian art, conventionally called "inlaid bronzes," again originated in the sixth century B.C. or even earlier, when stylized animals, already fashioned in red copper, were cast into the walls of a vessel, while turquoise and gold were also occasionally used to embellish the surface of bronze artifacts.[76] The sixty-five inlaid vessels from Leigudun tomb 1, which amounted to more than half the total number of the ritual vessels found in the burial, demonstrate the unprecedented popularity of inlay decor. Some of these works continued to bear cast-inlay copper motifs. Others are also inlaid with turquoise, gold, and some unknown materials for richer color combinations. The isolated block motifs on earlier inlaid objects have here dissolved into a series of thick spiral shapes embellished with hooks and scrolls and cover a much larger surface on a vessel. The further development of this rhythmic design is exemplified by some extraordinary objects from Baoshan 包山 in Hubei and Zhaoqing 肇慶 in Guangdong; their undulating patterns are filled with a variety of inlay substances and are further outlined with gold or silver threads for visual clarity (Fig. 10.11).

This curvilinear inlay style, and indeed the whole development of the colorful inlay decoration during the Warring States period, reflects strong influences from lacquerware, which had also gained great popularity during this period.[77] According to a 1986 statistic, more than 3,000 lacquer objects, most dating from the Warring States period, had been found in the area of Chu.[78] Unlike bronze vessels, which only appeared in the tombs of the powerful and rich, lacquer objects are somewhat ubiquitous in Chu burials. Even small graves could contain several dozen of them; large tombs such as Leigudun tomb 1 often had more than 200 exquisite lacquer objects. Indeed, the sudden

[75] The energy and intensity in the bronzes of Hou Yi are no longer felt from the objects found in a slightly later tomb in the same graveyard (Leigudun tomb 2). See *Jiang Han kaogu* 1981.1: 1–2; *Hubei Suizhou Leigudun chutu wenwu* (Hong Kong: China Resources Artland, 1984), nos. 14–17, 66–7. Generally speaking, although the lost-wax casting technique was continuously (and occasionally) used to produce intricate interlace patterns and openwork designs, the Suixian *zun* has remained the unsurpassed example of this style.

[76] For discussions of inlaid bronzes of the Eastern Zhou period, see Jenny So, "The Inlaid Bronzes of the Warring States Period," in *The Great Bronze Age of China*, ed. Wen Fong (New York: Metropolitan Museum of Art, 1980), pp. 305–20; Jenny So, *Eastern Zhou Ritual Bronzes*, pp. 33–5, 46–50; Jia E, "Guanyu Dong Zhou cuojin xiangqian tongqi de jige wenti de tantao," *Jiang Han Kaogu*, 1986.4: 34–48.

[77] Jenny So, *Eastern Zhou Ritual Bronzes*, p. 52.

[78] Chen Zhenyu, "Shilun Zhanguo shiqi Chuguo de qiqi shougongye," *Kaogu yu wenwu* 1986.4: 77–85. The author of this article estimated that "more than 3,000 tombs" had been discovered in the Chu area, significantly fewer than the "more than 4,000" excavated Chu tombs estimated in the 1984 publication *Xin Zhongguo de kaogu faxian he yanjiu* (Beijing: Wenwu, 1984), p. 304.

(a)

(b)

Figure 10.11. Inlaid bronzes, from the south: (a) *lei* with silver and lacquer inlays from Zhaoqing, Guangdong. Late fourth to early third century B.C. From *Wenwu* 1974.11: 71, fig. 5. (b) *zun* with gold and silver inlays from Baoshan tomb 2, Jingmen, Hubei province. Late fourth century B.C. From *Baoshan Chu mu* (Beijing: Wenwu, 1991), vol. 1, fig. 120a, b.

increase of lacquer objects in mid-Warring States tombs casts doubt on the frequently cited opinion that lacquerware was extremely expensive, even more so than bronze.[79] It is more likely that only a small group of specially commissioned lacquer objects, such as those unusually fine or large specimens from a number of royal mausoleums, were truly precious.[80] Commercial lacquerware became increasingly less costly in the south so that ordinary families were able to acquire some of its pieces.[81]

The popularization of lacquer objects was coupled with the formation of a new decorative style. Early Warring States lacquerwares derived many of their decorative motifs, often interlace designs, from bronze art. A typical example of this early trend is a covered *dou* 豆 vessel from Leigudun tomb 1 (Fig. 10.12). Carved and painted with ornate serpentine forms, it closely imitates sculpted and openwork patterns found on the bronze *zun* from the same tomb (Fig. 10.10). By the mid-Warring States period, however, many new motifs in lacquer decoration emerged, including animals, birds, clouds, and flowing geometric patterns. A curvilinear style gradually prevailed in the south, and the brushwork became increasingly free. In addition, coloristic effects were diligently pursued during this period; the full range of seven colors, red, black, yellow, blue, brown, gold, and silver, have only been observed on mid-Warring States lacquerwares.[82] Welcomed as this style clearly was, it must presumably have influenced other art forms with some force. That the art of inlay also reached its maturity in the fourth century B.C. is no matter of mere coincidence.

The flowing lacquer decoration seems to have been particularly similar to an inlay style developed in the south (Fig. 10.11), a style that differed quite markedly from that of some of the inlaid bronzes found north of the Yellow River. This northern style may also have evolved from the cast-inlay copper decoration of the sixth century B.C. By the early fifth century B.C., experiments had evidently been taking place with a broader range of inlay materials, as is demonstrated by vessels and a belt hook from Jinshengcun 金勝村 near Taiyuan 太原, Shanxi; these objects are inlaid with gold and an uniden-

---

[79] This argument is based on a passage in the Han text *Yan tie lun* 29 ("Sanbuzu"). Writing about 50 B.C., Huan Tan was describing the inlaid lacquerwares of his own time, rather than ordinary lacquer objects of the Warring States period. See Wang Liqi, *Yan tie lun jiaozhu* (rev. ed., Beijing: Zhonghua, 1992), p. 351.

[80] Remains of inlaid lacquerwares have been found in Eastern Zhou tombs at Jincun and in Zhongshan mausoleums at Pingshan. A very large lacquer *jian* vessel was reportedly taken from a Wei royal mausoleum at Guweicun. See Li Xueqin, *Eastern Zhou and Qin Civilizations*, pp. 357–8.

[81] Several burial sites in Qin and Ba-Shu, dating from the middle and late Warring States period, have also yielded a considerable number of lacquer objects. See Chen Zhenyu, "Shilun Hubei Zhanguo Qin Han qiqi de niandai fenqi," *Jiang Han kaogu* 1980.2: 37–50, 114; Li Zhaohe, "Bashu yu Chu qiqi chutan," in *Zhongguo kaogu xuehui dierci nianhui lunwenji* (Beijing: Wenwu, 1980), pp. 93–9.

[82] Early lacquerwares from Chu lack the colors blue, gold, and silver, while later objects also lack yellow. See Chen Zhenyu, "Shilun Zhanguo shiqi Chuguo de qiqi shougongye," pp. 81–2.

Figure 10.12. Lacquer *dou*, from tomb 1 at Leigudun, Suixian, Hubei. Second half of the fifth century B.C. From *Zeng Hou Yi mu* (Beijing: Wenwu, 1989), vol. 1, fig. 227.

tified pastelike substance.[83] A *dou* discovered from Changzhi 長治 in the same province, tentatively dated to the late fifth or early fourth century B.C., reflects a more advanced state of inlay decoration (Fig. 10.13).[84] It resembles an earlier *dou* reportedly from Hunyuan 渾源 in northern Shanxi, but abstract dragon patterns delineated in gold threads take the place of the copper inlays of animals and figures. Quite unlike the organic and spiraling images on southern inlaid bronzes, the decoration of this and other northern products is more geometric, being restricted within parallel registers.

An impressive *hu* 壺 vessel excavated from Liulige 琉璃閣 tomb 1 represents the next developmental stage of this style: more than half a meter tall, its surface is divided into seven registers, each filled with abstract linear patterns organized in alternating triangular and rectangular blocks. This horizontal design was further transformed into a diagonal grid, resulting in a series of brilliant inlaid vessels of the middle and the late fourth century, including those from the Royal City and also from the mausoleums of

[83] For the archaeological report on the Jinshengcun finds, see *Wenwu* 1989.9: 59–86. For inlaid bronzes in the north during the fifth century B.C., see Jenny So, *Eastern Zhou Ritual Bronzes*, pp. 41–2.

[84] *Wenwu* 1972.4: 38–46. The excavator dates Fenshuiling tomb 126, which originally contained the *dou*, to the middle of the third century. But as Lawton has argued, the *dou* was made earlier and was placed in the tomb as an heirloom. See *Chinese Art of the Warring States Period*, p. 42.

Figure 10.13. Inlaid bronze *dou*, from Fenshuiling, Changzhi, Shanxi. From *Xin Zhongguo chutu wenwu* (Beijing: Waiwen, 1972), pl. 72.

Zhongshan 中山 kings all covered with dazzling inlays organized in mazelike diagonal patterns (Fig. 10.14).[85]

The coexistence of these two inlay styles exemplifies a general situation in Warring States art. On the one hand, a distinctive art style was often an important attribute of a regional culture that was limited by its geographical boundaries. On the other hand, it was related to other regional styles in a broad, synchronic artistic movement. Although inlaid bronzes from north and south show different preferences for decorative motifs and formulas, they

---

[85] These inlaid vessels include two pairs of *dui* 敦 and a pair of *hu* (one is the *Chen Zhang* 陳璋 *hu* made before 314 B.C.) from Jincun and a *hu* from the Zhongshan mausoleum of King Cuo; see Jenny So, *Eastern Zhou Ritual Bronzes*, p. 56.

Figure 10.14. Inlaid *hu*, from tomb 1 at Zhong-shan. From *Chûgoku sengoku jidai no yû: Chûzan ôgoku bunbutsuten* (Tokyo: Tokyo National Museum, 1981), no. 6.

together contributed to the formation of a new art tradition: the art of mixed media. In both regions, the inlaid portion on an object constantly grew more conspicuous, and the decoration became increasingly complex and rich. As a result, a vessel gradually acquired a surface of gold, silver, turquoise, and lacquer. It is misleading to consider such an object a bronze, not only because its visual appearance is determined by the inlaid surface, rather than by the bronze base material, but also because the base material for inlay could be other substances than bronze, for example, iron and lacquer. Moreover, although the art of inlay was first associated with bronze decoration, it finally developed into an independent art genre. In fact, an inlaid work of the fourth century B.C., with its contrasting colors and fluent designs on a smooth surface, is more akin to a colorful lacquerware; the main difference is that it was not painted with a brush, but fashioned with a chisel.

It is interesting to compare an inlaid *hu* from a Zhongshan mausoleum (Fig. 10.14) with the bronze *zun* from Leigudun tomb 1 (Fig. 10.10). The difference between the two objects, separated as they are by about a hundred years, cannot be overstated. Indeed, although both vessels are products of the Eastern Zhou extravagant art tradition, they represent two stages of this art and two essentially different attitudes. The fifth-century Leigudun *zun* shows its extravagant quality through exaggerating decorative details. It is still made of pure bronze, but it is a debasement from traditional bronze art by the absence of a commemorative inscription and its distortion of symbolic imagery. This almost painful struggle against tradition disappears from the fourth-century Zhongshan *hu*; the solemnity of bronze finally gave way to colorful inlays and sensual pleasure. The extravagant art style gained its own ground, as it was no longer confined to the genre of bronze art. Once this style had obtained its independence, the pressure and burden of traditional norms were removed. The result was a splendid and balanced art characterized by the harmony of shape, pattern, and color.

SCULPTURE AND ORNAMENTS.   Leigudun tomb 1 also yielded important evidence for the achievement of sculpture in the early Warring States period. The pursuit of complex decoration, a tendency that is also demonstrated by the clay molds from the Houma foundries in Shanxi, led to frequent and sophisticated uses of the "cast-on" technique in bronze casting. Of a three-dimensional form, accessories such as a serpentine handle or a dragon-shaped base were made first and then cast on to a larger object. The making of these individual parts, from shaping a clay or wax model to casting the final bronze version, employed all the essential techniques and necessary steps for creating a free-standing bronze statue. It is thus in no way a matter of chance that some accessories of Leigudun bronzes likewise began to manifest the characteristics of sculpture. Although not yet completely self-contained, these images embody aesthetic values that are independent from the works to which they are attached and impress the viewer as three-dimensional forms of human figures or mythical animals.

The three most important examples of such sculpted bronze images are all associated with musical instruments, including the human-shaped caryatids of the bell set; the two winged monsters that support a set of stone chimes; and a hybrid creature with a bird's body and deer antlers, which may have been the stand for a drum.[86] The value of the set of bells, which may be taken as our chief example, lies not only in its inscriptions, which document a sophisticated musical system, but also in the complex shape and decor of each bell, sometimes produced by as many as thirty-eight pieces of mold. The three-tiered wooden frame, from which the bells are suspended, is itself

---

[86] See Zhu Jianhua, "Chu shu tanbi – Lujiao lihe xuangu, lugu, huzuo niaojia gu kao," *Jiang Han kaogu* 1991.4: 83–6.

Figure 10.15. Bronze figure (supporting bells), from tomb 1 at Leigudun. From *Zeng Hou Yi mu wenwu yishu* (Wuhan: Hubei Meishu, 1991), fig. 38.

a work of art. Fitted with intricate bronze finials, its horizontal wooden beams are supported by six bronze standing figures of gigantic size, as compared with the tiny figures sometimes found on earlier bronze ritual vessels (often serving as the feet of a tripod or a plate). Each of the three figures on the lower level weighs 359 kg and stands approximately 1 m high above a hemispherical base 0.35 m high (Fig. 10.15). The three figures on the second level are slightly shorter, about 80 cm each; tenons extending from the upper and lower ends secure these figures in position. These statues presumably represent persons of substantial rank; they are clothed identically with tight jackets and long skirts, both originally painted with black lacquer and again embellished with bands of red floral patterns. All six figures wear swords, a feature that has led some scholars to call them "warriors" or "palace guards."

The modeling of the figures shows intense artistic concerns. Although in actuality their straight bodies function as column-like caryatids, the artist created an illusion that these warriors effortlessly support the heavy frame with their two bent arms. Each figure has a rather large head, but not as disproportionately large as may be seen in some earlier or contemporary examples. What makes these bronze figures truly outstanding works of sculpture, however, are their faces, created with a surprisingly sophisticated understanding of human anatomy. The straight eyes and closed lips are defined by sharp contours, contrasting the smooth and subtle transition between the broad forehead, the high cheekbones, and the pointed chin. This naturalistic sculptural style must have been intended, because an entirely different style is employed to decorate the hemispherical bases. Densely covered with undulating curls and volutes derived from dragon motifs, these bases are stylistically homogeneous to many ritual objects in the Leigudun group. But here their prickly surfaces also serve to set off the naturalness of the figures they support.

These and other works from Leigudun tomb 1 attest to two large categories of Warring States sculpture, human figures and mythical animals, whose development followed quite separate paths. The naturalistic representation of the human-shaped caryatids is shared by a large group of Warring States human figures. Debris from the foundry at Houma has yielded complicated section molds for casting such figures; finished products from similar molds have been excavated from other sites in Shanxi dated to the late sixth and early fifth centuries B.C.[87] While these Shanxi figures often raise their arms to support objects (and hence are similar to the Leigudun figures), many other bronze figures, in either kneeling, squatting, or standing positions, extend their arms to hold hollow tubes or to clasp a tube with both hands. Several examples of this kind were reported to have come from Jincun 金村, Henan; others have been found through archaeological excavations, sometimes with a lamp holder inserted in the tube held by the figure.[88] All of these figures have stiff front poses, with extended arms like bent cylinders. Their detailed rendering of costume and, especially, headdresses, however, reveals a straightforward attempt at a naturalistic effect.

[87] *Shanxi chutu wenwu* (Taiyuan: Shanxi Renmin, 1980), nos. 87–9, 98, 103. See Jenny So, *Eastern Zhou Ritual Bronzes*, p. 65.

[88] For two excavated examples, see *Wenwu* 1976.3: fig. 4; *Baoshan Chu mu*, 2 vols. (Beijing: Wenwu, 1991), vol. 1, pp. 189–94.

Figure 10.16. Bronze dragon, from Xiadu. From Umehara Sueji, *Sengoku shiki dôki no kenkyû* (Kyoto: Tôhô bunka gakuin Kyôtô kenkyûjo, 1936), fig. LXXX.

Strange animals, often of a hybrid form, take a prominent place in Chinese mythology and religion. Such figures appear as an essential element in the descriptions that the *Shan hai jing* 山海經 (Classic of the mountains and the seas) regularly provides for sites that were inhabited by holy spirits or those that concealed inherent dangers. It is hardly surprising that the same themes recur in the art of the Warring States period and that the sculptures of mythical animals emphasize a very different set of qualities. This is in contrast with bronze figures of human beings, which represent warriors or servants. Like the hybrid creatures from Leigudun tomb 1, these works show little effort to portray living animals. Instead, their images resulted from fantasy and aimed to stir up the imagination. A bronze dragon, reportedly from Laomu Tai outside Wuyang, may have originally decorated the pavilion on the platform (Fig. 10.16). Half-feline and half-reptilian, the dragon has dorsal spikes and pinioned wings. Its body is covered by linear volutes filled with dots. But its sharp wings, horns, and fins convey a strong sense of three-dimensionality. The exaggerated curves of these projecting parts even create a feeling of movement, whereby the mythical animal, bending its cylindrical neck and tightening its sinews and muscles, is about to leap in the air.

The only large group of sculptures of both human figures and mythical animals from the middle to late Warring States period was found in the royal mausoleums of the Zhongshan kingdom at Pingshan 平山, Hebei. Like the earlier state of Zeng of the fifth century B.C., in the fourth century B.C. Zhongshan was one of the smaller peripheral states that contended for survival among its stronger neighbors. Zeng probably perished not long after the death of Zeng Hou Yi; Zhongshan was destroyed by Zhao in 296 B.C., some ten years after the construction of the last major mausoleum (tomb 1) near the capital of Lingshou 靈壽. From 1974 to 1978, extensive archaeological work at the site resulted in the discovery of more than thirty tombs dating from the Eastern Zhou period.[89] Among them, tomb 1 to the west of Lingshou is believed to have belonged to King Cuo 響, while the occupant of tomb 6, a mausoleum located in the western part of Lingshou within the city walls, was probably his father. A combined group of sculptures from these two tombs includes two bronze lamps with human and animal figures; an inlaid bronze table supported by dragons and phoenixes, remnants of three screen stands in the shapes of an ox, a rhinoceros, and a tiger; and a pair of winged mythical beasts without apparent practical function.

Three essential features of these works are their strong three-dimensionality, vivid imagery, and brilliant ornamentation. No longer do they just exhibit stiff frontal views of men and animals; instead, they can be appreciated from various angles. They also portray a far wider range of subjects. A bronze lamp from tomb 1 takes the shape of a gigantic tree whose individual branches support fifteen lamp holders (Fig. 10.17). The spiraling dragon climbing the central branch may be the mythological Zhulong 燭龍, literally "Lamp Dragon."[90] Other images on this tree lamp, however, are derived from the observed world of nature: birds perch on the tree singing, and monkeys reach out toward two men, who stand under the tree to feed the animals. The artist has captured a moment in life and created an atmosphere that is lively and delightful. A different visual strategy is employed in designing a lamp from tomb 6. Instead of emphasizing dramatic interactions between men and animals, a single standing male figure dominates the viewer's eyes. The serpents that he grasps in both hands support lamp holders. A distinctive feature of this work, which separates it from the other human-

[89] For the excavation report, see *Wenwu* 1979.1: 1–13. Exhibition catalogs of Zhongshan objects include *Chûgoku sengoku jidai no yû: Chûzan ôgoku bunbutsuten* (Tokyo: Tokyo National Museum, 1981) and *Zhongshan: Tombes des Rois Oubliés* (Paris: Galeries nationales du Grand Palais, 1985).

[90] For Zhulong's place in mythology, see Michael Loewe, *Ways to Paradise: The Chinese Quest for Immortality* (London: Allen & Unwin, 1979), p. 58.

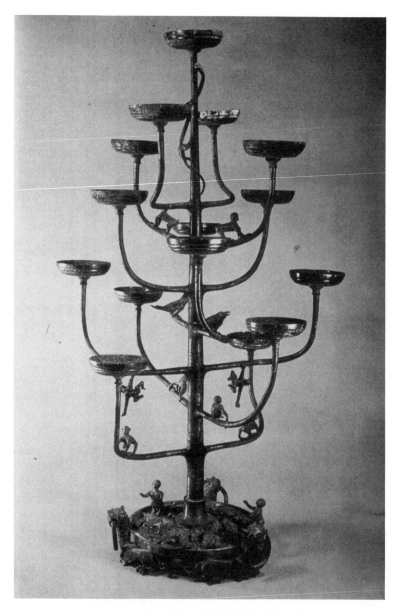

Figure 10.17. Tree-shaped lamp, from tomb 1 at Zhongshan. After *Wenwu* 1979.1: 17, fig. 1.

Figure 10.18. Tiger stand, from tomb 1 at Zhongshan. After *Wenwu* 1979.1: pl. 2:1.

shaped supporters discussed earlier, is its rich inlay, which serves both decorative and representational purposes. The man has a face made of silver and eyes of black gem. Inlaid patterns also represent the scales of the serpents and the fabric of the figure's elegant long robe.

Other sculpted works from the Zhongshan mausoleums, mostly animal images, have equally exquisite inlays but show more fantastic or foreign features. Among these, a small table stand consists of four dragons and four phoenixes; their bodies, wings, and horns intertwine, forming one of the most ingenious interlace designs from ancient China. With their horned square heads, gaping mouths, and winged feline bodies, a pair of mythical beasts from tomb 1 resembles the four dragons on this table stand but differs from three other animal sculptures, which show definite influences from the steppes. Explained as being parts of the basis of a screen, these three animal images must have been arranged in a row, with the ox and rhinoceros flanking a forceful tiger that is crushing a deer (Fig. 10.18). It is this tiger stand that best reveals the origin of these animal images: both the animal-combat motif and the emphasis on life motion are trademarks of steppe art. There were historical reasons for this stylistic connection: it was widely believed that the Zhongshan people were descended from the nomadic White Di 白狄, tribes that made incursions into the area of northern Shaanxi and northwestern Shanxi about the eighth century B.C.[91] It would be wrong, however, to view the tiger stand as merely a copy of steppe art. Created in the fourth century B.C. in Central China, it transforms the sort of combat scene that appears only on small plaques in the steppe into a monumental scale, half a meter long and weighing 26 kg. The original two-dimensional representation is molded into a brilliant three-dimensional form. The cultural and artistic fusion is also reflected by the creative use of inlay decoration; instead of forming abstract designs, the gold and silver inlays accentuate the animal's skin patterns.

The Zhongshan mausoleums also supply evidence for the coexistence of and interaction between tradition and innovation in late Warring States art. Forming a sharp contrast with the beautiful lamps and stands are ritual objects made entirely of bronze. Articles in this second group have neither inlaid decoration nor pictorial motifs, and their shapes show only minor differences from traditional ritual objects. A bronze axe, for example, is identified by its inscription as part of the insignia of royal power, a form of symbolism that can be traced back to the jade axes from Neolithic sites at Dawenkou 大汶口 and Liangzhu 良渚. A *ding* tripod and two *hu* vessels, all from King Cuo's tomb, bear long inscriptions documenting important political events and the king's merit (Fig. 10.19). The archaic literary style of the documents, as well as the very practice of inscribing such commemorative inscriptions on bronze vessels, seems to signify a deliberate effort to resurrect Western Zhou traditions. The radically different appearances of the two groups of Zhougshan objects, therefore, were intimately related to their divergent functions. In retrospect, we realize that all inlaid sculptures in the first group are objects of daily use or ornamental statues, serving as furnishings for a palace hall rather than an ancestral temple; their animal and human images resulted from a strong desire to forge a fantastic and exotic art outside the canon of ritual art. These two styles in Zhongshan art further imply different degrees of artistic freedom: while the design of ritual vessels was restricted by convention, utensils and ornaments eagerly embraced innovative elements such as foreign images, coloristic effects, and realistic styles.

It is in this light that we can understand the rapid development of the mirror and the garment hook, two objects of use that attracted wide attention during the Warring States period. Although bronze mirrors have been

---

[91] For the history of Zhongshan, see Liu Laicheng and Li Xiaodong, "Shitan Zhanguo shiqi Zhong-shanguo lishi shangde jige wenti," *Wenwu* 1979.1: 32–6; Li Xueqin and Li Ling, "Pingshan sanqi yu Zhongshanguo shi de ruogan wenti," *Kaogu xuebao* 1979.2: 147–70. The excavations of stone burials, gold earrings, and bronze daggers in the Zhongshan area suggest that the people who lived here continued using Di costume at least until the early Warring States period; see *Kaoguxue jikan* 5 (1987): 157–93; *Kaogu* 1984.11: 971–3; *Wenwu* 1986.6: 20–4.

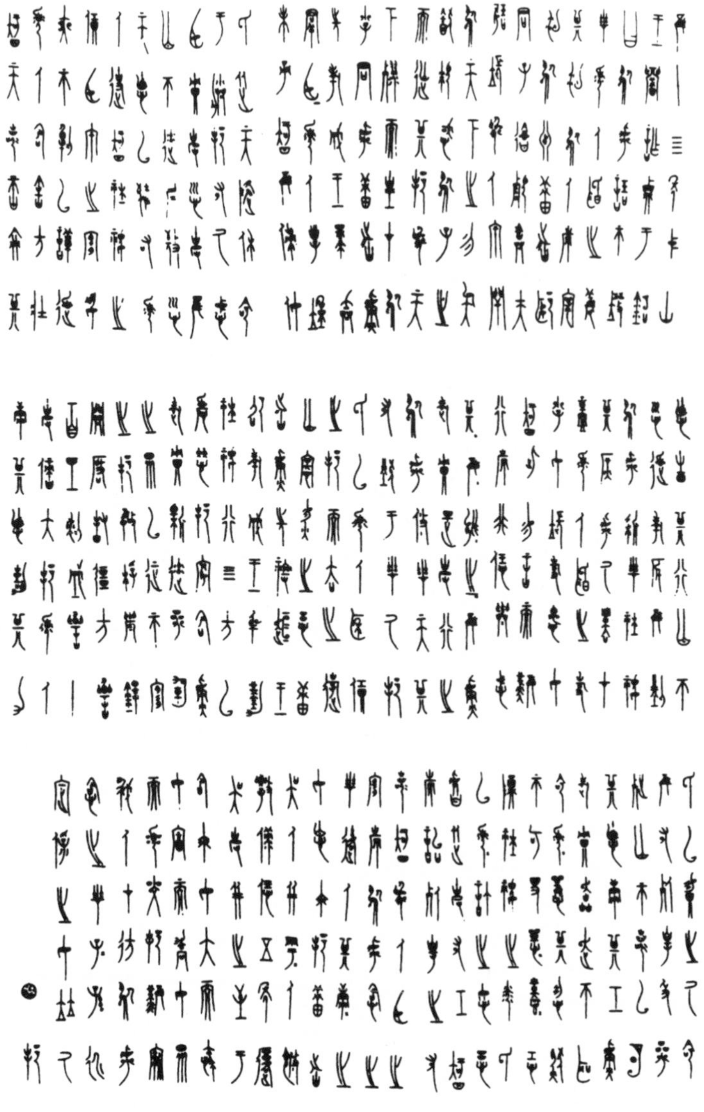

Figure 10.19. Inscription on a bronze *ding*, from tomb 1 at Zhongshan. After *Yin Zhou jinwen julu*, ed. Xu Zhongshu (Yibin: Sichuan cishu, 1984), #713.

found in late Shang tombs in Central China, these objects were not widely used until the sixth to fifth century B.C., since only a few mirrors of the Spring and Autumn period have been found through excavations.[92] However, more than a thousand Warring States mirrors are known; their abundance

[92] Among the three bronze mirrors excavated at Shangcunling in Henan, dated to the eighth to seventh centuries B.C., two are undecorated and the other bears animal images delineated in awkward lines;

and elaboration contrast sharply with the paucity and crudity of previous examples. Most of these mirrors came from the region of Chu, especially around Changsha 長沙, where about a quarter of 2,000 excavated tombs yielded mirrors. By contrast, only a limited number of tombs in Central and North China contained mirrors: 2 from the 212 Warring States tombs at Erligang 二里崗 in Zhengzhou 鄭州, 5 from the 112 tombs at Banpo 半坡 in Xi'an, 1 from the 59 tombs at Shaogou 燒溝 in Luoyang, and 1 from the 49 tombs at Handan in Hebei.[93]

Several classifications of Warring States mirrors that have been attempted were based on archaeological evidence, but even the most recent one, which suggests thirteen types and thirty-one subtypes, still does not exhaust all the varieties of designs on Warring States mirrors.[94] The difficulty in reaching a definitive typology lies in the material itself: although some major motif categories do exist, including trapezoid patterns, floral and leaf patterns, feather and scale patterns, curves and diamonds, and interlacing dragons (Fig. 10.20), it is incessant permutation, not standardization, that forms the main characteristic of Warring States mirrors. The repertoire of motifs expanded continuously; the patterns became increasingly more complex; and new techniques, such as openwork, inlay, and painting, were employed to broaden the decorative effect.

That the few mirrors from the northern tombs are often of a unique, ingenious design suggests that their owners were somewhat unusual. Among these examples, a mirror unearthed in the Qi capital of Linzi is among the largest of Warring States mirrors, about 30 cm in diameter, with three rings for hanging attached to the rim.[95] On the back, gold threads form cloud patterns, intermingled with silver and turquoise inlays. Three other inlaid mirrors, all reportedly from Jincun, exemplify three very different decorative styles (Fig. 10.21). The first mirror was constructed in two layers, with the reflecting surface fitted in the beveled edge of the base. Six dragons, inlaid with gold and silver in alternating sequence, form an undulating circle on the reverse side of the mirror.[96] On the second mirror, gold threads divide

see *Shangcunling Guoguo mudi* (Beijing: Kexue, 1959), pl. 27. As for examples dating from the late Spring and Autumn period, the Houma foundry has yielded some clay molds for casting mirrors, and finished products have been found at Houma and Xinjiang, Shanxi. See *Houma zhutong yizhi*, 2 vols. (Beijing: Wenwu, 1993), vol. 1, p. 194; and Wang Jinping, "Houma Xinjiang chutu liangmian Dong Zhou tongjing," *Wenwu jikan* 1995.2: 81, color pls. 1, 2.

[93] See Kong Xiangxing and Liu Yiman, *Zhongguo gudai tongjing* (Beijing: Wenwu, 1984), pp. 53–4.

[94] For studies of early Chinese mirrors, see Bernard Karlgren, "Early Chinese Mirrors," *BMFEA* 40 (1968) 79–98; Umehara Sueji, *Kan izen no kokyô no kenkyû* (Kyoto: Tôhô bunka gakuin Kyôto kenkyûjo, 1935); Liang Shangchun, *Yanku cangjing*, 4 vols. (Beijing: 1938–42); *Hunan chutu tongjing tulu* (Beijing: Wenwu, 1960); Lei Congyun, "Chu shi jing de leixing yu fenqi," *Jiang Han kaogu* 1982.2: 20–36; Kong Xiangxing and Liu Yiman, *Zhongguo gudai tongjing*.

[95] *Wenwu* 1972.5: 14–15, and pl. 1.

[96] See Lawton, *Chinese Art of the Warring States Period*, pp. 83–4.

Figure 10.20. Typical designs of Warring States mirrors. After Kong Xiangxing and Liu Yiman, *Zhongguo gudai tongjing* (Beijing: Wenwu, 1984), figs. 9–26. Drawings by Li Xiating.

the decorative area into three concentric circular bands, filled with patterned blue glass and fluted pale jade.[97] On the third mirror, delicate gold and silver threads and dots outline three groups of images: a phoenix, two beasts in combat, and a cavalryman fighting with a tiger. Once again, the combat

[97] See *Grenville L. Winthrop: Retrospective for a Collector* (Cambridge, Mass: Fogg Museum of Art, 1969), no. 55.

Figure 10.21. Inlaid mirrors, from Jincun, Henan: After (a) Freer Galley of Art (Thomas Lawton, *Chinese Art of the Warring States Period: Change and Continuity, 480–222 B.C.* [Washington, D.C.: Freer Gallery of Art, 1982], p. 84), (b) Harvard Art Museum (*Grenville L. Winthrop: Retrospective for a Collector* (Cambridge, Mass.: Fogg Museum of Art, 1969), no. 55), (c) M. Hosokawa Collection, Tokyo (Sherman E. Lee, *A History of Far Eastern Art*, 4th ed. [New York: Harry N. Abrams, 1982], color pl. 3). Drawings by Li Xiating.

motifs and the tiger's twisting torso indicate unmistakable influences from steppe art. Like the inlaid bronzes from the Zhongshan mausoleums, these exquisite mirrors, apparently made for the most privileged patrons, reveal a specific taste for luxurious materials and exotic images.

Although it has been suggested that the belt hook was introduced from the steppes during the Warring States period, actual belt hooks, some dating from the Spring and Autumn period, have been excavated mainly in Chinese contexts.[98] The Houma foundry of the state of Jin, for example, has yielded molds for casting belt hooks by the bushel, indicating some degree of mass production during the late Spring and Autumn and early Warring States periods.[99] In addition to serving the local clientele, the foundry may have also exported belt hooks to other regions. This is perhaps why belt hooks made in Jin were especially praised in the Chu text "Summoning the Soul" (Zhao hun 招魂).[100] The use of belt hooks prior to the Warring States period has been proven by excavated examples.[101] Most convincingly, the 260 Eastern Zhou tombs unearthed along the Zhongzhou Road 中州路 at Luoyang were classified in seven consecutive chronological groups; a number of bronze hooks were found there in burials that are dated to the middle and late Spring and Autumn period.[102] On the other hand, these finds challenge the conventional identification of belt hooks, which include any object with a small upturned hook at one end and a button on the underside of the other end. Such hooks, especially the earlier ones from Zhongzhou Road, were sometimes found beside the head of the deceased and were thus presumably used to fasten headdresses. Other small hooks were probably supporters for swords, knives, pouches, or other personal paraphernalia.[103] It is therefore more precise to call these objects "garment hooks," which would also include belt hooks.[104]

Like the bronze mirror, during the Warring States period garment hooks developed from practical personal objects to become lavishly decorated ornaments. The early hooks were small and without much surface decoration.

[98] Wang Renxiang, "Gudai daigou yongtu kaoshi," *Wenwu* 1982.10: 75–6. Jenny F. So and Emma C. Bunker, *Traders and Raiders on China's Northern Frontier* (Washington, D.C.: Arthur M. Sackler Gallery, Smithsonian Institution; and Seattle: University of Washington Press, 1995), pp. 81–4.

[99] *Kaogu* 1962.2: 55–62. *Houma zhutong yizhi*, vol. 1, pp. 159–74. For belt hooks of the Spring and Autumn period excavated in the Jin area, see *Wenwu* 1959.6: 49.

[100] *Chu ci*, 9 ("Zhaohun"), Zhu Xi (1130–1200), *Chu ci jizhu* (1235: rpt. Shanghai: Shanghai guji, 1979), p. 142; David Hawkes, *Songs of the South: An Ancient Chinese Anthology of Poems by Qu Yuan and Other Poets*, 2d ed. (Harmondsworth: Penguin, 1985), p. 228.

[101] For Spring and Autumn tombs that contained belt hooks, see Wang Renxiang, "Gudai daigou yongtu kaoshi," p. 76.

[102] *Luoyang Zhongzhoulu* (Beijing: Kexue, 1959), pp. 128–30.

[103] *Kaogu* 1963.9: 469; *Kaogu* 1973.3: 157.

[104] This term is employed by Thomas Lawton in *Chinese Art of the Warring States Period*, pp. 89–94. For discussions of the various kinds of garment hooks, see Wang Renxiang, "Gudai daigou yongtu kaoshi," pp. 77–81.

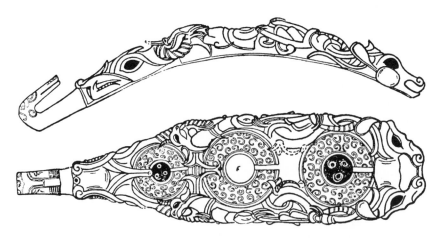

Figure 10.22. Gilt and inlaid garment hook from tomb 5 at Guweicun, Huixian, Henan. From *Huixian fajue baogao* (Beijing: Kexue, 1956), p. 104.

This situation changed dramatically during the fourth and third centuries B.C., when garment hooks acquired varieties of shapes, technical finishes, and colors. Richly inlaid with precious metals and stones, these objects best exemplify the development of the extravagant art tradition in the middle and late Warring States period. Some of the most beautiful garment hooks are said to have come from Jincun;[105] this provenance is confirmed by the recent find of an extraordinary gilded hook at the same site.[106] Splendid garment hooks found in other areas include an example from Guweicun 固圍村 tomb 5 in Huixian, Henan, on which intertwining animals, cast in bronze openwork designs, surround three jade rings fitted onto the surface. The round rear end of the object is marked by a large animal mask seen *en face*; the hook itself on the other end represents a slender animal head made of jade (Fig. 10.22).[107] Of particular interest are some unusually large hooks from late Chu tombs, including the inlaid iron hooks from Changtaiguan 長台關 tomb 1 at Xinyang 信陽, Henan (22.4 cm long) and Wangshan 望山 tomb 1 in Jiangling 江陵 (46.2 cm long). Such hooks, however, were probably used for interior decoration (e.g., as curtain hangers) rather than for personal ornamentation.[108]

The strong interest in personal ornamentation during the Warring States period also explains the development of textiles and jade carvings. Although

[105] Umehara Sueji, *Rakuyô Kinson kobô shûei* (Kyoto: Kobayashi shashin seibanjo, 1937), pls. 69–75.
[106] *Luoyang chutu wenwu jicui* (Beijing: Morning Glory 1990), no. 34.
[107] See *Huixian fajue baogao* (Beijing: Kexue, 1956), p. 104, fig. 123, pl. 74.
[108] See *Xinyang Chu mu* (Beijing: Wenwu, 1986), p. 63, pls. 64–5; *Wenwu* 1966.5: 36. Lawton suggests that the oversized hooks were likely "examples of ostenatious luxury items, perhaps awarded in recognition of merit"; *Chinese Art of the Warring States Period*, p. 90.

Figure 10.23. Patterns on textiles from Mashan, Jiangling. After *Wenwu* 1982.10: 1–8, color pl. and fig. 11. Drawings by Li Xiating.

only limited remains of textiles have been found, these materials reflect an amazing sophistication of design and technique.[109] The most significant finds of Warring States textiles were from a small tomb at Mashan 馬山 in Jiangling, Hubei province.[110] Silk fabrics found in the tomb include the cover of the coffin, a silk painting, bags of utensils, dresses on wooden figurines, and the nineteen layers of clothes and quilts used to wrap the corpse of the deceased. These materials have been classified into three groups: plain silk (with a broad range of density from 50 by 30 to 160 by 70 threads per sq. cm), brocades, and gauze. Some brocades integrate geometric patterns of figures, dragons, and birds. Others, especially embroidered pieces, show fluent curvilinear patterns of intertwining animals (Fig. 10.23). Both styles echo the patterns of lacquerware and inlaid bronzes.

The art of jade carving, the origin of which can be traced to prehistoric times, also underwent a profound transformation in both form and function. Some traditional ritual jades, such as the circular *bi* 璧, were still in wide production; but the tiny whorls covering their surfaces reflect the con-

---

[109] For a summary of these finds, see Li Xueqin, *Eastern Zhou and Qin Civilizations*, pp. 359–70.
[110] *Wenwu* 1982.10: 1–8. Chen Yaojun and Zhang Xuqiu, "Jiangling Mazhuan yihaomu chutu de Zhang-guo sizhipin," *Wenwu* 1982.10: 9–11.

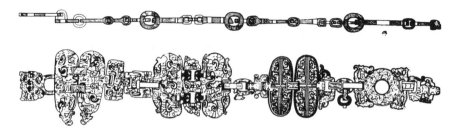

Figure 10.24. Jade ornament from tomb 1 at Leigudun, Suixian, Hubei. Second half of the fifth century B.C. From *Zeng Hou Yi mu* (Beijing: Wenwu, 1989), vol. 1, fig. 250.1.

temporary taste for ornamentation. The transformation of ritual jades was therefore apparently related to another major aspect of Warring States jades: the dominance of personal ornaments. Generally speaking, the production of ornaments had superseded that of ritual instruments, not only in number, but, of greater importance, in the creative energy that they generated. An early Warring States example of extraordinary workmanship was again from Leigudun tomb 1 (Fig. 10.24). Forty-eight cm long, this beltlike ornament consists of sixteen openwork segments lashed together by mortises and bronze hooks. Found next to the head of the deceased, it was likely to have been part of an elaborate headdress. Other jade ornaments of the Warring States period include pendants, garment hooks, and rings, as well as fittings on daggers and swords. Various dragon pendants with their gracefully curved bodies and projecting scrolling fins became widespread during the fourth century B.C.[111] A famous pectoral necklace from Jincun is formed by three such dragons, in combination with jade tubes that are decorated with scroll patterns, and a pair of jade dancers (Fig. 10.25). Made of highly polished white jade, the two dancers exemplify the increasing use of human images in personal ornamentation, a phenomenon parallel to the use of bronze figures in interior furnishing (Fig. 10.15).

PICTORIAL ART. One of the most important developments of Chinese art during the Eastern Zhou was the emergence of pictorial representation, first on bronze vessels and then on lacquerware and the walls of palace halls. Pictorial bronzes appeared during the sixth century B.C. and lasted for about a century.[112] Although these vessels differ radically from the ornately decorated bronzes of the same period (Figs. 10.11, 10.13, and 10.14), they reflect the same

---

[111] For the development of jade carving during the Eastern Zhou, see Jessica Rawson, *Chinese Jade from the Neolithic to the Qing* (London: British Museum, 1995), pp. 53–75.

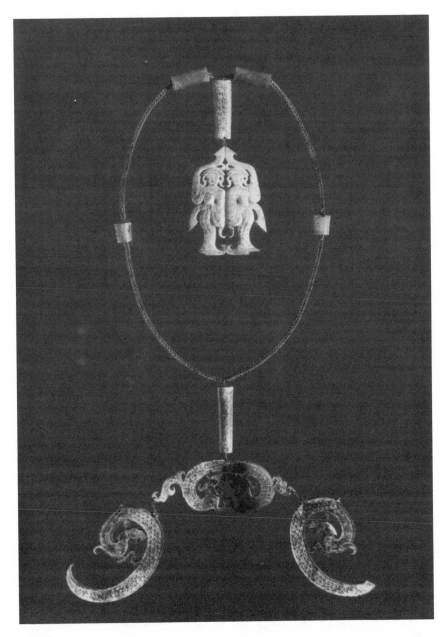

Figure 10.25. Jade and gold pectoral from Jincun, Henan. Ca. fourth century B.C., Freer Gallery of Art, Washington, D.C. From Thomas Lawton, *Chinese Art of the Warring States Period: Change and Continuity, 480–222 B.C.* (Washington, D.C.: Freer Gallery of Art, 1982), p. 132.

tendency toward the autonomy of decoration. In both cases, a bronze vessel supplies a surface for two-dimensional images, which have become the primary visual property of the object.

Various techniques, including casting, incising, and inlay, were employed to delineate pictorial images on bronze vessels. There also appeared at least three major compositional styles. One type of composition consists of inlaid copper images and combat scenes repeated in a series of rectangular frames (Fig. 10.26a). The orderly quality of this design disappears in the second composition, in which a jumbled array of images, animals, birds, and men, fight against one another in confusion. No ground line is seen; the figures and animals are scattered across a wide area of the vessel's surface (Fig. 10.26b). The third and last composition represents large-scale social activities in well-defined pictorial spaces, often centered on a multistoried building standing on the baseline (Fig. 10.26c). Some frequent scenes in this composition, such as shooting contests, the picking of mulberry leaves, sacrificial offerings, and musical and dance performances, probably represent some of the prevailing rituals at the time. Other scenes depict violent warfare: soldiers attack a city or do battle on a river. There are different opinions about the origin of these bronzes and compositions, and their discovery in widespread areas precludes any definitive conclusion. In any event, these objects belonged to a transitional stage in the development of pictorial art. Mainly because of the limitation of bronze as a painting medium, pictorial bronzes were soon replaced by painted lacquer objects, which provided far greater flexibility for artists to create vivid pictorial images.

Painted lacquer objects from Leigudum tomb 1 mark the beginning of this new stage. Among them, a duck-shaped box displays miniature paintings on its two sides, one a dance scene and the other a musical performance (Fig. 10.27). The work demonstrates the artist's awareness of the divergent functions and visual effects of representation and decoration. He painted the two pictorial scenes against an empty background within rectangular frames surrounded by the dense patterns that cover the rest of the vessel. Each picture thus appears as a window through which one glimpses an aspect of court entertainment. In a more general sense, this work signifies a fantastic iconography and the interplay between a variety of artistic styles, two principal features of Eastern Zhou lacquer paintings in the southern area of Chu. The two musicians on the lacquer box are not human figures, but a bird and

---

[112] Charles D. Weber has attributed these vessels to the period from about the third quarter of the sixth century through the mid-fifth century B.C. *Chinese Pictorial Vessels of the Late Chou Period* (Ascona: Artibus Asiae, 1968). Other studies of these vessels include Mary H. Fong, "The Origin of Chinese Pictorial Representation of the Human Figure," *Artibus Asiae* 51 (1989): 5–38; Esther Jacobson, "The Structure of Narrative in Early Chinese Pictorial Vessels," *Representations* 8 (Fall 1984): 61–83.

(a)

(b)

(c)

Figure 10.26. Three types of pictorial bronzes. Sources: (a) Charles D. Weber, *Chinese Pictorial Bronze Vessels of the Late Chou Period* (Ascona: Artibus Asiae, 1968), fig. 63b; (b) ibid., fig. 63a; (c) Wen Fong, ed., *The Great Bronze Age of China* (New York: Metropolitan Museum of Art, 1980), fig. 107.

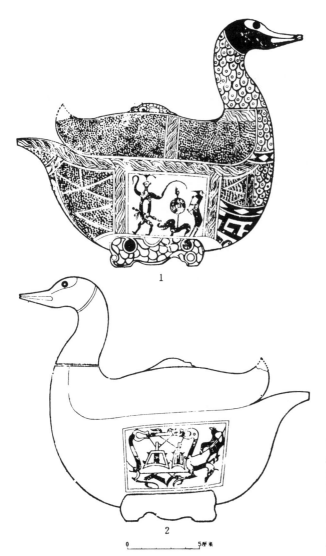

Figure 10.27. Duck-shaped lacquer box from tomb 1 at Leigudun, Suixian, Hubei. Second half of the fifth century B.C. From *Zeng Hou Yi mu,* vol. 1, fig. 224.

a beast. Such strange images and scenes, found on many Chu artifacts including a *se* 瑟 zither from Changtaiguan tomb 1 at Xinyang, have led scholars to relate them to the strong shamanistic tradition in Chu culture, reflected in literature in the vivid descriptions of gods and goddesses, the ancient legends, and the bizarre creatures to be found in the *Chu ci* 楚辭 (Verses of Chu).

    In this respect, the element of the fantastic seems to be linked with the mythical animal images in contemporary sculpture, but it is distinct from other illustrations that though often produced in the south, represent such scenes of daily life as human entertainment, processions, and occasions of greeting. The most outstanding example of this second tradition is a painted lacquer box from Baoshan tomb 2 at Jingmen 荊門, Hubei (Fig. 10.28).[113] Like the duck-shaped vessel from Leigudun, its decoration integrates both geometric and pictorial elements. On the vertical side of the cover, a series of lively human images construct a complex spatial system never, as far as is known, attempted before. The figures are shown either in profile or from the rear; the latter are situated in positions closer to the viewer, either on a chariot to shield a male master, or in the foreground to watch the master walking in front of them. The sense of depth in the painting is created by overlapping images, varying sizes, and separate ground levels. The composition, which is 87.4 cm long but only 5.2 cm high, is further divided by graceful trees into five sections, which may well illustrate the stages of a continuous narrative. The only grouping of two trees seems to indicate the beginning (and the end) of the picture. Reading from right to left, we find that an official in a white robe is taking a tour on a horse-drawn chariot; the horses increase speed and attendants run ahead of them; the chariot then slows down and is greeted by a kneeling figure. Meanwhile, a gentleman wearing a dark robe is on his way to meet the official. In the final scene, the official has descended from the chariot and meets the host; but somehow he is now dressed in a dark robe while the host wears a white robe.

This work shows remarkable advances in both spatial conception and temporal representation. Much like a later handscroll painting, it must be viewed section by section in a sequential order. In fact, various interpretations, including the one just proposed, are largely inspired by its horizontal format and sequential reading, which invite the viewer to read figures and scenes as components of a continuous narrative. This compositional style, as well as the picture's subject matter, thus continued that of the ritual scenes depicted on earlier pictorial bronzes (Fig. 10.26c). In both cases, the impression of the figures' rhythmic movement is enhanced when we shift our gaze along the horizontal baseline over the round surface.

It is possible that murals representing figurative images only appeared during the Eastern Zhou. Based on all excavated examples, Shang and Western Zhou ritual structures were probably decorated with the kinds of zoomorphic and geometric patterns that one finds on contemporary ritual vessels.[114] The recent excavation of the Qin palaces at Xianyang allow us, for the first time, to recognize the brilliance of palace painting during the late

---

[113] *Baoshan Chu mu*, 2 vols. (Beijing: Wenwu, 1991), vol. 1, pp. 144–6, 501–3. Also see Cui Renyi, "Jingmen Baoshan erhaomu chutu de yingbin chuxingtu chulun," *Jiang Han kaogu* 1988.2: 72–9; Chen Zhenyu, "Chu guo chema chuxingtu chulun," *Jiang Han kaogu* 1989.4: 54–63.

[114] For excavated examples of Shang and Western Zhou murals, see Wu Hung et al., *3000 years of Chinese Painting* (New Haven, Conn.: Yale University Press, 1997), pp. 18–19.

Figure 10.28. Pictorial scenes on a lacquer box from tomb 2 at Baoshan, Jingmen, Hubei. Late fourth century B.C. From *Baoshan Chu mu* (Beijing: Wenwu, 1991), vol. 1, fig. 120a, b.

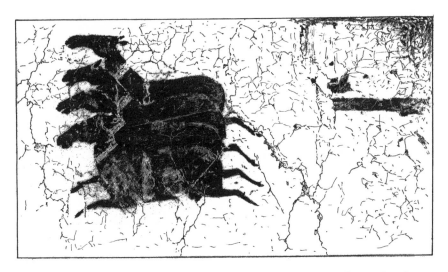

Figure 10.29. Horse chariot mural, in Xianyang Palace no. 3, Xianyang, Shaanxi. Late Eastern Zhou to Qin, third century B.C. After *Zhongguo meishu quanji, Huihua* (Beijing: Wenwu, 1986), 1, fig. 47. Drawing by Li Xiating.

Warring States period and the Qin. In addition to the fragmented murals in palace 1, large pictorial compositions were found along a corridor in palace 3. A surviving section shows a procession of seven chariots, each drawn by four galloping horses (Fig. 10.29); another fragment illustrates a well-proportioned palace lady dressed in a long skirt with a broad lower hem. These colorful images, painted without the help of outlines, are thought to be the earliest examples of the "boneless" (*mo gu* 沒骨) technique in Chinese painting.

ART AND ARCHITECTURE FOR THE DEAD

Ritual canons compiled during the Warring States period and the early Han make a basic distinction between *jili* 吉禮 (auspicious rituals) and *xiongli* 凶 禮 (inauspicious rituals) within the general practice of ancestral worship.[115] The former were conducted in the ancestral temple inside a town and were dedicated to deities of a living community; the latter were carried out in a graveyard and were associated with death and sorrow. This classification of rituals led in turn to a similar kind of classification of ritual architecture and instruments. Thus, the vessels used in ancestral temples were called *jiqi* 祭

---

[115] *Zhou li* 18 ("Chunguan Zongbo"), 1a–11a.

器 (sacrificial vessels), while those furnishing a burial were termed *mingqi*
(spirit vessels) or *guiqi* 鬼器 (vessels for ghosts).[116]

Even during the Shang and Western Zhou, temple and tomb coexisted as
twin centers of ancestral worship; but literary records and archaeological
excavations demonstrate that temple rituals were far more important than
grave sacrifices. This situation changed dramatically during the Eastern
Zhou. The increasing attention paid to funerary rituals and tomb furnishings is revealed by the compilations of detailed codes for mortuary rites; the
appearance of large-scale above-ground structures in graveyards; and the
growing importance of *mingqi*, objects designed and produced specifically
for burials. The Eastern Zhou and especially the Warring States period thus
appears to be a crucial transitional period in the history of Chinese art and
architecture, during which the focus of ritual art shifted from the lineage
temple to the family graveyard. This transition, the subject of the following
discussion, finally led to the complete dominance of funerary art during the
Qin and Han dynasties.[117]

Architecture: Graves and Graveyards

The *Zhou li* (Rites of Zhou) states that two kinds of graveyards coexisted
during the Zhou dynasty. The first, called *gongmu* 公墓 (royal cemetery), was
the burial site of kings and their descendants. The second, *bangmu* 邦墓
(public cemetery), belonged to a clan or lineage. It may be argued, however,
that the *gongmu* was a special kind of *bangmu*, because it also belonged to a
lineage (the royal one) and because, according to the ritual canon, its internal
organization reflected that lineage's genealogical hierarchy.[118] Archaeologists
have identified some large Eastern Zhou "public cemeteries." The common
characteristic of these burial sites is their systematization: tombs in a graveyard followed a coherent chronological sequence and exhibited a consistent
spatial orientation. For example, 558 tombs at Yutaishan 兩台山 in Jiangling
were densely located in a narrow graveyard 80 m wide by 1,050 m long. Sometimes two grave pits were so close that only a 30-cm earthen wall separated
them. Similar phenomena have been observed at other places, such as Shangcunling 上村嶺 in Sanmenxia 三門峽, Henan; Baqitun 八旗屯 in Fengxiang,

---

[116] *Li ji* 8 ("Tangong 1"), 9b, (Legge, *Li Chi*, vol. 1, p. 151). This classification of ancestral sacrifices may
have been related to a theory of the soul. A passage in the *Li ji*, 47 ("Jiyi"), 14b–15a, explains that *gui*
(ghost) means the *po* soul that remains underground after one's death, while the *shen* (spirit, divinity)
flies on high and becomes a divine being. "Once this opposition is established, two kinds of rituals
are framed in accordance and [different] sacrifices are regulated." See Wu Hung, *Monumentality in
Early Chinese Art and Architecture*, pp. 111–12.

[117] For a general observation of art and architecture in their religious context during the ancient and early
imperial periods, see Wu Hung, *Monumentality in Early Chinese Art and Architecture*, pp. 44–250.

[118] *Zhou li* 22 ("Chunguan Zongbo"), 1a–5b.

Shaanxi; and Erligang in Zhengzhou, Henan.[119] The internal regularity of these graveyards apparently resulted from the work of ritual specialists, perhaps the Tomb Officers (*Mudafu* 墓大夫) mentioned in the *Zhou li*.[120]

Such large clan or lineage cemeteries, however, seem to have been seriously challenged during the Warring States period. A symptom of their decline was the increasing independence of smaller groups of burials, presumably belonging to extended or nuclear families, inside a clan graveyard.[121] This phenomenon was most obvious in the cemeteries of royal lineages, which became increasingly fragmented during this period. Sometimes, as in the states of Qin, Yan, and Qi, changes in the capital site or an irregularity in the royal succession led to the establishment of new state cemeteries. Elsewhere, as in the cases of Zhongshan and Wei, a ruler's mausoleum was completely divorced from or only loosely related to the tombs of other members of the royal lineage. This change in burial pattern had a profound impact on funerary architecture: the basic unit of architectural design became increasingly smaller, focusing on individual mausoleums and the funerary parks (*lingyuan* 陵園) that housed them. The intense attention paid to individual tombs was reflected in the three essential aspects of a burial: its appearance above ground, its tomb chambers underground, and the selection and arrangement of its grave goods.

DESIGNS OF ROYAL CEMETERIES. The record in the *Liji* (Records of ritual) that "the ancients made graves only and raised no mounds over them" has been proven by archaeological excavations.[122] Except for some isolated cases in the southeast that indicated an indigenous custom,[123] Shang and Western Zhou tombs lacked tumuli and had very limited above-ground architectural components. Although sometimes a wooden-framed building, perhaps an offering shrine, was constructed over the grave pit, it was tiny and stood on level ground or on a low foundation.[124] This basic design survived in the Qin during the Spring and Autumn and early Warring States periods. Thirty-two Qin royal mausoleums in thirteen "funerary parks" were located near the state capital, Yong, at present-day Fengxiang in

---

[119] *Kaogu* 1980.5: 391–402.   [120] *Zhou li*, 22 ("Chunguan Zongbo"), 4b.

[121] See Ou Yan, "Zhanguo shiqi de muzang," *Beifang wenwu* 1989.3: 35.

[122] *Li ji* 6 ("Tangong 1"), 7a (Legge, *Li Chi*, vol. 1, p. 123).

[123] Tumuli built of pebbles and earth have been found over some middle Western Zhou burials in Jiangsu and Anhui. But these tombs had no pits and the grave goods were placed on a prepared ground. They thus differed markedly from vertical-pit graves and belonged to an indigenous tradition. For excavation reports, see *Kaogu xuebao* 1959.4: 59–90; *Kaogu* 1977.5: 292–7; *Kaogu* 1979.2: 107–18; *Kaogu* 1976.4: 274; *Wenwu ziliao congkan* 2 (1978): 66–9; *Kaogu* 1978.3: 151–4.

[124] For example, the building over the tomb of Fuhao 婦好 was only about 5 m on each side; neither walls nor other architectural remains have been observed around this structure. *Yinxu Fu Hao mu* (Beijing: Wenwu, 1980), pp. 4–6. Remains of small above-ground mortuary houses from the later Shang dynasty

Shaanxi.[125] The funerary parks shared a standard architectural plan, and the largest (*lingyuan* 1) may be taken as an example. This funerary park occupied an area of 200,000 sq. m and was surrounded by a continuous ditch, sometimes 7 m in depth. Within this enclosure, a group of tombs and sacrificial pits was centered on an enormous mausoleum (tomb 1), whose underground chamber was 40 m wide, 60 m long, and 24 m deep, with two sloping ramps stretching out toward the east and west. No trace of the tumulus remains. Instead, post holes and other architectural remains indicate a large wooden-framed structure that once stood in front of the mouth of the grave pit.

A later funerary park was excavated in 1950 at Guweicun in Huixian, Henan province. Generally believed to be the mausoleum of a king of Wei 魏 who died in the mid-Warring States period, the graveyard occupied a walled space of 600 m on each side.[126] There may have been an inner wall surrounding a foundation built of rammed earth. Running for 135 m north to south and 150 m east to west, this foundation once supported three individual halls built over three grave pits. The central and largest hall, presumably belonging to the king, measured 27.5 m on each side. It was a timber structure with a tiled roof; a row of posts divided the facade into seven bays. The other two halls, probably belonging to two royal consorts, both had a square floor plan but differed slightly in size, one stretching for 19 m and the other for 17.7 m on each side. Instead of seven bays, they have only five bays on the facade. Significantly, the social status of the deceased was symbolized by the size and form of his or her funerary shrine.

Regardless of their many differences, these two groups of Qin and Wei mausoleums followed the old convention by having no more than a wooden-framed ritual hall built above the ground. They thus retained a traditional appearance, while many contemporary tombs were designed to present a more startling image by erecting tall architectural forms, large tumuli, or terrace pavilions, over the grave pits. It was said that in his travels Confucius saw tomb mounds resembling raised halls or dikes, either covered with a roofed building or in the shape of an axe head.[127] One of these forms, that of a grave covered with a terrace building, is exemplified by a Zhongshan royal mausoleum at Pingshan. Belonging to King Cuo of the late fourth century B.C., it was surrounded by a series of sacrificial pits (Fig. 10.30) and was accompanied by another large tomb to the east, the occupant of which was probably the queen. As with the Wei tombs at Huixian, an elaborate

have also been found in Dasikong village; see Ma Dezhi et al. "1953 nian Anyang Dasikongcun fajue baogao," *Kaogu xuebao* 1953.9: 20.

[125] *Wenwu* 1983.7: 30–7; *Kaogu yu wenwu* 1987.4: 19–28.
[126] *Huixian fajue baogao* (Beijing: Kexue, 1956).
[127] *Li ji* 8 ("Tangong 1"), 16a–b (Legge, *Li Chi*, vol. 1, p. 156).

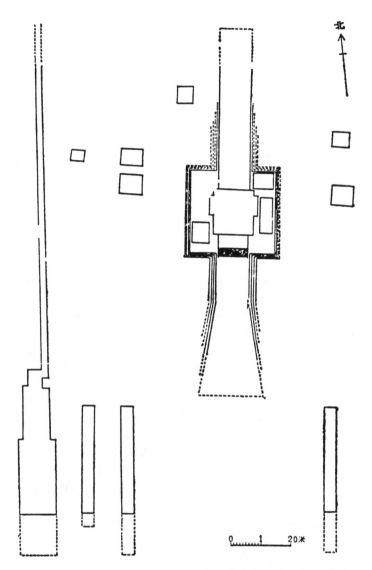

Figure 10.30. Plan of tomb 1 at Zhongshan, Pingshan, Hebei province. From *Wenwu* 1979.1: 2, fig. 3.

architectural complex surmounted the king's grave. But instead of standing on a flat foundation, it was built around an earthen pyramid, 110 m from north to south and 92 m east to west. Although the wooden-framed structure has long vanished, pebbles and fragmented tiles scattered on a 15-m-high mound disclose its past existence.

King Cuo's funerary park was never finished, however, as the kingdom of

Zhongshan perished before its completion. We know this because an engraved copy of the design of his funerary park was found in the tomb (Fig. 10.31); the inscription on this plan (*Zhaoyu tu* 兆域圖) records that another copy of the same design was stored in the palace. Inlaid on a bronze plate about a meter long and half a meter wide, this is the earliest known architectural drawing from ancient China. It details the situation, dimensions, and measurements of the royal cemetery and its various components. An edict inscribed on the plate warns that those who do not follow this design in building the funerary park would be executed without mercy. The severe tone of this edict, along with the appearance of such a funerary architectural plan, signifies an important psychological change: an individual person now saw his or her main interest in his or her own tomb rather than in the lineage temples dedicated to a deceased ancestor. The stern edict issued by the king vividly reflects both his desire to build a great mausoleum for himself and his anxiety about the disloyalty of his descendants.

A number of reconstruction plans of this funerary park have been made on the basis of this design and archaeological excavations (Fig. 10.32).[128] All proposals agree that the cemetery was originally planned to contain five tombs; the king's tomb is in the center, flanked by the tombs of two queens and again by the tombs of two concubines. Each grave is covered by an individual ceremonial hall of the terrace pavilion type. The king's hall, about 200 m square at the base, is built on a three-storied terrace; galleries surround the earthen core at the lowest level, and a free-standing square hall of considerable size stands on top of the pyramid. The five halls are major components of the central area of the funerary park, the *neigong* 內宮 (Inner Palace), which is enclosed by double walls. The outer wall that surrounds the whole structure is over 410 m by 176 m; the inner wall is 340 m by 105 m. Between the two walls and behind the five tombs are four square halls with different names, identifying them as ceremonial offices. This reconstruction demonstrates three basic features of a Warring States royal cemetery. First, each king had an independent funerary park containing his tomb and the tombs of his spouses. Second, a funerary park imitated a palace, with double walls defining the king's private domain and his court. Third, each grave in a funerary park was marked by an above-ground ceremonial structure.

While the Qin and Wei mausoleums at Fengxiang and Guweicun also shared these architectural conventions, the Zhongshan mausoleum signified the major development of mortuary architecture toward verticality during

---

[128] Identified as an example of a *Zhaoyu tu* 兆域圖. For reconstruction plans of the Zhongshan mausoleum, see Yang Hongxun, "Zhanguo Zhongshan wangling ji Zhaoyutu yanjiu," *Kaogu xuebao* 1980.1: 119–37; Fu Xinian, "Zhanguo Zhongshanwang Cuomu chutu de Zhaoyutu ji qi lingyuan guizhi de yanjiu," *Kaogu xuebao* 1980.1: 97–119.

the Warring States period. By building a terrace pavilion over the grave, the mausoleum became much more conspicuous. Two other groups of Warring States mausoleums, one outside the Qi capital of Linzi and the other near the Zhao capital of Handan, were constructed on natural hills and thus fulfilled the desire to achieve a monumental effect to an even greater extent. With such a natural setting these tombs can be properly called *shanling* 山 陵, a term that originally meant "mountains and hills" but, by the Warring States period, came to signify "mountain mausoleums."

The five funerary parks northwest of Handan are believed to be the burials of Zhao kings and their consorts.[129] All built on top of small hills, these mausoleums had large rectangular "grave platforms" (*lingtai* 陵台), ranging from 181 to 340 m in length. Funerary park 3, for example, was a walled architectural complex. A grave platform stood on a steep hill and supported a rectangular tomb mound that rose toward the sky. The particular shape of the mound has reminded scholars of the dike-shaped tumuli that Confucius saw in his travels,[130] but the tiles scattered on its surface also suggest that this was the earthen core of a terrace pavilion. Similarly, the six large tombs southeast of Linzi were also mountain mausoleums; each consisted of a large tumulus (sometimes even now more than 10 m high) above a rectangular platform. These tombs have been tentatively identified as the burials of six Tian Qi 田齊 rulers.[131]

There have been suggestions that the Eastern Zhou Chinese learned to build tomb mounds from the steppe people, who had constructed their tumuli called *kurgan*s at least as early as the sixth century B.C.[132] This opinion may be supported by the dates of the earliest known earthen tomb mounds in China. This architectural feature is seen in a number of large tombs constructed in the fifth century B.C., including a very large one at Hougudui 侯 古堆 in Gushi 固始, Henan, and several that were built inside the Yan capital of Wuyang.[133] Among these examples, the tumulus surmounting tomb 16 in Wuyang is best documented. Measuring 32 by 38 m at the base and 8 m in height, it was rectangular with rounded corners and a flat top. The mound was built of layers of rammed earth in increments of 8 to 22 cm thick. Several other tumuli found in the north had similar shapes and were constructed by

[129] *Kaogu* 1982.6: 597–605.

[130] *Li ji*, 8 ("Tangong 1"), 16b (Legge, *Li Chi*, vol. 1, p. 156).

[131] Zhang Xuehai, "Tian Qi liuling kao," *Wenwu* 1984.9: 20–2.

[132] See Sekino Takeshi, "Chûgoku ni okeru funkyû no seisei," in *Chûgoku kôkogaku kenkyû* (Tokyo: Tokyo University Press, 1963), pp. 563–91; Robert L. Thorp, "Burial Practices of Bronze Age China," in *The Great Bronze Age of China*, ed. Wen Fong, pp. 58–9.

[133] For archaeological reports, see *Wenwu* 1981.1: 1–8; *Kaogu xuebao* 1965.2: 79–102. Other tumuli of the same period have been found at Huainan 淮南, Anhui, and at Lünan 呂南, in Shandong. See *Kaogu* 1963.4: 204–12; *Kaogu xuebao* 1978.3: 317–36.

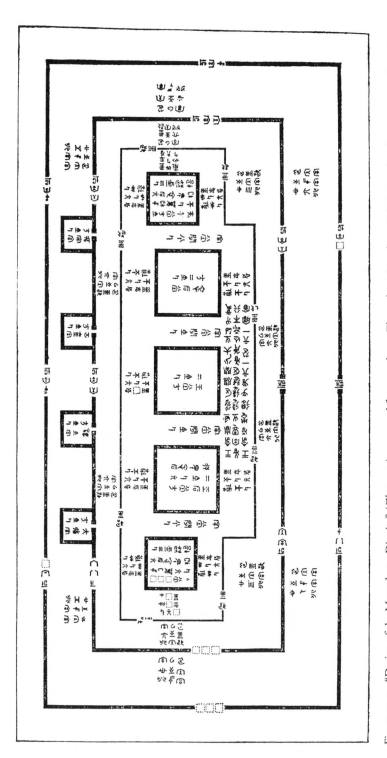

Figure 10.31. "Design of the Mausoleum District" (*Zhaoyu tu*), excavated from tomb 1 at Zhongshan, Pingshan, Hebei. Late fourth century B.C. From Yang Hongxun. "Zhanguo Zhongshan wangling ji Zhaoyutu yan jiu," *Wenwu* 1979.1: 23.

中山王𓊝陵園全景想像圖之二　王堂三層.用飛陛疊上王堂百積軼大

Figure 10.32. A reconstruction of tomb 1 at Zhongshan. From Fu Xinian, "Zhanguo Zhongshanwang Cuo mu chutu de Zhaoyutu jiqi lingyuan guizhi de yanjiu," *Kaogu xuebao* 1980.1: 110.

using the same technique, though some Chu tomb mounds in the south were not rammed solid and were hemispherical in shape.[134] While these may suggest certain regional variations, tumuli as a general architectural type became increasingly prevalent in various areas during the Warring States period. The term *ling* 陵 was first used for the mausoleum of Zhao Su Hou 趙肅侯, who died in 326 B.C.[135] This term then became the standard designation for royal mausoleums of the Warring States. In Qin, Huiwen 惠文 (d. 311 B.C.) was the title of the first ruler who assumed the title of king; it is perhaps not surprising that his tomb was also the first Qin royal mausoleum to be called a *ling*.[136]

Gong Ling 公陵 (Royal Mausoleum) and Yong Ling 永陵 (Eternal Mausoleum), being the resting places of King Huiwen and his son King Wu 武 of Qin, were not part of the royal cemetery at Yong; by their time Qin had moved its capital to Xianyang, and these two kings were buried near that site. Large tumuli distinguish their tombs from the earlier royal mausoleums at Fengxiang. Their examples were followed by the last three Qin kings before the First Emperor.[137] These three rulers, Zhao 昭 (r. 306–251 B.C.), Xiaowen 孝文 (r. 250 B.C.), and Zhuangxiang 莊襄 (r. 249–247 B.C.) were buried in Zhiyang 芷陽 in present-day Lintong 臨潼. According to archaeological surveys, their mausoleums continued two traditional features of the Fengxiang tombs: each funerary park was encircled by ditches and contained a ritual building. The difference, however, is that the graves in the Zhiyang group were marked by large tomb mounds.[138] It may be significant that the tomb mounds in Qin royal mausoleums began to appear not so long after the time when Shang Yang had instituted his political reforms, which included an estate system to regulate funerary design. According to this system, the height of a tomb mound and the trees planted on it should symbolize the rank of the deceased, such rank being determined not by his inherited status but by his contribution to public service.[139]

As with the development of contemporary palaces, the growing political significance and physical presence of the tomb was related to the social and religious transformation that was taking place during the Eastern Zhou. As

---

[134] For a survey of these and other archaeological excavations, see Wang Shimin, "Zhongguo Chunqiu Zhanguo shidai de zhongmu," *Kaogu* 1981.5: 459–66.

[135] *Shi ji*, 43, p. 1802.

[136] *Shi ji*, 6, pp. 288–9.

[137] *Shi ji*, 6, p. 289; *Kaogu yu wenwu* 1987.4: 86–8.

[138] *Kaogu yu wenwu* 1986.4: 19–28.

[139] *Shangjun shu*, 19 ("Jingnei") (Sibu beiyao ed.), 2b. According to *Zhou li*, 22 ("Chunguan Zongbo"), 2a, the *zhongren*, or the officer in change of tombs, was "to regulate the measurement of the tumuli and the number of trees [planted in the graveyards] according to the rank of the deceased." For Qin funerary systems, see Ma Zhenzhi, "Shilun Qin guo lingqin zhidu de xingcheng ji tedian," *Kaogu yu wenwu* 1989.5: 110–17.

discussed in earlier chapters, during this period the Zhou royal house grad-ually declined, and society was no longer united in a hierarchical genealogi-cal structure. Political struggles were waged by families and individuals who gained power from their control of economic resources and military force, not from noble ancestry. The old religious institutions and symbols could no longer convey political messages and were consequently replaced or com-plemented by new ideas. The lineage-temple system declined, and tombs belonging to families and individuals became symbols of the new social elite. In this sense, the Qin estate system of funerary architecture best reveals the essential difference between a Warring States mausoleum and a traditional ancestral temple: a temple represented a person's clan heritage, while the tomb demonstrated his personal accomplishments. As individual ambition increased, so did the height of the funerary structures soar. The *Lü shi chunqiu* 呂氏春秋 (Mr. Lü's Spring and Autumn [annals]), a miscellany com-piled at the end of the Warring States period, describes vividly the conse-quence of this development:

Nowadays when people make burials, they erect tumuli tall and huge as mountains and plant trees dense and luxuriant as a forest. They arrange tower-gates and court-yards and build halls and chambers with flights of steps for visitors. Their cemeter-ies are like towns and cities! This may be a way of making a display of their wealth to the world, but how could they serve the deceased [with such extravagance]![140]

In the great Lishan 驪山 mausoleum of the First Qin Emperor, tomb building reached its point of culmination.

UNDERGROUND TOMB STRUCTURES. Compared with the aboveground remains of Warring States tombs, far more materials are available for study-ing their underground sections. More than 6,000 large and small Eastern Zhou tombs are reported to have been discovered in China. But to understand general conventions and changes in mortuary customs, the most systematic data are provided by large burial sites covering long time spans. Among such sites, the 260 tombs discovered along Zhongzhou Road in Luoyang, dating from the Spring and Autumn to the end of the Warring States period, have allowed archaeologists to establish a developmental sequence of burial struc-ture and furnishings in the Zhou capital area.[141] Not far from Luoyang, some 600 tombs have been discovered in the territory of the state of Wei, includ-ing large burial sites at Huixian, Jixian 汲縣, Shaanxian 陝縣, and Zhengzhou.[142] These Wei tombs can be compared with the 81 Zhao tombs

---

[140] *Lü shi chunqiu* 10 ("An si"); Chen Qiyou, *Lü shi chunqiu jiaozhu* (Taipei: Huazheng, 1988), pp. 535–6.
[141] *Luoyang Zhongzhoulu*, pp. 128–30.
[142] For reports on these sites, see *Shanbiaozhen yu Liulige, Huixian fajue baogao, Zhengzhou Erligang* (Beijing: Kexue, 1959); *Wenwu* 1955.10: 3–23; *Kaogu* 1958.11: 74.

of the middle and late Warring States period at Baijiacun 百家村 and Qicun 齊村 in Handan and some 30 Hann tombs of the late Spring and Autumn to late Warring States period at Fenshuiling 分水嶺 in Changzhi 長治.[143] To the west, more than 500 Qin tombs have been excavated in Shaanxi province. In addition to the royal cemeteries at Fengxiang and Lintong, important finds include the 90 tombs at Baqitun and Gaozhuang 高莊 near Fengxiang 風翔 and the 219 tombs at Keshengzhuang 客省莊, Banpo 半坡, Beizhaizi 北寨子, and Lijiaya 李家崖 in the Xi'an 西安, Baoji 寶雞 area.[144] A periodization of Qin tombs has been attempted on the basis of these materials.[145]

In the east and northeast, large cemeteries are known inside and outside Linzi and Wuyang, the capitals of the Qi and Yan, respectively. But only a few tombs have been scientifically examined. Among group burials excavated in Shandong and Hebei, those at Dongyueshi 東岳石 in Pingdu 平度, Jiagezhuang 賈各莊 in Tangshan 唐山, Zhangguizhuang 張貴莊 in Tianjin 天津, and Huairou 懷柔 in Beijing are most significant, each site containing 20 to 30 middle- and small-sized tombs.[146] In comparison, archaeology of grave sites has achieved much greater success in the southern provinces of Hubei and Hunan, which were within the domain of Chu during the Warring States period. According to an estimate made in 1984, more than 4,000 Chu tombs have been discovered, over 70 percent of the total number of excavated Eastern Zhou burials.[147] Among these, 554 are at Yutaishan in Jiangliang and 297 at Zhaojiahu 趙家湖 in Dangyang 當陽.[148] While these two sites are situated in the Chu capital area, the 1,800 tombs discovered in Changsha, Hunan, provide important data regarding Chu burial customs in a regional center.[149]

Given how numerous and widespread these excavated tombs are, it is rather surprising to find that their construction basically followed the design of the vertical-pit grave, which had been firmly established in China since the Shang and Western Zhou dynasties. It may indeed be argued that during the greater part of the preimperial periods, the vertical-pit burial was one of the most important ritual conventions of the homogeneous Chinese cultural

---

[143] For reports on these sites, see *Kaogu* 1959.10: 535–6; 1962.12: 613–34; 1964.3: 37; *Kaogu xuebao* 1957.1: 103–18; 1974.2: 63–86; *Wenwu* 1972.4: 38–46.

[144] For reports on these sites, see *Wenwu ziliao congkan* 2 (1978): 75–91; 3 (1980): 67–85; *Kaogu* 1955.2: 34–7; *Wenwu* 1980.9: 10–14; *Kaogu yu wenwu* 1981.1: 12–38; *Fengxi fajue baogao*; *Kaogu xuebao* 1957.3: 63–92.

[145] Han Wei, "Lüelun Shaanxi Chunqiu Zhanguo Qin mu," *Kaogu yu wenwu* 1981.1: 83–93.

[146] For reports on these sites, see *Kaogu* 1962.10: 513–18; 1965.2: 65; *Kaogu xuebao* 1953.6: 62–5; *Wenwu* 1957.3: 66–9.   [147] See *Xin Zhongguo de kaogu faxian he yanjiu* (Beijing: Wenwu, 1984), p. 304.

[148] For reports on these sites, see *Kaogu* 1980.5: 391–402; Gao Yingqin and Wang Guanggao, "Danyang Zhaojiahu Chu mu de fenlei fenqi de niandai," *Zhongguo Kaogu xuehui di er ci nianhui lunwenji* (Beijing: Wenwu, 1981), pp. 41–50.

[149] For reports, see *Changsha fajue baogao*; *Kaogu xuebao* 1959.1: 41–60.

complex, albeit with many variations due to regional, temporal, or social differences. Radically different burial forms, such as cist graves, boat-coffin burials, and a type of burial known as *xuanguan zang* 懸棺葬 (in which a coffin is supported by wooden stakes against a cliff) were most frequently observed in the border regions and signified alien cultural identities.[150]

Although the vertical pit structure still generally dominated Warring States funerary architecture, this period also witnessed the beginning of two new burial conventions, denoted by archaeologists as the "cave-chamber tomb" (*dongshi mu* 洞室墓) and the "hollow-brick tomb" (*kongxinzhuan mu* 空心 磚墓; that is, a tomb built of hollow bricks). Both types emerged as variations of the vertical-pit grave. A hollow-brick tomb retained a vertical shaft, merely substituting a brick encasement for the customary wooden one. The horizontal coffin room of a cave-chamber grave, on the other hand, possibly developed from the wall niche of a vertical-pit grave.[151] Increasing archaeological information also shows that the hollow-brick tombs were mainly distributed in eastern Henan in the late Warring States period, while the cave-chamber graves first emerged in southern Shaanxi around the middle of the Warring States period.[152] Once having developed into the dominant burial structure in Qin, the cave-chamber type spread eastward into Henan; but there it could never challenge the traditional vertical-pit structure.[153] During the Warring States period, therefore, these two tomb types were strictly regional phenomena. Judging from the small size and poor furnishing of the excavated examples, both types enjoyed popularity mainly among commoners.

Vertical-pit tombs had many shapes. The walls of their rectangular shafts were either smooth, carved into steps, or furnished with niches for the placement of grave goods. The size of the tombs varied remarkably depending on the status of the deceased. Social factors also determined other formal and structural attributes of a burial, such as the layers of the coffin assemblage, the addition of ramps, and the accompanying sacrificial pits.[154] A striking phenomenon of Warring States vertical-pit graves is the enormous difference in their scale and furnishing. During the fourth and third centuries B.C. espe-

---

[150] For introductions to these different kinds of burials, see K. C. Chang, *The Archaeology of Ancient China*, 3d ed. (New Haven, Conn.: Yale University Press, 1977), pp. 387–470; Li Yujie, *Xian Qin sangzang zhidu yanjiu* (Luoyang: Zhongzhou guji, 1991), pp. 201–36.

[151] *Kaogu xuebao* 1955.9: 109–10; K. C. Chang, *The Archaeology of Ancient China*, pp. 359–61.

[152] See Ou Yan, "Zhanguo shiqi de muzang," pp. 29–35; Teng Mingyu, "Guanzhong Qin mu yanjiu," *Kaogu xuebao*, 1992.3: 281–300.

[153] For example, out of twenty-nine late Warring States tombs excavated along Zhongzhou Road in Luoyang, only three belonged to the cave-chamber type. Among the fifty-nine late Warring States tombs discovered at Shaogou, sixteen are cave-chamber graves. See Ye Xiaoyan, "Qin mu chutan," *Kaogu* 1982.1: 65–73; also see Han Wei, "Lüelun Shaanxi Chunqiu Zhanguo Qin mu," 83–93.

[154] For statements about the correspondence between funerary architecture and social status, see *Mozi*, 25

cially, the majority of tombs in a cemetery became crudely constructed and poorly equipped. For example, among the 260 tombs excavated along Zhongzhou Road in Luoyang, most burials containing bronze vessels and chariot fittings belonged to the Spring and Autumn period; the only exception was a tomb dated to the early fifth century B.C. The overwhelming majority of Warring States burials at this site, 88 in all, had no significant grave goods; some of these tombs were tiny, others did not even contain coffins.

Such changes in the tomb structure and furnishing have been explained in terms of the decline of the Zhou royal house.[155] But this interpretation ignores contemporary tombs in Luoyang, which were huge and extravagantly furnished. Several such tombs found in 1957 at the northeastern corner of the Royal City have been dated to the middle to late Warring States period. One of them had a rectangular pit 9 m by 10 m at the opening, with a 40-m-long ramp extending to the south. The walls of the tomb chamber and the ramp were painted with multicolored patterns; pebbles and charcoal surrounded and protected the coffins. Although it had been robbed several times, the excavators still found, among other things, exquisite jade figures and ornaments, as well as a stone tablet inscribed with the two characters *tianzi* 天子 (Son of Heaven) in ink.[156]

But even this tomb is inferior to the famous Jincun tombs. Found by chance in 1928 at Luoyang, these tombs yielded numerous objects of astonishing artistic quality (Figs. 10.21 and 10.25).[157] The eight large graves at Jincun, assigned the numbers I–VIII, had similar shapes, each with a rectangular pit and a ramp to the south. Three tombs, I, V, and VII, had additional horse pits flanking the ramps. Bishop White has left a detailed description of tomb V, which can be tentatively dated to the mid-Warring States period.[158] The ramp of the tomb was 250 feet long, connected with a 40-foot-square grave pit at the tomb opening. Inside the pit, an octagonal wooden burial chamber, with a door in front, was built above a thick layer of slate and surrounded by pebbles and charcoal. The interior was painted brown; bronze disks and glass ornaments decorated the upper edge of the walls. These richly furnished mausoleums are in sharp contrast with the small tombs along Zhongzhou Road, suggesting that very wide differences in the

---

("Jiezang"), 9b–10a (Burton Watson, trans., *Mo Tzu: Basic Writings* [New York: Columbia University Press, 1963], p. 67); *Xunzi* 19 ("Lilun"), (Sibu beiyao ed.), 6b–7a (Burton Watson, trans., *Hsün Tzu: Basic Writings* [New York: Columbia University Press, 1963], p. 97).

[155] See *Xin Zhongguo de kaogu faxian he yanjiu*, p. 281.

[156] For the excavation report, see *Kaogu* 1959.12: 653–7.

[157] For Jincun materials, see Umehara, *Rakuyô Kinson kobô shûei*; William Charles White, *Tombs of Old Loyang* (Shanghai: Kelly & Walsh, 1934).

[158] This date is based on similar tombs found in the Luoyang area. See Li Xueqin, *Eastern Zhou and Qin Civilizations*, p. 33.

style of burial arrangements set in during the fourth and third centuries B.C. Similar situations can be observed in other regions. For example, the 219 burials excavated at Keshengzhuang, Banpo, Baizhaizi, and Lijiaya in Shaanxi maintained the Qin burial conventions established during the Spring and Autumn and early Warring States period; it was only the scale of the tombs and the amount of furnishings that changed dramatically. With one exception, none of these tombs yielded any bronze vessels, weapons, musical instruments, or horse and chariot fittings. Many tombs had no furnishings at all, or merely a few pottery utensils and small ornaments.

These and other small vertical-pit graves found throughout the country were constructed to meet the minimum requirements for a burial. Large tombs, on the other hand, demonstrated far greater innovation and variation in both structure and furnishing. Although still vertical-pit graves, these were designed individually to satisfy their patrons' specific concerns with the afterlife. Most technical, architectural, and artistic innovations in burial practices during the Warring States period, therefore, were necessarily reflected in these large tombs. In terms of construction technique, the material of their walls and foundations was not only firmly rammed; sometimes it was also fired and plastered. Beginning in the fifth century B.C., the wooden burial chamber was frequently sealed with stone, charcoal, and clay. The layered wooden burial encasements called *guan* 棺 and *guo* 槨 became increasingly more complex, sometimes growing into a series of roomlike chambers that were intended for different purposes. The large grave also appeared as the focus of auxiliary burials of both human sacrifices and ritual offerings.

Very few large tombs of this period, however, have survived intact; still fewer have been scientifically excavated and thoroughly documented. Leigudun tomb 1 at Suixian, the burial of Zeng Hou Yi, is one rare example that not only yielded numerous works of art, but also provided invaluable information about a complete mortuary context.[159] Several objects from this tomb discussed earlier (Figs. 10.10, 10.24, and 10.27) belonged to an enormous set of funerary furnishings, the relationship of which with the tomb's structure provides important clues to understanding specific conceptions of the afterlife. This tomb was dug into a small hill. A group of wooden chambers, 13 m below ground level at the bottom of the vertical shaft, were built with large timbers and sealed by a fill of charcoal and then by a layer of clay. The configuration of these chambers differed from the typical design of

---

[159] Although this tomb was looted once, the robbers only pierced the northeast corner of the tomb's central chamber and took few, if any, objects out. For the excavation report, see *Zeng Hou Yi mu*; for an English introduction to the tomb, see Robert L. Thorp, "The Sui Xian Tomb: Re-Thinking the Fifth Century," *Artibus Asiae* 43, 5 (1981): 67–92.

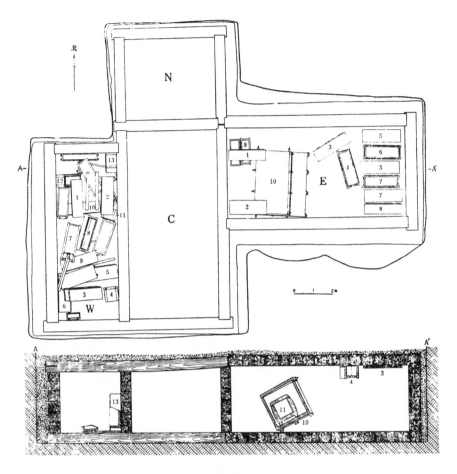

图五 曾侯乙墓平、剖面图
N.北室 C.中室 E.东室 1—8.陪葬棺 9.殉狗棺 10、11.墓主棺 W.西室 1—13.陪葬棺

Figure 10.33. Plan of tomb 1 at Leigudun, Suixian, Hubei. From *Zeng Hou Yi mu* (Beijing: Wenwu, 1989), vol. 1, fig. 5.

Warring States tombs. Instead of having a series of wooden boxes tightly packed one inside the other in a rectangular space, the four chambers in Leigudun tomb 1 were conceived as four adjacent rooms (Fig. 10.33). Over 3 m tall, these chambers were tall enough for an adult to enter. Rows of hooks fixed on the walls suggest that fabric hangings may have originally decorated these chambers. The function of each room is indicated by the objects it contained. The central room, 4.75 m wide by 9.75 m long, mirrored the formal audience hall in the residence of the deceased. Being the largest chamber of the four, it contained most of the ritual bronzes, as well as the very great set of bronze bells and an accompanying set of chimestones, two musical instruments that were essential for a ritual orchestra. The north chamber was an armory, storing most of the 4,500 items of weaponry, shields, and armor, as well as horse and chariot fittings. The west chamber supplied an underground harem, concealing the bodies of thirteen young women in their respective lacquer coffins. Eight more women and a dog were found in coffins in the east room, the main burial chamber that also housed Hou Yi's enormous coffin (Fig. 10.34a). The musical instruments buried here included five large zithers (*se* 瑟), two small zithers (*qin* 琴), two mouth organs (*xiao* 簫), and a flat drum. Unlike the ritual orchestra in the central chamber, these melodical instruments found inside the private quarter may have been used in informal performances that probably involved singing.[160]

Although these underground chambers reflect the internal divisions of a residence, they do not imitate their worldly counterparts to exact scale. For instance, small openings at the base of the interior walls symbolize doorways, but they are not life-size. There must have been a conscious decision to use such openings to link individual spaces in the tomb: not only do they penetrate all the partition walls between the four rooms, but the lord's outer coffin also bears a rectangular hole, 34 by 25 cm, and his inner coffin is painted with doors and windows with lattice patterns (Fig. 10.34). Similar openings in either architectural or painted form have been found in at least a dozen other Chu tombs.[161] Since these tombs were all later than Leigudun tomb 1, dating from the fourth to second centuries B.C., it is likely that the representation of these symbolic passageways in burials was a Warring States and early Han phenomenon, possibly related to a belief in the autonomous nature of the soul after death. According to this belief, when a person dies, his *hun* 魂 soul would fly away but his *po* 魄 soul would be attached to the corpse to be buried underground.[162] The series of doorways in Leigudun tomb 1 seems to indicate the mobility of the *po* within the tomb's physical confines.

Subsequent to Leigudun tomb 1, a series of large Chu tombs discovered in Henan, Hubei, and Hunan all had tomb mounds and large grave pits, sometimes 20 m square, at the tomb opening.[163] Usually, the overall rectangular wooden encasement was subdivided into a number of "chambers," or "rooms" (*shi* 室). The tomb of Chu You Wang 楚幽王 (r. 237–28 B.C.) had nine rooms, representing the highest level of these structures. The slightly

---

[160] See Lothar von Falkenhausen, "Chu Ritual Music," in *New Perspectives on Chu Culture During the Eastern Zhou Period*, ed. Thomas Lawton (Washington, D.C.: Arthur M. Sackler Gallery, 1991), p. 82.

[161] See Alain Thote, "The Double Coffin of Leigudun Tomb No. 1: Iconographic Sources and Related Problems," in Thomas Lawton, *New Perspectives on Chu Culture*, pp. 26–7.

[162] *Li ji*, 47 ("Jiyi"), 14a–15a (Legge, *Li Chi*, vol. 2, pp. 220–1).

[163] These large tombs are found at Tianxingguan, Tengdian 藤店, and Wangshan in Jiangling, Hubei

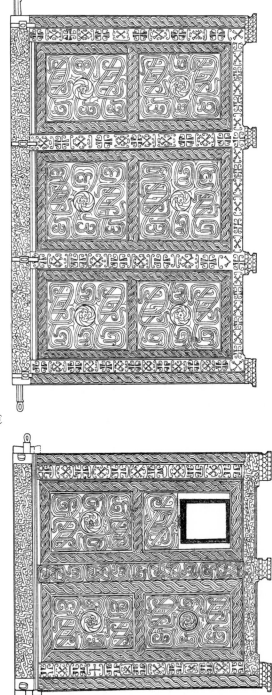

(a)

Figure 10.34. Coffins of Zeng Hou Yi in tomb 1 at Leigudun. (a) Outer coffin, (b) inner coffin. From *Zeng Hou Yi mu* (Beijing: Wenwu, 1989), vol. 1, figs. 14–15, 20–1. Drawings of outer coffin by Li Xiating.

(b)

Figure 10.34. (cont.)

less elaborate tombs, such as those discovered at Changtaiguan in Xinyang and at Tianxingguan 天星觀 in Jiangling, had seven rooms. Other Chu tombs, including some early Han examples, consisted of five or fewer rooms. It is possible that in Chu during this period, the number of rooms in a tomb symbolized the rank of the occupant.[164] As in Leigudun tomb 1, the symbolic functions of these rooms are suggested by their furnishings. At least seven Chu tombs, moreover, have yielded grave inventory lists (*qiance* 遣冊) written on bamboo strips, which help to identify not only individual items that were buried but also the internal divisions of the burial.

For example, twenty-seven bamboo strips found in Baoshan tomb 2 (316 B.C.) register grave goods.[165] Instead of forming a single continuous document, they were divided into four lists, stored in different compartments around the central burial chamber. The list in the east room identifies this place as the food chamber (*sishi* 飤室) and includes bronze vessels of the food chamber (*sishi zhi jin* 飤室之金) and food in the food chamber (*sishi zhi shi* 飤室之食). The list in the west room states, "Objects in this rear [compartment] of the casket are used in traveling," and it was in this room that the excavators found various intimate objects that one would take on a journey. The bronze and lacquer objects from the south chamber are identified as paraphernalia used in the *Dazhao* 大兆 ceremony, held in front of the ancestral temple of the deceased before the entombment of his coffin. The final list, also from the south chamber, registers the horses and chariots used in the funerary procession. It seems that the south chamber stored the equipment used in the funerary rituals, while the items in the other three chambers were intended to provide comforts for the life hereafter.

No comparable grave inventory lists have been found in northern tombs. Moreover, most known large tombs in the north had been looted before excavation, making a thorough investigation of their architectural design and symbolism difficult. Nevertheless, some of these examples, such as the two Zhongshan mausoleums at Pingshan, have left remains that are sufficient to demonstrate a coherent design. These two Zhongshan mausoleums (tombs 1 and 6) are among the largest vertical-pit graves ever discovered in ancient China.[166] As mentioned earlier, unlike most southern tombs that had round earthen tumuli, each of the graves at Zhongshan was surmounted by a multi-storied terrace pavilion (Fig. 10.32). Their underground sections also show

province, Niuxingshan 牛形山 in Xiangxiang 湘鄉, Hunan province, and Changtaiguan in Xinyang, Henan province. For a general introduction, see Peng Hao, "Chu mu zangzhi chulun," in *Zhongguo Kaogu xuehui di er ci nianhui lunwenji* (Beijing: Wenwu, 1982), pp. 33–40; Guo Dewei, "Chu mu fenlei wenti tantao," *Kaogu* 1983.3: 249–59; *Xin Zhongguo de kaogu faxian he yanjiu*, pp. 308–10.

[164] Guo Dewei, "Chu mu fenlei wenti tantao," pp. 251–4.   [165] *Baoshan Chu mu*, pp. 369–371.

[166] For the archaeological report, see *Wenwu* 1979.1: 1–13.

marked differences from southern tombs. Each mausoleum is an architectural complex, in which the main burial was accompanied by two groups of auxiliary burials, one for human companions and the other containing material offerings. In the case of King Cuo's mausoleum (Fig. 10.30), the main burial, tomb 1, was surrounded at the north side by small tombs of five women, whose heads were all directed toward the king in the central tomb.

The relatively rich furnishings in these five tombs have led the excavators to identify their occupants as the king's consorts. Following this line of argument, one may also assume that the sixth and last burial in this group belonged to a maid servant: it was located further away from the main burial and contained only coarse pottery vessels. The second group of auxiliary burials consisted of a series of sacrificial pits, arranged on a straight line south of the main burial. Two long wooden-framed trenches, located symmetrically in front of the king's tomb, constituted an underground royal stable. Each probably contained twelve horses and four chariots, as well as a tent and weapons. Next to the stable was a slightly shorter trench, again an underground post-and-beam structure, which stored the king's hunting facilities, including two hunting dogs with gold and silver neck rings. A boat pit lay further west. The three large and two small boats found in the surviving section were probably only part of the royal fleet. A long ditch extending to the north may have allowed water to flow into this underground harbor.

Each of the two Zhongshan tombs had two ramps along the north–south axis. In King Cuo's tomb, the wooden chamber, 14.9 m north–south by 13.5 m east–west, was sealed by stone walls, 1.5 to 2.1 m thick on the four sides and 90 cm on top. This stone envelope, however, failed to prevent tomb robbers, who not only looted but also burned the tomb's central chamber. Fortunately, two independent storage rooms (*ku* 庫) on either side of the central chamber remained intact and yielded a huge array of ritual objects and luxury goods (Figs. 10.14, 10.17, 10.18, and 10.19). The other Zhongshan mausoleum (tomb 6) was likewise looted; however, more architectural details have remained to suggest that the entire tomb was modeled on a palace structure. In particular, rows of columns built of clay bricks lined the ramps as well as the walls of the tomb chamber. Without any practical structural function, these columns served the symbolic role of transforming the tomb into a wooden-framed palace hall.

Art: Grave Furnishings

One of the most important phenomena in Warring States art was the development of *mingqi* (spirit articles) designed and manufactured specifically for tombs. Their development was twofold. First, although surrogates made for funerary purposes had appeared long before the fifth century B.C., it was only during the Warring States period that *mingqi* were widely produced and came into general use. Second, corresponding to the mass production of *mingqi*, there appears to have been an attempt to define these objects as an independent category within a larger assemblage of tomb furnishings; the other two categories, *shengqi* 生器 (articles of daily life) and *jiqi* (sacrificial equipment), were derived from possessions that belonged to the dead person during his or her lifetime.

The terms *mingqi* and *shengqi* were used by Xunzi 荀子 to designate two types of burial goods.[167] The same distinction recurs in the ceremonies held on the day before the burial in which objects that would be installed in the tomb were publicly displayed. According to the *Yi li* 儀禮 (Ceremonies and rites), these objects included *mingqi* as well as *shengqi*; the latter included daily utensils (*yongqi* 用器), musical instruments for entertainment (*yanyue qi* 燕樂器), weapons and armor (*yiqi* 役器), and intimate objects belonging to the dead person such as his cap, cane, and bamboo mat (*yanqi* 燕器).[168] These are the articles that the *Yi li* prescribes for the funeral ceremony of a *shi* 士 officer. When the deceased was a *dafu* 大夫 or had an even higher rank, however, he was entitled to bring with him not only *mingqi* and *shengqi*, but also sacrificial vessels previously used in his family temple.[169] This is why *mingqi* were sometimes also called "vessels for ghosts" (*guiqi* 鬼器) as opposed to sacrificial vessels, which were known as "vessels for the living" (*renqi* 人器).[170]

Spirit articles were therefore distinguished from objects of daily use on the one hand and from temple ritual vessels on the other, although all three kinds of objects could have been buried in a tomb. This classification of tomb furnishings, however, was probably not yet formulated in the early Warring States period, because identifiable spirit articles were still largely absent in many early Warring States burials, even in a huge example such as Leigudun tomb 1. Upon reflection, we realize that this tomb's north, central, and east chambers housed, respectively, weapons and armor, sacrificial vessels and ritual musical instruments, and intimate belongings of the dead. These objects had been used in three kinds of activities in which the deceased had engaged during his lifetime, ceremonies, entertainment, and warfare; now they were transported into his tomb to symbolize the continuation of these activities in the afterlife. However, few if any of these objects can be clearly

---

[167] *Xunzi*, 19 ("Lilun"), 11b (Watson, trans., *Hsün Tzu*, p. 104).   [168] *Yi li*, 13 ("Jixi li"), 11b–14b.
[169] See Zheng Xuan's commentary to *Yi li*, 13 ("Jixi li"), 14b.
[170] *Li ji*, 8 ("Tangong 1"), 9b (Legge, *Li Chi*, vol. 1, p. 151). For the significance of the ancestral temple for a living community, see Wu Hung, *Monumentality in Early Chinese Art and Architecture*, pp. 49–99.

distinguished as *mingqi* made specifically for the burial. The selection and arrangement of gravegoods in this tomb thus followed a more traditional classification of manufactured objects, whose three major categories were equipment used in ritual (*liqi* 禮器, or *jiqi*), weaponry (*rongqi* 戎器), and utensils of everyday life (*yongqi*).[171] But during the fifth century B.C., some tombs also began to contain large groups of spirit articles, indicating a new direction in Warring States funerary art.

SPIRIT VESSELS. The best representative of this new type of burial is tomb 16 at Wuyang, one of the thirteen large tombs within the walled compound at the northwestern corner of the city (Fig. 10.4).[172] The high status of the tomb is indicated by its location, the large tumulus, the two ramps, and the special firing treatment of the grave chamber that was intended to harden its walls of rammed earth. What the excavators found on the platform surrounding the coffin assemblage, however, were not bronze vessels, but a group of 135 painted pottery surrogates, which substituted for an entire array of ritual bronzes, including a bell set used in a ritual orchestra (Fig. 10.35). Similar painted *mingqi* ceramics have also been found in other Yan tombs, including those at Changping 昌平 near Beijing and at Luanhezhen 灤河鎮 in Chengde 承德, Hebei.[173]

These elaborate pottery imitations of ritual bronzes signified the acceptance of *mingqi* by members of the elite. On a more general level, spirit vessels were also produced to replace the real pottery objects that had furnished earlier graves. As scholars have noted, pottery vessels in Western Zhou and early Eastern Zhou graves were mostly hard and high-fired practical wares; from the fifth to third centuries B.C., however, most of the pottery vessels found in graves are soft and relatively low-fired, differing markedly from the vessels made for practical use that are found in habitation sites of the same period. These two types of pottery also differed from each other in visual appearance. Instead of adopting established ceramic types, the craftsmen shaped their spirit pottery vessels as imitations of bronze ritual vessels and ceremonial musical instruments.[174] But it would be misleading to view these surrogates simply as cheap replacements for more expensive and functional objects. Some of the excavated pottery *mingqi* have complex shapes and beautiful decoration, which must have required considerable labor and special skills to produce. Of greater importance, it was believed that, as a ghost vessel,

---

[171] For a discussion of this classification, see ibid., pp. 18–24.
[172] For the excavation report, see *Kaogu xuebao* 1965.2: 79–102.
[173] For reports on these sites, see *Wenwu* 1959.9: 53–5; *Kaogu* 1961.5: 244.
[174] See *Luoyang Zhongzhoulu*, pp. 78, 129; Robert L. Thorp, "The Mortuary Art and Architecture of Early Imperial China," Ph.D. dissertation, University of Kansas, 1979, pp. 54–8.

Figure 10.35. Painted pottery "spirit vessels" from tomb 16 at Wuyang. Fifth century B.C. From Li Xueqin, *Eastern Zhou and Qin Civilizations*, trans. K. C. Chang (New Haven, Conn.: Yale University Press, 1985), fig. 51.

a spirit article had to be different from a vessel for the living. Xunzi summarized this idea in his discussion of funerary rites: "The spirit articles prepared especially for the dead resemble real objects but cannot be used."[175] In other words, *mingqi* retained the form of real vessels while abandoning their original function and substance.

Leigudun tomb 1 and tomb 16 in Wuyang seem to reflect two tendencies in the fifth century B.C., since one contained real ritual vessels, while the other was furnished with surrogates. During the next century, however, a majority of excavated large tombs reflect a deliberate mixture of spirit articles, sacrificial vessels, and utensils. One such example is again seen in the mausoleum of King Cuo of Zhongshan. As mentioned earlier, artifacts from this tomb included two groups of objects with radically different functions and styles: one consisted of bronze ritual vessels, sometimes bearing long

---

[175] *Xunzi*, 16 ("Lilun"), 11b (Watson, trans., *Hsün Tzu*, p. 104).

Figure 10.36. Black pottery "spirit vessel" from tomb 1 at Zhongshan, Pingshan, Hebei. Late fourth century B.C. After *Chûgoku sengoku jidai no yû: Chûzan ôgoku bunbutsuten* (Tokyo: Tokyo National Museum, 1981), fig. 86. Drawing by Li Xiating.

commemorative inscriptions (Fig. 10.19); the other, including objects of daily use and ornamental sculptures, is characterized by brilliant inlay decoration and exotic animal images (Figs. 10.17, 10.18). The former can thus be identified as *jiqi*, the latter as *shengqi*. A third group of objects from the same tomb had a quite different appearance, consisting of shining, black pottery vèssels decorated with elegantly incised and scraped patterns (Fig. 10.36). However striking in visual effect, these are actually soft and low-fired ceramic wares; their black surface resulted from a special firing process.[176] Their shapes and modeling further confirm their identification as spirit articles. A duck-shaped *zun* vessel, for example, has a spout in the shape of a duck's head, which can barely pour water. A plate has a central column supporting a sculpted bird. Although its function is not clear, the form is clearly derived from a type of ritual vessel, exemplified by a bronze plate from the same mausoleum.

Additional evidence can also be derived from other tombs, where similar black pottery vessels have been found, for example, at Shaogou near Luoyang and at several locations in Huixian. The examples from Guweicun tomb 1 at Huixian, supposedly a royal mausoleum of Wei, included another black

[176] Li Zhiyan, "Zhongshan wangmu chutu de taoqi," *Gugong bowuyuan yuankan* 1979.2: 93–4.

pottery bird-column plate (*niaozhu pan* 鳥柱盤).[177] Such monochromatic spirit vessels probably evolved from painted ones. Grave pottery wares from an early Warring States tomb at the capital of Xue 薛, for example, included a painted bird-column plate.[178] Conversely, tomb 29 at Dongdoucheng 東斗城 village in Wuyang yielded a group of black grave vessels, but their shapes resemble the painted ones from nearby tomb 16.[179]

Spirit articles were not limited to these and other ceramic types. Sometimes, such pottery vessels are painted with lacquer patterns.[180] In other examples, even bronze spirit vessels were made to complement bronze sacrificial vessels in a burial. This second case is best exemplified by two sets of tripods from Baoshan tomb 2 at Jiangling, dated to 316 B.C.[181] Each set consists of seven tripods with similar shapes, all covered with lids. In each set, six tripods form three pairs in descending size; in addition, the seventh is the smallest in size and bears ring handles. While the formal resemblance of the two sets is obvious, they differ in manufacture and function. The tripods in one set are thick and heavy, blackened on the bottom from cooking. Those in the other set are thin and light, poorly cast and without traces of use. In fact, many bronzes from this tomb share the characteristics of this second set of tripods, leading the excavators to conclude that most of the fifty-nine bronzes from this tomb were actually spirit vessels.[182] The correspondence between the two sets of tripods, however, signifies a deliberate effort to furnish this tomb with objects of two complementary but distinct classes.

TOMB FIGURINES AND PAINTING.   Gradually, the concept of *mingqi* was applied to a wide range of objects with different materials and forms. For example, clothes made for the corpse were called spirit clothes (*ming yishang* 明衣裳).[183] Their use is best demonstrated in Mazhuan 馬磚 tomb 1 (Mashan zhuanchang 馬山磚廠), Jiangling, in which the deceased was dressed in many layers of clothes: first a pair of brocade trousers, and then a skirt and three robes. The body was further wrapped in garments and several brocade quilts, tied tightly with nine silk ribbons, and was finally covered with a silk robe and a quilt with embroidered dragon and phoenix patterns (Fig. 10.23).[184] With regard to other kinds of *mingqi* the *Li ji* states:

[The grave articles made of] bamboo should not be suited for actual use; those of earthenware should not be able to contain water; those of wood should not be finely

---

[177] *Kaogu xuebao* 1954.8: 139–44; *Huixian fajue baogao.*   [178] *Kaogu xuebao* 1991.4: 449–96.
[179] *Kaogu* 1965.11: 550–3.   [180] *Wenwu* 1959.9: 53–5.   [181] *Baoshan Chu mu*, pp. 330–3.
[182] Ibid., p. 96.
[183] *Yi li*, 35 ("Shisang li"), 11a; 36 ("Shisang li"), 8a. Such clothes may also include miniature robes made for funerary purposes; for an example, see *Wenwu* 1982.10: 5, pl. 2.3.
[184] For the excavation report, see *Wenwu* 1982.10: 1–8. Also see Peng Hao, "Jiangling Mazhuan yihaomu suojian zangshu lüeshu," *Wenwu* 1982.10: 12–15.

carved; the zithers should be strung, but not evenly; the mouth organs should be prepared, but not in tune; the bells and chimestones should be there, but have no stands.[185]

The concept of *mingqi* was therefore not determined by medium or form, but was based on ritual function and symbolism.

A type of *mingqi* that would develop into an extremely important art tradition during the subsequent Qin and Han dynasties is the funerary figurine. Although sculpted human figures have been found in Shang and Western Zhou tombs and even in prehistorical burials, it is unclear whether these images were specifically produced for funerary purposes; their accidental occurrences do not confirm any ritual convention. Only from the late Spring and Autumn and early Warring States period did grave figurines (*muyong* 墓俑) become a regular, though still small, component of tomb furnishing in both the north and south. The 209 tombs at Changsha dated to this period, for example, yielded 14 figurines.[186] But the appearance of such objects in other Chu burial sites tends to be later. Among the 84 tombs discovered at Deshan 德山 in Changde 長德, none of the early Warring States tombs contained figurines. The 7 figurines from 2 middle Warring States period tombs mark the emergence of this type of grave furnishing at Deshan. A total of 23 figurines from 5 late Warring States tombs further indicates the growing popularity of this art in the third century B.C.[187]

Funerary figurines have frequently been interpreted as substitutes for human sacrifices, which occurred during earlier periods. Archaeological excavations generally support this theory. First, in a Warring States tomb, figurines were often placed next to or around the deceased; this arrangement followed the burial pattern of human sacrifices. Second, Niujiapo 牛家坡 tomb 7, a late Spring and Autumn period burial at Changzi 長子 in Shanxi, contained three human victims along the east and south walls and four wooden figurines near the west and north walls. These seven figures together surrounded and protected the chief tomb occupant in the middle.[188] Third, figurines are identified in the grave inventory from Wangshan tomb 2 as "dead servants" (*wangtong* 亡僮) of the deceased master in the underworld.[189] Fourth, the appearance and popularity of tomb figurines were coupled with the general decline of human sacrifices for funerary purposes.

On the other hand, archaeological excavations also present a complex sit-

[185] *Li ji*, 8 ("Tangong 1"), 5b–6a (Legge, *Li Chi*, vol. 1, p. 148).   [186] See *Kaogu xuebao* 1959.1: 54.
[187] *Kaogu* 1963.9: 461–73.
[188] *Kaogu xuebao* 1984.4: 504–7.
[189] *Wenwu* 1966.5: 33–55; Li Xueqin, *Eastern Zhou and Qin Civilizations*, p. 422.

uation, in which human sacrifices and figurines coexisted in a burial. In a fifth century B.C. tomb at Langjiazhuang 郎家莊 near Linzi, for example, a total of twenty-six skeletons were found outside the main burial chamber.[190] Seventeen of them, all young females, were in wooden coffins in individual tombs surrounding the man buried in the middle. These women wore jewelry and possessed personal belongings; two were themselves accompanied by human sacrifices, and six had small pottery figurines. A similar arrangement was found in another Qi tomb, excavated more recently at Zhangqiu 章邱 and dating from the mid-Warring States period.[191] This repeated phenomenon seems to suggest that while the death of a prestigious nobleman could still have demanded human sacrifices, a lower-ranking person used figurines as substitutes.

The tomb at Langjiazhuang also challenges the general categorization of human sacrifice. Unlike the seventeen young women who were given their own burials, nine other victims in the tomb, including both men and women, had suffered violent deaths, being either killed or buried alive. Scholars have distinguished these two types of human victims as "companions in death" (renxun 人殉) and "human offerings" (rensheng 人牲).[192] It is possible that when funerary figurines first appeared, they were made to substitute for both types of human victims. Most figurines represent servants, drivers, and musicians and were therefore replacements of companions in death.

The features of a small number of examples, however, implied specific ritual or magical functions. Changtaiguan tomb 1, for example, has a transverse front room that runs the width of the entire structure (Fig. 10.37).[193] Behind it, five small rooms surround the coffin chamber in the center. As in Leigudun tomb 1, gravegoods indicate the function of each compartment, thereby suggesting the identities of the figurines stored there. The front room resembles an audience hall, furnished with bronze vessels and musical instruments in a ceremonial orchestra. Behind it, the deceased, wearing jade ornaments and a gold-inlaid belt hook, was buried in double coffins in the central room. This coffin chamber is flanked by a stable to the left and a kitchen to the right; the stable contained two driver figurines, the kitchen two cook figurines. The far left room behind the stable was probably a study, equipped with a large couch and a box of writing equipment and bamboo strips. Two exquisite figurines found in this room probably represent clerical assistants. Their black clothes are painted with extremely fine patterns; hair is glued to their heads and fabric to their sleeves (Fig. 10.38a–c). To the far right, the kitchen is backed by a storage room, in which a kneeling servant is guard-

[190] *Kaogu xuebao* 1977.1: 73–104.   [191] *Wenwu* 1993.3: 1–7.
[192] See Huang Zhanyue, *Zhongguo gudai de rensheng renxun* (Beijing: Wenwu, 1990), pp. 1–12.
[193] *Xinyang Chu mu*, pp. 18–20.

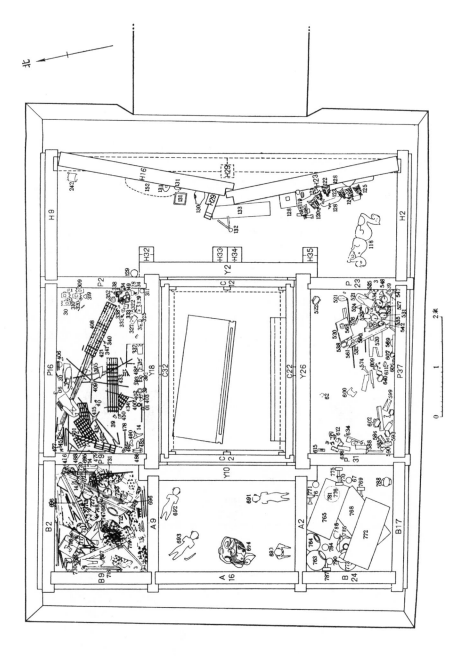

Figure 10.37. Plan of tomb 1 at Changtaiguan, Xinyang, Henan. From *Xinyang Chu mu* (Beijing; Wenwu, 1986), fig. 15.

ing large jars. The most mysterious room is the one at the center rear, directly behind the coffin chamber: a long-tongued creature with deer antlers, conventionally called a "tomb guardian beast" (*zhenmushou* 鎮墓獸) stood in the middle of the room (Fig. 10.39), surrounded by four human-shaped figurines at the four corners. Unlike other figurines in the tomb, these four figures have no robes and their bodies are crudely carved. One of them has a bamboo needle piercing the chest, thus provoking an intriguing question of its purpose or symbolism. It is possible that these were human sacrifices dedicated to a deity represented by the statue in the center.

Two kinds of Warring States figurines generally correspond to the geographical divisions of north and south. All figurines from the Chu region are made of wood, while most figurines from the northern states are of clay. The eleven figurines from Changtaiguan tomb 1 exemplify one of three major types of Chu figurines. Each of these eleven figures is carved from a single block of wood. But some of the figures' outstretched arms and hands were made separately and then attached to the body with dowels. Facial features were not carved but were painted; the same method is used to represent the patterns on clothes. Some figures are more carefully designed than others, as suggested by their well-proportioned bodies, the subtle modeling of their round shoulders,

Figure 10.38. Figurines from Chu. Sources: (a) *Xinyang Chu mu* (Beijing: Wenwu, 1986), fig. 40; (b) *Zhongguo gudai fushi yanjiu*, 2 vols. (Taipei: Longtian, 1981), vol. 1, fig. 12; (c) *Baoshan Chu mu* (Beijing: Wenwu, 1991), vol. 1, fig. 170.

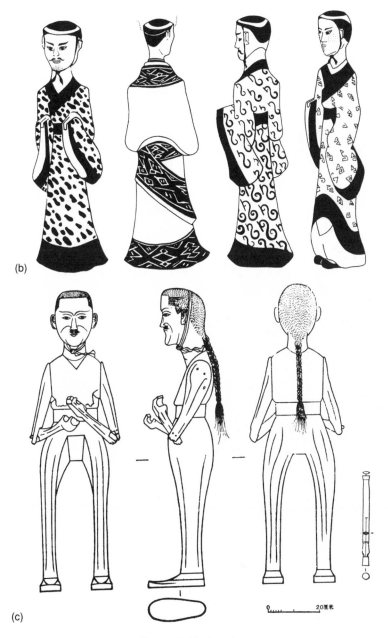

Figure 10.38. (*cont.*)

Figure 10.39. "Tomb guardian beast" from tomb
1 at Changtaiguan, Xinyang. From *Wenwu*
1957.9: frontispiece.

the flowing draperies, the richly painted fabric patterns, and the unconventional posture (Fig. 10.38a). A more stylized figurative type is demonstrated by
figurines from Changsha (Fig. 10.38b). Often taller and more cylindrical, these
figures have a shield-shaped face, with a broad forehead and a pointed and

slightly protruding chin. The neck is greatly elongated and connected to sloping shoulders. The figures are often dressed in robes drawn up in front. The stylization of these Changsha examples seems to contrast with the third type of Chu figurine, which reflects the most diligent effort made to imitate living persons. Two large figures from Baoshan tomb 2, for instance, are each more than a meter tall (Fig. 10.38c). Not only are their arms made of separate pieces of wood, but their ears, hands, and feet were all carved individually and then attached so as to achieve more complex gestures. This sculpted body, however, only served the role of a dummy for silk dresses. The torso below the neck is thus crudely carved, while the exposed parts received the most careful treatment. The head and face are subtly modeled and finely painted, with a mustache and a braid made of real hair attached.

A radically different style characterizes a majority of figurines from the north. Most of them are handmade from soft clay, painted either bright red, yellow, and brown, or entirely black like the color of some of the pottery *mingqi* (Fig. 10.36). Many are tiny: the figurines from Langjiazhuang tomb 1 are about 10 cm tall; examples of similar sizes have also been found at Fenshuiling in Shanxi, Huixian and Luoyang in Henan, and in several locations in Shandong.[194] The faces are rudimentary; what makes these figures special are their dramatic poses and gestures, which identify them as performers. The most significant group of this type of figurine was discovered in 1990 from a large tomb at Zhangqiu in Shandong.[195] As mentioned earlier, both human offerings and companions in death accompanied the deceased in this tomb, and a group of thirty-eight figurines further accompanied a female companion in death. Consisting of twenty-six figures, five musical instruments, and eight birds, these miniature sculptures originally constituted a large assemblage of musical and dance performers. There are ten female dancers, ranging from 7.7 to 7.9 cm in height. Their varying costumes and gestures indicate finer groupings in a dance formation. Two male musicians are drummers; the other three are playing bells, chimestones, and a zither. There are ten additional figures who have their hands folded in front of them, in a gesture that has led the excavators to identify them as the audience for the dance and musical performances.

Figurines from the north and south thus attest to quite different artistic and religious concerns. Most Chu figurines embodied household roles as servants, cooks, drivers, and clerical assistants in the underworld. They rarely formed a larger group on their own. Instead, each one was associated with other tomb furnishings, such as daily utensils, horse and chariots, kitchenware, or writing equipment, and was installed in a particular chamber in a tomb. We may thus

[194] *Kaogu xuebao* 1957.1: 116; *Huixian fajue baogao*, p. 45; *Kaogu* 1959.12: 656; 1960.7: 71; 1962.10: 516.
[195] *Wenwu* 1993.3: 1–7.

consider these figurines to be individual puppets taking their places on a series of stages that imitated various sections of a household. The Zhangqiu figurines, on the other hand, do not show a definable relationship with other gravegoods in the burial. Instead, these crudely modeled miniatures were integral elements of a large and self-contained representation of dance and musical performances, which possessed a definable meaning in the mortuary context: with performers, props, and audience, this group of figurines displayed a delightful aspect of the afterlife. In this sense, a group of clay figurines from a Qin tomb are similar to these Qi examples but have a different focus. By representing an ox-drawn carriage and a granary, they reveal a specific interest in agricultural activities, an interest that may have been related to the social status of the patrons who were buried in a small tomb.[196]

Generally speaking, all these styles and types reflect regional and cultural variations of a single category of artwork known as the grave figurine. There were, however, other types of sculpture that were strictly regional products. The best known of these is the tomb guardian beast, whose identity and meaning has been the focus of an intense debate among scholars, who have not been able to arrive at a definitive interpretation. Although examples of the tomb guardian beast have been found in Hunan and Henan, this type of object seems to have enjoyed its greatest popularity during the Warring States period in the Jiangling area in Hubei, where a single cemetery at Yutaishan yielded as many as 156 examples.[197] Without direct textual references, a study of this object must rely on formal and archaeological evidence. Its recurrent features, including the long tongue, the deer antlers, and the action of grasping and devouring snakes, seem to reflect shamanistic elements (Fig. 10.39).[198] Archaeological excavations suggest its association with higher-ranking tombs, since it has been found only in tombs with wooden encasements and ritual vessels. Each tomb always contained no more than one guardian beast, often accompanied by drums and situated in the front or the rear chamber of a tomb.[199] While some of these contextual features (such as its coexistence with the drum) seem to support the shamanistic connection, others may imply the sociological and religious significance of the statue as a symbol of social privilege and as a deity worshiped in a large household.

Like sculpture, the art of painting was much stimulated by the growing importance of the tomb in social and religious life. Many objects made for funerals required painted decoration. In addition to spirit articles and tomb

---

[196] *Wenwu ziliao congkan* 3 (1980): 67–85.

[197] For a typology of this object, see Chen Yaojun and Yuan Wenqing, "'Zhenmushou' lüekao," *Jiang Han kaogu* 1983.3: 63–7.

[198] See Qiu Donglian, "'Zhenmushou' biankao," *Jiang Han kaogu* 1994.2: 54–9. For an early study of these figures, see Albert Salmony, *Antler and Tongue: An Essay on Ancient Chinese Symbolism* (Ascona: Artibus Asiae, 1954).   [199] See *Wenwu* 1966.5: 33–55.

figurines, coffins and silk banners offered ideal two-dimensional surfaces for painting. According to the *Li ji*, "When a ruler succeeds to his state, he makes his coffin, and thereafter paints it with lacquer every year."[200] Although this passage does not specify the color or decor of the coffin, excavated lacquer coffins of the Warring States period, especially those of aristocrats, were embellished with rich combinations of pictorial and decorative images. In fact, no two Warring States coffins found in archaeological excavations share the same decoration. Sometimes, a limited number of geometric motifs were woven into a variety of designs; at other times, unusual images and compositions were created for a special coffin. The first situation is best demonstrated by the twenty-one small coffins found in Leigudun tomb 1. Although these were prepared for young women who followed their lord in death, they bear painted patterns in different configurations; even the windows painted on twelve of the coffins show varying lattice designs. The second situation, that of highly inventive decoration of special coffins, is demonstrated by the double coffins of Hou Yi himself (Fig. 10.34). Considering how much thought was given to the small coffins of his consorts and even of a dog, it is not surprising that the decoration of his own coffins would have required far greater attention and imagination. The huge outer coffin, measuring 3.2 m long, 2.1 m wide, and 2.19 m deep, is strengthened from inside by a bronze framework. On the surface, curvilinear and wave motifs form decorative bands to define a series of nearly square panels, filled with S-shaped interlacing patterns. The repetition and variation of six basic motifs creates a disciplined clarity. This geometric style seems in deliberate contrast to the decoration of the inner coffin, which is at once far more complex and dynamic. It utilizes not only geometric patterns but also zoomorphic and anthropomorphic images. Hybrid creatures are depicted either as individual guardian figures standing next to painted doors or as integral elements of large compositions. Rather than being purely decorative, these images seem to have carried some magic or symbolic significance in the funerary context.[201]

The Leigudun examples were followed by a series of painted coffins of the middle and late Warring States period, including the exquisite inner coffin from Baoshan tomb 2 (Fig. 10.40).[202] Archaeological excavations also provide evidence for the relationship between coffin paintings and other types of architectural decoration, such as the eleven geometric murals in Tianxingguan tomb 1.[203] The most important development of painting after the fifth century B.C., however, is exemplified by two third-century silk banners from

[200] *Li ji*, 8 ("Tangong" 1), 18b (Legge, *Li Chi*, vol. 1, pp. 156–7).

[201] For a discussion of the decoration of these two coffins, see Thote, "The Double Coffin of Leigudun Tomb No. 1."

[202] *Baoshan Chu mu*, vol. 1, pp. 61–3; color pl. 4.1–3; fig. 45a, b.   [203] *Kaogu xuebao* 1982.1: 76–7.

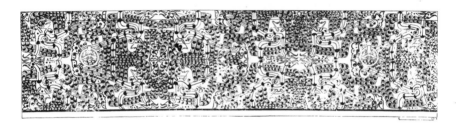

Figure 10.40. Painted coffin from tomb 2 at Baoshan, Jingmen, Hubei. Late fourth century B.C. From *Baoshan Chu mu* (Beijing: Wenwu, 1991), vol. 1, fig. 45a, b.

the vicinity of Changsha, which can, without hesitation, be called the earliest individual paintings known to survive in Chinese history (Fig. 10.41). Although there are different opinions regarding their ritual function and nomenclature, most scholars believe that both paintings represent an alternative form of the "name banner" (*mingjing* 名旌) that was used in funerary rites. According to ritual canons, a *mingjing* inscribed with the name of the deceased was hung beside the coffin during the *bin* 殯 ceremony.[204] Guests would arrive to pay their condolences to the dead, and the members of the family would demonstrate their extreme grief. The focus of this ritual homage was the name banner, which allowed the living "to recognize the dead and to express their love towards him."[205] The banner was finally put in the tomb to symbolize the otherworldly existence of the dead. It is logical that the name of the deceased that was written on a banner could be replaced by a portrait, which would better preserve his likeness.

It has been reported that a small silk painting was found on top of the coffin in Mashan tomb 1.[206] But this is all we know about this work. Among the two published Warring States silk paintings, the one from Chenjia

---

[204] For the identification of a similar painted banner from Mawangdui tomb 1 as a *mingjing*, see An Zhimin, "Changsha xin faxian de Xi Han bohua shitan," *Kaogu* 1973.1: 43–53; Ma Yong, "Lun Changsha Mawangdui yihao Han mu chutu bohua," *Kaogu* 1973.2: 118–25.

[205] *Yi li*, 12 ("Shisang li"), 9a. For a discussion of the ritual significance of the Name Banner, see Wu Hung, "Art in Its Ritual Context: Rethinking Mawangdui," *EC* 17 (1992): 111–45.

[206] *Wenwu* 1982.10: 3.

(a)　　　　　　　　　　　　　　(b)

Figure 10.41. Chu silk paintings: (a) from Chenjia dashan, Changsha (Li Xueqin, *Eastern Zhou and Qin Civilizations*, trans. K. C. Chang [New Haven, Conn.: Yale University Press, 1985], fig. 203); (b) from Zidanku, Changsha (*Zhongguo gudai fushi yanjiu*, 2 vols. [Taipei: Nantian, 1988], vol. 1, fig. 12).

dashan 陳家大山 with a female image (Fig. 10.41a) was reportedly found by the tomb robber on a bamboo suitcase next to the corpse; according to other accounts it was found either within a pottery vessel or inside the suitcase.[207] The position of the male image from Zidanku 子彈庫 is definite (Fig. 10.41b): according to the excavation report, this painting was discovered face upward on top of the coffin.[208] In this position it closely corresponded to the corpse inside the coffin. The identity of this painting as a portrait of the tomb occupant is confirmed by two additional pieces of evidence: first, like the gentleman in the painting, the deceased was a middle-aged male; second, the bronze sword worn by the deceased resembles the one worn by the gentleman in the painting. With a thin bamboo stick fixed on its upper edge and a ribbon attached in the middle of the stick, this painting must presumably have been hung during the funerary ritual before it was buried; such evidence again confirms the identity of this painting as a name banner.

The two paintings, on the other hand, do more than just preserve the likeness of the deceased. The figure in each work is the focus of a large composition, which includes other images to represent a specific situation. No consensus about the meaning of these two compositions has been reached, but a dominant opinion is that the pictures represent the transformation of the soul. The strongest evidence for this argument is that both figures seem

---

[207] Li Xueqin, *Eastern Zhou and Qin Civilizations*, p. 443.   [208] *Wenwu* 1973.7: 3–4.

to be taking a heavenly journey: the woman is standing on a crescent moon; the man is driving a dragon or a dragon boat. Additional animals and birds accompany these two figures. In one painting, a phoenix is fighting against a snakelike creature; in the other painting, a carp is swimming next to the gentleman's dragon boat, while a crane is standing on the dragon's tail. A great deal has been written on the magical power of these creatures in assisting a person to achieve immortality.[209] The two paintings also share drawing techniques and a figurative style: images are delineated by ink lines, and the principal figures are shown in profile. The main difference between these two works lies in the degree of artistry. Without much sense of volume, the female figure appears as a flat silhouette; the outlines are rather coarse and uneven, apparently executed by an unassured hand. The painter of the gentleman's portrait, on the other hand, had far better control of his brush and a higher artistic goal. Not only could he deal with more difficult tasks in representing his subject, with a convincing and subtle depiction of the figure's round shoulder, his delicate cap, and his gentle facial expression, but his ink lines have assumed a kind of independent aesthetic value since they can be appreciated for their smoothness, fluidity, dynamism, and harmonious configuration. In fact, this painting provides a superb example of the drawing style called "floating silk threads from antiquity" (*gaogu yousi miao* 高古游絲描) that would be followed and praised by artists and art critics of later ages.

A major factor separates this type of silk painting from decoration on lacquerware: each name banner was done by a single person, while according to the *Kaogong ji* the process of painting a lacquer object normally consisted of five stages from drawing sketches to applying colors, being executed by artisans with different specialties.[210] The superb quality of the Zidanku painting thus implies the existence of a superb artist. That such persons could and did exist may in turn have provided the basis for the literary characterization of an individual artist. We read in the *Zhuangzi* that the lord of Song once wanted to have a painting done and a large number of painters came for the job.[211] They all paid their respects to the patron and obediently demonstrated their skills. The painter who arrived last, however, ignored the official greeting and took off his clothes as if no one else were present. He was recognized as a true painter and given the assignment.

[209] See Huang Hongxin, "Chu bohua suokao," *Jiang Han kaogu* 1991.2: 45–9.
[210] *Zhou li*, 6 ("Dongguan Kaogong ji"), 7b.
[211] *Zhuangzi* (Sibu beiyao ed.) 7 (21 "Tianzi Fang"), 19b.

CHAPTER ELEVEN

THE CLASSICAL PHILOSOPHICAL WRITINGS

David Shepherd Nivison

SOURCES

In no case does one find a book, written by an identifiable person at an identifiable time prior to 221 B.C., when the Qin state completed its conquests to create the first empire. There is only one finished book, the *Lü shi chunqiu* 呂氏春秋 (Mr. Lü's Spring and Autumn [annals]), with a known data of completion (239 B.C.), and it bears the name not of its author but of the patron who engaged the nameless persons who actually wrote it.[1] All of the other "books," no matter whose names they bear, are either obviously layered texts that "grew" over centuries or are suspected to have been added to, taken from, rearranged, or pieced together after the main author (if there was one) died. For some, this editorial process continued into the Han era (206 B.C.–A.D. 220) and even later. In some cases, as in that of the *Guanzi* 管子 (Master Guan), the name on the text has to be understood as honorific or as outright fiction.[2]

Further, a large part of the literature known to have existed has been lost; and in both the lost and the surviving parts there are or were texts that may or may not be pre-Qin, as well as some that pretend to be but certainly are

---

[1] For this date, see *Lü shi chunqiu* (Sibu beiyao ed.), 12 ("Xu yi"), 9a. An English translation of the *Lü shi chunqiu* has just been completed by John Knoblock and Jeffrey K. Riegel (forthcoming). Valuable additional information and contrasting appraisals of authenticity on all of the texts treated here can be found in Michael Loewe, ed. *Early Chinese Texts: A Bibliographical Guide* (Berkeley: Society for the Study of Early China and the Institute of East Asian Studies, University of California, 1993). Texts are discussed by the following contributors: *Lun yu*, Anne Cheng; *Mozi*, A. C. Graham; *Mencius*, D. C. Lau; *Guanzi*, W. Allyn Rickett; *Gongsun Longzi*, A. C. Graham; *Zhuangzi*, H. D. Roth; *Xunzi*, Michael Loewe; *Han Feizi*, Jean Levi; *Laozi* William G. Boltz; *Lü shi chunqiu*, Michael Carson and Michael Loewe.

[2] The Guanzi ("Master Guan") of the *Guanzi* is Guan Zhong, chief minister under Qi Huan Gong (r. 685–643 B.C.). The book is probably material (some of it important for philosophy) produced in Qi in the third century B.C. by Jixia scholars and edited in the first century B.C. A translation in English by W. Allyn Rickett is currently in progress; see *Guanzi: Political, Economic, and Philosophical Essays from Early China*, vol. 1 (Princeton, N.J.: Princeton University Press, 1985).

not. Over all of the material we must examine, disagreement has raged, even as far back as the Han. One famous example is the *Shang shu* 尚書 (Venerated documents; also known as *Shu jing* 書經, Classic of documents). The pieces in it pretend to date from the third millennium B.C. down to the seventh century B.C. In fact, as Chinese scholars had suspected for a thousand years and have known for three centuries, about half of it was lost during the Han and reconstituted or forged in the third or fourth century A.D. Of the remainder, at most one or two short pieces are pre-Zhou (most scholars would deny even this). Other parts of it cannot have been written earlier than the third century B.C., which is probably the time when the book was put together; earlier, the various pieces circulated separately. Another famous example is the *Laozi* 老子, or *Dao de jing* 道德經 (Classic of the way and virtue). Claimed to be a sixth century B.C. text written by the Daoist sage of sages, it is probably a late-fourth-century amalgam.

Another even more important short text is the *Analects* (*Lun yu* 論語, Judgments and conversations) of Confucius. Probably all of it is pre-Qin. But certainly none of it was written down before Confucius died (479 B.C.), and it was added to repeatedly, the last parts probably after 250 B.C.[3] Somehow, out of this and other equally frustrating material, we have to reconstruct Confucius – who he was, what he did, and what he thought.

And so also must it be with others in the Warring States era "age of philosophers." In doing this one must try not just to delineate a sequence of persons, but to picture what was going on in a sequence of times, that picture in turn being dependent in part on how we conceive the persons. Only a comprehensive view can hope to defeat the obvious danger of circularity in this. A very ancient notion is that this pre-Qin era (but not farther back than Confucius) was an age of philosophers, a short burst (in the historian's mirror) of exuberant originality and variety, that settled into something steadier and less varied in the long subsequent centuries of empire. As we have learned more of the great richness and variety of later intellectual history, this idea has come to be seen as the illusion that it is.[4]

Nonetheless, there are, for us, beginnings. The repertory of Chinese philosophers begins with Confucius. There was a more or less anonymous literary tradition in this time reaching back at least five centuries (in an

---

[3] This statement draws on correspondence with E. Bruce Brooks. His new translation of the *Analects* makes the layering clear; *The Original Analects: Sayings of Confucius and His Successors, 0479–0249.* (New York: Columbia University Press, 1998).

[4] One must not, however, dismiss the idea that there was in early China an "axial age," when thinkers began to be critically aware of their traditions. See Heiner Roetz, *Confucian Ethics of the Axial Age: A Reconstruction Under the Aspect of the Breakthrough Toward Postconventional Thinking* (Albany: State University of New York Press, 1993). (Karl Jaspers, the author of the concept [see *The Origin and Goal of History* (New Haven, Conn.: Yale University Press, 1953)], even supposes that this is a worldwide phenomenon that occurred at approximately the same time in different civilizations.)

already archaic language), and a tradition of history, institutions, concepts, and customs stretching back much farther than that, that people like Confucius were beginning to do more than just take for granted: to be aware of, consciously study or neglect, treasure or disregard.

The Political Context

The world in time and space, as a Chinese of the late sixth century saw it, was the northern half of what we call China. It was made up of small political units we call states, the nominal domains of local lords, theoretically subject to a king who lived in Luoyang 洛陽, a city located near the confluence of the Luo and Yellow Rivers, more or less the center of what was then the Chinese world. A town was simply the seat of a lord, a state the extension of the town's (and lord's) dominance. The king was the present heir of the Zhou dynasty, which five centuries earlier had achieved paramount power in a "conquest" of the preceding world order, of much the same sort, called Shang or Yin. The Shang had been dominant in its turn for about five centuries, following a victory by its founding king, named Tang 湯, over a still earlier dynasty named Xia.[5] On the peripheries were peoples who did not observe Chinese customs and political allegiances; thought of as foreign, there were pockets of such peoples scattered through the whole country. In the late sixth century one's perspective probably did not extend farther back or out than this.

One would be aware of change. Not only was there the sequence of royal dynasties, but thirteen reigns previously in the present dynasty there was King You (r. 781–771 B.C.), who in 771 B.C. had been defeated and killed by an alliance of lords and non-Chinese peoples. He and his predecessors (You was the twelfth Zhou king) had ruled with real power from a city farther west, in the Wei 渭 valley near modern Xi'an 西安. After the 771 disaster a successor, King Ping, had been set up in Luoyang by the then most powerful local lord, Jin Wen Hou 晉文侯, but King Ping and his descendants were virtually powerless, and the whole "world" soon slipped into interstate anarchy, the more powerful states destroying and annexing many of the lesser ones, and wars became a constant prospect.[6]

One effect was that people looked back to the centuries when Zhou kings had had real authority, especially the beginnings of Zhou rule, as a kind of golden age, and they came to think of the ideal human situation as one in

---

[5] The existence of a "Xia Dynasty" is disputed by many. See, e.g., Sarah Allan, "The Myth of the Xia Dynasty," *JRAS* 1984: no. 2. 242–56. For another view, see also D. Nivision and K. Pang, "Astronomical Evidence for the *Bamboo Annals*' Chronicle of Early Xia," *EC* 15 (1990): 87–95.

[6] Jin Wen Hou (r. 780–746 B.C.) is not to be confused with the later *Ba* Jin Wen Gong (r. 636–628).

which order was maintained, for the good of all, from a world political center, to which it became natural to ascribe great efficacy for good, if it only did hold real authority. This was a way of thinking that was to dominate Chinese political philosophy.

Continuing disintegration was visible: In Lu 魯, Confucius's native state, three sons of an earlier ruler, Huan Gong 桓公 (r. 711–694), had established branch lineages that had in the next two centuries become independent powers each with its own military citadel, and the nominal lord had become virtually helpless. In much larger Jin 晉 to the west, a like process was occurring in the last decades of Confucius's life, dividing Jin first into six spheres of as many hereditary officers with their domains. Civil wars soon destroyed the state. The last nominal ruler of Jin disappears from the historical record after 370 B.C.

Counterbalancing such disintegration, however, powers that could hope to be strong enough to survive in the increasingly warlike environment had to tighten their internal organization. Traditional structures of hereditary office holding by aristocratic houses were beginning to become bureaucracies with appointed governors and officers whose qualifications need not be those of lineage, but could be ability and training. Warfare made this necessary; it also made it possible, by creating a growing class of employable persons whose fathers or grandfathers had been retainers or distant descendants of earlier lords, often of now extinct tiny states. This was the class of *shi* 士 (knights), next in social order and means above the peasantry.[7] They might not actually have military skills, but they tended to have military values, a sense of honor and an ideal of loyalty and service. A life well lived for such a person would be one committed to a lord able to discern ability and to employ people having it. Social mobility characterizes this situation. The *shi* were moving into roles that in an earlier age one had to be born into, and *shi* status could even be a stage on the way up for persons farther down. In Eastern Zhou China this is the background of most of the people who think – including "philosophers."

BASIC CONCEPTS

There are characteristic things that these people who think think about and want. They want to be employed, meaningfully. This requires that they prepare, by acquiring the right knowledge and skills, and (for many) also cultivating the right qualities of character. And they are concerned about what they should be trying to do if successful in seeking such employment: what policies should inform a good government? This concern never leads toward

---

[7] For more on the *shi*, see p. 583 above.

any semblance of democracy: it is always taken for granted that the only way to be effective is to gain the ear and the confidence of a lord. One's *shi* status makes that possible, as it is not for a farmer or artisan (nor, until much later, for a merchant). Against this interest, which takes many forms, others deliberately and consciously "drop out." Skeptical and speculative, they give us some of the most interesting (and entertaining) philosophical fare to be found anywhere.

There is a background of basic concepts and values that shapes all of these philosophers, even indirectly the dropouts. Family relationships and lineage had always been especially prominent in the way Chinese society worked. Intrafamily hierarchy demanded honor and obedience to one's parents (*xiao* 孝, filial piety). The obligation extended past the grave: rites and offerings were owed to ancestors. A parent at death must be mourned, and the rules were taxing, requiring various forms of ascetic behavior, extending into the third year after the death. This institution, especially emphasized by Confucius and his followers, was both old and entrenched, its beginnings veiled in prehistory. In any case, rites and sacrifices were a prominent feature of the background civilization. Since social and even political position both qualified one for and required of one such ritual performance, "rite" or "ritual" (*li* 禮), becomes a concept that extended far beyond religious performance, to include the forms that must be observed in all sorts of interpersonal and interrole relationships; these in turn included all of traditional rule-governed political behavior. Therefore, one type of subsequent philosophy – the Confucian – sees a cherishing of ritual as central to the cultivation of character and the maintenance of social order.

Other such concepts are often on the lips of the Confucians and figure in much subsequent discussion. A person of prominence such as a king or lord or teacher or family head who carefully observes sacrificial duties and adheres to the restraints of the *li* in his conduct acquires respect and status. The grateful spirits cause him to prosper. Such a one is regarded as having *de* 德, a vexing term conventionally translated "virtue." (Other translations are "potency" or "moral force.") The term has an important semantic spread that requires keeping in sight the Chinese original. Its meaning seems to grow out of a common idiom, in which its sense is "gratitude": if I do something for you that causes you to feel grateful and compelled to respond favorably, I "have *de* from" (i.e., in relation to) you. You come to feel this compulsion as a psychological force emanating from me; this for you, is my *de*.

The virtue of a person (especially) of prestigious position, such as a king, seems to be a subtle transformation of this feeling of obligation we naturally have toward someone who does us a favor, gives a gift, shows generosity in withholding judgment or punishment, or respects us and "counts us in" by listening to our opinions. The feeling gets projected on the giver, who is thus both regarded as virtuous and is felt to have a psychic attractive power. Such is "royal virtue," which a good king acquires and enhances by offerings to spirits, and by gifts of goods, authority and confidence to subordinates, as well as by opening his ears to advice. Conversely, he would squander this power by self-indulgence, lack of restraint, arrogance, or cruelty. This *de*-quality is reified as something in the self but not belonging to it, that one (if a king) is entrusted with (by Heaven) and has a duty (in all humility) to conserve and cultivate. Typically the form this cultivation will take will be one's modeling one's behavior on the idealized behavior of esteemed ancestors. Heaven gives *de*, yet also rewards the king seen to hold and cultivate it, by giving him the "mandate" to rule the world, a mandate (as Mencius, ca. 390–305, will say later) revealed not by any explicit "voice of God," but by the way people act – by the people's tacit acceptance of the king's authority, in a reign of good order and prosperity that seems to emanate from the royal person.[8]

Two things need to be noticed at once in a tradition of ethics that is centered on such a concept. First, the focus is not on how to define the good or the right, or to determine what is good or right; these things will seem unproblematic. The real problem seems to be how one becomes a person who has *de*; and this means that the moral tradition is centered from the start on self-cultivation and on how one conveys insight to a student or gets the student to change. Second, this concept of "virtue" is paradoxical, because the purpose of moral instruction is to inculcate virtue; yet a primary aspect of virtue (*de*) is being disposed to listen humbly to instruction; and it seems that one who has this characteristic must be virtuous already. Here it should be added that in the early stage of moral philosophy, moral education is conceived as the education of adult "disciples," not the moral conditioning of children (though the later literature of pedagogy is large). This "paradox of virtue" is especially visible (and distressing) in the matter of giving moral guidance to rulers; a bad ruler drives away would-be good advisers. But it is no less real in any teacher–student relationship. We repeatedly find Confucius frustrated by the unresponsive student (as, e.g., in *Analects* 5/9 and 6/10).[9]

Other concepts in the immediate background of the age of philosophers need notice. The word *dao* 道, originally meaning "way" or "road," is used everywhere by the philosophers to mean the way to do something, or

---

[8] For more on the *de* concept, see D. S. Nivison, *The Ways of Confucianism: Investigations in Chinese Philosophy*, ed. Bryan Van Norden (La Salle, Ill.: Open Court, 1997), chapters 2–3. The notion of the imitation of models is stressed in an analysis by Donald J. Munro, *The Concept of Man in Early China* (Stanford, Calif.: Stanford University Press, 1969), esp. pp. 101–12.

[9] References to the *Analects* will be given by book and chapter number, as is customary in most Western translations, following Legge's annotated edition and translations.

the (right moral) "Way," or (later) the "Way" of all nature. In the last sense, it forces new and curious senses on the word *de*, with which it is often paired.[10]

Another pair of terms, whose difficulty of translation measures their importance, *ren yi* 仁義, seems simply to be "morality" in *Mencius*; but the words also must be taken singly.[11] Translations proposed for *ren* 仁 include "benevolence," "Goodness," or "Manhood-at-its-best"; *yi* 義 is "righteousness," "sense of duty," and much else. The words in moral-philosophical senses seem not to be old, and perhaps are still being refined in Confucius's thought. The first term, cognate (as the philosophers saw) with *ren* 人 (man) in the idiom "other persons," seems to contrast with the second term as cognate with *wo* 我 (me), so perhaps "otherliness" contrasted with what I ought to do (and be ashamed of not doing – as in *Mencius* 2A/6).[12] In literature not much earlier than Confucius, *ren* seems to mean "having a pleasing grace," as of someone well born (*ren*, man, refers to well-born persons in contrast to the *min* 民, ordinary people). Thus, in the *Shang shu* chapter "Jin teng" 金縢 (Metal-bound coffer) in which Zhou Gong 周公 caused to be sealed the record of his divinatory offer of himself as substitute for his dying brother King Wu, the suppliant advertises himself as "*ren* and *qiao* 巧," apparently "graceful and clever" (in manner and speech).[13] The word *ren* (*nien) here brings to mind its graphic cognate *ning* 佞 (*nǐěng) "skillful in speech." Confucius forces the senses apart, giving *ning* a bad sense, and insisting on real *ren* as an interior virtue of character: "Clever (*qiao*) in word and fine in appearance; seldom indeed [is such a person truly] *ren*!" (*Analects* 1/3, 17/15). Therefore, "The gentleman (*junzi* 君子, literally "lord's son") desires to be cautious in speech but earnest in action" (*Analects* 4/24). One of the group of disciples was described as "*ren* but not *ning*" (5/5); Confucius retorts

---

[10] When Dao comes to be the ground of the universe, a thing's *de* 德 is said to be what the thing "gets" (*de* 得) from the *dao* to be itself, with whatever interactive efficacy that thing has (and so, its "power"): see *Guanzi* (Sibu beiyao ed.), 13 (36 "Xin shu A"), 3b. Note the related sense, a "power" or tendency in history, as in the expression *wu de* (the Five Powers).

[11] The translation is as in D. C. Lau, *Mencius: Translated with an Introduction* (Harmondsworth: Penguin, 1970), p. 236.

[12] For this sense, see Peter A. Boodberg, "Some Proleptical Remarks on the Evolution of Archaic Chinese," *HJAS* 2 (1937): 329–72. One earlier sense of *yi* (assuming 義 to equal 儀) may, however, have been simply dignified "proper behavior" in formal situations. Citations of the *Mencius* will be given simply to the book (with A signifying the *shang* portion and B the *xia* portion) and chapter, as is usual in Western translations.

[13] *Shang shu* 13 (6 "Jin teng"), 8a; see James Legge, *The Chinese Classics. Vol. 3: The Shoo King, or Book of Historical Documents*, 2nd ed. (Oxford: Clarendon Press. 1893–4; rpt. Hong Kong: Hong Kong University Press, 1960), p. 345). The graph for *ning* is a modification of the graph for *ren* 仁. In the standard text of the "Jin teng," the phrase is *ren ruo kao* 仁若考. B. Karlgren, on good evidence, emends *kao* to *qiao* 巧, but punctuates differently: *Glosses on the Book of Documents, BMFEA* 20 (1948): 39–315 (Rpt. Stockholm: Museum of Far Eastern Antiquities, 1970), p. 252 (no. 1570); *ruo* can be understood as *er* 而 (and), between verbs or adjectives (though Karlgren does not do so).

in effect, "I don't know about his being *ren*, but it is good that he isn't *ning*; people would hate him."

We see in this an elitist cultural climate, and most of the ancient philosophies reflect this fact: *junzi* (gentleman, or morally noble person) is one of the most common words in the *Analects* and contrasts with *xiao ren* 小人 (small man, or morally petty person). And we see something else distinctive of the development of philosophy in China, in contrast to ancient Greece: The sociopolitical changes that brought forward a class of men who were potentially "intellectuals," and so potentially philosophers, caused them to focus their attention on the ideal form of political and social (familial) relationships on the one hand, and on the other the qualities a man should have to serve in those relationships; and this focus was on political and moral philosophy. The natural world at first went unnoticed.

CONFUCIUS

"Confucius" is the Latinization of Kong Fuzi 孔夫子 (Master Kong), as he has been known by his followers; his personal name was Qiu 邱, his "capping" name (given at his attainment of majority) was Zhongni 仲尼. He is said to have been born in 551 B.C., in Lu 魯, a small state at the base of the Shandong Peninsula neighboring on the larger state of Qi 齊 to the east. His father was a military *shi* named Shuliang He 叔梁紇 (clan name Kong), who seems to have had little to do with him, except to give him an ancestry historians carry back to the lords of Song 宋, and before that to the kings of Shang. He is said by tradition to have been brought up by his mother and to have been a *shi* at first of quite humble economic status. He took no interest in a military career and devoted himself to learning the culture of the past, so as to qualify himself for service in a lord's retinue. Eventually he found himself teaching other young men who had the same aim. He was partially successful, both in gaining a position himself and in placing some of his students. Tradition has enormously exaggerated that success, some accounts making him reach the high position of prime minister of Lu. Actually, he seems to have at one time been in the retinue of a diplomatic mission to Qi and later to have held a minor official post in Lu. It was perhaps because he was taking the futile course of supporting the legitimate claims of the lord of Lu against the actual dominance of the "Three Huan" families that he had to leave the state for some years, traveling west to Wey 衛, Chen 陳, and Cai 蔡.[14]

---

[14] See D. C. Lau, *Confucius: The Analects* (Harmondsworth: Penguin, 1978), Appendix 1.

As a Writer and Transmitter

Tradition further has it than in old age he returned to Lu and left the world a literary opus, editing the major "classics," the *Shang shu* and the *Shi jing* 詩經 (Classic of poetry), writing a long philosophical commentary to the *Yi* 易 (Changes) and actually writing another classic, the *Chunqiu* 春秋 (Spring and Autumn [annals]), a chronicle of the Lu state.

Except for the last, these texts are not convincingly referred to as books until the third century. The commentary to the *Yi* is now generally regarded to be a much later creation. The cache of texts of the Wei kings buried around 299–296 B.C., which contained the *Zhushu jinian* 竹書紀年 (Bamboo annals), also had a copy of the *Yi* with only the base text, lacking the commentaries traditionally ascribed to Confucius, but with a commentary explaining the text in terms of the concepts of *yin* 陰 and *yang* 陽, as one would expect of a commentary of ca. 300 B.C.[15] Confucius has been magnified by legend, in many ways.

Most scholars, even including some premodern ones in China, also questioned the part played by Confucius in the composition of the *Chunqiu*. But this book cannot be so easily dismissed. The *Mencius*, put together by Mencius's disciples possibly before Mencius died (just before 300 B.C.), has Mencius saying explicitly (3B/9) that Confucius wrote – or "did," that is, used (*zuo* 作) – the *Chunqiu*. The claim is plausible: Confucius died in 479 B.C., and the chronicle stops in 481. The book reads like an official state chronicle, and probably that is what it is; but if Confucius could have had access to the official text, he might have copied it, perhaps abridging it slightly. And it is reasonable to suppose that he did have access to it. All the states had their chronicles. The *Zuo zhuan* 左傳 (Zuo's tradition) records stories – which may or may not be true – about official chroniclers in Qi and in Jin who risked death, and in three cases incurred it, to put in the record criticisms of the de facto rulers in their states.[16] Such stories presuppose that the texts were accessible to a serious public. So there is no difficulty in supposing that Confucius was able to copy out the text of the chronicle of Lu.

And he would have had a motive to do so. The *Analects* shows that a frequently used technique of moral teaching was to discuss and criticize some important person of the past. Having the actual text, or a paraphrase, of the state chronicle, which recorded the actions of persons of prominence not just

---

[15] For the Wei tomb text of the *Yi* with *yin–yang* commentary (long since lost), see Du Yu (A.D. 222–84). "Zuo Zhuan hou xu" 左傳後序 (following the text and notes on the *Zuo zhuan*, as in the *Shisan jing zhushu*).

[16] For these two stories, see *Zuo zhuan*, 36 (Xiang 25), 6b (Legge, *The Chinese Classics. Vol. 5: The Ch'un Ts'ew with the Tso Chuen*, [Hong Kong: Hong Kong University Press, 1960], p. 514); and *Zuo zhuan*, 21 (Xuan 2), 11b–12a (ibid., p. 290).

of Lu but also of other lands, would be useful. The Confucian belief has been that this was his purpose with the *Chunqiu*: the *Mencius* says (4B/21) that the book's subject matter is the doings of the lords Qi Huan Gong (r. 685–643 B.C.) and Jin Wen Gong (r. 636–628), but that "as for its *yi* 義, Confucius himself said 'I have ventured to appropriate it'" – i.e., in his moral teaching. Here *yi* seems to mean the "principles" of what is right illustrated by the chronicle (though not stated in it).

Hagiography goes much farther, however, and maintains that Confucius expressed his judgments of persons and doings by what he selected or omitted, and by subtle hints in wording. Whether he actually did so is another question. More that came to be believed requires a smile: the *Mencius* (3B/9) says that writing the book was "the business of the Son of Heaven" – that is, that its function was to make such judgments, which only the sovereign or his officer was entitled to do. By the Han dynasty, this had grown into the claim that Confucius *was* a sovereign, an "uncrowned king," and that the closing record in the chronicle, of the capture of a fabulous animal called a *lin* 麟 in 481, was a sign from Heaven that the Mandate of Heaven had passed to Confucius as, in a moral sense, founder of a new dynasty, who in the way he wrote the *Chunqiu* was describing a future utopia, pictured by the way he implicitly characterized the Lu state. That such a fantasy could have come into men's minds in antiquity shows how cautious one must be in weighing evidence of what Confucius did think.[17]

Did Confucius, the first philosopher, have a philosophy featuring new ideas of his own? It is not easy to find any. He himself said that he was "a transmitter, not a creator" (*Analects* 7/1). He did try to "reanimate the old" (2/11), he says, for example, by novel moralistic interpretations of lines in the Odes (the *Analects* provides examples: 1/15). There is a tone, a stance, that may be new: Confucius takes over a traditional aristocratic set of moral and social standards and claims or hopes that he and his followers, of relatively humble status but hoping to move up into positions of consequence, embody these values more reliably than the high-born who hitherto had a monopoly on high positions. He and his students ideally would be "knights (*shi*) of the Way" (4/9), each concerned above all else with the perfecting of his own moral character, concerned not with gaining office or "being known," but with making himself worthy of it (1/16), by cultivating in himself a quasi-military steadfastness and courage (2/24, 8/7). Confucius, with a sense of mission, thought of himself as having a virtue, a *de*, that Heaven had given him (7/23).

---

[17] See Fung Yu-lan, *A History of Chinese Philosophy. Vol. 2: The Period of Classical Learning*, trans. Derk Bodde (Princeton, N.J.: Princeton University Press, 1953), pp. 71–87.

Li

So also with Confucius's cherishing of *li* 禮 (ritual) in much more than its mere religious sense. Confucius has been seen as having a picture of the human moral being as whole (a philosophically healthy way of looking at ourselves), undivided into outer visible and inner psychic components.[18] The matter requires delicacy. One may reasonably argue that in Confucius we do catch moral philosophy moving from a naive stage of taking for granted that what you see is what is there to a new concern with genuineness. *Li* must not be mere form: "Ritual performed without reverence, the forms of mourning observed without grief – these are things I cannot bear to see!" (3/26). Confucius does not yet, as do Mencius and his contemporaries, argue about what is "outside" and what is "inside." But if the foregoing reflection on Confucius's concept of *ren* is even partly right, one must be careful. Perhaps the thing to say is that for the early Confucians ritual behavior is a "criterion" of moral quality and not a manifestation of something else inside us; one can "just see" if it is not genuine, just as one can just see that a forced smile is only a skillful grimace.[19]

Two ideas that can be documented in the *Analects*, and that are very important in later thought, need to be noted (but one has to be unsure that Confucius himself world recognize one of them). In *Analects* 5/12 (one of the earliest parts) we read, "Zi Gong said, 'What I do not want others to do to me, I also wish to avoid doing to others.'" "Zi Gong" 子貢 is the philosophical name of a disciple close to Confucius named Duanmu Si 端木賜; Confucius replies, putting him down sweetly, "Oh Si! This is not something you have attained to." Zi Gong's words, if restated as a rule of conduct (instead of being a description, as here, of his ideal of himself) would be one form of what we call the Golden Rule. Just such a formulation is found in two parts of the *Analects* (12/2, 15/24) that are generally agreed to be much later (perhaps late fourth century B.C.). At 15/24 Zi Gong (again) is presented as asking the Master, "Is there a single maxim that can be practiced throughout one's life?" Confucius is made to reply, "Surely, [the principle of] consideration [*shu* 恕]: What you do not want [done to] yourself, do not do to others." The similarity with the early 5/12 shows that the idea belongs to the Confucian circle even at the beginning, and also that it is not to be read as a decision procedure for discovering whether an act would be right.

---

[18] See Herbert Fingarette, *Confucius: The Secular as Sacred* (New York: Harper & Row, 1972), esp. chapter 3, pp. 37–56.

[19] This translation of *Analects*, 3/26, is taken from Arthur Waley, *The Analects of Confucius* (London: Allen & Unwin, 1938), p. 101; for the "criterion" interpretation, see Lee Jig-chuen, "Cong liangge jiaodu lai kan Lunyu zhong de dao," *Xinya xueshu jikan* 3 (1982): 171–7.

Consideration (shu)

Consideration (*shu*) is discussed again, at 4/15:

The Master said, "Shen!" [i.e., Zeng Shen 曾參, a prominent disciple]. "In my Way [*dao*] there is one [idea] that threads it together." Zengzi replied, "Yes." The Master left. The other disciples asked, "What did he mean?" Zengzi replied, "Our Master's Way is just *zhong* and *shu*."[20]

The disciples may have thought themselves answered, but we must ask, what did Zengzi mean? The literature on this extends down through centuries, the usual view being that *zhong* 忠, cognate with *zhong* 中 (inside), means "inner conscientiousness," contrasting with *shu* 恕 (cognate perhaps with *ru* 汝, "you," or *ru* 如, "like"), which is the extension of one's inner cultivated virtue to others. But then we would have just that inside–outside split that is supposed to be absent in basic Confucianism.

The ordinary meaning of *zhong* 忠 is "loyalty." Confucius himself shows what he would mean by it and how he would pair it with "consideration." In 5/19, he is asked to evaluate Dou Gouwutu, 鬭穀於菟, also called Zi Wen 子文, sometime prime minister (*lingyin* 令尹) of the great state of Chu in the south, who was "three times appointed *lingyin* without appearing pleased, and three times was dismissed without appearing displeased; and [on each dismissal] always explained the standing business of the *lingyin*'s office to the incoming *lingyin*. The Master replied, He was *zhong*, to be sure" – but Confucius will not grant that this makes him *ren* (good, otherly), having consideration for others who need help (6/30). *Zhong* obviously means "loyal," specifically in the sense of being strict with oneself in the matter of duty and holding oneself responsible to a standard in serving one's superior that one would expect the other to adhere to, if positions were reversed; whereas *shu* (consideration), is the converse, being lenient with others one is in a position to hurt, as you would hope they would be toward you if positions were reversed.[21]

We glimpse in these texts a characteristic teacher–disciple milieu. Moral instruction and guidance in self-cultivation is carried on by way of comments that probe into the behavior of others in the group, the teacher also some-

---

[20] *Analects*, 4/15: cf. Lau, *Analects*, p. 74. Book 4 is an early one; but this section is obviously designed to show Zengzi off and was probably added after the latter's death in 436 B.C., by his own disciples (E. Bruce Brooks, correspondence).

[21] Herbert Fingarette ("Following the 'One Thread' in the *Analects*," *Journal of the American Academy of Religion*, Thematic Issue, 47, 3S, *Studies in Classical Chinese Thought* (1979): 373–405) offers a different analysis. Taking *shu* not as a character ideal but as a decision procedure, he notes that any such formal "golden rule" will sometimes sanction actions that are obviously morally wrong, unless it is supplemented by a substantive moral rule, which in this case must be *zhong*, taken as *zhong xin* (loyalty and faithfulness).

times commenting on himself, even critically, as well as by evaluations of others outside and past. Sometimes it does not work, and the Master must stamp his foot:

Ran Qiu 冉求 said, "It is not that I am not pleased with your *dao* [Way], but rather that my strength is not enough." The Master said, "One whose strength is not enough collapses mid-Way; but now you just draw a line." (6/12)

That is, you just tell yourself, "I can't." Some are taught but don't respond (the paradox of virtue); others respond but can't act; yet others respond but just don't act (weakness of will). And yet others respond but tell themselves they can't act (self-deception). Ideals like *zhong* and *shu* were not easily realized.

Rectification of Names

A second theme always recognized as being genuinely a theme of Confucius is brought out in the following exchange:

Qi Jing Gong 齊景公 asked Confucius about government. Confucius replied, "Let the ruler be ruler, the subject be subject, the father be father, and the son be son." (12/11, in part)

This comes from a late stratum of the *Analects*, but the pithiness of the line sounds genuine (and surely is memorable), so maybe Confucius did say it. This is the prime locus of what is said to be one of Confucius's fundamental doctrines and to have been named by himself "the rectification of names" (*zheng ming* 正名), or such is the usual translation. In 13/3, which is at least as late, we find the disciple Zi Lu 子路 (Zhong You 仲由) asking his teacher what he, Confucius, would do first if he were given the direction of a state. "Zheng ming," replies Confucius. "You can't be serious!" says Zi Lu in effect. "How boorish you are!" says Confucius:

When names are not correct, what is said will not sound reasonable; when what is said does not sound reasonable, affairs will not culminate in success; when affairs do not culminate in success, rites and music will not flourish; when rites and music do not flourish, punishments will not fit the crimes.[22]

There is another similar account in the Han collection of stories *Shuo yuan* 説苑, which is just as obviously fabricated. In this story, Confucius serves as *si kou* 司寇 (supposedly "minister of crime") in Lu. As his first act, he actually executes a prominent man for deviousness in speech and similar faults. The disciple Zi Gong, aghast, objects; Confucius puts him down with a sharp

---

[22] The translation is that of Lau, *Analects*, pp. 118–19.

rebuke: "This is not within your understanding," thereupon justifying the execution with a long-winded literary argument.[23] The sneers at the disciples, the series of non sequiturs leading up to the endorsement of harsh government, come not from Confucius but from third-century Legalism. Nevertheless, the "rectification of names" has remained a standard ingredient in any description of the Master's views.

But the pithy "Let the ruler be ruler..." might come from Confucius, if we take it as calling not for straightening out terminology, but for a reform of the realities the terms are supposed to name. Confucius was a "transmitter" of traditional standards (let sons really be filial), and a legitimist (let the *tianzi* 天子 really be respected as Son of Heaven, the lord of Lu really acknowledged as having ruling authority). In a later time, when reform has become obviously impossible, it will go the other way, and Mencius will deny the use of the name, when the referent has failed to fit the meaning, as he does (1B/8) when he maintains that King Wu of Zhou did not commit regicide because the last Shang ruler had ceased to behave like a king. Straightening out the use of terms so that you can promulgate an unambiguous (and brutalizing) code of penal law is another idea entirely.

Attitude to History

One can often only guess at how much of the *Analects* to accept as evidence of what Confucius himself thought. In earlier parts of the book he is represented as deploring ritual and ceremonial performances by persons present and past who cannot pretend to the status the rituals imply: the Three Families, for example, performing rites appropriate only for the king (3/2); or Guan Zhong 管仲, chief minister under Qi Huan Gong 齊桓公, using in his household ceremonials proper to a head of state, which Guan Zhong was not (3/22). In one of the much later parts (16/2), Confucius laments the devolution of authority from the king to the regional lords, and in turn to their subordinate officers, a process he was able to observe easily in Lu itself. But the thrust of these statements is that these things ought to be made right (though Confucius is obviously not hopeful), not that there must be a radically new beginning.

The relatively near past had seen the abortive development of an arrangement ostensibly aimed at restoring royal dignity if not real authority. Qi Huan Gong under the guidance of ministers like Guan Zhong had so strengthened his state and military position that he was able to dominate the

---

[23] For the *Shuo yuan* story, see ibid., Appendix 1, pp. 189–90 (from *Shuo yuan* (Sibu beiyao ed.), 15 ["Zhi wu"], 8b). (For a different opinion, defending *Analects*, 13/3, see Angus Graham, *Disputers of the Tao: Philosophical Argument in Ancient China* [La Salle, Ill.: Open Court, 1989], p. 24, note.)

other major lords and bring them into an alliance in service to the king, who recognized him as a kind of lord protector (*ba* 霸) of the realm. The most dramatic episode was a confrontation with the armies of Chu 楚 in 656, resulting in a peaceful settlement, Chu agreeing to tender ritual forms of submission to the Zhou king. Confucius praises Guan Zhong and Duke Huan for these successes (14/15–17).

When he looks at history farther back, Confucius mentions the Three Dynasties – Xia, Shang, and the current Zhou (2/23, 3/9, 3/14); and since the concept of virtue is a prominent part of his moral thinking, one can assume that he accepted the standard view that a dynasty comes into being when Heaven recognizes the virtue of the founder and is superseded when this virtue is exhausted. Without having much to say about it, Confucius favors Zhou as a model of customs and culture, it being both more easily knowable (3/9) and better (3/14); perhaps here we see again his legitimist bias.

As for the still earlier mythicized "sage"-rulers Yao 堯, Shun 舜, and Yu 禹, their role as models in political philosophy has been to support programs of radical reform of the world, prepared to scrap legitimacy: Yao was thought to have set aside his own heir, finding his ablest subject and making him his chief minister, and then resigning the throne to him; and Shun was thought to have done likewise. These are not ideas of Confucius's time, and the texts in the *Analects* that have Confucius praising these men have to be suspected. The most prominent ones are at the end of a "book," 8/18–21. The end of a chapter would be the easiest place to add material; and Book 8, containing seven sections of sayings not by Confucius but by Zengzi, was itself probably added to the *Analects* by the latter's disciples after his death in 436 B.C.[24] There is a fair likelihood, therefore, that these model "sage emperors" enter Chinese "history," that is to say, Chinese philosophy, only at the end of the fifth century, just in time to be the hottest new ideas during the formative years of Mencius (probably born around 390 B.C.).

MOZI

Between the death of Confucius and the birth of Mencius falls the career of Mozi 墨子 (ca. 480–390). "Master Mo" was founder of an amazingly different philosophical movement. In his time, history had taken a turn that must have made any restorationist hopes ridiculous. Mozi was from Song, west of Lu; his movement probably was strongest at first in Chu; but what was the shape of his "world"? The strongest ruler after the Zhou collapse in 771 had been Jin Wen Hou, (r. 780–746) while the later Jin Wen Gong 晉公, of the

---

[24] See Nivison and Pang, "Astronomical Evidence," esp. p. 93, n. 18.

Quwo 曲沃, line had been the *ba* after Qi Huan Gong. By the 490s, Jin was effectively divided among six ministerial houses, and a civil war was going on that reduced these to four. War broke out again in 453, leaving three survivors, Zhao, Hann, and Wei. Fifty years later, in 403, the lords of these three new states obliged the Zhou "king" to accept the demise of Jin and to recognize them as among the regional lords (*zhuhou* 諸侯); on this, says the *Shi ji*, the "cauldrons of Zhou" (embodying the virtue of the dynasty) "shook."[25] A quarter century after this a coup d'état in Qi toppled that state's ruling house and established a new line. All now took it for granted that eventually the now purely nominal Zhou dynasty would inevitably be replaced by a new world power. But when and how, and by whom? Thus began the era of the Warring States, in which Mozi moved.

Nothing is known about Mozi the person. In the book *Mozi* he is sometimes given the personal name Di 翟. (His apparent surname Mo perhaps means "branded," suggesting that he had suffered corporal punishment.) Hints in the book named for him suggest that he may have been an artisan in origin, perhaps a carpenter. We find him, like Confucius, however, behaving like a *shi* turned teacher of young men who seek employment; and also like Confucius, Mozi knows and uses the classical literature and is able to quote and argue from he *Shang shu* and the *Shi jing*. And more explicitly than Confucius, Mozi argues that lordly employers should give offices to men who are worthy, rather than to men who have the right aristocratic connections.

Beyond this, everything is different. For Confucius, there is little more than the brief *Analects*, which must be carefully sifted, but which has been treasured down the ages, Confucius being honored as the greatest of sages. For Mozi, there is a substantial book containing not only conversations but systematic essays on morals and politics, and much more; but Mozi's philosophical-political movement, though deeply influencing the other major philosophers of the Warring States period, had died out completely by the Han dynasty, and the book (or most of it) survived to attract attention in relatively modern times only by accident.

Moral Values

Mozi's moral values, too, are sharply different. Confucius had been refining an aristocratic and traditional normative ethics, turning it into a "virtue ethic" in which a good polity and society are dominated and led by good men, and a good man is one who has cultivated admirable traits of charac-

---

[25] See *Shi ji*, 15, p. 709, for 403 B.C.

ter. For Mozi, a good government is one that realizes namable material benefits for the community, and a good man is one who has the abilities that would enable him to give effective service in such a government if employed and properly paid to remain loyal.[26]

Confucius treasures the rites for their value in cultivating virtue (while virtually ignoring their religious origin). Mozi sees ritual, and the music associated with it, as wasteful, is exasperated with Confucians for valuing them, and seems to have no conception of moral self-cultivation whatever. Further, Mozi's ethics is a "command ethic," and he thinks that religion, in the bald sense of making offerings to spirits and doing the things they want, is of first importance: it is the "will" of Heaven and the spirits that we adopt the system he preaches, and they will reward us if we do adopt it. He takes it for granted that we will not do what we should (in this sense) if we do not believe in spirits or Heaven or if we think that good fortune depends on "fate" rather than being a reward for good deeds. So people must believe in spirits and must not believe in fate. In his view of religion there is (as in his ethics) no inner feeling or awe.[27]

The basic goods in Mozi's consequentialist thinking are three: order (absence of conflict between persons, families, cities, states), material wealth for the community, and increase in population. They are interrelated: more basic wealth, then more reproduction; more people, then more production and wealth. Conflict will interfere with both, whereas if people have plenty, they will be good, filial, kind, and so on unproblematically. "Basic goods" are goods for social entities: there is no appeal to happiness or pleasure for individuals in Mozi's "utilitarianism."[28]

The *Mozi* as presently constituted has titles for seventy-one chapters, eighteen of which are missing and some others defective. The extant chapters are of markedly different kinds. Chapters 1–7 are obviously late. (Chapter 3 mentions an event in 286 B.C.)[29] They are also untypical (e.g., there is a stirring short chapter on self-cultivation). Chapters 8–39 present the core of Mozi's doctrines (eight of these chapters are now missing) and perhaps are based on writings by Mozi himself, although formally they describe his views and quote him. These are in groups of three chapters each which concern ten theses: "Promoting the Worthy," "Identification Upwards," "Impartial

---

[26] See chapters 8–10, "Shang xian."

[27] See especially the chapters titled "Tian zhi" (The Will of Heaven), "Ming gui" (On Spirits), and "Fei ming" (Against Fatalism).

[28] For the basic goods in Mo Zi's consequentialism, see, for example, the opening sentences of chapter 8 ("Promoting the Worthy," Part 1) and chapter 35 ("Against Fatalism," part 1), i.e., *Mozi* (Sibu beiyao ed.), 2 (8 "Shang xian A"), 1a; and 9 (35 "Fei ming A"), 1a (Burton Watson, *Mo Tzu: Basic Writings* [New York: Columbia University Press, 1963], pp. 18, 117).

[29] Chapter 3 ("On Dyeing"), *Mozi*, 1 (3 "Suo ran"), 5b, mentions the death of King Kang of Song. See D. C. Lau, *Lao Tzu: Tao Te Ching* (Harmondsworth: Penguin, 1963), pp. 157–8.

Caring," "Against Attacking," "Economy in Expenditures," "Simplicity in Funerals," "The Will of Heaven," "On Spirits," "Against Music," and "Against Fatalism." (There were two more chapters in this group, both titled "Against Confucians," one of which remains.) These chapters are the doctrinal texts of three schools of Mohists that started at different times and represent changes and sometimes compromises in original Mohist positions.[30]

This doctrinal aspect of the *Mozi* shows that Mozi was not just a philosopher. He started a highly disciplined movement that demanded of its members acceptance of a body of doctrine, and even the exact wording of the statements of this doctrine was so important that subtle disagreement led to schisms. Accounts in other texts show that Mohists were organized under a leader (called the *Juzi* 鉅子, chief master) who could order members on assignments, tax them for part of their salaries if they were placed in official positions, and even inflict the death penalty. He held his position for life and named his own successor.[31]

Chapters 40–5 are a highly dense and systematic (and badly garbled) presentation of principles of epistemology and methods of argument, a feature of no other ancient system of thought in China. They seem to be the work of a group of specialists of the late fourth and third centuries B.C.[32] This interest in the forms and methods of argument can already be seen in the earliest stratum of the *Mozi*, both in the apparently purposeful use of formal structure in arguments and at one point – in the chapters "Against Fatalism" (Fei Ming 非命) – in an explicit listing of the criteria that Mozi thinks must be met by a theory if it is to be sound: "A theory must be judged by three tests, . . . its origin, its validity, and its applicability." One judges its origin "by comparing the theory with the deeds of the sage kings of antiquity," its validity "by comparing the theory with the evidence of the eyes and ears of the people," and its applicability "by observing whether, when the theory is put into practice in the administration, it brings benefit to the state and the people."[33]

Chapters 46–50 are collections of conversations involving Mozi, a kind of Mohist analects. This group is probably later than the main group of chapters 8 through 39 and is probably partly of a fictional nature.[34]

[30] See Graham, *Disputers of the Tao*, pp. 35, 51–3.

[31] The Mohist organization and the powers of their leader are described and illustrated by Fung Yu-lan, *History of Chinese Philosophy*, vol. 1, pp. 81–4.

[32] These chapters are very difficult and have been much studied by modern Chinese scholars. For a recent translation (necessarily also an attempt to restore the original texts), see A. C. Graham, *Later Mohist Logic, Ethics, and Science* (Hong Kong: Chinese University Press; London: University of London, School of Oriental and African Studies, 1978).

[33] *Mozi*, 9 (35 "Fei ming A"), 1b; the translations are from Watson, *Mo Tzu*, p. 118.

[34] Not included in Watson; translations of these chapters can be found in Yi-pao Mei, *The Ethical and Political Works of Motse* (London: Arthur Probsthain, 1929; rpt. Taipei: Ch'eng Wen, 1974).

Chapters 51–71 (ten missing) are technical texts on defensive warfare. The basic Mohist texts "Against Attacking" (Fei gong 非攻) mark Mohists as pacifists of a sort: they condemned offensive warfare, but they considered it one of the functions of a state to provide weapons for defense. And they reasoned that if offensive war is bad, it is the duty of Mohists to aid states and cities being attacked. There are accounts of their doing this that show that some Mohists became specialists in the art of defense; these chapters appear to be the remains of texts expounding their art. One interesting idea in them is that soldiers on a city wall under attack are to be held responsible for each other, each soldier for the one on his right and the one on his left, to prevent treason. This is but one example of a concept of "group responsibility" that appears in another guise in the core chapters on political organization ("Shang tong" 尚同, Identification upwards), which require that the members of a community are to be punished if they fail to report wrongdoing in their midst. The group responsibility idea was taken over by specialists in government, later called "Legalists," and passed into imperial law down to modern times.

Impartial Caring

The Mohist doctrine that attracted the most attention among Mozi's opponents is the third, "impartial caring" (*jian ai* 兼愛), usually translated "universal love." Mozi puts the idea forward as the solution to all socially destructive conflict, from quarrels between individuals to wars between states. I am to "love" (*ai*) or care for your children or your father as I would my own, your family or city or state as I would my own; conflicts then will cease and all will be secure. One cannot reject this idea without contradicting oneself, because even if one rejected it verbally, if one were to go on a journey and had to leave one's family in the care of another, one would choose a person who did accept the ideal of impartial caring, and this amounts to accepting it yourself.[35] The taste for argument, leading your opponent through a thought experiment, and the assumption that if you can lead him step by step to your conclusion, he will be forced to accept it, are typical of Mohists.

There are, however, certain problems. One can see at least three. A Thrasymachus, inspecting the foregoing argument, would sneer and say (at least to himself) that in choosing the impartial caregiver as caretaker of my family, I am not approving his doctrine but merely exploiting the fact that he holds it. How is the altruist to avoid being exploited? For it to be rational for me to be altruistic myself, I must live in a community in which I can be sure

---

[35] *Mozi*, 4 (16 "Jian ai C"), 8a; Watson, *Mo Tzu*, p. 42.

that everyone else will be altruistic too. And given Mozi's simplistic non-psychology – having no self-cultivation, no possibility of relying on a culti-vated delight in a "good" for its own sake – he must find it to be the case, or make it be the case, that people have no choice. He points out that a ruler, simply by favoring something, can get his subjects to favor it (the *de* effect) and that "no good deed is not returned" by the receiver (another *de* effect).[36]

But one needs to be sure. For Mozi, a rational altruism requires an author-itarian political community. In "Shang tong" the Mohist develops a quasi-Hobbesian theory of the state. In the beginning each person had his own *yi* 義 (standard of right), that is, each wanted to benefit himself, and so life was brutish for all. So a ruler set up a government. (Mozi does not consider how this could have happened, any more than do Western contract theories.) A structure of lords, governors, and village heads is brought into being, and the village head orders his people to accept the standard of the head of the dis-trict, who orders all under him to accept the standard of the lord, who orders his people to accept the standard of the king. Finally, Mozi supposes, the king must do the same with respect to the will of Heaven. There are chap-ters ("Tian zhi" 天志, The will of Heaven) telling us what that is: it is that all shall care for each other impartially.

But the solution of this difficulty is too easy. We sense that something strange is going on: How, as a person in a village, am I to go about taking as my own the view of what is right held by the head of the district? For that matter, since it is going to come down to impartial caring, how am I to go about adopting that attitude toward you? Mozi talks as if adopting an atti-tude (or a belief, for that matter, as we read in the chapter on spirits) can be done on command, just as I might on command raise my arm. Countering the objection of a ruler who might tell him that this is just impossible, Mozi replies that it is simple: the sage kings of old did it, so just do it! It is not as if you were being asked to pick up Mount Tai 泰山 and jump over a river with it.[37] We see that Mozi's command ethic is also bizarrely voluntaristic. But this remains a problem, and it will have a major consequence in later moral psychology.

Yet another difficulty is this: Mozi is able to show me that it would be to my advantage to live in an altruistic world, if altruism were all that were involved and if there were some way to get there; and he can even make out a case for an enlightened ruler, that he as well as everybody would be better off if he ruled "impartially." For the sacrifices required, there would be obvious rewards through Heaven's favor. But what about Mozi's band of fol-lowers, who are expected to give up all personal interests in promoting Mozi's

---

[36] *Mozi*, 4 (16 "Jian ai C"), 11a–12b; Watson, *Mo Tzu*, pp. 47–9.
[37] *Mozi*, 4 (16 "Jian ai C"), 9b; Watson, *Mo Tzu*, p. 44.

vision? And what about Mozi himself? Why should they and he do this, if the only real good is what satisfies material needs?

By the fourth century B.C., there were other philosophers who noticed just this problem.

FOURTH CENTURY: YANG ZHU, ZI HUAZI

New problems reshaped old concepts. There is a famous story told in the *Shi ji* about two men of Zhao 趙 in the early third century B.C. Lian Po 廉頗 was a general, and Lin Xiangru 藺相如 a younger man who for daring diplomatic service had been accorded a status at court higher than Lian's. Lian Po, jealous, threatened to disgrace his imagined rival if the two met publicly. One day Lin Xiangru, with his retinue, saw Lian Po and his followers approaching on the same road. Lin Xiangru led his group aside to let the other pass, a gesture of deference. Afterward his retainers protested and were about to leave his service. When we joined you, they said, we thought you were a man of *gao yi* 高義 – a lofty sense of honor; we seem to have been wrong. Lin Xiangru explained that he was putting the interest of the state above petty quarreling. Word of this got back to Lian Po, who in a dramatic scene apologized, and the two swore blood brotherhood.[38]

Yi ("Honor") and Its Value

The word *yi* 義 is usually a moral term, "righteousness," "dutifulness," "morality." But Lin's men were not making a moral-philosophical point. For them *yi* meant "honor," including a disposition to insist on due respect. One's *yi* in this sense, they assumed, was something one was prepared to fight about, whatever the consequences.

The Mozi of the (probably fourth century B.C.) Mohist "Conversations," however, is making (not quite fairly) a moral-philosophical point in a remark about *yi* that sounds like this idea. He observes that one would decline the gift of a hat or shoes if in return one must let one's hands and feet be cut off; and one would decline the gift of the whole world if in return one had to give up one's life; one's hands and feet are thus more valuable than a mere thing, and one's life is more valuable – to oneself – than the whole world. "Yet people will fight to the death over a single *yan* 言 (word). This shows that *yi* is held more valuable than one's life."[39] It is clear from the context that Mozi is addressing the third and last of the three difficulties pointed out

---

[38] "Lofty [sense of] honor" (*gao yi*); see *Shi ji*, 81, p. 2443.
[39] *Mozi*, 12 (47 "Gui yi"), 1a; cf. Mei, *Motse*, p. 222.

above: Why should he and his followers give up everything else, even life if need be, to promote the Mohist *yi*? By *yan* (word), here he means a maxim; and by *yi* a philosophical principle expressed in a *yan*.

But we do not expect to find the old philosophers settling disputes among themselves with the knife. Mozi has borrowed and twisted a mode of argument seen in a new type of philosopher in the fourth century. Among them, the argument would have meant, "Yet people will fight to the death over a single word (i.e., an insult); this shows that honor (*yi*) is valued more than life." That this was a common thought is shown by the fact that another later fourth-century philosopher named Song Keng 宋牼 (or Song Xing 鈃), who shared many Mohist views and was a doctrinaire pacifist, held that it should be resisted, arguing that really "suffering insult is no disgrace," so men should not fight about it. Song's position would be analyzed destructively by Xunzi in the early third century.[40]

As an example of what Mozi's words ought to have meant, consider a certain Zi Huazi 子華子, said to be from Wei, whose writings survive only in quotations in the *Lü shi chunqiu*. He is one of a kind of thinker who argues that what is most important is *quan sheng* 全生 (keeping [one's own] life complete). He says, "The complete life is highest, the depleted life is next, death is next, and an oppressed life is lowest." He elaborates: when all our desires get what is appropriate for them, this is the complete life; when they get only part, this is a depleted life; when they get nothing, this is death; and when they are forced to endure what they detest, this is an oppressed life, which is worse than death.[41] An example of what is detested is disgrace; and the worst sort of disgrace is "not *yi*," "dishonor." And the implication is that it would be better to die than to suffer it.

But the most visible aspect of this kind of personal philosophy is what (rather surprisingly) is indicated by the first part of the remark given to Mozi here: you would value a part of your body more than gaining some valuable possession, and your life more that gaining the whole world. This should show you that if you are a ruler, you are short-sighted if you endanger yourself by war, and if you are a more ordinary person you are equally short-sighted if you risk yourself (too often a risk of life) in the scramble for advancement that taking any public office or position of service involves – up to and including the position of ruler of the whole world. (By this stage in the development of Chinese philosophy, arguments were often followed through to their logical conclusion, no matter what.) The best thing to do

---

[40] *Xunzi* (Sibu beiyao ed.), 12 (18 "Zheng lun"), 11a–14a; John H. Knoblock, *Xunzi: A Translation and Study of the Complete Works* (Stanford, Calif.: Stanford University Press, 1994), vol. 3, pp. 45–8.

[41] *Lü shi chunqiu*, 2 ("Gui sheng"), 4b–5a. For different interpretations of these texts, see Fung, *History of Chinese Philosophy*, vol. 1, p. 139; and Graham, *Disputers of the Tao*, pp. 62–3.

(this is obviously an elitist point of view) is to withdraw from all engagement in the public world and cultivate a lifestyle in which in the time alloted you, you are able to satisfy all your desires, optimally and appropriately – which is not to say excessively.

The Cultivation of Sheng

This viewpoint could lead to a simple-minded hedonism; Xunzi criticizes a certain Wei Mou 魏牟 who practices this. It is interesting, however, that the justification such hedonists claim is that if one happens to be the sort of person who cannot rein in one's cravings, forcing oneself to do so may be harmful to one's "life," that is, to one's nature.[42] But the notion of a "complete life" leads ordinarily to a moderate asceticism, satisfying desire but avoiding harmful excess. The good life, in short, is going to be one in which one "cultivates" one's person, in a sense, seeking to have one's most precious possession, one's *sheng* 生 (life) in the sense of natural tendencies and natural span, kept uninjured. One cultivates one's *sheng;* the word is cognate with (and probably the original form of) the word *xing* 性, which in the psychological turn taken by the Confucianism of the late fourth century B.C. seems to mean "human nature."

This philosophy of *sheng* is associated chiefly with a philosopher of the fourth century B.C. named Yang Zhu 楊朱, who has no surviving writings, though it is thought that some chapters in the *Lü shi chunqiu* and in the "Daoist" *Zhuangzi* 莊子 represent him or describe and elaborate a view like his.[43] It is probable that the author of the original parts of the *Zhuangzi* began as a disciple of Yang Zhu, or someone like him, but later underwent a kind of conversion experience that led him to a much more subtle view. There seem to be four aspects of Yangist thinking: (1) it involves withdrawal from the ordinary world and from any interest in either reforming it or conforming to its conventional demands; (2) it is selfcultivationist, in a way; (3) it places value on long life; and (4) it is inner-directed (though not mystical).

It is one kind of drop-out philosophy that can be seen in the increasingly complicated thought world of the fourth century B.C. Another is the stance of the hermit who, perhaps holding to a Confucian ideal of a perfect world, simply decides that the present age is hopeless and that all one can do is withdraw and perfect one's moral character. There are accounts in late sections of the *Analects* about Confucius encountering such persons (18/3–15), and there the motive of the recluse for avoiding political involvement is some-

---

[42] Fung, *History of Chinese Philosophy*, p. 140; *Lü shi chunqiu*, 21 ("Shen wei"), 6b. On Wei Mou, see also Knoblock, *Xunzi*, vol. 1, pp. 63–4.
[43] Graham, *Disputers of the Tao*, p. 55

times that it is hopeless (implying an ideal of service), sometimes that it is dangerous (implying first a concern for self).

The ease of overlooking the importance of this difference may explain a remark in the *Mencius* concerning the followers of Yang Zhu and the followers of Mozi (7B/26): "Those who desert the Mohist school are sure to turn to Yang; those who desert the Yang school are sure to turn to the *Ru* 儒 (Confucians)."[44] Mencius was actually deeply influenced by both Mozi and Yang Zhu, but when he criticizes them (as he does, sharply, 3B/9) he hits Mozi's doctrine of "impartial caring," which to him means to deny the natural family obligation one has of prior affection to parents, and Yang's contrasting selfishness, which implies denying the ultimate obligation of respect and service to rulers. A Yangist can be seen as reacting against Mozi's ideal of impartiality by saying, I am just not like that: I find that I naturally care more for what is nearer, my state rather than another, my family rather than another's, and my self rather than others in my family.[45] But a Yangist become a "self"-cultivating recluse can seem to be on the way to being a principled (even Confucian) recluse who simply thinks that the present age is hopeless.

Another detail in the stories in the *Analects* points to another possible dimension of drop-out behavior. In two cases, the hermits are farmers (18/5, 18/6). It became a common criticism of philosopher-types (even leveled at Mozi) that they ate the rice of idleness and accepted support that they had not earned. The implication is that a proper life would be spent producing one's own food. Following the trend of the time to push an idea as far as it would go, one would then conclude that even a really moral ruler would do the same, ploughing in the fields with his people, and that this must have been the way it was in really remote, really perfect antiquity. An ideal sage-ruler was invented, the "Divine Farmer," Shen Nong 神農, who behaved this way in a world "empire" that was essentially anarchic, and a cult of rather intellectual hermit-farmer followers of Shen Nong developed. Mencius had an interesting argument with one of them, a disciple of a certain Xu Xing 許行 (3A/4). Mencius argues for a division of labor and defends the role of the ruler, but is really defending himself:

There are those who work with their minds and those who work with their muscles. Those who work with their minds rule others, and those who work with their muscles are ruled by others. The latter feed others; the former are fed by others. This is a principle [*yi*] accepted everywhere in the world.[46]

[44] Cf. Lau, *Mencius*, p. 199.
[45] Cf. *Mozi*, 11 (46 "Geng zhu"), 12b; Mei, *Motse*, p. 219.
[46] *Mencius*, 3A/4 (cf. Lau, *Mencius*, p. 101).

The end of the fourth century B.C. was a time when "those who work with their minds" were often able to live quite well, for two reasons. One was that what caused the "Warring States" to be warring states was that it now seemed more and more obvious that eventually one of them would "roll up the other states like a mat," its ruler replacing the Zhou king to become real king of the world. This would be accomplished by becoming strong in war, and this in turn required becoming strong in organization, population, and production. If a man could become recognized as having talent in statecraft, he could have a very enviable career no matter what his background. Two men in particular, Gongsun Yang 公孫鞅 (or Shang Yang 商鞅) in Qin and Shen Buhai 申不害 in Hann, did this; both had books named for them, actually written (for the most part) later – the former (*Shang jun shu* 商君書, The book of Lord Shang) surviving almost complete, the latter (*Shen Buhai*, or *Shenzi* 申子) in fragments. Their ideas (which tended to ruthlessness) were taken up and refined by the best read of the ancient writers on statecraft, Han Feizi 韓非子 (d. 233 B.C.), who will be considered in due course.

The second reason is also a consequence of the deadly serious interstate competition. To win out in the long run, a ruler needed more than just a strong army. He would need prestige, the ability to inspire awe, the conviction among all people that he was the one destined to rule, whose side it would be wise to join now: in short, the winning ruler must have virtue (*de*). The best way to be seen as having it was to be conspicuously successful in attracting to one's court wise advisers, whom one would treat with great deference and place in sinecure positions. In this context, philosophy prospered as never before.

The Mutual Recognition of Kings: The Jixia Academy

Ying 罃 (嬰), a prince of the state of Wei, had succeeded (after a court struggle) as ruler of his state in 370 or 369 B.C. In 343 B.C., he was badly defeated by Qi in the battle of Maling 馬陵, and the Qi ruler in the flush of victory had declared himself "king" (*wang* 王), as Wei Wang 威王, effective in 342 B.C. [47] Undaunted, Ying in Wei declared himself king in 335 (probably mistaking this year as the 700th anniversary of the founding of the parent state of Jin), taking the title Huicheng Wang 惠成王. [48] The universal concept

[47] Qian Mu, *Xian Qin zhuzi xinian* (Shanghai: Shangwu, 1935; rev. rpt. Hong Kong: Hong Kong University Press, 1956), pp. 256–9, 265.
  [Editors' note: Other sources indicate that the battle of Maling took place in 341 B.C., and that King Wei of Qi's title as "king" (*wang*) was recognized in 334 B.C.]

[48] The date 335 B.C. is given in the "Present Text," *Bamboo Annals* (*Jin ben Zhu shu jinian*), which also gives (incorrectly) 1035 B.C. as the date of the enfeoffment of Tangshu Yu, in effect the first duke of Jin. (This text is widely but wrongly regarded as a fake. An English translation can be found in Legge, *The Shoo King*, Prolegomena, pp. 108–76).

had come to be that there could be only one legitimate *wang* in the world; thus, such a declaration amounted to a declaration of intent to conquer all the other states, a move not without danger. To forestall combinations against himself, a claimant therefore would enter into a diplomatic agreement with another claimant or claimants of "mutual recognition as king" (*xiang wang* 相王). The first such *xiang wang* treaty, in 334 between Wei and Qi, was followed by others through the 320s, with more and more rulers in the club. As this process went on – with the problem of how to make one's claim stick becoming more and more urgent and the likelihood that one could do it wholly by force becoming less and less clear – ambitious rulers sought prestige, patronizing philosophy. Over two decades, King Huicheng had Hui Shi 惠施, a quasi-Mohist who talked about "loving all things" and dazzled all with paradoxical ticks of reasoning, as prime minister. For their part the kings of Qi collected pampered intellectuals in what has come to be known as the Jixia 稷下 Academy, from the location of quarters given them in the Qi capital Linzi 臨淄. Both the Wei court and the Qi court were places where a writer or teacher with a reputation could expect a generous reception.

MENCIUS

It is in this scene that Mencius, the "second sage" in the Confucian tradition, first appears (as far as is known) on the Chinese world stage, being welcomed at the Wei court in 320 B.C. by King Huicheng at his capital Daliang 大梁, at modern Kaifeng 開封. (Hence he is known as King Hui of Liang.) Huicheng was already an old man, and Mencius may have been even older (the king greeted him as *sou* 叟, venerable sir). Mencius (the Latinization of Meng Zi 孟子, Master Meng) must already have had a well-established reputation. His personal name was Ke 軻, and he came from a very small state called Zou 鄒, next to Lu.

The *Mencius* is in seven parts, conventionally called "books." The *Shi ji's* account of Mencius says that these seven were written by Mencius with the help of a few of his disciples at the end of his life.[49] (There must have been at least minor editing later, probably with additions.)[50] Sometime in early Han, four more books were added, but were deleted by Zhao Qi 趙岐 (d. A.D. 201), the earliest commentator whose work survives. The text is one of the best preserved of Warring States works.

[Editors' note: According to other sources this ruler was titled Hui Hou from 369 B.C. first adopting the royal title *wang* in 344 B.C., and then declaring a new first year of reign in 334 B.C. Bearing the title Hui Wang until his death in 319, he is also referred to as Liang Hui Wang for this latter part of his reign, Liang being the name of his capital city. Incorrectly, the *Shi ji* lists Wei Xiang Wang as the ruler of Wei from 334 to 319 B.C.; see Calendar and Chronology and Chapter 9, both this volume.]

[49] *Shi ji*, 74, p. 2343.   [50] Lau, *Mencius*, pp. 220–2.

The first two books appear to be in chronological order, covering events and conversations from 320 through 314 B.C., when Qi invaded Yan. These show Mencius in conversations with two kings of Wei: Huicheng (d. 319) and Xiang 襄 (in 319–318); and with King Xuan 宣 of Qi (between 319 and 314). All of these rulers were obviously chiefly interested in how to promote their project of becoming king of all China, and Mencius adroitly plays on this interest to urge them that their best course is to adopt morally approvable policies – lightening taxes and enlisting the sympathy of their subjects by seeing to their economic welfare. The other books contain matter that cannot be dated and may be as much as thirty or forty years earlier. The books have been sectioned by later editors (Zhao Qi divided each book in two), and usually the sectioning is obviously right. The last book has very short sections and may consist of notes and recollections brought forward by disciples later on.

Especially important is the first half of Book 6, opening with the record of an argument with an older philosopher named Gaozi 告子 on human nature (*xing* 性). Book 2 opens with another especially interesting extended conversation between Mencius and one of his followers in Qi, Gongsun Chou 公孫丑, and here Gaozi appears again, apparently long dead, his words being quoted and criticized. He figures nowhere else in ancient philosophical literature except, in all probability, in one of the chapters in *Mozi*, but Mencius's disagreements with him have been near the center of attention in Confucian philosophy over the past eight centuries. We learn much of other philosophers in the Mencius. Mencius sometimes quotes and always praises Confucius and is said to have got his own training in Confucian principles through a student of Confucius's grandson Kong Ji 孔伋 (better known as Zi Si 子思).[51] He has a brief conversation with Song Xing, shows (without naming him) familiarity with Zi Huazi, and in one long section in Book 3 has a debate already mentioned, with a "follower of Sheng Nong," who held that all, even rulers, should produce their own food by farming. He attacks with spirit the central positions (as he understands them) of both Mozi and Yang Zhu, but (as will be shown) is also deeply influenced by both. And with Mencius the old problem of the "paradox of virtue" becomes acute. It is sharpened by what Mencius draws from Mozi and resolved by what he gets from Yang Zhu.

The Acquisition of De

The first conversation with King Xuan of Qi (1A/7) probably occurred in 319 B.C. Xuan wants to know, of course, how he can win some wars. Could

---

[51] *Shi ji*, 74, p. 2343 (translated in Lau, *Mencius*, p. 205).

Mencius discuss classic strategies with him? Mencius steers the king into talking about *de*, (virtue) instead – appropriately; giving the king an image of having *de* was what he and men like him were there for. You already have the virtue a true king needs, Mencius says, and calls Xuan's attention to an absurd incident a few days back, when Xuan had happened to see an ox being led past in the street, to a sacrifice, had been moved to pity, and had ordered a sheep to be substituted for it. The very absurdity of the act showed the genuine feeling behind it. Now, Mencius continues, all you have to do is (so to speak) to pick up this capacity over there, and put it down over here: apply it to your people and adopt policies that will make their lives bearable. I'm not asking you to do something difficult, like picking up Mount Tai and jumping over the sea with it, says Mencius; it's easy; just do it: "extend your compassion" (*tui en* 推恩). In the comparison with "picking up Mount Tai," Mencius is not just drawing from but actually quoting Mozi's argument for impartial caring.

Confucius had wanted rulers to be ritually correct and to love the good, so that their people would also. Mencius is more explicit about concrete policies: lowering taxes, lightening punishments, making sure the people are never in want (for the ordinary people cannot be expected to be good if they are ill housed and starving). Mencius advises his kings to adopt a policy of government by sympathy, giving a new twist to the Confucian Golden Rule: so manage your state that you share your pleasures with your people; then you will enjoy your pleasures more, just as it is more enjoyable to listen to music with others rather than alone (1B/1):

There is a way to get the World: get the people and you will get the world. There is a way to get the people: get their hearts and you will get the people. There is a way to get their hearts: acquire together with them the things you desire, and do not inflict on them the things you dislike. (4A/10)

Mencius here drops in place a bit of philosophical philology that was current in his time: "virtue" (*de* 德) is "getting" (*de* 得). As for military success, forget it. To seek domination by force will simply turn the world against you, whereas if you practice a benevolent government, all the world will want you to be their king, and no army will dare to oppose you: "The benevolent one has no enemy" (literally "no equal"; 1A/5, 2A/5, 7B/3). This too is Mohist pacifism; in his "Against Aggressive War," Mozi had said that if a ruler governs kindly, "in all the world he will have no enemy."[52]

But what do you do if the ruler who needs virtue is not hearing you? This was the paradox: "Can one talk with a cruel man? He is at ease with the

---

[52] *Mozi*, 5 (19 "Fei gong C"), 10b; Watson, *Mo Tzu*, p. 60.

danger [he brings on himself], mistakes disasters for advantages, delights in what will destroy him" (4A/9). Mozi had held in effect that one simply must show a person how to calculate where his real advantage lies. Mencius is always trying this – in the opening conversation with Huicheng, shaming the king for putting advantage (*li* 利) ahead of compassion and justice (*ren yi* 仁義) and then pointing out the advantages of putting compassion and justice first. But suppose he sees where his advantage lies. What is one to do when he says, "I can't." How is the teacher really to reach and motivate the student toward virtue, unless the student is motivated already, which is to be virtuous already? (The problem resembles the problem of the teacher of any kind of knowledge in Plato's *Meno*: the student will not recognize the lesson as a lesson, unless in some deep sense he knows what he is to be taught already.) Mencius's solution is to say that in appropriate situations we all have incipient stirrings of sympathy, shame, modesty. In this sense, he is saying that we are all potentially virtuous already. The teacher's task, then, is literally to educate, draw out of us a recognition of these potentialities; and this is exactly what he tries to do with King Xuan.

The Goodness of Human Nature and the Cultivation of Morality

Mencius's famous theory of the "goodness of human nature" is on the one hand his resolution of the deepest problem in Mozi – how can one move oneself to care, or to believe in caring, simply by an act of will, as one might obey an order (to oneself or by another) to move one's arm? Mencius believes we already have a head start. We will need some coaxing, perhaps (by a teacher), or must coax ourselves (self-cultivation), but we already have a "nature" (*xing*) to work on. On the other hand, *xing* is cognate with and originally identical with *sheng*, the tendency of life stressed by Yang Zhu, who argued that we must not damage our *sheng* by forcing it in directions that Heaven did not intend. For Yang, this meant measured satisfactions of desires, aimed at letting us live out our natural span. But here Mencius is Confucian: Heaven favors the moral and has so shaped our nature (*xing*) that if we help it to develop naturally we will become fully moral. Looking at the matter differently, a Mencian can also say that the fact that moral learning occurs at all shows that man's nature must be "good."[53]

In spelling out this idea, Mencius draws on the thought (and even the phrasing) of another philosopher of the Yangist persuasion already mentioned, Zi Huazi (who must have been a contemporary of Mencius). Echoing

[53] See *Mencius*, 6A/16, on "the honors bestowed by Heaven" (also 7A/1); note *Xunzi*, 17 (23 "Xing e"), 1b, quoting Mencius.

Zi Huazi, Mencius calls attention to the fact that as humans we all have natural likes: our eyes are pleased by beauty, our ears by fine music, our mouths by delicious foods. So also our "hearts" (xin 心) are pleased by li yi 理義 (order and right) (6A/7). Zi Huazi, in describing the oppressed life that is worse than death, had said that it is a life in which the mind and the senses are all forced to endure what they detest, the most detestable thing being bu yi 不義, which seemed to mean "dishonor." But Zi Huazi elsewhere also says that a successful king is one who has a natural taste for li and yi; and it is this phrase that Mencius slips into place here, insisting that we all (not just kings) naturally savor li and yi, adding that the sages of the past, like famous cooks, have merely "anticipated" our taste in laying down for us moral rules.[54]

In this way of putting the matter. Mencius uncovered a problem that has vexed Confucian moral philosophy ever since. If the sages and we have the same moral tastes, why do we need to heed them? Why can't we simply do some reflecting and discover or work out morality for ourselves? The alarmingly antinomian potential of this is sharpened by another problem, in another way in which Mencius describes the goodness of human nature. He gives a list of four natural virtues (2A/6, 6A/6), which are ren 仁 (benevolence), yi 義 (dutifulness), li 禮 (propriety), and zhi 智 ([moral] intelligence). We are not born with these, however, but with four dispositions of "heart" (xin 心), for example, a natural sense of pity (Mencius asks us to imagine how we would react if we were to see a baby about to crawl into a well), which is the basis of ren, and a natural sense of shame, which is the basis of yi (notice the tinge of meaning of "honor" that this word continues to have). But how do we get from here to there? Mencius calls the dispositions duan 端 (sprouts). The metaphor suggests that if we water them they will grow to maturity; and this seems to be what he is saying elsewhere (4A/27): there is a natural effect of reinforcement whenever we do a good act; we enjoy it, and with the enjoyment the tendency becomes irrepressible. But there is a danger: How can we be sure that the end result will be a cultivated nature that is disposed to just the rules that are required in a good Confucian society? At least two views can be distinguished. Perhaps this is the natural way one will develop – surely Mencius's view (we might say that the duan are the "deep structure" of morality). But this seems risky, and a different view appears, which holds that the duan are clues or hints of a full moral knowledge that is "in" us all the time, waiting for us to discover it. But of course, to a cautious and conservative moralist, this is going to seem even more dan-

---

[54] For discussion of the Zi Huazi texts, see A. C. Graham, "The Background of the Mencian Theory of Human Nature," Tsing-hua Hsueh-pao, n.s., 6, 1–2 (1967): 239–40. The texts are in Lü shi chunqiu, 2 ("Gui sheng"), 4b–5a, and 4 ("Wu tu"), 7a. Graham would not agree with this translation of bu yi as "dishonor."

gerous. This was an issue that excited Mencian ethics especially in the six-teenth century and later.

The developmental aspect of Mencius's picture is elaborated in the dialogue between him and Gongsun Chou in Book 2A, where Gaozi's ideas are criticized. In the debate in 6A, Gaozi is quoted as holding that the significant aspects of morality, which he calls *yi*, are outside our nature, meaning apparently that our acceptance of the moral rules we abide by is the result of conditioning (or even choice on our part) – a person is given a moral shape just as a piece of wood is shaped into a bowl – but also that when I do something a rule requires of me, the significant part of the cause of my behavior is not any disposition there may be in me to do it, but the objective social situation-stimulus. The "nature" (*xing*) for Gaozi is just the life process (*sheng*). The two disputants pursue this by comparing the grammatical form of phrases describing examples, with Mencius (who wants *yi* to be "inside") in this way forcing into the open crucial semantic distinctions: Is a white horse's white like an old horse's age, like an old man's elderliness (i.e., age) (namely, deserving of respect, an example of *yi*)? Natural affections, like appetites, Gaozi allows, are inside us; whether they constitute a significant part of our morality is not pursued.

Nourishment of Qi and Ethical Values

The Gongsun Chou dialogue (taking 2A/1 and 2A/2 together) begins with a discussion of the tensions involved in holding office, requiring courage, of which there are various kinds. The highest kind is confidence in the rightness of one's stance. One will need an "unmoved heart" (*bu dong xin* 不動心) for this. Mencius says that he attained this state at the age of forty and that Gaozi attained it at an earlier age. Gongsun Chou asks Mencius to explain his method and Gaozi's for attaining this state. Mencius then quotes an aphorism of Gaozi's: "What you do not get from words, do not seek in the heart; what you do not get from the heart, do not seek in *qi*."[55] Mencius dismisses the first line as obviously wrong, without bothering to explain it. He gives cautious assent to the second line, but stresses that one's *qi* 氣 – literally "vapor" or "energized air," here apparently moral and physical energy – should not be forced; the *zhi* 志 (will, perhaps motivated "heart") should lead the *qi*, but gently.

Mencius plays briefly on the *qi* concept (tantalizing later philosophers and modern scholarship): *qi* when properly nourished fills the space between

---

[55] *Mencius*, 2A/2 (Lau, p. 77, has a very different translation). See Nivison, *The Ways of Confucianism*, chapter 8, "Philosophical Voluntarism in Fourth-Century China."

Heaven and Earth. He himself is good at nourishing his "vast *qi*" (*hao ran zhi qi* 浩然之氣). In an analogy in 6A/8 he speaks of the "night air" (*ye qi* 夜氣) as having an invigorating effect on even deadened moral natures; but just as a mountain can be stripped of new plant growth by overgrazing, so we wither during the day, getting and spending. In 2A/2, if either the *zhi* or the *qi* is "unified" (while the other is not), or perhaps is "blocked" (frustrated), there is a disturbing physical effect. To be moral we need the *qi* in a healthy state, and this is achieved by "accumulating *yi*" through repeated good acts; otherwise the *qi* will "starve."[56]

Mencius is not hinting at a mysterious, otherwise unarticulated part of his philosophy here, but seems merely to be drawing on popular medical notions impressionistically to describe what moral vigor feels like. There were, however, among the Jixia philosophers in the Qi capital, those who urged a form of quietist self-cultivation philosophy involving "nourishing *qi*," and a poetic chapter in the *Guanzi* ("Nei ye" 內業, Inner training, i.e., self-cultivation) preserves some of this thinking; Mencius must have been familiar with it.[57]

One should always be concerned about one's moral development but should not force it, Mencius warns. There follows a famous imaginary story about a stupid farmer who tugged at his grain shoots to help them to grow and, of course, killed them. Some, to be sure, do not even weed their sprouts (*miao* 苗; obviously Mencius's *duan*, sprouts of virtue-potentiality), thinking there is "no use" in doing so. This language (and more about seeking and getting) is echoed in 7A/3: "Seek and you get it, neglect and you lose it; here seeking is of use in getting," that is, in the inner world of finding and nourishing the sprouts of morality in ourselves, unlike the outer world of our activities, where success depends on fate (*ming* 命) – one more of many jabs at the Mohists.

But what of Gaozi's first line, "What you do not get from words (*yan* 言), do not seek in the heart"? By "words" Gaozi means philosophical doctrines or moral maxims of conduct (Confucius' Golden Rule is labeled a *yan* in *Analects* 15/24). Gaozi's idea is that for moral guidance one cannot draw on one's intuitions, but must start by adopting a doctrine – another statement of his position in 6A that *yi* is "outside," but here the statement is starkly voluntaristic and shows Gaozi's point of departure; he is probably the Gaozi discussed at the end of the "Gong Meng" 公孟 chapter of *Mozi* and was probably in the Mohist circle, where he absorbed Mozi's voluntaristic command-ethic stance, later going his independent way. There, Mozi himself

---

[56] See Lau. *Mencius*, pp. 24–6, for a very interesting discussion of the *qi* concept.
[57] Graham, *Disputers of the Dao*, pp. 100–5.

criticizes Gaozi for "practicing *ren*" as a man might "stand on tiptoe to make himself tall" and as being unable to "govern himself." If would seem that Gaozi's concept of ethics was too much even for Mozi, who then – it would have to have been very late in his life – has almost the accent of a self-cultivationist.[58]

What was happening in Mohism can be seen from a discussion between Mencius and a Mohist named Yi Zhi 夷之 (*Mencius* 3A/5). Mencius criticizes Yi Zhi for burying his parents with lavish rites, contrary to Mohist doctrine, which not only preached economy, but held that one should care for all equally. Yi Zhi defends himself by saying that he does subscribe to the "universal love" doctrine, but that our practice of it must start with our parents. Thus, Mohists have now realized that one cannot simply obey the ethical command "love all equally"; one must first develop in oneself a capacity for loving, and then one can use this capacity as doctrine demands, spreading it out flat, so to speak. This looks very much like Mencius's own position in his opening interview with King Xuan (1A/7), which he modifies in his much more subtle discussion with Gongsun Chou in 2A/2. Mencius accuses Yi Zhi of having "two roots" (*er ben* 二本), by which Mencius seems to mean (1) *yan* (doctrine) and (2) *xin* (heart), the seat of familial affection (which would seem to be Gaozi's position). Mencius argues that really there is only the one root, the heart, in which Heaven has implanted our tendency to morality – which must lead us to prefer our family relationships over others, in due degree. Even so, and even when he is most anti-Mohist in saying this, he still will say (7A/15, 7A/45) that the family is a kind of nursery for developing capacities for love and respect, the basis of *ren* and *yi*, that one must then extend, apply outside one's family, appropriately. But how does one go about this "extending" (*tui* 推, *da* 達)? Is there not still an unsolved difficulty about learning to be moral if and to the extent that one is not moral already? Some people will say that they just can't. For Mencius, this is to deny, in self-deception, one's inner moral capacities, to "throw oneself away" (*zi qi* 自棄, 4A/11).

One striking difference between Confucius and Mencius was Mencius's taking for granted that a new world order was inevitably coming, which he hoped would be sensitive to the people's material welfare. Even more striking, however, is his explicit focus on the inner life, a tendency that is very much a part of his age: we see it in Song Xing, in the specialists in "inner training" cultivating *qi*, in the Yangists, even in later Mohists. In Mencius the tension between inner and outer is never far off: virtue is not something one has simply by acting correctly, but is one's inner psychic shape that

<hr />

[58] *Mozi*, 12 (48 "Gong meng"), 12a; Mei, *Motse*, pp. 241–2.

enables one to do the right thing in the right way. The good man does not "practice *ren yi*" but "acts according to *ren yi* (4B/19); "one must always be concerned" about one's nature's development, but "nourishing" does not allow "forcing" (2A/2); yet when faced with a clear moral obligation one must not put off the required act (3B/8).

Mencius repeatedly speaks of the dispositions of the heart as resources that one can develop and "use." But who or what does the using? "If you seek it you will find it," Mencius says of our moral "root." But who does the seeking? The heart? But the heart just is what is being sought. A disciple, Gong Duzi 公都子, seems to thrust this problem in Mencius's face (6A/15): "Why are some (morally) greater than others?" "He who follows the greater part of himself (*da ti* 大體) is a great man; he who follows the lesser is a small man." "But why do some follow the greater and some the lesser?" All the disciple gets out of Mencius is a picture of a person's psyche as a kind of political structure, the senses blindly drawn to their natural objects, the mind/heart (*xin*) alone autonomous, its function being to "reflect" (*si* 思), saying yes or no to this or that sense. Yet Mencius has also described the heart as on a par with the senses (6A/7), delighting in the right just as the eye delights in the beautiful. A writer in the *Guanzi* suggests that there is a "heart within the heart,"[59] but this just moves the problem to another level without resolving it. That the problem is unsolvable would not prevent other philosophers from noticing and worrying it.

In the end, Mencius believed that one has a religious duty to understand and cultivate one's "nature": "For a man to give full realization to his heart is for him to understand his own nature, and a man who knows his own nature will know Heaven (7A/1)."[60] Heaven implants in us our moral dispositions (6A/16), wants us to be moral, and operates in history through men's choices – for example, validating a ruler's authority via the people's acceptance of him (5A/5). This was in effect the Mandate of Heaven concept (but Heaven's purpose can be inscrutable; it tends to produce a "true king" every 500 years, but may not [2B/13]). The Han text "Zhong youg" 中庸 (Use of the mean), which continues the Mencian strand of Confucianism, applies the Mandate concept to the human psyche: it begins, "Heaven's Mandate (in us) is what is meant by our Nature."[61]

---

[59] *Guanzi*, 16 (49 "Nei ye"), 3b. See Benjamin I. Schwartz, *The World of Thought in Ancient China* (Cambridge, Mass.: Harvard University Press, 1985), p. 273.

[60] The translation is from Lau, *Mencius*, p. 182.

[61] This is the opening sentence in the "Zhong yong" (the title is often translated The Doctrine of the Mean). This and another shorter self-cultivation text, the "Da xue" (Great learning), are chapters in the Han book *Li ji* (Record of ritual), recognized as one of the Confucian Classics. These two, together with the *Analects* and the *Mencius*, were put together as the "Four Books" by Zhu Xi (1130–1200) and became basic texts for Neo-Confucianism. For a translation, see Legge, *The Chinese Classics*, vol. 1.

THE SOPHISTS

Hui Shi: The Fallacy of Absolute Terms

Some of Mencius's contemporaries who can in some sense be called philosophers were also men of consequence in the world of power. In addition to Shang Yang in Qin and Shen Buhai in Hann, there was another man of a very different type, who for over two decades held high office in Wei, under King Huicheng; he is Hui Shi, whose writings are unfortunately completely lost, except for a tantalizing set of ten propositions. Here are some of them:

The ultimately great has nothing outside it; call it the Greatest One. The ultimately small has nothing inside it; call it the Smallest One.
The dimensionless cannot be accumulated, yet its girth is a thousand miles.
Heaven is as low as the earth; the mountains are level with the marshes.
Simultaneously with being at noon the sun declines; simultaneously with being alive a thing dies.
The south has no limit yet does have a limit.
I go to Yue 越 today yet arrived yesterday.
I know the center of the world: north of Yan 燕 up in the north, south of Yue 越 down in the south, you are there.
Let concern spread to all the myriad things; heaven and earth count as one unit.[62]

POSSIBLE EXPLANATIONS. There can be only one "One," since "one" means "unique." Therefore, we cannot distinguish the infinitely large and the infinitely small. Other commonsense opposites fare the same; for example, life is a terminal disease. When we try to think of space or direction as such, we cannot think of it as either limited or unlimited. Absolute location in time or space is impossible, because we can say antithetical things, depending on when or where we say it. Therefore, one cannot make any distinctions on which favoring one thing (person, group) over others could be based, so, care impartially ("love universally").[63]

Huizi, it seems, is some kind of Mohist, but a strange one indeed. The fascination with the power of precisely constructed argument (not always achieved) that one sees in the early Mohist seems to have run off on its own, dragging the core doctrine after it.

One senses that for Huizi philosophy had become a game, and the

---

Confucian tradition credits the "Zhong yong" to Kong Ji (Zi Si), grandson of Confucius, and the "Da xue" to Confucius and Zeng Shen.

[62] *Zhuangzi* (Sibu beiyao ed.), 10 (33 "Tianxia"), 20b–21a. The translations given here are those of Graham, *Disputers of the Tao*, p. 78.

[63] There is an extensive discussion of these propositions in Joseph Needham, *Science and Civilisation in China. Vol. 2: History of Scientific Thought* (Cambridge University Press, 1969), pp. 189–91.

doctrinal purpose was only incidental. For others in the late fourth and early third centuries, the game was everything, and the purpose if any was invisible. Other paradoxes by nameless sophists are recorded from this time:

A wheel does not touch the ground. [Possibly because the tangent to a circle is a point, without dimension.]
The eye does not see. [You do.]
The shadow of a flying bird never moves. [Similarly, the space from which water is displaced by a swimming fish doesn't move; it just keeps changing.][64]

This kind of gamesmanship can produce extraordinarily important discoveries, in a philosophical tradition that becomes fascinated with it and savors such puzzles. In the West, it was to lead eventually to relativity theory in physics, to transfinite arithmetic, and to incompleteness proofs in mathematics. In China there were only short bursts of interest (there was another, in the third century A.D.), followed by centuries of disparagement, which ensured that any texts that might have given adequate explanations have either been lost or are usually badly garbled.

Six Mohist Chapters: Limits and Their Possibility

Some texts do survive sufficiently to have been partially reconstructed. Two are noteworthy: (1) six chapters, 40–5, in the Mozi; and (2) parts of a book called the *Gongsun Longzi* 公孫龍子, as a whole forged between A.D. 300 and 600, but still containing three very short genuine chapters. The later Mohists were not playing games. Their serious purpose was the defense, in argument, of Mohist doctrines. The six chapters are (40, 41) "Canons," (42, 43) "Explanations" (of the Canons), and (44, 45) "Major" and "Minor" theses (*qu* 取). Here is an example of Canon and Explanation that seems to have a relation to the fifth of Hui Shi's paradoxes listed earlier, "The south has no limit yet does have a limit" (implying that we cannot hope to determine which of these we ought to say):

Canon: Absence of a limit does not interfere with universality.
Explanation: (Objection:) If the south has a limit it is exhaustible; if not it is inexhaustible. If whether it has a limit or not cannot be known, then whether it is exhaustible or not, hence whether people fill it or not, and so necessarily whether the people can be exhausted or not, likewise cannot be known. Therefore necessarily it is a fallacy to say that the people can be completely loved.

(Elsewhere the Mohist will argue that while "he rides horses" implies only that he rides some of them, "he loves men" implies that he loves all of them.

---

[64] *Zhuangzi*, 10 (33 "Tianxia"), 22a. Graham, *Disputers of the Tao*, pp. 81–2 (modified). For much more, see Needham, *Science and Civilisation*, vol. 2, pp. 191–7.

"Completely loved" is literally "exhaustively loved." To "exhaust [*jin* 盡] X" here means to do something to all of X. The text continues.)

Answer: If people do not fill the limitless, then the people are limited, and there is no difficulty about exhausting the limited. If they do fill the limitless, then the limitless is exhausted.[65]

(And so can be by us too.) Therefore, claims the Mohist, the sophist's argument against the possibility of universal love fails. (There is a fallacy, of course. The rational numbers less than 10 do not "fill" the real numbers; yet the rationals – even less than 10 – are "limitless.")

Four Types of Argument

Chapter 45, "Xiao qu" 小取 (Minor theses), has been transmitted in the best condition, and has been worked on the most. Among the interesting things in it is a taxonomy of argument types; there are four:

a. Illustrating (*pi* 辟) is referring to some other thing for clarification.
b. Matching (*mou* 侔) is comparing sentences and developing them together.
c. Adducing (*yuan* 援) is saying, If it is so in your case, why should it not be so in mine too?
d. Inferring (*tui* 推) is using what is the same in something which he refuses to accept and in something which he does accept, in order to propose the former.[66]

We seem to have here four systematically differing argument modes: a material mode, about things; a formal mode, about sentences used; a defensive mode, my right to my position; and an aggressive mode, forcing you to adopt my position. We may notice that the word for this last mode, *tui*, is the word that Mencius used for "extending" one's compassion (*en* 恩), in talking with King Xuan. It would seem that Mencius was thinking of what he wanted the king to do as addressing a *tui* argument to himself, transferring his compassion for the ox to his people.

The "Xiao qu" then provides a demonstration of "matching" (and again we think of Mencius; for it is what he was doing in his argument with Gaozi, in comparing the phrases "a white horse's white" and "an old [elder] man's age [elderliness]"). The point is to show systematically that there are some matchings that work and some that do not. Thus, from "a white horse is a horse" it follows that "to ride a white horse is to ride a horse." That is a type

---

[65] The translation of this "Canon" and "Explanation" is taken from Angus C. Graham, "The Logic of the Mohist *Hsiao-ch'u*," *TP* 51 (1964): 12; *Mozi*, 10 (41 "Jing B"), 4b; *Mozi*, 10 (43 "Jing shuo B"), 16a–b. See also Needham, *Science and Civilisation*, vol. 2, pp. 165–84, and consult Graham, *Later Mohist Logic*.

[66] *Mozi*, 11 (45 "Xiao qu"), 5b–6a; Graham, "The Logic of the Mohist *Hsiao-ch'u*," p. 4 (Graham's translations).

that works. But here is a type that does not: while it is true that "a robber-man (*dao ren* 盜人) is a man (*ren* 人)," it does not follow that "having no robbers is having no men," or that "not loving robbers is not loving men," or that "killing (executing) robbers is killing men (i.e., murder)." And with this the Mohist (who accepts capital punishment but preaches universal caring) is back on home ground.[67]

Gongsun Long and the White Horse

Gongsun Long 公孫龍, a native of Zhao, is a horse of a different color. Probably born about 320 B.C., and eventually a client of the Lord of Pingyuan 平原 (308–251) in Zhao, he did have a serious side: he was an admirer of a certain Yin Wenzi 尹文子, who was an associate of Song Xing, and he shared the latter's engaged pacifism.[68] But his most famous short essay – which does survive – was probably written around 300 B.C., revealing its author as a young smart aleck. (One can reasonably assume that the Mohist text just examined, and also the *Mencius*, were both available to him in some way.) In this piece it is difficult to discern any other motive than to amaze his hearers: philosophy has become pure show, not without chicanery.

The "Essay on White Horse" (Bai Ma Lun 白馬論) opens as follows:

Question: Is it admissible that a white horse is not a horse?
Answer: It is admissible.
Question: Why?
Answer: "Horse" is that by which we name the shape. "White" is that by which we name the color. To name the color is not to name the shape. Therefore I say, A white horse is not a horse.[69]

The argument continues. But a satisfactory literal translation is impossible, because the outrageousness – the sophist's undeniable denial of a common philosophical paradigm – requires that the sophist and his victim understand differently the words *bai ma fei ma*, literally "white horse is-not horse." The victim understands them as everybody does and objects that "white" is merely a sample color; so the proposition is in effect saying that nothing counts as a horse unless it is colorless, which would mean that there are no horses. The sophist (on one of several explanations) means that the

---

[67] *Mozi* 11 (45 "Xiao qu"), 6a–b; Graham. "The Logic of the Mohist *Hsiao-ch'u*," p. 7.

[68] On the relation between Song Xing, Yin Wen, and Gongsun Long, see Qian Mu, *Xian Qin zhuzi xinian*, pp. 378–9; and Knoblock, *Xunzi*, vol. 1, p. 62; for the dates of Gongsun Long, see Qian Mu, *Xian Qin zhuzi xinian*, p. 619.

[69] *Gongsun Longzi* (Sibu beiyao ed.), 3b. The translation is Graham's in *Disputers of the Tao*, p. 85. (The *Han Feizi* [Sibu beiyao ed.], 11 [32 "Wai chu shuo, Zuo, Shang"], 4a, says that the "white horse" paradox was defended by a certain Ni Yue of Song, against the Jixia dialecticians – without mentioning Gongsun Long.)

entity "horse" (the shape) and the entity "white" (the color) should be taken as (ontologically) distinguishable, though interpenetrating (like "hard" and "white") in making up the whole object; but it is a mistake to identify a whole – here white plus horse – with one of its parts. For this, the sophist would have recourse to a stock ancient Chinese example: suppose one has a pair of things (that happen not to interpenetrate), call it "ox-horse," one being horse and one being ox; you would not want to say that an ox-horse is a horse. Therefore "white horse is-not horse" *is* "admissible."[70] Gongsun Long has been fantastically successful: his little game has now become world famous as a prime example of philosophical horseplay.

ZHUANGZI

Zhuangzi and Huizi were enjoying themselves on the bridge over the Hao 濠 River. Zhuangzi said, "The minnows are darting about free and easy! This is how fish are happy." Huizi replied, "You are not a fish. How do you know that the fish are happy?" Zhuangzi said. "You are not I. How do you know that I do not know that the fish are happy?" Huizi said, "I am not you, to be sure, so of course I don't know about you. But you obviously are not a fish; so the case is complete that you do not know that the fish are happy." Zhuangzi said, "Let's go back to the beginning of this. You said, How do you know that the fish are happy; but in asking me this, you already knew that I know it. I know it right here above the Hao."[71]

The Basis of Knowledge: Non-Involvement

Friends of these two amiable holiday philosophers are still scratching their heads about what is going on here. Perhaps Zhuangzi is making the point that what we "know" depends on our point of view, and there is no getting around this. Or perhaps Zhuangzi's point is this:

Your question was a rhetorical one; in asking it, you were supposing that even though you are not I, you still are able to know something about my mental state, namely (as you think) that I don't know that they are happy. But if you think you can know this about me, though not being me, you are in no position to object to my claim that I do know the fish are happy, even though I am not a fish. I just know it, right here![72]

[70] Graham, *Disputers of the Tao*, pp. 82–90. See also Chad Hansen, *Language and Logic in Ancient China* (Ann Arbor: University of Michigan Press, 1983). Hansen's book is developed out of his own interpretation of the "white horse" paradox, arguing that ancient Chinese "thing" words are "mass nouns."

[71] *Zhuangzi*, 6 (17 "Qiu shui"), 15a–b; Burton Watson, trans., *The Complete Works of Chuang Tzu* (New York: Columbia University Press, 1968), pp. 188–9; see also Graham, *Disputers of the Tao*, pp. 80–1.

[72] Harold Shadick and Chiao Chien, *A First Course in Literary Chinese* (Ithaca, N.Y.: Cornell University Press, 1968), vol. 1, p. 107.

Either interpretation assumes that for Zhuangzi "knowing" is simply a state of mind and that one cannot go beyond this to ask whether it has objective validity. If this is his view, something else of interest is that in making his antirationalist point, he uses subtle skill: he uses reason to undermine reason.

Very little can be confidently said about the life of Huizi's younger friend Zhuangzi (Zhuang Zhou 莊周). The *Shi ji*'s account has him born in Meng 蒙, in what is modern Henan. Perhaps born as early as 365 B.C., he must have lived until well after 300 B.C. Evidence in the parts of the *Zhuangzi* that are likely to be by Zhuangzi himself suggests that he had been reading, probably recently, parts of the *Mencius*, that Mencius and his disciples are said to have put together shortly before Mencius died (ca. 305). If this is right, Zhuangzi was probably still active in the 290s and 280s.[73]

The parts of the *Zhuangzi* that are likely to be by Zhuangzi are a riotous celebration of the life of non-involvement. But Zhuangzi did not write a book; the *Zhuangzi* is an editorial product: compositions or just jottings apparently by Zhuangzi have been loosely sorted into the first seven (so-called inner) chapters of the book, and genuine Zhuangist matter is scattered through other parts of it. There are those who think that the last chapter (33, "Tianxia" 天下 [The world], reviewing the Warring States philosophical scene) was written in the early Han and should be classed with other chapters that some scholars call "syncretist."[74] Another group of chapters (28–31) expresses a Yangist point of view. Yet another group (8–10 and part of 11) defends a "primitivist" view and appears to be by a single author; these must have been added later than the succession of King Jian of Qi in 264 B.C. (referred to indirectly in *Zhuangzi*, 10). This author offers an idyllic picture of precivilized humanity, "a time of Perfect Virtue" when "the gait of men was slow and ambling," people's innocence sensed by animals, who are unfrightened by them.[75]

Detachment, Emotions, and Their Origin

Chapter 4, "Ren jian shi" 人間世 (In the world of men), is safely assignable to Zhuangzi himself. The drift of the whole chapter seems to be that the sort

[73] See *Shi ji*, 63, p. 2143. Qian Mu, *Xian Qin zhuzi xinian*, p. 618, dates Zhuangzi to 365–290 B.C. But in *Zhuangzi*, 2 (5 "De chong fu"), 19b (Watson, trans., *Chuang Tzu*, p. 72), there appears to be a reference to the story that Confucius once went to see Laozi; D. C. Lau has a good argument that this story was invented not earlier than 286 B.C.; see D. C. Lau, *Lao Tzu*, pp. 156–8. This chapter is one that is probably by Zhuangzi.

[74] For Graham's views, see A. C. Graham, trans., *Chuang Tzu: The Seven Inner Chapters* (London: Allen & Unwin, 1981), pp. 28–9; idem, *Disputers of the Tao*, p. 173. Schwartz groups the "Tianxia" with the description of the "six schools" in the last chapter of the *Shi ji*, "both of which may be quite late" (*The World of Thought in Ancient China*, p. 250).

[75] Watson, trans., *Chuang Tzu*, p. 105 (*Zhuangzi* 4 [9 "Ma ti"], 7a); Watson's translation.

of prudent disengagement from the snares of the ordinary world of social and political life that a reflective person will want cannot be actual withdrawal: we are unavoidably "in the world of men."

The opening section is a narrative dialogue, like many one finds in the *Mencius*. But this one, like almost all dialogue material in the *Zhuangzi*, is fiction with a philosophical point. Confucius's favorite disciple Yan Hui 顏回 asks his master for advice. He wants to go to Wey and try to reform the young ruler, who is governing badly and hurting his people. Confucius objects: Yan is merely going to get himself executed, by provoking the lord of Wey with a display of his own virtue. "The Perfect Man of ancient times made sure that he had it in himself before he tried to give it to others." ("And suppose he just is the kind who delights in worthy men and hates the unworthy – then why do you need to try to make him any different?"; the paradox of virtue again.)[76] Confucius rants on, finally asking Yan how he plans to proceed. Yan tries, "If I am grave and empty-hearted, diligent and of one mind, won't that do?" Confucius snaps at him: "Goodness, how could that do!" That's just making a display of virtue. Yan tries again: Suppose he is "inwardly direct, but outwardly compliant," avoiding criticism by humble behavior while quoting the ancients (whose words will not be chargeable to him). "Goodness, how could that do!" says Confucius again, and continues: "You must fast!" Yan responds, But I'm poor; I'm always fasting! to which Confucius says, No! Not that way! "That's the fasting one does before a sacrifice, not the fasting of the mind!" Confucius then explains:

> Make your will one! Don't listen with your ears, listen with your mind [*xin* 心, heart]. No, don't listen with your mind, but listen with your *qi* 氣! The ears stop with [mere literal] listening; the mind stops with [recognizing] signs [*fu* 符, evidence], but *qi* is empty [*xu* 虛] and waits on all things. It is only the *dao* that accumulates in emptiness. Emptiness is the fasting of the mind.[77]

But this does not mean doing nothing:

> If he listens, then sing; if not keep still. . . . It's easy to keep from walking; the hard thing is to walk without touching the ground. . . . Look into that closed room, the empty chamber where brightness is born! . . . Let your ears and eyes communicate with what is inside, and put mind and knowledge on the outside.[78]

Confucius is onstage as a fast-talking Daoist mystic.

But there is calculated mischief in all of this: Mencius, in 2A/1–2, had dis-

---

[76] *Zhuangzi* 2 (4 "Ren jian shi"), 5a; contrast Watson, trans., *Chuang Tzu*, p. 55.

[77] *Zhuangzi*, 2 (4 "Ren jian shi"), 7a (Watson, trans., *Chuang Tzu*, pp. 57–8, modified); context and parallel structure require that "listening stops with the ears" be changed to "the ears stop with listening." For a different treatment, see Graham, trans., *Chuang-tzu*, pp. 66–9.

[78] *Zhuangzi*, 2 (4 "Ren jian shi"), 7b–8a; Watson, trans., *Chuang Tzu*, p. 58.

cussed how to conduct oneself with steadiness in a trying official position and was talking with his disciple Gongsun Chou. Zhuangzi does better, by making his little story be about Confucius and Confucius's most memorable disciple. Mencius and Gongsun Chou had picked apart Gaozi's program, which places "words" – what you "hear" – first, then "heart" (*xin*) and *qi* (spirit) last. Zhuangzi deftly reverses the order. As Mencius rambles on, he talks about what happens when the "will" (*zhi* 志) is "unified"; Zhuangzi has his Confucius say, "Make your will one!" Mencius warns that one's *qi* will "starve" unless one nourishes it by "accumulating *yi*." Zhuangzi's Confucius calls his program a "fast" that will result in "accumulating" dao. Any perceptive philosophically minded person in the early third century B.C. would instantly recognize the joke and would howl with laughter.

Zhuangzi is never just joking, however. In having Confucius advise Yan to "walk without touching the ground," Zhuangzi is making a deep philososophical point; and it is an insight that Zhuangzi himself had to learn. We watch him learning it in an episode (fiction again) in one of the "outer" chapters (20, "Shan mu" 山木, The mountain tree). Zhuangzi, wandering in a park with a crossbow, sees a strange huge bird and is about to shoot, when he notices a cicada enjoying itself in a spot of shade, unaware of a mantis about to snatch it – and then sees that the bird, in turn oblivious to danger, is about to snap up the mantis. The impulse to shoot driven from his mind, he is fascinated by the philosophical implications, every creature caught up in an interlocking web of danger because of its fixation on what interests it. He leaves in disgust. Just at this point the gamekeeper surprises him and heaps abuse on him. Zhuangzi goes home in a state of shock. He realizes that his own philosophy of detachment, by causing him to fix his attention on the foolish involvements of other beings rather than on his own safety, had "self-destructed": detachment had proved to be only another form of engagement. So a true saving detachment must be a detachment-in-engagement. In effect he has come to see that one must "walk without touching the ground." He quotes his "master": "When in the ordinary world, follow the ordinary ways."[79] The presence of Yangist-oriented chapters in the book suggests that his "master" may have been Yang Zhu or one of Yang's followers; so perhaps this is the distinctive turn that Yangism was taking, as it evolved into Zhuangzi's "Daoism."

In the *Zhuangzi* the transformation is complete. We live in a world of conflicting views, passionately pursued, one person's right is another's wrong, all

[79] Cf. Watson, trans., *Chuang Tzu*, pp. 218–19; and Graham, *Disputers of the Tao*, p. 173; *Zhuangzi*, 7 (20 "Shan mu"), 15a. The story is fiction, but this does not weaken its meaning. For a review of other analyses and a slightly different interpretation, see P. J. Ivanhoe, "Zhuangzi's Conversion Experience," *Journal of Chinese Religions* 19 (1991): 13–25.

is right (or wrong) from some view. Accept the confusion, even smile at it, but don't let it get at you. Modern scholars write furious articles trying to analyze Gongsun Long. Zhuangzi merely twits him (without bothering to name him): "To use a horse to show that a horse is not a horse is not as good as using a non-horse to show that a horse is not a horse." (Zhuangzi knows the game: We recall that ox [which is non-horse] combined with horse equals ox-horse, which is not horse.)[80]

Realizing the silliness of getting stirred up over differences of opinion means being content with uncertainty. If two people argue, how do I decide who is right? If I agree with either side, I am no fit judge; but also if I agree with neither I am no fit judge. Even the difference between dreaming and waking disintegrates in this contented scepticism. Zhuangzi dreams (or says he dreams) that he is a butterfly, then wakes (or says he does) to find himself "solid and unmistakable Zhuang Zhou." But which was the dream state and which waking? The most interesting (and maddest) chapter (2) in the book ends with this question, happily left unanswered.[81]

So it is even with the ultimate question, Who am I, really? At the opening of this chapter ("Qi Wu Lun" 齊物論, On equalizing things), a mystic emerges from a trance and describes the "piping of Earth," the howling wind in a mountain forest. Like it, the "piping of Heaven," "blowing on the 10,000 things in a different way, so that each can be itself – all take what they want for themselves, but who does the sounding?" From this arise men's fears and quarrels, bitter conflicts over right and wrong, until they fade away into death:

Joy, anger, grief, delight, worry, regret, . . . music from empty holes, mushrooms springing up in dampness, day and night replacing each other before us, and no one knows where they sprout from. . . . Without them we would not exist, without us they would have nothing to take hold of. . . . It would seem that they have some True Master, and yet I find no trace of him. . . . Which (of the parts of my body) should I feel closest to? I should delight in all parts, you say? But there must be one I ought to favor more. If not, are they all of them mere servants? But if they are all servants, then how can they keep order among themselves? Or do they take turns being lord and servant? It would seem that there must be some True Lord among them, but whether I succeed in discovering his identity neither adds to nor detracts from his reality.[82]

"Which should I favor more?" was Mencius's question in 6A/14. Who is the "True Lord" among them is the problem lurking behind Gong Duzi's question in 6A/15, why only some "follow the greater part" of themselves, the

---

[80] *Zhuangzi*, 1 (2 "Qi wu lun"), 15b; Watson, trans., *Chuang Tzu*, p. 40.

[81] *Zhuangzi*, 1 (2 "Qi wu lun"), 25b; Watson, trans., *Chuang Tzu*, p. 49.

[82] *Zhuangzi Zi*, 1 (2 "Qi wu lun"), 12a–13a; Watson, trans., *Chuang Tzu*, pp. 37–8, modified.

problem Mencius does not quite see (and no one knows how to solve). Zhuangzi has been attending to Mencius again.

Dao *and Its Comprehension*

Zhuangzi's Confucius in chapter 4 speaks of the *Dao*, the "Way," as "accumulating." Has the *Dao* become a "stuff" in this philosophy? Metaphorically only: a thing, but not a thing among things, rather the ground of all being, as well as the source of all insight. This metaphysical turn is the fundamental move to mysticism. The True is the Real: we must *understand* the True, and we must *be* the Real. But to put understanding into words is to "objectify," push it away from us, make it other than what we are, and so falsify our understanding of it. So the *Dao* cannot be talked about (and so cannot be learned, except by some kind of *via mystica* of self-change). This is a "truth" that, inconsistently, will be baldly stated in the first line of the *Laozi*; and also (but is he really serious?) by Zhuangzi: "The Great Way is not named." Everything is "One"; but (half-humorously) "the One and what I said about it make two, and two and the original One make three." Better, then, not to start at all.[83] To cope with this impossible situation Zhuangzi must "talk without talking," so to speak (the analogue in discourse, perhaps, of "walking without touching the ground"). He will be effective (and honest) in philosophical debate just so far as he can do it in a disguised (and partly dishonest) way. The result is stylistic exuberance, fantastic fiction, tongue-in-cheek humor. This enables him, in his "fast of the mind" prank, to show up the most vulnerable side of Mencius, that philosopher's sometimes oppressive stuffiness.

Locating the enlightened person "in the world of men" does not negate his feeling of this world as alien but heightens it, forcing a sharp tension between what is natural, spontaneous, "of Heaven," and what is artificial, conventional, prejudice- and concept-ridden, "of man." This has several important consequences. Thinking, the functioning of mind, thought of as conniving and scheming, being bound by received notions of right and wrong, of what is to be valued and what is to be feared, is thought of as unnatural and bad. Spontaneity and (curiously) the exercise of skills (carving something, catching cicadas on the sticky tip of a long pole), which require such concentration that they crowd out (and would be hobbled by) thinking about ulterior purposes, are ideals, good.

What is of "man," what is human, has to be accepted and lived with. Zhuangzi can even begin to look Confucian: we are all sons and subjects and

---

[83] *Zhuangzi*, 1 (2 "Qi wu lun"), 18b–19a; Watson, trans., *Chuang Tzu*, p. 43.

cannot escape these attachments. Again he appropriates Confucius, who is made to give this advice to a man who is being sent on a dangerous mission:

In the world, there are two great restraints [*jie* 節]: one is fate [*ming* 命] and the other is duty [*yi* 義]. That a son cares for his parents is fate; you cannot erase this from his heart. That a subject serves his lord is duty; His ruler is always his ruler wherever he goes. . . . Therefore in serving his parents if he is at ease no matter what the case, this is the height of filial piety. If in serving his ruler he is at east no matter what the task, this is the epitome of loyalty. And to serve your own mind so that sadness or joy do not sway or move it; to understand what you can do nothing about and to be content with it as with fate – this is the perfection of virtue [*de* 德]. As a subject and a son, you are bound to find things you cannot avoid. If you act in accordance with the state of affairs and forget about yourself, then what leisure will you have to love life and hate death?[84]

Note, however, that even with the moralistic language, the saving detachment – "serving your own mind" – is achievable *in spite of* the Confucian-required attachments; so Zhuangzi really does not begin to be Confucian.

Accommodation with Death

Another consequence of "detachment in involvement" is a freeing from the fear of death. Coupled with Zhuangzi's acceptance of uncertainty, this becomes the attitude that for all we know death may be better than life, a waking from a dream: "How do I know that loving life is not a delusion? How do I know that in hating death I am not like a man who, having left home in his youth, has forgotten the way back?"[85] Once unstuck from the conventional attitude that death is something dreadful, Zhuangzi moves on to an almost ecstatic acceptance of it; the fact that death follows life is fated, "a matter of Heaven," and anything that is "of Heaven" is good; the *Dao* is as much in this sequence as in the sequence of the seasons:

The Great Clod [namely, the *Dao*] burdens me with form, labors me with life, eases me in old age, and rests me in death. So if I think well of my life, for the same reason I must think well of my death.[86]

Similarly Zhuangzi banishes grief. His wife dies. When Huizi comes to condole, he finds his friend beating on a tub and singing. Zhuangzi explains, didactically:

When she first died, do you think I didn't grieve like anyone else? But I looked back at her beginning and the time before she was born. . . . In the midst of the jumble

---

[84] *Zhuangzi*, 2 (4 "Ren jian shi"), 9a–b; Watson, trans., *Chuang Tzu*, pp. 59–60, modified.

[85] *Zhuangzi*, 1 (2 "Qi wu lun"), 23a; Watson, trans., *Chuang Tzu*, p. 47.

[86] *Zhuangzi*, 3 (6 "Da zong shi"), 4b–5a; Watson, trans., *Chuang Tzu*, p. 80.

of wonder and mystery a change took place and she had a spirit. Another change and she had a body. Another change and she was born. Now there's been another change and she's dead. It's just like the progression of the four seasons, spring, summer, fall, winter. Now she's going to lie down peacefully in a vast room. If I were to follow after her bawling and sobbing, it would show that I don't understand anything about fate. So I stopped.[87]

But why should not grief be itself natural, therefore good, therefore the traditional ritual forms of expressing it beautiful and to be savored, their ordering of the emotions itself "of Heaven"? These are questions that would be asked by Xunzi, surely reflecting on Zhuangzi, who was the most immediately visible philosopher in his own formative years.[88]

Zhuangzi was, as it were, a volcanic eruption in the development of Chinese philosophy. Nothing would ever be the same again.

XUNZI

Xunzi (full name Xun Kuang 荀況; also known as Xun Qing 荀卿) lived a long time and was active through major events during the sixty years preceding the Qin conquest completed in 221 B.C. Variety in the views found in his essays requires that we either suppose them to be the work of several persons (as some do) or suppose (reasonably) that in the course of a long life through major historical changes and influences his views and interests evolved. Using the latter theory, we see at once that the essays in the *Xunxi* are not in chronological order. Important recent scholarship paces his life in seven periods as follows (important essays are as numbered in standard editions):[89]

ca. 310	Born in Zhao
1. ca. 295–284	Xunzi is a student in the Jixia community (in Qi) ("Jie bi" 解蔽, no. 21).
	(288: the kings of Qin and Qi assume the title of *di* for a short time; the dominance of Qi culminates in its annexation of Song, 286 B.C.; allied reaction, and occupation of Qi by Yan, 284–279.)

---

[87] *Zhuangzi*, 6 (18 "Zhi le"), 17a; Watson, trans., *Chuang Tzu*, p. 192.

[88] For this relationship of Xunzi to Zhuangzi, see D. S. Nivison, "Hsun Tzu and Chuang Tzu," in *Chinese Texts and Philosophical Contexts*, ed. Henry Rosemont, Jr. (La Salle, Ill.: Open Court, 1991), pp. 129–42.

[89] John H. Knoblock, "The Chronology of Xunzi's Works," *EC* 8 (1982–3): 29–52; see esp. the table on p. 46. The estimate of Xunzi's birthdate is taken from Knoblock, *Xunzi*, vol. 1, p. 5. The partial translation by Burton Watson, *Hsün Tzu: Basic Writings* (New York: Columbia University Press, 1963), is also valuable.

2. 284–275	Xunzi avoids turmoil in Qi and goes to Chu ("Quan xue" 勸學, no. 1; "Xiu shen" 修身, no. 2; "Li lun" 禮論, no. 19).
3. 275–265	Xunzi heads the restored Jixia Academy in Qi ("Tian lun" 天論, no. 17; "Yue lun" 樂論, no. 20; "Xing e" 性惡, no. 23).
4. 265–260	Xunzi, slandered in Qi, travels to Qin ("Wang zhi" 王制, no. 9 begun).
	(260: Qin defeats Zhao, massacres Zhao army, besieges the Zhao capital Handan 邯鄲.)
5. 260–255	Xunzi in Handan (Zhao), at the court of the Lord of Pingyuan ("Yi bing" 議兵, no. 15; part of "Yue lun," no. 20; "Wang Zhi" finished).
	(257: Qin defeated by Zhao–Wei–Chu alliance.)
6. 255–238	Xunzi is magistrate of Lanling 蘭陵 (Chu) ("Zheng ming" 正名, no. 22; "Fei xiang" 非相, no. 5).
	(247: Xunzi's student Li Si 李斯 goes to Qin; his student Han Fei 韓非, later a major philosopher, leaves soon afterward; 238: Xunzi's Chu patron Huang Xie 黃歇, Lord of Chunshen 春申, assassinated.)
7. 238–	Xunzi in retirement in Lanling.
	(233: Han Fei commits suicide in prison in Qin; during the next twelve years, Qin conquers all the states; Qi [the last to fall] surrenders, 221; Xunzi declines an invitation to the Qin court by Li Si, 219–218 [?].)
ca. 215	Xunzi dies.

Xunzi is the first philosopher in China who could be described as "academic" in the modern sense. He examined all of the leading thinkers of his time that he knew and wrote careful position papers that analyze and use or criticize their views (though not always naming them). In his student period the most influential thinkers, contemporary and earlier, with whom he had to deal were Mencius and Song Xing, in or close to the Jixia group, and Mozi, Yang Zhu, and Zhuangzi, outside it or earlier. Xunzi identified himself as Confucian at the outset, and Mencius, whom he could never have known personally, was always both a source and a rival. He always saw Mozi as an arch-enemy, failing to realize how deeply Mozi influenced him. On the (potentially paradoxical) problem that emerges out of late Mohist and Mencian reflection on early Mohist thinking, how a person can voluntarily commit himself to pursue a life directed toward goodness and virtue, and the related question of the analysis of human psychology, Xunzi is close to Mencius's rival Gaozi, but Xunzi expands the problem much farther than did the Gaozi in the *Mencius*.

The Mind and Its Capacity

One can first see this problem of commiting to goodness and virtue in the early essay "Jie bi" (Dispelling obsessions). The title and the opening discussion are obviously suggested by Mencius's analysis of mental structure in 6A/15 and by what seems to be Zhuangzi's critique of this in his second chapter, "Qi wu lun." Mencius had proposed that the "mind-heart" (*xin*) is a kind of inner ruler and seat of personal autonomy. The sense appetites react mechanically to attractive objects, which thus "cover" (*bi* 蔽), that is, blind or "obsess" them: only the *xin* can say yes or no and will do so only if it "reflects." Zhuangzi apparently sees that to locate the "I" in this way in an organ that must be made to perform its "function" (*guan* 官) is self-contradictory: one is forced to the question, where or what is the inner "True Lord"? Though perhaps not seeing this, Xunzi does see that the *xin* can be viewed as an organ on a par with the rest in one sense: it itself can be obsessed, so that it blindly pursues a wrong course thinking it to be right.

This leads Xunzi to analyze the capacities of the mind (and *xin* is *mind* now, not mind-heart): it is (potentially) "empty," in that there is no limit to what it can store; "unified," in that intellect can grasp accurately many diverse ideas without confusing them; and "still," in that though always active, both perceiving, imagining, dreaming, it can always distinguish what is real. Such is the mind when it functions ideally, as it must if it is just to see the right Way; it must then be as undisturbed as a pan of water. This is like Zhuangzi's "fast of the mind," but with strict consistency: one does not literally "empty" the mind; it must be "empty" while full, "still" while active (i.e., disengaged while engaged). But Xunzi describes the accomplished "sage" as rhapsodically as might a Daoist: "Broad and vast – who knows the limits of such a man? Brilliant and comprehensive – who knows his virtue? Shadowy and ever-changing – who knows his form?"[90] Usually, however, Xunzi is cool and analytical: "The mind must first understand the Way before it can approve it, and it must first approve it before it can abide by it and reject what is at variance with it."[91] But one wants to ask, if such clarity of mind is a necessary condition for seeing and accepting the Way, is it also a sufficient condition? Can we imagine a person who might really see that the way is the Way, and still reject it? Xunzi cannot, and for him, at this stage in his thinking, this is simply an aspect of our autonomy:

The mind is the ruler of the body and the master of its god-like intelligence. . . . Thus the mouth can be forced to speak or be silent . . . but the mind cannot be made to

---

[90] *Xunzi*, 15 (21 "Jie bi"), 5b; Watson, trans., *Hsün Tzu*, p. 129.
[91] *Xunzi*, 15 (21 "Jie bi"), 6a; Watson, trans., *Hsün Tzu*, p. 127.

change its opinion. What it considers right it will accept; what it considers wrong it will reject.[92]

That is, what I really think to be right I will *eo ipso* be accepting, whatever you may frighten me into saying. This is a way of thinking that has noteworthy implications in at least two later important essays, "Xing e" (Human nature is evil) and "Zheng ming" (Using terms correctly). It requires of us one of several important qualifications to his thesis that "the nature is evil" (attacking Mencius). Xunzi does not conceive of man as like a Miltonic Satan, deliberately choosing evil as his good, or as capable of going on an Augustinian pear-stealing rampage out of sheer pleasure in doing wrong as wrong.[93] At worst he supposes (too optimistically, perhaps) that a person may, in "obsession," mistake the wrong for the right, or choose it by just following impulse, because he is not balancing costs and benefits.

This second possibility is assumed in the last part of the "Zheng ming": granted that man is a desiring being, how can he do other than seek to satisfy his immediate personal cravings? This is possible because one can come to see that the unlimited satisfaction of all one's desires is not possible and that seeking to do so will only make one miserable; one would be made wretched by anxiety even if one got the things one wants. Seeing this – "doing arithmetic," Xunzi calls it (and one may just not do it) – one will see that the Confucian Way (*Dao*) of civilized life offers one what we would call "the best deal." "All men will abide by what they think is good and reject what they think is bad. It is inconceivable, therefore, that any man could understand that there is nothing in the world to compare to the Way, and yet not abide by it."[94]

This makes explicit what Xunzi was assuming in "Jie bi." But Xunzi does not quite reject the possibility of *akrasia*. Xunzi is talking here on a meta-moral level: he knows well that in the state in which we are, before the intervention of socialization, we will not "abide" by the Way in detail even if we see its advantages; the choice for the Way is a choice to remake ourselves, as he saw already in his second-period essays "Quan xue" (Encouragement to study) and "Xiu shen" (On cultivating one's person). In both, Xunzi is as voluntaristic as Mozi or Gaozi: "When you find good in yourself, steadfastly approve it; when you find evil in yourself, hate it as something loathsome."[95] The feelings can be commanded, and must be. In the "Quan xue" he writes: "The learning of the gentleman enters his ear, clings to his mind, spreads through his four limbs, and manifests itself in his actions. . . . The learning

[92] *Xunzi*, 15 (21 "Jie bi"), 6a; Watson, trans., *Hsün Tzu*, p. 129.
[93] See Philip J. Ivanhoe, *Confucian Moral Self Cultivation* (New York: Lang, 1993), p. 40, n. 11.
[94] *Xunzi*, 16 (22 "Zheng ming"), 9b; Watson, trans., *Hsün Tzu*, p. 152.
[95] *Xunzi*, 1 (2 "Xiu shen"), 7a–b; Watson, trans., *Hsün Tzu*, p. 24.

of the petty man enters his ear and comes out his mouth."[96] The method is to find a good teacher, place yourself at his feet, and let him guide you in the study of the Classics: the *Shi jing*, the *Shang shu*, and the *Chunqiu*; this is now clearly the age of books:

The gentleman . . . trains his eyes so that they desire only to see what is right, his ears so that they desire to hear only what is right, his mind so that it desires to think only what is right. When he has truly learned to love what is right . . . he follows this one thing in life, he follows it in death.[97]

The Origins of Morality and the Need for Li

"The basic nature (*xing* 性) of man is that which he receives from Heaven" (from "nature" in the ordinary sense.) "The dispositions (*qing* 情) are the substance of the nature and the desires (*yu* 欲) are the responses of the dispositions."[98] Xunzi has no doubt that this *xing*, which Mencius had pronounced "good" (and requires to be good if he is to do any effective teaching), is potential trouble. The trouble is inevitable at the level of social organization (i.e., from the point of view of a ruler), if there are not proper standards and restraining institutions, what Xunzi calls *li* 禮 (ritual) or *li yi* 禮義 (ritual and right), an expression he uses the way Mencius uses *ren yi* 仁義 (benevolence and right), which virtually means "morality":

What is the origin of ritual? I reply: man is born with desires. If his desires are not satisfied for him, he cannot but seek some means to satisfy them himself. If there are no limits and degrees to his seeking, then he will inevitably fall to wrangling with other men. From wrangling comes disorder and from disorder comes exhaustion. The ancient kings hated such disorder, and therefore they established ritual and right in order to curb it, to train men's desires and to provide for their satisfaction.[99]

Xunzi seems to be thinking out the problem of the origin of an ordered society and state structure in the same way that Mozi did. It was ordered from the top, a creation of rulers (Xunzi does not here ask how their position came to exist or how they came to occupy it), to lift mankind out of a natural state of destructive strife.

Morality thus was created because it was needed. But how does a deliberately invented "morality" become morality? And how can its sage-king inventors have created it if they, being men, had selfish natures like the rest of us? The questions are not explicitly formulated, but their logical pressure

---

[96] *Xunzi*, 1 (1 "Quan xue"), 4b–5a; Watson, trans., *Hsün Tzu*, p. 20.
[97] *Xunzi*, 1 (1 "Quan xue"), 6b–7a; Watson, trans., *Hsün Tzu*, pp. 22–3.
[98] *Xunzi*, 16 (22 "Zheng ming"), 9a; Watson, trans., *Hsün Tzu*, p. 151, modified.
[99] *Xunzi*, 13 (19 "Li Lun"), 1a; Watson, trans., *Hsün Tzu*, p. 89, modified.

on Xunzi, in his "Xing e" essay, is obvious. He has a complex answer, seen in that essay, as well as in his earlier "Li lun" and in his later "Zheng ming." Man is a combination of two elements, which he calls *xing* (nature) and *wei* 偽 (activity), the latter given two senses in definitions at the beginning of the "Zheng ming": a capacity for conscious intelligent action, to resolve a problem one has thought out; and also the cumulative result of the exercise of this capacity over time, in the individual as his habits, and in society as its customs and institutions. All people are alike in having a selfish *xing*; but we differ in respect to *wei*, the sage-kings happening to have much sharper *wei* than the rest of us. They saw that man's selfish *xing*, if nothing is done, will result in chaos, conflict, and misery. So the restraints of civilization, the "rituals," are necessary for truly human existence. This means an imposition of hierarchic order, which can be seen as an extension into the human realm of the cosmic order of Heaven.[100]

Xunzi is not a theist. His Heaven is not (as it was for most earlier thinkers and would be for many later ones in Han) a being with a human-like will or purpose, but seems to be for him simply the ultimate order of nature.[101] But Xunzi's attitude toward this order has a strong religious tone. What he seems to do is to read back into the whole order of the cosmos the notion of "rites" that flower out of it, seeing it as due the reverence appropriate in "rites" in the religious sense – since after all he sees that order as the matrix of everything that is valuable:

Through rites Heaven and earth join in harmony, the sun and moon shine, the four seasons proceed in order, the stars and constellations march, the rivers flow, and all things flourish; men's likes and dislikes are regulated and their joys and hates made appropriate. Those below are obedient, those above are enlightened.[102]

Emerging from his ecstatic vision, Xunzi says that "this is something that the *xiao ren* 小人, the 'small man,' cannot comprehend." The sage, however, does comprehend: he can see *li yi* as having a cosmic necessity that commands awe, and so gives himself intelligent reason to love it, thus moralizing himself at the same time that he gives morality to mankind. And as for us, Xunzi does assume that even with our "evil" nature, we are, as a species, able to learn to apprehend a prudential rule as a moral one; so he says (in "Wang zhi," The institutions of a king) that man in contrast to animals "has *yi* 義":

[100] Xunzi says that man desires goodness paradoxically because he sees that he lacks it (just as in other ways he "wants" what he lacks). See *Xunzi*, 17 (23 "Xing e"), 3b; Watson, trans., *Hsün Tzu*, pp. 161–2.
[101] Xunzi rejects the idea that strange natural phenomena are portents and regards prayers for rain, divination, and so on as mere ritual embellishments to life, without any other effect; see *Xunzi*, 11 (17 "Tian lun"), 13a; Watson, trans., *Hsün Tzu*, p. 85.
[102] *Xunzi*, 13 (19 "Li lun"), 4b–5a; Watson, trans., *Hsün Tzu*, p. 94.

Fire and water possess energy [*qi* 氣] but are without life [*sheng* 生]. Grass and trees have life but no consciousness [*zhi* 知]. Birds and beasts have consciousness but no sense of duty [*yi* 義]. Man possesses energy, life, consciousness, and in addition a sense of duty. Therefore he is the noblest being on earth.[103]

This is not at all to say that an individual person has a Mencian "nature" predisposed to (and only to) received morality. (For it can still be true that an "obsessed" mind can pursue a wrong end as sincerely as a right one.) But it is to say that man as a species forms and lives in ordered communities structured by moral rules of some kind. (And in the end, only one kind works.)

The Lessons and Values of the Past

At least one problem is untouched. Xunzi is trying to give a rational justification for morality (and to this extent his ethic is not a command ethic); so he is pushed toward affirming what Mencius affirms, that the sages are men like us and that we could become sages if we would. The logical push of this view makes it impossible for him to assert unambiguously that the sage's *wei* is transcendent or unique. But then, is not the *xing–wei* distinction just a word game? Why bother to distinguish them? Why not say that the "accumulated *wei* that results in *li yi*" (*li yi ji wei* 禮義積偽) just is the result of *xing*, and that the sage, in "making" institutions, is extracting them from his *xing*? No, Xunzi replies (to his own hypothetical objection); this would be like saying that a potter makes a pot out of a part of himself. The analogy blurs the issue, which Xunzi identifies. If you talk this way, then "what reason is there to pay any particular honor to Yao, Shun or the gentleman?"[104] Xunzi's worry is that the dangerous argument Mencius opens up in 6A/7 will stand: If the sages merely "anticipated" what all hearts have in common, then why could not anyone, if he thinks his *wei* is up to it, simply invent his own morality? The result would be just the chaos that *li yi* is supposed to block.

Xunzi has an escape from this predicament, which he does not quite dare to use. It is suggested in the way he puts the problem: it is the *ji wei*, the accumulated conscious problem solving of many sages, that becomes the moral order. Why not take the reasonable view that this was the work not of one sage but of many, over a long time? That is something that an individual, now, cannot do. Our due respect for the sages is really a respect for

---

[103] *Xunzi*, 5 (9 "Wang zhi"), 7b; Watson, trans., *Hsün Tzu*, p. 45, modified; Watson takes *zhi*, here translated "consciousness," as "intelligence"; but Xunzi is talking about the bare capacity of distinguishing animals from vegetable life; Knoblock, *Xunzi*, vol. 2, p. 103, has "awareness." For other examples of this "ladder of souls" idea in other philosophers (including Aristotle), see Needham, *Science and Civilisation*, vol. 2, pp. 21–6.

[104] *Xunzi*, 17 (23 "Xing e"), 5b; Watson, trans., *Hsün Tzu*, pp. 164–5.

the accumulated wisdom of the past. But to say this too quickly would be to allow that the moral order changes over time, in response to needs as they arise. This is just what the political philosophers later dubbed "Legalists" were saying, justifying their denial of any constraints from the past, in urging an amoral and savage political order that horrified Xunzi. To allow that different sages had different "ways," furthermore implying that we have to choose which to follow, also makes admissible positions (like those of the agrarian utopians with whom Mencius argued (3A/4) and who appealed to an imaginary far past) that reproach established conventions; and this kind of appeal to the past is also something that Xunzi must reject if the Way is to be validated.[105]

These problems lead him to his peculiar view of history, which he spells out in another essay assignable to his Lanling period, "Fei xiang" 非相 (Against physiognomy). What is important in a man is not his external form examined by the physiognomist, but his inner "heart" (mind) and "principles." A man is not just a "featherless biped," but a being capable of making distinctions, the most important being social ones, set in "rites and right," established by the sages. But there are many sage-kings of old: which should we follow, say the critics? This is always an unreal problem for Xunzi: "Things of the same class do not become contradictory even though a long time has elapsed because they share an identical principle of order."[106] So if one analyses problems into categories, one can be sure that within a category there is no essential change over centuries of time; but it is true that information from the very remote past becomes blurred and difficult to recover; therefore, while past models are essential guides for the present, we should "follow the later kings." The result is that Xunzi in effect simply shuts out the conceptual and philosophical problem, "How could morality have started?" by transforming it into a simple historical problem, which we can ignore because we should not expect to be able to know – the origins are too far back, and we do not need to know because we have all we need near at hand.

"Zheng ming"

The most famous of Xunzi's essays is probably his "Zheng ming." Its fame is partly due to the modern fashion of supposing that all "real" philosophy is "philosophy of language," and here is an old Chinese philosopher actually

[105] For example, in his "Yue lun" (A Discussion of Music), Xunzi argues against the Mohist claim that the sage-kings rejected music and that the Confucians are therefore wrong to encourage it (*Xunzi*, 14 [20 "Yue lun"], 2a–b; Watson, trans., *Hsün Tzu*, p. 115). In this essay, and typically, Xunzi argues that it is a mistake to suppose that the sage-kings had values and practices that differed from received civilized traditions; so they do not offer a choice of models.
[106] *Xunzi*, 3 (5 "Fei xiang"), 5a; Knoblock, *Xunzi*, vol. 1, p. 207; Knoblock's translation.

doing it. The chapter seems to lack coherence, suddenly shifting in the last third to the problem, "Why should we be moral?" and given our desiring "nature," How can we be? – and it is usually said that the whole is simply two separate essays glued together (perhaps by the Han editor Liu Xiang 劉向, 79–8 B.C.). But it has been noticed that the "Zheng ming" is Xunzi's Confucian-oriented adaptation of the scheme and subject matter of the Mohist "Canons."[107] Like them it begins with a set of definitions of crucial terms (crucial for Xunzi – including *xing* and *wei*). It then proceeds through the first, third, and fourth of the Mohist "disciplines":

Discourse – knowing how to connect names with objects. Here Xunzi seems to be reacting to Zhuangzi's observation in "Qi wu lun" that "things are so because they are called so" – the frightening discovery that there are no uses of "names" that are just naturally right, a fact that Xunzi admits: "Names have no intrinsic appropriateness." Intolerable confusion will result unless names are standardized.

Sciences – knowing objects. Xunzi's problem: "distinguishing between things that are the same and those that are different."

Argumentation – knowing names. Xunzi's problem: assigning names according to "sameness" and "difference" and making sure that one's opponents do not confuse matters, as they will and do.

This leads Xunzi to list sample fallacious claims in each of the three categories: for example, (1) "When you kill a thief you do not kill a man" (from the Mohist "Xiao qu"); (2) "Mountains and chasms are on the same level" (one of Huizi's paradoxes); and (3) "A [white] horse is not a horse" (Gongsun Long). If we still had sage-kings, they would straighten all this out by wise fiat (and put an end to useless and dangerously confusing philosophical disputes). We do not, so "the gentleman" has to use persuasion and a proper science of names; and descriptions follow, distinguishing the discourse of the sage, the gentleman, and the fool.

Then there follows in the "Zheng ming" the seeming departure into ethics, probing the problem of how desiring beings can become moral. Still, this last part does belong in the essay, for (as has recently been observed) the second Mohist discipline, skipped so far, was knowing how to act; and here it gets its play, but in prime position, placed at the end and occupying a third of the whole discussion. It is obvious that Xunzi's first interest is always moral philosophy.

Moral philosophy also includes political philosophy (for him, the appli-

---

[107] *Xunzi*, 16 (22 "Zheng ming"), 1a–11b; Watson, trans., *Hsün Tzu*, pp. 139–56. The comparison with Mohist "disciplines" was first noticed by Graham, *Disputers of the Tao*, pp. 261–7; for Graham on the Mohist discipline "knowing how to act," see *Disputers of the Tao*, pp. 156–60.

cation of morals to government and policy). The striking thing about Xunzi's "Wang zhi" (The government of the [ideal] king) is not its uncompromising stress on authority (What else was there?) – not excluding punishment – but its humanity.[108] The sociopolitical order is hierarchic (which, in Chinese terms, is simply to say that it is order). But where Aristotle carefully explains why some by nature must be slaves and some barbarians, with Xunzi there is none of that. We do find in him, as firmly but more explicitly than in Mencius, the principle that the ideal king will take care of the disadvantaged – the blind, deaf, crippled, maimed: "The government should gather them together, look after them, give them whatever work they are able to do, . . . provide them with food and clothing."[109] Environmental protection will be a concern of the sage-king. "When plants and trees are flowering or putting out new growth, no axes may be taken into the hills and forests, for they would destroy life and injure the growing things."[110] The guiding principle is always: "The ruler is the boat, and the common people are the water. It is the water that bears the boat up, and the water that capsizes it."[111]

HAN FEIZI, LAOZI, LEGALISM, AND DAOISM

The *Shi ji*, in its chapter on Laozi, Zhuangzi, Shen Buhai, and Han Feizi, credits the story of Laozi once being visited by Confucius and recognizes Zhuangzi as author of chapters (such as "Dao Zhi" 盜跖, Robber Zhi) that scholars now think to be written by others. These are reasons for being doubtful about the chapter as history, but perhaps the historian was better informed about Han Feizi. He was, it is said, a minor prince of the Hann state, who "delighted in the study of forms and names, law and methods, but the real basis of his thought was 'Huang Lao' 黃老 ideas. He had a speech impediment and was not good at discourse, but was a very good writer. Together with Li Si, he served [i.e., studied under] Xunzi."[112] The account goes on to say that Li Si considered Han Feizi abler than himself. Han Feizi was distressed at Hann's weakness, but was unable to get its king to listen to his ideas and expressed his frustration in essays such as "Gu fen" 孤憤 (Solitary

[108] On this point, see Henry Rosemont, Jr., "State and Society in the Hsun Tzu: A Philosophical Commentary," *MS* 29 (1970–1): 501–41.

[109] *Xunzi*, 5 (9 "Wang zhi"), 1b; Watson, trans., *Hsün Tzu*, p. 34.

[110] *Xunzi*, 5 (9 "Wang zhi"), 8a; Watson, trans., *Hsün Tzu*, p. 47.

[111] *Xunzi*, 5 (9 "Wang zhi"), 3a; Watson, trans., *Hsün Tzu*, p. 37.

[112] *Shi ji*, 63, p. 2146 (most of the narrative on Han Fei is translated in W. K. Liao, trans., *The Complete Works of Han Fei Tzu* (London: Arthur Probsthain, 1939), vol. 1, pp. xxvii–xxix). The analysis of Han Feizi's thought that follows treats most of the *Han Feizi* as Han Feizi's work, but how much of it is his is not certain; for important skeptical doubts, see Bertil Lundahl, *Han Fei Zi: The Man and the Work* (Stockholm: Institute of Oriental Languages, Stockholm University, 1992). "Huang Lao" (Huang Di and Laozi) refers to Daoist thought in Qin and Han, especially as applied to politics.

indignation), "Wu du" 五蠹 (The five vermin), and "Shui nan" 説難 (The difficulty of persuasion). Some of these got to Qin, where Li Si held high office; the Qin king admired them and, learning from Li Si that they were written by Han Feizi, he launched attacks against Hann until, at length, Han Feizi was sent to Qin as an envoy. But Li Si warned the king that if Han Feizi were employed, his loyalty was bound to be with Hann; and if he were allowed to return to Hann he would cause trouble later. So Han Feizi was arrested and imprisoned, and Li Si then persuaded him to take poison. Han Feizi accepted, unnecessarily; the Qin king (soon to be First Emperor) relented, though too late for Han Feizi: Li Si had accomplished his objective. Han Feizi died in 233 B.C., probably under the age of fifty.[113]

Han Feizi's essays, like Xunzi's, at first circulated separately, and were later assembled into a book after he died. They are usually coherent and well constructed, in a prose style that has been much admired. A pleasing feature of his writing is his use of engaging stories drawn from history, or invented, to give point to his arguments.

The Relations of Ruler and Minister

One entire essay, "He Shi" 和氏 (Mr. He), is such a story, with reflections at the end. A certain Bian He 卞和, a man of Chu, finds a rough jade, potentially of great value. Bian He presents it to the Chu king. The royal lapidaries look at it and say it is a mere rock; so Bian gets a foot cut off for attempted deception. In the next reign he tries again, only to lose his other foot. In the following reign, off in the mountains, he clasps his rough jade and weeps until he weeps blood. The king sends someone to inquire: "Many people have had their feet cut off; why are you weeping so bitterly?" Bian He replies that he is not upset about the loss of his feet, but about being called a liar and having a treasure pronounced a mere rock. The jade is then cut and polished and discovered to be the treasure Bian He claimed it was. Han Feizi's point is that, almost always, invaluable advice to a ruler is rejected as worthless or as deception, and the person offering the advice is savagely punished or loses his life.[114]

But this story illustrates a point that Han Feizi himself may have missed. Typically the Legalist philosopher is framing arguments on how a government should be run as advice to a prince. But in Han Feizi's thinking, a recurrent theme is that the "intelligent ruler" will so conduct himself that his ministers cannot take advantage of his preferences or wishes to realize their

[113] Qian Mu, *Xian Qin zhuzi xinian*, p. 620; *Shi ji*, 63, p. 2155.
[114] For this story, see *Han Feizi*, 4 (13 "He shi"), 10b–12a; Burton Watson, trans., *Han Fei Tzu: Basic Writings* (New York: Columbia University Press, 1964), pp. 80–3.

own selfish purposes, and he will be prudent if he assumes that their purposes are always selfish and not in his own interest. ("Ruler and minister differ in interest. Therefore, ministers are never loyal.")[115] So Han Feizi, as adviser to a prince, is in the position of saying, in effect, "Trust me, your adviser, when I tell you that you must distrust all advice" – a virtual liar's paradox: little wonder, then, that this stance spelled trouble.

There are also impossible difficulties in being a ruler, in Han Feizi's philosophy. Han Feizi stresses incessantly that a state will come to ruin unless ultimate control of everything is always in the ruler's hands. He must delegate authority to officials, of course, who have the system of law to control the people. It is therefore essential that the ruler keep control of his officials, by holding them strictly responsible for performance implied by their titles – keeping "names and realities" in exact accord. He must punish them when they do less or more, never showing the slightest leniency. He must distrust his ministers totally, always assuming that they will find ways to take advantage of him if they are able to guess his desires or fears.

To this end, the ruler must achieve an utter mysteriousness:

Do not let your power be seen; be blank and actionless. Government reaches to the four quarters, but its source is in the center. The sage holds to the source, and the four quarters come to serve him. In emptiness he awaits them (*xu er dai zhi* 虛而待之), and they come to serve him as needed.[116]

(In Zhuangzi's "fast of the mind," "*Qi* is empty and awaits all things [*xu er dai wu* 虛而待物].")

This is the way to listen to the words of others: Be silent as though in a drunken stupor. Say to your self: Lips! teeth! do not be the first to move; . . . If you show delight, your troubles will multiply; if you show hatred, resentment will be born. Therefore discard both delight and hatred, and with an empty mind become the abode of the Way.[117]

For Zhuangzi's "Confucius" it was the minister, but for Han Feizi it is the ruler, who is to "fast the mind," so that the *Dao*, the Way, will "accumulate in emptiness." "Hence it is said, 'So still he seems to dwell nowhere at all; so empty no one can seek him out.' The enlightened ruler reposes in nonaction above, and below his ministers tremble with fear."[118]

Han Feizi's idea is that if the system of government and order can be set going and the ruler can sit at the top of it in a pose of utterly trans-human

[115] *Han Feizi*, 10 (31 "Nei chu shuo xia: Liu wei," 2, "Li Yi"), 1a; W. K. Liao, trans., *Han Fei Tzu*, vol. 2, p. 2.
[116] *Han Feizi*, 2 (8 "Yang quan"), 8b; Watson, trans., *Han Fei Tzu*, p. 35, modified.
[117] *Han Feizi*, 2 (8 "Yang quan"), 10b–11a: Watson, trans., *Han Fei Tzu*, p. 38, modified.
[118] *Han Feizi*, 1 (5 "Zhu dao"), 10b; Watson, trans., *Han Fei Tzu*, p. 17.

self-control, all will operate like clockwork and the ruler will have to do nothing. But with all this, he must be omniscient, with the qualities like those of the sovereign who has perfect virtue (*de*): "If loyal ministers, though guiltless, still face peril and death, then good officials will go into hiding; and if evil ministers, though without merit, enjoy safety and profit, then corrupt officials will come to the fore. This is the beginning of downfall."[119] The ruler's position is as paradoxical as is that of the minister-adviser's predicament. He is to assume that all subordinates are potential traitors; yet he is lost unless he just knows, unerringly, who the really loyal ones are.

The Laozi, Zhuangzi, *the* Dao *and* De

The Daoist echoes in this philosophy are not all from Zhuangzi. The *Han Feizi* has two chapters (20, 21) of comments on the little book in verse and poetic prose traditionally arranged in eighty-one sections and called the *Laozi* (from its supposed author) or the *Dao de jing* (Classic of the way and virtue). This text is mentioned by Xunzi at the end of his "Tian lun" (Discussion of Heaven), probably belonging to his Jixia period ending in 265 B.C. There is nothing in the *Laozi* to identify an author, though its language and ideas suggest a late fourth- or early third-century date. The *Han Feizi* comments on only twenty-one of the eighty-one sections, so perhaps the *Laozi* was still incomplete when these comments were written. Some of them are Confucian in tone, and so must be Han Feizi's work at an early age or by someone else who accepted his viewpoint only in part.

A tradition quickly sprang up that the *Laozi* was written by a man called Lao Dan 老聃 (the *Han Feizi*'s name for him), or Li Er 李耳, a supposed elder contemporary of Confucius and keeper of archives in the royal Zhou capital, whom Confucius is supposed to have visited and consulted.[120] Thus, the proponents of Daoist philosophy, claiming it as their primary "classic," have insisted that the Master paid homage to their Master and to their views. In this century, iconoclastic challenge to this tradition has produced furious debate among Chinese scholars. Some still defend the *Shi ji*'s account; others consider the book to be a collage by nameless editors of scraps of earlier text.[121] The *Laozi* has been spectacularly successful, having been translated (into many languages) more often than any other Chinese text. It has become, forever, part of World Literature.

The reason for this success, in part, is the book's tone of terse and elusive

[119]   *Han Feizi*, 2 (6 "You du"), 2a–b; Watson, trans., *Han Fei Tzu*, p. 23.
[120]   Lau convincingly dates the origin of this fable to 286–240 B.C.; see D. C. Lau, *Lao Tzu*, p. 158.
[121]   For a representative of this view, see D. C. Lau, *Lao Tzu*, pp. 163–73; for the conservative view, see, e.g., Wing-tsit Chan, trans., *The Way of Lao Tzu* (Indianapolis, Ind.: Bobbs-Merrill, 1963), p. 35.

"wisdom," which is often so ambiguous that a new interpreter can always be persuaded that hitherto unseen profundities are almost within reach. For example, does the opening line mean "The Way that can be told is not the eternal Way" (i.e., the real Way is beyond description) or "The Way that may truly be regarded as the Way is other than a permanent way"? Or does the word *dao* mean here not "Way" at all, but "discourse"?[122]

There are teasing ideas in this text. It speaks of the relativity of concepts (2); of ideal government as "emptying men's minds and filling their bellies" (3) and "acting without acting" (3, also 37); of the usefulness of what isn't, for example, the space in a room (11). Much of it is recognizably primitivist: it was only when the *Dao* "declined" that morality developed (18) or "When the *Dao* was lost, then virtue (*de*); when virtue was lost, then benevolence (*ren*); when benevolence was lost, then right (*yi*); when right was lost, then ritual . . ." (38), a thought that could be a dialectic of history.

If the *Han Feizi* commentary offers one contemporary reading of the *Laozi*, the primitivist chapters in *Zhuangzi* (8–10, part of 11) offer another. They frequently quote or echo the *Laozi*. Both the *Laozi* and the primitivist author in the *Zhuangzi* deplore harsh government (as Han Feizi does not). Both insist that wisdom is the beginning of evil. But where the *Laozi* (19) merely says, "Cut off sageliness, throw away wisdom, and the people will benefit a hundredfold," in the *Zhuangzi* chapter "Qu qie" 胠篋 (Rifling trunks), there is rhetorical violence: "Cudgel and cane the sages, and let thieves and bandits go their way, then the world at last will be well ordered! . . . Gag the mouths of Yang and Mo, wipe out and reject benevolence and righteousness, and for the first time the Virtue of the world will reach the state of Mysterious Leveling."[123] Thus the transintellectual tone in the *Laozi* as magnified by this primitivist lens can even be seen as part of the background of Qin's attempt to suppress backward-looking moral philosophy after its conquest of the other states.

The *Dao* (the Way) in the *Laozi*, as in the *Zhuangzi*, is not just a philosophical truth but the Way of Nature, a Reality, transcending number but giving birth to the "One," creator of all else. It is frequently said to be beyond description, yet it is described as weak and "shadowy," "dim, dark" (21), but accomplishing everything, enabling everything to be what it is, simple, like an "uncarved block" (28, 32, 37, 57). The sage is like the *Dao* in these respects and is usually spoken of as (or as if he were) a ruler; ten or more of the sections are explicitly about the way of government of such a person, preternaturally effective because of being nonassertive, noncontriving, not even

---

[122] D. C. Lau, *Lao Tzu*, p. 57; J. J. L. Duyvendak, trans., *Tao Te Ching: The Book of the Way and Its Virtue* (London: John Murray, 1954), p. 17; Hansen, *Language and Logic in Ancient China*, p. 67.
[123] *Zhuangzi*, 4 (10 "Qu qie"), 10b, 12a; Watson, trans., *Chuang Tzu*, pp. 109, 111.

noticed by the people. There is an echo of pacifist resentment against the devastation of war (30, 31), but also the idea that "weakness" paradoxically has military value (68, 69, 73, 76). Enough of the book is not about government to allow the possibility that it is a book of counsel for any wise man who would survive by not pressing for too much (44, 52), be effective by being still, quiet; sometimes sexual imagery makes this point (28, 61): "The female gets the better of the male by stillness," by "taking the lower position" (so also with states). There are echoes of Yangism (13): one who values his body more than the world most deserves to be ruler of the world. Yangist life-enhancing asceticism and restraint are approved (12, 44). The *Dao* cuts down that which has risen too high (77) ("turning back is the way the *Dao* moves," 40); there is even a sinister suggestion, that a good strategy first strengthens what it will destroy (36) (so a survival strategy must avoid too much success). The sage is often said to be like a baby (10, 20, 28, 50, 55).

One translator has seen the book as an anti-Legalist text.[124] Han Feizi could not have. In the essays quoted, he is using the Daoist's idea of the *Dao*, effortlessly determining everything, as model for a virtually transcendent ruler whose power is absolute because he is silent, mysterious, but always holding in his hands the ultimate weapons of control, cutting back the powers of others who become too prominent: "The ruler of men must prune his trees from time to time and not let them grow too thick, for if they do they will block his gate." The idea is explicit in *Laozi* 36, one of the sections that the *Han Feizi* comments on.[125]

In this sometimes sinister but more often quietistic Daoism, interference with nature – scheming intentional action that meddles with the world – is the bane of human life, responsible for the deterioration of the human condition from primitive simplicity into constraining convention and greed (e.g., 38); instead, one should "do nothing [*wu wei* 無為: avoid scheming intentional action] and nothing will remain undone" (37). (In surely deliberate contrast, Xunzi makes *wei* 偽, the human capacity for intelligent intentional action, the source of all that is good in our civilized life.)[126] Han Feizi takes the quietist ideal and activates it, making being still, blank, and recessive the intentional tactics of a ruler in making his power absolute. The result is what has aptly been termed "purposive Daoism" – potentially frightful, because

[124] For this view, see, e.g., Arthur Waley, *The Way and Its Power: A Study of the Tao Te Ching and Its Place in Chinese Thought* (London: Allen & Unwin, 1934, rpt. 1949), pp. 86–8.

[125] *Han Feizi*, 2 (8 "Yang quan"), 14a; Watson, trans., *Han Fei Tzu*, p. 41; *Han Feizi*, 7 (21 "Yu lao"), 1b; W. K. Liao, *Han Fei Tzu*, vol. 1, p. 210; *Han Feizi*, 10 ("Nei chu shuo xia, Liu wei," 1 "Quan jie"), 1a; Liao, *Han Fei Tzu*, vol. 2, p. 1.

[126] For the relation between the Laozi's *wu wei* and Xunzi's *wei*, see Schwartz, *The World of Thought in Ancient China*, p. 309.

the Dao-model is explicitly transmoral: the sage, like "Heaven and Earth," is "ruthless, and treats the people as straw dogs" (*Laozi*, 5).[127]

Two recently unearthed texts of the *Laozi* (from Mawangdui 馬王堆) reveal that at first the sections beginning with *Dao* (1–37) and *De* (38–81) were in reverse order, thus giving first place to *de* (virtue, or power).[128] (The *Han Feizi*'s comments begin with section 38, lending credence to these comments being very early.) Yet the two halves are not consistently about *dao* and *de*, respectively. If such variety suggests an accretion of falling snow (whose "author" was the last editor who touched it), nonetheless, this seems to be an accretion around a core idea – not entirely new: Zhuangzi also uses it, in his own escapist philosophy. The term *de* in very early thinking seems to refer to a "power, whether benign or baleful, to move others without exerting physical force."[129] A ruler wants it and will rule more effectively if he relies on it rather than on force, though he does have force at his disposal (e.g., *Analects*, 2/3). Likewise a military commander: the *Zuo zhuan* quotes a lost military text as saying that "he who has *de* cannot be opposed."[130]

The next step in this dialectic is the reflection that such a commander is confronting another who uses physical force; so *de*, as other than physical force, must be (literal) weakness, and one has the delicious paradox that weakness is stronger than strength. Analogous paradoxes bloom in the *Laozi*: the soft is tougher than the hard; ugliness is more beautiful than beauty; silence shows more understanding than speech; stupidity is wiser than wisdom – all intellectualized primitivism. The ultimate paradox begins the text that Han Feizi would have had (perhaps catching his attention as a young man around 260 B.C.): *de* itself is superior as *de* if it denies itself (*shang de bu de* 上德不德, *Laozi*, 38). The *Zhuangzi* anticipates this idea in "Ren jian shi" (chap. 4), cryptically referring to "crippled virtue" in the account of "Crippled Shu," as well as in having Confucius counsel Yan Hui to hide his virtue. In another way, it is dramatized in the battles for prestige through self-abasement in Sima Qian's 司馬遷 biography of Wuji 無忌, Prince of Wei, in the *Shi ji*.[131] The Confucians themselves, insisting on the effective superiority of benevolence over harshness, were known as the "weak" ones (*ru* 儒). But for Han Feizi, weakness as a means to real power must in the end be only apparent weakness.

[127] For "purposive Taoism," see H. G. Creel, *What Is Taoism?* (Chicago: University of Chicago Press, 1970), chapter 3, "On Two Aspects of Early Taoism," pp. 37–47. *Laozi*, 5, is as translated by D. C. Lau, *Lao Tzu*, p. 61.

[128] The texts were in tomb 3 at the Mawangdui site (Changsha, Hunan), excavated in 1973–4, datable to 168 B.C. See Jeffrey K. Riegel, "A Summary of Some Recent *Wenwu* and *Kaogu* articles on Mawangdui Tombs Two and Three," *EC* 1 (1975): 10–15.

[129] Graham, *Disputers of the Tao*, p. 13.

[130] *Zuo zhuan*, 16 (Xi 28), 19b; Legge, *The Ch'un Ts'ew with the Tso Chuen*, p. 209.

[131] *Shi ji*, 77, pp. 2377–85.

Fa, Shu, *and* Shi

Han Feizi is like Xunzi in also being academic, criticizing and selecting from many other and earlier thinkers. His "purposive Daoist" strand is anticipated by Shen Dao 慎到 (ca. 350–275 B.C.), a Jixia thinker who is often described as Daoist. The last chapter of the *Zhuangzi* describes him as "discarding knowledge," "being indifferent to things," "condemning the sages." Among his sayings (there is a *Shenzi* 慎子, reconstituted from fragments): "Knowledge is not to know"; "A clod of earth does not miss the way."[132] Han Feizi remembers him for a concept expressed in some prose that is both wild poetry and political realism: an effective ruler is like a flying dragon borne up by the clouds, his ability to control being due to his "position" (*shi* 勢: the word means "power" or "circumstance," perhaps "power base"), but not just any power; we are to think of his being at the top of the pyramid of authority as having a magical force (almost an amoral *de*, virtue). Han Feizi has a chapter (40) on the concept, demystifying it.[133]

But Han Feizi uses the notion. Reviewing past thinking and policy on the strengthening of a state, he holds three things essential: *fa* 法, *shu* 術, and *shi*. *Fa* he says is the main idea of Gongsun Yang (or Shang Yang), prime minister of Qin who was killed after the death of his patron ruler in 338 B.C.; *shu* he assigns to Shen Buhai, prime minister of Hann, 351–337 B.C. There were books named for both men, the first surviving and translated into English, probably containing no material earlier than the third century.[134] For the second there are fragments, as well as a study in English.[135]

The word *fa* means "model," and when the model is a description of desired human behavior in certain situations, announced by the state with prescribed punishments for failure to abide by it, as in Shang Yang's *fa*, it is obviously a law. Han Feizi's concept seems to be "model" nonetheless, in this sense: a *fa* fixes the substance of an order (*ling* 令) issued by a magistrate covering a case that comes before him. For this reason, Han Feizi says that the *fa* are the means by which the officials control the populace.

In contrast, *shu* (arts, or methods) are uncodified strategies by which a ruler controls his officials. Shang Yang's system of *fa* included savage corporal punishments (some of them much worse than Mr. He's defooting), but also rewards for successful obedience; the population was divided into groups

---

[132] Fung, *History of Chinese Philosophy*, vol. 1, p. 153; for the *Shenzi*, see Paul M. Thompson, *The Shen Tzu Fragments* (Oxford: Oxford University Press, 1979).

[133] *Han Feizi*, 17 (40 "Nan shi"), 1a–b; Liao, *Han Fei Tzu*, vol. 2, pp. 199–206.

[134] J. J. L. Duyvendak, trans., *The Book of Lord Shang: A Classic of the Chinese School of Law* (London: Arthur Probsthain, 1928).

[135] H. G. Creel, *Shen Pu-hai: A Chinese Political Philosopher of the Fourth Century B.C.* (Chicago: University of Chicago Press, 1974).

of families mutually responsible for unreported crimes. The behavior desired was productivity in agriculture and victory in war. The *shu*, which the ruler keeps to himself, include holding on to the "handles" of life and death and holding officials precisely responsible for performance of their stated duties, without favoritism. The ruler's *shi* is his "position," whereby he "dominates the masses," without which he cannot apply *fa* and *shu*, and which he must guard vigilantly by applying them correctly.[136] The Legalists had a strictly mechanistic conception of the relation between successful policy and "human nature." Human beings are naturally selfish, have "likes and dislikes," and so may be moved to act (or not to) by the promise of rewards and by the threat of punishment. Han Feizi even says that people who are ostensibly motivated by morality (he always thinks of them as really self-serving) are a menace to the state.[137]

It has been suggested that we should think of these Legalists as developing a system of ideas that we would call applied social science (rather than philosophy).[138] Both Shang Yang (in the book) and Han Feizi have a strikingly "social-scientific" conception of history. Its moving force is the inevitably increasing stress caused by growth in population.[139] Times change: a benevolent near-anarchy was quite possible in very early ages, Han Feizi writes, but no longer: "The generosity with resources in ancient times was not benevolence, it was because resources were ample; the competition and robbery of today is not dishonesty, it is because resources are sparse."[140] Like Xunzi, Han Feizi objects to those who would take the very remote past as a model for the present; but his reason differs: times change, and one must look at the conditions of one's own time. Like the Daoist author of *Laozi*, 38, he sees historical changes as a stage-by-stage movement away from primitive simplicity. (So also Shang Yang: in the first stage of human life, "people knew their mothers but not their fathers.")[141] But unlike the Daoist poet in the *Laozi*, Han Feizi does not see this as deterioration: different times are simply different, neither better nor worse. What is called for now is severity. But even in taking this stance, Han Feizi sometimes sounds an almost Confucian note, for the implication is that severe policies in the long run are for the people's benefit, though (like a child having a boil lanced) they cannot be expected to realize it.[142] Order (as both Mozi and Xunzi would agree) is

---

[136] Fung, *History of Chinese Philosophy*, vol. 1, p. 320.
[137] *Han Feizi*, 2 (6 "You du"), 3b; Watson, trans., *Han Fei Tzu*, pp. 25–6.
[138] See Schwartz, *The World of Thought in Ancient China*, p. 333.
[139] See Graham, *Disputers of the Tao*, pp. 270–3.
[140] *Han Feizi*, 19 (49 "Wu du"), 2a; Liao, *Han Fei Tzu*, vol. 2, p. 278; translation from Graham, *Disputers of the Tao*, p. 273.
[141] Fung, *History of Chinese Philosophy*, vol. 1, p. 315; *Shang jun shu* (Sibu beiyao ed.), 2 (7 "Kai sai"), 10a; Duyvendak, trans., *The Book of Lord Shang*, p. 225.
[142] *Han Feizi*, 19 (50 "Xian xue"), 12b; Watson, trans., *Han Fei Tzu*, p. 128.

surely better than disorder. But Han Feizi's thesis is recognizable as yet another *Laozi*-like paradox: harshness is more benevolent than kindness.

THE *LÜ SHI CHUNQIU* AND CORRELATIVE THINKING

Han Feizi's colleague and nemesis Li Si was himself cut in two at the waist in the market place in 208 B.C., only five years after he had authored the First Emperor's edict for the "Burning of the Books," applying a policy earlier endorsed by Han Feizi in his "He shi." (To be sure, the burning may not have been very thorough.)[143] But while Qin destroyed, it also preserved. Lü Buwei 呂不韋 (d. 235 B.C.), a merchant in Hann, had befriended a Qin prince who was a diplomatic hostage. Lü Buwei's influence (and bribery) got the prince the throne of Qin in 249 B.C., and from that time and into the reign of King Zheng 政 (king of Qin from 246; First Emperor of Qin from 221; died 210 B.C.) Lü Buwei was first minister. According to the *Shi ji*'s account, Lü Buwei felt that Qin's prestige was suffering in comparison with that of other states, some of whose junior princes (the so-called four *junzi* 君子) were lavishly patronizing men of letters. So Lü Buwei drew together a large group of writers of different viewpoints, getting them to participate in the composition of an encyclopedic book that would systematically illustrate all of their theories.[144]

This *Lü shi chunqiu* 呂氏春秋 (Mr. Lü's spring and autumn [annals]) has the completion date of 239 B.C. and has chapters that one can identify as Yangist, Daoist, cosmologist, Confucian, and more. Mozi is mentioned favorably, as is Shen Buhai sometimes. The dominant Legalist political policies in the Qin state are not given favorable treatment in the book, and in general Confucian values are endorsed in it. This has led to puzzlement about Lü Buwei's deeper purpose, some actually seeing in the book an attempt by Lü Buwei's guest scholars to bring about a coup in favor of Lü Buwei; another view is that Lü Buwei was attempting to educate the young king and lead him toward a more desirable point of view. But it seems not unlikely that it was, as the *Shi ji* suggests, simply cultural splash, which passed the attention of later Qin censorship because it did augment the prestige of the new dynasty.[145] It has great value: all of what we know of Zi Huazi comes from it, for example, and it is one of the earliest systematic and detailed statements

---

[143] For doubts on the extent of the "burning of the books," see Jens Østergård Petersen, "Which Books Did the First Emperor of Ch'in Burn? On the Meaning of *Pai Chia* in Early Chinese Sources." *MS* 43 (1995): 1–52.

[144] For this see Kung-chuan Hsiao, *A History of Chinese Political Thought. Vol. 1: From the Beginnings to the Sixth Century* A.D., trans. F. W. Mote (Princeton, N.J.: Princeton University Press, 1979), pp. 556–70, esp. p. 557.

[145] Ibid., p. 557.

of the correlative cosmological thought that became very popular in the Han in the next century.

Yin–Yang and the Five Phases, or Powers

The *Lü shi chunqiu* contains 160 short chapters on philosophical and metaphysical topics, distributed into three groups. The first group is arranged according to the twelve months of the year. The first chapter in each "month" contains information duplicated in the "Yue ling" 月令 (Monthly ordinances) chapter of the Han Confucian collection *Li ji* 禮記 (Record of rites), counted as one of the "classics." The position of the sun in the lunar zodiac at the beginning of the month is given, as are the culminating asterisms at dawn and dusk (i.e., the "months" are solar, not lunar). There follows a list of the things that correspond to that month: musical tones, numbers, flavors, odors, and so on; then the prescribed ritual behavior of the Son of Heaven during the month, what he is to say and wear, where he is to dwell, and so on. In the first of the eight *lan* 覽 (surveys, the second category of chapter groups), titled "Beginnings [of Heaven and Earth]," the second essay sketches a theory of historical correspondences. At the beginning of a dynasty, Heaven will always display signs that indicate which of the so-called Five Phases (*wu xing* 五行), or Five Powers (*wu de* 五德), is to dominate in that era, with its associated color:

Founding ruler	*Phase*	*Color*
Huang Di	Earth	Yellow
Yu (Xia)	Wood	Green
Tang (Shang)	Metal	White
Wen (Zhou)	Fire	Red
(Yet to be)	Water	Black

More of this associationist "science" is found in the *Guanzi*:

The Yin and Yang are the great principles of Heaven and Earth. The four seasons are the great path of the Yin and the Yang. Punishment and reward are the harmonizers of the four seasons. When punishment and reward are in harmony with the seasons, there is good fortune; when they are not, there is misfortune. What is [the sovereign] to do in spring, summer, autumn and winter?[146]

The text continues with a multitude of correlations: Yang with warmth, pleasure, growth, fire, the sun, and so on; Yin with the intuitive opposites. The Five Phases are correlated with the four seasons by way of the four cardinal

---

[146] *Guanzi*, 14 (40 "Si shi"), 5a; Fung, *History of Chinese Philosophy*, vol. 1, p. 165 (modified).

directions, by postulating a cross-shaped world with earth and yellow at the "center." Another important text that develops correlations with a list of the Five Phases is the "Hong Fan" 洪範 chapter of the *Shang shu*.

The Yin and Yang concepts (supposed to be aspects or phases of universal *qi*), and the Five Phases may be independent notions that are brought together in third century B.C. thought. The philosopher best known for a fantastic elaboration of them in a system of historical phases is Zou Yan 騶 衍, probably born around 300 B.C., active ca. 250 B.C., and much in demand in royal courts. All of his works are lost even though he was very influential in the Han. He was Confucian (and Mencian) in his ethics; and Xunzi says that Mencius was charged with being sympathetic to this kind of thinking (which Xunzi himself abhors). All one finds in the *Mencius* is a tendency to think of history schematically and deterministically (a "great king arising" every 500 years: 2B/13, 7B/38), with no mention of the Five Phases or of Yin and Yang.[147]

Correlative Thinking and Science

Correlative thinking seems scientific but is actually close to the intuitive aesthetics of music and dance; it tended to crowd out any possibility of a vigorous development of genuine science in ancient China (as, also, in the West). There were discoveries in the fifth and fourth centuries B.C. that excited some philosophers. Mencius, for example, exclaimed, "Although Heaven is high, and the stars far away, if you just seek out the data (*gu* 故, causes) you can deduce the [dates of the] solstices of a thousand years [past or future] right where you sit" (4B/26). Mencius had in mind, probably, the nineteen-year and seventy-six-year (*zhang* 章 and *bu* 蔀) intercalation cycles.[148] Chinese astronomer-astrologers contemporary with Mencius had data in hand that should have enabled them to discover the precession of the equinoxes. Instead, the data were effaced by redrawing the boundaries of the lunar "zodiac" to conform to observed asterisms, which were then grouped into "Jupiter stations" with fancied astrological correlations with each of the Warring States. To ask "Why not true science?" is to ask the wrong question.

---

[147] *Xunzi* 3 (6 "Fei shi er zi"), 9a–b; Knoblock, *Xunzi*, vol. 3, pp. 214–16, 224, and 303, n. 48. (Knoblock puts this chapter in Xunzi's Zhao phase, 260–255 B.C.) The usual interpretation of the Chinese text has Xunzi himself charging that Mencius favored Five Phases thinking. Knoblock's view is that the *Xunzi* says only that others in Xunzi's time made this charge against Mencius, implying that Xunzi himself did not.

[148] The *zhang* and *bu* cycles were Chinese equivalents of the Metonic and Callippic intercalation cycles known in Greece (Meton of Athens was active in the late fifth century B.C.; Callippus was in the circle of Aristotle, late fourth century B.C.). These cycles were probably gotten by the Greeks from Babylon. The Chinese may have discovered them independently.

What needs explaining is the breakout that occurred in the West around 1600, liberating thought from this mold and leading to modern science.[149]

But even if correlative thinking is a universal tendency in human thought, one must ask why it became (relatively suddenly) the dominant aspect of Chinese thinking in the third and second centuries B.C. Several tendencies converged to make this happen.

First, the problem of reforming self and society structured a dialectic in moral thought from Confucius to the third century B.C. Confucius saw the reform of the world as turning on the moral cultivation of persons who would guide policy, but was frustrated by unresponsive students. (This was the paradoxical aspect of *de* [virtue].) Mozi was (at first anyway) blind to self-cultivation and thought that a rational analysis of the needs for change could be followed by persons simply choosing to adopt the requisite beliefs and attitudes (such as universal caring.) Mencius saw the impossibility of this, unless there was a core of moral-making dispositions in individuals, on which education and right action could be based, and concluded that Heaven had implanted in human beings the "sprouts" of morality. Xunzi feared this idea as potentially antinomian and viewed the moral order as the consequence of the wisdom of ancient rulers, who saw (much as had Mozi) that without order human selfishness made an acceptable human existence impossible; so Xunzi's sage-kings established rules of "rite and right." For Mozi the decreed standards had been a conforming to the Will of Heaven; but for Xunzi Heaven was simply Nature, and his Rites therefore, being necessary, were an extension into the human order, in all of its detail, of the order of Nature, seen as inevitable.

Though Xunzi rejected correlative thinking himself, his picture of the world thus provided a metaphysical basis for it. But Xunzi, needing the past as a model in order to ensure the authority of received morality, could not allow that different sages had had different Ways for men to choose from. Others, of a more common way of thinking, knew better: virtue understood as moral power or prestige underlay the universally held concept of history, accepted since before Confucius, as a sequence of dynasties with different institutions; but virtue in its nonmoral sense as the characteristic of a thing allowed a new direction for this old concept, the *de* of a thing being what it gets from the *dao* to be itself ("The virtue of the people is grass"). Dynastic change must be the work of Heaven (even Mencius thought this). So each

---

[149] Graham, *Disputers of the Tao*, pp. 317–25. Graham makes the fascinating suggestion that there are structural features in all human languages that steer the mind in the correlative direction. One must not overlook centuries of intermittent background achievement outside of Europe (to which China contributed), especially in mathematics, without which the scientific revolution would have been impossible.

dynasty must have its Heaven-assigned *de*, or tendency (*xing*) – the explanation for its unique institutions – reflected even in concurrent natural phenomena. This principle that accounted for the larger changes of history must also account for the minutiae of human life, month by month, even day by day. The correlative hypothesis thus explained the ancient manual of divination, the *Yi jing* 易經 (Classic of changes), and enabled the book to be read as a book of natural and moral philosophy, as it came to be, with the Han transition, becoming first among the "Classics."

And finally, correlative thinking in both structuring the behavior of the sovereign and ordering everything under him was suited to an era when for the first time a genuine universal empire (from the Chinese perspective) was taking shape.[150] Correlative ideas may well have been a welling up into the "high culture" of a way of thinking that had been latent in the populace for ages past. But whatever the source, Chinese philosophy turned to correlationist thought at this time because this had become (and was to remain in large part, down to modern times) the only way the Chinese could think about their world and themselves.

---

[150] Nathan Sivin, in an address at Stanford University on May 9, 1996, pointed out this relationship between correlative thought and the developing imperial state.

CHAPTER TWELVE

WARRING STATES NATURAL PHILOSOPHY AND OCCULT THOUGHT

Donald Harper

With the exception of the later Mohists (late fourth to third centuries B.C.), whose interest in geometry, optics, and mechanics was related to their investigation of logical demonstration, investigation of nature and its manifold phenomena was not the central philosophical concern of the various men from Kongzi 孔子 (Confucius) to Zhuangzi 莊子 and Han Feizi 韓非子, who were often acknowledged by the honorific *zi* 子 (master; and who were retrospectively identified as the *zhuzi* 諸子, collected masters, in Han times). While the masters of philosophy examined issues of the individual, society, the state, and world harmony – each offering his own version of the ideal and the means to reach it – the collection and interpretation of data concerning nature was the province of astrologers and almanac makers, diviners, physicians, musicians, and others with expertise requiring such knowledge.[1]

The link between the Warring States natural experts and earlier Zhou court functionaries is clear; even in the Former Han imperial court the position of scribe/astrologer (*shi* 史) was frequently hereditary, and that official's activities were circumscribed by state service. However, the mechanisms that led to the proliferation of masters and to their profuse philosophical discourse during the Warring States transformed the practice of astrology and other specialties as well. Like the masters, these experts saw themselves as participants in text-based traditions. A new technical literature became one basis for identifying astrology or medicine as fields of knowledge alongside other fields, thus freeing the transmission of knowledge from hereditary occupa-

---

[1] See A. C. Graham, *Disputers of the Tao: Philosophical Argument in Ancient China* (La Salle, Ill.: Open Court, 1989), pp. 137–70, for an excellent summary of later Mohist logic and scientific interests. As Graham notes, the influence of the later Mohists' causal form of explanation was short-lived, having been quickly overshadowed by correlative system building based on yin–yang and Five Phases concepts (p. 161).

tion and furthering the growth of learned traditions. At the courts of the Warring States nobility an increasing number of experts presented themselves in company with the masters of philosophy seeking patronage in return for their ideas and advice, and the availability of their writings ensured its increased dissemination among the elite at large.

The natural experts were vital participants in the intellectual and spiritual ferment of the Warring States period. They looked for order in natural phenomena and related this order to human activity in numerologically based classifications, resulting by the end of the Warring States in the formation of a correlative cosmology centered on the concepts of qi 氣 (vapor), yin–yang, and the Five Phases (Soil, Wood, Metal, Fire, Water); they abetted the rationalizing project being carried out by the masters of philosophy, although in the third century B.C. certain masters of philosophy voiced their disbelief in the validity of the Five Phases (by the first century A.D. yin–yang and Five Phases correlative cosmology had become the standard basis for understanding natural phenomena as well as all human activity).[2] At the same time, the natural experts embraced the magico-religious elements of Warring States culture. Varieties of divination, demonology, charms, incantations, and magico-religious operations (exorcism, propitiation, etc.) found a place in their practices and texts; in short, the natural experts were also occultists.

Studies in the history of Chinese philosophy have looked at the intellectual and spiritual temperament of the Warring States era mainly through the lens of the masters of philosophy, whose seeming humanistic outlook obscures the magico-religious and naturalistic points of view of the natural experts and occultists. Scholars in the field of Chinese science tend to focus on issues in the history of science at the expense of a broad view of Warring States thought and religion. More integrated studies of the entire Warring States intellectual and spiritual landscape are appearing, studies that set the magico-religious and occult elements alongside philosophy and science. New evidence of cross-fertilization between Warring States philosophy, cosmology, and religion has disproven older theories that rationalistic principles in Warring States philosophy were transformed into objects of religious devotion in the syncretistic Han era. Thus, we are beginning to know more about the interplay of ideas in Warring States culture, and a more coherent picture

---

[2] "The Five Phases have no regular conquest" is one of the later Mohist logical propositions in *Mozi* (Sibu beiyao ed.), 10 ("Jingxia"), 3a. *Han Feizi* (Sibu beiyao ed.), 5 ("Shixie"), 8a–b, associates the Five Phases with the deceptive ideas spread by divination and astrology. Two studies by A. C. Graham are essential introductions to the early history and characteristics of Chinese correlative cosmology: A. C. Graham, *Yin–Yang and the Nature of Correlative Thinking* (Singapore: Institute of East Asian Philosophies, 1986); and *Disputers of the Tao*, pp. 315–70. *Qi* (vapor), yin–yang, and the Five Phases are discussed later in this chapter.

of the transitions from early Chinese civilization into the medieval period is emerging.[3] Given that similar investigations are leading to reappraisals of Greek thought and religion, we may also look forward to comparative insights on magic, religion, philosophy, and science in the two ancient civilizations.[4]

DEFINITIONS AND SOURCES

With the aim of presenting Warring States ideas so as to elucidate a Warring States conception (and to avoid imposing modern points of view), one must decide on certain English terms that have general descriptive value, yet do not misrepresent the ideas under investigation. Like the study of aspects of scientific thought in other premodern contexts, the use of the word "science" to designate a specific body of knowledge or set of practices in early China is problematic, even though the subject of this chapter is directly relevant to the contemporary discipline known as the history of Chinese science. Natural philosophy, in the sense of systems of thought that take nature as their primary object of investigation and that develop theories to explain phenomena in terms of perceived regularities in the operation of nature itself, is gaining currency among historians of science writing in English.[5] The term is serviceable for correlative cosmology in its formative Warring States stage (one must assume that natural philosophy can be separated from its long history in the Western intellectual tradition). However, the term "natural philosophy" does not fully cover the diverse elements of Warring States correlative cosmology (which was not simply a means to learn about nature), nor does it acknowledge the evident interpenetration of correlative cosmology, magico-religious belief, and other forms of occult thought in the Warring States period. Even as correlative cosmology created the basis for naturalistic

---

[3] Li Ling, "An Archaeological Study of Taiyi (Grand One) Worship," *Early Medieval China* 2 (1995–6): 1–39, examines Warring States and Han archaeological evidence of Taiyi 太一 (Grand One) in astrological and magico-religious traditions, disproving the earlier hypothesis that Taiyi was originally a Warring States philosophical concept that became the name of an astral body in Han times and somewhat later was exalted as the supreme spirit of Heaven (see below, pp. 869–71). For recent studies of the relation between myth, religion, and cosmology, see Marc Kalinowski, "Mythe, cosmogenese et theogonie dans la Chine ancienne," *L'homme* 137, 1 (1996): 41–60; and John Major, "Myth, Cosmology, and the Origins of Chinese Science," *Journal of Chinese Philosophy* 5 (1978): 1–20.

[4] See especially G. E. R. Lloyd, *Magic, Reason and Experience* (Cambridge University Press, 1979), which breaks new ground in the study of Greek science; in G. E. R. Lloyd, *Demystifying Mentalities* (Cambridge University Press, 1990), pp. 105–34, the author offers a comparative treatment of Greek and Chinese concepts.

[5] See David C. Lindberg, *The Beginnings of Western Science* (Chicago: University of Chicago Press, 1992), pp. 1–4, for arguments in favor of adopting natural philosophy as a general term in the study of the premodern history of science.

explanations of phenomena, yin–yang and Five Phases theories did not lead to a conceptual opposition between natural philosophy on the one hand and occult thought on the other.[6]

Moreover, Warring States knowledge of nature encompassed more than what was channeled into yin–yang and Five Phases theories. To take the example of medicine, physiological and etiological theories that made the body a microcosm of the cosmos did not make extensive use of yin–yang and Five Phases theories before the Former Han. In addition to early theoretical developments, the formation of a learned medicine during the Warring States relied on popular lore (much of it based on magico-religious beliefs), practical experiences, and competition between several kinds of medical practitioners. The ideal term for the subject under investigation in this chapter would connote all of the preceding in equal measure. The use of "natural philosophy" and "occult thought," either singly or as a pair, is a kind of portmanteau expression intended to emphasize the inclusiveness of Warring States knowledge of nature; that is, the two terms are intended to be complementary, not to suggest opposite categories in the Warring States conception.

The terms "magico-religious" and "occult" raise no less thorny issues of definition in themselves. I take for granted the obsolescence of earlier theories that attempt to relate magic developmentally to either the history of religion or of science (with the implicit understanding that religion and science are more evolved civilizational forms); magic is also not simply degenerate religion.[7] Magic, whether from the perspective of ancient textual sources or that of modern investigation, may be said to concern human actions undertaken in the belief that spirits and divine powers are present in nature. In response to particular circumstances, humans tap the divine presence with voice, gesture, and select materials; the same is true with religion. Qualifications can be proposed, but it is difficult to justify the discreteness of religion except on relativistic grounds. When such grounds are expressed in an ancient text they are an invaluable record of how an individual or a group (social, religious, or political) judged the action in question; they do not define the action absolutely.[8]

---

[6] Marc Kalinowski, *Cosmologie et divination dans la Chine ancienne* (Paris: École française d'Extrême-Orient, 1991), p. 47, likens yin–yang and Five Phases correlative cosmology to the Hermetic traditions of Greco-Roman times and notes especially the "extreme diversity of the elements of which it is composed and . . . its multiple applications not only in the realm of the investigation of things in general, but also in that of politics, religion, and the arts."

[7] The history of late-nineteenth- and twentieth-century scholarly debate on magic and the current state of the debate are well treated in Stanley J. Tambiah, *Magic, Science, Religion, and the Scope of Rationality* (Cambridge University Press, 1990).

[8] Han sources attest to the fact that magico-religious activity deemed harmful to the person of the ruler and the state was to be prosecuted, even though the activity in itself was no different from contempo-

Divination exemplifies the interface between magico-religious and naturalistic thinking in early China. It was not by accident that by the end of the third century B.C., the *Yi jing* achieved new stature as a source of yin–yang cosmology. Features of Warring States astrology (the belief that astral bodies were the celestial manifestations of divine entities, the ominous consequences of celestial events in the subcelestial realm, etc.) similarly exhibit the fusion of magico-religious concerns with systematic calculations.

Although "magico-religious" and "occult" are often treated as roughly synonymous, there is one respect in which use of the term "occult thought" should be qualified in connection with the Warring States natural experts and occultists. Too little is known about the place of *wu* 巫 (shamans) and other religious officiants in Warring States culture and their relation to the natural experts and occultists. They are sometimes linked in written sources, for example in the compound *wu yi* 巫醫, either "shamans and physicians" or "shaman physician."[9] Despite flexible attitudes that might allow incantations within the body of medical knowledge along with drugs, by Warring States times physicians participated in the text-based alignment of knowledge, which distanced them socially and intellectually from the *wu*, who appear to have belonged to a substratum of religion.[10] In the hands of the physicians and other specialists magico-religious belief and practice became part of the knowledge recorded in texts and also made accessible to an elite readership. As a result, knowledge of not only astrology and divination but also incantation, demonology, and other magico-religious lore acquired a significance apart from religious belief and practice, influencing intellectual trends among the elite in a way that religion alone did not. It is with this broader intellectual context in mind that occult thought is paired with natural philosophy.

While natural philosophy and occult thought are useful terms to facilitate discussion, one cannot speak of Warring States natural philosophy and occult thought as a cohesive body of knowledge shared by members of a self-identified group who saw themselves as the "natural experts" and "occultists."

---

rary forms of religion; see Donald Harper, *Early Chinese Medical Literature: The Mawangdui Medical Manuscripts* (London: Kegan Paul, 1997), pp. 157–9. Although undocumented, similar attitudes about illicit magic or witchcraft probably existed in the Warring States. The nature of magic as "unsanctioned religion" is examined in C. R. Phillips, "*Nullum Crimen sine Lege*: Socioreligious Sanctions on Magic," in *Magika Hiera: Ancient Greek Magic and Religion*, ed. Christopher Faraone and Dirk Obbink (Oxford: Oxford University Press, 1991), pp. 260–76.

9   For an early example of the compound, see *Analects*, 13/22 (James Legge, *The Chinese Classics. Vol. 1: Confucian Analects, The Great Learning, and The Doctrine of the Mean* [rpt. Hong Kong: Hong Kong University Press, 1960], p. 273).

10   The question of *wu*-ism (or shamanism) is discussed in Donald Harper, "Warring States, Qin, and Han Periods," in "Chinese Religions: The State of the Field," ed. Daniel L. Overmyer, *JAS* 54, 1 (1995): 154–5. Cf. Lothar von Falkenhausen, "Reflections on the Political Role of Spirit Mediums in Early China: The *Wu* Officials in the *Zhou li*," *EC* 20: 279–300.

The latter terms are also used to facilitate discussion, not to denote a social identity recognized in the Warring States. The theoretical cohesion of yin–yang and Five Phases correlative cosmology was accomplished during the Han dynasty, not before. It was also during the Han that labels like *yin–yang jia* 陰陽家 (yin–yang specialist) and *fangshi* 方士 (recipe gentleman) were applied to third century B.C. men who disseminated correlative cosmology and various occult arts; neither term is attested to in pre-Han sources, and both probably belong to the Han reappraisal of the Warring States intellectual legacy.[11]

For most of the Warring States period the practitioners of various specialties (astrology, music, medicine, etc.) worked mainly within their specialties, aware of one another's ideas and subject to mutual influence, but not pursuing a common intellectual purpose. Their activities must also be set within the context of sociopolitical, intellectual, and spiritual change from the fifth to the fourth and third centuries B.C., as older Zhou religious attitudes and institutional forms gave way to increasingly reasoned speculation on mankind and the world at large. Basic concepts emerged gradually, and the meaning of key words changed as theoretical developments freighted them with added significance. In the fourth century B.C. yin–yang was not yet a technical term for a concept of dualism, nor did *wu xing* 五行 have the sense of the "five phases" of a naturalistic cycle.[12] By the mid-third century B.C. men like Zou Yan 騶衍 (305–240? B.C.; Zou Yan was one of those classified as yin–yang specialists in Han sources) were applying yin–yang and Five Phases correlative cosmology to political theory.[13] When in 221 B.C. Qin Shihuang declared Water the sign of Qin's ascendancy, adopting the Five Phases theory that the virtue of Water (*shuide* 水德) would succeed the virtue of Fire (*huode* 火德) assigned to Zhou rule (as Water conquers Fire), the basic ideas of yin–yang and Five Phases correlative cosmology had achieved sufficient currency to provide a cogent rationale of political power rooted in the natural cycle of the cosmos.[14]

Apart from a few fragments of questionable authenticity, none of the technical literature of Warring States natural philosophy and occult thought has

---

[11] Yin–yang *jia* and *fangshi* are discussed below, pp. 822–3, 827.

[12] See pp. 860–1 below.

[13] In the *Han shu* bibliographic treatise, the classification yin–yang specialist is used to group the writings of Zou Yan and others with those of the masters of philosophy (*Han shu*, 30, p. 1733). I agree with Graham, *Disputers of the Tao*, pp. 328–9, that the classification is retrospective and that in the third century B.C., Zou Yan was not recognized as one of the masters of philosophy.

[14] See Denis Twitchett and Michael Loewe, eds., *The Cambridge History of China. Vol. 1: The Ch'in and Han Empires* (Cambridge University Press, 1986), pp. 96–7, for arguments supporting the historicity of Qin Shihuang's adoption of Five Phases theory, which has been challenged. There is a full account of the political cycle linked to the conquest sequence of the Five Phases in *Lü shi chunqiu* (Sibu beiyao ed.), 13 ("Yingtong"), 4a; cf. Graham, *Disputers of the Tao*, pp. 329–30.

survived in the received record.[15] Occasional anecdotal evidence of the activities of astrologers and other experts in Warring States historical texts (like the *Zuo zhuan*, Zuo's tradition, and *Guo yu*, Sayings of the States, which record events prior to the Warring States period, but were most likely composed during the fourth century B.C.) and in philosophical texts (the *Lü shi chunqiu*, Mr. Lü's Spring and Autumn [annals], of ca. 239 B.C. is an important source) sheds some light, but the main received sources of information date from Han times. One should not discount the value of Han testimony, yet the pervasiveness of yin–yang and Five Phases correlative cosmology in Han thought and the vicissitudes of Han occult learning (while magicoreligious and occult arts continued to flourish, their acceptability was tempered by Han conceptions of orthodoxy) require that the later testimony be evaluated with caution lest a Han point of view color the account of Warring States natural philosophy and occult thought.

Archaeology is responsible for restoring essential evidence to twentieth-century scholars. Discoveries of manuscripts in tombs excavated since the 1970s have been particularly rich. As of 1995, tombs from the late fourth to the mid-second century B.C. have yielded silk and bamboo- or wooden-strip manuscripts with texts on subjects like divination, astrology, hemerology, demonology, and medicine. By analysis of the script and other features, it has been judged that some manuscripts from second century B.C. tombs were copied before the end of the third century B.C. – for example, several of the medical manuscripts from Mawangdui 馬王堆 tomb 3, in Changsha 長沙, Hunan (which is dated 168 B.C.). The contents of other manuscripts that were copied during the first half of the second century B.C. also reflect third century B.C. knowledge. In contrast to the greater part of the evidence in received literature, which is mostly anecdotal and frequently critical, the newly discovered texts are technical writings that belonged to the literate elite who patronized the natural experts and occultists; they give us direct access to the ideas of the Warring States experts themselves. The regularity with which these manuscripts have appeared in tombs ranging from Hunan and Hubei to Shandong, Anhui, and Gansu bears witness to the ubiquity of the literature of natural philosophy and occult thought, as well as to its distribution in the several geographical and cultural regions of the Warring States *oikoumene.*[16]

---

[15] I leave aside the *Shan hai jing* 山海經; see below, p. 822.

[16] See Donald Harper, "Warring States, Qin, and Han Manuscripts Related to Natural Philosophy and the Occult," in *New Sources of Early Chinese History: An Introduction to Reading Inscriptions and Manuscripts*, ed. Edward L. Shaughnessy (Berkeley: Society for the Study of Early China, and Institute of East Asian Studies, University of California, 1997), pp. 223–52, for a survey of the manuscripts discovered as of 1992. Harper, *Early Chinese Medical Literature*, pp. 22–30, provides a physical description of the Mawangdui medical manuscripts.

Other artifacts found in tombs contribute to our knowledge of the popularity among the elite of ideas broadly related to religion, natural philosophy, and occult thought and allow us to see how certain ideas developed over time. To give a single example, several lacquer clothes cases from the tomb of Zeng Hou Yi 曾侯乙, in Suixian 隨縣, Hubei (burial dated 433 B.C. or slightly later) bear astrological designs. The lid of one is inscribed with the names of the twenty-eight stellar lodges (*ershiba xiu* 二十八宿) arranged in a ring, the earliest attestation of the complete sequence of twenty-eight. The graph *dou* 斗 written inside the ring of stellar lodges represents the constellation *beidou* 北斗 (Northern Dipper; the Big Dipper) in its function as a celestial pointer; a sexagenary-cycle day designation written alongside the stellar lodge (*kang* 亢, Gullet) indicates that calendrical calculations expressed by reference to the stellar lodges and the Dipper were already being made in the fifth century B.C. The design of the lacquer lid anticipates the astrological instrument called *shi* 式 (cosmic board), specimens of which have been recovered from the Han tomb of Xiahou Zao 夏侯竈 (d. 165 B.C.).[17]

Were one to reconstruct the worldview of the Warring States elite based solely on the evidence of the tombs excavated to date, ideas related to natural philosophy and occult thought would occupy a prominent place – more prominent than would result from a reconstruction based on the received record, particularly were that record to be narrowed down to the writings attributed to the masters of philosophy. Although still limited by the scarcity of primary sources, an account of natural philosophy and occult thought adds depth and perspective to our perception of the Warring States period.

WARRING STATES NATURAL EXPERTS AND OCCULTISTS AND THEIR TEXTS

To judge from the *Zuo zhuan* and *Guo yu*, Spring and Autumn period statesmen, scribe/astrologers (*shi* 史), physicians (*yi* 醫), turtle and milfoil diviners (*bu* 卜), and musicians expounded their knowledge of the spirit world and nature at the courts of the various states, at times competitively. Under the year corresponding to 541 B.C., the *Zuo zhuan* recounts Zi Chan's 子產 (d. 522 B.C.) mission from Zheng 鄭 to Jin 晉 in response to news of the Jin ruler's illness. In Jin, the court scribe/astrologers had been unable to identify the two spirits named as the cause of the illness by the diviners. Zi Chan knew them: he identified one of them as a spirit of the stellar lodge *Shen* 參 (Triaster) and the other as a spirit of the Fen River 汾水, both of which were linked to the fortunes of the state of Jin and its rulers. The Jin ruler's illness

---

[17] Translations of the stellar lodge names follows Edward Schafer, *Pacing the Void: T'ang Approaches to the Stars* (Berkeley: University of California Press, 1977), pp. 76–7.

continues as the subject of the immediately following passage. The ruler of Qin sent Physician He 醫和 to Jin, and Physician He's diagnosis included a well-known discussion of the *liu qi* 六氣 (six vapors) in Heaven that underlie the phenomena of taste, color, sound, and illness (the first two *qi* are yin and yang in an early sense of "shade" and "sunshine"). The conclusion of each passage notes that Zi Chan and Physician He were praised and richly rewarded for their wisdom.[18] The *Guo yu* has the musician Zhou Jiu 州鳩 describe the astrological signs marking the date when King Wu of Zhou began the attack on Yin. Zhou Jiu did so during a presentation on music and harmony to King Jing of Zhou (r. 544–520 B.C.).[19]

One may question the historical accuracy of the personages and speeches recorded in the *Zuo zhuan* and *Guo yu*, but the portrayal must maintain at least the semblance of truth, if not for the Spring and Autumn period itself then at least for the fifth and fourth centuries B.C. when the narratives that constitute the received texts of the *Zuo zhuan* and *Guo yu* were composed. This period coincides with the rise of a more private type of literature as exemplified in the books of the masters of philosophy. By no later than the fourth century B.C., the technical literature of the natural experts and occultists also began to circulate.[20] The story of natural philosophy and occult thought is closely tied to this literature, which became more voluminous over the third, second, and first centuries B.C. and played a significant role in the growth and dissemination of ideas.

The contents of this technical literature may be considered in the light of the *Han shu* bibliographic treatise, which reproduces the general scheme of Liu Xin's 劉歆 (46 B.C.–A.D. 23) now lost catalog of the first century B.C. Han court library at Chang'an 長安.[21] Although it is impossible to make a count of the books that assuredly date to the Warring States rather than to the Former Han, the lists of titles in the bibliographic treatise attest to a diversity of literature that undoubtedly existed by the third century B.C. As will

---

[18] *Zuo zhuan*, 41 (Zhao 1), 20a–29a (Legge, *The Ch'un Ts'ew with The Tso Chuen*, pp. 580–1). See below, p. 862, for Physician He and the *liuqi*. For accounts of hexagram divination from the *Zuo zhuan*, see Kidder Smith, "*Zhouyi* Interpretation from Accounts in the *Zuozhuan*," *HJAS* 49 (1989): 424–41.

[19] *Guo yu* (Sibu beiyao ed.), 3 ("Zhouyu xia"), 18a. David W. Pankenier, "Astronomical Dates in Shang and Western Zhou," *EC* 7 (1981–2): 2–37, has used the *Guo yu* passage for astronomical confirmation of the date of King Wu's attack; cf. David S. Nivison, *The Riddle of the Bamboo Annals* (Stanford, Calif.: Private publication, 1995), pp. 132–6, for another argument.

[20] On the beginnings of private literature in China, see T. H. Tsien, *Written on Bamboo and Silk: The Beginnings of Chinese Books and Inscriptions* (Chicago: University of Chicago Press, 1962), pp. 9–11. Earlier writing consisted primarily of official records and collections like the *Shu jing* 書經 and *Shi jing* 詩經, which by the age of Confucius were revered as "Canons." The Chu Silk Manuscript of ca. 300 B.C. and Chu divination records from Baoshan 包山 tomb 2 (burial dated ca. 316 B.C.) are the earliest known examples of technical literature, whence the estimate of fourth century B.C. as its terminus ad quem.

[21] See Graham, *Disputers of the Tao*, p. 379; and Twitchett and Loewe, eds., *Cambridge History of China*, p. 651.

be discussed shortly, the treatise's classification scheme is not an accurate guide to the social and intellectual affiliations of the men who produced and transmitted the literature, but this in no way diminishes its primary value as our only comprehensive record of the literature itself.

The literature of natural philosophy and occult thought is distributed across four of the six major divisions of the *Han shu* bibliographic treatise. The division "*zhuzi*" 諸子 (Collected masters), which contains the works of the masters of philosophy arranged in ten sections that purport to represent the different philosophical traditions of the pre-Han era, lists "Yin yang jia" 陰陽家 (Yin–yang specialists) as the third section; the first and second sections are "Rujia" 儒家 (Ru specialists) and "Daojia" 道家 (Dao specialists), respectively. Zou Yan's name appears prominently under "Yin–yang specialists" as the author of two books, one in forty-nine fascicles (*pian* 篇) and the other in fifty-six.[22] In the division "Bingshu" 兵書 (Military books), "Bing yin yang" 兵陰陽 (Military yin–yang) is one of five sections of books related to military arts.[23] The entirety of the division "Shushu" 數術 (Calculations and arts) represents the literature of natural philosophy and occult thought. The sections are: "Tianwen" 天文 (Patterns of Heaven; astrology, including various celestial phenomena like comets, rainbows, and clouds); "Lipu" 曆譜 (Calendars and tables; the calendar, related astrological and hemerological calculations, and chronological tables); "Wu xing" 五行 (Five Phases; various systems of numerological calculation related to astrology and the calendar, including use of the *shi* 式 "cosmic board"); "Shigui" 蓍龜 (Milfoil and turtle; hexagram-divination and plastromancy);[24] "Zazhan" 雜占 (Miscellaneous divination; dream interpretation, demonology, incantation, and exorcism are among the topics); and "Xingfa" 形法 (Configuration models; geomancy and physiognomy).[25] Medical literature occupies the four sections of the division "Fangji" 方技 (Recipes and techniques).[26] Of the 278 titles listed in the four divisions of the bibliographic treatise, only 2 survive in received editions: the *Shan hai jing* 山海經 (Classic of mountains and seas; parts of the text being

---

[22] *Han shu*, 30, pp. 1733–5. The nine main traditions of *jia* (specialists) in the bibliographic treatise are summarized in Graham, *Disputers of the Tao*, pp. 379–81. The idea of organizing the Warring States masters of philosophy into groups of *jia* can be traced back to Sima Tan 司馬談 (d. 110 B.C.). Sima Tan identified six groups, leading off with yin–yang specialists (*Shi ji*, 130, pp. 3288–9); see Graham, *Disputers of the Tao*, pp. 377–8. The *jia* in the Han classification do not correspond to philosophical schools as formal organizations sharing core doctrines; except for the Ru followers of Confucius and the Mohists, school organization was not a significant feature of the Warring States philosophical tradition; see Twitchett and Loewe, eds., *Cambridge History of China*, pp. 651–3.

[23] *Han shu*, 30, pp. 1759–60.

[24] The *Yi jing* is the basic text of hexagram divination; in the bibliographic treatise the *Yi jing* also occupies pride of place in the first section of the division "Liuyi" 六藝 (Six arts), the canonical books as defined in the Han Ru tradition (*Han shu*, 30, pp. 1703–4).

[25] *Han shu*, 30, pp. 1763–75.

[26] *Han shu*, 30, pp. 1776–80.

dated to the Warring States), listed in the section "Configuration models" in the division "Calculations and arts," and the *Huang Di neijing* 黃帝內經 (Inner classic of Huang Di; compiled probably during the first century B.C., with later additions) in the division "Recipes and Techniques."[27]

Works classified in "Calculations and Arts" most obviously reflect the pairing of natural philosophy and occult thought. Appraisals that conclude each section and each division of the *Han shu* bibliographic treatise are also revealing. Both the yin–yang specialists (in the division "Collected Masters") and the yin–yang militarists (in the division "Military Books") are praised for their knowledge of the calendar and the cycles of Heaven with which to determine opportune times, but they are criticized for their exploitation of the powers of demons and spirits.[28] Sima Tan 司馬談 (d. 110 B.C.), in an earlier classification of the Warring States philosophical legacy into six groups of *jia* (specialists), expressed the same opinion of the yin–yang specialists, whom he admired for their skillful calibration of the seasonal cycle, yet deprecated for spreading superstition among the populace.[29]

Were we to recover the lost books whose titles are listed in the *Han shu* bibliographic treatise we would be better able to track developments across several centuries among the natural experts and occultists, as well as between them and the masters of philosophy. While excavated manuscripts and relevant artifacts restore parts of the intellectual mosaic effaced in the received record and improve the accuracy of our hypotheses, the extent of our understanding remains severely limited. Nevertheless, the evidence permits some general deductions concerning the emergence of yin–yang and Five Phases correlative cosmology during the third century B.C. and the status of natural philosophy and occult thought at the end of the Warring States continuing into the Qin and Han eras.

Sima Tan and the *Han shu* bibliographic treatise attribute the emergence of yin–yang ideas (by Han times the term yin–yang alone referred generally to correlative cosmology) to men with knowledge of celestial and seasonal cycles, that is, astrological and calendrical knowledge. The prestige of yin–yang and Five Phases correlative cosmology in Han thought explains the placing of yin–yang together with other Warring States philosophical traditions expounded by the masters, now organized in groups of *jia* (specialists). Having situated the yin–yang specialists within the division "Collected Masters," the *Han shu* bibliographic treatise acknowledges other yin–yang

[27] On the *Shan hai jing*, see Michael Loewe, ed., *Early Chinese Texts, A Bibliographical Guide* (Berkeley: Society for the Study of Early China and Institute of East Asian Studies, University of California, Berkeley, 1993), pp. 357–67. On the received text of the *Huang Di neijing*, see ibid., pp. 196–215.

[28] *Han shu*, 30, pp. 1734–5, 1760.

[29] *Shi ji*, 130, pp. 3288–9; cf. Graham, *Disputers of the Tao*, p. 377.

practitioners in the divisions "Military Books" and "Calculations and Arts" (with its separate sections for astrology, the calendar, and the Five Phases). The treatise's organization suggests a stratification of yin–yang and Five Phases correlative cosmology, with the yin–yang specialists as theoreticians and others as lesser practitioners.

This appears to be a Han conception, grounded in large part on the legendary reputation enjoyed by Zou Yan during the second and first centuries B.C. The *Shi ji* provides the most explicit testimony of this reputation. In a chapter that is nominally an account of Mencius (fl. 320 B.C.) and Xunzi (ca. 310–215? B.C.), Zou Yan is portrayed as the more influential intellectual figure at the Jixia Academy in Qi in the third century B.C. (Zou Yan was active ca. 250 B.C.) The *Shi ji* devotes three times more space to describing Zou Yan's theories and activities than it gives to Mencius or to Xunzi. Zou Yan is credited with having used yin–yang and the Five Phases to speculate inductively on phenomena in nature, with a theory of cosmogony, and with a theory of the cycles of political change extending back to Huang Di 黃帝. The stature Zou Yan enjoyed in Qi was matched by the respect accorded to him when he visited rulers in Liang 梁 (Wei 魏), Zhao 趙, and Yan 燕 (in contrast to the hardships experienced by Confucius and Mencius).[30]

Remarkably, there is no pre-Han corroboration of the *Shi ji* account. Given Zou Yan's theories and his enormous reputation according to the *Shi ji*, one might expect some form of acknowledgment from Xunzi, whom the *Shi ji* says came to the Jixia Academy after Zou Yan. Several essays in the *Xunzi* criticize the ideas of other masters of philosophy, but there is no mention of Zou Yan even though his ideas about Heaven would have conflicted with those of Xunzi. Indeed, none of the third and second century B.C. philosophical texts that identify masters of philosophy either in formal enumerations or in references to philosophical disputes – books like *Xunzi Zhuangzi, Han Feizi, Lü shi chunqiu, Huainanzi* – mention Zou Yan. Zou Yan appears once in the *Han Feizi*, where he is condemned along with other men who spread false faith in divination and astrology; otherwise, the received record is virtually silent.[31]

Zou Yan's historicity and his presence in Qi in the mid-third century B.C. are not in doubt. However, the contemporary masters of philosophy did not regard Zou Yan as one of their own number. As an exponent of cosmology, Zou Yan's place was among the astrologers and almanac makers; he belonged to the world of the natural experts and occultists, not to that of the masters

---

[30] *Shi ji*, 74, pp. 2344–5.
[31] *Han Feizi*, 5 ("Shixie"), 8a. Zou Yan is also mentioned once in *Zhanguoce* (Sibu beiyao ed.), 29 ("Yance" 1), 8b; cf. Graham, *Yin–Yang and the Nature of Correlative Thinking*, pp. 12–13.

of philosophy.[32] To reject the image of Zou Yan as it is presented in the *Shi ji* and codified in the *Han shu* bibliographic treatise (where the books attributed to him are in the section for yin–yang specialists in the division of "Collected Masters") is not to deny the role that Zou Yan may have played in the development of cosmological speculation and its assimilation into the philosophical mainstream. If the cosmological knowledge of the natural experts and occultists was primarily an applied knowledge intended to resolve particular situations as they arose (typical of astrology and divination), perhaps Zou Yan fashioned theories that demonstrated the relevance of cosmology to the state and the individual, thereby making it indispensable to philosophy.

At Warring States courts and among the elite generally, the applied knowledge of the natural experts and occultists was valued as much as the speculations of the masters of philosophy. Astrology, hemerology, medicine, and other arts were of immediate consequence in the pattern of daily life; the natural experts and occultists were there to dispense their wisdom as the occasion required. The words *shu* 數 (calculation) and *shu* 術 (art) in the division "Calculations and Arts" of the *Han shu* bibliographic treatise concretely express the expectation that the literature of natural philosophy and occult thought was demonstrably effective, containing models and methods to be applied to achieving beneficial ends. The significance of *fang* 方 (recipe) and *ji* 技 (technique) in the division "Recipes and Techniques" is comparable; medicine was perceived as a skill backed up by recipes. Although the textual evidence documenting the use of all four words in connection with natural philosophy and occult thought dates only to Han, it was probably applied knowledge that connected the various Warring States natural experts and occultists socially and intellectually, whether they were astrologers, diviners, or physicians; their mutual connection was reinforced by the varieties of technical literature that they each possessed.[33]

Ideas and attitudes arise in an environment, and one cannot isolate the natural experts and occultists from issues that also occupied the masters of philosophy and men in positions of political power. By the third century B.C. *shu* 術 (art) and related words acquired increased significance as part of the belief that knowledge and action could be formulated as a technique. Virtually any significant activity – such as statecraft, rhetoric, or mind cultivation – rested on its own particular skill. To be sure, *dao* 道 (way) as a central idea

---

[32] Graham, *Disputers of the Tao*, pp. 328–9; idem, *Yin–Yang and the Nature of Correlative Thinking*, pp. 12–13.

[33] See Harper, *Early Chinese Medical Literature*, pp. 45–54, for detailed discussion and text citations. See also, Chen Pan, "Zhanguo Qin Han jian fangshi kaolun," *BIHP* 17 (1948): 7–57.

in classical Chinese philosophy was more concerned with guiding the course of human life than with abstract questions of truth and reality, but the emphasis of the third century B.C. on defining techniques to quantify *dao* reflects both rationalizing tendencies in thought and the increasing specialization of knowledge.[34]

Within philosophy key questions regarding techniques were left unresolved: Were techniques genuine or spurious? Did they rely on reasoned principles or appeal to occult powers? Were they ethical or did they aim to deceive? The ambiguity is concisely expressed in a text included in the Mawangdui tomb 3 manuscript of the *Yi jing*, entitled *Yao* 要 (Essentials), which gives an apology by Confucius for his attachment to a book of divination; I attribute the sentiments to a third century B.C. point of view:

If men of later generations doubt me, Qiu [i.e., Confucius], perhaps it will be because of the *Yi*. I seek the virtue in it, no more. I am one who shares a path with scribe/astrologers and shamans, but whose final destination is different. How can the virtuous conduct of the gentleman be intended to seek fortune? Thus his performance of sacrificial worship is infrequent. How can his humaneness and sense of duty be intended to seek auspices? Thus his performance of turtle and milfoil divination is rare. Does not the turtle and milfoil divination of the incantors and shamans come after this?[35]

While Confucius is shown as admitting to "sharing a path" with men whose use of the *Yi jing* is to determine fortune, he insists that his motives are wholly ethical.

A comparable ambiguity lay at the heart of natural philosophy and occult thought. Within a framework of applied knowledge expressed in arts and recipes, as various theories arose (yin–yang and Five Phases among them) and contributed to an increasingly reasoned understanding of natural phenomena these theories did not in themselves exclude or invalidate an occult understanding. There were certainly skeptics who focused their attention on more naturalistic explanations. However, rejection of magico-religious and occult beliefs was a relative stand taken by individuals and was not necessitated in principle by the theories.[36]

---

[34] Statecraft as a *shu* (art) is associated with Shen Buhai 申不害 (d. 337 B.C.); see Graham, *Disputers of the Tao*, p. 268. For evidence of the *shu* of rhetoric and mind cultivation, the *Xunzi* may be cited: *Xunzi* (Sibu beiyao ed.), 3 ("Feixiang"), 6b, "the *shu* of speaking and persuasion"; and 1 ("Xiushen"), 8b, "the *shu* of cultivating vapor and nurturing the heart." On the idea of *dao* in classical Chinese philosophy, see Graham, *Disputers of the Tao*, pp. 222–3.

[35] Chen Songchang and Liao Mingchun, "Boshu *Ersanzi wen, Yi zhi yi, Yao* shiwen," *Daojia wenhua yanjiu* 3 (1993): 435.

[36] For evidence from the Han period, see Donald Harper, "The Conception of Illness in Early Chinese Medicine as Documented in Newly Discovered 3rd and 2nd Century B.C. Manuscripts," *Sudhoffs Archiv* 74 (1990): 211 (on the explicit rejection of the belief that demons and spirits cause illness in the *Huang Di neijing*, which stops short of denying that demons and spirits exist); and p. 225, n. 76 (on Wang Chong's 王充 [27–ca. 100] use of yin–yang and the Five Phases).

Enthusiastic eclecticism in natural philosophy and occult thought near the end of the third century B.C. is evidenced in the *Shi ji*'s accounts of men called *fangshi* 方士 (recipe gentlemen). Said to be followers of Zou Yan, the recipe gentlemen catered to the elite demand for esoteric, occult knowledge. Their appearance coincides with the first evidence of the *xian* 仙 cult (which promised immortal life as a transcendent being), and it was as teachers of alchemy and immortality that recipe gentlemen were patronized by Qin Shi-huang.[37] The name *fangshi* is first attested in the *Shi ji*, so we cannot be certain whether it originated among the occultists so named or was applied to them by the elite who patronized them, or whether it is another example of Han terminology like yin–yang specialist. Names aside, the recipe gentlemen represent a new addition to the natural philosophers and occultists. Unlike astrologers or physicians, who by and large worked within their specialties, the recipe gentlemen operated more as free agents with a reputation for occult arts. The influence of the recipe gentlemen on Han natural philosophy, occult thought, and religion was great; they had a hand in the spread of religious cults, expanded the range of occult belief and practice, and contributed to the investigation of nature. As yin–yang and Five Phases correlative cosmology became part of Han state orthodoxy (which for obvious reasons of political authority was hostile to the spread of occult arts among the populace) and as practitioners in fields such as astrology and medicine adapted to it, the recipe gentlemen blurred the boundaries that orthodoxy set between approved yin–yang and Five Phases theories and unapproved forms of occult thought.[38]

If we take a broad view of Warring States intellectual traditions, it appears that the natural experts and occultists developed theories to explain natural phenomena and applied them in the practice of their specialties without the masters of philosophy acting as catalysts. To be sure, the masters of philosophy were interested in the idea of nature. Every master drew upon aspects of nature in developing analogies for his particular philosophical argument, and all equated harmony in nature (whether conceived as Heaven, as Heaven and Earth, or as the *dao* [way] of the *Zhuangzi* and *Laozi*) with harmony in society. At times they acknowledged the learning of astrologers and physicians, as when the *Mencius* expresses admiration for the ability to calculate the solstices of a thousand years hence or when it describes *qi* (vapor) as what fills and nurtures the body.[39] However, speculation on natural phenomena

---

[37] *Shi ji*, 28, pp. 1368–70.

[38] Ngo Van Xuyet, *Divination, magie, et politique dans la Chine ancienne* (Paris: Presses universitaires de France, 1976), pp. 64–6, contrasts the *fangshi* with Han Ru orthodoxy.

[39] *Mencius*, 4B/26 (on the solstices) and 2A/2 (Legge, *The Works of Mencius*, pp. 331–2, 188–90), Mencius's ideas about *qi* were probably influenced by late-fourth century B.C. medical writings and philosophical writings like the *Guanzi* essay "Neiye"; see above, Chapter 11, p. 810, and below, pp. 880–1.

was tangential to their philosophical programs. When in the third century B.C. speculation on nature became a vital element of philosophy, it was in the form of nature-based political models of the sort described in the *Laozi*, as well as in several *Guanzi* essays that link the mechanics of government to the operation of the cosmos. At that point the concerns of political philosophy and correlative cosmology converged, as can be seen in the career of Zou Yan.[40]

The lives and works of the Warring States natural experts and occultists are mostly unknown to us. I offer brief discussions of three astrologers and one physician who lived between the fifth and third centuries B.C., not with the intent of presenting biography, but rather in order to connect Warring States natural philosophy and occult thought (treated by subject below) with the ideas and activities of particular individuals. All four were received at the courts of Warring States rulers, and each one transmitted his knowledge in texts. I claim no historical role for them in the development of particular ideas. However, I think they can be regarded as representative of the natural experts and occultists who shaped the course of thought alongside the masters of philosophy.

Zi Wei 子韋 of Song (fl. 480 B.C.) is named in the astrological treatise of the *Shi ji* as one of the men of old who "transmitted the calculations of Heaven" (*tianshu* 天數). The *Han shu* bibliographic treatise lists a book attributed to him, entitled *Song Sixing Zi Wei* 宋司星子韋 (Star Director Zi Wei of Song), first in the section for yin–yang specialists in the "Collected Masters" division. Although it is doubtful that the contents of the lost book were indeed fifth century B.C. writings of Zi Wei, his position at the head of the yin–yang specialists in the bibliographic treatise indicates his importance in the Han construction of a lineage of yin–yang specialists before Zou Yan.[41] The only Warring States record of Zi Wei is in an anecdote of the *Lü shi chunqiu*. As scribe/astrologer to Song Jing Gong 宋景公 (r. 516–477 B.C.), Zi Wei predicted that the baleful appearance of Mars in the stellar lodge *Xin* 心 (Heart) in 480 B.C. would not prove fatal for his ruler (Heart was

---

[40] See Graham, *Disputers of the Tao*, pp. 232–4, on spontaneity and government by *wu wei* 無為 (doing nothing) in the *Laozi*, and ibid., pp. 285–92, on Han Fei's use of the *Laozi*. Relevant *Guanzi* essays are translated and discussed in W. Allyn Rickett, *Guanzi: Political, Economic, and Philosophical Essays from Early China* (Princeton, N.J.; Princeton University Press, 1985), vol. 1, pp. 201–15 (the essay "Zhouhe"), and pp. 148–92 ("Xuangong"). See also the discussion of various *Guanzi* calendars in Graham, *Yin–Yang and the Nature of Correlative Thinking*, pp. 84–9. My understanding of the emergence of correlative cosmology accords with the views of Graham as expressed in *Disputers of the Tao* and *Yin–Yang and the Nature of Correlative Thinking* (see Graham's summary statement in the latter work, pp. 91–2).

[41] *Shi ji*, 27, p. 1343; *Han shu*, 30, p. 1733. The classification of Zi Wei as yin–yang specialist was not absolute, since he is also included among the transmitters of *shushu* (calculations and arts) in the appraisal of the division "Calculations and Arts" (*Han shu*, 30, p. 1775; the list includes many names in common with the *Shi ji* astrological treatise, indicating the prominence of astrology in defining calculations and arts).

astrologically correlated with the region of Song); on the contrary, Heaven would reward Jing Gong's moral virtue by adding twenty-one years to his lifespan.[42]

Shi Shen 石申 of Wei and Gan De 甘德 of Qi (according to the *Shi ji* astrological treatise) or Chu 楚 (according to the *Han shu* bibliographic treatise) are without doubt the most famous Warring States astrologers.[43] They are reputed to have compiled star catalogs in the fourth century B.C. that recorded celestial observations with coordinates in degrees along the celestial equator. Although the *Han shu* bibliographic treatise does not include astrological writings for either Shi Shen or Gan De (Gan De is credited with a work on dream divination), both men are quoted in the *Han shu* astrological treatise.[44] The major source for fragments of writings attributed to Shi Shen and Gan De is the eighth-century *Kaiyuan zhanjing* 開元占經 (Divination classic of the Kaiyuan Era; compiled by Gautama Siddhārta during Kaiyuan [A.D. 718–729], consisting chiefly of quotations from a *Shishi xingjing* 石氏星經 (Star classic of Mr. Shi). Recent scholarship has determined that the coordinates recorded in the *Shishi xingjing* represent observations made within a thirty-year range before or after 70 B.C., which undermines the authenticity of the *Kaiyuan zhanjing* quotations as well as the claim that observations with degree coordinates were made in the fourth century B.C. in China.[45] Nevertheless, certain observations of Venus attributed to Shi Shen and Gan De in the *Kaiyuan zhanjing* can be dated to the fourth century B.C. Which of the remaining *Kaiyuan zhanjing* quotations derive from writings of Shi Shen and Gan De is uncertain, but we at least have confirmation of the time when they were active. In the case of Shi Shen, the observations would have been made ca. 330 B.C., placing him in Wei (Liang) at the time when the court of King Hui 惠王 (r. 369–319 B.C.) was a center of intellectual activity. The date of the observations attributed to Gan De could have been either 313 or 305 B.C.[46] Thus, Gan De was active shortly after the founding of the Jixia Academy in Qi.

Wen Zhi 文摯 of Song appears in the *Lü shi chunqiu* as the physician who cured King Min 湣王 of Qi (r. 300–284 B.C.) at the cost of his own life. Causing the ruler to explode with anger was the only treatment, and King

---

[42] *Lü shi chunqiu*, 6 ("Zhile"), 8a–b.   [43] *Shi ji*, 27, p. 1343; *Han shu*, 30, p. 1775.

[44] See *Han shu*, 30, p. 1772, for Gan De's dream divination book. *Han shu*, 26, p. 1290, refers explicitly to the *jing* 經 (classic) of Gan De and of Shi Shen.

[45] See Y. Maeyama, "The Oldest Star Catalogue of China, Shih Shen's Hsing Ching," in *Prismata: Natur Wissenschaftsgeschichtliche Studien: Festschrift für Willy Hartner*, ed. Y. Maeyama and W. G. Salzer (Wiesbaden: Franz Steiner, 1977), pp. 211–45; and Kiyoshi Yabuuti, "The Observational Date of the *Shih-shih Hsing-ching*," in *Explorations in the History of Science and Technology in China*, ed. Li Guohao et al. (Shanghai: Shanghai guji, 1982), pp. 133–41.

[46] Michel Teboul, "Les premiers développements de l'astronomie chinoise des royaumes combattants au début de l'ère Chrétienne," *Bulletin de l'école française d'Extrême-Orient* 71 (1982): 152–5.

Min would not forgive the physician's offensive behavior (which was calculated to cure him). Wen Zhi was boiled alive in an open caldron for three
days and nights without suffering the least change in his facial complexion;
he finally died after he gave instructions to cover the caldron in order to "cut
off the vapor of yin and yang."[47] New evidence of Wen Zhi's medical practice has emerged in a bamboo-strip medical text from Mawangdui tomb 3
that has been assigned the title *Shi wen* 十問 (Ten questions). Wen Zhi
appears in the ninth of ten interviews between medical experts and patrons
seeking knowledge of macrobiotic hygiene (including breath cultivation,
exercise, dietetics, and sexual techniques). Wen Zhi's teaching confirms that
his practice embraced both healing and macrobiotic hygiene, the latter being
the reason for his ability to withstand the boiling caldron.[48]

The Mawangdui text shows Wen Zhi in better times advising King Wei
威王 of Qi (r. 356–320 B.C.), the eminent patron of learning and founder of
the Jixia Academy. King Wei, stating that he has no leisure to talk at length
"due to the sacrifices of the ancestral temple," would like to hear just the
"crux of the way in two or three words and no more." Wen Zhi replies that
his way fills 300 fascicles, but "sleep is foremost." Thus begins a discussion
of physical regimen, diet, drugs, and health, with King Wei an active participant. In *Shi wen* we see a Warring States physician addressing a ruler in
the exact manner of the masters of philosophy. The interview is idealized,
but no more so than interviews between Mencius and King Xuan 宣王 of
Qi (r. 319–301 B.C.) that figure prominently in the *Mencius*. Wen Zhi's interview in *Shi wen* (the manuscript was copied ca. 180 B.C.) probably originated
in a more extensive collection of writings attributed to Wen Zhi; as with the
Mencius, the interview was first committed to writing sometime after it took
place, either by Wen Zhi himself or by followers.

The name of a second physician deserves mention. Bian Que 扁鵲 is the
preeminent Warring States physician in the received record. The *Shi ji*
recounts events in his career at length, combining various medical themes
and the traditions of several physicians (including Wen Zhi) to produce an
image of Bian Que as an archetypal figure for Han medicine. Some may resist
consigning Bian Que to the realm of pure legend, but the historicity of a
Warring States physician named Bian Que remains doubtful.[49]

---

[47] *Lü shi chunqiu*, 11 ("Zhizhong"), 4a–b.

[48] *Mawangdui Han mu bo shu*, vol. 4 (Beijing: Wenwu, 1985), pp. 150–1; translated in Harper, *Early Chinese Medical Literature*, pp. 406–10.

[49] *Shi ji*, 105, pp. 2785–94; translated in R. F. Bridgman, "La medicine dans la Chine antique," *Mélanges chinois et bouddhiques* 10 (1952–5): 17–24. For detailed analysis of the *Shi ji* account of Bian Que, see Yamada Keiji, "Hen Shaku densetsu," *Tōhō gakuhō* 60 (1988): 73–158. Bian Que is mentioned in *Han Feizi*, 7 ("Yu Lao"), 2b–3a, and thus pre-Han textual sources do exist. Yamada notes that the *Shi ji* account probably was not fashioned whole by Sima Qian, but was based on traditions within medical circles in his day.

ASTROLOGY AND THE CALENDAR

Since the 1960s, excavated manuscripts and artifacts of the Warring States, Qin, and Han periods have provided abundant data to bear out Joseph Needham's characterization of Chinese astronomy as "polar and equatorial" and "arithmetical-algebraical": polar and equatorial because Heaven was organized around the polestar, which radiated outward to the constellations marking the celestial equator (the sun's path was noted but it was not the central fact informing spatial and temporal schemes); arithmetical-algebraic because the main purpose of observation was to detect celestial regularities and to express them in the numerical categories of the calendar.[50] The basic conception of the celestial regions predates the Warring States period. Between the fifth and third centuries B.C., astrologers and calendrical experts gave specificity to this conception with precise observations and theoretical elaboration. Their explanations of the macrocosmic operation of Heaven and Earth probably contributed most to the formation of the idea that all phenomena and human activity were linked in microcosmic synchronicity; that is, their role in the emergence of yin–yang and Five Phases correlative cosmology was seminal.

While correlative cosmology is a significant historical outcome, other aspects of Warring States astrology and the calendar should not be overlooked. First, new astrological and calendrical knowledge did not bring about the demise of celestial deities in religious belief; astrology remained closely connected to religious ideas about Heaven and the spirit world, whose influence was manifested in celestial and other phenomena. One could say that the new knowledge rendered the spirit world more easily subject to scrutiny as the movements of certain deities were detailed in astrological and calendrical systems devised specifically to keep track of the deities. Thus, the same ideas that supported a naturalistic understanding of phenomena also gave the spirit world a new modus operandi; the spirit world was incorporated, not eliminated.

Another aspect concerns the purpose of the calendar. The Warring States calendars preserved in the *Guanzi*, the *Lü shi chunqiu*, and other sources are of a type known as *yue ling* 月令 (ordinances of the months). The *yue ling* calendars focus on seasonal phenomena and the correct human activities to be observed throughout the year (especially those related to agriculture); unseasonal phenomena and incorrect conduct were thought to disturb the essential harmony between nature and mankind. The political nature of these

---

[50] Joseph Needham, *Science and Civilisation in China. Vol. 3: Mathematics and the Sciences of the Heavens and the Earth* (Cambridge University Press, 1959), p. 229.

calendars is clear in the twelve seasonal records that occur as the introductory sections to the first twelve chapters of the *Lü shi chunqiu*; astrological and calendrical data, including yin–yang and Five Phases correlations, are set forth as the foundation of an orderly state.[51]

Such *yue ling* calendars also figured in the evolving Warring States image of a king who fulfilled the ideal of Son of Heaven. The calendar provided a concrete plan for how to coordinate royal action with the cycles of Heaven. It became the playbook for a ritualized mimesis of Heaven, with the king playing the leading role; in speech, gesture, and movement, the king translated Heaven's harmonious operation into social reality. The *Guanzi* chapter entitled "Xuangong" 玄宮 (Dark palace; the name of the royal hall of government) preserves a remarkable example of a third century B.C. royal calendar whose contents are related to traditions documented in Han sources concerning the cosmo-ritual palace occupied by the ruler known as the *mingtang* 明堂 (bright hall). Inside the *mingtang* the ruler shifted clockwise from chamber to chamber with the passage of months and seasons, in each chamber performing the seasonally appropriate acts.[52]

In contrast to the received *yue ling* calendars, excavated almanacs of the fourth and third centuries B.C. show the Warring States elite to have been deeply concerned with the hemerological uses of the calendar in their daily lives. They expected that reliance on the calendar would optimize their fortunes in matters ranging from success in warfare and career to illness, marriage, and childbirth. The manuscripts reveal the side of astrology and the calendar criticized by Sima Tan when he accused the yin–yang specialists of feeding popular superstition.[53] Yet it was in the context of the almanacs that new ideas took shape and changed how the elite viewed their world. They still sought guidance in turtle and milfoil divination, but hemerology routinized decision making in ways that older forms of divination had not. The cycle of time expressed in the numerological systems of the calendar made fortune and misfortune predictable even

---

[51] Calendars that tabulate the days and months of a year or a period of years are known from Han times and probably existed in the Warring States period. *Huainanzi*, 5 ("Shize") is another early example of the *yue ling* calendar, translated in John Major, *Heaven and Earth in Early Han Thought: Chapters Three, Four, and Five of the Huainanzi* (Albany: State University of New York Press, 1993), pp. 217–68.

[52] See Rickett, *Guanzi*, pp. 148–92, for dating, analysis, and translation of the Xuangong calendar (the chapter name in the received text, "Youguan" 幼官, is an error), as well as for discussion of the *Lü shi chunqiu* seasonal records and other Warring States *yue ling* calendars; see also, Major, *Heaven and Earth in Early Han Thought*, pp. 217–24. For details on the *mingtang*, see Henri Maspero, "Le Ming T'ang et la crise religieuse chinoise avant les Han," *Mélanges chinois et bouddhiques* 9 (1948–51): 1–171; and William E. Soothill, *The Hall of Light: A Study of Early Kingship* (London: Lutterworth, 1951). The name *mingtang* occurs in Warring States texts, but it is uncertain whether it denotes the cosmo-ritual structure described in Han sources.

[53] *Shi ji*, 130, p. 3289.

without divination, and the calendar itself encouraged belief in a knowable world.[54]

Documentation of Warring States astrology and the calendar has been scant in comparison to the fuller record of Han astrological and calendrical ideas associated with yin–yang and Five Phases correlative cosmology.[55] Archaeologically excavated manuscripts and artifacts have contributed significant new evidence of Warring States astrology and the calendar, and this evidence is the focus of the discussion that follows.

The Structure of Heaven

We may take the lid of the lacquer clothes case from the tomb of Zeng Hou Yi as the basis for a description of a fifth century B.C. view of Heaven composed of the twenty-eight stellar lodges in an outer ring with the Northern Dipper functioning as the pointer for the polestar (see Fig. 12.1). Perhaps originally identified as the constellations where the moon lodged during a sidereal month, the stellar lodges define the celestial equator, which is arranged in four palaces (*gong* 宮; north, east, south, west) of seven stellar lodges each and associated with presiding spirits (Fig. 12.2).[56] The calendrical notation *jiayin sanri* 甲寅三日 "*jiayin* third day" by *Kang* 亢 (Gullet) indicates another correlation between the twenty-eight stellar lodges and the equal division of the celestial equator into twelve solar stations, each of which is identified by one of the twelve *dizhi* 地支 (earthly branches). Beginning with the first branch *zi* 子, which marks north and the winter solstice (positioned at the bottom of the circle), the branches are enumerated clockwise passing from the north to the east (vernal equinox at *mao* 卯), south (summer

---

[54] See Jiang Xiaoyuan, *Tianxue zhenyuan* (Shenyang: Liaoning jiaoyu, 1991), pp. 140–5, for criticism of the conventional judgment that the calendar served agriculture in early China; and pp. 167–87, for discussion of the hemerological aspects of the calendar in Warring States, Qin, and Han times.

[55] For Han ideas, see Major, *Heaven and Earth in Early Han Thought*; and Kalinowski, *Cosmologie et divination dans la Chine ancienne*.

[56] *Zeng Hou Yi mu* (Beijing: Wenwu, 1989), vol. 1, pp. 354–5; and vol. 2, color pl. 13. The dragon on the lid is the spirit of the east, the tiger the spirit of the west. The twenty-eight lodge names on the lid do not all correspond to the names recorded in received sources; see Wang Jianmin et al., "Zeng Hou Yi mu chutu de ershiba xiu qinglong baihu tuxiang," *Wenwu* 1979.7: 43–4. Scholars generally assume that the twenty-eight stellar lodges were originally linked to the sidereal month, as is the case with other twenty-eight-constellation systems in Eurasia. However, as Marc Kalinowski has observed (private communication), a functional relation between the lodges and the moon's motion is not described in early calendars and astrological writings. Current opinion tends in the direction of regarding the stellar lodge system as indigenous, rather than a foreign importation. For a recent speculation on its origin, see David S. Nivison, "The Origin of the Chinese Lunar Lodge System," in *World Archaeoastronomy*, ed. Anthony F. Aveni (Cambridge University Press, 1989), pp. 203–18. Schafer, *Pacing the Void*, pp. 75–84, discusses ancient and medieval lore concerning the stellar lodges and provides a convenient table identifying their arrangement by palace and presiding spirit (the approximate position of the lodges in Western constellations is also given).

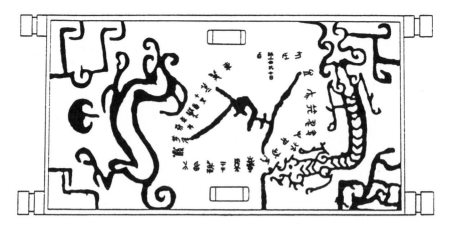

Figure 12.1. Zeng Hou Yi lacquer clothes-case lid. After *Zeng Hou Yi mu wenwu yishu*, fig. 186.

solstice at *wu* 午), and west (autumnal equinox at *you* 酉). The twelve branches assigned to the solar stations also designate the clockwise sequence of months. This sequence is the reverse of the actual path of the sun through the solar stations, which is counterclockwise.

The clothes-case lid attests to the early use of the handle of the Northern Dipper to mark the clockwise sequence of months. Observed regularly at dusk, the handle rotates clockwise through one-twelfth of the circle of the solar stations in unison with the branches and months of the calendar. Among the various Warring States calendars, some set the first month of the civil year at *zi*, corresponding to the beginning of the tropical year with the winter solstice; others set the first month of the civil year at *yin* 寅 to coincide with the beginning of spring. The fixed correlation between the solar station branches and the stellar lodges places *Kang* (Gullet) within the station marked *chen* 辰; depending on the calendar in use, the sexagenary cycle day "*jiayin* third day" recorded by the stellar lodge on the lid designates the third day in the fifth month (if the first month is *zi*) or third month (if the first month is *yin*) of the year in question (Fig. 12.2).[57]

---

[57] The lid depicts the Dipper and stellar lodges from the perspective of an observer on the ground looking up at the dome of Heaven, which is why the names of the stellar lodges are written in the reverse order of the astro-calendrical model in Figure 12.2. For further discussion of the disposition of the solar stations, branches, stellar lodges, and Dipper handle, see Kalinowski, *Cosmologie et divination dans la Chine ancienne*, pp. 68–74. For an overview of calendars in use before the Han, see Zhang Peiyu, *Zhongguo xian Qin shi libiao* (Jinan: Qi Lu, 1987), pp. 3–6.

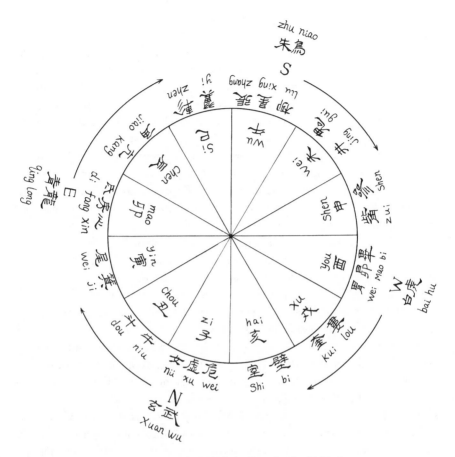

Figure 12.2. Astrological circle. Drawing by Li Xiating.

It happens that *jiayin* occurs as the third day in the fifth month (or third month) in 433 B.C., the same year attested to on an inscribed bell in the tomb. There has been disagreement over whether the bell, a gift from King Hui 惠王 of Chu (r. 488–432 B.C.), is a funerary gift sent at the time of Hou Yi's death or is unconnected with his death. The "*jiayin* third day" on the lid is not decisive evidence for a burial date ca. 433 B.C. First, it is not clear that the lacquer clothes case was made as a burial object; even if the date is placed in 433 B.C., the clothes case (like the Chu bell) may have belonged to the man in life. Then again, if the clothes case was made as a burial object, the date on the lid might belong to 402 B.C., when *jiayin* also occurs as the third day in the appropriate month. In support of the second possibility, carbon-

14 and tree-ring datings suggest a burial date closer to 400 B.C. than to 433 B.C.[58]

Uncertainty over the date recorded on the lid does not affect its significance as concrete evidence of the astro-calendrical correlations already described. For calendrical and hemerological calculations, the multiple applicability of the branches is especially noteworthy. In addition to indicating directions in space and months, the branches indicate hours of the day, days (in combination with the *tiangan* 天干, celestial stems, in the sexagenary cycle), and years (again using the sexagenary cycle). It remains to mention the astro-calendrical significance of Jupiter, whose role in annual calculations was comparable with that of the Dipper in monthly calculations. Jupiter's sidereal period of 11.86 tropical years (modern calculation) resulted in the application of the solar station branches to years in the rotation of Jupiter, which had the name Suixing 歲星 (Year Star) or Xing 星 (Star). Since Jupiter (like the sun) is seen to move counterclockwise against the stars, a clockwise correlate of Jupiter was devised to rotate opposite Jupiter. Sui 歲 (Year), Taisui 太歲 (Grand Year), and Tai Yin 太陰 (Grand Yin) are all attested as names for Jupiter's correlate in the *Huainanzi* (completed in the main by 139 B.C.) and other Han sources.[59]

A standard Warring States design for the cosmic structure can be readily associated with the astro-calendrical layout of the lacquer clothes-case lid, which serves as a fifth century B.C. point of reference for it. The design is first described in the *Huainanzi* astrological essay as consisting of two cords (*er sheng* 二繩) and four hooks (*si gou* 四鉤). The two cords are the cross formed by lines from *zi* 子 (north) to *wu* 午 (south) and from *mao* 卯 (east) to *you* 酉 (west). The hooks span the corners on the circumference of the circle defined by the central cross: *chou* 丑 and *yin* 寅 on either side at the northeast corner, *chen* 辰 and *si* 巳 at the southeast corner, *wei* 未 and *shen* 申 at the southwest corner, *xu* 戌 and *hai* 亥 at the northwest corner (Fig. 12.3).[60] In the form of a square, the cord-hook design appears prominently in the Mawangdui manu-

---

[58] The results of carbon-14 and tree-ring datings are summarized in *Zeng Hou Yi mu*, vol. 1, pp. 463–4. Qiu Xigui, "Tantan Suixian Zeng Hou Yi mu de wenzi ziliao," *Wenwu* 1979.7: 25, argues against identifying the Chu bell as a funerary gift. In identifying "*jiayin* third day," I have followed the table for the Yin *li* 殷曆 (Yin calendar) in Zhang Peiyu, *Zhongguo xian Qin shi libiao*, pp. 179, 185. The Yin *li* fixes the first month at *zi*. The various calendars documented in received sources do not commence in the same year on the same day with the same sexagenary cycle name, and it is often difficult to correlate archaeologically obtained calendrical data with known calendars; see Zhang Wenyu, "Zeng Hou Yi mu tianwen tuxiang 'jiayin sanri' zhi jieshi," *Jiang Han kaogu* 1993.3: 68, who argues that the indications of the Yin *li* for the fifth month should be applied to the calendar in use in Chu that fixed the first month at *yin* (making *chen* the third month rather than the fifth).

[59] See Major, *Heaven and Earth in Early Han Thought*, pp. 74, 92–4, 118–26, for discussion of Jupiter and its correlate in the *Huainanzi*.

[60] *Huainanzi* (Sibu beiyao ed.), 3 ("Tienwen"), 5b; Major, *Heaven and Earth in Early Han Thought*, pp. 84–6.

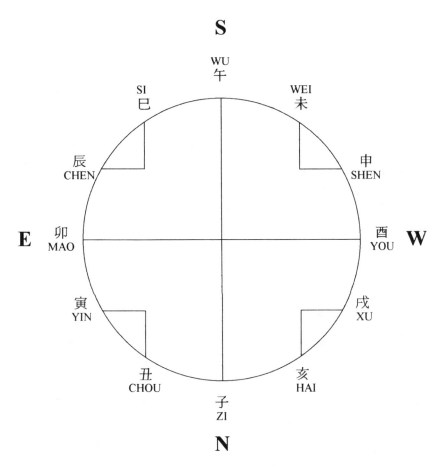

Figure 12.3. Cord-hook design.

scripts to map the sixty-year cycles of Tai Yin and *de* 德 (virtue) in the *Xingde* 刑德 (Punishment and virtue) texts, and also to indicate numerologically lucky directions in which to bury an afterbirth during each month in the medical text *Taichan shu* 胎產書 (Book of the generation of the fetus). In each instance the cord-hook design serves as a basic cosmic plan on which specific astro-calendrical and hemerological data are plotted (see Fig. 12.4).[61]

---

[61] Editors of the Mawangdui manuscripts have assigned the title *Xingde* to three texts whose main contents concern the astro-calendrical system known as *xingde* (punishment and virtue). *Xingde*, text B (dated to ca. 190 B.C.), is reproduced and transcribed in Fu Juyou and Chen Songchang, *Mawangdui Han mu wenwu* (Changsha: Hunan, 1992), pp. 132–43. Marc Kalinowski, "Mawangdui boshu *Xingde* shitan," *Huaxue* 1 (1995): 82–110, is a detailed examination of the contents of *Xingde*, text B. For the afterbirth burial diagram, see *Mawangdui Han mu bo shu*, vol. 4, p. 134; and Harper, *Early Chinese Medical Literature*, pp. 374–7.

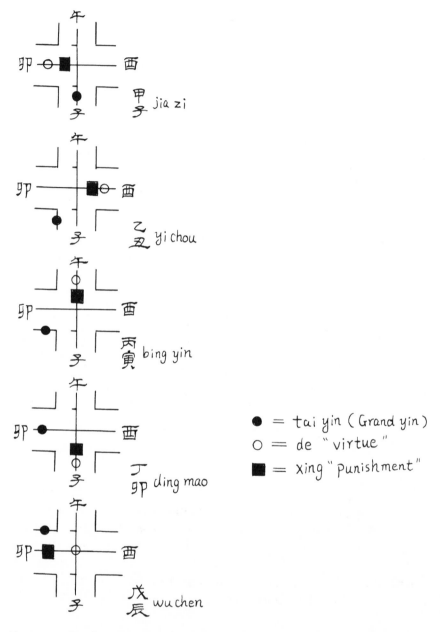

Figure 12.4. *Xingde*, text B; cord-hook diagrams for the sexagenary cycle. Drawing by Li Xiating.

The discovery of the design in other archaeological contexts cannot be unrelated. The *liubo* 六博 game board from Yutaishan 雨臺山 tomb 314, in Jiangling 江陵, Hubei (burial dated ca. mid-fourth century B.C.), is probably the oldest example of the cord-hook design. The bronze mirror conventionally called TLV in Western studies manifests the same design in a more explicitly cosmological form (excavated mirrors date mostly to the Han, but some may be pre-Han).[62] In a seemingly mundane application, the cord-hook design is incorporated in the slotted bottom of a bronze steamer (the steamer fits over the lower pot containing boiling water) from the tomb of Cuo 譽, king of Zhongshan (r. 327–313 B.C.).[63] It appears again on the boards lining the bottom of the coffins in several late fourth century B.C. Chu tombs.[64] Magico-religious, occult symbolism in the uses of the cord-hook design is obvious, even if in each case the exact significance of the symbolism defies precise description.

Astrological instruments called *shi* 式 (cosmic board) in Han sources represent the technical perfection of the cord-hook design and the stellar lodge and Dipper design on the lacquer clothes-case lid. The cosmic board was constructed as a working model of cosmic operations and was used as an aid in astro-calendrical calculations. One specimen excavated from the tomb of Xiahou Zao 夏侯竈 (who held the title of Ruyin Hou 汝陰侯; d. 165 B.C.), in Fuyang 阜陽, Anhui, is of the type known in later sources as *liuren shi* 六壬式 (six-*ren* cosmic board). The instrument is composed of two pieces: a disk (representing Heaven) bears the seven stars of the Northern Dipper in the center with the months and stellar lodges written around the circumference; the disk is mounted on a square plate (representing Earth) that has the cord-hook design, with branches, stems, and stellar lodges recorded in their proper directions around the four sides (see Fig. 12.5). In contrast to the lacquer clothes-case lid, which depicts the Dipper from the perspective of an observer on the ground looking up at the dome of Heaven, the Dipper on the Xiahou Zao instrument represents the Dipper as seen from above the dome of Heaven. The principle of its design is the same as that of a celestial globe; by rotating the disk one can follow the movement of the Dipper relative to a position on Earth over the course of the year. The actual use of the instrument involved numerological calculations based on the date (expressed

---

[62] The Yutaishan *liubo* game board is made of black lacquered wood with the designs in red lacquer; see *Jiangling Yutaishan Chu mu* (Beijing: Wenwu, 1984), pp. 103–104. A Han *liubo* game set from Mawangdui tomb 3 is illustrated in Fu Juyou and Chen Songchang, *Mawangdui Han mu wenwu*, p. 76. See Michael Loewe, *Ways to Paradise: The Chinese Quest for Immortality* (London: Allen & Unwin, 1979), pp. 60–85, for a comprehensive survey of TLV mirrors and the related *liubo* game board.

[63] See *Zhongguo wenwu kaogu zhi mei* (Beijing: Wenwu, 1994), vol. 6, p. 113.

[64] Kalinowski, "Mawangdui boshu *Xingde* shitan," p. 85.

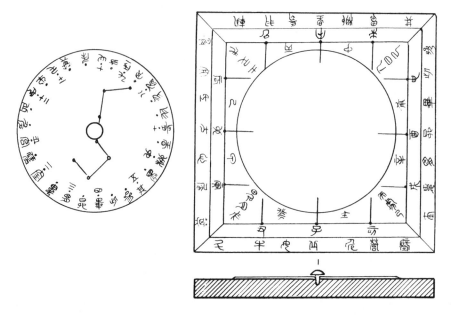

Figure 12.5. Six-*ren* cosmic board. After *Kaogu* 1978.5: 340. Drawing by Li Xiating.

in stems and branches) and the correspondences with the astro-calendrical configuration of Heaven on that date.[65]

Two other astrological instruments were discovered in the Xiahou Zao tomb. One consists of two disks: the upper disk with the Dipper on it rotates on a larger lower disk ringed with the stellar lodges (a number by each lodge indicates its extension along the celestial equator in degrees). We do not know how the instrument was used, but it is clearly another demonstrational model and not an instrument used for observation. The second is similar in construction to the six-*ren* cosmic board, but the disk is laid out with a representation of the *jiugong* 九宮 (nine palaces) of Heaven. The inscribed text on the square plate concerns lucky and unlucky aspects of the year keyed to solstices and equinoxes; the back of the plate has more text arranged around the cord-hook design. The instrument is another variety of cosmic board and

---

[65] The word *shi*, which also means "model," is not clearly attested to in the sense of the astrological instrument in Warring States texts. There are other Han specimens of the six-*ren* cosmic board, all similarly constructed. The most comprehensive study of them, including the method of employment as described in later sources, is Marc Kalinowski, "Les instruments astro-calendériques des Han et la méthode *liu ren*," *Bulletin de l'école française d'Extrême-Orient* 72 (1983): 309–419. See Donald Harper, "The Han Cosmic Board," *EC* 4 (1978–9): 1–10; Christopher Cullen, "Some Further Points on the *Shih*," *EC* 6 (1980–1): 31–46; Donald Harper, "The Han Cosmic Board: A Response to Christopher Cullen," *EC* 6 (1980–1): 47–56; and Loewe, *Ways to Paradise*, pp. 75–80.

was perhaps used to calculate the movement of Taiyi 太一 (Grand One), the polar deity most closely associated with the nine-palace astro-calendrical system in Han sources (Fig. 12.6).[66]

As of 1995, only one pre-Han astrological instrument has been discovered. It is a square wooden board with a handle found in Wangjiatai 王家臺 tomb 15, in Jiangling, Hubei, a burial dated ca. mid-third century B.C. On the front of the board the Five Phases are arranged in a cross in the middle (Soil at the center, surrounded by Fire, Metal, Water, and Wood); next are the twelve months in a ring around the Five Phases; the stellar lodges are arranged on the four sides. On the back is the cord-hook design.[67] Surely the board served as an aid in making some type of astro-calendrical calculation within the framework of yin–yang and Five Phases correlative cosmology.

The probability that the six-*ren* and nine-palace types of cosmic board were already in use in the third century B.C. is also great. The "Five Phases" section of the "Calculations and arts" division of the *Han shu* bibliographic treatise lists two books on cosmic board methods, and the yin–yang militarists (in the division "Military Books") are noted for their ability to "calculate punishment and virtue [*xingde* 刑德; an astro-calendrical system discussed below], follow the strike of the Dipper, and accord with the Five Conquerors (the Five Phases in the conquest sequence)."[68] The Dipper as an occult weapon is evoked in the *Huainanzi* astrological essay, in a passage that allies it with the deity Tai Yin (Grand Yin): "Where Grand Yin resides, it cannot be faced away from but can be faced towards; where the Dipper strikes, no one can oppose it." The astro-calendrical deities and systems encountered throughout the *Huainanzi* essay bear witness to the Warring States occult legacy, and it often seems that use of instruments like the six-*ren* cosmic board is implicitly understood in the text.[69] Recent scholarship on the "Tian wen" 天問 (Heaven questions) of the *Chu ci* anthology, a poetical treatment of cosmological matters that dates to the first half of the third century B.C., has also noted the likely influence of the cosmic board on that composition.[70] A second potential source of Warring States attestation is the

---

[66] See Yan Dunjie, "Guanyu Xi Han chuqi de shipan he zhanpan," *Kaogu* 1978.5: 334–7; Yin Difei, "Xi Han Ruyin Hou mu de zhanpan he tianwen yiqi," *Kaogu* 1978.5: 338–43; and Li Ling, *Zhongguo fangshu kao* (Beijing: Renmin Zhongguo, 1993), pp. 115–18. The system of degree measurement on the double-disk instrument is studied in Nivison, "The Origin of the Chinese Lunar Lodge System."

[67] For the reference, see *Wenwu* 1995.1: 42. The report calls the artifact *shi* 式 even though it is not an adjustable instrument like the Han cosmic boards (the artifact is described but not illustrated).

[68] *Han shu*, 30, pp. 1769, 1760.

[69] *Huainanzi*, 3 ("Tianwen"), 16a. For general observations on the astrological essay, see Major, *Heaven and Earth in Early Han Thought*, pp. 55–61.

[70] See Stephen Field, "Cosmos, Cosmograph, and the Inquiring Poet: New Answers to the 'Heaven Questions,'" *EC* 17 (1992): 83–110.

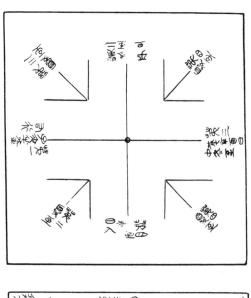

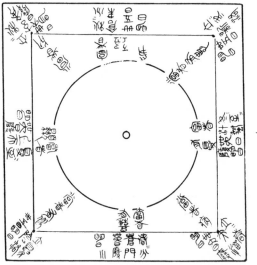

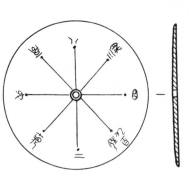

Figure 12.6. Nine-palace cosmic board. After *Kaogu* 1978.5: 341. Drawing by Li Xiating.

Han Feizi, where the practice of astro-calendrical calculations with instruments like the cosmic board appears to be the point of Han Fei's harangue on men who would place their trust in astral deities and astro-calendrical calculations to secure the state.[71]

As all who watch the sky know, the calendar and the sky are not forever fixed. The archaeological material discussed is notable for presenting a schematic model of Heaven for astro-calendrical calculations at the cost of observational precision. The purpose of the cosmic board was to provide calendrical data for numerological interpretation, not to measure the complex and changing arrangement of Heaven itself. Observational instruments certainly were used, as is evidenced by the stellar lodge degree measurements on the Xiahou Zao double-disk instrument; one hopes that future discoveries will provide artifacts to fill the gap in our knowledge of observation in Warring States astrology. However, the apparent dominance of calendrical concerns, which focused on determining opportune times for successful action, is also indicated in the excavated manuscripts. The concerns of observation and astro-calendrical calculations were not incompatible; rather, a pragmatic balance was maintained between improvements in observational precision and astro-calendrical calculations.

Almanacs and Other Astro-Calendrical Texts

The term "almanac" is applied here to texts whose contents concern mainly the determination of lucky and unlucky times based on astro-calendrical calculations, but which may include information on subjects ranging from incantations, demonology, and illness to dream divination and travel rituals – all considered important in dealing with the hazards encountered in daily life. To the extent that some of the texts focus on stem and branch numerology without reference to astrology, one could also characterize the literature as hemerological. Indeed, the title *Rishu* 日書 (Day book) is written on one of the bamboo-strip almanacs from Shuihudi 睡虎地 tomb 11, in Yunmeng 雲夢, Hubei (burial dated ca. 217 B.C.), the word *ri* (day) denoting hemerological arts.[72] None of the almanacs set out a day-by-day record for a single calendar year (the usual sense of the English word), yet their indications of dates and times expressed in stem and branch notation are meant to be generally applicable to any year. Calendrical texts in the form of tables for the days and months of a year or period of years (sometimes including

---

[71] *Han Feizi*, 5 ("Shixie"), 8a–b.
[72] See Donald Harper, "A Chinese Demonography of the Third Century B.C.," *HJAS* 45 (1985): 462–7, for a description of the two almanacs from Shuihudi tomb 11. The almanacs are reproduced in *Shuihudi Qin mu zhujian* (Beijing: Wenwu, 1990), and transcribed on pp. 175–255.

hemerological material, but without the broad contents of the almanacs) have been excavated from Han tombs and other sites and probably also existed in the Warring States period. As far as can be determined, the astrologers and calendrical experts responsible for such calendrical texts were the same men who compiled the almanacs.[73]

Mawangdui tomb 3 manuscripts provide examples of other types of astro-calendrical literature that would have existed by the late Warring States (all texts are on silk, and the titles have been assigned by the editors of the manuscripts). *Wuxing zhan* 五星占 (Five stars divination) identifies the Phases and spirits associated with the five planets (Wood/Jupiter, Metal/Venus, Fire/Mars, Soil/Saturn, Water/Mercury), discusses their omens, details their sidereal periods, and concludes with a record of the annual positions of each planet from the year of Qin Shihuang's accession to the throne of the state of Qin to the third year of Han Wendi (246–177 B.C.).[74] *Tianwen qixiang zazhan* 天文氣象雜占 (Miscellaneous astrological and meteorological divination) illustrates clouds, solar and lunar halos, rainbows, comets, and other astrologically significant phenomena; the final illustration depicts the Dipper as a bamboo stalk bent into the proper shape with the seven Dipper stars as the nodes. The illustrations are accompanied by text, sometimes simply naming the phenomenon, but often identifying what it portends (military portents dominate). Many portents are attributed to Renshi 任氏 (Mr. Ren) and Beigong 北宮, experts who are unknown in received literature.[75] *Xingde* 刑德 (Punishment and virtue), text B, is discussed below; in addition to detailing the *xingde* astro-calendrical system, one section of the text discusses portents like those illustrated in *Tianwen qixiang zazhan*. Based on its contents, the editors assigned the title *Yin-yang wu xing* 陰陽五行 (Yin–yang and Five Phases) to a final text that exists in two editions; knowledge of the contents awaits publication of the full text; however, two published photographs indicate that it includes calculations involving the polar deity Tianyi 天一 (Heaven One) and other spirits.[76]

Excavated manuscripts cast an irregular light over Warring States astrology and the calendar, but one is grateful for what illumination they provide in areas that were previously dark. From the earliest evidence of almanacs in the late fourth century B.C. to the various Mawangdui texts, one can detect

---

[73] See Jiang Xiaoyuan, *Tianxue zhenyuan*, pp. 167–87, for detailed discussion and sources.

[74] The *Wuxingzhan* is transcribed in *Zhongguo tianwenxue shi wenji* (Beijing: Kexue, 1978), pp. 1–14; and in Yamada Keiji, ed., *Shin hatsugen Chûgoku kagakushi shiryô no kenkyû* (Kyoto: Kyôto daigaku jinbun kagaku kenkyûjo, 1985), vol. 1 (*Yakuchû hen*), pp. 1–44.

[75] The text portion of *Tianwen qixiang zazhan* is transcribed in *Zhongguo wenwu* 1 (1979): 26–9; a reproduction of the entire manuscript is on pp. 1–4. See also, Yamada, ed., *Shin hatsugen Chûgoku kagakushi shiryô no kenkyû*, vol. 1, pp. 45–86. The illustrations of comets are studied in Michael Loewe, "The Han View of Comets," *BMFEA* 52 (1980): 1–31.

[76] See Fu Juyou and Chen Songchang, *Mawangdui Han mu wenwu*, pp. 144–5.

ideas that were continuous even as they underwent change and elaboration over time. When set alongside the evidence of the received record (e.g., the politically oriented *yue ling* calendars in the *Guanzi* and *Lü shi chunqiu*), the manuscripts tend to confirm the conclusion that the correlative cosmology built around yin–yang and Five Phases concepts belongs mostly to the third century B.C., but they also show that the logic underlying correlative cosmology was already emerging in many separate astro-calendrical systems. It would have been a small step to apply yin–yang and Five Phases interpretations to systems that had been evolved previously, uniting them into a universal theory. In addition, the manuscripts bear witness to magico-religious and occult ideas that continued to have a place in yin–yang and Five Phases correlative cosmology.

The Chu Silk Manuscript (removed from a tomb near Changsha, Hunan, in 1942 and dated to ca. 300 B.C.) is currently the oldest example of an almanac. Due to its state of preservation and the difficulty of identifying many of its graphs, the interpretation of the manuscript continues to be a subject of scholarly argument.[77] The manuscript is arranged in the form of a calendrical diagram with twelve figures representing the spirits of the months drawn around the perimeter, three figures for each season to a side; trees are drawn at the four corners. In the center of the silk are two texts written side by side but in reverse directions. The design is thought to represent a pattern similar to the cord-hook design or the cosmic board (Fig. 12.7).[78]

Brief statements next to each of the twelve figures indicate which activities are permitted and which prohibited during the month in question, and at least once unlucky days are identified. In the first month the days *renzi* 壬子 and *bingzi* 丙子 are unlucky; the second month is appropriate for military expeditions and construction work, inappropriate for giving a daughter in marriage; the eighth month is unlucky for taking a wife. The two central texts are rhymed expositions. The first is a cosmogonic myth – perhaps better described as an account of the creation of seasons and days – beginning from the appearance of Baoxi 包戲 (i.e., Fuxi 伏義) in a disordered world. To summarize the calendrical elements of the myth in brief, Baoxi takes a wife who bears four sons. Because the sun and moon do not yet exist, the sons take

---

[77] The complicated history of the Chu Silk Manuscript and of Chu Silk Manuscript studies is summarized in Li Ling, *Zhongguo fangshu kao*, pp. 168–79; see also, Li Xueqin, *Eastern Zhou and Qin Civilizations* (New Haven, Conn.: Yale University Press, 1985), pp. 435–9. The manuscript, which was removed by tomb robbers, is now in the Arthur M. Sackler Gallery at the Smithsonian Institution, Washington, D.C. For the most recent transcriptions of the manuscript, see Li Ling, *Zhongguo fangshu kao*, pp. 180–5; and Li Ling, *Changsha Zidanku Zhanguo Chu boshu yanjiu* (Beijing: Zhonghua, 1985), pp. 49–80.

[78] See Li Ling, *Chu boshu yanjiu*, pp. 30–6; cf. Li Xueqin, *Eastern Zhou and Qin Civilizations*, pp. 439–40.

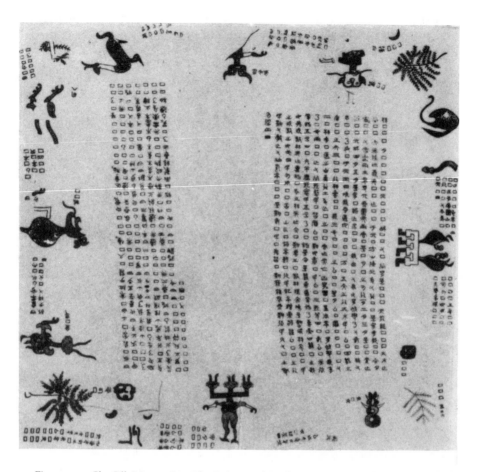

Figure 12.7. Chu Silk Manuscript. After Li Ling, *Changsha Zidanku Zhanguo Chu boshu yanjiu* (Beijing: Zhonghua, 1985).

turns measuring the passage of the year by pacing it out with their feet, thus demarcating the four seasons. The sun and moon are created after 1,100 years (presumably this marks the beginning of the luni-solar calendar). The divisions of night, dawn, daytime, and evening come about later due to the actions of Gong Gong 共工.[79]

---

[79] Some scholars identify the name of the wife as Nüwa 女媧, giving the mythical pair Fuxi and Nüwa; Li Xueqin, *Eastern Zhou and Qin Civilizations*, pp. 441–2, expresses reservations about the correctness of the identification. See Derk Bodde, "Myths of Ancient China," in *Mythologies of the Ancient World*, ed. Samuel Noah Kramer (Garden City, N.Y.: Doubleday, 1961), pp. 386–9, on Fuxi, Nüwa, and Gong-gong (rpt. Derk Bodde, *Essays on Chinese Civilization*, edited and introduced by Charles LeBlanc and Dorothy Borei [Princeton, N.J.: Princeton University Press, 1981], pp. 62–5).

The second text is a teaching on astrology and the calendar, which are together the keys to the relation between Heaven and the human community. Seasonal irregularity, retrograde motion of the planets, and comets are omens of natural catastrophes. Speaking directly, Di 帝 exhorts the people to model their conduct on Heaven's images. They must be respectful so that when Heaven bestows fortune, the spirits will join them; and when Heaven sends calamity, the spirits will be kind to them. Thus, the spirit world can shield the people from a sometimes unkind Heaven. Specifically, the text speaks of the year as possessing *de* 德 (virtue) and *te* 慝 (evil) (written 匿 in the manuscript). So long as the people's worship of the spirits is constant, which will be manifest in the brightness of the celestial asterisms, then even when the year is evil the spirits will intercede with their virtue. Li Ling has noted the parallel between "virtue and evil" in the Chu Silk Manuscript and the idea of *xingde* (punishment and virtue), which can be traced from old Zhou religious thinking about Heaven into Warring States astro-calendrical systems and political philosophy.[80]

Moving from the Chu Silk Manuscript to the almanacs of the third century B.C., one notices above all the elaboration of distinct astro-calendrical and hemerological systems (none are mentioned in the Chu Silk Manuscript), and the amount of material of various kinds included in the almanacs; almanacs were clearly a thriving genre. In comparison, the Chu Silk Manuscript is more archaic in its language, as well as in its outlook; Di's speech and the myth of the seasons are decidedly religious, as if the manuscript itself possessed iconic value. There is fragmentary evidence of astro-calendrical and hemerological systems in excavated texts of roughly the same date as the Chu Silk Manuscript. Thus, the late third century B.C. almanacs from Fangmatan 放馬灘 tomb I, in Tianshui 天水, Gansu (burial dated ca. 230–220 B.C.), and from Shuihudi have late fourth century B.C. antecedents.[81] However, the Fangmatan and Shuihudi almanacs reflect the flowering of

---

[80] Li Ling, *Chu boshu yanjiu*, pp. 57–8 (other identifications of 德 and 匿 have been made). My interpretation of the meaning of *de te* as a compound in the Chu Silk Manuscript is based on Rao Zongyi, "Chu boshu tianxiang zaiyi," *Zhongguo wenhua* 3 (1990): 68, who argues convincingly that it means "without virtue" or "evil" in contrast to *de* alone, which means "virtue." Rao Zongyi, "Shendao sixiang yu lixing zhuyi," *BIHP* 49 (1978): 496–9, examines the idea of *xingde* from the Western Zhou through the Warring States.

[81] Professor Li Ling (private communication) has informed me that astro-calendrical and hemerological material appears on a second silk manuscript from the same tomb as the Chu Silk Manuscript, also kept at the Sackler Gallery. Only a small portion of the folded silk has been opened, thus the contents of the full text are not known. In addition, bamboo strips from Jiudian 九店 tomb 56, Hubei, are reported to contain material similar to the Shuihudi almanacs (the date of the tomb is not specified, but is no later than the early third century B.C.); see *Zhongguo da baike quanshu: Kaoguxue* (Beijing: Zhongguo da baike quanshu), p. 230. He Shuangquan, "Tianshui Fangmatan Qin jian zongshu," *Wenwu* 1989.2: 23–31, summarizes the contents of the Fangmatan almanacs; the first almanac is transcribed in *Qin Han jiandu lunwenji* (Lanzhou: Gansu renmin, 1989), pp. 1–6. For the date of the Fangmatan tomb, see Li Xueqin, "Fangmatan jianzhong de zhiguai gushi," *Wenwu* 1990.4: 45.

natural philosophy and occult thought between the fourth and third centuries B.C., which was connected to intellectual and spiritual changes, as well as to the wider circulation of texts. Despite new ideas, the religious outlook of the Chu Silk Manuscript continued into the third century B.C. almanacs, where astral and other spirits remain a focus of attention. This outlook contrasts with the humanistic skepticism of the spirit world among many masters of philosophy. One thinks especially of Xunzi and his criticism of men who seek to know Heaven and its mysteries. The philosophy of Zhuangzi is one object of his attacks, but his "Tian lun" 天論 (Discussion of Heaven) chapter targets astrologers and calendrical experts when it condemns the belief that natural phenomena are omens from Heaven.[82]

The pair of almanacs from Shuihudi and another pair from Fangmatan show that Xunzi's skepticism was not necessarily shared by educated men in positions of power. Administrative writings and maps in tombs (the latter in the Fangmatan tomb) suggest that the tomb occupants held office locally. Their possession of almanacs was surely not an anomaly in otherwise staid lives as government servants; almanacs were simply popular among the elite, who referred to them as a matter of course. Indeed, the first Shuihudi almanac demonstrates the relevance of almanacs to men in government service in a section on "Officials" (*li* 吏) that identifies days by branch and indicates one's reception at court or government office at different times on that day. An audience held at daybreak on a *yin* 寅 day results in anger, but on a *mao* 卯 day in pleasure; an evening audience on a *zi* 子 day results in praise, but on a *chou* 丑 day in slander; and so forth.[83]

We have better knowledge of the Shuihudi almanacs due to the publication of a reproduction and full transcription. Some of the astro-calendrical and hemerological systems described in them are referred to in received writings like the astrological essay of the *Huainanzi* (chapter 3), but we know virtually nothing of the details. A good example is the system of *jianchu* 建除 (establishment and removal), which is based on the sequence of branches pointed to monthly by the Dipper handle during the year. In the first month, when according to the calendar the Dipper points to *yin* 寅, *yin* is designated the "establishment" position for the first month; any day in the first month with *yin* in its sexagenary cycle name is subject to the portents associated with "establishment," all of which are favorable. *Mao* 卯 is the "removal" position for the first month, and its portents are all unfavorable. After the "establishment" and "removal" positions, there are ten more such signs associated in sequence with the ten remaining branches. Month by month the

---

[82]   See John Knoblock, *Xunzi: A Translation and Study of the Complete Works* (Stanford, Calif.: Stanford University Press, 1988–94), vol. 3, pp. 4–6, 10–11.
[83]   *Shuihudi Qin mu zhujian*, pp. 207–208.

whole system shifts by one position down the sequence of branches. Thus, in the second month when the Dipper points to *mao*, *mao* is the "establishment" position, *chen* 辰 is the "removal" position, and so forth. The *Huainanzi* reference to the *jianchu* system is elliptical, only now becoming clear.[84]

Actual observation of celestial cycles and astral bodies has little place in the astro-calendrical systems of the almanacs. Even in a system based on the stars Xuange 玄戈 (Dark Dagger-axe) and Zhaoyao 招搖 (Far Flight), both stars in the vicinity of the Dipper handle and astrologically linked with it, the first almanac describes the stars as astral bodies that move opposite one another over the twelve months of the year: Zhaoyao's rotation is calculated in a counterclockwise direction through the branches of the solar stations; Xuange rotates clockwise through the stellar lodges. Their relative movement is reminiscent of the annual movement of Jupiter and its clockwise correlate, sometimes called Tai Yin (Grand Yin).[85]

Xingde, text B, from Mawangdui reveals the precision and complexity of the late Warring States astro-calendrical systems. As in the case of the *jianchu* system, its detailed accounts for the first time clarify passages in the *Huainanzi* astrological essay. Comparison with the rest of the *Huainanzi* shows its astrological essay to be a synopsis of astro-calendrical knowledge derived from the more technical literature now restored to us; the *Huainanzi* seems to assume the Han reader's knowledge of the technical literature, without which it would have been difficult to follow the astrological essay. Let me illustrate with one of several *Huainanzi* passages concerning Tai Yin (Grand Yin) and *xingde* (punishment and virtue):

When Tai Yin [Grand Yin] is at *jiazi* 甲子 [the beginning of the sexagenary cycle], *xing* "punishment" and *de* "virtue" join in the east palace [of Heaven]. They regularly shift to the position that is not conquered [according to the conquest sequence of the Five Phases]. After being joined for four years, they part for sixteen years and then rejoin. The reason for their parting is because *xing* "punishment" cannot enter the center palace [of Heaven], but shifts to Wood [in the east palace].[86]

The passage has been poorly understood due to the assumption that it is related to other astro-calendrical lore in the *Huainanzi* where Tai Yin is treated as Jupiter's clockwise correlate and *xingde* is treated as an aspect of

---

[84] Ibid., pp. 182–3 (from the first almanac); see Marc Kalinowski, "Les traités de Shuihudi et l'hémérologie chinoise a la fin des royaumes-combattants," *TP* 72 (1986): 198–9; and Michael Loewe, *Divination, Mythology and Monarchy in Han China* (Cambridge University Press, 1994), pp. 221–6 (Kalinowski's and Loewe's studies also provide a general survey of the contents of the almanacs). *Huainanzi*, 3 ("Tianwen"), 13b; see Major, *Heaven and Earth in Early Han Thought*, pp. 119–20.

[85] *Shuihudi Qin mu zhujian*, pp. 187–8; see Kalinowski, "Les traités de Shuihudi et l'hémérologie chinoise," pp. 219–20.

[86] *Huainanzi*, 3 ("Tianwen"), 14a; see Major, *Heaven and Earth in Early Han Thought*, p. 123.

the yin–yang cycle (*de*, virtue, is correlated with yang and the sun, *xing*, punishment, with yin and the moon; spring and summer are the *de* seasons, fall and winter the *xing* seasons).[87] *Xingde*, text B, provides the key to the above passage, which concerns a form of *xingde* calculation based not on yin–yang cycles, but on stem and branch numerology. The positions of Tai Yin and *de* over the sixty-year cycle are plotted on the cord-hook diagrams of *Xingde* (the positions of *xing* are added in Fig. 12.4). As shown on the diagrams and explained in the body of the text, beginning in a *jiazi* year when Tai Yin is positioned at *zi* (north, Water), *de* and *xing* begin their annual cycle at *mao* (east, Wood). While Tai Yin shifts clockwise one branch each year, over the next three years *xing* and *de* move to *you* (west, Metal; Metal conquers Wood, thus it is "the position that is not conquered"), then *wu* (south, Fire; Fire conquers Metal), and then *zi* (north, Water; Water conquers Fire). In the fifth year *xing* and *de* part because *xing* is not allowed to enter the "center palace" along with *de* (where Soil conquers Water); *xing* shifts back to *mao* (east, Wood), and it is sixteen years before both *xing* and *de* occupy the position *mao* in the east.[88]

Tai Yin in *Xingde*, text B, is not represented as Jupiter's correlate, but as another sort of calendrical entity whose cycle belongs to the *xingde* system. There was a formula for coordinating the counterclockwise movement of Jupiter through the stellar lodges with the clockwise movement of Tai Yin through the branch solar stations; it was an attempt to coordinate observation of Jupiter with the astro-calendrical calculation of Tai Yin, and the formula is given in the Mawangdui *Wuxing zhan*. But in the *Wuxing zhan* account of Jupiter's sidereal period, the record of the planet's actual movement among the stellar lodges does not conform to the formula. The salient point in these discrepancies is that Tai Yin did not have a single identity as Jupiter's correlate in Warring States astrology and the calendar; rather, its identity in several astro-calendrical systems was formed within the context of the system concerned. The same observation applies to *xingde*.[89]

---

[87] *Huainanzi*, 3 ("Tianwen"), 3b, 5b–6a; cf. Major, *Heaven and Earth in Early Han Thought*, pp. 73–4, 87–8. *Xingde* in connection with the yin–yang cycle is discussed in John Major, "The Meaning of Hsing-te," in *Chinese Ideas About Nature and Society: Studies in Honour of Derk Bodde*, ed. Charles Le Blanc and Susan Blader (Hong Kong: Hong Kong University Press, 1987), pp. 281–91, where he argues for translating *xing* as "recision" (the yin part of the cycle) and *de* as "accretion" (the yang part of the cycle). As is shown below, the yin–yang cycle was not the only astro-calendrical referent of *xingde*; in Warring States astrological usage, the words expressed the idea of the "punishment" and "virtue" associated with Heaven. On the use of the *xingde* system in Warring States military strategy, see Robin Yates, "New Light on Ancient Chinese Military Texts: Notes on Their Nature and Evolution, and the Development of Military Specialization in Warring States China," *TP* 74 (1988): 233–5.

[88] See Fu Juyou and Chen Songchang, *Mawangdui Han mu wenwu*, p. 137, for transcription of the relevant passage in *Xingde*, text B; and Kalinowski, "Mawangdui boshu *Xingde* shitan," pp. 83, 90–1, for full explication.

[89] Kalinowski, "Mawangdui boshu *Xingde* shitan," pp. 87–8.

The multiplicity of astro-calendrical functions is illustrated by another *xingde* system described for the first time in *Xingde*, text B. The stem and branch sexagenary cycle of days is divided among the *jiugong* 九宮 (nine palaces) of Heaven. In addition to *xing* and *de*, the portentous aspects of the days are determined by the locations in the nine palaces of six additional spirits, including Fengbo 風伯 (Wind Sire), Leigong 雷公 (Thunder Lord), and Yushi 雨師 (Rain Master). Thus, *Xingde*, text B, shows us two *xingde* systems operating concurrently (one for years, the other for days) in addition to the more generally known *xingde* system based on seasonal yin–yang cycles.[90]

Additional evidence of the merging of numerological calculation with the organization of the spirit world in Warring States astro-calendrical systems may be found in the Mawangdui *Yin-yang wu xing*. The published diagram from *Yin-yang wu xing*, edition B, shows the nine palaces in an inner square, with the polar deity Tianyi 天一 (Heaven One) in the center palace. An outer square is divided into palaces for the four directions. Inside each palace are, not seven stellar lodges, but seven deities. Many are known from sources like the *Huainanzi*: Tai Yin (Grand Yin), Tai Yang (Grand Yang), Taiyi (Grand One), Qinglong 青龍 (Azure Dragon; also the spirit of the east palace), Baihu 白虎 (White Tiger; also the spirit of the west palace), and others. There are also deities whose astrological connections are less known, like Beihai 北海 (North Sea) and Taishan 太山 (Grand Mountain). The full text has not been published, so it is not clear how the system works. However, the diagram alone clarifies an important point regarding the spirit world and astrology. Just as Tai Yin has a multiple identity, so also do Tai Yang, Qinglong, Baihu, and the others. Their multiple identity is sometimes elided in the *Huainanzi*. Furthermore, in some instances the *Huainanzi* treats several deities as one, as when it states that "of the most honored spirits of Heaven none is more honored than Qinglong (Azure Dragon), who is sometimes called Tianyi (Heaven One) and sometimes called Tai Yin (Grand Yin)." Based on the *Yin-yang wu xing* diagram, we see that the relation between the three deities in an astro-calendrical system is the basis for their joint identity in the *Huainanzi*.[91]

Yin–yang and Five Phases concepts are implicitly understood in many passages in the Shuihudi almanacs and Mawangdui astro-calendrical texts. However, neither the compound yin–yang nor *wu xing* (Five Phases) occurs as an independent term. The degree of elaboration of yin–yang and Five

[90] Fu Juyou and Chen Songchang, *Mawangdui Han mu wenwu*, p. 135; Kalinowski, "Mawangdui boshu *Xingde* shitan," pp. 94–9.

[91] The diagram from *Yin-yang wuxing*, edition B, is reproduced in Fu Juyou and Chen Songchang, *Mawangdui Han mu wenwu*, p. 145. *Huainanzi*, 3 ("Tianwen"), 16a; see Major, *Heaven and Earth in Early Han Thought*, p. 135.

Phases concepts is not clear. Correlation of Phases with stems, branches, and directions does not extend to seasons or other sets of five. Furthermore, only the conquest sequence of the Five Phases (attributed to Zou Yan in Han sources) is explicitly identified or implicitly understood: Water conquers Fire, Fire conquers Metal, Metal conquers Wood, Wood conquers Soil, Soil conquers Water. The production sequence of the Five Phases that correlates the Phases with the cycle of seasons from Wood/spring/east to Fire/summer/south, Soil/center, Metal/fall/west, and Water/winter/north is nowhere in evidence.[92] One is left with the impression that in their earliest forms the astro-calendrical systems relied principally on stem and branch numerological correlations linking temporal cycles and spatial relations. Subsequently, when Soil, Wood, Metal, Water, and Fire became the preeminent form of pentadic classification, the already established numerological correlations were easily fitted into the new pentadic model.[93]

TURTLE AND MILFOIL DIVINATION

Divination with turtle and milfoil remained important in the religious life of the Warring States elite. The bamboo-strip divination record from Baoshan 包山 tomb 2, Hubei (burial dated ca. 316 B.C.), documents routine divination to obtain judgments from the spirits and their approval of sacrificial offerings – continuing the pattern of divination coupled with propitiatory and exorcistic acts that is first recorded in the Shang bone and shell inscriptions. At the same time, the *Zuo zhuan* provides evidence that by the fourth century B.C., the *Zhou yi* (Zhou changes) had acquired the status of a book of wisdom; its tradition of milfoil divination served not just to resolve human doubts but also to provide moral guidance.[94] Ambivalence about the purpose of milfoil divination and the *Yi* is nicely expressed in the words put into the mouth of Confucius (see above) in the Mawangdui text *Yao* (Essen-

---

[92] The second Shuihudi almanac lists the correlations of stems and branches to phases, and for each phase identifies the phase it conquers (*Shuihudi Qin mu zhujian*, p. 239). The conquest and production sequences of the Five Phases are discussed later in this chapter.

[93] Kalinowski, "Mawangdui boshu *Xingde* shitan," p. 96, makes this point with regard to the arrangement of the sixty-day cycle in the *Xingde* nine-palaces diagram. See also, Kalinowski, "Les traités de Shuihudi et l'hémérologie chinoise," pp. 220–4, for general observations on the relation of the Shuihudi almanacs to yin–yang and Five Phases ideas. Graham has a similar interpretation of the development of Five Phases models.

[94] The Baoshan divination record is reproduced in *Baoshan Chu jian* (Beijing: Wenwu, 1991), and transcribed on pp. 32–7. See also, Li Ling, "Formulaic Structure of the Chu Divinatory Bamboo Slips," *EC* 15 (1990): 71–86; and idem, *Zhongguo fangshu kao*, pp. 255–78. On the moral aspects of the *Yi jing*, see Kidder Smith, "*Zhouyi* Interpretation from Accounts in the *Zuozhuan*," *HJAS* 49 (1989): 459–62; and Edward L. Shaughnessy, "The Composition of the *Zhouyi*," Ph.D. dissertation, Stanford University, 1983 (UMI 8320774), pp. 69–74. See Loewe, ed., *Early Chinese Texts*, pp. 216–28, for details on the textual history of the *Zhou yi* or *Yi jing* (the latter name is usually applied to the text once it achieved canonical status and acquired the ancillary writings known as the *Shiyi* 十翼, Ten wings).

tials) that Confucius "seeks the virtue" in the *Yi* and that he is "one who shares a path with scribe/astrologers and shamans, but whose final destination is different." Nevertheless, when asked whether he believes in milfoil divination with the *Yi* Confucius replies, "Of one hundred divinations I have performed, seventy have been on the mark."[95]

Yao is one of several lost writings that together with the Mawangdui manuscript edition of the *Xi ci* 繫辭, the cosmological commentary to the *Zhou yi*, bear witness to yet another facet of milfoil divination with the *Yi* during the third century B.C.: its sponsorship by Ru specialists and their involvement in cosmological speculation based on the correlation of the *Yi* hexagrams with yin–yang dualism. Ru specialists were not likely to have been responsible for devising the cosmological interpretation of the *Yi*. According to Du Yu 杜預 (A.D. 222–84) a manuscript of the *Yi* excavated in A.D. 279 from the tomb of King Xiang 襄王 of Wei (d. 296 B.C.) did not include the *Xi ci* and associated ancillary texts, but did include a lost text of "yin–yang explanations"; on the reasonable assumption that the yin–yang text dated to the end of the fourth century B.C., Ru specialists were probably receiving their yin–yang ideas from others.[96] Nor did the concept of yin–yang dualism originate in milfoil divination with the *Yi*. As will be discussed shortly, hexagrams in excavated manuscripts from the fourth and third centuries B.C. were composed not of six solid (yang) or broken (yin) lines, but of a column of six numbers: the numbers 1, 5, 6, and 8 are used in the Baoshan divination record; the numbers 1, 6, and 8 are used in a milfoil divination text from Wangjiatai tomb 15 (burial dated ca. mid-third century B.C.). While the Mawangdui hexagram text uses just two symbols for the hexagrams, and it is uncertain whether the symbols were perceived as numbers or lines, it is evident that the hexagrams themselves were not primary symbols of yin and yang until after the yin–yang concept had formed.

Milfoil divination and the *Yi* clearly played a more multifaceted role in Warring States intellectual and spiritual life than did turtle divination, which despite its prestige did not become involved in new Warring States patterns of thought. We know from the *Zuo zhuan* that milfoil divination with the *Yi* was performed by experts other than the traditional diviners by the fourth century B.C. and that it already had become an elite practice. Moreover, the *Yi* was a textual relic of Western Zhou tradition; one need not take a stand

---

[95]   Chen Songchang and Liao Mingchun, "Boshu *Ersanzi wen, Yi zhi yi, Yao* shiwen," p. 435.

[96]   For Du Yu's description of the *Yi* manuscript and related texts, see *Zuo zhuan*, "Houxu" 後序, 1a; see also, Chapter 11, this volume. Li Xueqin, *Zhouyi jingzhuan suyuan* (Changchun: Changchun, 1992), pp. 183–8, examines all contemporary testimony regarding the *Yi* manuscript from King Xiang's tomb. Li accepts traditions regarding Confucius's sponsorship of the *Yi* and offers a number of supporting arguments (see esp. pp. 49–62), but it is probably still best to consider the Mawangdui manuscript material as evidence of third century B.C. ideas.

on whether or not Confucius himself promoted the *Yi* in order to appreciate the multiple uses of the text in areas other than milfoil divination in Warring States times.

In connection with natural philosophy and occult thought, the Zhou milfoil diviners were learned in the omens exhibited by nature; it is often by means of the juxtaposition of images from nature with human affairs that the hexagram and line statements of the *Yi* guide those who consult the text. Interpreting the meaning of such images as part of the mystical system of the *Yi* has preoccupied *Yi jing* hermeneutics since the time of the Han scholiasts. Modern scholarship has made positive contributions to identifying probable natural phenomena behind some of the images. For example, the dragon in the Qian 乾 and Kun 坤 hexagrams seems to refer to the dragon spirit of the east palace of Heaven, manifest in its seven stellar lodges. Shared astro-calendrical significance might account for the placement of Qian and Kun together at the head of the received text of the *Yi jing*, and probably accounts as well for their cosmic symbolism prior to their association with pure yang and pure yin.[97]

Warring States milfoil diviners continued the traditions of their predecessors, practicing the divination method and observing the natural phenomena that gave context and meaning to human affairs. Other natural experts and occultists surely participated in the project of fitting the cosmological and dualistic insights of the *Yi* into the yin–yang framework as it appears in the *Xi ci*. One also cannot overlook the participation of masters of philosophy for whom the textual stature of the *Yi* gave authority to cosmological ideas.[98] Given that the processes leading toward the reinterpretation of the *Zhou yi* as a book of wisdom and cosmology were well underway by the end of the fourth century B.C., the Baoshan divination record is remarkable evidence of the continuation of turtle and milfoil divination in the old religious manner of spirit communication and sacrifice. Third century B.C. evidence from the almanacs indicates that the spirits were being reorganized into astro-calendrical and hemerological systems, which provided a new basis for dealing with them. It appears that between the fourth and third centuries B.C., the interface between the spirit world and the human community was being redefined.[99]

---

[97] Shaughnessy, "The Composition of the *Zhouyi*," pp. 266–87; cf. Michel Teboul, "Ancient Chinese Auroral Records: Interpretation Problems and Methods," in *History of Oriental Astronomy*, ed. G. Swarup et al. (Cambridge University Press, 1987), pp. 41–50, who argues that the dragon in Qian and Kun is connected to the Aurora Borealis. See Chapter 4, this volume, for further discussion of the connection between omens and milfoil divination in the *Yi*.

[98] See Li Xueqin, *Zhouyi jingzhuan suyuan*, pp. 98–109, for details concerning the involvement of Xunzi and his followers with the *Yi*.

[99] Similarly, the second text in the center of the Chu Silk Manuscript emphasizes the need to maintain regular worship of the spirits. Some might limit the late fourth century B.C. view of religion in the

The Baoshan divination record, which contains turtle and milfoil divinations made on behalf of the tomb occupant Shao Tuo 邵𧪒 over a period of several years, identifies the turtle diviners and milfoil diviners by name. They form two separate groups, and each diviner possessed his own materials: the turtle diviner Gu Ji's 盬吉 shell is named Baojia 寶家 (Precious Home); the set of milfoil stalks used by Wu Sheng 五生 is named Chengde 丞德 (Receive Virtue). The same subjects (Tuo's impending prospects, illness, and the like) were sometimes divined several times by both turtle and milfoil diviners, the divination entailing two stages: first, the presentation of the subject for a judgment of auspicious or inauspicious, followed by a second divination to verify that the sacrificial offerings were correct. The following divination dates to 316 B.C.:

In the year that the Great Director of Horses, Dao Gu, led the army of the domain of Chu to rescue Fu; in the month Xingyi 䏝屍 [fourth month]; on the day *jimao*. Wu Sheng divines for the Chief Minister of the Left, Tuo, with the Receive Virtue [milfoil]: "There is illness in the abdomen and heart, and rising vapor. [Tuo] finds food unpalatable. Would that he gradually be cured, and that there be no trouble." ☰ (1-1-1-6-1-8), ☰ (8-1-1-1-6-6). The prediction: "The divination is ever auspicious. The illness alters, the ailment has become more severe. According to its cause, let there be an elimination rite." "To be offered in prayer to King Jing and to [the kings] from Xiong Yi to King Wu, five oxen and five pigs. May Water and people who have drowned be attacked and expelled." Wu Sheng's prediction: "Auspicious."[100]

If one assumes that the odd numbers represent a yang, solid line, and the even numbers a yin, broken line, the two number hexagrams following the statement of the divination subject can be correlated with the *Yi* hexagrams "Xu" 需 (Await) and "Heng" 恒 (Constancy). The first prediction is based on the two hexagrams. The hexagrams formed after the second divination statement (concerning the spirits to receive offerings and those to be expelled) are not identified. A turtle divination on the same day performed by Gu Ji with the Precious Home shell recommends offerings to a longer list of Chu ancestors and other spirits, including the polar deity Taiyi (Grand One) and Dashui 大水 (Great Water; perhaps Great Water and Water designate Yangzi River spirits). Whereas Wu Sheng proposes that Water and the ghosts of drowning victims be exorcised, Gu Ji proposes exorcism of Sui 歲 (Year; the planet Jupiter or an astro-calendrical correlate of it).

Shao Tuo evidently died from the illness, which is the subject of four addi-

---

Chu Silk Manuscript and the Baoshan divination record (also a Chu text) to the region of Chu; in my judgment the two texts are evidence of broader trends.

[100] *Baoshan Chu jian*, p. 36. In addition to the notes to the transcription, my interpretation of the text (which contains many difficulties) relies on Li Ling's analysis of the Baoshan divination record in "Formulaic Structure of the Chu Divinatory Bamboo Slips," pp. 71–86, and in *Zhongguo fangshu kao*, pp. 255–75.

tional divinations in 316 B.C. – two turtle divinations and one milfoil divination on the same date as the two preceding divinations, and one turtle divination in the next month (the last entry in the divination record). Presumably turtle and milfoil divination were the chief methods of iatromancy available to Shao Tuo. The Shuihudi almanacs document third century B.C. astro-calendrical methods of iatromancy. One iatromantic section keys the occurrence of illness to the ten stems, and it is understood that the stems are correlated with the Five Phases: *jia* 甲 and *yi* 乙 with Wood; *bing* 丙 and *ding* 丁 with Fire; *wu* 戊 and *ji* 己 with Soil; *geng* 庚 and *xin* 辛 with Metal; *ren* 壬 and *gui* 癸 with Water. According to the almanac, when illness (*ji* 疾) arises on a *jia* or *yi* day it is caused by one's deceased parents and it manifests itself as an ailment (*bing* 病) on a *wu* or *ji* day; the principle is based on the conquest sequence of the Five Phases, according to which Wood conquers Soil. A break in the ailment and recovery can be expected on *geng* and *xin* days because Metal conquers Wood.

Allowance is made for exceptional situations when the person does not recover: "If there is not a recovery, Fan 煩 (Fever) occupies the east quarter [correlated with Wood]; when Sui 歲 (Year) is in the east quarter, azure color [correlated with Wood] accompanies death." Sui (Year) in the iatromantic system refers not to the planet Jupiter, but to an astro-calendrical correlate that occupies one of the four directions during each month; Fan (Fever) must represent a pathogenic entity plotted in the calendrical cycle (this meaning is not attested to in received literature). The person who has the bad luck to become ill on a *jia* or *yi* day when both Fan and Sui are positioned in the east is doomed and at death has the azure complexion appropriate to Wood. The predictions for the remaining stems follow the same pattern of Five Phases correlations, although different family members and spirits are blamed for causing the illness.[101]

Turtle and milfoil divination over illness continued to be practiced in the third century B.C. and was not eclipsed by the astro-calendrical iatromancy of the almanacs. But some fundamental premises had changed. In the Baoshan divination record, illness is a chance event due to unsatisfied spirits or demonic malevolence; divination ascertains the religious remedy, including sacrificial offerings to Taiyi (Grand One) and exorcism of Sui (Year). In the astro-calendrical systems of the almanacs, all illnesses arising on a particular day share a common etiology and follow a common progression. Having identified day one (perhaps retrospectively based on the day when

---

[101] *Shuihudi Qin mu zhujian*, p. 193. For a detailed study of iatromancy in the almanacs, which is related to early medical diagnosis and prognosis based on yin–yang and Five Phases correlative cosmology, see Donald Harper, "Iatromancy, Diagnosis, and Prognosis in Early Chinese Medicine," in *Innovation in Chinese Medicine*, ed. Elizabeth Hsu (Cambridge University Press, forthcoming).

the ailment became manifest), a person could anticipate what to expect and in the majority of cases be assured of a cure within a specified period of time – knowing all the while that other astro-calendrical factors like Fan and Sui might suddenly prove fatal. Even though illness was still associated with spirit intrusion, there was no need for propitiatory sacrifices or for exorcism; the calamitous activity of the spirit world had been subsumed within astro-calendrical operations (it is interesting that iatromancy in the almanacs also bypasses medical treatment; illness follows a predicted course with or without medical intervention). The case of iatromancy may be extended to other areas of human concern where, by the third century B.C., turtle and milfoil divination existed alongside the astro-calendrical and hemerological systems, which in turn were leading toward yin–yang and Five Phases correlative cosmology.

Hexagram names are not identified in the Baoshan divination record. However, the *Yi jing* hexagram names are attested to in the *Zuo zhuan* as well as in excavated manuscripts. Du Yu's report on the *Yi* manuscript from the tomb of King Xiang of Wei (d. 296 B.C.) states that the manuscript matched the received text of the hexagrams and hexagram and line statements. In the Mawangdui *Yi jing* manuscript, the sequence of the hexagrams is different, but the hexagram names as well as the hexagram and line statements by and large correspond to the received *Yi jing*. The hexagram names in the bamboo-strip milfoil divination text from Wangjiatai tomb 15 (mid-third century B.C.) mostly correspond to the received *Yi jing*. The unusual feature of this manuscript is that after giving the name, most of the hexagrams are identified by reference to famous divinations in early history; the hexagram and line statements of the received *Yi jing* do not appear. For example, "Jie" 節 (Moderation; recorded as the number hexagram ䷻ [1-1-6-6-1-6]) is the hexagram obtained when King Wu of Zhou divined about attacking Yin, and "Tongren" 同人 (Gathering Men; recorded as the number hexagram ䷌ [1-8-1-1-1-1]) is the hexagram obtained by Huang Di 黃帝 when he battled Yan Di 炎帝. The statements following "Jie" and "Tongren" occur among the preserved fragments of the lost *Guizang* 歸藏 (one of three pre-Han recensions of the *Yi* hexagrams, the third being the lost *Lianshan* 連山), and the Wangjiatai text is probably an edition of the *Guizang*.[102]

While the naming of the sixty-four hexagrams had already stabilized in the fourth century B.C., the Warring States method (or methods) of count-

---

[102] For the archaeological report on the Wangjiatai text, see *Wenwu* 1995.1: 40–1; for the identification with the *Guizang*, see Li Jiahao, "Wangjiatai Qin jian Yizhan wei *Guizang* kao," *Chuantong wenhua yu xiandaihua* 1997.1: 46–52. On Huang Di's battle with Yan Di, see Mark Edward Lewis, *Sanctioned Violence in Early China* (Albany: State University of New York Press, 1990), pp. 179–80. On the Mawangdui hexagram names and their sequence, see Edward L. Shaughnessy, "A First Reading of the Mawangdui *Yijing* Manuscript," *EC* 19 (1994):50–5.

ing the milfoil stalks and forming the hexagrams is unknown. The only known method is described in a section of the *Xi ci* that is not in the Mawangdui *Xi ci*. From fifty milfoil stalks, one stalk was initially removed and the remaining forty-nine were sorted in several sequences that invariably resulted in a remainder of thirty-six, thirty-two, twenty-eight, or twenty-four. Division by four produced a quotient of 9, 8, 7, or 6. The numbers 9 and 7 (odd) are yang and are represented in the hexagram with a solid line; 8 and 6 (even) are yin and are represented with a broken line (the standard term for the lines is *yao* 爻). Beginning with the bottom line, the procedure was performed six times to form a hexagram. With 9 and 6 having special significance as numerical manifestations of yang and yin respectively, the line statements of the hexagrams use 9 as the tag for a solid line and 6 as the tag for a broken line.[103]

The Warring States number hexagrams from Baoshan and Wangjiatai could not have been formed following this method. Nevertheless, numbers in the number hexagrams correlate with solid lines in the received *Yi jing* and even numbers correlate with broken lines (clearly proven by the Wangjiatai hexagrams, which identify the number hexagrams by their accepted name). The Baoshan number hexagrams use two odd numbers (1 and 5) and two even numbers (6 and 8); 7 and 9 are also attested in number hexagrams in another Chu manuscript from a late fourth century B.C. tomb at Tianxingguan 天星觀, Hubei. The choice of numbers seems to have been based on a decimal system, with 2, 3, and 4 purposely ignored. However, we do not know exactly how the numbers were related to the milfoil divination method employed at that time.[104] Inasmuch as the number hexagrams constitute a symbolic figure, the numbers may not be simply the remainders or quotients resulting from the sorting procedure, but perhaps represent the translation of the sorting procedure into a pattern of symbolically significant numbers.

Symbolic choices probably account for the reduction of odd numbers in the number hexagrams from Wangjiatai (third century B.C.) to just 1 (*yi* 一), at which point the number essentially represented the solid line. It would have been an equally small step from 6 (*liu* 六) and 8 (*ba* 八) – both graphs visually representing a point of division or parting – to a symbolic broken line.[105] With the Mawangdui *Yi jing* manuscript, it may no longer be appro-

---

[103] *Yi jing*, 7, 20a; see Richard Lynn, *The Classic of Changes: A New Translation of the I Ching* (New York: Columbia University Press, 1994), pp. 60–2 (the method is also explained in the Introduction, pp. 19–21).

[104] See Li Ling, *Zhongguo fangshu kao*, pp. 242–4, for evidence of a decimal system; p. 254 lists the number hexagrams from Baoshan tomb 2 and Tianxingguan tomb 1.

[105] *Shuo wen jie zi zhu* (rpt. Shanghai: Shanghai guji, 1981), 2A, 1b, defines *ba* 八 as "to separate" and analyzes the graph as a depiction of two figures facing away from one another.

priate to speak of number hexagrams. Even though the symbol ⅃ㄴ used in recording the hexagrams is associated graphically with 8 八, the hexagrams were probably already perceived as figures composed of solid and broken lines. Further, the line statements of the Mawangdui *Yi jing* manuscript use 9 and 6 as tags exactly as in the received *Yi jing*; and the Mawangdui *Xi ci* and related texts unequivocally place milfoil divination within the cosmological framework as we know it in the received *Yi jing*. Thus, with the Mawangdui texts we witness the point where archaeological evidence merges with received testimony.

The preceding description of a shift from number hexagrams to hexagrams using solid and broken lines during the Warring States is plausible, but there is too much that we do not know to permit a neat diachronic account of the development of the hexagram.[106] Likewise, barring new discoveries we cannot know anything more about the divination method itself and must simply acknowledge that we do not know the procedure used to produce the number hexagrams. From the standpoint of cosmological ideas, the Baoshan and Wangjiatai number hexagrams seem to be prima facie evidence that Warring States hexagrams did not exhibit the essential image of solid and broken lines. This conclusion would indicate that the hexagram itself was not yet the ideal representation of a cosmos based on the yin–yang concept. To be sure, dualistic notions of male and female, and of Heaven and Earth, are embedded in the hexagram and line statements – the original core of the *Yi*. Its intrinsic dualism made the *Yi* a perfect text to validate the new yin–yang concept.

The *Xi ci* is the oldest received text to claim that the *Yi* embraces the cosmos within its yin–yang system and that the *Yi* provides mankind with knowledge of the operation of the cosmos. Beyond simply validating the yin–yang concept, the intent of the *Xi ci* is to demonstrate that the *Yi* itself is the true manifestation of the yin–yang concept; that is, the *Xi ci* aims to refute other yin–yang claimants and establish the *Yi* as the foundation of cosmology.[107] The *Xi ci*'s argument belongs to the third century B.C. debate over cosmology, when yin–yang and Five Phases ideas were being taken up by natural experts and occultists, as well as by masters of philosophy. Several of the other Mawangdui texts shed light on the polemic behind the *Xi ci*. A passage from *Yao* (Essentials) is notable for referring to Water, Fire, Metal, Soil, and Wood (the reference is not to the concept of the Five Phases, but to the older idea of five "Processes" associated with the operation of Earth):

[106] The *Zuo zhuan* accounts of milfoil divination record the hexagrams using solid and broken lines, but this is probably the result of later editorial standardization and is not evidence of fourth century B.C. practice.

[107] See Willard J. Peterson, "Making Connections: 'Commentary on the Attached Verbalizations' of the *Book of Change*," *HJAS* 42 (1982): 67–116.

The *Yi* possesses the way of Heaven. Because it cannot be wholly assayed by means of sun, moon, stars, and chronograms, yin and yang are applied to it. The *Yi* possesses the way of Earth. Because it cannot be wholly assayed by means of Water, Fire, Metal, Soil, and Wood, the pliant and rigid are used to regulate it.[108]

On the one hand, the passage claims that yin and yang as manifested in the *Yi* transcend astro-calendrical data in grasping the totality of Heaven and that the qualities of pliant and rigid associated with the broken and solid lines of the hexagrams are the quintessence of Earth. At the same time, one detects criticism of other natural experts and occultists who have not yet acknowledged the *Yi*'s supremacy.

YIN–YANG AND FIVE PHASES

Yin and yang are most often left untranslated, leaving their exact meaning open to specification based on historical period and context. The growing acceptance of Five Phases as the translation of *wu xing* 五行 can be attributed to several factors. One is certainly the convenience of conventional renderings coupled with the sense that Phase is preferable to the previously used Element, whose connotations and denotations are firmly embedded in Western thought. Phase is also claimed to convey the main sense of *xing* in the more fully elaborated correlative cosmology of Han times; since it was the Han theories that were passed down through the centuries, the notion of *wu xing* as Five Phases would be appropriate for the greater part of China's history. Use of Five Phases to translate *wu xing* in pre-Han texts or to refer to ideas that come under the general heading of *wu xing* raises the problem of anachronism, which if properly acknowledged need not prevent its adoption as a conventional rendering. A brief description of Han yin–yang and Five Phases correlative cosmology is the best approach to the Warring States idea of *wu xing*, as well as that of yin–yang.

As the stuff that is everywhere in the cosmos and accounts for all phenomena, *qi* 氣 (vapor) was at the base of Han yin–yang and Five Phases correlative cosmology. Yin–yang and the Five Phases served to identify and classify the characteristics of *qi* as it moved in specific cycles of time or configurations of space. To the extent that the idea of a Phase strips Soil, Wood, Metal, Water, and Fire of their substantive properties and makes them simply aspects of the cycles of the universal *qi*, the translation sacrifices some of the connotation of *xing* even in Han usage. However, Phase does express the idea that the *wu xing* function within a continuous cosmological system that

---

[108] Chen Songchang and Liao Mingchun, "Boshu *Ersanzi wen, Yi zhi yi, Yao* shiwen," p. 435. *Yao* does not use the term *wu xing*, but it occurs in a related text, *Ersanzi wen* 二三子問 (Several disciples ask); see Chen Songchang and Liao Mingchun, "Boshu *Ersanzi wen, Yi zhi yi, Yao* shiwen," p. 426.

embraces everything and extends everywhere; the *wu xing* do not act on one another as individual entities.[109] Whether in Han astro-calendrical theory, medical theory, or political theory, yin–yang and the Five Phases explained how *qi* operates. The resultant knowledge was then applied to the matter at hand, be it seasonal forecasting, medical diagnosis, or government policy.

A correlative cosmology composed of three parts – *qi*, yin–yang, and the Five Phases – was well established by the first century B.C. After this time yin–yang and Five Phases correlative cosmology, as worked out in the Han, was the ruling theory; all categories of natural phenomena and human activity were susceptible to its theoretical interpretation. Looking back to the fourth century B.C., we find a different situation. The three parts of the Han ruling theory were not yet bound together. The idea of *qi* as the basic stuff of human life and of other things in nature was current. Yin and yang were associated with *qi*, but yin–yang had not yet become the label for the concept of dualism. *Wu xing* did refer to Soil, Wood, Metal, Water, and Fire – which were also called the *wu cai* 五材 (five materials) – but *xing* was understood as a "process" characteristic of each "material," not as a Phase in the cycle of *qi*. *Wu xing* was one of several pentadic classification schemes; it was not yet the label for the concept of pentadic organization. The formulation of correlative cosmology in the third century B.C. was a coalescence of ideas in which *qi*, yin–yang, and *wu xing* each gained considerable conceptual significance as a broad theory of nature gradually emerged from the various theories and practices of the natural experts and occultists.

The idea that *qi* and blood together are the essential components of human life is reliably documented only in the fourth century B.C. sources, by which time *qi* already referred to the omnipresent stuff of the phenomenal world. It is not clear whether *qi* was initially a word for atmospheric vapors (clouds, steam, etc.) that was generalized to encompass the source of human vitality and everything else; or whether *qi* was a term for the life-sustaining stuff received from food, drink, and air or breath, which was extended to the natural world. The graph 气, glossed as "cloud *qi*" 雲气 in Xu Shen's 許慎 (ca. 55 A.D.–ca. 149) etymological dictionary *Shuo wen jie zi*, suggests the former derivation;[110] but the meaning is not attested to in the

---

[109] A detailed rationale for regarding *wu xing* as Five Phases in Han correlative cosmology is offered by Nathan Sivin, *Traditional Medicine in Contemporary China* (Ann Arbor: University of Michigan Center for Chinese Studies, 1987), pp. 72–7. Sivin adduces a variety of Han sources by way of illustration; p. 76 cites the *Oxford English Dictionary* for his understanding of "phase" to mean, "any one aspect of a thing of varying aspects; a state or stage of change or development." Kalinowski, *Cosmologie et divination dans la Chine ancienne*, pp. 111, 138, n. 338, chooses "agent" to render *xing* as "the least objectionable among the generally accepted translations." Kalinowski notes that even in later usage, the *xing* are characterized as having *ti* 體 (body) and *xing* 形 (form) in addition to their function in schemes related to time and space.

[110] *Shuo wen jie zi zhu*, 1A, 39a.

oldest uses of this graph in Shang and Zhou inscriptions (where it means "beseech," "end," "food donation"). The graph 氣 – which became the standard graph for the word *qi* in its generalized meaning – may have had earlier associations with food and breath, from which the idea of "stuff" in nature arose. By the fourth century B.C. the word was already a fixture in discourse on nature; barring new evidence, the question of etymological derivation is moot.[111] It is becoming accepted not to translate *qi*, in part because the word is gaining currency in English. However, modern use of the word *qi* in Chinese and in English has distorted its original meaning sufficiently to justify the attempt at translation, no matter whether the choice is imperfect; "vapor" avoids potentially misleading associations with "air," "pneuma," or "energy" in Western thought while retaining the sense of *qi* as something material but simultaneously volatile and pervasive.

Physician He's 醫和 discussion of the *liu qi* (six vapors) in the *Zuo zhuan* serves as evidence of the fourth century B.C. understanding of yin and yang:

Heaven has six vapors. They descend to generate the five tastes; radiate to make the five colors; are called forth to make the five sounds; and in excess produce the six illnesses. The six vapors are: yin and yang, wind and rain, dark and bright. They divide to make the four seasons; form a sequence to make the five nodes; and make calamity when they exceed.[112]

According to Physician He, excess of yin vapor produces cold illnesses and excess of yang vapor produces hot illnesses. As distinct from *hui* 晦 (dark) and *ming* 明 (bright), yin signifies the "shade" associated with cold; yang signifies the "sunshine" associated with heat. Another *Zuo zhuan* passage refers to the unseasonal nature of "excess yang" in winter, "concealed yin" in summer, "chill wind" in spring, and "bitter rain" in fall. The ideal association of yin with winter and yang with summer is implicitly understood in the passage, and the absence of "dark" and "bright" indicates that the latter have been subsumed by yin and yang.[113] Whether counted as six or four, Heaven's vapors, whose interactions are responsible for various phenomena, are not the universal *qi* of Han theory.

[111] The relevant etymological and textual evidence is conveniently summarized in Onozawa Sei-ichi et al., eds., *Ki no shisō: Chūgoku ni okeru shizenkan to ningenkan no tenkai* (Tokyo: Tōkyō daigaku, 1978), pp. 14–17, 30–4; see also Sivin, *Traditional Medicine in Contemporary China*, pp. 46–8. The compound "blood and *qi*" occurs in *Analects*, 16/7 (Legge, *Confucian Analects*, pp. 312–13), but the passage is from no earlier than the fourth century B.C. Other occurrences of *qi* in received literature also cannot be dated earlier than the fourth century B.C.

[112] *Zuo zhuan*, 41 (Zhao 1), 26b–27b (Legge, *The Ch'un Ts'ew with the Tso Chuen*, 580–1). Cf. Graham, *Disputers of the Tao*, p. 325; and Sivin, *Traditional Medicine in Contemporary China*, pp. 55–6.

[113] *Zuo zhuan*, 42 (Zhao 4), 24b (Legge, *The Ch'un Ts'ew with the Tso Chuen*, p. 596). Cf. Graham, *Yin–Yang and the Nature of Correlative Thinking*, p. 88.

The inner chapters of the *Zhuangzi* (dating to the late fourth or early third centuries B.C.) occasionally use yin and yang as an independent pair, but the usage is always in connection with physiological ideas and represents a borrowing from an early medical use of yin and yang. Fluctuations of yin and yang vapor in the body are a cause of illness as well as of changes of temperament (yang vapor accounts for feelings of delight, yin vapor for anger).[114] While it is likely that a dualistic yin–yang concept related to cosmological classification arose by the end of the fourth century B.C. (the "yin–yang explanations" included with the *Yi* from King Xiang's tomb suggest the possibility), the first indisputable attestation is in third century B.C. texts that are not earlier than the period of Zou Yan's reputed activities.[115]

Soil, Wood, Metal, Fire, and Water are labeled as the *wu cai* 五材 (five materials) in the *Zuo zhuan*. In the fourth century B.C. they were understood to be the essential resources of the Earth provided by Heaven for human sustenance. As resources, they were also understood to be exhaustible.[116] The term *wu xing* referred to the materials from the perspective of their characteristic qualities; each "did something" or exemplified a "process." The "Hong fan" 洪範 chapter of the *Shang shu* (dateable to ca. 400 B.C.) provides one explanation of what the Five Processes do:

The first is called Water, the second Fire, the third Wood, the fourth Metal, the fifth Soil. Of Water one says that it wets and descends, of Fire that it flames and rises, of Wood that it bends and straightens, of Metal that it conforms to change; Soil is sown and harvested.[117]

In the *Zuo zhuan* the Five Processes belong to Earth just as the sun, moon, and asterisms belong to Heaven.[118] One passage specifically juxtaposes the "six vapors" of Heaven with the Five Processes of Earth. The passage is noteworthy for correlating the five tastes, five colors, and five sounds with the six vapors of Heaven as did Physician He. The Five Processes are important, but they are self-contained. Moreover, they lack a conceptual link to *qi* (vapor),

---

[114] *Zhuangzi* (Sibu beiyao ed.), 2 ("Ren jian shi"), 8b–9a and 10a; Graham, *Yin–Yang and the Nature of Correlative Thinking*, pp. 72–3.

[115] Even were one to allow an earlier date for the *Laozi*, chapter 42, statement that "the myriad things bear yin on their back and embrace yang," it is the only occurrence of yin and yang in the *Laozi*. And it retains the *Zhuangzi*'s physiological sense of the properties of the things of creation, at a low place in the hierarchy of the cosmogonic creation initiated by *dao*.

[116] *Zuo zhuan*, 38 (Xiang 27), 14b (Legge, *The Ch'un Ts'ew with the Tso Chuen*, p. 534); *Zuo zhuan*, 45 (Zhao 11), 18b (ibid., p. 634).

[117] *Shang shu*, 12, 5b (James Legge, *The Chinese Classics. Vol. 3 The Shoo King, or The Book of Historical Documents* [rpt. Hong Kong: Hong Kong University Press, 1960], pp. 325–6). Graham, *Yin–Yang and the Nature of Correlative Thinking*, p. 77, dates the "Hongfan" to ca. 400 B.C. and judges (p. 80) its correlation of the Five Processes with the "five tastes" as a later interpolation.

[118] *Zuo zhuan*, 53 (Zhao 32), 26a (Legge, *The Ch'un Ts'ew with the Tso Chuen*, p. 741).

which is clearly the reason for classifying the five tastes, five colors, and five sounds under the six vapors.[119]

However, there are indications in the *Zuo zhuan* that the Five Processes were acquiring broader significance. In a speech set in the year 513 B.C., Cai Mo 蔡墨, the scribe/astrologer of Jin, attributes the disappearance of dragons to the failure to maintain the tradition of the *shuiguan* 水官 (Water Office), which was responsible for watery creatures including the dragon. Cai Mo explains that the Water Office is one of the offices of the Five Processes, each of which has a presiding spirit who should receive appropriate sacrifices: the presiding spirit of Wood is Goumang 句芒; of Fire, Zhurong 祝融; of Metal, Rushou 蓐收; of Water, Xuanming 玄冥; of Soil, Houtu 后土.[120] In the *yue ling* calendars of the late third century B.C., four of these spirits were firmly associated with directions and seasons: Goumang/east/spring, Zhurong/south/summer, Rushou/west/fall, Xuanming/north/winter.[121] The *Zuo zhuan* reflects an earlier stage when deities were first being organized into astro-calendrical schemes. The spatial arrangement of the five spirits in Cai Mo's speech is clear: Houtu is situated at the center with the four other spirits in the directions indicated in the later calendars. Correlation of the spirits with the Five Processes marks an expansion of the earlier idea of the *wu xing* as five discrete processes. As part of the pentadic spatial plan the Five Processes exist in relation to one another, and they become subject to astro-calendrical correlations.

Mutual relations between the Five Processes in the form of the conquest sequence are also attested to in the *Zuo zhuan*. Cai Mo twice makes predictions based on the conquest of one *xing* by another that correlate them with stems and branches, the basic data of astro-calendrical calculations. We may tentatively conclude that stem and branch correlations for all Five Processes existed in the fourth century B.C. and that the conquest sequence was used by astrologers and calendrical experts. In the first example, the prediction is based on the correlation of the stem *geng* 庚 with Metal and of the branch *wu* 午 with Fire for a day *gengwu*, and Cai Mo observes that Fire conquers Metal. The second example is more complicated and presents Cai Mo as one of three scribe/astrologers who are requested to offer predictions following a turtle divination. Cai Mo's prediction is based on the correlation of *zi* 子 with Water; identification of Yan Di as the Fire Master (*huoshi* 火師) leads to the statement that Water conquers Fire.[122]

[119] *Zuo zhuan*, 51 (Zhao 25), 9a (ibid., p. 708).
[120] *Zuo zhuan*, 53 (Zhao 29), 5a–7a (ibid., p. 731).
[121] See the introductory sections to the first twelve chapters (*juan*) of the *Lü shi chunqiu*; cf. Jeffrey K. Riegel, "Kou-mang and Ju-shou," *Cahiers d'Extrême-Asie* 5 (1989–90): 68–73.
[122] *Zuo zhuan*, 53 (Zhao 31), 20b–21a (Legge, *The Ch'un Ts'ew with the Tso Chuen*, p. 738); *Zuo zhuan*, 58 (Ai 9), 17a–b (ibid., p. 819). According to the *Zuo zhuan*, the original turtle divination resulted in

The *Zuo zhuan*'s evidence of the conquest sequence fits well with the Shui-hudi almanacs, which apply the conquest sequence to the sexagenary cycle of stems and branches in various astro-calendrical systems. The absence of the production sequence (Wood produces Fire, Fire produces Soil, Soil produces Metal, Metal produces Water) in the excavated almanacs also speaks against the supposition that the spatial arrangement of the offices of the Five Processes in the *Zuo zhuan* assumes knowledge of the correlations between *xing*, directions, and seasons in the production sequence as given in later calendars. The order of the Five Processes in the "Hongfan" chapter of the *Shang shu* and their spatial arrangement in the *Zuo zhuan* both suggest coordination with cardinal points around the center: Water and Fire (first and second in the "Hongfan") form the north–south axis, Wood and Metal (third and fourth in the "Hongfan") the east–west axis, and Soil (fifth in the "Hongfan") is at the center. Only after Five Processes correlations were extended to the seasons (not attested to in either the *Zuo zhuan* or the excavated almanacs) would this prior spatial arrangement have served as the basis for the production sequence (Wood, Fire, Soil, Metal, Water).[123]

A final development was needed before Soil, Wood, Metal, Fire, and Water could function as rubrics for broad cosmological classification. There is no evidence that it occurred before Zou Yan, who (as reported in the *Shi ji*) proposed the theory of the mutual conquest of the *wu de* 五德 Five Virtues (understanding virtue here in the sense of the intrinsic power of something; the etymology of *de* is similar). Received sources consistently associate the term *wu de* with Zou Yan. The new term served to signify a virtue in Soil, Wood, Metal, Fire, and Water that could be extended beyond the substances and their characteristic processes, and so be applied to other pentadic sets. In the *Lü shi chunqiu*'s account of the cycle of political change since the reign of Huang Di (evidently a restatement of Zou Yan's theory), the change in the cosmic environment that introduces each succeeding age results from the *qi* (vapor) of the Five Virtues: Huang Di observed the vapor of Soil being ascendant and modeled his government on the symbolic correlations of Soil; Yu founded the Xia when he observed Wood vapor ascendant; Tang founded the Shang when he observed Metal vapor ascendant; King Wen founded the Zhou when he observed Fire vapor ascendant; the successor to Zhou would recognize the signs of Water vapor ascendant.[124]

"water meets fire" (the exact meaning of this sign in plastromancy is uncertain). Thus, all three scribe-astrologers deal with the water/fire symbolism, but only Cai Mo refers to it in terms of the conquest of one *xing* by another. The conquest sequence is enumerated earlier in this chapter.

[123] Graham, *Yin–Yang and the Nature of Correlative Thinking*, pp. 79–80, 82–4. As Graham observes, it is likely that the spatial arrangement was influenced by ritual considerations arising from the ruler's position in the north facing south with east and west on the left and right, respectively.

[124] *Shi ji*, 74, p. 2344; *Lü shi chunqiu*, 13 ("Yingtong"), 4a. See Graham, *Disputers of the Tao*, p. 329.

In the late third century B.C., *wu xing* correlative classification was expanding by imposing itself on the older "six vapors" correlations and by extending the range of phenomena it incorporated.[125] In concept the *wu xing* paralleled yin–yang: both provided a means to classify phenomena based on characteristics of vapor. At this point one can understand *wu xing* in the sense of Five Phases in a cycle defined by *qi*. However, one still cannot speak of a unified yin–yang and Five Phases correlative cosmology. In some areas of natural philosophy and occult thought, yin–yang ideas had already been incorporated, while Five Phases ideas were only beginning to be applied. The Mawangdui medical manuscripts offer an example from medicine. Some of the Mawangdui texts already structure physiology around a system of yin and yang vessels that contain vapor, and yin–yang ideas are the basis for understanding health and illness. The Five Phases are mentioned only once, in a description of gestation that lists them in the conquest sequence from the fourth month through the eighth month of pregnancy.[126] The integration of yin–yang and the Five Phases in medicine occurred gradually over the second and first centuries B.C. (as evidenced by the *Huang Di neijing*). The Han state orthodoxy that was fashioned around yin–yang and Five Phases correlative cosmology formed during the same period.[127]

RELIGION AND MAGIC

One consequence of the excavation of manuscripts related to natural philosophy and occult thought has been rediscovery of the religious beliefs and practices of the Warring States, Qin, and Han elite. The Shuihudi almanacs are especially rich in magico-religious lore, as is the silk Mawangdui manual of medical recipes assigned the title *Wushier bingfang* 五十二病方 (Recipes for fifty-two ailments). Before the discoveries of the manuscripts, the conventional wisdom was that the religion of the elite concerned family ancestral cults and ritual observances associated with state and family; in general, the spirit world was kept at a distance. If there was a popular religion, it was presumed to have been part of regional *wu* (shaman) cults. The mechanisms of interaction with the spirit world (incantation, exorcism, etc.) were, so far as was recorded in received sources, in the hands of shamans and religious officiants, whose activities paralleled those of astrologers, diviners, and related

---

[125] Graham, *Yin–Yang and the Nature of Correlative Thinking*, pp. 84–91, discusses the textual evidence in the calendrical essays of the *Guanzi* and in other third to second century B.C. texts.

[126] *Mawangdui Han mu boshu*, vol. 4, p. 136; Harper, *Early Chinese Medical Literature*, pp. 379–81.

[127] For medicine, see Harper, *Early Chinese Medical Literature*, pp. 86–90; and Yamada Keiji, "The Formation of the *Huang-ti Nei-ching*," *Acta Asiatica* 36 (1979): 67–89. For state orthodoxy, see Twitchett and Loewe, eds., *Cambridge History of China*, pp. 708–13.

experts.[128] In the excavated almanacs and other texts, we find detailed instructions on how to deal with the spirit world in the course of daily life, employing simple folkloristic devices as well as incantations and complicated ritual acts of a type previously thought to have been restricted to shamans and religious officiants. It is evident that by the third century B.C., such practices were in use among the elite, who surely gained some of their knowledge orally but could also expect to learn from the texts of the natural experts and occultists.[129]

Although the magico-religious content is mixed with astro-calendrical and hemerological systems in the almanacs and with other recipes in several Mawangdui recipe manuals, it exemplifies the literature listed in the "Miscellaneous Divination" section (of the "Calculations and Arts" division) in the *Han shu* bibliographic treatise, which includes titles such as *Qingdao zhifu* 請禱致福 (Favor-granting prayers to bring good fortune) and *Rengui jingwu liuchu bianguai* 人鬼精物六畜變怪 (Human and demonic spectral entities and the mutant prodigies of the six domestic animals).[130] The view of religion in the manuscripts is taken from the perspective of the literature of natural philosophy and occult thought; that is, the manuscripts are not in themselves religious literature, but rather represent the blending of ideas in Warring States natural philosophy and occult thought. The manuscripts do not inform us of the activities of shamans and religious officiants, nor do we learn from them the details of specific cults. However, their contents are a remarkable testament to the place of religion in elite life. Rather than isolating a world of strictly natural phenomena from a world inhabited by spirits and demons, the two worlds were merged in varying composites. In one form, the spirits were drawn into the astro-calendrical systems discussed above which made their influence more predictable. In another, incantations and other magico-religious techniques gave people a sense of control in their dealings with the spirit world. And there were advantages in combining magico-religious techniques with the astro-calendrical systems.[131]

[128] Graham, *Disputers of the Tao*, p. 47, echoes this understanding: "The tendency throughout the classical age [for Graham, the period from 500 to 200 B.C.] is to ignore the spirits of the dead and of the mountains and rivers after paying them their customary respects, and to regard Heaven as an impersonal power responsible for everything outside human control." The tendency identified by Graham is chiefly derived from the writings of the masters of philosophy, whose biases are now being revealed by the archaeological record.

[129] For general treatments of religion and magic in the excavated manuscripts, see Harper, "Warring States, Qin, and Han Manuscripts Related to Natural Philosophy and the Occult"; idem, "A Chinese Demonography of the Third Century B.C."; idem, *Early Chinese Medical Literature*, pp. 148–83; and Mu-chou Poo, "Popular Religion in Pre-Imperial China: Observations on the Almanacs of Shui-hu-ti," *TP* 79 (1993): 225–48.

[130] *Han shu*, 30, p. 1772.

[131] Mu-chou Poo, "Popular Religion in Pre-Imperial China," examines the Shuihudi almanacs from the standpoint of sociocultural background and underlying religious mentality, concluding (pp. 242–8)

If we leave aside for the moment the various deities incorporated into astro-calendrical systems, the following characterization of the spirit world is gleaned from the Shuihudi almanacs and the Mawangdui medical manuscripts. Tian Di 天帝 (God of Heaven) or Shang Di 上帝 (God on High) are standard names for the chief celestial deity, who oversees an animistic pantheon. One recipe to treat the painful rash caused by the sap of the lacquer plant in *Wushier bingfang* curses the spirit of the lacquer plant: "God of Heaven sent you down to lacquer bows and arrows. Now you cause scabby sores for the people down below. I daub you with pig feces."[132] The demonographic section of the first Shuihudi almanac, entitled "Jie" 詰 (Spellbinding), describes one case of demonic harassment in which the demon identifies himself as the "son of God on High" who intends to steal someone's daughter; the demon is exorcised with dog feces and reeds.[133] Spirits may also assume disguises, as when one "feigns being a rat and enters people's vinegar . . . or drink." Having made contact with its victims, the demon threatens them with announcements of their day of death.[134]

Most spirits may be beneficial or harmful depending on the circumstances; the spirit world is not clearly divided into benign spirits and evil demons. The purpose of a text such as the Shuihudi "Jie" was to teach people precautionary measures should they happen to encounter certain spirits or prodigies of nature. The idea of the spirit world was also influenced by the new ideas about nature. When the kitchen stove does not cook food, the cause is the "yang demon" (*yanggui* 陽鬼) who has taken the *qi* (vapor) of the stove; when "cloud vapor" (*yunqi* 雲氣) infiltrates the home it must be counteracted by building a fire; when wild beasts and domestic animals speak, it is because of the *qi* of "whirling wind" (*piaofeng* 飄風).[135] The final example is related to the belief that spirits themselves are manifestations of *qi* or *jing* 精 (essence; refined *qi*). The latter word used alone may have the sense of "genie" or "specter."[136] There were surely more exotic encounters with weird spirit powers; the almanacs and medical manuscripts show a spirit world that is contiguous with the everyday human environment, and they reflect basic beliefs shared by the elite and nonelite alike.

that the almanacs reflect views of elite and nonelite population throughout the various states at the end of the Warring States period.

[132] *Mawangdui Han mu boshu*, vol. 4, p. 68; Harper, *Early Chinese Medical Literature*, pp. 293–4.

[133] *Shuihudi Qin mu zhujian*, p. 215, translated in Donald Harper, "Spellbinding," in *Religions of China in Practice*, ed. Donald Lopez (Princeton, N.J.: Princeton University Press, 1996), p. 249, no. 57. For details on the Shuihudi demonography, see Harper, "A Chinese Demonography of the Third Century B.C."

[134] *Shuihudi Qin mu zhujian*, p. 213; Harper, "Spellbinding," p. 246, no. 22.

[135] *Shuihudi Qin mu zhujian*, pp. 212, 215; Harper, "Spellbinding," p. 245, nos. 11–12, p. 249, no. 61.

[136] See the definition of *mei* 魅 (a kind of goblin) in the *Shuo wen jie zi zhu*, 9A. 41a, as "the *jing* of an aged entity"; the longer *qi* and *jing* linger the more spiritually potent they become. See Harper, "The Conception of Illness in Early Chinese Medicine," pp. 224–5.

A short bamboo-strip text from Fangmatan reveals a heretofore unknown aspect of Warring States popular religion. The text is an official record dated in the thirty-eighth year of King Zhao 昭王 of Qin (269 B.C.), and it reports the case of a man named Dan 丹 who, having killed himself in 300 B.C. (his suicide was in anticipation of his likely execution), was resurrected three years later. Dan's former employer, the Wei general Xi Wu 犀武 (d. 293 B.C.), believed that Dan was not yet fated to die and submitted a written declaration to the Scribe of the Director of the Life Mandate (*siming shi* 司命史) in the underworld. The appeal was successful; however, Dan's resurrected body still bore the signs of his suicide and burial.[137] The account of the resurrection gives evidence of a belief current by the end of the fourth century B.C. to the effect that the underworld resembled a bureaucratic state and that dealings with the underworld bureaucracy conformed to the norms of Warring States bureaucracies; yet another channel was opened for communication with the spirit world. It was precisely this type of bureaucratized spirit world in Later Han (A.D. 25–220) popular religion that was among the elements that gave rise to religious Daoism in the second century A.D. The Fangmatan text is currently the only Warring States attestation of human transactions with a bureaucratized spirit world. It leaves many questions unanswered at the same time as it changes our understanding of religion in Warring States society.[138]

Archaeology has afforded us much fuller knowledge of the polar deity Taiyi (Grand One) in Warring States religion, natural philosophy, and occult thought. In the received record, Taiyi emerged as a prominent astrological deity in the Former Han period. Miu Ji's 謬忌 memorial to Wudi in 133 B.C. proposing the establishment of a state cult explains that "Taiyi is the most exalted of the spirits of Heaven; the *wu di* 五帝 are Taiyi's assistants" (the *wu di* were the gods of the five directions, whose cult had been established at the beginning of the dynasty). Miu Ji's elevation of Taiyi is mirrored in the *Shi ji* astrological treatise, in which the first sentence identifies the star corresponding to Kochab (β *Ursa minor*, the polestar at that time) as "the regular lodging of Taiyi." Several cult sites for worship of Taiyi were established during Wudi's reign, and the Taiyi cult survived the religious reforms of the first century B.C.[139]

---

[137] See Li Xueqin, "Fangmatan jian zhong de zhiguai gushi"; and Donald Harper, "Resurrection in Warring States Popular Religion," *Taoist Resources* 5, 2 (1994): 13–28.

[138] See Harper, "Resurrection in Warring States Popular Religion," for further speculations. Archaeological evidence is again crucial to our current knowledge of Later Han popular religion; see esp. Anna Seidel, "Traces of Han Religion in Funeral Texts Found in Tombs," in *Dôkyô to shûkyô bunka*, ed. Akizuki Kan'ei (Tokyo: Hirakawa, 1987), pp. 21–57.

[139] Miu Ji's memorial is quoted in *Shi ji*, 28, p. 1386; the astrological treatise reference is *Shi ji*, 27, p. 1289. Li Ling, "An Archaeological Study of Taiyi (Grand one) Worship," gives a detailed account of the Former Han Taiyi cult and related state cults; cf. Twitchett and Loewe, eds., *Cambridge History of China*, pp. 661–8.

Scattered references to Taiyi in pre-Han philosophical literature concern more a concept of cosmic oneness than a deity. The *Lü shi chunqiu* essay "Da yue 大樂 (Great music)" places Taiyi at the cosmic origin. When paraphrasing the passage from *Laozi*, chapter 25, that assigns the provisional name *da* 大 (great) to the ineffable *dao*, the *Lü shi chunqiu* uses *taiyi* in place of *da*.[140] In the absence of other pre-Han evidence, it had been argued that a Warring States philosophical concept *taiyi* was the basis for the Han invention of one of several astrological deities, but this has now been disproven by the Baoshan divination record and several artifacts with images that can be identified as the deity Taiyi.[141]

The Baoshan divination record names Taiyi several times as one of the spirits who receive sacrificial offerings.[142] The key to the iconographic image of Taiyi is provided by a Mawangdui silk painting that depicts a group of spirits in the upper part of the painting with three dragons below (Fig. 12.8). The large central figure is labeled Taiyi; flanking it are Leigong (Thunder Lord) on the left and Yushi (Rain Master) on the right; the dragon on the left side is labeled Qinglong (Azure Dragon), while the dragon on the right is Huanglong 黃龍 (Yellow Dragon). The painting, which has been referred to as the *Bibing tu* 避兵圖 (Repel weapon chart), includes explanatory text concerning military fortunes associated with the deities depicted.[143] The painting is an iconographic representation of some of the astro-calendrical deities from the Mawangdui *Xingde*, text B, and *Yin yang wu xing*, edition B, discussed earlier. The specific arrangement of Taiyi and the three dragons in the painting is a representation of the constellation Taiyi. The iconography can be identified with the *Shi ji* description of a Taiyi *feng* 太一鋒 (Grand One spear) used by Wudi in 112 B.C. when worshipping Taiyi prior to launching an attack on Nanyue 南越. During the ceremony the Taiyi spear was pointed in the direction of Nanyue in order to vanquish the enemy magically. The same iconography has been discovered on a late fourth century B.C. dagger-axe from a tomb at Cheqiao 車橋, in Jingmen 荊門, Hubei, which bears the inscription "*bing bi* Taisui" 兵避太歲 (weapon to repel Grand Year) (Fig. 12.9). Just as the Baoshan divination record makes offer-

[140] *Lü shi chunqiu*, 5 ("Da yue"), 4a. For other references in philosophical texts see Li Ling, "An Archaeological Study of Taiyi (Grand One) Worship," pp. 1–2.

[141] For the thesis that Taiyi as an astrological deity was a Han invention, see Qian Baocong, "Taiyi kao," *Yanjing xuebao* 12 (1932): 2454–66. Li Ling, "An Archaeological Study of Taiyi (Grand One) Worship," critically reviews Qian's thesis in the light of the new archaeological discoveries and proves the existence of the Warring States deity Taiyi.

[142] *Baoshan Chu jian*, pp. 34, 36. See Li Ling, "An Archaeological Study of Taiyi (Grand One) Worship," pp. 13–14, for discussion of the several different graphs used to write the name. Li Ling speculates that both *taiyi* and *siming* (Director of the Life-Mandate) in the Baoshan divination record are related to the deities of the same name in the "Jiuge" (Nine songs) of the *Chu ci* (p. 22).

[143] Li Ling, "An Archaeological Study of Taiyi (Grand One) Worship," pp. 14–15. See Fu Juyou and Chen Songchang, *Mawangdui Han mu wenwu*, p. 35, for a color reproduction of the painting.

Figure 12.8. *Bibing tu*. After Fu Juyou and Cheng Songchang, *Mawangdui Han mu wenwu* (Changsha: Hunan, 1992), p. 35.

ings to Taiyi and exorcises Sui (Year; Jupiter), the dagger-axe uses the iconography of Taiyi to avert the evil of Taisui. The exact relation between Taiyi in popular religion and in philosophical discourse remains uncertain, but clearly both identities coexisted.[144]

Among the varieties of magic employed in the Shuihudi almanacs and Mawangdui medical manuscripts, the incantations shed additional light on the conception of the spirit world in Warring States popular religion. The majority of incantations are exorcistic curses that threaten the offending demon with annihilation unless it ceases and desists. Indeed, the phrase

[144] *Shi ji*, 28, p. 1395. Li Ling, "An Archaeological Study of Taiyi (Grand One) Worship," pp. 18–19, also relates the iconography to several talismans inscribed on funerary jars from Later Han tombs.

Figure 12.9. *Taiyi* (Grand One) dagger-axe. After *Kaogu* 1963.3: 153. Drawing by Li Xiating.

"desist, if you do not desist" (*yi bu yi* 已不已) and related phrases, followed by the exact form of mayhem to be applied, are common in the Mawangdui recipe manual *Wushier bingfang* and also occur in the section "Jie" of the first Shuihudi almanac. Another formula utilizes the standard bureaucratic phrase "*kəgw*, I dare to declare to . . ." (*gao gan gao* 皋敢告; the first *gao* is an utterance, hence the use of Old Chinese reconstruction in the translation)[145] used in exchanges with a superior, typically addressing a superior spirit who is expected to deal with the offending demon. The incantation to exorcise demons who cause nightmares, recorded in both Shuihudi almanacs, begins: "*Kəgw*, I dare to declare you [the demon] to Qinqi 豹蹄 [the controller of nightmare demons]."[146]

Forms of magic related to Yu 禹, the flood hero and legendary founder of Xia, indicate his importance in Warring States magico-religious and occult traditions. Yu's legendary circumambulation and pacification of a world in chaos appear to have made Yu the archetypal pacifier of the spirit world that continued to exist alongside mankind. In the Shuihudi almanacs, Yu is closely associated with travel. The section "Yu xuyu" 禹須臾 (Promptuary of Yu) in the first almanac begins by listing the stem and branch sexagenary cycle in

[145] I use Li Fanggui's reconstruction of Old Chinese as given in Axel Schuessler, *A Dictionary of Early Zhou Chinese* (Honolulu: University of Hawaii Press, 1987), p. 190.

[146] *Shuihudi Qin mu zhujian*, pp. 210, 247. See Harper, *Early Chinese Medical Literature*, pp. 160–7, for additional discussion of incantation. On the nightmare incantation and bureaucratic style of address, see also Donald Harper, "Wang Yen-shou's Nightmare Poem," *HJAS* 47 (1987): 270–1; and Harper, "Warring States, Qin, and Han Manuscripts Related to Natural Philosophy and the Occult," p. 291, n. 60.

five groups of twelve signs each; embarking on a journey on the days in each of the five groups should be at a certain time of day to ensure luck and safety. This hemerological system is the antecedent to the *nayin* 納音 (contained [musical] note) system that is first detailed in the fourth century *Baopuzi*. As related in the *Baopuzi*, Six Dynasties Daoists utilized the *nayin* system in religious practices, including the precautions observed when traveling into the wilds.[147]

"Yu xuyu" concludes with a ritual to be performed before going out of the city gate:

When traveling, on reaching the threshold-bar of the capital gate, perform the Pace of Yu thrice. Advance one pace. Call out, "*Kəgw*, I dare make a declaration. Let so-and-so [to be filled in with the name of the traveler] travel and not suffer odium; he first acts as Yu to clear the road." Immediately draw five lines on the ground. Pick up the soil from the center of the lines and put it in your bosom.[148]

The Pace of Yu (Yu *bu* 禹步) is the basic magical dance step of Six Dynasties religious Daoism. Although the name is first attested to in received literature in the *Baopuzi*, Marcel Granet argued that the Daoist Pace of Yu went back to ancient shamanistic traditions. Granet pointed to accounts of Yu's lameness in Warring States philosophical texts as indirect evidence of an original shamanic trance-inducing limp like the one described in the *Baopuzi*. Occurrences of the Pace of Yu in both the Shuihudi and Fangmatan almanacs concern travel, but the Pace of Yu is employed seven times in the Mawangdui *Wushier bingfang* as part of the magical strategy for exorcising demons blamed for ailments. Granet is surely correct about its shamanic origins. However, the excavated manuscripts show that in the third century B.C., the Pace of Yu had already become part of the fund of magico-religious knowledge regularly employed by the elite. It was probably in this more popular milieu that the Pace of Yu found its way into religious Daoism.[149]

Parallels between popular magico-religious practices recorded in excavated manuscripts and the scant evidence of religious rites or shamanic performances in received sources show the common ground shared by both. Entries in "Jie" on shooting arrows from peachwood bows, scattering ashes, and fumigation with demonifuges to neutralize harmful demons have counterparts in the *Zuo zhuan* and in sections of the *Zhou li* (Rites of Zhou) that

---

[147] *Shuihudi Qin mu zhujian*, pp. 222–3; Kalinowski, "Les traités de Shuihudi et l'hémérologie chinoise," pp. 200–204.

[148] *Shuihudi Qin mu zhujian*, p. 223. See Harper, "Warring States, Qin, and Han Manuscripts Related to Natural Philosophy and the Occult," pp. 271–2, for more detailed treatment.

[149] Marcel Granet, "Remarques sur le Taoisme ancien," *AM* 2 (1925): 146–51; Harper, *Early Chinese Medical Literature*, pp. 167–9; idem, "Warring States, Qin, and Han Manuscripts Related to Natural Philosophy and the Occult," p. 240.

describe officers in the ideal state whose job is to rid the environment of noxious and demonic creatures. The same repertoire is applied to exorcising demons blamed for ailments in the *Wushier bingfang*. Clearly the elite were not only accustomed to observing religious officiants and shamans dealing with the spirit world, but they also expected to take matters into their own hands as necessary.[150]

MEDICINE

The formation of a learned medicine between the fourth and first centuries B.C. was accomplished by the *yi* 醫, translated here as "physician." Etymologically, *yi* is related to words for exorcism in Shang inscriptions, and the notion of *yi* as originally a medicine man is also evident in the Warring States legend that credits Shaman Peng 巫彭 with creating the profession of physician in antiquity. During the Warring States and through the Han the compound *wu yi*, either "shamans and physicians" or "shaman physician," was not necessarily pejorative. The recipes for magical treatments in the Mawangdui *Wushier bingfang* bear witness to the eclecticism of third and early second century B.C. medicine; the incantations and exorcistic rituals were part of the occult learning that medicine shared with other fields of natural philosophy and occult thought.[151] However, as a group, *yi* (physicians) were no longer *wu* (shamans) in the sense of the shamanic practitioners of Warring States religion. One finds the model for the physicians in Wen Zhi, who boasted to King Wei of Qi (r. 356–320 B.C.) that his "way consists of three hundred fascicles"; that is, Wen Zhi's medical knowledge was contained in texts, and it was on a par with the knowledge of other natural experts and occultists who gained the attention of rulers and the literate elite.[152]

To be sure, in the competition among medical practitioners – including diviners and astrologers who practiced iatromancy, shamans, and drug gatherers – certain physicians used the label "shaman physician" in accusations of malpractice. The *Lü shi chunqiu* essay "Jin shu" 盡數 (Fulfill the calculation), which represents the viewpoint of physicians committed to the new theories of *qi* (vapor) as the only valid basis for medical practice, concludes with words of condemnation for other practices:

[150] For general discussion of the varieties of magic in "Jie" and *Wushier bingfang*, see Harper, *Early Chinese Medical Literature*, pp. 159–72; and idem, "Warring States, Qin, and Han Manuscripts Related to Natural Philosophy and the Occult," pp. 243–9. For an example of exorcistic archery using jujube arrows and peachwood bows in the *Zuo zhuan*, see *Zuo zhuan*, 42 (Zhao 4), 23b (Legge, *The Ch'un Ts'ew with the Tso Chuen*, pp. 595–6). The exorcistic duties of certain state officers are detailed in *Zhou li*, 37, 6a–8b.

[151] See Harper, *Early Chinese Medical Literature*, pp. 43–4, 163. Shaman Peng's legendary position in medicine is cited in *Lü shi chunqiu*, 17 ("Wugong"), 9a.

[152] See Harper, *Early Chinese Medical Literature*, pp. 42–3.

The current age elevates turtle and milfoil divination, prayers, and sacrificial offerings. Thus illness and ailment come in ever greater numbers. By analogy it is like the archer who when he fails to hit the target adjusts the target. How does this improve his shooting? If you add boiling water to stop water from boiling, the boiling is all the more unceasing. Eliminate the fire and it will stop. Thus to purge [illness] with the poisonous drugs of the shaman–physicians [*wu yi*] – people of antiquity disparaged it because it was inconsequential.[153]

In the light of the Mawangdui medical manuscripts, which combine exorcistic cures and drugs – some of which possessed magical and exorcistic properties – in their contents, the "Jin shu" condemnation seems to have been aimed at the medical practices of certain physicians, as well as at the other medical practitioners.

The Han physician Chunyu Yi 淳于意 (216–ca. 150 B.C.) and the physicians whose views are represented in the oldest parts of the received recensions of the *Huang Di neijing* (ca. first century B.C.) furthered the skepticism of magico-religious ideas voiced in "Jin shu" in the course of elaborating a new medical paradigm based on *qi* (vapor).[154] The *Huang Di neijing* adheres to naturalistic theories in its explanations of illness and therapy. Illness is said to arise from pathogenic conditions of the vapor within the system of *mai* 脈 (vessels) and internal organs in the human body – the workings of which are explained by yin–yang and Five Phases theories – and illness is cured by correcting the vapor with acupuncture. The *Huang Di neijing* does not deny outright the existence of demonic phenomena, but its medical theories are consistent in disallowing the possibility that illness is demonically inspired and in rejecting magico-religious treatments; indeed, the only therapy of which the *Huang Di neijing* approves is use of the *jiu zhen* 九鍼 (nine needles) of acupuncture.[155]

The monolithic view of medicine in the *Huang Di neijing* is a Han construct and cannot be taken as representative of the entirety of medicine even in Han times. The Mawangdui medical manuscripts provide the earliest documentation of three broad lines of development in Warring States medicine. First, the recipe manual *Wushier bingfang* exemplifies the wealth of practical medical knowledge from drug treatments to fumigations and minor surgery that was inherited from earlier medicine and continued to grow in sophisti-

---

[153] *Lü shi chunqiu*, 3 ("Jin shu"), 5a (*shu*, "calculation," refers to a person's allotted lifespan). See Harper, *Early Chinese Medical Literature*, pp. 145–7, for arguments that "Jin shu" represents the physicians' viewpoint.

[154] Medical writings of Chunyu Yi are excerpted in *Shi ji*, 105, pp. 2794–817; translated in Bridgman, "La medicine dans la Chine antique," pp. 24–50. For the textual history of the *Huangdi neijing*, see Loewe, ed., *Early Chinese Texts*, pp. 196–215.

[155] See Harper, "The Conception of Illness in Early Chinese Medicine," p. 211, n. 4. On the supremacy of the nine needles of acupuncture, see *Lingshu* (Sibu beiyao ed.), 7 ("Bingchuan"), 2a; cf. Harper, *Early Chinese Medical Literature*, p. 68.

cation in the late Warring States, Qin, and Han periods. The kind of medical theory that informs the *Huang Di neijing* is not in evidence in the *Wushier bingfang*, and one finds magico-religious practices existing alongside the other forms of therapy in its recipes; all approaches to treating ailments are regarded as useful.

Second, there are several texts that describe a system of eleven *mai* (vessels) in the body and associate certain ailments with the condition of the vapor in certain vessels. The recommended treatment is to cauterize (*jiu* 灸) the vessels to correct the pathogenic vapor. The vessels are classified into yin and yang vessels using the nomenclature attested to later in the *Huang Di neijing* (which, however, proposes a twelve-vessel physiological model that is much more elaborate in terms of theory); Five Phases ideas are completely absent from manuscript accounts of the vessels. In addition, acupuncture is not mentioned. It is generally accepted that the Mawangdui vessel theory texts represent an earlier stage in the development of the theory and practice of acupuncture that is described in the *Huang Di neijing* and that cauterization preceded acupuncture as the therapeutic application of vessel theory.[156]

Third, there are Mawangdui texts on macrobiotic hygiene, known in received sources as *yang sheng* 養生 (nurturing life), with detailed information on dietetics, breath cultivation, exercise, and sex. These practices played a role in regular personal hygiene for the purpose of increasing vitality and extending life. Since human life depended entirely on the condition of the individual's *qi* (vapor), hygiene was essentially vapor cultivation. Two bamboo-strip manuscripts from Zhangjiashan 張家山 tomb 247, in Jiangling, Hubei (burial dated ca. mid-second century B.C.), entitled *Maishu* 脈 書 (Vessel book) and *Yinshu* 引書 (Pulling book; *daoyin* 導引 "guiding and pulling" refers to the hygienic exercise tradition), add to our knowledge of late Warring States macrobiotic hygiene. Together with the Mawangdui texts they provide new evidence of vessel theory. On the testimony of the *Huang Di neijing* it has been thought that vessel theory originally developed within the context of pathological theories, the system of vessels containing vapor serving as the basis for medical diagnosis and treatment. The Mawangdui and Zhangjiashan texts indicate that vessel theory may have developed first in connection with hygienic theories and that it was then applied to pathology.[157]

Vessel theory was the key to the new Warring States conception of the body, its health, and its ailments. Like *qi* (vapor), *mai* as the name for vessels

---

[156] See Harper, *Early Chinese Medical Literature*, pp. 84–94.

[157] On *Maishu* and *Yinshu*, see Harper, *Early Chinese Medical Literature*, pp. 30–33. *Maishu* is transcribed in *Wenwu* 1989.7: 72–4; *Yinshu* is transcribed in *Wenwu* 1990.10: 82–6 (reproductions of the original manuscripts have not been published).

in the body that carry both blood and vapor is first attested to in fourth century B.C. sources. Blood vessels were the original referent of *mai*, as indicated by the *Zuo zhuan* description of an excited horse with "ridges of swollen vessels bulging" and an analogy in the *Guanzi* that describes water as "the blood and vapor of the Earth – like what flows through the muscles and vessels."[158] The conception of the *mai* and their contents continued to acquire new meaning between the fourth and first centuries B.C., culminating in the *Huang Di neijing* idea of *jingmai* 經脈 (conduit vessels). The eleven vessels described in the Mawangdui vessel theory texts are definitely not a representation of the vascular system; while they contain blood as well as vapor, vapor is more important in terms of theory. Unlike the conduit vessels of the *Huang Di neijing* that are linked in an interconnected circulatory system that includes internal organs, the eleven vessels in the Mawangdui texts constitute separate channels for vapor in the body; cauterization applied to a vessel affects the vapor in that vessel. One text offers a basic differentiation between yang vessels that contain the vapor of Heaven and yin vessels that contain the vapor of Earth and that are the "vessels of death" (meaning that ailments associated with yin vessels are likely to be fatal).[159]

There were other physiological ideas. A passage in the Zhangjiashan *Maishu* identifies the six constituents of the body that each perform an essential function: bone is the "pillar" supporting the body, muscle is the binding, blood moistens, vessels provide channels through the body, flesh is the "attachment" that gives the body mass, and vapor is the "exhalation" that vitalizes it.[160] However, even in the excavated manuscripts it is evident that the theoretical focus is on vapor and the vessels that contain it. By the time of the *Huang Di neijing*, the vessels were regarded as the essential structure of the body, and any ideas about other body constituents were subsumed by vessel theory; physiological theory was vessel theory.

While vessel theory in its early stage of development was not tied to yin–yang and Five Phases concepts, its subsequent success had much to do with the parallel growth of correlative cosmology. Once yin–yang and Five Phases theories provided the basis for a coherent understanding of all phenomena, vessel theory facilitated the incorporation of correlative cosmology into medicine by providing an ideal schematic representation that allowed the broad application of yin–yang and Five Phases theories to the human

---

[158] *Zuo zhuan*, 14 (Xi 15), 4b (Legge, *The Ch'un Ts'ew with the Tso Chuen*, pp. 167–8). *Guanzi* (Sibu beiyao ed.), 14 ("Shuidi"), 1a. Graham, *Disputers of the Tao*, p. 356, argues convincingly that the *Guanzi* essay predates the crystallization of yin–yang and Five Phases theories in the third century B.C.

[159] See Harper, *Early Chinese Medical Literature*, pp. 82–90. The text that speaks of yin vessels as the vessels of death is assigned the title *Yin-yang mai sihou*. See *Mawangdui Han mu boshu*, vol. 4, p. 21; and Harper, *Early Chinese Medical Literature*, pp. 219–20.

[160] *Wenwu* 1989.7: 74; translated in Harper, *Early Chinese Medical Literature*, p. 80.

organism. The movement of vapor in the vessels resonated with the cycles of vapor in the cosmos. The body was not simply fashioned in the image of the cosmos – its various functions were synchronized concretely with the operation of the cosmos. This was precisely how Chunyu Yi envisioned the invention of the "model of the vessels" (*maifa* 脈法) by ancient sages: "They differentiated the vessels in man and named each one. Matching with Heaven and Earth, [the vessels] combine in man to form a trinity."[161] Despite Chunyu Yi's belief that vessel theory was yet another example of antique cosmological wisdom (according to the *Yi jing*, the hexagrams were also invented by ancient sages as a model of the cosmos), the Mawangdui vessel theory texts allow us to delineate an intermediate stage between the early, simpler idea of the vessels and the *Huang Di neijing* theory, which incorporates both yin–yang and Five Phases theories.[162]

Vessel theory redefined health and illness by making each dependent on the condition of vapor. One third century B.C. definition of health was the maintenance of a constant supply of free-flowing blood and vapor in the vessels. Thus, in the Mawangdui hygiene text *Shi wen* (Ten questions), the flood hero Yu is taught that "when blood and vapor ought to move yet do not move, this is called the calamity of blockage"; that is, stagnation in the vessels causes infirmity.[163] The Mawangdui vessel theory texts and the *Huang Di neijing* understand illness as a physiological dysfunction of the vapor in the vessels; therapy corrects the dysfunction and restores the organism to its original harmonious condition, thereby eliminating the signs of illness. There was a difficulty, however, in the fact that the conception of illness prior to vessel theory attributed illness to agents or pathogens that sicken their victims. Demons or pathogens of a more naturalistic origin were alike in being the entities that caused certain nameable ailments; therapy cured the ailments by eliminating the entities that caused them. From the standpoint of vessel theory, such ailments were no longer the primary noso-logical data, but were merely manifestations of the deeper dysfunction within the system of vessels. Moreover, long-standing medical treatments for these ailments were nugatory because they were not designed to correct the vapor in the vessels.

Stated in terms of modern research in the history of medicine, the con-flict that arose in late Warring States medicine was between an ontological explanation of illness (which holds that ailments have an existence of their own) and a physiological explanation, vessel theory being the Chinese coun-terpart to humoral pathology and other types of physiological explanation in

---

[161] *Shi ji*, 105, p. 2813.
[162] The sages' invention of hexagrams is described in *Yi jing*, 9 ("Shuo gua"), 1b.
[163] *Mawangdui Han mu boshu*, vol. 4, pp. 149–50; Harper, *Early Chinese Medical Literature*, pp. 404–5.

Western medicine.[164] The Mawangdui medical manuscripts bear witness to the coexistence of both ontological and physiological explanations in the third and second centuries B.C., with *Wushier bingfang* being the chief representative of the former and the vessel theory texts representing the latter. The ailment *tui* 癩 (inguinal swelling; referring to various kinds of swelling in the inguinal region, including hernias) provides a convenient example. The majority of recipes in *Wushier bingfang* attribute inguinal swelling to demonic agents who are to be exorcised. Wind and vapor as pathogens are also involved (the ontological nature of vapor-caused illness is related to Physician He's six vapors of Heaven, each of which causes specific categories of ailments when they are excessive). One recipe concludes by offering an alternative to the treatment in the recipe proper, stating that inguinal swelling can be treated by "cauterizing the Great Yin 太陰 and Great Yang 太陽" vessels. As the only reference to vessel theory and vessel cauterization in *Wushier bingfang*, its inclusion represents acknowledgment of vessel theory. However, in one of the vessel theory texts inguinal swelling is classified as an ailment associated with dysfunction in the Ceasing Yin 厥陰 vessel.[165]

The Mawangdui texts show that in the third and second centuries B.C., the exponents of vessel theory were still in the process of justifying the new physiological explanation of illness, which required changing older ontological ideas and reclassifying ailments in accordance with vessel theory. The *Huang Di neijing* is the prime evidence of the remarkable success of vessel theory pathology by the first century B.C. However, despite the privileged place accorded to both vessel theory and the physiological explanation of illness in the *Huang Di neijing*, ontological ideas were never supplanted in later Chinese medicine. In medieval recipe manuals and *materia medica*, ailments continued to be treated as localized entities that drugs and other therapies could control. As in *Wushier bingfang*, demonic illness and magical treatment remained part of the medicine practiced by physicians, demonic agents being comparable to the other entities responsible for illness.

The evidence of a Warring States medical tradition of macrobiotic hygiene comes primarily from Mawangdui and Zhangjiashan manuscripts. *Yinshu* opens with a maxim on the "way of Pengzu 彭祖," the paragon of longevity in late fourth and third century B.C. received literature, followed by a description of the daily hygienic routine appropriate for each season of the year. For example, in spring:

---

[164] On the ontological and physiological explanations of illness in Western medicine, see R. Hudson, "Concepts of Disease in the West," in *The Cambridge World History of Human Disease*, ed. K. Kiple (Cambridge University Press, 1993), pp. 45–6; and Paul Unschuld, "History of Chinese Medicine," in ibid., pp. 21–2 (Unschuld uses the term "functional" in place of physiological).

[165] *Mawangdui Han mu boshu*, vol. 4, p. 52; Harper, *Early Chinese Medical Literature*, pp. 69–71, 267.

After rising in the morning, eliminate water [urinate], scrub [the hands], rinse [the mouth], wash the teeth, and knock [the teeth]; unfasten the hair, stroll to the lower end of the hall to meet the purest of dew and to receive the essence of Heaven [practice breath cultivation], and drink one cup of water – these are the means to increase accord. Enter the palace [engage in sexual intercourse] from evening until greater midnight; increasing it injures vapor.[166]

What mattered most in hygiene was to nurture life (*yangsheng*) through activities that bolstered somatic harmony and to avoid activities that damaged the condition of the body's vapor (like untimely sexual intercourse). The chief clientele for macrobiotic hygiene were elite men or, as stated in *Maishu*, "those who ride in carriages and eat meat." The division between elite and nonelite in society is the point of a passage at the end of *Yinshu* that distinguishes between the noble and the ignoble. Noble people (*gui ren* 貴人) practice the techniques of breath cultivation to maintain the proper balance of vapor and thus avoid illness; ignoble people (*jian ren* 賤人), because they must engage in strenuous labor and are ignorant (they do not even know about the breathing techniques!), are prone to sickness and death.[167]

The Mawangdui and Zhangjiashan texts represent the baseline of hygiene taught by physicians like Wen Zhi, whose instruction of King Wei concludes with discussion of "eating vapor" (*shi qi* 食氣; i.e., breath cultivation). In addition to writings on breath cultivation, the Mawangdui texts include the earliest examples of sex manuals, dietetic recipe manuals, and an illustrated chart of *daoyin* 導引 (guiding and pulling) exercises (Fig. 12.10); the Zhangjiashan *Yinshu* provides a lengthy written account of similar hygienic exercises. The earliest received literature on macrobiotic hygiene dates to the end of the Han and later, and many of the practices described in the Mawangdui and Zhangjiashan texts were previously believed to have originated in the intellectual and spiritual syncretism of the Han period. We now know that the essential elements of macrobiotic hygiene were already articulated in Warring States medicine.[168]

Care of the body and physio-spiritual cultivation became important philosophical issues in the fourth century B.C. The *Guanzi* essay "Neiye" 內業 (Inward training) is the oldest received writing on the subject of the cultivation of vapor and meditation techniques. The essay was probably composed at the Jixia Academy in Qi in the late fourth century B.C. (around the time when Wen Zhi was active), and the influence of medical macrobiotic hygiene

---

[166] *Wenwu* 1990.10: 82; translated in full in Harper, *Early Chinese Medical Literature*, pp. 110–11.

[167] *Wenwu* 1989.7: 74; *Wenwu* 1990.10: 86.

[168] See Harper, *Early Chinese Medical Literature*, pp. 409–10 and 119–42; and Donald Harper, "The Sexual Arts of Ancient China as Described in a Manuscript of the Second Century B.C.," *HJAS* 47 (1987): 539–60, 580–1.

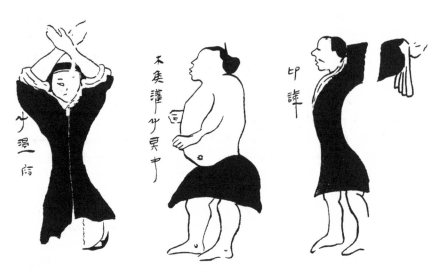

Figure 12.10. *Daoyin tu*. After Fu Juyou and Cheng Songchang, *Mawangdui Han mu wenwu* (Changsha: Hunan, 1992), p. 150. Drawing by Xu Datong.

is apparent.[169] A dodecagonal block of jade inscribed with a rhymed teaching entitled *xingqi* 行氣 (circulating vapor) – thought to be from the late fourth or early third century B.C. – also bears witness to medical hygiene at roughly the same time. The jade inscription describes the stages of breath cultivation from first swallowing the vapor to completion:

Swallow, then it travels; traveling, it extends; extending, it descends; descending, it stabilizes; stabilizing, it solidifies; solidifying, it sprouts; sprouting, it grows; growing, it returns; returning, it is Heaven.[170]

A similar cycle of downward movement of vapor internal regeneration, and final upward return is described in *Yinshu* in these terms: "Make a circuit in the vessels and follow along the skin's webbed pattern to benefit the heels and head."[171]

Passages in the *Zhuangzi* and *Laozi* also treat of macrobiotic hygiene in combination with meditative practices. However, the *Zhuangzi* ridicules people who emulate Pengzu and devote themselves to hygienic regimens in

---

[169] *Guanzi*, 16 ("Neiye"), 1a–6b. On the date and contents of the "Neiye," see Harper, *Early Chinese Medical Literature*, pp. 119–20, and Graham, *Disputers of the Tao*, pp. 100–105.

[170] The translation is based on the transcription and interpretation by Chen Banghuai, "Zhanguo Xingqi yuming kaoshi," *Guwenzi yanjiu* 7 (1982): 187–93; cf. Harper, *Early Chinese Medical Literature*, pp. 125–6.

[171] *Wenwu*, 1990.10: 85.

the hope of extending their lifespan.[172] The *Laozi* makes use of a multivalent, metaphoric vocabulary that includes macrobiotic cultivation within its range of reference. Several of the metaphors occur in the Mawangdui and Zhangjiashan texts, but they contain a much richer metaphorical vocabulary of their own that is not derived from the *Laozi*.[173] Now that we have recovered the first examples of medical literature on macrobiotic hygiene from the late Warring States to early Han periods, the conventional wisdom that traces Warring States macrobiotic hygiene to beliefs and practices broadly termed Daoist must be revised. Future research will clarify the cross-fertilization between macrobiotic hygiene in Warring States medicine and the macrobiotic ideas of certain masters of philosophy.

A similar caveat applies to the relation between medical macrobiotic hygiene and the *xian* 仙 cult. The formation of the *xian* cult in the late third century B.C. remains unclear, but eremitism, shamanic religion, and ideas about flight to spirit paradises each played a role, as did new ideas about a drug of deathlessness and alchemical elixirs. The goal of transcendence and immortality in the *xian* cult was based in part on prior ideas about longevity in macrobiotic hygiene, but the medical tradition did not promise immortality. Rather than adopt Pengzu, the *xian* cult attributed its macrobiotic traditions to a new pair of legendary adepts, Chisongzi 赤松子 and Wangzi Qiao 王子喬.[174]

The popularity of the *xian* cult during the second and first centuries B.C. led the Han elite to associate macrobiotic hygiene with *xian* ideas; hence the medical division of the *Han shu* bibliographic treatise lists books on macrobiotic hygiene in a section named "Shenxian" 神僊 (Divine transcendence).[175] One passage in the Mawangdui text *Shiwen* does speak of not dying and refers to *xingjie* 形解, an idea associated with the *xian* cult in the *Shi ji*. In *Shiwen*, *xingjie* appears to mean "release of the physical form"; that is, after long cultivation the practitioner's body becomes spirit-like and he is no longer bound to mundane existence. It is not clear whether the term is borrowed from the *xian* cult or vice versa, nor is it clear what *xingjie* meant in the early *xian* cult. By the first to second centuries A.D. it was assumed that

---

[172] *Zhuangzi*, 1 ("Xiaoyao you"), 3a–b, and 6 ("Keyi"), 1a; cf. Harper, *Early Chinese Medical Literature*, pp. 113–15.

[173] See Harper, *Early Chinese Medical Literature*, pp. 127–9; and Donald Harper, "*Laozi* V and Warring States Macrobiotic Hygiene," *EC* 20 (1995): 381–91.

[174] See Harper, *Early Chinese Medical Literature*, pp. 114–15. The relation between Daoism and the *xian* cult is also unclear. A. C. Graham, *Chuang Tzu: The Seven Inner Chapters and Other Writings from the Book of Chuang-tzu* (London: Allen & Unwin, 1981), p. 176, notes that in the whole of the *Zhuangzi* (which contains a variety of material down to the second century B.C.), there are only two passages concerning the pursuit of immortality. For discussion of the *xian* cult, see Needham, *Science and Civilisation in China. Vol. 5: Chemistry and Chemical Technology, Part 2: Spagyrical Discovery and Invention: Magisteries of Gold and Immortality* (Cambridge University Press, 1974), pp. 93–113.

[175] *Han shu*, 30, pp. 1779–80.

xingjie was synonymous with *shijie* 尸解 (often translated "release from the corpse"), a term first attested in the first century for the emergence of the immortal *xian* being from the slough of the physical body. There is no evidence in the Mawangdui and Zhangjiashan macrobiotic hygiene texts for this idea of an immortal being, nor is there a hint of other influence from the *xian* cult. The excavated texts represent the macrobiotic hygiene of third and early second century B.C. medicine and are unaffected by the Han mingling of macrobiotic and *xian* ideas.[176]

CONCLUSION

Our knowledge of the history of ideas and of religions in the ancient civilizations of the world is shaped primarily by writings that survived down the centuries, their survival having been due to conscious efforts at preservation and frequently to chance. The received texts of the masters of philosophy have constituted the main evidence of the intense intellectual and spiritual ferment of the Warring States period. To be sure, the influence of yin–yang and Five Phases theories on philosophy in the third century B.C. has been well known, and astrologers and physicians (to name just two categories among the Warring States natural experts and occultists) have not gone unnoticed. However, the scantness of evidence has made it difficult to ascertain the characteristics of Warring States natural philosophy and occult thought and to determine their place in the whole of Warring States thought. The current state of our knowledge is largely the result of the archaeological discovery of texts and artifacts related to natural philosophy and occult thought; we may be certain that future archaeological discoveries will add to our knowledge.

Among the Warring States traditions of astrology, divination, and medicine we have discussed – each of which played a role in the gradual formulation of correlative cosmology – two general characteristics are noteworthy. First, the development of naturalistic theories (yin–yang and Five Phases theories finally having become dominant) did not supplant magico-religious ideas. The Shuihudi almanacs and Mawangdui astrological texts provide ample evidence of how the two ways of thinking meshed; Mawangdui medical texts intersperse magical procedures without prejudice among the various types of effective medical treatment. There were significant changes in magico-religious belief and practice as new, naturalistic theories appeared, but the new theories did not establish an absolute division between a natu-

[176] *Mawangdui Han mu boshu*, vol. 4, p, 148; Harper, *Early Chinese Medical Literature*, pp. 124–5 and 398–9.

ralistic understanding of phenomena on the one hand and an occult understanding on the other.

Second, the natural experts and occultists shared with the masters of philosophy the tradition of transmitting knowledge in texts. The exact relationship between natural experts, occultists, and philosophers in Warring States society remains unclear; the general lack of interest in natural philosophy on the part of the masters of philosophy prior to the third century B.C. suggests that they focused their attention elsewhere. Whatever the differences between natural experts, occultists, and philosophers might have been, the textual traditions in which they all participated constituted a common bond. The writings of the Warring States natural philosophers and occultists were the basis for lineages of practice within the several fields of knowledge (the function of texts among the masters of philosophy was similar), and the writings also facilitated the exchange of ideas across fields. Moreover, the writings spread among the literate elite, who were targeted as an audience for the technical literature of natural philosophy and occult thought. While one must not discount the influence of orally transmitted knowledge, the influence of transmitted texts was surely greater.

In view of the prominent role played by texts in the Warring States period, archaeological discoveries of examples of the technical literature of Warring States natural philosophy and occult thought are of signal importance. The Baoshan divination record, the Shuihudi almanacs, and other relevant texts chart the growth of ideas across the fourth and third centuries B.C. The texts bear witness to an intellectual tradition that flourished alongside the speculations of the masters of philosophy. In addition to gaining a more precise view of the intellectual temperament of the Warring States period, we gain from the texts concrete evidence of the complex mingling of scientific and magico-religious traditions in the Warring States period.

CHAPTER THIRTEEN

THE NORTHERN FRONTIER IN PRE-IMPERIAL CHINA

Nicola Di Cosmo

The northern frontier of China has long been recognized as something more than a simple line separating natural zones, political entities, or ethnic groups.* This frontier has been represented as the birthplace of independent cultures and the habitat of peoples whose lifestyle, economic activities, social customs, and religious beliefs became, from the Bronze Age onward, gradually but increasingly distant from the civilization of the Central Plain. This distinct cultural region, often called the "Northern Zone" of China, comprises the interlocking desert, steppe, and forest regions from Heilongjiang and Jilin in the east to Xinjiang in the west.[1] The frontier between China and the north has also been envisaged as a bundle of routes and avenues of communications through which peoples, ideas, goods, and faiths flowed incessantly between West and East. In economic terms, it provided the Chinese with a source of foreign goods as well as a market for domestic production.

The process by which the northern frontier acquired these qualifications was a long one. While its complexities cannot be captured in a single image, the Great Wall – this symbolic and material line that came into existence as

* I wish to acknowledge funding received from the Milton Fund, which has made possible the collection of research material and a fact-finding trip to Xinjiang. Among the colleagues that have made suggestions and helped me with gathering sources, I wish to thank Robert Bagley, Emma Bunker, Louisa G. Fitzgerald Huber, Fred Hiebert, Jessica Rawson, and the archaeologists from Xinjiang: Wang Binghua, Wang Ping, Idris from the Institute of Archaeology, Dr. Zhao from the Society for Altaic Studies (Altai City), and the Ili Cultural Bureau. A special thanks to my friend Cui Yanhu for his help in organizing my research in Xinjiang, and to Yangjin Pak for his knowledgeable assistance. All mistakes are, of course, my own.
[1] For uses and definitions of the term "Northern Zone," see Lin Yün, "A Reexamination of the Relationship Between Bronzes of the Shang Culture and of the Northern Zone," in *Studies of Shang Archaeology*, ed. K. C. Chang (New Haven, Conn.: Yale University Press, 1986), pp. 237–73. See too William Watson, *Cultural Frontiers in Ancient East Asia* (Edinburgh: Edinburgh University Press, 1971), p. 63; idem, *Inner Asia and China in the Pre-Han Period* (London: School of Oriental and African Studies, 1969), p. 16.

a unified system of fortifications with the establishment of the Qin empire in 221 B.C. – can be seen as the culmination of a long process of cultural differentiation that embraces several aspects.

The first concerns the frontier's material culture. As Neolithic communities learned to use and transform their territory, different applications of economic potential and intellectual abilities created cultural, social, and economic differences that are visible through the relics of their civilizations. It was during the Bronze Age that a distinct northern culture emerged. During the latter part of the Shang dynasty (ca. 1200–1050 B.C.), northern China already featured a clearly discernible cultural complex undeniably distinct from that of the Central Plain (Zhongyuan 中原). This Northern Complex cannot be regarded as a single culture; rather different communities shared a similar inventory of bronze objects across a wide area. This inventory allows us to establish broad connections with bronze civilizations of North Asia, West Asia, and China.

Second, human adaptation to an environment more arid than that of the lower Yellow River and Wei 渭 River valleys, such as that of Inner Mongolia and Gansu, historically emphasized animal breeding over farming technology. Across the northern frontier a steady transition from an agriculture-based to a pastoral-based economy took place beginning in the late second millennium B.C. While hunting, fishing, and farming remained actively pursued, animal remains indicate the gradual expansion of domesticated cattle, sheep, and horses. Domesticated animals were not new, but larger herds demanded new ways of management. Beginning in about the eighth century B.C., throughout Inner Asia horse-riding pastoral communities appear, giving origin to warrior societies. Known by the Greeks as Scythians in the western end of Asia, their cultural expansion was by no means limited to the Pontic steppe to the north of the Black Sea, but extended across the Eurasian steppe belt. Equestrian pastoral peoples, who may be broadly defined as "early nomads," were present in northern China and can be regarded as cultural forerunners of the Xiongnu 匈奴, the Huns, and the later Turco-Mongol nomads. The use of the horse in war became widespread in northern China well before it was adopted by the Chinese. Finally, in literary records frontier peoples came to represent a sort of alter ego that contributed, by providing a contrasting image, to the formation of China's cultural identity.

The relationship between China and the nomads appears to have been of secondary importance to Chinese history until it exploded into one of its most critical issues, during the Qin–Han period. The emergence of the Xiongnu empire, in 209 B.C., struck the newly born Chinese empire with unprecedented strength, forcing upon it the realization that the north had become a major antagonist, politically, militarily, and culturally. Because of this, scholars have had great difficulties explaining the origin of the Xiongnu and related nomadic cultures in northern China.

Countless efforts to identify some of the alien peoples (Xianyun 獫狁, Rong 戎, Qiang 羌, and Di 狄 in particular) that figure prominently in pre-Han written records with pastoral nomadic cultures have so far failed to yield firm results. Pastoral nomads become historically identifiable only during the late Warring States period. This has created the impression that their sudden appearance on the stage of Chinese history was a product of the creation of a unified Chinese state. However, archaeological evidence has now shown that the presence of nomadic pastoralists on the northern frontier of China was by no means a sudden phenomenon and that the genesis of distinct northern cultures can be traced back to the Shang period, if not earlier.

The interface between China and the Northern Zone was a dynamic factor that featured prominently in their respective histories. From the Central Plain the geographical configuration and natural topography of the north could be modified by building roads and fortifications, by subjugating native peoples, and by establishing settlements. On the other side, northern peoples formed independent political entities that entered Chinese history in their own right as military opponents, political allies, and trading partners, stimulating innovations and cultural exchanges. However, written sources for this historical phenomenon are hazy at best. As northern peoples emerge from prehistorical obscurity, their history can be tentatively reconstructed only through succinct mentions of battles and alliances that supply more questions than answers. Recently, archaeological work has provided a referential framework that allows us to trace the cultural progress of the Northern Zone from the Shang through the Warring States periods. Though the temptation to cloak archaeological finds in historical garb should be avoided, and though the asymmetry between textual and material records leaves room for wide differences of interpretations, the contours of this broad phenomenon have become less blurred.

This chapter, however, cannot be a history of contacts between China and Central Asia over two millennia; neither can it say anything definitive about the evolution of ancient nomadic cultures in today's northern China. Rather, it aims to provide a broad narrative of the northern frontier with a particular question in mind: what was the genesis of the Xiongnu steppe empire as a historical phenomenon? This question, so fundamental for the history of China, is the leading issue that this chapter attempts to address.

PERIODIZATION OF THE NORTHERN ZONE CULTURES

The appearance of a distinct Xiongnu culture in northern China is commonly dated to the end of the fourth century B.C. Western scholars have often attributed it to patterns of continental migrations of Central Asian pastoral nomads, at times even identified linguistically as Altaic or Indo-European. By contrast, the traditional Chinese ethnogenealogy of the Xiongnu, traceable back to the *Shi ji*, refers to them as the descendants of ancient northern peoples.[2] Archaeological studies in China have by and large emphasized continuity and gradual evolution over sudden ruptures and influences from Central Asia, and Chinese scholars insist that the origin and evolution of the Xiongnu people be placed within the context of the autochthonous formation of pastoral cultures in northern China. Nevertheless, though detailed evidence is still wanting, connections between the Northern Zone and South Siberia, in particular the Karasuk and Tagar cultures, are beyond doubt, and it is safe to say that the evolution of pastoral cultures in northern China, while displaying an original and distinctive history, was not an isolated phenomenon. The Northern Zone cultural complex was an active participant in the continent-wide evolution of a North Eurasian pastoral nomadic culture whose fundamental character and premises it shared with other complexes across the Eurasian steppe and forest regions. Its position within this process is, however, not clear. Given the uncertainty of the connections, caution requires us to limit the scope of this study to the Sino-Mongolian frontier zone (Shanxi, Shaanxi, Hebei, northern Henan, and Inner Mongolia), flanked by northeastern (Liaoning and Heilongjiang) and northwestern extensions (Gansu, Ningxia, parts of Qinghai and Xinjiang). Within this broad Northern Zone, archaeological remains reveal the existence of regional and local features according to period and territorial distribution.

Various efforts have been directed at showing the internal coherence of the evolution of the Northern Zone, or "Ordos," culture. Excavations carried out in Inner Mongolia and adjacent areas have shown that the presence of pastoralists in the Northern Zone can be dated to the Shang period and can be divided into three stages of development: Bronze Age (Shang, Western Zhou, and Spring and Autumn periods); Early Iron Age (Warring States period); Iron Age (Former and Latter Han). Stages prior to the late Warring States period are referred to, by Chinese scholars, as early or proto-Xiongnu

---

[2] *Shi ji*, 110 (Beijing: Zhonghua shuju, 1985 [1959]), pp. 2879–82. This "genealogy" was rejected by both Bernhard Karlgren, "Some Weapons and Tools of the Yin Dynasty," *BMFEA*, 17 (1945): 141; and Otto Maenchen-Helfen, "Archaistic Names of the Hiung-nu," *Central Asiatic Journal* 6 (1961): 248–61.

cultures.[3] An alternative four-phase periodization, based on bronze typology, includes a first phase, the late Shang and early Western Zhou (thirteenth to ninth centuries B.C.), with bronzes characterized by dagger and knife terminals in the shape of animal and bird heads; a second phase, from the late Western Zhou to the mid-Spring and Autumn period (ninth to sixth centuries B.C.), represented by the bronzes of the Upper Xiajiadian 夏家店 culture; a third phase, from the late Spring and Autumn to the end of the Warring States (sixth to third century B.C.), characterized by rectangular bronze plaques with animal designs in relief or openwork, and by animal figures in the round; and a fourth phase, during the Former and Later Han dynasties, also featuring rectangular belt ornaments with animal motifs in openwork.[4]

This first periodization compresses approximately ten centuries (1500–500 B.C.) within the same category of "Bronze Age," thus obscuring the variety and complexity of socioeconomic, technological, and cultural changes that took place in the Northern Zone during that period. Moreover, both periodizations tend to convey the impression that such a development was wholly endogenous and to discard the extensive contacts between the Northern Zone and Central Asia as a powerful stimulus to change and development. Finally, these periodizations emphasize the material culture almost exclusively, with socioeconomic and historical considerations playing only ancillary roles. An approach that combines social and economic considerations and information drawn from historical records may provide a fuller appreciation of cultural progress in the Northern Zone. This progress can be divided into four periods.

The Second Millenium B.C.

A frontier, understood as a geographical area penetrated by cultures with different characteristics and cutting across various political and social units, can be discerned prior to and during the Shang dynasty, as some cultures of the Northern Zone are believed to have already been pastoral, though probably not yet engaged in pastoral nomadism, that is, a socioeconomic system based on a fixed migratory cycle and overwhelmingly dependent on animal products. More likely, the earliest representatives of the Northern Zone complex were mixed communities of shepherds and farmers that also practiced extensive hunting. At this early stage the frontier appears to have been a broad

[3] Tian Guangjin, "Jinnianlai Nei Menggu diqu de Xiongnu kaogu," *Kaogu xuebao* 1983.1: 7–24; idem, "Taohongbala de Xiongnu mu," *Kaogu xuebao* 1976.1: 131.
[4] Wu En, "Woguo beifang gudai dongwu wenshi," *Kaogu xuebao* 1990.4: 409–37. See also Emma Bunker, "Ancient Ordos Bronzes," in *Ancient Chinese and Ordos Bronzes*, ed. Jassica Rawson and Emma Bunker (Hong Kong: Museum of Art, 1990), pp. 291–307.

belt of cultural transition between the Shang civilization and the bronze cultures of Central Asia and South Siberia. Though northern peoples displayed different cultural traits, such as distinct ceramic objects, burial customs, habitations, and economic structures, certain characteristic elements, such as bronze weapons, became widely adopted throughout the Northern Zone, and this common metallurgical culture was different and independent from that of the Central Plain. The date of 1000 B.C. seems a suitable chronological marker to end this phase. The Zhou conquest caused a political realignment of the Central Plain, which affected foreign relations. The Zhou house had a very different relationship with some of the earlier enemies of the Shang; for instance, they intermarried with the Jiang 姜 clan, probably related to the Qiang.[5] Moreover, the early Zhou kings achieved a period of peace on the borders.

Western Zhou to Early Spring and Autumn (ca. 1000–650 B.C.)

During the Western Zhou, the appearance of a northeastern cultural complex characterized by advanced metallurgical techniques marked an expansion of the Northern Zone, in particular toward the east (Heilongjiang, Jilin, Liaoning). The Western Zhou court carried out intense political and military activities in the north, east, and west against peoples whose archaeological identification is still debated. Among the multitude of alien peoples, at times friendly and more often hostile, the funerary inventories are consistent with the emergence of aristocratic warrior elites and a broad productive basis, whose main force was represented by increasingly more specialized pastoralists.

Mid-Spring and Autumn to Early Warring States (ca. 650–350 B.C.)

A third phase of the history of the northern frontier can be dated from the middle or late seventh century to the mid-fourth century. This period witnessed the appearance of fully developed steppe pastoral nomads who may be regarded as the cultural ancestors of the Xiongnu and can be termed "early nomadic." Early nomadic cultures spread in the Eurasian steppe beginning from the eighth century B.C. and lasted through the third century. It is interesting that approximately the same chronology applies to the Scythians, known from Herodotus's *Histories* as the powerful nomadic warriors of the North Pontic steppe, and to the eastern steppe cultures variously termed

---

[5] On the relationship between Jiang and Zhou see Wang Zhonghan, ed., *Zhongguo minzu shi* (Beijing: Zhongguo shehui kexue, 1994), p. 125.

Altaic Scythian,[6] Scytho-Siberian, or Saka. Even though there were fundamental ways in which nomadic groups over such a vast territory differed, the terms "Scythian" and "Scythic" have been widely adopted to describe a special phase that followed the widespread diffusion of mounted nomadism, characterized by the presence of special weapons, horse gear, and animal art in the form of metal plaques. Archaeologists have used the term "Scythic continuum" in a broad cultural sense to indicate the early nomadic cultures of the Eurasian steppe.[7]

The term "Scythic" draws attention to the fact that there are elements – shapes of weapons, vessels, and ornaments, as well as lifestyle – common to both the eastern and the western ends of the Eurasian steppe region. However, the extension and variety of sites across Asia makes Scythian and Scythic terms too broad to be viable, and the more neutral "early nomadic" is preferable, since the cultures of the Northern Zone cannot be directly associated with either the historical Scythians or any specific archaeological culture defined as Saka or Scytho-Siberian.[8] Mentions of "proto-Xiongnu" cultures should also be avoided to eschew inferences of a close genetic relationship with any *single* group of nomads that would appear centuries later, since no such relationship can be confirmed to date, and since the early nomads of the Northern Zone could just as well be claimed to be the predecessors of other nomadic groups, such as the Dong Hu 東胡, Lin Hu 林 胡, and Wusun 烏孫.

These early nomadic communities achieved a dominant position throughout the Eurasian steppe region, and their metal culture displayed a singular uniformity of features. In the Northern Zone, the transition to pastoral nomadism occurred gradually. The Saka culture in Xinjiang, the Shajing 沙 井 culture in Gansu, the Ordos complex in Inner Mongolia, and the Upper Xiajiadian culture of Liaoning, all point to a transition from mixed agropastoral to predominantly or exclusively pastoral nomadic cultures. From the seventh century onwards, objects related to improved horse management and horse riding, such as the bit, cheekpieces, horse masks, and bell ornaments, became ever more widespread and sophisticated. Iron metallurgy is likely to

---

[6] See, e.g., S. I. Rudenko and N. M. Rudenko, *Iskusstvo skifov Altaia* (Moscow: Gos. muzeia izobrazitel'nikh iskusstv im. A. M. Pushkina, 1949); M. I. Artamanov, "Skifo-sibirskoie iskusstvo tsverinogo stili (osnovniie etapy i napravleniia)," in *Problemy skifskoi arkheologii*, ed. P. D. Liberov and V. I. Guliaev (Moscow: Nauka, 1971), pp. 24–54; and idem, *Sokrovishcha Sakov: Amu-Dar'inskii klad, altaiskie kurgany minusinskie bronzy, sibirskoe zoloto* (Moscow: Iskusstvo, 1973).

[7] William Watson, *Cultural Frontiers in Ancient East Asia*, p. 101; Roman Kenk, *Grabfunde der Skythenzeit aus Tuva, Süd-Sibirien* (Munich: Beck, 1986); and E. A. Novgorodova et al., *Ulangom: Ein skythenzeitliches Gräberfeld in der Mongolei* (Wiesbaden: Harrassowitz, 1982).

[8] For uses of the term "early nomads" for the eastern" steppe people of the Scythian period, see Mikhail P. Gryaznov, *The Ancient Civilization of Southern Siberia* (New York: Cowles, 1969), chapter 3, "The Age of the Early Nomads"; and idem, *Der Großkurgan von Aržan in Tuva, Südsibirien* (Munich: Beck, 1984), pp. 76–7.

have spread in the Northern Zone before its general appearance in the Central Plain, with iron objects found in Xinjiang in the ninth century B.C. and in Inner Mongolia and the northeast by no later than the mid-seventh century B.C.

The changes that were taking place in the north, however, were not immediately noticeable to historians and chroniclers in China. This was due in part to the mode of historical writing itself, not yet mature enough to be concerned with anthropological and ethnographic detail. But it is also possible that the nomads inhabited a "deep" frontier not yet discovered by the people of the Central Plain. The presence of mixed archaeological remains on the borders of China, and the lack of reference to mounted pastoralists in the Chinese sources, probably indicate that alien communities of mixed shepherds and agriculturalists acted as a buffer between the Central Plain and the nomadic lands.

Late Warring States to Qin (ca. 350–209 B.C.)

The fourth period starts in the late Warring States and leads to the foundation of the Xiongnu state in 209 B.C. In 307 B.C. King Wuling of Zhao 趙武靈王, influenced by the nomads, introduced cavalry into his army. The famous debate that accompanied this event provides the first historical information on pastoral nomads – known as Hu 胡 – along the northern borders of China. The reduction of the number of the contending states in China to a few strong ones, and the northward expansion of Qin, Zhao, and Yan 燕, resulted in the assimilation of several peoples, such as the Rong and the Di, within the orbit of the Zhongyuan. This eliminated the protective screen that those people had supplied between China and the unambiguously nomadic, warlike groups further north, who suddenly appear in the Chinese sources beginning at this time.

It is in this phase that China started to develop a knowledge of Inner Asia and a deeper understanding of the surrounding cultures. Even though, during the last phase of the Warring States, Hu nomads and Xiongnu played a relatively minor role in the history of the Central States, nevertheless their presence and activity on the Chinese northern border cannot be denied. The frontier reached its historical definition with the creation of the Great Walls, which separated the northern states of Qin, Zhao, and Yan from the nomads. Wall building was not limited to the northern regions, but the northern walls and fortresses remained and were strengthened after Qin's unification of the realm, whereas fortifications between states disappeared.

Qin continued to expand northward after 221 B.C. The colonization of the Ordos region led by General Meng Tian 蒙恬 in 215 B.C. caused a widespread dislocation of Xiongnu tribesmen from their ancestral land, the ensuing political and economic crisis creating among the Xiongnu the conditions for the rise of a new leadership. This led to the formation of a powerful northern empire, founded by Maodun 冒頓 in 209, just as China was about to plunge into a civil war. When the newly born Han dynasty came to confront the Xiongnu, it found that the balance of power had been reversed. The Xiongnu were able to impose their rule in the north, the Great Wall being declared the frontier between the people "with bows and arrows" and those "with hats and girdles."

THE NORTHERN FRONTIER IN THE SECOND MILLENNIUM B.C.

The Northern Zone Complex: Defining Characteristics

A cultural "complex" with characteristics unquestionably different from those of the Central Plain emerged during the Shang period in the Northern Zone. This term should not suggest a homogeneous culture, but rather a broad area in which different people shared certain common traits, in particular their bronze inventory. This metallurgical tradition typifies the north and marks the cultural boundary with the civilization of the Central Plain. Most characteristic of the Northern Zone complex are bronze weapons, probably indicating that the development of metallurgy was linked to the rise of military elites and to increased warfare – possibly resulting from competition for economic resources. Among the weapons, the most representative are daggers, knives, axes, mirrors, and a "bow-shaped" object.

DAGGERS. Daggers, or "short swords," are characterized for the most part by the integral casting of hilt and double-edged blade and by a relatively narrow and straight hand-guard (Fig. 13.1a). The early types, dated to the middle and late period of the Shang dynasty, display a characteristic curved hilt, often decorated with geometric designs, featuring a terminal in the shape of an animal head, usually a horse, ram, eagle, or ibex. Others have perforated hilts, or straight hilts with grooves ending in a rattle.

KNIVES. Whereas Shang bronze knives normally have short stems inserted into a handle of a different material, all northern-type bronze knives of this period have an integrally cast hilt (Fig. 13.1b). The spine of the knife has an arched shape and is wider than the grip. Between the blade and the grip there is often a small tongue. Pommels come in many shapes; the most characteristic are the mushroom, animal head, and various shapes of rings, or loops. Handles are decorated with geometric motifs similar to those of the daggers.

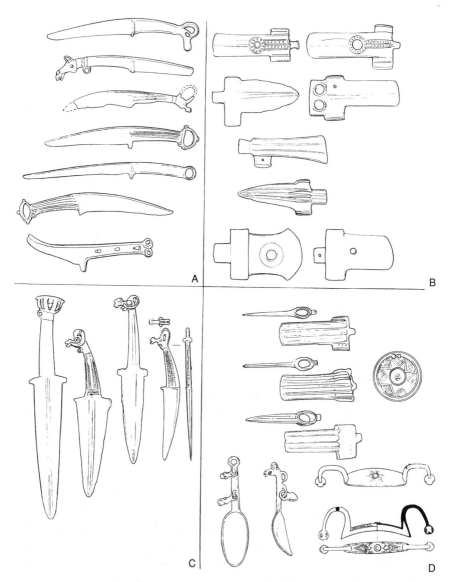

Figure 13.1. Northern Zone bronzes of the second and early first millennium B.C. A: Bronzes of the Karasuk culture, Southern Siberia. B, C, D: Respectively, daggers, knives, and axes of the Northern Zone complex. After: Wu En 烏恩. "Yin zhi Zhou chu de beifang qingtong qi" 殷至周初的北方青銅器, *Kaogu xuebao* 1985.2, figs. 1, 2, 3, 5. Drawings by Li Xiating.

AXES WITH TUBULAR SOCKETS. The axe's blade is typically long and thick, with a relatively narrow cutting edge clearly different from the fan-shaped axe of the Shang. Their main characteristic, however, is a tubular socket set perpendicularly to the blade (Fig. 13.1c and d). In early axes, the socket can be longer than the width of the body. This hafting system is very different from the predominant Shang method of attaching the handle to a protruding flat tang. Tubular axes have been found in Hebei (Chaodaogou 抄道溝, Qinglong 青龍 county), in Shanxi, (Gaohong 高紅, Liulin 柳林 county, and Chujiayu 褚家峪, Shilou 石樓 county), and at Shang sites, such as Dasikong 大司空.[9] In Gaohong two axes were found together with a dagger with a rattle pommel, a spearhead, a helmet, three knives each with a double-ring head, and other small objects.[10]

MIRRORS. Round bronze disks, usually defined as mirrors in Chinese archaeology, are also part of a northern heritage (Fig. 13.1d). Typically they have a smooth surface on one side; on the other, which may carry surface decoration, they have a central knob handle. A Qinghai mirror decorated on the back with a star-shaped design suggests a solar cult, possibly of Central Asian origin. Mirrors found in Anyang tombs, such as those in Fu Hao's 婦好 tomb, have decorative motifs that are not consonant with the artistic vocabulary of the Shang.[11] Other mirrors found in Shang burials in central Shaanxi together with a *ding* 鼎 vessel, curved knives, and gold earrings, suggest associations with non-Chinese cultures.[12] Finally, a mirror has been found in another burial together with two bronze *jue* 爵 vessels with the character Qiang 羌 inscribed on them.[13] This evidence connects the mirror to a distinctive northern culture, and possibly to the Qiang people. Only in the mid-seventh century did the bronze mirror become part of the Chinese native tradition.

"BOW-SHAPED" OBJECT. This curious object is comprised of a slightly bent decorated central bar and curved lateral sections. Various hypotheses have been adduced as to its use (Fig. 13.1d).[14] Found in the Yinxu 殷墟 culture

---

[9] *Kaogu* 1962.12: 644–65; Wu Zhenlu, "Baode xian xin faxian de Yindai qingtong qi," *Wenwu* 1972.4: 62–6; Yang Shaoshun, "Shanxi Liulin xian Gaohong faxian Shangdai tongqi," *Kaogu* 1981.3: 211–12; *Wenwu* 1981.8: 49–53; Ma Dezhi et al., "Yijiuwusan nian Anyang Dasikong cun fajue baogao," *Kaogu xuebao* 1955.9: 25–90.

[10] Yang Shaoshun, "Shanxi Liulin xian Gaohong faxian Shangdai tongqi."

[11] See pp. 194–202 above, "The Tomb of Fu Hao"; Diane M. O'Donoghue, "Reflection and Reception: The Origins of the Mirror in Bronze Age China," *BMFEA* 62 (1990): 5–25.

[12] Yao Shengmin, "Shaanxi Chunhua xian chutu de Shang Zhou qingtongqi," *Kaogu yu wenwu* 1986.5:12–22.

[13] *Wenwu* 1986.11: 7, fig. 11.5.

[14] Karlgren, "Weapons and Tools," p. 112, is probably wrong in considering it a kind of yoke, but right in rejecting the old hypothesis that it was a "banner bell." Max Loehr, "Weapons and Tools from

with end rattles and horse heads, and in the Minusinsk region with a much simpler decoration of knobs, it was probably invented in the Northern Zone and thereafter transmitted to both China and South Siberia.

Other objects also regarded as characteristic of this particular culture are a distinctive type of spoon (Fig. 13.1d) and helmet. The spoons have rings on the handle with attached pendants. The helmets are undecorated, the sides coming down to cover the ears; they have a ring on top and holes on the bottom to the right and left.[15]

ANIMAL STYLE. The term "Animal Style" indicates a decorative style and an artistic tradition shared across the Northern Zone from the thirteenth century onwards. Common both to the Karasuk culture of South Siberia (1200–800 B.C.) and the early nomadic cultures of Central Asia, the style consists of various representations of animals on bronze vessels, weapons, and tools. At this early stage the Animal Style is expressed in the Northern Zone mainly in the form of ornamental animal heads in the round attached to the end of knife handles and dagger hilts.[16]

Geographic Distribution

During the Shang, and in particular the late Shang period, the Northern Zone included the territory of northern Shaanxi, Shanxi, and northern Henan; in the east it reached as far as the Liaodong coast; in the north it reached western Liaoning and Inner Mongolia; and in the west it extended to Gansu, Ningxia, and Xinjiang (Map 13.1). That elements of the bronze culture of the Northern Zone are present as far as Transbaikalia, Mongolia, the Altai region, South Siberia (Minusinsk River basin), and Tuva is evidence of the extraordinary reach of this cultural complex. In recent years the excavation of archaeological sites in North China allows us to identify a number of cultures or cultural features located within the Northern Zone complex.

Anyang, and Siberian Analogies," *American Journal of Archaeology* 53 (1949): 138, relates it to bows and quivers. However, the "bow-shaped" object appears commonly on so-called deer stones – anthropomorphic steles with carvings representing stylized deer – attached to the belt. On this basis, Lin Yün, "A Reexamination," p. 263, suggests that it was used as a "reins-holder" by drivers of horse-drawn chariots and horse drivers. Yet the iconography of the deer stones does not show it in combination with chariots or horses. See also Qin Jianming, "Shang Zhou 'gongxingqi' wei 'qiling' shuo," *Kaogu* 1995.3: 256–8.

[15] A. Kovalev, "'Karasuk-dolche', Hirschsteine und die Nomaden der chinesischen Annalen im Alterum," in *Maoqinggou: Ein eisenzeitliches Gräberfeld in der Ordos-Region (Innere Mongolei)*, ed. Thomas Höllman and Georg W. Kossack (Mainz: Philipp von Zabern, 1992), pp. 60–1.

[16] On the animal style the following works may be consulted: Karl Jettmar, *Art of the Steppes* (New York: Crown, 1967); and Anatoly Martinov, *The Ancient Art of Northern Asia*, trans. and ed. Demitri B. Shimkin and Edith M. Shimkin (Urbana: University of Illinois Press, 1991). On the origin and earliest occurrences of the Animal Style, see Yakov A. Sher, "On the Sources of the Scythian Animal Style," *Arctic Anthropology* 25, 2 (1988): 47–60.

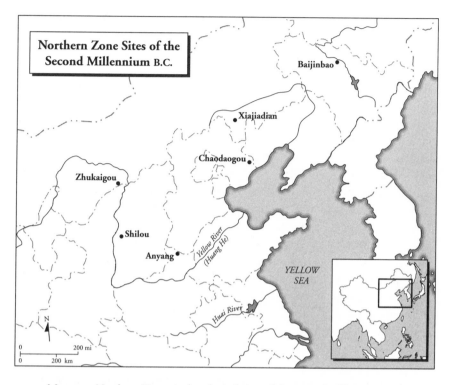

Map 13.1. Northern Zone: Archaeological sites of the second millennium B.C.

These are the Lower Xiajiadian culture, the northern-style bronzes, and Baijinbao 白金寶 (Heilongjiang) culture in the northeast; the Zhukaigou 朱開溝 and Chaodaogou cultures, together with mixed Shang and Northern Zone sites, in the north-central sector; and the Qijia 齊家, Xindian 辛店, and Siwa 寺洼 cultures in the northwestern portion, including present-day Gansu and Ningxia provinces.

LOWER XIAJIADIAN. Approximately contemporary with the last phases of the Zhukaigou culture, but located further east, is the Lower Xiajiadian culture (ca. 2000–1300 B.C.), essentially a pre-Shang culture, though partially overlapping with the early Shang. Lower Xiajiadian sites extend across southeastern Inner Mongolia, Liaoning, and northern Hebei, and reveal a Bronze Age culture at the initial phase of transition toward metalworking. People lived in settlements, the economy of which was firmly agricultural, based on millet. This was supplemented with hunting of deer and stock raising, as shown by remains of sheep, cattle, and, in particular, pigs. Metalwork was limited to small objects, such as rings, knives, and handles. In contrast, stone and bone production attained a high level. The southern limit of the Lower

Xiajiadian culture is located in Hebei (Yixian 易縣 and Laishui 淶水 counties). The whole Beijing region, however, forms a large belt where the Lower Xiajiadian and the Shang cultures met.[17]

NORTHEASTERN BRONZES. Bronzes found in the northeast that are typologically similar to the Northern Zone bronzes attributed to the Shang and early Western Zhou periods have been found mostly in cache and storage pits; they consist primarily of weapons: battle-axes, socketed axes, knives, and daggers. These findings are concentrated in western Liaoning; the eastern part of Liaoning seems to have been marginal to the distribution of northern-type bronzes. In eastern Liaoning, together with knives, socketed axes, battle-axes, and a distinctive type of socketed dagger, only one type of northern-style dagger has been found, with hollow hilt and blade in a single casting. Socketed daggers are not found in the rest of the Northern Zone. The battle-axes with long and narrow sockets and straight blades are similar to those found in Chaodaogou. Unusual items, which nevertheless belong to the same Northern Complex, are a dagger hilt that terminates in the shape of a human head, as well as vessel lids and chariot ornaments. In the northeast, as in the rest of the Northern Zone, bronzes are not associated with pottery.[18]

ZHUKAIGOU. The importance of the Zhukaigou culture lies in its role as the reputed progenitor of the "Ordos bronze culture" and, by extension, as the first Northern Zone culture. It extended to northern and central Inner Mongolia, northern Shaanxi, and northern Shanxi, with the Ordos region at its center.[19] Bronze objects dated to the last period of its existence (ca. 1500 B.C.) have been excavated. These point to the indigenous production of typical Northern Zone items, such as bronze daggers, together with typical Shang dagger-axes (ge 戈) and integrally cast knives with terminal ring and upward-turned point that reveal both Shang and northern features. The people of Zhukaigou were agriculturalists, with a main staple of millet. They also raised sheep, pigs, and cattle. The transition to metalworking occurred around the end of the third millennium, which also coincides with a higher level attained in the ceramic industry. It is in this period that certain motifs appear, such as the snake pattern and the flower-shaped edge of the li 鬲

[17] Li Jinghan, "Shilun Xiajiadian xiaceng wenhua de fenqi he leixing," in *Zhongguo Kaogu xuehui di yi ci (1979) nianhui lunwenji* (Beijing: Wenwu, 1980), pp. 163–70.
[18] Zhai Defang, "Zhongguo beifang diqu qingtong duanjian fenqun yanjiu," *Kaogu xuebao* 1988.3: 277–99. On the distribution of bronze cultures in Liaoning, see Xu Yulin, "Liaoning Shang Zhou shiqi de qingtong wenhua," in *Kaoguxue wenhua lunwenji*, ed. Su Bingqi (Beijing: Wenwu, 1993), vol. 3, pp. 311–34.
[19] *Kaogu* 1988.3: 301–32; Wu En, "Zhukaigou wenhua de faxian ji qi yiyi," in *Zhongguo kaoguxue luncong* (Beijing: Kexue, 1995), pp. 256–66.

vessel, the latter of which archaeologists regard as characteristic of later nomadic peoples of this area.[20] Interestingly in this area in the first half of the second millennium, people already used oracle-bone divination, a practice that came to be closely associated with Shang culture and statecraft. Shang ritual vessels, such as *ding* and *jue*, and weapons appear here during the Erligang and Erlitou periods.[21] This may suggest that around the mid-second millennium B.C., there was a northward movement of Shang culture or that contacts between the local people and the Shang increased.

CHAODAOGOU CULTURE. The Chaodaogou culture,[22] located between the bend of the Yellow River and the Liao 遼 River drainage basin, extends across northern Hebei, Shanxi, Shaanxi, and Henan. It is characterized mostly by funerary sites that have yielded identical or closely related objects, among which the most characteristic are bronze weapons, in particular daggers, knives, and axes. The type site is Chaodaogou (Qinglong 青龍 county, Hebei), excavated in May 1961.[23] The bronzes found here have contributed greatly to defining the Northern Zone as a distinct cultural complex. These are a dagger with decorated handle and ram-head pommel, an axe with tubular socket, and four knives each with arched back and a pommel in the form of a rattle, while a fifth knife has a ram-head knob. Another typical site of this culture is Linzheyu 林遮峪 (Baode 保德 county, Shaanxi), a burial ground that yielded a dagger with grooved hilt and rattle pommel, bronze plaques with spiral designs, small rattles in bronze, small bells, horse harness, two axes with tubular sockets, as well as bronze ritual vessels.[24]

BAIJINBAO CULTURE. Roughly contemporary with the Chaodaogou culture is the Baijinbao culture in Heilongjiang, which spans the late second and the early first millennium.[25] The type site of this culture is located in Zhaoyuan 肇源 county, Heilongjiang, and was excavated in 1974. Centered in the plain of the Sungari-Nonni River system, its distribution extends west

[20] Tian Guangjin and Guo Suxin, "E'erduosi shi qingtong qi de yuanyuan," *Kaogu xuebao* 1988.3: 260. On the snake motif, see Li Shuicheng, "Zhongguo beifang didai de shewenqi yanjiu," *Wenwu* 1992.1: 50–7.

[21] See Katheryn Linduff, "Here Today and Gone Tomorrow: The Emergence and Demise of Bronze Producing Cultures Outside the Central Plain." Paper presented at the Conference on Chinese History and Archaeology, Academia Sinica, Taipei, Taiwan, January 4–8, 1994.

[22] For the definition of Chaodaogou as an archaeological culture, see Kovalev, "'Karasuk-dolche', Hirschsteine und die Nomaden der chinesischen Annalen im Alterum," pp. 48–62.

[23] *Kaogu* 1962.12: 644–5.

[24] Wu Zhenlu, "Baode xian xin faxiande Yindai qingtong qi," *Wenwu* 1972.4: 62–6.

[25] On the Baijinbao type site, see *Kaogu* 1980.4: 311–24. On the relationship between Baijinbao and the Neolithic Hanshu 漢書 culture, see Du Xingzhi, "Shi lun Hanshu wenhua he Baijinbao wenhua," *Beifang wenwu* 1986.4: 21–5. For a general survey of the Baijinbao culture, see Jia Weiming, "Guanyu Baijinbao leixing fenqi de tansuo," *Beifang wenwu* 1986.1: 11–15, 52.

to the border between Inner Mongolia and Heilongjiang, south to Baicheng 白城 county in Liaoning, north to Ang'angxi 昂昂溪, Fuyu 富裕, and Nenjiang 嫩江 counties in Heilongjiang, and east to Harbin, Bin county 賓縣, and Bayan 巴彥 county.[26] Bronze objects are typically small and include knives, buttons, rings, and earrings. Casting molds have also been found. Two semisubterranean houses excavated at Baijinbao indicate settled life. Some tools are made of stone (polished axes, adzes, and scrapers), but most are made of bone or shell. The abundance of fishing- and hunting-related tools, such as harpoons, spears, projectile points, knives, and scrapers, indicate that fishing and hunting were the main activities of this culture, as we would expect in a region rich in rivers and forests. The chronology of the culture is based on the pottery, such as li 鬲 tripods, hu 壺 jars, and guan 罐 pots. The Baijinbao ceramics are characteristically embellished with a decor executed in dotted lines that includes geometric designs or animals, such as frogs, sheep, and deer. The finding of a typical Baijinbao guan pot in an Upper Xiajiadian (eleventh to fourth centuries B.C.) site in southeastern Inner Mongolia points to close relations between these two areas in the early Western Zhou period.[27] The latest date of the Baijinbao culture is believed to be the early Spring and Autumn period (eighth to seventh centuries B.C.).

NORTHERN CULTURES IN THE GANSU–NINGXIA REGION. The Gansu–Ningxia region has had a long and rich history of archaeological investigation. European surveys in the 1920s and 1930s by Sven Hedin, Teilhard de Chardin, and, especially, J. Gunnar Andersson recognized a number of early cultures and established an initial chronology for the cultures of Qijia, Yangshao 仰韶 (Machang 馬廠), Xindian, Siwa, and Shajing. Later Chinese excavations, in the 1930s and 1940s, however, led to the recognition of the Qijia as an Early Bronze Age culture.[28] Throughout the 1950s and 1960s extensive surveys and excavations were conducted in the Weihe 渭河, Jinghe 涇河, Taohe 洮河, and Huangshui 湟水 River valleys. Further studies in the 1970s and 1980s synthesized the material collected thus far and tried not only to establish a better chronology, but also to assess the extent of contacts with neighboring regions.[29]

The Qijia culture is regarded as one of the earliest bronze cultures and is dated as early as 2000 B.C. Though its main sites are located in present-day

[26] Tan Yingjie and Zhao Shandong, "Song Nen pingyuan qingtong wenhua chuyi," *Zhongguo kaogu xuehui di si ci nianhui lunwenji 1983* (Beijing: Wenwu, 1985), p. 199.

[27] Jia Hong'en, "Wengniute qi Dapaozi qingtong duanjian mu," *Wenwu* 1984.2: 50–4.

[28] On these cultures see K. C. Chang, *The Archaeology of Ancient China*, 4th ed. (New Haven, Conn.: Yale University Press, 1985), pp. 138–50.

[29] Shui Tao, "Xibei diqu shiqian kaogu yanjiu de huigu yu qianzhan," in *Kaoguxue wenhua lunji*, ed. Su Bingqi (Beijing: Wenwu, 1993), vol. 3, pp. 1–11.

Gansu province, such as in Huangniangniangtai 皇娘娘台, Qinweijia 秦魏家, and Dahezhuang 大何莊, its distribution is very broad, reaching north and east up to Inner Mongolia, the upper Yellow River valley, and the upper Weihe and Huangshui River valleys.[30] It was a sedentary culture, based on agriculture. Pig raising seems to have been important, given the relevance of the pig in sacrifices. Oracle divination was also practiced. An important feature of the Qijia culture is the presence of numerous domesticated horses. According to recent scholarship some of the metal artifacts recovered from Qijia sites, in particular knives and axes, might point to a connection with Siberian and Central Asian cultures, in particular the Seima–Turbino complex.[31] Though these connections are still hypothetical at present, it is plausible that future research may further corroborate the existence of early contacts between the Qijia culture and Central Asia.

During the second part of the Shang dynasty, three almost contemporary and intersecting cultures appeared in Gansu, Ningxia, and northern Qinghai, known as Siwa, Xindian, and Kayue 卡約. These cultures, succeeding the Early Bronze Age Qijia, show the presence of more advanced bronzes, in particular weapons.

The Xindian culture dates between the first half of the second millennium and the late Western Zhou period, and is regarded as later than Machang but earlier than Siwa. Its area of distribution is the Hehuang 河湟 River valley and the eastern part of Gansu. It originated in the late Qijia, with which the pottery bears evidence of cultural continuity. The early Siwa sites are distributed in the same area. They were contemporary neighboring cultures, located in close proximity, though each followed its own discrete development. The Xindian culture later expanded toward the west and came closer to the Kayue culture, by which it was possibly absorbed.[32]

The Siwa culture is dated to the middle and late second millennium; its eastern expansion may have resulted in a close interaction with the Zhou culture. It takes its name from the site of Siwashan 寺洼山 (in Lintao 臨洮 county, Gansu) and was discovered in 1924.[33] An important site is Xujianian 徐家碾 (in Zhuanglang 莊浪 county, eastern Gansu), a large cemetery where 104 graves were excavated, 7 of which contained human sacrifices. Two

[30] On the Qijia sites and their distribution, see Hu Qianying, "Shilun Qijia wenhua de butong leixing ji qi yuanliu," *Kaogu yu wenwu* 1980.3: 77–82, 33; Xie Duanju, "Shilun Qijia wenhua," *Kaogu yu wenwu* 1981.3: 79–80.

[31] Louisa G. Fitzgerald Huber, "Qijia and Erlitou: The Question of Contacts with Distant Cultures," *EC* 20 (1995): 17–67; see also An Zhimin, "Shilun Zhongguo de zaoqi tongqi," *Kaogu* 1993.12: 1110–19.

[32] Zhang Xuezheng et al., "Xindian wenhua yanjiu," in *Kaoguxue wenhua lunji*, ed. Su Bingqi (Beijing: Wenwu, 1993), vol. 3, pp. 122–52.

[33] K. C. Chang, *The Archaeology of Ancient China*, pp. 384–5; An Zhimin, "The Bronze Age in the Eastern Parts of Central Asia," in *History of Civilizations of Central Asia. Vol 1: The Dawn of Civilization: Earliest Times to 700 B.C.*, ed. A. H. Dani and V. M. Masson (Paris: UNESCO, 1992), pp. 327–8.

chariot and horse pits have also been found. The weapons recovered include dagger-axes, spearheads, and knives, all of whose shapes are similar to Western Zhou types.[34]

Relationship with the Shang Civilization

Much evidence of contacts between the Shang and the Northern Zone comes from the discovery of Northern Zone bronzes in Shang tombs excavated in the Anyang area. These include a bronze knife with animal-head pommel found at Houjiazhuang 侯家莊, another knife with a ring head together with a Shang pickaxe found at Xiaotun 小屯, and a pickaxe with shorter tubular socket unearthed together with a clay tripod and a piece of jade in 1953 at Dasikong.[35] Some of the most important evidence of contact between the Shang and northern cultures comes from the tomb of Fu Hao, the consort of King Wu Ding (ca. 1200 B.C.), excavated in 1976. It contained several items, such as a northern-style knife with an ibex head, that certainly did not originate in the Shang culture. There are also four bronze mirrors and a bronze hairpin with no equivalent in the Central Plain. Through laboratory "fingerprinting," a connection has been established between a large number of the jades found in the tomb of Fu Hao and nephrite sources in Xinjiang. Since opinions differed as to the provenance of the 755 jade objects excavated, many exquisitely crafted, over 300 pieces were sent to various laboratories in Beijing and Anyang, including that of the Chinese Academy of Social Sciences. Examination is reported to indicate that all but 3 pieces came from quarries in Xinjiang.[36]

Outside Anyang there are several other sites with mixed findings. For instance, in Yantou 墕頭 (Suide 綏德 county, Shaanxi) a Northern Zone knife has been found together with Shang bronze vessels and a *ge* dagger-axe, and a Western Zhou burial in Baifu 白浮 (Changping 昌平 county, Beijing) yielded a northern-style arched-back knife with geometric patterns on the handle and a ring pommel with three small knobs.[37] During the Yinxu period there was increased warfare between the Shang and the Northern Zone. By this period, the Northern Zone complex had evolved into a number of discrete cultural centers, which had established a network of contacts both between them and with the Central Plain.

[34] *Kaogu* 1982.6: 584–90.

[35] Li Ji, "Ji Xiaotun chutude qingtong qi," *Zhongguo kaogu xuebao* 4 (1949): 1–70. These were found in tomb M164. Kovalev, "'Karasuk-dolche', Hirschsteine und die Nomaden der chinesischen Annalen im Alterum," p. 54.

[36] Wang Binghua. "Xi Han yiqian Xinjiang he Zhongyuan diqu lishi guanxi kaosu," in Wang Binghua, *Sichou zhi lu kaogu yanjiu* (Urumqi: Xinjiang renmin, 1993), p. 167.

[37] *Wenwu* 1975.2: 82–4. For a description of finds from Shilou, a related site in Shanxi, see p. 225, this volume. *Kaogu* 1976.4: 246–58, 228.

THE CHARIOT. Numerous studies have suggested that the chariot was imported into China from the west, possibly around the thirteenth century B.C.[38] Wagons and carts were first made in the Near East in the third millennium B.C., as bronze tools and the domestication of the horse made possible the conception and technical realization of horse-drawn wheeled vehicles. Chariots should be distinguished from four-wheeled wagons and two-wheeled carts. Like wagons, carts were used to transport men and goods: they had solid or spoked wheels and a central axle on which the passenger box rested. Chariots had spoked wheels and a rear axle on which a box normally holding no more than two people rested.[39] Recent discoveries related to the Andronovo sites have revealed fully formed chariots with spoked wheels of the Sintashta–Petrovka culture, which may date, according to recent studies, as early as 2026 B.C.[40] These are technically and conceptually very similar to chariots found both in West Asia (such as the Lchashen site, Armenia, Russian Federation, in the Caucasus), and East Asia, such as the chariots unearthed at Anyang. Though based on preexisting models of wheeled vehicles, the war chariot seems to have been developed by the agropastoralists of the Andronovo culture. This successful culture was advanced in animal domestication and breeding and mastered the art of bronze metallurgy to the point that craftsmen were able to manipulate alloys so that the quality of the bronze would be harder or tougher according to the specific function of weapons and tools. Indeed, economic success and the development of the war chariot may have been the basic factors accounting for the rapid spread of this culture across the Eurasian steppe from the Urals to South Siberia.

The first Chinese chariots have been found in burials of the Shang dynasty at Anyang, together with horses and drivers, who served as sacrificial victims. This type of vehicle was used by the aristocracy for display, hunting, and war. It was made of a central pole with one horse harnessed on each side, and a box with two spoked wheels attached to the end of the pole. The box was typically rectangular or oval. The chariot appears in China already fully formed, unpreceded by stages of development.[41] There appear to have been

---

[38] Franz Hančar, *Das Pferd in prähistorischer und früher historischer Zeit* (Wien: Herold, 1956); Magdalene von Dewall, *Pferd und Wagen im fruhen China* (Bonn: Habelt, 1964); Edward L. Shaughnessy, "Historical Perspectives on the Introduction of the Chariot into China," *HJAS* 48, 1 (1988): 189–237; Stuart Piggott, "Chinese Chariotry: An Outsider's View." In *Arts of the Eurasian Steppelands*, ed. Philip Denwood. Colloquies on Art and Archaeology in Asia no. 7 (London: Percival David Foundation, 1978), pp. 32–51; M. A. Littauer and J. H. Crouwel, *Wheeled Vehicles and Ridden Animals in the Ancient Near East* (Leiden: Brill, 1979).

[39] Stuart Piggott, *The Earliest Wheeled Transport: From the Atlantic Coast to the Caspian Sea* (Ithaca, N.Y.: Cornell University Press, 1983), p. 95.

[40] David Anthony and Nikolai B. Vinogradov, "Birth of the Chariot," *Archaeology* 48, 2 (1995): p. 38.

[41] Yang Baocheng, "Yin dai chezi de faxian yu fuyuan," *Kaogu* 1984.6: 546–55; *Kaogu* 1984.6: 505–9.

no other wheeled vehicles, such as wagons or carts, pulled by cattle or equids. During the Zhou dynasty, chariots became a common feature of the funerary inventory of the richest tombs, and chariotry was the central core of both Zhou and foreign armies.

Few chariot remains have been found in the Northern Zone.[42] However, the presence of chariots in this region is documented by petroglyphs from South Siberia, the Altai region, the Tianshan 天山 Mountains, and the Yinshan 陰山 Mountains in Inner Mongolia. For instance, a rock carving from the Yinshan Mountains illustrates a hunting scene where a hunter was shooting game after having dismounted from a chariot with eight-spoked wheels, pulled by two horses.[43] This is identical with another drawing recovered from an incised bone fragment depicting the same scene, with the additional presence of two dogs, found at Nanshan'gen 南山根, dating to the eighth century B.C. or earlier. Their depiction, where chariot and horses are represented flat, is remarkably similar. If we can assume that petroglyphs in a similar style found in regions culturally and geographically akin can be attributed to the same period, then it is possible to hypothesize that the petroglyph from Yinshan is earlier than the eighth century B.C., thus providing a later chronological limit. The earlier limit should be the twenty-first century B.C., as this is the date of the earliest chariots found in the necropolises of the Andronovo culture.[44] The presence of similar drawings on deer stones, together with drawings of daggers with bent hilt common in the Northern Zone during the Shang period, suggest a dating of the petroglyphs to the mid-second millennium B.C.[45]

The petroglyphs, as well as the actual chariots found in the Sintashta burials, indicate essentially the same design and technical characteristics as the Chinese chariot, which is also very similar to a model found in the Caucasus at Lchashen and dated to the late second millennium B.C.[46] It is therefore probable that the war chariot with lightweight box and spoked wheels,

---

[42] For instance, the remains of wooden wheels found in Nuomuhong 諾木洪 (Dulan 都蘭 county, Qinghai) and tentatively dated to the mid-second millennium B.C. (*Kaogu xuebao* 1963.1: pl. 3); see also Jenny F. So and Emma C. Bunker, *Traders and Raiders on China's Northern Frontier* (Washington, D.C.: Arthur Sackler Gallery, Smithsonian Institution; and Seattle: University of Washington Press, 1996), p. 26.

[43] Gai Shanlin, "Cong Nei Meng Yinshan yanhua kan gudai beifang youmu minzu de lishi gongxian," in *Sichou zhi lu yanhua yishu*, ed. Zhou Jinbao (Urumqi: Xinjiang Renmin, 1993). For other examples of chariot petroglyphs, see Shaughnessy, "Historical Perspectives on the Introduction of the Chariot into China," pp. 202–203.

[44] Elena E. Kuzmina, "Les steppes de l'Asie centrale à l'Epoque du bronze: La culture d'Andronovo," *Dossiers d'archéologie* 185 (September 1993): 82–9.

[45] Wu En, "A Preliminary Study of the Art of the Upper Xiajiadian Culture." *The International Academic Conference of Archaeological Cultures of the Northern Chinese Ancient Nations (Collected Papers)*, ed. Zhongguo kaogu wenqu yanjiusuo (Huhhot, August 11–18, 1992).

[46] Two chariots were found in barrows 9 and 11. See Piggott, *The Earliest Wheeled Transport*, p. 95.

pulled by two horses, originated in Central Asia and was later adopted by the peripheral civilizations of China, Mesopotamia, and the Caucasus.[47]

Relationship with Northern and Central Asia

The relationship between the Northern Zone and the bronze cultures of South Siberia remains problematic.[48] From the twelfth to the eighth centuries B.C., a new culture known as Karasuk dominates the Altai Mountains and Minusinsk Basin. The Karasuk people, like their northern Chinese neighbors, had a mixed economy that, although mainly based on livestock, also relied on agriculture and other supporting activities.[49] Bones of antelope and deer point to extensive hunting, whereas cattle and horse remains show that the Karasuk were devoted to animal husbandry, their main productive activity. Their metal inventory presents many points in common with the Northern Zone bronzes of North China. Among the knives we find the type with hunched back. The daggers are also similar to the Ordos style, with a short guard. The pickaxes display tubular sockets for hafting such as those of the Northern Zone, though the blade presents a pointed cutting edge that may have been derived from a Shang prototype. Arrowheads are also similar to those found in Anyang.

The similarities triggered a long-standing dispute as to the influence, and primacy, of one culture over the other. Seminal work by Russian archaeologists in South Siberia[50] and subsequent analysis of the Karasuk and Shang affinities showed that the Anyang finds represented the earliest occurrences of certain Karasuk types. These studies also pointed to the presence of a new racial type in Karasuk, akin to the population of North China. As a result, the hypothesis that the appearance of a distinct bronze inventory pointed to

---

[47] This is the opinion of the majority of scholars. See in particular Shaughnessy, "Historical Perspectives on the Introduction of the Chariot into China"; Piggott, "Chinese Chariotry: An Outsider's View." Most Chinese scholars, however, either disagree or remain noncommittal as to the hypothesis of the exogenous origin of the chariot; e.g., see Lu Liancheng, "Chariot and Horse Burials in Ancient China," *Antiquity* 67, 257 (1993): 824–38.

[48] From the viewpoint of the development of metallurgy, the eastern zone of the steppe, of which one of the most dynamic centers was located in the Sayano–Altai region, embraced also Mongolia and Transbaikalia. This is what Chernyk defines as the Central Asian Metallurgical Province. The development of metallurgy and its diffusion throughout the region should probably be seen in connection with the development of nomadism, since more technologically advanced communities may have advanced more quickly along the road of pastoral specialization, and in turn their increased mobility may have facilitated the diffusion of their technology. For the extension and metallurgical development of this region in the Bronze Age, see E. N. Chernykh, *Ancient Metallurgy in the USSR*, trans. Sarah Wright (Cambridge University Press, 1992), pp. 270–1.

[49] A. P. Okladnikov, "Inner Asia at the Dawn of History" in *The Cambridge History of Inner Asia*, ed. Denis Sinor (Cambridge University Press, 1990), pp. 85–8.

[50] S. V. Kiselev, *Drevniaia istoriia Iuzhnoi Sibiri* (Moscow: Nauka, 1951).

a migration from China to Central Asia in the eleventh or tenth century B.C. was formulated.[51]

Recent studies, however, show that the Shang metallurgical tradition is separate from that of the Northern Zone complex.[52] That the Northern Complex was an independent cultural unit seems now to be generally accepted.[53] However, the Northern Zone acted as a filter as well as a link between China on the one hand and Central and North Asia on the other; many typical features, especially bronze decorations, originated here and were later transmitted elsewhere.[54]

Others see a closer relationship between the Northern Zone and South Siberia, regarding the Northern Zone together with the Sayano–Altai region, Mongolia, Transbaikalia, and northwestern China (Xinjiang), as part of the Central Asian Metallurgical Province. In view of the scarcity of archaeological information from Mongolia and Xinjiang, the full extent of the relationship among these areas, and between these areas and China, remains vague. Yet the similarity between some Central Asian forms and the Seima–Turbino knives with animal terminals and socketed celts may suggest an initial Western stimulus to the metallurgy that developed in the Sayano–Altai region and other zones of the Central Asian Metallurgical Province. There was also a possible symbiosis between Central Asian metallurgy and "true Chinese examples of high-quality casting," especially with respect to weapons and ritual objects. In a later period, typical artifacts of this broad Central Asian zone gradually penetrated the west.[55]

At the present stage of research it is only possible to say that the Northern Zone was home to a distinctive metallurgical culture with close ties not only with China, but also with areas to the West, in particular with the Sayano–Altai region. The economy of the Northern Zone peoples also resembles that of early pastoralists documented for the Karasuk people. It therefore seems that a process of gradual economic differentiation developed in which more mobile cultures specialized in raising livestock, whereas settled cultures retained mixed economic forms with emphasis on farming.

[51] Karl Jettmar, "The Karasuk Culture and Its South-Eastern Affinities," *BMFEA* 22 (1950): 116–23.
[52] Lin Yun, "A Reexamination," p. 272. On the relationship between Xinjiang and neighboring cultures, an excellent overview is provided by Chen Kwang-tzuu and Frederick T. Hiebert, "The Late Prehistory of Xinjiang in Relation to Its Neighbors," *Journal of World Prehistory*, 9, 2 (1995): 243–300.
[53] For a general survey of the Northern Zone bronzes and their archaeological importnace, see also Wu En, "Yin zhi Zhou chu de beifang qingtong qi," *Kaogu xuebao* 1985.2: 135–56.
[54] Tian Guangjin, "Jinnianlai Nei Menggu diqu de Xiongnu kaogu," *Kaogu xuebao* 1983.1: 23.
[55] Chernykh, *Ancient Metallurgy in the USSR*, pp. 269–73. The similarity between the Ordos–Karasuk and the Seima–Turbino artifacts is also recognized by Jettmar, "The Karasuk Culture and Its South-Eastern Affinities," p. 119.

Northern and Western Peoples in the Historical Records

According to the "Yu Gong" 禹貢 (Tribute of Yu) section of the *Shang shu* 尚書 (Venerated documents),[56] ever since the beginning of the Xia 夏 dynasty the Central Plain was surrounded by alien peoples, living in marshes or on mountains, who brought tribute to the Central Plain. Among the various tribute-bearing peoples are some whose description sounds familiarly nomadic, such as the felt-wearing people of Xiqing 西傾, Kunlun 崑崙, and Qusou 渠搜. The Xiqing are said to have lived by the Huan 桓 River, not far from the Shang. Among the tribute items are furs and hides, bronze and other metals, including iron, steel, and, possibly, gold, special wood to make bows, stone and whistling (possibly bone) arrowheads. Yet there is no reason to believe that the "Yu Gong" preserves genuine information about real pastoral nomads living next to the Central Plain in a remote past. At most, we might say that the "Yu gong" furnishes a mythical past with features contemporary with the period of its composition (possibly the third century B.C.), when mounted nomads had become a common sight on China's northern borders.

Shang oracle bones and written documents of the Zhou dynasty contain a considerable amount of data concerning the names of peoples against whom the Shang fought or with whom they entered into relations.[57] These people are usually referred to as *fang* 方 (country), preceded by a character probably indicating their ethnic name.[58] Given the paucity of information and the subsequent uncertainty in the identification of these people, we cannot be sure that they formed political unions. Certainly some of them were quite powerful and militarily threatening, but the repeated appearance of a certain name for a relatively long period does not mean that all the people recognized by the Shang under that name were at any given time organized, like the Shang, in a single political and social structure. It is more likely that these definitions indicated certain broadly similar ethnic groups that may or may not have had internal political cohesion.

The Gongfang 舌方 were probably located to the northwest of the Shang in northern Shaanxi, northern Shanxi, and possibly even the Ordos

---

[56] On the *Shang shu*, see Michael Loewe, ed., *Early Chinese Texts: A Bibliographical Guide* (Berkeley: Society for the Study of Early China and the Institute of East Asian Studies, University of California., 1993), pp. 376–89. Although it contains some of the very earliest of transmitted texts, much of it was written at a later date, the "Yu gong" probably dating as late as the Qin dynasty.

[57] On the relations between the Shang and surrounding states, and Shang historical geography, see Chen Mengjia, *Yinxu buci zongshu* (Beijing: Kexue, 1956), pp. 249–312; Li Xueqin, *Yindai dili jianlun* (Beijing: Kexue, 1959); Shima Kunio, *Inkyo bokuji kenkyû* (Hirosaki: Hirosaki daigaku Chûgokugaku kenkyûkai, 1958), pp. 349–423.

[58] Li Xueqin, *Yindai dili jianlun*, p. 80.

area.[59] They maintained frequent interaction with the Shang, especially during the reign of King Wu Ding, when several campaigns were undertaken against them. More resilient enemies may have been the Guifang 鬼方, who are said to have resisted Wu Ding's attacks for three years.[60] Another group mentioned often is that of the Tufang 土方, probably located in northern Shanxi and extinguished by Wu Ding's conquests. Another group becomes more important toward the end of the Shang, namely, the Renfang 人方, probably located in the middle and lower valley of the Huai 淮 River.[61] King Di Yi led several expeditions against them, and a chief of the Renfang is said to have been eventually captured and sacrificed to the gods.

The most constant enemy of the Shang was the Qiangfang 羌方, or simply Qiang.[62] Because of the presence of elements for "sheep" and "man" in the graph *qiang*, they are described in later sources as "shepherds."[63] Their territory extended through southern Shanxi, northern Henan, and northern Shaanxi. The Shang often mounted expeditions against them, capturing slaves and sacrificial victims. Qiang prisoners were also skilled in the preparation of oracle bones.[64] The Qiang also seem to have been horse breeders, as some groups among them are called Ma Qiang 馬羌 or Duo Ma Qiang 多馬羌 (Qiang with many horses).[65] Finally, the Qiang had a close relationship with the Zhou, who were intermittently at war with the Shang.

The many wars fought by the Shang in the north and west make it clear that the frontier was anything but static and may explain why contacts with the Northern Zone seem to have been particularly active during the Yinxu period. It is in the twelfth century that we have records of increased military activity. The Shang state, surrounded by hostile people, fought and possibly subjugated some of the northern groups, incorporating alien cultural traditions. Whether these people were ethnically or linguistically different cannot be said, but they certainly represented cultures that were neither purely local nor self-enclosed. Indeed, their hinterland extended far to the north and west. By attaining access to this northern complex, the Shang established indirect links with Central Asia. Even at this early stage of Chinese history, the pres-

---

[59] On the Gongfang in particular, and on Shang historical geography in general, see Edward L. Shaughnessy, "Historical Geography and the Extent of Early Chinese Kingdoms," *AM*, 3d series, 2 (1989): pt. 2, 1–13.

[60] K. C. Chang, *Shang Civilization* (New Haven, Conn.: Yale University Press, 1980), p. 12.

[61] Chen Mengjia, *Yinxu buci zongshu*, p. 304.

[62] Ibid., pp. 276–82.

[63] Duan Yucai, *Duan shi shuo wen jie zi zhu* (Shanghai: Sao Yeshan fang, 1928), 7, pp. 14b–15a; cf. Duan Yucai, *Kundoku Setsumon Kaiji chû*, ed. and trans. Ozaki Yûjirô 尾崎雄二郎, vol. 2, pp. 728–30 (Tokyo: Tôkai Daigaku, 1986).

[64] On the Qiang at Anyang, see Hu Houxuan, "Jiaguwen suojian Yindai nuli de fan yapo douzheng," *Kaogu xuebao* 1976.1: 8–10. On the Qiang in general, see Shirakawa Shizuka, "Kyôzoku kô," *Kôkotsu kinbungaku ronsô* 9 (1958): 1–16.

[65] Chen Mengjia, *Yinxu buci zongshu*, pp. 276–7.

ence of a different metallurgical tradition, the many layers of interaction between the north and the Central Plain (possibly responsible for the transmission of the chariot and other cultural features), and the presence of mixed communities bespeak the importance of the north in Shang history.

WESTERN ZHOU TO EARLY SPRING AND AUTUMN (CA. 1000–650 B.C.)

Transition to Pastoral Nomadism

At the end of the nineteenth century, the hypothesis was advanced that "the domestication of animals was possible only under the conditions of a sedentary way of life."[66] This presupposes both a long process of experimentation and accumulation of technical knowledge, and the existence of other sources of production to generate the surplus in fodder and grains needed to feed the animals. Human communities raised animals – sheep, cattle, onagers, pigs, and dogs – as a complement to farming. They then learned to use them either for direct productive activity or for other purposes, such as transportation.

Steppe oases provided a natural environment equally favorable to agriculture and animal husbandry. Surrounded by steppe pastureland, these areas imposed fewer restrictions on stock raising than valley agriculture, where an imbalance between the human and animal element could lead to disastrous consequences. The oasis dwellers specializing in stock breeding eventually separated themselves from their original environment and became nomadic pastoralists. In areas contiguous to farming communities, nomads remained to a certain extent dependent on them for agricultural and handicraft products. To a varying degree nomads also continued to practice some forms of agriculture in their winter quarters.[67]

The role of horses in the transition from sedentary herding to nomadic pastoralism is crucial. Possibly the first equid to be tamed was not the horse but the more docile onager.[68] Paleozoological evidence based on tooth bitwear suggests that the horse was first domesticated and possibly ridden in the

---

[66] S. I. Vejnshtein, "The Problem of the Origin and Formation of the Economic-Cultural Type of Pastoral Nomads in the Moderate Belt of Eurasia," in *The Nomadic Alternative*, ed. W. Weissleder (The Hague: Mouton, 1978), pp. 127–33. See also Anatoli Khazanov, *Nomads of the Outside World* (Cambridge University Press, 1984), p. 89.

[67] Iwamura Shinobu, "Nomad and Farmer in Central Asia," *Acta Asiatica* 3 (1962): 45–50; Nicola Di Cosmo, "Ancient Inner Asian Nomads: Their Economic Basis and Its Significance in Chinese History," *JAS* 53, 4 (1994): 1092–126.

[68] J. F. Downs, "Origin and Spread of Riding in the Near East and Central Asia," *American Anthropologist*, 63 (1961): 1193–6.

fourth millennium B.C. in the Ukraine.[69] Like the onager, it was first used as a draught animal, being mounted and ridden only later. The first communities to breed horses were mainly agricultural, also raising pigs, cattle, and sheep. The horse was, then, just another member of the animal stock of early farmer-pastoralists.

Although there are differences of opinion, it seems that horseback riding in the strictest sense of the word, that is, riding astride, spread in West and Central Asia around the early part of the second millennium B.C. or possibly at the end of the third millennium B.C.[70] The early pastoral communities were by no means nomadic in the sense that the later steppe nomads were, characterized by the military use of the horse. Although some were more or less mobile, following their herds on wheeled carts, or perhaps even mounted on horses, their pastoralism cannot be defined as nomadic – that is, a regular seasonal migratory cycle based on grass-producing environments at varying altitudes – but rather as "herder husbandry" or at most semi-nomadism. They still had settlements and depended on agricultural production. The vigorous expansion of the oasis civilizations of Central Asia in the third and second millennia B.C., based on coexisting agricultural and pastoral production and increasingly closer contacts with neighboring people, led to the spread of enhanced metalwork and transportation technology to the steppe, where the environment was more favorable to the development of a pastoral economy. By the third millennium B.C., farmer-herders had already begun to use various alloys and traveled in wheeled vehicles.[71] During this period "the struggle for forcible redistribution of pasture and accumulated wealth gives rise, at a certain stage, to a type of militarization of society that found expression and progress in the production of weapons."[72]

Archaeological and linguistic evidence shows that preconditions for the emergence of pastoral nomadism were present in the middle of the second millennium B.C. in both the European and Kazakh steppe. Nevertheless, the transition to pastoral nomadism practiced by horseback riders was not completed until the beginning of the first millennium B.C.[73]

[69] Marsha Levine, "Dereivka and the Problem of Horse Domestication," *Antiquity* 64 (1990): 727–40; Dmitriy Telehin, *Dereivka: A Settlement and Cemetery of Copper Age Horse Keepers on the Middle Dnieper* (Oxford: British Archaeological Reports International Series no. 287, 1986); David W. Anthony and Dorcas R. Brown, "The Origins of Horseback Riding," *Antiquity* 65 (1991): 22–38; Khazanov, *Nomads of the Outside World*, p. 91.

[70] Littauer and Crouwel, *Wheeled Vehicles and Ridden Animals in the Ancient Near East*, pp. 45–7, 65–8. Anthony and Vinogradov, "Birth of the Chariot," p. 40.

[71] Anthony and Vinogradov, "Birth of the Chariot," pp. 36–41.

[72] V. M. Masson and T. F. Taylor, "Soviet Archaeology in the steppe Zone: Introduction," *Antiquity* 63 (1989): 780.

[73] Aryan terminology appears in a Hittite work on horsemanship of the fourteenth century, concerned with the training of horses hitched to chariots, which may indicate that this type of training was a technique developed by steppe Indo-European peoples. See Pentti Aalto, "The Horse in Central Asian

The eventual emergence of pastoral nomadism has been attributed to several factors: the increasing number of livestock and the accumulated experience of a more progressive, mobile pastoral husbandry; changes in the climate leading to progressive desiccation as a result of which formerly sedentary cultivators and cattle breeders became full nomads; and finally transition to a nomadic life as a result of overpopulation.[74] It is also possible that nomadism emerged among forest hunters, who borrowed animals from their sedentary neighbors and then, after they began to use the horse, moved into the steppe.[75]

In South Siberia the transitional period that preceded the emergence of a more homogeneous nomadic culture is represented by the Karasuk cultural complex of the twelfth to the eighth centuries B.C. This period witnessed a rapid development of metallurgic technology based on a wide range of alloys and the use of stock breeding as the main economic activity. While no definite explanation can be provided for the appearance of the mounted steppe culture around the end of the second and beginning of the first millennium B.C., this is generally seen as the result of an internal process, rather than one caused by external factors, such as invasions or mass migrations. It was the combination of many factors over a long period of time that eventually produced an economic and cultural complex singularly well adapted to the arid conditions of the steppe. However, the speed with which people turned to fully developed pastoral nomadism is still subject to debate. For some, once the first pastoral communities emerged, the spread of nomadism ensued rapidly. By the eighth century B.C., many people in different parts of the steppe had taken to nomadism. At this time a military aristocracy was formed that concentrated in its hands a higher percentage of the common wealth (mostly weapons, ornaments, and, especially, animals) removed from the rest of the community. The rise of a warrior class is related to a general increase in aggressive warfare among pastoralists, aimed at securing pastures. Agricultural production was considerably reduced and was preserved only at the tribes' winter pastures. Others have proposed a far more gradual transition that required several centuries.[76]

Nomadic Cultures," *Studia Orientalia* 46 (1975): 4–7. See also Hančar, *Das Pferd in prähistorischer und Früher historischer Zeit,* pp. 551–63.

[74] G. E. Markov, "Problems of Social Change Among the Asiatic Nomads," in *The Nomadic Alternative,* ed. W. Weissleder (The Hague: Mouton, 1978), p. 306.

[75] Vejnshtein, "The Problem of the Origin and Formation of the Economic-Cultural Type of pastoral Nomads in the Moderate Belt of Eurasia," pp. 130–1.

[76] These various viewpoints are expressed in the following works: V. Masson, "Central Asia in the Early Iron Age: Dynamics of Cultural, Social and Economic Development," *Information Bulletin. UNESCO International Association for the Study of the Cultures of Central Asia* 9 (1985): 59–68; Gryaznov, *The Ancient Civilization of Southern Siberia,* pp. 131–2; Sergei Rudenko, *Kul'tura naseleniia tsentral'nogo Altaia v skifskoe vremia* (Moscow: Nauka, 1960), p. 197.

Evidence of Pastoralism in the Northern Zone

From the Western Zhou to the late Warring States period, an increasing number of horse fittings and ornaments is found throughout the Northern Zone. The amount and variety of horse gear, together with the presence of horse sacrifice within the funerary assemblage, betoken the growing importance of the horse in both the economic and symbolic spheres.

There are several indications that the early use of metal horse fittings and riding in the northeast may be related to the development of the Upper Xiajiadian culture. Since saddles are not found in burials and stirrups had not yet been invented, it is difficult to say whether horse-related findings are to be associated with horseback riding or with other uses of the horse, such as pulling a cart or a chariot. There is however an indication in the Upper Xiajiadian site at Nanshan'gen that horses were in fact ridden, as figures of horseback hunters are represented on a bronze ring in the act of pursuing a hare. This find shows the existence of horse-riding people in the northeast as early as the eighth to seventh century B.C. Other horse-related findings consist of bronze bits, cheekpieces, rein rings, ornaments, and chamfrons. With the exceptions of the cheekpieces, which were sometimes made of bone or wood, they were all made of bronze. The ornaments include disc-shaped ornaments, bells, *luan* 鑾 bells, and some head ornaments and masks. Iron ornaments appear regularly only in the Warring States and Former Han periods.

Throughout the geographic distribution of the Upper Xiajiadian culture – eastern Inner Mongolia, western Liaoning, Hebei, and the Beijing area – horse fittings appear prominently in Western Zhou and Spring and Autumn funerary assemblages. However, specific evidence of horse riding is not documented in the southern part of this area until the sixth century, which is the date assigned to special riding bits found in Yanqing 延慶, Beijing.[77] In the Central Plain we find no real evidence that horses were ridden before the fourth century B.C.[78] This may point either to a progressive southward movement of horse-riding communities or to a slow diffusion of horse riding toward the south.

---

[77] Emma C. Bunker, "Unprovenanced Artifacts Belonging to the Pastoral Tribes of Inner Mongolia and North China During the 8th–1st Century B.C.," in *The International Academic Conference of Archaeological Cultures of the Northern Chinese Ancient Nations (Collected Papers)*, ed. Zhongguo kaogu wenwu yanjiusuo (Huhhot, August 11–18, 1992); see also So and Bunker, *Traders and Raiders on China's Northern Frontier*, p. 29.

[78] H. G. Creel, "The Role of the Horse in Chinese History," *American Historical Review* 70, 3 (1965): 647–72, 649. See also C. S. Goodrich, "Riding Astride and the Saddle in Ancient China," *HJAS* 44, 2 (1984): 279–306.

EARLY IRON TECHNOLOGY. In the area of present-day Xinjiang we find the earliest appearance of iron of the Northern Zone. The cemetery site of Chawuhu 察吾乎 Pass reveals some of the earliest iron remains.[79] On the basis of multiple calibrated radiocarbon datings, this site has been attributed to a period from the tenth to the seventh century B.C. It consists of stone mounds with multiple burials encircled within a ring of stones. The funerary assemblage includes gold, bronze, and iron objects. Among the bronze objects are knives with ringheads, a spearhead, and horse bits. A bone cheekpiece in the form of a ramhead is representative of early Animal Style. Iron objects are few and small, such as an awl and a ring. The extensive evidence of animal sacrifices buried in sacrificial pits, either separate from or together with human remains, points to a culture that is no longer agricultural and has a surplus of animals to spare. Among the funerary objects no agricultural tools have been found.

The existence of iron in this region at a time that precedes its first appearance in the Central Plain (possibly in the sixth century B.C.), is confirmed by analogous findings in Qunbake 群巴克 (Luntai 輪台 county), the Pamirs, and the area near Urumqi.[80] Comparable iron and bronze knives found in the Chust culture in Ferghana, and skeletal remains of Europoid stock, point to a connection with the Pamirs and Ferghana regions.

The far northwest was not the only area close to the Northern Zone that had iron at an early period. Iron dated to the end of the second millennium B.C. has been found along the Amur River, in the Maritime Territory of Russia, while by the ninth century B.C. there was rather elaborate iron metallurgy, producing knives, daggers, and armor.[81] Direct connections between this area's ferrous metallurgy and that of the Northern Zone have not yet been established for the earlier period, but there are indications that relations existed between Transbaikalia and the Chinese northeast possibly following ancient routes of communication through the forests of Manchuria and the large waterways that run north to south: the Sungari, Nonni, and Liao Rivers.[82]

The question of the spread of iron technology in South Siberia is quite complex, and there is no unified opinion. The date usually assigned to the

---

[79] *Kaogu xuebao* 1988.1: 75–99.

[80] *Kaogu xuebao* 1981.2: 199–216.

[81] A. P. Derevianko, *Rannyi zheleznyi vek Priamur'ia* (Novosibirsk: Nauka, 1973); Pavel Markovich Dolukhanov et al., "Radiocarbon Dates of the Institute of Archaeology, 2," *Radiocarbon* 12 (1970): 130–55.

[82] At a later period, usually defined as Hunno–Sarmatian in Russian scholarship (second century B.C. to second century A.D.), there is evidence of close contacts between Heilongjiang and Transbaikalia; see D. L. Brodianskii, "Krovnovsko–Khunnske paralleli," in *Drevnee Zabaikal'e i ego kul'turnye sviazi*, ed. P. B. Konovalov (Novosibirsk: Academiia Nauk USSR, 1985), pp. 46–50.

Early Iron Age in Central Asia (Transoxiana) is the beginning of the first millennium B.C. The same date usually applies to the Early Iron Age in the
steppe regions of Kazakhstan, Tuva, South Siberia, and Mongolia, even
though sites of this period in the Kazakh steppe do not contain iron artifacts
and iron metallurgy developed in Mongolia only from the middle of the first
millennium B.C. Nevertheless, iron undoubtedly existed in Tuva at least from
the eighth century B.C., as documented by the finds of the Aržan royal burial
and other kurgans of the early nomadic period.[83]

In the part of the Northern Zone that is closer to China, and in particular in the north-central sector, iron was present at a time roughly comparable with the general period of diffusion throughout the steppe region. An
iron knife was found at the Taohongbala 桃紅巴拉 burial site (Ordos, Inner
Mongolia), chronologically close to the "Scythian" period of the western and
central Asian steppe regions.[84]

Distribution of Northern Cultures

NORTHEAST: UPPER XIAJIADIAN CULTURE. The Upper Xiajiadian
culture's geographical extension reaches in the north to the Sira Mören River
basin, up to the eastern side of the Great Khingan Mountains. The southern boundary is formed by the Luan 灤 River, Yan 燕 Mountains, and the
Qilaotu 七老圖 Mountains. The eastern boundary is the basin of the Liao
River; the western boundary is the area of Zhaowudameng 昭烏達盟 in Inner
Mongolia. It therefore extends over the three provinces of Inner Mongolia,
Liaoning, and Hebei (see Map 13.2). Its chronological limits have been the
object of considerable discussion among Chinese archaeologists.[85] The
general consensus today is that it lasted approximately eight centuries, from
the eleventh to the fourth century B.C.

The first excavation that identified the Upper Xiajiadian as a separate
culture took place at Chifeng 赤峰, in Inner Mongolia, where distinctive fea-

---

[83] On the Iron Age in Central Asia see: A Askarov, "The Beginning of Iron Age in Transoxiana," in
History of Civilizations of Central Asia. Vol I: The Dawn of Civilization: Earliest Times to 700 B.C., ed.
A. H. Dani and V. M. Masson (Paris: Unesco, 1992), p. 457; A. Askarov, V. Volkov, and N. Ser-Odjav,
"Pastoral and Nomadic Tribes at the Beginning of the First Millennium B.C.," in *ibid.*, pp. 459–75;
Grjaznov, *Der Großkurgan von Aržan in Tuva, Südsibirien*; Kenk, *Grabfunde der Skythenzeit aus Tuva,
Süd-Sibirien*. We should also note, however, that according to Martynova the presence of iron artifacts
in the Shestakocvo cemetery (Minusinsk region) is a completely new phenomenon associated with a
new cultural complex, attributed to the Hunnic (Xiongnu) culture and dated to the last two centuries
of the first millennium B.C. See Galina S. Martynova, "The Beginning of the Hunnic Epoch in South
Siberia," *Arctic Anthropology* 25, 2 (1988): 74.
[84] Tian Guangjin, "Taohongbala de Xiongnu mu," pp. 131–42.
[85] Jin Fengyi, "Xiajiadian shangceng wenhua ji qi zushu wenti," *Kaogu xuebao* 1987.2: 177–208.

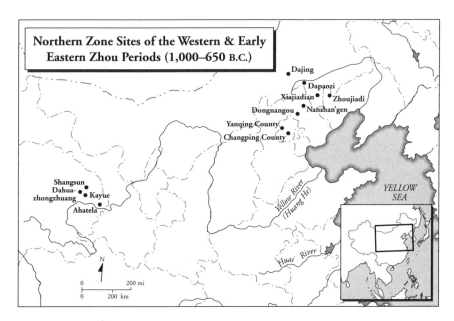

Map 13.2 Northern Zone: Archaeological sites of the Western and early Eastern Zhou periods (1000–650 B.C.)

tures were documented that differentiated it from the contemporary bronze culture of the Ordos region. Three chronological phases can be outlined based on characteristic objects such as the "wobbly," or curved-blade daggers.[86] Sites of the older period lasting throughout the Western Zhou period are located mostly in Linxi 林西 county in northern Liaoning. The type site for this period is the ancient mine of Dajing 大井, which we find in connection with a small settlement consisting of a few semisubterranean houses. The mine includes at least forty mining shafts, near one of which the remains of twelve smelting furnaces have been found. Most of the mining tools are made of stone, with very few small bronze objects (a drill and an arrowhead).[87] The extensive remains of wild animals suggest an economy still heavily dependent on hunting.

The cemetery at Dapaozi 大泡子 in the Onggut Banner (Wengniuteqi 翁牛特旗, Inner Mongolia) also belongs to this earlier phase. The pottery found here has a close relation to that of Baijinbao, in Heilongjiang. The northern location of these early sites, and the connection between the Dapaozi and

---

[86] On the classification of northeastern swords, see Lin Yun, "Zhongguo Dongbeixi tong jian chu lun," *Kaogu xuebao* 1980.2: 139–61; Jin Fengyi, "Lun Zhongguo dongbei diqu han quren qingtong duanjian de wenhua yicun," *Kaogu xuebao* 1982.4: 387–426 (part 1), and 1 (1983): 39–54 (part 2).

[87] *Wenwu ziliao congkan* 7 (1983): 138–46.

the Baijinbao pottery, may suggest a southward movement of northern peoples associated with a hoe-agriculture- and hunting-based economy.

The second phase of the Upper Xiajiadian culture (850–750 B.C.) is identified with the Nanshan'gen type site (in Ningcheng 寧城 county, Inner Mongolia), excavated in 1958 and 1961 (Fig. 13.2). Chronologically it is placed between the late Western Zhou and the early Spring and Autumn periods, with a lower limit of approximately 750 B.C. The graves are rectangular earthen pits with stone slabs lining the walls. The funerary assemblage reveals a considerable quantity of bronze objects and some golden ornaments. The characteristic Upper Xiajiadian assemblage of this phase includes bronze weapons, horse fittings, and mirrors. Animal bones of pigs, dogs, cattle, sheep, and deer have been found in considerable quantity. The contemporary settlement and the finding of a hoe indicates the presence of agriculture. But what is most remarkable about Nanshan'gen is the presence of horseback riding, suggested by the already mentioned bronze ring with two figures of horseback riders chasing a hare, and by a varied and sophisticated inventory related to horse and chariot technology: harness with cheekpieces, two different types of bit, and tinkling bells. Moreover, an incised bone plaque also recovered at Nanshan'gen shows a hunting scene with the use of chariots pulled by horses. The bronze weapons unearthed at sites of the second phase of Upper Xiajiadian include bronze daggers, knives, axes, spearheads, arrowheads, shields, and helmets. Human figures represented on the hilt of a dagger can be associated with the plates bearing designs of human faces that were unearthed at Shiertaiyingzi 十二台營子.

This period also boasts two additional important sites: Dongnangou 東南溝 (in Pingchuan 平川 county, Hebei), and the Zhoujiadi 周家地 cemetery (in Aohan 敖漢 Banner, Inner Mongolia).[88] The first was excavated in 1964–65. Of the eleven tombs excavated, only four had burial goods, which suggests the presence of different social groups. Their funerary assemblage, made primarily of bronze weapons, small ornaments, and bone beads, is far less rich than that at Nanshan'gen, but very similar in bronze typology. The second was excavated in 1981 and has been assigned to the Upper Xiajiadian culture of the Spring and Autumn period. Here are fewer weapons and more ornaments, such as bronze plaques and pendants. A special feature of the burial custom is that the face of the dead was covered with sackcloth decorated with turquoise beads and bronze buttons. This characteristic trait may have significance with respect to the ethnic distribution of northern peoples and is sometimes attributed to the Shan Rong 山戎.

In the Xiajiadian culture a special place was reserved for dogs, whose

---

[88] *Kaogu* 1977.1: 51–5; *Kaogu* 1984.5: 417–26.

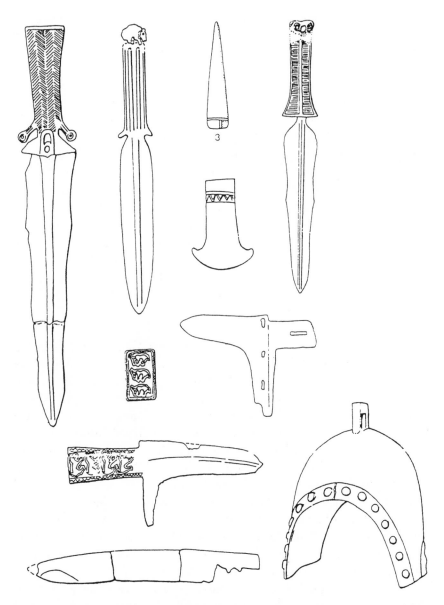

Figure 13.2. Bronze objects of the Upper Xiajiadian culture. After: Zhu Yonggang 朱永剛. "Xiajiadian shangceng wenhua de chubu yanjiu" 夏家店上層文化的初步研究. In *Kaoguxue wenhua lunji* 考古學文化論集 ed. by Su Bingqi 蘇秉琦, (Beijing: Wenwu, 1987), p. 109.

remains have been found in both dwelling sites and sacrificial pits. They also appear as a decorative motif on bronze weapons (a *ge* dagger-axe and a knife) and are depicted on the aforementioned bone plaque representing a hunting scene.

NORTH-CENTRAL REGION. The most representative Western Zhou sites of the so-called Ordos bronze culture of the north-central zone are Lingtai 靈台 in northern Gansu, and Changping 昌平 and Yanqing 延慶, both near Beijing, though Ordos-type finds are also present in Upper Xiajiadian sites, such as Dongnangou and Nanshan'gen tomb 101. During the Western Zhou and early Spring and Autumn periods the Ordos bronze culture went through considerable changes. A general increase in the volume of animal bones, and the presence of a larger number of domesticated animals in the funerary burials, suggest a general tendency toward the expansion of pastoral economies in the Northern Zone.[89] Bronze weapons remained prominent in funerary assemblages, but underwent stylistic modifications. For instance, the earlier animal-head and rattle pommels became rare and were gradually replaced by mushroom pommels.

GANSU–QINGHAI REGION. The Kayue culture of Gansu and Qinghai has been regarded in the past as the successor to the Xindian culture, but recent research has showed that the two were separate and to a certain degree contemporary cultural complexes. The Kayue culture, the first appearance of which is roughly the beginning of the Shang period, and which continues to the Han dynasty, shows a gradual evolution from a mixed farming and pastoral culture with settled life to a predominantly nomadic economy. This transition is reflected not only in an increased number of animal bones and sacrifices, but also in the composition of the animal stock. In the early period (Shangsun 上孫 type), the pig was the usual sacrificial offering, but it disappeared in the middle period (Ahatela 阿哈特拉 type), giving way to cattle and horse sacrifices.[90] In the third phase (Dahuazhongzhuang 大華中莊 type), bronze spears, knives, and *ge* dagger-axes replaced the earlier axes, showing a higher degree of ornamentation. Remains from a late Qijia or early Kayue site in Huangjiazhai 黃家寨 (Datong 大通 county, Qinghai), such as a decor of deer figures on a hollow bone tube, a bronze bird figure, and hooves of sacrificed horses, suggest early contacts with Siberian or Central Asian cultures.[91]

[89] Cui Xuan, "Nei Menggu xian Qin shiqi xumu yicun shulun," *Nei Menggu shehui kexue* 1 (1988): 69–74.
[90] Gao Donglu, "Lüelun Kayue Wenhua," in *Kaoguxue wenhua lunji*, ed. Su Bingqi (Beijing: Wenwu, 1993), vol. 3, pp. 153–65.
[91] *Kaogu* 1994.3: 193–205.

Historical Survey

For the period that stretches from the early Western Zhou to the middle of the Spring and Autumn period, historical documents reveal a complex situation on the northern borders. The Zhou fought various battles against foes who appear to have been their military equals. Some of these eventually forced the rulers of China to evacuate their capital.

The period opens with a series of hostilities between the Zhou and the Guifang 鬼方, one of the northern peoples whom the later historical tradition identifies as ancestors of the Xiongnu.[92] It ends, in 650 B.C., with the last mention of the Northern Rong 北戎, and with the rise of the Di 狄, who thereafter became the most important northern power. The middle of the seventh century B.C. is a turning point in the political balance of the northern frontier, possibly more significant in the history of the northern frontier than the end of the Western Zhou (771 B.C.).

GUIFANG. Records in the *Zhushu jinian* 竹書紀年 (Bamboo annals) state that a people by the name of Gui Rong 鬼戎, certainly the same as the Guifang, were already at war with the Zhou in Shang times, being attacked in the thirty-fifth year of King Wu Yi 武乙 (1119 B.C., according to the chronology given in that text) by the Zhou leader Jili 季歷.[93] The Guifang "proper" who appear during the reign of King Kang 康 (1005/03–978 B.C.) were probably located to the northeast of the Zhou territory. According to the inscription of the *Xiao Yu ding* 小盂鼎, cast in the twenty-fifth year of King Kang (979 B.C.), after two successful battles against the Guifang, captives were brought to the Zhou temple and offered to the king. The prisoners numbered over 13,000 and included four chiefs, the chiefs being executed. A large amount of booty was also collected. In general the Guifang do not seem to have posed any serious threat to the Zhou frontier and must have been either conquered by the Zhou at an early stage or dissolved politically, since their name soon disappears from the patchy sources at our disposal.

XIANYUN 玁狁. The *Shi jing* 詩經 (Classic of poetry) contains four songs that mention military engagements between the Zhou and the Xianyun. As examples of epic poetry, they relate feats of ancient heroes against alien foes. The song "Cai qi" 采芑 (Gathering sow thistle) extols the deeds of Fang Shu

---

[92] Wang Guowei, "Guifang Kunyi Xianyun kao." in *Haining Wang Jing'an xiansheng yishu*, vol. 5, *Guantang jilin*, chapter 13, "Shilin" 5, pp. 1–20.

[93] *Zhushu jinian* (Sibu beiyao ed.) 1, 17b (James Legge, *The Chinese Classics. Vol. 3: The Shoo King* [London: Henry Frowde, 1865], Prolegomena, p. 138).

方叔, who apparently led as many as 3,000 chariots in battle against the Xianyun.[94] The impression created in the songs is one of trepidation, urgency, and great relief and jubilation at the final victory of the Zhou troops. The song "Liu yue" 六月 (Sixth month) provides geographical information that allows us to place the battlefield very close to the center of the Zhou state,[95] between the lower reaches of the Jing 涇 and Luo 洛 Rivers and the Wei River valley. Although scholars dispute the exact date of the attacks, most place it during the reign of King Xuan 宣 (827/25–782 B.C.).

Written records place the first Xianyun incursions against the Zhou in 840 B.C., the fourteenth year of reign of King Li 厲,[96] when they reached the capital itself. Three years earlier the Western Rong (Xi Rong 西戎) had also launched an attack; it is possible that Xianyun and Western Rong may have been the same people, indicated in the first case by a generic term meaning "warlike tribes of the west" and in the second case by their actual ethnonym. They attacked again in 823 B.C, the fifth year of reign of King Xuan.[97] On the basis of their military tactics which were characterized by sudden attacks and could only have been carried out by highly mobile troops, most likely on horseback, some scholars have related the sudden appearance of the Xianyun to the general rise of mounted nomadism in the steppe region and to the specific appearance of Scythians and Cimmerians migrating from the west.[98] No definite evidence, however, supports the hypothesis that they were nomadic warriors.

In fact, new evidence indicates that the Xianyun fought, like the Zhou, on horse-drawn chariots. This is based on the inscription on the *Duo You ding* 多友鼎, unearthed in 1980 near Xi'an 西安, which tells of a Zhou military campaign, probably in 816 B.C., against Xianyun forces that had attacked a Jing 京 garrison in the lower Ordos region.[99] The Xianyun's pressure against the northern frontier was undoubtedly serious; however, there is no evidence that the large size of their armies or their increased mobility can be related to the emergence of a new type of warrior, namely, the mounted nomad armed with bow and arrow.

---

[94] *Shi jing*, 10/2, 8b (Legge, *The Chinese Classics. Vol. 4: The She King*, pp. 284–7).
[95] *Shi Jing*, 10/2, 2a (Legge, *The She King*, pp. 281–4).
[96] *Zhushu jinian*, 2, p. 8a (Legge, *The Shoo King*, Prolegomena, p. 154).
[97] This date is based on the *Xi Jia pan* 兮甲盤 inscription; Ma Chengyuan ed., *Shang Zhou qingtongqi mingwen xuan* (Beijing: Wenwu, 1988), no. 437 (Shaughnessy, *Sources of Western Zhou History*, p. 141); Guo Moruo, *Liang Zhou jinwenci daxi tulu kaoshi* (Beijing: Kexue, 1958), vol. 7, p. 143b.
[98] Yaroslav Průšek, *Chinese Statelets and the Northern Barbarians in the Period 1400–300 B.C.* (Dordrecht: Reidel, 1971), pp. 119–35.
[99] E. Shaughnessy, "The Date of the 'Duo You *Ding*' and Its Significance." *EC* 9–10 (1983–5): 55–69; Li Xueqin, "Lun Duo you ding de shidai ji yiyi," *Renwen zazhi* 1981.6: 87–92; Tian Xingnong and Luo Zhongru, "Duo you ding de faxian ji qi mingwen shishi," *Renwen zazhi* 1981.4: 115–18.

RONG 戎. The term *rong* 戎 is often applied in Chinese sources to warlike foreigners. Its general meaning relates to "martial" and "military," "war" and "weapons."[100] A widely accepted view is that the term "Rong" was used in Chinese sources as a blanket word that included many alien peoples around and within the territory occupied by the Zhou, without a specific ethnic connotation, thus including people not only of the north and west but also of the south – such as the Rong Man 戎蠻.[101] Because of the ambiguity of the term, it is not clear whether it was also used to indicate peoples known by other names, such as the Xianyun. It certainly appears to indicate more than a single people during the reign of King Mu 穆, who defeated the Quan Rong 犬戎 in the twelfth year of his reign and the following year attacked the Western Rong and the Xu Rong 徐戎.[102] These events bespeak a phase of expansion under King Mu, whose journey to the west was romanticized in the fourth century B.C. work *Mu Tianzi zhuan* 穆天子傳 (Biography of the Son of Heaven Mu).[103]

Based on the available records, relations between the Zhou and the Rong do not seem to have been hostile until the seventh year of King Yi 夷 (859 B.C.), when the Rong of Taiyuan 太原 attacked the area of the Zhou capital. At this time the Zhou royal family gradually came to depend on other noble families to defend the realm. In 854 Guo Gong 虢公 attacked the Rong, capturing a thousand horses. Under the reign of King Li 厲, the power of the dynasty was in decline, and both Western Rong and Xianyun launched attacks deep into Zhou territory.

A more energetic policy was followed by King Xuan (827/25–782), during whose period of reign the Zhou gradually incorporated some of the Rong within their own borders. In the fourth year of his reign, King Xuan ordered Qin to attack the Western Rong, who retreated. More expeditions against them finally led to their submission and to territorial gains.[104] Throughout the end of King Xuan's reign there were repeated engagements against the Rong. Particularly significant seem to have been the expedition in either 790 or 788 (the thirty-eighth year of King Xuan's reign) by Jin 晉 against the

---

[100] Everard D. H. Fraser and James H. S. Lockhart, *Index to the Tso Chuan* (London: Oxford University Press, 1930), p. 165. In the *Zuo zhuan, rong* is also used in the sense of "war chariot" in the phrase *yu rong* 御戎 (to drive a war chariot) and in the compound *rong che* 戎車 (war chariot).

[101] This opinion has been challenged by Edwin G. Pulleyblank, who regards the Rong as a Tibeto-Burman group related to the Qiang people, on the one hand, and to the founders of the Zhou dynasty, on the other. See Pulleyblank, "The Chinese and Their Neighbors in Prehistoric and Early Historic Times," in *The Origins of Chinese Civilization*, ed. David N. Keightley (Berkeley: University of California Press, 1983), pp. 416–23.

[102] *Zhushu jinian*, 2, pp. 4b–5a (Legge, *The Shoo King*, Prolegomena, p. 150).

[103] Loewe, *Early Chinese Texts*, pp. 342–6.

[104] *Hou Han shu*, 87, pp. 2871–2.

Northern Rong and the king's expedition the following year against the Rong of the Jiang 姜 clan, who were utterly destroyed.[105]

The final period of the Western Zhou, under the reign of King You 幽 (781–771 B.C.), was marked by increasing instability on the northern frontier and by a series of attacks by the Quan Rong. The Zhou defenses were overrun, the capital invaded, the king killed, and the court forced to move to the city of Luo 雒, marking the beginning of the Spring and Autumn period, in 770 B.C.

During the Western Zhou the various Rong were scattered over a broad area that encompassed the northern and western areas of the Wei River valley, the Fen 汾 River valley, and the Taiyuan 太原 region. They were therefore distributed in present-day northern Shaanxi, northern Shanxi, and Hebei, up to the Taihang 太行 Mountains. With few exceptions, their attacks against the Zhou do not seem to have been particularly effective. Like the Xianyun, they most probably used chariots, but a record for 714 B.C. shows that they also fought on foot.[106] There is no evidence to identify them with the later nomads. Rather, their military pressure on the Zhou borders might be attributed to unrecorded events taking place in the north that set a large number of people in motion and that may be related with the appearance of pastoral nomads. The later arrival of the Di populations along the northern borders of the Central Plain may have also been connected with large-scale migratory movements. Archaeological data concerning the development of horse riding in the northeast, north, and northwest may suggest that the pressure of the Rong, and later Di, on the Zhou northern frontier may have been the indirect effect of nomadic expansion in areas such as western Liaoning, Inner Mongolia, and Ningxia.

During the late Western Zhou, groups of Rong had settled in territory nominally controlled by the Zhou king and were interspersed among the political centers of the Central Plain. During the Eastern Zhou, some Rong tribes were located in the neighborhood of the state of Lu 魯. The Northern (Bei 北), or Mountain (Shan 山) Rong attacked the states of Zheng 鄭 in 714 B.C. and Qi 齊 in 706 B.C.[107] These names indicate relatively broad groups or confederations whose ethnic or political cohesiveness is difficult to determine. For instance, the Shan Rong included a people, known as the Wuzhong 無終, whose location has been traditionally placed by some near

---

[105] *Guo yu* (Sibu beiyao ed.), 1 ("Zhou yu shang"), 9a.

[106] *Zuo zhuan*, 4 (*Yin* 9), 14b (James Legge, *The Chinese Classics. Vol 5: The Ch'un Ts'ew with the Tso Chuen* [London: Trübner, 1872]) p. 28; Yang Bojun, ed., *Chunqiu Zuo zhuan zhu* [Beijing: Zhonghua, 1990], p. 65).

[107] *Zuo zhuan*, 4 (*Yin* 9), 14b (Legge, *The Ch'un Ts'ew with the Tso Chuen*, p. 28; Yang Bojun, ed., *Chunqiu Zuo zhuan zhu*, p. 65); *Zuo zhuan*, 6 (*Huan* 6), 21a (Legge, *The Ch'un Ts'ew with the Tso Chuen*, p. 49; Yang Bojun, ed., *Chunqiu Zuo zhuan zhu*, p. 113).

present-day Beijing, but who were probably located in the Taiyuan region, bordering on the state of Jin 晉.[108] However, other Wuzhong groups appear to have inhabited the region north of the state of Yan.[109] The record of a Wuzhong leader presenting the lord of Jin with tiger and leopard skins indicates that they may have been hunters who lived in or close to a forest environment, perhaps northern Hebei and Liaoning.[110]

The *Zuo zhuan* mentions repeated military clashes between Zhou and Rong forces during the reign of Lu Zhuang Gong 魯莊公 (693–662 B.C.). In 674, Zhuang Gong chased Rong raiders. Two years later Qi attacked them, and in 670 B.C. the Rong attacked the smaller state of Cao 曹. In 668 B.C., Zhuang Gong again attacked the Rong. In 666 B.C., Jin Xian Gong 晉獻公 took Rong women as wives.[111] Qi continued to battle Rong peoples, and in 664 B.C. Qi again obtained a victory against the Shan Rong.[112]

These events show that Rong communities were dispersed over a broad territory across the northern frontier of the Eastern Zhou and that a large number of them had even settled within or to the south of the state of Jin. It is possible that these Rong tribes retained a degree of autonomy or independence, but this was eroded and eventually eliminated by the relentless expansion of the Central States. By the mid-seventh century, the Rong, repeatedly defeated by Jin and hard pressed in the north by the rapidly growing power of the Di, were for the most part incorporated by Jin and Qi. By 662 the Di conquered the Taiyuan plains and replaced the Rong in this important economic zone to the north of Jin.[113]

The Quan Rong, located north of the Wei River valley were defeated by Guo 虢 in 660 and 658 B.C. At the same time, the Di intensified their attacks, first against Xing 邢 and then against Wey 衛. The people of Wey escaped from their city but were pursued by the Di and massacred near the Yellow

---

[108] Průšek, *Chinese Statelets*, p. 21.

[109] See map in ibid., p. 120.

[110] *Zuo zhuan*, 29 (Xiang 4), (22a; Yang Bojun, ed., *Chunqiu Zuo zhuan zhu*, p. 936; Legge, *The Ch'un Ts'ew with the Tso Chuen*, p. 424).

[111] In chronological order: *Zuo zhuan*, 9 (Zhuang 18), 14b, (Legge, *The Ch'un Ts'ew with The Tso Chuen*, p. 97; Yang Bojun, ed., *Chunqiu Zuo zhuan zhu*, p. 208); *Chunqiu*, 9 (Zhuang 20), 19a (Legge, *The Ch'un Ts'ew with the Tso Chuen*, p. 100; Yang Bojun ed., *Chunqiu Zuo zhuan zhu*, p. 214); *Chunqiu*, 10 (Zhuang 24), 3b (Legge, *The Ch'un Ts'ew with the Tso Chuen*, p. 107; Yang Bojun, ed., *Chunqiu Zuo Zhuan zhu*, p. 228); *Chunqiu*, 10 (Zhuang 26), 9a (Legge, *The Ch'un Ts'ew with the Tso Chuen*, p. 110; Yang Bojun, ed., *Chunqiu Zuo zhuan zhu*, p. 233); *Zuo zhuan*, 10 (Zhuang 28), 13a (Legge *The Ch'un Ts'ew with the Tso Chuen*, p. 114; Yang Bojun, ed., *Chunqiu Zuo zhuan zhu*, p. 239).

[112] *Zuo zhuan*, 10 (Zhuang 30), 18b (Legge, *The Ch'un Ts'ew with the Tso Chuen*, pp. 117–18; Yang Bojun, ed., *Chunqiu Zuo Zhuan zhu*, p. 246).

[113] The attacks of Qin against the Rong are related in a later entry in the *Zhu zhuan*, where it is said that Qin, greedy for land, had persecuted the Rong and forced them to migrate and seek the protection of Jin during the period of reign of Duke Hui 惠 (650–636 B.C.). See *Zuo zhuan*, 32 (Xiang 14), 8b (Legge, *The Ch'un Ts'ew with the Tso Chuen*, pp. 463–4; Yang Bojun, ed., *Chunqiu Zuo zhuan zhu*, pp. 1005–7).

River, only a few hundred people managing to survive.[114] The Di threat was so great that it prompted a renewed unity of the states of the Central Plain, which formed a league in 659 B.C. to save Xing.

The last mention we have of the Bei Rong is in the year 650 B.C., when they were attacked by Qi and Xu 許; the "Bei Rong" mentioned here possibly refers to the same people as the Shan Rong who attacked Yan 燕 in 664. After this event, the term "Rong" appears vestigially, often in compound with Di to indicate generic non-Chinese peoples to the north and west.

Culturally, the Rong seem to have had a keen sense of their difference from the Hua-Xia people. This is plainly expressed by a Rong leader, who is reported to have said that "in what we drink and eat, and in the way we dress, all of us Rong are different from the Chinese [Hua]. We do not exchange gifts with them, and do not understand each other's language."[115] However, it is not possible to identify them according to distinct ethnic or linguistic affiliations. Possibly they were hunting-farming communities that retained customs and forms of political organization markedly different from the Chinese. They were also associated with pastoral activities, but it is highly unlikely that they had a mature nomadic steppe economy. They also lacked unity, thus eventually becoming part of the Zhou political "galaxy," playing a gradually less important role in the political and military history of the Eastern Zhou.

MID-SPRING AND AUTUMN PERIOD TO THE MID-WARRING STATES (CA. 650–350 B.C.)

Development of Early Nomadic Cultures in Northern China

The first historical steppe nomads, the Scythians, inhabited the steppe north of the Black Sea from about the eighth century B.C. Pastoral nomadism was their main economic activity, and their society was ruled by a class of mounted warriors, who in Herodotus's *Histories* are called Royal Scythians. Below this aristocracy were other groups, such as the "agricultural," "nomadic," and "free" Scythians. Archaeologically, early nomadic cultures close to the Scythian, characterized by "specific equestrian armaments, horse trappings and the Animal Style,"[116] became dominant throughout the steppe region of Central Asia in the first half of the first millennium B.C. In the

---

[114] *Zuo zhuan*, 11 (Min 2), 9a (Legge, *The Ch'un Ts'ew with the Tso Chuen*, pp. 129–30; Yang Bojun, ed., *Chunqiu Zuo zhuan zhu*, pp. 265–6).

[115] *Zuo zhuan*, 32 (Xiang 14), 10b (Legge, *The Ch'un Ts'ew with the Tso Chuen*, p. 464; Yang Bojun, ed., *Chunqiu Zuo zhuan zhu*, p. 1007).

[116] Karl Jettmar, "The Origins of Chinese Civilization: Soviet Views," in *The Origins of Chinese Civilization*, ed. D. N. Keightley (Berkeley: University of California Press, 1983), p. 224.

northern area of the eastern steppe, which includes South Siberia, the Altai region, Mongolia, and Transbaikalia, evidence suggests that the early nomadic phase may have started as early as the eighth century B.C.[117]

Two separate centers existed in this region. To the east, in Transbaikalia and Mongolia's southern Gobi region, is a complex characterized by cist-stone tombs, bronze knives with characteristic human and animal decorations on the handle, and a Northern Asiatic anthropological type, similar to that of the Xiongnu burials of Noin Ula.[118] In Western Mongolia, the Altai region, and Tuva, there are timber-chamber burials similar to those of Pazyryk, as well as petroglyphs, bronze objects, and decorations in the Animal Style typical of the steppe region of Kazakhstan, Tuva, and South Siberia; the totemic sculptures known as "deer stones"; and a racial type with Europoid characteristics.[119]

This cultural separation can also be traced along the Chinese frontier. Anthropological studies have ascertained the Europoid character of nomadic cultures of Xinjiang, such as the Wusun 烏孫 and Saka.[120] Discoveries at burial sites in Ningxia show that around 500 B.C. the North Asian Mongoloid component of the population increased considerably and was associated with nomadic cultural forms.[121] This suggests the existence of two different anthropological and cultural complexes that came to share a similar way of life and cultural features. Unambiguous elements of horse-riding nomadic culture appear in the eastern steppe before the eighth century B.C., and specific early nomadic cultural features found in northern China – characteristic shapes and "animal" decorations of knives, daggers, and belt buckles – belong to the same cultural universe as the contemporary cultures of the South Siberian region. In the eighth and seventh centuries B.C., the needle of the Northern Zone's cultural orientation pointed to the north and west.

Questions concerning the historical context in which archaeological data from the Northern Zone should be read have suggested the movement of various Central Asian nomads to the Inner Asian borders of China, sometimes thought to have provided the impulse for the transition to nomadism

---

[117] Jettmar. *Art of the Steppes*, p. 143; Kiselev, *Dreviniaia istoriia Iuzhnoi Sibiri*, pp. 302–3.

[118] S. I. Rudenko, *Die Kultur der Hsiung-nu und die Hügelgräber von Noin Ula* (Bonn: Habelt, 1969), pp. 99–106.

[119] E. Nowgorodowa, "Mongolie de l'époque du 'style animale.'" in *Ethnologie und Geschichte. Festschrift für Karl Jettmar*, ed. Peter Snoy (Wiesbaden: Harrassowitz, 1983), pp. 440–4. On the Pazyryk culture, see S. I. Rudenko, *Frozen Tombs of Siberia: The Pazyryk Burials of Iron Age Horsemen* (London: Dent, 1970). On Siberian and East Asian animal styles, see Shu Takahama, "Early Scytho-Siberian Animal Style in East Asia," *Bulletin of the Ancient Orient Museum* 5 (1983): 45–51.

[120] Han Kangxin, "Xinjiang Kongjiaohe Gumugou mudi rengu yanjiu," *Kaogu xuebao* 1986.1: 361–84; Han Kangxin and Pan Qifeng, "Xinjiang Zhaosu Wusun mu gu renleixue cailiao de yanjiu," *Kaogu xuebao* 1987.4: 503–23.

[121] Han Kangxin, "Ningxia Pengpu Yujiazhuang mudi rengu zhongxi tedian zhi yanjiu," *Kaogu xuebao* 1995.1: 107–25.

in northern China.[122] However, it is more plausible that though the initial impulse may have come from large-scale migratory movements, the evolution toward fully developed pastoral nomadism soon acquired, in the various areas comprising the Northern Zone, a distinct local flavor, as it blended with pre-existing cultures. The chronological discrepancy between the *archaeological* existence of a more or less homogeneous "early nomadic" bronze culture in the steppe in the eighth century and the later *historical* appearance of mounted nomads in Chinese sources, in the fourth century B.C., may be due to the slow expansion of contacts between these cultures and China, hampered by the presence of intermediate sedentary peoples. Between the seventh and the fourth century B.C., contacts between the Central Plain and the far northwest were established.[123] The presence of Chinese silk and lacquer in the burials of the Altai culture of Pazyryk of the fifth century B.C. demonstrates the existence of at least indirect contacts. Moreover, the continued preference for, and even growth in the use of, bronze to produce funerary and ritual objects, even where iron metallurgy was available, separates the northern region, and the eastern steppe in general, from developments in western Central Asia, where ferrous metallurgy gradually replaced bronze.[124] The discovery of early Chinese knife-coins in Inner Mongolia dated to the sixth century has been interpreted as evidence of a certain degree of trade between China and the north.[125]

The archaeological cultures of northern China display a variety of centers that suggest two levels of development. At one level, represented by the metal production and use of ritual and functional tools and weapons similar to the early nomadic complex, they can be related to the continental phenomenon of the spread of nomadic pastoral societies. At a different level, represented by pottery and burial customs, we find a variety of local traditions. Possibly nomadic groups expanded and became dominant over communities that eventually adopted their technology. Alternatively, we may suppose a parallel development of the same technology within contiguous but different local traditions, as they progressed on the road of pastoral specialization.

[122] Gustav Haloun, *Seit wann kannten die Chinesen die Tocharer oder Indogermanen überhaupt* (Leipzig: Verlag der Asia Major, 1926); R. Heine-Geldern, "Das Tocharenproblem und die Pontische Wanderung," *Saeculum* 2 (1951): 225. According to Jettmar's more cautious opinion, the transition to nomadism was influenced by a general "contact" with a zone of unrest to the south and west of the steppes; movement in the area of the Volga River seems to have led this process, which was only realized over a fairly extended period of time. See Jettmar, *Art of the Steppes*, p. 215.

[123] On the issue of the first appearance of nomads in the Chinese sources, see Owen Lattimore, *Inner Asian Frontiers of China* (Boston: Beacon, 1962), pp. 60, 341; Pulleyblank, "The Chinese and Their Neighbors in Prehistoric and Early Historic Times," pp. 449–450; Yü Ying-shih, "The Hsiung-nu," in *The Cambridge History of Early Inner Asia*, ed. Denis Sinor (Cambridge University Press, 1990), p. 118.

[124] Chernykh, *Ancient Metallurgy in the USSR*, p. 271.

[125] William Watson, *Cultural Frontiers in Ancient East Asia*, pp. 101–2.

Major Archaeological Cultures

NORTHEASTERN ZONE. The heart of the late Bronze Age and Iron Age cultures, in Heilongjiang, is to be found at the confluence of the Sungari (Songhua 松花) and Nonni (Nenjiang) Rivers, known as Song–Nen Plain (see Map 13.3).[126] In this area rich in forests, arable land, and waterways, we find iron metallurgy that can be dated to the eighth century B.C. or even earlier, appearing together with the full blossoming of bronze production.

The two most important cultures for this period are Pingyang 平洋 and Hanshu 漢書 II, both of which present rich metal assemblages of bronze and iron. The Pingyang culture has been identified in burials in southwestern Heilongjiang and eastern Inner Mongolia,[127] but no settlements associated with this culture have been found. The type site is Pingyang (Tailai 泰來 county, Heilongjiang), which consists of two cemeteries, Zhuanchang 磚廠 and Zhandou 戰斗, excavated respectively in 1984 and 1985 and dating from the late Spring and Autumn to the middle Warring States period. The burials present very similar characteristics. Most of them are simple rectangular earthen pit graves, often used for multiple burials. A few tombs are T-shaped pit graves. Animal sacrifice was common, in particular dog and horse, with possible preference for the dog. The funerary inventory includes objects in bronze, iron, and gold, a large variety of pottery, and other tools made of bone or stone. Among the bronzes decorative elements prevail and include Animal Style plaques, buttons, and circular discs. The iron items are mostly objects of daily use, such as arrowheads, scrapers, and spearheads, though "tube ornaments" have also been found. The gold objects include three earrings and two plates. Most of the finds come from the first cemetery. Other burial goods include stone, agate, turquoise, bone, antler, ivory, and shell. The importance of archery is demonstrated by the discovery of more than 50 bow ends and 240 arrowheads.

On the basis of stratigraphic analysis and typological comparison with Baijinbao and Sanjiazi 三家子 (Qiqihaer 齊齊哈爾 city, Heilongjiang), archaeologists have proposed four phases of development, spanning from the late Spring and Autumn to the late Warring States. Some of the mortuary practices are similar to those found at Sanjiazi, such as the coexistence of primary

---

[126] Tan Ying-jie et al., "The Bronze Age in the Song Nen Plain," in *The Archaeology of Northeast China: Beyond the Great Wall*, ed. Sarah M. Nelson (London: Routledge, 1995), pp. 225–50. Tan Yingjie and Zhao Shandong, "Song Nen pingyuan qingtong wenhua chuyi," in *Zhongguo kaogu xuehui disici nianhui lunwenji 1983* (Beijing: Wenwu, 1985), pp. 196–202. Yang Hu, Tan Yingjie, Zhang Taixiang, "Heilongjiang gudai wenhua chulun," in *Zhongguo kaogu xuehui diyici nianhui lunwenji 1979* (Beijing: Wenwu, 1980), pp. 80–96. Li Chenqi et al., "Song Nen pingyuan qingtong yu chuxing zaoqi tieqi shidai wenhua leixing de yanjiu," *Beifang wenwu* 1994.1: 2–9.

[127] *Pingyang muzang* (Beijing: Wenwu, 1990).

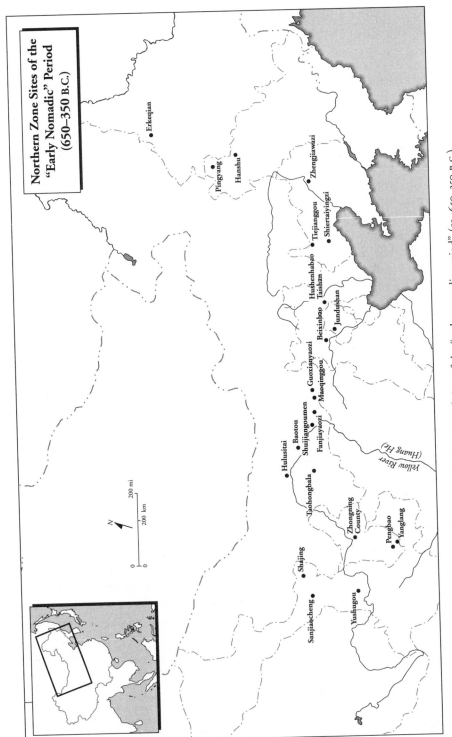

Map 13.3. Northern Zone: Archaeological sites of the "early nomadic period" (ca. 650–350 B.C.).

and secondary burials, animal sacrifice, and the custom of covering the deceased's face with bronze buttons. The latter custom is characteristic of sites that as we have seen above, are attributed to the Shan Rong. The type of assemblage suggests a mixed hunting-pastoral economy, with considerable use of metal. It is possible that this area was a center of metal production, but it is doubtful whether its people had achieved a full transition to pastoral nomadism. The artistic vocabulary, nonetheless, includes the classic motifs of the Animal Style plaques and small ornamental objects. This area, rich in rivers and forests, may have also been important as a route of communication between northeastern China and Transbaikalia and Mongolia.

The cemetery of Sanjiazi is dated to the Warring States period.[128] It is similar to Pingyang, and includes multiple burials in rectangular earthen pit graves, with evidence of sacrifices of horses and dogs. The metal remains include objects in bronze, iron, gold, and silver. Here, too, bronze is used almost exclusively for ornamental objects, whereas iron is also used for weapons and tools. As for precious metals, only one golden pendant and one silver earring have been found. A number of bow ends and bone arrowheads points to a developed hunting economy. Silk from China has also been found, suggesting that by the Warring States period, Heilongjiang had some relations with the Central Plain, possibly the state of Yan.

The presence of several semisubterranean dwellings and carbonized grains indicates that the Hanshu II culture was a settled one. Located in the same area as the Hanshu culture, it forms an independent complex, extending into the Song–Nen Plain.[129] It displays a bronze production that is varied and large, but is typically limited to small tools and ornaments, such as knives, arrowheads, awls, earrings, and buttons. Large bronze objects, such as daggers, are absent. Over fifty clay molds for bronze objects have been recovered, revealing local manufacture of spears, buckles, arrowheads, and horse-shaped ornamental plaques. Sandstone molds have also been found for axes and fishing hooks. But even more interesting is the recovery of iron-socketed axes and knives, which are similar to those found in the Central Plain during the Warring States period. The main economic activity was agriculture, but the presence of fishing hooks, boat-shaped pottery bowls, pots decorated with painted net patterns, and the large number of fish bones also suggests that fishing was widely practiced.

The burial site at Erkeqian 二克淺 (Nehe 訥河 county), excavated in 1985,[130] has also been associated with this culture. The metal funerary assemblage features mainly small bronze objects, such as knives, bells, plates, buttons, and

[128] *Kaogu* 1988.12: 1090–8.   [129] *Dongbei kaogu yu lishi* 1982.1: 136–40.
[130] An Lu and Jia Weiming, "Heilongjiang Nehe Erkeqian mudi ji qi wenti tantao," *Beifang wenwu* 1986.2: 2–8.

earrings, as well as some rusted iron objects, among which daggers and knives can be identified. The burials are rectangular earthen pits, in several cases with remains of a male and a female in the same burial and sacrifices of dogs and horses. At this site we find again two types of relics, one belonging to an earlier stratum, probably later than the Baojinbao culture, the other being roughly contemporary with the Hanshu II culture. The difference is marked not only in the pottery assemblage, which in the later burials includes more vessels and decorative patterns, but also in the metal assemblage. In the second, or upper, layer, an iron dagger has been found that is very similar in shape to the bronze daggers of the Northern Zone.[131] The earlier phase has been dated from the Spring and Autumn period, whereas the second phase seems to belong to the Warring States.

What the finds suggest is a pattern of cultural evolution, from the Spring and Autumn to the late Warring States, not dissimilar from the one observed in the Ordos region. This seems to emphasize two elements. The first is the creation of a wider and more stable network of contacts through which both artistic motifs and technical innovations could travel rapidly. This network included, in its southern fringes, adjacent parts of China, such as the state of Yan. The second is a more liberal use of iron; bronze was still widespread but increasingly limited to decorative objects. The molds indicate an advanced level of production and possibly show that these sites were centers of cultural diffusion within the Northern Zone.

In Liaoning and eastern Inner Mongolia the period ca. 650–350 B.C. corresponds to the last stage of the Upper Xiajiadian culture. It is best represented by the Shiertaiyingzi 十二台營子 site (Chaoyang 朝陽, Liaoning), a cemetery in use since the Western Zhou, whose upper layer is dated to the early and middle part of the Warring States period, that is, ca. 450–350 B.C. The metal inventory is entirely of bronze, and includes curved-blade daggers, mirrors with multiple knobs, knives, arrowheads, ornaments in various shapes, belt hooks, and buckles.[132] Because of the site's location, archaeologists often associate this culture with the people known in historical documents as Dong Hu 東胡, but without direct evidence such identification is purely speculative.

The cemetery found at Tiejianggou 鐵匠溝 (Aohan Banner, Inner Mongolia), which is located in the eastern part of Inner Mongolia and within the area of distribution of the Upper Xiajiadian culture, is representative.[133] Five tombs of this cemetery have been excavated; they can be divided into two

[131] Zhao Shantong, "Heilongjiang Guandi yizhi faxian de muzang," *Kaogu* 1965.1: 45–6.
[132] Zhu Gui, "Liaoning Chaoyang Shiertaiyingzi qingtong duanjianmu," *Kaogu xuebao* 1960.1: 63–71.
[133] This was excavated in May 1991. See Shao Guotian, "Aohanqi Tiejiangguo Zhanguo mudi diaocha jianbao," *Nei Menggu wenwu kaogu* 1991.1–2: 84–90.

groups. The first group (three tombs) yielded funerary objects such as bronze artifacts, pottery, and stone ornaments, whereas no burial goods were recovered from the second. The bronze objects include three knives and various Animal Style ornaments, belt hooks, buttons, earrings, and arrowheads. These burials are comparatively poor. Since a number of decorative and stylistic elements link this site with Xiaobaiyang 小白陽 (Xuanhua 宣化 county, Hebei), its occupants may been have southern immigrants, pushed north – and eventually subjugated – as a consequence of Yan's expansion. The area was conquered by Yan in 299 B.C., the terminal date of the site.

NORTH-CENTRAL ZONE. The north-central frontier in this period presents a fluid picture. Some sites display traits that already foreshadow the appearance of a Xiongnu culture. Others show a lesser degree of change with respect to the previous period. Though ethnic or historical attributions are highly speculative, these sites are frequently associated with the Shan Rong and the Di.

Archaeological sites attributed to the Shan Rong are scarcely consistent with any specific culture. Generally speaking, these are burial grounds whose system of interment differs from that of the Central Plain, and whose funerary inventory shows mixed derivation and cultural affiliation. Many of these sites are located to the northeast of the Central Plain. The cemetery sites at Hushiha Paotaishan 虎什哈炮台山 (Luanping 灤平 county, Hebei) and at Jundushan 軍都山 (Yanqing county, Beijing),[134] have been dated to the late Spring and Autumn and early Warring States periods and attributed to the Shan Rong. The chief common characteristic of these sites is that while they show a clear association with the culture of the Central Plain, several discoveries link them with Northern Zone cultures. The Hebei site, for instance, participates in the last phase of the Upper Xiajiadian culture, whereas in the Yanqing burials a great number of weapons and horse fittings are found that show a clear association with the Ordos–Xiongnu bronze culture. Similar objects are also found in northern Hebei. Moreover, there are several types of burials, such as earthen pits, stone chambers, and wooden coffins. In some cases there are combinations of both stone chambers and wooden coffins. One particular aspect of the burial custom consists of covering the face of the deceased with sackcloth decorated with bronze buttons, similar to the custom found in Heilongjiang.

Other cemeteries, to the north of the Beijing area, are also characterized by a combination of more than one burial practice. At a site in Baotou 包頭 county, Inner Mongolia, excavated in 1988 and attributed to the Lin Hu,

---

[134] *Wenwu ziliao congkan* 1983.7: 67–74; *Wenwu* 1989.8: 17–35, 43.

both rectangular earthen pits and catacomb-style burials were found.[135] Animals were sacrificed and buried with the deceased on secondary platforms. The funerary assemblage is dominated by bronze ornaments, such as buckles, plaques, rings, buttons, earrings, and other small ornaments. In addition to these, there are tools and weapons, such as a spoon, an arrowhead, belt hooks, buckles, and knives. The bronze buckles are in typical northern Animal Style, similar to finds from Maoqinggou 毛慶溝 (Inner Mongolia). The three-winged arrowhead found here has a very large distribution, including Inner Mongolia (Liangcheng 涼城 county), Hebei (Beixinbao 北辛堡, in Huailai 懷來 county), and Liaoning (Zhengjiawazi 鄭家窪子, Shenyang 瀋陽).[136] Similar specimens have also been found in Iron Age burials (sixth century B.C.) in Transbaikalia. Several elements, such as a bronze semiannular pendant, similar to a silver one found in Guyuan 固原 county, Ningxia, and the shape of the catacomb burials, common to the Xindian and Kayue cultures, also suggest contacts with the northwest. While the assemblage in Baotou exhibits similarities with later Xiongnu sites, it is remarkable for the absence of some of the most typical elements of later nomadic cultures: iron, gold, and horse fittings, as well as the daggers, pickaxes, and plaques typical of the Ordos bronzes.

Another Inner Mongolian site attributed to a northern people, the Northern Di, is that of Guoxianyaozi 嶹縣窯子 (Liangcheng county, Inner Mongolia), excavated in May–July 1983.[137] Archaeologists believe three phases of development can be identified, from the late Spring and Autumn to the early Warring States. The burial practices are similar to those at Jundushan. They include rectangular vertical earthen pits – sometimes provided with head niches and secondary platforms, wooden coffins, stone chambers, or a combination of both. Interments are single in extended supine position with the head to the east. Animal sacrifices were practiced, and males were typically buried with horses, deer, or sheep, whereas females were buried with sacrifices of cattle and sheep. However, we do not find in Guoxianyaozi the custom of covering the face of the deceased with sackcloth decorated with bronze buttons.

The assemblage consists mostly of bronze ornaments, such as buckles, plaques, buttons, bells, rings, and earrings. Among the tools, we find two knives and a pickaxe. The plaques are particularly abundant – forty-four – and are in both Geometric Style and Animal Style. The buckles and the button ornaments establish a context for this site that is typical of the Ordos region. Similar buckles were found at contemporary or later Ordos sites, such as Taohongbala 桃紅巴拉, Fanjiayaozi 范家窯子 (Helin'geer 和林格爾), and

---

[135] *Nei Menggu wenwu kaogu* 1991.1.: 13–24.
[136] On Zhengjiawazi, see *Kaogu xuebao* 1975.1: 141–56.   [137] *Kaogu xuebao* 1989.1: 57–81.

Xigoupan 西溝畔. Similar bronze bells have been found at Beixinbao.[138] Among the other materials, stone beads are particularly numerous, with some of turquoise and one of agate. The bone arrowheads are similar to the bronze examples found in Taohongbala and are probably a poorer prototype.

Despite all the similarities with the early Xiongnu sites, specimens of the most advanced technology available in the area at this time, such as the iron daggers and horse fittings found at Taohongbala and Maoqinggou, do not appear here. Although horses were bred and used in sacrifices, the people of Guoxianyaozi do not seem to have had a highly developed horse-riding culture. Their metal inventory indicates a people rather different from the typical early nomads and points to a pastoral-hunting community that had established contacts with other more powerful mounted nomads who were gradually penetrating the area and establishing themselves throughout the steppe belt of Inner Mongolia and especially in the Ordos region. In Yanqing the metal inventory is dominated by bronze weapons and horse fittings. Whereas ornaments such as plaques, belt hooks, buckles, and bells are reminiscent of the Guoxianyaozi site, the discovery of about a hundred daggers with straight blade, *ge* dagger-axes, and axes indicates a southern extension of a martial horse-riding community of the Ordos type. They are also likely to have had trade relations with the Central Plain, as knife-coins have been found from the late Spring and Autumn and early Warring States.

The earliest Xiongnu-type bronze and early iron sites in the Ordos region are the cemeteries of Taohongbala and Maoqinggou (Inner Mongolia). The excavation of Taohongbala has brought to light a large number of small ornamental objects, which include plaques, buckles, rings, button-like and pea-shaped bronze decorative elements, and ornaments with a double-bird motif.[139] Stylistic affinities connect Taohongbala not only with Warring States sites, but also with earlier Upper Xiajiadian sites. Similar bronze plaques have been found, for instance, at Nanshan'gen. Bronze daggers in the so-called Antennae Style (*chujiao shi* 觸角式) are widespread and found, among others, at Beixinbao (Hebei) and Fanjiayaozi (Inner Mongolia). The ring ornaments are similar to those seen in Fanjiayaozi. The metal inventory also includes a pair of gold earrings like those seen in Nanshan'gen and Beixinbao.

Taohongbala was originally regarded as a site of the Bai Di 白狄, and has only later come to be recognized as a Xiongnu site. This is undoubtedly due

---

[138] *Kaogu* 1966.5: 231–42.

[139] Tian Guangjin, "Taohongbala de Xiongnu mu." The site consists of seven tombs excavated in 1973. In the original report published in 1976, Taohongbala was dated to the Warring States and regarded as a Xiongnu site on the basis of typological similarities with Xiongnu sites in Inner Mongolia, such as Fanjiayaozi, and the presence of iron objects. In the reprint of 1986 the site is attributed to the late Spring and Autumn period on the basis of carbon dating to approximately the sixth to fifth century B.C.

to the difficulty of attributing a site to a people – the Xiongnu – who appear in the historical records only two centuries later. However, the pottery found here, and in particular the brown single-ear *guan* 罐 pots, handmade and fired at low temperature, shows continuity with the Xiongnu sites of the Warring States period, such as Xigoupan and Aluchaideng 阿魯柴登, which present a type of gray pottery that is a more refined development of the earlier brown variety. This suggests that radical changes in the population of the area, if they occurred at all, must be dated to the late Spring and Autumn rather than to the mid-Warring States period, when the Xiongnu make their appearance in the written sources.

The other important Xiongnu site is that of Maoqinggou,[140] which presents a four-phase chronological evolution. The first phase, dated to the late Spring and Autumn period, contains pottery and bronze items. The treatment of the body, shape of the burial, and animal sacrifice have clear parallels at the previously discussed Guoxianyaozi site. Other similarities are seen in the absence of iron and the presence of a large number of bronze ornamental plates. But there are several discordant elements, such as the presence, in Maoqinggou, of a bronze dagger with double-bird-head pommel, of a bronze bit, and of belthooks, all of which are missing in Guoxianyaozi. It is possible that the early people of Maoqinggou belonged to the same cultural milieu as those of Guoxianyaozi but were starting to develop in the direction of a more specialized pastoral nomadism.

The later period of Maoqinggou, inclusive of early, middle, and late Warring States – phases II, III, and IV, respectively – shows a great difference with respect to phase I, such that archaeologists have attributed the first period to the Di and the subsequent ones to the Loufan 樓煩, a people who were certainly horse-riding steppe nomads and culturally related to the Xiongnu. In these later burials a large number of iron objects, including daggers, pickaxes, one knife, ornamental plates, and belthooks, have been found (Fig. 13.3). The typical jar with a small mouth, round belly, and round bottom of the early period is replaced with a similar example with a flat bottom. In the upper layer a knife-coin has been found, which again indicates the existence of trade with China. The appearance of iron is incremental, used not only for weapons and tools but also for ornamental plates. This site is thought to have been abandoned at the beginning of the third century as a result of occupation by Zhao.

The site's economy shows both pastoral and agricultural elements. Remains of a settlement, kilns, and pottery are next to the cemetery, whose funerary goods show the same military and ornamental inventory that is

---

[140] See Tian Guanjin and Guo Suxin, eds., *O'erduosi qingtong qi*, pp. 227–315.

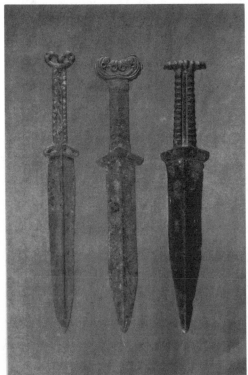

Figure 13.3. Bronze daggers and Animal Style plaque from Maoqinggou. From: Tian Guanjin 田廣金 and Guo Suxin 郭素新, eds., *O'erduosi qingtong qi* 鄂爾多斯青銅器, plates XXVI, XXVIII, LXVII (Beijing: Wenwu, 1986).

characteristic of the Northern Zone. The weapons are mostly bronze daggers and arrowheads in the earlier part of the site, with more iron objects in the later graves. Ornaments are in the animal style, with the bird as a favorite subject. Particularly common are the bronze plates with a double-bird design and a plate shaped in the form of a bird. Besides these, there are objects related to horse management, such as rein rings and bits. In sum, we find here an assemblage typical of an early nomadic culture and closely related to that of Taohongbala. The split between the earliest occupancy and the later tombs seems to support the hypothesis of a gradual affirmation of pastoral nomadism in this area. In the case of Maoqinggou, the shift must have taken place in the course of the sixth century. Given the similarities in mortuary practices and pottery types between the two phases, an internal evolution is likely to have occurred, though the new technology may also point to intrusive elements. However, the hypothesis that a new aristocracy of "Scythian-type" nomads might have extended its rule to this area is, at the present stage, insufficiently supported, requiring the existence of an original homeland that cannot presently be established.

Another site that can be attributed to the early nomads is Hulusitai 呼魯斯太 (Wulate Zhonghou Lianhe Qi 烏拉特中後聯合旗, Inner Mongolia).[141] This is dated to the early Warring States (fifth to fourth century B.C.) and belongs to a group of transitional sites between the late Spring and Autumn and the middle to late Warring States Xiongnu sites, which also include Fanjiayaozi and Shuijiangoumen 水澗溝門 (Tumote Youqi 土默特右旗, Inner Mongolia).[142] The assemblage is very similar to those at Taohongbala and Maoqinggou, but presents also more advanced elements, which are found in later Warring States Ordos sites (Zhunge'er 準格爾 Banner) such as Yulongtai 玉隆太, Xigoupan, and Sujigou 速機溝. The bronze tools and weapons such as bronze daggers, arrowheads, knives, axes, and pickaxes are very close to late Spring and Autumn types. Horse fittings are also similar to the earlier types. Innovations appear mostly in the area of ornamental objects, as in the case of decorative waist belts, which foreshadow the golden hu 胡 belt of the later period. Modifications in the production of traditional objects were also carried out, and certain features were standardized, as in the case of the wing-shaped dagger guard.[143] This site has been attributed to the Xiongnu.

This analysis of the Ordos and contiguous areas seems to indicate the existence of non-horse-riding communities living together, or in close proximity, with more advanced Scythic, early nomadic people already adept in the

---

[141] Ta la and Liang Jinming, "Hulusitai Xiongnu mu," *Wenwu* 1980.7: 11–12.
[142] On the latter see Tian Guanjin and Guo Suxin, eds., *O'erduosi qingtong qi*, pp. 220–1.
[143] Tian Guangjin, "Jinnianlai Nei Menggu diqu de Xiongnu kaogu."

use of the horse for riding and war. In Hebei, Liaoning, and Inner Mongolia, a radical transformation was taking place, which must surely be associated with the rise of new types of societies, both more mobile and militarily superior. It is not excluded that at least part of this transformation may have been caused by the arrival of northern people from Mongolia and Transbaikalia. They brought new types of burial systems,[144] such as the wooden and stone-cist coffins, and a new burial inventory, in which symbols of a warlike, horse-riding culture predominated. It is this movement that may have been responsible for the sudden acceleration of pressure on the northern frontier from people such as the Chi Di 赤狄, Bai Di, and Shan Rong in the mid-seventh century B.C.

The so-called pre-Xiongnu culture, therefore, should be seen as a synchronic evolution of different core areas where a true nomadic aristocracy established itself either by migration or internal evolution. Throughout the steppe and mountain areas of the northern region, increasingly homogeneous material culture, religious beliefs, and rituals were adopted, some of which coexisted and blended with the mortuary practices of preexisting and neighboring people. Due probably to increased contacts with China, the character of this aristocracy gradually began to shift from a notion of power and status symbolized by weapons and tools, to one in which wealth, accumulated in precious metals and stones, horses, and ornamental art, became its predominant pursuit.

NORTHWESTERN ZONE

GANSU. The Hexi 河西 Corridor, an arid region in northern Gansu between the Yellow River and the steppe region of the eastern Tianshan region, is home to the Shajing 沙井 culture, distributed over Minqin 民勤, Yongchang 永昌, Gulang 古浪, and Yongdeng 永登 counties.[145] Its chronology with respect to other regional cultures such as Siwa, Xindian, and Kayue, is not clear, but it is probably later than Xindian, partly overlapping with the Kayue culture, and probably dating from the Spring and Autumn to the Warring States. Its type site is Shajing cun 沙井村 (Minqin county) excavated in 1923–4 by Andersson.[146] It consists of a fortified dwelling site and a cemetery of forty graves. The settlement is surrounded by an earthen wall, and among the metal finds both in the settlement and in the funerary assemblage we find small bronze items: spearheads, arrowheads, knives, and orna-

---

[144] On Xiongnu burials, see S. Minyaev, "Niche Grave Burials of the Xiong-nu Period in Central Asia," *Information Bulletin. International Association for the Cultures of Central Asia*, 17 (1990): 91–99; S. Minyaev. "On the Origin of the Hiung-nu." *Information Bulletin. International Association for the Cultures of Central Asia* 9 (1985): 69–78.

[145] K. C. Chang, *The Archaeology of Ancient China*, pp. 407–8. See also *Kaogu yu wenwu* 1981.4: 34–6.

[146] J. C. Andersson, "Researches into the Prehistory of the Chinese," *BMFEA* 15 (1943): 197–215.

ments. Among the other remains, cowrie shells, turquoise beads, and marble
rings were used as ornaments. One of these, a three-lobed object with spiral
design, is similar to one found in a Warring States tomb at Luanping 灤平
county, Hebei.[147] A similar fortified settlement has also been found at Sanjiaocheng 三角城 (Yongchang county),[148] where a late Warring States date is
suggested by the presence of an iron hoe.

More iron objects have been unearthed at Yushugou 榆樹溝 (Yongdeng
county), which marks the southern extension of the Shajing culture. At this
site, one tomb has been excavated; it presents a number of features roughly
comparable to those of the Ordos sites of the Spring and Autumn period.
Animal sacrifices of horse, sheep, and cattle are evident. The bronze objects
include mainly ornaments in the animal style (eagle, deer, and dog), but also
a chariot axle end. The iron production is limited to tools, such as an object
in the shape of a spade, a spearhead, and a drill. The ornaments can be compared to those of Northern Zone sites of the Spring and Autumn and Warring
States periods such as Taohongbala (round ornaments), the Zhongshan 中山
state in Pingshan 平山, Hebei (openwork round ornaments with a whirlwind
design), and Xigoupan (eagle head). The appearance of a reddish, coarse-
grained jar with a double loop on the shoulders typical of Shajing shows the
affiliation of this site with the Shajing culture.

The presence of settlements and agricultural tools reveals a farming
culture. These people also bred animals, as indicated by the animal sacrifices.
The presence of fortifications suggests conflicts with neighboring peoples,
who were probably nomads. Moreover, ornaments closely related to those
of the Ordos and Hebei Northern Zone sites, such as cowrie shells and
turquoise beads, are evidence of trade with those areas.

NINGXIA. The ancient cemetery at Yanglang 楊郎 (Guyuan county,
Ningxia), dated to the Eastern Zhou period, shows strong similarities with
the early Ordos Xiongnu sites of Taohongbala and Maoqinggou.[149] The predominant burial style is the catacomb grave, so called because of its L-shaped
configuration, with the body placed in a lateral locule, or niche, typically
lower than the main shaft of the grave, and sealed with stones. Over 800
objects of bronze, iron, gold, silver, and bone, in addition to 2,000 beads,
were found. These were not specifically made for funerary purposes, but were
typically objects of daily use that had belonged to the dead. They reveal
strong local characteristics, particularly in the bone items and clothing ornaments. The graves are divided stratigraphically into two periods, the first
from the late Spring and Autumn and early Warring States, and the second

[147] K. C., Chang, *The Archaeology of Ancient China*, p. 407.
[148] *Kaogu* 1984.7: 598–601.
[149] *Kaogu xuebao* 1993.1: 13–56.

Figure 13.4. Bronze sword handle and Animal Style ornamental objects from Yanglang. After: Xu Cheng 許成, Li Jinzeng 李進增, "Dong Zhou shiqi de Rong Di qingtong wenhua" 東周時期的戎狄青銅文化 *Kaogu xuebao* 1993.1: 1–11, figs. 3 and 4. Drawings by Li Xiating.

from the late Warring States. Similarities across both periods point to continuous presence by the same people: grave shape and construction, body orientation, and burial custom.

The tombs of the first period contain a greater number of bronze artifacts. Among the weapons and tools we find *ge* dagger-axes, spearheads, daggers, knives, arrowheads, pickaxes, drills, and chisels, and a large number of ornaments, such as buckles, belt ornaments, earrings, and belt hooks (Fig. 13.4). The daggers, in the classic Antennae Style, are found only in graves of this period. At this time, iron was not widely used, though it was certainly known, as shown by the finding of fragments of an iron sword (tomb IM3). Horse and chariot fittings are present in the early period, but not in large quantity. Among the precious metals, only silver earrings are found in the earlier graves (tomb IIIM3).

Noteworthy in the funerary assemblage is the presence of bones of sacrificed animals, in particular skulls of horses, bovines, and sheep. Agriculture may also have been practiced, but evidence is limited. Pottery is also scarce. All data indicate that the people of Yanglang were predominantly pastoralists, whose considerable wealth is evident from the resources allocated to burial rituals in terms of labor, animals, and objects. Almost every grave contained funerary goods – usually more than ten objects and several with over fifty.

Similar sites have been found in Guyuan county, at Pengbao 彭堡 and Shilacun 石喇村.[150] The majority of the burials in Pengbao are T-shaped catacomb graves. The Pengbao cemetery is particularly important since, of the thirty-one graves excavated, twenty-seven were undisturbed. Animal sacrifice was practiced and documented by the presence of heads and hooves of horses, sheep, and cattle at both sites. The type of burials, divided between T-shaped catacomb types and vertical-pit graves may again point, as in the case of some Ordos sites, to a cultural admixture that possibly reflected the cohabitation, and even fusion, of different groups. Objects recovered from both types are very similar, including weapons, ornaments, and horse fittings, all in bronze. The absence of iron objects may indicate that these artifacts were deemed unsuitable as funerary objects. The *ge* dagger-axe is often present in assemblages of this period, as is the short straight-edge dagger. Horse technology was fairly advanced in Pengbao and included bronze bits, masks, and a bridle frontal piece. Though bronze weapons and tools are predominant, the greater role played by the mounted horse in this culture, the large selection of Animal Style ornaments, and some gold finds foreshadow the type of changes in the funerary assemblage that were to take place in the middle and late Warring States period.[151]

Another transitional site is a burial ground found in Zhongning 中寧 county.[152] The two graves excavated here in 1983 are attributed to the early Warring States period. The burials are single rectangular earthen pit graves,

[150] Zhong Kan, "Guyuan xian Pengbao Chunqiu Zhangguo muzang," *Zhongguo kaoguxue nianjian 1988* (1989): 255–6. Luo Feng, "Ningxia Guyuan Shilacun faxian yizuo Zhanguo mu," *Kaoguxue jikan 3* (1983): 130–1, 142. Luo Feng and Han Kongle, "Ningxia Guyuan jinnian faxian de beifang xi qingtong qi," *Kaogu* 1990.5: 403–18.

[151] On the Pengbao Yujiazhuang burial site, see *Kaogu xuebao* 1995.1: 79–107. On the physical characteristics of its inhabitants, see Han Kangxin, "Ningxia Pengbao Yujiazhuang mudi rengu zhongxi tedian zhi yanjiu," *Kaogu xuebao* 1995.1: 107–25.

[152] *Kaogu* 1987.9: 773–7.

with a body orientation from east to west, a type of burial close to that of the contemporary sites of Yanqing county and Maoqinggou. There is evidence of horse sacrifice, and the metal artifacts include bronze and gold. The bronzes consist of weapons and tools (daggers, knives, pickaxes, axes, and arrowheads), horse fittings, and ornaments. The weapons display traditional or even archaic features that would place them typologically in the late Spring and Autumn period or even earlier. The presence of a round golden plate and of many ornaments and horse fittings – bits, chamfrons, ornamental bells – however, suggests a later date, closer to the early Warring States period.

In general, these early nomadic sites in Ningxia share important cultural traits with the Ordos and suggest the presence of a similar military aristocracy. From the seventh to the sixth century the herds probably increased, as shown by the ample animal remains. Chamfrons and bits, though still limited in number, indicate a progressively more important role of the horse, used not only for transportation and herding, but also war. In all these aspects the Northern Zone resembles the general evolutional pattern of the Eurasian early nomadic universe.

XINJIANG. The silk and laquer of obvious Chinese provenance unearthed at Pazyryk and at the Alagou II cemetery show that the region to the far northwest of the Central Plain had a degree of interaction with China in this period. Archaeological studies have allowed a partial mapping of the presence of nomadic people referred to as Saka in Xinjiang from the eighth to third century B.C. (Map 13.4).[153]

The term Saka is the Iranian form of the Greek "Scythian," which entered Chinese sources as Sai 塞, read sǝk in ancient Chinese.[154] Historical information on the Saka is contained in the Han shu (History of the [Former] Han) biographies, "Zhang Qian Li Guangli zhuan" 張騫李廣利傳 and "Xiyu zhuan" 西域傳. According to these the Saka was the original inhabitants of the land (to the west of the Xiongnu) that were later invaded and conquered by the Wusun (the Great Yuezhi 月氏) and finally overtaken by the Xiongnu, in the course of their war against the Yuezhi.[155] The archaeological "Saka

---

[153] On the Saka culture in Xinjiang, see Wang Binghua, "Gudai Xinjiang Sairen lishi gouchen," Xinjiang shehui kexue yanjiu 1985.16: 8–19. This has been translated by Corinne Debaine-Francfort and published as "Recherches historiques préliminaires sur les Saka du Xinjiang ancien," Arts Asiatiques 42 (1987): 31–44.

[154] See Bernhard Karlgren, Analytic Dictionary of Chinese and Sino-Japanese (Paris: Librarie orientaliste Paul Geuthner, 1923), p. 233, idem, Grammata Serica Recensa, BMFEA 29 (1957): no. 908a, p. 240. A. F. P. Hulsewé and Michael Loewe, China in Central Asia: The Early Stage 125 B.C.–A.D. 23. An Annotated Translation of the Chapters 61 and 96 of the History of the Former Han Dynasty, Sinica Leidensia 14 (Leiden: Brill, 1979), p. 104.

[155] Han shu, 61, 2692; 96A, pp. 3897, 3884; 96B, p. 3901. See also Hulsewé and Loewe, China in Central Asia. Although in recent Chinese publications the characters 月氏 are given the reading "Yuezhi" (e.g., Wang Liqi, ed., Shi ji zhuyi [Xi'an: San Qin, 1988], vol. 4, p. 2591), scholars in China often read the

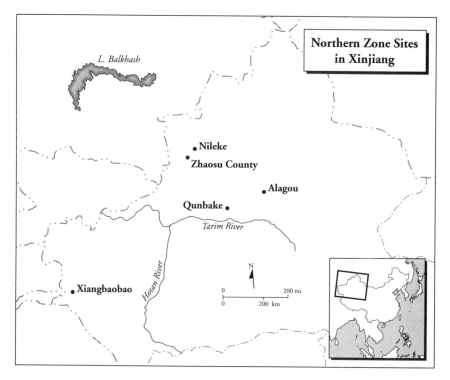

Map 13.4. Northern Zone: Archaeological sites in Xinjiang.

culture" has been based primarily on the discovery of a cache of bronzes in Xinyuan 新源 county (Ili 伊犁, Xinjiang), in 1983. However, no Saka sites have been excavated. One of the most interesting bronzes is a small statue (42 cm) of a genuflecting warrior, holding something (now lost) and wearing a high hat with a flat circular rim ending in a point turned downward in the front (Fig. 13.5a). The physical features of the man, who is naked with the exception of a kilt-type skirt, are unquestionably Europoid. Among the other finds are a square bronze basin with zoomorphic motifs, a large *fu* 釜 cauldron, and two heavy rings with facing animal heads (Fig. 13.5b). Most bronzes show clear connections with South Siberia, the Altai region, and Central Asia, but the cauldron, cast in sectional molds, points to a Chinese technique that

character 月 (*yue*) as *rou*, a variant of 肉; hence, the people's name is read Rouzhi, not Yuezhi. For instance, in the *Zhongguo Sichou zhi lu cidian*, ed. Xue Li (Urumqi: Xinjiang Renmin, 1994), the entry "Yuezhi Dudu fu" 月氏都督府 is listed under the reading *rou* (Index, p. 57); on the other hand, the same entry is found under *yue* in *Xinjiang lishi cidian*, ed. Ji Dachun (Urumqi: Xinjiang Renmin, 1993), p. 750. I could not find specific research to help with this issue, but the variant 月 for 肉 is attested to in the *Kangxi zidian*, section "Wei" 未, part 3 (xia 下).

Figure 13.5. Statuette of warrior (a), and bronze cauldron (b), Saka culture, Xinjiang. From Mu Shunying 穆舜英 et al., Zhongguo Xinjiang gudai yishu/The Ancient Art in Xinjiang, China 中國新疆古代藝術, pp. 44–6. (Urumqi: Xinjiang Art and Photography Press, 1994).

must presumably have been imported through the Northern Complex in the Western Zhou or Spring and Autumn periods.

North of the Tianshan Mountains of western Xinjiang, a poorly known culture represented by large earthen kurgans, all visible on the surface, has been attributed to the Wu Sun, a people who, according to historical sources, moved to this area from Gansu only during the Former Han under pressure from Xiongnu westward expansion. The anthropological type has been recognized as Europoid, and the dating has been thought to be around 550–250 B.C. One of the few excavated Wu Sun cemeteries (Xiata 夏塔, in Zhaosu 昭蘇 county, Xinjiang) has revealed different types of burial customs, dated to three different phases.[156] The earliest phase, probably pre-Han, exhibits a funerary chamber with earthen walls and an entrance reinforced with wooden poles, whereas the later tombs make greater use of timber. The assemblage includes small bronze and iron objects. Iron and gold objects appear in greater quantity in burials of the later period. Findings of silk, undated, may be contemporary with the Pazyryk finds and point to possible contacts with the Central Plain.

Another example of Saka culture is the Xiangbaobao 香寶寶 cemetery in

[156] Wenwu 1962.7–8: 98–102.

the Pamir region (Tashkurgan, Xinjiang),[157] where forty tombs have been investigated. Two different types of burial customs were evenly distributed: interment in stone kurgans, and cremation. The latter custom is attributed to the Qiang. The funerary assemblage includes only small bronzes, almost all ornamental, some of which, such as belt plaques, resemble ones from the Ordos region. In general, this site shows signs of partly settled, partly nomadic habitation and a relatively poor grave inventory. The people are Europoid of the Indo-Afghan type common to regions of Central Asia.

The later Saka phase, represented by the Alagou 阿拉溝 II culture of the Alagou necropolis (Toksun county, Xinjiang) to the south of the Tianshan range, is dated to the Warring States and Former Han periods.[158] The Alagou I phase, attributed to the Gushi 姑師 people, already displays elements characteristic of a pastoral culture. Alagou II, however, has a far richer funerary inventory, including large bronzes such as a square basin similar to the one found in Ili, decorative plaques in gold and silver, small iron knives, lacquer, and silk.

The decoration on the ornamental plaques, with facing tigers, recumbent felines, and wolf heads in gold and silver, belongs fully to the Ordos artistic idiom. This decorative art and the presence of luxury goods imported from China hint at the presence, in Xinjiang, of a possible evolution in the funerary inventory from bronzes used for practical or ritual purposes, such as weapons and vessels, to ornamental objects and the use of precious metals. A similar pattern can also be discerned in the Ordos region.

Archaeologists date the use of copper mines found in Xinjiang in Nileke 尼勒克 county (Ili) to the period 700–490 B.C. This dating places the mines in the context of the bronzes found in the Ili region and attributed to a Saka cultural sphere. The prolonged use of the mines indicates that these sites were centers of metallurgical production, and their extensive exploitation may have been an important, perhaps decisive, factor in the expansion of Saka culture in the region.

Metal Artifacts Associated with Early Nomadic Sites

BRONZE PRODUCTION. Bronze objects from Scythian sites in northern China comprise fairly typical nomadic objects, which have a wide distribution throughout the Eurasian steppe belt. Among these the most characteristic are the straight blade double-edged dagger, horse gear, large ritual cauldrons, ornamental plaques, and belt buckles.

The daggers from Ordos sites such as Taohongbala and Maoqinggou are

---

[157] *Kaogu xuebao* 1981.2: 199–216.   [158] *Wenwu* 1981.1: 18–22.

different from those of the Shang and early Zhou periods. A new and rapidly spread ornamental feature is the dagger pommel with facing bird heads, or Antennae Style. This motif is very common to the north and west, and is found widely in South Siberia.

Horse fittings increase in quantity, and new horse bits appear, showing signs of experimentation and technological progress. The considerable number of horse masks, or chamfrons – triangular and round bronze plates worn on the head of the horse for protection – indicate that the horse was not only used for transportation or herding, but also was ridden in battle.

Bronze cauldrons, most probably used to cook the meat of sacrificed animals, have a very wide distribution along the northern frontier, extending even into Central Asia and eastern Europe.[159] In northern China they are found in Heilongjiang, Hebei, Shanxi, Shaanxi, Gansu, and Xinjiang. They have a circular section, straight sides, a round bottom over a conic foot, and round handles often decorated with mushroom-shaped knobs. Other cauldrons have three feet with zoomorphic motifs. Pottery prototypes of these cauldrons can be seen at the Kokel' cemetery in Tuva (South Siberia).[160]

But the most characteristic elements of this culture are the Animal Style plaques and buckles. The animal combat motif, which shows West Asian influences,[161] appeared suddenly throughout the Ordos region. Most frequently this takes the form of wolves, tigers, and leopards attacking large herbivores, such as bucks and bulls, the whole scene being inscribed in rectangular or circular frames and represented in openwork over a flat surface. The boar is prominent in the animal "pantheon" of the steppe artistic vocabulary, as are birds of prey. Other popular features are small statuettes of animals in the round represented in various positions, such as the kneeling deer, coiled or crouched leopard, or recumbent horse, as well as bird-shaped plaques and double-bird designs. Plates decorated with abstract motifs were linked together to form a metal belt, a distinct component of Xiongnu attire commonly found in "pre-Xiongnu" and Xiongnu sites. Occasionally, ornamental objects were cast in gold and inlaid with turquoise, thus bearing a striking resemblance to Scytho-Siberian gold artifacts from South Siberia and Central Asia.

---

[159] On the bronze cauldron, see Liu Li, "Tong fu kao," *Kaogu yu wenwu* 1987.3: 60–5. For a comprehensive study on bronze cauldrons across Eurasia, see Miklós Érdy, "Hun and Xiong-nu Type Caldrons Finds Throughout Eurasia," *Eurasian Studies Yearbook* 67 (1995): 5–94.

[160] Roman Kenk, *Das Gräberfeld der hunno-sarmatischen Zeit von Kokel', Tuva, Süd-Sibirien* (Munich: Beck, 1984), pp. 60, 109–42.

[161] The Near Eastern origin of the animal style is rejected by several modern scholars, but western Asian motifs, in particular from Assyrian and Achaemenid art, are assumed to have played a role in the evolution of the animal style throughout Eurasia, including the Northern Zone. See Sher "On the Sources of the Scythic Animal Style." p. 55; and William Watson, *Cultural Frontiers in Ancient East Asia*, p. 112.

IRON METALLURGY. Iron appears fairly early in the Northern Zone, pointing to the introduction of iron metallurgy to China from the north. The earliest sites with iron are associated with the Scytho-Siberian sites in the Altai
Mountains (Xinjiang) and can be dated around the ninth century B.C. Typically these are small objects, suggesting that the use of iron was still rare.

In the central and eastern parts of the Northern Zone, iron objects came
into wider usage in the seventh century. One of the earliest weapon-related
uses of iron can be seen in the bronze-hilt iron swords found in Ningxia.[162]
Iron items have also been found in late Spring and Autumn burials in Inner
Mongolia. One iron sword has been found in burials 1 and 2 at Taohongbala, together with bronze weapons and horse ornaments. The earliest complete iron objects are daggers and pickaxes, confirming an early use of iron
for weapons and tools, whereas bronze was preferred for ornaments until a
much later date.

Both in the Ordos and in the Gansu–Ningxia regions, iron is far
more common in the Warring States period, with iron ornamental plates,
belthooks, and tools. Tomb 2 at Xigoupan yielded a sword, a ladle, a drill,
and several horse-related items, such as a horse bit and two cheekpieces. A
similar inventory has been recovered from a burial of the same period in the
Ordos region, at Yulongtai. Larger iron implements, such as a *ding* at tomb
2 at Budonggou 補洞溝, started to be made only in the Former Han period.

In the Ningxia area, the Yanglang site is particularly rich in iron tools and
weapons, dating partly to the late Spring and Autumn, but mostly to the late
Warring States period. The earliest finds, in grave I3, include an iron sword,
two rings, and two belt ornaments. From later burials other items have been
unearthed, such as a bronze-hilt iron sword, a complete iron sword, knives,
rings, horse bits, belt ornaments, cheekpieces, a spear, and an ornamental
plate. The bronze-hilted iron sword can be associated with the earlier site of
Langwozikeng 狼窩子坑, and only appears in the Ningxia–Gansu region.

Most iron objects in Gansu are also associated with Warring States or
possibly earlier sites. An interesting site is that of Yuanjia 袁家 (Pingzi 平子,
Ningxian 寧縣 county), where an iron spearhead has been recovered together
with bronze objects that include both weapons – a *ge* dagger-axe, a dagger,
arrowheads – and ornaments.[163] This site includes a horse sacrificial pit that
contained bronze bells, chariot finials, horse-head pole tops, and horse-head
ornamental plates. The presence of weapons, and Animal Style decorative
motifs, as well as the importance attributed to the horse, qualify this as a
typical early nomadic site. In Houzhuang 後莊 (Zhengning 正寧 county,

[162] *Kaogu xuebao* 1993.1: 13–56; Zhou Xinghua, "Ningxia Zhongwei xian Langwozikeng de qingtong duanjian muqun," *Kaogu* 1989.11: 971–80.
[163] On this and the following sites, see Liu Dezhen and Xu Junju, "Gansu Qingyang Chunqiu Zhanguo
muzang de qingli," *Kaogu* 1988.5: 413–24.

Gansu), a bronze-hilt iron sword has been found in a similar type of burial together with tools and horse-related ornaments, along with several bronze weapons. A clear relationship between the two sites can be established by the presence of almost identical *ge* dagger-axes and distinctive small ornamental statues representing a kneeling deer.

It is difficult to estimate the extent to which the use of iron was widespread in the Northern Zone. It does not seem, however, to have been limited to mounted pastoralists or associated exclusively with cultures in which the horse had attained a central role. Iron knives have been found in different burials belonging to the Shajing culture in Yongchang county, Gansu, where cattle and sheep sacrifices seem to predominate over the horses.[164] In a later Shajing burial site at Yushugou (Yongdeng county, Gansu), there are two iron spade-shaped objects, a spear, and a drill.[165] The rest of the bronze assemblage does not include weapons, but mostly ornaments and one chariot axle end. The ornaments show a connection between this site and the Ordos region (Xigoupan), the Ningxia area (Yanglang), and even the northern Chinese state of Zhongshan (Pingshan).

Bronze and, in the steppe, gold were considered to be more suitable for ornamental or ritual purposes. The use of bronze in the manufacture of hilts of iron swords suggests that it was appreciated for its hardness but not for its beauty;[166] this is possibly one reason why few iron artifacts are found in graves.

Historical Survey

DI 狄. The Di appear regularly in traditional sources from the mid-seventh century B.C. They were divided into two large groups: the Bai Di, located in the west, and the Chi Di, located in the east. Arguments as to a possible identification of Di people with "Scythian"-type early nomads have been based on very little textual evidence, such as the often quoted statement that "the Rong and the Di are continually changing their residence, they treasure material objects as valuable but give little importance to land; their land can be purchased."[167] But this is hardly a conclusive proof, and no horse riding is reported among the Di. On the contrary, they are described as foot soldiers.[168]

---

[164] *Kaogu xuebao* 1990.2: 205–37.

[165] *Kaogu yu wenwu* 1981.4: 34–6.

[166] Jessica Rawson, "Jade and Gold: Some Sources of Ancient Chinese Jade Design," *Oritentations* 26, 6 (1995): 26–37.

[167] *Zuo zhuan*, 29 (Xiang 4), 5b (Legge, *The Ch'un Ts'ew with the Tso Chuen*, p. 424; Yang Bojun, ed., *Chunqiu Zuo zhuan zhu*, p. 939).

[168] *Zuo zhuan*, 41 (Zhao 1), 19a (Legge, *The Ch'un Ts'ew with the Tso Chuen*, p. 579; Yang Bojun, ed., *Chunqiu Zuo zhuan zhu*, p. 1215).

The appearance of the Di on the northern borders of China suggests a large southbound migration of people displacing the sparse Rong communities, which were pushed further south and either fell under the control of the Chinese states, or survived semi-independently in the interstices between them. The relationship between the Di and the Chinese states was not just that of mere border conflicts. Throughout the Spring and Autumn period the Di played a complex, multifaceted role in interstate politics. They provided a safe haven for Chinese runaways, often victims of factional struggles or defeated pretenders to local lordships. From the frequent mentions of passionate appeals to all central states to unite against the Di, we can see that, militarily, they posed a threat that was perceived by the Zhou political community as being potentially more dangerous than the internal conflicts among the Chinese states. However, considerations of realpolitik often prevailed over feelings of cultural and ethnic brotherhood, and Chinese states attacked by the Di were often left to fend for themselves.

The most vicious wars against the Di were those waged by the state of Jin, bent since 660 B.C. on a campaign of annihilation that eventually paid off in 594 and 593 B.C., with the destruction of several Chi Di groups.[169] This attack probably took place in conjunction with an internal crisis of the Di, as there is evidence of famine and political dissent among them. In the following years, Jin engaged in all sorts of ploys and stratagems in its fight against them and completed its "subjugation" of the Di in 541 B.C.,[170] thus establishing Chinese political supremacy in the north. However, fighting continued against statelets set up by the Xianyu 鮮虞 – a tribe or state within the larger entity of the Di people – who were repeatedly attacked by Jin in the latter part of the sixth century. In this war, victories were by no means one-sided; in 507 B.C. Xianyu troops convincingly defeated the Jin army.

Foreign relations between Chinese states and the Di involved the establishment of marriage ties, and the Chinese custom of exchanging kin members from princely households as virtual hostages was also observed by the Di.[171] Regular treaties were concluded between Di and Chinese states, such as the one in 640 B.C. between Qi and the Di, both agreeing to join forces against Wey. Peace agreements were also ratified through treaties, as in 628, when the Di requested peace from Wey, or in 601, when peace was arranged between the Bai Di and Jin, who then proceeded to attack Qin.[172]

---

[169] *Zuo zhuan*, 24 (Xuan 16), 13a (Legge, *The Ch'un Ts'ew with the Tso Chuen*, p. 330; Yang Bojun, ed., *Chunqiu Zuo zhuan zhu*, pp. 767–8).

[170] Průšek, *Chinese Statelets*, p. 172.

[171] *Zuo zhuan*, 15 (Xi 24), 16b, (Legge, *The Ch'un Ts'ew with the Tso Chuen*, p. 191; Yang Bojun, ed., *Chunqiu Zuo zhuan zhu*, p. 416).

[172] On treaties, see *Zuo zhuan*, 14 (Xi 20), 25a (Legge, *The Ch'un Ts'ew with the Tso Chuen*, p. 178; Yang Bojun, ed., *Chunqiu Zuo zhuan zhu*, p. 387); *Zuo zhuan*, 17 (Xi 32), 10b (Legge, *The Ch'un Ts'ew with the Tso Chuen*, p. 220; Yang Bojun, ed., *Chunqiu Zuo zhuan zhu*, p. 489); *Zuo zhuan*, 22 (Xuan 8), 7a

In the political arena the Di did not behave differently from Chinese states, and generally do not seem to have been any more vicious or untrustworthy than any other political protagonist at this time. Indeed, the tactics adopted by Jin in its anti-Di campaigns, though highly effective, can hardly be commended as paragons of fair play.

Although it is not clear exactly in what way the Di differed from the Chinese, a difference was repeatedly noted by Chinese chroniclers. When in 661 B.C. the Di invaded the state of Xing 邢, Guan Jingzhong 管敬仲 said to Qi Hou 齊侯, "The Di and the Rong are like wolves and can never be satisfied; all the Xia states are closely related [to Qi], and none should be abandoned; to rest in idleness is a poison that should not be cherished."[173] According to an even more scathing judgment, the Di all conformed to the following "four evils":

Those whose ears cannot hear the harmony of the five sounds are deaf; those whose eyes cannot distinguish among the five colors are blind; those whose minds do not conform to the standards of virtue and righteousness are perverse; those whose mouths do not speak words of loyalty and faith are foolish chatterers.[174]

This clearly placed them beyond the pale of Chinese civilization.

In later sources we also find analogous remarks on the "diversity" of the Di. For instance, the state of Shu is described in the *Zhanguo ce* 戰國策 (Stratagems of the Warring States) as "a remote country of the west that still observes the old usages of the Rong and Di."[175] The state of Qin was accused by its enemies of sharing the same customs and moral qualitites as the Rong and Di: it had the heart of a tiger or a wolf, was greedy and cruel, untrustworthy when it came to making a profit, and did not behave according to protocol and virtuous conduct.[176]

By the time of the Warring States, the various Di peoples who had settled along the northern Chinese territories during the Zhou dynasty had developed into relatively small, independent frontier centers. The most important was the state of Zhongshan 中山, which in the written sources is referred to as a state of the Bai Di. Created by the Xianyu, it was attacked by Wei Wen Hou 魏文侯 in 408 B.C., conquered in 406 B.C., and ruled by Wei for about forty years. In 377 it regained its independence and continued to exist until

(Legge, *The Ch'un Ts'ew with the Tso Chuen*, p. 302; Yang Bojun, ed., *Chunqiu Zuo zhuan zhu*, p. 695).

[173] *Zuo zhuan*, 11 (Min 1), 1b (Legge, *The Ch'un Ts'ew with the Tso Chuen*, p. 124; Yang Bojun, ed., *Chunqiu Zuo zhuan zhu*, p. 256).

[174] *Zuo zhuan*, 15 (Xi 24), 21a (Legge, *The Ch'un Ts'ew with the Tso Chuen*, p. 192; Yang Bojun, ed., *Chunqiu Zuo zhuan zhu*, p. 425).

[175] *Zhanguo ce*, annotated by Liu Xiang 劉向 (Shanghai: Shanghai guji, 1978), vol. 1, p. 117; see also J. I. Crump, *Chan-Kuo Ts'e* (Oxford: Clarendon Press, 1970), p. 67. On the composition of the *Zhanguo ce*, see Loewe, *Early Chinese Texts*, pp. 1–11.

[176] *Zhanguo ce*, vol. 2, p. 869 (Crump, *Chan-Kuo Ts'e*, p. 436).

295 B.C. This state had fortified cities and an army with a thousand war chariots and very capable troops.[177] Archaeological research has shown that at least
from the end of the fifth century B.C., Zhongshan was fully within the sphere
of Chinese civilization. Its bronze production, especially at Pingshan 平山,
reveals its complete absorption within the culture of the Central Plain.[178] Still,
no matter how "Chinese" the rulers of Zhongshan were, references to their
diversity indicate that for a long time they were not accepted as one of the
states of the Hua-Xia cultural sphere.[179]

The fall of Zhongshan in 295 B.C. did not put an end to the history of
the Di. Some of these groups were attacked by General Tian Dan 田單 of
Qi during the reign of King Xiang 襄 of Qi (r. 283–265 B.C.).[180] Since by this
time Zhao had already conquered Zhongshan and Qi was cut off from
the northern territories, we must assume that either some Di people lived
between the states of Yan, Zhao, and Qi, or that either Zhao or Yan allowed
Qi to go through their territory to attack the Di people living in the north.

Either hypothesis would suggest that Di kingdoms continued to exist until
a later date and were gradually absorbed by the Chinese northern states. The
narrative of the war between Qi and the Di shows clearly that it was a long
siege war, which indicates that the Di were politically organized into city-
states. Though horses were imported from Dai, and this was often referred
to as Di territory, its inhabitants were probably not nomads. Taking advantage of the abundance of grassland, they may have bred horses for export and
military purposes. Horses had to be used for chariots by all armies, and by
the end of the fourth century B.C. Chinese states were already adopting
cavalry warfare, which meant a rising demand for horses. Because of their
closer relationship with the steppe areas, the people of Dai may have adopted
cavalry and bred horses even earlier. Though production of good horses
should not imply that the people of Dai were nomads, it points to closer
contacts between the northern Chinese frontier and peoples of the steppe.

In general, we can see that during the eighth, seventh, and sixth centuries
B.C., the Di settled in the great plains running from the loop of the Yellow
River and the Ordos territory to the Taiyuan plain, with some also living in
northern Hebei as far east as the state of Yan. They therefore may have created
an effective buffer, for several centuries, between the Zhou states and the
nomads of the northern territories.

The gradual encroachment of central states on the northern region, and

[177] Zhanguo ce, vol. 1, p. 436 (Crump, Chan-Kuo Ts'e, p. 200).
[178] Li Xueqin, "Pingshan muzangqun yu Zhongshan guo de wenhua," Wenwu 1979.1: 37–41; trans. in
     Chinese Archaeological Abstracts 3, ed. Albert Dien, Jeffrey Riegel, and Nancy Price (Los Angeles: Uni-
     versity of California, Institute of Archaeology, 1985), pp. 804–8.
[179] Zhanguo ce, vol. 3, pp. 1170–4 (Crump, Chan-Kuo Ts'e, pp. 574–6).
[180] Zhanguo ce, vol. 1, pp. 467–70 (Crump, Chan-Kuo Ts'e, pp. 213–14).

their subjugation and incorporation of Di and other frontier peoples, eventually brought China into direct contact with the nomads, primarily in the Ordos region. Relations between the Hu nomads and the state of Zhao prompted the adoption of cavalry. During the period between the end of the fourth century and the mid-third century, non-Chinese city-states continued to struggle for independence vis-à-vis China. Within the Chinese states a consciousness of the deep cultural divide between them and the Di did not soften even by the end of the Warring States. On the other hand, the differences between the Hua-Xia and Rong–Di peoples should not be confused with the conflict between China and the nomads. The written sources present the Rong and Di as communities politically organized on a tribal and territorial basis, centered around fortified settlements, often in the guise of city-states.

LATE WARRING STATES TO QIN (CA. 350–209 B.C.)

The final stage in the pre-imperial history of the northern frontier is a period of direct contacts between nomadic peoples and China. The acceleration of the northern expansion of the states of Zhao, Yan, and Qin caused the rapid absorption of the pastoral and semipastoral peoples who in the past had acted as buffers between the Central Plain and the northern steppe. As we have seen with the case of Zhongshan, from around the fifth century B.C. the differences between peoples such as the Di and the central states became less and less relevant, both in terms of political structures and cultural foundations. The people who inhabited these border regions were mostly settled; they lived in fortified cities, and continued to export pastoral products, animal husbandry having long become their main economic pursuit. It was probably due to pressure from the northern nomads that in the mid-fourth century B.C., the state of Zhongshan started the construction of frontier fortifications that was the prelude to the building of the Great Wall. Thus, we can take this approximate date as the beginning of our fourth phase in the history of the northern frontier.

The evidence available today, from both the written sources and archaeological investigation, suggests that it was the shrinkage of the intermediate area inhabited by semipastoral people, gradually converted to or absorbed within the Chinese sphere, that eventually brought the northern states into direct contact with the nomads. Contacts may have occurred long before, but firm evidence of a strong impact of northern nomads upon historical developments in the south must be dated to the end of the fourth century B.C. This is epitomized by the appearance of a new type of foreigner, the Hu 胡. This term, whatever its origin, soon came to indicate an "anthropological type" rather than a specific group or tribe, which the records allow us to identify as early steppe nomads. The Hu were the source of the introduction of cavalry in China.

Aside from military developments, trade relations and diplomatic contacts that are scarcely hinted at in the written sources can now be documented archaeologically. The large amount of gold found in third century B.C. Xiongnu tombs in the Ordos region reveals a possible shift from a purely military aristocracy to a leadership that engaged in trade as well as war and profited greatly from commerce with China. Politically, the nomads appear on the historical scene in 318 B.C., and the Chinese recording of the native term used by the Xiongnu for their leader, *shanyu* 單于, betrays the existence of diplomatic exchanges.[181]

The combined direct and circumstantial evidence of military fortifications, trade, and diplomatic exchanges points to the middle to late fourth century B.C. as the period when closer relations were established. These remained essentially stable during this period and clearly bore advantages for both sides, though increased friction occurred between Zhao and the Xiongnu toward the middle of the third century. During the third century the expansionist power of stronger and larger Chinese states in the south kept pressing the nomads, pushing the frontier progressively northward. Finally, as soon as the First Emperor of Qin had concluded his unification of the central states, he dispatched a powerful army to the Ordos with orders to occupy and colonize it. The fierce and proud Xiongnu reaction to Qin's encroachment led to the foundation of a new leadership and the creation of an immense nomadic power that would soon become a formidable opponent of the young Chinese empire.

Archaeological Cultures of the Northern Zone During the Late Warring States

The "closing in" between the northern cultures and the Chinese zone accelerated rapidly during the last part of the Warring States. From the fourth to the third centuries B.C., contacts with China became more significant. In art, the distinctive elements of early nomadic cultures, though still predominant and retaining their northern flavor, blended with different symbols – trees, mountains – which affected substantially earlier stylistic models.[182]

---

[181] *Zhanguo ce*, vol. 3, p. 1129. The correct reading of the character 單, normally read *dan*, has been the object of some debate. Though the reading *shanyu* 單于 has been accepted for some time. Chinese scholars usually prefer *chanyu*. See Wang Liqi, ed., *Shi ji zhuyi*, vol. 4, p. 2317.

[182] Esther Jacobson, "Beyond the Frontier: A Reconsideration of Cultural Interchange Between China and the Early Nomads," *EC* 13 (1988): 201–40. The presence of distinctive Chinese motifs in northern art has led some to believe that there was a Chinese production of artistic metalwork specifically

The sites thus far attributed to the Xiongnu are mostly concentrated in the Ordos region. They are also the richest sites in the Northern Zone. Other sites, similar in style, funerary inventory, and material culture, have also been excavated in the northeast and northwest, particularly in Ningxia. A common characteristic is the variety of burial styles on the same site, which may indicate increasing social differentiation or, alternatively, the cohabitation of different groups merging into a more composite society, as a result of forced displacement, migrations, or simply an enlargement of the range of action of human communities because of widespread adoption of a horse-based nomadic economy. Precious metals predominate in the aristocratic burials of this period, thus revealing the presence of a social elite no longer purely military in nature. Fewer weapons were buried, and the use of iron became more common. But these changes, as profound as they are, do not appear to be intrusive. The consensus today is that the nomadic cultures of the Northern Zone in the late Warring States were directly linked to earlier inhabitants such as those of the lower strata of Taohongbala and Maoqinggou. There is no doubt, however, that the culture represented by these earlier sites expanded tremendously and, in certain areas such as the northeast, replaced earlier cultures such as Upper Xiajiadian.

The Ordos region was the central area of the flourishing of nomadic culture in the fourth and third centuries B.C. The sites are of two types: those used before the Warring States, which show a degree of continuity with the earlier periods, and those that can be dated only to this later period. The sites of Taohongbala and Maoqinggou are representative of the first group, whereas Yulongtai, Xigoupan, Aluchaideng, and others belong to the second (Map 13.5).

Iron technology became far more widespread, with a much broader inventory of iron objects. However, iron did not completely replace bronze artifacts. In particular, iron was used for certain types of weapons and horse fittings. Antennae Style iron daggers, similar to earlier bronze daggers, and iron swords similar to those of the Central Plain are found both over a broader area and in larger numbers with respect to the preceding period. Horse bits and chamfrons came more frequently to be made out of iron. Furthermore, the bronze pickaxe was generally replaced with one of iron.

Another characteristic of the period is a tendency toward standardization. Traditional weapons and implements started to acquire standard features, such as the hole in the handle of bronze knives and a wavy line decoration

designed for the northern markets or that there were Chinese artisans among the nomads. For a full illustration of this viewpoint, see So and Bunker, *Traders and Raiders on China's Northern Frontier*.

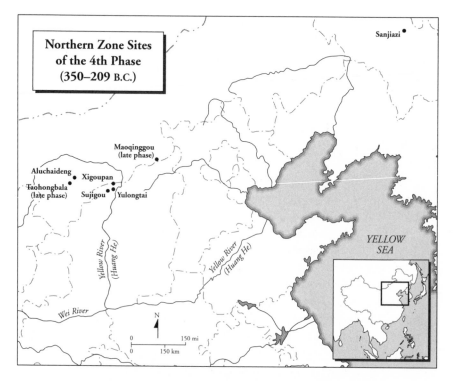

Map 13.5. Northern Zone: Archaeological sites of the fourth phase (350–309 B.C.).

on the shoulders of pots. Among the decorative features of this period, we see a decisive increase in Animal Style belt buckles and plates. Often these plates, round or rectangular, depict human activities.[183] Scenes of animal combat both realistic and stylized became more common, as well as artistically sophisticated.

By far the most stunning feature of this period is the presence of extraordinarily rich burial sites, with hundreds of precious objects, mostly gold and silver ornaments. In Aluchaideng (Hangjin 杭錦 Banner, Inner Mongolia),[184] located to the north of Taohongbala, two ancient tombs of the late Warring States period were unearthed. They are remarkable for the extraordinary number of precious objects and the artistic value of the ornaments (Fig. 13.6). Altogether 218 gold and 5 silver objects were found. Among these the most important are a gold headdress set, or crown, composed of 4

---

[183] Emma Bunker, "The Anecdotal Plaques of the Eastern Steppe Regions," in *Arts of the Eurasian Steppelands*. ed. Philip Denwood (London: Percival David Foundation, 1978), pp. 121–42.

[184] Tian Guangjin and Guo Suxin, "Nei Menggu Aluchaideng faxian de Xiongnu yiwu," *Kaogu* 1980.4: 333–8, 364, 368; idem, "Aluchaideng faxian de jin yin qi," in *O'erduosi qingtong qi*, pp. 342–50.

Figure 13.6. Gold ornaments, Xiongnu culture, Aluchaideng. From Tian Guanjin 田廣金 and Guo Suxin 郭素新, eds., *O'erduosi qingtong qi* 鄂爾多斯青銅器, plates I, IV, XVI (Beijing: Wenwu, 1986).

pieces (a skullcap and three headbands); 4 rectangular ornamental gold plates illustrating a tiger assaulting a bull or cow; 12 ornamental plaques with designs of tigers and birds inlaid with precious stones; 55 Animal Style ornamental plates with representations of tigers, birds, sheep, hedgehogs, and 2 tiger heads; and 45 rectangular gold buckles. In addition, ornaments in the shape of buttons, small tubular objects, and necklaces were also found. Because of its richness, this site is regarded as a royal burial of a chieftain of the Lin Hu people, who presumably inhabited this region in the late Warring States.

A closely related site excavated in 1979 and in 1980 is located at Xigoupan (Zhunge'er Banner, Inner Mongolia).[185] The first investigation revealed three tombs of the late Warring States period, while the second brought to light eight tombs and a nearby settlement dated to the Former Han period. That the first three tombs present a widely varied funerary assemblage, even though they belong to the same period, is a possible indication of growing social differentiation. Tomb 2 is the richest, with funerary goods dominated by gold and silver ornaments. Although fewer in number compared with Aluchaideng, they are equally impressive and include several Animal Style ornamental plates and decorative objects, at times depicting either realistic or fantastic animals. Decorations in silver, lead, and bronze are also present. Weapons and tools, such as a sword, a ladle, horse bits, and cheekpieces, are made of iron. Tomb 1 contains a few bronze objects and iron remains. Tomb 3 contains bronze ornaments typical of an earlier stage, including weapons, buckles, and other ornamental objects, comparable with the Taohongbala assemblage.

The sharp differentiation in the funerary assemblage seems to reflect distinction in social status rather than ethnic differences and may refer to the establishment of a rich aristocracy. The iron objects appear to be mostly weapons and tools of daily use, with no evident ritual or economic significance. From an early period, agricultural tools such as hoes, adzes, and pick-axes were made of iron, becoming progressively more common.[186] The existence of a settlement in the vicinity of the cemetery shows the presence of an agricultural or seminomadic people. It is possible that commoners or poor members of the tribe were buried with just a few iron tools. On the other hand, richer people were buried with finer and more prestigious bronze weapons and ornaments, which had a long tradition as mortuary objects. Only the highest elite accumulated enough wealth to be accompanied in death by an ostentatious array of glittering gold and silver jewelry, some of which was imported from China, as is clear from the presence of a Chinese inscription on the back of a golden plaque, and of Chinese characters on silver rein rings. The latter may refer to a workshop located in the state of Zhao. The inscription on the plaque, which indicates its weight, has been

---

[185] *Wenwu* 1980.7: 1–10. *Nei Menggu wenwu kaogu* 1981.1: 15–27.

[186] From Wuhuan 烏桓 burials of the Han period in Xichagou 西岔沟 (Xifeng 西豐, Liaoning), an iron axe, iron pickaxe, iron adze, iron hoe, and other agricultural implements have been recovered. See Lin Gan, "Guanyu Yanjiu Zhongguo gudai beifang minzu wenhua shi de wo jian," *Nei Menggu daxue xuebao* 1988.1: 3.

attributed to the state of Qin. It is possible that such objects were used as currency in commercial exchanges with the nomads, from whom China imported horses, cattle, and other typical pastoral products.

Stylistically, on both Aluchaideng and Xigoupan ornaments we find a vast gamut of animals depicted in relief or in the round, including horses, cattle, sheep, tigers, eagles, deer, and fantastic beasts. Reclining horses and kneeling deer are particularly representative of this period, as are scenes of animal combat.

Other Xiongnu graves of the late Warring States period were less richly adorned, such as those at Yulongtai (Zhunge'er Banner, Inner Mongolia), excavated in 1975.[187] The burial custom was identical with that seen at Tao-hongbala and included sacrifices of horse and sheep. The funerary assemblage consisted of bronze, iron, and silver artifacts, but no pottery. Horse fittings included a bit and bridle stopper, both in iron, in addition to cheek-pieces made of bone. The silver necklace is typical of later objects, and the iron artifacts, such as the pickaxe and horse bit, are more developed than those found in Taohongbala. The number of chariot fittings, which include seven animal-shaped finials in bronze representing lambs, antelope, deer, and horses, and two axle ends, indicate that the chariot was still in use. Other weapons and tools – two knives, one adze, two axes, and one arrowhead – are all in bronze.

A similar but richer tomb was investigated in 1984 in the Ordos region at Shihuigou 石灰溝 (Yijinhuoluo 伊金霍洛 Banner, Inner Mongolia),[188] in which there was an abundance of silver objects: ornamental plaques, buttons, and various other animal-shaped decorations. A new type of Animal Style motif is represented by the combat between two tigers. The inlay technique was advanced, as we find an iron-set gilded bronze ornament in the shape of a turtle, and gold- and silver-inlaid iron artifacts. Generally the style and motifs belong to the repertory of the mature Warring State Ordos art. However, iron-set gilded bronze and gold- and silver-inlaid iron objects are rare and betray a different origin. It is possible that the technique came from China, while the artifacts were made locally, but the very rarity of these finds strongly suggests that they were imported, which would confirm the development of steady commercial relations between the Central Plain and the adjacent northern steppe areas.

Finally, a site of some interest is Sujigou (Zhunge'er Banner).[189] This site

[187] Kaogu 1977.2: 111–14.   [188] Nei Menggu wenwu kaogu 1992.1–2: 91–6.
[189] Gai Shanlin, "Nei Menggu Yikezhaomeng Zhunge'er qi Sujigou chutu yibi," Wenwu 1965.2: 44–5, rpt. in Tian Guangjin and Guo Suxin, eds., O'erduosi qingtong qi, pp. 372–4. In the original report, this site was dated to the Han; that dating was omitted in the reprint.

Figure 13.7. Animal Style bronze ornaments, Xiongnu culture, from Sujigou. From Tian Guanjin 田廣金 and Guo Suxin 郭素新, eds., O'erduosi qingtong qi 鄂爾多斯青銅器, plates XI, XII, XIV (Beijing: Wenwu, 1986).

had been disturbed in the past, and only objects found by local residents were recovered, in the early 1960s. The singular fact is that the objects are mostly bronze pole tops in the shape of animals, including a crane head, a sheep head, a feline cub, two kneeling horses, and a wolf head (Fig. 13.7). Their style shows yet another instance of the variety of applications of Animal Style ornaments in the Ordos culture.

The progressive increase in the use of iron can be seen by looking at Former Han sites such as Budonggou (Yikezhaomeng 伊克昭盟, Inner Mongolia), where there is a vast inventory of iron tools and weapons. Iron was mostly reserved for vessels such as tripods and cauldrons, for weapons such as swords, knives, and arrowheads, for horse fittings such as horse bits, rings, and chamfrons, and, finally, for ornamental objects such as belt plates. Bronze was still the principal material to be used for decorative and ornamental purposes.

Related sites, from the viewpoint of their material culture, have been found in northern Shaanxi, as at Nalin'gaotu 納林高兔 (Shenmu 神木 county, Shaanxi). Dated to the late Warring States, a Xiongnu grave excavated here in 1956 yielded a large number of gold, silver, and bronze ornamental objects.[190] Here too animal sacrifices were practiced, and skulls of horses, cattle, and sheep accompanied the deceased. The subjects of the ornamental plaques are mostly tigers and deer. One gold object represents a fantastic animal in the shape of a deer. A gilded silver dagger handle that is particularly rare, and possibly imported, is the only military object recovered from the tomb. Other sites in Shenmu county, such as Lijiapan 李家畔 and Laolongchi 老龍池, lack silver and gold ornaments; their metal inventory is limited to a few buckles, ornaments, and one dagger.

In Yanglang we observe a situation similar to that of Maoqinggou and Taohongbala. Namely, the later tombs, dated to the late Warring States period, show a predominance in the use of iron, then widely available for weapons, tools, and ornaments. Though not on the scale of the Ordos, some gold objects appear in the funerary assemblage. Finally, examples of both horse gear (bits, chamfrons, bronze and bone cheekpieces, and harness ornaments) and chariot fittings (shaft ornaments, axle cuffs, and hubs) increase dramatically in number. Ornamental pole tops and plaques representing animal combat are also typical of this later assemblage.

In the Northern Zone, and particularly in the area closer to the Great Wall (from Ningxia and Gansu to Inner Mongolia and the northeast), then, the composition of metal assemblages seems to indicate a common pattern of development: a phase in which bronze weapons predominated – a sign of the formation of a warrior aristocracy – gave way to a stage marked by the extensive presence of horse fittings and ornaments, which point to technological advances in transportation and warfare, as well as to changes in the taste and possibly social and political functions of the elite. During this time not only do we find the widespread use of iron and more elaborate func-

---

[190] Dai Yingxin and Sun Jiaxiang, "Shaanxi Shenmu xian chutu Xiongnu wenwu," *Wenwu* 1983.12: 23–30.

tional goods, but social status is more often expressed through the presence of precious objects. Artifacts related to chariots, usually regarded as typical status symbols of ancient China, and to horses, which of course held primary importance in nomadic societies, came together to represent power and wealth enjoyed in life. This change in funerary assemblage may very well point to the emergence of a new class of aristocrats, whose position in society was proportional to their success in managing relations with China and other neighbors.

Such relations were not only political and diplomatic; they also carried strong commercial connotations. A tendency toward a commercialization of relations with China can also be found in earlier sites in Yanqing county (Beijing) dated to the Spring and Autumn period and attributed to the Shan Rong.[191] Here the presence of gold is consistent and regular. Even more significantly, coins have been found that indicate a degree of monetary exchange. This area was subsequently incorporated into the state of Yan, though it continued to have a dual cultural composition for a long time. These sites can be seen as the first instance of a trend toward commercialization of the frontier and the possible transformation of the upper echelons of nomadic society from a purely warrior aristocracy into diplomatic and commercial agents that monopolized or to some degree controlled border exchanges with China to their own profit. This trend reached its highest point during the late Warring States period, thanks to the establishment of more direct contacts between nomads and the northern Chinese states.

Relations Between Northern Nomads and Central States

The earliest textual evidence of direct contact between the Xiongnu and China is found in the year 318 B.C.,[192] when the Xiongnu are said to have been part of a joint force with Hann 韓, Zhao, Wei 魏, Yan 燕, and Qi 齊 that attacked Qin. Further and more detailed evidence of a direct connection between the Hu nomads and Chinese states can be found in the famous debate held in 307 B.C. at the court of King Wuling of Zhao 武靈 (r. 325–299 B.C.). In the course of this debate the monarch supported the adoption of mounted cavalry and archery against the myopic conservatism of his advisors.[193] This change in military thinking was not due exclusively to the need to repel nomadic assailants – though this may have been a consideration – but mostly to the king's eagerness to gain an advantage against other Chinese states by employing new military tactics and technology. The king's main

---

[191] *Wenwu* 1989.8: 17–35, 43.   [192] *Shi ji*, 5, p. 207.   [193] *Zhanguo ce*, vol. 2, p. 653–67.

goal was to turn part of his Chinese troops into mounted warriors, to be deployed on the borders with both Chinese (Hann, Qin, and Yan) and northern nomadic states (Hu and Loufan).[194] Since the greatest threat to the existence of Zhao came from other Chinese states, primarily Qin, it is questionable whether many of his new military units were used to contain the various nomads.

During the late Warring States period, Yan, Zhao, and Qin expanded their territory mostly at the expense of the northern peoples, who were in a position of military inferiority. Under King Zhao 昭 (r. 306–251 B.C.), Qin expanded into the territory of the Yiqu Rong 義渠戎, possibly the remnant of semipastoral tribes, acquiring the later commanderies of Longxi 隴西, Beidi 北地, and Shang 上, and building "long walls" as a protection against the Hu. During the reign of King Wuling, Zhao defeated the Lin Hu and Loufan to the north and also built a wall from Dai 代, at the foot of the Yinshan Mountains, to Gaoque 高闕, thereby establishing the commanderies of Yunzhong 雲中, Yanmen 雁門, and Dai 代. To the east, the state of Yan entertained diplomatic relations with the Hu through General Qin Kai 秦開, then attacked them by surprise, defeating the Dong Hu and pushing them back "a thousand *li*." Yan also built a wall that went from Zaoyang 造陽 to Xiangping 襄平 to protect itself against the Hu and created the commanderies of Shanggu 上谷, Yuyang 漁陽, Youbeiping 右北平, Liaoxi 遼西, and Liaodong 遼東. At this point Qin, Zhao, and Yan, three of the seven states of "the people who wore caps and girdles," bordered on the Xiongnu.[195]

The militarization of the frontier was due to the robust territorial expansion of the three northern Chinese states, all determined to protect their newly acquired lands. The state of Yan expanded mainly in the northeast and occupied both the maritime region north of the Liaodong Gulf and the Liaodong Peninsula, including, to the west, a large portion of what is today Hebei province. After conquering Zhongshan in 295 B.C., Zhao continued its drive to the north and built a series of fortifications along the northern bank of the great bend of the Yellow River, where it encircles the Ordos steppe in a great loop, thus creating a Chinese enclave deep into nomad territory. The state of Qin also expanded into the Ordos, in the Hetao 河套 region. Its line of fortifications ran from the Shang commandery in eastern Hetao to Longxi commandery in southern Gansu, along a northeast to southwest line. Longxi was the westernmost point of China's northern frontier.

---

[194] *Zhanguo ce*, vol. 2, p. 657.   [195] *Shi ji*, 110, pp. 2885–6.

In the course of the third century, Zhao continued to engage in a war of attrition with the Xiongnu. Entrusted by the state of Zhao with the defense of the northern border in the commanderies of Dai and Yanmen, General Li Mu 李牧 assumed a defensive posture; he was criticized for his passivity, even though the frontier was not penetrated by Xiongnu attacks. Under pressure of criticism and intimations of cowardice, Li Mu led an army of 1,300 war chariots, 13,000 cavalry, 50,000 select infantry, and 100,000 expert archers against the Xiongnu. He succeeded in drawing them into a trap, crushing them. This feat vindicated his honor and was followed by victories over the Dong Hu and the Lin Hu.[196]

Several factors possibly contributed to this shift toward aggressive military policies. Soldiers stationed on the frontier pressed their commanders into active engagements in order to profit from the spoils of war. Court politics could also have an effect on frontier defense. The pattern of military relations between nomads and Chinese in this period should therefore not be seen as a unilateral series of nomadic raids against Chinese soldiers and settlers, but rather as a war of attrition carried out between displaced nomads and a body of occupation troops who would often take the initiative and launch raids into nomadic territory.

Chinese Knowledge of the Northern Peoples

In the sources that can be dated to the Warring States period, there is little indication that the Central Plain statesmen and intellectuals were interested in the life and history of their northern neighbors. In most of the best-known pseudogeographical treatises of this period, such as the *Shan hai jing* 山海經 (Classic of the mountains and seas),[197] the space surrounding the Central Plain was the abode of surreal beings, inhabitants of a fantastic world. The rationalist attitude of the Han historians tended to reject information and accounts of this sort as being purely fictitious and untrustworthy. Other works were less inclined to supernatural description; nevertheless, the information they provide is far from reliable. This is true of the *Mu Tianzi zhuan* 穆天子傳, a biographical work of the fourth century B.C. that describes the travels of King Mu of Zhou (r. 956–918 B.C.) to visit the Queen Mother of the West, Xi Wang Mu 西王母.[198] In philosophical and historical works, such as the *Lü shi chunqiu* 呂氏春秋 (Mr. Lü's Spring and

[196] *Shi ji*, 81, pp. 2449–50 (William H. Nienhauser, Jr., ed., *The Grand Scribe's Records. Vol. 7: The Memoirs of Pre-Han China, by Ssu-ma Ch'ien* [Bloomington: Indiana University Press, 1994], p. 271).
[197] Loewe, *Early Chinese Texts*, 357–67.
[198] Ibid., 342–6.

Autumn [annals]), the northern peoples lack distinctive ethnographic features. Only the collection of fictionalized historical accounts known as the *Zhanguo ce* provides us with a description of their riding gear and their ability as archers.

However, from information that enters the texts anecdotally and almost unconsciously, we can grasp a few glimpses of Chinese acquaintance with the nomads, and of a knowledge of them that must have been widespread. A pre-Qin notion of the political organization of the nomads can be seen in a sentence of the *Zhanguo ce*, where it is said that Hu and Yue 越 (a people of the south) were divided into many groups that did not understand each other's languages; yet when threatened by a common enemy, they would all unite and fight together.[199] This statement seems to imply that by the end of the fourth century, the terms Hu (for the north) and Yue (for the south) were used as broad "anthropological" categories applied to various political entities – clans, tribes, or even states – that claimed different origins and spoke different languages; in case of need, however, these barriers could be overcome, and a political unity found. Applied to the nomads, this seems to refer to the formation of tribal confederations, whose first historical example was the creation of the Xiongnu empire.

Commercial and diplomatic interaction between the Central Plain and the Hu is documented both in the *Zhanguo ce* and in the *Mu Tianzi zhuan*. The former mentions the importation from the north of horses and furs.[200] The second, while a fictional account, mentions information that must have originated in actual practices and customs. In his encounters with several foreign chiefs and dignitaries, King Mu conducted gift exchanges that must have been characteristic of fourth century B.C. relations between China and northern pastoralists. While the information in this work points unquestionably to dealings with peoples who were predominantly pastoral, it also shows the existence of mixed products from both herding and farming activities. The largest "gift" received by King Mu was a herd of cattle and a flock of sheep numbered by the thousand. Even more valuable, and always mentioned at the head of any list of gifts, are horses, numbering in the several hundreds. Both cultures valued horses, which had long been used in China for military and ceremonial purposes, but it was the north that provided a surplus for sale to China. A third item, which appears often but not always, is that of cereals, such as millet. Other items include wine and other animals, such as dogs and goats. The gifts presented by King Mu in exchange include

---

[199] *Zhanguo ce*, vol. 3, p. 1110.
[200] *Zhanguo ce*, vol. 1, p. 178, and vol. 2, p. 608.

mostly precious artifacts. The mention of a silver deer, a silver bird, and golden deer presumably refers to the small sculptures or plaques with animals shown in relief that appear so commonly in Ordos art. Other items include necklaces of gold or precious stone beads, peals, gold bullion, belts adorned with precious shells, and sometimes fine horses in a team (four of the same color), probably meant to be hitched to a royal carriage and used for display. Finally, women were exchanged as wives, a detail that points to the role of bride giving as an instrument of diplomacy.[201]

The information contained in the *Mu Tianzi zhuan* substantiates the pattern of exchanges mentioned earlier – in particular the importation of horses. On the other hand, references to precious gifts of Animal Style objects are supported by archaeological finds in Xiongnu tombs of golden plaques and other objects manufactured in China. It is possible to discern a model of diplomatic and economic exchange beneath the fiction.

The Rise of the Xiongnu

In 215 B.C., the First Emperor of Qin ordered a campaign against the Hu (Xiongnu) in the Ordos region. This was not prompted by any real threat or any preexisting situation of belligerence. The alleged reason for the expedition was a preemptive strike to prevent the fulfillment of a prophecy according to which "Hu" was going to bring about the downfall of the dynasty.[202] In fact, the First Emperor was pursuing a policy of territorial expansion, as land was needed both to demobilize and resettle the great number of men who had been serving in the Qin army, as well as defeated enemy troops, and to resettle the dispossessed families of war refugees. The operation was undertaken on a massive scale. General Meng Tian was sent north with an army numbering as many as 300,000 troops, according to some records, or 100,000 according to others. His task was to invade and seize the whole Hetao region, thus making the northern bend of the Yellow River into the new northern frontier of the Qin empire. Forty-four fortified counties were built along the river and settled with convicts sentenced to guard the borders. Moreover, a road was built between Jiuyuan 九原 (near present-day Baotou, Inner Mongolia) and Yunyang 雲陽 in order to link the

---

[201] See Rémi Mathieu, *Le Mu Tianzi zhuan: Traduction annotée – Étude critique* (Paris: Collège de France, Institut des hautes études chinoises, 1978).

[202] *Shi ji*, 6, p. 252. In fact, the son of the First Emperor, the short-lived last ruler of Qin, was called Huhai 胡亥 (William H, Nienhauser, Jr., ed., with Tsia-fa Cheng, Zongli Lu, and Robert Reynolds, trans., *The Grand Scribe's Records. Vol. 1: The Basic Annals of Pre-Han China by Ssu-ma Ch'ien* [Bloomington: Indiana University Press, 1994], p. 271).

border with the metropolitan area. Border defenses were erected throughout the north from Lintao, in the western part of Gansu, to Liaodong.[203] Beyond the Yellow River, Meng Tian extended Qin control over the Yang 陽 Mountains in Inner Mongolia.[204] The leader of the Xiongnu, Touman 頭曼, fled north. In 211 B.C., Qin transferred 30,000 families of colonists to Beihe 北河 and Yuzhong 榆中, north of the Yellow River in what is today Inner Mongolia.[205]

It is within this context of political and military emergency, compounded with the economic crisis derived from the loss of pasturelands, that the unification of the Xiongnu took place. The formation of a tribal confederation under a single charismatic leader was accomplished in various phases. The first phase saw the emergence of a new leader. This was Maodun, son of Touman, who claimed the title of *shanyu* in 209 B.C. His rise took place initially as the result of an act of patricide and seizure of power, accomplished after having created an efficient, blindly loyal, militarily disciplined corps of personal bodyguards. The account of the killing of Touman by his son suggests a struggle between an old aristocracy, evidently unable to meet the challenge presented by the Chinese invasion, and the junior leaders, who joined together irrespective of established hierarchies. Values consisting primarily of military prowess, obedience to the leader, and personal ambition were embraced by the new leadership. The first task the young leader faced was the challenge posed by other nomadic confederations, the Dong Hu and the Yuezhi.

As a loose confederation of tribes, the Xiongnu had existed at least a century before the unification of China. The rise of Maodun, therefore, does not bring about the creation of a new historical subject, but rather points to its political reorganization in order to meet a military challenge. Meng Tian's seizure of the Ordos and displacement of the Xiongnu must have caused widespread relocation and migration, upsetting the established territorial makeup and balance of power among the peoples of the Northern Zone. This crisis produced a violent change of leadership, which allowed the Xiongnu not only to overcome the crisis, but also to defeat their enemies and consolidate their position over the steppe region in Inner Mongolia and eastern Manchuria. In 210 B.C., the death of the First Emperor and the forced suicide of General Meng Tian paralyzed the Qin politically and militarily

---

[203] *Shi ji*, 110, p. 2886.

[204] *Shi ji*, 88. pp. 2565–6. On archaeological investigations of the Great Wall, see Tang Xiaofeng, "Nei Menggu xibei bu Qin Han chang cheng diaocha ji," *Wenwu* 1977.5: 16–22 (trans. as "A Report of the Investigation on the Great Wall of the Qin-Han Period in the Northwest Sector of Inner Mongolia," in *Chinese Archaeological Abstracts* 3, pp. 959–65).

[205] *Shi ji*, 6, p. 259 (Nienhauser, ed., *The Grand Scribe's Records*, vol. 1, p. 151).

and threw China into renewed civil war, preventing Chinese armies from taking effective action against the Xiongnu. Soon the defense line established by Qin was overtaken by the nomads, determined to reconquer their lost territories. The subsequent growth of the Xiongnu state into an empire marked the beginning of a new stage in the history of the northern frontier, which had now been defined for many centuries to come.

CHAPTER FOURTEEN

THE HERITAGE LEFT TO THE EMPIRES

Michael Loewe

This chapter attempts to identify some of the institutions that were devised and the advances that were achieved principally in the Spring and Autumn and Warring States periods and without which no idea of a united empire could have been implemented. In some instances it may be seen how an experiment in administrative or economic practice that was carried out within the confines of a particular region could later be adopted or adapted to suit the needs of a mighty empire. But it is in no way suggested here that those who initiated such steps so as to control a people or organize its labors saw them as instruments devised to lead toward such a unification.

While the unification of Qin and Han should be seen as a definite break and reaction against the practices of the past, it would be erroneous to judge it as a sudden and immediately effective change. For some time, earlier methods of statecraft and the lessons of the past continued to exert their influence, affected as they had been by the ambitions that many had entertained to exercise power and their struggles to do so in the face of the antagonism of their rivals. Alliances could be formed or abandoned with scant attention to personal integrity; loyalties could shift from master to master as circumstance might require. Only rarely were kings or their senior advisers brought face to face with moral aspects of their behavior. Ideas of what had come to be regarded as the normal policies of princes persisted into imperial times; they may well have accounted for the suspicions that some of the emperors entertained of their immediate followers and supporters, seeing them as potentially disloyal rebels.

From their predecessors the empires inherited religious beliefs and practices and concepts of monarchy. Familiar with some of the events of China's history, the emperors and their ministers drew on the precepts of China's teachers and their writings and called on existing forms for the promulgation of their orders. Thanks partly to earlier experiments in preparing documents, their clerks drew up the records that were needed to administer a mighty empire; and the empires could learn much from the experience of organizing and controlling armed forces and of building lines of defenses that the kings and their generals had gained in the previous centuries. The kings of the past had shown how cities could be planned, royal tombs built, and ancestral shrines dedicated so as to enhance the prestige and display the majesty of a ruling house. Wide divergences of terrain and occupation, of ethnic origins, cultural habits, and political affiliation, had indeed yet to be reconciled; but a distinction between those who lived under the aegis of a civilized dispensation and those who were not so blessed had already appeared; a hierarchical view of the peoples of the world itself betrayed a view of the human race as forming a unity.

A number of the methods and organs needed to operate and legitimate a unified government of China had appeared in the preceding centuries. They included a means of collecting revenue, of conscripting men for service, of controlling crime, and of erecting defenses against an external enemy. They required religious sanction and intellectual support; they depended on written and other types of communications; and they gave rise to a display of royal power. It remained the task of the founders of the empires to adapt the political structure of the old kingdom of Qin 秦 to suit the new political and social scene; to determine which intellectual masters and which religious precedents would strengthen their command of loyalties; and to establish the administrative organs that would be strong enough to sustain different economic practices and to override varying cultural standards.

The telling developments of the early empires are seen in the greater stress that came eventually to be placed on achieved merit rather than on circumstances of birth, and in the evolution of forms for recruiting and training the many more officials that were now needed. They are seen in the concentration of military forces under a single command, even if, for reasons of security, their immediate control was allocated to two generals; they are exemplified in the formation of a single set of defense lines, as against the many walls that some of the kingdoms had erected against their neighbors. On a different level the empires saw the need for measures not known previously; their leaders were ready to take steps either to suppress subversive writings or to promote literature of an approved type, in order to strengthen the support that an emperor and his ministers required. In such ways they might eventually hope that the government of mankind within a single political framework would be accepted as the norm.

THE CREATION OF EMPIRE AND ITS HAZARDS

Born in 259 B.C., Zhao Zheng 趙政 (originally named Ying Zheng 嬴政) succeeded his father as king of Qin in 246, before attaining his majority. Lü
Buwei 呂不韋, who served as his Chancellor (*xiang* 相) for a short time before
committing suicide (235 B.C.), had assembled a group of men of letters whose
writings are preserved in the received text of the *Lü shi chunqiu* 呂氏春秋
(Spring and Autumn [annals] of Mr. Lü) and which include a variety of opinions derived from eclectic sources on subjects such as cosmology, ethical concepts, and historical fiction. On a personal side it was alleged by some that
it was Lü Buwei who had sired Zhao Zheng, but such a charge is open to
doubt, being voiced by those who wished to discredit Zhao Zheng's claim
to succeed as king and to become emperor later. Attached to Lü Buwei's staff
was Li Si 李斯 (ca. 280–208 B.C.) who, along with Han Fei 韓非 (ca. 280–ca.
233 B.C.), had been a pupil of Xunzi 荀子 (ca. 310–ca. 215 B.C.). The principles and aims of government that Li Si advocated were strictly practical, being
addressed to meet the needs of expediency rather than to take account of
ethical principle. It was largely due to Li Si's encouragement and advice that
in the short period between 230 and 221, Qin succeeded in vanquishing and
taking over the territories of the six kingdoms of Hann 韓, Zhao 趙, Wei 魏,
Chu 楚, Yan 燕, and Qi 齊 and proclaimed the first of China's empires, with
the explicit hope that it would last for eternity.[1]

Such success owed much to the practice of internal discipline, the growth
of military strength, and the operation of the institutions that Shang Yang
商鞅 (ca. 385–338 B.C.) had inaugurated. But the collapse of the Qin empire
within less than a dozen years was perhaps a foretaste of developments and
events that were to recur in the following 2,000 years of imperial history,
demonstrating all too clearly the fragile nature of those dynasties. Both in
the immediately ensuing future and in the later empires, the weakness of
emperors, the rivalries of their principal advisors, the jealousies of their consorts, and competition for the imperial succession played their part in endan-
gering and disrupting a regime.

At one point during the decade of civil warfare that had preceded his
victory, Liu Bang 劉邦 (king of Han 漢 from 206, emperor of Han from 202)
had contemplated dividing the rule of China with his principal adversary
Xiang Yu 項羽. Possibly he had in mind a precedent that had occurred in
288 B.C., when for a short time the kings of Qin and Qi had agreed to adopt

---

[1] For the part played by Li Si in the creation of the Qin empire, see Derk Bodde, *China's First Unifier*
(Leiden: Brill, 1938; rpt. Hong Kong: Hong Kong University Press, 1967); and idem, "The State and
Empire of Ch'in," in *The Cambridge History of China*, ed. Denis Twitchett and Michael Loewe (Cam-
bridge University Press, 1986), vol. 1, pp. 52–72.

titles which implied that they ruled on terms of equality. Once established, the new empire drew extensively on the institutions of the kingdom and then the empire of Qin, with some measure of compromise with other forms and social distinctions that harked back to Zhou. But moments of instability and crisis were to be all too frequent at a time when the concept of empire had yet to gain general acceptance as the normal way of government.

A mere eight years after Liu Bang's death in 195, the Lü 呂 family (with which Lü Buwei was not connected) supplanted the imperial authority that had been vested in the house of Liu 劉. A succession quarrel that followed the death of the Empress Lü ended with the enthronement of Wendi 文帝 (r. 180–157 B.C.). Involved in questionable and perhaps illegal activities, Wendi's half-brother Liu Chang 劉長 died on his way to exile in 174. Jingdi 景帝 (r. 156–141) faced and suppressed a rebellion in which seven kings challenged imperial authority. Liu An 劉安, a grandson of Liu Bang, staged a conspiracy and plot to rebel in 122 and avoided a painful death by suicide. Chang'an 長安, capital of the empire, witnessed scenes of violence and bloodshed in 91, when, following charges of witchcraft and imprecation, armed fighting broke out in its streets between the adherents of two different families of imperial consorts, thus seriously prejudicing the survival of the dynasty.[2]

Notwithstanding these moments of crisis, the first century of Han rule was marked by a consolidation of internal strength, as seen in the increasingly wider implementation of imperial orders and by the territorial advances that had brought Han authority to bear in the newly penetrated regions of the northeast, northwest, and southwest. In a major change of policy that took effect from ca. 135 B.C., imperial government moved from a laissez-faire tolerance of economic growth toward an imposition of controls; a defensive policy in regard to other peoples gave way to positive steps in expansion.[3] Although the young Jia Yi 賈誼 (201–169 B.C.) had warned Wendi of the dangers that had brought about the fall of the Qin empire, the motives and aims espoused by the officials of Wudi 武帝 (r. 140–87 B.C.) were essentially those of Shang Yang and Li Si, as means of tightening internal discipline, increasing the supply of staple goods, and reinforcing military strength. Perhaps from 90 B.C. a second change of emphasis took place, when it became apparent that the effort spent in implementing such policies had been exhausted and that retrenchment had to take the place of expansion. A few decades later senior officials were looking to the ideals ascribed to the house of Zhou as their model and blaming the ways of Qin for the cruelty that

---

[2] For this incident, see Michael Loewe, *Crisis and Conflict in Han China* (London: Allen & Unwin, 1974), pp. 37–90.
[3] See Twitchett and Loewe, eds., *The Cambridge History of China*, vol. 1, pp. 152–70.

they brought to the people of China. Thanks partly to Wang Mang 王莽, sole emperor of the Xin 新 dynasty from A.D. 9 to 23, and to the work of certain scholars such as Liu Xiang 劉向 (79–8 B.C.) and his son Liu Xin 劉歆 (46 B.C.–A.D. 23), by the time of the Later Han dynasty (A.D. 25–220) new ideas were affecting public life. Precedents for decisions were sought in Zhou; Qin's so-called Legalist principles drew little but protest; it was the ideals ascribed to the kings of Western Zhou that commanded respect.

THE LESSONS OF THE PAST

In certain respects, students of pre-imperial China today can call on fuller information and can assess it more accurately than the founding fathers of the Qin and Han dynasties. They possess a more comprehensive and clearer picture of China's physical geography and its relation to the growth and distribution of material resources. Archaeology has revealed evidence of a type that was unknown and that serves to confirm or amplify that of the oral tradition and the written records that were available in 200 B.C. Had writers such as Sima Tan 司馬談 (d. ca. 110 B.C.), Sima Qian 司馬遷 (ca. 145–ca. 86 B.C.), or Ban Gu 班固 (A.D. 32–92) seen the oracular inscriptions of the shells and bones of the Shang kings, it is by no means certain that they would have been able to recognize their value as documents or to place them in their historical context. Nor can it be told how far they would have been able to appreciate the value of bronze inscriptions, had they been faced with the array that is available for study today. The statement that the famous tripod or tripods found in 113 B.C. were unlike other vessels insofar as they carried no inscriptions, either in relief or intaglio, may perhaps imply a familiarity with such items; it does not necessarily show that their inscriptions were being read and understood.[4]

Alive as the men of letters of Qin and Han were to the passage of dynasties and the fall of kingdoms, they would have lacked the critical ability to distinguish attested fact from myth or fiction. Their view of history was formed before any work such as the *Shi ji* 史記 (Records of the historian) had been compiled; they had no example of a written account of human experience, drawn up in majestic, sequential terms; and they drew on oral traditions with little means with which to verify their statements or to reconcile their inconsistencies.

There were indeed a number of works written before imperial times that had been compiled specifically as chronicles. They recorded the deeds or sayings of the dukes (*gong* 公) and kings (*wang* 王) of pre-imperial times;

---

[4] *Shi ji*, 28, p. 1392; *Han shu*, 25A, p. 1225.

they listed events in chronological sequence; and the purpose that they fulfilled was perhaps mainly ritual. In some of these the compilers paid deference to the kings of Zhou as meriting the respect due to recognized, or even hallowed, authority. In the case of the only one that survives in full, the *Chunqiu* 春秋 (Spring and Autumn [annals]), which is a chronicle of the dukes of Lu 魯 from 722 to 481 B.C., the terse nature of the entries and the particular choice of expressions laid it open to later interpretation as a deliberate attempt to impose a moral judgment on some of the personalities concerned or on their decisions and deeds. By contrast with such formal accounts, designed as a record for the court, there existed a large body of other writings which, while including some material of a factual nature, also carried much that was anecdotal or fictional. Their tales were sometimes intended to draw attention to feats of arms or to the wiles of those who were set to outwit their adversaries by intellectual means. Insofar as such works treated of kings and their advisers, and the relations between different kingdoms, they could be regarded as being of a historical nature.

But a new stage of Chinese historiography opened with the creation of the *Shi ji* by Sima Tan and his son Sima Qian. Their work was intended to review the history of mankind as a whole, without limitation to the activities of a particular court or area. The compilers incorporated material of both types, formal and informal, at times adding their own judicious comments on their validity. They framed their work so as to include special studies of the principal individuals who were concerned in China's cultural development, dynastic fortunes, and political or military incidents; they saw their way to isolating certain subjects, such as religious cults, astronomical observations, or regulation of the calendar, and treating them in their own special chapters. As yet they were not bound by the inhibitions under which their successors labored. They were not required to display their masters as paragons of fine behavior, whose predecessors had rightly deserved destruction. As yet they were not obliged to portray the past in terms of the steady influence exerted on mankind by the force of Confucian teaching.[5]

Those who, in imperial times, were intent on studying the past might thus have had at hand copies of chronicles of the states, as exemplified in the *Zhushu jinian* 竹書紀年 (Bamboo annals), the *Chunqiu*, or the *Shi ben* 世本 (Generations' roots), or in historical records such as those found at Mawangdui 馬王堆; fictional accounts of the negotiations conducted between the

---

[5] For China's early historiography, see P. van der Loon, "The Ancient Chinese Chronicles and the Growth of Historical Ideals," in *Historians of China and Japan*, ed. W. G. Beasley and E. G. Pulleyblank (London: Oxford University Press, 1961), pp. 24–30; and entries by Tsuen-hsuin Tsien, Anne Cheng and Chang I-jen, and William Boltz in *Early Chinese Texts: A Bibliographical Guide*, ed. Michael Loewe (Berkeley: Society for the Study of Early China and the Institute of East Asian Studies, University of California, 1993), pp. 1–11, 67–76, and 263–8.

rulers of the different states by way of their advisers, as seen in the original version of the *Zhanguo ce* 戰國策 (Stratagems of the Warring States) and again in recently discovered manuscripts, may have added further color to the somewhat dry records. While there is considerable evidence to show a familiarity with the *Chunqiu* at least from the time of Dong Zhongshu 董仲舒 (ca. 179–ca. 104 B.C.), the first direct reference to the *Zuo zhuan* 左傳 (Zuo's tradition) to be made in Han times is found in a memorial dated not before 6 B.C.[6]

Nonetheless, in at least three respects, those who responded to a call to gather at one of the courts to join in literary exercises, such as that of the king of Huainan 淮南 (before 122 B.C.), or those who filled the role of the Academicians (*boshi* 博士) were more fortunate than many of their successors. Provided that they had access to the books and documents that were eventually to be held in the palace library, they could call on a large body of material that has since been lost. Second, they may have been able to consult certain contemporary official documents of an archival nature, in the form of lists and genealogies, that have long disappeared beyond recall. Finally, those scholars and historians who were writing before the end of the Former Han period were not yet inhibited by some of the steps introduced to standardize the texts of early literature; to formalize the interpretation to be put upon them; and to restrict the growth of individual criticism, in the interests of maintaining an orthodox point of view.

The structure of the Qin empire derived from the principles advocated by Shang Yang of Wey 衛, Shen Buhai 申不害 (b. ca. 400 B.C.) of Zheng 鄭, and Han Fei of Hann 韓 and from the practices of the Qin kingdom; much of this was inherited by the Han empire. It will be noted that these three political theorists were not natives of Qin. In addition, the presence of a few other senior experienced statesmen from some of the other kingdoms may have ensured that a knowledge of their ways of government was not necessarily denied to the counselors and rulers of empire. Thus, the first and second Qin emperors were served by Li Si, who had been a native of Chu; and the distinguished military family of Meng 蒙, whose members included the generals Meng Tian 蒙恬 and Meng Yi 蒙毅 (both died 210), had been reared in Qi 齊. Some knowledge of the traditions of these other kingdoms may well have been available to those who pondered on China's history as the empire was being formed.

Two outstanding elements may be observed in the view of China's history as this seems to have been conceived in early imperial times, one deriving from age-old mythology, one from a concern for genealogy; both provided

---

[6] *Han shu*, 73, p. 3127.

an intellectual or perhaps a psychological framework from which the leaders of the realm had been able to draw support and comfort over the centuries. Rulers and noblemen and their advisers could see in mythology a means with which to strengthen their own position of authority; and they were able to trace their ancestry to persons of renown. Mythological history told of primeval progenitors such as Fu Xi 伏羲, or named ideal monarchs such as Yao 堯 and Shun 舜. Descent from Fu Xi or Huang Di 黃帝 could be claimed on behalf of the Han emperors or of Wang Mang. Other subjects which recur frequently enough in this connection may be seen in the three idealized regimes of Xia 夏, Shang 商 and Zhou 周; or the Three August Ones (*San huang* 三皇) and Five Monarchs (*Wu di* 五帝), however variously these famous personages may have been identified. Genealogy was to become a matter of major significance so as to ensure that religious rites were observed correctly, to determine the degrees of kinship and social structure, and to support a claimant's right to power or property.

A few examples may suggest how far some of the founders of the empire were familiar with accounts of their past or how ready they were to make use of their knowledge. In 246 B.C., Li Si commented on the failings of Qin Mu Gong 秦穆公 (r. 659–621 B.C.) who, while possibly acting as *Ba* 霸, had not been able to unite what were later to become the six states.[7] He explained that this was due to the large number of leaders of the land at the time; it was before the decline of Zhou had set in, when the Five *Ba* were rising up in turn, one after the other, each one showing his respect for that house. There followed Zhou's manifest weakness, in the time of Qin Xiao Gong 秦孝公 (r. 361–338 B.C.), and it was then that there followed the amalgamation of the many units into the six major states. Li Si claimed that from the time of Xiao Gong onwards, six rulers of Qin had asserted their superiority over the lesser leaders of the day.

The debate which is recorded for 213 B.C., and which touched on some of the recurrent problems that would confront imperial government, started by way of congratulations that no less than seventy academicians were offering to their emperor; but a call on the past obtruded at its crucial point. Chunyu Yue 淳于越, one of those taking part, observed that the long-lasting success of the Shang and Zhou dynasties had depended on the support received from those sons and brothers of the king who had been commissioned to rule over certain territories on a hereditary basis; he suggested that similar provisions should be made for the empire. In rebutting the proposal Li Si, the chancellor, perhaps showed a more mature sense of the past. He pointed out the difference between earlier days, marked by a multiplicity of rulers, and the

---

[7] *Shi ji*, 87, p. 2540.

present state of unity, and he saw no reason for adopting precedents from those earlier times in the completely different circumstances of the day. It was on this opposition to traditionalism that he based his proposal to prevent free access to the literature and historical records of the past, a proposal which has come to be known as the Burning of the Books.[8]

Li Si also referred to historical events right at the end of his career, when he was faced by the open antagonism of Zhao Gao 趙高 (d. 207 B.C.). In his memorial of 210 B.C. to the Second Emperor, he cited precedents that showed the dangers that beset a state if its ruler placed an excessive trust in advisers of Zhao Gao's type and character. Li Si's references to certain personages of the sixth to third centuries B.C. are not entirely consistent with what is related in other records that have survived. Also in 210, Zhao Gao himself cited historical precedents. These were mentioned in his successful attempt to persuade Ying Huhai 嬴胡亥, one of the younger sons of the First Emperor, to cooperate in the conspiracy to have him elected in place of the more rightful heir to the throne. Zhao Gao referred to two cases, frequently cited by way of warning, that were of a much more extreme nature, in which the two monarchs Jie 桀 and Zhou 紂, last monarchs of the Xia and Shang dynasties, respectively, had actually been assassinated. Li Si's reaction to Zhao Gao's proposal had been to refute it with a more recent example of what had occurred, namely in Jin 晉 during the seventh century. Meanwhile, Meng Tian, another of Zhao Gao's victims, answered the Second Emperor's charge of disloyalty by telling of the false accusations made against Zhou Gong 周公 and the latter's vindication. On another occasion, in 208 B.C., the Second Emperor himself, who had been taught something of the operation of Qin's laws by none other than Zhao Gao, called on the lesson that he had learned from one of Han Fei's references to the practices of Yao and Shun.[9]

Certain parts of the traditional story were to assume a regular place in Chinese historiography. Writing shortly after the start of the Han empire, Lu Jia 陸賈 (ca. 228–140 B.C.) mentioned what was to become a paradigm: that of the extreme difference between the regimes of Yao and Shun on the one hand and those of Jie and Zhou on the other. The contrast was seen in terms of the relationship between effective government and moral values. Some elements of the story could be of immediate value, to be cited by way of support for actions that ran counter to an established rule. An example of such an exploitation may be seen in the references made in Wang Mang's

---

[8] *Shi ji*, 6, p. 254 (Édouard Chavannes, trans., *Les mémoires historiques de Se-ma Ts'ien* [vols. 1–5, Paris: Ernest Leroux, 1895–1905; rpt., with vol. 6, ed. Paul Demiéville, Paris: Adrien Maisonneuve, 1969], vol. 2, p. 169); see also Bodde, *China's First Unifier*, pp. 23, 80; and Twitchett and Loewe, eds., *The Cambridge History of China*, vol. 1, p. 69.

[9] *Shi ji*, 87, pp. 2549–50, 2559 (Bodde, *China's First Unifier*, pp. 31, 47); *Shi ji*, 88, p. 2569.

time to the selfless part played by Zhou Gong in acting as regent without wishing to seize the throne for himself or to Yao's abdication in favor of Shun.[10]

In a long memorial of 134 B.C., in which he advised Han Wudi to refrain from mounting an expedition against the Xiongnu 匈奴, Zhufu Yan 主父偃 expressed what may well have been becoming a standard view of the past.[11] The house of Zhou had kept the world in order for some 300 years, of which the reigns of Kings Cheng (1042/35–1006 B.C.) and Kang (1005/03–978 B.C.) had been the highest point, with no need to apply the punishments of state for 40 years. There followed a period of decline, again for 300 years, in which the Five *Ba* had arisen to take each other's place, constantly assisting the Son of Heaven to his advantage, eliminating evil, and setting the world to rights. With the disappearance of the *Ba*, the Son of Heaven was left isolated; the leaders of the land behaved in an arbitrary manner, the strong overwhelming the weak, and the many the few. Unauthorized rule was set up in Qi; the six high-ranking ministers split Jin, together forming the Warring States (*Zhanguo* 戰國), and thereby inaugurating an era of popular suffering. This view of the Five *Ba*, who are variously named, as acting in the interests of Zhou is seen in works such as the *Xunzi* 荀子 and, much later, the *Baihu tong* 白虎通 (Comprehensive discussions in the White Tiger Hall).[12] Jia Yi refers to them when he traces the rise of Qin after their disappearance, without necessarily implying a criticism;[13] by contrast, Meng Ke 孟軻 (i.e., Mencius; fl. 320 B.C.) viewed them as interlopers who had been displacing the rightful Son of Heaven from his proper seat of authority.[14]

The term *Zhanguo* may itself reveal something of the view that was taken of the centuries which immediately preceded the creation of the empires. An early occurrence of the phrase is seen in one of the chapters of the *Guanzi* 管子, of uncertain date.[15] In this passage the term does not imply any spe-

---

[10] See *Xin yu* 新語 (Sibu beiyao ed.), A ("Wuwei"), 6b–8a; *Han shu*, 99A, p. 4094; 99B, p. 4108 (Homer H. Dubs, *The History of the Former Han Dynasty*, 3 vols. [Baltimore: Waverly, 1938–55], vol. 3, pp. 251, 280).

[11] *Shi ji*, 112, p. 2957; *Han shu*, 64A, p. 2799.

[12] *Xunzi*, 11 ("Wang ba"), Liang Qixiong, *Xunzi jianshi* (Beijing: Guji, 1956), p. 139 (John Knoblock, *Xunzi: A Translation and Study of the Complete Works*, 3 vols. [Stanford, Calif.: Stanford University Press, 1988–94], vol. 2, p. 151); Ban Gu 班固 (A.D. 32–92), *Baihu tong* (Han Wei congshu, Chen Rong ed.), A ("Hao"), 12a–b (Tjan Tjoe Som, *Po hu t'ung: The Comprehensive Discussions in the White Tiger Hall*, 2 vols. [Leiden: Brill, 1949–52], vol. 1, p. 236).

[13] *Shi ji*, 6, p. 283 (Chavannes, *Mémoires historiques*, vol. 2, p. 232).

[14] *Mencius* 2A/3 (James Legge, *The Chinese Classics*, 5 vols., 2d rev. ed. [Oxford: Clarendon Press, 1893–94], vol. 2, *The Works of Mencius*, p. 196), and 6B/7 (Legge, *The Chinese Classics*, vol. 2, p. 435). See also Liu Xiang's preface to the *Zhanguo ce*, and *Han shu* 14, p. 391, for the view of the Five *Ba* as serving Zhou and supporting it at a time of weakness.

[15] *Guanzi* (Sibu beiyao ed.), 9 (23 "Bayan"), 9a (W. Allyn Rickett, *Guanzi: Political, Economic, and Philosophical Essays from Early China* [Princeton, N. J.: Princeton University Press, 1985], vol. 1, p. 361). For the dating of different parts of the *Guanzi*, see Loewe, ed., *Early Chinese Texts*, p. 244.

cific period; in general terms it denotes states that are in contention with one another on terms of parity, to be overcome by means of overlordship (*ba* 霸) if they are numerous or by correct monarchy (*wang* 王) if they are few. In his critique of the first Qin emperor, Jia Yi wrote of how, having separated the Warring States, that monarch had established his rule over the world.[16] A passage in the introduction to the *Shi ji*'s table of the rise and fall of monarchies from 475 to 207 B.C. mentions the changes in the grasp of power of the warring states.[17] Right at the close of the Former Han period, Liu Xiang adopted the expression *Zhanguo* in the title of the work *Zhanguo ce* that he had compiled on the basis of a number of existing records; from then on the term certainly came to denote a particular period of time, however this may have been defined. For Liu Xiang it was the 245 years that followed after the Spring and Autumn period until the rise of Chu and Han, that is, from 454 to 209 B.C.[18] As seen below, a different reckoning was accepted later.

Many of those who wrote before the empires had been created treated earlier times, and particularly those of the kings of Western Zhou, as a golden age that was followed by decay and decline. Ignoring, or unappreciative of, the social, economic, and political changes that had marked the face of China for perhaps half a millennium, they looked back nostalgically to those days, supposing that a restoration of their institutions would spell a new era of happiness and prosperity. Uncritical respect for the long-lost past continued to haunt China's historiography; it was only exceptionally that a writer such as Wang Chong 王充 (A.D. 27–ca. 100) could shake free of such inhibitions and express the view that in principle the present was not necessarily inferior to the past.

Nonetheless, the contribution made by Sima Tan and Sima Qian to the formation of China's ideas of its own past cannot be stressed too strongly. As distinct from references in earlier texts, in their majestic account of the origins of human society and the succession of the world's rulers, they fastened on Huang Di as the earliest of the monarchs, following the decline of the time of the culture hero Shen Nong 神農. They ignored claims that might have been made on behalf of figures of mythology such as Fu Xi to be the founders of sovereignty, and traced the succession of monarchs in two collateral lines, each springing from Huang Di; and they treated Huang Di in human rather than in divine terms. At several points Sima Qian expressed his reservations about the validity and weaknesses of the received traditions of these early times. He paid tribute to the *Chunqiu* for clarifying the chronological sequences of earlier days. He rarely used the terms *Chunqiu* or

---

[16] *Shi ji*, 6, p. 283 (Chavannes, *Mémoires historiques*, vol. 3, p. 232).
[17] *Shi ji*, 15, p. 686 (ibid., vol. 3, p. 27).
[18] *Zhanguo ce*, preface.

Zhanguo to denote periods, choosing as his distinctive epochs those of the *San dai* 三代 (Three Dynasties, from Huang Di to 842 B.C.), the *Shier zhuhou* 十二諸侯 (Twelve Lords, 841–477 B.C.), and the *Liu guo* 六國 (Six States, 475–207 B.C.). But by the time when the *Han shu* 漢書 was being compiled (after A.D. 36, and mainly before 92), the usage was set; the expressions *Chunqiu* and *Zhanguo* were both used to denote specific periods, the *Chunqiu* being reckoned at 242 years (722–481 B.C.).[19]

Along with these great merits, the fathers of Chinese history lacked a sense of causation, as compared with their colleagues of other civilizations, of whose existence they knew nothing. They left a legacy to their successors of treating China's history in periods that were determined by the rise and fall of dynastic houses. Political and official change was all important; social and economic developments, or the lives of the great majority of China's inhabitants, were matters of low priority. Their followers who compiled the standard histories for subsequent houses assumed, and were obliged to assume, that imperial unity was the norm; only exceptionally would a critic such as Xun Yue 荀悦 (A.D. 148–209) or Sima Guang 司馬光 (1019–86) perceive the need to present the facts of history in a more coordinated fashion that brought out the importance of chronological sequence and the contemporaneous incidence of certain actions and decisions.[20]

RELIGIOUS RITES

If the kings of Shang and Zhou had depended largely on their religious functions to display their authority and to forge a link between superhuman powers and mankind that would command acknowledgement and respect, so too were the emperors of the Han and later dynasties actively engaged in performing the state cults in order to demonstrate the essential nature of the position that they held in the cosmic order. How far they drew on earlier precedents in this respect may be difficult to judge. When all allowance is made for the strength of the traditions and of the oral transmission of ideas and ceremonies, it must still be acknowledged that too long an interval separated the centuries of Western Zhou from the unified empires to determine how far the memories or accounts of those early times necessarily molded

---

[19] *Shi ji*, 1, p. 46 (Chavannes, *Mémoires historiques*, vol. 1, pp. 94–6); 13, p. 487; see also the titles of *Shi ji* chapters 13 (p. 487), 14 (p. 509), and 15 (p. 685), and *Shi ji*, 27, p. 1344; *Han shu*, 1B, p. 81 (Dubs, *History of the Former Han Dynasty*, vol. 1, p. 148); 21A, p. 973; 26, p. 1300; 27B(2), p. 1500; 29, p. 1692, for a memorial ascribed to Jia Rang 賈讓 at the start of the reign of Aidi (acceded 6 B.C.); 100A, pp. 4227–8.

[20] For the place taken by Xun Yue and Sima Guang in Chinese historiography, see A. F. P. Hulsewé, "Notes on the Historiography of the Han Period," and E. G. Pulleyblank, "Chinese Historical Criticism: Liu Chih-chi and Ssu-ma Kuang," in *Historians of China and Japan*, ed. Beasley and Pulleyblank, pp. 43, and 151–9.

the observances of the imperial age. Nonetheless, it may probably be assumed that at least from the first century A.D. the rites of Zhou, as conceived at the time, were seen as the ideal which rulers of the day should seek to emulate. To what extent the detailed accounts of some of those rites that are preserved in the compendia on *li* 禮 (rites) reflect actual practice may likewise never be known. Nor can it be said how far those books, or the versions that were available in the initial stages of the empires, acted as a model for the imperial courts. It may nonetheless be suggested that considerable attention was paid to such precedents for imperial observance.

In introducing their chapters on state religion, the authors of the *Shi ji* and the *Han shu* drew on the tradition of primaeval practices and the achievements of the monarchs of mythology.[21] In writing about the inauguration of ordained rites in place of the earlier devotions to various spirits, or about the activities of the shamans, they credited Zhuan Xu 顓頊 with responsibility for commissioning officials to serve the spirits of Heaven and Earth. They recounted how the deified culture heroes introduced shrines to the soil and the crops; they wrote of the worship paid to Shang Di 上帝, the spirits of the constellations and the climate, and of the devotional visits that were paid to the sacred mountains. The chapters mention the work of Shun, but not that of Yao; the attention that Yu 禹 paid to religious matters; and a variety of events that thereafter accompanied a laxity in these matters. It was to the influence of Zhou Gong, with the exercise of true kingship and the beginning of the cultural gifts of civilized behavior and music, that fully ordered religious rites could be traced. As in other aspects of Chinese civilization, so here writers were quick to notice the hierarchies. Under the dispensation of Zhou, the Son of Heaven was responsible for the worship of the supreme powers; those of lesser rank could pay their respects to the lesser spirits of their localities.

Of highest importance in the great multiplicity of acts of worship were those that were rendered to the supreme deity of all, whom emperors were later to see as the source of their own authority. Tradition here was extensive, but it may be questioned how far the empires were aware of the devotions paid by the kings of Shang to Di 帝 or Shang Di. It is more likely that in early Han times they realized that the kings of Zhou had seen their supreme godhead in Tian 天. The final suspension of Zhou's acts of worship, which presumably included those to Tian, had occurred only in 249 B.C., perhaps within the memory of some of the founding fathers of the Han empire.[22]

---

[21] *Shi ji*, 28, pp. 1355–6; *Han shu*, 25A, pp. 1189–93.
[22] *Han shu*, 25A, p. 1200.

It is also possible to identify a number of other elements that had grown up within the tradition by the time of the empires. There were precedents for services paid in the remote past to the Four Mountain Peaks (*yue* 嶽): Hengshan 衡山 (of the south), Huashan 華山 (of the west), Hengshan 恆 山 (of the north) and Song Gao 嵩高 (of the center). Some writers of the Han period discerned a direct relationship between the performance of some unspecified religious rites, as practiced before the Zhou dynasty, and the fortunes of dynastic rule. They ascribed to the kings of Zhou the use of special halls of worship, named Ming tang 明堂 and Biyong 辟雍; they wrote of the services paid by those kings to the Lord of the Grain (*Hou ji* 後稷) at the city's bounds, as matching those to Tian, and those to King Wen in the Ming tang as matching those to Shang Di. Various other rites were maintained. Those of an obscene nature were banned.[23]

As in the view of dynastic destinies, so too in respect of religious practices were the events of 771 B.C. seen as marking a turning point. The inauguration of Qin's worship of the White Di (Bai Di 白帝), of the west, is dated to 770 B.C.[24] Although the *Shi ji*'s account of this practice may be couched in anachronistic terms, it perhaps indicates that in early imperial times it was believed that the worship of one of several *di* was started by the states that were coexisting with Zhou, and which could in no case claim a right to worship Tian. Qin's further worship of the Green Di (Qing Di 青帝) of the east, is recorded for 672 B.C.; and that of the White Di was reaffirmed in 374 B.C.[25] Meanwhile at his accession in 677 B.C., De Gong 德公 of Qin had chosen Yong 雍 as his seat of residence, where shrines to a number of deities had developed.[26]

The tradition whereby an acknowledged and duly established ruler would undertake the arduous ascent of Mount Tai 泰 and perform the *feng* 封 and *shan* 禪 ceremonies is ascribed, again perhaps in anachronistic terms, to a statement of Guan Zhong 管仲 of Qi in 651 B.C. He traced a number of examples of monarchs who had performed the feat, from the mythical Wu Huai 無懷 to King Cheng of Zhou, and by adroit argument he dissuaded Qi Huan Gong from embarking on the task. This account perhaps suggests a belief in early imperial times that these rites should be performed only by those whose sovereignty lay beyond question.[27]

Such were some of the precedents that may have been in the minds of those who ordered and conducted the religious rites of the Qin and Former Han empires. In accounts that somewhat surprisingly assume that the rulers

---

[23] *Han shu*, 25A, pp. 1191–3.
[24] *Shi ji*, 14, p. 532; for the sequence of changes in religious practices, see *Han shu*, 25A, pp. 1194–1200.
[25] *Shi ji*, 28, p. 1365 (Chavannes, *Mémoires historiques*, vol. 3, p. 429).
[26] *Shi ji*, 28, p. 1360 (ibid., p. 422).   [27] *Shi ji*, 28, p. 1361 (ibid., p. 423).

of Qin subscribed to the theory of the Five Phases and their influence on dynastic power, the *Shi ji* and the *Han shu* record that these rulers declared their fealty to the patron element or phase of Water, which would have implied the worship of the Black Di (Hei Di 黑帝). Elsewhere we are informed that at the time when Han had just been founded, services had been maintained to the four *di*, of white, green, yellow and red, and that it was only at the insistence of Han Gaodi 漢高帝, at the outset of his reign, that those to the Black Di were added.[28] In time the Han emperors were perhaps to revive part of the earlier tradition by establishing their worship of the five *di* at Yong, supposedly at regular intervals from 134 B.C. There does not seem to have been a direct precedent for their worship of Houtu 后土 (Presiding spirit of the soil) at Fenyin 汾陰 (114 B.C.) or of Taiyi 太一 at Ganquan 甘泉 (113 B.C.). It was only comparatively late in imperial times, from perhaps 33 B.C., that steps were taken to introduce imperial cults that were addressed to Tian, supreme god of the Zhou.[29]

It is not certain that when the First Emperor made his ascent of Mount Tai in 219 B.C., he actually performed the *feng* and *shan* ceremonies; it is related that the rites which were conducted there were comparable with those of the worship to Shang Di at Yong. Other rites which were continued after the growth of the empire included those to a whole host of spirits, including those of the mountains and rivers.

Two principal cults of immortality attracted devotions in pre-imperial times, the one by way of the Blessed Isle of Penglai 蓬萊, the other dependent on the grace of the Queen Mother of the West (Xi Wang Mu 西王母). The belief that the precious elixir, together with certain other gifts, could be acquired by undertaking a journey to Penglai and its neighboring islands had induced kings Wei 威 (r. 356–320 B.C.) and Xuan 宣 (r. 319–301 B.C.) of Qi and King Zhao 昭 (r. 311–279 B.C.) of Yan 燕 to send parties of men to attempt the feat, only to find that the islands vanished at their approach.[30] Such precedents may have been in mind when the First Emperor of Qin was advised to send out an expedition for the same purpose in 219 B.C., only to be angered by its costly failure to achieve any results.[31] Han Wudi made a similarly abortive attempt ca. 130 B.C.[32] References to the Queen Mother of the West found in texts such as the *Zhuangzi* 莊子 and the *Shan hai jing* 山

---

[28] *Shi ji*, 6, p. 237 (Chavannes, *Mémoires historiques*, vol. 2, p. 128); *Shi ji*, 15, p. 757; 26, p. 1259 (Chavannes, *Mémoires historiques*, vol. 3, p. 328); *Shi ji*, 28, p. 1366 (ibid., p. 430); *Han shu*, 25A, pp. 1200–1201, 1210. For an evaluation of the references in the *Shi ji*, see Twitchett and Loewe, eds., *The Cambridge History of China*, vol. 1, pp. 96–7.

[29] For the Han cults at Yong and elsewhere, see Loewe, *Crisis and Conflict in Han China*, pp. 166–70; for the Han imperial cults to Tian, see ibid., pp. 170–9.

[30] *Han shu*, 25A, p. 1204.   [31] *Shi ji*, 6, p. 247 (Chavannes, *Mémoires historiques*, vol. 2, p. 152).

[32] *Han shu*, 25A, p. 1216.

海經 (Classic of the mountains and the seas) allude not only to her possession of the gift of immortality, but also to her power of controlling the operation of the cosmos. Major attempts to procure the elixir through her intermediacy do not appear to have started in imperial times before 3 B.C.[33]

Other religious activities that were not backed by royal or official sponsorship, or which could even call for suppression, survived from pre-imperial times to be evidenced in the Han period. The practice of burying sacred vessels, valuables, treasures, items of utility, consumable supplies, and sundry texts for the benefit of a deceased person continued, so as to provide spiritual blessing, material enjoyment, or a means of entertainment in the life of the world to come. Shamans fulfilled their role as intermediaries between two worlds, as may be seen in the *Chu ci* 楚辭 (Verses of Chu) and as is told of the Yangzi River area in Han times. Many of the forms of seeking guidance by way of divination or by consulting oracles, often to ascertain the likelihood of military success, persisted then, as with the manipulation of the yarrow stalks and creation of their resulting hexagrams, or by observation of the natural signs inherent in the winds or the clouds. Powerful spirits of nature who had called for worship included He Bo 河伯 (Lord of the River). In Warring States times his power had been recognized as demanding regular appeasement by the sacrifice of virgin brides, who were floated downstream to sink in the depths of his domain. His image still gave cause for alarm in Han times, when no less a person than Wudi invoked his name at a time when floods menaced the peace of the realm (109 B.C.).[34]

THE TEACHINGS OF THE MASTERS

Detailed attention has been given in the preceding chapters of this volume to the teaching of the early masters and the development of various modes of thought, whether these were concerned principally with ethical precepts, political theories, or the reactions against the deliberate organization of human beings and their efforts. But it is perhaps questionable how far it may be assumed that exclusive schools, of types categorized as Confucian, Legal-

---

[33] See Michael Loewe, *Ways to Paradise: The Chinese Quest for Immortality* (London: Allen & Unwin, 1979), pp. 86–96, 98–101.

[34] For a reference to shamanism in Chu, see *Han shu*, 28B, p. 1666. For the large number of references to He Bo and the identification that came to be drawn with Bing Yi 冰夷 (馮夷), see Yuan Ke and Zhou Ming, *Zhongguo shenhua ziliao cuibian* (Chengdu: Sichuan sheng Shehui kexueyuan, 1958), pp. 217–25; and Yuan Ke, *Shan hai jing jiaozhu* (Shanghai: Guji, 1980), p. 316, n. 2. For a description of the sacrifice and an account of its suppression in the fifth century B.C., see Chu Shaosun's 褚少孫 (ca. 104–30 B.C.) addendum to *Shi ji*, 126, p. 3211. Perhaps the most evocative reference to He Bo is to be seen in the "Jiu ge" section of the *Chu ci* (*Chu ci buzhu* [Sibu beiyao ed.], 2, 19b; David Hawkes, *The Songs of the South: An Ancient Anthology of Poems by Qu Yuan and Other Poets* [2d ed., Harmondsworth: Penguin, 1985], pp. 113–14). For mention of He Bo in Wudi's song of 109 B.C., see *Han shu*, 29, p. 1683.

ist, or Daoist, could be distinguished at the start of the imperial age. The academic assemblies, such as the famous one of Jixia 稷下, had not necessarily produced a united viewpoint or given rise to a single tradition. Mo Di's 墨翟 followers had indeed formed themselves into a school or set of sects; but apart from those of their writings that concerned military strategy, their principles were hardly of a type to commend themselves to the masters of the newly founded empires, who, so far from being responsive to philanthropic motives, were anxious to vaunt their victories and expand their strength, rather than to attend to humanitarian calls. Nor should it be assumed that the soldiers who fought to found the Qin and Han empires or the officials who set about the task of administration were as yet consciously familiar with the precepts of the earlier masters or the writings ascribed to them, or that they deliberately sought to frame their institutions with such principles in mind. Several decades had to pass before their memorials would be colored by citations from such works.

Somewhat surprisingly the earliest reference to Confucius that is attributed to a leading figure in imperial times is ascribed to Zhao Gao.[35] This was the eunuch on whose machinations and deceits the destiny of empire depended and who, of all those persons mentioned in that tale, would seem to have been least responsive to Confucius's ethical ideals. The reference that he made was designed to lend authority to his own purpose of manipulating the imperial succession; it may perhaps be classified as a case of the devil quoting scripture.

Citations next appear in the essays of Jia Yi, whose views are far from being typical of his age, as far as the limited sources for the period may indicate. It is only in the memorials of Dong Zhongshu 董仲舒 that were probably submitted ca. 140 that an ordered statement of political principles for imperial times included a firm reliance on a number of citations that may be in seen in the *Analects*.[36] This was just at the time when deliberate preference was being given to the scholarly school (*Rujia* 儒家) rather than to those who cultivated adherence to the *Dao*. Certain chapters of the *Shi ji* (completed ca. 90 B.C.) and the final comments to other chapters refer to Confucius, often in relation to his work as a teacher or editor, or to his civilizing influence, and at least one such allusion may be paralleled in the *Analects*.[37] The earliest members of the imperial family to be credited with a familiarity with that work are Liu Qu 劉去, the infamous king of Guangchuan 廣川 from 91 to 70 B.C., and the twelve-year-old Liu Shi 劉奭, as yet the Heir Apparent

[35] *Shi ji*, 87, p. 2549 (Bodde, *China's First Unifier*, p. 27).
[36] For references by Jia Yi, see *Han shu*, 48, pp. 2248, 2253; for those by Dong Zhongshu, see *Han shu*, 56, pp. 2500, 2501, 2503, 2504, 2508.
[37] E.g., see *Shi ji*, 23, p. 1159, which carries Confucius's famous statement on the "Rectification of names."

and destined to reign as Yuandi from 49 to 33 B.C. Citations, without specific acknowledgement either to Confucius or to the *Analects*, first appear in
imperial decrees for 23 and 16 B.C. and A.D. 5.[38]

As will be discussed below, Laozi's 老子 name is coupled frequently
enough in early Han times with that of Huang Di, but strict evidence of a
general familiarity with his writings among men of affairs is not so certain.
Two copies of the book that is associated with Laozi's name, and which is
known today as the *Daode jing* 道德經 (Classic of the way and virtue),
were found in tomb 3 Mawangdui (168 B.C.), together with certain ancillary
texts. It is perhaps questionable how far this single example may be taken
to suggest that the text or texts were circulated on a comparatively wide
basis and that acquaintance with their mode of thought was not uncommon.
It was thanks to the insistence of the Empress Dou 竇 (d. 135 B.C.) that Wendi
and Jingdi, while still heirs apparent, were obliged to "read" in both
Huang Di and Laozi.[39] Allusions to Laozi's teachings, together with a few
citations, stem from the hands of Sima Tan or Sima Qian.[40] But citations
that are attributed to others are extremely rare. On an earlier occasion (ca.
180 B.C.), Sima Jizhu 司馬季主, a specialist in divination, is said to have
quoted from the *Laozi* and from a saying of Zhuangzi.[41] The next occasion
on which the *Laozi* was quoted is seen in a memorial submitted to the throne
by Liu An, king of Huainan, perhaps in 135 B.C. Citations from the *Laozi*
abound in the collection of writings that was in the main completed by 139
B.C.[42]

Both the Second Emperor of Qin and Li Si (Chancellor of the Left in 208
B.C.) were ready to cite from Han Fei, who had been a fellow student of Li
Si when they were studying with Xunzi.[43] In Han times, famous statesmen
such as Jia Yi and Chao Cuo 晁錯 (executed 155 B.C.) were familiar with the
principles of Han Fei and Shen Buhai; and despite the discrimination ordered
against such writings in a decree of 140 B.C., Dongfang Shuo 東方朔 (fl. 135
B.C.), anxiously seeking office, was ready to quote liberally from Shang Yang,
as well as from Han Fei.[44] That a number of Han officials a little later were

[38] For an account of Liu Qu and his barbaric cruelties, see *Han shu*, 53, p. 2428; for Liu Shi and his advisors, see *Han shu*, 71, p. 3039, and Michael Loewe, *Divination, Mythology and Monarchy in Han China*
(Cambridge University Press, 1994), pp. 268–74. For the decrees that are mentioned, see *Han shu*, 10,
pp. 313, 320; and 12, p. 358 (Dubs, *History of the Former Han Dynasty*, vol. 2, pp. 390, 402, and vol. 3,
p. 83).

[39] *Shi ji*, 49, p. 1975.

[40] *Shi ji*, 63, p. 2143, and 105, p. 2817.

[41] *Shi ji*, 127, pp. 3218–19.

[42] *Han shu*, 64A, p. 2784; in the *Huainanzi*, see esp. chapter 12.

[43] *Shi ji*, 87, pp. 2553, 2555 (Bodde, *China's First Unifier*, pp. 12, 36, 39).

[44] *Han shu*, 62, p. 2723, and 65, p. 2864.

well acquainted with Shang Yang's principles is clear from the *Yan tie lun* 鹽 鐵論 (Discourses on salt and iron), an account of a debate that was held in 81 B.C.[45]

The empires inherited two traditional approaches to the world and its values that are sometimes symbolized under the terms of two modes of thought, those of the *Daojia* 道家 and the *Rujia*. The latter group of thinkers expressed a marked emphasis on the need to maintain the established religious and other rites and to abide by the conventional social hierarchies of family and state. But here again some caution is necessary before it may be assumed that these ideas of *li* necessarily affected the ordering of public affairs significantly.

In a famous passage, the author of the *Shi ji* noted the survival of scholars who were familiar with the rites and music in Lu 魯 at the start of the Han era. He attributed this to little less than divine intervention and named a number of specialists in the *Zhou yi* 周易 (Zhou changes), *Shi jing* 詩經 (Classic of poetry), *Shang shu* 尚書 (Venerated documents), the *Li* 禮, and the *Chunqiu* who were active at the start of Wudi's reign. Two well-known incidents in the reign of the first of the Han emperors illustrate the need felt by some, perhaps exceptionally, to bring civilizing ideas to bear on the activities of the court and the decisions of government. But considerable evidence may be cited to testify to the intolerance which each group of thinkers entertained for the other and for the changes whereby they were in turn granted a favored position at the court. That the distinction could have political implications may be seen in the rejection of a suggestion that was made ca. 140 B.C. to build a Ming tang, on the grounds that it would serve the purposes of the *Rujia* and their traditions.[46] Despite the provision made for the study of the *li* in a decree of 136 B.C. and the discovery of parts of these texts at the court of Liu De 劉德, king of Hejian 河閒 (r. 155–129 B.C.), written documentation of the rites was evidently hard to come by in 110 B.C., when it was needed to assist the emperor in his conduct of ceremonies on Mount Tai.[47] Despite the existence of a whole tradition of this type of scholarship,

---

[45] *Yan tie lun*, 2 (7 "Fei Yang"); Wang Liqi, *Yan tie lun jiaozhu*, 2 vols. (rev. ed., Beijing: Zhonghua shuju, 1992), vol. 1, pp. 93–113 (Esson M. Gale, *Discourses on Salt and Iron* [Leiden: Brill, 1931; rpt. Taipei: Ch'eng-wen, 1967], pp. 40–9); and Loewe, *Crisis and Conflict*, pp. 99, 105, 109.

[46] For the prevalence of scholarship in Lu at the start of Wudi's reign, see *Shi ji*, 121, pp. 3117–18; for Lu Jia's advice to Gaodi and his subsequent writings, and the orders given to Shusun Tong (ca. 228–ca. 140 B.C.) to put the *li* in order, see *Han shu*, 43, p. 2113, and 22, p. 1030; *Shi ji*, 63, p. 2143, alludes to the relationship of the two groups of scholars denoted as *Daojia* and *Rujia*; for the Ming tang, see *Han shu*, 25A, p. 1215.

[47] For the decree of 136 B.C., see *Han shu*, 6, p. 159 (Dubs, *History of the Former Han Dynasty*, vol. 2, p. 32); for the discovery at the court of Liu De, see Loewe, ed., *Early Chinese Texts*, p. 26; *Shi ji* 12, p. 473.

in A.D. 4 Wang Mang had to make special efforts to have copies of these and other classical works collected.[48] It was mainly the masters of Later Han who were to bend their minds to the task of producing standardized versions of the texts of the *Rujia*, thus formulating much of China's tradition.

The ideas of yin and yang as two complementary forces and of the Five Phases (*wu xing* 五行) as the stages of a universal cycle had certainly been formulated and discussed in the centuries before the empires, but it ought not to be assumed that the subsequent development of correlative thinking exercised a major influence before perhaps 50 B.C. There remains one further major mode of thought whose origins and spread require consideration in view of the large number of references to Han officials and others who are described as its followers. This is known as Huang Lao.

Huang Lao Thought and Xing Ming

Three references in the *Shi ji* mention together the two sets of ideas that may be termed Huang Lao 黃老 thought and "forms and names" (*xing ming* 刑名), that is, matching description with reality.[49] Shen Dao 慎到 (ca. 350–ca. 275 B.C.) of Zhao, who was a member of the Jixia Academy, Tian Pian 田駢 and Jiezi 接子 of Qi, and Huan Yuan 環淵 of Chu, all probably of the fourth century B.C., are said to have studied the methods (*shu* 術) of Huang Lao and *Daode* 道德. Fragments of Shen Dao's writings survive.[50] Other reputed forerunners of Huang Lao thought include Shen Buhai and Han Fei. According to the *Shi ji*, while Shen Buhai's learning was based on Huang Lao, it took its principal ideas from *xing ming*. Of Han Fei the *Shi ji* writes that while being well pleased with the study of the models (*fa* 法) and methods of *xing ming*, he derived the basis of his thought from Huang Lao. There are also a large number of references in both the *Shi ji* and the *Han shu* to devotees of Huang Lao who held prominent positions in public life during the first century of Former Han.[51]

Huang Lao does not feature as one of the six major schools singled out for comment and description in the *Shi ji*, nor is it possible to name a master of that school who left his doctrines to a company of named disciples. None of our surviving texts includes indications that permit the positive identifi-

---

[48] For Wang Mang, see *Han shu*, 99A, p. 4069 (Dubs, *History of the Former Han Dynasty*, vol. 3, p. 192). For the growth of scholarly traditions and different interpretations of the various versions of texts during Former Han, see *Han shu*, 88, p. 3614; Tjan Tjoe Som, *Po Hu T'ung*, vol. 1, pp. 82–9.

[49] *Shi ji*, 63, p. 2146 (twice), and 74, p. 2347.

[50] For Shen Dao, see P. M. Thompson, *The Shen Tzu Fragments* (Oxford: Oxford University Press, 1979).

[51] The references are conveniently assembled in Aat Vervoorn, *Men of the Cliffs and the Caves: The Development of the Chinese Eremitic Tradition to the End of the Han Dynasty* (Hong Kong: Chinese University Press, 1990), p. 268, n. 31.

cation of their source as deriving from a school named Huang Lao. However, it has been suggested and accepted by a number of scholars that four of the texts which first came to light from tomb 3 of Mawangdui may be identified with an item that appears under the title of *Huang Di si jing* 黃帝四經 (Four classics of Huang Di) in the list of books in the Han imperial library that was compiled by Liu Xiang and Liu Xin.[52] While the date of the tomb is fixed at 168 B.C. and the copy of these texts may be dated to the reign of Han Huidi (r. 195–188 B.C.) or Han Wendi (r. 180–157 B.C.), it may perhaps be assumed that the original creation of the works in question can be ascribed to earlier, pre-imperial origins, but it cannot be said how far back they can be traced. It may also be noted that in passages where they mention Huang Di, including accounts of his consultation with his assistants, there is considerable affinity and even overlap with certain passages in the *Huainanzi* 淮南子.[53]

The principal ideas of the four texts may be summarized as follows. *Dao* is absolute, generative, and creative of all things, including *fa* 法 (the model) and *li* 理 (the pattern). *Xing* 刑 (forms or reality) exist first, to be followed by their description (*ming* 名). It is part of the duty of the monarch to cultivate the power of all-round vision (*guan* 觀), thus enabling him to take a penetrating view of reality. The concept of balance (*cheng* 稱) bears a great significance in metaphysical reality and in the practical application of a monarch's rule. Finally, it is essential for a monarch to follow the model in his task of reigning on earth.[54]

According to one view, Huang Lao thought takes its place as one of three aspects of the Daoist tradition, as may be observed from the bibliographical list of the *Han shu*: one of these was concerned with political theory, and is now seen only in the *Guanzi*; one centered around the contemplation of *Dao* in its majesty and in its pervasive influence over the universe, as may be seen in the *Laozi* and the *Zhuangzi*; the third was the philosophy of Shen Buhai and the four newly found texts and may be identified as Huang Lao. These

---

[52] The four texts are named *Jing fa* 經法, *Shiliu jing* 十六經, *Cheng* 稱, and *Dao yuan* 道原. For the original ascription of these texts to Huang Lao, see Tang Lan, "Huang Di si jing chu tan," *Wenwu* 1974.10: 48–52; and idem, "Mawangdui chutu Laozi yi ben juan qian gu yi shu de yanjiu: Jian lun qi yu Han chu Ru Fa douzheng de guanxi," *Kaogu xuebao* 1975.1: 7–38. Other early studies include Jan Yun-hua, "Tao Yuan or Tao: The Origin," and "Tao, Principle and Law," *Journal of Chinese Philosophy* 7, 3 (1980), pp. 195–204, and pp. 205–28; and Cheng Wu, "Han chu Huang Lao sixiang he Fajia luxian," *Wenwu* 1974.10: 43–7, 64. For a longer study, see R. P. Peerenboom, *Law and Morality in Ancient China: The Silk Manuscripts of Huang-Lao* (Albany: State University of New York Press, 1993).

[53] For a comparison of these passages, see Michael Loewe "Huang Lao Thought and the *Huainanzi*," *JRAS*, 3d series, 4, 3 (1994), pp. 386–7.

[54] For summaries of the ideas ascribed to Huang Lao, see Tu Wei-ming, "The Thought of Huang-Lao: A Reflection on the Lao Tzu and Huang Ti Texts in the Silk Manuscripts of Ma-wang-tui," *JAS* 39, 1 (1979): 103–6; and John S. Major, *Heaven and Earth in Early Han Thought: Chapters Three, Four, and Five of the Huainanzi* (Albany: State University of New York Press, 1993), p. 12.

texts write of *fa* (the mold or model), in its relation to *Dao* and place great importance on *li* (the pattern). These were terms which formed the keynote of the four texts; they are rarely seen in the *Laozi*. Another interpretation sees the four texts neither as Legalist nor as "legalized Daoism," but as representative of a unique system of thought.[55] In yet another, it is suggested that Tian Pian and Shen Dao were responsible for developing Legalism from a Daoist basis.[56] It may perhaps be suggested here that whereas the *Daojia* concentrated on the search for ultimate reality, the *Fajia* 法家 concentrated on the models that derived from *Dao* and their application to practical life, thus leading to the formulation of laws, sanctions, and punishments. While a complete understanding of the term Huang Lao may still be elusive and while it is not possible to assess its place in pre-imperial times, it may be noted that from the earliest days of the Han empire, leading personalities are stated to have been devoted to its ideas, beginning with Cao Shen 曹參, Chancellor of State (*Xiangguo* 相國) from 193 to 190 B.C., and the Empress Dou, mother of Jingdi.

THE TRADITION OF KINGSHIP

At the outset of the empires, sovereignty was conceived as little more than the imposition of force to secure obedience, and as such its incumbent was open to challenge by any one of his contemporaries who was strong enough to threaten his position. Such a situation had been witnessed among the kingdoms of the preceding centuries and it was due to reappear in the succession of coups d'état that ensued after the collapse of Qin's imperial authority. It was perhaps the frequency of such changes of power, brought about by force, trickery, or deceit, that partly accounted for the constant suspicion that Liu Bang entertained for the strongmen who had helped him to win his way to the throne. It was left to the subsequent Han emperors and their advisers to frame concepts which, harking back as they did to the ideals ascribed to the kings of Zhou, provided imperial sovereignty with what was both a source from which it derived and a master to whom its incumbent was responsible.

Several decades had to elapse before such ideas could mature and take their place within a cosmic scheme whose integral parts included a place for the rightful rule of the peoples of the earth and the authority of their emperor to command their obedience. That such ideas came to be formulated was largely due to the synthesis achieved shortly after 140 B.C. by Dong Zhongshu. They were in due course to be strengthened by a growing familiarity

[55] Tu Wei-ming, "The Thought of Huang-Lao," p. 107.
[56] Xu Fuguan, *Zhongguo renxing lun shi* (Taizhong: Donghai Daxue, 1963), pp. 430–40; Jan Yun-hua, "Tao Yuan or Tao: The Origin," p. 197.

with some of the writings of the masters of the Spring and Autumn and Warring States periods.

Although its precise significance may not be entirely clear and may have varied considerably, monarchy as vested in the *wang* 王 was practiced in China from Shang times at least. The authority of the king may have been seen to depend primarily on his religious functions or else on his powers as a military leader; the command that he exercised over his subjects may have been due to moral considerations or to administrative coercion. Ideally, by Zhou times he had come to be seen as an essential link that bound mankind and its destiny to the beneficent guidance of superior powers, and he was the sole dignitary who was entitled to perform certain sacrificial acts. Some early writers saw the true king behaving according to norms that contrasted sharply with the ambitions of a self-willed despot; some saw him as charged with a mission or as the successful victor in a battle to suppress a wicked rival or to remove a cursed predecessor whose conduct demanded elimination. By contrast with the heavenly appointed *wang*, the *ba* could call on no divine protection. Some owed their position, or claimed to have done so, to a specific charge received from the king of Zhou. Some had assumed their powers by means of force and could hardly claim recognition as leaders who were serving a moral cause; the contrast between their position and that of the true kings was made abundantly clear in a famous passage of the Mencius:

> King Xuan of Qi asked, "Is it right for me to learn about the deeds of Qi Huan Gong and Jin Wen Gong?"
>
> Mencius answered: "Of Confucius's pupils there was not one who talked about such matters. For that reason no account survived for transmission to later generations and I, for my part, have no information to give you. If we are not to stop talking, may we discuss the role of a true king?"[57]

By the fourth and third centuries none of the seven major kings who ruled their realms somewhat uneasily side by side could claim the rights that were the due of the one and only king of Zhou, whose line indeed survived until 256 B.C.

The first twenty years of the empires saw the adoption of three forms of polity in rapid succession. In the first instance, Qin's establishment of imperial unity, with the title of *Huangdi* 皇帝 (emperor), deliberately chosen to signify its superiority over all predecessors, had been organized entirely on a provincial basis, with governors who were subject to appointment and dismissal on personal grounds. Second, Xiang Yu set up a puppet king of Chu as a figurehead, whose honorific title included the term *di*; Xiang Yu himself was the king of one kingdom and the overlord of eighteen others, under the

---

[57] Mencius 1A/7 (Legge, *The Works of Mencius*, p. 137).

term *bawang* 霸王. In the third case, Liu Bang's empire comprised provincial units, as had been the regular rule in Qin; but in this case they were surrounded by an arc of subordinate hereditary kingdoms, acting as a protective barrier against invaders.

All three types lacked the divine and moral authority that had graced the kings of Zhou. The term *wang* had lost much of its character, coming to signify the monarch's authority as a realistic ruler rather than as an intermediary between territorial power and its reliance on a heavenly dispensation. It was only comparatively late, perhaps ca. 40 B.C., that some of the leaders of the Han empire made studied attempts to recapture some of those earlier ideals or qualities. But on occasion, citation of earlier, pre-imperial precedents could be of some value to those who wished to take steps that ran counter to normal practice of imperial times, and attention may be drawn to three aspects of the tradition that could be recalled in this way. One concerned the principle of hereditary succession, whereby the monarch nominated his successor; another is seen in the part played by a regent when an infant took his father's place on the throne; and the third provided for the acceptance of a king's authority following the abdication of his predecessor.

Nomination of a successor could sometimes override the need to choose the eldest son, as may be seen in the very first of all cases in the empire, when the First Emperor of Qin deliberately chose to displace his eldest son, Fusu 扶蘇, in favor of his younger son Huhai.[58] As yet a Chinese emperor felt no compunction or need to call for historical precedent or intellectual authority to support his action. On the next occasion when such a question arose, at the death of Han Zhaodi 昭帝 in 74 B.C., care was taken to assert a principle: if the eldest son lacked the necessary moral qualities it was right to enthrone one of his younger brothers.[59] On the same occasion precedents for the deposal of an unfit monarch, which were justified for similar reasons, were quoted from Zhou times. When Zhaodi had himself been enthroned, while still a minor, he had been put under the protection of a triumvirate who acted as his assistants, though there does not seem to be a direct reference to the term regent on this occasion.[60] At a later stage, when Wang Mang established himself as regent or acting emperor (A.D. 6), he was careful to compare himself with Zhou Gong.[61] His subsequent nomination of Shun as

---

[58] For manipulation of the royal succession in Qin in favor of a younger son who was to reign as King Zhuangxiang 莊襄王 (249–247 B.C.), see *Shi ji*, 84, p. 2506; for the accession of Huhai as the Second Emperor of Qin, in place of his brother Fusu, see *Shi ji*, 87, pp. 2548–52 (Bodde, *China's First Unifier*, pp. 26–34).

[59] For this principle, and the precedent cited from Zhou times, see *Han shu*, 68, p. 2937; and Loewe, *Divination, Mythology and Monarchy in Han China*, p. 100.

[60] *Han shu*, 7, p. 217 (Dubs, *History of the Former Han Dynasty*, vol. 2, p. 131).

[61] *Han shu*, 99A, pp. 4079, 4094 (Dubs, *History of the Former Han Dynasty*, vol. 3, pp. 221, 253).

one of his ancestors drew attention to the precedent whereby he had legitimately accepted his position on the throne, for Shun had succeeded in the same way after the abdication of Yao. The documents whereby the first of the Wei 魏 emperors claimed to be taking the place of Han Xiandi 獻帝 in A.D. 220 quoted the same precedent.[62]

A SENSE OF UNITY

An attempt has been made above to show how far the founders of the early empires and their successors could call on well-founded and well-tried religious and intellectual precedents that they could adopt or adapt to suit the social and political circumstances of their own time. It will be seen below how on several occasions those same senior statesmen or men of letters proclaimed that by contrast with their predecessors, their regimes had established a unified control of the world. The questions of how valid their claim was, how effectively a concept of unity could be implemented, and how successfully the idea of imperial unity could be practiced lie beyond the scope of this chapter.

It is, however, proper to ask what precedents, if any, existed before 221 B.C. from which a concept of unity may be seen to derive and to which philosophical traditions, masters of learning, or manipulators of politics it could be traced. It may also be asked what divisive factors, which had been widely apparent before the unification, survived to threaten or disrupt it in the future. Such questions involve a number of considerations. Mythology provides accounts of the origins of different groups of the human race, while literature includes a variety of terms that convey different degrees of assimilation to a cultured way of life. Attention is also due to the hierarchies devised so as to satisfy political or administrative concepts and to the place that was assigned to monarchy as a unifying factor within the scheme of the universe. It may also be asked how far these ideas remained no more than an ideal or to what extent they corresponded with reality.

In conceptual terms two interrelated questions are involved: first, the ways in which Chinese writers of the pre-imperial period saw their own communities or states as being distinct from those that existed beyond the pale; and second, the degree to which those communities or states were conscious of

---

[62] For references to the example of Shun to support the practice of abdication, see *Han shu*, 99A, p. 4095 (ibid., p. 255). For Wang Mang's definite choice of Shun as a figure in his line of descent, see Michael Loewe, "Wang Mang and His Forebears: The Making of the Myth," *TP* 80, 4–5 (1994): 197–222. For later references to the examples of Yao and Shun, see the series of documents cited in the extensive notes to *San guo zhi*, 2 (Wei shu: Wendi), pp. 67, 73; and Carl Leban "Managing Heaven's Mandate: Coded Communication in the Accession of Ts'ao P'ei, A.D. 220," in *Ancient China: Studies in Early Civilization*, ed. David T. Roy and Tsuen-hsuin Tsien (Hong Kong: Chinese University Press, 1978), p. 330.

a unifying factor which bound them together. Such a unifying factor would need to override major differences of a number of types. Some of these differences arose from ethnic origins, while others concerned religious practices. Yet other differences, which were inherent in conditions of climate and terrain, governed agricultural and other economic enterprises. Different intellectual concepts affected the growth of different cultural styles and the scale of advance in practical and technological terms.

Mythology

A sense of distinction from other peoples is brought out in mythology and in the choice of certain expressions to denote them. It is also seen in geographical and administrative concepts, and it appears in idealized political notions. Mythology often distinguishes the peoples of different localities by drawing attention to their strange bodily features. These are sometimes of a hybrid form, as may be seen in many pages of the *Shan hai jing*, whose chapters are variously dated to between the Warring States period and after Han.[63] Later writings, which were compiled for very different purposes, tell of the origins of peoples who were not fully assimilated to the culture and way of life of the empire: for example, of the Man Yi 蠻夷, who were descended from the union of the dog Panhu 槃瓠 and the daughter of an early monarch; or of the five families of the Man peoples of Bajun 巴郡 and Nanjun 南郡, whose forefathers came from the Red Cave or the Black Cave; or, in the case of the Ailao Yi 哀牢夷, of the ten sons born to a fisherwoman. One of these sons survived to respond to the call of a dragon who purported to be the father.[64] These were peoples who had not received the blessings that the culture heroes had conveyed to the Chinese as a means of advancing their standards and both ennobling and easing their way of life.

Terminology

It may be questioned how far the four terms Man 蠻, Yi 夷, Rong 戎, and Di 狄 that are used regularly to denote the non-Chinese peoples of the south, east, west, and north carried an implication of living creatures that should

---

[63] For an account of the evidence in the *Shan hai jing*, see Yuan Ke, *Zhongguo gudai shenhua* (rev. ed., Beijing: Zhonghua, 1960), pp. 241–63; Yuan Ke and Zhou Ming, *Zhongguo shenhua ziliao cuibian*, pp. 282–313; Loewe, ed., *Early Chinese Texts*, pp. 357–67; see also Loewe, *Divination, Mythology and Monarchy in Han China*, pp. 38–54.

[64] Fan Ye (A.D. 398–446) et al., *Hou Han shu* and *Xu Han zhi*, 86, pp. 2829, 2840, 2848; Steven F. Sage, *Ancient Sichuan and the Unification of China* (Albany: State University of New York Press, 1992), p. 50.

not properly be classified as human beings.[65] A more certain sense of distinction between the Chinese and other peoples is seen in the use of the terms Xia 夏, Hua 華, and, perhaps, *zhongguo* 中國, and reference may be made here to a telling passage in the observations of a man of deep learning and love of his own traditions, in a much later and highly sophisticated age. In one of his essays ("Yuan dao" 原道) in which he deliberately contrasted the heritage of a Chinese way of life and its values with those of other peoples, Han Yu 韓愈 (768–824) wrote:

When Confucius composed the *Spring and Autumn* [*Annals*], if the leaders of the land adopted alien (*yi* 夷) modes of behavior he treated them as aliens; but once they had advanced into the countries of the center (*zhongguo* 中國) he treated them as he did the inhabitants of the center. As the classics (*jing* 經) have it, "Even if the alien peoples (*yidi* 夷狄) have an acknowledged prince, they are inferior to the many Xia who may not."

The passage continues by citing the statement of the *Classic of Poetry* to the effect that it was Zhou Gong who had withstood the Rong and Di barbarians and repressed Jing 荆 and Shu 舒.[66]

Han Yu was writing after some thousand years in which imperial unity had come to be regarded as the norm, which all those who took part in public life accepted as proper, even if it was for no more than a part of those centuries that it had been achieved effectively. Two concepts underlay his views: first that of the distinction between the civilized peoples of the Tang empire, on the one hand, and those who had been denied such gifts; and second the principle that, provided that a group of people had achieved a degree of civilization, it deserved treatment as such and should be regarded as being a part of a unity.

The passage from the classics that Han Yu cites is found in the *Analects*,[67] and a few examples from the *Chunqiu* and its ancillary texts may be quoted to illustrate the principle that he enunciates. For the year 661 B.C., the *Zuo zhuan* includes the following telling statement, which is attributed to Guan Jingzhong 管敬仲: "The alien peoples (Rong, Di) are wild dogs and wolves and it is not right that they should receive submission; the many Xia (*zhu xia* 諸夏) are closely related and it is not right that they should be abandoned." The remark was prompted by the statement that the men of Qi had gone to the relief of Xing 邢, which was under attack by the Di. In an entry

---

[65] For the terms used to describe these peoples, see pp. 907–8, 947–9.

[66] See Ma Tongbo, *Han Changli wenji jiaozhu* (Shanghai: Gudian wenxue, 1957), p. 10. Han Yu's citation is from the *Shi jing*, 20(2) ("Bi gong": Mao no. 300), 10b; see Bernhard Karlgren, *The Book of Odes* (Stockholm: Museum of Far Eastern Antiquities, 1950), p. 260.

[67] *Analects*, 3/5 (Legge, *The Chinese Classics. Vol. 1: Confucian Analects, The Great Learning, and the Doctrine of the Mean* [rpt. Hong Kong: Hong Kong University Press, 1960], p. 156).

for 633 B.C., the same text explains the phraseology adopted by the *Chunqiu* as being due to a Chinese prince's adoption of alien (*yi*) modes of behavior; and for 569 B.C. a clear contrast is drawn between the many aliens (*zhu rong* 諸戎) and the many states blessed with elegance (*zhu hua* 諸華).[68] In practical terms, however, the failure of Chinese states to respond to an appeal to unite against the Di may perhaps suggest a lack of a conscious feeling of Chinese unity.[69]

The term *zhongguo* is used in several ways in early writings, perhaps without the precision that it came to acquire in later times. It recurs in the poem "Min lao" 民勞, whose opening lines are rendered: "The people for their part are sorely worn out and it is right that they should be given some rest. Treat the states of the center with kindness and thereby bring peace to those of the four quarters."[70] The traditional commentators, led by Mao 毛, take *zhongguo* to refer to the seat of the monarch (*jingshi* 京師) and explain the "four quarters" (*si fang* 四方) as the many Xia. A passage of the *Shang shu*, where the monarch's strength of character (*de* 德) is seen as being all important, reads as follows, bringing in the idea of a center to which other peoples bring their tribute:

(Feng 封 answered:) The king should say "The earlier kings took pains to exert their spiritual qualities, thereby persuading those who were distant to come into their own fold. The many states brought them their gifts, and their leaders came in from all quarters, as if they were close kinsfolk."[71]

The difference between the states of the center and others is brought out in two passages from the *Guo yu* (Sayings of the states), which may perhaps be dated from the fifth century, with the implication that those of the center shared a set of values in common. As distinct from the peoples of states such as Jin 晉, the Man, Yi, Rong, and Di are said for long not to have responded in submission to a cultural and ethical lead, and to be such that they were not of use to the lands of the center. In a second passage, the behavior of armies is compared with that of the four alien peoples – arrogant, oblivious of others, and lacking in respect.[72]

In a somewhat exceptional and particular way, a speaker in the *Zhuangzi* uses the term *zhongguo* with scorn to deprecate the home of Confucius's school, that is, the state of Lu. He observes that he has been told that the

---

[68] *Zuo zhuan*, 11 (Min 1), 1b (Legge, *The Chinese Classics. Vol. 5: The Ch'un Ts'ew with the Tso Chuen* [rpt. Hong Kong: Hong Kong University Press, 1960], pp. 123–4); 16 (Xi 27), 10a (ibid., pp. 200–201) and 29 (Xiang 4), 22a (ibid., pp. 422, 424).
[69] See Chapter 13.
[70] *Shi jing*, 17/4 ("Min lao": Mao no. 253), 10b.
[71] *Shang shu*, 14 ("Zi cai"), 27a.
[72] *Guo yu* (Sibu congkan ed.), 17 ("Chu yu" A), 1a, and 2 ("Zhou yu" B), 6b. For the dating of these parts of the *Guoyu*, see Loewe, ed., *Early Chinese Texts*, p. 264.

men of quality (*junzi* 君子) of the *zhongguo*, while being well versed in the approved modes of behavior and in a sense of right, are limited in their understanding of human emotions or intellect.[73] In the *Xunzi* the term is used by contrast with the outlying regions of the north, south, east, and west whose local and sometimes exotic products are not to be found in the states of the center, which nonetheless are able to acquire them to their own advantage.[74]

A passage of the *Han Feizi* 韓非子 reads:

> As is known, however rich the country, and however strong the forces of Yue 越 may be, the rulers of the countries of the center all understand why it would be of no advantage to themselves, and would say that it is not a country which they personally would be able to control.[75]

The subsequent passage makes it clear that the contrast here is with a land where the rightful ruler's powers have been eclipsed by those of his ministers. In another passage of the *Han Feizi*, an official of Qin Mu Gong 秦穆公 (r. 659–621 B.C.) advises his ruler that the situation of the Rong was remote and that they were ignorant of the sounds of the central states. His intention was that they should be beguiled into submission by the delights of Chinese music.[76] Two other chapters of the work include warnings against the danger of being beholden to Yue to come to the rescue of the weaker members of the *zhongguo*. In a speech that is attributed to Li Si and that is now included in the *Han Feizi*, Hann is twice stated to lie within the central states.[77]

Zones and Hierarchies

An idealized notion of the unity of the human race is seen in the manner whereby some texts divide its component elements into hierarchies, as may be seen most clearly in the references to the nine or the five concentric zones of the world and its inhabitants. Fictionalized as such schemes were, they nonetheless reflected a concept of two distinct types of area or human being, one being inner and one being outer.[78] While it may be doubted whether the

---

[73] *Zhuangzi* (Sibu congkan *Nan hua zhenjing*), 7 ("Tian Zifang"), 30a; Guo Qingfan, *Zhuangzi jishi* (1894; rpt. Taipei: Huazheng, 1991), p. 704.

[74] *Xunzi*, 9 ("Wang zhi"), pp. 107–8 (Knoblock, *Xunzi*, vol. 2, p. 102).

[75] Liang Qixiong, *Hanzi qianjie* (Beijing: Zhonghua, 1960), 11 ("Gu fen"), p. 84 (W. K. Liao, trans., *The Complete Works of Han Fei Tzu*, 2 vols. [London: Arthur Probsthain, 1939, 1959], vol. 1, p. 101).

[76] *Han Feizi*, 10 ("Shi guo"), p. 74 (Liao, *The Complete Works of Han Fei-Tzu*, vol. 1, p. 186).

[77] *Han Feizi*, 27 ("Yong ren"), p. 221 (Liao, *The Complete Works of Han Fei-Tzu*, vol. 1, p. 274), and 40 ("Nan shi"), p. 397 (Liao, *The Complete Works of Han Fei-Tzu*, vol. 2, p. 206).

[78] See Lien-sheng Yang, "Historical Notes on the Chinese World Order," in *The Chinese World Order*, ed. John King Fairbank (Cambridge, Mass.: Harvard University Press, 1968), pp. 21–2.

Chinese were unique in their view of their own superiority over others thanks to their civilization, this idea persisted in Shang and Zhou times, and even in the Warring States, despite the intense divisions of the day.[79]

A division between an inner and an outer zone may perhaps be traced back as far as Shang times, but a considerable time passed before this concept is seen in literature.[80] Two major passages in the *Zhou li* 周禮 (Rites of Zhou), which must reflect comparatively late concepts, carry highly stylized accounts of the world and its divisions, classified in three ways. Ethnic distinctions are seen in the account of the four peoples of the Yi, the eight of the Man, the seven of the Min 閩, the nine of the Mo 貉, the five of the Rong, and the six of the Di. In geographical terms, the world is divided into the nine major provinces (*zhou* 州) of southeast, due south, south of the Yellow River, due east, east of the river, due west, northeast, within the river, and due north, each characterized by its own type of terrain and natural produce. A third criterion depends on the distance from the center and the corresponding status that the inhabitants enjoyed. According to this, nine zones of submission (*jiu fu* 九服, or *jiu ji* 九畿) extended outwards from a tenth division, that is, the central zone of the king. The Man and the Yi were situated in the sixth and seventh zones, and the two that were further remote were designated as *zhen* 鎮 (under garrison) and *fan* 蕃, or 藩 (on the edge).[81]

A concept of five zones is seen in two passages of the *Shang shu*. In one, Yu 禹 the Great claims that he "assisted in establishing the five dependencies as far as 5,000 (*li*)." More specifically the second reference spells out the distances of the five, which are named *dianfu* 甸服, *houfu* 侯服, *suifu* 綏服, *yaofu* 要服, and *huangfu* 荒服. The *dianfu* is interpreted as the zone of the Son of Heaven. Two of these terms (*hou* and *dian*) are also seen as the names of the second and third zones of the nine, as in the *Zhou li*; the fourth is assigned to the Yi, and the fifth to the Man peoples.[82]

The passages of the *Zhou li* may perhaps be regarded as an attempt to explain all domains as being within the single *oikumene* of the Son of Heaven. Insofar as members of the human race are distinguished in such formalized hierarchies they are regarded as participants in the same unity. At the same time, just as some areas and their peoples are separated further and further from the royal domain, so are those who partook of the life within that

[79] Wang Gungwu, "Ming Relations with Southeast Asia: A Background Essay," in *The Chinese World Order*, p. 36.

[80] See K. C. Chang, *Shang Civilization* (New Haven, Conn.: Yale University Press, 1980), pp. 210–20.

[81] *Zhou li*, 33 ("Zhifang shi"), 9a (Édouard Biot, *Le Tcheou-li ou rites des Tcheou*, 3 vols. [Paris: Imprimerie nationale, 1851; rpt. Taipei: Ch'eng-wen, 1966], vol. 2, p. 263, and 29 ("Da sima"), 5a (Biot, *Le Tcheou-li*, vol. 2, p. 163).

[82] *Shangshu*, 5 ("Yiji"), 11a; 6 ("Yu gong"), 30a (Bernhard Karlgren, "Glosses on the Book of Documents," *BMFEA* 20 [1948]: 159, gloss 1384); *Shi ji*, 2, p. 75 (Chavannes, *Mémoires historiques*, vol. 1, p. 146).

domain seen as sharing values and traditions in common. But one highly sophisticated and critical writer, the author of the *Xunzi*, perhaps had somewhat different ideas of a practical nature in mind. Some of his contemporaries maintained that Chu and Yue's failure to accept the institutions of government demonstrated that Tang 湯 and Wu 武 had not been capable of implementing their prohibitions and their orders. Xunzi disputed their conclusion. He argued:

Tang and Wu were the most skilled persons in all the world at laying down their prohibitions and orders. They resided in their seats, in the one case at Bo 亳 and in the other at Hao 鄗, both being areas of 100 *li*. All beneath the skies formed a unity; the leaders of the land acted as their loyal subordinates, and whatever the area to which they reached, none failed to stand in awe of them and submit to their will, responding in obedience to their influence. How may it be said that Chu and Yue did not accept the institutions of government?[83]

The passage continues by describing how the institutions of true kings lay down regulations for different equipment to be used, in accordance with the nature of the land that is in question, and for dues to be levied in different grades, dependent on the distance that is involved:

It would be absurd to think that these were uniform, and for that reason the peoples of Lu, Wey and Qi made use of different types of vessels. Where the lay of the land varies, so too must the tools needed to work it vary. For that reason the many lands of the Xia are subject to the duties of one and the same zone and share modes of behavior in common; but the lands of the Man, Yi, Rong and Di, while bearing duties of the same zone, are not subject to the same institutions of government.

The five zones are then named in almost identical terms as those of the received text of the *Shang shu*, that is, Dian, Hou, Bin 賓, Yao, and Huang. The Man and the Yi are placed in the Yao zone, the Rong and the Di in the Huang zone. The text describes in descending hierarchical order the forms of religious dues that are rendered in each case. Finally the author dismisses, as the product of a shallow mind, any idea that the men of Chu and Yue could be expected to take part in types of worship suitable for those of the center.

A Cosmic System

In a cosmic sense, unity is seen in the expression of Warring States times "*Tian dao huan di dao fang* 天道圜地道方" (The way of Heaven is circular, that of Earth is square).[84] This conveys the idea of a cohesive system whereby

---

[83] *Xunzi*, 18 ("Zheng lun"), p. 239 (Knoblock, *Xunzi*, vol. 3, pp. 25, 38).
[84] Chen Qiyou, *Lü shi chunqiu jiaoshi*, 2 vols. (Shanghai: Xuelin, 1984), 3 (5 "Huan dao"), p. 171.

the circle of Heaven encloses the square Earth within its circumference. Those who looked to *Dao* but had no hand in organizing human effort corporatively could perhaps discern an idea of unity in the order of nature, whereby man constitutes no more than a part of the whole universe. But a somewhat different idea of unity may perhaps be seen in the *Huainanzi*, a work of the Han period which is usually described as Daoist and which gives its own account of the development of civilized rule thanks to the holy kings of mythology. So far from practicing the art of noninterference (*wu wei* 無 為), these monarchs exerted themselves positively so as to improve the lot of human beings. Their achievements included the expulsion of recalcitrant evil doers to deserted regions beyond the confines of the world that they were ruling. Monarchy had been established not so as to gratify their personal ambitions, but as a means of preventing oppression of one section of humanity by another, for example, of the weak by the strong, and with a view to treating all members of the human race in a uniform manner.[85]

Imperial Claims and Harsh Realities

The claim of unification that was made on behalf of Qin from 221 B.C. onwards rested on practical considerations, as may be seen from a number of documents. It is one of the ironies of history that, while all succeeding dynasties depended on Qin's precedents, achievements, and institutions, few failed to denigrate the regime as wicked. The initial proclamation of the First Emperor recited the tale of conquest of the other kings and the surrender of their territories. In their reply, Li Si, who was still Superintendent of Trials (*tingwei* 廷尉), and his colleagues reminded the emperor that in the past there had been no certainty whether, outside the royal domain of 1,000 *li*, those of the *houfu* 侯服 and the *yifu* 夷服 and other leaders of the lands (*zhuhou* 諸侯) would pay court to the Son of Heaven, who was unable to control them. The contrast with the present situation could not be more clear, with all territories being administered as commanderies (*jun* 郡) and counties (*xian* 縣) and the models of government and their orders deriving from a unified system. In a further statement in which he reiterated these claims, Li Si argued against restoring a system of making over lands to be held on a hereditary principle, for in such circumstances all the leaders could not be kept under control.[86]

The claim of unity is likewise expressed in the texts of some of the inscriptions that the First Emperor had engraved. For example, the one set up in

[85] Liu Wendian, *Huainan honglie jijie*, 2 vols. (Shanghai: Shangwu, 1923; rpt. Taipei: Shangwu, 1968), 19.1a–3b.

[86] *Shi ji*, 6, pp. 236, 239 (Chavannes, *Mémoires historiques*, vol. 2, pp. 124, 131).

219 B.C. reads, with reference to 221 B.C., "For the first time he united all under Heaven in such a way that none did not submit."[87] An inscription set up at Langye 琅邪 (Shandong) includes a specific reference to the unity of purpose that had been achieved in the empire, the standardization of military equipment and the uniformity of the script. Inscriptions on standard weights and measures likewise refer to the achievement of 221 B.C. The theme is also voiced in the proposal made in 214 B.C. by Li Si, by then Chancellor (*chengxiang* 丞相), for the destruction of certain types of literature. He mentioned the single source from which the orders of government derived: the contrast between the internecine rivalries of the past and the settled state of the whole world of the empire. The disruption known in the past and the failure to unify, together with the habit of citing inapplicable precedents and indulgence in private types of learning, demanded a further, consciously planned measure of unification of an intellectual nature; this would be achieved by imposing restrictions on certain types of writing.[88]

In imperial times a major change may be seen in the attitude regarding the unity of the human race and towards those who were not heirs to the Chinese tradition. Positive policies of expansion in the second century B.C. had brought Han officials into contact with leaders of other peoples who were in a position to thwart or challenge imperial interests. Beyond the confines of the commanderies in the northwest lay wide areas of an intermediate nature, whose inhabitants were perhaps nomads, perhaps stock breeders, or perhaps tillers of the soil. An uneasy compromise allowed the local chieftains the freedom to exert their authority; recognition by the Han court was intended to discourage them from damaging Chinese property or dislocating Chinese enterprises. Meanwhile the duly accredited Chinese officials who were posted in the Dependent States (*shuguo* 屬國) watched the interests of the Chinese settlers and their home government, hearing lawsuits, sentencing criminals, rounding up deserters, and collecting tax.

Occasions when a Chinese princess had been given in marriage to one of the chieftains of Central Asia or when a prince from one of the remote areas was held as a hostage in Chang'an 長安 betrayed the principle that imperial governments had perforce to accept: that they were obliged to negotiate with the rulers of other communities, be they the *shanyu* 單于 of the Xiongnu 匈奴 or the *kunmi* 昆彌 of the Wusun 烏孫.[89] Some of these communities were

---

[87] *Shi ji*, 6, p. 243 (Chavannes, *Mémoires historiques* vol. 2, p. 141).

[88] *Shi ji*, 6, pp. 247, 254 (Chavannes, *Mémoires historiques* vol. 2, pp. 144, 171); *Shoseki meihin sôkan*, series I, no. 15, "Shin kenryô mei" 秦權量銘 (Tokyo: 1959; unpaginated), includes photographs of a number of bronze vessels whose inscriptions carry the text of the First Emperor's decree of 221 B.C.

[89] For hostages and matrimonial alliances, see A. F. P. Hulsewé and Michael Loewe, *China in Central Asia: The Early Stage, 125 B.C.–A.D. 23* (Leiden: Brill, 1979), pp. 60–2.

subject to the authority of the Han Protector General (*duhu* 都護); to others the Han court was willing to send envoys. By this stage concepts such as those of the Man, Yi, Rong, and Di had become anachronistic, and the term *zhu xia* was obsolete. Nevertheless a man of letters could still invoke some of these traditional expressions with reference to the past, as may be seen in the arguments that Du Qin 杜欽 put forward in the time of Chengdi 成帝 (r. 33–7 B.C.) against involvement with peoples situated at a great distance from Chang'an, where access lay by way of perilous paths:

When the holy kings divided the world into nine provinces and made the regulations for the five zones, their efforts were directed to making the inner regions prosperous without seeking anything beyond. But now the envoys who are sent out on missions carry the commands of the Most Honourable [i.e., the Han emperor] to escort merchants of the barbarians [Man Yi]. Large numbers of officers and soldiers are made to toil, being sent out on journeys over dangerous and arduous roads; and the resources on which we rely are dissipated and exhausted for a cause which brings no [material] advantage. This is no long-term plan. Those of our envoys who have already received their emblems of authority should be permitted to proceed as far as Pishan and then to return.[90]

We may also look a little further forward to a grandiloquent boast made on behalf of the Han dynasty in highly rhetorical terms, after two centuries and more of imperial rule. How far the statement could justly be applied, either over the time that had already elapsed or indeed at the time when it was formulated, is of less significance here than the place that its concepts took in the minds of some of China's historians. In revealing something of a sense of unity that fitted the imperial ideal, Ban Gu 班固 (A.D. 32–92) draws attention to Zhou's loss of power and guidance and to the time when the carriages of the leaders of the land drove side by side and the horses of the Warring States galloped hither and thither:[91] "Then the Seven Mighty leaders roared with anger, splitting asunder the many Xia; and while the dragons were locked in conflict the tigers were embattled with one another." Ban Gu further referred to Shang Yang of Qin, who held hard to his three techniques with which to spur on Xiao Gong, and Li Si, who exploited the situation around him to bring pressure to bear on the First Emperor. But, he insists, these were achievements of no more than momentary duration, whereas now the mighty Han has swept away all the filth and removed all wild growth, restoring the heritage of the kings to an extent that is more glorious than that of Fu Xi and Shen Nong, and on a scale that is broader than that of Huang Di and Yao. "In its rule of all beneath the skies it sheds light like the

---

[90] *Han shu*, 96A, p. 3887; Hulsewé and Loewe, *China in Central Asia*, p. 111 (translation modified).
[91] *Han shu*, 100A, pp. 4227–8.

sun, it imposes its awe thereon like the holy spirits, it embraces it like the ocean, it nurtures it like the spring." The resulting unity is seen in the way that "all arises from the same source and all flows out towards the same ends, bathed in supreme virtue, blessed with almighty harmony."

Such an ideal, in which all are the willing subjects of the one and only Son of Heaven, would sound fine enough in the theoretical terms that suited the first century A.D.; it could hardly have been entertained seriously in the stirring days of the Warring States, when indeed, for a short time in 288 B.C., a compromise had actually been arranged whereby two powerful kings, one of Qin and one of Qi, each included the term *di* in their titles.[92] In practice, unity could be seen as the imposition of commands on recalcitrant elements and the forceful suppression of opposition. The dangers of such measures were all too apparent to writers such as Jia Yi.

However proud the boasts of Li Si and the First Emperor of Qin may have been, there are signs of centrifugal tendencies that persisted. Pretenders to the old houses of the Warring States period arose at the outset of the movements against the empire, from 210 B.C., when a call to restore a kingdom such as Chu could evoke considerable popular support. An old antagonism between Chu and Qi reappeared in the intrigues and fighting of those troubled times.[93] In the dispensations that they each tried to establish, both Xiang Yu and Liu Bang incorporated kingdoms that bore the old, honorable names of pre-imperial days, some of which were to reemerge as dynastic titles as late as the tenth century.[94]

Writing from the point of view of northerners who enjoyed the sophisticated standard of living of Luoyang 洛陽 during the first century A.D., the authors of the *Han shu* remarked on some of the characteristic features that distinguished parts of their empire, such as the vulgar music of Zheng and Wey, the uncouth religious rites of Chu, or the love of swordsmanship and cheap view of life in Wu 吳 and Yue.[95] Some peoples, such as those of Yelang 夜郎 in the far west, were still classified as Yi 夷; remarks were made on habits such as their style of hairdressing.[96]

A shared mythology, the worship of the same gods, use of the same lan-

---

[92] That is, *di* of the west and *di* of the east; *Shi ji*, 5, p. 212; 15, p. 739; 43, p. 1816; 44, p. 1853; 46, pp. 1898–9; and 72, p. 2325; see also *Shi ji*, 69, p. 2270, for the concept of Qin as *di* of the west, Yan as *di* of the north, and Zhao as *di* of the center.

[93] For antagonism between Qi and Chu, see, for example, allusions to the dispute between Tian Rong 田榮 and Xiang Yu, as in *Shi ji*, 7, p. 317 (Chavannes, *Mémoires historiques*, vol. 2, pp. 291–2), and *Han shu*, 1A, p. 33 (Dubs, *History of the Former Han Dynasty*, vol. 1, p. 74).

[94] See Twitchett and Loewe, eds., *The Cambridge History of China*, vol. 1, p. 125 (map 3) for the inclusion of kingdoms bearing these names in the Han empire.

[95] *Han shu*, 28B, pp. 1665–7.

[96] *Han shu*, 95, p. 3837.

guage,[97] the impact of a strong personality, the exercise of force, the threat of a common enemy, and the driving force of hunger may be included among the factors that encourage cohesion and unity among a numerous and mixed population. That some of these factors, divisive as they could also be, were operative from time to time in pre-imperial China can hardly be doubted, but their efficacy must remain in question. Nor can it be estimated how far the growth of trade acted as a unifying factor. Compelling differences can hardly be ignored, whether of terrain, climate, ethnic origin, or religion; whether seen in the pace of intellectual development or the advance of technology; whether manifest in a cultural standard of living, in the degrees of wealth, or in types of occupation. It may well be asked in what sense, if any, the inhabitants of Chinese villages and cities of pre-imperial days would be willing to claim to share a brotherhood with others up and down the land. Did a landed aristocrat of the royal entourage of Qi or Zhao see himself as a member of the same community as the peasant laboring on the wheels or pumps of the Min 岷 River to raise water for the terraced farms of Shu 蜀? Did the skilled bronzesmith who produced exquisite vessels for the kings of Zhongshan 中山 see himself as a colleague of the learned scholar of the Jixia Academy? And were there any elements in common between the prayer reciter who solemnly intoned the formulas at the ancestral shrines of Zhou and the shamaness who screeched her answers to the countryfolk of the rivers and hills of Chu?

INSTITUTIONAL NORMS AND ADMINISTRATIVE PRACTICE

It need hardly be stressed that the scale of organization and the complexity of the institutions designed to lead mankind and to control and coordinate its working efforts form a conspicuous feature of the imperial age. Nor need it be stressed that these were the cumulative results of a long-drawn-out process of experiment, trial and error, punctuated by incidents of both success and failure, marked by periods of both advance and decline. At the outset of the Qin and Han empires the forms of government and methods of administration that were to be accepted as the norm had yet largely to be framed; in setting about their task of doing so, the new masters of a unified China necessarily called on existing precedents.

It is however not possible to estimate the scale of written documentation to which they could look to find them. Nor is it to be assumed that at the outset of the imperial age, all those who took the decisions on which the

---

[97] For the value of language as a unifying factor, see Hawkes, *Songs of the South*, p. 16.

structure of empire rested were necessarily capable of reading the literary works that were available at the time, including as these did some texts which do not now survive and excluding the results of the later recensions that lie upon our shelves today. How far records of the administration of the pre-imperial kingdoms were available is also open to question.

In all probability the scale of the destruction of literature that is said to have occurred in 214 B.C. has been exaggerated. It is likely that records of the ethical precepts of Confucius and his pupils and some of the writings that took shape later as the compendia on ritual were at hand, irrelevant or unpalatable as their lessons may have seemed to be. Perhaps with greater confidence it may be accepted that those who built the Qin and Han empires were well versed in the discourses on the methods of government known now in texts such as the *Guanzi, Shang jun shu, Xunzi*, or *Han Feizi*, or at least in parts of those texts. Others, who perhaps kept their own counsel, may have found that works such as the *Laozi* or *Zhuangzi*, with their rejection of determined attempts to organize mankind, were more appealing. The question has been raised above of how far these and the many other books that existed at the time brought their influence to bear on the statesmen and officials of the empire.

In two respects it is likely that more resources are available for the study of certain aspects of pre-imperial history now than there were in those early times. Although the *Zuo zhuan* had been compiled perhaps up to two centuries before the foundation of the empires, it is questionable how far that text was in circulation. Second, students of Shang and Western Zhou today have at their disposal the wealth of material from the oracular documents and inscriptions on bronze vessels that still lay underground in 221 B.C.; had these been on display in the imperial palaces or shrines in Qin and Han times, their script would probably have baffled such scholars as were trying to read them.

The Concept and Practice of Law

Few studies of any one of the world's cultures can proceed far without involving the term "law" or "laws," and it need hardly be stressed how widely the concepts that underlie this term vary. Early China for its part has little that may compare directly with the concept that evolved in Israel or with the principles and problems that became manifest in Greece. Unlike the children of Israel, the early Chinese who have left a record behind them did not ascribe the gift of law to a transcendent and beneficent god; nor did they, as in the Greek tradition, look to certain individuals as lawgivers or philosophers, such as Solon or Plato, to whom their way of life owed its sense of justice; nor was there any ancient document that had been hallowed in the tradition to correspond with the Torah, the code of Hammurabi, or the inscriptions of Gortyna. Israel's majestic monotheism uniquely combined a belief in the omnipotent divinity with the moral code that his commands comprised. For Greece, Sophocles took as a powerful theme for one of his plays the conflict between certain immutable principles ascribed to the gods and the expedients whereby a ruler maintained his authority.[98]

As far as may be told from surviving records, Chinese thought had not as yet appreciated these distinctions, and attention can focus only on three main aspects of these questions, that is, the origin of legal authority, its nature and purpose as revealed in its terms, and the growth of documentation. By the beginning of the Warring States the people of China had experienced several centuries of government of increasing complexity and sophistication. But while the rulers of mankind and their officials had long imposed their authority by seeking obedience to their commands, they left insufficient records of their principles or systems to show how their concepts and practices had developed or how they had differed in the various dispensations of Western Zhou and the succeeding kingdoms. It is however clear that a major change which affected imperial practice took place during the fourth century, thanks to the work and influence of Shang Yang.

However successfully the kings of Shang and Western Zhou had been able to claim that their position and orders rested on the support of superhuman authorities, the rulers and leaders of the later centuries, whether entitled *wang* (王) or *gong* (公), were hardly able to do so, challenging as they did each other's right to practice sovereignty and unable to pretend that any of them was the sole monarch destined to rule over mankind. But if they could not point to a source of power to which they could ascribe the prime origin of their own commands, neither were they inhibited by the need to obey such an authority or godhead; there was no concept of law that could override a monarch's own decisions. Possibly the principle that the issue of orders derived from his will was deliberately strengthened at the outset of the imperial era by the adoption of the new terms *zhi* 制 (edict) and *zhao* 詔 (decree) to denote his commands, thereby investing them with a new type of dignity.

As yet the emphasis had been on the negative side, insofar as the orders that a monarch prescribed tended to lay down the punishments to be inflicted in case of disobedience. Different types of punishment, including those of mutilation and the death penalty, were to be taken over as precedents when the imperial age dawned; others, such as a sentence to hard labor,

---

[98] See Sophocles' *Antigone*, where Creon's brash statement (lines 665–6) that "whomsoever the city sets up must be obeyed, however just or unjust his decisions may be" is followed by the tragedy that an Athenian audience would relish.

exclusion from holding office, or suppression of a hereditary nobility were also to be introduced. At the same time, although negative in character, some of these early prescriptions that found their place in the laws of Qin in fact bore a positive purpose; for example, by laying down the penalties for failure to follow rules for agricultural work, they were in fact providing positive directions for certain types of economic activity. By Han times, there are clear indications that the conduct of the laws and their penalties was, at least in theory, subject to a hope of conforming with the system of the cosmos, as seen in the theory of the Five Phases and in the concept of resonance (*ganying* 感應).[99] But it must remain open to question how far such intentions may be traced back to pre-imperial times, how influential they were before ca. 50 B.C., and how far it may be said that a concept of natural law underlay any such concepts.[100]

As recent discoveries have shown,[101] by the later decades of the Qin kingdom and the early days of the empire, royal and then imperial commands were being promulgated to a considerable extent and in an elaborate way, covering all manner of human activity in which the government was concerned. Such commands, which had reached written form, were known under the general terms of either *lü* 律 or *ling* 令, rendered usually as "Statutes" and "Ordinances" respectively; these terms were retained in the administrative practice of the Han and subsequent empires. Both types of order included provisions designed to implement the decisions of the king or emperor and his officials in a positive way, together with the sanctions and punishments, often of a rigorous and to modern eyes a cruel type, that were intended to deter criminal practices and ensure obedience to the will of the government.

Despite the claims that the first of the Han emperors had taken steps to simplify a complex system and to moderate the excesses of Qin practice, Han in fact accepted much of the heritage left by its short-lived predecessor. These included an extremely detailed code and a fully laid down system for procedure in criminal cases, with the possibility of submitting some of these to a senior official, or even to the emperor himself, for final decision. The necessary regulations, surviving as they do either in whole or fragmentary form, are complex, and it is difficult to believe that they were compiled as a first

---

[99] For *ganying*, see Charles Le Blanc, *Huai-nan Tzu* 淮南子, *Philosophical Synthesis in Early Han Thought: The Idea of Resonance (Kan-ying* 感應), *with a Translation and Analysis of Chapter Six* (Hong Kong: Hong Kong University Press, 1985).

[100] For the question of natural law, see Joseph Needham, *Science and Civilisation in China. Vol. 2: History of Scientific Thought* (Cambridge University Press, 1969), pp. 526–7.

[101] For the legal manuscripts discovered at Shuihudi, which may be dated to the last decades of the kingdom or the first decade of the empire of Qin, see A. F. P. Hulsewé, *Remnants of Ch'in Law* (Leiden: Brill, 1985), and Xu Fuchang, *Shuihudi Qin jian yanjiu* (Taipei: Wenshizhe, 1993). For comparable documents found in an undated tomb of the Qin period, see *Wenwu* 1995.1: 37.

venture in legal codification without precedents that had been evolved in the pre-imperial era.[102] There is, however, little evidence to show that the law-makers of the early empires had access to accounts of earlier ventures of this type that pre-dated Shang Yang. While indications of legal procedures may now be seen on a few bronze inscriptions, perhaps of Western Zhou date, such statements would not have been available to those officials of the Qin and Han empires whose duties included those of framing regulations or judging criminal cases. In the absence of full documentary evidence, the few passages of early literature that concern these matters are in no way sufficient to provide a comprehensive idea of any concepts of law that might have existed in these early centuries. Nevertheless their use of certain terms is suggestive.

The two key terms that appear regularly are *fa* 法 and 刑 *xing*. Of these, *fa* denoted a model, to be taken as an exemplar on which the proper government of man was based; *xing* signified the punishments that might be necessary as an administrative measure. *Fa*, said in one passage to control the people in the same way as the potter molds his clay or the smith shapes his metal, was abstract, and of permanent value, and to be admired; *xing* were expedients, as required in times of need, and to be deplored as a necessary evil. The contrast between these two is brought out vividly in the earliest passage that is relevant, being a document of perhaps the early part of the Spring and Autumn period that is to be found in the *Shang shu*. The "Lü xing" 呂刑 (Punishments of Lü) criticizes the actions of the Miao 苗 people in instituting a set of oppressive punishments (*xing*) and denoting these as a model (*fa*); further point is added to the criticism in the implication that these orders were to be committed to writing.[103]

Direct protests against such action are voiced in accounts of two incidents, of 536 and 513 B.C. In the first of these the order to have the text of the punishments inscribed on bronze vessels drew the criticism that the existence of written orders of this type would decrease the trust and authority that a ruler can reasonably expect to enjoy from his people, and that a set of written punishments, which properly arise only from conditions of a disorderly administration, would not act as a deterrent against strife. Possibly the criticism arose from a further, implicit reason: that by being inscribed on a sacred vessel, the set of punishments in question would thereby acquire a measure of religious sanction or authority that they did not merit. The passage indeed proceeds to refer to the punishments of the approved norms and punishments (*yi xing* 儀刑) created by King Wen of Zhou 周文王, and it is notice-

---

[102] See Hulsewé, *Remnants of Ch'in Law*, p. 12.

[103] *Shang shu*, 19 ("Lü xing"), 16a (Karlgren, *Book of Documents*, p. 74); for the comparison with the potter and the smith, see *Guanzi*, 17 (53 "Jin cang"), 11a.

able that the expression *yi fa* 儀法 is sometimes quoted in place of *yi xing*. In 513 B.C. no less a person than Confucius commented that Jin's action in casting a bronze tripod with a text of the written set of punishments would be likely to disrupt social hierarchies.[104] The *Analects* records one statement to the effect that treating all the population according to the same terms of the punishments is a poor way of government as compared with guidance in the light of principles or possibly the right model. Elsewhere punishments and exemption therefrom (i.e., *fa* 罰; for this expression see below) take their place at the end of a series of administrative actions starting with the need to ensure the correct use of terms. Mencius's remarks on punishments include the need to reduce them to a minimum and to avoid their action as a trap into which the population is all too prone to fall.[105]

While there was evidently a clear distinction between *fa* and *xing*, it seems that there was no appreciation of the value of written documents as a means of protecting a people from the oppression of officials, or of formulating the rights, duties, and privileges of different members of society. Shang Yang and perhaps others saw the models on which the governance and control of human beings rested as a gift from certain unnamed sages, and shortly before the unification the author of a text entitled *Jingfa* 經法 that was found recently at Mawangdui and is identified by some as a statement of Huang Lao thought, wrote that "*dao* generated *fa*; it is the model which, by drawing its line of successes and failures, clarifies the difference between crooked and straight; those who hold fast to *dao* while producing the model do not venture to offend against it."[106] A passage from the *Guanzi*, whose date is perhaps uncertain, elaborates this basic statement by ascribing the origin of a control of affairs to the model, that of the model to the exercise of power (*quan* 權), and that of the exercise of power to *dao*.[107] *Fa* also plays its part as a model in connection with medical practice. Basic documents that described the operation of certain bodily features were termed *Maifa* 脈法 (Theory of the pulse), *Bingfa* 病法 (Theory of illness), or *Zhenfa* 診法 (Theory of the curative needle); it was in accordance with the principles

---

[104] For 536, see *Zuo zhuan*, 43 (Zhao 6), 16a–19a (Legge, *The Ch'un Ts'ew with the Tso Chuen*, pp. 607, 609). In his note to this, Du Yu (222–84) cites a passage from the *Shi jing* that includes the term *yi fa*, which does not however appear in the received text (*Shi jing*, 16(1) ["Wen wang"], 14a: Mao no. 235); for 513, see *Zuo zhuan*, 53 (Zhao 29), 11a (Legge, *The Ch'un Ts'ew with the Tso Chuen*, pp. 729, 732).

[105] *Analects*, 2/3 (Legge, *Confucian Analects*, p. 156) and 13/3 (ibid., p. 264); *Mencius*, 1A/7 (Legge, *The Works of Mencius*, pp. 147–8), and 3A/3 (ibid., p. 240).

[106] This statement is to be found as the opening sentence in the passage entitled *Dao fa* 道法; see *Mawangdui Han mu boshu*, vol. 1, transcription p. 43.

[107] See *Guanzi*, 13 (36 "Xinshu" A), 4a (W. Allyn Rickett, *Kuan-tzu: A Repository of Early Chinese Thought* [Hong Kong: Hong Kong University Press, 1965], p. 175); see *Mawangdui Han mu boshu*, vol. 1, transcription p. 44, n. 1.

enunciated therein that a physician would determine the treatment that he would prescribe for the particular case that he was treating.[108]

The connection between *Dao* and *fa* has involved considerable discussion, insofar as it can imply that the *Fajia* owed their origin to what is loosely termed a Daoist way of thought. *Fajia* should perhaps be taken to have denoted those who specialized in the models for living and ordering humanity that derived from *Dao*; the *Daojia* chose rather to concentrate on those very principles than to bend their attention to the ordering of a way of life. Confusion however arose during the Han period, when a revulsion set in against the practices of first the kingdom and then the empire of Qin. These practices came to be characterized as the result of the counsels of Shang Yang and Han Fei and their espousal of a rigorous set of laws and punishments. As a result, the term *Fajia* acquired a pejorative connotation, which stood in contrast with the approved principles and methods of government said to derive from the *Rujia*. The relationship between the *Rujia* and the *Daojia* has been discussed above.

Of all of China's pre-imperial thinkers who are known to us, Xunzi may perhaps be regarded as the one who was the most capable of political analysis and the formulation of political ideas. To him, abstractions such as *fa* took a subordinate place after that of the living rulers of mankind. For the best of models would not necessarily bring blessings to humanity in the absence of the right sort of ruler; and history could show examples of evil men who had inherited a kingdom, only to see it fall into ruin despite the fine models that they had inherited from their predecessors. Alive to the same distinction between the models and the punishments, he called for the need to understand the principles of the model before setting its individual provisions right; and while noting the uselessness of applying punishments without restraint, he agreed that severe measures of that type were needed to discourage crime.[109]

Shang Yang has always been cited and rightly regarded as a statesman who exercised a major influence on the development of the laws in China, and the two expressions whereby his actions are described are significant. *Gengfa* 更法 conveys the idea of a change of the model that is brought about by means of renewal. *Bianfa* 變法, a term that has received much greater attention, implies a change of the model by way of departure from something already established, even to the point of breaking the mold.[110] As a new depar-

---

[108] See *Shi ji*, 105, pp. 2797, 2804, 2811.

[109] See *Xunzi*, 10 ("Fu guo"), p. 130; 12 ("Jundao"), pp. 158–9; 14 ("Zhi shi"), p. 185; and 18 ("Zheng lun"), pp. 234–7 (Knoblock, *Xunzi*, vol. 1, pp. 132, 175; vol. 2, p. 207; and vol. 3, pp. 34–6).

[110] The initial chapter of the *Shang jun shu*, which is entitled "Gengfa," refers to the proposed action as *bianfa*. See *Shang jun shu* (Sibu beiyao ed.), 1, 1a, 2a.

ture, his proposals aroused the fears of his master (Qin Xiao Gong, r. 361–338 B.C.) that he himself, as ruler, would be subject to criticism. The *Shang jun shu* 商君書, which is named for Shang Yang and may be accepted as deriving from his own views or those of his immediate followers, retains the distinction between *fa* and *xing*. In a number of passages, *fa* is also paired with *li* (ritual).

One of Shang Yang's innovations is seen in the principle that, once established, the punishments for crime should be applicable to all members of the country irrespective of their status or position. The punishments should be neither administered nor suspended simply so as to accord with the arbitrary will of the ruler, whether to satisfy anger or to indulge in favoritism. The *xing* were to become part of the accepted structure of the state with a recognized place in its institutions, and without being subject to the previous criticisms, for example, as in the "Lü xing" 呂刑 or by Confucius. Such results, however, could not always be achieved, as is illustrated in a famous incident when, in place of applying punishments, including that of tattooing, to the Heir Apparent, these were duly executed on his mentors. As yet, hierarchies of class, whether deriving from kinship or privilege, could not be ignored; and no sanctions existed which could limit the power of the ruler.

In several passages, the *Shang jun shu* alludes to the models of government as being essential to the proper ordering of the state and as a means of ensuring that the inhabitants concentrate on their proper occupations. These are the models set up by the sages in such a way that they will be known and understood universally. The statement that officials are bound by the model in their treatment of the population may perhaps be taken as a rare glimpse of a view of law as a means of affording protection from official oppression.[111]

Early concepts of crime and punishment allowed scope for the redemption of crime by means of payment, as is denoted by the term *fa* 罰. The "Lü xing" gives a schedule of punishments and charges for the redemption from certain punishments, including those of mutilation, and enjoins rulers to investigate such cases thoroughly. Another passage of the *Shang shu*, which may be dated no earlier than the late Spring and Autumn period, uses the term *shu* 贖 to refer to redemption by means of payment.[112] By Han times both terms were being used, in a somewhat distinct sense. *Shu* denoted redemption from punishment by payments, such privileges being granted by

---

[111] See *Shang jun shu*, 3 (8 "Yi yan"), 1a, and 5 (26 "Ding fen"), 14b (J. J. L. Duyvendak, trans., *The Book of Lord Shang: A Classic of the Chinese School of Law* [London: Arthur Probsthain, 1928; rpt., Chicago: University of Chicago Press, 1963], pp. 234, 327).

[112] *Shang shu*, 3 ("Shun dian"), 14a and 19 ("Lü xing"), 26a (Karlgren, *Book of Documents*, pp. 5, 77).

special permission; *fa* denoted a fine, that is, an established penalty fixed as such in the first place.[113]

Documentation

The growing sophistication of government during the Warring States period demanded convenient means and materials for compiling the increasingly large number of documents that officials were being required to handle. In an entry for 501 B.C., the *Zuo zhuan* refers to a set of penal laws inscribed on bamboo. The expression *zhu bo* 竹帛 (bamboo and silk), which is seen in texts such as the *Mozi* 墨子, denotes two types of stationery, one being in use for normal purposes and one which was more costly and that was presumably reserved for more special copies. For the principal work of the administration, such as the registration of land or records of taxation, it is to be presumed that boards, or more usually narrow strips of bamboo and wood, served the needs of the official, equipped as he was with a knife with which to make erasures and corrections or to peel a surface that had been used once already and was needed for a second time.[114]

Traditionally, as one of the measures required for the unification, Li Si is credited with evolving the type of script that would accommodate to the needs of government more easily than other materials, and that would be suited to the use of a soft brush.[115] Material finds give some idea of the development of different styles and means of writing following the era of the bronze vessels and their inscriptions. Probably the earliest examples are the ten pillar-like stones, usually termed the "Stone Drums," which originally carried about 700 characters of rhymed verse and which are probably to be dated no earlier than the fifth century B.C.[116] Other examples of writings on stone include texts of oaths, which are dated to 497 B.C. and derived from Jin (Fig. 14.1).[117] The only text on silk that survives from pre-imperial times

---

[113] See Hulsewé, *Remnants of Han Law*, pp. 205–14. For the somewhat different terminology in Qin documents and the calculation of the sums due in terms of suits of armor or other objects, see ibid., p. 18.

[114] For the history of documentation, see Akira Fujieda, *Moji no bunka shi* (Tokyo: Iwanami, 1971; rpt. 1991); Tsuen-Hsuin Tsien, *Written on Bamboo and Silk: The Beginnings of Chinese Books and Inscriptions* (Chicago: University of Chicago Press, 1962); and Edward L. Shaughnessy, ed., *New Sources of Early Chinese History: An Introduction to Reading Inscriptions and Manuscripts* (Berkeley: Society for the Study of Early China, and Institute of East Asian Studies, University of California, 1997), Chapter 5. Other references to the use of these materials are seen in *Zuo zhuan*, 55 (Ding 9), 19a–b (Legge, *Ch'un Ts'ew with the Tso Chuen*, pp. 771–2); and *Mozi* (Sibu beiyao ed.), 2 (10 "Shang xian" C), 11a; *Shi ji*, 10, p. 436 (Chavannes, *Mémoires historiques*, vol. 2, p. 494).

[115] See Bodde, *China's First Unifier*, pp. 147–61; and Tsien, *Written on Bamboo and Silk*, pp. 68–9.

[116] For a tentative dating in the fifth century B.C., see Gilbert L. Mattos, *The Stone Drums of Ch'in* (Monumenta Serica Monograph, no. 19; Nettetal: Steyler, 1988), pp. 75–112, 369. For an earlier dating, see Tsien, *Written on Bamboo and Silk*, pp. 64–7.

[117] These texts are reproduced in *Wenwu* 1983.3: 83–6 and pls. 5–8; see also Chang Gan, " 'Hou ma meng shu' congkao" *Wenwu* 1975.5: 12–19, and *Wenwu* 1975.5: 20–6.

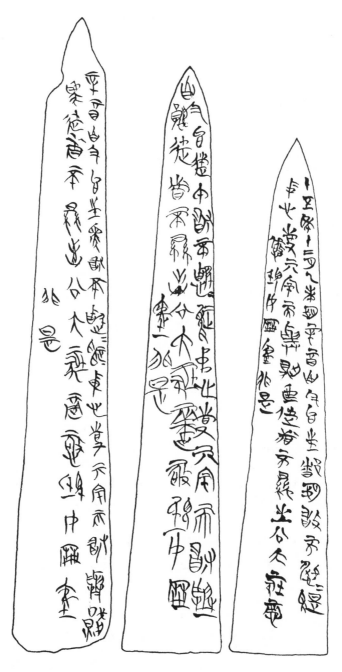

Figure 14.1. Oaths of alliance, written on stone, affirming the duties of ministers serving the ruler of Jin, 497 B.C. Found at Wenxian, Henan. *Wenwu* 1983.3: 84.

is of a religious, shamanistic, and philosophical nature, being found in a tomb within the area of Chu 楚 and dated to the fourth century (Fig. 12.7).[118] Wooden strips from Cili 慈利, Hunan, in the old land of Chu, include one group from the middle of the Warring States period which relates incidents that occurred in the history of Chu and Yue 越.[119] Another group of texts, including some of a mantic and some of a legal content, were found in tomb 2 at Baoshan 包山, also in Chu, and are dated to ca. 316 B.C.[120] These documents are of the same form as that of the normal stationery that was used by the clerks and officials of the Han empire. The width of the strips was sufficient to carry a single column of characters; the length was considerably longer than the standard strip of one foot (i.e., 23 cm) normally used in Han times.

It was doubtless records that had been made out in this form that Xiao He 蕭何 managed to save for the future task of administration when Liu Bang took over the Qin capital of Xianyang 咸陽 in 206 B.C.[121] Our sources specify that Xiao He collected maps, registers, and other documents, and some idea of the maps that may have been available at this time may be seen in some recent finds. Examples of such documents on silk, paper, or wood have been discovered at two sites (Fig. 14.2). One of these sites, which is in Gansu, may be dated shortly before the unification; other examples were found at Mawangdui.[122]

The Calendar and Registers of the Population and the Land

Effective government of the early and, indeed, the later empires rested on the preparation, maintenance, and distribution of three key documents; the calendar, the register of inhabitants, and the register of the land. Without these, officials would not be able to collect revenue, organize the corporate work required by provincial and local needs, or conscript manpower. By con-

---

[118] A detailed study of the Chu Silk Manuscript in English is to be found in Noel Barnard, *Studies on the The Ch'u Silk Manuscript. Part 2: Translation and Commentary* (Canberra: Australian National University, 1973). For the most authoritative study, see Li Ling, *Changsha Zidanku Zhanguo Chu boshu yanjiu* (Beijing: Zhonghua, 1985).

[119] The historical texts from Cili are described in *Wenwu* 1990.10: 45.

[120] See *Wenwu* 1988.5: 10, 27, and pl. 2.

[121] Xiao He's action is recorded in *Han shu*, 1A, p. 23 (Dubs, *History of the Former Han Dynasty*, vol. 1, p. 58).

[122] Facsimiles of the recently found maps, from Fangmatan 放馬灘 (Gansu) and Mawangdui will be found in Cao Wanru et al. eds., *Zhongguo gudai ditu ji* (Beijing: Wenwu, 1990), pls. 4–19, 20–8, Chinese text, pp. 1–2, English text pp. 17–18; see also He Shuangquan, "Tianshui Fangmatan Qin mu chutu ditu chutan" (*Wenwu* 1989.2: 12–22), p. 17 and color pl. 1; and Fu Juyou and Chen Songchang, *Mawangdui Han mu wenwu* (The Cultural Relics Unearthed from the Han Tombs at Mawangdui" [Changsha: Hunan, 1992]), pp. 151–3. For a critical examination of one of the maps from Mawangdui, see Hans Bielenstein, "Notes on the *Shui ching*," *BMFEA* 65 (1993): 264–5, and maps 1, 2.

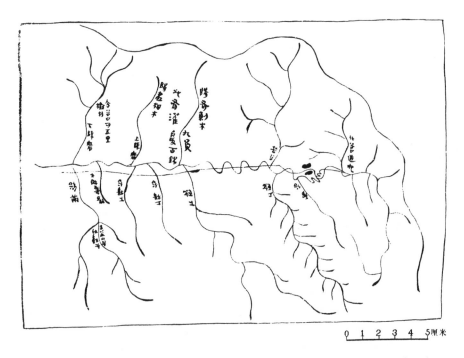

Figure 14.2. Map, on wood, showing topographical features and place-names, found at Fangmatan, Gansu. Late Warring States. *Wenwu* 1989.2: 15, fig. 5.

trast with imperial practice, for which there is much that is known or can be inferred from the standard histories, there is far less reliable information for pre-imperial days. As a description of the institutions that were operated in those years, the *Zhou li* is of highly doubtful value and should be regarded as little more than an account of the received tradition that was current in some circles in Han times. How far the statements of that text may be taken to record the functions, duties, or responsibilities of the officials who are ascribed to Western Zhou can only remain subject to question. Nor can it be said to which period or to which areas of China the statements of the text should be applied.

Regulation of the lunisolar calendar depended on astronomical observation and mathematical skills. To ensure the coincidence, or near coincidence, of the periods of the sun and the moon, it was necessary to determine the points at which the intercalary month, which was requisite after every thirty-two or thirty-three months, should be inserted.[123] It was also necessary to

[123] For the somewhat general and vague statement that two intercalary months were inserted every five years, see *Yi jing*, 7 ("Xici zhuan"), 21b.

determine to which months there should be assigned thirty and to which twenty-nine days; and it was also necessary to fix the starting point of the year. The catalog of the Han imperial library, which was drawn up by Liu Xiang 劉向 (79–8 B.C.) and Liu Xin 劉歆 (46 B.C.–A.D. 23), included entries for a number of written calendars or treatises that explained their workings.[124] These were named as those of the five schools of Huang Di, and as those of Zhuan Xu, Xia, Yin, Zhou, and Lu. Recognition that the royal calendar of Zhou should be accorded supreme priority, insofar as it derived from the decisions of the Son of Heaven, is seen in its retention in the *Chunqiu* and in the *Zhushu jinian*. One feature of that last-named document perhaps illustrates a growing concern with the enumeration of the years; from 784 B.C., and more particularly from 370 B.C., years are entered whether or not any events were worthy of record.[125]

According to one statement, at the outset of the dynasty Han had adopted the calendar of the legendary ruler Zhuan Xu. That several calendars were available is seen from the almanacs that were buried at Shuihudi 睡虎地, in the former territory of Chu, ca. 217 B.C. These documents apparently took note of two calendrical systems: first, that of Xia, which was used by Chu; and second, that of Zhuan Xu, which was in use in Qin. In at least one instance there is evidence to show that Qin's legal documents made use of the calendar of Zhou.[126] One feature of imperial usage, which may also be traced back to pre-imperial times, is seen in the precursor of the system of regnal titles (*nian hao* 年號). In 334 and 324 B.C., changes were introduced in Wei and Qin, respectively; from that point on the reigning monarchs started counting their years from a new point of origin.[127] Identical changes were in time introduced, in one case at least retrospectively, for the Han emperors Wendi and Jingdi, for 163, 149, and 143 B.C.; but it cannot be told how far the examples of the Warring States were in the minds of imperial

---

[124] References to the calendrical documents that were in the Han imperial library appear in *Han shu*, 30, pp. 1765–6; see also *Han shu*, 21A, p. 979, for Liu Xiang's work of coordination.

[125] For entries in the *Zhushu jinian*, see B, 16a and 28a (Sibu congkan ed.), and Loewe, ed., *Early Chinese Texts*, p. 40.

[126] *Han shu*, 21A, pp. 973–4, refers to the antiquity of calendrical reckoning, to the six calendars in question, and to Han's adoption of that of Zhuan Xu. For the use of the Xia and Zhuan Xu calendars in Chu and Qin and the changes that were introduced, as well as for the special terms used to denote the months in Chu, see Zeng Xiantong, "Chu yue ming chu tan," *Zhongshan daxue xuebao* 1980.1: 97–107. Strip no. 742 from Shuihudi distinguishes the almanac that starts at that point from other examples by the notation Qin 秦, thereby presumably differentiating it from other almanacs made out with the calendar of Chu in mind. For the Chu calendar, see Wang Shengli, "Guanyu Chu guo lifa de jianzheng wenti," *Zhongguo shi yanjiu* 1988.2: 137–42; Zeng Xiantong, "Chu yue ming chu tan"; and Rao Zongyi and Zeng Xiantong, *Yunmeng Qin jian rishu yanjiu* (Hong Kong: Chinese University Press, 1982), p. 46. For the use of the calendar of Zhou by Qin Wu Wang, see Li Xueqin, "Qingchuan Haojiaping mudu yanjiu," *Wenwu* 1982.10: 68.

[127] For these changes, see *Shi ji*, 5, p. 207 (Chavannes, *Mémoires historiques*, vol. 2, p. 70).

advisers, either then or when the system of regnal titles proper was introduced, again retrospectively, to take effect in the histories from 140 B.C.[128]

As in earlier times, so in the Han empire officials and others were required to submit detailed counts annually, giving the number of households and individuals in the counties, commanderies, and kingdoms, and the area of the land, classified according to its value or use. The earliest example of these counts that is available is the summary of those that were compiled for A.D. 1–2. Supplementary evidence to show how officials set about some of this work may be seen in the *Jiu zhang suan shu* 九章算書, a mathematical textbook that, while not being compiled until Han times, in all probability drew on the experience of the earlier centuries.[129]

In principle it is unlikely that the imperial officials had no precedents on which they could draw by way of assistance in compiling their sets of figures. A few references in early texts such as the *Zhou li*, which cannot be applied to an area or to a time that may be identified, suggest that responsibility for doing so may have been recognized as the duty of named officials.[130] One such reference mentions the inclusion on the registers of all persons, including infants from the age of seven or eight months onwards. Perhaps the two most telling citations are to be found in the *Zuo zhuan* and the *Guanzi*. In its record for 548 B.C., the *Zuo zhuan* implies the need for documents of this type in view of their requirement for taxation.[131] Documents of imperial times show that by then individuals were being identified on the registers and elsewhere in terms of their place of origin, age, height, and social status.[132]

Other measures that the officials of Chu are reported to have taken include: counting items of armor and offensive weapons; recording details of arable land; assessing the resources of the mountains and forests and the area of lakeland; marking off areas designated for special purposes or treatment, and perhaps for taxation at concessionary rates (e.g., hilly land or brackish soil); measuring the land subject to stagnant water; calculating the tax to be collected; and drawing up the dues for wagons and carriages and a register of horses. The passage in the *Guanzi* writes that the registers of the house-

[128] For the changes of 163, 149, and 143 B.C., see *Han shu*, 4, p. 128, and 5, pp. 144, 150, with notes in *Han shu buzhu*, 4.16a (Dubs, *History of the Former Han Dynasty*, vol. 1, pp. 260, 316, 326). For the introduction of regnal titles, see ibid., vol. 2, pp. 121–2.

[129] The figures for the Han empire are included in *Han shu*, 28; for problems involved in measuring differently shaped plots of land, see *Jiu zhang suan shu*, chapter 1; for the dating of the *Jiu zhang suan shu*, see Loewe, ed., *Early Chinese Texts*, pp. 17–19.

[130] References in the *Zhou li* are seen in 3, 5b, 3, 22b and 35, 24a (Biot, *Le Tcheou-li ou rites des Tcheou*, vol. 1, pp. 51, 68, and vol. 2, p. 353).

[131] See *Zuo zhuan* 36 (Xiang 25), 14a, b (Legge, *The Ch'un Ts'ew with the Tso Chuen*, pp. 512, 517). The passage in the *Guanzi* is from 17 (53 "Jincang"), 11a, which Luo Genze, *Guanzi tanyuan* (Shanghai: Zhonghua, 1931), p. 112, dates from late Warring States to early Han.

[132] E.g., see document UD 2, item 2, in Michael Loewe, *Records of Han Administration* (Cambridge University Press, 1967), vol. 2, p. 179.

holds and the accounts of the arable land are the means of understanding how the capacity for wealth varies.

There exists one record for the compilation of a register of households for 375 B.C., linked with arrangements for the joint responsibilities of the groups of inhabitants for crime; it is hardly surprising that this account is recorded for Qin.[133] The figure of 70,000 households which is quoted by Su Qin 蘇 秦 as the population of the great city of Linzi 臨淄 in Qi, during the fourth century B.C., must take its place in a highly rhetorical context and can in no sense be accepted as being trustworthy or derived from accurate counting.[134] It may nonetheless reflect some attempt at assessing the extent of a city's population at that time. Certificates for tax exemption for Chu survive uniquely in a set of five inscriptions in bronze, inlaid with gold, of 323 B.C. These valuable texts known as the *E jun qi jie* 鄂君啟節 record details of communications between two cities, by both land and water.[135] Another document of a unique nature, recently found from a site in Sichuan, carries the text of the "Wei tian lü" 為田律 (Statute for the formation of arable plots). Dated to 309 B.C., this strip lays down the statutory measurements for plots of lands together with rules for the establishment of boundaries and waterways and the upkeep of bridges.[136]

It is not suggested that precisely these documents, or precisely these types of document, were available for consultation by those who drew up the forms for the records to be made in the administration of the empires; they simply serve as evidence, however slight, of some of the types that may have been in use and available for reference so as to form precedents for adoption.

The Offices of State

The centuries of the Spring and Autumn and the Warring States periods saw the start of a protracted process that characterized much of China's intellectual development and administrative history. At first, those who possessed

[133] *Shi ji*, 6, p. 289 (Chavannes, *Mémoires historiques*, vol. 2, p. 240).

[134] Su Qin's statement about Linzi occurs in the advice that he gave to the king of Qi; see *Zhanguo ce* (Sibu beiyao ed.), 8 (Qi 1), 8b, (J. L. Crump, *Chan-Kuo Ts'e* [Oxford: Clarendon Press, 1970], p. 157). Some support may perhaps be given to Su Qin's statement by (a) the claim that ca. 135 B.C. the population of Linzi amounted to 100,000 households (*Shi ji*, 52, p. 2008) and (b) the comparable figure of 80,800 households that is given for the Han capital city of Chang'an for A.D. 1–2 (*Han shu*, 28A, p. 1543). For archaeological reports on the site of the city, see Qun Li, "Linzi Qi guo gu cheng kantan jiyao," *Wenwu* 1972.5: 45–54 (for the walls), and *Kaogu* 1988.9: 784–5 (for the drainage system).

[135] For the first reports on the *E jun qi jie*, see Guo Moruo, "Guanyu E jun qi jie de yanjiu," *Wenwu* 1958.4: 3–6, and Yin Difei and Luo Changming, "Shouxian chutu de E jun qi jie," *Wenwu* 1958.4: 8–11. For some of the many subsequent studies, see Li Xueqin, *Eastern Zhou and Qin Civilizations*, trans. K. C. Chang (New Haven: Conn.: Yale University Press, 1985), p. 167, n. 42.

[136] For a line drawing of the statute of 309 B.C., see *Wenwu* 1982.1: 11; for transcription and preliminary comments, see Yu Haoliang, "Shi Qingchuan Qin mu mudu," *Wenwu* 1982.1: 22–4; Tian Yichao and

estates or held a title such as *gong* 公 or *wang* 王 took their own decisions and controlled their own affairs; or they might depute one of their kinsmen or their favorites to specific tasks of administering their land or leading some of their forces in battle. But not all officials or officers received their entitlement to exert authority in this way. In addition there are many examples of men who attained powerful positions thanks to their merits rather than the circumstances of their birth or proximity to a seat of control; some of these positions were passed on within the family on a hereditary basis, and recompense for services rendered usually took the form of landed estates. It was the achievement of the empires to evolve a system whereby individuals who showed promise of intellectual gifts and administrative skills were trained and appointed to posts for which they received a salary paid in money. They were subject to promotion, demotion, or dismissal; they owed responsibility to their immediate superiors; and they were charged with the duty of supervising their juniors. This major change involved a long process, which developed in a manner that was by no means rigorous or regular. Its culmination was seen during the Qing dynasty (1644–1911); its seeds had been sown before the Qin empire had been founded.

The structure of government as inherited from Qin and operated in the Han empire comprised senior officials in two divisions. The Three Senior Statesmen, sometimes termed the Three Excellencies (*san gong* 三公), included the Chancellor (*chengxiang*), Imperial Counsellor (*yushi dafu* 御史大夫), and, for a time, the Supreme Commander (*taiwei* 太尉). These three ranked higher than the Nine Ministers (*jiu qing* 九卿), each of whom bore specialist responsibilities for an aspect of administration. In all cases these were senior authorities who were backed by a large number of assistants and clerical staff and to whom others, such as the many counselors, were subordinated. But although some of the titles of these imperial officials had also been borne by officials of the preceding kingdoms, no more than a general similarity of function and status may be assumed to have persisted during the long decades in which imperial government was evolved.

Thus, the Chancellor of the Qin and Han empires was the most senior of all imperial officials, sometimes enjoying enhanced status by conferment of the title of Chancellor of State (*xiangguo* 相國). In Qin, Shang Yang acted in an advisory or consultative capacity, that is, as Chancellor, for ten years

Liu Zhao, "Qin tian lü kaoshi," *Kaogu* 1983.6: 545–8; and Luo Kaiyu, "Qingchuan Qin du Wei tian lü suo guiding de Wei tian zhi," *Kaogu* 1988.8: 728–31, 756. See also Yang Kuan, "Shi Qingchuan Qin du de tianmu zhidu," *Wenwu* 1982.7: 83–5; Sage, *Ancient Sichuan and the Unification of China*, pp. 131–2, 258–9, nn. 36, 37, for interpretation of the document as giving "specific details of a land redistribution plan [for Shu 蜀] supervised by Gan Mao and other Qin officials." By contrast, Hulsewé (*Remnants of Ch'in Law*, pp. 211–12) treats the strip to meticulous examination as one of the surviving statutes that were applicable to the whole of the kingdom of Qin.

from ca. 359 B.C.[137] He was followed by Zhang Yi 張儀 in 328 B.C. and by Yue Chi 樂池 in 318 B.C., and the posts of Chancellors of the Left and the Right were first established in 309.[138] In 249 B.C., Lü Buwei, named as Chancellor of State, was sent to conquer East Zhou; at the time of King Zheng's accession in 246 B.C., when the kingdom of Qin had already been greatly extended, Lü Buwei was Chancellor, with the very large estate of 100,000 households; he was dismissed in 237 B.C.[139]

However, it was by no means only in Qin that senior officials bore this title. Sunshu Ao 孫叔敖, who served in Chu at times between 613 and 591 B.C. is referred to as Chancellor.[140] Shen Buhai was Chancellor of Hann in 351 B.C.,[141] and Fei Yi 肥義 is described as Chancellor of State of Zhao for 299 B.C., followed by Yu Qing 虞卿 during the reign of Xiao Cheng Wang 孝成王 (265–245 B.C.),[142] and the terms *chengxiang* or *xiang* are used for Wei in 262 B.C. and Yan in 251 B.C.[143] Usage in Qi is not so clear. In one peculiar case the Heir Apparent of the kingdom of Wei acted as the Chancellor. By contrast with these examples in which a title that was used in imperial times may be seen in the earlier kingdoms, a different tradition usually persisted in Chu, where the senior functionary was termed the *lingyin* 令尹.[144]

The complement of Han imperial officials included a few permanently established generals (*jiangjun* 將軍); other officers who had been appointed to conduct a particular campaign carried the same title, modified by a reference to the particular occasion or purpose for which they had been appointed. Senior military officers termed *jiang* appeared in the Warring States of Wei and Qin; Wei Ran 魏冉 was the first general to be appointed as *jiangjun* in Qin, in the time of Zhao Wang 秦昭王 (r. 306–251 B.C.).

Titles of other posts that formed part of the imperial government feature in the records of the Warring States period or even earlier. In the time of Shang Yang, the teachers of the Heir Apparent of Qin (*fu* 傅 and *shi* 師) bore the brunt of punishment for the crimes committed by their pupil; similar posts existed in Chu as early as 528 B.C.[145] The title of *neishi* 內史, which is rendered as Metropolitan Superintendent for imperial times, is mentioned in the record of Zhou for 563 B.C., for Qin as early as 626–624 B.C., and for Zhao ca. 408 B.C.[146] At the same time, Zhao also had an official who bore

---

[137] *Shi ji*, 68, p. 2233.   [138] *Shi ji*, 5, p. 209 (Chavannes, *Mémoires historiques*, vol. 2, p. 75).

[139] *Shi ji*, 6, p. 223 (ibid., p. 101), and 15, pp. 750, 753.

[140] *Shi ji*, 119, p. 3099; for Sunshu Ao, see Knoblock, *Xunzi*, vol. 1, p. 199.

[141] *Shi ji*, 15, p. 723.   [142] *Shi ji*, 43, pp. 1812, 1828.

[143] *Shi ji*, 65, p. 2167; for Yan, see *Shi ji*, 34, p. 1555, and 80, p. 2435.

[144] *Shi ji*, 44, p. 1851. For the appointment of a chancellor in Chu in 262, see *Shi ji*, 78, p. 2394.

[145] *Shi ji*, 68, p. 2231; 40, p. 1712.

[146] *Zuo zhuan*, 31 (Xiang 10), 7a (Legge, *Ch'un Ts'ew with the Tso Chuen*, pp. 443, 446); *Shi ji*, 5, p. 193; 43, p. 1798.

the title of Superintendent of the Capital (*zhongwei* 中尉), perhaps also seen as an official who advised the king of Qin to embark on the conquest of Shu in 316 B.C.[147] Of the Nine Ministers, the post of Superintendent of Trials (*tingwei*) was held by Li Si for perhaps twenty years before the unification;[148] that of Superintendent of the Guards (*weiwei* 衛尉) had appeared in Qin; that of Superintendent of Transport (*taipu* 太僕) in Wei, Hann, Qi, and Qin, and that of the Lesser Treasury (*shaofu* 少府) in Hann.

A *yezhe* 謁者, that is, the Imperial Messenger of later times, had been appointed in Qin during the first half of the third century B.C.;[149] and the title was also known in Wei, Qi, and Chu. The title of Gentlemen of the Palace (*langzhong* 郎中) had appeared in Zhao, Hann, Qi, Qin, and Chu. There was a *taishi* 太史, or official concerned with recording astronomical phenomena, during the first half of the third century in Qi,[150] and possibly in Chu. A number of other officials of a lower rank with specialist responsibilities who had a place in the imperial government seem to have had their counterparts in Chu, where they were termed *yin* 尹, being charged with the care of such diverse matters as the outskirts of the city, jade, divination, music, or the gates.[151]

Commanderies (*jun* 郡) and counties (*xian* 縣) formed the regular and normal units of provincial government of the Qin empire and these were adopted by Han, along with the assignment of certain areas to the kings (*zhuhouwang* 諸侯王) and the nobles (*liehou* 列侯). Counties had in fact made their appearance in the early parts of the Spring and Autumn period in the kingdoms of Qin, Jin, and Chu as a means of bringing newly acquired territories under the control of the central governments of those kingdoms.[152] Administration in this way was basically different from that of areas which were in the hands of major landowners as estates. As the years of the Spring and Autumn period passed, the number of counties grew; there are records of Qin's establishment of these units for defensive purposes on its eastern borders for 456, 398, 379 and 374 B.C.[153]

---

[147] Chang Qu (fourth century A.D.), *Huayang guozhi* (Sibu beiyao ed.), 3 ("Shu zhi"), 2b.

[148] *Shi ji*, 87, p. 2546.   [149] *Shi ji*, 79, p. 2402.

[150] *Shi ji*, 82, p. 2456.

[151] For the officials (*yin*) who were responsible for the outskirts, see *Zuo zhuan*, 46 (Zhao 13), 4a (Legge, *Ch'un Ts'ew with the Tso Chuen*, pp. 642, 648); for jade, see *Xin xu* (Sibu congkan ed.), 5 ("Zashi di wu"), 16b; for divination, see *Zuo zhuan*, 46 (Zhao 13), 8b (Legge, *Ch'un Ts'ew with the Tso Chuen*, pp. 644, 649), and *Shi ji*, 40, p. 1709; for music, see *Zuo zhuan*, 55 (Ding 5), 4a (Legge, *Ch'un Ts'ew with the Tso Chuen*, pp. 759, 761); and for the gates, see *Zuo zhuan*, 60 (Ai 16), 6a (Legge, *Ch'un Ts'ew with the Tso Chuen*, pp. 845, 847). See also Yang Kuan, *Zhangguo shi*, 2d rev. ed. (Shanghai: Shanghai Renmin, 1980), pp. 205–9.

[152] For the consignment of newly annexed territories in Chu to officials entitled *yin* 尹, see p. 574 above.

[153] See Yang Kuan, *Zhangguo shi*, pp. 209–10, for Pinyang 頻陽, Pu 蒲, Lantian 藍田, and Yueyang 櫟陽 (*Han shu*, 28A, pp. 1545, 1570, 1543, 1545).

Commanderies were likewise set up, primarily for defensive purposes against non-assimilated peoples, in the first instance by Jin. Initially units of this type were situated in land that was less populous and less valuable than that of the counties; but in time there evolved a system whereby the counties became component units of the commanderies, being subordinated to their control. This first appeared in the three kingdoms that replaced Jin; for example, in Wei in 328 B.C. The practice was soon followed in Qin, Chu, and Yan. Acquiring territories from its neighbors or rivals, Qin formed thirty-seven cities of Zhao into Taiyuan commandery 太原郡 (248 B.C.) and twenty cities of Wei, together with the important city of Puyang 濮陽 of Wey, into Dongjun 東郡 (242 B.C.). Commanderies were established as defensive measures against internal rivals; counties were set up in the areas around the walled cities, to the point that the terms xian 縣 and cheng 城 were used interchangeably. Commanderies were not found in Qi, which centralized its defensive and administrative system in five major cities (du 都).

Commanderies were under the jurisdiction of a governor (shou 守), who had the power and authority to call up able-bodied men for service. In Qin, the title of shou of Shu was borne in the early part of the third century by Li Bing 李冰, the engineer who set up a system of water control in Sichuan; one of his colleagues was the Governor of Hanzhong 漢中. The senior official of the county was the ling 令 (Magistrate).[154]

Military Organization

Sources of information regarding military matters are notoriously scanty, partly by reason of what is said to have been the prevailing view of such activity. As against the pride vested in a brave stand against fearful odds, or a successful feat of arms, that runs through much of Greek and Roman civilization, in traditional Chinese terms warfare was regarded as an activity in which to engage only in the last resort and only when necessity demanded; no heroic view was taken of martial valor. But for all this, China was far from being unaccustomed to the calls for service that were imposed or the manner in which a battle or siege could bring one kingdom into creation or despoil its neighbor of its territories.

The generals who led the forces of the Qin and Han empires were able to call on a rich fund of experience learned during the fighting of the previous centuries. In some instances they were members of families that had supplied commanding officers in the past, perhaps on a hereditary basis, as in the case

---

[154] For Li Bing, see Joseph Needham, *Science and Civilisation in China. Vol. 4:3: Civil Engineering and Nautics* (Cambridge University Press, 1971), pp. 288–96.

of Meng Tian, his father Meng Wu 蒙武, and his grandfather Meng Ao 蒙驁. Military leaders who were literate could call on a number of treatises on strategy or tactics, or on records of omens that spelled out the outcome of a battle. These may be seen in works such as the *Sunzi bing fa* 孫子兵法 (Sunzi's art of war) and *Sun Bin bing fa* 孫臏兵法 (Sun Bin's art of war), parts of which may possibly be dated to the fifth century, or in texts such as the *Yu Liaozi* 尉繚子 (or Wei Liaozi)[155] and *Liu tao* 六韜 (Six quivers) of the Warring States period. By the end of Former Han, the imperial library included twelve items of pre-imperial origin that were classified as *Bing quan* 兵權 (The use of armed force).[156] But although the lessons learned from the warfare of the pre-imperial kingdoms may well have been present in the minds of some of these officers, no descriptions of such battles survive, if indeed they were ever composed.

When Meng Tian was dispatched north to supervise the construction of the unified system of defenses (214 B.C.), he may well have been renovating walls that had been built by Qin in the first half of the third century.[157] Further afield, defensive walls had been built by the small kingdom of Zhongshan 中山 (369 B.C.) and by Qi (by 368 B.C.), Wei (351 B.C.), Zhao (333 B.C.), and Yan (first half of the third century B.C.). In some cases these may have been built or manned by convicted criminals, who were working out their sentences.[158] In imperial times a regular system provided for the conscription of able-bodied males to serve both in the armed forces and the labor gangs, and it was in this way that the ranks of the defensive garrisons were filled; but it is open to question how effectively any of the pre-imperial kingdoms was able to operate such a system. There seems to have been one in force in Qin just before the empire was created. Lao Ai 嫪毐 forged the seals needed to call out conscripts from the counties to serve in the rebellion that he was mounting; to counter this the government of Qin also called out a force from similar sources.[159]

There was, however, one means whereby military prowess was encouraged and which the empires inherited from the earlier kingdoms. As is described in a famous chapter of the *Han Feizi*, the will of government was implemented by reliance on the two "handles" of rewards and punishments.

[155] The reading *Yuliaozi* rather than *Weiliaozi* is attested to in Luo Zhufeng, ed., *Hanyu da cidian* (12 vols. and index [Shanghai: Shanghai cishu, 1986–93]), vol. 2, p. 1279, and in Morohashi Tetsuji, *Dai Kan Wa jiten* (12 vols. and index [Tokyo: Suzuki ippei, 1955–60]), vol. 4, p. 3432 (7440: 43, 44).

[156] See *Han shu*, 30, pp. 1756–7.

[157] For the construction of walls, see *Shi ji*, 43, p. 1799; 44, p. 1845; and 110, pp. 2885–96.

[158] For the presence of convicted criminals working on the walls, see *Shi ji*, 15, p. 758. For the walls built by Qin, see Huang Linshu, *Qin huang changcheng kao* (Kowloon: Zaoyang, 1973); for subsequent developments throughout the imperial age, see Arthur Waldron, *The Great Wall of China: From History to Myth* (Cambridge University Press, 1990).

[159] *Shi ji*, 6, p. 227 (Chavannes, *Mémoires historiques*, vol. 2, pp. 108–10).

Rewards consisted partly of the conferment of a mark of social status that could bring with it certain privileges of a valuable nature, such as mitigation or exemption from punishment in case of crime or exemption from statutory service. From precedents that may go back to the sixth century, a system of seventeen orders of honor (*jue* 爵), in ascending order of merit, was regularized in Qin during the time of Shang Yang; that it had been the practice in some form in other kingdoms, such as Chu and Zhao, may be inferred from references to some of the titles of the orders that duly appeared in the system that Qin was adopting in the fourth century. These orders of honor were conferred specifically for success on the field of battle, the degree of the order corresponding with the number of enemy servicemen that the recipient had killed. There are instances of conferment by the king of Chu in the interregnum between the Qin and Han empires; by Han times the system comprised twenty orders, of which the highest was held on a hereditary basis. The enumeration of military services rendered by those who fought to found the Han empire includes details of battle honors in the form of the number of prisoners taken, counties occupied, or enemy slain, with particular attention to the ranks of those who were defeated. This practice would seem to reflect the system of rewards and punishments that had been instituted by Shang Yang. Two major changes took place with the passage of time: the orders came to be bestowed for acts of civil rather than military merit; and it became possible to acquire them, with their attendant privileges, by means of purchase.[160]

Attempts at Economic Control

While economic theory, as such, could hardly find a place in the memorials submitted by officials of early imperial times, it is nonetheless possible to discern several ways in which imperial policies were directed in practical ways to the more intense exploitation of natural resources or to the solution or alleviation of daily problems. Some of the measures that were adopted rested on precedents cited for earlier periods. Although it may be open to question how far such precedents were matters of myth or imagination rather than fact, those of the former type may well have exerted just as much influence on the minds of imperial officials. The most valuable source of information on these matters is to be found in the *Yan tie lun*, where protagonists argue variously about the merits of allowing the population

---

[160] For the orders of honor, see Nishijima Sadao, *Chûgoku kodai teikoku no keisei to kôzô: Nijû tô shakusei no kenkyû* (Tokyo: Tokyo Daigaku, 1961); Michael Loewe, "The Orders of Aristocratic Rank of Han China," *TP* 48 (1960): 97–174; and *Han shu*, 40, p. 2051; 41, pp. 2086–7.

freedom of action or of imposing controls in the interests of imperial strength.[161]

Conscious attempts to increase agricultural production are seen in the decrees of Wendi and in the new methods of tillage that were advocated by Zhao Guo 趙過 (ca. 90 B.C.).[162] Such ideas accompanied a sharp distinction drawn between the fundamental occupations (*ben* 本) of agriculture and sericulture and those of manufacture, mining, and commerce, which were deemed to be of lower priority (*mo* 末). Such a distinction was by no means new to the imperial age, having been expressed in texts such as the *Guanzi*.[163] Mencius, however, while stressing the need for promoting agriculture, recognized the interdependence of the three occupations of farmer, manufacturer, and merchant, and such a view is reiterated in the *Yan tie lun*.[164] Examples of rich men who made their fortunes by means other than agriculture are given for both pre-imperial and Han times.[165]

Reference has been made above to a text of 913 B.C. which concerned the transfer of land (see p. 327). More recently Shang Yang had given legal recognition to the acquisition of land by purchase, rather than by direct gift of a monarch. By the second century, Dong Zhongshu was protesting against the cumulative effects of such freedom, which had resulted in a marked disparity between the rich landowners and the poor peasantry. In 7 B.C., Shi Dan 師丹 was advocating measures to restrict the extent of land holdings. In both cases the writers drew on what they believed or alleged to have been the golden precedent of pre-imperial times that was known as the "well-field system."[166] The extent to which such a system had been practiced was hardly relevant; its importance lay in the ideal that it portrayed from the golden age of the past.

Coins had taken various forms in the kingdoms of pre-imperial times, as bronze imitations of spades or knives, or as small discs, also in bronze; small golden ingots had been in use to some extent in Chu. It was probably on

---

[161] Translations of a number of chapters of the *Yan tie lun* are to be found in Gale, *Discourses on Salt and Iron*; for a summary of the debates recorded in the text, see Loewe, *Crisis and Conflict in Han China*, pp. 91–112.

[162] For early examples of Wendi's decrees, see *Han shu*, 4, pp. 117, 118 (Dubs, *History of the Former Han Dynasty*, vol. 1, pp. 242, 245). For Zhao Guo, see *Han shu*, 24A, p. 1138 (Nancy Lee Swann, *Food and Money in Ancient China* [Princeton, N. J.: Princeton University Press, 1950], p. 184).

[163] *Guanzi*, 15 (48 "Zhi guo"), 14a–b; see also *Han shu*, 24A, p. 1128 (Swann, *Food and Money*, p. 153).

[164] *Mencius*, 3A/4 (Legge, *The Works of Mencius*, pp. 248–9); *Guanzi*, 8 (20 "Xiaokuang"), 6b–8b; *Yan tie lun*, 1 (1 "Ben yi"), p. 3 (Gale, *Discourses on Salt and Iron*, p. 6).

[165] *Shiji*, 129; *Han shu*, 91 (Swann, *Food and Money*, pp. 413–64).

[166] For Dong Zhongshu's statement, see *Han shu*, 24A, p. 1137 (Swann, *Food and Money*, p. 179); for Shi Dan, see *Han shu*, 24A, p. 1142 (Swann, *Food and Money*, p. 200).

the basis of Qin's practice that the Han government finally (ca. 115 B.C.) introduced the state's monopoly of minting coin. When Wang Mang experimented with a multi-denominational currency he pointed to the tradition of such a system in ancient times.[167] Advocates of the state monopolies of salt and iron sought their precedents in the action ascribed to Guan Zhong of Qi in the seventh century.[168] In reviving attempts to stabilize prices and provide a steady supply of staple goods, Wang Mang invoked an example from the days of Zhou.[169]

CITIES, PALACES, AND ROYAL SHRINES AND TOMBS

Throughout pre-imperial and early imperial times, and indeed for many centuries later, the great majority of the population dwelled in the countryside, dependent for their living on the fruits of the earth and the unending labor needed to wrest these gifts from a harsh terrain or an unpredictable climate. Nonetheless, it was from the cities that there emerged some of the more significant and permanent features of Chinese culture.

By the time of the early empires, Chinese cities had acquired many of their characteristics. Choice of a site by means of divination and the removal of a king's seat from one city to another are seen from the earliest times. Already in the days of Shang, at what may have been a royal capital at Erligang 二里崗, a city may have been built to a square or rectangular design and oriented in general terms so as to meet the points of the compass. Various settlements or cities, such as Qishan 岐山, Feng 豐, and Hao 鎬, served as capitals where the kings of Western Zhou could assert their authority and demonstrate its power by the performance of religious rites. It was perhaps partly because such centers had acquired a rich symbolical significance that the migration of the kings of Zhou to Luoyang in 771 B.C., while being due to force majeure, was seen at least in later times as marking a curtailment of royal and spiritual authority in the face of superior material powers on earth.

Distinctions of occupation and social status were present in Chinese cities from Shang times onwards, as may be seen in the separation of sites for a royal residence and the quarters for craftsmen and their workshops. In time the cities came to possess a reputation as centers where wealth could be easily acquired without the intensive effort that the farms demanded. Hearsay accounts could attract those who were gullible, who found an agricultural way of life demanding and unrewarding, or who were anxious to enjoy the

---

[167] *Han shu*, 24B, p. 1177 (Swann, *Food and Money*, p. 324).
[168] *Yan tie lun*, 3 (14 "Qingzhong"), p. 178 (Gale, *Discourses on Salt and Iron*, p. 85).
[169] *Han shu*, 24B, p. 1179 (Swann, *Food and Money*, pp. 334–5).

comforts and fleshpots of easier conditions. Officials of Warring States times would complain that too many persons were fleeing from the countryside, where they would be engaged in productive labor, to seek a livelihood from secondary and unessential occupations in the towns. Such warnings recur in a number of proposals submitted by imperial officials in the interest of improving the standard of living in Han times.

With the more sophisticated conditions of the Spring and Autumn and the Warring States periods, the many cities that had developed formed eagerly sought prizes of war. Protected by their array of doubled walls, they guarded considerable resources of wealth and acted as the sites from which a kingdom's business could be controlled. They could include some of the centers of economic enterprise, such as the seats of the magnates and later the imperial commissions who managed the production of salt, iron, or textiles. Some housed a royal mint, which turned out coins inscribed with the name of the site where they had been cast. Xingyang 滎陽, whose name recurs in the tale of the fighting between the states and in the civil wars that preceded the formation of the Han empire, was of exceptional importance thanks to the abundant stores accumulated in the famous Ao 敖 granary nearby.

The strategic and psychological importance of the cities of Warring States times may be seen in the attention paid in literature to their defense and capture. Tactics are described in texts such as the *Mozi* or the *Sunzi*; romantic accounts of the stratagems whereby a city could be taken, perhaps by diverting a river to bring about its inundation, are seen in works such as the *Zhanguo ce*. Despite a change of name or removal from one site to another, the early cities provided a measure of continuity, whether on the part of the royal houses that had founded them or of the conquerors who had taken possession by storm. They provided the precedents without which the later magnificent capitals of Xianyang, Chang'an, and Luoyang could hardly have been conceived.

Linzi, in eastern China, forms an excellent example of the continuity of ancient urban settlements. By the end of Former Han it was listed as the principal city and county of the commandery of Qi 齊, with the note that it housed two official commissions, responsible for the manufacture of robes and iron goods. The site and the city already had a long history. Some time in the ninth century B.C., according to one tradition, Xian Gong 獻公 of Qi had moved his seat of residence and government from Pugu 薄姑 to Linzi; according to others the move had been from Yingqiu 營丘, which, according to yet others, was to be identified with Linzi. By the Spring and Autumn and Warring States periods the city was featuring as an important and flourishing site, acting as the capital of the Qi kingdom of Tian He 田和 (fl. 390

B.C.). It is perhaps best known from the description, deliberately couched in rhetorical terms, by Su Qin in one of his addresses to King Xuan of Qi 齊宣王 (r. 319–301 B.C.). Anxious to impress the monarch with Linzi's wealth and prosperity, he singled out some of its activities of leisure times, or signs of its obvious opulence, such as the general addiction to music, its cockfights, its games of *liubo* 六博, the frequency of carriages on its streets, and the press of its inhabitants.

Excavations confirm the continuity of settlement in the city that the Qin and Han empires inherited. It had in fact consisted of two sections, each walled; the smaller one, to the southwest, is sometimes referred to as the Huan Gong Tai 桓公台, after one of Qi's most famous rulers of the seventh century; this was clearly the site of a well-established seat of authority. The larger section included no traces of major buildings; probably it accommodated the populace, and it included sites of metalworking and other crafts. The sites of eleven out of a reported total of thirteen gates have been identified on the walls of the two sections. Some of the major streets measured up to 20 m in width; one of two drainage systems, which made use of a natural waterway, ran for a length of 2,800 m from south to north, at a width of some 30 m. Some of the remains of the walls are dated to late Western Zhou, but between then and the Han empire they had been subjected to considerable repair and renovation.[170]

Other examples are seen in the old city of Zheng 鄭, which was adopted as the capital of Hann when it took over Zheng in 375 B.C.; or Handan 邯鄲, which, like Linzi, consisted of two units comprising an original palace settlement and a walled city. Unlike Linzi these had not been formed into a single unit.[171]

According to one of the political manipulators of the Warring States period, Anyi 安邑 was the main support of Wei, Jinyang 晉陽 that of Zhao, and Yanying 鄢郢 that of Chu. As did others, so did these three cities retain their importance as administrative and cultural centers right into imperial times, as may be seen from the list of provincial units of the Han empire for A.D. 1–2. Yangdi 陽翟, associated in the tradition with Yu 禹 the Great and the site where Han Jing Hou 韓景侯 had moved at the end of Western Zhou, had become the capital of Yingchuan 潁川 commandery.[172] Jinyang, capital of Taiyuan commandery and site of a salt commission, was identified

---

[170] *Han shu*, 28(A), p. 1583; *Han shu buzhu*, 28A(2).79b–80b (notes); *Shi ji*, 32, p. 1482; Takigawa Kametarô, *Shiki kaichû kôshô* (Tokyo: Tôhô bunka gakuin, 1932–4), 32, p. 11; Qun Li, "Linzi Qi guo gu cheng kantan jiyao," pp. 45–54; *Zhanguo ce* 8 (Qi 1), 8b (Crump, *Chan-Kuo Ts'e*, p. 157); for the results of excavations of Linzi, see Yang Kuan, *Zhongguo gudai ducheng zhidu shi yanjiu* (Shanghai: Guji, 1993), pp. 65–70.

[171] For Zheng, see *Xin Zhongguo de kaogu faxian he yanjiu* (Beijing: Wenwu, 1984), p. 274; for Handan, see *Kaogu* 1980.2: 142–6.

[172] *Han shu*, 28A, p. 1560.

in Han times as the Tang guo 唐國 of the *Shi jing*; later it featured as the subject of a famous siege whose tale was told with delight by the fiction writers of the Warring States period.[173] Jimo 即墨, whose mints had turned out some of the knife-shaped coins of Qi, had become the capital of Jiaodong 膠東 kingdom.[174] Anyi with its salt and iron commissions had served as an administrative center for Wei from 562 to 339 B.C. and was the capital of the Han commandery of Hedong 河東.[175] Handan, adopted as the capital of Zhao in 386 B.C., was the first city of that small remnant of territory that still bore the proud title of Zhao guo 趙國.[176] Ji 薊, to the south of present-day Beijing, had been a famous city of Yan and was the capital of its successor, known as Guangyang 廣陽.[177] Down in Chu, King Wen 文王 moved from Danyang 丹陽 to Ying in 689 B.C., and that remained a royal capital with little interruption for four centuries, until 278 B.C.; it was known as Jiangling 江陵 in Han, being the capital of Nan 南 commandery.[178] In 241 B.C., King Xiaolie 孝烈王 of Chu moved to Shouchun 壽春, known for its earlier association with Qu Yuan 屈原 (fourth century B.C.). Liu An, king of Huainan, had adopted it as his capital and assembled a group of literary men there prior to his rebellion and death in 122 B.C. In time it became the capital of the Han commandery of Jiujiang 九江.[179] Continuity is also seen at the site of Yunmeng 雲夢, which has yielded artifacts of the Spring and Autumn, middle Warring States, and early Former Han periods.[180]

According to records which may at times be dubious, there were precedents in all the major pre-imperial kingdoms for the construction of major buildings, such as palaces or imposing ornamental terraces (i.e., *tai* 臺), that doubtless served as material symbols of royal majesty. Thus, King Ling 靈 of Chu (r. 540–529 B.C.) built just such a terrace, named Qianxi 乾谿,[181] and the Jieshi 碣石 palace of Yan was built by King Zhao 昭 (r. 311–279 B.C.) at the time of a visit by Zou Yan the cosmologist.[182] According to one report, King Xuan of Qi had built a mansion that extended for 100 *mu*.[183] This

173 *Han shu*, 28A, p. 1551; *Shi jing*, 6(1) and (2), for the poems named for Tang (Mao nos. 114–25) (Karlgren, *Book of Odes*, pp. 73–80); *Han Feizi*, 10 ("Shi guo"), p. 72 (Liao, *Complete Works of Han Fei Tzu*, vol. I, p. 79).

174 *Han shu*, 28B, p. 1635.

175 *Han shu*, 28A, p. 1550; *Shi ji*, 44, p. 1836.

176 *Han shu*, 28B, pp. 1631, 1656; *Shi ji*, 43, p. 1798; *Kaogu* 1980.2: 142.

177 *Han shu*, 28B, p. 1634.

178 *Han shu*, 28B, p. 1666. King Wen of Chu (r. 689–677 B.C.) had settled his capital at Ying, but this had been moved to Yan under King Hui (r. 488–432 B.C.); Yanying was sometimes used as a term to denote Chu's capital.

179 *Han shu*, 28A, p. 1569; see also *Shi ji*, 15, p. 752, and *Han shu*, 28B, p. 1668.

180 *Wenwu* 1994.4: 42.

181 *Xin yu* (Sibu beiyao ed.), B ("Huai lü"), 5a.

182 *Shi ji*, 74, p. 2345.

183 *Lü shi chunqiu*, 20 (7 "Jiao zi"), p. 1405. 100 *mu* was equivalent to 11.3 English acres.

rhetorical figure may at least be taken as an indication of the very large area that the building covered. Wei had planned to build a terrace, perhaps bearing religious connotations, that was to reach to the heavens, being named Zhongtian 中天 (Straight to the skies).[184] A whole variety of royal or ducal buildings are recorded for Qin, beginning with the Xichui 西垂 Palace in which Wen Gong 文公 resided from the first year of his reign (765 B.C.).[185] At a later stage Qin had evidently built a palace called Ganquan; the name persisted in Han imperial times as the site of Wudi's summer retreat.[186]

Archaeology has revealed the remnants of one of the many palaces built for one of the kings of Qin, at Xianyang. It has been inferred that this consisted of two principal buildings that were constructed east and west of a natural ditch in symmetrical design, the two being connected by means of a covered way, with the ditch acting as the main drain for the complex. The remains of the building, which has been excavated, showed that it had comprised two stories, with five rooms on the upper and six rooms on the lower floor; access from the upper floor to a yet higher level was by way of an inclined ramp. The skill of the builders is demonstrated by the small degree of variation in maintaining the necessary levels of the structure, there being an error of no more than 1 cm in a length of 50 m. Some of the rooms on the lower floor were used for residential purposes, with one being equipped for washing. The largest room, on the upper floor, measured 13.4 by 12 m. The walls carried columns of at least two types and there were traces of the paintings with which they had been adorned. Corridors gave access from one room to another, and the whole was equipped with four pits for drainage. Piping had been constructed in such a way that a siphon effect speeded the flow of the water and prevented blockages. This building is believed to have originated in the Warring States period, later to be repaired and perhaps extended by the First Emperor of Qin.[187]

A major change occurred between Western and Eastern Zhou in the situation and function of royal shrines and graves.[188] In Shang and Western Zhou times the shrine was situated within the city. It acted as a sacred center, being devoted to the memory of the original ancestors of the royal house and serving to strengthen the cohesion of its kin. This structure was planned on a comparatively large scale and acted as a repository for the memorial tablets of the king's forebears. By contrast, the tombs of these monarchs were situ-

---

[184] *Xin xu* (Sibu congkan ed.), 6 ("Ci she"), 1b.

[185] *Shi ji*, 5, p. 179 (Chavannes, *Mémoires historiques*, vol. 2, p. 15).

[186] *Shi ji*, 6, p. 227 (ibid., p. 113).

[187] For reports on this site, see *Wenwu* 1976.11: 12–24, 25–30; Tao Fu, "Qin Xianyang gong di yihao yizhi fuyuan wenti de chubu tantao," *Wenwu* 1976.11: 31–41; and *Wenwu* 1976.11: 42–44. See, above, p. 673 and fig. 10.9.

[188] For the different practices of Western Zhou and later, see Wu Hung, "From Temple to Tomb: Ancient Chinese Art and Religion in Transition," *EC* 13 (1988): 78–115.

ated in the open fields, being monuments on a smaller scale that were concerned solely with the attention due to the person immediately deceased. But with the change of emphasis that took place in Eastern Zhou, the kings came to be buried in tombs that were of a much more majestic and significant type, being surrounded by a park and surmounted by a tumulus. The new style is perhaps seen in practice for the kings of Qin, when the names of tombs began to incorporate the term *ling* 陵.[189] Construction of one such tomb, named Shou Ling 壽陵, was started in 335 B.C.; three kings of Qin were buried in similarly named tombs in 311, 307, and 250 B.C. However, the term did not feature in connection with the burial of the predecessors of the *wang*, that is, those entitled *gong*. It was used regularly in the designations of the burial sites of Han emperors.

The change signified a decline in the importance of the shrine as a sacred center and its growth as a symbol of a king's power. Signs of the transition may be seen in the arrangements made for the burial of the kings of Zhongshan, a small kingdom, which was finally overcome by its neighbors in 296 B.C. These graves, which date from ca. 300 B.C., were intended either for the kings themselves or for their immediate relatives. Some were situated within the capital city of Lingshou 靈壽; some lay outside, to the west. The funerary equipment that was buried in the tombs included some exquisite pieces of bronze inlay work and some notable inscriptions; fortunately it also included a bronze plaque which carried the plan that was made for the construction of a complex site. Although the mausoleum was never completed as planned, the artifacts found on the site permit the identification of one of the tombs as being intended for King Cuo 譽 (r. 323–309 B.C.) and his consorts and suggest the degree of accuracy with which it had been designed. As compared with the earlier practice, the change is seen in the manner in which the coffin chambers were surmounted by a high tumulus, with halls of worship being erected on the summit.[190]

The great attention that was paid to the imperial tombs of Qin and Han owed much to precedents of this type, as may be seen in the hillock built over the tomb of the First Emperor of Qin, that still survives as a conspicuous landmark.[191] This lay outside the capital city, as did the tombs of the Han

---

[189] For the use of the term *ling* in the designation of Qin tombs, see *Shi ji*, 6, pp. 224, 288 (Chavannes, *Mémoires historiques*, vol. 2, pp. 104, 240); 43, p. 1802; and 85, p. 2511.

[190] For the mausoleum of the king of Zhongshan and his consorts, see *Chûgoku sengoku jidai no yû: Chûzan ôgoku bunbutsuten* (*Treasures from the Tombs of Zhong shan guo kings: An Exhibition from the People's Republic of China* [Tokyo: Tokyo National Museum, 1981]); *Zhongshan: Tombes des Rois Oubliés* (Paris: Galeries nationales du Grand Palais, 1985); and Cao Wanru et al. eds., *Zhongguo gudai ditu ji* pls. 1–3, Chinese text p. 1, English text p. 17. See, above, Figs. 10.30, 10.31 and 10.32.

[191] For the tomb of the First Emperor of Qin at Lishan, see Lothar Lederose and Adele Schlombs, *Jenseits der Grossen Mauer. Der Erste Kaiser von China und seine Terracotta-armee* (Gütersloh-München: Bertelsmann Lexicon, 1990).

emperors. But in the imperial age these also fulfilled the same role as that of the shrines built for the kings of Western Zhou within their cities; they now constituted a center for asserting the cohesion of the imperial realm and the kinship of its ruling house. One further way in which some of the tombs and shrines of the emperors of Former Han came to display their prime position is seen in an ingenious arrangement whereby they were situated alternately to the west and east sides of that of the founder, which retained its prime place in the center. This was the Zhao Mu 昭穆 system, named after two kings of Western Zhou, and providing for the continuity of service to the first monarch of the royal or imperial kin. It also symbolized the ordered succession of deceased kings or emperors, taking their place first as the last descendant of the house and finally as the ancestor to whom services were due from all followers. The system asserted genealogical origins and continuity. It affirmed the legitimacy of royal and imperial rule, and it provided for the perpetual devotions due to the founder of the house. How much it owed to traditional practice of the early kings of Zhou may be open to question; certainly in Former Han times it was regarded as doing so.[192] As part of his determined effort to assert the legitimacy of his rule, Wang Mang invoked the system in a particularly conspicuous way, so as to display that his line was descended from the monarchs of mythology and the kings of Western Zhou.[193]

The well-established practice of providing costly funerals had provoked criticism in Warring States times.[194] Equally strong protests were voiced in Han times, as may be seen most conspicuously in the valedictory decree of Wendi and in a set of comparisons and contrasts that is included in the *Yan tie lun*.[195] Such protests called attention to the evil effects of extravagance and of the consumption of materials in a time of need and complained that, so far from wishing to honor their deceased relatives by these means, mourners were adopting them simply in order to impress their neighbors.

Discoveries of the valuable treasures, consumable supplies, and utilities that were buried in Han tombs have shown that good reason existed for these strictures. They also demonstrate that, while funerary practice of early imperial times drew on traditional mythology and well-established concepts, it also developed its own characteristic features. Bronze vessels were buried to serve the purposes of ritual, while beautiful jades indicated the status that the deceased person had enjoyed in life and provided a noble ornamentation

---

[192] For the Zhaomu system, see Li Hengmei, *Lun Zhaomu zhidu* (Taipei: Wenjin, 1992), and Loewe, *Divination, Mythology and Monarchy in Han China*, pp. 276–9, 284.

[193] See Loewe, "Wang Mang and His Forebears: The Making of the Myth."

[194] *Mozi*, 25 ("Jie zang"); *Lü shi chunqiu* 10 ("Jie sang") (Chen Qiyou, *Lü shi chunqiu jiaoshi*, pp. 524–35.

[195] *Han shu*, 4, p. 142 (Dubs, *History of the Former Han Dynasty*, vol. 1, p. 267); *Yan tie lun*, 6 (29 "San bu zu"), p. 353.

for the hereafter. Bronze mirrors and, less frequently, silk paintings, which bore the symbols or invocations for a future life, accompanied the dead to escort their souls to paradise. Documents showed the professional occupation in which an official or scholar had been engaged and perhaps provided reading matter for the long years to come. Other texts, that were of a more practical nature, together with the necessary instruments instructed the dead how to proceed should they wish to consult an oracle, treat an illness, or fight an enemy. Figurines or fresco paintings provided simulacra of the deceased persons' colleagues in office, the jesters and musicians who had entertained them, or the servants who had attended to their comforts and needs. Clothing, food, and drink, as well as lacquered vessels and a plentiful supply of ready money, were included in the tombs to satisfy the requirements of daily life; the figures of horse and carriage that decorated the tombs showed the style of living to which the dead person had been accustomed.[196]

CONCLUSION

The empires had yet to work out an elusive compromise that was achieved only too rarely: the viable balance between a rigorous, disciplined mode of government and attention to the ethical values of the humanities. From the outset they faced one question, seen indeed before the days of empire had dawned, but not fully resolved over twenty centuries. Each dynastic house would need to choose between two principles that lay behind its way of government. Emperors could either rely on the ties of kinship to their own ancestors so as to ensure loyalty in the face of ambition, or they could exercise their government by controlling the appointments of their chief advisers on the grounds of merit. Neither principle was wholly effective.

But the empires did find a way to fill one deficiency that had become manifest after the end of the Western Zhou period. Those kings had embodied the link that was seen to be essential between the temporal authority that they exerted on earth and the superhuman power of a cosmic order from which it derived. In the effective absence during the Spring and Autumn and the Warring States periods of a single earthly ruler who commanded universal respect, that link had been severed. It was only after a hundred years or so of an imperial dispensation that steps were taken to restore this element of dynastic rule without which few houses could hope to survive for long.

A number of questions that may be raised and that will long await an answer concern the senses in which a unified China could have contributed

---

[196] For examples of funerary goods of the Han period, see Michèle Pirazzoli-t'Serstevens, *The Han Dynasty* (New York: Rizzoli, 1982). For the interpretation of certain types of object, see Loewe, *Ways to Paradise.*

more to human welfare than a multiplicity of political units. The tales of dynastic intrigue, plot and counterplot, and violence recur on the pages of imperial history too frequently to allow the unmodified conclusion that the existence of empire added substantially to the peace of mankind. An imperial system of tax and service that was more stringent and efficient than the imposition of dues that varied from area to area could perhaps be more just; and yet it might allow wider scope for corruption. The more intensely coordinated efforts of an imperial government's call for talent, which were practiced over a wider catchment area, could perhaps offer greater opportunities for social mobility; but the existence of a number of royal courts and palaces could perhaps lead to a wider patronage of the arts. Imperial suppression of religious rites and other practices in the name of uniformity may well have demanded as its price the elimination of a living culture with a rich folklore, particularly in southern areas. Fortunately, it is only too evident that such measures were by no means universally effective.

BIBLIOGRAPHY

Aalto, Pentti. "The Horse in Central Asian Nomadic Cultures." *Studia Orientalia* 46 (1975): 1–9.

Akatsuka Kiyoshi 赤塚忠. *Chûgoku kodai no shûkyô to bunka: In ôchô no saishi* 中國古代の宗教と文化：殷王朝の祭祀. Tokyo: Kadokawa shoten, 1977.

Allan, Sarah. *The Heir and the Sage*. San Francisco: Chinese Materials Center, 1981.

Allan, Sarah. "The Myth of the Xia Dynasty." *JRAS* 1984 no. 2: 242–56.

Allan, Sarah. *The Shape of the Turtle: Myth, Art, and Cosmos in Early China*. Albany: State University of New York Press, 1991.

Allard, Francis. "Interaction and Social Complexity in Lingnan During the First Millennium B.C." *Asian Perspectives* 33, 2 (1994): 309–26.

Amano Motonosuke 天野元之助. "Indai no nôgyô to sono shakai kôzô" 殷代の農業とその社會構造. *Shigaku kenkyû* 史學研究 62 (1956): 1–16.

Ames, Roger T. *The Art of Rulership: A Study in Ancient Chinese Political Thought*. Honolulu, University of Hawaii Press, 1983.

An Lu 安路 and Jia Weiming 賈偉明. "Heilongjiang Nehe Erkeqian mudi ji qi wenti tantao" 黑龍江訥河二克淺墓地及其問題探討. *Beifang wenwu* 北方文物 1986.2: 2–8.

An Zhimin. "The Bronze Age in the Eastern Parts of Central Asia." In *History of Civilizations of Central Asia. Vol 1: The Dawn of Civilization: Earliest Times to 700 B.C.*, ed. A. H. Dani and V. M. Masson. Paris: Unesco, 1992, pp. 319–36.

An Zhimin. 安志敏. "Changsha xin faxian de Xi Han bohua shitan" 長沙新發現的西漢帛畫試探. *Kaogu* 考古 1973.1: 43–53.

An Zhimin 安志敏. "Shilun Huanghe liuyu xinshiqi shidai wenhua" 試論黃河流域新石器時代文化. *Kaogu* 考古 1959.10: 565.

An Zhimin 安志敏. "Shilun Zhongguo de zaoqi tongqi" 試論中國的早期銅器. *Kaogu* 考古 1993.12: 1110–19.

An Zhimin 安志敏. "1952 nian qiuji Zhengzhou Erligang fajue ji" 1952年秋季鄭州二里崗發掘記. *Kaogu xuebao* 考古學報 8 (1954): 65–108.

An Zhimin 安志敏. "Zhejiang Rui'an Dongyang zhishimu de diaocha" 浙江瑞安東陽支石墓的調查. *Kaogu* 考古 1995.7: 585–8.

An Zhimin 安志敏. "Zhongguo xinshiqi shidai kaoguxue shang de zhuyao chengjiu" 中國新石器時代考古學上的主要成就. *Wenwu* 文物 1959.10: 21.

An Zhimin 安志敏, Jiang Bingxin 江秉信, and Chen Zhida 陳志達. "1958–1959 nian Yinxu fajue jianbao" 1958–1959年殷虛發掘簡報. *Kaogu* 考古 1961.2: 63–76.

An Zhisheng, Wu Xihao, Wang Pinxian, Wang Shuming, Dong Guangrong, Sun Xiangjun, Zhang De'er, Lu Yanchou, Zheng Shaohua, and Zhao Songlin. "Changes in the Monsoon and Associated Environmental Changes in China Since the Last Interglacial." In *Loess, Environment and Global Change (The Series of the XIII Inqua Congress)*, ed. Tungsheng Liu. Beijing: Science, 1991, pp. 1–29.

Andersson, J. G. "An Early Chinese Culture." *Bulletin of the Geological Society of China*, Series A, 5, 1 (1923): 1–68.

Andersson, J. G. "Hunting Magic in the Animal Style." *BMFEA* 4 (1932): 221–317, pl. xxxvi.

Andersson, J. G. "Researches into the Prehistory of the Chinese." *BMFEA* 15 (1943): 1–298.

Andersson, J. G. "Selected Ordos Bronzes." *BMFEA* 5 (1933): 143–54, pl. xvi.

Anhui sheng bowuguan, ed. *Anhui sheng Bowuguan cang qingtongqi* 安徽省博物館藏青銅器. Shanghai: Shanghai Renmin meishu, 1987.

Anthony, David W., and Dorcas R. Brown. "The Origins of Horseback Riding." *Antiquity* 65 (1991): 22–38

Anthony, David, and Nikolai B. Vinogradov. "Birth of the Chariot." *Archaeology* 48, 2 (1995): 36–41.

Artamanov, M. I. "Skifo-sibirskoie iskusstvo tsverinogo stili (osnovniie etapy i napravleniia)." In *Problemy skifskoi arkheologii*, ed. P. D. Liberov and V. I. Guliaev. Moscow: Nauka, 1971, pp. 24–54.

Artamanov, M. I. *Sokrovishcha Sakov: Amu-Dar'inskii klad, altaiskie kurgany minusinskie bronzy, sibirskoe zoloto*. Moscow: Iskusstvo, 1973.

Askarov, A. "The Beginning of Iron Age in Transoxiana." In *History of Civilizations of Central Asia. Vol. 1: The Dawn of Civilization: Earliest Times to 700 B.C.*, ed. A. H. Dani and V. M. Masson. Paris: Unesco, 1992, pp. 441–58.

Askarov, A., V. Volkov, and N. Ser-Odjav. "Pastoral and Nomadic Tribes at the Beginning of the First Millennium B.C." In *History of Civilizations of Central Asia. Vol. 1: The Dawn of Civilization: Earliest Times to 700 B.C.*, ed. A. H. Dani and V. M. Masson. Paris: Unesco, 1992, pp. 459–75.

Ba Shu qingtongqi 巴蜀青銅器 Ed. Sichuan sheng bowuguan. Chengdu: Ziyunzhai, 1991.

Bagley, Robert W. "Changjiang Bronzes and Shang Archaeology." In *Proceedings: International Colloquium on Chinese Art History, 1991, Antiquities, Part 1*. Taipei: National Palace Museum, 1992, pp. 209–55.

Bagley, Robert W. "An Early Bronze Age Tomb in Jiangxi Province." *Orientations* 24, 7 (1993): 20–36.

Bagley, Robert W. "P'an-lung-ch'eng: A Shang City in Hupei." *Artibus Asiae* 39 (1977): 165–219.

Bagley, Robert W. "Replication Techniques in Eastern Zhou Bronze Casting." In *History from Things: Essays on Material Culture*, ed. Steven Lubar and W. David Kingery. Washington: Smithsonian Institution Press, 1993, pp. 234–41.

Bagley, Robert W. "Sacrificial Pits of the Shang Period at Sanxingdui in Guanghan County, Sichuan Province." *Arts Asiatiques* 43 (1988): 78–86.

Bagley, Robert W. "A Shang City in Sichuan Province." *Orientations*, 21, 11 (1990): 52–67.

Bagley, Robert W. "Shang Ritual Bronzes: Casting Technique and Vessel Design." *Archives of Asian Art* 43 (1990): 6–20.

Bagley, Robert W. *Shang Ritual Bronzes in the Arthur M. Sackler Collections*. Cambridge, Mass.: Harvard University Press, 1987.

Bagley, Robert W. "What the Bronzes from Hunyuan Tell Us About the Foundry at Houma." *Orientations* 26, 1 (1995): 46–54.

Bai Rongjin 白榮金. "Xi Zhou tongjia zuhe fuyuan" 西周銅甲組合復原. *Kaogu* 考古 1988.9: 849–51, 857.

Bailey, H. W. "Recent Work in 'Tocharian.'" *Transactions of the Philological Society* 1947: 126–53.

Bao Quan 保全. "Xi'an Laoniupo chutu Shang dai zaoqi wenwu" 西安老牛坡出土商代早期文物. *Kaogu yu wenwu* 考古與文物 1981.2: 17–18.

Bao Quan 保全. "Xi Zhou ducheng Feng Hao yizhi" 西周都城豐鎬遺址. In *Zhou wenhua lunji* 周文化論集, ed. Shaanxi Lishi bowuguan. Xi'an: San Qin, 1993, pp. 321–3.

Baoshan Chu mu 包山楚墓. 2 vols. Beijing: Wenwu, 1991.

Baoshan Chu jian 包山楚簡. Beijing: Wenwu, 1991.

Barnard, Noel. "Chou China: A Review of the Third Volume of Cheng Te-K'un's *Archaeology in China*." *MS* 24 (1965): 307–442.

Barnard, Noel. "A Recently Excavated Inscribed Bronze of Western Chou Date." *MS* 17 (1958): 12–46.

Barnard, Noel. *Studies on the Ch'u Silk Manuscript. Part 1: Scientific Examination of an Ancient Chinese Document as a Prelude to Decipherment, Translation, and Historical Assessment. Part 2: Translation and Commentary.* Canberra: Australian National University, 1972, 1973.

Barnard, Noel, and Sato, Tamotsu. *Metallurgical Remains of Ancient China.* Tokyo: Nichiosha, 1975.

Barnes, Gina L. *China, Korea, and Japan: The Rise of Civilization in East Asia.* London: Thames & Hudson, 1993.

Bartoli, Matteo. *Saggi di linguistica spaziale.* Turin: Rosenberg & Sellier, 1945.

Baxter, William H. *A Handbook of Old Chinese Phonology.* Trends in Linguistics: Notes and Monographs, no. 64. Berlin: de Gruyter, 1992.

Baxter, William H. "'A Stronger Affinity . . . than Could Have Been Produced by Accident': A Probabilistic Comparison of Old Chinese and Tibeto-Burman." In *The Ancestry of the Chinese Language*, ed. William S. Y. Wang. Journal of Chinese Linguistics monograph series, no. 8. Berkeley: *Journal of Chinese Linguistics*, 1995, pp. 1–39.

Baxter, William H. "Zhou and Han Phonology in the *Shijing*." In *Studies in the Historical Phonology of Asian Languages*, ed. William G. Boltz and Michael C. Shapiro. Amsterdam Studies in the Theory and History of Linguistic Science, series 4: *Current Issues in Linguistic Theory*, no. 77. Amsterdam: John Benjamins, 1991, pp. 1–34.

Beasley, W. G., and E. G. Pulleyblank, eds. *Historians of China and Japan.* London: Oxford University Press, 1961.

Bielenstein, Hans. "Notes on the *Shui ching*." *BMFEA* 65 (1993): 257–83.

Bilsky, Lester. *The State Religion of Ancient China.* 2 vols. Taipei: Chinese Association for Folklore, 1975.

Biot, Édouard. *Le Tcheou-li ou rites des Tcheou.* 3 vols. Paris: Imprimerie nationale, 1851; rpt. Taipei: Ch'eng-wen, 1966.

Birrell, Anne. *Chinese Mythology: An Introduction.* Baltimore: Johns Hopkins University Press, 1993.

Blakeley, Barry B. *Annotated Genealogy of Spring and Autumn Period Clans. Vol. 1: Seven Ruling Clans.* Taipei: Chinese Materials Center, 1983.

Blakeley, Barry B. "Functional Disparities in the Socio-Political Traditions of Spring and

Autumn China, Parts I, II, III." *JESHO* 20, 2 (1977): 108–43; 20, 3 (1977): 307–43; 22, 1 (1979): 81–118.

Blakeley, Barry B. "In Search of Danyang I: Historical Geography and Archaeological Sites." *EC* 13 (1988): 116–52.

Blakeley, Barry B. "King, Clan, and Courtier in Ancient Ch'u." *AM*, 3d series, 5, 2 (1992): 1–39.

Blakeley, Barry B. "On the Location of the Chu Capital in Early Chunqiu Times in Light of the Handong Incident of 701 B.C." *EC* 15 (1990): 49–70.

Blakeley, Barry B. "Recent Developments in Chu Studies: A Bibliographical and Institutional Overview." *EC* 11–12 (1985–7): 371–87.

Blanford, Yumiko. "Studies of the 'Zhanguo Zonghengjia Shu' Silk Manuscript." Ph.D. dissertation, University of Washington, 1989.

Blanford, Yumiko. "A Textual Approach to 'Zhanguo Zonghengjia Shu': Methods of Determining the Proximate Original Word Among Variants." *EC* 16 (1991): 187–207.

Blunden, Caroline, and Mark Elvin. *Cultural Atlas of China.* New York: Facts on File, 1983.

Bodde, Derk. *China's First Unifier.* Leiden: Brill, 1938; rpt., Hong Kong: Hong Kong University Press, 1967.

Bodde, Derk. "Myths of Ancient China." In *Mythologies of the Ancient World*, ed. Samuel Noah Kramer. Garden City, N.J.: Doubleday, 1961, pp. 367–408.

Bodde, Derk. *Statesman, Patriot, and General in Ancient China.* New Haven, Conn.: American Oriental Society, 1940.

Bodde, Derk, and Clarence Morris. *Law in Imperial China: Exemplified by 190 Ch'ing Dynasty Cases.* Cambridge, Mass.: Harvard University Press, 1967.

Bodman, Nicholas C. "Proto-Chinese and Sino-Tibetan: Data Towards Establishing the Nature of the Relationship." In *Contributions to Historical Linguistics. Cornell Linguistic Contributions, III*, ed. Frans van Coetsem and Linda. R. Waugh. Leiden: Brill, 1980, pp. 34–199.

Boltz, William G. "East Asian Writing Systems (Introduction)." In *The World's Writing Systems*, ed. Peter T. Daniels and William Bright. Oxford: Oxford University Press, 1996, pp. 189–90.

Boltz, William G. "Notes on the Reconstruction of Old Chinese." *Oriens Extremus* 36, 2 (1993): 185–207.

Boltz, William G. *The Origin and Early Development of the Chinese Writing System.* American Oriental Series, vol. 78. New Haven, Conn.: American Oriental Society, 1994.

Bonfante, G., and Thomas Sebeok. "Linguistics and the Age and Area Hypothesis." *American Anthropologist* 46 (1944): 382–6.

Bonner, Joey. *Wang Kuo-wei: An Intellectual Biography.* Cambridge, Mass.: Harvard University Press, 1986.

Boodberg, Peter A. "Marginalia to the Histories of the Northern Dynasties." *HJAS* 4 (1939): 230–83.

Boodberg, Peter A. "Some Proleptical Remarks on the Evolution of Archaic Chinese." *HJAS* 2 (1937): 329–72.

Bowman, Sheridan. *Radiocarbon Dating.* London: British Museum, 1990.

Braidwood, Robert. *The Near East and the Foundation for Civilization.* Eugene: Oregon State Museum, 1952, pp. 11–15.

Braidwood, Robert. *Prehistoric Man.* 6th ed. Chicago: Natural History Museum, 1964.

Bridgman, R. F. "La medicine dans la Chine antique." *Mélanges chinois et bouddhiques* 10 (1952–5): 1–213.

Brodianskii, D. L. "Krovnovsko-Khunnskie paralleli." In *Drevnee Zabaikal'e i ego kul'turnye sviazi*, ed. P. B. Konovalov. Novosibirsk: Akademiia Nauk USSR, 1985, pp. 46–50.

Brooks, E. Bruce, and A. Taeko Brooks. *The Original Analects: Sayings of Confucius and His Successors, 0479–0249.* New York: Columbia University Press, 1998.

Buck, David S., ed. and trans. "Archaeological Explorations at the Ancient Capital of Lu at Qufu in Shandong Province." *Chinese Sociology and Anthropology* 19, 1 (1986): 1–76.

Buck, John Lossing. *Land Utilization in China.* Nanking: University of Nanking, 1937.

Bunker, Emma. "The Anecdotal Plaques of the Eastern Steppe Regions." In *Arts of the Eurasian Steppelands*, ed. Philip Denwood. London: Percival David Foundation, 1978, pp.121–42.

Bunker, Emma C. "Ancient Ordos Bronzes." In *Ancient Chinese and Ordos Bronzes*, ed. Jessica Rawson and Emma Bunker. Hong Kong: Museum of Art, 1990, pp. 291–307.

Bunker, Emma C. "Unprovenanced Artifacts Belonging to the Pastoral Tribes of Inner Mongolia and North China During the 8th–1st Century B.C." In *The International Academic Conference of Archaeological Cultures of the Northern Chinese Ancient Nations (Collected Papers)*, ed. Zhongguo kaogu wenwu yanjiusuo. Huhhot, August 11–18, 1992.

Cai Yunzhang 蔡運璋. "Guo Wen gong mukao – Sanmenxia Guo guo mudi yanjiu zhi er" 虢文公墓考 — 三門峽虢國墓地研究之二. *Zhongyuan wenwu* 中原文物 1994.3: 42–5, 94.

Cai Yunzhang 蔡運璋. "Lun Guozhong qi ren – Sanmenxia Guo guo mudi yanjiu zhi yi" 論虢仲其人 — 三門峽虢國墓地研究之一. *Zhongyuan wenwu* 中原文物 1994.2: 86–9, 100.

Cai Yunzhang 蔡運章. "Luoyang Beiyao Xi Zhou moshu wenzi lüelun" 洛陽北窯西周墨書文字略論. *Wenwu* 文物 1994.7: 64–9, 79.

Cai Zhemao 蔡哲茂. "Yin buci Yi Yin jiu shi kao: Jianlun ta shi" 殷卜辭 '伊尹 jiù 虽示' 考 —兼論它示. *BIHP* 58, 4 (1987): 755–808.

The Cambridge Encyclopedia of Human Evolution. Ed. Steve Jones, Robert Martin, and David Pilbeam. Cambridge University Press, 1992.

Cammann, Schuyler. "The Evolution of Magic Squares in China." *JAOS* 80 (1960): 116–24.

Cammann, Schuyler. "The Magic Square of Three in Old Chinese Philosophy and Religion." *History of Religions* 1 (1961): 37–80.

Cammann, Schuyler. "Old Chinese Magic Squares." *Sinologica* 7 (1963): 14–53.

Cann, R. L., M. Stoneking, and A. C. Wilson. "Mitochondrial DNA and Human Evolution." *Nature* 325 (1987): 31–6.

Cao Bingwu 曹兵武. "Henan Huixian ji qi fujin diqu huanjing kaogu yanjiu" 河南輝縣及其附近地區環境考古研究. *Hua Xia kaogu* 華夏考古 1994.3: 61–7, 78.

Cao Dingyun 曹定雲. "Fu Hao nai Zi Fang zhi nü" 婦好乃子方之女. In *Qingzhu Su Bingqi kaogu wushiwu nian lunwenji* 慶祝蘇秉琦考古五十五年論文集. Beijing: Wenwu, 1989, pp. 381–5.

Cao Dingyun 曹定雲. "Fu Hao Xiao Ji guanxi kaozheng – cong Fu Hao mu Simu Xin mingwen tanqi" 婦好小己關係考証—從婦好墓司母辛銘文談起. *Zhongyuan wenwu* 中原文物 1993.3: 70–9.

Cao Dingyun 曹定雲. "Lun Yinxu Houjiazhuang 1001-hao mu muzhu" 論殷墟侯家莊1001號墓墓主. *Kaogu yu wenwu* 考古與文物 1986.2: 44–51.

Cao Dingyun 曹定雲. "Yinxu Fuhao mu mingwen zhong renwu guanxi zongkao" 殷墟婦好墓銘文中人物關係綜考. *Kaogu yu wenwu* 考古與文物 1995.5: 44–54.

Cao Fazhan 曹發展 and Chen Guoying 陳國英. "Xianyang diqu chutu Xi Zhou qingtongqi" 咸陽地區出土西周青銅器. *Kaogu yu wenwu* 考古與文物 1981.1: 8–11.

Cao Guicen 曹貴岑. "Henan Xichuan Heshangling Xujialing Chu mu fajueji" 河南淅川何尚嶺許家嶺楚墓發掘記. *Wenwu tiandi* 文物天地 1992.6: 10–12.

Cao Jinyan 曹錦炎. "Zhejiang chutu Shang Zhou qingtongqi chulun" 浙江出土商周青銅器初論. *Dongnan wenhua* 東南文化 1989.6: 104–12.

Cao Mingtan 曹明檀 and Shang Zhiru 尚志儒. "Shaanxi Fengxiang chutu de Xi Zhou qing-tongqi" 陝西鳳翔出土的西周青銅器. *Kaogu yu wenwu* 考古與文物 1984.1: 53–65.

Cao Wanru 曹婉如 et al., eds. *Zhongguo gudai ditu ji* 中國古代地圖集. Beijing: Wenwu, 1990.

Cao Wei 曹瑋. "Zhouyuan Xi Zhou tongqi fenqi" 周原西周銅器分期. *Kaoguxue yanjiu* 考古學研究 2 (1994): 144–65.

Cavalli-Sforza, L. Luca, Paolo Menozzi, and Alberto Piazza. *The History and Geography of Human Genes*. Princeton, N.J.: Princeton University Press, 1994.

Chan, Wing-tsit, trans. *The Way of Lao Tzu*. Indianapolis, Ind.: Bobbs-Merrill, 1963.

Chang Cheng-lang. "A Brief Discussion of Fu Tzu." In *Studies of Shang Archaeology: Selected Papers from the International Conference on Shang Civilization*, ed. K. C. Chang. New Haven, Conn.: Yale University Press, 1986, pp. 103–19.

Chang Gan 長甘. "'Houma meng shu' congkao" 侯馬盟書叢考. *Wenwu* 文物 1975.5: 12–19.

Chang, K. C. *The Archaeology of Ancient China*, 1st ed.. New Haven, Conn.: Yale University Press, 1963; 3rd ed. 1977; 4th ed. 1986.

Chang, K. C. *Art, Myth, and Ritual: The Path to Political Authority in Ancient China*. Cambridge, Mass.: Harvard University Press, 1983.

Chang, K. C. "A Classification of Shang and Chou Myths." In K. C. Chang, *Early Chinese Civilization: Anthropological Perspectives*. Cambridge, Mass.: Harvard University Press, 1976, pp. 149–73. Originally published in *Bulletin of the Institute of Ethnology* (Academia Sinica) 14 (1962): 47–94.

Chang, Kwang-chih. *Early Chinese Civilization: Anthropological Perspectives*. Cambridge, Mass.: Harvard University Press, 1976.

Chang, K. C. "An Essay on Cong." *Orientations* 20, 6 (1989): 37–43.

Chang, K.C. "Sandai Archaeology and the Formation of States in Ancient China: Processual Aspects of the Origin of Chinese Civilization." In *The Origins of Chinese Civilization*, ed. David N. Keightley. Berkeley: University of California Press, 1984, pp. 495–521.

Chang, Kwang-chih. "Shamanism in Human History." *Bulletin of the Department of Archaeology and Anthropology* 49 (1993): 1–6.

Chang, K. C. *Shang Civilization*. New Haven, Conn.: Yale University Press, 1980.

Chang, K. C. "Shang Shamans." In *The Power of Culture: Studies in Chinese Cultural History*, ed. Willard J. Peterson. Hong Kong: Chinese University Press, 1994, pp. 10–36.

Chang, K. C. "Some Dualistic Phenomena in Shang Society." In K. C. Chang, *Early Chinese Civilization: Anthropological Perspectives*. Cambridge, Mass.: Harvard University Press, 1976, pp. 93–114. Originally published in *JAS* 24 (1964): 45–61.

Chang, K. C., ed. *Studies in Shang Archaeology*. New Haven, Conn.: Yale University Press, 1986.

Chang, K. C., et al., *Fengpitou, Tapenkeng, and the Prehistory of Taiwan*. Yale University Publications in Anthropology 73, New Haven, Conn.: Yale University Press, 1969.

Chang, T. T. "Domestication and Spread of the Cultivated Rices." In *Foraging and Farming: The Evolution of Plant Exploitation*, ed. D. R. Harris and G. C. Hillman. London: Unwin Hyman, 1989, pp. 408–17.

Chang, Te-tzu. "The Origins and Early Cultures of the Cereal Grains and Food Legumes." In *The Origins of Chinese Civilization*, ed. David N. Keightley. Berkeley: University of California Press, 1983, pp. 65–94.

Chang, T. T. "Rice: *Oryza sativa* and *Oryza glaberrima* (Gramineae-Oryzeae)." In *Evolution of Crop Plants*, ed. J. Smartt and N. W. Simmonds. London: Longman Scientific & Technical, 1995, pp. 147–55.

Chang Yuzhi 常玉芝. *Shangdai zhouji zhidu* 商代周祭制度. N.p.: Zhongguo Shehui kexueyuan, 1987.

Changsha fajue baogao 長沙發掘報告. Beijing: Kexue, 1957.

Chao Fulin 晁福林. "Guanyu Yinxu buci zong de shi he zong de tantao" 關于殷墟卜辭中的示和宗的探討. *Shehui kexue zhanxian* 社會科學戰線 1989.3: 158–66.

Chao, Lin. *The Socio-Political Systems of the Shang Dynasty.* Nankang, Taipei: Institute of the Three Principles of the People, 1982. Academia Sinica, Monograph no. 3.

Chavannes, E. "Les livres chinois avant l'invention du papier." *JA* series 10, 5 (1905): 5–75.

Chavannes, Édouard, trans. *Les mémoires historiques de Se-Ma Ts'ien.* Vols. 1–5. Paris: Ernest Leroux, 1895–1905; rpt., with vol. 6 (ed. Paul Demiéville). Paris: Adrien Maisonneuve, 1969.

Chavannes, Édouard. *Le Tai chan: Essai de monographie d'un culte chinois.* Paris: Annales du Musée Guimet, 1910.

Chavannes, Édouard. "Le traité sur les sacrifices Fong et Chan de Se ma Ts'ien traduit en Français par Édouard Chavannes." *Journal of the Peking Oriental Society* (Peking: Typographie du Pei-T'ang, 1890), in-8: xxxi–95.

Che Guangjin 車廣錦. "Fajue Yancheng yizhi de zhuyao shouhuo" 發掘淹城遺址的主要收獲. In *Nanjing Bowuyuan jianyuan 60 zhounian jinian wenji* 南京博物院建院60週年紀念文集. Nanjing: n.p., 1992, pp. 178–80.

Chen Banghuai 陳邦懷. "Zhanguo Xingqi yuming kaoshi" 戰國行氣玉銘考釋. *Guwenzi yanjiu* 古文字研究 7 (1982): 187–93.

Chen De'an 陳德安. *Shang dai Shu ren mibao: Sichuan Guanghan Sanxingdui yiji (Zhongguo kaogu wenwu zhi mei 3)* 商代蜀人秘寶：四川廣漢三星堆遺蹟（中國考古文物之美3）. Beijing: Wenwu, 1994.

Chen Hanping 陳漢平. *Xi Zhou ceming zhidu yanjiu* 西周冊命制度研究. Shanghai: Xuelin, 1986.

Chen Kwang-tzuu and Frederick T. Hiebert. "The Late Prehistory of Xinjiang in Relation to Its Neighbors." *Journal of World Prehistory* 9, 2 (1995): 243–300.

Chen Mengjia 陳夢家. "Shangdai de shenhua yu wushu" 商代的神話與巫術. *Yanjing xuebao* 燕京學報 20 (1936): 485–576.

Chen Mengjia 陳夢家. "Shouxian Cai Hou mu tongqi" 壽縣蔡侯墓銅器. *Kaogu xuebao* 考古學報 1956.2: 95–123.

Chen Mengjia 陳夢家. "Xi Zhou tongqi duandai, 1–6" 西周銅器斷代. *Kaogu xuebao* 考古學報 1955.9: 137–75; 1955.10: 69–142; 1956.1: 65–114; 1956.2: 85–94; 1956.3: 105–27; 1956.4: 85–122.

Chen Mengjia 陳夢家. *Yinxu buci zongshu* 殷虛卜辭綜述. Beijing: Kexue, 1956.

Chen Mengjia 陳夢家. *Yin Zhou qingtongqi fenlei tulu* 殷周青銅器分類圖錄 (*In Shû seidôki bunrui zuroku: A Corpus of Chinese Bronzes in American Collections*), edited from the original Chinese edition (1962) by Matsumaru Michio 松丸道雄. 2 vols. Tokyo: Kyûko, 1977.

Chen Pan 陳槃. *"Chunqiu dashibiao: Lieguo juexing ji cunmiebiao" zhuanyi.* 春秋大事表：列國爵姓及存滅表譔異. Zhongyang Yanjiuyuan Lishi Yuyan Yanjiusuo zhuankan 中央研究院歷史語言研究所專刊52. Originally published 1969; Taipei: Academia Sinica, 1988.

Chen Pan 陳槃. "Zhanguo Qin Han jian fangshi kaolun" 戰國秦漢間方士考論. *BIHP* 17 (1948): 7–57.

Chen Peifen 陳佩芬. "Ji Shanghai Bowuguan suocang Yue zu qingtongqi – Jianlun Yue zu qingtongqi de wenshi" 記上海博物館所藏越族青銅器—兼論越族青銅器的文飾. *Shanghai bowuguan jikan* 上海博物館集刊 4 (1987): 221–32.

Chen Ping 陳平. "Shilun Guanzhong Qin mu qingtong rongqi de fenqi wenti" 試論關中秦墓青銅容器的分期問題. *Kaogu yu wenwu* 考古與文物 1984.3: 58–73; 1984.4: 63–73.

Chen Qianwan 陳千萬. "Gucheng Xindian chutu de Chunqiu tongqi" 谷城新店出土的春秋銅器. *Jiang Han kaogu* 江漢考古 1986.3: 13–16.

Chen Qianwan 陳千萬. "Zhong Zi Bin fou chutan" 中子賓缶初探. *Jiang Han kaogu* 江漢考古 1985.3: 56–61.

Chen Qiyou 陳奇猷. *Han Feizi jishi* 韓非子集釋. Shanghai: Renmin, 1974.

Chen Qiyou 陳奇猷. *Lü shi chunqiu jiaoshi* 呂氏春秋校釋. 2 vols. Shanghai: Xuelin, 1984; rpt., Taipei: Huazheng, 1988.

Chen Quanfang 陳全方. "Zao Zhou ducheng Qi yi chutan" 早周都城歧邑初探. *Wenwu* 文物 1979.10: 44–9.

Chen Quanfang 陳全方. *Zhouyuan yu Zhou wenhua* 周原與周文化. Shanghai: Shanghai Renmin, 1988.

Chen Shou 陳壽. "Tai Bao gui de fuchu he Tai Bao zhuqi" 太保簋的復出和太保諸器. *Kaogu yu wenwu* 考古與文物 1980.4: 23–30.

Chen Shuxiang 陳樹祥. "Shixi Panlongcheng de xingshuai" 試析盤龍城的興衰. *Hubei sheng Kaogu xuehui lunwen xuanji* 湖北省考古學會論文選集 2 (1991): 54–9.

Chen Songchang 陳松長 and Liao Mingchun 廖名春. "Boshu *Ersanzi wen, Yi zhi yi, Yao shiwen*" 帛書二三子問易之義要釋文. *Daojia wenhua yanjiu* 道家文化研究 3 (1993): 424–35.

Chen Xiandan 陳顯丹. "Guanghan Sanxingdui qingtongqi yanjiu" 廣漢三星堆青銅器研究. *Sichuan wenwu* 四川文物 1990.6: 22–30.

Chen Xu 陳旭. "Zhengzhou Xiaoshuangqiao Shang dai yizhi de niandai he xingzhi" 鄭州小雙橋商代遺址的年代和性質. *Zhongyuan wenwu* 中原文物 1995.1: 1–8.

Chen Yaojun 陳躍鈞 and Ruan Wenqing 阮文清. "Zhenmushou lüekao" 鎮墓獸略考. *Jiang Han kaogu* 江漢考古 1983.3: 63–67.

Chen Yaojun 陳躍鈞 and Zhang Xuqiu 張緒球. "Jiangling Mazhuan yihaomu chutu de Zhangguo sizhipin" 江陵馬磚一號墓出土的戰國絲織品. *Wenwu* 文物 1982.10: 9–11.

Chen Yuanfu 陳元甫. "Jiangzhe diqu shishi tudun yicun xingzhi xinzheng" 江浙地區石室土墩遺存性質新證. *Dongnan wenhua* 東南文化 1988.1: 20–3.

Chen Yuanfu 陳元甫. "Tudunmu yu Wu Yue wenhua" 土墩墓與吳越文化. *Dongnan wenhua* 東南文化 1992.6: 11–21.

Chen Zhenyu 陳振裕. "Chu guo chema chuxingtu chulun" 楚國車馬出行圖初論. *Jiang Han kaogu* 江漢考古 1989.4: 54–63.

Chen Zhenyu 陳振裕. "Shilun Hubei Zhanguo Qin Han qiqi de niandai fenqi" 試論湖北戰國秦漢漆器的年代分期. *Jiang Han kaogu* 江漢考古 1980.2: 37–50.

Chen Zhenyu 陳振裕. "Shilun Zhanguo shiqi Chuguo de qiqi shougongye" 試論戰國時期楚國的漆器手工業. *Kaogu yu wenwu* 考古與文物 1986.4: 77–85.

Chen Zhenyu 陳振裕 and Yang Quanxi 楊權喜. "Xiangyang Shanwan wuzuo Chu mu de niandai ji qi xiangguan wenti" 襄陽山灣五座楚墓的年代及其相關問題. *Jiang Han kaogu* 江漢考古 1983.1: 19–24, 71.

Chen Zhida 陳志達. "Yinxu wuqi gaishu" 殷墟武器概述. In *Qingzhu Su Bingqi kaogu wushiwu nian lunwenji* 慶祝蘇秉琦考古五十五年論文集, Beijing: Wenwu, 1989, pp. 326–37.

Cheng, Te-k'un. *Archaeology in China. Vol. 1: Prehistoric China*. Cambridge: Heffer, 1959.

Cheng, Te-k'un. *Archaeology in China. Vol. 2: Shang China*. Cambridge: Heffer, 1960.

Cheng Wu 程武. "Han chu Huang Lao sixiang he fajia luxian: Du Changsha Mawangdui san hao Han mu chutu boshu zhaji" 漢初黃老思想和法家路線: 讀長沙馬王堆三號漢墓出土帛書札記. *Wenwu* 文物 1974.10: 43–7, 64.

Chernykh, E. N. *Ancient Metallurgy in the USSR.* Trans. Sarah Wright. Cambridge University Press, 1992.

Childe, V. Gordon. *Man Makes Himself.* 1936; New York: New American Library Edition, 1951.

Childs-Johnson, Elizabeth. "The *Jue* and Its Ceremonial Use in the Ancestor Cult of China." *Artibus Asiae* 48, 3–4 (1987): 171–96.

Chinese Academy of Architecture, ed. *Ancient Chinese Architecture.* Beijing: China Building Industry Press, 1982.

The Chinese Bronzes of Yunnan. Foreword by Jessica Rawson. London: Sidgwick & Jackson Limited, in association with Beijing: Cultural Relics Publishing House, 1983.

Chu Ko-chen (*see too* Zhu Kezhen 竺可楨). "A Preliminary Study on the Climatic Fluctuations During the Last 5,000 Years in China." *Cycles* 25 (1974): 243–61.

Chûgoku sengoku jidai no yû: Chûzan ôgoku bunbutsuten 中國戰國時代の雄：中山王國文物展. Tokyo: Tokyo National Museum, 1981.

Chûka Jimmin Kyôwakoku kodai seidôki ten 中華人民共和國古代青銅器展. Tokyo: Nihon Keizai Shimbunsha, 1976.

Chunhua xian wenwuzhi 淳化縣文物誌. Shaanxi sheng wenwuzhi bianzuan weiyuanhui et al., eds. Xi'an: Shaanxi Renmin jiaoyu, 1991.

Coblin, W. South. *A Sinologist's Handlist of Sino-Tibetan Lexical Comparisons.* Monumenta Serica monograph series 18. Nettetal: Steyler, 1986.

Conroy, G. C. *Primate Evolution.* New York: Norton, 1990.

Cook, E. T., and A. Wedderburn, eds. *The Works of John Ruskin.* 39 vols. London, 1904.

Creel, H. G. "The Beginning of Bureaucracy in China: The Origin of the *Hsien.*" *JAS* 23 (1964): 155–84.

Creel, H. G. "The Role of the Horse in Chinese History." *American Historical Review* 70, 3 (1965): 647–72.

Creel, Herrlee Glessner. *The Birth of China: A Study of the Formative Period of Chinese Civilization.* New York: Reynal & Hitchcock, 1937; 6th printing, New York: Ungar, 1967.

Creel, Herrlee G. *The Origins of Statecraft in China: The Western Chou Empire.* Chicago: University of Chicago Press, 1970.

Creel, Herrlee G. *Shen Pu-hai: A Chinese Political Philosopher of the Fourth Century* B.C. Chicago: University of Chicago Press, 1974.

Creel, Herrlee G. *What Is Taoism?* Chicago: University of Chicago Press, 1970.

Crump, J. I. *Chan-Kuo Ts'e.* Oxford: Clarendon Press, 1970.

Cui Lequan 崔樂泉. "Shandong diqu Dong Zhou kaoguxue wenhua de xulie" 山東地區東周考古學文化的序列. *Hua Xia kaogu* 華夏考古 1992.4: 72–97.

Cui Renyi 崔仁義. "Jingmen Baoshan erhaomu chutu de yingbin chuxingtu chulun" 荊門包山二號墓出土的迎賓出行圖初論. *Jiang Han kaogu* 江漢考古 1988.2: 72–9.

Cui Xuan 崔璇. "Nei Menggu xian Qin shiqi xumu yicun shulun" 內蒙古先秦時期畜牧遺存述論. *Nei Menggu shehui kexue* 內蒙古社會科學 1988.1: 69–74.

Cullen, Christopher. "Some Further Points on the *Shih.*" *EC* 6 (1980–1): 31–46.

Dai Yingxin 戴應新. "Shaanbei he Jin xibei Huang he liang'an chutu de Yin Shang tongqi ji youguan wenti de tansuo" 陝北和晉西北黃河兩岸出土的殷商銅器及有關問題的探索. In

Kaoguxue yanjiu: Jinian Shaanxi sheng kaogu yanjiusuo chengli sanshi Zhounian 考古學研究：記念陝西省考古研究所成立三十週年, ed. Shi Xingbang 石興邦 et al. Xi'an: San Qin, 1993, pp. 219–35.

Dai Yingxin 戴應新 and Sun Jiaxiang 孫嘉祥. "Shaanxi Shenmu xian chutu Xiongnu wenwu" 陝西神木縣出土匈奴文物. *Wenwu* 文物 1983.12: 23–30.

Dai Zhen 戴震. *Kaogongji tu* 考工記圖. 1746; rpt. Shanghai: Shangwu, 1955.

Dangyang Zhaojiahu Chu mu. 當陽趙家湖楚墓. Hubei sheng Yichang diqu bowuguan and Beijing daxue Kaoguxi eds. Beijing: Wenwu, 1992.

Dawenkou 大汶口. Beijing: Wenwu, 1974.

de Mailla, Joseph. *Histoire générale de la Chine ou annales de cet empire.* Paris: 1777–83.

Debaine-Francfort, Corinne. "Archéologie du Xinjiang des origines aux Han; IIème partie." *Paléorient* 15, 1 (1989): 183–213.

Debaine-Francfort, Corinne. "Recherches historiques préliminaires sur les Saka du Xinjiang ancien." *Arts Asiatiques* 42 (1987), 31–44.

Deng Cong 鄧聰, ed. *Nan Zhongguo ji linjin diqu gu wenhua yanjiu* 南中國及鄰近地區古文化研究. Hong Kong: Xianggang Zhongwen daxue, 1994.

Derevianko, A. P. *Rannyi zheleznyi vek Priamur'ia.* Novosibirsk: Nauka, 1973.

Di Cosmo, Nicola. "Ancient Inner Asian Nomads: Their Economic Basis and Its Significance in Chinese History." *JAS* 53, 4 (1994): 1092–126.

Dien, Albert, Jeffrey Riegel, and Nancy Price, eds. *Chinese Archaeological Abstracts. 3: Eastern Zhou to Han. Monumenta Archaeologica* 10. Los Angeles: University of California, Institute of Archaeology, 1985.

Ding Yi 丁乙. "Zhouyuan jianzhu yicun he tongqi jiaocang" 周原建築遺存和銅器窖藏. *Kaogu* 考古 1982.4: 398–401, 424.

Ding Shan 丁山. *Shang Zhou shiliao kaozheng* 商周史料考證. Hong Kong: Longmen Lianhe, 1960.

Dirlik, Arif. *Revolution and History: Origins of Marxist Historiography in China, 1919–1937.* Berkeley: University of California Press, 1978.

Dobson, W. A. C. H. *Early Archaic Chinese: A Descriptive Grammar.* Toronto: University of Toronto Press, 1962.

Dobson, W. A. C. H. "Linguistic Evidence and the Dating of the Book of Songs." *TP* 51 (1964): 322–34.

Dolukhanov, Pavel Markovich, et al. "Radiocarbon Dates of the Institute of Archaeology, 2." *Radiocarbon* 12 (1970): 130–55.

Dong Chuping 董楚平. *Wu Yue wenhua xintan* 吳越文化新探. Hangzhou: Zhejiang Renmin, 1988.

Dong Yue 董說. *Qi guo kao* 七國考. Punctuated edition. Beijing: Zhonghua, 1956.

Dong Zuobin 董作賓. *Yinli pu* 殷曆譜. 2 vols. Nanqi, Sichuan: Academia Sinica, 1945.

Dong Zuobin 董作賓. *Zhongguo nianli zongpu* 中國年曆總譜. Hong Kong: Hong Kong University Press, 1960.

Dongbei kaogu yu lishi 1982.1: 136–40. "Da'an Hanshu yizhi fajue de zhuyao shouhuo" 大安漢書遺址發掘的主要收獲.

Dongnan wenhua 東南文化 1988.3–4: 13–50. "Jiangsu Dantu Beishanding Chunqiu mu fajue baogao" 江蘇丹徒北山頂春秋墓發掘報告.

Downer, Gordon B. "Derivation by Tone Change in Classical Chinese." *BSOAS* 22 (1959): 258–90.

Downs, J. F. "Origin and Spread of Riding in the Near East and Central Asia." *American Anthropologist* 63 (1961): 1193–6.

Drews, Robert. *The Coming of the Greeks.* Princeton, N.J.: Princeton University Press, 1988.

Du Naisong 杜迺松. "Cong lieding zhidu kan keji fuli de fandongxing" 從列鼎制度看克己復禮的反動性. *Kaogu* 考古 1976.1: 17–21.

Du Naisong 杜迺松. "Tan Jiangsu diqu Shang Zhou qingtongqi de fengge yu tezheng" 談江蘇地區商周青銅器的風格與特征. *Kaogu* 考古 1987.2: 169–74.

Du Xingzhi 都興智. "Shi lun Hanshu wenhua he Baijinbao wenhua" 試論漢書文化和白金寶文化. *Beifang wenwu* 北方文物 1986.4: 21–5.

Du Zhengsheng 杜正勝. *Bian hu qi min: Chuantong zhengzhi shehui jiegou zhi xingcheng* 編戶齊民：傳統政治社會結構之形成. Taipei: Lianjing, 1991.

Du Zhengsheng 杜正勝. *Zhou dai chengbang* 周代城邦. Taipei: Lianjing, 1979.

Duan Shaojia 段紹嘉. "Shaanxi Lantian xian chutu Er Shu deng yiqi jianjie" 陝西藍田縣出土弔叔等彝器簡介. *Wenwu* 文物 1960.2: 9–10.

Duan Qingbo 段清波 and Zhou Kunshu 周昆叔. "Chang'an fujin hedao bianqian yu wenhua fenbu" 長安附近河道變遷與文化分布. In *Huanjing kaogu yanjiu* 環境考古研究, ed. Zhou Kunshu 周昆叔 and Gong Qiming 龔啟明 Beijing: Kexue, 1991, pp. 47–55.

Duan Yucai 段玉裁. *Duan shi shuo wen jie zi zhu* 段氏説文解字注. Shanghai: Sao Yeshan fang, 1928.

Duan Yucai 段玉裁 *Kundoku Setsumon Kaiji chû* 訓讀説文解字注. Ed. and trans. Ozaki Yûjirô 尾崎雄二郎. Tokyo: Tôkai daigaku, 1986.

DuBois, Eugene. "On Pithecanthropus Erectus: A Transitional Form Between Man and the Apes." *Scientific Transactions of the Royal Dublin Society* 6 (1896): 1–18.

DuBois, Eugene. *Pithecanthropus Erectus: Eine Menschenahnliche Ubergangsform aus Java* (Batavia); rpt. in *Jaarboek van het Mijnwezen* 24 (1894): 5–77.

Dubs, H. H. "The Date of the Shang Period." *TP* 40 (1951): 322–35.

Dubs, Homer H. *The History of the Former Han Dynasty.* 3 vols. Baltimore: Waverly, 1938–55.

Dubs, Homer H. *The Works of Hsüntze: Translated from the Chinese with Notes.* London: Arthur Probsthain, 1928.

Duyvendak, J. J. L., trans. *The Book of Lord Shang: A Classic of the Chinese School of Law.* London: Arthur Probsthain, 1928; rpt. Chicago: University of Chicago Press, 1963.

Duyvendak, J. J. L., trans. *Tao Te Ching: The Book of the Way and Its Virtue.* London: John Murray, 1954.

E Bing 鄂兵. "Hubei Suixian faxian Zeng guo tongqi" 湖北隨縣發現曾國銅器. *Wenwu* 文物. 1973.5: 21–3.

Eberhard, Wolfram. *A History of China: From the Earliest Times to the Present Day.* London: Routledge & Kegan Paul, 1950.

Eberhard, Wolfram. *Lokalkulturen in alten China.* Vol. 1, Leiden: Brill, 1942. Vol. 2, Peking: The Catholic University of Peking, 1942. English translation of vol. 2: *The Local Cultures of South and East China,* trans. A. Eberhard. Leiden: Brill, 1968.

Elman, Benjamin. *From Philosophy to Philology.* Harvard East Asian Monographs, no. 110. Cambridge, Mass.: Council on East Asian Studies, Harvard University, 1984.

Eno, Robert. "Was There a High God *Ti* in Shang Religion?" *EC* 15 (1990): 1–26.

Erdy, Miklōs. "Hun and Xiong-nu Type Caldron Finds throughout Eurasia." *Eurasian Studies Yearbook* 67 (1995): 5–94.

Erdy, Miklōs. "The Xiongnu Type Cauldrons Throughout Central Eurasia and Their Occurrence on Petroglyphs." In *The International Conference on Archaeological Cultures of the Northern Chinese Ancient Nations,* ed. Nei Menggu Wenwu kaogu yanjiusuo, Huhhot, August 11–18, 1992.

Erlitou taoqi jicui 二里頭陶器集粹. Zhongguo Shehui kexueyuan Kaogu yanjiusuo, ed. Beijing: Zhongguo Shehui kexue, 1995.

Fairbank, John King. *The Chinese World Order.* Cambridge, Mass.: Harvard University Press, 1968.

Falkenhausen, Lothar von. "Ahnenkult und Grabkult im Staat Qin: Der religiöse Hintergrund der Terrakotta-Armee." In *Jenseits der Großen Mauer: Der Erste Kaiser von China und seine Terrakotta-Armee,* ed. Lothar Ledderose and Adele Schlombs. München: Bertelsmann, 1990, pp. 35–48.

Falkenhausen, Lothar von. "Chu Ritual Music." In *New Perspectives on Chu Culture During the Eastern Zhou Period,* ed. Thomas Lawton. Washington, D.C.: Arthur M. Sackler Gallery, 1991, pp. 47–106.

Falkenhausen, Lothar von. "Issues in Western Zhou Studies: A Review Article." *EC* 18 (1993): 139–226.

Falkenhausen, Lothar von. "The Moutuo Bronzes: New Perspectives on the Late Bronze Age in Sichuan." *Arts Asiatiques* 51 (1996): 29–59.

Falkenhausen, Lothar von. "On the Historiographical Orientation of Chinese Archaeology." *Antiquity* 67 (1993): 839–49.

Falkenhausen, Lothar von. "Reflections on the Political Role of Spirit Mediums in Early China: The *Wu Officials in the Zhou li.*" *EC* 20 (1995): 279–300.

Falkenhausen, Lothar von. "The Regionalist Paradigm in Chinese Archaeology." In *Nationalism, Politics, and the Practice of Archaeology,* ed. P. Kohl and C. Fawcett. Cambridge University Press, 1995, pp. 198–217.

Falkenhausen, Lothar von. "Serials on Chinese Archaeology Published in the People's Republic of China: A Bibliographical Survey," *EC* 17 (1992): 247–95.

Falkenhausen, Lothar von. "Shangma: Demography and Social Differentiation in a Late Bronze Age Community in North China." Forthcoming.

Falkenhausen, Lothar von. "Shikin no onsei: Tô Shû jidai no shun taku dô nado ni tsuite" 四金之音聲：東周時代の錞鐸鐃などについて. *Sen'oku hakkokan kiyô* 泉屋博古館紀要 6 (1989): 3–26.

Falkenhausen, Lothar von. "Sources of Taoism: Reflections on Archaeological Indicators of Religious Change in Eastern Zhou China." *Taoist Resources* 5, 2 (1994): 1–12.

Falkenhausen, Lothar von. *Suspended Music: Chime-Bells in the Culture of Bronze Age China.* Berkeley: University of California Press, 1993.

Fan Weiyue 樊維岳. "Lantian chutu yizu Xi Zhou zaoqi tongqi taoqi" 藍田出土一組西周早期銅器陶器. *Kaogu yu wenwu* 考古與文物 1987.5: 12–13.

Fan Wenlan 范文瀾. *Zhongguo tongshi* 中國通史. Beijing: Renmin, 1978.

Fan Yuzhou 范毓周. "Jiaguwen yueshi jishi keci kaobian" 甲骨文月食記事刻辭考辯. *Jiaguwen yu Yin Shang shi* 甲骨文與殷商史 2 (1986): 310–37.

Fan Yuzhou 范毓周. "Yin dai Wuding shiqi de zhanzheng" 殷代武丁時期的戰爭. *Jiaguwen yu Yin Shang shi* "甲骨文與殷商史 3 (1991): 175–239.

Fang Guoxiang 方國祥. "Anhui Congyang chutu yijian qingtong fangyi" 安徽樅陽出土一件青銅方彝. *Wenwu* 文物 1991.6: 94.

Fang Shanzhu 方善柱. "Xi Zhou niandai xue shang de jige wenti" 西周年代學上的幾個問題. *Dalu zazhi* 大陸雜誌 51, 1 (1975): 15–23.

Feng Hanji 馮漢驥. "Sichuan Peng xian chutu de tongqi" 四川彭縣出土的銅器. *Wenwu* 文物 1980.12: 38–47.

Feng Shi 馮時. "Henan Puyang Xishuipo 46 hao mu de tianwenxue yanjiu" 河南濮陽西水坡 46號墓的天文學研究. *Wenwu* 文物 1990.3: 52–60, 69.

Feng Shi 馮時 "Yinli suishou yanjiu" 殷曆歲首研究. *Kaogu xuebao* 考古學報 1990.1: 19–42.

Feng Xiahong and Samuel Epstein. "Climatic Implications of an 8000-Year Hydrogen Isotope Time Series from Bristlecone Pine Trees." *Science* 265 (19 August 1994), pp. 1079–81.

Fengxi fajue baogao 灃西發掘報告. Beijing: Wenwu, 1962.

Ferguson, David K. "The Impact of Late Cenozoic Environmental Changes in East Asia on the Distribution of Terrestrial Plants and Animals." In *Evolving Landscapes and Evolving Biotas of East Asia Since the Mid-Tertiary*, ed. Nina G. Jablowski and So Chak-lam. Hong Kong: Centre of Asian Studies, The University of Hong Kong, 1993, pp. 145–96.

Feuerwerker, Albert, ed. *History in Communist China*. Cambridge, Mass.: M.I.T. Press, 1968.

Field, Stephen. "Cosmos, Cosmograph, and the Inquiring Poet: New Answers to the 'Heaven Questions.'" *EC* 17 (1992): 83–110.

Fingarette, Herbert. *Confucius: The Secular as Sacred*. New York: Harper & Row, 1972.

Fingarette, Herbert. "Following the 'One Thread' in the *Analects*." *Journal of the American Academy of Religion*, thematic issue, 47, 3S, *Studies in Classical Chinese Thought*, Sept. 1979: 373–405.

Finley, M. I. "Schliemann's Troy: One Hundred Years After." *Proceedings of the British Academy* 60 (1974): 393–412.

Fleagle, J. G. *Primate Adaptation and Evolution*. San Diego: Academic, 1988.

Fogg, Wayne H. "Swidden Cultivation of Foxtail Millet by Taiwan Aborigines: A Cultural Analogue of the Domestication of *Setaria italica* in China." In *The Origins of Chinese Civilization*, ed. David N. Keightley. Berkeley: University of California Press, 1983, pp. 95–115.

Fong, Mary H. "The Origin of Chinese Pictorial Representation of the Human Figure." *Artibus Asiae* 51 (1989): 5–38.

Fong, Wen., ed. *The Great Bronze Age of China: An Exhibition from the People's Republic of China*. New York: Metropolitan Museum of Art, 1980.

Fortes, Meyer. "Some Reflections on Ancestor Worship in Africa." In *African Systems of Thought*, ed. M. Fortes and G. Dieterlen. London: Oxford University Press, 1965, pp. 122–42.

Franklin, Ursula Martius. "The Beginnings of Metallurgy in China: A Comparative Approach." In *The Great Bronze Age of China: A Symposium*, ed. George Kuwayama. Los Angeles: Los Angeles County Museum of Art; distributed by University of Washington Press, 1983, pp. 100–123.

Franklin, Ursula Martius. "On Bronze and Other Metals in Early China." In *The Origins of Chinese Civilization*, ed. David N. Keightley. Berkeley: University of California Press, 1983, pp. 279–96.

Fraser, Everard D. H., and James H. S. Lockhart. *Index to the Tso Chuan*. London: Oxford University Press, 1930.

Fu Juyou 傅舉有 and Chen Songchang 陳松長. *Mawangdui Han mu wenwu* 馬王堆漢墓文物. Changsha: Hunan, 1992.

Fu Sinian 傅斯年. "Yi Xia dong xi shuo" 夷夏東西説. In *Qingzhu Cai Yuanpei xiansheng liushiwu sui lunwenji* 慶祝蔡元培先生六十五歲論文集. Nanjing: Institute of History and Philology, Academia Sinica, 1933, pp. 1093–134.

Fu Sinian 傅斯年, Li Ji 李濟, et al. *Chengziyai* 城子崖, Nanjing: Institute of History and Philology, Academia Sinica, 1934.

Fu Xinian 傅熹年. "Shaanxi Fufeng Shaochencun Xi Zhou jianzhu yizhi chutan" 陝西扶風召陳村西周建築遺址初探. *Wenwu* 文物 1981.3: 34–45.

Fu Xinian 傅熹年. "Zhanguo Zhongshanwang Cuo mu chutu de Zhaoyu tu ji qi lingyuan guizhi de yanjiu" 戰國中山王響墓出土的兆域圖及其陵園規制的研究. *Kaogu xuebao* 考古學報 1980.1: 97–119.

Fufeng Qijiacun qingtongqi qun 扶風齊家村青銅器群. Shaanxi sheng bowuguan and Shaanxi sheng wenwu guanli weiyuanhui ed. Beijing: Wenwu, 1963.

Fujieda Akira 藤枝晃. *Moji no bunka shi* 文字の文化史. Tokyo: Iwanami, 1971; rpt. 1991.

Fung, Yulan. Derk Bodde, trans. *A History of Chinese Philosophy. Vol. 1: The Period of the Philosophers.* Princeton, N.J.: Princeton University Press, 1952.

Fung, Yulan. Derk Bodde, trans. *A History of Chinese Philosophy. Vol. 2: The Period of Classical Learning.* Princeton, N.J.: Princeton University Press, 1953.

Gai Shanlin 蓋山林. "Cong Nei Meng Yinshan yanhua kan gudai beifang youmu minzu de lishi gongxian" 從內蒙陰山山岩畫看古代北方游牧民族的歷史貢獻. In *Sichou zhi lu yanhua yishu* 絲綢之路岩畫藝術, ed. Zhou Jinbao 周菁葆. Urumqi: Xinjiang Renmin, 1993.

Gai Shanlin 蓋山林. "Nei Menggu Yikezhaomeng Zhunge'er qi Sujigou chutu yipi tongqi" 內蒙古伊克昭盟準格爾旗速機溝出土一批銅器. *Wenwu* 文物 1965.2: 44–5. Rpt. as "Zhunge'er qi Sujigou chutu de tongqi" 準格爾旗速機溝出土的銅器. In *O'erduosi qingtong qi* 鄂爾多斯青銅器, ed. Tian Guangjin 田廣金 and Guo Suxin 郭素新. Beijing: Wenwu, 1986, pp. 372–4.

Gale, Esson M. *Discourses on Salt and Iron.* Leyden: Brill, 1931; rpt. Taipei: Ch'eng-wen, 1967.

Gao Chongwen 高崇文. "Shilun Jinnan diqu Dong Zhou tongqimu de fenqi yu niandai" 試論晉南地區東周銅器墓的分期與年代. *Wenbo* 文博 1992.4: 17–33.

Gao Ciruo 高次若 and Liu Mingke 劉明科. "Baoji Rujiazhuang xin faxian tongqi jiaocang" 寶雞茹家庄新發現銅器窖藏. *Kaogu yu wenwu* 考古與文物 1990.4: 11–16.

Gao Donglu 高東陸. "Lüelun Kayue wenhua" 略論卡約文化. In *Kaoguxue wenhua lunji* 考古學文化論集, ed. Su Bingqi 蘇秉琦. Beijing: Wenwu, 1993, vol. 3, pp. 153–65.

Gao Guangren 高廣仁. "Shilun Dawenkou wenhua de fenqi" 試論大汶口文化的分期. *Kaogu xuebao* 考古學報 1978.4: 399–419.

Gao Ming 高明. *Gu wenzi leibian* 古文字類編. Beijing: Zhonghua, 1982.

Gao Ming 高明. "Zhongyuan diqu Dong Zhou shidai qingtong liqi yanjiu" 中原地區東周時代青銅禮器研究. *Kaogu yu wenwu* 考古與文物 1981.2: 68–82, 1981.3: 84–103, 1981.4: 82–91.

Gao Quxun 高去尋. *Houjiazhuang (Henan Anyang Houjiazhuang Yin dai mudi) di er ben, 1001 hao da mu* 侯家莊（河南安陽侯家莊殷代墓地）第二本，1001號大墓. 2 vols. Taipei: Academia Sinica, 1962.

Gao Quxun 高去尋. "Huanghe xiayou de quzhizang wenti: *Di'erci tanjue Anyang Dasikongcun nandi jianbao* fulun zhi yi" 黃河下游的屈肢葬問題：第二次探掘安陽大司空村南地簡報附論之一. *Zhongguo kaogu xuebao* 中國考古學報 2 (1947): 121–66.

Gao Wei 高煒, Gao Tianlin 高天麟, and Zhang Daihai 張岱海. "Guanyu Taosi mudi jige wenti" 關於陶寺墓地幾個問題. *Kaogu* 考古 1983.6: 531–6.

Gao Xisheng 高西省. "Shaanxi Fufeng xian Yijiabao Shangdai yizhi de diaocha" 陝西扶風縣壹家堡商代遺址的調查. *Kaogu yu wenwu* 考古與文物 1989.5: 5–8.

Gao Yingqin 高應勤. "Zhaojiahu Chu mu xingzhi yu leibie zongshu" 趙家湖楚墓性質與類別綜述. *Jiang Han kaogu* 江漢考古 1991.1: 29–39, 56.

Gao Yingqin 高應勤 and Wang Guanghao 王光鎬. "Danyang Zhaojiahu Chu mu de fenlei yu fenqi" 丹陽趙家湖楚墓的分類與分期. *Zhongguo Kaoguxuehui di er ci (1980) nianhui lunwenji* 中國考古學會第二次(1980)年會論文集. Beijing: Wenwu, 1982, pp. 41–50.

Gao Zhixi 高至喜. "Hunan faxian de jijian Yuezu fengge de wenwu." 湖南發現的幾件越族風格的文物. *Wenwu* 文物 1980.12: 48–51.

Gao Zhixi 高至喜. "Hunan sheng bowuguan cang Xi Zhou qingtong yueqi" 湖南省博物館藏西周青銅樂器. *Hunan kaogu jikan* 湖南考古集刊 2 (1984): 29–34.

Gao Zhixi 高至喜. "Ji Changsha Changde chutu nuji de Zhanguo mu: Jian tan youguan nuji gongshi de jige wenti" 記長沙常德出土弩機的戰國墓：兼談有關弩機弓矢的幾個問題. *Wenwu* 文物 1964.6: 33–45.

Gao Zhixi. "Shang and Zhou Period Bronze Musical Instruments from South China." *BSOAS* 55 (1992): 262–71.

Gao Zhixi 高至喜. "Shang wenhua bu guo Changjiang bian" 商文化不過長江辨. *Qiusuo* 求索 1981.2: 107–12.

Gaocheng Taixi Shang dai yizhi 藁城臺西商代遺址. Hebei sheng Wenwu yanjiusuo, ed. Beijing: Wenwu, 1985.

Gaojiabao Ge guo mu 高家堡戈國墓. Shaanxi sheng Kaogu yanjiusuo. Xi'an: San Qin, 1995.

Ge Yinghui 葛英會. "Zhou ji buci zhong de zhixi xian bi ji xiangguan wenti" 周祭卜辭中的直系先妣及相關問題. *Beijing daxue xuebao: Zheshe ban* 北京大學學報：哲社版, 1990.1: 121–8.

Gettens, Rutherford John. *The Freer Chinese Bronzes. Vol. 2: Technical Studies.* Washington, D.C.: Smithsonian Institution, 1969.

Goepper, Roger, et al. *Das Alte China, Menschen und Götter im Reich der Mitte.* Essen: Kulturstiftung Ruhr, 1995.

Goffman, Erving. *The Presentation of Self in Everyday Life.* 1959; rpt. Harmondsworth: Allen Lane and Penguin Press, 1990.

Gombrich, E. H. *The Sense of Order: A Study in the Psychology of Decorative Art.* Ithaca, N.Y.: Cornell University Press, 1979.

Gong Hwang-cherng. "The System of Finals in Sino-Tibetan." In *The Ancestry of the Chinese Language,* ed. William S-Y. Wang. Journal of Chinese Linguistics monograph series, no. 8. Berkeley: *Journal of Chinese Linguistics,* 1995, pp. 41–92.

Gong Qiming 鞏啟明 and Jiang Jie 姜捷. "Shiwen Longshan wenhua de shehui xingzhi" 試問龍山文化的社會性質. In *Jinian Chengziyai yizhi fajue liushi zhounian guoji xueshu taolunhui wenji* 紀念城子崖遺址發掘六十週年國際學術討論會文集, ed. Zhang Xuehai 張學海. Jinan: Qi Lu, 1993, pp. 77–89.

Gong Qiming 鞏啟明 and Wang Shejiang 王社江. "Jiangzhai yizhi zaoqi shengtai huanjing de yanjiu" 姜寨遺址早期生態環境的研究. In *Huanjing kaogu yanjiu* 環境考古研究, eds. Zhou Kunshu 周昆叔 and Gong Qiming 鞏啟明. Beijing: Kexue, 1991, pp. 78–84.

Goodrich, C. S. "Riding Astride and the Saddle in Ancient China." *HJAS* 44, 2 (1984): 279–306.

Gosei Tadako 五井直弘. "Shunjû jidai no Shin no daifu Ki shi Yôzetsu shi no ôzato ni tsuite" 春秋時代の晉の大夫祇氏羊舌氏の邑について. *Chûgoku kodaishi kenkyû* 中國古代史研究. Tokyo: Chûgoku kodaishi kenkyûkai, 1968.

Graham, Angus C. "The Background of the Mencian Theory of Human Nature." *Tsing-hua Hsueh-pao,* n.s., 6, 1–2 (1967): 215–71.

Graham, Angus C., trans. *Chuang-tzu: The Seven Inner Chapters and Other Writings from the Book Chuang-tzu.* London: Allen & Unwin, 1981.

Graham, A. C. *Disputers of the Tao: Philosophical Argument in Ancient China.* La Salle, Ill.: Open Court, 1989.

Graham, A. C. *Later Mohist Logic, Ethics, and Science.* Hong Kong: Chinese University; and London: University of London, School of Oriental and African Studies, 1978.

Graham, Angus C. "The Logic of the Mohist *Hsiao-ch'u.*" *TP* 51 (1964): 1–54.

Graham, A. C. *Yin–Yang and the Nature of Correlative Thinking.* Singapore: Institute of East Asian Philosophies, 1986.

Granet, Marcel. *La pensée chinoise.* 1934; rpt. Paris: Albin Michel, 1968.

Granet, Marcel. "Remarques sur le Taoisme ancien." *AM* 2 (1925): 146–51.

Grenville L. Winthrop: Retrospective for a Collector. Cambridge, Mass.: Fogg Museum of Art, 1969.

Gryaznov M. P. *The Ancient Civilization of Southern Siberia.* New York: Cowles, 1969.

Grjaznov, Michail P. *Der Großkurgan von Aržan in Tuva, Südsibirien.* Munich: Beck, 1984.

Gu Donggao 顧棟高. *Chunqiu dashi biao* 春秋大事表. In *Huang Qing jingjie xubian* 皇清經解續編, ed. Wang Xianqian 王先謙. 360 vols. Nanjing, 1888; rpt. Beijing: Zhonghua, 1993, vol. 34.

Gu Jiegang 顧頡剛. "Gansu changcheng yiji" 甘肅長城遺跡. In *Shi lin za zhi* 史林雜識. Beijing: Zhonghua, 1963.

Gu Jiegang 顧頡剛. "*Yizhoushu* Shifu pian jiaozhu xieding yu pinglun" 逸周書世俘篇校注寫定與評論. *Wenshi* 文史 2 (1962): 1–42.

Gu Jiegang 顧頡剛, ed. *Gu shi bian* 古史辨. 7 vols. Shanghai: Pushe, 1926–41.

Gu Jiegang 顧頡剛 and Liu Qiyu 劉起釪. "Shangshu Xibo kan Li jiaoshi yilun" 尚書西伯戡黎校釋議論. *Zhongguo lishi wenxian yanjiu jikan* 中國歷史文獻研究輯刊 1 (1980): 46–59.

Gu Zuyu 顧祖禹 (1631–92). *Dushi fangyu jiyao* 讀史方輿紀要. 6 vols. Shanghai: Shangwu, 1936.

Guan Baiyi 關百益. *Xinzheng guqi tulu* 新鄭古器圖錄. 2 vols. Shanghai: Shangwu, 1929.

Guan Baiyi 關百益. *Zhengzhong guqi tukao* 鄭冢古器圖考. 4 vols. Shanghai: Zhonghua, 1940.

Guan Donggui 管東貴. "Zhongguo gudai shi ri shenhua zhi yanjiu" 中國古代十日神話之研究. In *Cong bijiao shenhua dao wenxue* 從比較神話到文學, ed. Gu Tianhong 古添洪 and Chen Huihua 陳慧樺. Taipei: Dongda, 1977, pp. 83–149.

Guan Xiechu 管燮初. "Shang Zhou jiagu he qingtongqi shang de guayao bianshi" 商周甲骨和青銅器上的卦爻辨識. *Guwenzi yanjiu* 古文字研究 6 (1981): 141–9.

Guo Baojun 郭寶鈞. *Shanbiaozhen yu Liulige* 山彪鎮與琉璃閣. Kaoguxue zhuankan, series 2, no. 11. Beijing: Kexue, 1959.

Guo Baojun 郭寶鈞. *Shang Zhou tongqiqun zonghe yanjiu* 商周銅器群綜合研究. Beijing: Wenwu, 1981.

Guo Baojun 郭寶鈞. *Xunxian Xincun* 濬縣辛村. Kaoguxue zhuankan, series 2, no. 13. Beijing: Kexue, 1964.

Guo Baojun 郭寶鈞 "Yijiuwuling nian chun Yinxu fajue baogao" 一九五〇年春殷墟發掘報告. *Kaogu xuebao* 考古學報, 1951.5: 1–61.

Guo Baojun 郭寶鈞, and Lin Shoujin 林壽晉. "Yijiuwuer nian qiuji Luoyang dongjiao fajue baogao" 一九五二年秋季洛陽東郊發掘報告. *Kaogu xuebao* 考古學報 9 (1955): 91–116.

Guo, Dashun. "Hongshan and Related Cultures." In *The Archaeology of Northeast China Beyond the Great Wall*, ed. Sarah M. Nelson. London: Routledge, 1995, pp. 21–65.

Guo Dewei 郭德維. "Chu mu fenlei wenti tantao" 楚墓分類問題探討. *Kaogu* 考古 1983.3: 249–59.

Guo Keyu 郭克煜. *Lu guo shi* 魯國史. Beijing: Renmin, 1994.

Guo Moruo 郭沫若. "Guanyu E jun qi jie de yanjiu" 關于鄂君啟節的研究. *Wenwu* 文物 1958.4: 3–6.

Guo Moruo 郭沫若. *Liang Zhou jinwenci daxi tulu kaoshi* 兩周金文辭大系圖錄考釋. Tokyo: Bunkyûdô, 1935; 2nd rev. ed., Beijing: Kexue, 1958.

Guo Moruo 郭沫若. *Nuli zhi shidai* 奴隸制時代. Beijing, Renmin: 1954.

Guo Moruo 郭沫若. *Qingtong shidai* 青銅時代. Shanghai: Qunyi, 1946. Originally published, Chongqing: Wenzhi, 1945.

Guo Moruo 郭沫若. *Zhongguo shi gao* 中國史稿. Beijing: Renmin, 1964.

Guo Moruo 郭沫若, ed., Hu Houxuan 胡厚宣, ed. in chief. *Jiagu wen heji* 甲骨文合集. 13 vols. N.p.: Zhonghua 1978–82.

Guo Qingfan 郭慶藩. *Zhuangzi jishi* 莊子集釋. 1894; rpt. Taibei: Huazheng, 1991.

Guo Shengqiang 郭勝強. "Lüelun Yindai de zhijiu ye" 略論殷代的制酒業. *Zhongyuan wenwu* 中原文物 1986.3: 94–5.

Hadingham, Evan. "The Mummies of Xinjiang." *Discover*, April 1994, pp. 68–77.

Haidai kaogu 海岱考古 1989.1: 254–74. "Qingzhou Shi Sufutun Shang dai mu fajue baogao" 青州市蘇埠屯商代墓發掘報告.

Haidai kaogu 海岱考古 1989.1: 274–82. "Linzi Liangchun mudi fajue jianbao" 臨淄兩醇墓地發掘簡報.

Haidai kaogu 海岱考古 1989.1: 283–91. "Linzi Donggu mudi fajue jianbao" 臨淄東古墓地發掘簡報.

Haloun, Gustav. *Seit wann kannten die Chinesen die Tocharer oder Indogermanen überhaupt?* Leipzig: Verlag der Asia Major, 1926.

Han Kangxin 韓康信. "Ningxia Pengtao Yujiazhuang mudi rengu zhongxi tedian zhi yanjiu" 寧夏彭堡于家莊墓地人骨種系特點之研究. *Kaogu xuebao* 考古學報 1995.1: 107–25.

Han Kangxin 韓康信. "Xinjiang Kongquehe Gumugou mudi rengu yanjiu" 新疆孔雀河古墓溝墓地人骨研究. *Kaogu xuebao* 考古學報 1986.1: 361–84.

Han Kangxin 韓康信 and Pan Qifeng 潘其風. "Xinjiang Zhaosu Wusun mu gu renleixue cailiao de yanjiu" 新疆昭蘇烏孫墓古人類學材料的研究. *Kaogu xuebao* 考古學報 1987.4: 503–23.

Han Mingxiang 韓明翔 et al., eds. "Lintong Nanluo Xi Zhou mu chutu qingtongqi" 臨潼南羅西周墓出土青銅器. *Wenwu* 文物 1982.1: 87–9.

Han Wei 韓偉. "Fengxiang Qin gong lingyuan zuantan yu shijue jianbao" 鳳翔秦公陵園鑽探與試掘簡報. *Wenwu* 文物 1983.7: 30–7.

Han Wei 韓偉. "Guanyu Qin ren zushu wenhua yuanyuan guanjian" 關於秦人族屬文化淵源管見. *Wenwu* 文物 1986.4: 23–28.

Han Wei 韓偉. "Lüelun Shaanxi Chunqiu Zhanguo Qin mu" 略論陝西春秋戰國秦墓. *Kaogu yu wenwu* 考古與文物 1981.1: 83–93.

Han Wei 韓偉. "Majiazhuang Qin zongmiao jianzhu zhidu yanjiu" 馬家莊秦宗廟建築制度研究. *Wenwu* 文物 1985.2: 30–8.

Han Wei 韓偉. "Qin gong miaoqin zuantantu kaoshi" 秦宮廟寢鑽探圖考釋. *Kaogu yu wenwu* 考古與文物 1985.2: 53–6.

Han Wei 韓偉 and Wu Zhengfeng 吳鎮烽. "Fengxiang Nanzhihui Xicun Zhou mu de fajue" 鳳翔南指揮西村周墓的發掘. *Kaogu yu wenwu* 考古與文物 1982.4: 15–38.

Hančar, Franz. *Das Pferd in prähistorischer und früher historischer Zeit.* Wien: Herold, 1956.

Hansen, Chad. *Language and Logic in Ancient China.* Ann Arbor: University of Michigan Press, 1983.

Harper, Donald. "The Bellows Analogy in *Laozi* V and Warring States Macrobiotic Hygiene." *EC* 20 (1995): 381–91.

Harper, Donald. "A Chinese Demonography of the Third Century B.C." *HJAS* 45 (1985): 459–98.

Harper, Donald. "The Conception of Illness in Early Chinese Medicine, as Documented in Newly Discovered 3rd and 2nd Century B.C. Manuscripts." *Sudhoffs Archiv* 74 (1990), 210–35.

Harper, Donald. *Early Chinese Medical Literature: The Mawangdui Medical Manuscripts.* Sir Henry Wellcome Asian Series, vol. 2. London: Kegan Paul, 1997.

Harper, Donald. "The Han Cosmic Board." *EC* 4 (1978–9): 1–10.

Harper, Donald. "The Han Cosmic Board: A Response to Christopher Cullen." *EC* 6 (1980–1): 47–56.

Harper, Donald. "Iatromancy, Diagnosis, and Prognosis in Early Chinese Medicine." *Innovation in Chinese Medicine*, ed. Elizabeth Hsu. Cambridge University Press, forthcoming.

Harper, Donald. "Resurrection in Warring States Popular Religion." *Taoist Resources* 5, 2 (1994): 13–28.

Harper, Donald. "The Sexual Arts of Ancient China as Described in a Manuscript of the Second Century B.C." *HJAS* 47 (1987): 539–93.

Harper, Donald. "Spellbinding." In *Religions of China in Practice*, ed. Donald Lopez. Princeton, N.J.: Princeton University Press, 1996, pp. 241–50.

Harper, Donald. "Wang Yen-shou's Nightmare Poem." *HJAS* 47 (1987): 239–83.

Harper, Donald. "Warring States, Qin, and Han Manuscripts Related to Natural Philosophy and the Occult." In *New Sources of Early Chinese History: An Introduction to the Reading of Inscriptions and Manuscripts*, ed. Edward L. Shaughnessy. Berkeley: Society for the Study of Early China and Institute of East Asian Studies, University of California, 1997, pp. 223–52.

Harper, Donald. "Warring States, Qin, and Han Periods." In "Chinese Religions: The State of the Field," ed. Daniel L. Overmyer. *JAS* 54.1 (1995): 152–60.

Hawkes, David. "The Quest of the Goddess." In *Studies in Chinese Literary Genres*, ed, Cyril Birch. Berkeley: University of California Press, 1974, pp. 42–68.

Hawkes, David. *The Songs of the South: An Ancient Chinese Anthology of Poems by Qu Yuan and Other Poets*. 2nd ed., Harmondsworth: Penguin, 1985.

Hayashi Minao 林巳奈夫. *Chûgoku In Shû jidai no buki* 中國殷周時代の武器. Kyôto: Kyôto daigaku Jinbun kagaku kenkyûjo, 1972.

Hayashi Minao 林巳奈夫. "Inkyo Fukô bo shutsudo no gyokki jakkan ni taisuru chûshaku 殷墟婦好墓出土の玉器若干に對する注釋." *Tôhô gakuhô* 東方學報 (Kyoto) 58 (1986): 1–70. Rpt. in Hayashi Minao, *Chûgoku kogyoku no kenkyû* 中國古玉の研究. Tokyo: Yoshikawa kôbunkan, 1991, pp. 515–76.

Hayashi Minao 林巳奈夫. "In Seishû jidai no chihôkei seidôki" 殷西周時代の地方型青銅器. *Kôkogaku Memoir* 考古學ナモアール 1980: 17–58

Hayashi Minao 林巳奈夫. "In Seishû jidai reiki no ruibetsu to yôhô 殷西周時代禮器の類別と用法. *Tôhô gakuhô* 東方學報 (Kyoto) 53 (1981): 1–108.

Hayashi Minao 林巳奈夫. "In Shû jidai no tuzô kigô" 殷周時代の圖象記號. *Tôhô gakuhô* 東方學報 (Kyoto) 39 (1968): 1–117.

Hayashi Minao 林巳奈夫. *In Shû seidôki sôran. Pt. 1: In Shû jidai seidôki no kenkyû* 殷周青銅器綜覽：殷周時代青銅器の研究. 2 vols. Tôkyô: Yoshikawa kôbunkan, 1984.

Hayashi Minao 林巳奈夫. In Shû seidôki sôran, Pt. 2: *In Shu seidôki monyô no kenkyû* 殷周青銅器紋樣の研究. Tokyo: Yoshikawa kôbunkan, 1986.

Hayashi Minao 林巳奈夫. *In Shû seidôki sôran. Pt. 3: Shunjû Sengoku jidai seidôki no kenkyû* 殷周青銅器綜覽：春秋戰國時代青銅器の研究. Tôkyô: Yoshikawa kôbunkan, 1988.

Hayashi Minao 林巳奈夫. "In Shû seido iki no meishô to yôto" 殷周青銅彝器の名稱と用途. *Tôhô gakuhô* 東方學報 (Kyoto) 34 (1964): 199–298.

He Fan 何凡. "Guoren baodong xingzhi bianxi" 國人暴動性質辨析. *Renwen zazhi* 人文雜誌 1983.5: 76–7.

He Jiejun 何介鈞. "Hunan Shang Zhou shiqi gu wenhua de fenqu tansuo" 湖南商周時期古文化的分區探索. *Hunan kaogu jikan* 湖南考古輯刊 2 (1984): 120–7.

He Jiejun 何介鈞. "Shilun Daxi wenhua" 試論大溪文化. *Zhongguo kaogu xuehui dierci nianhui lunwenji* 中國考古學會第二次年會論文集. Beijing: Wenwu, 1982, pp. 116–23.

He Jisheng 何紀生. "Lüelun Guangdong Dong Zhou shiqi de qingtong wenhua ji qi yu jiheyinwentao de guanxi" 略論廣東東周時期的青銅文化及其與幾何印文陶的關係. *Wenwu jikan* 文物集刊 3 (1981): 212–24.

He Shuangquan 何雙全. "Tianshui Fangmatan Qin jian zhongshu" 天水放馬灘秦簡綜述. *Wenwu* 文物 1989.2: 23–31.

He Shuangquan 何雙全. "Tianshui Fangmatan Qin mu chutu ditu chutan" 天水放馬灘秦墓出土地圖初探. *Wenwu* 文物 1989.2: 12–22.

He Tianxing 何天行. *Hangxian Liangzhu zhen zhi shiqi yu heitao* 杭縣良渚鎮之石器與黑陶. Shanghai: Wu Yue yanjiuhui, 1937.

He Yeju 賀業矩. "Shilun Zhou dai liangci chengshi jianshe gaochao" 試論周代兩次城市建設高潮. In *Zhongguo jianzhushi lunwen xuanji* 中國建築史論文選集, ed. Li Runhai 李潤海. Taipei: Mingwen, 1983.

He Youqi 何幼琦. "Di Yi, Di Xin jinian he zheng Yi fang de niandai" 帝乙帝辛紀年和征夷方的年代. *Yindu xuekan* 殷都學刊 1990.3: 1–9.

Hebei sheng chutu wenwu xuanji 河北省出土文物選集. Beijing: Wenwu, 1980.

Heine-Geldern, R. "Das Tocharenproblem und die Pontische Wanderung." *Saeculum* 2 (1951): 225.

Henan kaogu sishi nian (1952–1992) 河南考古四十年. Henan sheng Wenwu yanjiusuo, ed. Zhengzhou: Henan Renmin, 1994.

Henning, W. B. "Argi and the 'Tocharians.'" *BSOAS* 9, 3 (1938): 545–71.

Henricks, Robert G. *Lao-Tzu Te-Tao Ching: A New Translation Based on the Recently Discovered Ma-wang-tui Texts*. New York: Ballantine, 1989.

Higuchi Takayasu 樋口隆康. "Kanan shutsudo no Shô (In) shiki dôki no kenkyû" 華南出土の商（殷）式銅器の研究. *Museum* 301 (April 1976): 4–16.

Ho, Ping-ti. *The Cradle of the East: An Inquiry into the Indigenous Origins of Techniques and Ideas of Neolithic and Early Historic China, 5,000–1,000 B.C.* Hong Kong: Chinese University of Hong Kong Press, and Chicago: University of Chicago Press, 1975.

Höllmann, Thomas O., and Georg W. Kossack, eds. *Maoqinggou: Ein eisenzeitliches Gräberfeld in der Ordos-Region (Innere Mongolei)*. Mainz: Philipp von Zabern, 1992.

Hopkirk, Peter. *Foreign Devils on the Silk Road*. London: John Murray, 1980.

Horai, Satoshi, Kenji Hayasaka, Rumi Kondo, Kazuo Tsugane, and Naoyuki Takahata. "Recent African Origin of Modern Humans Revealed by Complete Sequences of Hominoid Mitochondrial DNA." *Proceedings of the National Academy of Sciences, USA* 92 (1995): 532–36.

Hou, Ching-lang. *Monnaies d'offrandes et la notion de trésorerie dans la religion chinoise*. Paris: Collège de France Institut des Hautes Études Chinoises, 1975.

Houma mengshu 侯馬盟書. Beijing: Wenwu, 1976.

Houma zhutong yizhi 侯馬鑄銅遺址. 2 vols. Beijing: Wenwu, 1993.

Howells, William. *Getting Here: The Story of Human Evolution*. Washington, D. C.: Compass, 1993.

Hsia Nai. "The Classification, Nomenclature, and Usage of Shang Dynasty Jades." In *Studies of Shang Archaeology: Selected Papers from the International Conference on Shang Civilization*, ed. K. C. Chang. New Haven, Conn.: Yale University Press, 1986, pp. 207–36. Chinese versions of the article appear in *Kaogu* 考古 1983.5: 455–67, and *Yinxu Fu Hao mu*, 2nd. ed. Beijing: Wenwu, 1984, pp. 241–54.

Hsiao, Kung-chuan. F. W. Mote, trans. *A History of Chinese Political Thought, Vol. 1: From the Beginnings to the Sixth Century A.D.* Princeton, N.J.: Princeton University Press, 1979.

Hsu, Cho-yun. *Ancient China in Transition*. Stanford, Calif.: Stanford University Press, 1965.

Hsu, Cho-yun. *Han Agriculture*. Seattle, Wash.: University of Washington Press, 1980.

Hsu, Cho-yun, and Katheryn M. Linduff. *Western Chou Civilization*. New Haven, Conn.: Yale University Press, 1988.

Hu Daojing 胡道靜. "Shi shu pian" 釋菽薾. *Zhonghua wenshi luncong* 中華文史論叢 1963: 111–19.

Hu Dianxian 胡淀咸. "Zeng guo de laiyuan" 曾國的來源. *Wenwu yanjiu* 文物研究 3 (1988): 53–6.

Hu Houxuan 胡厚宣. "Chonglun Yu yi ren wenti" 重論余一人問題. *Guwenzi yanjiu* 古文字研究, 6 (1981): 15–33.

Hu Houxuan 胡厚宣. "Jiaguwen Sifang feng ming kaozheng" 甲骨文四方風名考證. *Jiaguxue Shangshi luncong chuji* 甲骨學商史論叢初集. Chengdu: Qi Lu daxue yanjiusuo, 1944.

Hu Houxuan 胡厚宣. "Jiaguwen suojian Yindai nuli de fan yapo douzheng" 甲骨文所見殷代奴隸的反壓迫斗爭. *Kaogu xuebao* 考古學報 1976.1: 1–18.

Hu Houxuan 胡厚宣. "Qihou bianqian yu Yindai qihou zhi jiantao" 氣候變遷與殷代氣候之檢討. *Zhonguo wenhua yanjiu huikan* 中國文化研究彙刊 4 (1944): 1–84, 289–90. Reprinted in Hu Houxuan, *Jiaguxue Shangshi luncong erji* 甲骨學商史論叢二集. Chengdu: Qi Lu daxue yanjiusuo, 1944, vol. 2, pp. 1–64.

Hu Houxuan 胡厚宣. "Zhongguo nuli shehui de renxun he renji (xia pian)" 中國奴隸社會的人殉和人祭（下篇）. *Wenwu* 文物 1974.8: 56–67, 72.

Hu Lingui 呼林貴 and Xue Dongxing 薛東星. "Yaoxian Dingjiagou chutu Xi Zhou jiaocang qingtongqi" 耀縣丁家溝出土西周窖藏青銅器. *Kaogu yu wenwu* 考古與文物 1986.4: 4–5.

Hu Qianying 胡謙盈. "Lun Nianzipo yu Qi yi Feng yi Xian Zhou wenhua yizhi (muzang) de niandai fenqi" 論碾子坡與歧邑豐邑先周文化遺址（墓葬）的年代分期. In *Kaoguxue yanjiu: Jinian Shaanxi sheng kaogu yanjiusuo chengli sanshi zhounian* 考古學研究：紀念陝西省考古研究所成立三十週年, ed. Shi Xingbang 石興邦 et al. Xi'an: San Qin, 1993, pp. 332–55.

Hu Qianying 胡謙盈. "Shilun Qijia wenhua de butong leixing ji qi yuanliu" 試論齊家文化的不同類型及其源流. *Kaogu yu wenwu* 考古與文物 1980.3: 77–82, 33.

Hu Qianying 胡謙盈. "Tai Wang yiqian de Zhoushi guankui" 太王以前的周史管窺. *Kaogu yu wenwu* 考古與文物 1987.1: 70–81.

Hu Xiaolong 胡小龍. "Qiantan Sanmenxia Shangcunling Guo guo mudi chemakeng" 淺談三門峽上村嶺虢國墓地車馬坑. *Hua Xia kaogu* 華夏考古 1993.4: 96–7, 86.

Hua Jueming 華覺明. *Shijie yejin fazhan shi* 世界冶金發展史. Beijing: Kexue jishu wenxian, 1985.

Hua Jueming 華覺明, Feng Fugen 馮富根, Wang Zhenjiang 王振江, and Bai Rongjin 白榮金. "Fu Hao mu qingtongqi qun zhuzao jishu de yanjiu" 婦好墓青銅器群鑄造技術的研究. *Kaoguxue jikan* 考古學集刊 1 (1981): 244–72.

Hua Jueming 華覺明 and Guo Dewei 郭德維. "Zenghou Yi mu qingtong qiqun de zhuhan jishu he shilafa" 曾侯乙墓青銅器群的鑄銲技術和失蠟法. *Wenwu* 文物 1979.7: 46–8.

Hua Xia kaogu 華夏考古 1988.1: 30–44. "Pingdingshan shi Beizhicun Liang Zhou mudi yihao mu fajue jianbao" 平頂山市北滍村兩周墓地一號墓發掘簡報.

Hua Xia kaogu 華夏考古 1992.3: 114–30. "Xichuan xian Heshangling Chunqiu Chu mu de fajue" 淅川縣何尚嶺春秋楚墓的發掘.

Hua Xia kaogu 華夏考古 1992.3: 92–103. "Pingding shan Ying guo mudi jiushiwu hao mu de fajue" 平頂山應國墓地九十五號墓的發掘.

Hua Xia kaogu 華夏考古 1992.3: 104–113. "Sanmenxia Shangcunling Guo guo mudi M2001 fajue jianbao" 三門峽上村嶺虢國墓地M2001發掘簡報.

Huang Hongxin 黃宏信. "Chu bohua suokao" 楚帛畫瑣考. *Jiang Han kaogu* 江漢考古 1991.2: 45–9.

Huang Linshu 黃麟書. *Qin huang changcheng kao* 秦皇長城考. Kowloon: Zaoyang wenxueshe, 1973.

Huang Ranwei 黃然偉. *Yin Zhou qingtongqi shangci mingwen yanjiu* 殷周青銅器賞賜銘文研究. Hong Kong: Longmen, 1978.

Huang Shengzhang 黃盛璋. "Tongqi mingwen Yi Yu Ze de diwang ji qi yu Wu guo de guanxi" 銅器銘文宜虞夨的地望及其與吳國的關係. *Kaogu xuebao* 考古學報 1983.3: 295–305.

Huang Tianshu 黃天樹. *Yinxu wang buci de fenlei yu duandai* 殷墟王卜辭的分類與斷代. Taipei: Wenjing, 1991.

Huang Yukun and Chen Jiajie. "Sea Level Changes Along the Coast of the South China Sea Since Late Pleistocene." In *The Palaeoenvironment of East Asia from the Mid-Tertiary: Proceedings of the Second Conference. Vol. 1: Geology, Sea Level Changes, Palaeoclimatology and Palaeobotany*, ed. Pauline Whyte, Jean Aigner, Nina G. Jablonski, Graham Taylor, Donald Walker, Wang Pinxian, and So Chak-lam. Hong Kong: Center of Asian Studies, University of Hong Kong, 1988, pp. 289–318.

Huang Zhanyue 黃展岳. "Lun Liang Guang chutu de xian Qin qingtongqi" 論兩廣出土的先秦青銅器. *Kaogu xuebao* 考古學報 1986.4: 409–34.

Huang Zhanyue 黃展岳. "Wo guo gudai de renxun he rensheng: Cong renxun rensheng kan Kong Qiu keji fuli de fandongxing" 我國古代的人殉和人牲：從人殉人牲看孔丘克己復禮的反動性. *Kaogu* 考古 1974.3: 153–63.

Huang Zhanyue 黃展岳. "Yin Shang muzang zhong renxun rensheng de zaikaocha: Fulun xunsheng jisheng" 殷商墓葬中人殉人牲的再考察：附論殉牲祭牲. *Kaogu* 考古 1983.10: 935–49.

Huang Zhanyue 黃展岳. *Zhongguo gudai de rensheng renxun* 中國古代的人牲人殉. Beijing: Wenwu, 1990.

Huang Zhongye 黃中業. "Cong kaogu faxian kan Shang wenhua qiyuan yu woguo beifang" 從考古發現看商文化起源于我國北方. *Beifang wenwu* 北方文物 1990.1: 14–19.

Hubei sheng Jing Sha tielu kaogudui ed. *Baoshan Chu jian* 包山楚簡. Beijing: Wenwu, 1991.

Hubei Suizhou Leigudun chutu wenwu 湖北隨州擂鼓墩出土文物. Hong Kong: China Resources Artland, 1984.

Huber, Louisa G. Fitzgerald. "Qijia and Erlitou: The Question of Contacts with Distant Cultures." *EC* 20 (1995): 17–67.

Hudson, R. "Concepts of Disease in the West." In *The Cambridge World History of Human Disease*, ed. K. Kiple. Cambridge University Press, 1993, pp. 45–52.

Huixian fajue baogao 輝縣發掘報告. Beijing: Kexue, 1956.

Hulsewé, A. F. P. "Notes on the Historiography of the Han Period." In *Historians of China and Japan*, ed. W. G. Beasley and E. G. Pulleyblank. London: Oxford University Press, 1961, pp. 31–43.

Hulsewé, A. F. P. *Remnants of Han Law. Vol. 1: Introductory Studies and an Annotated Translation of Chapters 22 and 23 of the History of the Former Han Dynasty*. Leiden: Brill, 1955.

Hulsewé, A. F. P. *Remnants of Ch'in Law: An Annotated Translation of the Ch'in Legal and Administrative Rules of the 3rd Century B.C. Discovered in Yün-meng Prefecture, Hu-pei Province, in 1975*. Leiden: Brill, 1985.

Hulsewé, A. F. P. "Weights and Measures in Ch'in Law." In *State and Law in East Asia: Festschrift Karl Bünger*, ed. D. Eikemeier and Herbert Franke. Wiesbaden: Harrassowitz, 1981, pp. 25–39.

Hulsewé, A. F. P., and Michael Loewe. *China in Central Asia: The Early Stage 125 B.C.–A.D. 23. An Annotated Translation of the Chapters 61 and 96 of the History of the Former Han Dynasty*. Sinica Leidensia 14. Leiden: Brill, 1979.

Hummel, Arthur W. *The Autobiography of a Chinese Historian, Being the Preface to* A Symposium on Ancient Chinese History (*Ku Shih Pien*). Leiden: Brill, 1931.

Hunan bowuguan wenji 湖南博物館文集 1 (1991): 142–51. "Yueyang xian Yingkou chutu Chunqiu renxiang dongwuwen qingtong you" 岳陽縣篔口出土春秋人像動物紋青銅卣.

Hunan chutu tongjing tulu 湖南出土銅鏡圖錄. Beijing: Wenwu, 1960.

Hunan kaogu jikan 湖南考古輯刊 1 (1982): 25–31. "Zixing Jiushi Chunqiu mu" 資興舊市春秋墓.

Hunan kaogu jikan 湖南考古輯刊 2 (1984): 35–7. "Changsha xian chutu Chunqiu shiqi Yue zu qingtongqi" 長沙縣出土春秋時期越族青銅器.

Hunan kaogu jikan 湖南考古輯刊 3 (1986): 27–30. "Xinshao Liuyang Zhuzhou Zixing chutu Shang Zhou qingtongqi" 新邵瀏陽株洲資興出土商周青銅器.

Iijima Taketsugu 飯島武次. "Xian Zhou wenhua taoqi yanjiu" 先周文化陶器研究. *Kaoguxue yanjiu* 考古學研究 1 (1992): 229–55.

Inoue Satoshi 井上聰. "Shangdai miaohao xinlun" 商代廟號新論. *Zhongyuan wenwu* 中原文物, 1990.2: 54–60.

Itô Michiharu 伊藤道治. "Bokuji ni mieru sorei kannen ni tsuite" 卜辭に見える祖靈觀念について *Tôhô gakuhô* 東方學報 (Kyoto) 26 (1956): 1–35.

Itô Michiharu 伊藤道治. *Chûgoku kodai kokka no shihai kôzô* 中國古代國家の支配構造. Tokyo: Chuô kôronsha, 1987.

Itô Michiharu 伊藤道治. *Chûgoku kodai ôcho no keisei* 中國古代王朝の形成. Tokyo: Sôbunsha, 1975.

Itô Michiharu. "Part One: Religion and Society." In *Studies in Early Chinese Civilization: Religion, Society, Language, and Palaeography. Vol. 1: Text; Vol. 2: Tables and Notes*, ed., Itô Michiharu and Ken'ichi Takashima. Hirakata: Kansai Gaidai University Press, 1996, pp. 1–178.

Itô Michiharu 伊藤道治. "Yindai shi de yanjiu" 殷代史の研究. In *Riben kaoguxue yanjiuzhe: Zhongguo kaoguxue yanjiu lunwenji* 日本考古學研究者：中國考古學研究論文集, ed. Higuchi Takayasu 通口隆康, trans. Cai Fengshu 蔡鳳書. Hong Kong: Dongfang, 1990, pp. 205–60.

Ivanhoe, Philip J. *Confucian Moral Self Cultivation*. New York: Lang, 1993.

Ivanhoe, Philip J. "Zhuangzi's Conversion Experience." *Journal of Chinese Religions* 19 (1991): 13–25.

Iwamura, Shinobu. "Nomad and Farmer in Central Asia." *Acta Asiatica* 3 (1962): 45–50.

Jacobson, Esther. "Beyond the Frontier: A Reconsideration of Cultural Interchange Between China and the Early Nomads." *EC* 13 (1988): 201–40.

Jacobson, Esther. "The Structure of Narrative in Early Chinese Pictorial Vessels." *Representations* 8 (Fall 1984): 61–83.

James, T. G. H., ed. *An Introduction to Ancient Egypt*. London: British Museum, 1979.

Jan Yun-hua. "The Silk Manuscripts on Taoism." *TP* 63 (1977): 65–84.

Jan Yun-hua. "Tao, Principle and Law." *Journal of Chinese Philosophy* 7, 3 (1980): 205–28.

Jan Yun-hua. "Tao Yuan or Tao the Origin." *Journal of Chinese Philosophy* 7, 3 (1980): 195–204.

Jaspers, Karl. *The Origin and Goal of History*. New Haven, Conn.: Yale University Press, 1953.

Jettmar, Karl. *Art of the Steppes*. New York: Crown, 1967.

Jettmar, Karl. "The Karasuk Culture and Its South-Eastern Affinities." *BMFEA* 22 (1950): 83–123, 16 pl.

Jettmar, Karl. "The Origins of Chinese Civilization: Soviet Views." In *The Origins of Chinese Civilization*, ed. D. N. Keightley. Berkeley: University of California Press, 1983, pp. 217–36.

Ji Dachun 紀大椿, ed. *Xinjiang lishi cidian* 新疆歷史詞典. Urumqi: Xinjiang Renmin, 1993.

Ji Dewei 吉德煒 (David N. Keightley). "Zhongguo gudai de jiri yu miaohao" 中國古代的吉日與廟號. *Yinxu bowuyuan yuankan* 1 (1989): 20–32.

Ji Naijun 姬乃軍 and Chen Mingde 陳明德 "Shaanxi Yanchang chutu yipi Xi Zhou qingtongqi 陝西延長出土一批西周青銅器 *Kaogu yu Wenwu* 孝古與文物 1993.5: 8–12.

Ji Xianlin 季羨林. *Dunhuang Tulufan Tuhuoluo yu yanjiu daolun* 敦煌吐魯番吐火羅語研究導輪. Dunhuangxue daolun congkan 敦煌學導輪叢刊, no. 6, ed. Lin Congming 林聰明, Taibei: Xinwenfeng, 1993.

Jia E 賈峨. "Guanyu Dong Zhou cuojin xiangqian tongqi de jige wenti de tantao" 關於東周錯金瓖嵌銅器的幾個問題的探討. *Jiang Han kaogu* 江漢考古 1986.4: 34–48.

Jia Hong'en 賈鴻恩. "Wengniute qi Dapaozi qingtong duanjian mu" 翁牛特旗大泡子青銅短劍墓. *Wenwu* 文物 1984.2: 50–4.

Jia Weiming 賈偉明. "Guanyu Baijinbao leixing fenqi de tansuo" 關於白金寶類型分期的探索. *Beifang wenwu* 北方文物 1986.1: 11–15, 52.

Jian Bozan 翦伯贊. *Zhongguo shi gangyao* 中國史綱要. Beijing: Renmin, 1983.

Jiang Han kaogu 江漢考古 1981.1: 1–2."Suizhoushi Leigudun erhao mu chutu yipi zhongyao wenwu" 隨州市擂鼓墩二號墓出土一批重要文物.

Jiang Han kaogu 江漢考古 1982.2: 37–61. "Hubei Huangpi Lutaishan liang Zhou yizhi yu muzang" 湖北黃陂魯台山兩周遺址與墓葬.

Jiang Han kaogu 江漢考古 1983.2: 1–35. "Xiangyang Shanwan Dong Zhou muzang fajue baogao" 襄陽山灣東周墓葬發掘報告.

Jiang Hongyuan 蔣鴻元 et al. *Xinzheng chutu guqi tuzhi* 新鄭出土古器圖誌. 3 vols. N.p. [Kaifeng]: 1923.

Jiang Tingyu 蔣廷瑜 and Lan Riyong 籃日勇. "Guangxi xian-Qin qingtongwenhua chulun" 廣西先秦青銅文化初論. In *Zhongguo Kaoguxuehui di si ci nianhui (1983) lunwenji* 中國考古學會第四次年會(1983)論文集. Beijing: Wenwu, 1985, pp. 252–63

Jiang Weidong 蔣衛東. "Zhenmushou yiyi bian" 鎮墓獸意義辨. *Jiang Han kaogu* 江漢考古 1991.2: 40–4.

Jiang Xiaoyuan 江曉原. *Tianxue zhenyuan* 天學真原. Shenyang: Liaoning Jiaoyu, 1991.

Jiang Zudi 蔣祖棣. "Lun Feng Hao Zhou wenhua yizhi taoqi fenqi" 論豐鎬周文化遺址陶器分期. *Kaoguxue yanjiu* 考古學研究 1 (1992): 256–86.

Jiangling Yutaishan Chu mu 江陵雨台山楚墓. Hubei sheng Jingzhou diqu bowuguan ed.. Zhongguo tianye kaogu baogaoji 中國田野考古報告集. Kaoguxue zhuankan 考古學專刊, series 4, no. 27. Beijing: Wenwu, 1984.

Jin Fengyi 靳楓毅. "Lun Zhongguo dongbei diqu han quren qingtong duanjian de wenhua yicun" 論中國東北地區含曲刃青銅短劍的文化遺存. *Kaogu xuebao* 考古學報 1982.4: 387–426; 1983.1: 39–54.

Jin Fengyi 靳楓毅. "Xiajiadian shangceng wenhua ji qi zushu wenti" 夏家店上層文化及其族屬問題. *Kaogu xuebao* 考古學報 1987.2: 177–208.

Jin Zhengyao 金正耀 et al. "Guanghan Sanxingdui yiwu keng qingtongqi de qian tongweisu bizhi yanjiu" 廣漢三星堆遺物坑青銅器的鉛同位素比值研究. *Wenwu* 文物 1995.2: 80–5.

Jones, Steve, Robert Martin, and David Pilbeam, eds. *The Cambridge Encyclopedia of Human Evolution*. Cambridge University Press, 1992.

Kaizuka Shigeki 貝塚茂樹. *Kyôto daigaku jinbun kagaku kenkyûjo zô kôkotsu moji. Honbun hen* 京都大學人文科學研究所藏甲骨文字. 本文編. Kyoto: Kyôto daigaku jinbun kagaku kenkyûjo, 1960. Rpt. as Kaizuka Shigeki and Itô Michiharu 伊藤道治. *Kôkotsu monji kenkyû: Honbun hen* 甲骨文字研究：本文編. Kyoto: Dôhôsha, 1980.

Kalinowski, Marc. *Cosmologie et divination dans la Chine ancienne*. Paris: École française d'Extrême-Orient, 1991.

Kalinowski, Marc. "Les instruments astro-calendériques des Han et la méthode de *Liu ren*." *Bulletin de l'école française d'Extrême-Orient* 72 (1983): 309–419.

Kalinowski, Marc. "Mawangdui boshu Xingde shitan" 馬王堆刑德試探. *Huaxue* 華學 1 (1995): 82–110.

Kalinowski, Marc. "Mythe, cosmogenese et theogonie dans la Chine ancienne." *L'homme* 137.1 (1996): 41–60.

Kalinowski, Marc. "Les traités de Shuihudi et l'hémérologie Chinoise a la fin des Royaumes Combattants." *TP* 72 (1986): 175–228.

Kanaya Osamu 金谷治. *Shin Kan shisô shi kenkyû* 秦漢思想史研究. 2nd rev. ed. Kyoto: Heiraku, 1981.

Kane, Virginia. "The Independent Bronze Industries in the South of China Contemporary with the Shang and Western Zhou Dynasties." *Archives of Asian Art* 28 (1974–5): 77–107.

Kao, Chih-hsi. "An Introduction to the Shang and Chou Bronze *Nao* Excavated in South China." In *Studies of Shang Archaeology: Selected Papers from the International Conference on Shang Civilization*, ed. K. C. Chang. New Haven, Conn.: Yale University Press, 1986, pp. 275–99.

Kao, Ch'ü-hsün. "The Royal Cemetery of the Yin Dynasty at An-yang." *Bulletin of the Department of Archaeology and Anthropology, National Taiwan University* 13–14 (1959): 1–9.

Kaogu 考古 1955.2: 33–9. "Baoji he Xi'an fujin kaogu fajue jianbao" 寶雞和西安附近考古發掘簡報.

Kaogu 考古 1958.11: 67–78. "1957 nian Henan Shanxian fajue jianbao" 1957 年河南陝縣發掘簡報.

Kaogu 考古 1959.10: 531–6. "1957 nian Handan fajue jianbao" 1957 年邯鄲發掘簡報.

Kaogu 考古 1959.11: 588–91. "Shaanxi Weishui liuyu diaocha jianbao" 陝西渭水流域調查簡報.

Kaogu 考古 1959.12: 653–7. "Luoyang Xijiao yihao Zhanguo mu fajueji" 洛陽西郊一號戰國墓發掘記.

Kaogu 考古 1960.7: 71. "Henan Linxian faxian Chunqiu Zhanguo muzang" 河南林縣發現春秋戰國墓葬.

Kaogu 考古 1961.5: 244. "Chengde shi Luanhe zhen de yizuo Zhanguo mu" 承德市灤河鎮的一座戰國墓.

Kaogu 考古 1961.6: 289–97. "Shandong Linzi Qi gucheng shijue jianbao" 山東臨淄齊故城試掘簡報.

Kaogu 考古 1961.7: 345–54. "Zhejiang Jiaxing Majiabang xinshiqi shidai yizhi de fajue" 浙江嘉興馬家濱新石器時代迹址的發掘.

Kaogu 考古 1962.1: 20–2. "1960 nian qiu Shaanxi Chang'an Zhangjiapo fajue jianbao" 一九六〇年秋陝西長安張家坡發掘簡報.

Kaogu 考古 1962.2: 55–62. "Houma Niucun gucheng nan Dong Zhou yizhi fajue jianbao" 侯馬牛村古城南東周遺址發掘簡報.

Kaogu 考古 1962.10: 509–18. "Shandong Pingdu Dongyueshi cun xinshiqi shidai yizhi yu Zhanguo mu" 山東平度東岳石村新石器時代遺址與戰國墓.

Kaogu 考古 1962.12: 613–34. "Hebei Handan Baijia cun Zhanguo mu" 河北邯鄲百家村戰國墓.

Kaogu 考古 1962.12: 644–5. "Hebei Qinglong xian Chaodaogou faxian yi pi qingtong qi" 河北青龍縣抄道溝發現一批青銅器.

Kaogu 考古 1963.10: 544–6. "Shanxi Xiangfen Zhaokang cun fujin guchengzhi diaocha" 山西襄汾趙康村附近古城址調查.

Kaogu 考古 1963.4: 204–12. "Anhui Huainanshi Caijiagang Zhaojiagudui Zhanguo mu" 安徽淮南市蔡家崗趙家孤堆戰國墓.

Kaogu 考古 1963.9: 461–73. "Hunan Changde Deshan Chu mu fajue baogao" 湖南常德德山楚墓發掘報告.

Kaogu 考古 1963.9: 474–9. "Shanxi Xiaxian Yuwangcheng diaocha" 山西夏縣禹王城調查.

Kaogu 考古 1964.3: 111–37. "Shanxi Changzhi Fenshuiling Zhanguo mu di er ci fajue" 山西長治分水嶺戰國墓第二次發掘.

Kaogu 考古 1964.9: 441–7, 474. "Shaanxi Chang'an Fengxi Zhangjiapo Xi Zhou yizhi de fajue" 陝西長安灃西張家坡西周遺址的發掘.

Kaogu 考古 1964.10: 498–503. "Anhui Shucheng chutu de tongqi" 安徽舒城出土的銅器.

Kaogu 考古 1965.2: 62–9. "Bohaiwan liang'an guwenhua yizhi diaocha" 渤海灣兩岸古文化遺址調查.

Kaogu 考古 1965.3: 105–5. "Jiangsu Luhe Chengqiao Dong Zhou mu" 江蘇六合程橋東周墓.

Kaogu 考古. 1965.9: 447–50. "Shaanxi Chang'an Zhangjiapo Xi Zhou mu qingli jianbao" 陝西長安張家坡西周墓清理簡報.

Kaogu 考古 1965.11: 548–61. "1964–1965 nian Yan Xiadu muzang fajue baogao" 1964–1965 年燕下都墓葬發掘報告.

Kaogu 考古 1965.11: 562–70. "Yan Xiadu di 22 hao yizhi fajue baogao" 燕下都第22號遺址發掘報告.

Kaogu 考古 1965.12: 599–613. "Shandong Qufu kaogu diaocha shijue jianbao" 山東曲阜考古調查試掘簡報.

Kaogu 考古 1965.12: 622–35. "Shandong Zouxian Tengxian guchengzhi diaocha" 山東鄒縣滕縣古城址調查.

Kaogu 考古 1966.5: 231–4. "Hebei Huailai Beixinbao Zhangguo mu" 河北懷來北辛堡戰國墓.

Kaogu 考古 1973.1: 30–4, 41. "Guangxi Gongcheng xian chutu de qingtongqi" 廣西恭城縣出土的青銅器.

Kaogu 考古 1973.3: 151–61. "Hubei Jiangling Paimashan Chu mu fajue jianbao" 湖北江陵拍馬山楚墓發掘簡報.

Kaogu 考古 1974.1: 1–5. "Shaanxi Chang'an Xinwangcun Mawangcun chutu de Xi Zhou tongqi" 陝西長安新旺村馬王村出土的西周銅器.

Kaogu 考古 1974.2: 116–120. "Jiangsu Luhe Chengqiao erhao Dong Zhou mu" 江蘇六合程橋二號東周墓.

Kaogu 考古 1974.5: 309–321. "Beijing fujin faxian de Xi Zhou nuli xunzangmu" 北京附近發現的奴隸殉葬墓.

Kaogu 考古 1975.1: 27–46. "1973 nian Anyang Xiaotun nandi fajue jianbao" 1973 年安陽小屯南地發掘簡報.

Kaogu 考古 1976.1: 31–48. "Shaanxi Qishan Hejiacun Xi Zhou muzang" 陝西歧山賀家村西周墓葬.

Kaogu 考古 1976.2: 121–8. "Fengxiang xian Qin gongdian shijue ji qi tongzhi jianzhu goujian" 鳳翔縣秦宮殿試掘及其銅制建築構件.

Kaogu 考古 1976.4: 246–58, 228. "Beijing diqu de you yi zhongyao kaogu shouhuo: Changping Baifu Xi Zhou muguomu de xin qishi" 北京地區的又一重要考古收獲：昌平白浮西周木槨墓的新啓示.

Kaogu 考古 1976.4: 274. "Jiangsu Lishui faxian Xi Zhou mu" 江蘇溧水發現西周墓.

Kaogu 考古 1977.1: 20–36. "Anyang Yinxu nuli jisikeng de fajue" 安陽殷墟奴隸祭祀坑的發掘.

Kaogu 考古 1977.1: 51–5. "Hebei Pingchuan Dongnangou Xiajiadian shangceng wenhua muzang" 河北平川東南溝夏家店上層文化墓葬.

Kaogu 考古 1977.1: 71–2. "Shaanxi Chang'an Fengxi chutu de Pu yu" 陝西長安灃西出土的逋盂.

Kaogu 考古 1977.2: 111–14. "Nei Menggu Zhunge'er qi Yulongtai de Xiongnu mu" 內蒙古准格爾旗玉隆太的匈奴墓.

Kaogu 考古 1977.5: 292–7. "Jiangsu Jurong xian Fushan Guoyuan Xi Zhou mu" 江蘇句容縣浮山果園西周墓.

Kaogu 考古 1977.5: 341–50. "Anyang Yinxu wu hao mu zuotan jiyao" 安陽殷墟五號墓座談紀要.

Kaogu 考古 1978.3: 151–4. "Jiangsu Jintan Aodun Xi Zhou mu" 江蘇金壇鰲墩西周墓.

Kaogu 考古 1978.5: 297–300. "Hunan Hengyang Xiangtan faxian Chunqiu muzang" 湖南衡陽湘潭發現春秋墓葬.

Kaogu 考古 1979.1: 20–2. "Henan Lingbao chutu yi pi Shang dai qingtongqi" 河南靈寶出土一批商代青銅器.

Kaogu 考古 1979.2: 107–18. "Jiangsu Jurong Fushan Guoyuan tudun mu" 江蘇句容浮山果園土墩墓.

Kaogu 考古 1980.1: 18–31. "Shanxi Xiangfen xian Taosi yizhi fajue jianbao" 山西襄汾縣陶寺遺址發掘簡報.

Kaogu 考古 1980.2: 142–6. "Hebei Handan shiqu gu yizhi diaocha jianbao" 河北邯鄲市區古遺址調查簡報.

Kaogu 考古 1980.4: 311–24. "Heilongjiang Zhaoyuan Baijinbao yizhi di yi ci fajue" 黑龍江肇源白金寶遺址第一次發掘.

Kaogu 考古 1980.5: 391–402. "Jiangling Yutaishan Chu mu fajue jianbao" 江陵雨台山楚墓發掘簡報.

Kaogu 考古 1981.1: 13–18. "1976–1978 nian Chang'an Fengxi fajue jianbao" 1976–1978 年長安灃西發掘簡報.

Kaogu 考古 1981.2: 111–18. "Henan Luoshan xian Mangzhang Shang dai mudi di yi ci fajue jianbao" 河南羅山縣蟒張商代墓地第一次發掘簡報.

Kaogu 考古 1981.6: 496–9, 555. "Sichuan Peng xian Xi Zhou jiaocang tongqi" 四川彭縣西周窖藏銅器.

Kaogu 考古 1982.1: 107, 102. "Shaanxi Tongchuan faxian Shangdai qingtongqi" 陝西銅川發現商代青銅器.

Kaogu 考古 1982.2: 142–6. "Hubei Suixian Liujiaya faxian gudai qingtongqi" 湖北隨縣瀏家崖發現古代青銅器.

Kaogu 考古 1982.6: 584–90. "Gansu Zhuanglang xian Xujianian Siwa wenhua muzang fajue jiyao" 甘肅庄浪縣徐家碾寺注文化墓葬發掘紀要.

Kaogu 考古 1982.6: 597–605. "Hebei Handan Zhao wangling" 河北邯鄲趙王陵.

Kaogu 考古 1983.1: 1–3. "Guangdong Fengkai Huangyandong dongxue yizhi" 廣東封開黃岩洞洞穴遺址.

Kaogu 考古 1983.1: 30–42. "1978–1980 nian Shanxi Xiangfen Taosi mudi fajue jianbao" 1978–1980 年山西襄汾陶寺墓地發掘簡報.

Kaogu 考古 1983.4: 289–92. "Yantai shi Shangkuang cun chutu Ji guo tongqi" 煙台市上夼村出屺土國銅器.

Kaogu 考古 1983.5: 389–97. "Shaanxi Wugong xian xinshiqi shidai ji Xi Zhou yizhi diaocha" 陝西武功縣新石器時代及西周遺址調查.

Kaogu 考古 1983.5: 430–41, 388. "1975–1979 nian Luoyang Beiyao Xi Zhou zhutong yizhi fajue" 1975–1979 年洛陽北窰西周鑄銅遺址發掘.

Kaogu 考古 1984.4: 302–32, 348. "Chunqiu zaoqi Huang Jun Meng fufu mu fajue baogao" 春秋早期黃君孟夫婦墓發掘報告.

Kaogu 考古 1984.4: 333–7. "Shandong Tengxian faxian Teng hou tongqi mu" 山東滕縣發現滕侯銅器墓.

Kaogu 考古 1984.5: 405–16, 404. "1981–1983 nian Liulihe Xi Zhou Yan guo mudi fajue jianbao" 1981–1983 年琉璃河西周燕國墓地發掘簡報.

Kaogu 考古 1984.5: 417–26. "Nei Menggu Aohan qi Zhoujiadi mudi fajue jianbao" 內蒙古敖漢旗周家地墓地發掘報告.

Kaogu 考古 1984.6: 505–9. "Yinxu Xiqu faxian yizuo chema keng" 殷墟西區發現一座車馬坑.

Kaogu 考古 1984.6: 510–14. "Hubei Suixian faxian Shang Zhou qingtongqi" 湖北隨縣發現商周青銅器.

Kaogu 考古 1984.7: 582–90. "Yanshi Erlitou yizhi 1980–1981 nian III qu fajue jianbao" 偃師二里頭遺址 1980–1981 年 III 區發掘簡報.

Kaogu 考古 1984.7: 598–601. "Gansu Yongchang Sanjiaocheng Shajing wenhua yizhi diaocha" 甘肅永昌三角城沙井文化遺址調查.

Kaogu 考古 1984.9: 779–83. "Chang'an Fengxi zao Zhou muzang fajue jilüe" 長安灃西早周墓葬發掘記略.

Kaogu 考古 1984.11: 971–3. "Hebei Xinle xian Zhongtongcun Zhanguo mu" 河北新樂縣中同村戰國墓.

Kaogu 考古 1984.12: 1069–71. "Shanxi Xiangfen Taosi yizhi shou ci faxian tongqi" 山西襄汾陶寺遺址首次發現銅器.

Kaogu 考古 1985.3: 284–6. "Pindingshan shi chutu Zhoudai qingtongqi" 平頂山市出土周代青銅器.

Kaogu 考古 1985.9: 848–9. "Shanxi Jixian chutu Shang dai qingtongqi" 山西吉縣出土商代青銅器.

Kaogu 考古 1985.10: 865–74. "Nei Menggu Aohan qi Xinglongwa yizhi fajue jianbao" 內蒙古敖漢旗興隆洼遺址發掘簡報.

Kaogu 考古 1986.1: 22–7, 11. "Chang'an Zhangjiapo Xi Zhou Jingshu mu fajue jianbao" 長安張家坡西周井叔墓發掘簡報.

Kaogu 考古 1986.3: 197–209. "1979–1981 nian Chang'an Fengxi Fengdong fajue jianbao" 1979–1981 年長安灃西灃東發掘簡報.

Kaogu 考古 1986.11: 977–81. "1984 nian Fengxi Dayuancun Xi Zhou mudi fajue jianbao" 1984 年灃西大原村西周墓地發掘簡報.

Kaogu 考古 1986.12: 1067–72. "Anyang Xuejiazhuang dongnan Yin mu fajue jianbao" 安陽薛家庄東南殷墓發掘簡報.

Kaogu 考古 1987.1: 15–32. "1984–85 nian Fengxi Xi Zhou yizhi muzang fajue baogao" 1984–85 年灃西西周遺址墓葬發掘報告.

Kaogu 考古 1987.5: 410–13, 430. "Hubei Gucheng Zaoyang chutu Zhou dai qingtongqi" 湖北谷城棗陽出土周代青銅器.

Kaogu 考古 1987.5: 414–28. "Hebei Yixian Yan Xiadu dishisanhao yizhi di yi ci fajue" 河北易縣燕下都第 13 號遺址第一次發掘.

Kaogu 考古 1987.8: 701–6, 762. "Shandong Linyi Zhongqiagou faxian sanzuo Zhou mu." 山東臨沂中洽溝發現三座周墓.

Kaogu 考古 1987.9: 773–7. "Ningxia Zhongning xian qingtong duanjian mu qingli jianbao" 寧夏中寧縣青銅短劍墓清理簡報.

Kaogu 考古 1987.12: 1062–70, 1145. "Anyang Wuguancun Beidi Shang dai jisi keng de fajue" 安陽武官村北地商代祭祀坑的發掘.

Kaogu 考古 1987.12: 1071–85. "Houma Chengwanglu jianzhuqun yizhi fajue jianbao" 侯馬呈王路建築群遺址發掘簡報.

Kaogu 考古 1988.1: 15–23. "Luoyang laocheng faxian sizuo Xi Zhou chemakeng" 洛陽老城發現四座西周車馬坑.

Kaogu 考古 1988.3: 301–32. "Neimenggu Zhukaigou yizhi" 內蒙古朱開溝遺址.

Kaogu 考古 1988.7: 601–15. "1982–1983 nian Shaanxi Wugong Huangjiahe yizhi fajue jianbao" 1982–1983 年陝西武功黃家河遺址發掘簡報.

Kaogu 考古 1988.9: 769–77, 799. "1984 nian Chang'an Puducun Xi Zhou muzang fajue jianbao" 1984 年長安普渡村西周墓葬發掘簡報.

Kaogu 考古 1988.9: 784–7. "Linzi Qi guo gu cheng de paishui xitong" 臨淄齊國故城的排水系統.

Kaogu 考古 1988.10: 882–93. "Anyang Guojiazhuang xinan de Yindai chemakeng" 安陽郭家莊西南的殷代車馬坑.

Kaogu 考古 1988.10: 894–909. "Shanxi Houma Niucun gucheng Jin guo jisi jianzhu yizhi" 山西侯馬牛村古城晉國祭祀建築遺址.

Kaogu 考古 1988.12: 1090–8. "Qiqihaer shi Dadao Sanjiazi muzang qingli" 齊齊哈爾市大道三家子墓葬清理.

Kaogu 考古 1989.1: 10–19. "Henan Xinyang xian Shihegang chutu Xi Zhou zaoqi tongqiqun" 河南信陽縣獅河港出土西周早期銅器群.

Kaogu 考古 1989.1: 20–5, 9. "Henan Xinyang shi Pingxi wuhao Chunqiu mu fajue jianbao" 河南信陽市平西五號春秋墓發掘簡報.

Kaogu 考古 1989.10: 893–905. "1987 nian Anyang Xiaotuncun dongbeidi de fajue" 1987 年安陽小屯村東北地的發掘.

Kaogu 考古 1989.12: 1057–66. "1988 nian Henan Puyang Xishuipo yizhi fajue jianbao" 1988 年河南濮陽西水坡遺址發掘簡報.

Kaogu 考古 1990.1: 20–31. "Beijing Liulihe 1193 hao da mu fajue jianbao" 北京琉璃河 1193 號大墓發掘簡報.

Kaogu 考古 1990.6: 504–10. "Shaanxi Chang'an Zhangjiapo M170 hao Jingshu mu fajue jianbao" 陝西長安張家坡 M170 號井叔墓發掘簡報.

Kaogu 考古 1991.5: 390–1. "Anyang Guojiazhuang 160 hao mu" 安陽郭家莊 160 號墓.

Kaogu 考古 1991.8: 684–703, 736. "Xinjiang Luntai xian Qunbake muzang di er san ci fajue jianbao" 新疆輪台縣群巴克墓葬第二三次發掘簡報.

Kaogu 考古 1991.9: 781–802. "Hubei Xiangyang Tuanshan Dong Zhou mu" 湖北襄陽團山東周墓.

Kaogu 考古 1992.4: 294–303. "1987 nian Yanshi Erlitou yizhi muzang fajue jianbao" 1987 年偃師二里頭遺址墓葬發掘簡報.

Kaogu 考古 1993.6: 488–99. "1991 nian Anyang Huayuanzhuang dongdi nandi fajue jianbao" 1991 年安陽花園莊東地南地發掘簡報.

Kaogu 考古 1993.6: 507–17. "Anhui Tongling shi gudai tongkuang yizhi diaocha" 安徽銅陵市古代銅礦遺址調查.

Kaogu 考古 1993.7: 656–7, 670. "Anhui Lu'an xian faxian yizuo Chunqiu shiqi muzang" 安徽六安縣發現一座春秋時期墓葬.

Kaogu 考古 1993.10: 880–901. "1991 nian Anyang Hougang Yin mu de fajue" 1991 年安陽後岡殷墓的發掘.

Kaogu 考古 1994.3: 193–205. "Qinghai Datong Huangjiazhai mudi faxian baogao" 青海大通黃家寨墓地發現報告.

Kaogu 考古 1995.9: 788–91, 801. "Luoyang dongjiao C5M906 hao Xi Zhou mu" 洛陽東郊 C5M906 號西周墓.

Kaogu xuebao 考古學報 1953.6: 57–116. "Hebei sheng Tangshanshi Jiagezhuang fajue baogao" 河北省唐山市賈各庄發掘報告.

Kaogu xuebao 考古學報 1954.8: 139–44. "Luoyang Shaogou fujin de Zhanguo mu" 洛陽燒溝附近的戰國墓.

Kaogu xuebao 考古學報 1955.9: 91–116. "1952 nian qiuji Luoyang dongjiao fajue baogao" 1952 年秋季洛陽東郊發掘報告.

Kaogu xuebao 考古學報 1957.1: 93–102. "Changsha chutu de sanzuo daxing muguo mu" 長沙出土的三座大型木槨墓.

Kaogu xuebao 考古學報 1957.1: 103–18. "Shanxi Changzhi Fenshuiling gumu de qingli" 山西長治分水嶺古墓的清理.

Kaogu xuebao 考古學報 1957.3: 63–92. "Xi'an Banpo de Zhanguo muzang" 西安半坡的戰國墓葬.

Kaogu xuebao 考古學報 1959.1: 41–60. "Changsha Chu mu" 長沙楚墓.

Kaogu xuebao 考古學報 1959.2: 15–36. "Luoyang Jianbin Dong Zhou chengzhi fajue baogao" 洛陽澗濱東周城址發掘報告.

Kaogu xuebao 考古學報 1959.4: 59–90. "Anhui Tunxi Xi Zhou muzang fajue baogao" 安徽屯溪西周墓葬發掘報告.

Kaogu xuebao 考古學報 1963.1: 17–44. "Qinghai Dulan xian Nuomuhong Dalitaliha yizhi diaocha yu shijue" 青海都蘭縣諾木洪搭里他里哈遺址調查與試掘.

Kaogu xuebao 考古學報 1965.1: 83–106. "Hebei Yixian Yan Xiadu gucheng kancha he shijue" 河北易縣燕下都古城勘察和試掘.

Kaogu xuebao 考古學報 1965.2: 79–102. "Hebei Yixian Yan Xiadu dishiliuhao mu fajue" 河北易縣燕下都第十六號墓發掘.

Kaogu xuebao 考古學報 1974.2: 63–86. "Changzhi Fenshuiling 269 270 hao Dong Zhou mu" 長治分水嶺 269 270 號東周墓.

Kaogu xuebao 考古學報 1975.1: 141–56. "Shenyang Zhenjiawazi de liangzuo qingtong shidai muzang" 沈陽鄭家窪子的兩座青銅時代墓葬.

Kaogu xuebao 考古學報 1977.1: 73–104. "Linzi Langjiazhuang yihao Dong zhou xunren mu" 臨淄郎家庄一號東周殉人墓.

Kaogu xuebao 考古學報 1977.2: 99–130. "Gansu Lingtai Baicaopo Xi Zhou mu" 甘肅靈台白草坡西周墓.

Kaogu xuebao 考古學報 1978.1: 39–93. "Hemudu yizhi di yi qi fajue baogao" 河姆渡遺址第一期發掘報告.

Kaogu xuebao 考古學報 1978.2: 211–58. "Pingle Yinshanling Zhanguo mu" 平樂銀山嶺戰國墓.

Kaogu xuebao 考古學報 1978.3: 317–36. "Junan Dadian Chunqiu shiqi Ju guo xunrenmu" 莒南大店春秋時期莒國殉人墓.

Kaogu xuebao 考古學報 1978.4: 449–66. "Shenyang Xinle yizhi shijue baogao" 瀋陽新樂遺址試掘報告.

Kaogu xuebao 考古學報 1979.1: 27–146. "1969–1977 nian Yinxu xiqu muzang fajue baogao" 1969–1977 年殷墟西區墓葬發掘報告.

Kaogu xuebao 考古學報 1980.3: 329–85. "Shandong Zhucheng Chengzi yizhi fajue baogao" 山東諸城呈子遺址發掘報告.

Kaogu xuebao 考古學報 1980.4: 457–502. "1967 nian Chang'an Zhangjiapo Xi Zhou muzang de fajue" 1967 年長安張家坡西周墓葬的發掘.

Kaogu xuebao 考古學報 1981.2: 199–216. "Pamier gaoyuan gu mu" 帕米爾高原古墓.

Kaogu xuebao 考古學報 1981.3: 287–302. "Zhongguo zaoqi tongqi de chubu yanjiu" 中國早期銅器的初步研究. English translation by Julia Murray, "A Preliminary Study of Early Chinese Copper and Bronze Artifacts." *EC* 9–10 (1983–5): 261–89.

Kaogu xuebao 考古學報 1981.4: 491–518. "Anyang Xiaotun cun bei de liang zuo Yin dai mu" 安陽小屯村北的兩座殷代墓.

Kaogu xuebao 考古學報 1982.1: 71–116. "Jiangling Tianxingguan yihao Chu mu" 江陵天星觀一號楚墓.

Kaogu xuebao 考古學報 1982.3: 325–50; 1982.4: 477–508. "Chu du Jinancheng de kancha yu fajue" 楚都紀南城的勘察與發掘.

Kaogu xuebao 考古學報 1984.4: 503–29. "Shanxi Changzhi xian Dong Zhou mu" 山西長治縣東周墓.

Kaogu xuebao 考古學報 1985.2: 209–22. "Shenyang Xinle yizhi di er ci fajue baogao" 瀋陽新樂遺址第二次發掘報告.

Kaogu xuebao 考古學報 1986.2: 153–97. "Luoshan Tianhu Shang Zhou mudi" 羅山天湖商周墓地.

Kaogu xuebao 考古學報 1987.1: 99–117. "Yinxu 259 260 hao mu fajue baogao" 殷墟 259 260 號墓發掘報告.

Kaogu xuebao 考古學報 1987.3: 359–96. "Gansu Gangu Maojiaping yizhi fajue baogao" 甘肅甘谷毛家坪遺址發掘報告.

Kaogu xuebao 考古學報 1988.1: 75–99. "Xinjiang Hejing xian Chawuhu goukou yi hao muzang" 新疆和靜縣察吾乎溝口一號墓葬.

Kaogu xuebao 考古學報 1988.3: 301–32. "Nei Menggu Zhukaigou yizhi" 內蒙古朱開溝遺址.

Kaogu xuebao 考古學報 1988.4: 455–500. "Dangyang Caojiagang wu hao Chu mu" 當陽曹家崗五號楚墓.

Kaogu xuebao 考古學報 1989.1: 57–81. "Liangcheng Guoxian Yaozi mudi" 涼城崞縣窯子墓地.

Kaogu xuebao 考古學報 1990.2: 205–37. "Yongchang Sanjiaocheng yu Hamadun Shajing wenhua yicun" 永昌三角城與蛤蟆墩沙井文化遺存.

Kaogu xuebao 考古學報 1991.4: 449–95. "Xue guo gucheng kancha he muzang fajue baogao" 薛國故城勘查和墓葬發掘報告.

Kaogu xuebao 考古學報 1992.1: 97–128. "1986–1987 nian Anyang Huayuanzhuang nandi fajue jianbao" 1986–1987 年安陽花園莊南地發掘簡報.

Kaogu xuebao 考古學報 1992.3: 365–92. "Tengzhou Qianzhangda Shangdai muzang" 滕州前掌大商代墓葬.

Kaogu xuebao 考古學報 1993.1: 13–56. "Ningxia Guyuan Yanglang qingtong wenhua mudi" 寧夏固原楊郎青銅文化墓地.

Kaogu xuebao 考古學報 1993.2: 207–37. "Jiangsu Dantu Nangangshan tudunmu" 江蘇丹徒南崗山土墩墓.

Kaogu xuebao 考古學報 1995.1: 79–107. "Ningxia Pengbao yujiazhuang mudi" 宁夏彭堡于家庄墓地.

Kaogu yu wenwu 考古與文物 1980.2: 17–20. "Shaanxi Chunhua Shijiayuan chutu Xi Zhou Da ding" 陝西淳化史家原出土西周大鼎.

Kaogu yu wenwu 考古與文物 1981.1: 12–38. "Shaanxi Fengxiang Gaozhuang Qin mu fajue jianbao" 陝西鳳翔高庄秦墓發掘簡報.

Kaogu yu wenwu 考古與文物 1981.4: 34–6. "Gansu Yongdeng Yushugou de Shajing Muzang" 甘肅永登榆樹溝的沙井墓葬.

Kaogu yu wenwu 考古與文物 1982.5: 12–20. "Fengxiang Majiazhuang Chunqiu Qin yi hao jianzhu yizhi diyici fajue jianbao" 鳳翔馬家庄春秋秦一號建築遺址第一次發掘簡報.

Kaogu yu wenwu 考古與文物 1983.1: 5–11. "Shanxi Wenxi Qiujiazhuang Zhanguo muzang fajue jianbao" 山西聞喜邱家庄戰國墓葬發掘簡報.

Kaogu yu wenwu 考古與文物 1985.1: 12–18. "Fufeng Qijiacun qi ba hao Xi Zhou tongqi jiaocang qingli jianbao" 扶風齊家村七八號西周銅器窖藏清理簡報.

Kaogu yu wenwu 考古與文物 1985.2: 7–20. "Qin du Yongcheng zuantan yu shijue jianbao" 秦都雍城鑽探與試掘簡報.

Kaogu yu wenwu 考古與文物 1986.1: 1–7. "Gansu Chongxin Yujiawan Zhou mu fajue jianbao" 甘肅崇信于家灣周墓發掘簡報.

Kaogu yu wenwu 考古與文物 1987.2: 1–8. "Tongchuan shi Wangjiahe mudi fajue jianbao" 銅川市王家河墓地發掘簡報.

Kaogu yu wenwu 考古與文物 1987.4: 17–18. "Shaanxi Fengxiang Shuigou Zhou mu qingliji" 陝西鳳翔水溝周墓清理記.

Kaogu yu wenwu 考古與文物 1987.4: 19–28. "Qin dongling diyihao lingyuan tanchaji" 秦東陵第一號陵園探查記.

Kaogu yu wenwu 考古與文物 1987.4: 86–8. "Qin Dongling Kancha chuyi" 秦東陵勘查初議.

Kaogu yu wenwu 考古與文物 1988.1: 57–60. "Shanxi Houma Jin guo yizhi Niucun gucheng de shijue" 山西侯馬晉國遺址牛村古城的試掘.

Kaogu yu wenwu 考古與文物 1989.3: 13–19. "Houma Jin guo taoyao yizhi kantan yu fajue" 侯馬晉國陶窯遺址勘探與發掘.

Kaoguxue jikan 考古學集刊 2 (1982): 181–93. "Yinxu jinshu qiwu chengfen de ceding baogao (1): Fu Hao mu tongqi ceding" 殷墟金屬器物成份的測定報告（一）：婦好墓銅器測定.

Kaoguxue jikan 考古學集刊 5 (1987): 157–93. "Hebei Pingshan Sanji gucheng diaocha yu muzang fajue" 河北平山三汲古城調查與墓葬發掘.

Kaoguxue yanjiu 考古學研究 1 (1992): 124–228. "Yicheng Quwo Kaogu kanchaji" 翼城曲沃考古勘察記.

Karlbeck, Orvar. "Anyang Moulds." *BMFEA* 7 (1935): 39–60.

Karlgren, Bernhard. *Analytic Dictionary of Chinese and Sino-Japanese.* Paris: Librairie orientaliste Paul Geuthner, 1923; rpt. New York: Dover, 1974.

Karlgren, Bernhard. "The Book of Documents." *BMFEA* 22 (1950): 1–81.

Karlgren, Bernhard. *The Book of Odes.* Stockholm: Museum of Far Eastern Antiquities, 1950.

Karlgren, Bernhard. "Early Chinese Mirrors." *BMFEA* 40 (1968): 79–98.

Karlgren, Bernhard. *Études sur la phonologie chinoise.* Göteborg: Elanders, 1915–26.

Karlgren, Bernhard. "Glosses on the Book of Documents." *BMFEA* 20 (1948): 39–315; rpt. Stockholm: Museum of Far Eastern Antiquities, 1970.

Karlgren, Bernhard. "Grammata Serica." *BMFEA* 12 (1940): 1–71.

Karlgren, Bernhard. "Grammata Serica Recensa." *BMFEA* 29 (1957): 1–332.

Karlgren, Bernhard. "New Studies on Chinese Bronzes." *BMFEA* 9 (1937): 1–117.

Karlgren, Bernhard. "Some Weapons and Tools of the Yin Dynasty." *BMFEA* 17 (1945): 101–44.

Karlgren, Bernhard. "Yin and Chou in Chinese Bronzes." *BMFEA* 8 (1936): 9–156.

Keightley, David N. "Akatsuka Kiyoshi and the Culture of Early China: A Study in Historical Method." *HJAS* 42 (1982): 139–92.

Keightley, David N. "Archaeology and Mentality: The Making of China." *Representations* 18 (1987): 91–128. (Chinese versions: "Cong kaogu qiwu kan Zhongguo siwei shijie de xingcheng" 從考古器物看中國思維世界的形成, *Zhongguo wenhua yu Zhongguo zhexue* 中國文化與中國哲學 1988: 466–500; "Kaoguxue yu sixiang zhuangtai: Zhongguo de chuangjian" 考古學與思想狀態：中國的創建, trans. Chen Xingcan 陳星燦, *Hua Xia kaogu* 華夏考古 1993.1: 97–108.)

Keightley, David N. "The *Bamboo Annals* and Shang-Chou Chronology." *HJAS* 38 (1978): 23–38.

Keightley, David N. "The Late Shang State: When, Where, and What?" In *The Origins of Chinese Civilization*, ed. David N. Keightley. Berkeley: University of California Press, 1983, pp. 523–64.

Keightley, David N. "Public Work in Ancient China: A Study of Forced Labor in the Shang and Western Chou." Ph.D. dissertation, Columbia University, 1969.

Keightley, David N. "Religion and the Rise of Urbanism." *JAOS* 93, 4 (1973): 527–38.

Keightley, David N. "The Religious Commitment: Shang Theology and the Genesis of Chinese Political Culture." *History of Religions* 17 (1978): 211–24.

Keightley, David N. "Shang China Is Coming of Age: A Review Article." *JAS* 41 (1982): 549–57.

Keightley, David N. "Shang Divination and Metaphysics." *Philosophy East and West* 38 (1988): 367–97.

Keightley, David N. "The Shang State as Seen in the Oracle-Bone Inscriptions." *EC* 5 (1979–80): 25–34.

Keightley, David N. *Sources of Shang History: The Oracle-Bone Inscriptions of Bronze Age China*. Berkeley: University of California Press, 1978. (2nd printing, with minor revisions, 1985.)

Keightley, David N. "Sources of Shang History: Two Major Oracle-Bone Collections Published in the People's Republic of China." *JAOS* 110, 1 (1990): 39–59.

Keightley, David N., ed. *The Origins of Chinese Civilization*. Berkeley: University of California Press, 1983.

Kemp, Barry J. *Ancient Egypt: Anatomy of A Civilization*, London: Routledge, 1989.

Kenk, Roman. *Das Gräberfeld der hunno-sarmatischen Zeit von Kokel', Tuva, Süd-Sibirien*. Munich: Beck, 1984.

Kenk, Roman. *Grabfunde der Skythenzeit aus Tuva, Süd-Sibirien*. Munich: Beck, 1986.

Keyser, Barbara. "Decor Replication in Two Late Chou Bronze Chien." *Ars Orientalis* 11 (1979): 127–62.

Khazanov, Anatoli. *Nomads of the Outside World*. Cambridge University Press, 1984.

Kimura Masao 木村正雄. *Chûgoku kodai teikoku no keisei: Toku ni sono seiritsu no kiso jôken* 中國古代帝國の形成：特にその成立の基礎條件. Tokyo: Fumeitô, 1967.

Kiselev, S. V. *Drevniaia istoriia Iuzhnoi Sibiri*. Moscow: Nauka, 1951.

Klein, Richard G. *The Human Career: Human Biological and Cultural Origins*. Chicago: University of Chicago Press, 1989.

Knoblock, John H. "The Chronology of Xunzi's Works." *EC* 8 (1982–3): 29–52.

Knoblock, John H. *Xunzi: A Translation and Study of the Complete Works*. 3 vols. Stanford, Calif.: Stanford University Press, vol. 1, 1988; vol. 2, 1990; vol. 3, 1994.

Koga Noboru 谷賀登. *Kan Chôanjô to senpaku kenkyû teiri seido* 漢長安城と阡陌鄉亭里制度. Tokyo: Yôsankaku, 1980.

Kolb, Raimund Theodor. *Die Infanterie im alten China: Ein Beitrag zur Militärgeschichte der Vor-Zhan-Guo-Zeit*. Mainz: Philip von Zabern, 1991.

Komai Kazuchika 駒井和愛. "En koku no sôryûmon gatô" 燕國の雙龍文瓦當. In *Chûgoku kôkogaku ronsô* 中國考古學論叢. Tokyo: Keiyûsha, 1974, pp. 323–7.

Komai Kazuchika 駒井和愛. *Kyokufu Rojô no iseki* 曲阜魯城の遺跡. *Kôkogaku kenkyû* 考古學 研究 2 (1950).

Komai Kazuchika 駒井和愛 and Sekino Takeshi 關野雄. *Hantan* 邯鄲. *Archaeologia Orientalis*, series B, 7 (Tokyo, 1954).

Kong Xiangsheng 孔祥生 and Liu Yiman 劉一曼. *Zhongguo gudai tongjing* 中國古代銅鏡. Beijing: Wenwu, 1984.

Korit, Robert L., Hiroshi Akashi, and Walter Gilbert. "Absence of Polymorphism at the ZFY Locus on the Human Y Chromosome." *Science* 268 (1995): 1183–5.

Kovalev, A. "'Karasuk-dolche,' Hirschsteine und die Nomaden der chinesischen Annalen im Alterum." In *Maoqinggou: Ein eisenzeitliches Gräberfeld in der Ordos-Region (Innere Mongolei)*, ed. Thomas Höllman and Georg W. Kossack. Mainz: Philipp von Zabern, 1992: 46–87.

Kunstausstellung der Volksrepublik China. [East] Berlin: Staatliche Museen Berlin, 1951.

Kuzmina, Elena E. "Les steppes de l'Asie centrale à l'Epoque du bronze: La culture d'Andronovo." *Dossiers d'archéologie* 185 (1993): 82–9.

Lao Bomin 勞伯敏. "Huzhou Xiagucheng chutan" 湖州下菰城初探. In *Zhongguo Kaoguxuehui di wu ci nianhui (1985) lunwenji* 中國考古學會第五次年會 (1985) 論文集. Beijing: Wenwu, 1988, pp. 31–9.

Lattimore, Owen. *Inner Asian Frontiers of China*. 1940; rpt. Boston: Beacon Press, 1962.

Lau, D. C. *Confucius: The Analects: Translated with an Introduction*. Harmondsworth: Penguin, 1978.

Lau, D. C. *Lao Tzu: Tao Te Ching*. Harmondsworth: Penguin, 1963.

Lau, D. C. *Mencius: Translated with an Introduction*. Harmondsworth: Penguin, 1970.

Lawton, Thomas. *Chinese Art of the Warring States Period: Change and Continuity, 480–222 B.C.* Washington, D.C.: Freer Gallery of Art, 1982.

Lawton, Thomas. "A Group of Early Western Chou Period Bronze Vessels." *Ars Orientalis* 10 (1975): 111–21.

Le Blanc, Charles. Huai-nan Tzu 淮南子: *Philosophical Synthesis in Early Han Thought: The Idea of Resonance (Kan-ying* 感應*), with a Translation and Analysis of Chapter Six*. Hong Kong: Hong Kong University Press, 1985.

Le Coq, Albert von. *Buried Treasures of Chinese Turkestan*. London: Allen & Unwin, 1928. Rpt. with an introduction by Peter Hopkirk. Oxford: Oxford University Press, 1985.

Leban, Carl. "Managing Heaven's Mandate: Coded Communication in the Accession of Ts'ao P'ei, A.D. 220." In *Ancient China: Studies in Early Civilization*, ed. David T. Roy and Tsuen-hsuin Tsien. Hong Kong: Chinese University Press, 1978, pp. 315–42.

Lederose, Lothar, and Adele Schlombs. *Jenseits der Grossen Mauer: Der Erste Kaiser von China und seine Terracotta-armee*. Gütersloh München: Bertelsmann Lexicon, 1990.

Lee, Jig-chuen 李植全. "Cong liangge jiaodu lai kan Lunyu zhong de dao" 從兩個角度來看 論語中的道. *Xinya xueshu jikan* 新亞學術集刊 3 (1982): 171–7.

Lee, Sherman E. *A History of Far Eastern Art*, 4th ed. New York: Harry N. Abrams, 1982.

Leeming, Frank. "Official Landscapes in Traditional China." *JESHO* 23 (1980): 153–204.

Lefeuvre, J. A. "An Oracle Bone in the Hong Kong Museum of History and the Shang Standard of the Center." *Journal of the Hong Kong Archaeological Society* 7 (1976–8): 46–68.

Lefeuvre, J. A. "Les inscriptions des Shang sur carapaces de tortue et sur os: apercu historique et bibliographique de la découverte et des premières études." *TP* 61 (1975): 1–82.

Legge, James. *The Chinese Classics. Vol. 1: Confucian Analects, The Great Learning, and the Doctrine of the Mean*. 2nd ed. Oxford: Clarendon, 1893; rpt. Hong Kong: Hong Kong University Press, 1960.

Legge, James. *The Chinese Classics. Vol. 2: The Works of Mencius.* 2nd ed. Oxford: Clarendon, 1895; rpt. Hong Kong: University of Hong Kong Press, 1960.

Legge, James. *The Chinese Classics. Vol. 3: The Shoo King, or Book of Historical Documents.* London: Henry Frowde, 1865; 2nd ed. Oxford: Clarendon, 1893–4; rpt. Hong Kong: University of Hong Kong Press, 1960.

Legge, James. *The Chinese Classics. Vol. 4: The She King.* London: Trübner, 1871; rpt. Hong Kong: Hong Kong University Press, 1960.

Legge, James, trans. *The Chinese Classics. Vol. 5: The Ch'un Ts'ew with the Tso Chuen.* London: Trübner, 1872; rpt. Hong Kong: Hong Kong University Press, 1960.

Legge, James. trans. *Li Chi, Book of Rites.* 2 vols. 1885; rpt. New York: University Books, 1967.

Lei Congyun 雷從雲. "Chu shi jing de leixing yu fenqi" 楚式鏡的類型與分期. *Jiang Han kaogu* 江漢考古 1982.2: 20–36.

Lei Xueqi 雷學淇. *Zhushu jinian yizheng* 竹書記年義證. 1810; rpt. Taipei: Yiwen, 1977.

Levi, Jean. *Les fonctionnaires divins: Politique, despotisme et mystique en Chine ancienne.* Paris: Seuil, 1989.

Levine, Marsha. "Dereivka and the Problem of Horse Domestication." *Antiquity* 64 (1990): 727–40.

Lewis, Mark Edward. *Sanctioned Violence in Early China.* Albany: State University of New York Press, 1990.

Li Anmin 李安民. "Chu wenhua de li yu dengji yanjiu" 楚文化的禮與等級研究. *Dongnan wenhua* 東南文化 1991.6: 198–206, 72.

Li Bing-yuan, Yang Yi-chou, Zhang Qing-song, and Wang Fu-bao. "On the Environmental Evolution of Xizang (Tibet) in Holocene." In *Quaternary Geology and Environment of China,* ed. Liu Tung-sheng. Beijing: China Ocean; and Berlin: Springer-Verlag, 1985, pp. 234–40.

Li Boqian 李伯謙. "Shilun Wu Yue wenhua" 試論吳越文化. *Wenwu jikan* 文物集刊 3 (1981): 133–43.

Li Boqian 李伯謙. "Zhongguo qingtong wenhua de fazhan jieduan yu fenqu xitong" 中國青銅文化的發展階段與分區係統. *Hua Xia kaogu* 華夏考古 1990.2: 82–91.

Li Changqing 李長慶 and Tian Ye 田野. "Zuguo lishi wenwu de you yici zhongyao faxian" 祖國歷史文物的又一次重要發現. *Wenwu* 文物 1957.4: 5–9.

Li Chenqi 李陳奇 et al. "Song Nen pingyuan qingtong yu chuxing zaoqi tieqi shidai wenhua leixing de yanjiu" 松嫩平原青銅與雛形早期鐵器時代文化類型的研究. *Beifang wenwu* 北方文物 1994.1: 2–9.

Li, Chi. *The Beginnings of Chinese Civilization: Three Lectures Illustrated with Finds at Anyang.* Seattle: University of Washington Press, 1957.

Li, Chi. *Anyang.* Seattle: University of Washington Press, 1977.

Li, Chung 李眾. "Studies on the Iron Blade of a Shang Dynasty Bronze *Yüeh*-axe Unearthed at Kao-ch'eng, Hopei, China." *Ars Orientalis* 11 (1979): 259–89. Translation of "Guanyu Gaocheng Shang dai tong yue tie ren de fenxi" 關於藁城商代銅鉞鐵刃的分析. *Kaogu xuebao* 考古學報 1976.2: 17–34.

Li Cong-xian, Li Ping, and Wang Li. "Postglacial Marine Beds in the Coastal and Deltaic Areas in East China." In *Quaternary Geology and Environment of China,* ed. Liu Tung-sheng. Beijing: China Ocean Press; and Berlin: Springer-Verlag, 1985, pp. 30–5.

Li Feng 李峰. "Guo guo mudi tongqiqun de fenqi ji qi xiangguan wenti" 虢國墓地銅器群的分期及其相關問題. *Kaogu* 考古 1988.11: 1035–43.

Li Feng 李峰. "Shilun Shaanxi chutu Shangdai tongqi de fenqi yu fenqu" 試論陝西出土商代銅器的分期與分區. *Kaogu yu wenwu* 考古與文物 1986.3: 53–63.

Li Feng 李峰. "Xian Zhou wenhua de neihan ji qi yuanyuan tantao" 先周文化的內涵及其淵源探討. *Kaogu xuebao* 考古學報 1991.3: 265–84.

Li Guoliang 李國梁. "Wannan chutu de qingtongqi" 皖南出土的青銅器. *Wenwu yanjiu* 文物研究 4 (1988): 161–6.

Li Hancai 李漢才. "Qinghai Huangzhong xian faxian gudai shuangma tong yue he tong jing" 青海湟中縣發現古代雙馬銅鉞和銅鏡. *Wenwu* 文物 1992.2: 16.

Li Hengmei 李衡眉. *Lun Zhao Mu zhidu* 論昭穆制度. Taipei: Wenjin, 1992.

Li, Hui-lin. "The Domestication of Plants in China: Ecogeographical Considerations." In *The Origins of Chinese Civilization*, ed. David N. Keightley. Berkeley: University of California Press, 1983, pp. 21–63.

Li Ji 李濟. "Heitao wenhua zai Zhongguo shanggushi zhong suo zhan de diwei" 黑陶文化在中國上古史中所佔的地位. *Bulletin of the Department of Archaeology and Anthropology* 考古人類學刊 21–2 (1963): 1–12.

Li Ji 李濟. "Ji Xiaotun chutu de qingtong qi" 記小屯出土的青銅器. *Zhongguo kaogu xuebao* 中國考古學報 1949.4: 1–70.

Li Ji 李濟, Liang Siyong 梁思永, and Dong Zuobin 董作賓, eds. *Chengziyai: Shandong Licheng Xian Longshan Zhen zhi heitao wenhua yizhi* 城子崖：山東歷城縣龍山鎮之黑陶文化遺址. Nanjing: Academia Sinica, 1934.

Li Jiahao 李家浩. "Wangjiatai Qin jian Yizhan wei *Guizang* kao" 王家臺秦簡易占為歸藏考. *Chuantong wenhua yu xiandaihua* 傳統文化與現代化 1997.1: 46–52.

Li Jian 李監 and Zhang Longhai 張隆海. "Linzi chutu de jijian qingtongqi" 臨淄出土的幾件青銅器. *Kaogu* 考古 1985.4: 380–1.

Li Jingchi 李鏡池. *Zhouyi tanyuan* 周易探源. Beijing: Zhonghua, 1978.

Li Jinghan 李經漢. "Shilun Xiajiadian xiaceng wenhua de fenqi he leixing" 試論夏家店下層文化的分期和類型. In *Zhongguo Kaogu xuehui di yi ci (1979) nianhui lunwenji* 中國考古學會第一次 (1979) 年會論文集. Beijing: Wenwu, 1980, pp. 163–70.

Li Ling. "An Archaeological Study of Taiyi (Grand One) Worship." *Early Medieval China* 2 (1995–6): 1–39.

Li Ling 李零. *Changsha Zidanku Zhanguo Chu boshu yanjiu* 長沙子彈庫戰國楚帛書研究. Beijing: Zhonghua, 1985.

Li Ling 李零. "Chu guo tongqi mingwen biannian huishi" 楚國銅器銘文編年匯釋. *Gu wenzi yanjiu* 古文字研究 13 (1986): 353–97.

Li Ling 李零. "Chu guo zuyuan shixi de wenzixue zhengming" 楚國族原世系的文字學證明. *Wenwu* 文物 1991.2: 47–54, 90.

Li Ling 李零. "Chu Shuzhisun Peng jiujing shi shui?" 楚叔之孫倗究竟是誰? *Zhongyuan wenwu* 中原文物 1981.4: 36–7.

Li Ling 李零. "Chunqiu Qin qi shitan: Xinchu Qin Gong zhong bo ming yu guoqu zhulu Qin zhong guiming de duidu." 春秋秦器試探一新出秦公鐘鎛銘與過去著錄秦鐘簋銘的對讀. *Kaogu* 考古 1979.6: 515–21.

Li Ling. "Formulaic Structure of Chu Divinatory Bamboo Slips." *EC* 15 (1990): 71–86.

Li Ling 李零. "Lun Dong Zhou shiqi de Chu guo dianxing tongqiqun" 論東周時期的楚國典型銅器群. *Guwenzi yanjiu* 古文字研究 19 (1992): 136–78.

Li Ling. Lothar von Falkenhausen, trans. "On the Typology of Chu Bronzes." *Beiträge zur Allgemeinen und Vergleichenden Archäologie* 11 (1991): 57–113.

Li Ling 李零. "Shi Ji zhong suojian Qin zaoqi duyi zangdi" 史記中所見秦早期都邑葬地. *Wenshi* 文史 20 (1982): 15–23.

Li Ling 李零. *Zhongguo fangshu kao* 中國方術考. Beijing: Renmin Zhongguo, 1993.

Li Longzhang 李龍章. "Hunan Liang Guang qingtongshidai Yue mu yanjiu" 湖南兩廣青銅時代越墓研究. *Kaogu xuebao* 考古學報 1995.3: 275–312.

Li Mengcun 李孟存 and Chang Jincang 常金倉. *Jin guo shi gangyao* 晉國史綱要. Taiyuan: Shanxi Renmin, 1988.

Li Min 李民. "Shi Shang shu Zhou ren zun Xia shuo" 釋尚書周人尊夏説. *Zhongguo shi yanjiu* 中國史研究 1982.2: 128–34.

Li, Paul Jenkuei. "Is Chinese Genetically Related to Austronesian?" In *The Ancestry of the Chinese*, ed. William S. Y. Wang. Journal of Chinese Linguistics monograph series, no. 8. Berkeley: Journal of Chinese Linguistics, 1995, pp. 93–112.

Li Shuicheng 李水城. "Zhongguo beifang didai de shewenqi yanjiu" 中國北方地帶的蛇紋器研究. *Wenwu* 文物 1992.1: 50–7.

Li Xiaoding 李孝定. *Jiagu wenzi jishi* 甲骨文字集釋. Zhongyang yanjiuyuan lishi yuyan yanjiusuo zhuankan zhi wushi 中央研究院歷史語言研究所專刊之五十. 8 vols. Nangang, 1965.

Li Xiating 李夏庭. "Hunyuan yiqi yanjiu" 渾源彝器研究. *Wenwu* 文物 1992.10: 61–75.

Li Xiating 李夏庭 et al. *Art of the Houma Foundry*, ed. Robert W. Bagley. Princeton, N.J.: Princeton University Press, 1996.

Li Xingjian 李行健. "Ye shuo jiang he – cong jiang he hanyi de bianhua kan ciyi de fazhan he ciyu de xunshi" 也説江河 – 從江河含義的變化看詞義的發展和詞語的訓釋. *Yuyanxue luncong* 語言學論叢 14 (1987): 70–85.

Li Xixing 李西興. "Guanyu Zhou Xuanwang zhi si de kaocha" 關於周宣王之死的考察. In *Xi Zhou shi lunwenji* 西周史論文集. 2 vols. Xi'an: Shaanxi Renmin jiaoyu, 1983, vol. 2, pp. 966–76.

Li, Xueqin. "Are They Shang Inscriptions or Zhou Inscriptions?" *Early China* 12 (1985–7): 173–6.

Li, Xueqin 李學勤. "Chu Bronzes and Chu Culture." In *New Perspectives on Chu Culture on the Eastern Zhou Period*, ed. Thomas Lawton. Washington, D.C.: Smithsonian Institution, 1991.

Li Xueqin 李學勤. "Cong xinchu qingtongqi kan Changjiang xiayou wenhua fazhan" 從新出青銅器看長江下游文化發展. *Wenwu* 文物 1980.8: 35–40, 84.

Li, Xueqin. *Eastern Zhou and Qin Civilizations*, trans. K. C. Chang. New Haven, Conn.: Yale University Press, 1985.

Li Xueqin 李學勤. "Fangmatan jian zhong de zhiguai gushi" 放馬灘簡中的志怪故事. *Wenwu* 文物 1990.4: 43–7.

Li Xueqin 李學勤. "Guangshan Huang guo mu de jige wenti" 光山黃國墓的幾個問題. *Kaogu yu wenwu* 考古與文物 1985.2: 49–52.

Li Xueqin 李學勤. *Jianbo yi ji yu xueshu shi* 簡帛佚籍與學術史. Taipei: Shibao wenhua, 1994.

Li, Xueqin. "Liangzhu Culture and the Shang Dynasty *Taotie* Motif." In *The Problem of Meaning in Early Chinese Ritual Bronzes*, ed. Roderick Whitfield. London: School of Oriental and African Studies, 1993, pp. 56–66.

Li Xueqin 李學勤. "Lun Duo You ding de shidai ji yiyi" 論多友鼎的時代及意義. *Renwen zazhi* 人文雜誌 1981.6: 87–92.

Li Xueqin 李學勤. "Lun Fu Hao mu de niandai ji youguan wenti" 論婦好墓的年代及有關問題. *Wenwu* 文物 1977.11: 32–7. Rpt. in Li Xueqin, *Xin chu qingtongqi yanjiu* 新出青銅器研究. Beijing: Wenwu, 1990, pp. 18–26.

Li Xueqin 李學勤. "Lun Han Huai jian de Chunqiu tongqi" 論漢淮間的春秋銅器. *Wenwu* 文物 1980.1: 54–8.

Li Xueqin 李學勤. "Lun Zhong Chengfu gui yu Shen guo" 論仲再父簋與申國. *Zhongyuan wenwu* 中原文物 1984.4: 31–2, 39.

Li Xueqin 李學勤. "Pingshan muzangqun yu Zhongshan guo de wenhua" 平山墓葬群與中山國的文化. *Wenwu* 文物 1979.1: 37–41.

Li Xueqin 李學勤. "Qingchuan Haojiaping mudu yanjiu" 青川郝家坪木牘研究. *Wenwu* 文物 1982.10: 68–72.

Li Xueqin 李學勤. *Xin chu qingtongqi yanjiu* 新出青銅器研究. Beijing: Wenwu, 1990.

Li Xueqin 李學勤. *Yindai dili jianlun* 殷代地理簡論. Beijing: Kexue, 1959.

Li Xueqin 李學勤. "Yinxu jiagu fenqi xinlun" 殷墟甲骨分期新論. *Zhongyuan wenwu* 中原文物, 1990.3: 37–44.

Li Xueqin 李學勤. "Zeng guo zhi mi" 曾國之迷. *Guangming ribao* 光明日報 October 4, 1978. Rpt. in Li Xueqin, *Xinchu qingtongqi yanjiu* 新出青銅器研究. Beijing: Wenwu, 1990, pp. 146–50.

Li Xueqin 李學勤. *Zhouyi jingzhuan suyuan* 周易經傳溯源. Changchun: Changchun, 1992.

Li Xueqin 李學勤. *Zhongguo meishu quanji: Gongyi meishu bian 4, Qingtongqi (shang)* 中國美術全集：工藝美術編 4，青銅器（上）. Beijing: Wenwu, 1985.

Li Xueqin 李學勤 and Li Ling 李零. "Pingshan sanqi yu Zhongshan guo shi de ruogan wenti" 平山三器與中山國史的若干問題. *Kaogu xuebao* 考古學報 1979.2: 147–70.

Li Yujie 李玉潔. *Xian Qin sangzang zhidu yanjiu* 先秦喪葬制度研究. Luoyang: Zhongzhou guji, 1991.

Li, Yu-ning, ed. *Shang Yang's Reforms and State Control in China.* White Plains, N.Y. Sharpe, 1977.

Li Zhaohe 李昭和. "Bashu yu Chu qiqi chutan" 巴蜀與楚漆器初探. *Zhongguo kaogu xuehui di er ci nianhui lunwenji* 中國考古學會第二次年會論文集. Beijing: Wenwu, 1980, pp. 93–9.

Li Zhiyan 李知宴. "Zhongshan wangmu chutu de taoqi" 中山王墓出土的陶器. *Gugong bowuyuan yuankan* 故宮博物院院刊 1979.2: 93–4.

Li Zizhi 李自智. "Jianguo yilai Shaanxi Shang Zhou kaogu shuyao" 建國以來陝西商周考古述要. *Kaogu yu wenwu* 考古與文物 1988.5–6: 60–70.

Li Zizhi 李自智. "Yin Shang liang Zhou de chema xunzang" 殷商兩周的車馬殉葬. In *Zhou wenhua lunji* 周文化論集. Xi'an: San Qin, 1993, pp. 168–86.

Lian Shaoming 連邵名. "Yinxu buci suojian Shang dai de wangji" 殷墟卜辭所見商代的王畿. *Kaogu yu wenwu* 考古與文物, 1995.5: 38–43, 66.

Liang Qixiong 梁啟雄. *Hanzi qianjie* 韓子淺解. Beijing: Zhonghua, 1960.

Liang Qixiong 梁啟雄. *Xunzi jianshi* 荀子簡釋. Beijing: Guji, 1956.

Liang Shangchun 梁上椿. *Yanku cangjing* 巖窟藏鏡. 4 vols. Beijing: 1938–42.

Liang Siyong 梁思永. "Xiaotun Longshan yu Yangshao" 小屯龍山與仰韶. In *Qingzhu Cai Yuanpei xiansheng liushiwu sui lunwenji* 慶祝蔡元培先生六十五歲論文集. Nanjing: Institute of History and Philology, Academia Sinica, 1933, pp. 555–67.

Liang Siyong 梁思永 and Gao Quxun 高去尋. *Houjiazhuang 1001-hao damu* 侯家莊 1001-號大墓. 2 vols. Taipei: Academia Sinica, 1962.

Liang Xingpeng 梁星彭 and Feng Xiaotang 馮孝堂. "Shaanxi Chang'an Fufeng chutu Xi Zhou tongqi" 陝西長安扶風出土西周銅器. *Kaogu* 考古 1963.8: 413–15.

Liangzhu wenhua yuqi 良渚文化玉器. Zhejiang sheng Wenwu kaogu yanjiusuo, Shanghai shi Wenwu guanli weiyuanhui, and Nanjing bowuyuan, eds. Beijing: Wenwu and Liangmu, 1989.

Liao Genshen 廖根深. "Zhongyuan Shang dai yinwentao yuanshici shaozao diqu de tantao" 中原商代印紋陶原始瓷燒造地區的探討." *Kaogu* 考古 1993.10: 936–41.

Liao, W. K., trans. *The Complete Works of Han Fei Tzu.* 2 vols. London: Arthur Probsthain, 1939, 1959.

Lieberman, D. E., D. R. Pilbeam, and B. A. Wood. "A Probablistic Approach to the Problem of Sexual Dimorphism in *Homo Habilis*: A Comparison of KNM-ER 1470 and KNM-ER 1813." *Journal of Human Evolution* 17 (1988): 503–12.

Lin Gan 林幹. "Guanyu Yanjiu Zhongguo gudai beifang minzu wenhua shi de wo jian" 關於研究中國古代北方民族文化史的我見. *Nei Menggu daxue xuebao* 1988.1: 1–13.

Lin Shoujin 林壽晉. *Xian Qin kaoguxue* 先秦考古學 Hong Kong: Chinese University Press, 1991.

Lin Shoujin 林壽晉. *Zhanguo ximugong sunjie he gongyi yanjiu* 戰國細木工榫接合工藝研究. Xianggang Zhongwen daxue Zhongguo wenhua yanjiusuo Zhongguo kaogu yishu yanjiu zhongxin zhuankan 1. Hong Kong, 1981.

Lin Xiaoan 林小安. "Cong jiagu keci lun Xian Zhou qiyuan" 從甲骨刻辭論先周起源. *Kaogu yu wenwu* 考古與文物 1991.2: 66–9.

Lin Yun 林澐. "Cong Wu Ding shidai de jizhong Zi buci shilun Shangdai de jiazu xingtai" 從武丁時代的幾種子卜辭試論商代的家族形態. *Guwenzi yanjiu* 古文字研究 1 (1979): 314–36.

Lin Yun 林澐. "Jiaguwen zhong de Shangdai fangguo lianmeng" 甲骨文中的商代方國聯盟. *Guwenzi yanjiu* 古文字研究 6 (1981): 67–92.

Lin, Yün. "A Reexamination of the Relationship Between Bronzes of the Shang Culture and of the Northern Zone." In *Studies of Shang Archaeology: Selected Papers from the International Conference on Shang Civilization*, ed. K. C. Chang. New Haven, Conn.: Yale University Press, 1986, pp. 237–73.

Lin Yun 林澐. "Shangdai bingzhi guankui" 商代兵制管窺. *Jilin daxue shehui kexue xuebao* 吉林大學社會科學學報, 1990.1: 11–17.

Lin Yun 林澐. "Shang wenhua qingtongqi yu beifang diqu qingtongqi guanxi zhi zai yanjiu" 商文化青銅器與北方地區青銅器關係之再研究. In *Kaoguxue wenhua lunji (1)* 考古學文化論集 (1), ed. Su Bingqi 蘇秉琦. Beijing: Wenwu, 1987, pp. 129–55.

Lin Yun 林澐. "Xiaotun nandi fajue yu Yinxu jiagu duandai" 小屯南地發掘與殷墟甲骨斷代. *Guwenzi yanjiu* 古文字研究 9 (1984): 111–54. (For an English translation see Laura Skosey, "Lin Yun's 'The Xiaotun *Nandi* Excavation and the Periodization of Yinxu Oracle Bones.'" Master's thesis, Far Eastern Languages and Civilizations, University of Chicago, 1987.)

Lin Yun 林澐. "Zhongguo Dongbeixi tong jian chu lun" 中國東北系銅劍初論. *Kaogu xuebao* 考古學報 1980.2: 139–61.

Lin Yun 林澐. "Zhou dai yongding zhidu shangque" 周代用鼎制度商榷. *Shixue jikan* 史學集刊 1990.3: 12–23.

Lindberg, David. *The Beginnings of Western Science*. Chicago: University of Chicago Press, 1992.

Linduff, Kathryn. "Here Today and Gone Tomorrow: The Emergence and Demise of Bronze Producing Cultures Outside the Central Plain." Paper presented at the Conference on Chinese History and Archaeology, Academia Sinica, Taipei, Taiwan, January 4–8, 1994.

Linyi Fenghuangling Dong Zhou mu 臨沂鳳凰嶺東周墓. Ji'nan: Qi Lu, 1987.

Littauer, M. A., and J. H. Crouwel. *Chariots and Related Equipment from the Tomb of Tutankhamun*. Oxford: Griffith Institute, 1985.

Littauer, M. A., and J. H. Crouwel. *Wheeled Vehicles and Ridden Animals in the Ancient Near East*. Leiden: Brill, 1979.

Liu Binhui 劉彬徽. "Chu guo qingtong liqi chubu yanjiu" 楚國青銅禮器初步研究. *Zhongguo Kaoguxuehui di si ci Nianhui (1983) lunwenji* 中國考古學會第四次年會 (1983) 論文集. Beijing: Wenwu, 1985, pp. 108–22.

Liu Binhui 劉彬徽. "Chu guo youming tongqi biannian gaishu" 楚國有銘銅器編年概述. *Guwenzi yanjiu* 古文字研究 8 (1984): 331–72.

Liu Binhui 劉彬徽. "Chu mu chutu tongqi de niandai lüeshuo" 楚墓出土銅器的年代略説. *Zhongyuan wenwu* 中原文物 1989.4: 23–4, 37.

Liu Binhui 劉彬徽. "Lun Dong Zhou shiqi yongding zhidu zhong Chu zhi yu Zhou zhi de guanxi" 論東周時期用鼎制度中楚制與周制的關係. *Zhongyuan wenwu* 中原文物 1991.2: 50–8.

Liu Dashen 劉大申, Gao Shenlan 高申蘭, and Pu Haiying 浦海英. "Zhongguo xuanguan dili fenbu yu xianzhuang" 中國懸棺地理分布與現狀. *Jiangxi wenwu* 江西文物 1991.1: 8–14.

Liu Dezhen 劉得禎 and Xu Junju 許俊巨. "Gansu Qingyang Chunqiu Zhanguo muzang de qingli" 甘肅慶陽春秋墓葬的清理. *Kaogu* 考古 1988.5: 413–24.

Liu Dezhen 劉得禎 and Zhu Jiantang 朱建唐. "Gansu Lingtai xian Jingjiazhuang Chunqiu mu" 甘肅靈台縣景家庄春秋墓. *Kaogu* 考古 1981.4: 298–301.

Liu Hexin 劉合心. "Shaanxi sheng Zhouzhi xian faxian Xi Zhou yü qi yijian" 陝西省周至縣發現西周玉室器一件. *Wenwu* 文物 1975.7: 91.

Liu Hexin 劉合心. "Shaanxi sheng Zhouzhi xian jinnian zhengji de jijian Xi Zhou qingtongqi" 陝西省周至縣近年征集的幾件西周青銅器. *Wenwu* 文物 1983.7: 93.

Liu Hexin 劉合心. "Shaanxi Zhouzhi chutu Xi Zhou Tai Shi gui" 陝西周至出土西周太師簋. *Kaogu yu wenwu* 考古與文物 1981.1: 128.

Liu Huaijun 劉懷君 and Ren Zhoufang 任周芳. "Meixian chutu Wang zuo Zhong Jiang bao ding" 眉縣出土王作仲姜寶鼎. *Kaogu yu wenwu* 考古與文物 1982.2: 5–6, 13.

Liu Huaijun 劉懷君 and Ren Zhoufang 任周芳. "Meixian chutu yipi Xi Zhou jiaocang qing-tong yueqi" 眉縣出土一批西周窖藏青銅樂器. *Wenbo* 文博 1987.2: 17–25.

Liu Jianguo 劉建國. "Jiangnan Zhou dai qingtong wenhua" 江南周代青銅文化. *Dongnan wenhua* 東南文化 1994.3: 20–41.

Liu Jianguo 劉建國. "Jiangsu Dantu Liangshan Chunqiu shixuemu" 江蘇丹徒糧山春秋石穴墓. *Kaogu yu wenwu* 考古與文物 1987.4: 29–38.

Liu Jianguo 劉建國. "Lun Chu li wenhua tezheng de liangchongxing: Jianji Chu wenhua yu Zhongyuan wenhua de guanxi" 論楚鬲文化特征的兩重性：兼及楚文化與中原文化的關係. *Zhongyuan wenwu* 中原文物 1989.4: 4–13.

Liu Jianguo 劉建國. "Lun tudunmu de fenqi" 論土墩墓的分期. *Dongnan wenhua* 東南文化 1989.4–5: 96–115.

Liu Junshe 劉軍社. "Bianjiazhuang Qin guo mudi fajue de zhuyao shouhuo ji qi yiyi" 邊家庄秦國墓地發掘的主要收獲及其意義. *Baoji wenbo* 寶雞文博 1 (1991): 12–18.

Liu Laicheng 劉來成 and Li Xiaodong 李曉東. "Shitan Zhanguo shiqi Zhongshan guo lishi shang de jige wenti" 試談戰國時期中山國歷史上的幾個問題. *Wenwu* 文物 1979.1: 32–6.

Liu Li. "Chiefdoms in the Longshan Culture." Ph.D. dissertation, Harvard University, 1994.

Liu Li. "Settlement Patterns, Chiefdom Variability, and the Development of Early States in North China." *Journal of Anthropological Archaeology* 15 (1996): 237–88.

Liu Li 劉莉. "Tong fu kao" 銅釜考. *Kaogu yu wenwu* 考古與文物 1987.3: 60–5.

Liu Muling 劉牧靈. "Xinle yizhi de gu zhibei he gu qihou" 新樂遺址的古植被和古氣侯. *Kaogu* 考古 1988.9: 846–8.

Liu Pingsheng 劉平生. "Nanling gu tongkuang kaogu zai huo xin chengguo" 南嶺古銅礦考古再獲新成果. *Dongnan wenhua* 東南文化 1990.3: 29.

Liu Qiyi 劉啟益. "Wen Wang qianzhi Feng Wu Wang mie Shang qianhou tongqi lizheng" 文王遷至豐武王滅商前後銅器例證. In *Kaoguxue yanjiu* 考古學研究, ed. Shi Xingbang 石興邦 et al. Xi'an: San Qin, 1993, pp. 376–97, 218.

Liu Qiyu 劉起釪. "Chonglun Pan Geng qian Yin ji qian Yin de yuanyin" 重論盤庚遷殷及遷殷的原因. *Shixue yuekan* 史學月刊 1990.4: 1–5.

Liu Shizhong 劉詩中, Cao Keping 曹柯平, and Tang Shulong 唐舒龍. "Changjiang zhongyou diqu de gu tongkuang" 長江中游地區的古銅礦. *Kaogu yu wenwu* 考古與文物 1994.1: 82–8.

Liu Wendian 劉文典. *Huainan honglie jijie* 淮南鴻烈集解. 2 vols. Shanghai: Shangwu, 1923; rpt., Taipei: Shangwu, 1968.

Liu Xing 劉興. "Dongnan diqu qingtongqi fenqi" 東南地區青銅器分期. *Kaogu yu wenwu* 考古與文物 1985.5: 90–101.

Liu Xing 劉興. "Tan Zhenjiang diqu chutu qingtongqi de tese" 談鎮江地區出土青銅器的特色. *Wenwu ziliao congkan* 文物資料叢刊 5 (1981): 112–16.

Liu Xing 劉興. "Tantan Zhenjiang diqu tudunmu de fenqi" 談談鎮江地區土墩墓的分期. *Wenwu ziliao congkan* 文物資料叢刊 6 (1982): 79–85.

Liu Xing 劉興. "Zhenjiang diqu chutu de yuanshi qingci" 鎮江地區出土的原始青瓷. *Wenwu* 文物 1979.3: 56–7.

Liu Xing 劉興. "Zhenjiang diqu jinnian chutu de qingtongqi" 鎮江地區近年出土的青銅器. *Wenwu ziliao congkan* 文物資料叢刊 5 (1981): 106–11.

Liu Yao 劉耀. "Longshan wenhua yu Yangshao wenhua zhi fenxi" 龍山文化與仰韶文化之分析. *Zhongguo kaogu xuebao* 中國考古學報 2 (1947): 251–82.

Liu Yiman 劉一曼. "Shilun Yinxu jiagu shuci" 試論殷墟甲骨書辭. *Kaogu* 考古 1991.6: 546–54, 572.

Liu Ying 劉瑛. "Ba Shu tongqi wenshi tulu" 巴蜀銅器文飾圖錄. *Wenwu ziliao congkan* 文物資料叢刊 7 (1983): 1–12.

Liu Zhao 劉釗. "Anyang Hougang Yin mu suochu bing xing shi yongtu kao" 安陽後崗殷墓所出柄形飾用途考. *Kaogu* 考古 1995.7: 623–5, 605.

Liulihe Xi Zhou Yan guo mudi, 1973–1977 琉璃河西周燕國墓地. Beijing: Wenwu, 1995.

Lloyd, G. E. R. *Demystifying Mentalities.* Cambridge University Press, 1990.

Lloyd, G. E. R. *Magic, Reason and Experience.* Cambridge University Press, 1979.

Loehr, Max. "The Bronze Styles of the Anyang Period." *Archives of the Chinese Art Society of America* 7 (1953): 42–53.

Loehr, Max. *Chinese Bronze Age Weapons.* Ann Arbor: University of Michigan Press, 1956.

Loehr, Max. *Ritual Vessels of Bronze Age China.* New York: Asia House Gallery, 1968.

Loehr, Max. "Weapons and Tools from Anyang, and Siberian Analogies." *American Journal of Archaeology* 53 (1949): 126–44.

Loewe, Michael. "China's Sense of Unity in the Early Empires." *TP* 80 (1994): 6–26.

Loewe, Michael. *Crisis and Conflict in Han China.* London: Allen & Unwin, 1974.

Loewe, Michael. *Divination, Mythology and Monarchy in Han China.* Cambridge University Press, 1994.

Loewe, Michael. "The Han View of Comets." *BMFEA* 52 (1980): 1–31.

Loewe, Michael. "The Orders of Aristocratic Rank in Han China." *TP* 48 (1960): 97–174.

Loewe, Michael. "Huang Lao Thought and the *Huainanzi.*" *JRAS* 3rd series, 4, 3 (November 1994): 377–95.

Loewe, Michael. *Records of Han Administration.* 2 vols. Cambridge University Press, 1967.

Loewe, Michael. "Wang Mang and His Forbears: The Making of the Myth." *TP* 80, 4–5 (1994): 197–222.

Loewe, Michael. *Ways to Paradise: The Chinese Quest for Immortality.* London: Allen & Unwin, 1979; rpt. Taibei: Southern Materials Center, 1994.

Loewe, Michael, ed. *Early Chinese Texts: A Bibliographical Guide.* Berkeley: The Society for the Study of Early China and the Institute of East Asian Studies, University of California, 1993.

Long Hui 龍晦. "Mawangdui chutu Laozi yi ben qian gu yi shu tan yuan" 馬王堆出土老子乙本前古佚書探原. *Kaogu xuebao* 考古學報 1975.2: 23–32.

Lu Benshan 盧本珊 and Liu Shizhong 劉詩中. "Tongling Shang Zhou tongkuang kaicai jishu chubu yanjiu" 銅嶺商周銅礦開採技術初步研究. *Wenwu* 文物 1993.7: 33–8.

Lu Liancheng. "Chariot and Horse Burials in Ancient China." *Antiquity* 67: 257 (1993): 824–38.

Lu Liancheng 盧連成. "Lun Shangdai Xi Zhou ducheng xingtai" 論商代西周都城形態. *Zhongguo dili luncong* 中國地理論叢 1990.3: 143–60.

Lu Liancheng 盧連成. "Lun Shangdai Xi Zhou ducheng xingtai (xu bian)" 論商代西周都城形態（續編）. *Zhongguo dili luncong* 中國地理論叢 1991.1: 59–81.

Lu Liancheng 盧連成. "Xi Zhou Feng Hao liang jing kao" 西周豐鎬兩京考. *Zhongguo dili luncong* 中國地理論叢 1988.3: 115–52.

Lu Liancheng 盧連成. "Xian Zhou wenhua yu zhoubian diqu de qingtong wenhua" 先周文化與週邊地區的青銅文化. In *Kaoguxue yanjiu* 考古學研究, ed. Shi Xingbang 石興邦 et al. Xi'an: San Qin, 1993, pp. 243–79.

Lu Liancheng 盧連成 and Hu Zhisheng 胡智生. *Baoji Yu guo mudi* 寶雞弓國墓地. 2 vols. Beijing: Wenwu, 1988.

Lu Liancheng 盧連成 and Hu Zhisheng 胡智生. "Baoji Rujiazhuang Zhuyuangou mudi youguan wenti de tantao" 寶雞茹家庄竹園溝墓地有關問題的探討. *Wenwu* 文物 1983.2: 12–20.

Lu Liancheng 盧連成 and Luo Yingjie 羅英杰. "Shaanxi Wugong xian chutu Chu gui zhuqi" 陝西武功縣出土楚簋諸器. *Kaogu* 考古 1981.2: 128–33.

Lu Liancheng 盧連城 and Yang Mancang 楊滿倉. "Shaanxi Baoji xian Taigongmiao faxian Qin Gong zhong Qin Gong bo" 陝西寶雞縣太公廟發現秦公鐘秦公鎛. *Wenwu* 文物 1978.11: 1–5.

Lu Liancheng 盧連成 and Yin Shengping 尹盛平. "Gu Ze guo yizhi mudi diaochaji" 古夨國遺址墓地調查記. *Wenwu* 文物 1982.2: 48–57.

Lu Yuanjun 盧元駿. *Xin xu jinzhu jinyi* 新序今註今譯. Taipei: Shangwu (rpt. Tianjin: Guji, 1988).

Lu Zhirong 呂志榮. "Shilun Shaan-Jin beibu Huang he liang'an diqu chutu de Shangdai qingtongqi ji youguan wenti" 試論陝一晉北部黃河兩岸地區出土的商代青銅器及有關問題. In *Zhongguo kaoguxue yanjiu lunji: Jinian Xia Nai xiansheng kaogu wushi zhounian* 中國考古學研究論集：紀念夏鼐先生考古五十週年. Xi'an: San Qin, 1987, pp. 214–25.

Lucas, A., and J. R. Harris. *Ancient Egyptian Materials and Industries*. 4th ed. London: Edward Arnold, 1962.

Lundahl, Bertil. *Han Fei Zi: The Man and the Work*. Stockholm: Institute of Oriental Languages, Stockholm University, 1992.

Luo Feng 羅豐. "Ningxia Guyuan Shilacun faxian yizuo Zhanguo mu" 寧夏固原石喇村發現一座戰國墓. *Kaoguxue jikan* 3 (1983): 130–1, 142.

Luo Feng 羅豐 and Han Kongle 韓孔樂. "Ningxia Guyuan jinnian faxian de beifang xi qingtong qi" 寧夏固原近年發現的北方系青銅器. *Kaogu* 考古 1990.5: 403–18.

Luo Genze 羅根澤. *Guanzi tanyuan* 管子探源. Shanghai: Zhonghua, 1931.

Luo Kaiyu 羅開玉. "Qingchuan Qin du Wei tian lü suo guiding de Wei tian zhi" 青川秦牘為田律所規定的為田制. *Kaogu* 考古 1988.8: 728–31, 756.

Luo Xizhang 羅西章. "Fufeng chutu Shang Zhou qingtongqi" 扶風出土商周青銅器. *Kaogu yu wenwu* 考古與文物 1980.4: 6–22, 53.

Luo Xizhang 羅西章. "Zhouyuan chutu taozhi jianzhu cailiao" 周原出土陶質建築材料. *Kaogu yu wenwu* 考古與文物 1987.2: 9–17, 65.

Luo Xizhang 羅西章. "Zhouyuan qingtongqi jiaocang ji youguan wenti de tantao" 周原青銅器窖藏及有關問題的探討. *Kaogu yu wenwu* 考古與文物 1988.2: 40–7; reprinted in *Zhou wenhua lunji* 周文化論集. Xi'an: San Qin 1993, pp. 199–206.

Luo Xizhang 羅西章 et al., eds. *Fufeng xian wenwuzhi* 扶風縣文物誌. Xi'an: Shaanxi Renmin jiaoyu, 1993.

Luo Xizhang 羅西章, Wu Zhenfeng 吳鎮烽, and Luo Zhongru 雒忠如. "Shaanxi Fufeng chutu Xi Zhou Bo Dong zhuqi" 陝西扶風出土西周伯 *冬* 諸器. *Wenwu* 文物 1976.6: 51–60.

Luo Zhewen 羅哲文. "Lintao Qin changcheng Dunhuang Yumen guan Jiuquan Jiayuguan kancha jian ji" 臨洮秦長城敦煌玉門關酒泉嘉峪關勘察簡記. *Wenwu* 文物 1964.6: 46–57.

Luo Zhufeng 羅竹風, ed. *Han yu da ci dian* 漢語大詞典. Vols. 1–12 and Index. Shanghai: Shanghai cishu, 1986–93.

Luoyang chutu wenwu jicui 洛陽出土文物集粹. Beijing: Morning Glory, 1990.

Luoyang fajue baogao: 1955–1960 nian Luoyang Jianbin Kaogu fajue ziliao 洛陽發掘報告. 1955–1960 年洛陽澗濱考古發掘資料. Beijing: Yanshan, 1989.

Luoyang Zhongzhoulu 洛陽中州路. Beijing: Kexue, 1959.

Lynn, Richard. *The Classic of Changes: A New Translation of the I Ching.* New York: Columbia University Press, 1994.

Ma Chengyuan 馬承源. "Changjiang xiayou tudunmu chutu qingtongqi de yanjiu" 長江下游土墩墓出土青銅器的研究. *Shanghai bowuguan jikan* 上海博物館集刊 4 (1987): 198–220.

Ma Chengyuan 馬承源, ed. *Shang Zhou qingtongqi mingwen xuan* 商周青銅器銘文選. Beijing: Wenwu, 1988.

Ma Daokuo 馬道闊. "Anhui sheng Lujiang xian chutu Chunqiu qingtongqi: Jiantan Nan Huaiyi wenhua" 安徽省盧江縣出土春秋青銅器：兼談南淮夷文化. *Dongnan wenhua* 東南文化 1990.1–2: 74–8.

Ma Dezhi 馬得志 et al. "Yijiuwusan nian Anyang Dasikong cun fajue baogao" 一九五三年安陽大司空村發掘報告. *Kaogu xuebao* 考古學報 1955.9: 25–90.

Ma Shizhi 馬世之. "Shilun Shang dai de chengzhi" 試論商代的城址. In *Zhongguo Kaogu xuehui di wu ci nianhui lunwen ji 1985* 中國考古學會第五次年會論文集 1985, ed. Zhongguo Kaogu xuehui. Beijing: Wenwu, 1988, pp. 24–30.

Ma Tongbo 馬通伯. *Han Changli wenji jiaozhu* 韓昌黎文集校注. Shanghai: Gudian wenxue, 1957.

Ma Xilun 馬璽倫. "Shandong Yishui faxian yizuo Xi Zhou muzang" 山東沂水發現一座西周墓葬. *Kaogu* 考古 1986.8: 756–8.

Ma Yong 馬雍. "Lun Changsha Mawangdui yihao Han mu chutu bohua" 論長沙馬王堆一號漢墓出土帛畫. *Kaogu* 考古 1973.2: 118–25.

Ma Zhenzhi 馬振智. "Shilun Qin guo lingqin zhidu de xingcheng ji tedian" 試論秦國陵寢制度的形成及特點. *Kaogu yu wenwu* 考古與文物 1989.5: 110–17.

MacNeish, Richard S., and Jane Libby, eds. *Preliminary (1994) Report of the Sino-American Jiangxi (PRC) Origin of Rice Agriculture Project* (draft copy). Publication in Anthropology, no. 13. El Paso: El Paso Centennial Museum, University of Texas at El Paso, 1995.

Maenchen-Helfen, Otto. "Archaistic Names of the Hiung-nu." *Central Asiatic Journal* 6 (1961): 248–61.

Maeyama, Y. "The Oldest Star Catalogue of China, Shih Shen's *Hsing Ching*." In *Prismata: Natur Wissenschaftsgeschichtliche Studien: Festschrift für Willy Hartner*, ed. Y. Maeyama and W. G. Salzer. Wiesbaden: Franz Steiner, 1977, pp. 211–45.

Mair, Victor H. "Mummies of the Tarim Basin." *Archaeology* March–April, 1995, pp. 28–35.

Major, John S. "The Five Phases, Magic Squares, and Schematic Cosmography." In *Explorations in Early Chinese Cosmology*, ed. Henry Rosemont, Jr. JAAR Thematic Issue 50/2. Chico, Calif.: Scholars Press, 1984, pp. 133–66.

Major, John. *Heaven and Earth in Early Han Thought: Chapters Three, Four, and Five of the Huainanzi*. Albany: State University of New York Press, 1993.

Major, John. "The Meaning of Hsing-te." In *Chinese Ideas About Nature and Society: Studies in Honour of Derk Bodde*, ed. Charles Le Blanc and Susan Blader. Hong Kong: Hong Kong University Press, 1987, pp. 281–91.

Major, John. "Myth, Cosmology, and the Origins of Chinese Science." *Journal of Chinese Philosophy* 5 (1978): 1–20.

Makeham, John. *Name and Actuality in Early Chinese Thought*. Albany: State University of New York Press, 1994.

Mallory, J. P. *In Search of the Indo-Europeans*. London: Thames & Hudson, 1989.

Markov, G. E. "Problems of Social Change Among the Asiatic Nomads." In *The Nomadic Alternative*, ed. by W. Weissleder. The Hague: Mouton, 1978, pp. 305–11.

Martin, L. "Relationships Among Extant and Extinct Great Apes and Humans." In *Major Topics in Primate and Human Evolution*, ed. B. Wood, L. Martin, and P. Andrews. Cambridge University Press, 1986, pp. 161–87.

Martin, R. D. *Primate Origins and Evolution: A Phylogenetic Reconstruction*. London: Chapman & Hall, 1990.

Martinov, Anatoly. *The Ancient Art of Northern Asia*. Trans. and ed. Demitri B. Shimkin and Edith M. Shimkin. Urbana: University of Illinois Press, 1991.

Martynova, Galina S. "The Beginning of the Hunnic Epoch in South Siberia." *Arctic Anthropology* 25.2 (1988): 61–83.

Maspero, Henri. "La chronologie des rois de Ts'i au IVe siècle avant notre ère." *TP* 25 (1928): 367–86.

Maspero, Henri. "Le Ming T'ang et la crise religieuse chinoise avant les Han." *Mélanges chinois et bouddhiques* 9 (1951): 1–171.

Masson, V. M. "Central Asia in the Early Iron Age: Dynamics of Cultural, Social and Economic Development." *Information Bulletin. Unesco International Association for the Study of the Cultures of Central Asia* 9 (1985): 59–68.

Masson, V. M., and T. F. Taylor. "Soviet Archaeology in the Steppe Zone: Introduction." *Antiquity* 63 (1989): 779–83.

Masubuchi Tatsuo 増淵龍夫. *Chûgoku kodai no shakai to kokka* 中國古代の社會と國家. Tokyo: Kôbundô, 1962.

Mathieu, Rémi. *Etudes sur la mythologie et l'ethnologie de la Chine ancienne; Traduction annotée du* Shanhai jing. 2 vols. Paris: Collège de France, 1983.

Mathieu, Rémi. *Le Mu Tianzi zhuan: Traduction annotée: Étude critique*. Paris: Collège de France, Institut des hautes études chinoises, 1978.

Mathieu, Rémi. "Mu t'ien tzu chuan 穆天子傳." In *Early Chinese Texts: A Bibliographical Guide*, ed. Michael Loewe. Berkeley: Society for the Study of Early China and Institute of East Asian Studies, University of California, Berkeley, 1993, pp. 342–6.

Matsumaru Michio 松丸道雄. "Inkyo bokujichû no denryôchi ni tsuite: Indai kokka kôzô kenkyû no tame ni" 殷墟卜辭中の田獵地について：殷代國家構成研究のために. *Tôyô bunka kenkyûjo kiyô* 東洋文化研究所紀要 31 (1963): 1–163.

Matsumaru Michio 松丸道雄. "In Shû kokka no kôzô" 殷周國家の構造. *Iwanami kôza: sekai rekishi* 岩波講座：世界歴史 4 (1970): 49–100.

Matsumaru Michio 松丸道雄. *Sei Shû seidôki to sono Kokka* 西周青銅器とその國家. Tokyo: Tokyo daigaku, 1980.

Matsumaru Michio 松丸道雄 and Takashima Ken'ichi 高島謙一. *Kôkotsumonji jishaku sôran* 甲骨文字字釋綜覽. Tokyo: Tokyo University Press (1993, not for sale), 1994.

Mattos, Gilbert L. "Eastern Zhou Bronze Inscriptions." In *New Sources of Early Chinese History: An Introduction to the Reading of Inscriptions and Manuscripts*, ed. Edward L. Shaughnessy. Berkeley: Society for the Study of Early China and Institute of East Asian Studies, University of California, Berkeley, 1997, 85–123.

Mattos, Gilbert L. *The Stone Drums of Ch'in*. Monumenta Serica Monographs, no. 19. Nettetal: Steyler, 1988.

Mawangdui Han mu bo shu 馬王堆漢墓帛書. *Vol.* 1, ed. Guojia Wenwu ju guwenxian yanjiushi. Beijing: Wenwu, 1980; *Vol.* 3, ed. Mawangdui Han mu boshu zhengli xiaozu. Beijing: Wenwu, 1983; *Vol.* 4, 1985.

Mayr, Ernst. *The Growth of Biological Thought*. Cambridge, Mass.: Harvard University Press, 1982.

Meacham, William. "Continuity and Local Evolution in the Neolithic of South China: A Non-nuclear Approach." *Current Anthropology* 18 (1977): 419–40.

Mei Tsu-lin and Jerry Norman. "The Austroasiatics in Ancient South China: Some Lexical Evidence." *Monumenta Serica* 32 (1976): 274–301.

Mei, Y. P. *The Ethical and Political Works of Motse*. London: Arthur Probsthain, 1929.

Meng Huaping 孟華平. "Lun Daxi wenhua" 論大溪文化. *Kaogu xuebao* 考古學報 1992.4: 293–412.

Meng Xianwu 孟憲武. "Anyang Sanjiazhuang Dongwangducun faxian de Shang dai qingtongqi ji qi niandai tuiding" 安陽三家莊董王度村發現的商代青銅器及其年代推定. *Kaogu* 考古 1991.10: 932–8.

Miaodigou yu Sanliqiao 廟底溝與三里橋. Beijing: Kexue, 1959.

Miller, Roy A. "The Far East." In *Current Trends in Linguistics*, vol. 13, pt. 2, "Historiography of Linguistics," ed. Thomas Sebeok. The Hague: Mouton, 1975, pp. 1213–64.

Minyaev, S. "Niche Grave Burials of the Xiong-nu Period in Central Asia." *Information Bulletin. International Association for the Cultures of Central Asia* 17 (1990): 91–9.

Minyaev, S. "On the Origin of the Hiung-nu." *Information Bulletin. International Association for the Cultures of Central Asia*, 9 (1985): 69–78.

Misra, V. H., and Peter Bellwood, eds. *Recent Advances in Indo-Pacific Prehistory: Proceedings of the International Symposium Held at Poona, Dec. 19–23, 1978*. Leiden: Brill, 1985.

Moorey, P. R. S. *Ancient Mesopotamian Materials and Industries: The Archaeological Evidence*. Oxford: Clarendon Press, 1994.

Moorey, P. R. S. "The Archaeological Evidence for Metallurgy and Related Technologies in Mesopotamia, c. 5500–2100 B.C." *Iraq* 41, 1 (Spring 1982): 13–38.

Moorey, P. R. S. *A Century of Biblical Archaeology*. Louisville, Ky: Westminster/John Knox Press, 1991; and Cambridge: Lutterworth, 1991.

Moorey, P. R. S. "The Emergence of the Light, Horse-drawn Chariot in the Near East c. 2000–1500 B.C." *World Archaeology* 18 (1986): 196–215.

Morohashi Tetsuji 諸橋轍次. *Dai Kan Wa jiten* 大漢和辭典. 12 vols. and index. Tokyo: Suzuki ippei, 1955–60.

Mou Yongkang 牟永抗. "Zhejiang yinwentao: Shitan yinwentao de tezheng yiji yu ciqi de guanxi" 浙江印紋陶：試談印紋陶的特征以及與瓷器的關係. *Wenwu jikan* 文物集刊 3 (1981): 261–9.

Mou Yongkang 牟永抗 and Mao Zhaoting 毛兆廷. "Jiangshan xian Nanqu gu yizhi muzang diaocha shijue" 江山縣南區古遺址墓葬調查試掘. *Zhejiang sheng Wenwu kaogu yanjiusuo xuekan* 浙江省文物考古研究所學刊 1 (1981): 57–84.

Mozi jian gu 墨子閒詁. Annotated by Sun Yirang 孫詒讓. In *Xin bian zhu zi ji cheng* 新編諸子集成, vol. 6. Taipei: Shijie, 1974.

Munro, Donald J. *The Concept of Man in Early China*. Stanford, Calif.: Stanford University Press, 1969.

Mu Shunying 穆舜英 et al. *Zhongguo Xinjiang gudai yishu/The Ancient Art in Xinjiang, China* 中國新疆古代藝術 (Urumqi: Xinjiang Art and Photography Press, 1994).

Needham, Joseph. *The Development of Iron and Steel Technology in China*. Cambridge: Heffer, 1964.

Needham, Joseph. *Science and Civilisation in China. Vol. 2: History of Scientific Thought*. Cambridge University Press, 1969.

Needham, Joseph. *Science and Civilisation in China. Vol. 3: Mathematics and the Sciences of the Heavens and the Earth*. Cambridge University Press, 1959.

Needham, Joseph, with the research assistance of Wang Ling and Lu Gwei-djen. *Science and Civilisation in China. Vol. 4: Physics and Physical Technology. Part 3: Civil Engineering and Nautics*. Cambridge University Press, 1971.

Needham, Joseph. *Science and Civilisation in China. Vol. 5: Chemistry and Chemical Technology. Part 2: Spagyrical Discovery and Invention: Magisteries of Gold and Immortality*. Cambridge University Press, 1974.

Nei Menggu wenwu kaogu 內蒙古文物考古 1981.1: 15–27. "Xigoupan Handai Xiongnu mudi diaochaji" 西溝畔漢代匈奴墓地調查記.

Nei Menggu wenwu kaogu 內蒙古文物考古 1991.1: 13–24. "Baotou Xiyuan Chunqiu mudi" 包頭西園春秋墓地.

Nei Menggu wenwu kaogu 內蒙古文物考古 1992.1–2: 91–6. "Yijinhuoluo qi Shihuigou faxian de E'erduosi shi wenwu" 伊金霍洛旗石灰溝發現的鄂爾多斯式文物.

Nelson, Sarah Milledge, ed. *The Archaeology of Northeast China: Beyond the Great Wall*. London: Routledge, 1995.

Ngo Van Xuyet. *Divination, magie, et politique dans la Chine ancienne*. Paris: Presses universitaires de France, 1976.

Ni Jinbin 倪進斌. "Tongling gudai gongye wenxue chutan" 銅陵古代工業文學初探. *Dongnan wenhua* 東南文化 1991.2: 104–5.

Ni Zhenkui 倪振逵. "Yancheng chutu de tongqi" 淹城出土的銅器. *Wenwu* 文物 1959.4: 3–5.

Nie Gaozhong and He Deming. "A New Explanation Regarding the Provenances of Materials of China's Xiashu Loess." In *Loess, Environment and Global Change (The Series of the XIII Inqua Congress)*, ed. Liu Tungsheng. Beijing: Science Press, 1991, pp. 213–27.

Nienhauser, William H., Jr., ed., with Tsai-fa Cheng, Zongli Lu, and Robert Reynolds, trans. *The Grand Scribe's Records. Vol. 1: The Basic Annals of Pre-Han China by Ssu-ma Ch'ien*. Bloomington: Indiana University Press, 1994.

Nienhauser, William. H., Jr. *The Grand Scribe's Records. Vol. 7: The Memoirs of Pre-Han China by Ssu-ma Ch'ien*. Bloomington: Indiana University Press, 1994.

Nishijima Sadao 西島定生. *Chûgoku kodai teikoku no keisei to kôzô: Nijû tô shakusei no kenkyû* 中國古代帝國の形成と構造：二十等爵制の研究. Tokyo: Tokyo daigaku, 1961.

Nivison, David S. "1040 as the Date of the Chou Conquest." *EC* 8 (1982–3): 76–8.

Nivison, David S. "The Dates of Western Chou." *HJAS* 43.2 (1983): 481–580.

Nivison, David S. "Hsun Tzu and Chuang Tzu." In *Chinese Texts and Philosophical Contexts*, ed. H. Rosemont, Jr. La Salle, Ill.: Open Court, 1991, pp. 129–42.

Nivison, David S. "The Origin of the Chinese Lunar Lodge System." In *World Archaeoastronomy*, ed. Anthony F. Aveni. Cambridge University Press, 1989, pp. 203–18.

Nivison, David S. *The Riddle of the Bamboo Annals*. Stanford, Calif.: Private publication, 1995.

Nivison, David S. *The Ways of Confucianism: Investigations in Chinese Philosophy*, edited and with an introduction by Bryan Van Norden. La Salle, Ill.: Open Court, 1997.

Nivison, David S. "Western Chou History Reconstructed from Bronze Inscriptions." In *The Great Bronze Age of China: A Symposium*, ed. George Kuwayama. Los Angeles: Los Angeles County Museum of Art, 1983, pp. 44–55.

Nivison, David S., and Kevin Pang. "Astronomical Evidence for the *Bamboo Annals*' Chronicle of Early Xia." *EC* 15 (1990): 87–95.

Norman, Jerry. *Chinese*. Cambridge University Press, 1988.

Norman, Jerry. "Pharyngealization in Early Chinese." *JAOS* 114, 3 (1994): 397–408.

Norman, Jerry, and Mei, Tsu-lin. "The Austroasiatics in Ancient South China: Some Lexical Evidence." *MS* 32 (1976): 274–301.

Novgorodova, E. A., et al. *Ulangom: Ein skythenzeitlisches Gräberfeld in der Mongolei*. Wiesbaden: Harrassowitz, 1982.

Nowgorodowa, E. "Mongolie de l'époque du 'style animale'." In *Ethnologie und Geschichte. Festschrift für Karl Jettmar*, ed. Peter Snoy. Wiesbaden: Harrassowitz, 1983, pp. 440–4.

O'Donoghue, Diane N. "Reflection and Reception: The Origins of the Mirror in Bronze Age China." *BMFEA* 62 (1990): 5–183.

Ogura Yoshihiko 小倉芳彦. *Chûgoku kodai seiji shisô kenkyû* 中國古代政治思想研究. Tokyo: Aoki, 1970.

Okamura Hidenori 岡村秀典. "Go Etsu izen no seidôki" 吳越以前の青銅器. *Koshi shunjû* 古史春秋 3 (1986): 63–89.

Okamura Hidenori 岡村秀典. "Shin bunka no hennen" 秦文化の編年. *Koshi Shunjû* 古史春秋 2 (1985): 53–74.

Okladnikov, A. P. "Inner Asia at the Dawn of History." In *The Cambridge History of Inner Asia*, ed. Denis Sinor. Cambridge University Press, 1990, pp. 41–96.

Okura Yoshihiko 小倉芳彦. "I i no toriko: *Saden* no Ka I kannen" 裔夷の俘：左傳の華夷觀念. *Chûgoku kodaishi kenkyû* 中國古代史研究 2 (1965): 153–88. Also in Okura's *Chûgoku kodai seiji shisô kenkyû* 中國古代政治思想研究. Tôkyô: Aoki, 1970, pp. 131–61.

Onozawa Seiichi 小野澤精一 et al., eds. *Ki no shisô: Chûgoku ni okeru shizenkan to ningenkan no tenkai* 氣の思想：中國における自然觀と人間觀の展開. Tokyo: Tôkyô daigaku, 1978.

Ou Tansheng 歐潭生. "Gushi Hougudui Wu Taizi Fuchai furen mu de Wu wenhua yinsu" 固始侯古堆吳太子夫差夫人墓的吳文化因素. *Zhongyuan wenwu* 中原文物 1991.4: 33–8.

Ou Yan 甌燕. "Shilun Yan Xiadu de niandai" 試論燕下都的年代. *Kaogu* 考古 1988.7: 645–9.

Ou Yan 甌燕. "Zhanguo shiqi de muzang" 戰國時期的墓葬. *Beifang wenwu* 北方文物 1989.3: 29–35.

Pang Pu 龐樸. "Huo li gouchen" 火曆鉤沉. *Zhongguo wenhua* 中國文化 1 (1989): 3–23.

Pankenier, David W. "Astronomical Dates in Shang and Western Zhou." *EC* 7 (1981–2): 2–37.

Pankenier, David W. "The *Bamboo Annals* Revisited: Problems of Method in Using the Chronicle as a Source for the Chronology of Early Zhou, Part 1." *BSOAS* 55 (1992): 272–97. "Part 2: The Congruent Mandate Chronology in *Yi Zhou shu*," 498–510.

Pankenier, David W. "*Mozi* and the Dates of Xia, Shang, and Zhou: A Research Note." *EC* 9–10 (1983–5): 175–83.

Peerenboom, R. P. *Law and Morality in Ancient China: The Silk Manuscripts of Huang-Lao*. Albany: State University of New York Press, 1993.

Pei Anping 裴安平 and Cao Chuansong 曹傳松. "Hunan Lixian Pengtoushan xinshiqi shidai zaoqi yizhi fajue baogao" 湖南澧縣彭頭山新石器時代早期遺址發掘報告. *Wenwu* 文物 1990.8: 17–29.

Peng Bangjiong 彭邦炯. "Shangdai "zhongren" de lishi kaocha: Guanyu zhongren de xin tansuo" 商代 `眾人' 的歷史考察：關於眾人的新探索. *Tianfu xinlun* 天府新論 1990.3: 77–85.

Peng Hao 彭浩. "Chu mu zangzhi chulun" 楚墓葬制初論. In *Zhongguo kaogu xuehui di er ci nianhui lunwenji* 中國考古學會第二次年會論文集, ed. Zhongguo Kaogu xuehui. Beijing: Wenwu, 1982, pp. 33–40.

Peng Hao 彭浩. "Jiangling Mazhuan yihao mu suojian zangsu lüeshu" 江陵馬磚一號墓所見葬俗略述. *Wenwu* 文物 1981.10: 12–15.

Peng Hao 彭浩. "Woguo Liang-Zhou shiqi de Yue shi ding" 我國兩周時期的越式鼎. *Hunan kaogu jikan* 湖南考古集刊 2 (1984): 136–41, 119.

Peng Shifan 彭適凡. "Jiangxi diqu chutu Shang Zhou qingtongqi de fenxi yu fenqi" 江西地區出土商周青銅器的分析與分期. In *Zhongguo Kaogu xuehui di yi ci nianhui lunwenji 1979* 中國考古學會第一次年會論文集 1979, ed. Zhongguo Kaogu xuehui. Beijing: Wenwu, 1980, pp. 181–94.

Peng Shifan 彭適凡 and Yang Rixin 楊日新. "Jiangxi Xin'gan Shang dai da mu wenhua xingzhi chuyi" 江西新干商代大墓文化性質芻議. *Wenwu* 文物 1993.7: 10–18.

Peng Shifan 彭適凡, Zhan Kaixun 詹開遜, and Liu Lin 劉林. *Changjiang zhongyou qingtong wangguo: Jiangxi Xin'gan chutu qingtong yishu (The Bronze Kingdom in Mid Yangtze: The Art of Bronze Unearthed at Xin'gan in Jiangxi)* 長江中游青銅王國：江西新干出土青銅藝術. Hong Kong: Liangmu, 1994.

Petersen, Jens Østergård. "What's in a Name? On the Sources Concerning Sun Wu." *AM*, 3d series, 5, 1 (1992): 1–32.

Petersen, Jens Østergård. "Which Books *Did* the First Emperor of Ch'in Burn? On the Meaning of *Pai Chia* in Early Chinese Sources." *MS* 43 (1995): 1–52.

Peterson, Willard J. "Making Connections: 'Commentary on the Attached Verbalizations' of the *Book of Change*." *HJAS* 42 (1982): 67–116.

Phillips, C. R. "*Nullum Crimen sine Lege*: Socioreligious Sanctions on Magic." In *Magika Hiera: Ancient Greek Magic and Religion*, ed. Christopher Faraone and Dirk Obbink. Oxford: Oxford University Press, 1991, pp. 260–76.

Piggott, Stuart. "Chariots in the Caucasus and in China." *Antiquity* 48 (1974): 16–24.

Piggott, S. "Chinese Chariotry: An Outsider's View." In *Arts of the Eurasian Steppelands*, ed. Philip Denwood. Colloquies on Art and Archaeology in Asia, no. 7. London: Percival David Foundation, 1978, pp. 32–51.

Piggott, Stuart. *The Earliest Wheeled Transport: From the Atlantic Coast to the Caspian Sea.* Ithaca, N.Y.: Cornell University Press, 1983.

Piggott, Stuart. *Wagon, Chariot and Carriage.* London: Thames & Hudson, 1992.

Pingyang muzang 平洋墓葬. Beijing: Wenwu, 1990.

Pirazzoli-t'Serstevens, Michèle. *The Han Dynasty.* New York: Rizzoli, 1982.

Pirazzoli-t'Serstevens, Michèle. "Pour une archéologie des échanges. Apports étrangers en Chine – Transmission, réception, assimilation." *Arts Asiatiques* 49 (1994): 21–33.

Poo, Mu-chou. "Ideas Concerning Death and Burial in Pre-Han China." *Asia Major*, 3d series, 3, 2 (1990): 25–62.

Poo, Mu-chou. "Popular Religion in Pre-imperial China: Observations on the Almanacs of Shui-hu-ti." *TP* 79 (1993): 225–48.

Pope, Geoffrey G. "Replacement Versus Regionally Continuous Models: The Paleobehavioral and Fossil Evidence from East Asia." In *The Evolution and Dispersal of Modern Humans in Asia*, ed. Takeru Akazawa, Kenichi Aoki, and Tasuku Kimura. Tokyo: Hokusensha, 1992, pp. 3–14.

Postgate, Nicholas, Tao Wang, and Toby Wilkinson. "The Evidence for Early Writing: Utilitarian or Ceremonial?" *Antiquity* 69 (1995): 459–80.

Powers, Martin. "Artistic Taste, the Economy and the Social Order in Former Han China." *Art History* 9, 3 (September 1986): 285–9.

Průšek, Yaroslav. *Chinese Statelets and the Northern Barbarians in the Period 1400–300 B.C.* Dordrecht: Reidel, 1971.

Psarras, Sophia-Karin. "Exploring the North: Non-Chinese Cultures of the Late Warring States and Han." *MS* 42 (1994): 1–125.

Pulleyblank, E. G. "Ablaut and Initial Voicing in Old Chinese Morphology: **a* as an Infix and Prefix." *Proceedings of the Second International Conference on Sinology*, Section on Linguistics and Paleography. Taibei: Academia Sinica, 1989, pp. 1–21.

Pulleyblank, E. G. "Chinese and Indo-Europeans." *JRAS* (April 1966): 9–39.

Pulleyblank, E. G. "The Chinese and Their Neighbors in Prehistoric and Early Historic Times." In *The Origins of Chinese Civilization*, ed. David N. Keightley. Berkeley: University of California Press, 1983, pp. 411–66.

Pulleyblank, E. G. "Chinese Historical Criticism: Liu Chih-chi and Ssu-ma Kuang." In *Historians of China and Japan*, ed. W. G. Beasley and E. G. Pulleyblank. London: Oxford University Press, 1961, pp. 135–66.

Pulleyblank, E. G. "Close/Open Ablaut in Sino-Tibetan." *Lingua* 14 (1965): 230–40.

Pulleyblank, E. G. "European Studies on Chinese Phonology, the First Phase." In *Europe Studies China: Papers from an International Conference on the History of European Sinology*, ed. Ming Wilson and John Cayley. London: Han-shan Tang, 1995, pp. 339–67.

Pulleyblank, E. G. "The Ganzhi as Phonograms and Their Application to the Calendar." *Early China* 16 (1991): 39–80.

Pulleyblank, E. G. "The Historical and Prehistorical Relationships of Chinese." In *The Ancestry of the Chinese*, ed. William S.-Y. Wang. Journal of Chinese Linguistics monograph series, no. 8. Berkeley: Journal of Chinese Linguistics, 1995, pp. 145–94.

Pulleyblank, E. G. "An Interpretation of the Vowel Systems of Old Chinese and Written Burmese." *AM*, n.s., 2 (1963): 200–221.

Pulleyblank, E. G. *Lexicon of Reconstructed Pronunciation in Early Middle Chinese, Late Middle Chinese, and Early Mandarin.* Vancouver: University of British Columbia Press, 1991.

Pulleyblank, E. G. "The Locative Particles yu 于, yu 於 and hu 乎." *JOAS* 106 (1986): 1–12.

Pulleyblank, E. G. *Middle Chinese: A Study in Historical Phonology.* Vancouver: University of British Columbia Press, 1984.

Pulleyblank, E. G. "The Old Chinese Origin of Type A and B Syllables." *Journal of Chinese Linguistics* 22 (1994): 73–100.

Pulleyblank, E. G. "Some New Hypotheses Concerning Word Families in Chinese." *Journal of Chinese Linguistics* 1 (1973): 111–25.

Pulleyblank, E. G. "The Typology of Indo-European." *Journal of Indo-European Studies* 21 (1993): 63–118.

Pulleyblank, E. G. "Why Tocharians?" *Journal of Indo-European Studies* 23 (1995): 415–30.

Pulleyblank, E. G. "Zou 鄒 and Lu 魯 and the Sinification of Shandong." In *Chinese Language, Thought and Culture: Nivison and His Critics*, ed. P. Ivanhoe. La Salle, Ill: Open Court, 1996, pp. 39–57.

Qi Sihe 齊思和 "Xi Zhou dili kao" 西周地理考. *Yanjing xuebao* 燕京學報 30 (1936): 63–106.

Qi Wentao 齊文濤 (Wang Entian 王恩田). "Gaishu jinnianlai Shandong chutu de Shang Zhou qingtongqi" 概述近年來山東出土的商周青銅器. *Wenwu* 文物 1972.5: 3–18.

Qi Wenxin 齊文心. "Wang zi benyi shitan" 王字本意試探 *Lishi yanjiu* 歷史研究 1991.4: 141–5.

Qian Baocong 錢寶琮. "Taiyi kao" 太一考. *Yanjing xuebao* 燕京學報 12 (1932): 2449–78.

Qian Mu 錢穆. *Xian Qin zhuzi xinian* 先秦諸子繫年. 2 vols. Shanghai: Shangwu, 1935; rev. rpt. Hong Kong: Hong Kong University Press, 1956.

Qian Mu 錢穆. "Zhou chu dili kao" 周初地理考. *Yanjing xuebao* 燕京學報 10 (1931): 1955–2008.

Qin Han jiandu lunwenji 秦漢簡牘論文集. Gansu sheng wenwu kaogu yanjiusuo, ed. Lanzhou: Gansu Renmin, 1989.

Qin Jianming 秦建明. "Shang Zhou gongxingqi wei qiling shuo" 商周弓形器為旂鈴說. *Kaogu* 考古 1995.3: 256–8.

Qin Xiaoli 秦小麗. "Shilun Kexingzhuang wenhua de fenqi" 試論客省庄文化的分期 *Kaogu* 考古 1995.3: 238–55.

Qiu Donglian 邱東聯. "Zhenmushou biankao" 鎮墓獸辯考. *Jiang Han kaogu* 江漢考古 1994.2: 54–9.

Qiu Shihua 仇士華 et al. "Youguan suowei Xia wenhua de tan shisi niandai ceding de chubu baogao" 有關所謂夏文化的碳十四年代測定的初步報告. *Kaogu* 考古 1983.10: 923–8.

Qiu Xigui. "An Examination of Whether the Charges in Shang Oracle-Bone Inscriptions Are Questions." Trans. Edward L. Shaughnessy. *EC* 14 (1989): 77–114 and 165–72.

Qiu Xigui 裘錫圭. "Guanyu Shangdai de zongzu zuzhi yu guizu he pingmin liangge jieji de chubu yanjiu" 關於商代的宗族組織與貴族和平民兩個階級的初步研究. *Wenshi* 文史 17 (1983): 1–26.

Qiu Xigui 裘錫圭. "Hanzi xingcheng wenti de chubu tansuo" 漢字形成問題的初步探索, *Zhongguo yuwen* 中國語文 1978.3: 162–71.

Qiu Xigui 裘錫圭. "Jiagu buci zhong suo jian de tian mu wei deng zhiguan de yanjiu: Jianlun Hou Dian Nan Wei deng jizhong zhuhou de qiyuan" 甲骨卜辭中所見的田牧衛等職官的研究：兼論侯甸男衛等幾種諸侯的起源. *Wenshi* 文史 19 (1983): 1–13.

Qiu Xigui 裘錫圭. "Jiaguwen zhong suo jian de Shangdai nongye" 甲骨文中所見的商代農業. *Nongshi yanjiu* 農史研究 8 (1985): 12–41.

Qiu Xigui 裘錫圭. "Lun Lizu buci de shidai" 論歷組卜辭的時代. *Guwenzi yanjiu* 古文字研究 6 (1981): 263–321. (Errata list at *Guwenzi yanjiu* 古文字研究 8 [1983]: 237.)

Qiu Xigui 裘錫圭. "Tantan Suixian Zeng Hou Yi mu de wenzi ziliao" 談談隨縣曾侯乙墓的文字資料. *Wenwu* 文物 1979.7: 25–31.

Qu Wanli 屈萬里. "He zi yiyi de yanbian" 河字意義的演變 *BIHP* 30 (1959): 143–55.

Qu Wanli 屈萬里 *Xiaotun dier ben: Yinxu wenzi – Jiabian kaoshi* 小屯第二本：殷虛文字：甲編考釋. Taipei: Academia Sinica, 1961.

Qu Yingjie 屈英傑. *Xian Qin ducheng fuyuan yanjiu* 先秦都城復原研究. Ha'erbin: Heilongjiang Renmin, 1991.

Qufu Lu guo gucheng 曲阜魯國故城. Ji'nan: Qi Lu, 1982.

Qun Li 群力. "Linzi Qi guo gu cheng kantan jiyao" 臨淄齊國故城勘探紀要 *Wenwu* 文物 1972.5: 45–54.

Rao Zongyi 饒宗頤. "Chu boshu tianxiang zaiyi" 楚帛書天象再議. *Zhongguo wenhua* 中國文化 3 (1990): 66–73.

Rao Zongyi 饒宗頤. "Shendao sixiang yu lixing zhuyi" 神道思想與理性主義. *BIHP* 49 (1978): 489–513.

Rao Zongyi 饒宗頤. *Yindai zhenbu renwu tongkao* 殷代貞卜人物通考 (*Oracle Bone Diviners of the Yin Dynasty*). 2 vols. Hong Kong: Chinese University Press, 1959.

Rao Zongyi 饒宗頤 and Zeng Xiantong 曾憲通. *Yunmeng Qin jian rishu yanjiu* 雲夢秦簡日書研究. Hong Kong: Chinese University Press, 1982.

Rawson, Jessica. "The Ancestry of Chinese Bronze Vessels." In *History from Things: Essays on Material Culture*, ed. Steven Lubar and W. David Kingery. Washington: Smithsonian Institution Press, 1993, pp. 51–73.

Rawson, Jessica. "Ancient Chinese Ritual as Seen in the Material Record." In *Court and State Ritual in China*, ed. J. P. McDermott. Cambridge University Press, forthcoming.

Rawson, Jessica. "Ancient Chinese Ritual Bronzes: The Evidence from Tombs and Hoards of the Shang (*c.* 1500–1050 B.C.) and Western Zhou (*c.* 1050–771 B.C.) Periods." *Antiquity* 67, 257 (December 1993): 805–23.

Rawson, Jessica. *Chinese Jade: From the Neolithic to the Qing*. London: British Museum Press, 1995.

Rawson, Jessica. "Jade and Gold: Some Sources of Ancient Chinese Jade Design." *Orientations* 26.6 (June 1995): 26–37.

Rawson, Jessica, ed. *Mysteries of Ancient China: New Discoveries from the Early Dynasties*. London: British Museum, 1996.

Rawson, Jessica. "Die rituellen Bronzegefäße der Shang- und Zhou-Perioden." In *Das alte China: Menschen und Götter im Reich der Mitte*, ed. Roger Goepper. Essen: Kulturstiftung Ruhr, 1995, pp. 76–94.

Rawson, Jessica. "Shang and Western Zhou Designs in Jade and Bronze." In *International Colloquium on Chinese Art History, 1991: Proceedings, Antiquities, Part 1*, Taipei: National Palace Museum, 1992, pp. 73–105.

Rawson, Jessica. "Statesmen or Barbarians? The Western Zhou as Seen Through Their Bronzes." *Proceedings of the British Academy* 75 (1989): 71–95.

Rawson, Jessica. *Western Zhou Ritual Bronzes from the Arthur M. Sackler Collections*. Cambridge, Mass.: Harvard University Press, 1990.

Ren Shinan 任式楠. "Xinglongwa wenhua de faxian ji qi yiyi" 興隆窪文化的發現及其意義. *Kaogu* 考古 1994.8: 710–18.

Ren Song 韌松 and Fan Weiyue 樊維岳. "Ji Shaanxi Lantian xian xin chutu de Ying Hou zhong" 記陝西藍田縣新出土的應候鐘. *Wenwu* 文物 1975.10: 68–9.

Rickett, W. Allyn. *Guanzi: Political, Economic, and Philosophical Essays from Early China*, vol. 1. Princeton, N.J.: Princeton University Press, 1985.

Rickett, W. Allyn. *Kuan-tzu: A Repository of Early Chinese Thought*. Hong Kong: Hong Kong University Press, 1965.

Riegel, Jeffrey, and John Knoblock. *Lü shi chunqiu: A New Translation*. Stanford, Calif.: Stanford University Press, forthcoming.

Riegel, Jeffrey K. "Ju-tzu Hsi 孺子瘨 and the Genealogy of the House of Wei 魏." *EC* 3 (1977): 46–51.

Riegel, Jeffrey K. "Kou-mang and Ju-shou." *Cahiers d'Extrême-Asie* 5 (1989–90): 55–83.

Riegel, Jeffrey K. "A Summary of Some Recent *Wenwu* and *Kaogu* Articles on Mawangdui Tombs Two and Three." *EC* 1 (1975): 10–15.

Roetz, Heiner. *Confucian Ethics of the Axial Age: A Reconstruction Under the Aspect of the Breakthrough Toward Postconventional Thinking*. Albany: State University of New York Press, 1993.

Rong Mengyuan 榮孟源. *Zhongguo lishi jinian* 中國歷史紀年. Beijing: Sanlian, 1956.

Rosemont, Henry, Jr. "State and Society in the Hsun Tzu: A Philosophical Commentary." *MS* 29 (1970–1): 501–41.

Rosemont, Henry, Jr., ed. *Chinese Texts and Philosophical Contexts: Essays Dedicated to Angus C. Graham.* La Salle, Ill.: Open Court, 1991.

Rosen, Sydney. "In Search of the Historical Kuan Chung." *JAS* 35.3 (1975): 431–40.

Roth, Harold D. *The Textual History of the Huai-nan Tzu.* Ann Arbor, Mich.: The Association for Asian Studies, 1992.

Rudenko, S. *Frozen Tombs of Siberia: The Pazyryk Burials of Iron Age Horsemen.* London: Dent, 1970.

Rudenko S. *Kul'tura naseleniia tsentral'nogo Altaia v skifskoe vremia.* Moscow: Nauka, 1960.

Rudenko, S. I. *Die Kultur der Hsiung-nu und die Hügelgräber von Noin Ula.* Bonn: Habelt, 1969.

Rudenko, S. I., and N. M. Rudenko. *Iskusstvo skifov Altaia.* Moscow: Gos. muzeia izobrazitel'nikh iskusstv im. A. M. Pushkina, 1949.

Rui Yifu 芮逸夫. "Miaozu de hongshui gushi yu Fuxi Nüwa de chuanshuo" 苗族的洪水故事與伏犧女媧的傳説. *Renleixue jikan* 人類學集刊 I (1938): 155–94.

Ruvolo, M., T. R. Disotell, M. W. Allard, W. M. Brown, and R. L. Honeycutt. "Resolution of the African Hominoid Trichotomy by the Use of a Mitochondrial Gene Sequence." *Proceedings of the National Academy of Sciences, USA*, 88 (1991): 1570–4.

Sagart, Laurent. "Chinese and Austronesian: Evidence for a Genetic Relationship." *Journal of Chinese Linguistics* 21.1 (1993): 1–62.

Sagart, Laurent. "Some Remarks on the Ancestry of Chinese." In *The Ancestry of the Chinese*, ed. William S. Y. Wang. Journal of Chinese Linguistics monograph series, no. 8. Berkeley: Journal of Chinese Linguistics, 1995, pp. 195–223.

Sage, Steven F. *Ancient Sichuan and the Unification of China.* Albany: State University of New York Press, 1992.

Salmony, Albert. *Antler and Tongue: An Essay on Ancient Chinese Symblism.* Ascona: Artibus Asiae, 1954.

Salmony, Albert. *Sino-Siberian Art in the Collection of C. T. Loo.* Paris: C. T. Loo, 1933.

San Jin kaogu 三晉考古 I (1994): 139–53. "Wenxi xian Shangguocun 1989 nian fajue jianbao" 聞喜縣上郭村 1989 年發掘簡報.

San Jin kaogu 三晉考古 I (1994): 154–84. "Houma Beiwu gucheng kantan fajue jianbao" 侯馬北塢古城勘探發掘簡報.

San Jin kaogu 三晉考古 I (1994): 208–12. "Houma Xinanzhang jisi yizhi diaocha shijue jianbao"侯馬西南張祭祀遺址調查試掘簡報.

San Jin kaogu 三晉考古 I (1994): 123–38. "1976 nian Wenxi Shangguocun Zhou dai muzang qingliji" 1976 年聞喜上郭村周代墓葬清理記.

Sanxingdui yu Ba Shu wenhua 三星堆與巴蜀文化. Ed. Li Shaoming 李紹明, Lin Xiang 林向, and Zhao Dianzeng 趙殿增. Chengdu: Ba Shu, 1993.

Sauer, Carl O. *Agricultural Origins and Dispersals.* New York: American Geographical Society, 1952.

Sawyer, Ralph, trans. *The Seven Military Classics of Ancient China.* Boulder: Westview Press, 1993.

Sawyer, Ralph, trans. *Sun Pin: Military Methods.* Boulder: Westview, 1995.

Sawyer, Ralph trans. *Sun Tzu: Art of War.* Boulder: Westview, 1994.

Schafer, Edward H. *Pacing the Void: T'ang Approaches to the Stars.* Berkeley: University of California Press, 1977.

Schafer, Edward H. "Ritual Exposure in Ancient China." *HJAS* 14 (1951): 130–84.

Schmandt-Besserat, Denise. *Before Writing*, Part 1: "From Counting to Cuneiform." Austin: University of Texas Press, 1992.

Schneider, Laurence A. *Ku Chieh-kang and China's New History*. Berkeley: University of California Press, 1971.

Schuessler, Axel. *A Dictionary of Early Zhou Chinese*. Honolulu: University of Hawaii Press, 1987.

Schunk, Lutz. *Dokumente zur Rechtsgeschichte des alten China: Übersetzung und historisch-philologische Kommentierung juristischer Bronzeinschriften der West-Zhou-Zeit (1045–771 v.Chr.)*. Doctoral dissertation. Westfalischen Wilhelms-Üniversitat zu Munster, 1994.

Schwartz, Benjamin I. *The World of Thought in Ancient China*. Cambridge, Mass.: Harvard University Press, 1985.

Schwentner, Ernst. *Tocharische Bibliographie, 1890–1958*. Deutsche Akademie der Wissenschaften zu Berlin. Institut für Orientforschung. Veröffentlichung no. 47. Berlin: Akademie, 1959.

Scientia Sinica 21, 4 (1978): 516–32. "Development of Natural Environment in the Southern Part of Liaoning Province During the Last 10,000 Years."

Seidel, Anna. "Buying One's Way to Heaven: The Celestial Treasury in Chinese Religions." *History of Religions* 17, 3–4 (1978): 419–31.

Seidel, Anna. "Traces of Han Religion in Funeral Texts Found in Tombs." In *Dôkyô to shûkyô bunka* 道教と宗教文化,ed. Akizuki Kan'ei 秋月觀暎. Tokyo: Hirakawa, 1987, pp. 21–57.

Sekino Takeshi 關野雄. *Chûgoku kôkogaku kenkyû* 中國考古學研究. Tokyo: Tokyo University Press, 1963.

Sekino Takeshi 關野雄. "Chûgoku ni okeru funkyû no seisei" 中國における墳丘の生成. In *Chûgoku kôkogaku kenkyû* 中國考古學研究. Tokyo: Tokyo University Press, 1963, pp. 563–91.

Shaanxi chutu Shang Zhou qingtongqi 陝西省出土商周青銅. Ed. Shaanxi sheng kaogu yanjiusuo et al., eds. 4 vols. Vol. 1, Beijing: Wenwu, 1979; vol. 2, 1980; vol. 3, 1980; vol. 4, 1984.

Shadick, Harold, and Chiao Chien. *A First Course in Literary Chinese*. 3 vols. Ithaca, N.Y.: Cornell University Press, 1968.

Shanbiaozhen yu Liulige 山彪鎮與琉璃閣. Beijing: Kexue, 1959.

Shandong wenwu xuanji (pucha bufen) 山東文物選集（普查部分）. Shandong sheng bowuguan et al., eds. Beijing: Wenwu, 1959.

Shang Chengzuo 商承祚. *Hunyuan yiqitu* 渾源彝器圖. Jinling daxue Zhongguo wenhua yanjiusuo jikan 金陵大學中國文化研究所輯刊 1 (1936).

Shang Zhiru 尚志儒 and Zhao Congcang 趙從倉. "Fengxiang Majiazhuang yihao jianzhu yizhi fajue jianbao buzheng" 鳳翔馬家庄一號建築遺址發掘簡報補正. *Wenbo* 文博 1986.1: 11–13.

Shang Zhiru 尚志儒. "Qin guo xiaoxingmu de fenxi yu fenqi" 秦國小型墓的分系與分期. *Shaanxi sheng Kaogu xuehui di yi jie nianhui lunwenji* 陝西省考古學會第一屆年會論文集 (i.e., *Kaogu yu wenwu congkan* 考古與文物叢刊 3 [1983]): 58–67.

Shang Zhitan 商志潭. "Sunan diqu qingtongqi hejin chengfen de tese ji xiangguan wenti" 蘇南地區青銅器合金成份的特色及相關問題. *Wenwu* 文物 1990.9: 48–55.

Shang Zhitan 商志潭 and Tang Yuming 唐鈺明. "Jiangsu Dantu Beishanding Chunqiu mu chutu zhongding mingwen shizheng" 江蘇丹徒背山頂春秋墓出土鐘鼎銘文釋證. *Wenwu* 文物 1989.4: 51–9.

Shangcunling Guo guo mudi 上村嶺虢國墓地. Beijing: Kexue, 1959.

Shangma mudi 上馬墓地. Beijing: Wenwu, 1994.

Shanxi chutu wenwu 山西出土文物. Ed. Shanxi sheng Wenwu gongzuo weiyuanhui. Taiyuan: Shanxi Renmin, 1980.

Shanxi kaogu sishi nian 山西考古四十年. Ed. Shanxi sheng Kaogu yanjiusuo. Taiyuan: Shanxi Renmin, 1994.

Shanxi sheng kaogu xuehui lunwenji 山西省考古學會論文集, Ed. Shanxi sheng kaogu xuehui and Shanxi kaogu yanjiusuo. *Vol.* 2. Taiyuan: Shanxi renmin, 1994.

Shao Guotian 邵國田. "Aohanqi Tiejiangguo Zhanguo mudi diaocha jianbao" 敖漢旗鐵匠國戰國墓地調查簡報. *Nei Menggu wenwu kaogu* 內蒙古文物考古 1992.1–2: 84–90.

Shaughnessy, Edward L. *Before Confucius: Studies in the Creation of the Chinese Classics*. Albany, N.Y.: State University of New York Press, 1997.

Shaughnessy, Edward L. "The Composition of the *Zhouyi*." Ph.D. dissertation, Stanford University, 1983. University Microfilms International, no. 8320774.

Shaughnessy, Edward L. "The 'Current' Bamboo Annals and the Date of the Zhou Conquest of Shang." *EC* 11–12 (1985–7): 33–60.

Shaughnessy, Edward L. "The Date of the 'Duo You *Ding*' and Its Significance." *EC* 9–10 (1983–5): 55–69.

Shaughnessy, Edward L. "The Duke of Zhou's Retirement in the East and the Beginnings of the Minister-Monarch Debate in Chinese Political Philosophy." *EC* 18 (1993): 41–72.

Shaughnessy, Edward L. "Extra-Lineage Cult in the Shang Dynasty: A Surrejoinder." *EC,* 11–12 (1985–7): 182–94.

Shaughnessy, Edward L. "A First Reading of the Mawangdui *Yijing* Manuscript." *EC* 19 (1994): 2–27.

Shaughnessy, Edward L. "From Liturgy to Literature: The Ritual Contexts of the Earliest Poems in the *Book of Poetry*." *Hanxue yanjiu* 漢學研究 13.1 (1994): 133–64.

Shaughnessy, Edward L. "Historical Geography and the Extent of Early Chinese Kingdoms." *Asia Major*, 3d series, 2, 2 (1989): 1–22.

Shaughnessy, Edward L. "Historical Perspectives on the Introduction of the Chariot into China." *HJAS* 48, 1 (1988): 189–237.

Shaughnessy, Edward L. "The Last Years of Shang King Wu Ding: An Experiment in Reconstructing the Chronology of Ancient China." Unpublished manuscript (7 May 1990).

Shaughnessy, Edward L. "Marriage, Divorce and Revolution: Reading between the Lines of the *Book of Changes*." *JAS* 51, 3 (1992): 587–99.

Shaughnessy, Edward L. "Micro-Periodization and the Calendar of a Shang Military Campaign." In *Chinese Language, Thought and Culture, Essays Dedicated to David S. Nivison*, ed. P. J. Ivanhoe. La Salle, Ill.: Open Court, 1996, pp. 58–93.

Shaughnessy, Edward L. "'New' Evidence on the Zhou Conquest." *EC* 6 (1980–81): 57–81.

Shaughnessy, Edward L. "On the Authenticity of the *Bamboo Annals*." *HJAS* 46.1 (1986): 149–80.

Shaughnessy, Edward L. "The Origin of an *Yijing* Line Statement." *EC* 20 (1995): 223–40.

Shaughnessy, Edward L. "Recent Approaches to Oracle-Bone Periodization." *EC* 8 (1982–3): 1–13.

Shaughnessy, Edward L. *Sources of Western Zhou History: Inscribed Bronze Vessels*. Berkeley: University of California Press, 1991.

Shaughnessy, Edward L. "Western Zhou Bronze Inscriptions." In *New Sources of Early Chinese History: An Introduction to the Reading of Inscriptions and Manuscripts*, ed. Edward L. Shaughnessy. Society for the Study of Early China monograph series, no. 3. Berkeley: Institute of East Asian Studies and Society for the Study of Early China, 1997, pp. 57–84.

Shaughnessy, Edward L. "Zhouyuan Oracle-Bone Inscriptions: Entering the Research Stage?" *EC* 11–12 (1985–7): 146–63.

Shaughnessy, Edward L., ed. *New Sources of Early Chinese History: An Introduction to the Reading of Inscriptions and Manuscripts.* Society for the Study of Early China monograph series, no. 3. Berkeley: Institute of East Asian Studies and the Society for the Study of Early China, 1997.

Shen Bin 申斌. "Fu Hao mu yuqi cailiao tanyuan" 婦好墓玉器材料探源. *Zhongyuan wenwu* 中原文物 1991.1: 73–8.

Shen Yinhua 沈銀華. "Hubei sheng Hanchuan xian faxian yipi Chunqiu shiqi qingtongqi" 湖北省漢川縣發現一批春秋時期青銅器. *Wenwu* 文物 1974.6: 85.

Sher, Yakov A. "On the Sources of the Scythic Animal Style." *Arctic Anthropology* 25, 2 (1988): 47–60.

Shi ben bazhong 世本八種. Shanghai: Shangwu, 1977.

Shi ji zhuyi 史記注譯. Ed. Wang Liqi 王利器. 4 vols. Xi'an: Sanqin, 1988.

Shi Ming 史明. "Xi Zhou Chunqiu shidai lizhi de yanbian he Kong Qiu keji fuli de fandong shizhi" 西周春秋時代禮制的演變和孔丘克己復禮的反動實質. *Kaogu* 考古 1974.2: 81–8.

Shi Nianhai 史念海. *He shan ji* 河山集. 3 vols. Beijing: Sanlian, vol. 1, 1963; vol. 2, 1981; Beijing: Renmin, vol. 3, 1988.

Shi Quan 石泉. *Gudai Jing Chu dili xintan* 古代荊楚地理新探. Wuhan: Wuhan daxue, 1988.

Shisan jing zhushu fu jiaokanji 十三經注疏附校勘記. Annotated by Ruan Yuan 阮元. 2 vols. Beijing: Zhonghua shuju, 1980.

Shi Xingbang 石興邦. "Chang'an Puducun Xi Zhou muzang fajueji" 長安普渡村西周墓葬發掘記. *Kaogu xuebao* 考古學報 8 (1954): 109–26.

Shi Xingbang 石興邦. "Huanghe liuyu yuanshi shehui kaogu shang de ruogan wenti" 黃河流域原始社會考古上的若干問題. *Kaogu* 考古 1959.10: 568.

Shi Xingbang 石興邦 et al., eds. *Kaoguxue yanjiu: Jinian Shaanxi sheng Kaogu yanjiusuo chengli sanshi zhounian* 考古學研究:紀念陝西省考古研究所成立三十週年. Xi'an: San Qin, 1993.

Shi Yafeng and Wang Jingtai. "The Fluctuations of Climate, Glaciers, and Sea Level Since Late Pleistocene in China." In *Sea Level, Ice, and Climatic Change*, ed. I. Allison. Washington, D.C.: International Association of Hydrological Sciences, 1981, pp. 281–93.

Shi Yan 史言. "Meixian Yangjiacun da ding" 眉縣楊家村大鼎. *Wenwu* 文物 1972.7: 3–4.

Shi Zhangru 石璋如. *Xiaotun diyiben: Yizhi de faxian yu fajue: Yibian: Jianzhu yicun* 小屯第一本：遺址的發現與發掘. 乙編：建築遺存 Nangang: Academia Sinica, 1959.

Shi Zhangru 石璋如. "Yin che fuyuan shuoming" 殷車復原說明." *BIHP* 58 (1987): 253–80.

Shima Kunio 島邦男. *Inkyo bokuji kenkyû* 殷墟卜辭研究. Hirosaki: Hirosaki daigaku Chûgoku gaku kenkyûkai, 1958.

Shirakawa Shizuka 白川靜. *Kinbun tsûshaku* 金文通釋. Kobe: Hakutsuru bijutsukan, 1962–84.

Shirakawa Shizuka 白川靜. "Kyôzoku kô" 羌族考. *Kôkotsu kinbungaku ronsô* 甲骨金文學論叢 9 (1958): 1–16.

Shiyi jia zhu Sunzi 十一家注孫子. Shanghai: Guji, 1978.

Shoseki meihin sôkan 書跡名品叢刊. Tokyo: Nigensha, 1959.

Shouxian Cai Hou mu chutu yiwu 壽縣蔡侯墓出土遺物. Ed. Anhui sheng Wenwu guanli weiyuanhui and Anhui sheng bowuguan. Kaoguxue zhuankan 考古學專刊, series 2, no. 5. Beijing: Kexue, 1956.

Shui Tao 水濤. "Xibei diqu shiqian kaogu yanjiu de huigu yu qianzhan" 西北地區史前考古研究的回顧與前瞻. In *Kaoguxue wenhua lunji* 考古學文化論集, ed. Su Bingqi 蘇秉琦. Beijing: Wenwu, 1993, vol. 3, pp. 1–11.

Shuihudi Qin mu zhujian 睡虎地秦墓竹簡. Ed. Shuihudi Qin mu zhujian zhengli xiaozu. Beijing: Wenwu, 1990.

Shuowen jiezi gulin 説文解字詁林. Ed. Ding Fubao 丁福保. Preface dated 1928. Shanghai: yixue; rpt. Shanghai: Shangwu, 1937; Taibei: Shangwu, 1970.

Sivin, Nathan. *Traditional Medicine in Contemporary China.* Ann Arbor, Mich.: University of Michigan Center for Chinese Studies, 1987.

Skosey, Laura A. "The Legal System and Legal Tradition of the Western Zhou (1045 B.C.E.–771 B.C.E.)." Ph.D. dissertation, University of Chicago, 1996.

Smith, Kidder. "*Zhouyi* Interpretation from Accounts in the *Zuozhuan.*" *HJAS* 49 (1989): 421–63.

So, Jenny F. *Eastern Zhou Ritual Bronzes from the Arthur M. Sackler Collection.* New York: Adams, 1995.

So, Jenny F. "The Inlaid Bronzes of the Warring States Period." In *The Great Bronze Age of China*, ed. Wen Fong. New York: Metropolitan Museum of Art, 1980, pp. 305–20.

So, Jenny F., and Emma C. Bunker. *Traders and Raiders on China's Northern Frontier.* Seattle: Arthur Sackler Gallery, and Seattle: University of Washington Press, 1995.

Song Shaohua 宋少華. "Changsha chutu Shang Chunqiu qingtongqi" 長沙出土商春秋青銅器. *Hunan bowuguan wenji* 湖南博物館文集 1 (1991): 133–6.

Song Zhenhao 宋鎮豪. "Xia Shang renkou chutan" 夏商人口初探. *Lishi yanjiu* 歷史研究, 1991.4: 92–106.

Soothill, William E. *The Hall of Light: A Study of Early Kingship.* London: Lutterworth, 1951.

Steinhardt, Nancy S. *Chinese Imperial City Planning.* Honolulu: University of Hawaii Press, 1990.

Stephen, Barbara. "Formal Variation in Shang Dynasty Vehicles." In *Proceedings: International Colloquium on Chinese Art History, 1991, Antiquities, Part 1.* Taipei: National Palace Museum, 1992, pp. 107–35.

Stephen, Barbara. "Shang Bronzes with Ancient Repairs." In *1961 Annual, Art and Archaeology Division, The Royal Ontario Museum, University of Toronto.* Toronto: Royal Ontario Museum, 1962, pp. 8–14.

Stumpfeldt, Hans. *Staatsverfassung und Territorium im antiken China: Über die Ausbildung einer territorialen Staatsverfassung.* Freiburger Studien zu Politik und Gesellschaft überseeischer Länder, vol. 8. Düsseldorf: Bertelsmann Universitätsverlag, 1970.

Su Bingqi 蘇秉琦 and Yin Weizhang 殷瑋璋. "Guanyu kaoguxue wenhua de quxi leixing wenti" 關於考古學文化的區系類型問題. *Wenwu* 文物 1981.5: 10–17. Rpt. in *Su Bingqi kaoguxue lunshu xuanji* 蘇秉琦考古學論述選集. Beijing: Wenwu, 1984, pp. 225–34.

Su Rongyu 蘇榮譽, Hua Jueming 華覺明, Li Kemin 李克敏, and Lu Benshan 盧本珊. *Zhongguo shanggu jinshu jishu* 中國上古金屬技術. Ji'nan: Shandong Kexue, 1995.

Su Rongyu 蘇榮譽 and Peng Shifan 彭適凡. "Xin'gan qingtongqi qun jishu wenhua shuxing yanjiu" 新干青銅器群技術文化屬性研究. *Nanfang wenwu* 南方文物 1994.2: 30–6.

Suixian Zeng Hou Yi mu 隨縣曾侯乙墓. Beijing: Wenwu, 1980.

Sun Bin bingfa 孫臏兵法. Beijing: Wenwu, 1975.

Sun Haibo 孫海波. *Xinzheng yiqi* 新鄭彝器. 2 vols. Kaifeng: Henan sheng Tongzhiguan, 1937.

Sun Hua 孫華. "Guanzhong Shangdai zhu yizhi de xin renzhi: Yijiabao yizhi fajue de yiyi" 關中商代諸遺址的新認知：壹家堡遺址發掘的意義. *Kaogu* 考古 1993.5: 426–43.

Sun Hua 孫華. "Xin'gan Dayangzhou da mu niandai jianlun" 新干大洋洲大墓年代簡論. *Nanfang wenwu* 南方文物 1992.2: 35–40.

Sun Ji 孫機. "Zhongguo gudai mache de jijia fa" 中國古代馬車的繫駕法. *Ziran kexue shi yanjiu* 自然科學史研究 3, 2 (1984): 169–76.

Sun Ji 孫機. "Zhongguo gu duzhou mache de jiegou" 中國古獨輈馬車的結構. *Wenwu* 文物 1985.8: 25–40.

Sun Miao 孫淼. *Xia Shang shigao* 夏商史稿. Beijing: Wenwu, 1987.

Sun Shoudao 孫守道 and Guo Dashun 郭大順. *Wenming shuguangqi jisi yizhen: Liaoning Hongshan wenhua tanmiaozhong (Zhongguo kaogu wenwu zhi mei 1)* 文明曙光期祭祀遺珍：遼寧紅山文化壇廟冢（中國考古文物之美1）. Beijing: Wenwu, 1994.

Sun Shoudao 孫守道 and Guo Dashun 郭大順. "Niuheliang Hongshan wenhua nüshen touxiang de faxian yu yanjiu" 牛河梁紅山文化女神頭像的發現與研究. *Wenwu* 文物 1986.8: 18–24.

Sun Yirang. 孫詒讓. *Zhou li zhengyi* 周禮正義. 14 vols. Rpt. Beijing: Zhonghua, 1987.

Sun Zuoyun 孫作雲. *Shijing yu Zhoudai shehui yanjiu* 詩經與周代社會研究. Beijing: Zhonghua, 1966.

Sussman, Robert. "A Current Controversy in Human Evolution." *American Anthropologist* 95 (1993): 9–96.

Swann, Nancy Lee. *Food and Money in Ancient China: The Earliest Economic History of China to A.D. 25; Han shu 24 with Related Texts, Han shu 91 and Shih-chi 129*. Princeton, N.J.: Princeton University Press, 1950.

Swisher III, C. C., G. H. Curtis, T. Jacob, A. G. Getty, A. Suprijo, and Widiasmoro. "Age of the Earliest Known Hominids in Java, Indonesia." *Science* 263 (1994): 1118–21.

Sylwan, Vivi. "Silk from the Yin Dynasty." *BMFEA* 9 (1937): 119–26.

Takahama, Shu. "Early Scytho-Siberian Animal Style in East Asia." *Bulletin of the Ancient Orient Museum* 5 (1983): 45–51.

Ta la 塔拉 and Liang Jingming 梁京明. "Hulusitai Xiongnu mu" 呼魯斯太匈奴墓. *Wenwu* 文物 1980.7: 11–12.

Taiping yulan 太平御覽. Compiled by Li Fang 李昉 et al. 984; rpt. Beijing: Zhonghua, 1960.

Takigawa Kametarô 瀧川龜太郎. *Shiki kaichû kôshô* 史記會注考證. Tokyo: Tôhô bunka gakuin, 1932–4; rpt. Beijing: Wenxue guji, 1955.

Tambiah, Stanley J. *Magic, Science, Religion, and the Scope of Rationality*. Cambridge University Press, 1990.

Tan Derui. *The Splendid Craft of Lost Wax Casting in Ancient China* (in Chinese and English). Shanghai: Shanghai Scientific and Technological Literature Publishing House, 1989.

Tan Derui 譚德叡 and Huang Long 黃龍. "Wu Yue wenhuaxi qingtong jishu diaocha baogao" 吳越文化系青銅技術調查報告. Paper presented at the International Symposium on Wu-Yue Bronzes, Shanghai, August 1992.

Tan Derui 譚德叡, Lian Haiping 廉海萍, Wu Zejia 吳則嘉 Su Limin 蘇立民, Li Jing 李靖, Zhang Guoying 張國英, Tang Jingjuan 唐靜娟, and Xu Zhizheng 許志正. "Wu Yue lingxing wenshi tongbingqi jishu chutan" 吳越菱形紋飾銅兵器技術初探. *Nanfang wenwu* 南方文物 1994.2: 120–6.

Tan Sanping 談三平 and Liu Shuren. 劉樹人 "Taihu diqu shishi tudun fenbu guilü yaogan chubu yanjiu" 太湖地區石室土墩分布規律遙感初步研究. *Dongnan wenhua* 東南文化 1990.4: 100–103.

Tan Ying-jie et al. "The Bronze Age in the Song Nen Plain." In *The Archaeology of Northeast China: Beyond the Great Wall*, ed. Sarah Milledge Nelson. London: Routledge, 1995, pp. 225–50.

Tan Yingjie 潭英杰 and Zhao Shandong 趙善恫. "Song Nen pingyuan qingtong wenhua chuyi" 松嫩平原青銅文化芻議. In *Zhongguo kaogu xuehui di si ci nianhui lunwenji 1983* 中國考古學會第四次年會論文集 1983. Beijing: Wenwu, 1985, pp. 196–202.

Tang Aihua 唐愛華."Xinxiang bowuguan cang Xi Zhou Ze Bo yan" 新鄉博物館藏西周夨伯甗. *Wenwu* 文物 1986.3: 93.

Tang Jigen 唐際根. "Yinxu yi qi wenhua ji qi xiangguan wenti" 殷墟一期文化及其相關問題. *Kaogu* 考古 1993.10: 925–35.

Tang Jigen 唐際根. "Zhongguo yetieshu de qiyuan wenti" 中國冶鐵術的起源問題. *Kaogu* 考古 1993.6: 556–65, 553.

Tang Jinyu 唐金裕, Wang Shouzhi 王壽芝, and Guo Changjiang 郭長江. "Shaanxi sheng Chenggu xian chutu Yin Shang tongqi zhengli jianbao" 陝西省城固縣出土殷商銅器整理簡報. *Kaogu* 考古 1980.3: 211–18.

Tang Lan 唐蘭. "Huang Di si jing chu tan" 黃帝四經初探. *Wenwu* 文物 1974.10: 48–52.

Tang Lan 唐蘭. "Mawangdui chutu Laozi yi ben juan qian gu yi shu de yanjiu: Jian lun qi yu Han chu ru fa douzheng de guanxi" 馬王堆出土老子乙本卷前古佚書的研究：兼論其與漢初儒法斗爭的關系. *Kaogu xuebao* 考古學報 1975.1: 7–38.

Tang Lan 唐蘭. "Shaanxi sheng Qishan xian Dongjiacun xin chu Xi Zhou zhongyao tongqi mingci de yiwen he zhushi" 陝西省歧山縣董家村新出西周重要銅器銘辭的譯文和注釋.*Wenwu* 文物 1976.5: 55–9, 63.

Tang Lan 唐蘭. *Xi Zhou qingtongqi mingwen fendai shizheng* 西周青銅器銘文分代史徵. Beijing: Zhonghua, 1986.

Tang Lan 唐蘭. "Yi Hou Ze gui kaoshi" 宜侯夨簋考釋. *Kaogu xuebao* 考古學報 1956.2: 79–83.

Tang Lan 唐蘭. "Yong yu mingwen jieshi" 永盂銘文解釋. *Wenwu* 文物 1972.1: 58–62.

Tang Lingyu 唐領余, Li Minchang 李民昌, and Shen Caiming 沈才明. "Jiangsu Huai bei diqu xinshiqi shidai renlei wenhua yu huanjing" 江蘇淮北地區新石器時代人類文化與環境. In *Huanjing kaogu yanjiu* 環境考古研究, eds. Zhou Kunshu 周昆叔 and Gong Qiming. Beijing: Kexue, 1991, pp. 164–72.

Tang Xiaofeng 唐曉峰. "Nei Menggu xibei bu Qin Han chang cheng diaocha ji" 內蒙古西北部秦漢長城調查記. *Wenwu* 1977.5: 16–22.

Tang Yunming 唐雲明. "Taixi yizhi qiqi de yuanyuan ji yizhi wenhua xingzhi de tantao" 臺西遺址漆器的淵源及遺址文化性質的探討. *Huaxia kaogu* 華夏考古 1988.2: 62–8.

Tao Fu 陶復. "Qin Xianyang gong di yihao yizhi fuyuan wenti de chubu tantao" 秦咸陽宮第一號遺址復原問題的初步探討. *Wenwu* 文物 1976.11: 31–41.

Tao Zhenggang 陶正剛. "Shanxi chutu de Shang dai tongqi" 山西出土的商代銅器. In *Zhongguo Kaogu xuehui di si ci nianhui lunwenji 1983* 中國考古學會第四次年會論文集 1983. Beijing: Wenwu, 1985, pp. 57–64.

Tao Zhenggang 陶正剛 and Hou Yi 侯毅. *Jin guo qingtong kuibao* 晉國青銅愧寶. Zhongguo wenwu kaogu zhi mei, vol. 4. Taibei: Guangfu, 1994.

Teboul, Michel. "Ancient Chinese Auroral Records: Interpretation Problems and Methods." In *History of Oriental Astronomy*, ed. G. Swarup et al. Cambridge University Press, 1987, pp. 41–50.

Teboul, Michel. "Les premiers développements de l'astronomie chinoise des Royaumes Combattants au début de L'ère Chrétienne." *Bulletin de l'école française d'Extrême-Orient* 71 (1982): 147–67.

Telehin, Dmitriy. *Dereivka: A Settlement and Cemetery of Copper Age Horse Keepers on the Middle Dnieper.* Trans. V. K. Pyatkovskiy, ed. J. P. Mallory. Oxford: British Archaeological Reports, International series, no. 287, 1986.

Teng Mingyu 滕銘予. "Feng Hao diqu Xi Zhou muzang de ruogan wenti" 豐鎬地區西周墓葬的若干問題. *Kaoguxue wenhua lunji* 考古學文化論集 3 (1993): 201–29.

Teng Mingyu 滕銘予. "Guanzhong Qin mu yanjiu" 關中秦墓研究. *Kaogu xuebao* 考古學報 1992.3: 281–300.

Thatcher, Melvin P. "Central Government of the State of Chin in the Spring and Autumn Period." *Journal of Oriental Studies* 23, 1 (1985): 29–53.

Thatcher, Melvin P. "A Structural Comparison of the Central Government of Ch'i, Ch'u and Chin." *MS* 33 (1977–8): 140–61.

Thompson, P. M. *The Shen Tzu Fragments*. Oxford: Oxford University Press, 1979.

Thorp, Robert L. "The Archaeology of Style at Anyang: Tomb 5 in Context." *Archives of Asian Art* 41 (1988): 47–69.

Thorp, Robert L. "Burial Practices of Bronze Age China." In *The Great Bronze Age of China*, ed. Wen Fong. New York: Metropolitan Museum of Art, 1980, pp. 51–64.

Thorp, Robert L. "Erlitou and the Search for the Xia." *EC* 16 (1991): 1–38.

Thorp, Robert L. "The Growth of Early Shang Civilization: New Data from Ritual Vessels." *HJAS* 45 (1985): 5–75.

Thorp, Robert L. "The Mortuary Art and Architecture of Early Imperial China." Ph.D. dissertation, University of Kansas, 1979.

Thorp, Robert L. "The Sui Xian Tomb: Re-thinking the Fifth Century." *Artibus Asiae* 43, 5 (1981): 67–92.

Thote, Alain. "The Double Coffin of Leigudun Tomb no. 1: Iconographic Sources and Related Problems." In *New Perspectives on Chu Culture During the Eastern Zhou Period*, ed. Thomas Lawton. Washington, D.C.: Authur M. Sackler Gallery, 1991, pp. 23–46.

Tian Guangjin 田廣金. "Jinnianlai Nei Menggu diqu de Xiongnu kaogu" 近年來內蒙古地區的匈奴考古. *Kaogu xuebao* 考古學報 1983.1: 7–24.

Tian Guangjin 田廣金. "Taohongbala de Xiongnu mu" 桃紅巴拉的匈奴墓. *Kaogu xuebao* 考古學報 1976.1: 131–42.

Tian Guangjin 田廣金 and Guo Suxin 郭素新. "Aluchaideng faxian de jin yin qi" 阿魯柴登發現的金銀器. In *O'erduosi qingtong qi* 鄂爾多斯青銅器, ed. Tian Guangjin and Guo Suxin. Beijing: Wenwu, 1986, pp. 342–50.

Tian Guangjin 田廣金 and Guo Suxin 郭素新. "Nei Menggu Aluchaideng faxian de Xiongnu yiwu" 內蒙古阿魯柴登發現的匈奴遺物. *Kaogu* 考古 1980.4: 333–8, 364, 368.

Tian Guangjin and Guo Suxin. "O'erduosi shi qingtong qi de yuanyuan" 鄂爾多斯式青銅器的淵源. *Kaogu xuebao* 考古學報 1988.3: 257–75.

Tian Guangjin 田廣金 and Guo Suxin 郭素新, eds. *O'erduosi qingtong qi* 鄂爾多斯青銅器. Beijing: Wenwu, 1986.

Tian Xingnong 田醒農 and Luo Zhongru 雒忠儒. "Duo You ding de faxian ji qi mingwen shishi" 多友鼎的發現及其銘文試釋. *Renwen zazhi* 人文雜誌 1981.4: 115–18.

Tian Yichao 田宜超 and Liu Zhao 劉釗. "Qin tian lü kaoshi" 秦田律考釋. *Kaogu* 考古 1983.6: 545–8.

Tjan Tjoe Som. Po hu t'ung 白虎通. *The Comprehensive Discussions in the White Tiger Hall*. 2 vols. Leiden: Brill, 1949–52.

Tôdô Akiyasu 藤堂明保, *Kanji gogen jiten* 漢字語源辭典. Tokyo: Gakutôsha, 1969.

Tôdô Akiyasu. "Some Notes on the Ch'iang Tribes 羌族." *Acta Asiatica* 16 (1969): 39–50.

Tong dian 通典. Compiled by Du You 杜佑. Rpt. Taipei: Xinxing, 1963.

Tong Enzheng 童恩正. "Shi lun wo guo cong dongbei zhi xinan de biandi banyuexing wenhua zhuanbodai" 試論我國從東北至西南的邊地半月形文化傳播帶. In *Wenwu chubanshe chengli sanshi zhounian jinian: Wenwu yu kaogu lunji* 文物出版社成立三十週年紀念：文物與考古論集. Beijing: Wenwu, 1986, pp. 17–43.

Treistman, Judith M. "China at 1000 B.C.: A Cultural Mosaic." *Science* 160 (1968): 853–6.

Treistman, Judith M. *Prehistory of China.* Garden City, N.J.: Natural History Press, 1972.

Trigger, Bruce. *Beyond History: The Methods of Prehistory.* New York: Holt, Rinehart, & Winston, 1968.

Trigger, Bruce G. *A History of Archaeological Thought.* Cambridge University Press, 1989.

Trigger, Bruce G. *Gordon Childe: Revolutions in Archaeology.* London: Thames & Hudson; and New York: Columbia University Press, 1980.

Trigger, B. G., B. J. Kemp, D. O'Connor, and A. B. Lloyd. *Ancient Egypt: A Social History.*: Cambridge University Press, 1983.

Tsien, Tsuen-hsuin. *Written on Bamboo and Silk: The Beginnings of Chinese Books and Inscriptions.* Chicago: University of Chicago Press, 1962.

Tu, Wei-ming. The Thought of Huang-Lao: A Reflection on the Lao Tzu and Huang Ti Texts in the Silk Manuscripts of Ma-wang-tui. *JAS* 39, 1 (1979): 95–110.

Twitchett, Denis, and Michael Loewe, eds. *The Cambridge History of China. Vol. 1: The Ch'in and Han Empires.* Cambridge University Press, 1986.

Umehara Sueji 梅原末治. *In bo hakken mokki in'ei zuroku* 殷墓發現木器印影圖録. Kyoto: Benridô, 1959.

Umehara Sueji 梅原末治. *Kan izen no kokyô no kenkyû* 漢以前の古鏡的研究. Kyoto: Tôhô bunka gakuin Kyôto kenkyûjo, 1935.

Umehara Sueji 梅原末治. *Rakuyô Kinson kobô shûei* 洛陽金村古墓聚英. Kyoto: Kobayashi shashin seibanjo, 1937.

Umehara Sueji 梅原末治. *Sengoku shiki dôki no kenkyû.* 戰國式銅器の研究. Kyoto: Tôhô bunka gakuin Kyôto kenkyûjo, 1936.

Unschuld, Paul. "History of Chinese Medicine." In *The Cambridge World History of Human Disease*, ed. K. Kiple. Cambridge University Press, 1993, pp. 20–7.

van der Loon, P. "The Ancient Chinese Chronicles and the Growth of Historical Ideals." In *Historians of China and Japan*, ed. W. G. Beasley and E. G. Pulleyblank, London: Oxford University Press, 1961, pp. 24–30.

van Riper, A. Bowdoin. *Men Among Mammoths.* Chicago: University of Chicago Press, 1993.

Vandermeersch, Leon. *Wangdao ou la voie royale: Recherches sur l'esprit des institutions de la Chine archaique. Tome 1: Structures culturelles et structures familiales.* Paris: École francaise d'Extrême Orient, 1977.

Vavilov, N. I. *The Origin, Variation, Immunity and Breeding of Cultivated Plants.* Trans. K. Starr Chester. New York: Ronald, 1952.

Vejnshtein, S. I. "The Problem of the Origin and Formation of the Economic-Cultural Type of Pastoral Nomads in the Moderate Belt of Eurasia." In *The Nomadic Alternative*, ed. W. Weissleder. The Hague: Mouton, 1978, pp. 127–33.

Vervoorn, Aat. *Men of the Cliffs and Caves: The Development of the Chinese Eremitic Tradition to the End of the Han Dynasty.* Hong Kong: Chinese University Press, 1990.

Vollmer, John. "Textile Pseudomorphs on Chinese Bronzes." In *Archaeological Textiles*, ed. Patricia L. Fiske. Washington, D.C.: Textile Museum, 1974, pp. 170–4.

von Dewall, Magdalene. *Pferd und Wagen im frühen China.* Bonn: Habelt, 1964.

von Lochow, Hans Juergen. *Sammlung Lochow, Chinesische Bronzen II.* Beijing: [Fu Jen], 1944.

Wagner, Donald B. *Iron and Steel in Ancient China.* Leiden: Brill, 1993.

Waldron, Arthur. *The Great Wall of China: From History to Myth.* Cambridge University Press, 1990.

Waley, Arthur. *The Analects of Confucius.* London: Allen & Unwin, 1938.

Waley, Arthur. *The Book of Songs: The Ancient Chinese Classic of Poetry*. London: Allen & Unwin, 1937; rpt. New York: Grove, 1960.

Waley, Arthur. *The Way and Its Power: A Study of the Tao Te Ching and Its Place in Chinese Thought*. London: Allen & Unwin, 1934; rpt. 1949.

Wan Shuying 萬樹瀛 and Yang Xiaoyi 楊孝義. "Tengxian chutu Qi Xue tongqi" 滕縣出土杞薛銅器. *Wenwu* 文物 1978.4: 94–6.

Wang Binghua 王炳華. "Gudai Xinjiang Sairen lishi gouchen" 古代新疆塞人歷史鉤沉. *Xinjiang shehui kexue yanjiu* 新疆社會科學研究 16 (1985): 8–19

Wang Binghua 王炳華. "Xi Han yiqian Xinjiang he Zhongyuan diqu lishi guanxi kaosu" 西漢以前新疆和中原地區歷史關系考溯. In Wang Binghua, *Sichou zhi lu kaogu yanjiu* 絲綢之路考古研究. Urumqi: Xinjiang Renmin, 1993, pp. 164–182.

Wang Entian 王恩田. "Henan Gushi Gouwu furen mu: Jiantan Fan guo dili weizhi ji Wu fa Chu luxian." 河南固始句吳夫人墓：兼談番國地理位置及吳伐楚路線. *Zhongyuan wenwu* 中原文物 1985.2: 59–62, 64.

Wang Fei 王飛. "Yongding zhidu xingshuai yiyi" 用鼎制度興衰異議. *Wenbo* 文博 1986.6: 29–33.

Wang Gesen 王閣森 and Tang Zhiqing 唐致卿. *Qi guo shi* 齊國史. Ji'nan: Shandong Renmin, 1992.

Wang Guimin 王貴民. "Jiu Yinxu jiaguwen suojian shishuo Sima zhiming de qiyuan" 就殷墟甲骨文所見試說司馬職名的起源. In *Jiaguwen yu Yin Shang shi* 甲骨文與殷商史, ed. Hu Houxuan 胡厚宣. Shanghai: Shanghai guji, 1983, pp. 173–90.

Wang Gungwu. "Ming Relations with Southeast Asia: A Background Essay." In *The Chinese World Order*, ed. John King Fairbank. Cambridge, Mass.: Harvard University Press, 1968, pp. 34–62.

Wang Guowei 王國維. *Guan tang ji lin* 觀堂集林. 2nd. rev. ed. Beijing: Zhonghua, 1959.

Wang Guowei 王國維. "Guifang Kunyi Xianyun kao" 鬼方昆夷獫狁考. In *Haining Wang Jing'an xiansheng yishu* 海寧王靜安先生遺書. N.p: 1936, vol. 5, ch. 13.

Wang Hui 王暉. "Zhou chu Tangshu shou feng shiji san kao" 周初唐叔受封事跡三考. In *Xi Zhou shi lunwenji* 西周史論文集. Xi'an: Shaanxi Renmin jiaoyu, 1993, pp. 933–43.

Wang Jianmin 王健民 et al. "Zeng Hou Yi mu chutu de ershiba xiu qinglong baihu tuxiang" 曾侯乙墓出土的二十八宿青龍白虎圖象. *Wenwu* 文物 1979.7: 40–5.

Wang Jiayou 王家祐. "Ji Sichuan Peng xian Zhuwajie chutu de tongqi" 記四川彭縣竹瓦街出土的銅器. *Wenwu* 文物 1961.11: 28–31.

Wang Jinping 王金平. "Houma Xinjiang chutu liangmian Dong Zhou tongjing" 侯馬新絳出土兩面東周銅鏡. *Wenwu jikan* 文物季刊 1995.2: 81.

Wang Kelin 王克林. "Houma Dong Zhou shesi yiji de tantao" 侯馬東周社祀遺跡的探討. *Shanxi wenwu* 山西文物 1983.1: 8–14.

Wang Kelin 王克林. *Xia shi luncong* 夏史論叢. Ji'nan: Qi Lu, 1985.

Wang Liqi 王利器. *Shi ji zhu yi* 史記注譯. 4 vols. Xi'an: San Qin, 1988.

Wang Liqi 王利器. *Xin yu jiaozhu* 新語校注. Beijing: Zhonghua, 1986.

Wang Liqi 王利器. *Yan tie lun jiaozhu* 鹽鐵論校注. 2 vols. Rev. ed. Beijing: Zhonghua, 1992.

Wang Pinxian 汪品先, Min Qiubao 閔秋寶, Bian Yunhua 卞云華, and Cheng Xinrong 成鑫榮. "Wo guo dongbu disiji haiqin diceng dechubu yanjiu" 我國東部第四紀海侵地層的初步研究. *Dizhi xuebao (Acta Geologica Sinica)* 地質學報 1981.1: 1–12.

Wang Qing 王青. "Shilun shiqian Huanghe xiayou de gaidao yu gu wenhua de fazhan" 試論史前黃河下游的改道與古文化的發展. *Zhongyuan wenwu* 中原文物 1993.4: 63–72.

Wang Renxiang 王仁湘. "Gudai daigou yongtu kaoshi" 古代帶鉤用途考釋. *Wenwu* 文物 1982.10: 75–81.

Wang Rulin 王儒林 and Cui Qingming 崔慶明. "Nanyang shi Xiguan chutu yipi Chunqiu qingtongqi" 南陽市西關出土一批春秋青銅器. *Zhongyuan wenwu* 中原文物 1982.1: 39–41.

Wang Shaoquan 王少泉. "Xiangfan shi Bowuguan shoucang de Xiangyang Shanwan tongqi" 襄樊市博物館收藏的襄陽山灣銅器. *Jiang Han kaogu* 江漢考古 1988.3: 96–7, 62.

Wang Shengli 王勝利. "Guanyu Chu guo lifa de jianzheng wenti" 關于楚國歷法的建正問題. *Zhongguo shi yanjiu* 中國史研究 1988.2: 137–42.

Wang Shihe 王世和, Zhang Hongyan 張宏顏, Fu Yong 傅勇, Yan Jun 嚴軍, and Zhou Jie 周杰. "Anban yizhi baofen fenxi" 案皮遺址孢粉分析. In *Huanjing kaogu yanjiu* 環境考古研究, ed. Zhou Kunshu 周昆叔 and Gong Qiming 鞏啟明. Beijing: Kexue, 1991, pp. 56–65.

Wang Shimin 王世民. "Guanyu Xi Zhou Chunqiu gaoji guizu liqi zhidu de yixie kanfa" 關於西周春秋高級貴族禮器制度的一些看法. In *Wenwu yu kaogu lunji* 文物與考古論集. Beijing: Wenwu, 1986, pp. 158–66.

Wang Shimin 王世民. "Zhongguo Chunqiu Zhanguo shidai de zhongmu" 中國春秋戰國時代的冢墓. *Kaogu* 考古 1981.5: 459–66.

Wang Shouzhi 王壽芝. "Shaanxi Chenggu chutu de Shang dai qingtongqi" 陝西城固出土的商代青銅器. Wenbo 文博 1988.6: 3–9.

Wang Xianqian 王先謙. *Han shu bu zhu* 漢書補注. Changsha, 1900; rpt. in reduced facsimile, Taipei: Yiwen, 1955.

Wang Xianqian 王先謙. *Shi ming shuzheng bu* 釋名疏證補. Shanghai: Shanghai Guji, 1984.

Wang Xianqian 王先謙. *Xunzi jijie* 荀子集解. Taipei: Lantai, 1972.

Wang Xiantang 王獻唐. *Linzi fengni wenzi xumu* 臨淄封泥文字序目. Ji'nan: Shandong shengli tushuguan, 1936.

Wang Xueli 王學理. *Qin du Xianyang* 秦都咸陽. Xi'an: Shaanxi Renmin, 1985.

Wang Xueli 王學理. "Qin du Xianyang yu Xianyang gong bianzheng" 秦都咸陽與咸陽宮辯正. *Kaogu yu wenwu* 考古與文物 1982.2: 67–71.

Wang Xueli 王學理 et al. "Qin du Xianyang fajue baodao de ruogan buchong yijian" 秦都咸陽發掘報導的若干補充意見. *Wenwu* 文物 1979.2: 85–6.

Wang Xueli 王學理, Shang Zhiru 尚志儒, and Hu Lingui 呼林貴, eds. *Qin wuzhi wenhua shi* 秦物質文化史. Xi'an: San Qin, 1994.

Wang Yi 王逸. *Chu ci jizhu* 楚辭集注. Shanghai: Shanghai Guji, 1979.

Wang Yongbo 王用波. "Si xing duan ren qi de fenlei yu fenqi" 耜形端刃器的分類與分期. *Kaogu xuebao* 考古學報 1996.1: 1–61.

Wang Youqiao 王幼僑. *Xinzheng guqi fajianji* 新鄭古器發見記. Kaifeng: Henan sheng jiaoyuting, 1924.

Wang Yuxin 王宇信. *Jiaguxue tonglun* 甲骨學通論. Beijing: Zhongguo Shehui kexue, 1989.

Wang Yuxin. "Once Again on the New Period of Western Zhou Oracle-Bone Research: With a Brief Description of the Zhouyuan Sacrifice Inscriptions." *EC* 12 (1985–7): 164–72.

Wang Yuxin 王宇信. "Wuding qi zhanzheng buci fenqi de changshi" 武丁期戰爭卜辭分期的嘗試. In *Jiaguwen yu Yin Shang shi* 甲骨文與殷商史, ed. Wang Yuxin. Shanghai: Shanghai Guji, 1991, pp. 142–74.

Wang Yuxin 王宇信. *Xi Zhou jiagu tanlun* 西周甲骨探論. Beijing: Zhongguo Shehui kexue, 1984.

Wang Yuxin 王宇信, Zhang Yongshan 張永山, and Yang Shengnan 楊升南. "Shilun Yinxu wu hao mu de Fu Hao" 試論殷墟五號墓的婦好. *Kaogu xuebao* 考古學報 1977.2: 1–22.

Wang Yuzhe 王玉哲. "Shangzu de laiyuan diwang shitan" 商族的來源地望試探. *Lishi yanjiu* 歷史研究, 1984.1: 61–77.

Wang Yuzhe 王玉哲. "Xian Zhou zu zui zao laiyuan yu Shanxi" 先周族最早來源於山西. *Zhonghua wenshi luncong* 中華文史論叢 1982.3: 1–24.

Wang Zhonghan 王鍾翰, ed. *Zhongguo minzu shi* 中國民族史. Beijing: Zhongguo shehui kexue, 1994.

Watson, Burton, trans. *The Complete Works of Chuang Tzu*. New York: Columbia University Press, 1968.

Watson, Burton, trans. *Han Fei Tzu: Basic Writings*. New York: Columbia University Press, 1964.

Watson, Burton, trans. *Hsün Tzu: Basic Writings*. New York: Columbia University Press, 1963.

Watson, Burton, trans. *Mo Tzu: Basic Writings*. New York: Columbia University Press, 1963.

Watson, Burton, trans. *Records of the Grand Historian*. 3 vols. New York: Columbia University Press, 1961, 1993.

Watson, William. *Archaeology in China*. London: Parrish, 1960.

Watson, William. *China Before the Han Dynasty*. New York: Praeger, 1961.

Watson, William. *Cultural Frontiers in Ancient East Asia*. Edinburgh: Edinburgh University Press, 1971.

Watson, William. *Inner Asia and China in the Pre-Han Period*. London: School of Oriental and African Studies, 1969.

Weber, Charles D. *Chinese Pictorial Bronze Vessels of the Late Chou Period*. Ascona: Artibus Asiae, 1968.

Wei Jingwu 魏京武 and Wang Weilin 王煒林. "Hanjiang shangyou diqu xinshiqi shidai yizhi de dili huanjing yu renlei de shengcun" 漢江上游地區新石器時代遺址的地理環境與人類的生存. In *Huanjing kaogu yanjiu* 環境考古研究, ed. Zhou Kunshu 周昆叔 and Gong Qiming 鞏啟明. Beijing: Kexue, 1991, pp. 85–95.

Weidenreich, Franz. *Apes, Giants, and Men*. Chicago: University of Chicago Press, 1957.

Weld, Susan Roosevelt. "Covenant in Jin's Walled Cities: The Discoveries at Houma and Wenxian." Ph.D. dissertation., Harvard University, 1990.

Weld, Susan. "The Covenant Texts from Houma and Wenxian." In *New Sources of Early Chinese History: An Introduction to Reading Inscriptions and Manuscripts*, ed. Edward L. Shaughnessy. Society for the Study of Early China monograph series, no. 3. Berkeley: Institute of East Asian Studies and Society for the Study of Early China, 1997 pp. 125–60.

Wen Guang 聞廣 and Jing Zhichun 荊志淳. "Fengxi Xi Zhou yuqi dizhi kaoguxue yanjiu" 灃西西周玉器地質考古學研究. *Kaogu xuebao* 考古學報 1993.2: 251–80.

Wen Shaofeng 溫少峰 and Yuan Tingdong 袁廷棟. *Yinxu buci yanjiu: Kexue jishu pian* 殷墟卜辭研究：科學技術篇. Chengdu: Sichuan Renmin, 1983.

Wen Yiduo 聞一多. "Shuo yu" 説魚. In *Wen Yiduo quanji* 聞一多全集. 4 vols. 1948; rpt. Beijing: Sanlian, 1982. vol. 1, pp. 117–38.

Wenbo 文博 1987.4: 5–20. "Shaanxi Fufeng Qiangjia yihao Xi Zhou mu" 陝西扶風強家一號西周墓.

Weng Wan-go, and Yang Boda. *The Palace Museum: Peking*. New York: Abrams, 1982.

Wenhua Dageming qijian chutu wenwu 1. 文化大革命期間出土文物. Ed. Chutu wenwu zhanlan gongzuozu. Beijing: Wenwu, 1972.

Wenwu 文物 1955.5: 58–69. "Jiangsu Dantu xian Yandunshan chutu de gudai qingtongqi" 江蘇丹徒縣煙墩山出土的古代青銅器.

Wenwu 文物 1955.10: 3–23. "Zhengzhou Gangdu fujin gu muzang fajue jianbao" 鄭州崗杜附近古墓葬發掘簡報.

Wenwu 文物 1957.3: 66–9. "Tianjin dongjiao faxian Zhanguo mu jianbao" 天津東郊發現戰國墓簡報.

Wenwu 文物 1958.12: 32–3. "Houma diqu gu chengzhi de xin faxian" 侯馬地區古城址的新發現.

Wenwu 文物 1959.1: inside front cover. "Anhui Funan faxian Yin Shang shidai de qingtongqi" 安徽阜南發現殷商時代的青銅器.

Wenwu 文物 1959.6: 45–6. "Houma Dong Zhou shidai shaotao yaozhi fajue jiyao" 侯馬東周時代燒陶窯址發掘記要.

Wenwu 文物 1959.6: 47–9. "Houma diqu Dong Zhou Liang Han Tang Yuan muzang fajue jianbao" 侯馬地區東周兩漢唐元墓葬發掘簡報.

Wenwu 文物 1959.9: 53–5. "Beijing Changpingqu Songyuancun Zhanguo muzang fajue jilüe" 北京昌平區松園村戰國墓葬發掘記略.

Wenwu 文物 1962.4–5: 59–65. "Gu Weicheng he Yuwang gucheng diaocha baogao" 古魏城和禹王古城調查報告.

Wenwu 文物 1962.7–8: 98–102. "Zhaosu xian gudai muzang shijue jianbao" 昭蘇縣古代墓葬試掘簡報.

Wenwu 文物 1964.4: 41–7. "Shandong Changqing chutu de qingtongqi" 山東長清出土的青銅器.

Wenwu 文物 1964.7: 20–7. "Shaanxi sheng Yongshou xian Wugong xian chutu Xi Zhou tongqi" 陝西省永壽縣武功縣出土西周銅器.

Wenwu 文物 1966.5: 33–55. "Hubei Jiangling sanzuo Chu mu chutu dapi zhongyao wenwu" 湖北江陵三座楚墓出土大批重要文物.

Wenwu 文物 1972.2: 47–53. Hubei Sheng Bowuguan. "Hubei Jingshan faxian Zeng guo tongqi." 湖北荊山發現曾國銅器.

Wenwu 文物 1972.3: 65–8. "Hubei Zhijiang Bailizhou faxian Chunqiu tongqi" 湖北枝江百里洲發現春秋銅器.

Wenwu 文物 1972.4: 38–46. "Shanxi Changzhi Fenshuiling 126 hao mu fajue jianbao" 山西長治分水嶺126號墓發掘簡報.

Wenwu 文物 1972.5: 3–18. "Gaishu jinnianlai Shandong chutu de Shang Zhou qingtongqi" 概述近年來山東出土的商周青銅器.

Wenwu 文物 1972.5: 45–54. "Linzi Qiguo gucheng kantan jiyao" 臨淄齊國故城勘探記要.

Wenwu 文物 1972.8: 17–30. "Shandong Yidu Sufutun di yi hao nuli xunzang mu" 山東益都蘇埠屯第一號奴隸殉葬墓.

Wenwu 文物 1972.10: 20–37. "Luoyang Pangjiagou wuzuo Xi Zhou mu de qingli" 洛陽龐家溝五座西周墓的清理.

Wenwu 文物 1973.7: 3–4. "Xin faxian de Changsha Zhanguo Chu mu bohua" 新發現的長沙戰國楚墓帛畫.

Wenwu 文物 1974.11: 69–79. "Guangdong Zhaoqing shi Beiling Songshan gu mu fajue jianbao" 廣東肇慶市北嶺松山古墓發掘簡報.

Wenwu 文物 1975.2: 82–4. "Shanxi Suide Yantoucun faxian yipi jiaocang Shangdai tongqi" 陝西綏德嫣頭村發現一批窖藏商代銅器.

Wenwu 文物 1975.5: 20–6. "Hou ma meng shu zhushi si zhong" 侯馬盟書注釋四種.

Wenwu 文物 1975.5: 89–90. "Shaanxi Changwu xian wenhua dageming yilai chutu de jijian Xi Zhou tongqi" 陝西長武縣文化大革命以來出土的幾件西周銅器.

Wenwu 文物 1975.6: 64–8. "Zhengzhou xin chutu de Shang dai qianqi da tong ding" 鄭州新出土的商代前期大銅鼎.

Wenwu 文物 1975.7: 51–71. "Jiangxi Qingjiang Wucheng Shang dai yizhi fajue jianbao" 江西清江吳城商代遺址發掘簡報.

Wenwu 文物 1976.1: 49–59. "1963 nian Hubei Huangpi Panlongcheng Shang dai yizhi de fajue" 1963年湖北黃陂盤龍城商代遺址的發掘.

Wenwu 文物 1976.2: 5–15. "Panlongcheng 1974 niandu tianye kaogu jiyao" 盤龍城1974年度田野考古紀要.

Wenwu 文物 1976.3: 52–4. "Henan Sanmenxia shi Shangcunling chutu de jijian Zhanguo tongqi" 河南三門峽市上村嶺出土的幾件戰國銅器.

Wenwu 文物 1976.5: 26–44. "Shaanxi sheng Qishan xian Dongjiacun Xi Zhou tongqi jiaoxue fajue jianbao" 陝西省岐山縣董家村西周銅器窖穴發掘簡報.

Wenwu 文物 1976.11: 12–24. Qin du Xianyang kaogu gongzuo zhan. "Qin du Xianyang di yihao gongdian jianzhu yizhi jianbao" 秦都咸陽第一號宮殿建築遺址簡報.

Wenwu 文物 1976.11: 25–30. "Qin du Xianyang ji ge wenti de chutan" 秦都咸陽幾個問題的初探.

Wenwu 文物 1976.11: 42–4. "Qin du Xianyang wadang" 秦都咸陽瓦當.

Wenwu 文物 1977.1: 21–31. "Zhengzhou Shang dai chengzhi shijue jianbao" 鄭州商代城址試掘簡報.

Wenwu 文物 1977.4: 63–71. "Jiaoxian Xi'an yizhi diaocha shijue jianbao" 膠縣西菴遺址調查試掘簡報.

Wenwu 文物 1977.8: 1–7. "Shaanxi Lintong faxian Wu Wang zheng Shang gui" 陝西臨潼發現武王征商簋.

Wenwu 文物 1977.8: 13–16. "Henan sheng Xiangxian Xi Zhou mu fajue jianbao" 河南省襄縣西周墓發掘簡報.

Wenwu 文物 1977.11: 1–8. "Beijing shi Pinggu xian faxian Shang dai muzang" 北京市平谷縣發現商代墓葬.

Wenwu 文物 1977.12: 23–33. "Liaoning Kezuo xian Shanwanzi chutu Yin Zhou qingtongqi" 遼寧喀左縣山灣子出土殷周青銅器.

Wenwu 文物 1977.12: 86–7. "Shaanxi sheng Qishan xian faxian Shang dai qingtongqi" 陝西省岐山縣發現商代青銅器.

Wenwu 文物 1978.3: 43–5. "Shaanxi Fengxiang Chunqiu Qin Gong lingyin yizhi fajue jianbao" 陝西鳳翔春秋秦公陵蔭遺址發掘簡報.

Wenwu 文物 1979.1: 1–13. "Hebei sheng Pingshan xian Zhanguo shiqi Zhongshan guo muzang fajue jianbao" 河北省平山縣戰國時期中山國墓葬發掘簡報.

Wenwu 文物 1979.11: 1–11. "Shaanxi Fufeng Qijia shijiu hao Xi Zhou mu" 陝西扶風齊家十九號西周墓.

Wenwu 文物 1980.1: 51–3. "Henan Luoshan xian faxian Chunqiu zaoqi tongqi" 河南羅山縣發現春秋早期銅器.

Wenwu 文物 1980.4: 27–38. "Fufeng Yuntang Xi Zhou guqi zhizao zuofang yizhi shijue jianbao" 扶風雲塘西周骨器製造作坊遺址試掘簡報.

Wenwu 文物 1980.4: 39–55. "Fufeng Yuntang Xi Zhou mu" 扶風雲塘西周墓.

Wenwu 文物 1980.6: 12–20. "Fujian Chong'an Wuyishan Baiyan yadongmu qingli jianbao" 福建崇安武夷山白巖崖洞墓清理簡報.

Wenwu 文物 1980.7: 1–10. "Xigoupan Xiongnu mu" 西溝畔匈奴墓.

Wenwu 文物 1980.8: 13–15. "Jiangxi Jing'an chutu Chunqiu Xu guo tongqi" 江西靖安出土春秋徐國銅器.

Wenwu 文物 1980.9: 10–14. "Fengxiang xian Gaozhuang Qin mu fajue jianbao" 鳳翔縣高庄秦墓發掘簡報.

Wenwu 文物 1980.10: 13–20: "Henan sheng Xichuan xian Xiasi Chunqiu Chu mu" 河南省淅川縣下寺春秋楚墓.

Wenwu 文物 1980.11: 1–25. "Jiangxi Guixi yamu fajue jianbao" 江西貴溪崖墓發掘簡報.

Wenwu 文物 1981.1: 1–8. "Henan Gushi Hougudui yi hao mu fajue jianbao" 河南固始侯固堆一號墓發掘簡報.

Wenwu 文物 1981.1: 9–14. "Henan Xinyang shi Pingqiao Chunqiu mu fajue jianbao" 河南信陽市平橋春秋墓發掘簡報.

Wenwu 文物 1981.1: 18–22. "Xinjiang Alagou shuxue muguo mu fajue jianbao" 新疆阿拉溝豎穴木槨墓發掘簡報.

Wenwu 文物 1981.3: 10–22. "Fufeng Shaochen Xi Zhou jianzhu qun jizhi fajue jianbao" 扶風召陳西周建築群基址發掘簡報.

Wenwu 文物 1981.7: 52–64. "Luoyang Beiyaocun Xi Zhou yizhi 1974 nian de fajue jianbao" 洛陽北窯村西周遺址1974年的發掘簡報.

Wenwu 文物 1981.8: 46–8. "Hubei Suixian faxian Shang dai qingtongqi" 湖北隨縣發現商代青銅器.

Wenwu 文物 1981.8: 49–53. "Shanxi Shilou Chujiayu Caojiayuan faxian Shang dai tongqi" 山西石樓褚家峪曹家垣發現商代銅器.

Wenwu 文物 1981.9: 18–24. "Shandong Jiyang Liutaizi Xi Zhou zaoqi mu fajue jianbao" 山東濟陽劉台子西周早期墓發掘簡報.

Wenwu 文物 1982.1: 1–21. "Qingchuan xian chutu Qin geng xiu tian lü mu du" 青川縣出土秦更修田律木牘.

Wenwu 文物 1982.8: 42–50. "Yan Xiadu di 23 hao yizhi chutu yipi tongge" 燕下都第23號遺址出土一批銅戈.

Wenwu 文物 1982.9: 49–52. "Shanxi Changzhi shi jianxuan zhengji de Shang dai qingtongqi" 山西長治市揀選徵集的商代青銅器.

Wenwu 文物 1982.10: 1–8. "Hubei Jiangling Mashan Zhuanchang yihaomu chutu dapi Zhangguo shiqi de sizhipin" 湖北江陵馬山磚廠一號墓出土大批戰國時期的絲織品.

Wenwu 文物 1982.10: 16–17. "Jiangling Yueshan Dadui chutu yipi Chunqiu tongqi" 江陵岳山大隊出土一批春秋銅器.

Wenwu 文物 1983.3: 28–34. "Shanxi Houma Chengwang gucheng" 山西侯馬呈王古城.

Wenwu 文物 1983.3: 49–59. "Zhengzhou xin faxian Shang dai jiaocang qingtongqi" 鄭州新發現商代窖藏青銅器.

Wenwu 文物 1983.3: 78–89, 77. "Henan Wenxian Dong Zhou mengshi yizhi yi hao kan fajue jianbao" 河南溫縣東周盟誓遺址一號坎發掘簡報.

Wenwu 文物 1983.4: 1–14, 28. "Zhengzhou Shang dai chengnei gongdian yizhi qu di yi ci fajue baogao" 鄭州商代城內宮殿遺址區第一次發掘報告.

Wenwu 文物 1983.7: 30–7. "Fengxiang Qin Gong lingyuan zuantan yu shijue jianbao" 鳳翔秦公陵園鑽探與試掘簡報.

Wenwu 文物 1983.11: 68–71. Huaining Xian Wenwu Guanlisuo. "Anhui Huaining xian chutu Chunqiu qingtongqi" 安徽淮寧縣出土春秋青銅器.

Wenwu 文物 1983.12: 1–6. "Shandong Linqu faxian Qi Xun Zeng zhu guo tongqi" 山東臨朐發現齊鄩曾諸國銅器.

Wenwu 文物 1984.1: 10–37. "Shaoxing 306 hao Zhanguo mu fajue jianbao" 紹興306號戰國墓發掘簡報.

Wenwu 文物 1984.5: 1–10. "Jiangsu Dantu Dagang Muzidun Xi Zhou tongqimu fajue jianbao" 江蘇丹徒大港母子墩西周銅器墓發掘簡報.

Wenwu 文物 1984.5: 16–20. "Jiangsu Wuxian Heshan Dong Zhou mu" 江蘇吳縣何山東周墓.

Wenwu 文物 1984.7: 1–15, 66. "Shaanxi Wugong Zhengjiapo Xian Zhou yizhi fajue jianbao" 陝西武功鄭家坡先周遺址發掘簡報.

Wenwu 文物 1984.7: 1–16. "Jin Yu E san sheng kaogu diaocha jianbao" 晉豫鄂三省考古調查簡報.

Wenwu 文物 1984.7: 16–29. "Fufeng Liujia Jiangrongmu fajue jianbao" 扶風劉家姜戎墓發掘簡報.

Wenwu 文物 1984.7: 30–41. "Fufeng Beilü Zhouren mudi fajue jianbao" 扶風北呂周人墓地發掘簡報.

Wenwu 文物 1984.7: 49. "Hunan Leiyang xian chutu Xi Zhou yong zhong" 湖南耒陽縣出土西周甬鐘.

Wenwu 文物 1984.9: 1–10. "Shandong Yishui Liujiadianzi Chunqiu mu fajue jianbao" 山東沂水劉家店子春秋墓發掘簡報.

Wenwu 文物 1984.9: 14–19. "Qi gucheng wuhao Dong Zhou mu ji daxing xunmakeng de fajue" 齊故城五號東周墓及大型殉馬坑的發掘.

Wenwu 文物 1984.12: 29–32. "Henan sheng Pingding shan shi chutu Xi Zhou Ying guo qingtongqi" 河南省平頂山市出土西周應國青銅器.

Wenwu 文物 1985.2: 1–2. "Fengxiang Majiazhuang yi hao jianzhu yizhi fajue jianbao" 鳳翔馬家庄一號建築遺址發掘簡報.

Wenwu 文物 1985.3: 1–11. "Shandong Shouguang xian xin faxian yipi Ji guo tongqi" 山東壽光縣新發現一批紀國銅器.

Wenwu 文物 1985.6: 1–15. "Leiyang Chunqiu Zhanguo mu" 耒陽春秋戰國墓.

Wenwu 文物 1985.12: 15–20. "Shandong Jiyang Liutaizi Xi Zhou mudi di er ci fajue" 山東濟陽劉台子西周墓地第二次發掘.

Wenwu 文物 1986.1: 1–31. "Xi Zhou Hao jing fujin bufen muzang fajue jianbao" 西周鎬京附近部分墓葬發掘簡報.

Wenwu 文物 1986.6: 20–4. "Hebei Lingshou xian Xichatoucun Zhanguo mu" 河北靈壽縣西岔頭村戰國墓.

Wenwu 文物 1986.8: 1–17. "Liaoning Niuheliang Hongshan wenhua nüshen miao yu jishi zhongqun faijue jianbao" 遼寧牛河梁紅山文化女神廟與積石冢群發掘簡報.

Wenwu 文物 1986.8: 56–68. "Fufeng Huangdui Xi Zhou mudi zuantan qingli jianbao" 扶風黃堆西周墓地鑽探清理簡報.

Wenwu 文物 1986.11: 1–18. "Shanxi Lingshi Jingjiecun Shang mu" 山西靈石旌介村商墓.

Wenwu 文物 1987.2: 1–16. "Shanxi Hongdong Yongningbao Xi Zhou muzang" 山西洪洞永凝堡西周墓葬.

Wenwu 文物 1987.6: 73–81. "Jin guo shigui zuofang yizhi fajue jianbao" 晉國石圭作坊遺址發掘簡報.

Wenwu 文物 1987.10: 1–15. "Guanghan Sanxingdui yizhi yi hao jisikeng fajue jianbao" 廣漢三星堆遺址一號祭祀坑發掘簡報.

Wenwu 文物 1987.12: 24–37. "Jiangsu Zhenjiang Jianbi Wangjiashan Dong Zhou mu" 江蘇鎮江諫壁王家山東周墓.

Wenwu 文物 1988.1: 1–31. "Zhejiang Yuhang Fanshan Liangzhu mudi fajue jianbao" 浙江余杭反山良渚墓地發掘簡報.

Wenwu 文物 1988.1: 32–51. "Yuhang Yaoshan Liangzhu wenhua jitan yizhi fajue jianbao" 余杭瑤山良渚文化祭壇遺址發掘簡報.

Wenwu 文物 1988.5: 1–14. "Jingmen shi Baoshan Chu mu fajue jianbao" 荊門市包山楚墓發掘簡報.

Wenwu 文物 1988.5: 25–9. "Bao shan 2 hao mu zhujian gaishu" 包山2號墓竹簡概述.

Wenwu 文物 1988.6: 1–22. "Xi'an Laoniupo Shangdai mudi de fajue" 西安老牛坡商代墓地的發掘.

Wenwu 文物 1988.11: 14–23, 54. "Shaanxi Long xian Bianjiazhuang wuhao Chunqiu mu fajue jianbao" 陝西隴縣邊家庄五號春秋墓發掘簡報.

Wenwu 文物 1989.1: 1–14. "Henan Wuyang Jiahu xinshiqi shidai yizhi di er zhi liu ci fajue jianbao" 河南舞陽賈湖新石器時代遺址第二至六次發掘簡報.

Wenwu 文物 1989.3: 57–62. "Hubei Zhijiang Yaojiagang Gaoshanmiao liangzuo Chunqiu Chu mu" 湖北枝江姚家港高山廟兩座春秋楚墓.

Wenwu 文物 1989.5: 1–20. "Guanghan Sanxingdui yizhi er hao jisikeng fajue jianbao" 廣漢三星堆遺址二號祭祀坑發掘簡報.

Wenwu 文物 1989.7: 72–4. "Jiangling Zhangjiashan Han jian Maishu shiwen" 江陵張家山漢簡脈書釋文.

Wenwu 文物 1989.8: 17–35, 43. "Beijing Yanqing Jundushan Dong Zhou Shanrong buluo mudi fajue jilüe" 北京延慶軍都山東周山戎部落墓地發掘紀略.

Wenwu 文物 1989.9: 59–86. "Taiyuan Jinshengcun 251 hao Chunqiu damu ji chemakeng fajue jianbao" 太原金勝村251號春秋大墓及車馬坑發掘簡報.

Wenwu 文物 1990.2: 1–28. "1987 nian Jiangsu Xinyi Huating yizhi de fajue" 1987 年江蘇新沂花廳遺址的發掘.

Wenwu 文物 1990.10: 25–32. "Hubei Dangyang Zhaoxiang si hao Chunqiu mu fajue jianbao" 湖北當陽趙巷四號春秋墓發掘簡報.

Wenwu 文物 1990.10: 37–47. "Hunan Cili Shiban cun sanshiliu hao Zhanguo mu fajue jianbao" 湖南慈利石板村36號戰國墓發掘簡報.

Wenwu 文物 1991.10: 1–26. "Jiangxi Xin'gan Dayangzhou Shang mu fajue jianbao" 江西新干大洋洲商墓發掘簡報.

Wenwu 文物 1993.3: 1–7. "Shandong Zhangqiu Nülangshan Zhanguo mu chutu yuewu taoyong ji youguan wenti" 山東章邱女郎山戰國墓出土樂舞陶俑及有關問題.

Wenwu 文物 1993.3: 11–30. "1992 nian chuntian Tianma Qucun yizhi muzang fajue baogao" 1992 年春天天馬曲村遺址墓葬發掘報告.

Wenwu 文物 1993.6: 56–60. "Hubei sheng Huangzhou shi Xiayaozui Shang mu fajue jianbao" 湖北省黃州市下窯嘴商墓發掘簡報.

Wenwu 文物 1993.7: 1–9. "Zhangshu Wucheng yizhi di qi ci fajue jianbao" 樟樹吳城遺址第七次發掘簡報.

Wenwu 文物 1993.10: 1–27. "Baoji shi Yimencun er hao Chunqiu mu fajue jianbao" 寶雞市益門村二號春秋墓發掘簡報.

Wenwu 文物 1994.1: 4–28. "Tianma Qucun yizhi Beizhao Jin hou mudi di er ci fajue" 天馬曲村遺址北趙晉侯墓地第二次發掘.

Wenwu 文物 1994.3: 4–40. "Sichuan Mao Xian Moutuo yi hao shiguanmu ji peizang keng qingli jianbao" 四川茂縣牟托一號石棺墓及陪葬坑清理簡報.

Wenwu 文物 1994.8: 1–21. "Tianma Qucun yizhi Beizhao Jin hou mudi di sici fajue" 天馬曲村遺址北趙晉侯墓地第四次發掘.

Wenwu 文物 1994.8: 22–33, 68. "Tianma Qucun yizhi Beizhao Jin Hou mudi disanci fajue" 天馬曲村遺址北趙晉侯墓地第三次發掘.

Wenwu 文物 1995.1: 4–31. "Shangcunling Guo guo mudi M2006 de qingli" 上村嶺虢國墓地 M2006的清理.

Wenwu 文物 1995.1: 37–43. "Jiangling Wangjiatai 15 hao Qin mu" 江陵王家台15號秦墓.

Wenwu 文物 1995.7: 4–39. "Tianma Qucun yizhi Beizhao Jin hou mudi diwu ci fajue" 天馬曲村遺址北趙晉侯墓地第五次發掘.

Wenwu cankao ziliao 文物參考資料 1954.3: 60–2. "Henan Jiaxian faxian de gudai tongqi" 河南郟縣發現的古代銅器.

Wenwu chubanshe chengli sanshi zhounian jinian: Wenwu yu kaogu lunji 文物出版社成立三十週年紀念：文物與考古論集. Ed. Wenwu chubanshe bianjibu. Beijing: Wenwu, 1986.

Wenwu kaogu gongzuo sanshinian (1949–1979) 文物考古工作三十年 (1949–1979). Ed. Wenwu bianji weiyuanhui. Beijing: Wenwu, 1979.

Wenwu kaogu gongzuo shinian (1979–1989) 文物考古工作十年 (1979–1989). Ed. Wenwu bianji weiyuanhui. Beijing: Wenwu, 1990.

Wenwu ziliao congkan 文物資料從刊 1 (1977): 1–47. "Zhengzhou Shang dai cheng yizhi fajue baogao" 鄭州商代城遺址發掘報告.

Wenwu ziliao congkan 文物資料叢刊 2 (1978): 66–9: "Jiangsu Lishui Wushan Xi Zhou erhaomu qingli jianbao" 江蘇溧水烏山西周二號墓清理簡報.

Wenwu ziliao congkan 文物資料叢刊 2 (1978): 70–4. "Henan Xinye gu muzang qingli jianbao" 河南新野古墓葬清理簡報.

Wenwu ziliao congkan 文物資料叢刊 2 (1978): 75–91. "Zhaoyi Zhanguo muzang fajue jianbao" 朝邑戰國墓葬發掘簡報.

Wenwu ziliao congkan 文物資料叢刊 3 (1980): 56–66: "Henan Xinzheng Zheng Han gucheng de zuantan he shijue" 河南新鄭鄭韓故城的鑽探和試掘.

Wenwu ziliao congkan 文物資料叢刊 3 (1980): 67–85: "Shaanxi Fengxiang Baqitun Qinguo muzang fajue jianbao" 陝西鳳翔八旗屯秦國墓葬發掘簡報.

Wenwu ziliao congkan 文物資料叢刊 7 (1983): 67–74. "Liangpingxian Hushenhabao Taishan Shanrong mudi de faxian" 梁平縣虎什哈炮台山山戎墓地的發現.

Wenwu ziliao congkan 文物資料叢刊 7 (1983): 138–46. "Liaoning Linxi xian Dajing gu tongkuang 1976 nian shijue jianbao" 遼寧林西縣大井古銅礦1976年試掘簡報.

Wenwu ziliao congkan 文物資料叢刊 8 (1983): 77–94. "Shaanxi Qishan Hejiacun Xi Zhou mu fajue baogao" 陝西岐山賀家村西周墓發掘報告.

Wertime, Theodore A., and James D. Muhly, eds. *The Coming of the Age of Iron.* New Haven, Conn.: Yale University Press, 1980.

Wheatley, Paul. *The Pivot of the Four Quarters: A Preliminary Enquiry into the Origins and Character of the Ancient Chinese City.* Edinburgh: Edinburgh University Press, 1971.

White, William Charles. *Tombs of Old Loyang.* Shanghai: Kelly & Walsh, Ltd., 1934.

Whitfield, Roderick, ed. *The Problem of Meaning in Early Chinese Ritual Bronzes.* Colloquies on Art and Archaeology in Asia, no. 15. Percival David Foundation of Chinese Art. London: School of Oriental and African Studies, 1993.

Whyte, Robert O. "The Gramineae, Wild and Cultivated, of Monsoonal and Equatorial Asia." *Asian Perspectives* 15 (1972): 127–51; 21 (1978): 182–205.

Winkler, Marjorie G., and Pao K. Wang. "The Late Quaternary Vegetation and Climate of China." In *Global Climates Since the Last Glacial Maximum,* ed. H. E. Wright, Jr., J. E. Kutzbach, T. Webb III, W. F. Ruddiman, F. A. Street-Perrott, and P. J. Bartlein. Minneapolis: University of Minnesota Press, 1993, pp. 221–64.

Winthrop, Grenville L. *Retrospective for a Collector.* Cambridge, Mass.: Fogg Museum of Art, 1969.

Wittfogel, Karl A. *Oriental Despotism: A Comparative Study of Total Power.* New Haven, Conn.: Yale University Press, 1963.

Wolpoff, M. H. "Multiregional Evolution: The Fossil Alternative to Eden." In *The Human Evolution: Behavioural and Biological Perspectives on the Origin of Modern Humans,* ed. P. Mellars and C. Stringer. Edinburgh: Edinburgh University Press, 1989, pp. 62–108.

Wolpoff, M. H., et al. "Modern Human Origins." *Science* 241 (1988): 772–3.

Wu En 烏恩. "A Preliminary Study of the Art of the Upper Xiajiadian Culture." In *The International Academic Conference of Archaeological Cultures of the Northern Chinese Ancient*

Nations (Collected Papers), ed. Zhongguo kaogu wenwu yanjiusuo. Huhhot, August 11–18, 1992.

Wu En 烏恩. "Woguo beifang gudai dongwu wenshi" 我國北方古代動物紋飾. *Kaogu xuebao* 考古學報 1990.4: 409–37.

Wu En 烏恩. "Yin zhi Zhou chu de beifang qingtong qi" 殷至周初的北方青銅器. *Kaogu xuebao* 考古學報 1985.2: 135–56.

Wu En 烏恩. "Zhukaigou wenhua de faxian ji qi yiyi" 朱開溝文化的發現及其意義. In *Zhongguo kaoguxue luncong* 中國考古學論叢. Beijing: Kexue, 1995, pp. 256–66.

Wu, Hung. "The Art of Xuzhou: A Regional Approach." *Orientations* 21.10 (October 1990): 40–9, 80.

Wu, Hung. "Art in its Ritual Context: Rethinking Mawangdui" *EC* 17 (1992): 111–45.

Wu, Hung. "From Temple to Tomb: Ancient Chinese Art and Religion in Transition." *EC* 13 (1988): 78–115.

Wu, Hung. *Monumentality in Early Chinese Art and Architecture*. Stanford, Calif.: Stanford University Press, 1995.

Wu, Hung, et al. *3,000 Years of Chinese Painting*. New Haven, Conn.: Yale University Press, 1997.

Wu Mingsheng 吳銘生. "Hunan Dong Zhou shiqi Yueren muzang de yanjiu" 湖南東周時期越人墓葬的研究. *Hunan kaogu jikan* 湖南考古集刊 5(1989): 161–4.

Wu Rukang. 吳汝康 "A Revision of the Classification of the Lufeng Great Apes." *Acta Anthropologica Sinica* 6 (1987): 265–71.

Wu Rukang 吳汝康 et al. *Beijing yuanren yizhi zonghe yanjiu* 北京猿人遺址綜合研究. Beijing: Kexue, 1985.

Wu Rukang 吳汝康, Wu Xinzhi 吳新智, and Zhang Senshui 張森水. *Zhongguo yuangu renlei* 中國遠古人類. Beijing: Kexue, 1993.

Wu Weitang 吳維棠. "Cong xinshiqi shidai wenhua yizhi kan Hangzhou wan liang an de quanxinshi gu dili" 從新石器時代文化遺址看杭州灣兩岸的全新世古地理 *Dili xuebao* 地理學報 *(Acta Geographica Sinica)* 38.2 (1983): 113–27.

Wu Yuming 吳聿明. "Beishanding siqi ming shikao cunyi"北山頂四器銘釋考存疑. *Dongnan wenhua* 東南文化 1990.1–2: 68–70.

Wu Zhenfeng 吳鎮烽. "Shaanxi Shang Zhou qingtongqi de chutu yu yanjiu" 陝西商周青銅器的出土與研究. *Kaogu yu wenwu* 考古與文物 1988.5, 6: 71–89.

Wu Zhenfeng 吳鎮烽. "Zhou wangchao jiena yi zu rencai chutan" 周王朝接納異族人才初探. In *Xi Zhou shi lunwenji* 西周史論文集. 2 vols. Xi'an: Shaanxi Renmin jiaoyu, 1983, vol. 2, pp. 805–18.

Wu Zhenfeng 吳鎮烽 and Luo Zhongru 雒忠如. "Shaanxi sheng Fufeng xian Qiangjiacun chutu de Xi Zhou tongqi" 陝西省扶風縣強家村出土的西周銅器. *Wenwu* 文物 1975.8: 57–62.

Wu Zhenlu 吳振錄. "Baode xian xin faxian de Yindai qingtong qi" 保德縣新發現的殷代青銅器. *Wenwu* 文物 1972.4: 62–66.

Xia Hanyi 夏含夷 (Edward L. Shaughnessy). "Cong Jufu xu gai mingwen tan Zhou wangchao yu Nan Huai Yi de guanxi" 從駒父盨蓋銘文談周王朝與南淮夷的關係. *Hanxue yanjiu* 漢學研究 5, 2 (1987): 567–73.

Xia Hanyi 夏含夷. "Xi Zhou zhi shuaiwei" 西周之衰微. In Xia Hanyi, *Wen gu zhi xin lu* 溫故知新錄. Taipei: Daohe, 1997, pp. 149–56.

Xia Hanyi 夏含夷. "Zaoqi Shang Zhou guanxi ji qi dui Wu Ding yihou Yin Shang wangshi shili fanwei de yiyi" 早期商周關係及其對武丁以後殷商王室勢力範圍的意義. *Jiuzhou xuekan* 九州學刊 2, 1 (1987): 20–32.

Xia Nai 夏鼐. *Kaoguxue he kejishi* 考古學和科技史. Beijing: Kexue, 1979.

Xia Nai 夏鼐. "Wuchan jieji wenhua dageming zhong de kaogu xin faxian" 無產階級文化大革命中的考古新發現. *Kaogu* 考古 1972.1: 29–42.

Xia Nai 夏鼐 and Yin Weizhang 殷瑋璋. "Hubei Tonglüshan gu tongkuang" 湖北銅綠山古銅礦. *Kaogu xuebao* 考古學報 1982.1: 1–14.

Xiang Chunsong 項春松 and Li Yi 李義. "Ningcheng Xiaoheishigou shiguomu diaocha qingli baogao" 寧城小黑石溝石槨墓調查清理報告. *Wenwu* 文物 1995.5: 4–22.

Xiao Jiayi 肖家儀. "Jiangsu Wujiang xian Longnan yizhi baofen zuhe yu xianmin shenghuo huanjing de chube yanjiu" 江蘇吳江縣龍南遺址 龍 粉組合與先民生活環境的初步研究. *Dongnan wenhua* 東南文化 1990.5: 259–63.

Xiao Menglong 蕭夢龍. "Chulun Wu wenhua" 初論吳文化. *Kaogu yu wenwu* 考古與文物 1985.4: 61–72.

Xiao Menglong 蕭夢龍. "Wu guo wanglingqu chutan" 吳國王陵區初探. *Dongnan wenhua* 東南文化 1990.4: 95–9, 55.

Xiao Qi 肖琦. "Shaanxi Longxian Bianjiazhuang chutu Chunqiu tongqi" 陝西隴縣邊家庄出土春秋銅器. *Wenbo* 文博 1989.3: 79–81.

Xichuan Xiasi Chunqiu Chu mu 淅川下寺春秋楚墓. Ed. Henan sheng Wenwu yanjiusuo, Henan sheng Danjiang Kuqu Kaogu fajuedui, and Xichuan xian bowuguan. Beijing: Wenwu, 1991.

Xie Duanju 謝端琚. "Shilun Qijia wenhua" 試論齊家文化. *Kaogu yu wenwu* 考古與文物 1981.3: 79–80.

Xin Zhongguo chutu wenwu 新中國出土文物. Beijing: Waiwen, 1972.

Xin Zhongguo de kaogu faxian he yanjiu 新中國的考古發現和研究. Ed. Zhongguo Shehui kexueyuan Kaogu yanjiusuo. Beijing: Wenwu, 1984.

Xing Jiaming. "The Relationship Between Environment Changes and Human Activities Since Late Quaternary in North China." In *The Palaeoenvironment of East Asia from the Mid-Tertiary. Proceedings of the Second Conference: Vol. 2: Oceanography, Palaeozoology and Palaeoanthropology,* ed. Pauline Whyte. Hong Kong: Center of Asian Studies, University of Hong Kong, 1988, pp. 1076–83.

Xinyang Chu mu 信陽楚墓. Beijing: Wenwu, 1986.

Xiong Chuanxin 熊傳新. "Hunan faxian de qingtongqi" 湖南發現的青銅器. *Wenwu ziliao congkan* 文物資料叢刊 5 (1981): 103–5.

Xiong Chuanxin 熊傳新 and Wu Mingsheng 吳銘生. "Hunan gu Yuezu qingtongqi gailun" 湖南古越族青銅器概論. In *Zhongguo Kaogu xuehui di si ci nianhui (1983) lunwenji* 中國考古學會第四次年會 (1983)論文集. Beijing: Wenwu, 1985, pp. 152–66.

Xiong Jianhua 熊建華. "Xiangtan xian chutu Zhou dai qingtong tiliangyou" 湘潭縣出土周代青銅提梁卣. *Hunan kaogu jikan* 湖南考古集刊 4 (1987): 19–21.

Xu Cheng 許成 and Li Jinzeng 李進增. "Dong Zhou shiqi de Rong Di qingtong wenhua" 東周時期的戎狄青銅文化 *Kaogu xuebao* 1993.1: 1–11.

Xu Fuchang 徐富昌. *Shuihudi Qin jian yanjiu* 睡虎地秦簡研究. Taipei: Wenshizhe, 1993.

Xu Fuguan 徐復觀. *Zhongguo renxing lun shi* 中國人性論史. Taizhong: Donghai Daxue, 1963.

Xu Hengbin 徐橫賓. "Guangdong qingtongqi shidai gailun" 廣東青銅器時代概論. In *Guangdong chutu xian Qin wenwu* 廣東出土先秦文物, ed. Guangdong sheng bowuguan and Xianggang Zhongwen daxue Wenwuguan. Hong Kong: Art Gallery, Chinese University of Hong Kong, 1984, pp. 45–63; English translation ibid., pp. 64–85.

Xu Jinxiong 許進雄. *Yin buci zhong wuzhong jisi de yanjiu* 殷卜辭中五種祭祀的研究. Taipei: Guoli Taiwan daxue wenxueyuan, 1968.

Xu Peigen 徐培根 and Wei Rulin 魏汝霖. *Sun Bin bingfa zhushi* 孫臏兵法注釋. Taipei: Liming wenhua shiye, 1967.

Xu Shaohua 徐少華. *Zhoudai nantu lishi dili yu wenhua* 周代南土歷史地理與文化. Wuhan: Wuhan daxue, 1994.

Xu Tianjin 徐天進. "Shilun Guanzhong diqu de Shang wenhua" 試論關中地區的商文化. In *Jinian Beijing daxue kaogu zhuanye sanshi zhounian lunwenji (1952–1982)* 紀念北京大學考古專業三十周年論文集 (1952–1982),ed. Beijing daxue kaoguxi. Beijing: Wenwu, 1990, pp. 211–42.

Xu Wei 許偉. "Jin zhong diqu Xi Zhou yiqian gu yicun de biannian yu puxi" 晉中地區西周以前古遺存的編年與譜系. *Wenwu* 文物 1989.4: 40–50.

Xu Xitai 徐錫台. "Qishan Hejiacun Zhoumu fajue jianbao" 岐山賀家村周墓發掘簡報. *Kaogu yu wenwu* 考古與文物 1980.1: 7–12.

Xu Xitai 徐錫台. "Zao Zhou wenhua de tedian ji qi yuanyuan de tansuo" 早周文化的特點及其淵源的探索 *Wenwu* 文物 1979.10: 50–9.

Xu Xitai 徐錫台. "Zao Zhou wenhua de tezheng ji qi yuanyuan de zai tantao: Jian lun Wen Wu shiqi qingtongqi de tezheng" 早周文化的特征及其淵源的再探討：兼論文武時期青銅器的特征. In *Kaoguxue yanjiu* 考古學研究, ed. Shi Xingbang 石興邦 et al. Xi'an: San Qin, 1993, pp. 280–320.

Xu Xitai 徐錫台. *Zhouyuan jiaguwen zongshu* 周原甲骨文綜述. Xi'an: San Qin, 1987.

Xu Xusheng 徐旭生. "1959 nian xia Yuxi diaocha Xiaxu de chubu baogao" 1959 年夏豫西調查夏墟的初步報告. *Kaogu* 考古 1959.11: 592–600.

Xu Xusheng 徐旭生. *Zhongguo gushi de chuanshuo shidai* 中國古史的傳說時代. Rev. ed. Beijing: Kexue, 1960.

Xu Yongsheng 許永生. "Cong Guo guo mudi kaogu xin faxian tan Guo guo lishi gaikuang" 從虢國墓地考古新發現談虢國歷史概況. *Hua Xia kaogu* 華夏考古 1993.4: 92–5.

Xu Yu-lin. "The Houwa Site and Related Issues." In *The Archaeology of Northeast China: Beyond the Great Wall*, ed. Sarah Milledge Nelson. London: Routledge, 1994, pp. 65–88.

Xu Yulin 許玉林. "Liaoning Shang Zhou shiqi de qingtong wenhua" 遼寧商周時期的青銅文化. In *Kaoguxue wenhua lunwenji* 考古學文化論文集, ed. Su Bingqi 蘇秉琦. Beijing: Wenwu, 1993, vol. 3, pp. 311–34.

Xu Zhengguo 徐正國. "Zaoyang Dongzhaohu zaici chutu qingtongqi" 棗陽東趙湖再次出土青銅器. *Jiang Han kaogu* 江漢考古 1984.1: 106.

Xu Zhongshu 徐中舒, ed.. *Han yu da zi dian* 漢語大字典. Vols. 1–7 and index. Chengdu: Sichuan cishu and Hubei cishu, 1986–90.

Xue Yao 薛堯. "Jiangxi chutu de jijian qingtongqi" 江西出土的幾件青銅器. *Kaogu* 考古 1963.8: 416–8.

Yabuuti, Kiyoshi. "The Observational Date of the *Shih-shih Hsing-ching*." In *Explorations in the History of Science and Technology in China*, ed. Li Guohao et al. Shanghai: Shanghai guji, 1982, pp. 133–41.

Yamada Keiji 山田慶兒. "The Formation of the *Huang-ti Nei-ching*." *Acta Asiatica* 36 (1979): 67–89.

Yamada Keiji 山田慶兒. "Hen Shaku densetsu" 扁鵲傳說. *Tôhô gakuhô* 東方學報 (Kyoto) 60 (1988): 73–158.

Yamada Keiji 山田慶兒, ed. *Shin hatsugen Chûgoku kagakushi shiryô no kenkyû* 新發現中國科學史資料の研究. 2 vols. Kyoto: Kyôto daigaku jinbun kagaku kenkyûjo, 1985.

Yan Dunjie 嚴敦傑. "Guanyu Xi Han chuqi de shipan he zhanpan" 關於西漢初期的式盤和占盤. *Kaogu* 考古 1978.5: 334–7.

Yan Wenming 嚴文明. *Yangshao wenhua yanjiu* 仰韶文化研究. Beijing: Wenwu, 1989.

Yan Yiping 嚴一萍. "Fu Hao liezhuan" 婦好列傳. *Zhongguo wenzi* 中國文字 3 (1981): 1–104.

Yan Yiping 嚴一萍. "Jiao 'Zheng Renfang ripu'" 校正人方日譜. *Zhongguo wenzi* 中國文字 11 (1986): 173–7.

Yan Yiping 嚴一萍. *Yin Shang shi ji* 殷商史記. 3 vols. Taipei: Yiwen, 1989.

Yang Baocheng 楊寶成. "Shilun Zeng guo tongqi de fenqi" 試論曾國銅器的分期. *Zhongyuan wenwu* 中原文物 1991.4: 14–20.

Yang Baocheng 楊寶成. "Yin dai chezi de faxian yu fuyuan" 殷代車子的發現與復原. *Kaogu* 考古 1984.6: 546–55.

Yang Baocheng 楊寶成 and Yang Xizhang 楊錫璋. "Cong Yinxu xiaoxing muzang kan Yindai shehui de pingmin" 從殷墟小型墓葬看殷代社會的平民. *Zhongyuan wenwu* 中原文物, 1983.1: 30–4.

Yang Boda 楊伯達. *Zhongguo meishu quanji: Gongyi meishu bian 9, yuqi* 中國美術全集：工藝美術編9，玉器. Beijing: Wenwu, 1986.

Yang Bojun 楊伯峻, ed. *Chunqiu Zuo zhuan zhu* 春秋左傳注. 4 vols. Beijing: Zhonghua, 1981.

Yang Debiao 楊德彪. "Shilun Wannan tudun mu" 試論皖南土墩墓. *Wenwu yanjiu* 文物研究 4 (1988): 81–8.

Yang Hong 楊泓. *Zhongguo gu bingqi luncong* 中國古兵器論叢. Beijing: Wenwu, 1980.

Yang Hongxun 楊鴻勛. "Fengxiang chutu Chunqiu Qin Gong tonggou: Jingang." 鳳翔出土春秋秦宮銅構：金釭 *Kaogu* 考古 1976.2: 103–8.

Yang Hongxun 楊鴻勛. *Jianzhu kaoguxue lunwen ji* 建築考古學論文集. Beijing: Wenwu, 1987.

Yang Hongxun 楊鴻勛 (Tao Fu). "Qin Xianyang gong di yi hao yizhi fuyuan wenti de chubu tantao" 秦咸陽宮第一號遺址復原問題的初步探討. *Wenwu* 文物 1976.11: 31–41.

Yang Hongxun 楊鴻勛. "Xi Zhou Qi yi jianzhu yizhi chubu kaocha" 西周岐邑建築遺址初步考察. *Wenwu* 文物 1981.3: 23–33.

Yang Hongxun 楊鴻勛. "Zhanguo Zhongshan wangling ji Zhaoyutu yanjiu" 戰國中山王陵及兆域圖研究. *Kaogu xuebao* 考古學報 1980. 1: 119–37.

Yang Hsi-chang. "The Shang Dynasty Cemetery System." In *Studies of Shang Archaeology: Selected Papers from the International Conference on Shang Civilization*, ed. K. C. Chang. New Haven, Conn.: Yale University Press, 1986, pp. 49–63.

Yang Hu 楊虎, Tan Yingjie 潭英杰, and Zhang Taixiang 張泰湘. "Heilongjiang gudai wenhua chulun" 黑龍江古代文化初論. In *Zhongguo kaogu xuehui diyici nianhui lunwenji 1979* 中國考古學會第一次年會論文集 1979. Beijing: Wenwu, 1980, pp. 80–96.

Yang Huaijen, Chen Xiqing, and Xie Zhiren. "Sea Level Changes Since the Last Deglaciation and Their Impact on the East China Lowlands." In *The Palaeoenvironment of East Asia from the Mid-Tertiary: Proceedings of the Second Conference. Vol. 1: Geology, Sea Level Changes, Palaeoclimatology and Palaeobotany*, eds. Pauline Whyte, Jean Aigner, Nina G. Jablonski, Graham Taylor, Donald Walker, Wang Pinxian, and So-Chak-lam. Hong Kong: Center of Asian Studies, University of Hong Kong, 1988, pp. 356–74.

Yang Kuan 楊寬. "Chunqiu shidai Chu guo xianzhi de xingzhi wenti" 春秋時代楚國縣制的性質問題. *Zhongguo shi yanjiu* 中國史研究 1981.4: 19–30.

Yang Kuan 楊寬. *Gushi xintan* 古史新探. Beijing: Zhonghua, 1965.

Yang Kuan 楊寬. "Lun Xi Zhou jinwen zhong liu shi ba shi he xiangsui zhidu de guanxi" 論西周金文中六師八師和鄉燧制度的關係. *Kaogu* 考古 1964.8: 414–19.

Yang Kuan 楊寬. "Shi Qingchuan Qin du de tianmu zhidu" 釋青川秦牘的田畝制度. *Wenwu* 文物 1982.7: 83–5.

Yang Kuan 楊寬. *Zhanguo shi* 戰國史. Shanghai: Shanghai Renmin, 1955; 2nd rev. ed., Shanghai: Shanghai Renmin, 1980.

Yang Kuan 楊寬. *Zhongguo gudai ducheng zhidu shi yanjiu* 中國古代都城制度史研究. Shanghai: Guji, 1993.

Yang Kuan. *Zhongguo lidai chi du kao* 中國歷代尺度考. Shanghai: Shangwu, 1955.

Yang Lien-sheng. "Historical Notes on the Chinese World Order." In *The Chinese World Order*, ed. John King Fairbank, Cambridge, Mass.: Harvard University Press, 1968, pp. 21–2.

Yang Lixin 楊立新. "Wannan gudai tongkuang de faxian ji qi lishi jiazhi" 皖南古代銅礦的發現及其歷史價值. *Dongnan wenhua* 東南文化 1991.2: 131–7.

Yang Quanxi 楊權喜. "Dangyang Jijiahu kaogu shijue de zhuyao shouhuo" 當陽季家湖考古試掘的主要收獲. *Jiang Han kaogu* 江漢考古 1980.2: 27–30.

Yang Quanxi 楊權喜. "Xiangyang Shanwan chutu de Ruo guo he Deng guo tongqi" 襄陽山灣出土的鄀國和鄧國銅器. *Jiang Han kaogu* 江漢考古 1983.1: 51–3.

Yang Shaoshun 楊紹舜. "Shanxi Liulin xian Gaohong faxian Shangdai tongqi" 山西柳林縣高紅發現商代銅器. *Kaogu* 考古 1981.3: 211–12.

Yang Shaoshun 楊紹舜. "Shanxi Shilou Chujiayu Caojiayuan faxian Shangdai tongqi" 山西石樓褚家峪曹家垣發現商代銅器. *Wenwu* 文物 1981.8: 49–53.

Yang Shenfu 楊深富. "Shandong Rizhao Guheya chutu yipi qingtongqi" 山東日照崮河崖出土一批青銅器. *Kaogu* 考古 1984.7: 594–7, 606.

Yang Shengnan 楊升南. "Cong Yinxu buci zhong de shi zong shuo dao Shangdai de zongfa zhidu" 從殷墟卜辭中的示宗說到商代的宗法制度. *Zhongguo shi yanjiu* 中國史研究 1985.3: 3–16.

Yang Shengnan 楊升南. "Lüelun Shang dai de jundui" 略論商代的軍隊. In *Jiagu tanshi lu* 甲骨探史錄, ed. Hu Houxuan 胡厚宣. Beijing: Sanlian, 1982, pp. 340–99.

Yang Shengnan 楊升南. "Shangdai de caizheng zhidu" 商代的財政制度. *Lishi yanjiu* 歷史研究 1992.5: 81–94.

Yang Shengnan 楊升南. "Yinxu jiaguwen zhong de he" 殷墟甲骨文中的河. *Yinxu bowu yuan yuankan* 殷墟博物苑苑刊, 1 (1989): 54–63.

Yang Shengnan 楊升南. "Zhou zu de qiyuan ji qi boqian" 周族的起源及其播遷. *Renwen zazhi* 人文雜誌 1984.6: 75–80.

Yang Xiangkui 楊向奎. *Zhongguo gudai shehui yu gudai sixiang yanjiu* 中國古代社會與古代思想研究. Shanghai: Renmin, 1964, pp. 162–3.

Yang Ximei 楊希枚. "Henan Anyang Yinxu muzang zhong renti guge de zhengli he yanjiu" 河南安陽殷墟墓葬中人體骨骼的整理和研究. *BIHP* 42 (1970): 231–65.

Yang Xizhang 楊錫璋. "Anyang Yinxu Xibeigang damu de fenqi ji youguan wenti" 安陽殷墟西北岡大墓的分期及有關問題. *Zhongyuan wenwu* 中原文物 1981.3: 47–52.

Yang Xizhang 楊錫璋. "Yinren zun dongbei fangwei" 殷人尊東北方位. In *Qingzhu Su Bingqi kaogu wushiwu nian lunwenji* 慶祝蘇秉琦考古五十五年論文集, ed. Qingzhu Su Bingqi kaogu wushiwu nian lunwenji bianjizu. Beijing: Wenwu, 1989, pp. 305–14.

Yanzhou Xiwusi 兗州西吳寺. Ed. Guojia Wenwuju kaogu lingdui peixunban. Beijing: Wenwu, 1990.

Yao Shengmin 姚生民. "Shaanxi Chunhua xian chutu de Shang Zhou qingtongqi" 陝西淳化縣出土的商周青銅器. *Kaogu yu wenwu* 考古與文物 1986.5: 12–22.

Yao Xiaosui 姚孝遂. "Du Xiaotun nandi jiagu zhaji" 讀小屯南地甲骨劄記. *Guwenzi yanjiu* 古文字研究 12 (1985): 107–24.

Yao Xiaosui 姚孝遂 and Xiao Ding 肖丁. *Yinxu jiagu ke ci lei zuan* 殷墟甲骨刻辭類纂. Beijing: Zhonghua, 1985.

Yates, Robin. "New Light on Ancient Chinese Military Texts: Notes on Their Nature and Evolution, and the Development of Military Specialization in Warring States China." *TP* 74 (1988): 211–48.

Yates, Robin. "Siege Engines and Late Zhou Military Technology." In *Explorations in the History of Science and Technology in China*, ed. Hu Daojing, Li Guohao, Zhang Mengwen, and Cao Tianqin. Shanghai: Shanghai Chinese Classics, 1982, pp. 409–52.

Ye Wansong 葉萬松. "Jin shinian Luoyang shi Wenwu gongzuodui kaogu gongzuo gaishu" 近十年洛陽市文物工作隊考古工作概述. *Wenwu* 文物 1992.3: 40–5, 54.

Ye Wenxian 葉文憲. "Xian Zhou shi yu Xian Zhou wenhua yuanyuan bianxi" 先周史與先周文化淵源辨析. In *Xi Zhou shi lunwenji* 西周史論文集. Xi'an: Shaanxi Renmin jiaoyu, 1983, pp. 376–86.

Ye Xiaojun 葉曉軍. *Zhongguo ducheng fazhan shi* 中國都城發展史. Xi'an: Shaanxi Renmin, 1988.

Ye Xiaoyan 葉小燕. "Qin mu chutan" 秦墓初探. *Kaogu* 考古 1982.1: 65–73.

Yin Difei 殷滌非. "Xi Han Ruyin Hou mu de zhanpan he tianwen yiqi" 西漢汝陰侯墓的占盤和天文儀器. *Kaogu* 考古 1978.5: 338–43.

Yin Difei 殷滌非. "Anhui Tunxi Zhou mu di er ci fajue" 安徽屯溪周墓第二次發掘. *Kaogu* 考古 1990.3: 210–13, 288.

Yin Difei 殷滌非 and Luo Changming 羅長銘. "Shouxian chutu de E jun Qi jin jie" 壽縣出土的鄂君啟金節. *Wenwu* 文物 1958.4: 8–11.

Yin Shengping 尹盛平. "Cong Xian Zhou wenhua kan Zhou zu de qiyuan" 從先周文化看周族的起源. In *Xi Zhou shi yanjiu* 西周史研究. *Renwen zazhi congkan* 人文雜誌叢刊, no. 2. Xi'an: 1984, pp. 221–31.

Yin Shengping 尹盛平. "Gu Ze guo yizhi mudi diaochaji" 古夨國遺址墓地調查記. *Wenwu* 文物 1982.2: 48–57.

Yin Shengping 尹盛平, ed. *Xi Zhou Wei shi jiazu qingtongqi qun yanjiu* 西周微氏家族青銅器群研究. Beijing: Wenwu, 1992.

Yin Shengping 尹盛平 and Zhang Tian'en 張天恩. "Shaanxi Longxian Bianjiazhuang yi hao Chunqiu Qin mu" 陝西隴縣邊家庄一號春秋秦墓. *Kaogu yu wenwu* 考古與文物 1986.6: 15–22.

Yin Weizhang 殷瑋璋. "Xin chutu de Taibao tongqi ji qi xiangguan wenti" 新出土的太保銅器及其相關問題. *Kaogu* 考古 1990.1: 66–77.

Yin Zhiyi 殷之彝. "Shandong Yidu Sufutun mudi he Ya Chou tongqi" 山東益都蘇埠屯墓地和亞醜銅器. *Kaogu xuebao* 考古學報 1977.2: 23–34.

Yin Zhou jin wen jicheng 殷周金文集成. Ed. Zhongguo Shehui kexueyuan Kaogu yanjiusuo. Beijing: Zhonghua, 1986–96.

Yinxu de faxian yu yanjiu 殷墟的發現與研究. Ed. Zhongguo Shehui kexueyuan Kaogu yanjiusuo. Beijing: Kexue, 1994.

Yinxu fajue baogao, 1958–1961 殷墟發掘報告, 1958–1961. Ed. Zhongguo Shehui kexueyuan Kaogu yanjiusuo. Beijing: Wenwu, 1987.

Yinxu Fu Hao mu 殷墟婦好墓. Ed. Zhongguo Shehui kexueyuan Kaogu yanjiusuo. Beijing: Wenwu, 1980; 2nd ed. 1984.

Yinxu qingtongqi 殷墟青銅器. Ed. Zhongguo Shehui kexueyuan Kaogu yanjiusuo. Beijing: Wenwu, 1985.

Yinxu yuqi 殷墟玉器. Ed. Zhongguo Shehui kexueyuan Kaogu yanjiusuo. Beijing: Wenwu, 1982.

You Lian-yuan. "Characteristics and Evolution of the Longitudinal Profiles in the Middle and Lower Reaches of the Changjiang (Yangtze) River Since Late Pleistocene." In *Quaternary Geology and Environment of China*, ed. Liu Tung-sheng. Beijing: China Ocean; and Berlin: Springer-Verlag, 1985, pp. 261–8.

Yu Haoliang 于豪亮. "Shi Qingchuan Qin mu mudu" 釋青川秦墓木牘. *Wenwu* 文物 1982.1: 22–4.

Yu Weichao 俞偉超. "Gushi fenqi wenti de kaoguxue guancha (yi)" 古史分期問題的考古學觀察(一). *Wenwu* 文物 1981.5: 45–58.

Yu Weichao 俞偉超. *Xian Qin Liang Han kaoguxue lunji* 先秦兩漢考古學論集. Beijing: Wenwu, 1985.

Yu Weichao 俞偉超. "Zhongguo gudai ducheng guihua de fazhan jieduanxing: Wei Zhongguo Kaoguxuehui di wu ci nianhui er zuo" 中國古代都城規劃的發展階段性：為中國考古學會第五次年會而作. *Wenwu* 文物 1985.2: 52–60.

Yu Weichao 俞偉超. *Zhongguo gudai gongshe zuzhi de kaocha: Lun Xian Qin Liang Han de dan dan dan"* 中國古代公社組織的考察：論先秦兩漢的單僤彈. Beijing: Wenwu, 1988.

Yu Weichao 俞偉超 and Gao Ming 高明. "Zhou dai yong ding zhidu yanjiu" 周代用鼎制度研究. *Beijing daxue xuebao* 北京大學學報 1978.1: 84–98 (part 1); 1978.2: 84–97 (part 2); 1979.1: 83–96 (part 3).

Yu Xingwu 于省吾. "Lüelun Xi Zhou jinwen zhong de liu shi he ba shi ji qi tuntian zhi" 略論西周金文中的六師和八師及其屯田制. *Kaogu* 考古 1964.3: 152–5.

Yu Xiucui 余秀翠. "Dangyang faxian yizu Chunqiu tongqi" 當陽發現一組春秋銅器. *Jiang Han kaogu* 江漢考古 1983.1: 81–2, 73.

Yü, Ying-shih. "The Hsiung-nu." In *The Cambridge History of Early Inner Asia*, ed. Denis Sinor. Cambridge University Press, 1990, pp. 118–149.

Yuan Guangkuo 遠廣闊. "Guanyu Peiligang wenhua yizhi xiqian de jige wenti" 關於裴李崗文化一支西遷的幾個問題. *Hua Xia kaogu* 華夏考古 1994.3: 41–8.

Yuan Ke 袁珂. *Shan hai jing jiaozhu* 山海經校注. Shanghai: Guji, 1980.

Yuan Ke 袁珂. *Zhongguo gudai shenhua* 中國古代神話. Rev. ed., Beijing: Zhonghua, 1960.

Yuan Ke 袁珂 and Zhou Ming 周明. *Zhongguo shenhua ziliao cuibian* 中國神話資料萃編. Chengdu: Sichuan sheng Shehui kexueyuan, 1958.

Yunnan Jinning Shizhaishan gumuqun fajue baogao 雲南晉寧石寨山古墓群發掘報告. Ed. Yunnan sheng bowuguan. 2 vols. Beijing: Wenwu, 1959.

Zeng Hou Yi mu 曾侯乙墓, Ed. Hubei sheng bowuguan. 2 vols. Beijing: Wenwu, 1989.

Zeng Hou Yi mu wenwu yishu 曾侯乙墓文物藝術. Wuhan: Hubei meishu, 1992.

Zeng Lin 曾琳, Xia Feng 夏鋒, Xiao Menglong 蕭夢龍 and Shang Zhitan 商志潭. "Su'nan diqu qingtongqi hejin chengfen de ceding" 蘇南地區青銅器合金成份的測定. *Wenwu* 文物 1990.9: 37–47.

Zeng Xiantong 曾憲通. "Chu yue ming chu tan: jian tan Zhaogu mu zhujian de niandai wenti" 楚月名初探：兼談昭固墓竹簡的年代問題. *Zhongshan Daxue xuebao* 1980.1: 97–107.

Zeng Zhaomin 曾昭岷 and Li Jin 李瑾. *Zeng guo he Zeng guo tongqi zongkao* 曾國和曾國銅器綜考. *Jiang Han kaogu* 江漢考古 1980.1: 69–84.

Zeng Zhongmao 曾中懋. "Sanxingdui chutu tongqi de zhuzao jishu" 三星堆出土銅器的鑄造技術. *Sichuan wenwu* 四川文物 1994.6: 68–9, 77.

Zhai Defang 翟德芳. "Zhongguo beifang diqu qingtong duanjian fenqun yanjiu" 中國北方地區青銅短劍分群研究. *Kaogu xuebao* 考古學報 1988.3: 277–99.

Zhang Bingquan 張秉權. "Jiaguwen zhong suo jian ren di tongming kao" 甲骨文中所見人地同名考. In *Qingzhu Li Ji xiansheng qishi sui lunwenji* 慶祝李濟先生七十歲論文集. Taipei: Qinghua xuebaoshe, 1967, pp. 687–776.

Zhang Binquan 張秉權. *Xiaotun di er ben: Yinxu wenzi – Bingbian* 小屯第二本殷墟文字丙編. Taipei: Academia Sinica, 1955–.

Zhang Bingquan 張秉權. "Yindai de nongye yu qixiang" 殷代的農業與氣象. *BIHP* 42 (1970): 267–336.

Zhang Changping 張昌平. "Zeng guo tongqi de fenqi ji qi xiangguan wenti" 曾國銅器的分期及其相關問題. *Jiang Han kaogu* 江漢考古 1992.3: 60–6.

Zhang Changshou 張長壽. "Guanyu Jingshu jiazu mu di 1983 nian 1986 nian Fengxi fajue ziliao zhi yi" 關於井叔家族墓地 1983 年 1986 年灃西發掘資料之一. In *Kaoguxue yanjiu:*

Jinian Shaanxi sheng kaogu yanjiusuo chengli sanshi zhounian 考古學研究：紀念陝西省考古研究所成立三十週年, ed. Shi Xingbang 石興邦 et al. Xi'an: San Qin, 1993, pp. 398–401.

Zhang Changshou 張長壽. "Lun Jingshu tongqi: 1983–1986 nian Fengxi fajue ziliao zhi er" 論井叔銅器 1983-1986年 灃西發掘資料之二. *Wenwu* 文物 1990.7: 32–5.

Zhang Changshou 張長壽. "Xi Zhou de zang yu 1983–1986 nian Fengxi fajue ziliao zhi ba" 西周的葬玉 1983-1986年 灃西發掘資料之八. *Wenwu* 文物 1993.9: 55–9.

Zhang Changshou 張長壽 and Liang Xingpeng 梁星彭. "Guanzhong Xian Zhou qingtongqi wenhua de leixing yu Zhou wenhua de yuanyuan" 關中先周青銅器文化的類型與周文化的淵源. *Kaogu xuebao* 考古學報 1989.1: 1–23.

Zhang Changshou 張長壽 and Zhang Xiaoguang 張孝光. "Yin Zhou chezhi lüeshuo" 殷周車制略説. In *Zhongguo kaoguxue yanjiu: Xia Nai xiansheng kaogu wushi nian jinian lunwenji* 中國考古學研究：夏鼐先生考古五十年紀念論文集, ed. Zhongguo kaoguxue yanjiu. 中國社會科學院考古研究所. Beijing: Wenwu, 1986, pp. 139–62.

Zhang Guangzhi 張光直 (K. C. Chang). "Shang wang miaohao xin kao" 商王廟號新考. *Zhongyang yanjiuyuan minzuxue yanjiusuo jikan* 中央研究院民族學研究所集刊 15 (1963): 65–95. Reprinted in Zhang Guangzhi, *Zhongguo qingtong qi shidai* 中國青銅器時代. Hong Kong: Zhongwen daxue, 1982, pp. 85–106.

Zhang Guangzhi 張光直. "Xinshiqi shidai de Taiwan haixia" 新石器時代的台灣海峽. *Kaogu* 考古 1989.6: 541–50, 569.

Zhang Guangzhi 張光直. "Yangshao wenhua zhong de wuxi ziliao" 仰韶文化中的巫覡資料 *BIHP* 64 (1993): 611–25.

Zhang Guangzhi 張光直. "Zhongguo dongnan haian yuangu wenhua yu Nandao minzu qiyuan wenti" 中國東南海岸遠古文化與南島民族起源問題. *Nanfang minzu kaogu* 南方民族考古 1987.1: 1–14.

Zhang Guangzhi 張光直. "Zhongguo xinshiqi shidai wenhua duandai" 中國新石器時代文化斷代. *BIHP* 20 (1959): 259–309.

Zhang Guoshuo 張國碩. "Yinxu chengqiang shangque" 殷墟城牆商榷. *Yindu xuekan* 殷都學刊 1989.2: 26–30.

Zhang Jian 張劍. "Luoyang bowuguan cang de jijian qingtongqi" 洛陽博物館藏的幾件青銅器. *Wenwu ziliao congkan* 文物資料叢刊 3 (1980): 41–5.

Zhang Juzhong 張居中. "Henan Wuyang jiahu xinshiqi shidai yizhi di er zhi liu ci fajue jianbao" 河南舞陽賈湖新石器時代遺址第二至六次發掘簡報. *Wenwu* 文物 1989.1: 1–14, 47.

Zhang Juzhong 張居中. "Huanjing yu Peiligang wenhua" 環境與裴李崗文化. In *Huanjing kaogu yanjiu* 環境考古研究, ed. Zhou Kunshu 周昆叔 and Gong Qiming 鞏啟明. Beijing: Kexue, 1991, pp. 122–9.

Zhang Min 張敏. "Ningzhen diqu qingtong wenhua puxi yu zushu yanjiu" 寧鎮地區青銅文化譜系與族屬研究. In *Nanjing Bowuyuan jianyuan 60 zhounian jinian wenji* 南京博物院建院60週年紀念文集. N.p. [Nanjing], 1992, pp. 119–77.

Zhang Peiyu 張培瑜. "Yinxu buci lifa yanjiu zongshu" 殷墟卜辭曆法研究綜述. *Xian Qin shi yanjiu* 先秦史研究 12, 3 (1986): 1–14.

Zhang Peiyu 張培瑜. *Zhongguo xian Qin shi libiao* 中國先秦史曆表. Jinan: Qi Lu, 1987.

Zhang Tianen 張天恩. "Bianjiazhuang Chunqiu Qin mudi yu Qian yi de diwang" 邊家庄春秋秦墓地與汧邑的的地望. *Wenbo* 文博 1990.5: 227–31, 251.

Zhang Weihua 張維華. "Zhao changcheng kao" 趙長城考. *Yu gong* 禹貢 7, 8–9 (1937): 40–68.

Zhang Wenjun 張文君 and Gao Qingshan 高青山. "Jin xinan san xian shi guwenhua yizhi de diaocha" 晉西南三縣市古文化遺址的調查. *Kaogu yu wenwu* 考古與文物 1987.4: 3–18.

Zhang Wenyu 張聞玉. "Zeng Hou Yi mu tianwen tuxiang 'jiayin sanri' zhi jieshi" 曾侯乙墓天文圖象甲寅三日之解釋. *Jiang Han kaogu* 江漢考古 1993.3: 66–8.

Zhang Xishun 張希舜, ed. *Shanxi wenwu guan cang zhenpin* 山西文物館藏珍品. Taiyuan: Shanxi Renmin, n.d.

Zhang Xuehai 張學海. "Lun sishinianlai Shandong xian Qin kaogu de jiben shouhuo" 論四十年來山東先秦考古的基本收獲. *Haidai kaogu* 海岱考古 1 (1989): 325–43.

Zhang Xuehai 張學海. "Tian Qi liuling kao" 田齊六陵考. *Wenwu* 文物 1984. 9: 20–2.

Zhang Xuezheng 張學正 et al. "Xindian wenhua yanjiu" 新店文化研究. In *Kaoguxue wenhua lunji* 考古學文化論集, ed. Su Bingqi 蘇秉琦. Beijing: Wenwu, 1993, vol. 3, pp. 122–52.

Zhang Yachu 張亞初. "Shangdai zhiguan yanjiu" 商代職官研究. *Guwenzi yanjiu* 古文字研究 13 (1986): 82–116.

Zhang Yachu and Liu Yu. "Some Observations About Milfoil Divination Based on Shang and Zhou *Bagua* Numerical Symbols." Edward L. Shaughnessy, trans. *EC* 7 (1981–2): 46–55.

Zhang Yongshan 張永山. "Lun Shangdai de zhong ren" 論商代的眾人. In *Jiagu tanshi lu* 甲骨探史錄, ed. Hu Houxuan 胡厚宣. Beijing: Sanlian, 1982, pp. 192–264.

Zhang Zhaowu 張肇武. "Henan Pingdingshan shi chutu Xi Zhou Ying guo qingtongqi" 河南平頂山市出土西周應國青銅器. *Wenwu* 文物 1984.12: 29–32.

Zhang Zhenglang 張政烺. "Buci poutian ji qi xiangguan zhu wenti" 卜辭裒田及其相關諸問題. *Kaogu xuebao* 考古學報 1973.1: 93–120.

Zhang Zhiheng 張之恒. "Huanghe zhongxiayou jizuo Longshan wenhua chengzhi de xingzhi" 黃河中下游幾座龍山文化城址的性質. In *Jinian Chengziyai yizhi fajue liushi zhounian guoji xueshu taolunhui wenji* 紀念城子崖遺址發掘 六十週年國際學術討論會文集, Zhang Xuehai 張學海 ed. Ji'nan: Qi Lu, 1993, pp. 90–8.

Zhang Zhongpei 張忠培. "Liangzhu wenhua de niandai he qi suo chu shehui jieduan" 良渚文化的年代其所處社會階段. *Wenwu* 文物 1995.5: 47–57.

Zhang Zhongpei 張忠培. "Qijia wenhua yanjiu (xia)" 齊家文化研究（下）. *Kaogu xuebao* 考古學報 1987.2: 153–76.

Zhang Zhongpei 張忠培. *Zhongguo beifang kaogu wenji* 中國北方考古文集. Beijing: Wenwu, 1986.

Zhang Zongxiang 張宗祥. *Jiaozhu sanfu huangtu* 校注三輔黃圖. Beijing: Gudian wenxue, 1958.

Zhangjiashan Han jian zhenglizu. "Zhangjiashan Han jian *Yinshu* shiwen" 張家山漢簡引書釋文. *Wenwu* 文物 1990.10: 82–6.

Zhanguo zong heng jia shu 戰國縱橫家書. Beijing: Wenwu, 1976.

Zhao Congcang 趙從倉. "Fengxiang chutu yipi Chunqiu Zhanguo wenwu" 鳳翔出土一批春秋戰國文物. *Kaogu yu wenwu* 考古與文物 1991.2: 2–13.

Zhao Congcang 趙從倉. "Shaanxi Fengxiang faxian Chunqiu Zhanguo de qingtongqi jiaocang" 陝西鳳翔發現春秋戰國的青銅器窖藏. *Kaogu* 考古 1986.4: 337–43.

Zhao Shantong 趙善桐. "Heilongjiang Guandi yizhi faxian de muzang" 黑龍江官地遺址發現的墓葬. *Kaogu* 考古 1965.1: 45–6.

Zhao Yongfu 趙永福. "1961–62 nian Fengxi fajue jianbao" 1961–62 年灃西發掘簡報. *Kaogu* 考古 1984.9: 784–9.

Zhao Zhiquan 趙芝荃. "Lun Erlitou yizhi wei Xia dai wanqi duyi" 論二里頭遺址為夏代晚期都邑. *Hua Xia kaogu* 華夏考古 1987.2: 196–204, 217.

Zhejiang sheng wenwu kaogusuo xuekan 浙江省文物考古所學刊 1981, 1–34. "Tongxiang xian Luojiajiao yizhi fajue baogao" 桐鄉縣羅家角遺址發掘報告.

Zheng Hongchun 鄭洪春 and Jiang Zudi 蔣祖棣. "Chang'an Fengdong Xi Zhou yicun de kaogu diaocha" 長安灃東西周遺存的考古調查. *Kaogu yu wenwu* 考古與文物 1986.2: 1–6.

Zheng Jiexiang 鄭傑祥 and Zhang Yafu 張亞夫. "Henan Huangchuan xian faxian yipi qing-tongqi" 河南潢川縣發現一批青銅器. *Wenwu* 文物 1979.9: 91–3.

Zheng Ruokui 鄭若葵. "Yinxu Dayi Shang zuyi buju chutan" 殷墟大邑商族邑布居初探. *Zhongyuan wenwu* 中原文物 1995.3: 84–93, 83.

Zheng Zhenduo 鄭振鐸, ed. *Quan guo jiben jianshe gongcheng zhong chutu wenwu zhanlan tulu* 全國基本建設工程中出土文物展覽圖錄. Beijing: Guoji, 1955.

Zheng Zhenxiang 鄭振香. "The Excavation of Tombs Number 17 and 18 and Their Signifi-cance." *EC* 7 (1981–2): 55–9.

Zheng Zhenxiang 鄭振香. "Yinxu fajue liushi nian gaishu" 殷墟發掘六十年概述. *Kaogu* 考古 1988.10: 929–41.

Zheng Zhenxiang 鄭振香. "Zao qi Shu wenhua yu Shang wenhua de guanxi" 早期蜀文化與商文化的關係. *Zhongyuan wenwu* 中原文物 1993.1: 6–11, 46.

Zheng Zhenxiang 鄭振香 and Chen Zhida 陳志達. *Yinxu dixia guibao: Henan Anyang Fu Hao mu (Zhongguo kaogu wenwu zhi mei 2)* 殷墟地下瑰寶河南安陽婦好墓（中國考古文物之美2）. Beijing: Wenwu, 1994.

Zhengzhou Erligang 鄭州二里崗. Beijing: Kexue, 1959.

Zhengzhou Shang cheng kaogu xin faxian yu yanjiu 1985–1992 鄭州商城考古新發現與研究 1985–1992. Ed. Henan sheng Wenwu yanjiusuo. Zhengzhou: Zhongzhou Guji, 1993.

Zhong Kan 種侃. "Guyuan xian Pengbao Chunqiu Zhanguo muzang" 固原縣彭堡春秋戰國墓葬. *Zhongguo kaoguxue nianjian 1988* (1989): 255–6.

Zhongguo da baike quanshu: Kaoguxue 中國大百科全書：考古學. Beijing: Zhongguo da baike quanshu, 1986.

Zhongguo gudai fushi yanjiu 中國古代服飾研究. 2 vols. Taipei: Nantian, 1988.

Zhongguo kaogu wenwu zhi mei 中國考古文物之美. 10 vols. Beijing: Wenwu, 1994.

Zhongguo kaoguxue zhong tan shisi niandai shuju ji 1965–1991 中國考古學中碳十四年代數據集 1965–1991. Ed. Zhongguo Shehui kexueyuan Kaogu yanjiusuo. Beijing: Wenwu, 1991.

Zhongguo kexue 中國科學 1977.6: 603–14. "Liaoning sheng nanbu yiwan nian lai ziran huan-jing zhi yanbian" 遼寧省南部一萬年來自然環境之演變.

Zhongguo Kexueyuan Kaogu yanjiusuo, ed. *Changsha fajue baogao* 長沙發掘報告. Zhongguo tianye kaogu baogaoji, Kaoguxue zhuankan, series 4, no. 2. Beijing: Kexue, 1957.

Zhongguo Kexueyuan Kaogu yanjiusuo. *Fengxi fajue baogao: 1955–1957 nian Shaanxi Chang'an xian Fengxi xiang kaogu fajue ziliao* 灃西發掘報告：1955–1957年陝西長安縣灃西鄉考古發掘資料. Zhongguo tianye kaogu baogaoji, Kaoguxue zhuankan, series 4, no. 12. Beijing: Wenwu, 1962.

Zhongguo Kexueyuan Kaogu yanjiusuo. *Hui Xian fajue baogao* 輝縣發掘報告. Zhongguo tianye kaogu baogaoji, no. 1. Beijing: Kexue, 1956.

Zhongguo Kexueyuan Kaogu yanjiusuo. *Shangcunling Guo guo mudi (Huanghe Shuiku kaogu baogao zhi san)* 上村嶺虢國墓地（黃河水庫考古報告之三）. Zhongguo tianye kaogu baogaoji, Kaoguxue zhuankan, Series 4, no. 10. Beijing: Kexue, 1959.

Zhongguo Kexueyuan Kaogu yanjiusuo. *Kaoguxue zhuankan yi zhong di shiwu hao: Chang'an Zhangjiapo tongqi qun* 考古學專刊乙種第十五號：長安張家坡銅器群. Beijing: Wenwu, 1965.

Zhongguo meishu quanji, Huihua 中國美術全集 繪畫. Beijing: Wenwu, 1986.

Zhongguo qingtongqi quanji: 13, Ba Shu 中國青銅器全集：13, 巴蜀. Ed. Zhongguo qingtongqi quanji Bianji weiyuanhui. Beijing: Wenwu, 1994.

Zhongguo Shehui kexueyuan Kaogu yanjiusuo, ed. *Chang'an Zhangjiapo Xi Zhou tongqi qun* 長安張家坡西周銅器群. Beijing: Wenwu, 1965.

Zhongguo Shehui kexueyuan Kaogu yanjiusuo, ed. *Xin Zhongguo de kaogu faxian he yanjiu* 新中國的考古發現和研究. Kaoguxue zhuankan, series A, no. 17. Beijing: Wenwu, 1984.

Zhongguo Shehui kexueyuan Kaogu yanjiusuo, ed. *Kaoguxue zhuankan, yi zhong di ershi jiu hao, Kaogu jinghua: Zhongguo Shehui kexueyuan Kaogu yanjiusuo jiansuo sishi nian jinian* 考古學專刊 • 乙種第二十九號 • 考古精華：中國社會科學院考古研究所建所四十年紀念. Beijing: Kexue, 1993.

Zhongguo Shehui kexueyuan Kaogu yanjiusuo, ed. *Yin Zhou jinwen jicheng* 殷周金文集成. 18 vols. Beijing: Zhonghua, 1984–1996.

Zhongguo Sichou zhi lu cidian 中國絲綢之路辭典. Ed. Xue Li 雪犁. Urumqi: Xinjiang Renmin, 1994.

Zhongguo tianwenxue shi wenji 中國天文學史文集. Beijing: Kexue, 1978.

Zhongguo wenwu 中國文物 1 (1979): 26–9. "Xi Han boshu Tianwen qixiang zazhan shiwen" 西漢帛書天文氣象雜占釋文.

Zhongguo wenwu bao 中國文物報 389 (June 26, 1994): front page. "Xue gucheng kantan shijue huo zhongda chengguo" 薛故城勘探試掘獲重大成果.

Zhongguo wenwu dituji: Henan fence 中國文物地圖集：河南分冊. Ed. Guojia wenwuju Beijing: Zhongguo ditu, 1991.

Zhongguo wenwu jinghua 1990 中國文物精華 1990. Beijing: Wenwu, 1990.

Zhongguo wenwu kaogu zhi mei 中國文物考古之美. 11 vols. Beijing: Wenwu, 1994.

Zhongshan: Tombes des Rois Oubliés. Paris: Galeries nationales du Grand Palais, 1985.

Zhongyuan wenwu 中原文物 1982.1: 42–6. "Xichuan xian Maoping Chu mu fajue jianbao" 淅川縣毛坪楚墓發掘簡報.

Zhongyuan wenwu 中原文物 1981.4: 14–15. "Xinyang shi Pingqiaoxi sanhao Chunqiu mu fajue jianbao" 信陽市平橋西三號春秋墓發掘簡報.

Zhongyuan wenwu 中原文物 1988.1: 14–20. "Luoshan Mangzhang Houli Shang Zhou mudi di san ci fajue jianbao" 羅山蟒張後李商周墓地第三次發掘簡報.

Zhongyuan wenwu 中原文物 1991.1: 87–95. "Zhengzhou Shang cheng wai hangtu qiangji de diaocha yu shijue" 鄭州商城外夯土牆基的調查與試掘.

Zhou Benxiong 周本雄. "Hebei Xushui xian Nanzhuangtou yizhi shijue jianbao" 河北徐水縣南庄頭遺址試掘簡報. *Kaogu* 考古 1992.11: 961–7.

Zhou Daming 周大鳴. "Lun Ningzhen diqu gudai wenhua yu qita wenhua de guanxi" 論寧鎮地區古代文化與其他文化的關係. *Nanfang wenwu* 南方文物 1992.1: 30–5.

Zhou Dao 周到 and Zhao Xinlai 趙新來. "Henan Hebi Pangcun de qingtongqi" 河南鶴壁龐村的青銅器. *Wenwu ziliao congkan* 考古資料叢刊 3 (1980): 35–40.

Zhou Feng 周鋒. "Quanxinshi shiqi Henan de dili huanjing yu qihou" 全新世時期河南的地理環境與氣候. *Zhongyuan wenwu* 中原文物 1995.4: 111–14.

Zhou Hongxiang 周鴻翔. *Shang Yin diwang benji* 商殷帝王本紀. Hong Kong: Wanyou tushu, 1958.

Zhou Houqiang 周厚強. "Hubei Xi Zhou taoqi de fenqi" 湖北西周陶器的分期. *Kaogu* 考古 1992.3: 236–44.

Zhou Kuangming 周匡明. "Qianshanyang can juan pian chutu de qishi" 錢山漾殘絹片出土的啟示. *Wenwu* 文物 1980.1: 74–7.

Zhou Kunshu 周昆叔 and Gong Qiming 鞏啟明, eds. *Huanjing kaogu yanjiu* 環境考古研究. Beijing: Kexue, 1991.

Zhou Shirong 周士榮. "Cansangwen zun yu wushi xuexingyue" 蠶桑紋尊與武士靴形鉞 *Kaogu* 考古 1979.6: 566–7, 563.

Zhou wenhua lunji 周文化論集. Ed. Shaanxi Lishi bowuguan. Xi'an: San Qin, 1993.

Zhou Xiaolu 周曉陸 and Zhang Min 張敏. "Beishan siqi ming kao" 北山四器銘考. *Dongnan wenhua* 東南文化 1988.3–4: 73–82.

Zhou Xinghua 周興華. "Ningxia Zhongwei xian Langwozikeng de qingtong duanjian muqun" 寧夏中衛縣狼窩子坑的青銅短劍墓群. *Kaogu* 考古 1989.11: 971–80.

Zhou Ya 周亞. "Wu Yue diqu tudunmu qingtongqi yanjiuzhong de jige wenti: Cong Anhui Tunxi tudunmu bufen qingtongqi tanqi" 吳越地區土墩墓青銅器研究中的幾個問題：從安徽屯溪土墩墓部分青銅器談起. Paper presented at the International Symposium on Wu-Yue Bronzes, Shanghai, August 1992.

Zhou Yongzhen 周永珍. "Liang Zhou shiqi de Ying guo Deng guo tongqi ji dili weizhi" 兩周時期的應國鄧國銅器及地理位置. *Kaogu* 考古 1982.1: 48–53.

Zhou Yongzhen 周永珍. "Zeng guo yu Zeng guo tongqi" 曾國與曾國銅器. *Kaogu* 考古 1980.5: 436–43.

Zhu Bao 珠葆. "Chang'an Fengxi Mawangcun chutu Xunan tong ding" 長安灃西馬王村出土鄦男銅鼎. *Kaogu yu wenwu* 考古與文物 1984.1: 66–8.

Zhu Fenghan 朱鳳瀚. "Guanyu Yinxu buci zhong de Zhou hou" 關於殷墟卜辭中的周侯. *Kaogu yu wenwu* 考古與文物 1986.4: 68–9.

Zhu Fenghan 朱鳳瀚. "Lun Yinxu buci zhong de dashi ji qi xiangguan wenti" 論殷墟卜辭中的大示及其相關問題. *Guwenzi yanjiu* 古文字研究 16 (1989): 36–48.

Zhu Fenghan 朱鳳瀚. *Shang Zhou jiazu xingtai yanjiu* 商周家族形態研究. Tianjin: Tianjin Guji, 1990.

Zhu Fenghan 朱鳳瀚. "Yinxu buci suo jian Shang wangshi zongmiao zhidu" 殷墟卜辭所見商王室宗廟制度. *Lishi yanjiu* 歷史研究 1990.6: 3–19.

Zhu Gui 朱貴. "Liaoning Chaoyang Shiertaiyingzi qingtong duanjianmu" 遼寧朝陽十二台營子青銅短劍墓. *Kaogu xuebao* 考古學報 1960.1: 63–71.

Zhu Hua 朱華. "Wenxi Shangguocun gumuqun shijue" 聞喜上郭村古墓群試掘. *San Jin kaogu* 三晉考古 1 (1994): 95–122.

Zhu Jianhua 祝建華. "Chu su tanmi: Lujiao lihe xuangu lugu huzuo niaojia gu kao" 楚俗探秘：鹿角立鶴懸鼓鹿鼓虎座鳥架鼓考. *Jiang Han kaogu* 江漢考古 1991.4: 83–6.

Zhu Kezhen 竺可楨 (see too Chu Ko-chen). "Zhongguo jinwuqian nian lai qihou bianqian de chubu yanjiu" 中國近五千年來氣候變遷的初步研究. *Kaogu xuebao* 考古學報 1972.1: 15–38.

Zhu Xi 朱熹. *Chu ci jizhu* 楚辭集注 (1235). Shanghai: Shanghai Guji, 1979.

Zhu Yonggang 朱永剛. "Xiajiadian shangceng wenhua de chubu yanjiu" 夏家店上層文化的初步研究. In *Kaoguxue wenhua lunji* 考古學文化論集 ed. Su Bingqi 蘇秉琦 (Beijing: Wenwu, 1987), pp. 99–128.

Zou Heng 鄒衡. "Jiangnan diqu zhu yinwentao yizhi yu Xia Shang Zhou wenhua de guanxi" 江南地區諸印紋陶遺址與夏商周文化的關係. *Wenwu jikan* 文物集刊 3 (1981): 46–51.

Zou Heng 鄒衡 "Lun zaoqi Jin du" 論早期晉都. *Wenwu* 文物 1994.1: 29–34.

Zou Heng 鄒衡. "Shilun Zhengzhou xin faxian de Yin Shang wenhua yizhi" 試論鄭州新發現的殷商文化遺址. *Kaogu xuebao* 考古學報 1956.3: 77–104.

Zou Heng 鄒衡. *Xia Shang Zhou kaoguxue lunwenji* 夏商周考古學論文集. Beijing: Wenwu, 1980.

Zou Houben 鄒厚本. "Jiangsu nanbu tudunmu" 江蘇南部土墩墓. *Wenwu ziliao congkan* 文物資料叢刊 6 (1982): 66–72.

Zou Youkuan 鄒友寬, Lu Benshan 盧本珊, Liu Shizhong 劉時中, and Xia Zongjing 夏宗經. "Tongling Xi Zhou liucao xuankuangfa moni shiyan yanjiu" 銅陵西周溜槽選礦法模擬實驗研究. *Dongnan wenhua* 東南文化 1993.1: 244–8.

Zuo Zhongcheng 左忠誠. "Weinan shi you chu yipi Shangdai qingtongqi" 渭南市又出一批商代青銅器. *Kaogu yu wenwu* 考古與文物 1987.4: 111.

INDEX

References to figures, maps, and tables are in bold type. Chinese characters for names and terms are given on their first occurrence in the text of each chapter.

abdication, of Yao, 991
Academia Sinica, 127, 130
Academicians (*boshi*), 973
Acheulean hand-axe complex, 40–1
acupuncture, 875
administration: jurisdictions, of Shang, 287, and kinship, 17; procedures of, 603; provincial, 574–5; of Qi, 554; structures of, 573, 574–5, 647–9, 655; state, 572–4
Afanasievo culture, 87
affixes, of language, 91
Africa, as origin of human evolution, 42–1
afterlife, 496
agate, 423, 431
Agnean dialect, 83
agrarian reforms of Shang Yang, 613
agriculture: attempts to increase production, 1023; beginnings of, 42–7; encouragement of, 613, 1023; Li Kui's theory of, 605; in Northern zone, 886; regional cultures and, 47–54; seed plants, 43–7; Shang, 277–81; use of bronze tools in, 577–8
Ailao Yi, 992
Alagou, Xinjiang, 941, 944
aliens, concept of, 549–50
alliances of Warring States, 632–45
almanacs, 843–52
Altai region, 925, 926
Altar to the Soil, 665

altruism, 755, 764
Aluchaideng, Inner Mongolia, 945, 953, 954–5, 957
amulets, 430, 443
An Zhimin, 56n.55, 132n.9
Analects (*Lun yu*), 7, 16, 19, 95–8, 591, 641, 746, 752, 755, 759, 767, 768, 983, 993
ancestors, 256; banquets for, 386; character of worship to, 258, 260; cults of, 649; five-ritual cycle, 245, 250–1; influence of, 375; and sacrifices, 430; Shang, 233, **234–5**, 255–62; status of, 368; tablets and temples of, 257–8, 665, 707–8; titles of, 249
Andersson, J. G., 4, 39, 49, 55, 127, 900, 937
animal guardian, of tombs (*zhenmushou*), 507–8, 519, 533, **534**, 538, 736, **738**, 740
animal husbandry, 280–1, 654, 886, 911
animals: motifs, 68, 152–3, 398; domesticated, 46; jade, **199**; mythical, 687–9, 691, 704–5; and northern peoples, 889; sacrificial, 184, 193, 212–13, 258, 280, 281, 938, 940; shapes, 420, 423, 430, 443, **447**. *See also* Animal Style; dogs; dragons; horses; human sacrifice
Animal Style, 896, 913, 924, 927, 929, 932, **935, 939**, 945, 946, 957, **958**
Antennae Style, 933, 939–40, 945, 953
Anyang, 124, 180–208, 404; chariots at, 903; contacts with neighbors, 158, 221; dates